Matthew Sturgis

OSCAR

A Life

An Apollo Book

This is an Apollo book, first published in the UK in 2018 by Head of Zeus Ltd
This paperback edition published in the UK in 2019 by Apollo

Typeset by Adrian McLaughlin

Printed and bound in Great Britain
by CPI Group (UK) Ltd, Croydon CR0 4YY

Head of Zeus Ltd
First Floor East
5–8 Hardwick Street
London ECIR 4RG

WWW.HEADOFZEUS.COM

For Rebecca,
always

Contents

Preface and Acknowledgements

Oscar Wilde is part of our world. Leaving my Airbnb in New York on my way to inspect a previously overlooked Wilde letter in the library at Columbia, I passed a chalkboard outside an Irish bar scrawled with the legend, 'Work is the curse of the Drinking Classes'. Opposite me on the Uptown subway sat a girl whose mobile-phone case carried the slogan, 'To live is the rarest thing in the world'. And then, to make my morning complete, walking through the university portals was a student sporting a T-shirt that declared, 'Genius is born, not paid'. All three quotations were duly – and (as is not always the case) correctly – credited to 'Oscar Wilde'.

Such encounters are by no means exceptional. Indeed, seeing the world as I have done over recent years through a Wildean prism, it seems to me that rare is the newspaper or magazine that does *not* contain a stray reference to Wilde or his work. And it is not simply his epigrams that have survived in the age of Twitter and shortening attention spans. His plays are still performed. His books are still read. His image is widely reproduced, and instantly recognized. He regularly appears, as a character, on both stage and screen. He has even been turned into a detective by Gyles Brandreth.

The position he holds is an extraordinary one; it spans high and popular culture, it bridges the past and the present. Among British writers he stands, in terms of visibility, with Shakespeare and Jane Austen. In America perhaps Mark Twain shares something of this glamour. The French might look to Baudelaire and Proust. Wilde, however, seems likely to outstrip them all. His prominence increases with each year. His defiant individualism, his refusal to accept the limiting constraints of society, his sexual heresies, his political radicalism, his commitment to style and his canny engagement

with what is now called 'celebrity culture', all conspire to make him ever more approachable, more exciting and more 'relevant'.

All this is impressive, and extraordinary, but does it mean that we need another biography of Wilde?

Soon after I began work on this book, I went to dinner at the house of some friends. My host had piled on my chair a selection of books about Wilde drawn from his own shelves. There was Hesketh Pearson's 1946 *Life of Oscar Wilde*, Montgomery Hyde's 'definitive biography' from 1976, and, of course, the book that supplanted it: Richard Ellmann's monumental green volume – *Oscar Wilde*, published in 1987.

And it was not, moreover, as if my host's collection was anything like complete. It was just a gathering from the shelves of a general reader. There were dozens of other books that might have been added to the already tottering pile – lesser biographical accounts, the memoirs of contemporaries, literary studies. Surely the story had been told (and retold), the details fixed (and refixed). The tale had become familiar.

But appearances, as Oscar knew, can be deceptive. To anyone with a more than general interest in Wilde it had been clear for some time that there was a pressing need for a new and full biography. The reasons for this are threefold. In the thirty years since Ellmann's book appeared, much new material has come to light, much interesting research has been carried out, and the deficiencies in Ellmann's biography have become ever more apparent.

As to the new material: there have been some amazing discoveries. The full transcript of the libel trial that Wilde launched against the Marquess of Queensberry was unearthed; so too were the detailed 'witness statements' of many of those involved in the case. At the Free Library of Philadelphia, Mark Samuels Lasner and Margaret Stetz discovered (hiding in plain sight) one of Wilde's early notebooks, his annotated typescript of *Salomé* and a long letter concerning his *Ballad of Reading Gaol*. Numerous other previously unknown letters were gathered up in the magnificent, and much expanded, new edition of Wilde's letters, produced by Rupert Hart-Davis and Wilde's grandson Merlin Holland in 2000.

Scholarship, too, has been busy. Oxford University Press has started to produce *The Complete Works of Oscar Wilde* in its scholarly Oxford English Texts series; there are seven volumes so far, including two tomes of Wilde's journalism, all with critical introductions and exhaustive notes. There have been many excellent specialist studies – articles, pamphlets, books and websites – on specific aspects of Wilde's life: his working practices, his medical

history, his sex life, his family background, his Irishness, his schooldays, his classical education, his reading, his American tour, his Liberal politics, his British lectures, his role as an editor, his fairy tales, his women friends, his love of Paris, his seaside holiday at Worthing, his Neapolitan sojourn; his final days. There have been dedicated biographies of important figures in Wilde's life: his mother; his wife; the Marquess of Queensberry; Lord Alfred Douglas; such collaborators as Charles Ricketts, Pierre Louÿs and Aubrey Beardsley; such friends as Carlos Blacker, More Adey, Frank Miles and Lillie Langtry. The Oscar Wilde Society has grown and thrived over the last twenty-five years, producing an impressive and regular stream of publications. The Oscholars website has provided another useful forum for research. The need to bring together all this scattered and disparate new information – to assess it and integrate it into the record of Wilde's life – has grown more pressing with each year.

And, of course, knowledge prompts knowledge. The many additions to the record of Wilde's life provided by such scholarship have encouraged new avenues of research. Certainly they have encouraged me to re-investigate the great Wildean archives, to search out new material, to track down forgotten references and to avail myself of the possibilities allowed by the groundbreaking digitalization of historical newspaper archives. (To anyone who can recall the long journey out to the British Library Newspaper Archive at Colindale, and the eye-wearying trawl through flickering reels of microfilm in search of an elusive review, or paragraph, the ease and efficiency of the new process seems quite miraculous – if not almost indecent.)

In tandem with this growth in knowledge about the incidents of Wilde's life, it has become more and more apparent that Ellmann's book – for all its many and great virtues – is not quite satisfactory. As scholars have engaged with his text, its deficiencies as a record of Wilde's life have become only too apparent. The German academic Dr Horst Schroeder began to compile a hand-list of 'Additions and Corrections to Richard Ellmann's Oscar Wilde', soon after the book's appearance. It was published in 1989. And, having continued his investigations, Dr Schroeder issued an expanded edition in 2002, running to over 300 pages. It is, though, by no means exhaustive. Almost every scholar who has written on Wilde during the last three decades has had to correct or amend the picture framed for them by Ellmann. Certainly that was my experience in working on my biographies of Aubrey Beardsley and Walter Sickert, both of whom knew Wilde well.

There are good reasons for this. Ellmann was overtaken in his work on the biography by a debilitating illness. He was racing to finish the book before he died. It was published posthumously. But beyond this sad circumstance it should also be noted that his approach was that of a literary critic rather than an historian. The Life is seen largely through the prism of the Work. Of course, in examining the life of a writer, there are virtues in such an approach – but it has its limits too. And it does seem to have inclined Ellmann not to pay as much attention as he might have done to the facts and the chronology of Wilde's life, or to the testing and assessing his historical sources. The errors, for the most part, might be small enough, but they are many, and they inevitably distort the unfolding narrative.

Ellmann's determinedly literary approach also has its subtly warping effect. He frames his story – as others have done – in the terms of Greek tragedy, foreshadowing the narrative arc from the outset, and suggesting an awful inevitability to its course. And by deploying quotations from Wilde's works as a running commentary on all the incidents of his life, fact and fiction, early hopes and later achievement, actual experience and reflection upon experience, truth and legend, often become blurred and confused. Because, it seems, Mrs Cheveley (in Wilde's 1894 play *An Ideal Husband*) remarked that she had forgotten her schooldays, Ellmann seems content to race past Oscar's six years at the Portora Royal School in scarcely more than a couple of pages. Wilde, of course, created myths about himself, and adopted poses, and there is always a fruitful tension to be explored between these masks and the truths that stand behind them. But there are moments – in the pages of Ellmann – when our hero seems almost to be parading through his life as the 'Oscar Wilde' of later legend.

This is a feature of many books about Wilde. Indeed it is a constant challenge to avoid it. The established persona of 'Oscar Wilde' – the unflappable epigrammatic Aesthete – is so compelling, that it is hard not to be seduced by it. At its most extreme this can lead to such cheerful distortions as Hesketh Pearson's claim that Wilde 'sinned against his nature', during his youth, by shooting, fishing and playing tennis 'with some approach to gusto'. But it can distort in lesser ways too. The picture tends to be complicated further by the fact that in the years after Wilde's death so many myths grew up around him – spurious anecdotes, invented epigrams, inaccurate newspaper reports, misremembered incidents. Biographers have sometimes been more ready to perpetuate these tales than to question them.

In writing this book I have sought to return Wilde to his times, and to the facts. To view him with an historian's eye, to give a sense of contingency, to chart his own experience of his life as he experienced it.

In this enterprise I owe a huge debt to all the scholars who have been working on Wilde over the last three decades. Some I have encountered only in their work: Karl Beckson, Ian Small, Josephine M. Guy, John Stokes, Bobby Fong, Joseph Donohue, Mark Turner, J. Robert Maguire, Stefano Evangelista, Kerry Powell, Joel Kaplan, Antony Edmonds, amongst them.

Others I have been fortunate to know. In the generous sharing of scholarship, I owe personal debts to Merlin Holland, Joseph Bristow, Thomas Wright, John Cooper, Michael Seeney, Geoff Dibb, Don Mead, Iain Ross, Franny Moyle, Horst Schroeder, Margaret Stetz, Mark Samuels Lasner, Julia Rosenthal, Neil McKenna, John Stratford and Ashley Robins.

I am grateful to the staffs of the: William Andrews Clark Memorial Library (UCLA); Harry Ransom Center, University of Texas at Austin; British Library; London Library; Bodleian Library; the National Archives, Kew; Trinity College Dublin Library; Glasgow University Library; National Library of Congress, Washington; New York Public Library; Columbia University Library; Fales Library (NYU), Morgan Library & Museum (New York); Houghton Library (Harvard); Beinecke Library (Yale); Archive of American Art at the Smithsonian Institution (Washington); Mark Samuels Lasner Collection at University of Delaware; Massachusetts Historical Society Library (Boston); National Library of Australia; Toronto University Library; Brotherton Library (Leeds); University College Library (Oxford); Magdalen College Archive (Oxford); Biblioteca della Società Napoletana di Storia Patria; Biblioteca Universitaria di Napoli; library of the Institut de France (Paris), public library at Bad Homburg; public library at Leadville, Colorado.

To many others who have shared information or assisted in other ways: Amelia Gosztony, Michael Claydon, Clive Fisher, Steven Halliwell, John Nicoll, Robert Whelan, Roy Foster, Rupert Smith, David Macmillan, Edward Farrelly, Greg Gatenby, Kitty and Ted Drier, Tony and Jane Worcester, David White (*Somerset Herald*), Oliver Forge, Reg Gadney, Patrick Gibbs, Gyles Brandreth, Rebecca Jewell, Phil Shaw, Michael Tuffley, Peter Hyland, Gordon Cooke, Hugo Chapman, Audrey Curtis, Sophie Hopkins, Penny Fussell, John Nightingale, Robin Darwall-Smith, David Waller, Sile O'Shea, Megan Dunmall, Ellen O'Flaherty, Louise Turner, Scott Morrison, John Mexborough, Oliver Parker, Paul Vincent, Donna Clarke, Desmond Hillary, Alan Black, Devon Cox, Jill Hamilton, A. N. Wilson, Tim and Jean Sturgis,

Alexander Fygis-Walker, Charles Martin, Linda Kelly, Brendan Walsh, Silvia Melchior and Veronika Binoeder.

I owe a huge debt to my agent, Georgina Capel, for her vision and dedication in bringing this project to fruition; also to Georgina Blackwell and her colleagues at Head of Zeus for welcoming the book with such insight and enthusiasm.

And most of all to my wife, Rebecca Hossack, for her love and support, and for welcoming Oscar Wilde into our shared life during these last seven years.

Proem

There was a great pressure for admission. The body of the court was filled with barristers in their wigs and gowns. The galleries and passages were densely crowded with the public and the press. No libel case had so excited the town in a generation. Fashionable society was abuzz. The newspapers headlined the story in their largest type. The name of Wilde had been enough to assure huge interest; the lurid revelations of the opening days' evidence had increased that interest to a new pitch. And more was expected to follow. The potent mix of celebrity, sex and scandal would be brought to the boil. Counsel might complain at the prejudicial reporting of the morning papers, but the chief justice brushed all objections aside.[1]

The scene was the Court of Common Pleas in Dublin, on 17 December 1864. The 'great libel case' occasioning such intense interest had been brought by an attractive young woman of literary pretensions, Mary Travers, against Lady Wilde, the celebrated wife of Dublin's leading eye-and-ear doctor, Sir William Wilde. It marked the culmination of a fourteen-month campaign of vilification, annoyance and aggravation against the parents of the ten-year-old Oscar Wilde.

Mary Travers, daughter of the eccentric professor of medical jurisprudence at Trinity College Dublin, had been, since her late teens, a patient of Dr Wilde's, as well as a friend of the family. The doctor had taken a lively interest in her well-being and development, and perhaps something more. He had accompanied her to exhibitions, bought her clothes, lent – or given – her small sums of money, encouraged her literary ambitions, advised her on her reading, invited her to family meals and included her on family excursions. If there was an element of infatuation in all this, Dr Wilde had

– at the beginning of the 1860s – tried to break the connection, perhaps unsettled by signs of Miss Travers' increasingly unstable temperament. Twice he offered her money so that she might join her brothers in Australia. On both occasions she took the money but failed to make the voyage.

She became, instead, ever more demanding of Dr Wilde's attention, and increasingly resentful of his wife's refusal to engage. Alive to slights, she convinced herself that both the Wildes were determined to insult and humiliate her. But, according to her own account, the gravest insult occurred in October 1862. During a consultation in Dr Wilde's surgery, while he was examining the mark of a burn on her neck, she lost consciousness – perhaps choked by her bonnet strap. Coming round, she found Dr Wilde distraught and apologetic. She also found – so she claimed – that, during her period of unconsciousness, she had been 'violated'.

This discovery did not, however, terminate her relationship with the Wildes. She continued to see the doctor and to write to his wife, but with ever-growing intemperance and hostility. She put garlic into the surgery soap-tray at Merrion Square as part of a series of planned 'annoyances'. She continued to expect money, writing to the doctor on one occasion, 'if you do not choose to send it promptly as usual, see what will happen'. She wrote a barbed review of Lady Wilde's latest book, piqued at the success it was enjoying. She threatened suicide, and sent a mocked-up press cutting announcing her own death.

And then, in October 1863, she printed a pamphlet entitled *Florence Boyle Price: or A Warning* – a barely fictionalized record of her various complaints, with the Wildes figuring as the overweening 'Dr and Mrs Quilp' – he with 'a decidedly animal and sinister expression about his mouth', she 'an odd sort of undomestic woman' inclined to spend 'the greater portion of her life in bed'. The tale of how the doctor had used chloroform – concealed in 'a handsome scent bottle' – to subdue the young Miss Price in order that he might have his way with her, was told with the lurid relish of a penny dreadful. A thousand copies were produced.

The pamphlets were widely circulated in Dublin. The Wildes strove to ignore the attack, and for a while it appeared that they had weathered the storm. But the elevation of Dr Wilde to a knighthood at the beginning of 1864 fired Miss Travers' ire and resentment. In April of that year, with Sir William due to give a public lecture at the Metropolitan Hall on 'Ireland Past and Present', Miss Travers arranged for a troop of newsboys to distribute the pamphlet (together with extracts from some of Sir William's

letters to her) outside the venue. One rang a hand-bell, hired from a local auctioneers; all carried placards emblazoned with the names of Sir William and his wife. Miss Travers directed operations from the seclusion of a cab, parked nearby.

From then on the campaign became unceasing. A letter appeared in *Saunders's News-Letter* – signed 'Inquirer', but written by Miss Travers – feigning an innocent concern about the events of the evening, and suggesting a legal solution: 'A number of boys were selling a pamphlet, and through curiosity I purchased one in which [Sir William's] name most disreputably figured. Can it be possible the occurrence therein related took place? If untrue, the knight ought to take action and punish the offender. The pamphlet is six months in circulation and its accuracy has not been questioned.'[2]

Scurrilous verses alluding to Sir William's supposed sexual improprieties – and his several illegitimate children – began to be published in the *Dublin Weekly Advertiser*; others were pushed through the letterbox at 1 Merrion Square. When Lady Wilde fled down to Bray, Miss Travers tracked her there. She engaged the local newspaper boys to parade along the esplanade, directly outside the Wildes' house, again carrying placards and offering the pamphlet for sale. Harassed to the limit of her endurance, Lady Wilde wrote to Miss Travers' father:

> SIR – You may not be aware of the disreputable conduct of your daughter
> at Bray, where she consorts with all the low newspaper boys in the place,
> employing them to disseminate offensive placards, in which my name is
> given, and also tracts, in which she makes it appear that she has had an
> intrigue with Sir William Wilde. If she chooses to disgrace herself that is
> not my affair; but as her object in insulting me is the hope of extorting
> money, for which she has several times applied to Sir William Wilde,
> with threats of more annoyance if not given, I think it right to inform
> you that no threat or additional insult shall ever extort money for her
> from our hands. The wages of disgrace she has so basely treated for and
> demanded shall never be given to her. JANE. F. WILDE.

Although Professor Travers replied to the letter, he did not destroy it; and his daughter, finding it among his papers, at once grasped its potential. She had become fixed on the idea of getting Sir William into court, and this seemed an opportunity. Taking the letter to a firm of Dublin solicitors, she instructed them to bring a libel action against Lady Wilde – claiming that

such phrases as 'disreputable conduct', 'consorted with all the low news-paper boys', 'intrigue' and 'wages of disgrace', traduced her character and her chastity. And although Lady Wilde was the author of these slurs, Sir William was listed as the co-defendant in the action, since husbands – at that date – were held to be legally responsible for their wives' civil mis-demeanours. Miss Travers demanded £2,000 in damages.* The Wildes, it seems, sought to compromise the matter out of court, but Miss Travers was implacable. Forced to fight, they instructed their solicitors to enter a defence of justification and privilege.[3]

An extraordinary array of legal talent was deployed on both sides. Miss Travers was to be represented by Sergeant Armstrong, the leading figure of the Irish Bar, supported by Mr Heron QC and the brilliant Isaac Butt QC (an old friend of the Wildes), as well as by two juniors. Lady Wilde engaged Sergeant Sullivan (a future lord chancellor of Ireland), together with two supporting QCs and two further juniors. The trial began on Monday 12 Dec-ember, and lasted six days.

Miss Travers had the opportunity to air her grievances in open court. She told, in compelling detail, of Sir William's attentions to her, his letters (sometimes cajoling, sometimes railing), his desire that she should call him 'William', his attempt to embrace her, his contrition when she objected. Led by her counsel, she described the incident in October 1862, when she had lost consciousness in Dr Wilde's surgery. She reported his frantic imprecations when she had come to: 'Do be reasonable, and all will be right,' he had, apparently, pleaded. 'I am in your power... spare me, oh, spare me... strike me if you like. I wish to God I could hate you, but I can't. I swore I would never touch your hand again. Attend to me and do what I tell you. Have faith and confidence in me and you may remedy the past and go to Australia. Think of the talk this may give rise to. Keep up appear-ances for your own sake.' And she informed the hushed courtroom, that – yes – during her period of unconsciousness, she had been 'violated'; or, as Sergeant Armstrong glossed it, she 'went in to the room a maid, but out a maid she never departed'.[4]

These were the details feasted upon by the press and the public. But there was much that was incoherent in Miss Travers' testimony, and much

---

*   Although it is difficult to fix exact equivalents between old and current monetary amounts, most late nineteenth-century sums should be multiplied by between 80 and 120 to give an idea of their value at the time of writing.

that was odd about her behaviour. Sergeant Sullivan did his best to point up these inconsistencies: her failure to mention the alleged rape at the time, her inability to recall the exact date of the incident, her continued relationship with Sir William after the event, her uncertainty as to whether there had been any further 'transactions' of a similar sort. But no direct denial could be made, as Sir William – despite his nominal status as co-defendant – had been advised not to go into to the witness box.

Instead it was left to Lady Wilde, dressed in black (as a show of mourning for her brother, recently deceased in America), to give an account of Miss Travers' campaign of harassment. Cross-examined by Isaac Butt, her performance was assured. Perhaps too assured. She adopted a lofty disdain towards Miss Travers and her claims. She refused to countenance the notion that Sir William had had 'an intrigue' or 'underhand sort of love affair' with the plaintiff. She showed a turn of humour. Having been quizzed about the mock death notice that Miss Travers had sent her, she remarked, 'I think I saw her next in August 1863, after her death.' It drew a laugh from the public gallery, but rather shocked the jury. Although Butt tried to draw her into a discussion upon the supposed immorality of the German novel that she had recently translated, the judge stopped that line of questioning.

For some onlookers at least there would have been a spice of dramatic irony in this courtroom duel. The married Isaac Butt, for all his assumed tone of moral indignation, was (like Sir William Wilde) known to have fathered several illegitimate children. And, though he might seek to portray Lady Wilde as cold and unfeeling, it was rumoured that he had had a dalliance – if not an affair – with her in the years before her marriage. But in the theatre of the Four Courts everyone had their role to play.

There was a 'general expectation' that the case would be settled in favour of the Wildes.[5] The judge, in his address to the jury, emphasized the oddities of Miss Travers' behaviour in relation to the supposed rape, suggesting that, given her continued friendship with Sir William, it might be reasonable to conclude 'that if intercourse existed at all it was with her consent, or certainly not against her consent… and that the whole thing is a fabrication'.

But this had to be set against the eloquent summing-up delivered by Isaac Butt on the Friday afternoon – described in the press as 'one of the most powerful appeals ever addressed to a jury in Dublin'.[6] He portrayed Miss Travers as an isolated and vulnerable young woman callously treated by the proud and powerful Wildes. Sir William, in refusing to give evidence, had not played 'the part of a man' – and Butt was 'sorry an Irish gentleman should

have acted so'. Lady Wilde's attempts to rise above Miss Travers' baiting (and Isaac Butt's questioning), were set down as heartlessness – unworthy of a mother, a wife, a woman or a Christian. That she should have responded to Miss Travers' account of a suicide attempt with the terse rejoinder 'the intelligence has no interest for Lady Wilde', called forth a torrent of rhetorical mock-indignation: 'Oh! Shame on genius! Oh! shame on the heart of a woman; shame – shame above all on the heart of an Irishwoman.'

Such emotive appeals – for all their obvious theatricality – had their effect. The jury, after several hours' deliberation, found for Miss Travers – although they undercut the force of their verdict by awarding her only a farthing's damages, rather than the £2,000 she had sought. The Wildes, nevertheless, were burdened with the costs of the case – which were 'expected to be very heavy'.[7]

The extraordinary week-long drama was at an end. In its combination of salacious detail and impassioned advocacy it was deemed – outside of Ireland – to have been a peculiarly Irish spectacle. 'Irishmen are impetuous and demonstrative,' declared *The Times* of London, 'and forensic eloquence is such a characteristic of their race that we can readily believe it to have been powerfully displayed even in a cause like this; but Englishmen will probably wonder how so much interest could have been excited or so much professional energy employed.'[8]

THE STAR CHILD

1854–1874

AGE 1–20

Oscar Wilde as a schoolboy.

1

A Small Unruly Boy

*'He rarely spoke of his childhood, beyond saying that he had
been very, very happy.'*

ROBERT SHERARD

I n May 1855 – nine years before the Travers trial – Sir William Rowan
Hamilton, Ireland's astronomer royal, wrote to a friend about his busy
social life in Dublin: 'A very odd and original lady… had also lately a baby:
such things you know will happen, at least in Ireland; and on my being asked
to hand her in to dinner… when I met her for the first time in my life, she
told me of this "young pagan," as she called him… and she asked me to be a
godfather, perhaps because I was so to a grandson of Wordsworth the Poet…
and because she is an admirer of Wordsworth. However, I declined.'

The refusal did not, it seems, provoke any resentment. The 'odd and
original lady' paid Sir William a visit soon afterwards, when he had an open
day at his observatory. 'My visitress,' he reported, 'told me, as we drank a
glass of wine to the health of her child, that he had been christened on the
previous day, by a long baptismal name, or string of names, the two first
of which are Oscar and Fingal! the third and fourth [O'Flahertie and Wills]
sounding to me as a tremendous descent, but I daresay she prefers them.'[1]

Oscar Fingal O'Flahertie Wills Wilde, the 'young pagan' under discussion, had been born on 16 October 1854 at 21 Westland Row, Dublin, a neat

Georgian terraced house, close to the Westland Row Railway Station, and backing on to the open space of Trinity College park. And the long string of baptismal names had been bestowed upon him at a service – conducted by his uncle – in the neighbouring church of St Mark.[2]

'Oscar' and 'Fingal' were names touched with poetry and romance; they were, as his mother declared, 'grand, misty and Ossianic'. In the Celtic epic ascribed to the ancient bard Ossian (but written in 1760 by James Mac-Pherson), 'Oscar' figured as the great but doomed hero of Irish legend, while 'Fingal' was his no less heroic grandfather, leader of the mythic warrior troop the Fianna. The name O'Flahertie, if not quite so poetical, was scarcely less imbued with legendary association. The O'Flaherties were the great family of the west of Ireland: they had been lords of Connemara and kings of Connaught. And the young Oscar Wilde could claim kinship with them through his paternal great-grandmother. Wills, too, was a family name of sorts – though one with 'Anglo' rather than 'Irish' resonances. It had been adopted by Oscar's father, his grandfather, and – indeed – had also been given to Oscar's older brother, William, at his birth two years previously. The Wills family had been influential landholders around Castlerea since the beginning of the eighteenth century; and it seems to have been a desire for genteel association, rather than any ties of blood, that prompted the Wildes' serial adoption of the name. Taken together the names made up an impressive list. Certainly it impressed Sir William Rowan Hamilton. They were names that carried both hopes and expectations. They proclaimed, too, the affiliations – and, indeed, the pretensions – of the child's parents.[3]

Oscar Wilde's father and mother were figures of note on the Dublin scene. Although both were still in their thirties as the time of Oscar's birth, they were already marked out as real 'celebrities': 'Surgeon Wilde' and his wife 'Speranza'. And if they were famed in Dublin, their reputations also carried beyond the Pale. Their names were known across Ireland, in England, on continental Europe, and even in America.

William Wilde was not only the leading aural and ophthalmic surgeon in Dublin, and a leader in medical research, he was also the author of popular books on travel and history, an acknowledged expert on Irish archaeology, topography, ethnology and folklore, and a leading light of both the British Association for the Advancement of Science and the Royal Irish Academy (RIA). His wife, Jane, was a poet, and – to a large portion of the Irish populace – a national heroine. She may have been 'odd and original', but she was also, as Sir William Rowan Hamilton noted, 'quite a genius, and thoroughly

aware of it'. She contributed erudite articles to Dublin's periodical press, read Greek for pleasure, and produced acclaimed translations from both French and German.

In any setting the Wildes were a conspicuous couple. She was magnificent (indeed one observer described her as 'rather too magnificent'):[4] almost six feet tall, upright and commanding; not perhaps conventionally beautiful, but with a clear complexion, fine brows, dark eyes, blue-black hair and a delight in billowing white crinolines and flowing shawls. She was apt to put people in mind of a Roman goddess or Roman matron, or of the Ossianic heroine Deugala.[5] He was of medium height, but beside his towering wife appeared smaller. Also he stooped slightly as a result of his long hours of work. While she was stately and ponderous, he – 'like a Skye terrier' – was all sinewy energy and eager bustle. He walked in a curious fashion, pumping his elbows as he went. His eyes were bright. There was a slightly simian cast to his features, emphasized by his side whiskers. His dark hair, already flecked with wolfish grey, was thick and unruly. He had, too, a distinctive sallow complexion that caused some to think that he looked 'dirty'. Men considered him ugly; women found him attractive.[6]

Even in a city famed for its talk, both the Wildes were celebrated as brilliant exponents: he a wonderful conversationalist and raconteur, she 'amusingly fearless and original' and fond of making 'a sensation'. The home they created together at Westland Row had a reputation for being sociable, hospitable, intellectual, stimulating and unconventional. Some found the Wilde ménage rather over-stimulating and too unconventional, but few could deny that it rested upon a ground of real substance and achievement. They were recognized as the 'Jupiter-Æsculapius and Juno-Minerva' of their own Olympus.[7]

William Robert Wills Wilde had been born (in 1815) and raised in Co. Roscommon in the west of Ireland, the third son of a modestly well-to-do provincial doctor from the established Anglo-Irish protestant class. His mother, Amelia née Fynn, though, came of old Irish stock (the Fynns of Ballymagibbon in Co. Mayo were renowned for their wide estates, their ancient name, their connection to the O'Flaherties and their mental instability).[8] In an Ireland that was too often divided along established lines, between indigenous Catholic Celts and Anglo-Protestant incomers, William Wilde embraced the connections and ambiguities of his heritage. He saw great benefit in the 'fusion' of the races, and thought that there could not be a better intermixture 'than the Saxon and the Celt'.[9]

While both his older brothers entered the established Church of Ireland (and one of his two sisters also married a clergyman), William followed his father's profession. As a young man of seventeen he was sent to study medicine – or, rather, surgery – in Dublin. And after five years of training at the city's leading medical institutions, and five years of amiable sociability among his fellow medical students, he was appointed a licentiate of the Royal College of Surgeons of Ireland.

It was an achievement gained in the face of considerable distractions. He suffered from recurrent bouts of asthma. On the eve of his final exams he contracted a near-fatal fever, and was only brought through by a course of strong ale (one glass taken every hour) prescribed by his sometime tutor and long-time friend, Dr Graves. And, on top of these health worries, the unmarried twenty-two-year-old also learnt that he was due to become a father. Any – or all – of these considerations might have encouraged him to accept a position as medical attendant to a wealthy and consumptive Scots merchant who was about to depart in his steam yacht for a restorative nine-month cruise to the Holy Land. The newly qualified doctor's duties were not onerous, and he found time during the frequent stopovers to compile material for his first book, a two-volume travelogue, which was published to considerable acclaim on his return to Dublin.

Narrative of a Voyage to Madeira, Teneriffe, and along the shores of the Medi-terranean (or 'Wilde's *Madeira*', as it was more conveniently known) revealed the author as a young man of extraordinary energy, erudition and pluck. His literary style was lively and engaging; his range of interest boundless: birdlife, plant specimens, antiquities, the health-giving effects of climate, the habits of stray dogs, modes of capital punishment, modes of dress, Napoleonic battle sites, royal tombs, the beautifully shaped eyes of the young women in Bethlehem, the beautifully shaped fingers of the young women in the tobacco-factories at Corunna. He visited Algerian slave markets, ascended a pyramid at the risk of his life, dissected a dolphin (to discover how marine mammals suckled their young without drowning them), and – at Tyre – carried out a thorough investigation into the true origins of the 'Tyrhennian purple' dye.

At Mycenae, in the Greek Peloponnese, he was struck by a resemblance between the vast un-mortared stonework of the so-called 'Treasury of Atreus' and the great Neolithic tumulus at Newgrange in Co. Meath. It suggested to him that there must be a common ancestry between the Aryan peoples of pre-classical Greece and the early Celts of prehistoric

Ireland.[10] William Wilde had a particular enthusiasm for the early history of Ireland. During his childhood in rural Roscommon he had often accompanied his father on his medical rounds among the local peasantry. These trips had given him a love of the topography, the antiquities, the history and the folklore of the country. It was a world of mystery: unexplained ruins of ancient stone and earth littered the landscape, place names echoed with the figures of a lost heroic age, and the colourful superstitions of the local people seemed to preserve the world-view of Ireland's pre-Christian past.

And, as a medical student in Dublin, William Wilde had been delighted to find others who shared his antiquarian interests. Their common enthusiasm reflected a new spirit of cultural nationalism, less political and revolutionary than that espoused by some of their contemporaries, but no less challenging to the established hierarchies. The celebration of Ireland's pre-Christian Celtic past seemed to trump all the later divisions of creed, nationality and political allegiance, and to offer a vision of an Ireland united in itself and separate from England. A focus for these enthusiasts was provided by the RIA, an institution dedicated to the collection, investigation and analysis of Irish antiquities. William Wilde was elected a member at the young age of twenty-three.[11]

His love of Ireland, however, was never limiting or parochial. He used the money he earned from his book (a very useful £250) to complete his medical education at some of the foremost centres of learning in Europe. Partly as a result of his travels in Egypt, where he had seen many people suffering from ophthalmic trachaea, he decided to specialize in diseases of the eye. He spent three months at the Royal London Ophthalmic Hospital (Moorfields); he travelled to Vienna and studied at the Allgemeine Krankenhaus, the city's great general hospital, where classes were still conducted in Latin; and he visited institutions in Prague, Dresden, Heidelberg and Berlin, before returning to Dublin – in 1841 – to establish his practice in Westland Row (initially at No. 15, then at 21).

Wilde's energy was prodigious. He quickly built up a fashionable practice as both an ophthalmic and aural surgeon. As an act of civic philanthropy he opened a dispensary for poor patients in the converted stables next to the house, transforming it in 1844 into St Mark's Hospital for Diseases of the Eye and Ear, on Mark Street. On both the professional and the philanthropic fronts he was perhaps aided by the fact that he was an active Freemason.[12] He contributed regularly to the prestigious Dublin *Journal of Medical Science*

before – at the age of thirty – becoming its editor, and transforming it into the yet more respected *Quarterly* publication. His pioneering interest in medical statistics led to him being made medical commissioner for the census of 1841 (and assistant commissioner for the subsequent censuses of 1851, 1861 and 1871).

And there was more. He produced an overview of Austrian intellectual life (*Austria: Its Literary, Scientific and Medical Institutions*); he attended the natural history and ethnology sessions of the British Association. He continued his investigations into the antiquities of Ireland, giving regular updates to the RIA. He revised his *Madeira* for a second edition. He contributed articles on diverse topics to the *Dublin University Magazine* (a publication co-founded, and briefly edited, by Isaac Butt). He published *The Last Years of Dean Swift's Life*, the first work to suggest that the author of *Gulliver's Travels* had not gone mad during his final years. He produced a discursive account of *The Beauties of the Boyne and the Blackwater* (1849) based on his ramblings in the west of Ireland (he had taken Lord Macaulay over the battlefield of the Boyne when the author was researching his *History of England*).

And all this was accomplished against a background of committee meetings, convivial club dinners, occasional lectures and a busy social life. He seems to have taken some part in the education of the illegitimate son he had fathered at the end of his student days. Henry Wilson (as he was obliquely named) was acknowledged as an unspecified 'cousin', and brought up to follow his father's profession. William Wilde also sired at least two more children out of wedlock, girls – Emily (born 1847) and Mary (born 1849) – who were adopted as wards by his eldest brother, Rev. Ralph Wilde, sometime vicar of Kilsallaghan, outside Dublin. Their mother was reputed to be the keeper of a 'black oak shop' in the city.[13] The notion, though, that Dr Wilde was an inveterate 'runner after girls' with an illegitimate 'family in every farmhouse' was probably the exaggerated invention of Dublin gossip.[14] By the beginning of the 1850s he seems to have been in want of a wife. There was a courtship – or at least a flirtation – with the Shakespearean actress Helena Faucit. But it came to nothing, and he turned his attentions elsewhere.

Jane Francesca Elgee was a worthy mate. In 1851 she was twenty-nine and famous. Over the previous five years she had achieved a popular renown as one of Ireland's heroic voices, exposing the horrors of the Famine, and expressing a nationalist outrage at the failure of the British government to

address it. Although she came of a thoroughly conventional middle-class Protestant Dublin family, brought up among people high in both the established church and the British army, she had been seized by the radical nationalist spirit of the times, her 'patriotism kindled' by reading the poetry of the recently deceased Thomas Davis, one of the founders of the 'Young Ireland' movement.[15] The fire soon took hold.

The youngest of four children, brought up by a widowed mother, Jane was of a strongly romantic and literary disposition. She was proud of her connection to the Gothic novelist Charles Maturin, author of *Melmoth the Wanderer*, a bizarre Faustian tale revered by Goethe, Balzac and the young Romantics. Maturin had married her mother's sister, and although he had died in 1824 he remained a key presence in Jane's imaginative life. In search of additional support for her artistic nature, Jane had also convinced herself that the Elgee name derived from the Italian 'Algiati' – and from this (imaginary) connection she was happy to make the short leap to claiming kinship with Dante Alighieri (in fact the Elgees descended from a long line of Durham labourers).[16] Her childhood was spent among books and poetry. Tennyson and Elizabeth Barrett Browning became her favourites, 'leaving, of course, the great God, Wordsworth, undisturbed on his throne'.[17] An excellent linguist, she became familiar not just with English authors, but also with the whole range of classical and modern European literature. It was, though, in Ireland's nationalist cause that she found a subject to inspire her own creativity – and her own sense of an exalted destiny.

Confronted by the injustice and tragedy of the Famine and its aftermath, she began to write impassioned letters and impassioned verses indicting her own landlord class – 'the spoilers of our land' – in ringing cadences. They were sent to *The Nation*, the leading weekly paper of Irish radicalism, the voice of the 'Young Ireland' movement. Not daring to use her own name, for fear of outraging her family, she signed her letters 'John Fanshaw Ellis' and her verses 'Speranza', the Italian word for 'hope'. The *Nation*'s editor, Gavan Duffy, was impressed, and through the pages of his paper Speranza's poems were carried into thousands of humble Irish homes; they were read round fires and declaimed by ballad sellers: 'The Voice of the Poor', 'The Stricken Land', 'A Lament for the Potato'.

In her 1847 ballad 'The Brothers' she commemorated young John and Henry Sheares, who had been hanged for their part in the thwarted Irish rebellion of 1798, and imagined them calling to the next generation to take up their fight for 'Fatherland':

> Oh! they preach to us, those still and pallid features –
> Those pale lips yet implore us, from their graves,
> To strive for birthright as God's creatures,
> Or die, if we can but live as slaves.

Jane's family was shocked when, inevitably, her alias was exposed and they discovered what she was up to. But she was unrepentant. There was too much excitement and drama in her new role. She had found her calling: 'I should like to rage through life,' she declared; 'this orthodox creeping is too tame for me – ah, this wild rebellious ambitious nature of mine. I wish I could satiate it with Empires, though a St Helena were the end.'[18] An Irish revolt seemed a real possibility – at least in the radical circles of literary Dublin. In July 1848, with Duffy and some of the other leaders of the movement imprisoned, Jane added her voice to the calls for armed insurrection. Writing anonymously in the *Nation* she cried out for 'a hundred thousand muskets glittering brightly in the light of heaven'. The results were calamitous. The people, exhausted by their privations, did not rise. The government suspended *habeus corpus*. There was one minor insurrection in Tipperary ('the Battle of the Widow McCormack's Cabbage Patch') in the course of which two 'rebels' were shot. At the subsequent trial of Gavan Duffy (where he was defended by Isaac Butt), Jane's inflammatory leader was one of the planks in the prosecution's case. Jane had the considerable courage to go to the solicitor general and admit her own authorship. This act of bravery added new lustre to her reputation: it rapidly became mythologized into the story that she had actually stood up in open court, and interrupted the prosecution's address with the ringing declaration, 'I am the culprit, if culprit there be.'[19]

During the course of the trial Jane was certainly impressed by Isaac Butt. The thirty-five-year-old lawyer, though a recent convert to the Nationalist cause, was an impassioned advocate (he secured Duffy's acquittal). Jane romanticized him as 'the Mirabeau of the Young Ireland movement, with his tossed masses of black hair, his flashing eyes, and splendid rush of cadenced oratory'.[20] There were rumours that the attraction was mutual. Years later, John Butler Yeats, writing to his son William, reported: 'When she was Miss Elgee, Mrs Butt found [Jane] with her husband when the circumstances were not doubtful, and told my mother about it.'[21] The incident, however, seems to have been as transitory as the 1848 uprising.

Following the chastening collapse of the Young Ireland movement, Jane

withdrew from the political front line, concentrating instead upon sexual politics and literary work. She became an ardent supporter of women's rights, and an able translator. She produced, in 1849, an English version of Wilhelm Meinhold's weird Gothic romance *Sidonia the Sorceress*. Over the following two years she published translations of Lamartine's *Pictures of the First French Revolution* (1850) and *The Wanderer and his home* (1851). Not that these high-minded endeavours ever obscured her relish for the less exalted aspects of life: one female writer friend recalled how, at their first meeting, Jane 'spoke much about poetry... but still more about fashion'.[22]

Among Jane's several contributions to the Dublin press was an enthu-siastic review – in the *Nation* – of William Wilde's *Beauties of the Boyne and the Blackwater*. It is uncertain whether this encomium initiated a new, or reflec-ted an existing, friendship, but in November 1851 Jane was married to the book's author. The marriage was timely. She had been left orphaned by the death of her mother at the beginning of the year, and life for an unmarried woman in the middle years of the nineteenth century was still fraught with practical problems. Her relatives certainly were relieved to see her settled.

Speranza had once joked that 'genius should never wed'. And it was a stricture that might apply as much to her husband as to herself. Nevertheless, they both strove to accommodate themselves to their new state. They shared a pleasure in socializing and entertaining. Literary production was not abandoned. William, while working on his analysis of the 1851 census returns, also published *Irish Popular Superstitions* (dedicated 'to Speranza') and an important textbook on aural surgery, which helped establish the speciality of 'otology' (the branch of medicine relating to the diseases of the middle ear and mastoid). Jane continued her translation work with a version of Dumas *père*'s *Glacier Land*, before embarking on a new edition – if not a new translation – of Swedenborg's *The Future Life*.

Some adjustment, though, was of course necessary. William Wilde was not an easy man. He had, as Jane confided to a friend, 'a strange, nervous, hypochondriacal *home nature* which the world never sees – only I and often it makes me miserable, for I do not know how to deal with fantastic evils though I could bear up grandly against a real calamity... My husband so brilliant to the world envelops himself... in a black pall and is grave, stern, mournful and silent as the grave itself... And yet the next hour if any excitement arouses him he will throw himself into the rush of life as if life were eternal here. His whole existence is one of unceasing mental activity.'[23] But his brilliance excused much, and brought other rewards.

In 1853 he was appointed 'surgeon oculist-in-ordinary to the Queen in Ireland', and besides his own flourishing practice, he took on a lucrative role as medical advisor to the Victoria Assurance Company.[24]

The Wildes' first child, a son, was born on 26 September 1852. Although known as Willie almost from the first, he was christened William Charles Kingsbury (Wills) Wilde (Charles had been the name of Jane's father; Kingsbury her mother's maiden name). Another son arrived just thirteen months later: the 'young pagan' Oscar, his string of names providing a suitably Irish counterbalance to the Anglocentric designations of his older brother.

Jane embraced the cares of motherhood with self-dramatizing irony and enthusiasm. As she apostrophized to a friend, soon after Willie's birth, 'Oh Patriotism, on Glory, Freedom, Conquest, the rush, the strife, the battle and the Crown, ye Eidolons of my youth, where are you? Was I nobler then? Perhaps so, but the present is the truer life. A mere woman, nothing more. Such I am now... How many lives we live in life!... as someone said seeing me over little saucepans in the nursery, "Alas! the Fates are cruel / Behold Speranza making gruel!"... Well, I will rear Him a Hero perhaps the President of the future Irish Republic. *Chi sa*? I have not fulfilled my destiny yet. Gruel and the nursery cannot end me.'[25]

When Oscar was barely a year old, the Wildes moved the short distance from Westland Row to 1 Merrion Square. Although literally just around the corner, the new address marked a definite upward shift in both status and scale. The square, with its generously proportioned houses and large central garden, had been built in the 1760s as a fashionable Dublin enclave for the country's great landowning families. But, with the Acts of Union in 1800 marking the demise of the old Irish Parliament, many of these Anglo-Irish aristocrats found it more desirable to have their town houses in London, close the seat of real political power. Over the following decades the large Merrion Square houses became, instead, the preserve of Dublin's successful professional men – a home-grown aristocracy of talent and wit. With William's ever-growing practice and Jane's vivid sense of self-worth the square seemed an entirely appropriate setting for the unfolding drama of Wilde family life. Jane was thrilled: 'This move is very much to my fancy,' she declared complacently. 'We have got fine rooms and the best situation in Dublin.'

Number 1 certainly was impressive. Standing on the northwest corner of the square, it was larger than the other houses, augmented along its

Merrion Street flank by a two-storey addition, comprising the front door and a stone-flagged hallway on the ground floor, with, above it, a light-filled conservatory and a room in which Dr Wilde could see his patients. A door and staircase at the rear of the building gave separate access to this consulting room, while there was a larger room on the ground floor, at the back, where William could carry out operations. The principal rooms of the house were 'fine' indeed – high-ceilinged, with delicate mouldings and marble fireplaces, and with views across the square at the front. The Wildes filled them with books and pictures. There were Turkey carpets laid on the broad Irish-oak floorboards. A bust of Charles Maturin was one of the adornments of the ground-floor library. Six live-in servants were required to run the new establishment, their quarters confined to the basement. The nursery was at the top of the house.

Here were installed the two boys. Jane hoped they would 'flourish' in their commodious new environment, and they did. Willie, in his mother's words, was becoming 'slight, tall and *spirituelle* looking with large beautiful eyes full of expression', while the one-year-old Oscar was 'a great stout creature who minds nothing but growing fat'.[26] Jane was a devoted mother. Much of the passion and exalted vision that she had for the 'Fatherland' was converted into love and exalted vision for her children. William Wilde also took an active share of parenthood, despite both his professional cares and the huge project he had taken on to catalogue the collection of the RIA.[27] A fresh excitement enlivened the house in April 1857 when Jane gave birth to another child: a much-longed-for daughter, christened Isola Francesca Emily. She at once became the pet of the family.

There are occasional glimpses of the infant Oscar. A sense of self, and of self-dramatization, seem to have come to him early. One visitor recalled the two-year-old boy entertaining a group of guests in the Merrion Square drawing room, by repeatedly declaiming his own euphonious name: 'Oscar, Fingal, O'Flahertie, Wilde... Oscar, Fingal, O'Flahertie, Wilde.'[28] A photograph survives of him at this time, stout, assured, and dressed – according to the custom of the age – in a splendid dress of blue velvet.[29] There was, however, nothing girlish in his manner. The young Swedish writer Lotten von Kraemer, who visited Merrion Square in August 1857, accompanied by her father, the governor of Uppsala, considered him a 'little brown-eyed wildcat'. She recalled William Wilde coming into the room, leading the 'golden haired' Willie by the hand, and carrying Oscar – 'a small unruly boy' – upon his arm. The young brothers were already part of the bustling

life of the house. The Kraemers, when they attended an informal dinner that Sunday, were amazed to find the boys still up and about; and having kissed their father goodnight, they were charged with fetching a book from the library.[30]

By the following year both Oscar and Willie were, in their mother's partial estimation, growing 'tall and wise'. In the same letter Jane remarked of the ten-month-old Isola, 'she has blue eyes and promises to have an acute intellect – those two gifts are enough for any woman'.[31] Exaggeration, romance and the life of the mind were all part of atmosphere at Merrion Square. And so was literature. Jane read to her children from the first, and poetry in particular. As they leaned their heads against her, she unfolded the enchantments of Tennyson's 'The Lady Clare' and Longfellow's *Hiawatha*.[32] Poe's 'The Raven' was another of her favourites.[33] She also introduced her sons to the rich heritage of Irish verse, from the misty grandeur of 'Ossian' and the melancholy lyrics of Tom Moore to the stirring nationalist ballads by Thomas Davis, Denis Florence MacCarthy and, indeed, herself (of his mother's poems, Oscar's favourite was the ballad of the Sheares brothers).[34] And it was from his mother's reading that he began to perceive both the music and the magic of words.

Family life was full of affection, encouragement and caresses. Lotten von Kraemer noted how William Wilde's eyes rested upon his children 'with pleasure', and how he stroked Oscar's hair before sending him on his way.[35] When Jane travelled to London, she carried with her the memory of the boys' 'quick kiss and warm hug at parting'.[36] Her trip to the English capital, however, had been to find a trained nursery governess for the children. And with the arrival of this new helper (the first of a succession), together with the medical qualification of William Wilde's illegitimate son Henry Wilson, travel became a possibility for the Wilde parents. Inspired by their growing friendship with the Kraemers, they made regular trips to Sweden and Scandinavia over the coming years, leaving the children behind in the care of servants.[37]

But there were also holidays *en famille*, to villages and resorts near Dublin, or to 'the grand wild scenery' of Connemara, in the far west, where William had built a little fishing lodge, set – as Jane put it – 'on the edge the Atlantic'.[38]* Dr Wilde's enthusiasm for building increased with the years.

---

* The house stood (and still stands) beside Loch Fee, on the small peninsula of Illaunroe, meaning the 'red island'. William Wilde was very proud of the sash windows, which he

In 1861 he designed and built a terrace of four 'very handsome' houses at Bray, the favoured seaside retreat near Dublin; three were to be let, and one used by the family.[39]

Over one holiday, spent at the lovely village of Enniskerry at the foot of Glencree (perhaps in 1860 or 1861, before the completion of the Bray houses), Jane befriended Fr Lawrence Prideaux Fox, one of the Oblates of the Immaculate Heart charged with running the nearby – and recently established – St Kevin's Reformatory. He was an energetic and entertaining man, with literary and artistic interests: he knew Charles Dickens and Cardinal Newman, and was renowned for his 'talent as a decorator': at Inchicore, the oblate foundation on the outskirts of Dublin where he was based, he had originated a celebrated 'crib'.[40] During that Glencree vacation he and Speranza 'enjoyed many a pleasant hour' of conversation.

Religion was a subject much in her thoughts. She was working on a translation of the controversial German romance *Eritis Sicut Deus* ('You shall be as God'). The book – which had first appeared anonymously in 1854 – dramatized the crisis of faith, and the response to it of German philosophy, through the story of Robert and his beautiful wife, Elizabeth. The former renounces God in favour of a self-created aesthetic creed of art-worship and sensual indulgence, only to encounter despair; the latter briefly follows him down this path, but, having been brought to the brink of madness, recovers her faith – and with it, her sanity, and her happiness.[41] Although Jane herself had (as her son later described it) 'a very strong faith in that aspect of God we call the Holy Ghost', she was impatient of all religious dogma, and particularly of 'any notion of priest and sacrament standing between her and God'.[42] Nevertheless she maintained an aesthetic appreciation of many aspects of Catholic worship. In an article written for the *Dublin University Magazine* in 1850 she had praised the contemporary Catholic Church in Ireland for its inspired patronage of the arts, noting that 'Catholicism alone has comprehended the truth that Art is one of the noblest languages of religion'.[43]

During the Glencree holiday she took the children to services at the small Gothic-revival church next to the reformatory. There was a tribune that allowed visitors to attend without coming into contact with the reformatory

---

had installed, claiming they were 'the only sash-windows in Connemara'. When, however, he came to show them off to a visiting friend, 'he found that they would neither open nor shut'.

inmates. Fr Fox recalled that it was not long before she asked him to instruct Oscar and his brother: 'After a few weeks I baptised these two children, Lady Wilde herself being present on the occasion.' The priest subsequently called on William Wilde to tell him what had been done. The doctor, who was 'bitterly opposed to reformatories' as a means of dealing with the numerous boys convicted for petty crimes in the troubled aftermath of the famine, had never been particularly easy with Fr Fox, but in this instance he merely remarked that he did not care what his sons 'became so long as they became as good as their Mother'.[44] Oscar retained a memory of this second christening, but it was not backed up with any further Catholic teaching or contact during his childhood.[45]

Other spiritual forces impressed him rather more. He vividly recalled being awakened one night by a series of piercing shrieks. He thought it was a dog in pain. The next day, however, news arrived that a relative had died, and he was told that the cries of the night before must have been those of the Banshee – the fairy harbinger of death.[46] Irish lore and legend were always part of the family's shared imaginary world, and they became more so when in 1862 William Wilde bought 170 acres of land along the shore of Lough Corrib close to the little town of Cong, in Co. Mayo, in the far west. The land had special meaning for him, having once belonged to his maternal Fynn relatives. But it was also – he believed – the site of the legendary battle of Moytura (Magh-Tura) where the two ancient Celtic peoples of Ireland, the Dananns and the Firbolgs, had fought for supremacy. He began work on a handsome dwelling there, to be called 'Moytura House'. Set in 'a picturesque situation' looking over the lough, the two-storey building, whitewashed and steep gabled, would become a second home for the family. It had spacious rooms in which to entertain. There was a rose garden with a sundial, and a walled kitchen garden filled with fruit trees.*

In days spent playing together, Oscar developed a happy 'boyish comradeship' with his older brother – a relationship smoothed and lightened by Oscar's conciliatory nature.[47] At one juncture he even gave Willie his favourite teddy bear: 'Whenever afterwards I got angry with him,' he later explained, 'I used to threaten him with an "I shall take back my bear, Willie."' It was a saying that retained a currency between the brothers well beyond the end of their childhood.[48] But, though he was ready to accommodate himself

---

* Although William Wilde was pleased with his mansion, some considered it 'so singular in its construction' that it was dubbed by the Dublin wits 'Wilde's eye-sore'.

to others, Oscar's individuality of outlook was also becoming apparent. On one Connemara holiday he ran away from the family and hid in a cave.[49] On another occasion – at Merrion Square – he and Willie were having their evening bath in front of the fire in the nursery, their little nightshirts hanging to warm on the fender. While the nurse was momentarily out of the room, the boys noticed a brown spot appear on one of the shirts. It deepened slowly and then burst into flame. While Willie shouted for the nurse to come to the rescue, Oscar clapped his hands in delight at the conflagration. And when the nurse rushed in, snatched the flaming garment from the fender and pushed it into the fire, Oscar 'cried with rage at the spoiling of the pageant and the end of the fun'. This, he would later explain, revealed something of the difference between him and Willie.[50]

Oscar and his brother began their educations at home. A succession of governesses, usually foreign, introduced them at least to both French and German.[51] But they learnt rather more at the parental board. The Merrion Square house was often filled with interesting people and interesting talk; and – as the Kraemers noticed – the young Wilde children were excluded from little of it.

The social gatherings chez Wilde, lit by the energy and charisma of the host and hostess, overflowed with intellectual merriment and wit. There were regular Saturday dinner parties for what Jane described 'ten or twelve clever men': they would dine at half past six and part at eleven.[52] Sometimes the meal would be followed by poetry or music. The company would include not only 'the brilliant genius of Ireland' (the leading literary, scientific and antiquarian lights of Dublin), but also 'celebrities of Europe and America'.[53] The 'earliest hero' of Oscar's childhood was the 'tall and stately' Smith O'Brien – one-time leader of the Young Ireland movement – who became a regular visitor, having returned to Dublin from exile in Tasmania.[54] In the summer of 1861, when Dublin hosted the annual meeting of the National Association, the Wildes kept open house for the Swedish contingent, giving a series of happy informal dinners at which Irish and Scandinavian delegates could meet and talk 'merrily, freely and easily'.[55]

For many foreign visitors the conversation at Merrion Square was a revelation. Lotten von Kraemer recalled that her first dinner seated beside Dr Wilde gave her 'an idea of what English "table talk" really must be. So very striking was his easy and humorous way of entertainment.'[56] The adjective 'English' was ill-chosen. The ease and humour of Merrion Square discourse was distinctly Irish. Even among men of science, facts were never allowed

to dominate diversion. Dr William Stokes, William Wilde's great friend and mentor (who lived in the square at No. 5), pronounced it as 'the golden rule of conversation, *to know nothing accurately*'.[57] Many things, though, were known with assumed inaccuracy. Conversation ranged across 'all the current topics and literature and science of the day'.[58] Ideas were taken up, played with and discarded. Nothing was sacred: at the Wilde's table 'every creed' was both 'defended and demolished'. And Oscar, while still a young boy, heard it all. He came to consider 'that the best of his education in boyhood was obtained from this association with his father and mother and their remarkable friends'.[59]

If Oscar was aware of his parents' brilliance, he was also conscious of their rising social prestige. The purchase of the Moytura estate had made his father a landowner. And at the beginning of 1864 there was a further advance when William Wilde received his knighthood. According to the citation, the award was given less in consideration of his European-wide medical reputation, than in recognition of his services 'to statistical science... in connection with the Irish census'. If Dr Wilde was gratified to become 'Sir William', his wife was even more delighted to be transformed into 'Lady Wilde'. She found no difficulty in accommodating her National-ist sentiments to the glory of royal recognition. Oscar's pleasure in this development, however, took place at one remove. He was away from home.

2

A Fair Scholar

'Knowledge came to me through pleasure.'

A t the end January 1864 Oscar and his brother were sent away to school, leaving the six-year-old Isola at home.[1] It was an escape from the nursery and the rule of governesses. The Portora Royal School at Enniskillen in Co. Fermanagh, 100 miles north of Dublin, was an ancient foundation, established in 1608 by James I for the education of the town's recently transplanted Scotch Presbyterian population. It had, however, during the course of the nineteenth century, transformed itself into a far more outward-looking institution. And, under the enlightened stewardship of Rev. William Steele (beginning in 1857), it emerged as a small but flourishing – and academically renowned – 'public school'. The position of Enniskillen at the heart of the expanding Irish railway network made it a convenient location. Boarding pupils arrived from across the country, the sons of colonial officials, Irish gentry, established clergy and professional men.[2]

The Wildes had connections with Portora (the art master, William 'Bully' Wakeman, was a friend of the family, and had provided some illustrations for Sir William's book on the Boyne), but the reputation of the place, both academic and social – it was known to some as 'the Eton of Ireland' – would have been quite enough to commend it. The school was handsomely

housed in a fine Georgian mansion on the top of the hill outside the town, with beautiful views out over Lower Lough Erne. When the Wilde brothers arrived, they were among 175 pupils: 112 boarders and 63 dayboys. The boys, ranging in age from ten (according to the prospectus) to seventeen, were divided into distinct lower and upper schools.[3]

The headmaster, Dr Steele, was a remarkable man: intellectually distinguished, liberal-minded, frank, even noble (he encouraged Catholics to attend the school, though few came). Aged forty-four in 1864, he had still a 'lithe, vigorous frame', a quick step and an eye that 'gleamed with energy and bright intelligence'.[4] And he stood at the heart of the life of his school. He took morning prayers and roll call.[5] He was 'almost always present at the boys' dinner, which he himself carved'.[6] He managed – as one of Oscar's contemporaries recorded – to achieve 'the happy mean' between being too distant and being too familiar 'in his constant association with the boys, and the many unobtrusive ways by which he showed his interest and watchfulness in what was going on among them'.[7] As he made his rounds, his approach was usually heralded 'by the vigorous shaking of a large bunch of keys, which he held in outstretched hand', so that all had timely warning of his proximity.[8] He treated the boys (and, indeed, the masters) 'as if they were gentlemen' – and hoped that, as a result, they would behave as such. On the whole they did.[9]

Steele considered that classics and mathematics provided the best basis for the education of the young. Other subjects should certainly be taught – English, French, history and geography – but they were of lesser importance in the curriculum. To learn French properly, he believed, it was really necessary 'to go to France', while 'at the age when boys are at school, they are not capable of receiving a philosophic knowledge of history or geography'.[10] Steele himself was an excellent preceptor, with a real love of the classics. Anxious to have the boys 'well grounded in first principles', he mainly taught Latin and Greek in the lower school.[11] He was a firm believer, too, in the virtues of examinations and prizes – and he instituted a popular annual midsummer prize-giving and sports day, a gala end to the first half of each year. There were only two terms – or 'halves' – in each school year, one running from the end of January to the middle of June, the other from late August to late December.[12]

It was not, however, just energy and imagination that Steele poured into the school. He also expended his own money on improving the place. Impatient with the bureaucracy of the school board, and needing additional

accommodation for the ever-growing number of boarders, he filled in the spaces between the original house and its two free-standing wings (creating the so-called 'Stone Hall' and 'Master's Hall'). He built a sanatorium, and modernized the school's plumbing. In 1864 he was planning an ambitious new scheme: a spacious hall to accommodate the entire lower school, with three dedicated classrooms underneath.[13]

Steele appreciated the school's splendid setting, and devoted care to 'the beautifying of the grounds'.[14] The lough – a vast stretch of water running some twenty-five miles from Enniskillen to Belleek – was also a great asset. It provided a focus for recreation and sport, for swimming and rowing. Boys could take out boats to explore the islands. And rowing races became a feature of the school sports days. There were other organized games – football, athletics, racquet sports, cricket (on a newly laid-down cricket pitch) – as Steele embraced the new post-Arnoldian public school ethos.

The ethos, whatever its general benefits, was not one that the newly arrived Oscar Wilde found immediately congenial. At nine years old he was almost a full year younger than the designated entrance age. And there was little in his character that suited him to the rough and tumble of boarding-school life: slight, imaginative, independent and dreamy, he drifted to the edge of things. He made no firm friends. Games – the great motor of schoolboy existence – held no interest for him ('I never liked to kick or be kicked,' he claimed).[15] Work, too, at first failed to engage his energies. He distinguished himself mainly by being hopeless at mathematics.[16]

Willie, by contrast, thrived. Good at lessons, fond of games, sociable, boisterous, kind-hearted, he began at once to establish a position and a reputation among both his peers and his masters. He secured a lower school prize at the end of his first half – although, that year, the prize day, at which he would have received his award, had to be cancelled at short notice following the tragic drowning of two pupils in a boating accident on the lough. The incident was the first of a succession of painful dramas that would punctuate Oscar and Willie's schooldays.

The closing weeks of the Christmas half brought the second such blow: the lurid pantomime of the Mary Travers case. Even at Portora the brothers would have felt the reverberations. The Dublin press was readily available in Enniskillen, and the town's three local papers also carried full details of the court proceedings together with much disparaging comment.[17] The case offered a rich subject for discussion to both pupils and staff. Nevertheless, the relative youth of the Wilde boys (Oscar just ten, Willie barely twelve),

as well as the almost immediate arrival of the Christmas holidays, probably preserved them from too much prurient ribbing from their schoolfellows.

At home that Christmas they would have been bolstered by the parental line on the debacle – that it was a 'disagreeable' incident now mercifully passed. Lady Wilde wrote to her Swedish friend, Rosalie Olivecrona:

> The simple solution of the affair is this – that Miss Travers is half mad – all her family are mad too… It was very annoying but of course no one believed her story – all Dublin now calls on us to offer their sympathy and all the medical profession here and in London have sent letters expressing their entire disbelief of the, in fact, impossible charge. Sir Wm. will not be injured by it and the best proof is that his professional hours never were so occupied as now. We were more anxious about our dear foreign friends who could only hear through the English papers which are generally very sneering on Irish matters – but happily all is over now and our enemy has been signally defeated in her efforts to injure us.[18]

The papers – both popular and medical – while lamenting the whole 'melancholy transaction', had indeed been broadly supportive.[19] They condemned the 'demoniacal' Miss Travers for her 'scandalous, unwomanly, vulgar and degrading' conduct, while saluting Sir William's professional eminence and his wife's injured dignity. The few public voices of dissent (led by the ophthalmologist Arthur Jacob in the *Dublin Medical Press*) could be put down to professional rivalry.[20] Private reactions were more varied. Not quite 'all Dublin' did side with the Wildes. There were a good many who enjoyed the discomfort of so conspicuous a pair. Tall poppies were there to be cut down. To unsympathetic viewers the case confirmed that 'Sir William Wilde was a pithecoid [ape-like] person of extraordinary sensuality and cowardice [for "funking" the witness box] and that his wife was a highfalutin' pretentious creature whose pride was as extravagant as her reputation founded on second-rate verse-making.'[21] For others the debacle simply provided an opportunity for humour and chaff. The students of Trinity College Dublin delighted in the details of the case; one undergraduate ditty began:

> An eminent oculist lives in the Square,
> His skill is unrivalled, his talent is rare,

And if you will listen I'll certainly try
To tell how he opened Miss Travers's eye.[22]

But any sense of embarrassment was to be outfaced. Dublin society was not large enough to allow for escape (the Wildes continued to meet Isaac Butt on what appear to have been terms of friendship, or at least civility).[23] The family still had many friends and admirers. There was much sympathy for Speranza.[24] And as for Sir William – whatever the exact truth of the matter – there were many men in his circle who were reluctant to condemn him for such peccadillos. Dublin retained something of its permissive eighteenth-century air, and was little inclined to moral censure. Sir William's practice continued to prosper, which was just as well since he was faced with the vexing business of raising the legal costs.

It had been a bruising episode for the whole family, but Oscar and Willie were able to return to school at the beginning of 1865 with at least some feeling of reassurance – and some sense that their privileged place in the world remained secure.* Portora provided distraction from the cares of home. The boys enjoyed it in different ways. Willie's enthusiastic engagement with the details of school life seemed to license his younger brother's more detached stance. Little interested in lessons, Oscar escaped into his own books, and his own thoughts. It was said of him that he got 'quicker into a book than any boy that ever lived'.[25] Literature gave him a realm over which he could hold sway: from his earliest childhood, he recalled, 'I used to identify myself with every distinguished character I read about'.[26] Oscar's intelligence, nevertheless, did make itself known. In the summer of 1866 he was awarded a lower school classics prize (Willie, as in the two previous years, also gained one – together, on this occasion, with Mr Robinson's special 'prize in classics' and a drawing prize).

---

*   Oscar's understanding of the case – as he later described it – was that his mother had behaved with 'extraordinary' nobility throughout the proceedings, giving her testimony with a 'perfect serenity' devoid of all 'common womanly jealousy' that convinced the jury that her father must be 'guiltless' of any improper association. It had been hoped that, following the trial, Miss Travers would 'emigrate to some near relative in a distant colony'. But she remained in Dublin, and that June (1865), sued *Saunders's News-Letter* for suggesting that she had 'concocted' her 'infamous story' about Sir William Wilde. On this occasion, though she was again defended by Isaac Butt, the jury found against her, leaving her to pay costs. It was her last legal adventure, and the last time she annoyed the Wildes. She seems to have remained in Ireland, dying in 1919, aged eighty-three, in a home for decayed gentlewomen at Normanstown, Co. Meath.

Away from school, the long summer holidays were spent largely at Moytura. The house offered the family a retreat from Dublin life – and Dublin gossip. The place became Sir William's great passion. It was there that Oscar, under his father's instruction, learnt to be not merely an Irishman but a countryman and a Celt.* He became imbued with the 'wild magnificent beauty' of the western landscape, its bare hills and changing skies. The 'intensity of nature' on such a scale impressed him.[27] There was boating on Lough Corrib. Oscar learnt to fish for the 'great melancholy carp' that never moved from the bottom of the lake, unless lured from the depths by the magic of Gaelic song. Oscar – though he does not seem to have progressed far in the old Irish language – always retained a memory of one of these airs, with its mournful opening, *Athá mé in mu codladh, agus ná dúishe mé* ('I am asleep, and do not wake me').[28] He learnt to shoot. And he came to know some of the neighbouring landowning families who had children of his own age: the Martins at Ross House and the Moores of Moore Hall. Oscar and Willie, as they grew into their teens, would sometimes row up the lough to Carra to spend the day at Moore Hall. Old Mr Moore was greatly impressed by them, thinking his own four sons 'dunces' in comparison.[29]

Oscar's developing imagination was stimulated, too, by exploring the ancient Celtic remains in the locality. He and Willie assisted their father with the book he was preparing on the area's history and antiquities – 'taking rubbings and measurements' of archaeological sites – as well as listening to mythic tales about the days of yore.[30] Sir William's 'passion for the past' was supported by that rare gift 'which converts a piece of stone into a text for a glowing romance'. Rambling across the countryside with Oscar and Willie, he would linger happily over some 'piece of antiquity, filled with the actual delight of building up pictures of the past and its departed glories'.[31] All around were scenes of ancient heroism, where Nuada, king of the Dananns, had led his victorious forces against the Firbolgs. This was a world – both historic and ethnological – that the young Oscar readily adopted as part of his own identity. From his father he learnt to see himself as an heir to the 'bold, honourable, daring' and 'intellectually superior' Danann Celts. It was a rich inheritance, given William Wilde's belief (shared by

---

*   When Lady Wilde had published her collected verses – *Poems by Speranza* – at the end of 1864, it was dedicated to 'My Sons, Willie and Oscar Wilde' with the epigraph: 'I made them indeed, / Speak plain the word COUNTRY. I taught them, no doubt, / That a country's a thing men should die for at need!'

many of his antiquarian fellows) that these Celts came of the same stock as the ancient Greeks, and shared many of their exalted characteristics. Lady Wilde was delighted to suppose that the Celts held in common with the Greeks a love of 'glory, beauty and distinction' – and that, like the Greeks, they hated 'toil' and despised 'trade': for both peoples the 'highest honours were given to learning and poetry'.[32]

Ireland's medieval past was also much in evidence at Moytura, and offered its own stimulus to the imagination. When, during the summer of 1866, Oscar and his father came across a curious stone-built ruin at Inishmain near Lough Mask, Sir William persuaded himself that it must have been the 'penitentiary' for the nearby abbey. An image of it – drawn by Mr Wakeman – was duly published in his book, together with a gratifying caption explaining that the structure had been discovered 'by the author and his son Oscar'.[33]

But, whatever the excitements of the past, the cares of the present always threatened to break in: 1866 ended with the sad death – by drowning – of Dr Steele's eldest son, Frederick, another victim of the cold waters of Lough Erne. A highly promising classicist, he had just won a scholarship from Portora to Trinity College Dublin. His death cast a pall over the school. For Oscar, though, this tragedy was soon eclipsed by an even greater one. On 23 February 1867 his sister, Isola, died suddenly. Recovering from a brief bout of fever, she had been sent to recuperate at Edgeworthstown, some 65 miles west of Dublin, where her uncle, Rev. William Noble (married to Sir William's sister), was rector. Her condition, however, had worsened and, following 'a sudden effusion on the brain', she died. She was just nine years old.

It was a devastating blow. Isola had been a remarkable little girl. The doctor who attended her at Edgeworthstown Rectory thought her 'the most gifted and loveable child' that he had ever seen.[34] Sir William was 'crushed by sorrow' at her death. She had been his idol.[35] 'Isola was the radiant angel of our home,' Lady Wilde lamented to Lotten von Kraemer, 'and so bright and strong and joyous. We never dreamed the word *death* was meant for her.'[36] During her brief life she had become the happy pivot around which so many familial relationships turned. That dynamic was destroyed.

There seems to have existed a special bond between the twelve-year-old Oscar and his young sister.[37] She had offered him, perhaps, a more sympathetic companionship than the prosaic Willie. He spoke of her as 'embodied

sunshine', a 'wonderful creature, so gay and high spirited'. Certainly he was
'inconsolable' at her loss. Taken to Edgeworthstown (maybe for the funeral)
his lonely grief sought vent 'in long and frequent visits' to her grave in the
village cemetery. He carefully preserved a lock of 'My Isola's hair', decorating
the envelope in which it was held with elaborate images of love, hope and
redemption: linked initials, radiant crosses, lettered scrolls, laurel wreaths,
a jewelled crown. Nor was pictorial art the only way in which he strove
to express his emotion. He found solace, too, in verse, producing several
'touching, albeit boyish, poetic effusions'. They were a first hint that Oscar
might be a 'votary of the Muses'.[38]

The Edgeworthstown doctor was struck by the intensity of Oscar's feeling. He was impressed too by the boy's intelligence. As he later recalled,
he instituted 'in conversation with his uncle, a comparison between [Oscar]
and his elder brother, Willie, a very clever lad, and our assigning the meed
of superiority in mental depth to "Ossie".' It was a shrewd observation, for
in the conventional sphere of school life Willie continued to dominate. He
was, again, a serial award winner at the 1867 prize day, while Oscar received
only a single 'highly commended'.[39] Dr Steele would frequently hold Willie
up as an example to his younger brother.[40] Oscar, however, was becoming
increasingly sure of his own developing mental powers. His mother too,
always on the alert for excellence, seems to have recognized their special
force. When quizzed by a friend about her two schoolboy sons, she is
reported to have said, 'Oh, Willie is all right, but as for Oscar, he will turn
out something wonderful.'[41]

She had a chance to assess the boys at close quarters during the summer
holidays of 1867, when she took them over to France for three weeks (Sir
William remained at Moytura). It was a release from the sadness of life
at home, and, for Oscar, a thrilling introduction to a new country and a
new culture. From that first encounter, so he later claimed, he became
'passionately fond of the French character' – a character, he liked to believe,
'having some kinship with that peculiar to the Irish nation'.[42] The little
party visited Paris, then the most exciting city in the world. An *Exposition
Universelle* was in full swing, housed in a vast temporary 'palais' on the
Champs de Mars, surrounded by amusement parks and pleasure gardens.
Among the displays of scientific invention, mechanical innovation and
cultural diversity there was a Swedish peasant village, some Chinese violin
players, a promotion for Steinway pianos and a revelatory exhibition of
Japanese art. The family returned home lit up by the experience, and with

a distinct sense that, beside the brilliance of Paris, Dublin might be only 'a little provincial town'.[43]

Almost from the moment of their return, the pace of Oscar's progress seemed to quicken. Although there is no evidence that the visit had a beneficial effect on his French, his thorough mastery of the rudiments of Latin and Greek was confirmed when his career in the lower school closed with him winning three classics prizes at the 1868 prize day.[44] He also gained an award for drawing.

Oscar arrived in the upper school as a very young looking thirteen-year-old. To one contemporary – who entered Portora at that time – 'he was then, as he remained for some years after, extremely boyish in nature, very mobile, almost restless when out of the school-room'. Almost everything, though, about the teenage Oscar carried some suggestion of his growing sense of self, of style and of humour. All three qualities are discernible – beneath the schoolboy concerns and erratic punctuation – in the illustrated letter he sent his mother on 5 September 1868 (the first of his letters to survive, and the only one from his schooldays):

DARLING MAMA,

The hamper came today, I never got such a jolly surprise, many thanks for it, it was more than kind of you to think of it. The grapes and pears are delicious and so cooling, but the blancmange got a little sour, I suppose by the knocking about, but the rest came all safe.

Don't forget please to send me the *National Review*, is it not issued today?

The flannel shirts you sent in the hamper are both Willie's, mine are one quite scarlet and the other lilac, but it is too early to wear them yet, the weather is so hot.

We went down to the *horrid* regatta on Thursday last. It was very jolly. There was a yacht race.

You never told me anything about the publisher in Glasgow. What does he say and have you written to Aunt Warren on the green note paper?

We played the officers of the 27th Regiment now stationed in Enniskillen a few days ago and beat them hollow by about seventy runs.

You may imagine my delight this morning when I got Papa's letter saying he had sent a hamper.

Now dear Mamma, I must bid you goodbye as the post goes very soon.

Many thanks for letting me paint. With love to Papa, ever your affectionate son,

OSCAR WILDE.

He gives signs of a dandified assurance in his discrimination over his own 'quite scarlet' and lilac shirts, and reveals an artistic concern at being allowed to continue his painting lessons. There is a neat paradoxical turn in the '*horrid*' regatta having been so 'very jolly', a subversive mischief in his hope that 'Aunt Warren' (his mother's ultra-conventional sister, Emily Thomasine Warren, wife of an officer in the British army) might have received a letter on Nationalist-tinged green notepaper; and a playful cod-melodrama in his vision of 'ye hamperless boy'.

Oscar allied himself with his 'darling' mama's interests, both literary and patriotic. The *National Review*, which he hoped to receive, was a new Dublin-based periodical that had published her verse 'To Ireland' in the previous number; the poem would be used as the 'dedication' in a new edition of her collected poetry produced by Cameron and Ferguson, the Glasgow publishers he mentions.[45] More than this, though, he accepted his mother's whole vision of the world: grand, extravagant and bright with possibility. He accepted (and always retained) her vision of herself as 'one of the great figures of the world' and her vision of himself as 'something wonderful'.[46] All his letters to her from school, it seems, reflected elements of this shared understanding. Certainly Lady Wilde loved the promise that they showed – recalling them as 'wonderful and often real literature'.[47] They were, however, a private performance.

Willie remained always the larger public presence. Two years above Oscar, he had grown into 'something of a character' – 'clever, erratic and full of vitality'.[48] He was steeped in the life of the school. Although he took only a modest part in games, he knew all about football and cricket.[49] He may not have been a systematic scholar, but he was still a good one. He was approved of by the masters and liked by his schoolfellows. He made a point of being 'kind and friendly with the younger boys'. He played the piano, with real feeling – and tolerable accuracy – and would entertain the juniors with impromptu recitals. He told a good story. There was a pleasant air of Falstaffian absurdity about him: he was apt to be boastful and prone to be teased about it.[50] His nickname was 'Blue Blood'. He had – together with Oscar – inherited his father's swarthy open-pored complexion; and on account of it, was, like his father, often considered to look 'dirty'. On one

occasion, defending himself from this charge, he had claimed that he only looked grubby because – as an O'Flahertie and thus a descendant of the kings of Connaught – his blood was blue, rather than red.[51]

The two brothers maintained a cordial distance. School life did not bring them together. Willie treated Oscar 'always... as a younger brother'.[52] But Oscar – quietly confident of his own powers – refused to be patronized.[53] Although the headmaster might frequently hold Willie up to him as an example, Oscar was unimpressed. He merely smiled. As he recalled, 'I never for a moment regarded [Willie] as my equal in any intellectual field... and in my own opinion always went about "crowned".'[54]

Oscar began to cultivate a certain sense of refined singularity. 'I always wanted everything about me to be distinctive', he claimed.[55] His look – having been distinctly scruffy – became distinctly smart.[56] He grew 'more careful in his dress than any other boy'.[57] The lilac shirt was only one element in the campaign. He took to wearing his Sunday hat throughout the week.[58] His hair – 'long, straight, fair' and swept back from his forehead – proclaimed a determined otherness.[59] Indeed his hair length, perhaps more than anything, marked him out in the memory of his peers: 'he had a good wisp of hair' was still said of him in Enniskillen, some thirty years after he left the school.[60] Every aspect of school life, though, offered scope for the same sort of calculated individualism. Rather than using the conventional school textbooks, he began to affect 'handsome editions of the classics'.[61] He worked at his handwriting, in an effort to achieve a script that was 'clear and beautiful and peculiar to me'.[62]

Much of Oscar's time was still spent – when not dreaming away the hours – in reading for his own pleasure. He devoured, as he put it, 'too many English novels, and too much poetry'.[63] He read with phenomenal speed, developing a rare ability to absorb (and retain) information almost as quickly as he turned the pages.

He took in the English classics, coming to know Walter Scott, Jane Austen, Thackeray and Stevenson.[64] He read both Dickens, the great sentimental comic moralist of the age, and Disraeli, the less-regarded 'silver fork' literary and political dandy. And, in line with his desire to be 'distinctive' in all things, he declared a preference for the latter.[65] In this heresy, as in so much else, he drew encouragement from his mother. She lent him copies of Disraeli's books, and shared his delight in their 'epigrammatic style' and aristocratic settings.[66] Oscar also indulged a taste for the 'romantic' Gothic tales of Wilhelm Meinhold, reading his mother's translation of *Sidonia the*

Sorceress, and Lady Duff Gordon's version of *The Amber Witch*.[67] He developed, too, an enthusiasm for the tales of that 'lord of romance', Edgar Allan Poe, along with a reverence for 'uncle' Maturin's stupendously bizarre *Melmoth the Wanderer*.[68]

His love of poetry developed through reading Shakespeare and the English Romantics, together with his mother's great favourites, Tennyson and Elizabeth Barrett Browning. Not long after leaving school he would solemnly declare *Hamlet, In Memoriam* and Barrett Browning's verse-novel *Aurora Leigh* to be 'much the greatest work[s] in our literature'.[69] And it was probably his mother's influence, too, that gave him a precocious interest in the impassioned free verse of Walt Whitman.[70]

Oscar's immersion in literature did not shut him off from his contemporaries. Even if he was considered 'somewhat reserved and distant in his manners', he was neither unsociable nor unpopular.[71] He might have had no 'very special chums', but he was well liked and sometimes admired.[72] To those who knew him best he appeared 'generous, kindly [and, for the most part,] good tempered'.[73] He would take an occasional outing on Lough Erne, though he was a poor hand at an oar.[74] He could sometimes be induced to join in schoolboy larks – even breaking his arm while playing 'chargers' mounted on the back of a senior boy.[75] The incident marked what he called his 'first introduction to the horrors of pain, the lurking tragedies of life'. And he hated it. Physical pain, he would always assert, was 'a thousand times worse than mental suffering'.[76]

Sex seems to have played little part in Oscar's schooldays. Awareness of it came to him late: he later gave '16 as the age at which sex begins'. 'Of course,' as he explained, 'I was sensual and curious, as boys are, and had the usual boy imaginings; but I did not indulge in them excessively.'[77] In contrast to many of England's larger public schools, sex between pupils was all but unknown at Portora: 'Nine out of ten boys only thought of football or cricket or rowing. Nearly every one went in for athletics – running and jumping and so forth; no one appeared to care for sex. We were healthy young barbarians and that was all.'[78] In later life Oscar would recall the touching devotion of one junior boy – 'a couple of years younger than I' – who clearly had a schoolboy crush on him, about which Oscar – wrapped up in the drama of his own thoughts and plans – was entirely oblivious. Oscar enjoyed the boy's company because he provided an audience: 'My friend,' he explained, 'had a wonderful gift for listening.'[79] Audiences were becoming important to Oscar.

As his school career advanced, Oscar developed into, if not quite the class clown, an accomplished performer. He had more scope after Willie left for Trinity College Dublin in the autumn of 1869. At the informal gatherings around the stove in the Stone Hall on winter afternoons, Oscar was 'at his best'. He might amuse the other boys by striking 'stained-glass attitudes' – twisting his limbs into 'weird contortions' in imitation of saints and other 'holy people' (this, apparently, was also a party-trick of his father's).[80] His speed-reading offered scope for entertainment too. Often 'for a wager' he would 'read a three-volume novel in half an hour so closely as to be able to give an accurate résumé of the plot'; if allowed a whole hour, he could recount, in addition, the incidental scenes and the most pertinent dialogue.[81]

But, above all, he talked – fluently, amusingly, interestingly and well.[82] He entertained the gatherings in the Stone Hall. He amused his friends. He diverted the masters. His 'descriptive power' was 'far above the average' but his real gift was for comedy. He had a way with exaggeration that could transform even the most mundane occurrence into a vision of romance guyed by humour.[83] One of his contemporaries liked to recall an incident when he and Oscar, along with two other boys, had been in Enniskillen and had played a prank on a street orator, knocking off his hat with a stick. This jape provoked a minor outcry, and the boys had to flee the scene, back up the hill to Portora. Oscar, in the scramble to escape, had collided with an old man and knocked him over. Yet, in his vivid – and solemnly humorous – retelling of the incident, the aged cripple was transformed into 'an angry giant' barring the path, with whom Oscar had to fight 'through many rounds, and whom he eventually left for dead in the road after accomplishing prodigies of valour on his redoubtable opponent'.[84]

He developed, too, a relish for the recondite, and a penchant for the extravagant. In 1869, when reports of the prosecution for heresy of Rev. W. J. E. Bennett were filling the newspapers, and being eagerly discussed at Portora, Oscar was 'full of the mysterious nature of the Court of Arches' – the ancient ecclesiastical court at St Mary-le-Bow in London – where the case was being heard. Bennett, an extreme Anglo-Catholic ritualist, had outraged Protestant theology in a pamphlet claiming that the actual and perfect body of Christ was both present and visible in the Eucharist – and Oscar delighted in the drama of the proceedings. The reverberations of the Travers case had done nothing to put him off the law. He announced to his schoolfellows, gathered around the Stone Hall stove, that 'there was nothing he would like better in after life than to be the hero of such a

cause célèbre and to go down to posterity as the defendant in such a case as "Regina versus Wilde"!'[85]

Oscar's 'pungent wit' found expression in other ways as well. He enjoyed subverting authority, making fun of those aspects of school life that had least appeal to him: he 'never had a good word for a mathematical or science master' and the musketry instructor and drill sergeant were held in contempt[86] – though it was always admitted that 'there was nothing spiteful or malignant in anything he said against them'.[87] Only once did he overstep the mark, when he 'cheeked' the headmaster and got into 'an awful row'.[88]

He also had 'an uncanny gift for giving nicknames'. But although these 'used to stick to his victims... they did not rankle, as there was always a gaiety and no malice about them'.[89] This was an impressive and telling achievement. His own nickname was 'Grey-crow' – though its origins and relevance remain obscure. It apparently related in some way to one of the islands on Lough Erne, and perhaps connects with the comment of a contemporary, who remembered Oscar – grown, after his sixteenth birthday, suddenly 'tall for his age' and heavy – 'flop[ping] about ponderously'.[90] He, however, rather resented the name, and it was used only by those who wished to annoy him. For the most part he was called 'Oscar' – another distinction among peers more used to addressing each other by their surnames.[91] During the 1870 prize-giving, however, at which he won the prestigious Carpenter Prize for Greek Testament, his full name – 'Oscar Fingal O'Flahertie Wills Wilde' – became known, when it was read out by the headmaster, leading to much 'schoolboy chaff'.[92] The glory of the prize was, however, surely worth the teasing.

In academic terms Oscar's passage into the upper school marked a considerable advance. There had been, as was customary, a small intake of new pupils joining that year, attracted by Portora's growing reputation for excellence, and also by the chance of gaining one of the school's 'royal scholarships' to Trinity College Dublin. Among the boys entering the school in 1868 were Edward Sullivan (son of Sir Edward, the Wildes' counsel during the Travers trial) and the even more gifted Louis Claude Purser.[93] Purser, arriving from Midleton College, Cork, was amazed by the quality of the teaching at Portora – principally of classics and mathematics, but of English too, and French 'in its higher branches'. More than this, though, he found 'a far greater width of culture and diffusion of ideas' than at his previous schools. Indeed he thought the tenor of the Portora upper school 'more like a college of a university than a middle-class school'.[94]

Oscar responded well to this atmosphere, albeit in his own fashion. He developed, as Purser recalled, 'a real love for intellectual things, especially if there was a breath of poetry in them, and he often used to inveigle some of the masters (who were, I think, rather highly educated men) into spending the time usually devoted to "learning us our lessons" in giving a disquisition on some subject he would artfully suggest – for he had engaging manners when he liked – by some apparently innocent question'. On one occasion he asked 'What is a Realist?', drawing forth 'a disquisition on Realism and Nominalism and Conceptualism in which we all asked questions and which proved most illuminating'.[95]

Although Oscar always remained 'very exceptionally below the average in mathematics' (requiring frantic cramming before each set of school exams), in all the other school subjects – there being 'next to no "science" in those pre-historic days' – he did more than tolerably well. If – as Purser put it – he was 'not of outstanding general excellence among his fellow schoolboys... there was no one who could have been said to have been markedly his superior'. He gained a thorough and enduring knowledge of the Bible (both the King James version, and the Greek Testament), even winning a scripture prize in 1869.[96] Writing, though, was not, as yet, a particular forte: neither his 'English Essays' nor his 'Classical Composition' were 'exceptionally distinguished'.[97] His literary bent – and love of poetic things – seems to have found its expression away from the classroom, in humorous poems and poses.*

---

* One of these survives – the earliest of Wilde's extant poems – a ditty addressed to a Miss ffrench, whom he appears to have met at the Galway Ball.

> Does my Angelina Fancy
> That her Edwin is untrue [?]
> Does she think that he's forgetful
> Prone the "Galway Ball" to rue [?]
>
> *Canto the 2nd*
> Maiden let that foolish fancy
> Leave thy loving, trusting heart
> Never shall thy image, never!
> From this mind of mine depart
>
> *Here endeth ye 2nd Canto the Poet being too sorrowful to go on.*
> Never shall this fateful passion
> Leave this love inspired breast[.]
> Write then but a line to cheer me
> Write, if, but to give me rest[.]

Reading, though, absorbed him more. A new world of the imagination was opening up to him. As he later recalled, 'I was nearly sixteen [i.e. in 1870] when the wonder and beauty of the old Greek life began to dawn upon me. Suddenly I seemed to see the white figures throwing purple shadows on the sun-baked palaestra; "bands of nude youths and maidens... moving across a background of deep blue as on the frieze of the Parthenon." I began to read Greek eagerly for love of it all, and the more I read the more I was enthralled.'[98] As ever, he tended to identify with the subjects of his reading, and he noticed – 'with some wonder' – that it was the men of creative intellect rather than the men of military action with whom he identified most readily: 'Alcibiades or Sophocles' rather than 'Alexander or Caesar'.[99]

They were interesting exemplars. The sketch of Alcibiades in William Smith's workaday *Smaller History of Greece*, the textbook used at Portora, certainly conjured up subversive visions of transgression licensed by genius: 'From early youth the conduct of Alcibiades was marked by violence, recklessness, and vanity. He delighted in astonishing the more sober portion of the citizens by his capricious and extravagant feats. He was utterly destitute of morality, whether public or private. But his vices were partly redeemed by some brilliant qualities. He possessed both boldness of design and vigour of action.'[100]

This great enthusiasm for the world of ancient Greece – perhaps heightened by his sense of Celtic affinity with Greek culture – carried Oscar's studies forward seemingly without effort. He must have worked hard, but – as he later put it – 'knowledge came to me through pleasure, as it always comes, I imagine'.[101] His rare natural abilities at last had a subject with which to

---

No fair jewels can I give thee
No bright diamonds from the mine
Love's my offering, pure, unsullied
To a heart alas! Not mine[.]

*Here the poet's tears / Were so frequent as /
To stop his writing any more.'*

Another purported schoolboy rhyme, concerned Wilde's dislike for cricket. It began:

Never more will I play
With the soaring and gay
But cruel in its fall –
The mean old cricket ball.

engage. The progress he made was 'astounding' to both peers and masters. Even Dr Steele was impressed.[102] And Oscar himself always considered that it was during this period, 1870–1, that he 'laid the foundations' for 'whatever classical scholarship' he possessed.[103]

Oscar's particular brilliance showed itself most clearly on 'the literary side' of his studies, as distinguished from 'the scholastic'. Purser recalled 'his appreciation of the literary merits of any author that he took the trouble to study appealed strongly to him, and his remarks and criticisms thereon were always deserving of attention': but he was less interested in such features as 'grammar, textual criticism, history, "antiquities" & co.'[104] He also enjoyed the element of performance that the syllabus required. According to Edward Sullivan 'the flowing beauty of his oral translations in class' was 'a thing not easily forgotten'.[105]

Oscar's studies came to command his full attention. The life of books interested him more than real life.[106] On the summer holidays at Moytura he cut a self-absorbed figure. One visitor (the son of the local doctor) found Oscar 'very dull company', remote, unsmiling and aloof, with his thoughts doubtless engaged on 'Greek poetry'– a striking contrast to the gay, ebullient undergraduate Willie, who enjoyed a drink, and sang to his own accompaniment at the piano.[107]

Since his arrival in the upper school Oscar had been recognized as 'a fair scholar' – but in his final year at Portora he emerged as one of the leading figures in a very able classical sixth form – along with Purser, the McDowells (J. and R.) and E. Galbraith. They seem to have been a tight-knit and supportive group, enjoying their proficiency and challenging each other to extend it. They were all signatories of a joint letter to the assistant master, Rev. Benjamin Moffett, complaining at the impossibility of some test he had set them. And, as Purser recalled, the group was both surprised and impressed by Oscar's stellar performance in one part of the classical gold medal exam – 'walking easily away from us all in the *viva voce* examination on the Greek play [*The Agamemnon* of Aeschylus]'.[108] He gained 25 per cent higher marks than his nearest rival.[109] The literary quality of the great work appealed to him, and he had 'made it up thoroughly' – but 'to the neglect perhaps of other (to him less interesting) portions of the long examination'.[110]

In the event – when all the different parts of the 'long examination' were tallied up – it was Purser who came out on top. At the 1871 prize-giving he also took the Frederick Steele memorial prize medal, as well as being

first prizeman in both mathematics and holy scripture. Oscar, along with everyone else, trailed in his wake. Not that he was so very far behind: he was one of three classical prizewinners from the head class (with Galbraith and J. McDowell); he shared the assistant master's prize in ancient history (with Galbraith) and was also awarded a drawing prize for a sensitive water-colour of Lough Erne.[111] In all, it marked a hugely impressive, and very satisfying, end to his school career. He would be going on to Trinity after the summer holidays.

Dr Steele, in bidding Oscar farewell, added – perhaps from force of habit – that if he kept up his hard work, he might yet be 'as big a credit to the school as Willie'. Oscar was quietly amused.[112] Willie, though, was doing well at Trinity: he got honours in classics in his junior freshman year; and he cut a rather glamorous figure when he re-visited Portora, possibly to see Oscar's prize day triumph.[113]

Oscar's own mind was already turning towards Dublin and university life. There were exciting possibilities – scholarly, artistic and social. He ima-gined that he would have his own room in the family house at Merrion Square. He hoped the Trinity dons would be friendly, and wished that they might all be poets. He could barely wait to begin. Swept up as he was in this new enthusiasm, Portora – despite all it had given him over the previous seven years – started to fade from his mind even before he had left it. He barely registered his little friend – the junior boy who had a crush on him – who insisted on coming to see him off at the station. And he was startled when the boy planted a tearful farewell kiss on his lips, as the train pulled out, heading for Dublin and the future.[114]

3

Foundation Scholarship

'He seemed to be able to master everything he tackled.'

HORACE WILKINS

Wilde matriculated at Trinity College Dublin on 10 October 1871, six days before his seventeenth birthday. In the three-day entrance examination, which took place immediately afterwards, he secured the second-highest marks of the forty-four candidates, excelling in Greek and history, and limping through the compulsory maths paper (Purser was ranked first overall).[1] Wilde followed up this success in the subsequent 'exam for royal school exhibitions', by gaining one of Portora's 'royal scholarships', together with Purser and Robert McDowell. The names of all three were duly inscribed on the honours board back at Portora.[2]

Although Trinity marked a new era for Wilde, the college was, in many ways, a return to familiar ground. He had been born almost within its precincts, and had grown up close to its gates. Its leading lights frequented his parents' home. His father, though not an alumnus, had been awarded an honorary degree, and interested himself in the life of the place.[3] His brother, entering his third year, was a notable figure on the campus. Familiarity, however, is not perhaps what a freshman most wants at the outset of his university career.

Wilde's great hopes for his time at Trinity suffered a succession of blows. Lodging at home in Merrion Square, surrounded by art and books and adult conversation, the undergraduate life of the college registered as coarse and unsympathetic. His hopes of discovering kindred spirits were rapidly disappointed. The camaraderie of the small classical sixth form was lost. He pronounced the prevailing atmosphere 'barbaric': like school but 'with coarseness superadded'.[4] Of the thousand-plus undergraduates at Trinity, the vast majority seemed 'simply awful', 'even worse than the boys at Portora': they thought of 'nothing but cricket and football, running and jumping; and they varied these intellectual exercises with bouts of fighting and drinking'. The other new element in the equation, Oscar noted, was sex. Those students who 'had any souls... diverted them with coarse amours among barmaids and the women of the streets'.[5] Willie seems to have entered enthusiastically into this aspect of university life; he even delivered a memorable speech, at one of the college debating societies, in defence of prostitution.[6]* Oscar was not interested. A natural fastidiousness – 'a peculiar refinement of nature' – began to make itself apparent. Contemporaries noted his aversion to the 'suggestive story', and, indeed, to all gross and crude expression. He quickly gained the reputation among his peers of being 'one of the purest minded men that could be met with'.[7] Sex would come to him, like so much else, first through literature.

To his new college-mates his most conspicuous traits were his size and his clumsiness. The spurt of growth that had occurred at the end of his Portora days had continued, leaving him struggling to catch up with his new self. He was remembered as an 'ungainly, overgrown, moping, awkward lad' who was 'continually knocking things over... and at whom everybody laughed'.[8]

In the face of all this, work offered a refuge, and also the chance of distinction. His triumph in the entrance exams was soon followed by other awards.[9] Wilde's Portora training carried him a long way, but he also found himself challenged by his new academic environment. He had been

---

*   Willie's enthusiasm for sexual adventures was – like his Christian name – something that he shared with his father. This could lead to complications. One (possibly apocryphal) anecdote relates how a girl wrote to Willie at Merrion Square to say that he was responsible for her unborn child. Sir William opened the letter by mistake, and – when his son came down to breakfast – declared, 'Here is the most disgraceful letter.' To which Willie, having read the letter over, remarked gravely, 'Well, sir, what are you going to do about it.'

fortunate in his timing. The classics at Trinity were undergoing a revival – coming even to match the university's established reputation as a centre of mathematical excellence. At the forefront of this renaissance were two young dons of undeniable energy and brilliance, Robert Yelverton Tyrrell and John Pentland Mahaffy. Wilde was swept into their orbit. They exerted a huge influence upon his development, they extended his horizons, and dominated his appreciation of university life. The two men – as Wilde came to say – 'were Trinity to me'.[10]

Tyrrell and Mahaffy – both Irishmen and Trinity graduates – were very different characters, and very different classicists. Tyrrell, in the year of Wilde's matriculation, had, at the impressively young age of twenty-seven, been made professor of Latin. Although a punctilious scholar – who knew what he knew 'perfectly' – his knowledge was concentrated within a limited range.[11] He 'did not affect to know or care much about' archaeology, anthropology, history or philosophy: it was literature that engaged him – and, despite his Latin professorship, Greek literature at that.[12]

He wore his learning lightly. His lectures were inspirational: 'stimulating joint examinations' of a subject, rather than magisterial pronouncements.[13] On occasion he might enter the lecture hall carrying an obviously uncut copy of the book upon which he was supposed to discourse, before leading his listeners into unexpected 'realms of poetry and imagination'.[14] Critical suggestions were 'lightly thrown off', while from his excellent memory he would quote apt parallels from authors both ancient and modern.[15] *The Times* obituarist would hail his 'scintillating wit', and suggested that if 'no teacher was ever less systematic; none succeeded so well in inspiring his pupils with his love of classical poetry'.[16] He delighted, particularly, in the beauties of form. Indeed in all things he was an arch-stylist: a 'model of disciplined elegance' not just in writing, but also in conversation and in dress.[17] Yet there was also something engagingly approachable and 'bohemian' in his make-up.[18] Still a bachelor during Wilde's time at Trinity, he was very popular with the students, and 'eminently happy' in his 'less formal relations' with them.[19]

The Rev. John Pentland Mahaffy, newly appointed professor of ancient history, was a rather more daunting figure. He, too, was still a young man, only five years older than Tyrrell, but – over six feet tall, 'stalwart', bewhiskered, and sporting a clerical collar – he had an air of imposing dignity.[20] It was an air that he cultivated. Although always aware of his own prowess, his occasionally supercilious manner was tempered by a bracing sense of humour, and undercut by an inability to enunciate the letter 'R'.

He had taken holy orders soon after winning his fellowship in 1864, but he was – as he liked to say – not a clergyman 'in any offensive sense of the word'. Indeed there were those who doubted he was even a believer. He loved the world and he loved his place in it. Country house parties, convivial dinners, formal banquets: these were his favoured settings. He was 'happiest among his fellow men and women, provided they had done something or were personages of interest'. And, though his detractors might say that he was most interested in the titled, if not the royal, in fact his sympathies were wide. He certainly did know numerous peers and several princes, but he claimed, too, never to have travelled on a train without discovering something of interest in his fellow passengers.

As a classicist, Mahaffy offered a different outlook. It was said that while Tyrrell was interested in Greek and Latin, Mahaffy was interested in the Greeks and Romans (or, as he would have called them, the 'Gweeks and Wo-mans'). Greek history – social and cultural as much as political – was his particular study. He had, as Wilde remarked, 'saturated himself in Greek thought and Greek feeling'. Unlike some of his library-bound colleagues, though, he was ready to look beyond the literary sources, embracing ethnology, anthropology and the new discoveries of archaeology. He evolved – and passed on – challenging revisionist views: asserting, for instance, the artistic superiority of Euripides over the (earlier and then more generally acclaimed) Sophocles, and the cultural superiority of Plato's fourth-century BC Athens to the famed Athens of Pericles in the century before. He (like Matthew Arnold and others) had a profound sense of the 'modernity' of the Greeks, and a belief that the nineteenth century could learn much from the Hellenic past.[21]

His lectures – unlike those of Professor Tyrrell – may have been delivered 'loftily to a silent class', but they were no less stimulating for that. He possessed 'that quality which marks the true teacher – the power of communicating the power of enthusiasm'.[22] He was respected by most of the students, feared by some – and lampooned by a few. He was not allowed to forget his remark, 'take me all round, I am the best man in Trinity College'. But if he was conceited, it was admitted that he did have plenty to be conceited about.

Wilde was attracted to both men, and they in their turn responded to his eager interest and energy. Wilde considered Tyrrell not only wonderfully 'crammed with knowledge' but also 'intensely sympathetic'; and he always recalled the young tutor's great kindness during those difficult early days

of college life.[23] Of Mahaffy, Wilde was less in awe than many of his contemporaries. He had the advantage of knowing 'the General' already.
Mahaffy was often a guest at 1 Merrion Square. And it was doubtless this
sense of an existing connection that prompted Oscar – like his brother Willie
– to choose Mahaffy as his college 'tutor' at the time of his matriculation.[24]
Mahaffy, for his part, was impressed by his young pupil's accomplishments:
as he later remarked, Oscar's 'aptitude for, and keen delight in, Hellenic
studies attracted me towards him. He was one of the few students I knew
who could write a really good Greek composition. In Greek you have to
diagnose the substance that underlies the form of the English you are transposing. And again, Wilde was one of the few students who could grasp
the nuances of the various phases of the Greek Middle Voice and of the
vagaries of Greek conditional clauses.'[25]

Mahaffy and Tyrrell, in their different ways, stimulated Wilde's intellect
and his imagination. From Tyrrell Wilde gained a more 'intimate knowledge of the [Greek] language' and from Mahaffy a deeper 'love of the Greek
thought and feeling'.[26] He adopted many of Mahaffy's critical positions
(favouring Euripides above Sophocles, for instance) – and came to flatter
him as 'my first and best teacher... the scholar who showed me how to love
Greek things'.[27]

Both tutors also encouraged Wilde to talk, and to talk well. Talk was
highly prized at Trinity, as it was in Dublin generally. It was considered not
only a vital social accomplishment, but the measure by which a man might be
judged.[28] Tyrrell, with his distinctive 'piping voice', was a fine talker himself:
droll, self-deprecatory, ironical, generous in his praise of others. Though
accounted witty, he was always controlled, stuck to topics he knew well and
was not, essentially, 'imaginative'.[29] Mahaffy, however, was a phenomenon.
He loved conversation; he had made a study of it, and would write a book
about it. The distinctive elements of his own talk were exuberance, fluency,
breadth of reference, imagination and a tendency to overstatement. Always
more interested in ideas than style, he would be 'boastful, provocative,
versatile, and bold to tread in areas where he was not an expert'.[30] It was
in many ways a dazzling performance. One listener considered that 'until
you heard Mahaffy talk, you hadn't realised how language could be used to
charm and hypnotize'.[31]

Among Mahaffy's most celebrated witticisms were the observations 'in
Ireland the inevitable never happens, and the unexpected constantly occurs',
and 'never tell a story because it is true: tell it because it is a good story'.[32]

Examples of Tyrrell's wit are harder to recover, although when asked –
apropos some archiepiscopal banquet – if it were true that he had 'got drunk
at the Archbishop's dinner-table', he is said to have replied, 'Oh no, I took
the obvious precaution of coming drunk'.[33] Of Browning's translation of
Aeschylus' *Agamemnon* he remarked that he found 'the Greek most useful
in understanding it', while he criticized Matthew Arnold for 'preaching the
doctrine of "Avoid Excess" excessively'.[34]

Wilde was impressed by the example of both men. He noted their use of
paradox and their subversion of expectation. He enjoyed Tyrrell's facetious
use of biblical allusion (Tyrrell complained of one embittered classical don
that 'had he been at the Wedding Feast at Cana, he would have soured the
wine – thereby weakening our faith'). Mahaffy, though, he found utterly
compelling; 'a really great talker in a certain way – an artist in vivid words
and eloquent pauses'.[35] And admiration encouraged emulation. Wilde
always claimed that at Trinity he 'did nothing... but talk'.[36] And, in the
absence of congenial classmates, it was with Tyrrell and Mahaffy that
much of that talking was done.[37] He proved an apt pupil. The beginning
that he had made at Portora was built upon. Certainly Tyrrell remembered
him as 'a most brilliant talker', though he noted an occasional affectation
of 'superciliousness' from 'trying to imitate Mahaffy'.[38] Mahaffy, accepting
such emulation as his due, found Wilde a 'delightful' conversationalist,
especially 'on matters of scholarship': his views 'always so fresh and unconventional',[39] his approach 'all verve and *joie de vivre*'.[40]

Neither of Wilde's Trinity mentors believed in a narrow academic focus,
and their example encouraged pupils to look beyond the set curriculum.
During his first terms Wilde regularly attended lectures on philosophy and
English literature.[41] The world of 'the Phil' (the Philosophical, or junior
debating society), however, failed to engage him. Although he was elected
during his first term (a notable distinction) and attended some meetings,
he 'hardly ever took any part in their discussions'. He did not seem to
hold 'any pronounced views on social, religious or political questions'.[42]
Besides, Willie, who was on the council – and through whose influence
Oscar doubtless secured his early election – was perhaps too prominent
there to encourage competition.[43]

Both Tyrrell and Mahaffy had a strong belief in the virtues of sport,
extolling the classical ideal of a healthy mind in a healthy body. Tyrrell
played tennis and racquets, and hockey; Mahaffy – a brilliant shot, an expert
angler and a keen admirer of the landed classes – considered country

pursuits among the 'cardinal virtues', citing the example of the ancient Macedonians to support his view.[44] His other sporting passion – and one that he shared with Tyrrell – was cricket. Mahaffy had captained the Trinity XI as an undergraduate, and continued to play as a don. Wilde, for his part, could never rise to more than a spectator's interest in the game, but he did play the newly popular 'lawn tennis' with real enthusiasm.[45] He also greatly enjoyed shooting and fishing, but they were diversions for the holidays in the far west, at Illaunroe and Moytura.

In Dublin he buried himself in books, just as he had done at school. Away from work, he devoted himself to 'the best English writers'. He continued to read Poe and Whitman, and he made a great new discovery: Swinburne.[46] At the beginning of the 1870s the thirty-something-year-old Algernon Swinburne was a daring and divisive figure: admired by the few, excoriated by the many. He had achieved a first, modest, success some five years earlier with his published drama in classical Greek form, *Atalanta in Calydon*. But he had followed this up with an electrifying first collection, *Poems and Ballads* (1866). Lyrics such as 'Dolores' ('our Lady of Pain'), 'Hermaphroditus', 'Faustine', 'Anactoria' (spoken in the voice of the Greek poet Sappho), 'Laus Veneris' (the lament of Tannhauser, trapped forever with Venus in her suffocating mountain lair), 'Itylus' (the song of Aedon, legendary queen of Thebes, who accidentally killed her own daughter, and was transformed into a nightingale) and 'Hymn to Proserpine' (ruing the victory of Christianity over the pagan gods in such resonant couplets as 'Thou has conquered, O pale Galilean; the world has grown grey from thy breath; / We have drunken of things Lethean, and fed on the fullness of death') conjured up vivid worlds – Hellenic and Medieval – peopled with *femmes fatales* and *hommes damnés*, and coloured with the burning hues of thwarted love and transgressive lust. On every page conventions were overthrown, taboos ignored and certainties undermined. The pagan and the republican were exalted above the Christian and the royal, and sexual pleasure was linked inextricably to sensual pain.

All this, moreover, was achieved in a swirling current of intoxicating verse, more suggestive than descriptive. Swinburne was a master of metre, an artist in rhythm and rhyme. The glorious melodic Choruses of *Atalanta in Calydon* echo and re-echo with the unceasing flow of assonance and alliteration:

> When the hounds of spring are on winter's traces,
> The mother of months in meadow or plain

Fills the shadows and windy places
With lisp of leaves and ripple of rain.

The poems have an almost hectic force that carries the reader ineluctably
from line to line; in 'Dolores' the poet asks:

Could you hurt me, sweet lips, though I hurt you?
Men touch them, and change in a trice
The lilies and languors of virtue
For the raptures and roses of vice.

Although some said that 'sound' often outran 'sense', none could deny
the music of Swinburne's verse. His poetry demanded to be uttered, even
sung. Wilde was swept away on the tide. He became 'an intense admirer',
constantly reading and re-reading Swinburne's poems.[47] Everything about
them was calculated to appeal to his youthful mind. There were the
settings: a classical world he knew well, a medieval one he was excited to
discover. There were the sentiments: daringly contrary to all the accepted
norms and established values. There was the skilful adaptation of classical
metres to English verse, and the rapturous love of words. Wilde judged
Swinburne 'the greatest master of the English language living': language,
he suggested, was to him 'what the beautiful musical instrument is to the
musician – the violin from which he draws the tunes he wishes'.[48] And
then there was the erotic charge: Swinburne – for Wilde – was the first
English poet to 'sing divinely the song of the flesh'.[49] It was a beguiling air,
wonderfully different from the coarse ditties, and coarser experiences, of
the average Trinity student, separated from sordid reality, and heightened
by the mingled senses of transgression and hopelessness.

Wilde steeped himself in Swinburne's poetry. *Atalanta in Calydon* he
loved.[50] He was impressed too by *Poems Before Sunrise*, Swinburne's stirring
1871 collection about the heroic struggle for Italian unification – a unification
only achieved in the year before the book's publication.[51] But it was *Poems and
Ballads* that held the first rank in his affections. He described its verse as 'very
perfect and very poisonous' – and he drank the poison in great draughts.[52]
The volume became for him a 'golden book' – the first of several – a constant
source of reference, consolation and inspiration. He later claimed that he
would rather have written it 'than anything else in literature'.[53]

Immersion in Swinburne's verse also carried Wilde into an exciting new

cultural world: the realm of the Pre-Raphaelites. Among Swinburne's closest friends and allies were the painter Dante Gabriel Rossetti (a founder member of the Pre-Raphaelite Brotherhood), and Rossetti's two young disciples, William Morris and Edward Burne-Jones. It was a world of close connections: both Rossetti and Morris, besides their painting (and designing) practice, were also poets, and their verse, though different in some ways from Swinburne's – and from each other's – still shared many common elements: a fascination with past ages, a weary yet exquisite sensibility, a relish for sensual detail. Certainly to hostile critics they all seemed to belong to the same 'Fleshly School of Poetry', as it had been memorably dubbed by Robert Buchanan. It was a school variously condemned as 'sub-Tennysonian', 'erotic', 'hysteric' and 'aesthetic'.[54] To one conservative critic the common artistic and moral deficiencies of its practitioners might be traced back to a shared allegiance to Liberalism and a shared artistic debt to Keats.[55]

Of course such critical abuse became an incitement to exploration for the undergraduate Wilde. He came to love William Morris, whose grand Chaucerian-style epic The Earthly Paradise retold the Greek and Scandinavian myths.[56] In the 'precious melodies' of Rossetti, he found another writer able to draw 'the quintessential music out of words', as well as a 'dominant personality' that radiated 'strength and splendour'.[57] And – following the artistic genealogy mapped out by the critics and indeed by Rossetti himself – he was led back to Keats, the 'spiritual leader' of the Pre-Raphaelites: the doomed, maligned and half-forgotten Romantic who had died half a century before at the age of twenty-five.[58] Keats, the 'god-like boy', became Wilde's enduring touchstone of poetic excellence.[59]

For Rossetti and his circle the pictorial was inextricably linked to the poetic, the two arts fed and supported each other. Immersion in the poetry of Keats and Rossetti, of Morris and Swinburne, soon made Wilde aware of the artistic achievements of the Pre-Raphaelite school – the paintings of Burne-Jones, Simeon Solomon, Ford Madox Ford and of Rossetti himself. All employed the same medieval and classical subjects, the same overloading of sensual detail; all shared the same genius for colour and – as one critic pointed out – the same want of perspective.[60]

But if Wilde was intrigued by tales of Pre-Raphaelite art, he must also have endured some frustration. There was scant first-hand knowledge of such work in Dublin, and no opportunity for seeing it. The recently established National Gallery of Ireland had no examples among its modest gathering of Old Masters and classical casts.[61] Even in London, Rossetti had for many

years refused to exhibit his pictures publicly. Nevertheless photographic reproductions were available. And Swinburne wrote enthusiastically about the work of his friends. His booklet, *Notes on the Royal Academy Exhibition, 1868*, contained glowing accounts of numerous works *not* in the Royal Academy show. There was lavish praise for – and lush descriptions of – several Rossetti paintings. There was also a rapt account of the daring impressionistic works – 'symphonies' in colour – by the American-born 'genius' James McNeil Whistler (another friend and neighbour).[62] Wilde's artistic horizons began to expand. 'The knowledge of the beautiful is personal,' he would suggest, 'and can only be acquired by one's own eyes and ears.'[63] At Trinity Wilde's eyes and ears were always open, straining to catch new sights and sounds.

The strongly aesthetic approach to experience that Wilde encountered in the poems and pictures of the Pre-Raphaelites found an echo in the work of another young writer: John Addington Symonds. His 1873 volume *Studies of the Greek Poets* provided an elegant overview of Greek literature; it too was 'perpetually' in Wilde's hands.[64] Wilde was beguiled by the music of its prose, and stimulated by the boldness of its ideas. Two in particular struck home. In a chapter on 'The Genius of Greek Art', Beauty – 'the true province of the Greeks, their indefeasible domain' – was identified by Symonds as not only a key element in their world-view, but as the very basis and sanction of their morality. 'Beauty to the Greeks was one aspect of the universal Synthesis, commensurate with all that is fair in manners and comely in morals. It was the harmony of man with nature in a well-balanced and complete humanity, the bloom of health upon a conscious being, satisfied, as flowers and beasts and stars are satisfied, with the conditions of temporal existence.'[65] 'Individualism', too, was exalted. The ideal of Greek life, Symonds averred, 'imposed no commonplace conformity to one fixed standard on individuals, but each man was encouraged to complete and realise the type of himself to the utmost'.[66]

Wilde also noted Symonds' habit of likening modern writers to classical ones. Keats was compared with Theocritus for his expression of 'the sensuous charms of rustic idleness' (Theocritus, in due course, joined Keats as one of Wilde's favourite poets).[67] And Walt Whitman was praised as being 'more truly Greek than any other man of modern times... Hopeful and fearless, accepting the world as he finds it, recognizing the value of each human impulse, shirking no obligation, self-regulated by a law of perfect health'.[68]

Although Mahaffy disagreed with some of the specifics in Symonds'

'very brilliant but inaccurate book', his own general outlook was not dissimilar.[69] He loved to draw parallels between past and present. And his focus, too, was strongly upon the aesthetic elements of Greek life. Indeed Wilde came to recognize that his tutor, like Symonds, 'took deliberately the artistic standpoint towards everything'. It was an attitude that chimed with his own burgeoning sensibility. And under Mahaffy's daily influence it became 'more and more' Wilde's own considered 'standpoint'.[70]

This 'artistic' outlook encouraged, and directed, Wilde's creative energies. He continued to draw and paint in his own time.[71] He was also writing verse. One of his college notebooks contains a ringing sixty-line piece of Swinburnian declamation, titled 'Ye Shall be Gods':

> Before the dividing of days
> Or the singing of summer or spring
> God from the dust did raise
> A splendid and goodly thing:
> Man – from the womb of the land,
> Man – from the sterile sod
> Torn by a terrible hand –
> Formed in the image of God.
> But the life of man is a sorrow
> And death a relief from pain,
> For love only lasts till tomorrow
> And life without love is vain.

It borrows its metre from *Atalanta in Calydon* and its vision of a cruel Venus from *Poems and Ballads*. In a further obeisance to Swinburne's determined Hellenism, alternate verses are headed, as in a Greek chorus, 'strophe' and 'apostrophe'. The same notebook also contains another yearning stanza, addressed to some implacable *femme fatale*, as well as a few lines of cod-medieval verse-drama involving 'Rosamund' and 'Violetta' (Swinburne's first published play, issued in 1860, had been titled *Rosamond*).[72] Wilde was overflowing with Swinburnian literary schemes.

There was, however, no forum where he felt that he could share his ideas and enthusiasms. It was not that his new heroes were completely unknown at Trinity. Willie's friend Bram Stoker had read a paper on Rossetti's poetry at the Philosophical Society in the session before Wilde's matriculation. And it is probable that Wilde listened to the lecture on Keats given at the

society by John Todhunter, the young professor of English literature from Alexandra College, Dublin.[73]

Professor Tyrrell had started a college literary magazine called *Kottabos* (after an ancient Greek drinking game) – but it was focused almost exclusively on translations, usually from or into Greek and Latin. They were learnedly droll productions by dons and gifted pupils, playful variations upon the usual examination exercises: Tennyson in the style of Horace, Horace in the style of Tennyson. Tyrrell excelled in these performances, as well as in such *jeux d'esprit* as an account of Dublin life in the manner of Herodotus or a captain's address to his cricket team in the style of Xenophon. Wilde admired his skill but recognized the danger in such purely imitative work. He later remarked of Tyrrell: 'If he had known less he would have been a poet. Learning is a sad handicap.'[74] Oscar was perhaps further discouraged from seeking to make his debut in *Kottabos* by the fact that – as at 'the Phil' – Willie had got there before him. The 'Hilary 1872' issue contained W. C. K. W.'s deft translation of Victor Hugo's 'Amica Silentia Luna', and subsequent issues carried further works from his pen.[75]

Of like-minded friends there seem to have been few. That informal exchange among peers, which Mahaffy identified as such an important part of university life, was almost completely lacking from Wilde's experience of Trinity.[76] The majority of his fellow undergraduates remained – in his eyes – boors. 'When I tried to talk,' he recalled, 'they broke into my thoughts with stupid gibes and jokes. Their highest idea of humour was an obscene story.'[77] Art had no interest for most of them. When Wilde did read out one of his poems in the semi-formal setting of a 'class symposium' an oaf – 'the bully of the class' – laughed sneeringly at it. This was too much for the normally amiable Wilde. As a contemporary reported:

> I never saw a man's face light up with such savagery… He strode across the room and standing in front of the man asked him by what right he sneered at his poetry. The man laughed again and Wilde slapped him across the face. The class interfered, but inside of an hour the crowd was out behind the college arranging for a fight… No one supposed that Wilde had a ghost of a show, but when he led out with his right it was like a pile-driver. He followed the surprised bully up with half a dozen crushers and that ended it.

The incident impressed his fellow students, and 'Wilde's stock was high'.[78]

But it did not seem to bring him a circle of real friends, still less of literary confreres.

Purser he saw only occasionally, at exam time. Another student, Edward Carson, whom Wilde had encountered as a toddler, when they had been under the supervision of the same nanny during a seaside holiday, impressed him with his diligence, if not his academic achievements[79] (Carson's arena was 'the Phil' rather than the examination schools). They went about together a bit, but – as Mahaffy recorded – 'there was no camaraderie between them. They were utterly different types. Carson was the plodding quiet student' whose intellect would blossom later on in life, whereas Wilde had both brilliance and an irrepressible sense of fun.[80] The connection cannot have been encouraged when Wilde pointed out Carson to a female friend with the remark, 'There goes a young man destined to reach the very top of affairs,' only for his companion to reply, 'Yes. And one who will not hesitate to trample on his friends in getting there.'[81] Edward Sullivan arrived from Portora in Trinity term 1872, and he must have been one of the 'two or three people' who made Trinity bearable.[82]

Wilde found his social life largely outside the college. Merrion Square remained a hub of excitement. Shortly before Oscar began at Trinity, his mother had started to hold regular Saturday afternoon receptions. It was, she claimed, the only way that she could satisfy the many friends who wanted to see her, since – following Isola's death – she had ceased altogether to attend dinners, soirees, theatres, concerts and other evening parties.* These 'conversazione' – running from three o'clock until six – became popular, indeed celebrated, events: 'generally we have about a hundred assembled', she told her friend Lotten von Kraemer. 'I find them pleasurable for many clever men drop in, who would not come in the evening. We hear very good music, and often recitations. There is a table for the coffee and wine in the corridor and I have no further trouble... everything is *sans gêne*.'[83]

The grand high-ceilinged reception rooms at Merrion Square provided a fit setting, though there was often a throng on the stairs. Lady Wilde, magnificent in shawls and crinolines, might be encountered 'elbowing her way through the crush and crying out, "How ever am I to get through all these people."' The crowd was an impressive one: political leaders, actors,

---

* Sir William Wilde endured another great personal tragedy at the end of 1871, when his two illegitimate daughters, Emily and Mary Wilde, who were in the care of his brother, died from burns sustained when their crinoline dresses caught fire. They were aged just twenty-four and twenty-two.

poets, journalists, doctors, and scientists. 'It was,' reported one newspaper, 'like a Paris *salon* in a Dublin house.'[84] The occasions were 'devoid of that snobbism generally so fatal to social gatherings in Ireland'.[85] Talent was the sole basis for inclusion: 'Father Healy's humorous face was often seen there. W. J. Fitzpatrick, the biographer of Lever, melancholy and aristocratic, and Professor Mahaffy, observant and cynical, were constant visitors. Dr Tisdall sometimes recited with a fun all his own.'[86]

Principally, though, there was talk, 'stimulating and brilliant';[87] true to the spirit of a Paris *salon*, no one took any interest in the refreshments. Lady Wilde was, of course, a great talker herself; 'remarkably original, sometimes daring, and always interesting'.[88] But, more importantly, she encouraged others. She could draw out the shy, and deflect the boring. At her gatherings 'everyone talked their best'.[89] For Oscar these Saturday afternoon receptions offered a stimulating theatre – for practising his conversational gambits, for trying out ideas, for sharing enthusiasms, for experiencing the adult world. His gifts were challenged and honed. There were other forums, too, from vice-regal receptions to private dinner parties. As Edward Sulllivan recalled, Oscar 'mixed freely at... Dublin society functions of all kinds and was always a very vivacious and welcome guest at any house he cared to visit'.[90]

Such diversions, however, never dulled Wilde's capacity for study. Although he claimed that his reading 'was done at odd hours', this must be doubted.[91] His formidable academic triumphs continued. Through the ceaseless round of examinations, he never dropped below the 'first rank'.[92] In the final honour examination in classics at the end of his junior freshman year (1872) he was top of the whole class: 'first of the first'.[93] His excellent grounding at Portora and his photographic memory were powerful weapons, but so too were his verbal gifts. At Trinity the examiners still placed a particular premium on 'elegant and fluent viva voce translations' as a 'test of intelligence'.[94]

The following year Wilde put in for a coveted 'foundation scholarship', open to all members of the university 'up to MA standing' – a gruelling course of papers in Latin, Greek and English composition. Only ten were awarded. He, though, was successful, ranked sixth of the fifty candidates, behind his old schoolfellow Purser, but ahead of William Ridgeway, who would later become professor of archaeology at Cambridge. He scored the highest mark in both English composition and Greek translation.[95] The scholarship brought glory, along with £20 a year, free tuition and the right to a set of rooms in college.[96]

Oscar found accommodation on the north side of the quad known as 'Botany Bay'.[97] Although he never entertained there, and the rooms were remembered by a contemporary as 'exceedingly grim and ill-kept', they did bring him more into the life of the college.[98] There was, too, a greater scope for self-expression following Willie's graduation in December 1873. Willie gained his own glory with a gold medal (or first class) in 'ethics and logics', the final part of his honours course. His impressive debating achievements at the historical and philosophical societies had encouraged him to consider taking up the law – perhaps as a prelude to a political career. He had already been admitted to the King's Inns in Dublin, while still an undergraduate – a common occurrence with Trinity students wishing to follow a legal career. And he continued to 'keep terms' there, as well as at the Middle Temple in London.[99]

Living in Botany Bay, Oscar began to take a small part in college activities. He even spoke at 'the Hist', to which he had been elected in November 1873 (proposed by Willie). At the meeting on 21 January 1874 he supported the motion that 'The principle of Trades-Unionism is sound'.[100] The experiment, however, was not repeated. Among friends, he joined in the occasional game of cards. And he seems not to have shied away from all conviviality, though he was considered, at least by Irish university standards, 'an extremely moderate drinker'.[101] While never striking his contemporaries as 'a very exceptional person', he did become more generally known.[102] His love of the arts was acknowledged and (following his triumph over the class bully) respected.[103] If he was occasionally chaffed on account of his enthusiasms, the fun was mild.[104] He began to be generally liked.[105] He was recognized by friends and acquaintances as being not merely 'kind-hearted' and 'good natured' but also very funny. His attitude to college life was both amused and amusing.[106]

He had an eye for the comic detail. One incident with a college tutor – a broken-down young don, Townsend Mills, who was coaching him for an exam – entertained him richly. On seeing Mills come into his rooms wearing a tall hat covered in funereal black crape, he hastened to express his condolences, only for Mills to reply, with a smile, that no one was dead – 'it was only the vile condition of his hat that had made him assume so mournful a disguise'.[107] Oscar shared his mother's gift for dramatic overstatement, and her delight in shocking bourgeois sensibilities. Certainly he startled one college friend by inviting him to a Merrion Square reception with the decidedly Swinburnian line, 'I want to introduce you to my mother,

we have founded a Society for the Suppression of Virtue.'[108] Although
he was always delighted to achieve an *épat* there remained a playfulness
about his provocations. He relished his own absurdities. Indeed the notion
of the notably 'pureminded' Wilde being involved in a movement for the
'Suppression of Virtue' must have had a comical aspect of its own.

At Trinity he also developed his trope of treating trivial matters with
mock gravity or exaggerated force. One evening, when a tremendous row
was heard coming from his rooms, the two neighbours who rushed to
his assistance were amazed to discover him 'jumping about the floor in a
half-dressed condition': '"There's a huge fly in my room, a great buzzing
fly", he explained; "I can't sleep till I drive it out."' His reluctance simply to
squash the insect was regarded as quaintly ridiculous.[109] If he frequently
made grand claims, he then deftly undercut them. Visitors to his Botany
Bay rooms would find – conspicuously propped on an easel – an unfinished
landscape in oils, to which Wilde would claim he had just added 'the butterfly'. But this casual assumption of kinship with Whistler (who had taken
to signing his work with a stylized butterfly) was subverted by the 'humorously unconvincing way' in which Wilde delivered his aside.[110]

Wilde's aesthetic enthusiasms, for all their self-conscious Swinburnian
'fleshliness', were balanced by a contrary impulse: a fascination with the
Catholic Church. The details are obscure, but he seems to have come under
the influence of a local group of Jesuits, making friends with some of them,
and attending occasional services.[111] There was, no doubt, an aesthetic
element even in this new interest. Certainly the 'artistic side' of Catholicism's
rites and rituals had a great appeal. But, so too, Wilde claimed, did 'the fragrance of its teachings'.[112] And these were things that he failed to find in the
Church of Ireland.[113] Perhaps too the delicious sense of 'sin' explored in
Swinburne's verses required the teachings of the Roman Catholic Church
to provide both a proper context and a proper dynamic. Sin only made sense
when set between the possibilities of absolution and damnation. Tannhauser,
the doomed hero of 'Laus Veneris', made an abortive pilgrimage to Rome to
seek forgiveness, before returning to the Venusberg.

Wilde considered conversion. His father, though, forbade it.[114] It is hard
to know why – having been unperturbed by news of the infant Oscar's
baptism by Fr Fox – Sir William should now disapprove so strongly of the
connection. He himself does not appear to have been a man of great religious
convictions – even if both his brothers, and his brother-in-law, were Anglican
clergymen. It may be that his objections were more social and practical.

Although Roman Catholics had long since achieved emancipation, the old prejudices of the Anglo-Irish ruling class persisted in many quarters. Sir William himself seems not to have harboured such views: his dinner table was a meeting place for all.[115] But he perhaps considered that conversion would put Oscar at a disadvantage at the outset of his career. Strong anti-Catholic prejudices still prevailed at the universities. Although Catholics had been able to study at Trinity since 1793, it was only in 1873 that they were allowed to hold fellowships, or even scholarships. In his disapproval Sir William was supported by Mahaffy, and – very probably – by Tyrrell as well. Tyrrell, though a proclaimed agnostic, held a poor view of 'the effect of Roman Catholicism on the Irish people'. Mahaffy was an altogether more voluble critic of the Church of Rome.[116]

It was perhaps as a means of removing Oscar from the sphere of Jesuit influence that Mahaffy suggested that he should be sent to finish his studies at Oxford. The motive for this momentous scheme may, though, equally well have been academic. It was not that Mahaffy ever admitted the superiority of the ancient English universities, but he did concede that they offered a stimulating alternative – and an opportunity for professional advancement.[117] Oscar's father had, it appears, some initial doubts about the plan. It would, apart from anything else, carry additional expense, at a time when he was still recovering from his ambitious building operations at Moytura (in February 1872 he had taken a £1,000 mortgage on the Merrion Square house). Nevertheless his reservations were assuaged by Mahaffy, as well as by an Oxford contact, Sir Henry Acland, Regius Professor of Medicine, stalwart of the British Association, and a long-time friend of Dr William Stokes.[118]

Oscar himself must surely have been excited at the idea. Oxford was the university of Swinburne, Burne-Jones and Morris; and it was there that Rossetti had enlisted their help in decorating the debating chamber of the Oxford Union. Oxford would be an escape from the boors of Trinity and the provincial familiarity of Dublin. It might also offer a new stage for glory.

In February 1874 Oscar had surpassed even his earlier academic triumphs by winning the prestigious Berkeley gold medal for Greek – answering a series of papers on that year's set text, Auguste Meineke's monumental seven-volume compendium, *Fragments of the Greek Comic Poets*.* It was a

---

* Besides detailed textual queries, the questions included: 'Give an instance of real humour (if there be in your opinion any) in the fragments of Old Comedy' (set by Tyrrell), and 'What evidence do the Comic Fragments give us as to the peculiarities of dinner parties in various cities? (set by Mahaffy). Sadly Wilde's answers do not survive.

signal distinction, one achieved by neither Mahaffy nor Tyrrell – though the medal had been won, in 1862, by Townsend Mills, who coached Oscar for the exam, and, rather further back, by Oscar's great-uncle Ralph Wilde. Sir William was justly proud of his son's achievement, writing to Sir John Gilbert, president of the RIA, 'We are asking a few old friends upon Moytura cheer [i.e. for whiskey] on Thursday, and also to cheer dear old Oscar on having obtained the Berkeley Gold Medal last week with great honour. You were always a great favourite of his, and he hopes you will come.'[119] The medal itself was a handsome (and valuable) thing, cast in solid gold from a die presented to Trinity by the distinguished eighteenth-century philosopher of 'Immaterialism', Bishop Berkeley. It would be an enduring, and material, memento of Wilde's time at Trinity.

Although, from the outside, Oxford University might appear to exist as a singular institution, it was (and remains) an agglomeration of self-governing colleges. Wilde had to decide to which college he wanted to apply. Mahaffy's closest Oxford connection was A. H. Sayce, a brilliant young Assyrologist at Queen's. But Oscar chose Magdalen. It did not have the intellectual reputation of Balliol, the social cachet of Christ Church, or the historical associations of Merton or New College, but it was known to be beautiful. A Dublin neighbour, Louis Perrin, had recently matriculated there,[120] and John Addington Symonds had briefly been a fellow. The *Oxford University Gazette* (17 March 1874) announced that the college would be awarding at least two 'demyships' – or scholarships – in classics that year, each worth £95 per annum and tenable for five years.

Wilde travelled over to Oxford that summer, presenting himself to the college president, Rev. Frederic Bulley, on Monday 22 June, armed with his birth certificate (to prove he was under twenty years old) and a testament of 'good conduct'. The following day he sat the scholarship exam along with eighteen other candidates. He unsettled at least one of them by the 'reams of foolscap' that he got through. The young man was not to know that this was because Wilde's flowing cursive hand – now even more individual and distinctive than in Portora days – only ran to about four words a line.[121]

Wilde then joined his mother and brother 'a-pleasuring' in London (Sir William was busy in Ireland, preparing for the meeting of the British Association at Belfast later that summer). The news that Oscar had won a scholarship followed him up to town. It must have lent a pleasing glow to his first proper exploration of the English capital – or, as his mother called it, that truly 'great and mighty city – the capital of the world'. Dublin's

local heroes were replaced with titans of international renown. In a round of literary visits they went to Cheyne Row, and called on Thomas Carlyle, the aged and sometimes cantankerous 'Sage of Chelsea'.[122] Lady Wilde had corresponded with him during a visit he made to Ireland in the 1840s; they had shared their enthusiasm for Tennyson, and she had received from him a book inscribed with a stanza of Goethe in his own translation:

> Who never ate his bread in sorrow,
> Who never spent the darksome hours
> Weeping and watching for the morrow,
> He knows you not, ye gloomy powers.

These were lines that she often turned to in times of trouble, though the youthful Oscar affected to find them depressing.[123] He preferred the singing cadences of Carlyle's *History of the French Revolution*, whole passages of which he could recite from memory. 'How great he was!' Wilde later remarked of the author: 'He made history a song for the first time in our language. He was our English Tacitus.'[124]

After almost a month in London the three Wildes crossed over to the continent, travelling to Geneva, and then returning via Paris, where they put up at the Hôtel Voltaire, on the Left Bank. The hotel had, during the mid-1850s, been the home of Swinburne's great hero, Baudelaire, the poet who, in his *Fleurs du Mal*, had expressed so vividly the beauties of ugliness, corruption and sin. And it was under the influence of these twin guides (with additional notes from Poe and Rossetti) that Oscar began his own elaborately rhymed poem upon the Sphinx – a jewelled and sensual account of the monstrous Egyptian temptress, whose strange image lay close at hand in the Louvre.[125]

Back in Dublin later that summer Mahaffy invited Oscar to look over the manuscript of his latest book, *Social Life in Ancient Greece*. Much of the book's recondite information about Greek customs was drawn from Meineke's *Fragments*, and Wilde's exceptional knowledge of that work must have been a useful resource (Mahaffy, in his preface, would thank his former student for the 'many improvements and corrections' he had made 'all through' the volume.[126] The shared enterprise gave Wilde an even clearer sense of Mahaffy's defiantly 'artistic standpoint'. In one passage, for instance, Mahaffy described how late Greek commentators had 'degraded' Homer (the great delineator of human character and human passion) 'into a moral

teacher' by accrediting him 'with definite theories of life and duty'. It was, Mahaffy suggested, 'the same *sort* of blunder that we should make were we to dilate on the moral purpose of Shelley and Keats, and insist upon classing them with the school of Mr Tupper and Mr Watts'.[127] The notion that, in art, aesthetic considerations might stand, not just apart, but above moral obligations, was a novel and arresting one for the Victorian mind.

Even more arresting, though, was Mahaffy's treatment of the usually suppressed subject of pederasty or *paiderastia* – the erotically charged, and usually sexual, relationship between an older male 'lover' and a younger male 'beloved', that had been such a feature of ancient Greek life. The topic had for generations been taboo even among scholars, but a rising spirit of objective rigour, pioneered by German academics, had begun to bring it into the light. K. O. Müller's 1830 study of the ancient 'Dorians', or Spartans, had been perhaps the first work to broach the subject with anything approaching frankness. In warlike Sparta pederasty had been martial and educational in origin, but elsewhere in Greece it had evolved other emphases.

Amongst the Athenians of the fifth and fourth centuries BC it became a vital element of intellectual life, certainly as described by Plato. Pederasty underpinned several of his dialogues, and stood at the heart of his *Symposium* – where Socrates and his friends debated its exact nature and correct expression. Socrates, in his own contribution to the discussion, described how the priestess Diotima had mapped out the matter for him, explaining that Love was always drawn towards the Beautiful, the Good and the immortal. And the activity that brings man closest to these goals is creation – either physical (the conceiving of children) or mental (creating ideas and works of art). To achieve the former a man finds a beautiful women to love, to achieve the latter – and higher – goal he seeks a beautiful youth, a young male whose physical beauty and willingness to learn will stimulate his ideas and, through conversation, help them to gain form and expression.[128]

Mahaffy, considering the subject too central to ignore, devoted half a dozen pages to 'the peculiar delight and excitement felt by the Greeks in the society of handsome youths'. Aware that he was on dangerous ground, he sought to obscure the sexual element in the equation, framing these attachments as 'romantic and chivalrous' and essentially chaste – not so very different from 'romantic friendships' between modern men and women. Nevertheless he did admit that, occasionally, they might become allied with 'passion', that there were sometimes 'excesses' – and, indeed, that in places such as Thebes and Elis 'no one objected to such relations being even

physical'. He emphasized the civic virtues of the practice, and suggested that if the nineteenth century considered it unnatural, 'the Greeks would answer probably, that all civilization was unnatural'.[129] For Wilde it was a first intriguing encounter with a subject that, over the coming years, was to emerge as a fine but contentious strand in both classical scholarship and intellectual life. He would, though, be exploring it elsewhere.

At the end of the summer he made ready to depart for Oxford. Mahaffy dispatched his brilliant pupil with his blessing, and a quip that perhaps carried a first hint of competitive rivalry. 'Go to Oxford,' he said. 'You're not clever enough for us here in Dublin.'[130]

The Nightingale and the Rose

1874–1878

AGE 20–24

Oscar Wilde at Oxford, 1876.

1

Young Oxford

'He was very cheery and festive.'

BULMER DE SALES LA TERRIÈRE

The loveliness of Oxford in the 1870s was something remarkable. The ancient university dominated the little town: a medieval air still pervaded its colleges and quadrangles, its domes and towers, the honey-coloured stonework of its buildings, the 'dreaming spires' of its churches. Broad Street and 'the High' were cobbled thoroughfares. The city, not hemmed by suburbs, gave on to the gentle Oxfordshire countryside, 'that characteristic landscape,' as one contemporary recalled it, 'whose loveliness sinks into the soul rather than strikes the eye'.[1]

Wilde, alive to beauty and imbued with the spirit of romance, responded to its charms. 'My very soul seemed to expand within me to peace and joy,' he would remember. 'Oxford was paradise to me.' And in this paradise Magdalen held a special place. Perhaps the most beautiful of all the colleges, it was set slightly apart, at the bottom of the meandering 'stream-like' High Street, bounded on one side by the crenelated wall of its little deer park, and on the other by the stream of the river Cherwell. Over its 'venerable and picturesque' buildings, its fritillary-starred walks, its grey cloister and its vaulted chapel, rose Waynflete's graceful Gothic tower – from the summit of which surpliced choristers would greet the spring at sunrise on May

morning. Arriving there for his first term, Wilde accounted himself 'the happiest man in the world'.[2]

He was assigned a pair of rooms on the second floor of the 'Chaplain's' stair, close up against the stained-glass windows of the chapel transept.[3] His fellow undergraduates were, he found, not boisterous Irish louts, but well-connected young men, a few, like him, reading for Honours, most studying for a less onerous 'Pass' degree, but almost all carrying on the cheerful codes and camaraderie of their English public schools in the charmed, emancipated world of Oxford. The change in atmosphere – both social and physical – after Trinity seemed nothing short of 'astounding'.[4]

Although Wilde was slightly older than the other freshmen of his year (matriculating on 17 October 1874, the day after his twentieth birthday), his fresh-faced youthfulness disguised the fact. Not that he was otherwise inconspicuous. At six feet plus, he was taller than most of his fellows, and bigger, with a 'sprawling' ungainly air. His thick brown hair was 'much too long' and far too unpredictable, 'sometimes parted in the middle, sometimes at the side'.[5]* In an age of neat moustaches and trim side whiskers, his colourless 'moon-like' face was strikingly clean-shaven;[6] this 'hairlessness' seemed to some observers a 'natural attribute', rather than being due to the razor.[7] The clothes that he had brought with him were deemed both formal and unfashionable: 'though doubtless counted unexceptional on Dublin's Dame Street or College Green', they had, as one of his contemporaries observed, 'a quaint look of "doing the High" [the regular Sunday post-evensong promenade along Oxford's High Street]'. By the other Magdalen undergraduates he was soon being referred to, not unkindly, as 'our queer-looking freshman'.[8]

Wilde, though, seems to have been blithely unaware of his otherness. His excitement in his new surroundings, his limited social knowledge, and his self-conceit, might carry him into a few awkward situations – but they also carried him cheerfully beyond them. He was deemed guilty, during his first weeks, of the 'sin' of 'presumptuous affability'. Ignorant of established Oxford etiquette, he would present his card (freshly printed, and bearing the legend 'Mr. Oscar O'Flahertie Wilde, Magd. Coll.') to new acquaintances regardless of their age or standing. At his first dinner in hall, he caused

---

* The exact brownish shade of Wilde's hair is hard to fix. Referred to as 'fair' during his schooldays, it had clearly darkened over time. In was subsequently described variously as 'of an indistinctive brown colour' and 'mouse coloured and stringy'.

'consternation' by doing just this to an out-of-college guest (a third-year student of 'great athletic repute') next to whom he had happened to sit, and with whom he had got on well. He also hastened to leave cards with members of other colleges, whom he knew – or knew of – through family connections, without 'waiting for their seniorities to make the first call'.[9]

Despite these minor solecisms, his overtures were not rebuffed. He reconnected with J. E. C. Bodley (a second-year student at Balliol, whom he had encountered in Dublin over the summer) and was drawn into a lively circle of friends – mainly Balliol and Oriel men. They welcomed him as 'a good natured though unsophisticated young Irishman'. And it was – apparently – through such 'out-of-college' connections that Wilde came to be better known to his fellow Magdalen undergraduates.[10]

Magdalen was, then, a relatively small college, with fewer than a hundred undergraduates.[11] And within this body Wilde and the other 'demys' were a select and conspicuous group, distinguished by their flowing gowns and their bundles of books. They dined together in the hall at their own table. Not that Magdalen was a notably academic place (Balliol was *the* academic college); Wilde was one of only three undergraduates reading for Honours in classics in his year.[12] At Magdalen, it was said, 'more importance was attached to social ability' than to scholastic excellence or even 'athletic superiority'.[13] Wilde was well able to adapt himself to the environment. His '*bonhomie*, good-humour, [and] unusual capacity for pleasant talk' gradually achieved for him a popularity extending beyond the circle of his fellow scholars.[14]

Wilde did not shirk collegiate expectations. With his fellow classical demy G. T. Atkinson, he tried out for the college boat. It was not altogether a success. They were 'tubbed' by a ferociously Philistine rowing coach, Wilde at 'stroke', Atkinson at 'bow'. Progress, in both senses of the word, was slow. Wilde strove manfully in the face of much good-natured ridicule from his peers. But, despite some patient encouragement, he proved incapable of mastering even a rudimentary technique. His mind was inclined to wander. On one occasion, meeting the Varsity Eight coming downstream towards them, they were urged to put their backs into it and pull to the side. Wilde, however, took no notice. Ignoring the uncomplimentary remarks of the two coxes, he observed to Atkinson that 'he saw no *a priori* reason for rowing with a straight back' and did not believe that the Greeks had done so during their naval victory over the Persians at Salamis. The incident marked the end of his competitive rowing career.[15] It became his line that he did not see the point in going backwards to Iffley Lock every evening.[16]

Some other aspects of college life proved equally unsatisfactory. The classics dons at Magdalen were an uninspiring lot, certainly when compared to Tyrrell and Mahaffy. And 'college lectures', the small group-tutorials through which they taught, could be dreary affairs. W. D. Allen, the young ancient history tutor, would sometimes dictate his 'notes' to the assembled students, through his half-open bedroom door, while his 'huge mastiff stretched himself on the hearthrug'. On cold days, if there was skating, his door would be closed, and a card with some excuse pinned to it. John Young Sargent, the Latin tutor, would hold drowsy evening tutorials around his fire, at which he often seemed to be thinking less of his charges 'than of a silver tankard of beer which was warming on the hearth'.[17]

Wilde, with his three years at Trinity behind him, felt under-stretched by the work. Although some of his contemporaries were dimly aware of his previous career in Dublin, he did not advertise the details, content that his apparently effortless accomplishments should be put down to genius.[18] He dazzled with his fluent Greek translations, and – by claiming never to have done such exercises before – he greatly impressed Sargent with his Latin verse compositions. Not infrequently, though, he skipped lectures altogether.[19]

The wider intellectual life of Oxford was more enticing. There was a sense of anxious inquiry abroad, a search for new modes of thought and understanding. To many commentators it seemed that the advances in science and textual criticism had undermined not only the literal truths of the Bible but the religious and moral certainties that underpinned life and regulated conduct. In the face of Darwin and German philology, the sea of faith was receding. That this was taking place at a moment when Britain's material wealth was advancing at such speed only tended to exacerbate the problem. The nation appeared in danger of being overcome by commercialization, complacency and cultural stagnation.

In seeking ways past these difficulties, Oxford men had offered a variety of solutions. Matthew Arnold (sometime fellow of Oriel, and professor of poetry from 1857 to 1867) set up 'culture' in the place of religion, proposing the great works of the European canon as the foundation for the traditional moral scheme once supported by the Gospels. Benjamin Jowett, master of Balliol, looked to the philosophy of Plato to provide a transcendent alternative to Christian theology.[20] T. H. Green (who became the university's professor of moral philosophy in 1877) thought the want might be supplied by Aristotle's *Ethics* and a dedication to social responsibility. Friedrich Max

Müller, the German-born professor of comparative philology at All Souls, sought the common roots of belief through his work on ancient Sanskrit texts, opening up the new disciplines of comparative linguistics, comparative mythology and comparative religion. And then there was Ruskin, the inaugural Slade Professor of Art, who found a spiritual assurance in Beauty – in the visual worlds of both Nature and of Art.

Wilde was drawn by these currents. He bought Arnold's essays and Jowett's translations of Plato; he read Green and was befriended by the lively and music-loving Max Müller.[21] But among Oxford's competing celebrities it was Ruskin who appealed most strongly. He had a charisma and energy about him: critic, polemicist, visionary, reformer, artist and poet – the champion of Turner and defender of the Pre-Raphaelites. Wilde had already been taught by his mother to revere the great man, and he was excited to find himself, now, in such proximity.[22] Still in his mid-fifties, Ruskin cut an eccentric figure about the town, daunting yet also approachable. He might be glimpsed, handsome, beak-nosed and bewhiskered, perhaps crossing the street with an arm on the shoulder of the young Prince Leopold (Queen Victoria's youngest son, then an undergraduate at Christ Church), 'his braided gown slipping off his shoulders and trailing in the puddles'.[23]* During Wilde's first term Ruskin gave a series of public lectures on the early Italian Renaissance – eight talks on 'The Aesthetic and Mathematic schools of Art in Florence' beginning with Cimabue and Giotto and ending with Fra Angelico and Botticelli. Wilde attended assiduously.

The lectures had a huge impact: they introduced him to the artists who had inspired the Pre-Raphaelites, and fired him with an eagerness to see Italy and its masterpieces. But, even more than this, they vouchsafed him a new vision. Ruskin appealed to Wilde 'immensely'. His enthusiasm and his 'fine rhetoric', with its 'rhythm and colour... and marvelous music of words' – both on the lecture platform and printed page – were intoxicating.[24] He was, Wilde thought, a 'sort of exquisite romantic flower; like a violet filling the whole air with the ineffable perfume of belief'.[25] That belief was fixed upon the importance of 'Beauty' – its divine origin in the forms of nature,

---

* Wilde's friend Bodley encountered Ruskin one evening walking unsteadily over Magdalen Bridge. For a moment he thought Ruskin might be drunk, but then realized that the Slade Professor was in fact walking with his eyes closed. On being asked the reason, Ruskin replied that he had 'just seen a very beautiful sunset and wished to keep it in his mind's eye, uncontaminated by any other sights, until he could be alone in his rooms'.

its distillation in the visual arts, its moral force and its vital connection with Life.

Wilde recognized Ruskin as 'the Plato of England – a Prophet of the Good and True and Beautiful, who saw as Plato saw that the three are one perfect flower'.[26] Wilde was ready to embrace the vision. Full of the beauties of Oxford and the wonders of art, he found Ruskin's 'theory of the effect of beautiful associations' particularly suggestive.[27] It was an idea that he had also encountered in Plato's *Republic* – where children were to be raised in 'a simple atmosphere of all fair things, where beauty, which is the spirit of art, will come on eye and ear like a fresh breath of wind that brings health from a clear upland, and insensibly and gradually draw the child's soul into harmony with all knowledge and all wisdom, so that he will love what is beautiful and good, and hate what is evil and ugly (for they always go together) long before he knows the reason why'.[28] Wilde determined to become Ruskin's disciple.[29]

He was not alone in his enthusiasm. Ruskin's lectures, held twice a week at noon in the theatre of the University Museum, attracted audiences in excess of 600 interested undergraduates and ardent 'visitors' (mainly female).[30] Art and Beauty were clearly subjects with a wide appeal.

Ruskin had, the previous year, instituted a project to divert the energies of Oxford undergraduates away from useless sports and into useful labour by building a stretch of road across some marshy ground between the nearby villages of Upper and Lower Hinksey. Although most of the athletes had ignored his call, a small band of high-minded followers – mainly Balliol men – had embarked on the task, and were still carrying it on under Ruskin's occasional direction. Wilde (naturally 'luxurious' as he admitted) was rather reluctant to commit himself to an undertaking that involved early rising and hard physical work; nevertheless he does seem to have visited the 'diggings' that winter and to have introduced himself to his new hero, establishing a connection that he hoped might be further 'utilized in the future'.[31]

In his excitement at the broad horizons opened up by Ruskin's teaching, Wilde rather ignored immediate academic concerns. He neglected to prepare properly for 'Responsions' (or the 'Little Go'), a simple examination sat by all Oxford freshmen at the end of their first term. Although it is hard to believe that the Greek and Latin parts of the exam offered any sort of challenge to him, there was also a compulsory mathematics paper. And it was almost certainly this element that resulted in his failure to pass. Failure was an embarrassment as much as a setback. The college authorities were

not amused. At the end-of-term interview, or 'terminal examination', the Magdalen president, Dr Bulley, placed Wilde in the 'not commended' category, a severe mark of official displeasure.[32] And official disapprobation was reinforced at the start of the following term, when Wilde was formally 'admonished' by the president. It is likely that he was threatened with the loss of his demyship should he fail 'Responsions' a second time. He re-sat the exam later that term, and passed.[33]

This minor victory does not, however, seem to have been achieved through any significant re-engagement with academic work. Rather it occurred against a background of ever increasing distraction. At the beginning of 1875 Wilde, to the amusement of his friends, effected a radical change of look. He cropped his hair and changed his wardrobe. With his new tall-collars, his 'Union-Jack-like' check-suits, his 'horsey' birds-eye blue neckties, his 'curly brimmed hat' (perched jauntily on one ear), he strove to 'out-Oxford' the sporting undergraduates of the 'Young Oxford' set. He even adopted some of their slang – though not their 'severer' sporting practices.[34]

This was a pose perfected for pleasure. And over the next couple of terms Wilde seems to have dedicated himself to the heedless life of the fun-loving Oxford undergraduate. It was, as one of his companions recalled, a merry round of 'card playing, singing, room-visiting [and] wine bibbing'. And Wilde, 'cheery and festive', was in the thick of it.[35] He opened an account at Spiers, the emporium on the High Street, equipping his rooms during the course of the year with two china jugs, some candle ornaments, a claret decanter, eight tumblers, six port glasses and two packs of playing cards.[36]

He discovered the dangerous pleasures of 'credit'. Surrounded by wealthy and well-born young men, he chose to imagine that he was wealthy and well-born too. 'No one seemed to know anything about money,' he recalled, 'or care anything for it. Everywhere the aristocratic feeling; one must have money, but must not bother about it.' And Wilde did not bother. Although he had his demyship, and money from his father too, he began to run up debts with the town's tradesmen, and learnt to ignore their pleas for payment. At Oxford – as Wilde experienced it – 'the realities of sordid life were kept at a distance'.[37]

The diary that Bodley kept during 1875 gives a vivid glimpse into this careless world. There were convivial gatherings at the Mitre for illicit dinners and slap-up breakfasts of salmon and devilled kidneys. They hosted small lunch parties and long whist drives. There were 'constitutional' strolls along the river, and boating trips upon it. There were excursions into the

countryside on horse or by carriage: Sunday afternoon pony-and-trap races to Woodstock (which allowed Wilde to imagine himself a Greek charioteer); or more sedate jaunts by tandem cart, when Wilde, delighting in the back seat, 'would practise the post-horn with indifferent success' in between jumping down to open gates with 'a singular lack of agility'. He was particularly proud, too, of a 'dove-coloured dustcoat', in which he could look splendid when perched atop a large 'drag' coach.[38] Although on one occasion Bodley returned to Balliol to find Wilde and Barton boxing in his rooms, Wilde's friends took little part in organized games. They did, nevertheless, watch them, going down to the river to see the Eights, or to the running track to watch the sports. Wilde was often 'to be met with on the cricket field' albeit in a spectating role. And there is even a photograph of him surrounded by the Magdalen cricket team.[39]

By long-established university tradition, theatrical performances were banned at Oxford during term time, but the Victoria Theatre on George Street was permitted to mount 'concerts' and 'music hall entertainments'. They were popular undergraduate events, with rich potential for mayhem. Bodley records one rumbustious evening at the 'Vic' (29 January 1875) to hear some Tyrolese singers:

> Two boxes next to one another. Grand bally-rag, hats and umbrellas playing a not inconsiderable part. During performance, Wilde, of Magdalen, climbed into our box to tell me his brother from Trinity, Dublin was there. [Willie was over in England keeping Hilary term at the Middle Temple.] After chaffing the Tyrolese we leaped on the stage at the end of the concert. Old Wilde [i.e. Willie] was first introduced to me and then proceeded with Strauss to play on the piano a vague *valse*, a rush of affrighted carpenters and curtain. Three Tyrolese proceeded with us to Mitre. They yodeled and I and Welsh sang. I, Fitz, Childers, Williamson and Sharpe stand the damages. After calling at the Clarendon [Hotel] with Wilde we proceeded erratically home.[40]

Late hours out of college, and evening visits to licensed premises, were against university regulations, and led to regular run-ins with the proctors (the university law officers), as well as frequent fines – especially for Wilde. Indeed he gained a heroic reputation as 'the unluckiest undergraduate of his year' for such setbacks.[41] It was, though, considered part of the fun.

Among the friends there was much good-natured 'ragging' and 'chaff'.

Bodley and Childers made fun of Wilde's 'innocence', and Wilde retaliated with the jest that Bodley only knew eight anecdotes, which he kept 'carefully numbered and told in rotation'.[42] Practical jokes were played and spoof telegrams sent. Bodley reported that 'Wilde does not like to have the heads of cods and the "London Journal" sent him. The former, he said, he dropped stealthily into the Cherwell, feeling quite like Wainwright [the murderer].'* On outings to Blenheim Park, Wilde – the stoutest member of the group – would be seized by his companions and rolled down the grassy slope in front of the palace, 'an amusement into which he entered with the greatest good humour'.[43]

Aside from these many impromptu diversions the great focus of undergraduate sociability was Freemasonry. This arcane and supposedly ancient movement, which promoted fraternal fellowship and good works from behind a veil of allegorical ritual, was just then enjoying a special vogue at Oxford, enhanced by the enthusiastic support of Prince Leopold. Bodley was a keen member of the main university lodge, the 'Apollo', as were many of Wilde's college compeers (Magdalen was particularly noted for its Masonic sympathies).[44] Wilde soon joined up. Proposed by Frankland Hood (president of the Magdalen Junior Common Room), seconded by Bodley and approved by ballot, he was initiated into the Apollo Lodge on 23 February 1875, along with William Grenfell, a rising star at the university boat club.[45] Wilde 'lost no time in becoming the most enthusiastic of newly initiates', rising rapidly through the 'degrees'; he was passed to the 'second degree' on 24 April, and made a Master Mason on 25 May.[46] He was intrigued by the symbolic rituals, and delighted by both the 'gorgeousness' of the accoutrements and the elegance of the costume.[47] Officers of the Apollo Lodge preserved the tradition of wearing black knee-breeches, tailcoats, white tie, silk stockings and pumps.[48]

Although Freemasonry has moral and philosophical aspects, and the subscriptions paid by the initiates went to support 'some very deserving

---

* Henry Wainwright, a London tradesman, was tried for the murder of his mistress during the autumn of 1875. He had killed and buried her the previous year, but subsequently tried to move her dismembered body with the aid of his brother. He was convicted, and hanged on 21 December 1875. The case was widely reported, and – as Bodley's diary records – was much talked about at Oxford ('[Barton] was as usual full of chaff about the Wainwright case and the "fatal gift of beauty".') It is not – as has been previously supposed – a reference to Thomas Griffiths Wainewright, the eighteenth-century artist and poisoner about whom Wilde would later write.

charities', among most Oxford undergraduates of the 1870s it was acknowledged to be largely 'an excuse for more banquets and a big ball at the
"Commem"!'[49] Meetings were generally followed by a dinner, and much
merriment: songs were sung (Wilde lending 'his well-meaning but unsteady
monotone' to the chorus) and tricks were played.[50] At the 'festal board'
following his initiation, Wilde – who got 'very festive' as the evening wore
on – was prompted by Bodley to make a toast to 'J and B' as the foundation
of the order. Not realizing that the initials stood for 'Jakin and Boaz', the
twin columns that – according to Masonic tradition – supported the portico
of Solomon's Temple, Wilde provoked 'yells of laughter' from his more
initiated confreres, by proposing the health of 'John the Baptist' with the
remark, 'I have heard that [he] was the founder of this Lodge.' Adding to
the hilarity, he went on, 'I hope we shall emulate his life but not his death.
Therefore we ought to keep our heads.'[51]

Wilde's commitment to art was in no way diminished by the busy round
of student fun. It remained his great subject and his great interest. When
Bodley's family came to Oxford during Eights Week in 1875, it was noted with
amusement that Wilde 'talked "Art" at Agnes', as they walked back together
from the river (FitzGerald, one of Wilde's Oriel friends, meanwhile, amused
the other sister, Beta, with 'strange stories').[52] He continued to write verse,
Swinburne remaining 'his one poet', and certainly his greatest influence.[53]

Swinburne's distinctive rhythms swing through the impressive 'Chorus
of Cloud-Maidens' that Wilde translated from Aristophanes' *Clouds* during
his first year, perhaps feeling that a translation would have more chance of
publication than an original poem.

> Let us seek the watchtowers undaunted,
> Where the well-watered cornfields abound,
> And through murmurs of rivers nymph-haunted
> The song of the sea-waves resound.[54]

When Ruskin returned to Oxford in the summer of 1875, after a term of
absence, Wilde again sought him out. He seems to have spent time working on the Hinksey Road 'diggings' – breaking stones and laying levels; he
even, so he claimed, 'had the honour of filling Mr. Ruskin's especial wheel-
barrow', and was taught by the great man how to push a barrow along
a plank ('a very difficult thing to do').[55] As a road-maker he enjoyed the
privilege of being invited to breakfast in Ruskin's rooms at Corpus.[56] It was

a thrilling chance to hear Ruskin's matchless talk, and to forge a real, and enduring, connection with the great man. Such occasions also brought Wilde into closer contact with some of the established clique of Balliol 'diggers', idealistic young men such as Alfred Milner, Arnold Toynbee, Leonard Montefiore and Charles Stuart-Wortley.

It may also have been through Ruskin that Wilde came, at this time, to know a promising young artist called Frank Miles.[57] It was the beginning of an important friendship. Miles, only two years older than Wilde, was the youngest son of an independently wealthy high Anglican clergyman. Of a delicate constitution, he had been educated at home, developing keen interests in art, architecture, botany and gardening. He was, in his early twenties, already responsible (together with his mother) for a lavish decorative scheme at Canon Miles's church – All Saints, Bingham, near Nottingham – and for a glorious flower garden at the adjacent rectory.[58] Despite being colour-blind, he had abandoned a fledgling architectural career to concentrate on painting. He had made his debut at the Royal Academy Summer Exhibition in 1874 (with 'A study of reflections'), and was building a reputation for his tinted drawings of 'beautiful female heads' of 'the most perfect and charming expressiveness'.[59] Already in 1875 sets of autotype reproductions were being published and displayed in shop windows, 'attaining great popularity'.[60]

How Frank Miles came to know Ruskin is not recorded, although the Miles family's work on Bingham church was exactly the sort of artistic scheme likely to have appealed to the Slade Professor (Ruskin had examples of Mrs Miles's work on display at his drawing school in Oxford, so it may be that she and her son spent time there).[61] Certainly by 1875 Frank had secured the Slade Professor's interest – and Wilde's friendship. Bodley's diary for 8 May records: 'Wilde and Miles called, which roused my spirits a little' (Bodley and Wilde had then gone on to lunch with 'Fitz' at Oriel). 'Miles came in. He had been to Ruskin, who was charmed with one or two of his drawings.' Ruskin maintained his encouragement, writing several times to Miles, hailing him as 'the coming Turner' and suggesting that 'with his love for his mother and his ability to paint clouds he must get on'.[62]

There was a certain metropolitan glamour attached to Miles, which surely impressed Wilde. He was well connected, debonair and had his foot upon the ladder of fame. He was exhibiting – for the second time – at the Royal Academy that summer. His name was in the papers. He knew the London celebrities and could pass on inside stories about them (he impressed Bodley with tales of Henry Irving's early life as a city clerk).[63] For Wilde it

was a first exciting glimpse of what might be achieved by youthful talent and ambition beyond the cloistered world of the university.

Wilde's own horizons were expanding. At the beginning of the summer holidays, inspired by Ruskin's lectures on Renaissance art, he made his first trip to Italy. With a fine sense of self-dramatization, he prepared for the adventure by acquiring a 'very striking pair of trousers'. When his old Trinity friend, Edward Sullivan (on whom he called prior to his departure), made some 'chaffing remark' about them, Wilde begged him in 'that most serious style of which he was so excellent a master not to jest about them. "They are my Trasimene trousers, and I mean to wear them there."'[64]

Italy, like Oxford, seduced Wilde from the first. Everything about the country conspired to ravish the senses and the imagination: the beauty of its landscape, the colour of its everyday life, the drama of its history and the glories of its art. Italy was, he recognized, 'the land for which my life had yearned'.[65] Wilde diligently chronicled his sightseeing across the cities of northern and central Italy in detailed – and often illustrated – letters to his parents, emphasizing archaeological particulars for his father and human dramas for his mother. Sadly the account of his trip to Lake Trasimene in his 'striking' trousers is missing. The first surviving letter in the sequence records his visit to the archaeological museum in Florence, where he felt keenly how much his father would have been interested by the Etruscan goldwork (finer even than Irish examples). And, as a devotee of Ruskin, he noted approvingly that 'everything, even the commonest plate or jug [was of] the greatest delicacy and of beautiful design'.[66] It was, though, in the churches and galleries of Florence that – as he put it – 'the whole splendour of Italian art was revealed' to him.[67]

In Florence Wilde met up with Mahaffy, who was travelling with a young student called William Goulding. Together the three of them went on to Bologna, Venice ('beyond description'), Padua ('quaint'), Verona and Milan ('a second Paris'). There were excellent meals (at Biffi in Milan) and mediocre theatrical excursions (a very 'indifferent' *Hamlet* in the amphitheatre at Verona, and a new opera 'absolutely without merit' at La Scala.) There were literary pilgrimages (to the Armenian monastery in the Venetian lagoon where Byron used to stay, and to the house in Padua where Dante was said to have lodged with Giotto). And, above all, there was looking at art and architecture.[68]

Wilde's artistic enthusiasms reflected his Ruskinian allegiance: Venetian Gothic, Giotto (notably the 'great picture of Heaven and Hell' in the

Scrovegni chapel, supposedly inspired by the painter's famous house-guest), Fra Angelico, Bellini and Titian. Wilde, however, often marked his judgements with a personal stamp: he described a 'lovely Madonna' at Milan by Bernadino Luini (another Ruskin star) as surrounded by 'trellised roses that Morris and Rossetti would love'. Among his favourite paintings in Venice were Titian's 'Assumption of the Virgin' – 'certainly the best picture in Italy' – and 'Dives and Lazarus' by Veronese, 'containing the only *lovely* woman's face' he had seen on his travels.* The city's baroque churches he found 'inartistic', although better than Milan's bristling Gothic cathedral – 'an awful failure'.[69]

The beauties of Italy demanded a poetic response. Recording a (real or imagined) pre-dawn walk up the myrtle-wooded hill behind Florence, to the little early Renaissance church of San Miniato, Wilde distilled his memory of hearing a nightingale's song into a sensual lyric of regret for the passing of time and love, and the nightingale:

SAN MINIATO
(June 15th)

I.

See, I have climbed the mountain side
Up to this holy house of God,
Where the Angelic Monk has trod
Who saw the heavens open wide.
The oleander on the wall
Grows crimson in the morning light;
The silver shadows of the night
Lie upon Florence as a pall.
The myrtle-leaves are gently stirred,
By the sad blowing of the gale,
And in the almond-scented vale
The lonely nightingale is heard.

---

* Wilde was disappointed by Italian female beauty, telling his mother, 'After marriage the Italian women degenerate awfully, but the boys and girls are beautiful. Amongst married women the general types are "Titiens" and an ugly sallow likeness of "Trebelli Bettini".' Titiens and Bettini were generously proportioned opera divas of the period.

II.

The day will make thee silent soon
O! nightingale sing on for love,
While yet upon the shadowy grove
Fall the bright arrows of the moon.
While yet across the silent lawn
In golden mist the moonlight steals,
And from love-wearied eyes conceals
How the long fingers of the dawn
Come climbing up the Eastern sky
To grasp and slay the shuddering night,
All careless of my heart's delight,
Or if the nightingale should die.[70]

Although the setting of the poem, beside the church of San Miniato, seems almost accidental, and Fra Angelico, 'the Angelic Monk', never worked in that particular 'holy house of God', the combination does suggest something of how Italy – and Florence in particular – gave Wilde a new appreciation of 'the spiritual in art': a sense of the artistic richness and artistic harmony of the country's Catholic tradition. He was thrilled to encounter 'the splendour of a religion which is preached through colour and in glow'.[71]

The 'glow', however, could only be enjoyed for so long. Out of funds towards the end of June, Wilde had to part from his companions. While they went south from Milan to Rome, he headed for home, full of 'Italy and its gorgeous art' as well as a few regrets. Stopping at Arona, on Lake Maggiore, he began a poem, ruing that Rome must be – for the moment, at least – left 'unvisited'.[72]

The rest of the summer was passed in Ireland. There were amusements to hand. Wilde received a scolding letter from an outraged mother who had come into her drawing room to discover her seventeen-year-old daughter, Fidelia, sitting on Oscar's knee. Frank Miles came over to Dublin for a visit, and cemented their friendship with the gift of a pencil sketch: a portrait of a soulful-eyed, smooth-cheeked and perhaps even lightly moustachioed, Oscar.[73] It was a rather different image from the vision of Wilde as a saturnine countryman sketched by Henry Buxton Lawrence later that summer, out in the west. Wilde had gone to Moytura for 'peace, virtue and quiet' – although all three may have been disturbed by Willie, who was there,

anxious to escape his own romantic entanglements in Dublin. Poetry was not forgotten. Oscar suggested a couple of lines for a patriotic ode that his mother was writing to honour the centenary of Daniel O'Connell: 'you will be handsomely remunerated,' his mother joked, having sent the poem off to the Boston *Pilot*, America's leading Catholic paper. 'Why not make a little money by giving me delicious lines with a glowing word and a classical allusion.'[74] And when Wilde returned (sans moustache) to Oxford towards the end of October, on the boat over to Holyhead he composed a little cod-medieval ballad. 'The Dole of the King's Daughter' was a tale of fatal love and early death steeped in the Pre-Raphaelite spirit of Swinburne, Rossetti and Morris, beginning:

> Seven stars in the still water,
> And seven in the sky;
> Seven sins on the King's daughter,
> Deep in her soul to lie.[75]

Back at Magdalen he had been allocated a new, and better, set of rooms, on the ground floor of the cloisters. Picturesque and panelled, they looked out over the Cherwell, towards the water-meadows and Addison's Walk. Some considered them 'the jolliest rooms in the college'.[76] Wilde set about making them jollier. And if, in his furnishing scheme, he did not aspire to 'exotic splendour', he did display more taste – and more daring – than the average undergraduate.[77] While most of his contemporaries were content to hire pictures at Rymans ('stags crossing a lake', Swiss mountains, or 'sloppy' but innocuous portraits of 'maidens'), he put up 'some really beautiful framed drawings' given him by Frank Miles, 'of mostly nude subjects'.[78] There was an ever increasing array of bibelots gathered on the flat surfaces, dominated in due course by two 'very large' blue Sèvres-style vases.[79]

This elegant and well-appointed new setting offered distinct possibilities for entertaining. Wilde lost no time in purchasing six port glasses, four plain tumblers and four 'soda water tumblers' from Spiers' emporium.[80] He began to hold regular Sunday evening gatherings for his college friends. They were 'gay and hilarious' occasions, 'but not uproarious'. Bowls of punch were provided, and 'long church warden pipes with a brand of choice tobacco'. Wilde's sense of 'Irish hospitality' had, from the outset, a tendency to run 'beyond his modest means'. There was a piano, and the

brilliant young college choirmaster – and fellow Freemason – Walter Parratt could be relied upon to play it. Songs would be sung; one of Wilde's friends, Cholmley Jones, later became a noted opera singer. 'Sometimes,' as one guest recalled, 'the general cheerfulness degenerated into a scuffle or romp, to the imminent danger of our host's bric-a-brac.' But generally decorum was maintained.[81]

Wilde had things to celebrate that term. The November 1875 issue of the *Dublin University Magazine* contained his poem 'Chorus of Cloud Maidens', translated from Aristophanes. It was a proud moment: a first appearance in print. His name was given below the poem as 'Oscar O'F. Wills Wilde', with the additional legend '*Magdalen College Oxford*'.[82] The poem was both an achievement in itself and an assertion of fraternal power. Willie, for the past three years, had been publishing poems regularly in Professor Tyrrell's *Kottabos*.[83] The *Dublin University Magazine*, however, carried greater weight. Its past contributors included many of Ireland's most celebrated poets, and both Wilde parents. Despite its name it was not a 'university' publication, nor exclusively a Dublin one. Established in 1833 and subtitled 'A Literary and Political Journal', it was produced in both London and Dublin, and had 90 per cent of its circulation outside the Irish capital.[84]

Willie, though, was advancing on other fronts. Tall, handsome and bearded, he was set – as his mother proudly declared – 'to shine in society and in life'. He had been called to the Irish bar that April and was, Lady Wilde told her friend Lotten von Kraemer, 'ready to spring forth like another Perseus to combat evil'. His ambition, though, she went on, was 'to enter parliament – & this hope of his I think may be realized – There is the fitting arena for talent, eloquence & the power that comes of high culture & great mental training'.[85] To another friend, however, Lady Wilde almost unconsciously sounded a faint note of caution, remarking that Willie could be 'anything' he chose, 'if he cares to work'. The qualification was significant.[86]

Willie was already showing a tendency to extend the licence of his student years into his new life. Leisure had more attractions than work. There were drunken evenings and late nights, in his 'usual' round of dinners and balls. He became an habitué of Dublin's newly established skating rink. He continued to flirt and philander. Lady Wilde's hopes that he might marry, and marry soon, showed no signs of being fulfilled; the failed affair that had kept him away from Dublin over the summer was only one embarrassment among several.[87] He was gaining a reputation, even among Oscar's Oxford

contemporaries, as 'a damned compromising acquaintance' – though a very entertaining one.[88]

Oscar, for his part, seemed ready to match at least some of the 'uproarious' aspects of his brother's behaviour. At around ten o'clock on the evening of 1 November 1875 one of the university proctors – a young Oriel don called Lancelot Shadwell – was summoned to the Clarendon Hotel. As he reported to his co-proctor, J. R. Thursfield (of Jesus College), he there found four undergraduates 'at supper in the coffee-room': Fitzgerald and Harter of Oriel, Baillie Peyton Ward of Christ Church and Wilde of Magdalen.

> I took their names and ordered them to finish their supper at once or as soon as possible and go to their colleges. … I was told they had been about the streets all evening. Their manner to me was as impertinent as it well could be and the chief joke at their command seemed to be getting me to mention the College at which they were to call [the following morning; i.e. Oriel]. In answer to repeated enquiries Where? Where? I told them Fitzgerald could inform them. (He had [already] been to my rooms and was fined £1 for dining at the Mitre.)

Having walked around for quarter of an hour, Shadwell returned to find the revellers just as they had been. He ordered them to leave at once. They were more impertinent than ever. 'Wilde strutted about the room with his hat on till I told him that it would be proper for him to remove it.' One of the Oriel men lit up a cigar. Even by the general standards of undergraduate insubordination it was a noteworthy display. Shadwell decided to hand the offenders over to Thursfield for reprimand, as he found they were also on his list (perhaps on account of their antics earlier in the evening); he suggested only 'that it is a case for severe penalty and that they should be gated on the 5th [Guy Fawkes' Night]'.[89]

The incident seems to have marked both the nadir and a turning point of Wilde's undergraduate career. It was followed by an 'especially painful' proctorial interview, and – it is to be supposed – a heavy fine. Thursfield, however, was not perhaps totally unsympathetic. A brilliant classicist himself, and still in his early thirties, he reminded Wilde that 'Moderations were at hand', and impressed on him the need to apply himself to these examinations.[90] For Wilde, conscious of his powers and desirous of success, it was a timely warning.

2

Heart's Yearnings

'Thou knowest all: – I seek in vain
What lands to till or sow with seed.'

OSCAR WILDE, 'THE TRUE KNOWLEDGE'

There were, at Magdalen, some good influences to encourage Wilde in his new commitment to work. William Ward, a fellow classical demy in the year above, had rooms almost directly over Wilde's set, and the two scholars soon established a ready friendship. An Old Radleian, and scion of a line of Bristol solicitors, Ward had taken a 'first' in 'Mods' the previous year. His interests included both philosophy and Freemasonry. But he combined these with a self-deprecatory humour. He was – according to another Magdalen contemporary – 'a very charming little fellow'.[1] His nickname, 'Bouncer', was borrowed from a diminutive but lively character in the great comic novel of 1850s Oxford life, *The Adventures of Mr Verdant Green*. Ward provided not just an academic example to follow, but also a foil and a stimulus to Wilde's intellect. On delightful rides 'through the greenwood' he would 'rouse [Wilde] to talk or think' – and to laugh at himself.[2] Wilde, to Ward's amusement, proved a 'most shocking rider' – wrapped up in his arguments, he would tumble off almost every time they went out.[3]

'Bouncer' Ward also drew Wilde into his circle of Magdalen friends.

These included the Harding brothers, James (another classicist, in Ward's year) and Reginald, who had just matriculated that October. In the camaraderie of their college clique, the younger Harding soon acquired the nickname 'Kitten', perhaps from Wilde, after the music hall song, 'Beg your Parding, Mrs Harding, Is my Kitting in your Garding?' As a result, his older brother became known as 'Puss'. Wilde was called 'Hosky'. At the end of the Michaelmas term, 'Puss' Harding and 'Bouncer' Ward deepened Hosky's interest in Freemasonry by inducting him into the university's other lodge, the Churchill.[4] Ward also introduced Wilde to an amiable Magdalen passman, David Hunter-Blair, or 'Dunskie', as he was known, after his family's Scottish estate.[5]

Hunter-Blair was immediately taken with Wilde's attractive personality – 'the large features lit up with intelligence, sparkling eyes, and broad cheerful smile' – and impressed by his 'extraordinary conversational abilities'. And the three of them – Ward, Hunter-Blair and Wilde – would often linger on after the other guests had departed from Wilde's Sunday evening gatherings, and talk into the night. They ranged far and wide, conversing – as Hunter-Blair recalled – unrestrainedly 'about everything and other things as well'. Wilde 'was always the protagonist in these midnight conversations, pouring out a flood of... untenable propositions, quaint comments on men and things, and sometimes... "dropping into poetry", spouting yards of verse, either his own, or that of other poets whom he favoured... We listened and applauded and protested against some of his preposterous theories.'[6]

There was one topic to which they returned often: religion. Hunter-Blair, an Old Etonian and heir to a baronetcy, had, that April, converted to Roman Catholicism, while on a visit to Rome. Wilde, still full of the spiritual beauties of Florentine art, was 'greatly interested' in the step his new friend had taken. He asked numerous questions, and confessed to his own earlier Catholic leanings – regretting that his father had been (and would still be) so opposed to them. 'Lucky you, my dear Dunskie, to be as you are independent of your father and free to do what you like. My case is very different.'[7] Although Wilde's manner, as so often, was 'half in jest and half in earnest', Hunter-Blair was convinced of his real interest in – and sympathy for – the Catholic faith.

And, indeed, Wilde took to attending occasional services with Hunter-Blair at the little chapel of St Ignatius on the Marston Road, where there was excellent music and a sympathetic priest. Wilde also accompanied his friend to the inauguration of Oxford's grand new Catholic church,

St Aloysius, at the foot of the Woodstock Road, where Cardinal Manning preached the sermon, taking as his text the university motto *Dominus Illuminatio Mea* ('The Lord is my light'). And although Manning's words – 'a fierce denunciation of the tone and teaching of the University' – rather depressed Wilde, and indeed Hunter-Blair, there was an inescapable glamour about the occasion, and the cardinal.[8] A photograph of Manning was added to the clutter of Wilde's rooms, along with a cheap print of the pope (Pius IX) and a plaster-of-Paris Madonna.[9]

'Romanism' also provided Wilde with a new vehicle for self-dramatization. He was 'wearying of his sporting pose'; the role of the convert – or, at least, the putative convert – was rich in potential. It gave him, most importantly, a new and vital subject for his verse. The battle between faith and doubt was a worthy theme – and one that, in the late nineteenth century, might have a wide interest. Alongside his Pre-Raphaelite pastiches, his Greek translations and his conventional lyrics he began to write 'personal poetry... full of the feeling of Roman Catholicism'.[10] He reworked his poem 'San Miniato' into a hymn to the Blessed Virgin Mary ('could I but see thy face / Death could not come too soon'). His poem on 'Rome Unvisited' became a lament over his failure to see the pope ('Him who holds the awful keys... The gentle Shepherd of the Fold... The only God-anointed King').[11]

Hunter-Blair was encouraged by these signs. The priest at St Ignatius's, however, though impressed by Wilde as a person, was less sanguine, perceiving that despite his 'genuine attraction towards Catholic belief and practice', the time was not right – 'the finger of God had not yet touched him'; Wilde was, for the moment, 'in earnest about nothing except his quite laudable ambition to succeed in the schools', and even that, the priest noted, 'he keeps in the background'.[12]

Despite his academic goals, Wilde did not focus exclusively on the curriculum. Ruskin was lecturing again that term, 'on the Discourses of Joshua Reynolds'.[13] The lectures were less formal than his previous performances. Reynolds' work formed 'little more than a starting point' for Ruskin's impassioned 'excursions in many and various directions' – from the horrors of the industrial townscape to the frivolous prettiness of Mendelssohn's 'Oh for the wings of a dove'. Although some listeners found the effect disconcerting, even on occasions 'grotesque', for Wilde it was a chance to bathe again in Ruskin's glorious eloquence.[14]

But the moral message of Ruskin's teaching was now being tempered by a rather different strain of thought. Wilde had a made a new discovery:

the work of Walter Pater. In 1873, Pater, a thirty-four-year-old classics don at Brasenose College, had published a small volume of *Studies in the History of the Renaissance*. Its eight essays, and more importantly its 'Preface' and 'Conclusion,' carried the themes of Ruskin's discourse into new territories – territories recently opened up by the French writer Théophile Gautier. Following Gautier's lead, Pater ignored the moral and social claims of art and beauty proclaimed by Ruskin and suggested instead a purely sensory, indeed sensual, engagement with the world. Confronted with the state of flux revealed by modern science, he abandoned the search for certainties and absolutes, for overarching systems of belief, and retreated to the line of his own consciousness. Embracing the spirit of relativism, he suggested that man should simply concern himself with his own fleeting sensations and impressions. And that, for want of any other possible goal, he should devote himself to experiencing the greatest number of the finest sensations with the highest degree of discrimination:

Not the fruit of experience but experience itself is the end. A counted number of pulses only is given to us of variegated, dramatic life. How may we see in them all that is to be seen in them by the finest senses? How can we pass most swiftly from point to point, and be present always at the focus where the greatest number of vital forces unite in the purest energy? To burn always with this hard gem-like flame, to maintain this ecstasy, is success in life.[15]

Such impressions and sensations might be found in all aspects of changing life – some disposition of 'hand or face; some tone on the hills or sea… some mood of passion or insight or intellectual excitement'. But, they were to be met with most surely and most intensely – not in nature – but in 'the poetic passion, the desire of beauty, the love of art for art's sake' – for, as Pater put it, 'art comes to you frankly professing to give nothing but the highest quality to your moments as they pass, and simply for that moment's sake'.[16] It was a purely aesthetic creed that acknowledged no limitations of 'abstract morality', in the quest for experience. If Ruskin, viewing art from a moral standpoint, held out a vision of art for life's sake, Pater, treating morals (and everything else) from the standpoint of art, offered a vision not just of 'art for art's sake', but of life for art's sake too.

The book had provoked a degree of anxiety, if not alarm, at its first appearance. It was thought particularly to be dangerous to the young. The

bishop of Oxford even preached a sermon against it. Such strictures, though, were unlikely to deter the interested. Wilde discovered the volume early in his Oxford career, though it took him time to unpack its secrets. In due course it became for him another sacred text – 'the golden book of spirit and sense, the holy writ of beauty'.[17] He delighted in the control and formal elegance of its language. He judged that it contained 'a page or two of the greatest prose in all literature' – passages from which he might learn 'the highest form of art: the austerity of beauty'.[18] And although he considered that Pater's ideas derived in part from Ruskin's sense of the vital connection between art and life, he recognized, too, that they led in rather different directions.[19]

There was a different colouring, too, to Pater's aesthetic preferences. While Ruskin, in *The Stones of Venice*, had proclaimed the moral and spiritual superiority of Gothic to Renaissance architecture, and while he had praised Giotto and the early Trecento painters over later masters in his lectures on Florentine art, Pater adopted a different perspective. He favoured 'late' periods to 'early' ones. In the recurring pattern of austere development, balanced perfection and elaborated decline by which nineteenth-century historians tended to mark out the trajectories of past cultures, Pater was inclined to find worth and beauty in the latter phases of each cycle.[20] As he charted the course of the Renaissance he fixed approvingly upon the products of its late phases with their subtle notes of perversity and decay: the 'refined and comely decadence' of late Provençal poetry, or the art of Leonardo da Vinci with its 'interfusion of extremes of beauty and terror', its 'fascination of corruption', its delineation of 'strange thoughts, and fantastic reveries and exquisite passions'.[21] To a devotee of Swinburne, such as Wilde, this endorsement of the beauties of pain, strangeness and decay was both comprehensible and beguiling.

And as Pater expanded the range of aesthetic possibilities, he also hinted at alternative modes of conduct. His chapter about the eighteenth-century art historian Johann Winckelmann drew upon the writings of Plato to give, not a vision of quasi-Christian spiritual life, such as Jowett might endorse, but a coded account of Greek pederasty and its virtues.[22] The topic remained controversial. That very year, 1875, Mahaffy had felt obliged, following hostile reviews, to remove all mention of pederasty from the second edition of his *Social Life in Greece*. At the same moment John Addington Symonds was drawing similar critical fire for his incautious references to the subject in the second series of his *Studies of the Greek*

Poets. It was ground on which most classicists still refused to stray. Jowett considered that he had avoided the question by claiming Plato's pederasty was little more than a 'figure of speech' and was easily transposable, for modern readers, into a love of women: 'Had [Plato] lived in our own times he would have made the transposition himself.'[23]

While Pater's book was considered dangerous, Pater himself was deemed only slightly less so. Steeped in the Socratic tradition described by Plato, he had sought to achieve something of its flavour by gathering a select circle of bright young men for tea parties at the house that he shared with his two sisters in north Oxford. It was an atmosphere that delicately blurred the border between pedagogy and pederasty. This was a perilous game. Early in the previous year, 1874, prior to Wilde's arrival at Oxford, Pater had been embroiled in a largely suppressed scandal over his relationship with a Balliol undergraduate, William Money Hardinge.[24]* Whether Wilde (or anyone else not closely involved) knew the details of the case is uncertain. Montefiore, Milner, Toynbee, and Hardinge's other friends, had all resolved to keep 'an absolute silence' upon the subject. Nevertheless some hint of danger lingered around Pater's name – and probably (as far as Wilde was concerned) added to his attractiveness.

* Hardinge's friends (and, it seems, Pater's too) had been alarmed to discover letters between the two men in which they addressed each other as 'darling'. Pater by temperament was both cautious and discreet. Hardinge was anything but. A flamboyant figure with literary aspirations, who larded his conversation and his poetry with 'allusion to *unnatural* profligacy', he had – in the brief year since his matriculation – achieved a Varsity-wide 'notoriety' as 'the Balliol Bugger'. And although there was an element of pose in his behaviour – a desire to 'startle' – his letters all but confirmed the charge against him. As his friend Alfred Milner wrote to another college mate, 'When a man confesses to lying in another man's arms kissing him & having been found doing it… When verses are written from one man to another too vile to blot this paper, what hope can you have that a criminal act, if not committed already, may not be committed any day?' Leonard Montefiore, another of Hardinge's contemporaries, had mentioned these concerns to a friend among the Balliol dons. Jowett, the head of the college, was informed. He acted quickly to suppress the matter, anxious to preserve the good name of Balliol without destroying the reputations of either Hardinge or Pater. Hardinge was sent down until the end of the year. Pater (a former protégé of Jowett's) was summoned for a 'dreadful' interview – one that left him 'crushed [and] despairing'. Although there was no threat of exposure, Jowett does appear to have used his influence to prevent Pater being awarded a valuable university proctorship. It was an injury added to insult. The debacle left Pater with a sense of anger and pain at how circumscribed his life and relations must be for the future. Embracing the notion of himself as a victim of unjust forces, he made the glorification of suffering one of his enduring literary themes.

Pater and Ruskin, ancient Greece, Freemasonry and Roman Catholicism: Wilde was accumulating creeds and perspectives. But among these contending ideas, he seemed inclined neither to make a choice nor seek a synthesis; he preferred to play with each in turn. Although he might hesitate to commit himself at St Ignatius's, religion continued to fascinate him. By early December he was confiding to Bodley that he was 'swaying between Romanism (Manningism) and Atheism'.[25] And essentially he kept on swaying throughout the rest of his time at Oxford. It was a performance that provoked the interest, amusement and exasperation of his friends.

Over Christmas 1875 Oscar was back in Ireland. The atmosphere at Merrion Square was not cheerful. Sir William's health seemed to be failing. There was even talk of letting the house, and retreating full time to Moytura.[26] Oscar, escaping the gloom, went to stay with an old Dublin friend, Richard Trench, up at Clonfin. The house, in Co. Longford, belonged to Trench's uncle and aunt. 'With horses, dogs, guns, plenty to eat and lots of whiskey' they contrived to 'make the time fly pretty pleasantly'.[27] There was scope for poetry too. Wilde, 'swaying' away from 'Romanism' over the holiday season, began work on another exercise in Pre-Raphaelite lubricity, anatomizing his beloved in cloying detail:

> As a pomegranate, cut in twain,
> White-seeded is her crimson mouth,
> Her cheeks are as the fading stain
> Where the peach reddens to the south.

The poem, finished after his return to Oxford, and titled 'The Rose of Love and With a Rose's Thorns', was accepted by Tyrrell for a forthcoming issue of *Kottabos*.[28] It would be one of eight poems that Wilde published that year: four in the *Dublin University Magazine*, two in *Kottabos*, one in the *Irish Monthly* (a Jesuit-run journal) and one that appeared in both the *Month* and the Boston *Pilot* (his first American publication). It was an impressive achievement for an undergraduate. His mother was justly proud, thrilled that the family 'muse was not yet worn out'. She detected 'the evident spirit of a *Poet Natural*' in his work. Not that she was uncritical. Reading the first section of his reworked 'San Miniato', with its new closing stanza

> O! crowned by God with love and flame,
> O! crowned by Christ the holy one,

> O! listen, ere the searching sun
> Show to the world my sin and shame

she remarked 'I would have left out "Shame" – Sin and repentance are highly poetical, "Shame" is not – any other monosyllable would do that expressed moral weakness.'[29]

To an Irish audience the flurry of publications confirmed Oscar as the worthy offspring of the illustrious Speranza. Lady Wilde delightedly reported the general hymn of praise to Oscar's 'poesie' at one of her 'matinee' receptions,[30] while the verses, even though confined to Irish periodicals, gave Wilde a standing as a poet among his Oxford contemporaries. To confirm and enhance his status, he allowed his hair to grow long again.[31]

The published poems ranged from the Swinburnian lushness of 'The Rose of Love' to the graceful lyricism of 'Spring Days to Winter' – a poem featuring that most poetical of birds, the 'throstle' ('What,' Lady Wilde demanded, 'is a throstle?').[32] There was also a translation from Euripides' *Hecuba*. But the most frequently recurring note was one of Catholic soul-yearning. It pulsed through the two 'brief and Tennysonian' compositions (as Wilde called them), 'Tristitiae' and 'The True Knowledge'; it was present in his reworked version of 'San Miniato' and, most conspicuously, in his poem on 'Rome Unvisited'.[33]

These religious compositions attracted considerable attention in Dublin circles. The poet Aubrey De Vere (a Catholic convert and friend of Lady Wilde's) interested himself in them, suggesting corrections and using his influence to secure their publication.[34] Their appearance in print first prompted and then strengthened the rumour that Oscar had actually converted 'to the true and ancient church'.[35] Nor was their appeal limited to the Irish capital. 'Rome Unvisited' garnered 'high praise' from Cardinal Newman and even an anonymous verse tribute in the pages of the New Zealand *Tablet*.[36] Mahaffy, predictably, was less enthusiastic about the Catholic sentiment – '[he] say's "This thing won't do,"' Lady Wilde reported. 'All very well up to 25, after that stuff and nonsense.'[37]

Wilde's poetic achievements usefully distracted attention from his academic efforts. Although he was eager to succeed in his exams, he was equally keen not to appear so. He cultivated his pose as a 'dilettante' – and with considerable success.[38] Nevertheless a few of his close friends were aware that he was doing a huge amount of work 'surreptitiously'. Hidden away in his tiny back bedroom, he would often work through the small hours,

surrounded by a seemingly 'hopeless confusion' of books.[39] He stayed up during the Easter vacation to continue his reading, together with his fellow demy Atkinson. The only two undergraduates left in college, they dined (very badly) in each other's rooms, at least until they realized they had almost nothing in common, after which they fed alone. Wilde had amused Atkinson one night in hall, with his assertion that he would dress for dinner even if he were alone on a desert island; and perhaps he was true to his word on the occasion of these solitary repasts.[40]

The regime of study was interrupted by news from Merrion Square: Sir William was seriously ill. Oscar returned home to find his father confined to bed, and palpably fading. He was only sixty-one. There was, as Lady Wilde recorded, 'no pain – thank God, no suffering'; just 'quietness and stillness, and the gradual diminution of strength'.[41] The sober scene of the sickroom was given an unexpected twist by the arrival each morning of a woman 'dressed in black and closely veiled'. She would enter the room, unhindered by Lady Wilde or anyone else, and silently take her place at the head of the bed. She was one of Sir William's mistresses (possibly the mother of his two dead daughters), yet Lady Wilde, rising far above feelings of 'vulgar jealousy', made no objection; not – as Oscar admiringly observed – because she did not love her husband, but 'because she loved him very much', and recognized that it would be a 'comfort' for him to have the woman there.[42] Although hostile rumour claimed that Oscar and Willie vexed their father's last days by coming in late and traipsing noisily up the stairs, they were beside his bed when – on the afternoon of 19 April 1876 – he quietly passed away, Lady Wilde holding his hand.[43]

The grief of the moment was briefly obscured by practical imperatives: there was the large and public Dublin funeral, attended by the lord mayor, and a host of medical and antiquarian dignitaries; there were letters of condolence to answer and newspapers to read; laudatory obituaries appeared across the Irish press, although the World, a new English society weekly, noted that the 'London papers generally have given very scant recognition' to the passing of 'one of the kindest-hearted and most genial of Irishmen'.[44] But the true awfulness of Sir William's death could not be denied. Lady Wilde was bereft, confessing to one friend that she felt 'like one shipwrecked', her eyes 'blinded with tears', her mind filled with many sad bewildering cares and anxieties, her life 'broken [and] desolate'.[45] Oscar too was overwhelmed by grief. He had revered and loved his father, and cherished both his approval and his advice.[46] Over the coming months he

tried to resolve his sense of loss into verse, hoping – among other things – that the radiant 'glory' now about Sir William's head would prevent him from seeing too clearly his son's many inadequacies: 'that I / Am weak where thou dids't think me strong / And foolish where you feigned me wise'.[47]

To these emotional woes others were soon added. When Sir William's will was proved it was discovered that he had almost no money.[48] This was an appalling shock, and one that threatened the foundations of the Wildes' stable family life. It had always been assumed that Sir William was a wealthy man, and, indeed, at the height of his powers he was earning some £3,000 a year. But he had never been prudent, entertaining on a grand scale in Dublin, and pouring money into ambitious building schemes and charitable works. For the last few years, absorbed in his scholarly pursuits and Moytura estates, he had neglected his medical practice, leaving much of the work to his illegitimate son, Henry Wilson. Instead of earning money he had, as Lady Wilde lamented, been living on capital 'until all is gone'.[49] Scarcely a year before his death, he had taken out two large loans of £1,000, one secured against the Merrion Square house, the other against his Bray properties.[50] What the money had been spent on remained a mystery, but it was gone.[51] Instead of a secure inheritance for his family, he had left 'large debts', and very little with which to meet them.[52]

The £2,500 that Sir William had borrowed from his wife's marriage settlement back in 1862 had been entirely 'sunk' in Moytura.[53] The property was left to Willie, as the eldest son, together with the house in Merrion Square. Lady Wilde, however, was to receive, during her lifetime, the rents from the Moytura estate. These, however, amounted to barely £150 a year, far less than the annual £200 that Sir William had apparently promised his relict. And even that amount was dependent upon the rents being actually paid – something that, in an era of Irish agricultural depression and tenant recalcitrance, very rarely occurred.

Oscar, for his part, inherited the four terraced houses at Bray, a half-share (with Henry Wilson) in the little fishing lodge at Illaunroe, and also a part-interest in a property at Clonfeacle (in Co. Armagh) that had come into the family via the Maturins.[54] The excitement of being a property owner was tempered by the fact that the Bray houses (like 1 Merrion Square) were heavily mortgaged. Interest payments (and possibly principal repayments too) were falling due and there was no money available to meet them.[55]

Willie, as a fledgling barrister, was not yet earning more than the occasional fee. Lady Wilde's writing brought in very little (the *Dublin University*

Magazine, which published one of her several sorrow-filled lyrics on Sir William's death, had ceased even to pay its contributors).[56] She felt paralysed by grief, worry and exhaustion. She had hopes that the government might give her a pension either on her own account or in recognition of Sir William's contributions to Irish public life. Her own fiery Nationalist past, however, counted against her. On learning that the prime minister, Disraeli, required recipients to be 'loyal, orthodox, moral, and to praise the English!', she declared, '*Jamais* – my descending to this level. Fancy! I have stood a priestess at the altar of freedom!'[57]

'It is all a horrid dream,' she lamented to Oscar. 'Were I young like you I would take a pupil to read with. Youth can earn, age cannot.'[58] Oscar, though, was too busy preparing for his exams to think of taking a pupil. And although the houses at Bray could produce some rent (as much as £120 a year each, when let), he now required such funds to cover the expenses of his Oxford life. No one in the family had either the knowledge or the will to deal with the situation. Debts continued to accumulate. Outgoings continued to flow. Tradesmen went unpaid. When the bailiffs arrived at Merrion Square Lady Wilde retreated to the drawing room with her copy of Aeschylus.[59]

From such scenes Oscar escaped back to Oxford to prepare for Mods – and, also, the compulsory (and generally resented) oral 'Divinity' exam that preceded it. The classics papers began on 2 June, a punishing schedule of unseen translations, textual criticisms, historical essays and compositions in prose and verse.[60] Having learnt – from Mahaffy, Tyrrell and J. A. Symonds – the habit of bringing the ancient and modern worlds into dialogue, he was delighted to find that the Oxford examiners encouraged the same perspective, and that he might be allowed to match his classical erudition with his love of contemporary verse. He was doubtful, though, about his performance in the Logic paper, and even feared he might miss the hoped-for First.[61]

The college authorities had more confidence in him. The results of the exam would not be known for over a month, but Wilde's diligence in preparation was recognized. He had the distinction of being 'specially commended' at his terminal examination on 16 June (ever since the debacle of his first term, he had been consistently in the middle 'commended' category). With this endorsement, and the ordeal of the exams over, Wilde threw himself into Oxford's summer pleasures.

'Commemoration week' was coming on. There were breakfasts, picnic lunches, outings, dinners and dances. There was female company to be

entertained. Ward's mother and sisters (Gertrude and Florence) came up for 'Commem', as did the Hardings' mother and sister ('the child Amy') together with a German friend. Wilde spent much time going about with them. He took the Wards sightseeing round the colleges ('I am more charmed than ever with Worcester Chapel,' Wilde informed 'Kitten' Harding). They visited Radley, William Ward's old school, and played lawn tennis there. Wilde liked Mrs Ward 'immensely' and found the older sister Gertrude 'very charming indeed'. He drew comment by his marked attention to her on a group out-ing to Blenheim (where the nineteen-month-old Winston Churchill lay, unaware, in the nursery).[62] At a dance held by the Alfred Masonic lodge, he impressed – or amused – Florence Ward with his soulfulness. 'I think Wilde found me very green,' she confided to her diary, 'and tried to puzzle me by asking me such questions as "whether I found the world very hollow?"'[63]

When Ward gave a little dinner party in his rooms, Wilde 'took the top of the table' after Ward and 'Puss' Harding had to leave early in order to prepare for the Magdalen concert. He had to contend with Amy Harding having drunk too much Mosel cup – and getting into 'very excellent spirits'. He hosted a reciprocal dinner two days later.[64] Wilde was a punctilious host – insisting that the 'scout' (his college servant) wore felt slippers, and that he use the back bedroom as his pantry, so that the vulgar sound of corks popping could be avoided.[65]

For all Wilde's anxieties about the hollowness of the world, a spirit of infectious jollity predominated. Mr Guggenheim, the Oxford photographer, had much trouble in taking a large group picture in the Magdalen cloister – including the Wards, Wilde and numerous other undergraduates – because people kept 'bursting' with laughter. One elderly visitor who went on the picnic excursion to Blenheim was amazed at all the good-natured chaff that the Magdalen friends indulged in – and put up with. Jokes were many: spraying with soda-water syphons, practising on the post-horn, dressing up in drag. At another lunch party given by Wilde that week, one of his college friends (Bulmer de Sales la Terrière), arriving early and finding himself alone in Wilde's rooms, took the opportunity of discreetly 'clothing' the Frank Miles nudes that adorned the walls with 'some penny postage stamps' that were at hand. This intervention was only noticed once the lunch had begun. There were ladies in the party. As the prankster recalled, 'First one looked up, giggled and blushed, and then another, till the whole party was convulsed.' Even Wilde laughed.[66]

In the carefree period immediately after sitting his exams Wilde also saw

something of Frank Miles. He had come up to Oxford for a few days at the beginning of June, bringing with him a new friend, Lord Ronald Gower (they had met at a party given by Millais). Gower was thirty years old, the youngest son of the Duke of Sutherland; he had recently abandoned a career in Liberal politics to pursue his passions for sculpture and writing. Miles took him to Magdalen; 'there,' Gower recorded in his diary, 'I made the acquaintance of young Oscar Wilde… A pleasant cheery fellow, but with his long-haired head full of nonsense regarding the church of Rome.'[67]

Wilde was rather more impressed by the encounter. Gower was a figure of fascination: urbane and dandified, well connected, 'handsome, nobly born and passably rich'. He was a man of real artistic attainments.[68] His cultural interests were eclectic and intriguing. He had recently published a guidebook to the art galleries of Holland and Belgium, a set of auto-lithographed portraits by the sixteenth-century French court artist Clouet, and the preface to a volume on the life of the rakish Restoration poet the Earl of Rochester.[69] He was amusing, too, even if he did – in the first instance – employ his gifts of ridicule and sarcasm to try and laugh Wilde out of his 'Catholic proclivities'.[70]

If friendship with Frank Miles had given Wilde a first sense of connection to the exciting worlds of London 'society' and cultural achievement, the meeting with Lord Ronald Gower enhanced and strengthened that sense. It was, though, a realm that still lay just out of reach, even if it seemed to be getting closer. Wilde was thrilled when, passing through London soon afterwards, he called on Miles and found him sketching Lady Desart, 'the most lovely and dangerous woman in London'.[71] It was a rare hint of perilous excitement. Wilde filled most of the time before his *viva voce* (the oral part of his exam) by visiting his father's older brother, John, the vicar of West Ashby, near Horncastle, in Lincolnshire. He spent some happy summer days at the vicarage. Throwing himself into the life a country parish, he 'examined schools in geography and history, *sang* glees, *ate* strawberries', made himself 'the "bellus homo" of a tea party', and played a great deal of lawn tennis.[72]

'My uncle is milder than ever,' Wilde reported to Ward, 'says "Dear me now, wouldn't you have found the penny post more convenient than a telegram?" about six times a day.' Nevertheless he was roused by his nephew's professed interest in Catholicism. After they had argued 'fiercely' on the subject, 'he revenged himself on Sunday by preaching on Rome in the morning and humility in the evening'.[73]

Wilde returned to Oxford on 3 July, allowing himself – as he thought – a couple of days to prepare for his *viva*. But the very next morning, while lying in bed 'with Swinburne (a copy of)' he was roused by the clerk of schools, wanting to know why he had not presented himself. Arriving at the schools at about one, he was 'ploughed immediately in Divinity'. The failure was something of a badge of honour; it was, apparently 'considered poor form if one passed "Divvers" on the first attempt'.[74]

The serious part of the *viva* went rather better: on the *Odyssey* they discussed 'epic poetry in general, *dogs* and women'; in Aeschylus they talked of 'Shakespeare, Walt Whitman and the *Poetics*'; then followed an altogether 'delightful' discussion about his essay on poetry in the Aristotle paper.[75] When Bodley learnt that Wilde had been asked by the examiner 'what Aristotle would have said to Walt Whitman' he instantly offered to bet that 'Oscar had either been ploughed or taken a First'.[76] Wilde, fortunately for Bodley, was not on hand to take the bet. From the tenor of the questioning at the *viva*, he gauged at once that he had got his First, and – as he admitted to Ward – 'swaggered horribly' during the interview. His papers were indeed exceptional: the most brilliant of his year.[77]

The news was confirmed two days later in *The Times*. It was a real, and gratifying, achievement. Wilde was 'overwhelmed' with telegrams and messages of congratulation. His mother was 'in great delight'. Wilde, however, kept returning to the thought that his father 'would have been so pleased about it'. Exaggerating an emotion that was nonetheless real, he told Ward, 'I think God has dealt very hardly with us. It has robbed me of any real pleasure in my First.'[78]

Pleasure, in fact, was never very far away. Wilde spent a few days in London, seeing Oxford friends. There was a visit to the zoo and a trip to the 'Pro-Cathedral' to hear Cardinal Manning ('more fascinating than ever'). Conscious of his continued 'swaying', Wilde declared, 'I must do something decided.' But he could not decide what.[79]

Then, equipped with a splendid new 'Levant Morocco leather' travelling bag, he moved on for a week with the Miles family in 'the enchanted isle of Bingham Rectory'.[80] Wilde was swept up by the beauty of it all: the garden, with its white lilies and long rose-walks ('only that there are no serpents or apples it would be quite Paradise'); the decorated church ('simply beautiful'); and Frank's four sisters ('all very pretty indeed… My heart is torn in sunder with admiration for them all').[81] He made himself generally *'charming'*, played more lawn tennis ('I am *awfully* good'), attended more garden parties,

ate basketfuls more strawberries.[82] Canon Miles, Frank's father, proved a stimulating and informative companion; a 'very advanced Anglican', he had known both Manning and Newman during his Oxford days.[83]

Cardinal Newman ranked in fascination alongside Cardinal Manning. Wilde regarded him as one of the Catholic Church's 'great men' – 'like St Augustine, a good philosopher as well as a good Christian'.[84] It became one of Wilde's fantasies that he might one day visit Newman and, unable to resist 'that divine man', he would at last commit, finding 'a quiet peace in his soul'. But, of course, the belief that an interview might actually lead to decisive action made Wilde doubt that it would ever take place; his courage would fail him.[85] Before departing Oxford, Wilde had bought several of Newman's works, and planned to read them over the course of the summer holidays.[86] But there seems to have been a good deal of affectation in this regime of theological study. Certainly all that he retained from his reading of Newman was the memory of a passage about a 'snapdragon under the windows' of Trinity College, Oxford.[87]

Back in Dublin other demands and interests soon began to draw him away from Catholic piety. He spent time out at Howth with 'that dear Mahaffy', helping him correct the proofs of his new book, *Rambles and Studies in Greece*. He toyed with other literary projects, undertaking to edit an unfinished work of his father's – a 'memoir' of the Irish topographical artist Gabriel Beranger, and starting on a review of J. A. Symonds' *Studies in the Greek Poets (Second Series)*. There was more tennis, and regular sea bathing; Wilde confessed to 'always feeling slightly immortal when in the sea'. And sometimes in the early evening he would go for a ride.[88]

There was also the matter of his Bray houses. He had already missed the best selling season (June) but, in consultation with his solicitors, decided to put the properties up for auction in early September, offering them as four separate lots. In the meantime, though, he had to pay for them to be advertised in the press.[89] He was able to escape from these practical concerns when Frank Miles came over in the second week of August, and together they headed west for a fortnight's sport and recreation.

Exhilarated by the beauties of the landscape, Wilde immediately felt 'years younger'. At Moytura there was sailing on the lough, and painting too. Miles did some 'wonderful sunsets' and Wilde, encouraged to emulation, produced a sensitive crepuscular watercolour of Lough Corrib, dotted with islands and bounded by purple hills.[90] The pair moved on to Illaunroe, where Wilde hoped to make Miles – who had never fired a gun in his life

– 'land a salmon and kill a brace of grouse'. In the event, the sport consisted mainly of sea trout and hares. It is doubtful that Miles added much to the bag; his energies were channelled into painting a mural, depicting himself and Oscar as two fishing putti, above the legend 'tight lines'.[91] Lady Wilde had suggested they supplement their diet with 'chopped nettles', advising they 'make a good drink' or could be eaten 'like spinach'.[92]

When the weather was 'too bright for fishing', Wilde would reluctantly lay down his 'rod and gun' and pick up his 'quill'. He worked on his Symonds' review – but never finished it (the Beranger project was never started; Lady Wilde eventually took it on). Wilde's critique of Symonds' book focused on the chapter about women in Homer. And certainly women were on Wilde's mind. It had been a summer of romance. There had been the lovely Miles sisters at Bingham. One of the attractions of London was a girl described by an Oxford contemporary as 'your little friend with the smiling countenance'.[93] Perhaps she was the 'Eva' from whose cousin Wilde received a long, rambling and conspiratorial letter, asking him about his 'intentions' and offering to further his suit.[94] And then in Dublin, shortly before leaving for Moytura, he had met 'an exquisitely pretty girl' – Florence Balcombe, the eighteen-year-old daughter of a retired lieutenant-colonel. She had, Wilde informed 'Kitten' Harding, 'the most perfectly beautiful face I ever saw and not a sixpence of money'. They were potent ingredients for a doomed romance.[95]

Wilde presented her with his Moytura painting, made a charming little portrait drawing of her, and – later in the year – gave her a silver cross, inscribed with his name (one of their first dates had been to an afternoon service at Dublin's Anglican cathedral).[96] Curiously, though, Wilde does not seem to have rushed to compose any verse for, or about, his new love. He did write one unpublished 'Love Song', and several unfinished erotic reveries, but it is hard to connect them to any individual, least of all to the exquisitely pretty Miss Balcombe.[97] Perhaps there is a trace of her in some of the would-be aphorisms he scrawled in one of his Oxford notebooks: 'Love – a Godlike intoxication. The wine which God gives us to make us greet him on the road'; 'Love is always partly a misunderstanding'; and – less promisingly – 'Love itself is the worst misunderstanding of all.'[98]

He could, though, look the part of the love-struck poet. He cut a romantic figure, 'leaning over the bulwarks looking seawards', when he went to see Willie off on the boat over to England in early September. Willie introduced him to a girl he was trying to impress as 'my brother the

poet'.[99]* Oscar perhaps wished that he were travelling too. There had been plans to visit Rome with Frank Miles and Lord Ronald Gower ('we would have been a great Trinity') but at the last moment Gower had had to cry off. Instead Oscar was obliged to linger in Dublin – consoling himself, perhaps, with the presence of 'Florrie' – before heading north to Clonfin, to end the holidays with a final bout of 'sport'.[100]

Wilde started his third year at Oxford oppressed by financial anxieties. At auction the four Bray houses had failed to reach their reserve of £3,500 and so remained unsold. Instead of yielding money they were demanding expenditure. Perhaps at the agent's suggestion, a programme of repairs was put in hand. Wilde received from the local contractor a daunting six-page 'Estimate for Painting, Papering, Repairing & Whitening Ceilings & co & co'. And, as a local property owner, he also felt obliged to contribute £1 to a fund for 'White's widow and orphan' following 'the late disaster at Bray'.[101] Oscar wrote to his mother, lamenting that he would have to give up all thought of a fellowship, after his degree, as he would not be able to afford it.

Lady Wilde, overwhelmed by far greater financial troubles, was not impressed. She wrote with some asperity:

> I should be sorry that you had to seek a menial situation and give up the chance of the Fellowship but I do not see that, so far, your state is one that demands pity or commiseration – from May last (just five months) you have received cash for your own private personal expenses £145 and the rents of Bray and the sale of your furniture may bring you over the year till Spring. Then you can sell your houses for £3,000. £2,000 of which [after repayment of the mortgage] will give you £200 a year for ten years. A very ample provision to my thinking... £2,000 is a splendid sum to have in hand – and with your college income in addition I do not think you will need to enter a shop or beg for bread – I am very glad indeed you are so well off.[102]

As fiscal advice it displayed an alarming want of foresight: Lady Wilde's notion of financial planning seemed to be spending capital at a fixed rate,

---

* The girl was the eighteen-year-old Ethel Smyth (future composer and suffragist). By the end of the journey back to London Willie had proposed to her – despite the fact that Ethel had been violently sick on the crossing, and that Willie had, only a few weeks earlier, been courting a girl called Maud Thomas. The engagement was kept secret at Willie's insistence, and broken off after a few weeks. Ethel kept the ring.

in the hope that something would turn up before funds ran out completely. It was, however, a simple method, and both Oscar and Willie were ready to grasp it – in principle. It is doubtful, though, that Oscar ever regarded £200 a year as 'ample' – or even adequate – provision. Among his extravagances of the moment was a fine array of Masonic regalia, acquired when, proceeding into the Apollo Rose Croix Chapter, he was 'perfected into the 18th Degree of the Rose Croix'. He ran up a bill for over £13 on a special 'apron and collar', 'jewel', sword, belt, and sword-strap, along with an embossed case.[103]

Financial constraint was not the only thing encouraging Wilde to look beyond academe for his future. Although he certainly considered that an Oxford fellowship would be, in its way, a 'great honour', his first literary achievements, his contacts with Miles and Lord Ronald Gower, and his growing knowledge of London, had all made him eager for a larger stage. When Ward and Hunter-Blair – both in their final term, and both contemplating their long-destined careers as, respectively, 'a blameless lawyer' and a 'Scottish laird' – quizzed Wilde one evening as to his own ambitions, he replied with sudden seriousness, 'God knows, I won't be a dried up don, anyhow. I'll be a poet, a writer, a dramatist. Somehow or other I'll be famous, and if not famous, I'll be notorious.' Then, undercutting this call to action and self-assertion, he added, 'Or perhaps I'll lead the [life of pleasure] for a time, and then – who knows – rest and do nothing. What does Plato say is highest end that man can attain to here below?... to sit down and contemplate the good. Perhaps that will be the end of me too.'[104]

Ward's final examinations (which he sat that November) did not go as planned, and despite excellent philosophy papers he did not achieve his expected First. Wilde consoled him with the observation that 'it is a great thing to do well in the subjects worth doing well in'. And he still hoped that Ward might return and read for a fellowship. Ward, however, was determined to leave Oxford behind and visit Italy. As a parting gift Wilde and 'Kitten' Harding presented him with a gold ring – 'a memento of friendship, from two friends to another'.[105] 'Bouncer' would be a loss to Wilde's Magdalen life.

3

○○○○○○○○○

Hellas!

'The spirit of the god still dwelt within the marble.'

OSCAR WILDE

Wilde's exploration of the world beyond Oxford was continued at every opportunity. After the Michaelmas term ended, and before returning to Dublin for Christmas, he plunged into London's cultural round. He visited exhibitions, concerts; and, above all, theatres. Despite the attractions of pictorial art and music, plays and players tended to dominate his talk. And Henry Irving dominated above all. Irving's performance as Macbeth, at the Lyceum, made a huge impression on him. As Edward Sullivan recalled, 'he was fascinated by it'; though he feared that the general public 'might be similarly affected – a thing which he declared, would destroy his enjoyment of an extraordinary performance'.[1]

Wilde paid a very enjoyable visit to Lord Ronald Gower at Windsor, taking with him a new friend, Arthur May. 'He is quite charming in every way and a beautiful artist,' Wilde told Harding, 'and we have rushed into friendship.'[2] Gower's well-appointed new 'lodge' on the edge of Windsor Great Park was full of beautiful and curious things: fine French furniture, Old Master drawings, eighteenth-century portraits, and one of Marie Antoinette's fans.[3] Wilde, though, was developing his own ideas about interior decoration. It was a subject with which not only Ruskin but also the Pre-Raphaelites

had long engaged. In a desire to escape from the ugliness of ill-designed mass-produced furniture, with its machine-tooled ornamentation and ostentatious opulence, Morris, Rossetti and Burne-Jones had collaborated in the early 1860s on the quasi-medieval decor for Morris's 'Red House' at Bexleyheath, devising painted settles, decorative murals, carved tables and embroidered wall hangings. And the three friends were all involved in the company that Morris had established in the wake of this project, to produce furniture, fittings, fabrics, stained glass and wallpapers that reflected their shared passion for past ages and their shared respect for the traditions of hand-craftsmanship.

A rarified taste to begin with, supported by a few wealthy patrons, examples of Morris & Co.'s decorative work had gradually become more widespread, and more visible. One of the firm's first commissions had been to design the dining room at the new South Kensington Museum (now the V&A). And by the mid-1870s increasing numbers of individuals with moderate means but advanced tastes were using Morris-designed fabrics, papers and furniture – together with carefully chosen antique, modern and oriental objects – to adorn their rooms in what was being termed the 'Aesthetic' style.

The various distinctive elements of this decor had, by 1877, become well enough defined to be laid out – and lampooned. In September of that year *Punch* ran a decorator's guide to the Aesthetic fad, by its in-house expert, 'Mr Fernando F. Eminate'. He explained: 'It's a wide term, but I think I may say that the outcome of aestheticism is a mixture of antique quaintness, dingy and washed out colour, and oddity combined with dis-comfort.' Among his specific recommendations were: 'sage green' and 'dull yellow' colour-schemes; 'rugs in the most dull and neutral tones' over bare boards or matting; curtains 'with grotesque patterns', wallpapers 'of sombre or sickly ground', and 'spidery' design; a recess filled with 'delft and blue china'; and – for pictures – either 'E. B[urne]. Jones, or an occasional nocturne of Whistler's.'[4]

If this advanced decorative style was most closely associated with the newly developed west London suburb of Brompton, it was also recognized as flourishing in north Oxford, where the wives of many newly married dons – 'anxious to be up to date' – furnished their houses 'with Morris papers, old chests and cabinets and blue pots'.[5] Nor was the style confined to the details of home decor. There was an understanding that the so-called Aesthetics who did up their drawing rooms in low tones and Morris papers

were adherents of a new creed, a creed with a 'passionate' belief in the importance of culture, and the value of art (medieval, oriental or Greek). It was a creed that also found expression in 'eccentricities of attire' – long, flowing corsetless robes for the women; velvet jackets and capes for the men – in 'dishevelled hair' for both sexes; in esoteric jargon ('intense' was the adjective of choice); and in a 'general appearance of weary passion'.[6]

Wilde, steeped in the Pre-Raphaelite vision, and instinctively up to date, had lately become a devotee: 'aesthetic to the last degree' as one new acquaintance described him. And although he was too overflowing with enthusiasms to suggest a 'general appearance of weary passion', when it came to decor he was now 'passionately fond of secondary colours, low tones [and] Morris wallpapers'.[7] With Ward having gone down, Wilde was given his fine three-room first-floor set at the beginning of 1877, and he set about making them beautiful. A suitably 'neutral' grey carpet was set on the stained floorboards. Although it is not known whether he hung Morris wallpapers above the panelled wainscot, he filled the 'inner room' with china, pictures, a portfolio (for unframed works) and a piano. He acquired some 'Venetian hock glasses', six 'ruby champagne tumblers' and a pair of green 'Rumanian claret decanters'. 'The whole get up', he confessed to Ward, 'is much admired and a little made fun of on Sunday evenings.' Wilde kept up his tradition of informal Sunday evening entertaining – and, to do full justice to the splendour of the rooms, also laid on frequent 'breakfasts, lunches, etc'.[8]

He was, though, finding rather a want of stimulating company in college. As he complained to Ward, 'Kitten' Harding, for all his charms, 'never exerts my intellect or brain *in any way*'. And although he had hopes for some of the new demys, as well as for 'Gussy' Creswell who, like Ward, was both an Old Radleian and 'Psychological', the majority of the younger set, while 'capital good fellows', talked mostly 'nonsense or smut'.[9]

In the face of such puerility, art – its contemplation and creation – offered a welcome refuge. Closeted in the 'too charming' seclusion of his new rooms, with 'the sunshine, the crowing rooks and waving tree branches and the breeze at the window', Wilde did 'nothing but write sonnets and scribble poetry'. The literary successes of the previous year had to be built upon. And they were. Wilde would publish a further twelve poems during 1877, all but two of them sonnets. The discipline of the sonnet form, with its fourteen lines and fixed rhyme patterns was, he considered, an admirable exercise and 'trial of strength' for a young poet like himself.[10]

A love of beauty, though, was not to be confined to the page, the canvas, the concert hall, or the details of room decoration; it could touch every part of life. Symonds, in his *Studies of the Greek Poets* (1873) had urged his readers to 'seek some living echo' of the beauty of Greek sculpture by visiting 'the field where boys bathe in early morning, or the playgrounds of our public schools in summer, or the banks of the Isis when the eights are on the water'.[11] Wilde embraced the notion, going to the running track to watch the athletes train, and declaring of one sportsman that 'his left leg is a poem'.[12] At the university sports in March he singled out the running of F. Bullock Webster in the three-mile race as 'the most beautiful thing I ever saw'.[13] Nor was this self-consciously Hellenic admiration confined to the athletics field; Wilde was soon praising the 'Greek face' of one the new demys – as 'Greek' became a key term of approbation in his Aesthetic lexicon.[14]

He was not alone in such views. The celebration of male beauty was becoming something of a fad at Oxford. Wilde's Brasenose contemporary, Charles Edward Hutchison, produced an anonymous pamphlet in 1880 on 'Boy Worship' – declaring that it was not restricted to the self-conscious 'aesthetes', but had 'many an ardent follower' among the sportsmen too (the term 'boy' was, it seems, a broad one, encompassing both the oarsmen in the Varsity boat and the young choristers of the college chapel). Although such enthusiasms might claim to be a mode of Aesthetic contemplation, they could shade by degrees into sexual yearning and even sexual contact. Many undergraduates, after all, had come from large public schools where sexual relations between boys were commonplace.

Wilde was certainly aware of this possibility, but not approving. When he spotted his fellow Magdalen undergraduate Charles Todd sitting in a private box at the theatre with one of the young college choristers, he wrote to Ward: 'In our friend *Todd's* ethical barometer, at what height is his moral quicksilver?... Myself I believe Todd is extremely moral and only mentally spoons the boy [a thirteen-year-old], but I think he is foolish to go about with one, if he *is* bringing this boy about with him... *don't tell anyone about it like a good boy – it would do neither us nor Todd any good.*'[15] For Wilde male beauty provided scope not only for admiration but also for creation: he began one slightly bathetic poem upon a 'Choir Boy', and completed a rather more successful one, 'Wasted Days', inspired by the image of a 'fair slim boy' painted on a tile by Violet Troubridge, one of 'Gussy' Creswell's young cousins.[16]

But if a decorated tile, a chorister or a long-distance runner could produce an Aesthetic response, an art exhibition might furnish a spiritual one. Wilde remained, as ever, teetering on the brink of Catholicism, caught 'in the wiles of the Scarlet Woman'.[17] When he took 'Kitten' Harding up to London to the 'Old Masters' at the Royal Academy, he was delighted to note that it brought out his friend's 'Popish tendencies'. The show that year included a good scattering of Italian religious works, amid the usual round-up of British portraits and Dutch landscapes.[18] It was perhaps on that same visit that Wilde, calling at Miles's studio, was introduced to Ronald Gower's sister, Constance, wife of the Duke of Westminster. She was his first duchess, and he was greatly impressed, pronouncing her 'the most fascinating, Circe-like brilliant woman' he had ever met, 'something too charming'.[19]

Amid such distractions – social, cultural and spiritual – Wilde's academic work drifted. He had been put up for the 'Ireland scholarship' – the university's premier classics prize – but did not get it ('What stumped me was Philology'). He hated the taste of failure, and rued the fact that he had not worked harder.[20] But, although he resolved to reform and read hard for Greats, it would be on his terms.[21] At the end of term, that March, with all the students assembled in the college hall and the dons ranged at the high table, Wilde was called up by Dr Bulley for his 'terminal examination'. Mr Allen, the Roman history tutor, was asked, 'How do you find Mr Wilde's work?'. When Allen answered, 'Mr Wilde absents himself without apology from my lectures, his work is most unsatisfactory', the president remarked, in his distinctive courtly manner, 'That is hardly the way to treat a gentleman, Mr Wilde.' The temptation to make an *épat* was too great: Wilde replied, 'But, Mr President, Mr Allen is *not* a gentleman.' Consternation followed. For an undergraduate to make such an assertion about a tutor in a formal and semi-public setting had an electric effect. The fact that it was true did nothing to lessen the impact. Wilde was told to leave the hall.[22]

He already had a reputation within the college for subverting authority. There had been frequent run-ins with the proctors; or the incident in the college chapel, when – with Prince Leopold and Mrs Liddell (wife of the dean of Christ Church) in the congregation – Wilde was scheduled to read the first lesson. Reaching the lectern he turned over the pages of the Bible, then began in a languorous voice, 'The Song of Solomon...' Before he could get very far into that great hymn to female loveliness, the dean swooped down from his stall, and 'thrusting his beard into Wilde's face, cooed out, "You have the wrong lesson, Mr Wilde. It is Deuteronomy

XVI."' The incident at collections, however, was of a new order, and set the dons firmly against the 'bad boy' of the college.[23]

Wilde chose not to care. He could convince himself that the Magdalen Senior Common Room was a backwater, dwarfed by the beckoning ocean of London life and London opportunity. The same month as the Mr Allen incident, Wilde forged his first permanent London connection. He was elected to the St Stephen's Club in Westminster, flatteringly put up by David Plunket – solicitor general for Ireland, MP for Dublin University and uncle of his friend Barton. Although the club, founded in 1870 by Disraeli and others, was a Tory institution, it also had artistic sympathies: Whistler was a member. So too was Hunter-Blair. Wilde was conscious of the honour, but slightly annoyed that it had come so soon. The entrance subscription was a hefty £42.[24]

Saddled with this expense, and – once again – 'irretrievably broke', he felt unable to contemplate a trip to Rome that Easter to meet up with Ward and Hunter-Blair. He was sad to lose the opportunity. Hunter-Blair was disappointed too; he still nursed hopes of Wilde's conversion, and thought that a visit to Rome 'to see something of Catholicism at headquarters' might prove decisive. Placing the matter in the hands of 'Lady Luck', if not St Peter, he told Wilde that – since he was travelling via the South of France – he would stake 'a couple of pounds' on the tables at Monte Carlo; 'and if it is predestined that you are to come to Rome, I shall certainly win the money'. Wilde subsequently received a telegram with the extraordinary news that his friend had realized nearly £60. Alive to the drama of the moment he set off almost at once. 'This is an era in my life,' he told Harding. 'I wish I could look into the seeds of time and see what was coming.' He might have been surprised.[25]

On reaching London, Wilde discovered that Professor Mahaffy was passing through town on his way to the continent, en route for a tour of Greece. He was with two students, Goulding (his, and Wilde's, companion of the year before) and young George Macmillan, who had gone straight from Eton into the family publishing firm. Wilde resolved to travel with them down to Genoa. The journey proved to be spiritual as much as physical. From the moment they left Charing Cross, Mahaffy set about trying to divert Wilde from Rome and Roman Catholicism, 'using every argument he can', as Macmillan reported to his father. 'At first he tried hard to persuade him to come to Greece with us, pointing out to him by the way all the worst faults of Popery. Finding this not altogether effective, though it had some weight, he changed tack, and [by the time they reached Genoa] when

Wilde began to say that perhaps he would come, Mahaffy said, "I won't take you. I wouldn't have such a fellow with me," which of course, as Wilde is somewhat of a wilful disposition, has raised in him a firm determination to come, and I quite expect he will, and hope so.'[26]

Still debating his final decision, Wilde lingered in Genoa with Macmillan and Goulding, while Mahaffy called on his sister and invalid mother, who were staying in the town. He and his companions marvelled at the great Renaissance palaces, the general profusion of white marble doorways, the sparkling Mediterranean, the gaily painted houses ('blue, orange, deep red') and the gardens full of 'camellias, oranges, lemons, olives, and luxuriant shrubs'. They visited the Palazzo Rosso, and saw Guido Reni's languorously posed painting of the martyred St Sebastian. Macmillan thought it 'about the most beautiful picture' he had ever seen.[27] He was not alone in his verdict. Wilde, ignoring the fact that Ruskin dismissed Guido's art as sentimental and insincere, allowed himself to be seduced by the remote sensuality of the image: the 'lovely brown boy with crisp, clustering hair and red lips, bound by his evil enemies to a tree, and though pierced by arrows, raising his eyes with divine impassioned gaze towards... the opening heavens'.[28] Guido's 'Sebastian' acceded to Wilde's personal pantheon, joining the Greek youths of Plato and the Parthenon frieze as an ideal of adolescent male beauty, in all its 'bloom of vitality and radiance'.[29]

Easter was approaching and the city was *en fête*. Wilde framed the moment in his 'Sonnet written in Holy Week at Genoa', suggesting that he had been recalled from the sensual paganism of the 'sweet and honied hours' spent in the Scaglietto Gardens to a remembrance of the Passion's 'bitter pain' on hearing 'a little child' pass by singing an Easter hymn.[30] But, not untypically, having made this poetic declaration, setting the Catholic above the Hellenic, he decided to put off Christian Rome for the moment and go to pagan Greece. Mahaffy was delighted to have swayed his former pupil from 'the Jesuits' and 'cheat[ed] the Devil of his due'.[31]

The party left Genoa on Good Friday by train, crossed Italy to Ravenna (where Wilde was amazed at the sixth-century mosaics) and then travelled down to Brindisi to find their ship. They were, as Macmillan described them, a diverse but happy band: Mahaffy – the 'General' – 'amusing and interesting'; Goulding 'very full of spirits – delightfully innocent of what we call culture but still thoroughly entering into the delight of what we see – whether scenery, pictures, palaces etc. In fact a downright honest wild Irishman, with no end of fun in him and no particular harm'; and the 'aesthetic' Wilde,

resplendent in a new brownish-yellow coat.[32] Wilde might be 'capable of talking a good deal of nonsense' on Aesthetic topics but, for all that, he was deemed 'a very sensible, well-informed and charming man'.[33]

They set sail from Brindisi on the evening of Easter Sunday (1 April, 1877), and woke at dawn to see 'the low mountainous coast' of Epiros (or 'Thessaly' as Wilde dubbed it with more poetic feeling than geographical accuracy).[34] They put in at Corfu, and from there Wilde wrote with breezy unconcern to Mr Bramley, the dean of Magdalen. Term was due to begin in two days' time; he would not be there. 'The chance,' he explained of visiting Mycenae and Athens in 'such good company' as Dr Mahaffy's, 'was too great for me.' Surely to see Greece with such a guide was 'quite as good as going to lectures'. The country was still very little visited in the 1870s. He hoped Mr Bramley would not mind if he were 'ten days' late for term. Although he failed to mention his plan to take in Rome on the way home, his stated expectation that he would be reaching Athens around 17 April made it clear that his absence would be rather longer than ten days.[35] Magdalen's grey quadrangles no doubt seemed very far away.

The colour of life, bright at Genoa, intensified still further as they touched upon the Greek world, even at its very edge. Mahaffy considered a market day in Corfu, among 'the most picturesque sights in Europe'. For the young classicists it was thrilling to hear Greek words being spoken, to see Greek letters on the shop signs. The streets were thronged with people: 'royal-looking peasant lads, clothed in sheepskins', their 'brown throats and limbs' set off by 'scarlet fezes' and thick clustering curls'.[36] The beauty of these young men was striking. Macmillan thought they 'might well have sat to Phidias'. For Wilde they seemed the living type of Plato's Charmides or Guido's St Sebastian.[37]

That year the Greek Orthodox Easter fell a week later than the Western festival, so they found themselves once more in Holy Week. And Wilde, keeping up his sonnet sequence, produced at Corfu another poem balancing the pagan and Christian powers. This time he reversed the dynamic, imagining that though the classical deities are supposed dead, and 'Mary's Son is King', perhaps somewhere in the 'sea-trancèd isle' a 'God lies hidden in the asphodel' waiting to spring forth.[38] Although the poem suggested lingering to 'watch a-while' in the hope of seeing this lurking deity, the party moved on. They sailed the next day, 3 April, via the island of Zante (still gratifyingly 'woody' as Homer had described it) for Katakolo, on the northwest coast of the Peloponnese.[39]

This was the land about which Wilde had read and dreamed and thought since his days at Portora, the cradle of Alcibiades and Plato, of Homer, Euripides and Alexander the Great. 'Hellas! Hellas!' as Wilde called it in the sonnet which described the moment when, with the red sun setting into the sea, he 'stood upon the soil of Greece at last!'

The fact that Katakolo was an unlovely little port, and the surrounding landscape unexceptional, could be ignored. Wilde (like his companions) was not just arriving upon an actual shore, but returning to a land of the imagination. There were other accommodations to be made. For classicists, imbued with an idea of Greece's majesty, the 'smallness' of the country came as a shock (Mount Parnassus was visible from Zante). At Olympia – the first stop on their ride across the Peloponnese – they had to overlook the archaeologists' ugly earthworks and rude wheelbarrows, and confront the fact that the temples were built not of gleaming Parian marble but of coarse pitted stone. Macmillan's initial disappointment on this score transformed itself within a few hours into an admiration for the 'rugged grandeur' of the work.[40] Much else, however, struck them with an immediate sense of wonder. Dr Gustav Hirschfeld, director of the excavations at Olympia, showed them a 'colossal head' of Apollo that had just been unearthed. Mahaffy considered it among 'the grandest relics of the highest and purest Greek Art'.[41] And perhaps it first gave Wilde that sense of how – in the finest Hellenic sculpture – 'the spirit of the god still dwelt within the marble'.[42]

Their trip across the Peloponnese took eight days. They visited the great temple of Apollo upon its high and lonely eminence at Bassae. They wandered in the vast theatre at Argos (subject of another sonnet). They saw ancient Mycenae with its cyclopean remains. Although Wilde surrendered himself to Greece and its classical and pagan associations, he could not quite forget Christian Rome. Even in the theatre at Argos he recalled – amid the ruins – the pope, captive in the Vatican and 'half-dethroned for Gold!'[43] And 'topping the crest of a hill near Olympia' he was struck by the sight of a young peasant lad with a small lamb 'slung around his neck' – the very image of Jesus as 'the Good Shepherd'.[44]

There were other pleasures and distractions too. It was a week of Arcadian scenery, of spring flowers – young corn, scarlet anemones and purple cistus – of glorious profiles and stupendous hair. They put up with short rations during the fast of Holy Week, subsisting on sour cheese, resined wine ('a liquor we could only liken to furniture polish'), Easter eggs ('pink!!!') and 'the invigorating powers of Greek air'. They enjoyed life in the saddle. Goulding

had hoped to knock the 'swagger' out of Wilde once he got him on to a horse, but Oscar seems to have kept up well. He was fortunate perhaps that Greek horse owners were not keen on having their mounts ridden above a gentle amble. On the ride to Megalopolis, the horse provider, who was accompanying them on foot, finding his wishes ignored, pulled a knife to try and enforce his point. He was immediately trumped by a member of the party – almost certainly not Wilde – producing a revolver.[45]

Brigands, a serious danger in northern Greece, were not much in evidence. The few they met were 'disposed to be friendly'.[46] There was one anxious moment, when the three younger members of the group rode on ahead and lost sight of Mahaffy. When he failed to catch up to them, they began to fear the worst. But, before they could raise the alarm, he re-appeared, much put out at having spent a fruitless hour searching for his greatcoat and rug which had fallen from his saddle while he negotiated a 'short-cut'.[47]

Crossing by sea from Epidaurus (via Aegina), the group of travellers reached Athens on 13 April.[48] George Macmillan at once declared himself 'in the Seventh Heaven', and Wilde was probably upon the same exalted plain. To anyone familiar with ancient Greek history and literature it was a thrilling thing to stand upon the Acropolis, before the Parthenon, the Erechtheion, and the little temple of Athena Nike, to walk – as Macmillan put it – on 'the very pavement... trodden by so many mighty spirits'.[49] This was the literal and figurative high point of the trip. Something of Wilde's wonder was caught (albeit in fictionalized form) by one of his female friends:

> He was speaking to her of Greece, of Athens – the city of the early morning – rising in the cool, pale, steady light of dawn, a new Aphrodite, from out of the lapping circle of the waves. He spoke to her of the Parthenon, the one temple – not a building – a temple, as complete, as personal as a statue. And that first sight of the Acropolis, the delicate naked columns rising up in the morning sunshine: It was like coming upon some white Greek goddess. It made one feel.[50]

The Acropolis was followed by other wonders. They viewed the plain of Marathon. They visited monuments and museums, delighting in the little terracotta 'Tanagra' statuettes, so 'remarkable for the marvellous modernness of their appearance'.[51] Wilde acquired a 'white walking stick' cut from the olive groves of the Academia. It was not his only souvenir: he also had himself photographed – looking suitably Byronic – in Greek

national dress. Mahaffy's name opened all doors, securing them a private view of the extraordinary golden treasures that Schliemann had brought back from his excavations at Mycenae. The Irish contingent registered their 'strong resemblance to various old Irish things' – suggestive of that common ancestry between Greek and Celt.[52] Treasure of a different kind had been waiting for Wilde at the Athens *poste restante*: an Easter card from Florence Balcombe.[53]

Wilde and his companions left Athens on Saturday 21 April, seventeen days after the start of the Oxford term.[54] They travelled by steamer to Naples. Wilde was amused to hear, from his adjoining cabin, the 'piously inclined' Macmillan unleash a volley of 'oaths and profanity' at the legions of mosquitoes and fleas by which he was being tormented.[55] And neither Macmillan's woes nor Wilde's amusement ended there. During a 'frightful storm' that assailed the ship as they passed through the Aegean, the young publisher was 'sent crashing neck and crop into the keys of a piano in the small saloon'.[56]

From Naples Wilde hastened on alone to Rome, where Ward and Hunter-Blair were waiting for him at the Hotel d'Inghilterra. It was a happy reunion. Together they toured the ancient remains, expertly guided by Hunter-Blair's friend George Gilbert Murray, professor of humanities at Glasgow. But, after Greece, Wilde had perhaps supped full of ruins. It was, Hunter-Blair recalled, 'Rome, Christian and Catholic' which chiefly occupied his attention and 'evoked his enthusiasm'. The 'inexhaustible treasures' laid up by early Christian martyrs and high Renaissance popes were eagerly explored.

Nor was Rome's Christian present ignored. Hunter-Blair, ever anxious about Wilde's soul, was hopeful that the visit might 'do something to guide [his] wandering steps into the Fold'. The friends would often dine, at some local restaurant, together with Grissel and Ogilvie-Fairlie, two young Oxonian converts, who, like Hunter-Blair, had been made 'papal chamberlains'. And another Vatican contact, Monsignor Edmund Stoner, arranged a private audience with Pope Pius for Wilde and Hunter-Blair. In a memorable moment, the aged pontiff placed his hands on Wilde's head in benediction, and 'expressed the hope and wish that he would soon follow his [friend] into the City of God'. Wilde sat silent in the carriage on the drive back to the Inghilterra. But instead of making any decisive step, he retreated to his room and wrote a sonnet.[57]

That evening the three friends drove out to the great basilica of S. Paolo fuori le Mura. Wilde insisted that they stop at the beautiful non-Catholic

cemetery, by the Pyramid of Cestius, in the lee of the city wall. It was where Keats was buried (and Shelley too). Wilde wished to pay homage to the author of 'Endymion', who had died of tuberculosis in an apartment close to the Spanish Steps. His simple tombstone bore the epitaph 'This grave contains all that is mortal of a young English poet, who on his death bed, in the bitterness of his heart, at the malicious power of his enemies, desired these words to be engraven... Here Lies One Whose Name Is Writ In Water.' Keats's bitterness was supposedly towards his critics. It was said that their harsh reviews had hastened his end. And Wilde, standing by the grave, with its carpet of spring flowers, was struck by the idea that Keats too was a martyr, 'worthy to lie in the City of Martyrs... a Priest of Beauty slain before his time'. He saw him as 'a lovely Sebastian', slain 'by the arrows of a lying and unjust tongue'.[58]

The power of this vision was slightly undercut, Wilde felt, by the proximity of a recently erected marble tablet, set in the cemetery wall. It carried 'some mediocre lines of poetry' in praise of Keats, and a medallion profile that made the poet appear 'ugly', 'hatchet-faced' and thick-lipped – quite unlike Wilde's personal vision of him as an ideal Greek type of male beauty, to rank alongside Apollo, Charmides or Guido Reni's St Sebastian. But Wilde refused to let this 'marble libel' destroy the moment. To Hunter-Blair's disgust, he prostrated himself upon the hallowed turf.[59]

If Wilde could divine the spiritual in the aesthetic, Rome also helped him appreciate the worldly in the religious. The opulence of papal splendour dazzled him. And though he might still hesitate actually to become a Catholic, he was sure that he would like to be cardinal. It became his stated ambition – or one of them. To have been a prince of the church, certainly at the time of the Renaissance, would have allowed him to blur the line between popery and paganism. For Wilde one of the chief pleasures of his Roman sojourn was finding 'the Greek gods and the heroes and heroines of Greek story, throned in the Vatican'. Among the masterpieces of antiquity assembled by Julius II and his successors, a marble statue of a long-limbed athlete scraping the sweat from his body (a version of the 'Apoxymenos' carved by Lysippus, one-time court-sculptor to Alexander the Great) became Wilde's especial favourite.[60]

The sheer abundance and variety of Rome's art treasures amazed Wilde; he would later joke that the city was 'the Whiteleys of art'. Exposure extended his Aesthetic tastes, or perhaps corrupted them. Having already strayed from the approved Ruskinian canon in admiring Guido Reni, he

developed an enthusiasm for the similarly 'sensual' and 'impure' Correggio. The artist's 'Danae' was one of the jewels of the Borghese Collection.[61] But if Wilde had hoped his travels would 'mark an era in his life' by producing a resolution to his spiritual waverings, he was disappointed: they simply heightened his sense of both paganism and popery, imbuing them with brighter colours and quicker fire.

Wilde could air his new enthusiasms with a new companion. Through Ward and Hunter-Blair he met a young American called Julia Constance Fletcher; they went riding together in the Campagna. She lived in Rome with her mother and stepfather, an American-born painter, Eugene Benson. Although not yet twenty, Fletcher had already written one novel (published – under the pseudonym 'George Fleming' – by Macmillan & Co.) and was working on another. Clever, amusing, well-travelled and well-read, Wilde found himself 'much attracted to her in every way'.[62] Her vision of him can be caught in the pages of the romance that she was writing that spring. *Mirage* (a three-volume novel about a party of travellers on a tour of Syria) contains, in the character of 'Claude Davenant', a portrait of an Oxford-educated poet, recently returned from Greece.

> His face was almost an anachronism. It was like one of Holbein's portraits; pale, large-featured, individual; a peculiar and interesting countenance, of singularly mild yet ardent expression. Mr Davenant was very young – probably not more than two and twenty; but he looked younger. He wore his hair rather long, thrown back, and clustering about his neck like the hair of a mediaeval saint. He spoke with rapidity, in a low voice, with peculiarly distinct enunciation; he spoke like a man who made a study of expression. He listened like one accustomed to speak.

Fletcher certainly registered, and seems to have enjoyed, the elements of Wilde's developing pose: the mind set on higher things (Davenant repeatedly falls off his horse while lost in thought); the air of hieratic inscrutability (when asked what one of his poems 'means', he replies in his 'most languid tone', 'Ah, but I never explain things'); the divided allegiance between 'those two stars of the material and the spiritual life – the Venus of the Greeks and the Virgin of the Italians'; and – most distinctively – the adoption of the Aesthetic viewpoint upon every question. Davenant spends all his money on an old textile ('I should call it an inspiration, a poem in colour') to prevent

one of the other travellers buying it and re-backing it with 'a new piece of stuff'. He insists on a young messenger boy being brought into a bare waiting room because 'He's got a beautiful face... and it will be something to look at.' He admits that he rarely visits his sister, ever since she married a man who furnished his Elizabethan manor house with gilt-encrusted Louis Quinze furniture ('I'm sorry, for I was very fond of my sister').

Fletcher not only appreciated Wilde's humour; she also shared his intellectual curiosity. Walter Pater was one of her heroes. She would dedicate *Mirage* to 'The author of *The Renaissance*'. Wilde promised to send her some of Pater's uncollected articles – as well as, for comparison, one of J. A. Symonds' books (Fletcher found Symonds rather 'redundant in style – less an artist – less daring than Pater. I can imagine Mr Symonds to be married, and his wife's relations reading his book').[63]

Wilde finally returned to England and Oxford at the end of April. Full of the joys of Greece and Rome, he was shocked to discover that the college authorities – at last losing patience – had passed a resolution, rusticating him until the end of the academic year (October), and docking half his demyship (£47.50). During his suspension he would be expected to prepare a set amount of work, and any failure on this score would result in the loss of his demyship.[64] That he should be sent down from Oxford for being – as he put it – 'the first undergraduate to visit Olympia' confirmed all his worst thoughts about the ungentlemanly Mr Allen and 'that old woman in petticoats' the dean. He railed against the verdict, consulted the 'statutes', and appealed to the schools clerk, but in vain.[65] The Magdalen authorities were not to be moved. He secured just one small concession: if he returned in October with the prescribed work satisfactorily completed, half the fine would be remitted.[66]

Wilde retreated in disgust. He passed a 'delightful' couple of weeks in London 'with Frank Miles and a lot of friends'.[67] It was stimulating to be in artistic company and in town – and at the start of the 'season' too. There were concerts to attend: Wagner at the Albert Hall, Anton Rubinstein playing at St James's.[68] The Royal Academy summer exhibition opened on 5 May: Lord Ronald Gower had two sculptures in the show, and Frank Miles a view of 'Lough Muck, Connemara'. That year, however, the Royal Academy had a rival.

The great cultural excitement of the summer was the opening of the new Grosvenor Gallery on Bond Street. It was to be a novel type of exhibition space: luxurious, well appointed and up to date. The wealthy and artistic

Sir Coutts Lindsay, supported by his wealthy and artistic young wife, had poured his energy, taste and resources into creating a modern 'Temple of Art'. It was also a temple to the new Aesthetic style. Every detail of its opulent decor proclaimed the allegiance: damask wall hangings in the approved Aesthetic shades of 'sage green' and 'dead crimson'; dadoes of 'dull green and gold'; salvaged Palladian doorways; rich 'Turkey carpets' and artfully placed 'Japanese China'.[69]

The inaugural exhibition, carefully selected by the Lindsays, confirmed the Aesthetic connection. Pictures were hung 'on the line', rather than being crammed on to the walls (as at the Academy). They included works by many of the heirs to the Pre-Raphaelite tradition: Holman Hunt, Millais (including a portrait of Lord Ronald Gower), Walter Crane, and indeed the Lindsays themselves. But the most arresting works in the show were those by Burne-Jones and Whistler. The former had contributed three large closely worked canvases – the 'Beguiling of Merlin', the 'Days of Creation' and the 'Mirror of Venus' – and the latter offered something completely different. Whistler eschewed both detail and narrative in a succession of low-toned impressionistic 'symphonies' (usually landscapes), 'harmonies' and 'arrangements' (usually portraits).

The private view on 30 April was a glittering occasion. 'Everybody', as the papers reported excitedly, 'was there': aristocrats, politicians (Gladstone among them), artists, writers, actors, distinguished prelates, and 'a dream of fair women'.[70] Wilde, thanks to his connections, was there too, delighted to be in the midst of London's celebrities. It was an opportunity to meet literary figures such as Mahaffy's friend Lord Houghton (biographer of Keats), and to make the acquaintance of Whistler.[71] As an introduction to London's fashionable cultural life it could not be bettered. But if Wilde hoped to be noticed, he found that he was not the most conspicuous figure making a debut that season.

A new beauty had appeared in the London firmament: a young woman of grave yet languorous demeanour, fair-skinned, grey-eyed and with corn-gold hair. Her features had a definite sculptural quality: the arched brow, the full chin, the nobly chiselled mouth, the 'augustly pillared' throat. Beauty, like everything else, has its fashions. And to the eye of the time she seemed the ideal of female loveliness: a Greek statue come to life.[72] Frank Miles had been among the first to notice her, one night at the theatre, and among the first to meet her, at a reception hosted by Lady Sebright in Lowndes Square. She was Mrs Langtry, twenty-three-year-old daughter of a Channel

Island clergyman, recently married to a portly and undistinguished yachting enthusiast. Her great ambition was to make her way in society. She was not rich: she arrived in London with one black dress and no jewellery except for her wedding ring. Nor was she well connected. But in Lady Sebright (the friend of a friend) she found an able sponsor.[73]

By the end of that first Lowndes Square 'At Home', Lillie Langtry had acquired numerous aristocratic admirers and two artists eager to celebrate her beauty – and to catch something of its reflected glory. Besides Frank Miles, Millais was also present that evening. And as a fellow Channel Islander (and a Royal Academician) he secured both the honour of taking her in to dinner, and the promise of a portrait sitting.

Miles, however, not to be outdone, made an impromptu pencil sketch of her as she stood. He planned to reproduce it as the first salvo in a campaign to establish her fame. It was a campaign in which he wanted to enlist Wilde's assistance.[74] An introduction was effected: Wilde thought her 'the loveliest woman in Europe'.[75] And when Lord Ronald Gower called on Miles, not long afterwards, he reported that the artist was 'quite in ecstasies' about Mrs Langtry, declaring that 'he with his pencil and his friend Oscar Wilde with his pen, will make her the Joconde [Mona Lisa] and Laura of this century!'[76] The surprise is that Wilde, who had been writing poems all year, did not at once dash off a sonnet in her honour.[77] Instead he returned to Dublin.

4

Specially Commended

QUESTION: *'What are the sweetest words in the world?'*
OSCAR WILDE: *'Well Done!'*

Both Lady Wilde and Mahaffy were outraged at the actions of the Magdalen authorities. Mahaffy took it as almost a personal insult. Willie, typically, supposed that there must be some scandal behind it all, and wrote from Moytura to ask Oscar about the 'real' reason for his rustication.[1] Exiled from Oxford, Wilde devoted himself to literature and the intellect. He agreed to give a series of lectures on classical subjects to the young women of Dublin's Alexandra College. It would be a noteworthy undertaking: Mahaffy himself had given a similar course of lectures in 1869.[2] Wilde continued to write his verse – although, conscious of the need to enhance his standing, he put quite as much energy into building up his network of literary contacts. To the roster of periodicals willing to publish his work, he added the *Illustrated Monitor,* another Dublin-based Catholic magazine.[3] He attended an open meeting of the Catholic University Literary Society at which 'the foundation of an Irish National literature' was discussed by a gathering of Dublin's cultural worthies.[4] He dined out regularly, delighted that everyone thought he was a fellow of Magdalen and listened to him.[5]

But his horizons now reached beyond the Irish shore. With a precocious grasp of the power of association, he set about establishing links to the

wider literary world. His poems were his calling cards. Having written a sonnet on the 'Recent Massacre of Christians in Bulgaria', he sent a copy to Gladstone; the former Liberal prime minister, then in opposition, was campaigning against Turkish atrocities in the Balkans. 'I am little more than a boy,' Wilde claimed disingenuously, 'and have no literary interest in London, but perhaps if *you* saw any good stuff in the lines I send you, some editor (of the *Nineteenth Century* perhaps or the *Spectator*) might publish them.'[6] Gladstone's 'sympathetic' words of praise encouraged Wilde not only to send the politician another poem ('a poor return on your courtesy') but also to submit some verses to both the *Nineteenth Century* and the *Spectator*, with a note that Gladstone 'saw some promise in them'.[7] Such promise, however, was not quite enough to secure their publication.

His sonnet 'On the Grave of Keats', accompanied by a plea for a better monument to the poet's memory, Wilde sent off to Lord Houghton, Buxton Forman (editor of both Keats and Shelley), and William Michael Rossetti, brother of Dante Gabriel, and another Keats enthusiast. The responses were perhaps more polite that enthusiastic. Lord Houghton pointed out that – as his biography made clear – Keats's life was *not* the tragedy of neglect suggested by Wilde's poem, before adding that the medallion portrait at Rome, so objected to by Wilde, was in fact 'very like' the poet, and 'having been put up by enthusiastic friends' it would not do to try and displace it.[8]

He had better success with an article he wrote for the *Dublin University Magazine*, an extended review of the Grosvenor Gallery exhibition. It was an assured performance. The 'art critic' was a new role for him, though one endorsed by the examples of Ruskin and Swinburne; and Wilde readily assumed an equality with his heroes. When the *Dublin University Magazine* editor suggested some alteration to his strictures on Alma-Tadema's draughtsmanship, Wilde replied insufferably, 'I and Lord Ronald Gower and Mr Ruskin, and all artists of my acquaintance, hold that Alma-Tadema's drawing of men and women is disgraceful. I could not let an article signed with my name state he was a powerful drawer.'[9]

The review, when it appeared in July 1877, was a mixture of lush description, discerning praise and lofty qualification. Almost every sentence subtly proclaimed the author's own connections, accomplishments and allegiances: Millais's portraits of the daughters of the Duke of Westminster were endorsed as 'very good likenesses', while his portrait of Lord Ronald Gower 'will be easily recognized', though it is not in the same class as the artist's picture of Ruskin 'which is in Oxford' (not on public display, but

at the home of Sir Henry Acland). William Blake Richmond's painting of 'Electra at the Tomb of Agamemnon' captured 'exactly that peculiar opal blue' of a Greek sky – even if the treatment of the women's dresses showed clearly that Richmond had not studied Aeschylus' 'elaborate and pathetic' account of the scene in the *Choephorae*. A postscript gratuitously recorded that Whistler – creator of the famous 'Peacock Room' – was, unlike the reviewer, unaware of the peacock-patterned mosaics at Ravenna.[10]

If Wilde hailed Whistler as 'The Great Dark Master', he used the artist's low-toned images principally as grounds for humour. His comment upon 'Nocturne in Black and Gold' ('The falling rocket'), and its companion piece 'Nocturne in Blue and Silver', carried facetiousness dangerously close to derision: 'These pictures are certainly worth looking at for about as long as one looks at a real rocket, that is, for somewhat less than a quarter of a minute.' The most generous praise was lavished upon the works of Burne-Jones.

The article gave Wilde a first small toehold in the art world of the day. To reinforce his position, he hastened to send copies of the review to many of the artists mentioned. And much to his gratification he received several 'delightful letters' back.[11] The art world, though, was changing even as he began to engage with it. Ruskin's review of the same Grosvenor exhibition, for the *Fors Clavigera*, had not been as temperate as Wilde's. His comments on Whistler's 'Nocturne in Black and Gold' had provoked a libel action. Whistler won the case but was awarded only a farthing's damages, and had to pay his own costs. The debacle bankrupted the painter, and created a rift at the heart of the English art scene. Sides were taken. Burne-Jones, who – against his will – appeared as a witness for Ruskin, found himself on the other side of the line from his former friend, Whistler. It was awkward terrain that Wilde would have to negotiate.

The art world, though, was not Wilde's only concern in writing about the Grosvenor show. His review can also be read as a carefully contrived letter of introduction to Walter Pater. Wilde has been at Oxford for three years without, apparently, seeking to meet Pater; perhaps he was moved to do so now in part by a desire to keep up with Julia Constance Fletcher's Paterian enthusiasms. Pater is quoted once, and would have been quoted again but for the editorial blue pencil. He is also cited as one of the select band – along with Swinburne, Symonds and Morris – contributing to 'that revival of culture and love of beauty which in a great part owes its birth to Mr Ruskin'. There are mentions in the article of Heraclitus, the philosopher who provided the epigraph to Pater's celebrated 'Conclusion'; of

Correggio, an artist whose work adorned Pater's study at Brasenose; and of Simeon Solomon, a painter, and friend of Pater's, who no longer exhibited following his conviction, in 1873, for attempted sodomy in a public urinal off Oxford Street.

Wilde sent a copy of the review to Pater at Oxford, and received a gracious letter of recognition:

DEAR MR WILDE

Accept my best thanks for the magazine and your letter. Your excellent article on the Grosvenor Gallery I read with very great pleasure; it makes me much wish to make your acquaintance, and I hope you will give me an early call on your return to Oxford.

I should much like to talk over some of the points with you, though on the whole I think your criticism very just, and it is certainly very pleasantly expressed. It shows that you possess some beautiful, and for your age quite exceptionally cultivated, tastes; and a considerable knowledge also of many beautiful things. I hope you will write a great deal in time to come.

Very truly yours

WALTER PATER[12]

It was a trophy too precious to be parted from. Wilde copied it out when excitedly relaying news of its contents to Ward and Harding.[13]

Wilde's literary efforts also had their effect closer to home. They aided his courtship of Florence Balcombe. On receiving the copy of the *Monitor* containing 'Urbs Sacra Aeterna' Florrie wrote to congratulate Wilde on his 'sublime' sonnet: 'I can quite understand the priests going into ecstasies over it... We want to hear you read it yourself to us. Do come tomorrow evening if you can.' She added as a playful postscript, 'Was it quite right to send the *Monitor* to a good Protestant home like ours?'[14] The one person not impressed by the flow of spiritual poems was Hunter-Blair. Finally losing patience with Wilde's continued failure to commit to the Catholic Church, he declared 'Do not send me your sonnets. I do not care to see them.' They, nevertheless, remained friends.[15]

Home life showed signs of improvement. Oscar's half-brother Henry Wilson, buoyed by his position at St Mark's, had agreed to buy the Merrion Square house, and to allow Lady Wilde and her sons to continue in residence, at least for the moment. It was a happy solution that seemed to offer the

possibility of a continued family life in Dublin. The vision, however, had no sooner been conjured up, than it vanished. On 9 June 1877 Wilson was taken ill. Three days later he was dead.[16] The blow was a hard one.

All the Wildes were 'very much attached' to their so-called 'cousin'. He had, moreover, both the practicality and the earning power to assist the family through the upheaval of Sir William's death. But now he was gone. And there was worse to come. His will was, as Oscar reported, 'an unpleasant surprise, like most wills'.[17] Oscar and Willie had always understood that they were to be his heirs, but the bulk of his £8,000 fortune was left to St Mark's Hospital. Willie did receive £2,000. But Wilson, 'bigotedly intolerant of Catholics' and sensing Oscar 'on the brink' of conversion, had all but disinherited him. Oscar received just £100, together with Wilson's half-share in Illaunroe, and that only on condition he remained a 'Protestant'. It was 'a terrible disappointment'. Oscar had, so he claimed, become used to suffering 'in mind' from his 'Romish leanings', and had turned those sufferings into verse. Now, though, he was suffering 'in pocket'. It was not a subject for poetry.[18]

In the short term Willie's £2,000 windfall meant that Merrion Square could be kept on. Despite his round of pleasures, Willie was making small advances in his legal career (at least he was invited to dinner with Mr Larkin, a prominent Dublin solicitor), and he continued to think of a political future. One well-connected friend told Lady Wilde, much to her gratification, that 'he knew Willie would be returned MP for many places [in Ireland], by mere love of Speranza's name'. He advised Willie 'to start next election on Free Liberal principles'.[19]

Oscar matched his brother's ambition. Alongside his poetry and his art criticism, he was hoping to publish a paper on ancient Greece, perhaps derived from one of his Alexandra College lectures.[20] He was, though, rather aware that, among all these plans, he was not getting on with the prescribed work for his Magdalen tutors. He intended to rectify this during a summer of quiet – and sport – in the west of Ireland. He even hoped that Ward, recently returned from Constantinople, might join him, as an encouragement to study. In the event, though, he had to console himself with his old Irish friends, Dick Trench and Jack Barrow.

Very little reading got done. When not out with rod and gun, or indulging in 'Pool, Ecarté and Potheen Punch', there was a new claim upon Wilde's attention. The subject for the following year's Newdigate Prize poem had been announced in the *Oxford University Gazette* at the beginning

of June: by extraordinary good fortune it was 'Ravenna' – a city that Wilde had visited earlier that year. The prize (worth £21), for a poem 'in heroic couplets', was accounted the university's blue riband of literature. It had been won by both Matthew Arnold and Ruskin (as well as by many wholly forgotten young men). And Wilde was anxious to add his name to the roll of honour.[21]

Over the ensuing months he brought all his resources to bear, in order to give himself the best possible chance of winning. His opening lines proclaimed the fact that he had actually been to Ravenna. He pushed home this advantage with his evocations of the spirit of the place – glimpsed first 'across the sedge and mire', a 'holy city rising clear, / Crowned with her crown of towers'. He plundered his existing poems for what he considered his best lines and choicest images (the 'throstle' makes a re-appearance). And conscious of the probable political sympathies of the judges, he praised unified Italy's new king, rather than the defiant and dethroned pope in the Vatican: 'for at last / Italia's royal warrior hath passed / Rome's lordliest entrance, and hath worn his crown / In the high temples of the Eternal Town!'[22]

In August Wilde was at Clonfin again, for the grouse shooting. He joined a jolly house party that included some members of the Fox family, American relations of his hostess, over from Chicago. The daughter, Selena 'Teenie' Fox, had brought with her a 'mental photograph' album, in which the house-guests were invited to write down their 'Tastes, Habits, and Convictions'. Wilde filled in the questionnaire with fluent aplomb: 'What is your favorite game?' – 'Snipe and Lawn Tennis.'

He listed his least favourite traits in others as 'vanity, self-esteem and conceitedness', before cheerfully giving his own most 'distinguishing characteristic' as 'inordinate self-esteem'. It was an answer supported by many of his other entries. Favourite poets: 'Euripides, Keats, Theocritus and myself'; idea of happiness: 'absolute power over men's *minds*, even if accompanied by chronic toothache'; idea of misery: 'living a poor and respectable life in an obscure village'; dream: 'getting my hair cut'; desired characteristic in a spouse: 'devotion to her husband'. He gave as one of his 'favourite amusements' 'writing sonnets', and as his 'favorite occupation' 'reading my own sonnets'.

It is a sprightly performance, by a young man eager both to test and show off his powers. For him the 'sweetest words in the world' were 'Well Done!' and the 'saddest' – 'Failure!'. He considered the 'sublimest passions of which human nature is capable' to be 'ambition' and (less obviously)

'asceticism'. And – reiterating his comments to Ward and Hunter-Blair – he gave as his 'aim in life' 'success; fame or even notoriety'.[23]

Although at the beginning of the summer the local estate agents had managed to rent one of the Bray cottages (for £75 pa minus commission), Wilde was still anxious to sell the properties outright. And, back in Dublin in the last week of September, he was approached directly by a family friend, John Quain, with an offer of £2,800 for all four houses. Wilde was inclined to accept. At almost the same moment, another party made an offer (of £2,700) through Wilde's agents, Messers Battersby. Apprised of this, Wilde called at Battersby's office, to explain that he already had a higher offer; the Battersby clerk asked if Wilde might settle the matter in favour of their client for £2,900. Wilde replied that if he received formal notification of such an offer by the following Monday morning (eleven o'clock, 1 October) he would accept it. Monday, however, arrived without an offer having been received, so Wilde agreed the sale to Mr Quain for £2,800.

It should have been a small moment of triumph, or at least achievement. But the sale was halted. The other would-be purchasers, Watson & Pim (acting for a Mr Kernihan, the tenant of one of the Bray cottages), insisted that Messers Battersby, as Wilde's appointed agents, had accepted their offer of £2,900 on Wilde's behalf, before the Monday morning deadline. And that, even if Wilde himself knew nothing about it, the purchase should be theirs. To support this claim Messers Battersby lodged a registered 'memorial' of their 'sale' to Watson & Pim. As neither side consented to yield, Wilde was forced to begin legal proceeding to get this claimed agreement between Battersby and Watson & Pim set aside. It was a slow, expensive and uncertain business.[24]

Nor was it his only financial setback. Returning to Oxford to start his fourth year in October, he learnt that the college authorities would be upholding 'the loss of the emoluments of his Demyship for the year ending Michaelmas 1877'. It could, though, have been even worse. He arrived back without having completed the work assigned by his tutor, and had to use his powers of persuasion to convince the 'officers' not to impose any 'further penalty'.[25] Unpaid bills also began to be called in. He was twice summoned before the vice-chancellor's court and ordered to settle accounts (with his tailor, Joseph Muir, and with G. H. Ormond, the 'Jeweller' from whom he had purchased his Masonic regalia) – as well as to pay the accompanying costs.[26]

Despite these irritations, Wilde was happy to be back at Oxford, and back in his beautiful rooms. They were a fit setting in which to receive Walter

Pater; Wilde had lost no time in following up Pater's letter, calling on the author of *The Renaissance*, and inviting him to return the visit. The occasion, though, was nearly sabotaged by Bodley, who, turning up by chance and finding Wilde delicately laying the table, announced his intention of staying. Wilde was moved to protest, 'No, no! Impossible to have a Philistine like you. I have Walter Pater coming to lunch.'[27]

Other meetings followed. There were tea parties, walks, lunches, exchanges of books and photographs. Pater lent Wilde a copy of Flaubert's *Trois Contes*, with its jewelled account of Herodias and Salome.[28] Art was their common ground. Bodley, who did see them together on occasion, found it 'hard to follow the exquisite jargon that rippled between them'.[29] He nevertheless considered Pater a corrupting influence upon the 'blameless' and 'impressionable' Wilde. And certainly there was a slightly cloying homoerotic charge about his company. Mark Pattison, the rector of Lincoln, has provided a glimpse of the milieu in his diary of 5 May 1878: 'To Pater's to tea, where Oscar Browning, who is more like Socrates than ever. He conversed in one corner with 4 feminine looking youths "paw dandling" there in one fivesome, while the Miss Paters & I sat looking on in another corner – Presently Walter Pater, who I had been told, was "upstairs" appeared, attended by 2 more youths of similar appearance.' Although it is unlikely that Wilde, on the verge of his exams, was present on that occasion, it was through Pater that he came to know the Socratic Cambridge don Oscar Browning at around this time.[30]

Pater, for all the diffidence of his manner, challenged and stimulated Wilde. At their first meeting he asked, 'Why do you always write poetry? Why do you not write prose? Prose is so much more difficult.' It was a notion that Wilde took some time to comprehend and respond to.[31] And, in this, it was like much else of Pater's thought. The daring theories of *The Renaissance* opened up vistas to be explored over the coming years. In the meantime Wilde came to consider his new mentor as 'a sort of silent, sympathetic elder brother'. Pater's reticence, he claimed, encouraged him to talk: 'He was an admirable listener, and I talked to him by the hour. I learned the instrument of speech with him for I could see by his face when I had said anything extraordinary. He did not praise me but quickened me astonishingly, forced me always to do better than my best – an intense vivifying influence, the influence of Greek art at its supremest.'[32]

He was not, though, the only influence. Walks and talks with Pater were matched by walks and talks with Ruskin.[33] The Slade Professor was back in

Oxford in Michaelmas Term 1877, giving a series of lectures, ostensibly on his book *Modern Painters*. They were memorable affairs – each one 'more like a talk than a lecture', with many digressions and diversions; he might 'give a loving exposition on a picture by Turner', or 'a description of some delicate architectural drawing of his own', or a diatribe against 'modern times', and then 'suddenly break off into an appeal to his hearers to fall in love with each other at the earliest opportunity'.[34] In the crowded hall, Wilde cut a distinctive figure, always leaning against a door to one side of the hall, 'conspicuous' – according to one contemporary – 'for something unusual in his dress. Still more for his splendid head.'[35]

He delighted in 'the fire of passion, and the marvel of music' that Ruskin brought to the performance. He relished his ideas on the horrors of the modern industrial age, and extended them further. In hall one evening Wilde diverted his companions with a vision in which 'all the factory chimneys and vulgar workshops [were] herded together in some out-of-the-way island' so that Manchester might be given back to the shepherds and Leeds to the stock-farmers and 'England [made] beautiful again'.[36]

Beauty, the great theme of Ruskin's (and Pater's) discourse, was much in Wilde's thoughts. He constantly sought to understand its range and define its power. One page of his commonplace book – gleaned from Plato, from Swinburne's *Essays and Studies*, and from the French writers who stood behind many of Swinburne's ideas – runs:

'Rien n'est vrai que le beau' [Nothing is true but the beautiful]

Beauty may be strange, quaint, terrible, she may play with pain as with pleasure, handle a horror till she leaves it a delight.

Art is one though the service of art is diverse – Beauty also may become incarnate in a myriad of diverse forms but the worship of beauty is simple and absolute.

As it is the crown and prize of life – the flower which fadeth not, the joy which never disappoints – so it [is] the aim of early education.

Let a boy says Plato from his childhood find things of beauty a delight... and in another place he says the end of music is the love of beauty... And these expressions come in a scheme of the noblest education –

La beauté est parfait [beauty is perfect]

La beauté peut tout chose [beauty can do all things]

La beauté est la seule chose au monde qui n'existe pas à demi [beauty is the only thing in the world that does not exist by halves].'[37]

Wilde expressed his own personal commitment to the cult of Beauty with increasing flamboyance. He was evolving a distinct and distinctive persona. The decor of his rooms became yet more studied and conspicuous. To the eclectic mix of 'odds and ends' were now added 'Greek rugs' – brought back by Ward from Constantinople – and 'Tanagra figures', souvenirs of his own Peloponnesian travels.[38] He seems to have raided Merrion Square for a Guido Reni print, a marble head of the pope, and a selection of 'small china'.[39] He even had plans for a gilt ceiling. When faced with financial worries, extravagance was always his first resort. He assembled the key markers of the new Aesthetic look, ordering reproductions of several of Burne-Jones's pictures, including the three paintings that had dominated the Grosvenor Gallery exhibition. He also built up a collection of 'blue and white china' – even if his enthusiasm rather outran his connoisseurship. He confessed that, in purchasing one china service, he had been badly 'taken in'.[40]

The regular gatherings in his rooms took on an ever more Aesthetic flavour: less cosy collegiate affairs than assemblies of like-minded devotees. Wilde gathered about him what he described as 'an aesthetic clique', fellow undergraduates who shared his enthusiasms for art and literature and home decoration.[41] Women, too, were admitted. He began hosting 'Beauty Parties', as he called them; tea parties to which the daughters of dons – suitably chaperoned – were invited. Margaret Bradley (daughter of the master of University College) thought that she was asked principally on account of her resemblance to 'the portrait of the young Shelley'. Marian Willets, stepdaughter of the first Oxford professor of Chinese, was another regular attendee; she met her future husband at one gathering, and Wilde also presented her with one of his Burne-Jones reproductions. As the host, Wilde dominated these occasions. May Harper (daughter of the new principal of Jesus College) noted that people 'were beginning to sit at his feet'.[42]

Though he still 'dressed like other people' Wilde somehow contrived to look 'remarkable'. His size helped, of course, and his hair, and also, on occasion, a 'wide-brimmed soft hat'.* But there was something in the growing confidence of his manner too. When May Harper saw him in the street, shortly after their first meeting, her aunt remarked, 'Look, isn't this

---

* Wilde sometimes regretted that his figure did not show his clothes off to better advantage. He told Margaret Bradley, as they sat out a dance at a 'Commem' ball, 'Isn't it sad for me when I love beauty so much, to have a back like this?' Not rising to the bait, she suggested that he join the Volunteers.

your eccentric friend.' Wilde saluted them by sweeping off his hat and giving 'a very deep bow'. He was, May remarked, 'already noticeable everywhere'.[43] Not content with his growing reputation as a published poet, Wilde asserted his claims as a painter. The easel, from his days at Trinity, was re-erected, possibly with the same unfinished landscape upon it. He let it be thought that he had spent time studying painting in Paris, and even claimed that he might – should other means fail – renounce literature and 'live in a garret and paint beautiful pictures'. Some artists, he explained, 'feel their passion too intense to be expressed in the simplicity of language, and find crimson and gold a mode of speech more congenial because more translucent'.[44]

He developed his love of flowers, another key Aesthetic marker, sanctioned by the designs of William Morris, the paintings of Burne-Jones and the verse of Rossetti. Flowers took up a prominent place in his life and his verse. The poems on which he was working grew thick with primrose, snowdrop, violet, crocus, rose, harebell, meadowsweet, white anemone and 'bright-starred daffodil' – even if sometimes the music of words trumped sense and observation. One Oxford friend claimed to have found Wilde, at work on a poem, poring over a botanical guide, picking out 'the names of flowers most pleasing to the ear' regardless of when or where they bloomed.[45]

But there was much real engagement too. His recipe for a perfect dinner party was 'very little to eat, very little light, and a great many flowers'.[46] When confined to his rooms by illness he told 'Kitten' Harding that the only thing that could console him was flowers. 'Could you steal a branch of that lovely red blossoming tree outside the New Buildings for me? I am sick at heart for want of some freshness and beauty in life.'[47] The restorative power of floral beauty became one of Wilde's extravagant Aesthetic notions. He kept his rooms filled with lilies. And if he did not actually spend hours at a time standing 'in an early Florentine attitude' contemplating a single bloom, he let it be thought that he did.[48] He had a special cult for the daffodil ('our most perfect flower'), telling May Harper that he had once 'lived upon daffodils for a fortnight'. Not quite yet having the full courage of his absurdities, he then 'looked round suspiciously' to gauge her reaction to this new line. Finding that she was smiling, he added hastily, 'I don't mean I ate them.'[49]

Wilde was refining and developing his wit. The innocent world of undergraduate 'chaff' was not completely superseded. He could still write to Ward a passage such as:

Now of course Jupp and I are not on speaking terms, but when we were I gave him a great jar; the Caliban came into Hall beaming and sniggering and said, 'I'm very glad they've given the £15 exhibition to *Jones*'... So I maliciously said, 'What the old Jugger [Edward Cholmeley Jones, a Magdalen music scholar] got an Exhibition! very hot indeed.' He was *too sick* and said, 'Not likely, I mean Wansborough Jones [a fellow demy]' – to which I replied, 'I never knew there was such a fellow up here.' Which confined Jupp to his gummy bed for a day and prevented him dining in hall for two days.[50]

But now such lumbering banter was matched by more ingenious flights.

Wilde's Oxford notebooks show him experimenting with epigrammatic formulae, condensing his knowledge, making his ideas memorable: 'the danger of metaphysics is that men are often turning *nomina* into *numina*'; 'in History what we are to look for are not Revolutions but Evolutions'; 'nothing is easier than to accumulate facts, nothing is so hard as to use them'.[51] In conversation he began to play with paradox, deploying 'commonplaces turned upside down'. Margaret Bradley recalled him telling one unfortunate, 'I remember your name, but I forget your face.'[52]

In talking of his Aesthetic enthusiasms, he evolved a mode of 'extravagant' expression (as he termed it), colouring his utterances with romance.[53] But, with Wilde, fun was never far away: the extravagancies were almost invariably undercut with humour, the Romantic vision guyed by playful absurdity, or subtle satire. This became Wilde's distinctive mode of discourse. If he made fun of himself, it was not because he did not believe in his vision, only that he wanted his words to be enjoyed and remembered. At one Sunday evening gathering, he informed the assembled company that 'I find it harder and harder every day to live up to my blue china.'[54] As a witty distillation of the Ruskinian belief that Art and Beauty had a moral force, the comment struck home. It soon acquired a currency throughout the university, raising Wilde to a new level of notoriety among his peers, and provoking in various measure merriment, approbation and outrage.[55] A sermon was even preached against it in the university church, beginning (so Wilde claimed), 'When a young man says, not in polished banter but in sober earnestness, that he finds it difficult to live up to the level of his blue china, there has crept into the cloistered shades a form of heathenism which it is our bounden duty to fight against and to crush out if possible.'[56]

Some of Wilde's Oxford contemporaries grew irritated by his pose, but for the most part his good humour, and his wit, won him acceptance and even admiration.* His rooms were never 'ragged' by the college hearties.[57] Indeed, in the spring of 1878, he was actually invited to attend the Magdalen Boat Club dinner, proposing one of the toasts.[58]

His tutors, however, were not impressed: Wilde's work had been minimal since his return from rustication. They were convinced he was heading for a Third. He did not disabuse them of the notion. Instead he began an intensive – but surreptitious – regime of reading and revision. He filled the margins of his textbooks with comments. He compiled detailed notebooks. He stayed up in the vacation to read with his friend Milner.[59]

Not that he ignored all distractions. The Boat Race was held on the last day of term (13 April). Wilde went up to London. On the following day, Palm Sunday, he attended – as he sometimes did – the Brompton Oratory. Although Hunter-Blair might have ceased to interest himself in Wilde's spiritual wanderings, the wanderings had continued. Wilde's social success at Oxford seems to have provoked a reaction, a sudden sense of the affected unreality of his existence. He sought an interview with one of the Oratory priests, Fr Sebastian Bowden (an Old Etonian, former soldier, with a reputation for securing fashionable converts). Wilde spoke to him 'as a dreamer and a sceptic with no faith in anything, and no purpose in life'. He told, too, of his financial setbacks – his exclusion from Henry Wilson's will, and the legal impasse over the sale of the Bray houses. Fr Bowden urged him to answer the 'sting of conscience' and convert, accepting the 'loss of his fortune' as God's proof of the 'hollowness of the World'. He backed up his words with a letter the following day, urging Wilde to take the decisive step:

Do so promptly and cheerfully and difficulties disappear and with your conversion your true happiness would begin. As a Catholic you would find yourself a new man in the order of nature as of grace. I mean that you would put from you all that is affected and unreal as a thing unworthy of your better self and live a life full of the deepest interests as a man who feels he has a soul to save and but a few fleeting hours in which to save it. I trust then you will come on Thursday and have

---

*   One of his few implacable enemies was Rhoda Broughton, a young Irish-born writer, who moved to Oxford in 1878. She – as Margaret Bradley reported, 'loathed him'. Ill-equipped to deal with such hostility, the kind-hearted Wilde was no match for her quick, acerbic wit.

another talk; you may be quite sure I shall urge you to do nothing but what your conscience dictates. In the meantime pray hard and talk little.[60]

Thursday came. Wilde did not return to the Oratory. He sent in his stead a box of lilies – the symbol of purity and the Virgin Mary, but also the floral emblem of the Aesthetic movement.[61] Having finally brought matters to a point of crisis, he had made his decision: he would not be converting. Bodley ungenerously suggested this was because Wilde felt his conversion would not be shocking enough. He was not the hope of some ancient Protestant house, turning against the long-held traditions of his aristocratic forefathers, only the son of a Dublin doctor. By converting he would simply become 'one more Irish Papist'.[62] To Hunter-Blair, however, the matter was more mysterious. He remained convinced of Wilde's sincere attraction to Catholicism, and could not understand how he could see the right and not choose it.[63]

Wilde certainly was drawn to Catholicism – aesthetically, spiritually, sentimentally – but, then, he was drawn to so many things. The drama of indecision had lent an excitement to his student years, and had given him a rich subject for his verse, but it could only be maintained for so long. Although Fr Bowden might frame conversion as a new beginning, Wilde could not but see it as an end – and not the end he wanted. He was on the brink of life, full of hopes and plans. His 'two great gods' were 'Money and Ambition'. He might write to Ward that he craved 'earnestness and purity' of life, but it is hard to believe.[64] His actions showed that he did not really believe it himself. He recognized that – for him – the formal acceptance of any exclusive creed must (as he later expressed it) be an 'error', one that would arrest his intellectual development, and substitute 'a theory of life' for 'life itself'.[65] He wanted to proliferate creeds, not choose from among them. Henceforth when quizzed about his religion he would reply, 'I don't think I have any. I am an Irish Protestant.'[66]

Having decided not to 'go over to Rome', Wilde went down to Bournemouth instead, for a few days of ozone, inspiration and rest.

Returning to Oxford, refreshed in body and spirit, he attended a fancy-dress ball given by Mr and Mrs Herbert Morrell at Headington Hill Hall. There were some 300 guests, but Wilde stood out, resplendent in doublet and hose as 'Prince Rupert'. He danced with May Harper and told her that he was 'perfectly happy that night because he had buckles on his shoes'. He also confided to her that 'it was the sorrow of his life' that he had 'dark hair'.[67] The disappointment, however, of not being a blond (or, perhaps, a

redhead) did little to mar the evening. Wilde always recalled it as a night of particular triumph – a 'gratifying proof' of the 'exceptional position' he had gained.[68] 'I went as Prince Rupert, and I talked as he charged, but with more success, for I turned all my foes to friends. I had the divinest evening.' Everyone came around him, he recalled, and made him talk. He hardly danced at all.[69] To fix and extend the moment, he not only had himself photographed in costume, he also acquired the outfit so that he could wear it in his rooms.[70]

Wilde's high spirits lasted until the end of the month, not even dampened by having to retake the compulsory 'rudiments of faith and religion'. Registering for the exam, he shocked the senior proctor by replying to his inquiry as to whether he intended taking 'divinity or substituted matter' (the option for non-Anglicans), 'Oh, the Forty-nine Articles'. 'The Thirty-nine, you mean, Mr Wilde,' corrected the proctor. 'Oh,' Wilde answered, affecting a tired drawl, 'is it really?' On the day of the examination itself, he arrived late, confident that, as his name began with a 'W', he would not be called for some time. On being reprimanded by Dr Spooner, one of the examiners, he replied airily, 'You must excuse me; I have no experience of these pass examinations.' As a punishment he was set to copying out from the Greek Testament the long twenty-seventh chapter from the Acts of the Apostles, describing St Paul's voyage across the Mediterranean to Rome. After a while he was told he could stop, but it was noticed, almost half an hour later, that he was still working away. When asked, 'Didn't you hear us tell you, Mr Wilde, that you needn't copy out any more?' He answered, 'Oh, yes. I heard you, but I was so interested in what I was copying, that I could not leave off. It was all about a man named Paul, who went on a voyage, and was caught in a terrible storm, and I was afraid that he would be drowned, but, do you know, Mr Spooner, he was saved, and when I found that he was saved, I thought of coming to tell you.' Perhaps not surprisingly he was ploughed again.[71]

The following day, 1 June 1878, Wilde began the written exams for 'Literae Humaniores' or 'Greats'. He was not convinced that he had done well, though – as ever – he managed to unnerve his fellow candidates with his pose of blithe assurance, 'striding up to the desk for fresh paper after the first hour; then handing in his book half an hour before time was up'. Wilde's claim to have done scarcely any reading or revision was accepted by many, and added to the general belief that he must be 'a genius'.[72]

The belief received additional support the week after Wilde had sat his

exams. On 10 June it was announced that his poem had won the Newdigate Prize. It was a delicious moment of triumph. His mother was ecstatic:

> Oh Gloria, Gloria! Thank you a million times for the telegram. It is the first pleasant throb of joy I have had this year – How I long to read the poem – Well, after all we have genius. That is something. Attorneys can't take that away. O, I hope you will have some joy in your heart – You have got honour & recognition – And this at only 22 [Oscar was almost 24] is a grand thing. I am proud of you – & I am happier than I can tell – This gives you a certainty of success in the future. You can now trust your own intellect & know what it can do – I should so love to see the smile on your face now –
>
> Ever & ever, with joy & pride, your loving Mother.[73]

Willie raced round to 'all the Dublin papers' to let them know of their townsman's achievement. Paragraphs duly appeared, and were copied in the regional press.[74] Other letters of congratulation poured in.[75] Augustus M. Moore (brother of George Moore) even composed an ode 'To Oscar Wilde, author of *Ravenna*', which was published in the *Irish Monthly*.[76] Approbation was general, though Hunter-Blair was amused at Wilde's claim to have arrived in Ravenna on horseback (rather than by train) and disgusted about his desertion of the pope for King Victor Emmanuel; and the reviewer in the *Irish Monthly* thought Wilde had been too generous in his comments on Byron's moral reputation.[77]

Wilde hoped that Macmillan & Co. might publish the poem, but George regretted that it would not be suitable for the firm. Wilde had to fall back on the conventional expedient of having it printed by Shrimpton's, the booksellers in the Broad. As was customary the Oxford professor of poetry – then John Campbell Shairp – went through the text before publication, suggesting amendments. Wilde listened courteously to his advice, and even took notes, but then printed the poem exactly as written. The book may have been a small paper-bound pamphlet, but it was an excitement still to see his name on a title page for the first time. Of the 'few hundred copies' printed by Shrimpton's, Wilde bought 'no fewer than 175'.[78]

He dedicated the work to Julia Constance Fletcher – or, as he put it, to 'My Friend George Fleming, Author of "The Nile Novel" and "Mirage".' Miss Fletcher was over from Italy with her stepfather, and when she came up to Oxford Wilde could meet her as a fellow author with a book (or, at

least, a booklet) to his name. He hosted a dinner for her in his rooms, and effected an introduction to her literary hero, Pater.[79]

At the 'terminal examination' that June Wilde was not only 'specially commended'; he also received a marble bust of 'the young Augustus'. It had been bequeathed by a former member of the college, to be given to the next Magdalen undergraduate to win the Newdigate. Wilde was photographed with the sculpture, and several friends, in the Magdalen cloister. Willie was part of the small group. He had come over for 'Commem' Week. Together the brothers attended both the University College ball and the Freemasons' ball (24 and 25 June). Oscar, with his Newdigate victory secured, was becoming an Oxford celebrity. It is possible that there was even a portrait drawing of him published at this time.[80] Certainly he made himself conspicuous, wearing a 'tall white hat' on the back of his head.[81] On the day after the Freemasons' ball he gave a reading from 'Ravenna' as part of the Encaenia in the Sheldonian Theatre.

This annual awards ceremony was usually a rowdy event, with frequent interruptions from the undergraduate audience. Many prizewinners dreaded having to appear. Not Wilde. Following a tedious recital of the prizewinning English essay – 'On the Symptoms of the Decline of Races' – which had been listened to 'somewhat impatiently' – he received the 'rapt attention' of the audience (as the Oxford and Cambridge Undergraduates' Journal reported). There was already a 'great curiosity' about him, and his reading enhanced it. He delivered the lines 'remarkably well'. The poem, far from being interrupted, was 'frequently applauded', and he sat down to a great ovation. Afterwards people 'crowded round to praise' him, while men of 'great distinction' (Mahaffy among them) flattered him with 'extraordinary compliments'. For a young man whose favourite words were 'Well Done!' it was a signal afternoon.[82]

It provided a welcome comfort during the stressful annoyance of his legal suit over sale of the Bray houses. The case of Wilde v. Watson & Pym was heard in Dublin's vice-chancellor's court over three days (8, 11 and 12 July 1878). Having submitted his evidence in an affidavit, Wilde did not attend in person; indeed, he seems to have gone up to London in the hope of distraction.[83] He was represented by three barristers, two of them QCs. The judgement, he feared, hung in the balance. With characteristic exaggeration he told Ward that he was 'ruined', and that 'the world' was 'too much' for him.[84] In fact, when the vice-chancellor gave his decision on 17 July, he found in Wilde's favour, allowing the sale to Mr Quain to proceed. He also awarded

Wilde his costs. They were considerable. It is uncertain, though, when – or whether – he was able to recover them.[85]

From these practical concerns Wilde was summoned back to Oxford for his *viva*. His anxieties about his showing in the written exams proved unfounded. His papers were, once again, the best in the year.[86] The examiners, rather than quizzing him on his answers, congratulated him. He had secured his First.[87]

If the Newdigate proclaimed to the world that he was a poet, the achievement of a Double First was an undeniable confirmation of his brilliancy and intellectual power. Although Wilde himself might disparage most of his fellow prizemen as 'sluggish and syllogistic Scotchmen', he was justly proud of his achievement.[88] It gave him a special and recognized position in any gathering of educated Englishmen. And it provided him – at least in his own mind – with a foundation upon which all his extravagant poses and calculated absurdities could rest. It offered a shield against easy criticism: whatever foolishness he might indulge in, it was now that much harder for critics to dismiss him as a fool.

An additional pleasure was the surprise of it. The Magdalen dons, he reported to Ward, 'are "astonied" beyond words – the Bad Boy doing so well in the end... I am on the *best* terms with everyone including [the ungentlemanly] *Allen*! who I think is remorseful of his treatment of me'.[89] The college authorities insisted that Wilde stay up for the Gaudy Dinner on 22 July, at which Herbert Warren, the newest fellow, delivered the speech, and 'nice things' were said.[90] Wilde's success in Greats did not mark the end of his university career. His demyship had been awarded for five years, and he still had to pass his Divinity exam before he could take his degree. Nor had he given up entirely the idea of seeking a prize fellowship. He would return the following term.

In the meantime, though, there was the summer to enjoy. With Frank Miles he paddled from Oxford to Pangbourne in a 'birchbark canoe' and 'shot rapids and did wonders everywhere'.[91] He then returned to Dublin. The British Association was in town for its annual conference, and Willie, assuming his father's mantle, was much involved with arrangements. Oscar found himself drawn in. He helped escort one group, including 'a large number of ladies', on a day trip to Howth. Willie, who had begun contributing paragraphs to the *World*, ensured that an item appeared, reporting as one of the highpoints of the afternoon 'an introductory address by the Newdigate Prizeman of this year' before the ancient cromlech, during which he pointed

out that his legendary namesake, Oscar, son of Ossian, was buried on the site. The prizewinning poet also described how 'the ancient Irish believed a bard could, by poetic invective, bring down temporal misfortune on the object of his satire'. In Ireland, at least, it was understood that poets had real power.[92] Not everyone, though, was impressed by the self-confident young prizewinner. Otho Lloyd, an Oxford contemporary, encountered Oscar at one of the British Association receptions, startling T. H. Huxley's beautiful and artistically inclined daughter with the languidly delivered observation, 'To think that we are all walking about here, *potential skeletons*': Dr Huxley appeared and, 'without a world of apology, led his daughter away'.[93]

The conference over, Oscar and Willie went to Illaunroe. They extended their stay in the west into October, joining a house party gathered by Arthur Edward Guinness and his wife at the newly refurbished Ashford Castle. In the play of wit, ideas, poetry and lawn tennis, Oscar seems to have been at the heart of things, at least to judge from another paragraph that Willie sent to the *World*:

> Sundry charming little New Republics are to be met with in the Far West, and I must specially congratulate Lady Olive Guinness on her first big party in the new house at Ashford. I hear brilliant accounts of garden parties and the ball, and how the counties came to dance to Slappofski's music; and certainly, with lakes and mountains and steam-yachts and excellent company and a real live poet (not to speak of the Lawn Tennis-onians), the western pilgrims are having an excellent time of it.[94]

Besides sport and sociability, the summer gave Oscar and Willie a chance to make plans. It was resolved that their future – and their mother's too – should be in England. Oscar's years at Oxford, and his growing circle of London connections, had already shifted the focus of his interests and his ambitions away from Ireland. He craved a larger stage and bigger cast than Dublin could offer. Willie, though he still harboured parliamentary ambitions (and was encouraged to believe that his name and connections might secure an Irish seat), felt the same pull. He was becoming disillusioned with the law as a career. He saw that you needed to have 'an attorney of kin to get on' – 'brilliancy' on its own was not enough.[95] From his limited experience, journalism seemed easier of access, and more immediately rewarding. Newspapers and periodicals were proliferating, readerships were growing. And the centre of this world was London. Willie was encouraged by the

notion that many publications, 'tired of the old stagers', were looking for 'young men'.[96] He had already won the approval of Edmund Yates, editor of the World, and attracted the attention of the editor of the Athenaeum, who had been impressed by Willie's showing at the British Association. The MP David Plunket (Oscar's sponsor at the St Stephen's Club) was offering his support, and another contact suggested that he could 'readily make £1,200 a year in London by Press work'.[97]

Lady Wilde, for her part, felt there was nothing to hold her in Dublin.[98] She had allied herself to her sons, and believed that her future must lie where they chose to go. Despite all the blows that had fallen, her spirit remained undimmed. And Oscar, indeed, drew strength from her unfailing optimism.[99] As a first step Merrion Square and its contents would be sold. Although Oscar's experiences with the Bray properties suggested that this might not be a speedy business, the process was put in hand.[100]

Oscar's own sense of uncoupling from Dublin life was heightened when, on passing through the city on his way back to Oxford, he learnt that Florence Balcombe had become engaged. Her fiancé was Willie's old Trinity friend Bram Stoker, who had been working in Dublin as a civil servant and part-time drama critic. Oscar had, for some time, scarcely been an ardent suitor, if a suitor at all. Despite having been in Ireland for most of the summer, he had spent his time away from Dublin and from Florrie. Even so he allowed himself the luxury of feeling slightly heartbroken. He wrote with a show of restrained fortitude to wish her joy, and to ask whether she might return the little cross inscribed with his name that he had given her, to serve 'as a memory of two sweet years – the sweetest of all the years of my youth'. He chose to imagine that, since he was leaving Ireland, they would never meet again – unaware that Florence was herself also relocating to London, Stoker having agreed to become manager for Henry Irving at the Lyceum Theatre.[101]

The spurned and lovelorn poet was a useful role. Having just relinquished the part of the wavering Catholic convert, heartbreak provided Wilde with both a new poetic voice and a new poetic subject. During the coming months he seems to have explored – or, perhaps, evolved – his feelings in a sequence of poems, ruing the transience of love, savouring the anguish of regret and the pleasures of recall:

> But surely it is something to have been
> The best belovèd for a little while,

To have walked hand in hand with Love, and seen
His purple wings flit once across thy smile.
Ay! Though the gorgèd asp of passion feed
On my boy's heart, yet have I burst the bars,
Stood face to face with Beauty, known indeed
The Love which moves the Sun and all the stars![102]

Back at Oxford, Wilde had to give up his beautiful rooms in college and take lodgings in the High Street (at No. 71, above a chemist's shop). He began reading for a prize fellowship. These were a very recent innovation, instituted by a government commission that was even then sitting on the university. Worth around £200 a year, they were tenable for seven years, and had to be competed for by open examination. Very few, however, were being offered, as the colleges adjusted to the new system. And this, as one of Wilde's contemporaries recalled, resulted in 'a large and increasing number of first-class men waiting about and competing for whatever were offered'.[103] In the coming year only Trinity and Merton announced that they would be offering classical fellowships. Competition would be severe.

To give a specific focus to his continuing studies, Wilde also resolved to enter the chancellor's essay prize. The subject for 1879 was 'The Rise of Historical Criticism'. From the evidence of his notebooks – and indeed of a manuscript draft – he worked hard, mapping out the progress of classical historiography from Herodotus to Polybius. Perhaps because he felt it was a line more likely to appeal to the examiners (or maybe simply for the intellectual challenge), he reversed his usual preference for the poetic over the scientific, and described the development of 'Historical Criticism' as a progress from the 'fatal legacy' of Greek mythology – which concealed 'the rational order of nature in a chaos of miracles' – to the more scientific, fact-based approach of the later classical period.[104]

Wilde also assumed the mask of the conscientious Anglican examinee. On 22 November 1878 he was re-examined in the 'rudiments of faith and religion', and passed. As a result he was able, the following week, to receive his degree.[105] At the end-of-term collections the Magdalen authorities not only agreed to remit his old 1877 fine, they also awarded him a discretionary college prize worth £10.[106] The cheque might be the final monetary reward of Wilde's student career, but Oxford would never cease enriching his life in other, less tangible, ways.

-PART III-

THE HAPPY
PRINCE

1879–1881

AGE 24–27

Oscar Wilde, 1881.

1

A Dream of Fair Women

'The passion for beauty is merely the intensified desire for life.'

OSCAR WILDE

Having gained his degree, Wilde turned his attention to London and the future. His stated ambitions remained the grand, if nebulous, ideals of the previous year: 'success, fame or even notoriety'.[1] The means of achievement were equally vague. He knew only that he would not be entering any conventional profession. As he explained to Ward (dutifully embarked on his legal career), the drudgery of business 'made men not themselves, wearers of masks of which their faces by natural mimicry took the dull shape and lifeless likeness'. Life in Wilde's hands was to be 'a work of art' – something to be contemplated and fashioned.[2] He would wear a different mask. Literature offered possibilities. He had told his Oxford friends that he might become 'a poet, a writer, a dramatist'.[3] Beyond this, however, he seems to have had no definite plan. It was enough that he was an Oxonian, armed with intelligence, a prize poem, self-conceit, ambition, optimism, and a passionate desire 'to eat of the fruit of all trees in the garden of the world'.[4] He also had some money, having augmented the amount he received from the sale of the Bray houses with an additional £250 raised on the Clonfeacle property.[5]

Bolstered by these arrangements, he took rooms at 13 Salisbury Street, the rambling Dickensian rooming-house, just off the Strand, where on the second floor Frank Miles lived and had his studio. It was recalled by visitors as a dark old-world mansion of eccentric tenants, 'antique staircases, twisting passages, broken down furniture and dim corners' presided over by a spinsterish landlady, who occupied rooms on the ground floor together with her aged and infirm parents.[6] Wilde thought the place 'untidy and romantic'.[7] He established himself on the floor below Miles, transforming his main room, a large panelled chamber running across the full width of the house, into a vision of Aesthetic splendour. The panelling was painted white, providing a fitting background for the various artistic accoutrements he had assembled during his Oxford days: the blue and white china, the Moorish tiles, the rugs and hangings. To give added colour to the scene, fan-like displays of peacock feathers contrasted with sprays of sunflowers and lilies.[8]

Sharing the same house gave Wilde access to Miles's rich social milieu, which blended the arts, haute bohemia and the more advanced elements of fashionable society. Writers, painters, actors, 'professional beauties', society women, men-about-town (like Lord Ronald Gower): all were drawn to Miles's studio. Even royalty was not excluded: Miles had sold one of his early drawings of Lillie Langtry to Prince Leopold, who had called often while the sittings were in progress; and the prince's artistically inclined sister, Princess Louise, was also a visitor. For Wilde, young and new to London, Miles's friendship brought him into contact with an exalted realm that would otherwise have been beyond his reach. It was a realm that he romanticized – and yearned to conquer.

His own London connection comprised a modest enough circle of Oxford contemporaries and family friends, some more useful than others. Tom Taylor, the elderly editor of *Punch* (and a contact of Lady Wilde's) took a kindly interest in him, even writing to one artistic hostess asking if she might send Wilde an invitation to her ball.[9] Mrs Tennant (the mother of an Oxford contemporary) gave cosmopolitan receptions at Richmond Terrace. The president of the British Association, Professor Spottiswoode, and his hospitable wife, were warmly supportive, entertaining Wilde both in London, and at Combe Bank, their house in Kent. The professor also endorsed Wilde's application for a ticket to the British Museum Reading Room.[10]

If Wilde arrived in London as an Oxonian, he came as an Irishman too – and an Irishman aligned, like his mother, with the ideals of nationalist

self-assertion and political liberty. He was recognized as such by others. The designation marked him as an outsider, and also set him firmly on one side of the great political fault-line that ran through late Victorian society, the question of 'Home Rule' for Ireland. Nevertheless there was support to be gleaned from the association. Wilde 'hunted up' the capital's expatriate 'Irish brigade', a heterodox group composed mainly of literary and political types, and dominated by the novelist, MP, and 'delightful conversationalist', Justin McCarthy.[11] But it extended even to the fringes of the Irish aristocracy. The social highlight of Wilde's first London season was the ball he attended given by Lady Olive Guinness at Carlton House Terrace. It was a lone – and tantalizing – glimpse of real grandeur.[12]

Wilde's Hibernian connections were reinforced and augmented when his mother came over from Dublin at the beginning of May, Willie having finally sold Merrion Square and most of its contents. Lady Wilde and Willie settled together in a small white-stucco-fronted house in Ovington Square, Knightsbridge. There Lady Wilde soon began, on a modest scale, to host Saturday afternoon receptions for 'good literary and artistic people' gathered from her own London-Irish contacts, and those of her children. Her parties were among the few occasions where both Willie and Oscar might be seen together in London. One visitor recorded how Lady Wilde would sit, enthroned, between her dutiful and supportive boys. Otherwise Oscar sought to set a certain distance between himself and his brother in the public sphere. He wanted to assert his uniqueness. It was soon being said that he paid Willie to wear a beard in order that they should not be mistaken for each other.[13]

Certainly from the outset Oscar's social and literary ambitions were set higher than those of his brother. He threw himself into the fashionable round of gallery private views and theatrical first nights. He was keen to see and be seen. But he was also interested in the cultural riches on offer. His connection with the Stokers gave him an entrée at the Lyceum, where Henry Irving had established the capital's most exciting and innovative theatre company, with Ellen Terry as its leading lady. Wilde became a friend of the 'house', and may even have contributed – occasionally and anonymously – to *The Theatre*, an ostensibly independent magazine (in fact founded by the publicity-savvy Irving), which gave prominent coverage to Lyceum productions.[14] For the stage-struck Wilde it was thrilling to find himself so close to the heart of things. Irving became the first of his London 'heroes'.[15]

The Lyceum was also becoming a focus for young people of talent and ambition. Among them was the twenty-one-year-old actor Norman Forbes-Robertson.[16] Tall, spare and elegant, with a smile and a spirit that both regularly drew the epithet 'radiant', he was a happy companion, interested in poetry and knowledgeable about painting.[17] Wilde met him soon after arriving in London and claimed him as a friend and confidant.[18] Norman was one of ten picturesque Forbes-Robertson siblings, children of the art critic John Forbes-Robertson (an older brother, Johnston, was rapidly emerging as one of the leading actors of the new generation). The family held crowded Friday evening gatherings at their home off Bedford Square, bohemian parties that brought together the worlds of art and the stage. Wilde became a regular attendee, excited to find himself in such stimulating company.[19] Many were excited by him too.

As a social presence he was something fresh and unexpected. He looked – and behaved – differently from most of his contemporaries, even the avowedly Aesthetic ones; among them, to judge by the cartoons of the period, drooping beards, drooping shoulders, tweed capes, and wide-brimmed hats predominated. Wilde cut a different figure. The physical attributes that had served to mark him out from his fellow undergraduates at Oxford – height, beardlessness, slightly-too-long-hair – seemed almost more conspicuous in a London setting.

His 'customary apparel', though not outlandish, had the stamp of self-conscious style: light-coloured trousers; black frock coat, with only the lower button fastened, to allow a glimpse of brightly flowered waistcoat beneath; white silk cravat, held together by an old intaglio amethyst set as a pin.[20] The lack of facial hair gave to his visage an especial prominence, reinforced by the pallour of his complexion. It showed off his 'great eager eyes' to advantage, but also made his few large pale freckles oddly noticeable, and did nothing to hide his prominent and 'greenish hued' teeth.[21] A few found the effect – at least on first meeting – 'grotesque' or even 'revolting'.[22] One new acquaintance called him 'slab-faced'.[23] Others, though, subsuming the parts to the whole, could refer to him as 'a young man of beautiful appearance… more like the incarnation of Apollo than an ordinary human being'.[24] His refusal to adopt the conventional masculine tropes was disorientating to many. Julian Hawthorne – the son of the novelist Nathaniel Hawthorne – was not alone in being repelled by 'a sort of horribly feminine air' that he detected about Wilde. This unsettling 'effeminacy' seems, though, to have been regarded as disturbing to social norms, rather than to the sexual ones.[25]

In Hawthorne's case the disquiet was soon obliterated by awe at Wilde's conversation. Certainly, from the first, Wilde was recognized as 'an admirable talker' – fluent, vivid, assured, and with a 'wonderful "Stage Presence"'.[26] The move from Oxford to London did nothing to diminish his self-confidence, or his sense of command. He would give dramatic point to his gestures – 'which were many and varied' – with a pair of 'pale lavender' gloves carried in one hand. It helped, too, that he had developed, as a friend put it, 'one of the most alluring voices I have ever listened to, round and soft, and full of variety and expression'.[27] 'Exquisite' in 'timbre and cadence', it was marked by 'a peculiar inflection characteristic of Oxford men', as well as by more personal 'tricks of emphasis', including a 'slight susurration... the sucking up of his breath – something much less than a hiss' with which Wilde would mark the end of a story.[28] All trace of his Irish accent had been effaced – if not the ease of his Celtic manner.* There was, moreover, a remarkable positive energy about all he said. He spoke 'with enormous gusto, evidently enjoying thoroughly his own imagination and turns of speech'. And his enjoyment was transferred to others. His 'sense of humour (as distinct from wit) was great and very infectious'; so too was his laugh – a 'very full and hearty', and frequent, eruption.[29]

Wilde arrived in the capital as an enthusiast, and one whose enthusiasms were both unforced and contagious.[30] He was, at this stage of his career, 'really ingenuous'.[31] Those who met him recalled him as 'invariably smiling, eager, full of life and the joy of living and, above all, given to unmeasured praise of whatever and whoever pleased him'. This 'gift of enthusiastic admiration' was, in the society of those days, something both 'unexpected and delightful'. It won him many friends, especially among the acting profession, and it opened many doors. If Wilde could not praise, he 'shrugged his shoulders and kept silent' – at least in public.[32] In private he could be engagingly acerbic, making fun of 'friend and foe alike'. One

---

*   The most complete account of Wilde's voice was provided by his sometime sister-in-law: 'Voice – (light baritone) without a trace of Irish accent or "brogue," of wide gamut – varied in pace – sometimes hurrying, bright, animated and gay, but more usually measured and deliberate, and even languid (unlike his brother Willie, who spoke very rapidly); its tones were rounded and velvety in character, sometimes slightly throaty and purring; enunciation very distinct and studied; he gave full value to the double letter, in a way unusual in England, in such words as "adding", "yellow" etc., and lingers caressingly on the vowels.'

disagreeable old lady was dismissed as 'that old woman who keeps the artificial roses in place on her bald head with tin tacks'.[33]

He did, though, in talking of art, maintain the 'extravagant' expression that he had evolved at Oxford. This amused some and annoyed others. Quite a few doubtless followed the actor-manager Squire Bancroft in regarding such excesses as 'the affectations of youth'. The literal-minded, however, often failed to register the element of self-satirizing humour, and were tempted, on first meeting, to dismiss Wilde as a mere 'poseur'.[34] Julian Hawthorne was so unsettled that he felt the need to intervene. 'Wilde,' he said, coming away from a party one evening, 'why should you waste yourself in these fantastic make-believes? The very tones of your voice are a give-away; you'll be found out sooner or later... Can't you, for a few minutes, at least, be sincere?' Wilde unsettled him yet further by replying: 'I am always absolutely sincere!'[35] He understood already that a mask might reveal, rather than conceal. Very soon he began to achieve a reputation – in London drawing rooms at least – as a young man 'full of love of the arts'. It was a love that ran from literature to the stage, from music to dress, from painting to home decoration.[36]

He was fortunate in coming to know – almost from his first days in London – some of the leading figures of the Aesthetic movement. He developed a friendship with the pre-eminent Aesthetic architect – and designer of avant-garde 'Anglo-Japanese' furniture – E. W. Godwin. Godwin, besides being a friend of the Forbes-Robertsons, and the former lover of Ellen Terry, was designing a studio house for Frank Miles in Chelsea's newly fashionable Tite Street. Wilde met the artist and illustrator Walter Crane, a fellow regular at Combe Bank, and impressed him with his 'genuine love of beauty'. He also met Whistler again. The timing, however, was not propitious. Whistler, bankrupted by the costs of his recent legal battle with Ruskin, was on the verge of departing for an unknown period to Venice, where he hoped to recoup his fortunes by producing a series of etchings for the Fine Art Society. The White House (which Godwin had created for him in Tite Street) was up for sale.[37]

More immediately fruitful was Wilde's connection with the unconventional Sickert family in Kensington.[38] Mrs Sickert took him under her wing. She had a ready sympathy for outsiders, being, herself, the illegitimate offspring of a Cambridge mathematician and an Irish dancer; while her husband, Oswald, a Paris-trained painter, was Danish by birth. The eldest of their six children was the nineteen-year-old Walter, a mercurial youth

who, despite ambitions to be a painter, was trying to make a career on the stage, 'walking on' at the Lyceum as one of 'Mr Irving's Young Men'.

Wilde, on coming to London, had also hoped to make 'literary friends'.[39] Progress on this front, however, was slow. If the poetic calling cards that he had sent out to Gladstone, Michael Rossetti and others were followed up in person, the results were disappointing – though he does seem to have built upon his slight acquaintance with the hospitable Lord Houghton.[40] And he did manage to meet Matthew Arnold, and perhaps George Eliot too. He attended Eliot's funeral at Highgate Cemetery in December 1880, taking a large wreath of lilies, which he attempted – with limited success – to attach to the coffin as it passed by on its carriage.[41] And among the younger men he made some slight headway. He was introduced to Henry James, and expressed an admiration for his novels.[42] He managed to disconcert the literary critic Edmund Gosse. When, at their first encounter, Gosse responded to Wilde's generous enthusiasm with the self-deprecatory remark, 'I was afraid you would be disappointed,' Wilde had replied, 'Oh no, I am never disappointed in literary men, I think they are perfectly charming. It is their works I find so disappointing.'[43] He established rather more of a bond with the beautiful and fashionable Mrs Singleton, who wrote what was considered daringly outspoken verse under the pen name 'Violet Fane'.[44] And he was befriended too by Charles G. Leland, a middle-aged American comic writer and folklorist, who was then living in London, pursuing – among other projects – an interest in industrial design. Leland hoped to get Wilde elected to the Savile, the most literary of London's clubs, though nothing came of the plan.[45]

The most important of Wilde's early London friendships, however, was neither literary nor artistic. It was with Lillie Langtry. He met her again in Miles's studio. She had achieved much in the two years since her arrival on the London scene, and was now an established celebrity; the acknowledged doyenne of 'professional beauties' and the all-but-acknowledged mistress of the Prince of Wales. Crowds gathered to watch her pass, artists vied to paint her. Here was 'success, fame, even notoriety' – and all at the age of twenty-five. Wilde was both impressed and smitten. When Miles boasted to a friend that he had 'discovered... Mrs Langtry', Wilde remarked gravely: 'A more important discovery than America, in my opinion.[46] Langtry, for her part, was intrigued by Wilde; attracted by the 'splendour' of his eyes, she registered, beneath the bubbling of youthful enthusiasm, both real intelligence and the outline of a 'remarkably fascinating and compelling personality'.[47]

A rapport was quickly established between them. If Wilde admired Langtry's beauty and envied her fame, she was drawn by his energy and his intellect. Both might be useful to her. Although at the apogee of her success, she was very aware that her position was tenuous. About to embark on her third 'season', the tide of her fortunes was almost imperceptibly on the turn. Her relationship with the Prince of Wales was unlikely to be sustained. She was beset with difficulties – financial, marital and romantic. To have, at such a juncture, a new ally who was brilliant, amusing and optimistic, was a very welcome thing.[48]

Wilde's own hopes for fame quickly concentrated themselves on his writing. He decided that his primary literary ambition was to be recognized as a poet. After his campaign of undergraduate sonnet-writing, he had been working on some longer compositions: 'The Burden of Itys', with its vision of the Greek gods disporting themselves in the Oxfordshire countryside; 'The Garden of Eros', charting his poetic debts to Keats, Swinburne, Morris and Rossetti; and a highly sensual Keatsian classical fantasy titled 'Charmides'. Although they were not suitable for periodical publication, they would lend bulk and interest to a slim volume. That was Wilde's goal. Initial attempts, though, to interest a publisher in such a venture proved disappointing. A succession of editors refused even to read his work. Wilde was obliged to acknowledge that, in the estimation of the London book trade, he was still an unknown.[49] It was a first indication that progress might be slower than he had expected. Other options needed to be considered.

While many of his poetry-writing contemporaries sought to take their first step into the wider literary world by writing a novel (always a more commercially attractive proposition for a publisher), Wilde turned in a different direction.[50] He began working on a play. The theatre after all was one of his great passions. Drama, in his estimation, was 'the meeting place of art and life', dealing 'not merely with man, but with social man, with man in relation to God and to humanity.' More prosaically, it was popular – *the democratic* art' of the day: a stage success would bring with it both real fame and real money.[51]

Wilde was also interested to discover that many actors, and some writers, had parallel careers in the visual arts. Johnston Forbes-Robertson had studied painting at the Royal Academy, and continued to exhibit, while the playwright W. G. Wills – a member of the Irish Wills family to which the Wildes had long felt a bond of connection – maintained a successful

sideline as a portrait painter.[52] And such examples encouraged him to maintain his undergraduate notion that he might someday follow the same path.[53] There is no evidence, though, that he ever did anything towards actually achieving this fantasy.

More effort was put into avoiding the lure of popular journalism. Although writing for the newspapers offered ready rewards, it was scarcely a passport to 'fame', as almost all articles were unsigned. Journalism, moreover, was the preserve of his brother. Willie had made a bright start in his new profession. Even before moving to England he had kept up a steady stream of 'scraps' for the *World*, and on his arrival in London he was given a much larger role on the paper. He combined this with other commissions, such as contributing to the fashionable weekly *Vanity Fair*, and writing theatre reviews for the *Irish Daily News*.[54] For Oscar, the grander role of cultural critic – as played by Arnold, Pater, Swinburne or Ruskin – had more attractions. But its forums, the great monthly journals, were beyond his reach. If he perhaps hoped, one day, to write on artistic subjects for *Blackwood's*, the *Nineteenth Century* or the *Fortnightly Review* – he had, at the moment, to settle for contributing an overview of the 1879 Grosvenor Gallery summer exhibition to the *Irish Daily News*. It was a vivid indication of how far he had to travel.

Nevertheless the review (signed 'O. F. W.') did give Wilde a chance to praise a catalogue of admired heroes and would-be allies across the whole spectrum of the Aesthetic movement, from Burne-Jones and G. F. Watts ('the most powerful of all our living English artists') to William Blake Richmond and Whistler (that 'wonderful and eccentric genius'). It also allowed him to puff such friends and connections as Eugene Benson (Julia Constance Fletcher's stepfather), Johnston Forbes-Robertson (who had painted a 'very lifelike' portrait of the actor Hermann Vezin), 'Mrs Valentine Bromley' (née Ida Forbes-Robertson, another of the talented siblings), Mary Stuart-Wortley (sister of an Oxford friend) and W. G. Wills. And although the *Irish Daily News* scarcely circulated outside Dublin, Wilde took care to send copies of his article to the various artists mentioned – with apologies for the 'shocking' quality of the printing.[55]

At the outset of his London life Wilde did receive one very fortunate break. He secured the interest of Edmund Yates, Willie's employer at the *World*. Yates was planning to bring out a new literary monthly called *Time*, a companion to the weekly *World*, and was in search of contributors. He wrote to Willie, asking to be put *'en rapport'* with Oscar – 'the Newdigate

man, of whom I hear so much and so favourably'[56] (one of those who had been telling Yates about Oscar may well have been Violet Fane, herself a regular contributor to the *World*). Yates – recognized as a 'brilliant talker' himself – was pleased to meet another inspired conversationalist.[57] Wilde was duly asked to a write a poem for the inaugural number of *Time*.

He produced the appropriately titled 'Conqueror of Time' – a sixty-line poem about a 'white flower' grown from a seed found in a sarcophagus at the British Museum, which endures as 'the child of all eternity'.[58] The magazine and Wilde's contribution – both extensively trailed in the *World* and other papers – appeared in April 1879: it marked his first appearance in an English (rather than an Irish) periodical, and his formal debut on London's literary scene.

Yates was an adept at building up the reputations of his star contributors. The *World* of 4 June carried an account of Mrs Douglass-Murray's 'fancy ball' in Portland Place, mentioning among those who 'pre-eminently looked the character': Violet Fane as a 'Hindoo Princess', 'Mr. Whistler in a "nocturne" of black velvet, as a Spaniard of the Middle Ages' and 'Oscar Wilde as a Venetian noble'.[59] It was distinguished company, and Wilde was distinguished by association. The report may well have been written up by Willie. Certainly Willie's journalistic positions enabled him to do 'a good deal to make Oscar's name known' in London circles. And he entered into the game with enthusiasm, reporting – either in the press or among friends and colleagues – 'every clever thing that Oscar said or that could be attributed to him', and helping to form the beginnings of 'a sort of myth around him'.[60]

Despite these promising first steps in the capital, Wilde was concerned to keep open a second professional front: academia. He continued to work on his prize essay (though it is by no means certain that he ever handed it in).[61] He corresponded with George Macmillan about doing some translation work for his firm – selections from Herodotus and perhaps a play by Euripides. And he involved himself in Macmillan and A. H. Sayce's plans to establish a Hellenic society for the encouragement of ancient Greek archaeology.[62] He inquired about the archaeological studentships that had recently been founded at Athens.[63] And he determined to apply for the next open fellowship that was offered at Oxford.[64]

Oxford remained a significant element in Wilde's life. He still, it seems, had rooms there. He kept in touch with Pater and continued to use him as

a sounding board for his ideas. Once (according to Wilde's own account), while seated on a bench together 'watching the students bathing in the river' and talking of how 'the enchanting perfume of romance [might] be wedded to the severe beauty of classic form' to achieve a new 'synthesis of art', Pater – overcome by Wilde's inspired eloquence – slipped from his seat, knelt down and kissed his hand.[65] But if Wilde saw old friends, he also made new ones. He found a kindred spirit, and admiring disciple, in Rennell Rodd, a Balliol undergraduate of poetical sensibilities and Aesthetic leanings. Rodd had started a little poetry magazine, *Waifs and Strays*, to which Wilde agreed to contribute.[66] And Wilde, as he seems often to have done with new friends, took Rodd down to Windsor to see Lord Ronald Gower.[67] Cambridge too was on Wilde's horizon. He made several 'charming' visits to the ebullient Oscar Browning at King's College, though he confessed to Reggie Harding, 'I wish he was *not* called Oscar' (Wilde misled Browning by telling him that he – like his host – had been 'named after the King of Sweden').[68]

In London Wilde and Miles started entertaining together. Apparently reviving Wilde's Oxford practice, they hosted 'tea and beauty' parties, graced though by the celebrated, and often aristocratic, 'professional beauties' of Miles's connection, rather than by the daughters of Oxford dons. These 'bachelor at homes' were held in Wilde's Aesthetically adorned room, and were – according to one youthful visitor – 'about the most amusing things in their way in all London'.[69] The decor created its own sensation: the flowers, the feathers, and the fact that many of the theatrical and literary celebrities who attended had inscribed their names on the white panelling. Not that all the guests were famous. The twenty-one-year-old Laura Troubridge, taken along by her cousin, Charlie Orde, an Oxford friend of Wilde's, wrote in her diary: 'Great fun, lots of "intense" young men, such duffers, who amused us awfully.'[70]

But for most guests the chance of seeing Mrs Langtry was the great draw. Wilde often mentioned her probable attendance when sending out invitations, and he kept up a constant propaganda for her. Likening her to a classical statue, he would tell everyone that she was 'the loveliest thing that had ever come out of Greece'.[71] On overhearing one visitor inquire which of the ladies present was the famous beauty, he remarked dramatically, 'What an absurd question! If the sun shone I should know it was the sun.'[72] The guest, in any case, should have been assisted by the fact that the room was decked with numerous photographs of Langtry.[73]

There would sometimes be an artistic focus to the parties: after Miles had won the Turner Medal at the Royal Academy for his painting of 'An Ocean Wave', the canvas was proudly exhibited as the centrepiece of the next 'at home'.[74] And the same honour was accorded Edward Poynter's sumptuous portrait of Lillie Langtry, which the artist had presented to the sitter.[75] The combination of art and female beauty was, Wilde recognized, a potent one, claiming both attention and admiration. He resolved to harness its power. For his second appearance in *Time* he abandoned the abstract and composed an extended hymn of sensual praise to Lillie Langtry. She may not have been mentioned by name, but was clearly recognizable as 'The New Helen' of the title – 'Lily of love, pure and inviolate! / Tower of ivory! Red rose of fire!'[76] Wilde would later reinforce the connection between Langtry and Helen of Troy through such assertions as 'Yes, it was for such ladies [as Langtry] that Troy was destroyed, and well might Troy be destroyed for such a woman.' Or his dedicatory inscription in a book that he gave her, 'To Helen formerly of Troy, now of London.'[77]

Langtry, though, was not the only beauty eulogized by Wilde. At the end of May, Sarah Bernhardt arrived in England with the Comédie-Française for a groundbreaking season at the Gaiety Theatre in London. Bernhardt, at thirty-four, was already the greatest theatrical star of the age – the embodiment of Parisian sophistication and sexual allure. Wilde and Norman Forbes-Robertson went down to Folkestone to meet her – and the rest of the troupe – off the boat.

There was a crowd gathered. Forbes-Robertson, pressing forward, presented Bernhardt with a gardenia. One of the company remarked to the actress (in French), 'they'll make a carpet of flowers for you soon'. Wilde, sensing his cue, exclaimed, 'Here is one!' and flung down an armful of lilies on the ground in front of her. As she rather reluctantly walked over the blooms, he shouted, 'Hip, hip, hurrah! A cheer for Sarah Bernhardt!' – drawing an enthusiastic response from the crowd. Bernhardt was impressed by her youthful cheerleader, with his 'luminous eyes and long hair'.[78]

Wilde attended the company's opening night on 2 June, when Bernhardt won a rapturous reception for her interpretation of Racine's *Phèdre*. He thought it 'the most splendid creation' he had ever witnessed.[79] To the general clamour of press adulation he added a poetic tribute. His sonnet, beginning 'How vain and dull our common world must seem / To such a one as Thou', appeared the following week, not in *Time* but in its sister paper, the *World*, ensuring it an even wider notice. Willie wrote enthusiastically to

a female friend asking whether she had seen that 'Os' had 'poured out his soul' at Bernhardt's feet in the paper.[80]*

Having allied his name and his muse to two great luminaries – Langtry and Bernhardt – 'Os' promptly turned his attention to a third: the beautiful Ellen Terry. He produced one sonnet in praise of her performance in W. G. Wills's *Charles I* and another apostrophising her rendition of Portia in *The Merchant of Venice*. Both were published in the *World*.[81] By such tributes Wilde established himself as the laureate of female loveliness, securing a ready readership, and catching the reflected glow of his subjects' glamour.

He worked hard to reinforce these connections, and to win the friendship of his heroines. Ellen Terry was sent a copy of his first sonnet with the assurance that 'no actress has ever affected me as you have'.[82] Wilde became Bernhardt's 'devoted attendant' during her London sojourn; he was delighted to have a chance to show off his French.[83] The actress came several times to Salisbury Street, adding, after one jolly supper party, her scrawled signature to the whitewashed panelling.[84]† Time spent with Bernhardt taught Wilde that she was not only 'a great genius' but also 'a great woman'. She, for her part, appreciated her attendant's tact and his perceptiveness. 'Most men who are civil to actresses and render them services have an ulterior motive,' she later recalled. 'It is not so with Oscar Wilde. He… did much to make things pleasant and easy for me in London, but he never appeared to pay court.'[85] The compliment, though it might appear backhanded, suggests something of Wilde's great appeal to beautiful women: he treated them as people and as friends.

It helped, too, no doubt that he could present himself still as the heartbroken former lover of Florence Stoker: one who (as he put it in his poem 'Humanitad') must eschew the 'noble madness' of love, and 'From such sweet ruin play the runaway' even if he could never quite forget the beauty

---

* Willie also passed on an overheard 'fragment' of critical reaction to the poem, and its reference to 'the heavy fields of scentless asphodel' that, according to Greek mythology cover a portion of Hades:

   Crutch (to Tooth Pick): 'Say, what the deuce is *asphodel*?'

   Tooth Pick: 'Don't know – forget it – *some* sort of extinct *vegetable* I fancy!'

   ('Tooth Pick' and 'Crutch' were the generic nicknames for society swells of the period.)

† Bernhardt also wrote her name on the glass of a drawing that Wilde had bought for 5 guineas at the sale of Whistler's affects from the White House. The picture had been catalogued as a 'portrait of Sarah Bernhardt', and the actress wrote it was 'very like' her. Whistler, when he subsequently saw the work, declared that Bernhardt had never sat for him.

'Which for a little season made my youth / So soft a swoon of exquisite indolence'.[86] His memories drove him to send 'Florrie' – anonymously, via Ellen Terry – a floral crown to wear on her stage debut, wanting 'to think that she was wearing something of mine... That anything of mine might touch her'. He ended his letter with the melodramatic cry, 'She thinks I never loved her, thinks I forget. My God how could I!'[87]

Lillie Langtry might have tempted him to forget his former love, though she did not encourage it. She wanted an accomplice, not another lover. Wilde offered her much. He became her unofficial secretary, writing her letters, doing her chores.[88] He advised her on what to wear, and encouraged her in her extravagances. She occasionally demurred; Wilde once complained: 'The Lily is so tiresome. She *won't* do what I tell her... I assure her that she owes it to herself and to us to drive daily through the Park dressed entirely in black in a black victoria drawn by black horses and with "Venus Annodomini" emblazoned on her black bonnet in dull sapphires. But she won't.'[89] He fostered her sense of intellectual independence. A solitary girl in a family of boys, she had picked up the rudiments of classical learning; Wilde urged her to continue her studies. He gave her Latin lessons, took her regularly to the British Museum and accompanied her to Charles Newton's lectures on Greek art at University College, London where the excited students would line up to greet their arrival.[90] He brought his intellectual mentor, Ruskin, to see her. She noted Wilde's unusual attitude of 'extreme reverence and humility' as the 'master' discoursed upon 'Greek art', and vehemently denounced Japanese culture as an inferior caricature of Chinese. Wilde noticed that Ruskin had 'made [Langtry] cry and escape the room' with his remark 'Beautiful women like you hold the fortunes of the world in your hands to make or mar.'[91]

To his position as amanuensis and tutor, Wilde did bring an element of courtly love. Mrs Langtry was both his muse and the supposedly unapproachable object of his adoration. Poems and flowers were the currency of his worship. Both were welcome. On one occasion he bought an array of 'Jersey lilies' for her at Covent Garden, and, while he was waiting for a hansom cab, a street urchin, fascinated by the orange blooms, exclaimed, 'How rich you are!' (the story – with its apparent conflation of beauty and wealth – delighted Ruskin).[92] Of course, Wilde was not rich in any financial sense, and often he had to fall back on the expedient of buying a single amaryllis for Langtry, and carrying it to her, rather than taking a cab.[93]

But, for all the elegant formality of such gestures, Wilde does seem to have

become more than a little infatuated. Perhaps he even dared to approach the unapproachable. When he was composing 'The New Helen' he certainly haunted the streets around her house. One night Mr Langtry returned home late to find him curled up asleep on the doorstep.[94] And some of Wilde's unpublished poems hint maybe at a thwarted romance. 'Roses and Rue' – the manuscript of which is inscribed 'To L. L.' – recounts the poet's passion for a tremulous bird-like beauty, who, despite allowing a few snatched kisses, deems him unworthy of her attention: 'You have only yourself to blame' she tells him, 'That you have no fame'. To this the poet replies, 'I had wasted my boyhood, true, / But it was for you, / You had poets enough on the shelf, / I gave you myself!' There was, though, probably rather more fond imagining in such verses than recollection of actual events.[95]

When Wilde's ardour grew 'too persistent' Langtry became irritated. It was not what she needed. As one of Wilde's friends later remarked, 'He was not at all the kind of game she was after.'[96] To supplement her affair with the Prince of Wales, which was beginning to cool, she had taken up not only with his cousin, the dashing Prince Louis of Battenberg, but also with the youthful Lord Shrewsbury. And in tandem with these two illustrious liaisons, she embarked on a clandestine relationship with a childhood friend of hers called Arthur Jones.[97] These players might sometimes resent Wilde's privileged access to 'the New Helen', and her obvious enjoyment of his company, but it is doubtful that they considered him seriously as a rival for her favours.[98]

She kept Wilde in his place. 'I'm afraid that often I said things which hurt his feelings in order to get rid of him,' she later recalled. He was dismissed once for suggesting that 'man is constant in his infidelity and woman puts him to shame because she is, by nature, fickle'. On that occasion Wilde pleaded for forgiveness with a serenade. But, following another 'frank' deposal, Langtry noted, while sitting in her box at the theatre, 'a commotion in the stalls – it was Oscar, who, having perceived me suddenly, was being led away in tears by his friend, Frank Miles'.[99] A word, though, she knew could always bring him back. After one slight she wrote winningly, 'I cannot forgive myself so must implore you to forgive me instead.'[100]*

---

* After another 'silly quarrel' she sought to make it up with Wilde by presenting him with her much-cherished stuffed peacock. The gift, however, was deliberately double-edged, as she had just learnt that peacocks were supposed to be unlucky. Perhaps fortunately for Wilde, when the present was delivered, Frank Miles assumed it was intended for him, and carried it off to his studio.

Wilde remained in Langtry's thrall. Whatever his privileges and his knowledge, he was still a slave. He did not resent it. It was enough that their relationship made him both envied and conspicuous. The publication of 'The New Helen' had secured him an acknowledged position as 'her bard'.[101] And when the society versifier Frederick Lampson composed his own poetic tribute to Mrs Langtry, one stanza opened with the regret, 'I cannot rhyme like Oscar Wylde'.[102]

During the summer of 1879 Wilde made a short cultural tour of Belgium, armed no doubt with Lord Ronald Gower's guide to the country's art galleries.[103] He travelled with his new friend Rennell Rodd. Together they visited Tournai, where they were drawn by a Gothic tomb, depicting a knight in armour and bearing the words *Une heure viendra qui tout paiera*, which Rodd rendered poetically as 'An hour will come that shall atone for all'. For Wilde the 'strange legend' made 'one think how, perhaps, passion does live on after death'.[104] In the museum at Brussels, it was Rubens's 'masterpiece' 'Christ Bearing the Cross' that created the deepest impression, with its sparkling colours and swift dynamic action: 'That,' Wilde declared, despite the somber subject matter, 'is joy in art.'[105]

Wilde also spent time with Rodd's family at the fashionable riverside resort of Laroche in the Belgian Ardennes. Besides Rodd's rather conventional parents and younger sister, it was a decidedly literary gathering at the Hôtel Meunier that July. Also in residence were Jacques Peck, a twenty-year-old Dutch poet with a passion for Keats and Shelley, and Xavier de Reul, a widowed geologist, novelist, poet and art historian, who was holidaying with his two young children and a female relative, the twenty-one-year-old Mathilde Thomas. Even in such company Wilde was conspicuous. De Reul's eight-year-old son, Paul, remembered him vividly as 'Grand et blême, face glabre, cheveux longs, noirs et plats, il se vêtait de blanc, – blanc des pieds à la tête, depuis le large et haut chapeau de feutre jusqu'à la canne, un sceptre d'ivoire, au pommeau tourné, avec lequel j'ai joué bien souvent. Nous l'appelons Pierrot.'* He already seemed 'an artist in attitudes'.[106]

In an ambience of shared enthusiasm and endeavour, Wilde recited some of his poems, perched on one of the flat gravestone-like rocks that littered the Val du Bronze. And although young Paul found his drawling,

---

* 'Tall and pale, clean-shaven, long hair, black and straight, he was clothed in white – white from head to foot, from the wide-brimmed tall felt hat to his cane, an ivory sceptre, with a turned pommel, which I played with often. We called him Pierrot.'

monotone delivery pricelessly comic, the others seem to have been more impressed. Jacques Peck – breaking off from writing sonnets to Mathilde – produced a glowing verse vignette of Wilde as 'l'adolescent Anglais, d'intelligence plein, de gaîté, d'allégresse. Au cœur poète, qui hait tout ce qui est mauvais'.[107]★

Later on that summer, Wilde visited the Sickerts at Dieppe, where they had taken a house. He had been invited by Mrs Sickert, and he seems to have enjoyed the happy informality of the family seaside holiday. It was remembered as a time of ceaseless laughter. Wilde made a special friend of Helena, the lone daughter of the family. She was fifteen years old and determined to go to Cambridge (the scientific university); Wilde discussed poetry and ideas with her. He also delighted her two infant brothers, Oswald and Leo, with his fantastical tales. When Helena affected to cast doubt on the veracity of his more improbable stories, he would appeal to her in mock anguish, 'You don't believe me Miss Nelly. I *assure* you... well, it's as good as true.'[108] One afternoon he was prevailed upon to recite his prize poem, 'Ravenna', as the company sat beneath the apple trees in the orchard; and he submitted good-humouredly to occasional interruptions from Mrs Sickert's old schoolteacher, Miss Slee, as she corrected minor points in his pronunciation.[109]

The carefree summer days could not, however, be continued indefinitely. Wilde returned to London in September to the sad news that his friend Leonard Montefiore had died suddenly in America. He was just twenty-six, barely a year older than Wilde.[110] But if life itself might be uncertain, the practicalities of existence were only too definite: Wilde was running into debt.[111] His income was minimal, his outgoings constant, his tastes extravagant. The two stated tenets of his personal economic credo were 'give me the luxuries, anyone can have the necessities' and 'nothing succeeds like excess'.[112] And though he might be able to put off creditors with tales of unpaid Irish rents, there was little sign of relief.[113] Occasional poems published in the papers earned very little. He began to borrow, at first from his mother (who could ill afford it), and then from a moneylender called Edwin Levy.[114]

Against the background of such cares, Wilde sat the open fellowship exam at Trinity College, Oxford.[115] He had studied for it, but his months in

★ 'The English youth, full of intelligence, of gaiety, of joy. At heart a poet who hates everything that is bad.'

London had perhaps inevitably separated him from the narrow concerns of academe. One of his fellow candidates recalled his disconcertingly urbane presence in the examination hall on the first afternoon:

> The paper was on Metaphysics and was drawn up foolishly, consisting mainly of such vague questions as 'What is the relation between metaphysics and ethics?', 'metaphysic and religion?', 'metaphysic and art?' etc, etc. Soon after the paper was given out, Wilde rose and stretched himself before the hall-fire: and then addressed us loftily but pleasantly – 'Gentlemen, this paper is really the work of an uncultured person. I observe the word "metaphysic" appears in every question, a word that is never heard in polite society'.[116]

He failed to win the fellowship. And although he remained anxious to find some sort of position with 'an assured income', he did not even apply for the next fellowship to become available (at Merton, in December).[117] He put in instead for the 'archaeological studentship' at Athens, and sought Sayce's support for the application, as he had heard that there were many other 'competitors'.[118] Too many, as it turned out. After that rebuff he thought to follow in the footsteps of Matthew Arnold and applied to join the school inspectorship, asking Oscar Browning for his endorsement.[119] Again, though, he was unsuccessful.

He considered teaching. The Latin lessons he was giving to Lillie Langtry had awakened his didactic instincts – instincts further stimulated by his friendship with Harry Marillier, a pupil at Christ's Hospital school who used his uncle's ground-floor rooms at 13 Salisbury Street as an occasional retreat; Wilde encouraged the bright, blue-robed fourteen-year-old in his classical studies, reading Euripides with him on his half-holidays. Marillier would bring Wilde cups of coffee in return for these lessons and the informal chat that accompanied them. If Wilde were ever occupied when Marillier called, he would give the boy half a crown and send him off to the theatre.[120] In an effort to turn his teaching skills – and his experience of Greece and Italy – to account, Wilde offered himself as a 'travelling tutor' at the rate of £30 a month. It is uncertain, though, whether he found any takers.[121]

Despite these setbacks, and his own continuing financial anxieties, Wilde could show an impressive concern for the plight of others. He involved himself in fundraising initiatives, writing to Constance Westminster – Ronald Gower's sister – for help with one 'most deserving and sad case' (the duke

duly sent £10).[122] On another occasion, after disastrous flooding at Lambeth, on the south bank of the Thames, Wilde went – together with Rennell Rodd – to see what could be done for the poor families who had been washed out of their homes. Rodd recalled Wilde's encounter, in one 'miserable tenement', with an old bedridden Irish woman: he cheered her with 'his merry humour' and assisted her 'with little necessaries for which, as he said, she had more than compensated him by praying that "the Lord would give him a bed in glory"'.[123]

Such interventions no doubt drew upon the traditions of practical charity that Wilde had encountered at Oxford in the teachings of T. H. Green. They were also likely to have won the approval of Ruskin, another great champion of the poor. Wilde saw a good deal of his old and increasingly infirm mentor during the latter part of 1879. And he remained in awe of Ruskin's great-spirited engagement with society and its problems, thinking that 'like Christ he bears the sins of the world' (Wilde, for his own part, always felt 'like Pilate, washing his hands of all responsibility').[124] He took Ruskin to the Lyceum to see Irving's Shylock.* Afterwards Wilde went on to a large ball given by Millais and his wife, to celebrate their daughter's wedding. 'How odd it is,' he remarked to Reggie Harding, alive to the fact that 'Effie' Millais had, in the 1850s, been married to Ruskin, but had left him to elope with the painter.[125]

Wilde secured Ruskin's attendance at one of Lady Wilde's Ovington Square 'at homes'.[126] He also brought the great critic to the Tennants' house in Richmond Terrace, to see Dolly Tennant's drawings of children. Ruskin was impressed by the pictures and delighted by the vivacious twenty-four-year-old artist. He cancelled the planned afternoon visit to Lillie Langtry, telling Mrs Tennant that he had lost his heart to Dolly and her sister, Evie, 'those two dear girls'.[127] To Wilde he later confided, 'I *do* think that Dorothy and I "got on" in a little way, and I think we shall get on a little further – you had best look out – I always take all the love I can possibly get, from *such* girls (not that I've seen her like before).'[128] He felt that she had the potential to become great, if she worked.[129]

Wilde's own plans of working his way towards greatness were not unfolding as quickly as he had hoped. At the end of November 1879 he

---

* Wilde took Ruskin backstage after the performance to meet Irving. Ruskin praised Irving's acting as 'noble, tender and true' – as was reported in the *Theatre Magazine* – though he later clarified the point that he did not approve of Irving's revolutionary portrayal of Shylock as 'a victim to the support of the principles of legitimate trade'.

wrote ruefully of going to see his friends the Hick-Beaches 'to kill time and pheasants and the *ennui* of not having set the world quite on fire as yet'.[130] One society lady recorded a telling exchange when Wilde's friend and champion, Mrs Spottiswoode, arrived at a tea party announcing that she could only stay a minute, 'as I am on the way to Oscar Wilde's, to meet Mrs Langtry and several other professional beauties'. An eminent professor, surprised at hearing the name 'Oscar Wilde' spoken without the prefix 'Mr', inquired, 'Who is Oscar Wilde?', to which Mrs Spottiswoode, even more surprised, replied, 'Oscar Wilde is a poet.' Asked what he had written, however, she foundered, until the young man whom she had brought with her came to her aid, 'Hmm – ha – Oscar Wilde has not written much *yet*... But his university prize poem is great.' This elicited from the professor 'a sardonic look'. And, from the hostess, the confession 'I found myself rather out in the cold yesterday, because I owned to ignorance about this Oscar Wilde. But if his works are still in the future, I don't see that I need have been glared at as I was.'[131]

2

The Jester and the Joke

'He's a deuced sight cleverer than they think.'

CHARLES READE

The world, clearly, was not yet alight. Indeed by the close of his first year in London, notwithstanding an advertised connection with Lillie Langtry, and the fading glory of his Newdigate poem, Oscar Wilde was perhaps best known for being less well known than his friends and supporters thought he should be.

Nevertheless the tide was beginning to turn. Wilde was working hard – at fostering connections and following up invitations. With no regular employment, he had, as one ungracious observer put it, nothing else to do but 'trot round London and jump down people's throats'. He strove to make himself agreeable, and succeeded.[1] He was helped by the fact that conventional society– once closed, aristocratic and partisan – was beginning both to broaden and to open up. Although there were subtly graded hierarchies within the so-called 'upper ten thousand', and many of the ancient landed families continued to hold themselves aloof, old divisions were gradually eroding and new money was finding a place. Different political creeds were allowed to mix at receptions and dinners. The professions were gaining access to fashionable drawing rooms. Artists might be admitted. Even the stage was sometimes allowed. A few advanced

hostesses (wealthy if not actually aristocratic) led the way, throwing open their houses 'to everyone who was interesting and distinguished'.[2] Wilde benefited from this new mood: if he was not yet 'distinguished' he was undeniably 'interesting'.

Women, moreover, liked him, and women ruled society. It was they who drew up the dinner party guest lists and sent out the invitations. Men might consider Wilde 'effeminate' and 'affected', they might resent the way professional beauties treated him as a favourite, they might joke about him in their smoking rooms, but they found themselves welcoming him into their homes. Their wives appreciated Wilde's flow of conversation, his depth of culture, his intelligence, his views on interior decoration and opinions on dress; they welcomed his flattery and they enjoyed his good humour.[3] He improved their parties. To sit next to Wilde at dinner was accounted a treat. One aristocratic lady who encountered him at 'a Huxley dinner' soon after he left Oxford, considered that she had 'never met so wonderful and brilliant a creature'.[4]*

Women were charmed, too, by Wilde's fondness for children. The seven-year-old Violet Maxse, daughter of Mrs Cissie Maxse, was just one of many young girls whom he enthralled with tales and jokes.'[5] Older girls found him equally engaging. His perceived 'effeminacy' made him attractive, rather than otherwise, to the opposite sex. Laura Troubridge and one of her sisters 'both fell awfully in love' with him, thinking him – as Laura recorded in her diary – 'quite delightful.'[6] Wilde certainly welcomed such admiration. He induced Gussie Greswell to bring the Troubridge girls to his Salisbury Street tea parties in exchange for introducing Gussie to Sarah Bernhardt.[7]

But if Wilde enjoyed female attention, he made few efforts seriously to follow it up. The memory of Florence Balcombe continued to linger.

---

*   There were occasional missteps. Wilde disgraced himself by accepting an invitation to
     dinner from a 'Mrs Smith' and then – on receipt of a better invitation, which offered the
     chance to meet Robert Browning – writing to his hostess 'grieved' that he was unable
     to keep the engagement as he found he 'had to go North that evening'. The Browning
     dinner was an intimate affair at the house of some friends who lived near Regent's Park.
     Wilde and Browning were deep in conversation when – to Wilde's horror – 'Mrs Smith'
     was announced. Having received Wilde's second letter, she had not proceeded with
     plans for her own dinner party. She was not amused to discover Wilde ensconced. 'Is
     this what you call "Going North"?' she remarked. But, although she threatened never
     to speak to him again, by the end of the evening Wilde had soothed her ruffled feelings,
     and 'they were as great friends as ever'.

Julia Constance Fletcher, whom he admired so much, had suffered a disappointment in love, and seemed out of reach. With Francesca (Frankie) Forbes-Robertson he achieved a special rapport, but it was the basis for an enduring friendship rather than a romance. The tragic death of Leonard Montefiore did bring Wilde close to Leonard's sister, Charlotte. And, according to family tradition, he even proposed to her. But she, despite a genuine fondness, turned him down, eliciting the scrawled response, 'I am so sorry about your decision. With your money and my brain we could have gone so far.'[8]

Wilde, for the most part, preferred the more distant glamour of the great. When the celebrated Polish-born actress Helena Modjeska arrived in London, from America, early in February 1880, he elected himself her champion.[9] He introduced her to important people, composed a poem to her beauty, talked up her productions, arranged for her the use of Frank Miles's studio so that she could have her portrait painted, acted as one of her 'henchmen' when she was running a stall at a charity bazaar, proposed adapting a play for her, and 'translated' her Polish poem 'Sen Artysty' ('The Artist's Dream') into English, for publication in *Routledge's Christmas Annual*. And he made her laugh; she was delighted with his description of her achievement in making an English society audience cry when reciting a poem to them in incomprehensible Polish, as having 'tickled with [her] voice the tendrils of their nervous system'.[10] Though swept up by his enthusiasm, she remained somewhat bemused by her young champion: 'What has he done, this young man, that one meets him everywhere?' she inquired. 'Oh yes, he talks well, but what has he *done*? He has written nothing, he does not sing or paint or act – he does nothing but talk. I do not understand.'[11]

Of all the subjects upon which Wilde talked it was art that proved the most important, and the most useful in advancing his name. Having failed to establish himself as a newspaper art critic, a tenured academic, a successful writer or a travelling tutor, he became a sort of cultural chaperone, a self-elected arbiter of taste, squiring fashionable women around art galleries and exhibitions.[12] Women were interested in art, or thought that they should be. And in 1880 they were particularly interested in Aesthetic art. For so long the taste of a small initiated coterie, Aestheticism was finally achieving a social vogue. It was a vogue that Wilde both contributed to and benefited from. Anyone who had visited his rooms at Salisbury Street knew that he was a devotee. And he soon became a conspicuous figure, at

the Grosvenor and the Royal Academy, not merely looking at the pictures himself, but pointing them out to 'a herd' of eager female 'worshippers', and 'explaining his theories to willing ears'.[13]

Wilde's knowledge and taste were widely admired. The novelist Charles Reade cautioned those who dismissed Wilde as a poseur that 'he's a deuced sight cleverer than they think... He knows a lot about art and nearly every-thing about painting.' Reade recounted how he had run across the 'airy young gentleman' at the Royal Academy one morning – and witnessed him 'spot, with unerring accuracy, every picture worth looking at. It's true there were not many; but such as they were he spotted 'em.'[14] Wilde's humour was enjoyed too. He greatly amused one young listener with his statement that there was 'really no objection to be urged' against the rather conventional pictures gathered at the Royal Academy, 'except that they are not paintings, and are not art at all'.[15]

Wilde, all the while, sought to enhance his own Aesthetic credentials by drawing closer to the circles of the Pre-Raphaelites – the precursors and creators of the movement. He was taken up first by the painter and poet William Bell Scott, a great friend of both Rossetti and Swinburne – and 'one of the so-called Fathers of Pre-Raphaelitism'. Scott's wife was a serial promoter of 'promising young men' and thought that in Wilde – 'a wonder-ful young Irishman just up from Oxford' – she had found a new tyro. At one of her 'afternoons' – at Bellvue House on Cheyne Walk, Chelsea – Wilde met the Alfred Hunts and their seventeen-year-old daughter, Violet.

Mr Hunt he admired as a delicate water-colourist and fringe member of the Pre-Raphaelite group, and Mrs Hunt (a popular novelist) too, but Violet he admired most of all; with her mass of auburn hair, her large eyes and expressive mouth, she was – as Ellen Terry put it – 'out of Botticelli by Burne-Jones'.[16] Wilde became a friend of the family, inviting them to his Salisbury Street tea parties, visiting them at their Chelsea home and initiating a flirtation with Violet ('the sweetest Violet in England').[17] He encouraged her to write, and if he did not actually propose, he flattered her with the (half-recycled) line, 'We will rule the world – you and I – you with your looks and I with my wits.'[18]

Wilde also came to know Arthur Hughes, another Pre-Raphaelite painter. He spent happy Saturdays at the Hughes family's welcoming home at Wandle Bank, on the southern outskirts of London. There would be danc-ing in the studio, cheerful suppers and long walks through the meadows to the little river Wandle. Other regular guests included the Tom Taylors, the

Sickerts and the actor Corny Grain.[19] Wilde delighted the family; one of the three Hughes daughters, the 'farouche' eighteen-year-old Agnes, thought him 'the most amusing, comprehending and kindly' of all the friends who visited. He told them ghost stories and amused them with his extravagances. He used to drive all the way down from London in a hansom cab: 'Such vulgar things, dear Agnes, and *soh* useful!' Sometimes he brought friends with him: one he announced as 'such a gifted boy – he's painted his coal scuttle white, and it looks *soh* lovely!' Wilde, for his part, was impressed by the 'soft, flowing' Aesthetic dresses that Agnes made for herself, in 'clear colours and just off the ground'.[20]

It was perhaps through the Hughes family that Wilde came to know Edward Burne-Jones at this time.[21] Certainly when Sarah Bernhardt returned to London, in June 1880, Wilde arranged for the star-struck painter to meet her. And then, building up the web of connection, he sought Burne-Jones's assistance in getting access to the collection of Pre-Raphaelite pictures owned by William Graham; not for himself, but on behalf of the French artist Jules Bastien-Lepage, who was also in town that summer painting a portrait of Henry Irving.[22]

Wilde's most significant new connection, however, came from outside the cultural sphere. George Lewis was a forty-seven-year-old criminal and divorce lawyer: Jewish, wily, discreet, and with a growing reputation for taking on those cases 'where the sins and follies of the wealthy classes threaten exposures and disaster' – and keeping them safely out of court. The Prince of Wales employed him when dealing with his mistresses. As a result Lewis had come to know Lillie Langtry, and it was perhaps through her that Wilde met him.* Lewis, however, was not only a fixer, he also loved to bring people together, to make useful connections, to launch interesting schemes. He and his astringently vivacious second wife were establishing a remarkably vital meeting place for painters, politicians, writers and lawyers at their opulent house on Portland Place. For a 'young man with a future' it was the place to be.[23]

And Wilde remained convinced that he did have a future. It was during 1880 that his public profile began to change. Aside from occasional mentions

---

* Lady Augusta Fane records a, doubtless apocryphal, anecdote that has Wilde calling on Lewis and being shown into a room where several women were waiting. He complains to the manservant, 'This is the room for women with a past. I want the room kept for men with a future.' The mot, however, certainly reflects Wilde's sentiments, and could be a distant echo of something he did say.

in the *World*, the spread of his reputation had – up until then – largely depended upon word of mouth. Now a new element entered the equation: *Punch*. The comic weekly of middle-class humour and middle-class prejudice had been mocking the 'Aesthetic Craze' for the previous five years – in skits, parodies and, most particularly, in the cartoons of Gerald du Maurier. Indeed for many people, du Maurier's drawings, featuring such imaginary denizens of 'passionate Brompton' as the 'tender young bard', the Hon. Fitz-Lavender Belairs, the precious art critic, Prigsby, and the loose-robed, wildly-coiffed, Burne-Jones-profiled, Mrs Cimabue Brown – defined the movement. And as Aestheticism became both more prevalent and more fashionable, du Maurier intensified the attack. At the beginning of 1880 he added two new figures to his cast.

On 14 February *Punch* published 'Mutual Admiration Society', a du Maurier cartoon depicting 'the poet, Jellaby Postlethwaite', accompanied by 'the painter, Maudle', arriving at one of the Cimabue Brown's receptions and receiving a warm encomium from his hostess: 'Oh, look at his grand head and poetic face, with those flowerlike eyes, and that exquisite sad smile! Look at his slender willowy frame, as yielding and fragile as a woman's.' She describes him as 'the great poet' – though an accompanying note adds that he is 'quite unknown to fame'.

Du Maurier did not intend Wilde as the specific subject of this caricature. His 'Aesthetic' characters were stock 'types' (even if it was said that Mrs Cimabue Brown was partly based on Alice Comyns Carr, wife of Joe, manager of the Grosvenor Gallery). Self-regarding versifiers were not uncommon in the period. And the lean, bent figure of Postlethwaite did not look anything like Wilde, even if he was clean-shaven and longish-haired.[24] Nevertheless Wilde's growing reputation as a poet and Aesthete – extolled by enthusiastic friends, but largely 'unknown to fame' – meant that some people did make a connection. And this connection was not broken over subsequent weeks, as the 'intense' yet languorous Postlethwaite became a recurring figure in du Maurier's Aesthetic pantheon.[25]

Wilde recognized an opportunity. He not merely encouraged the idea of a link, he insisted upon it. Ignoring the lack of physical resemblance, he claimed that he was, in fact, the model for Postlethwaite. By taking the generalized ridicule of du Maurier's caricature, and accepting it as a personal tribute, Wilde was seeking to draw a bright clear beam of attention on to himself. *Punch* had a wide circulation and a deep influence. If Wilde could become identified in the public mind with the Aesthetic 'Postlethwaite', he

might assume Postlethwaite's position as Aestheticism's exemplary poet – perhaps even its exemplary figure.

The position, after all, was vacant. By 1880 the acknowledged figureheads of the Aesthetic movement were still the old-established Pre-Raphaelite coterie of Rossetti, Swinburne, Morris and Burne-Jones, with the additions of Godwin and their one-time friend Whistler. For a press that increasingly desired to frame issues in terms of personalities this was proving a drawback. Almost all these figures had withdrawn from public view or become respectable. With the exception of Whistler, none of them now even evinced any notable 'eccentricity of costume or manner'.[26] Rossetti was a virtual recluse. Swinburne had retired to Putney. Morris was taken up by business and politics. Burne-Jones, though his art was regularly lampooned, shied away from all personal publicity. Godwin was too busy. The press needed a new face, a new personality – a living embodiment of Aestheticism. Wilde – by projecting himself as the model for 'Postlethwaite' – might claim that role.

This was an original idea, and a bold ploy for a young man to adopt at the outset of his career. To most serious-minded Victorians, engaged in the high calling of the Arts, the notion of welcoming ridicule and accepting satire was incomprehensible. Wilde, though, thought differently. With what one of his contemporaries described as a 'keen insight into his age' he understood that 'the curiosity one raises is one of the ingredients of fame'.[27] And it mattered little how such curiosity was piqued. He had, since his schooldays, always been prepared to subvert his own pretensions with humour. If he had often made fun of himself, this was a merely a case of extending the privilege to others. He, of course, insisted on his own complicity in the game. He made a point of seeking out du Maurier and being civil to him, even offering (so he said) to sit for the artist so that he might be able to get a better likeness. He refused to be affronted by any of the jokes made at his expense, affecting only an Aesthetic concern for the artistic quality of the cartoons. He let it be thought that he actually supplied du Maurier with material for his drawings.[28]

Du Maurier, for his part, found himself swept along. He *did* begin to borrow from Wilde. On 17 June, Postlethwaite (in his fourth *Punch* appearance) was depicted sitting alone at a café table, on which stood a lily in a vase: to the waiter's inquiry, 'Shall I bring you anything else, Sir?', he replies, 'Thanks, no! I have all I require, and shall soon be done.' The notion of an Aesthetic poet being sustained by contemplating a flower carries an echo of Wilde's remark to May Harper that he had once 'lived upon daffodils

for a fortnight'. And it seems likely that du Maurier was re-using some version of this Wildean comment.[29] There was an even clearer debt when, a few months later, du Maurier depicted an 'Aesthetic bridegroom' (looking passably like Wilde) together with his 'intense bride', contemplating their 'six mark' Chinese teapot, with the caption: 'Oh, Algernon, let us live up to it.' The recycling of Wilde's celebrated Oxford mot was recognized – and commented on – by many.[30]

Whistler, back in London from Venice towards the end of the year, and encountering Wilde and du Maurier together at an exhibition, asked, 'I say, which one of you two invented the other, eh?' The remark was calculated primarily as an insult to du Maurier (a contemporary and one-time friend of Whistler's) but it did also reflect the growing congruity in the popular imagination between the Aesthetic 'Postlethwaite' and the Aesthetic Wilde.[31] And during the course of 1880, as 'Postlethwaite' became more like Wilde, Wilde became more like 'Postlethwaite'.[32] With remarkable 'clearsightedness' he set about projecting 'the character'.[33] He amplified his persona. His mannerisms became more flamboyant, his postures more languishing, his talk more studiedly affected. Perhaps he even used the key Aesthetic terms (as recorded in *Punch*) – 'consummate', 'utter', 'supreme', 'too-too'. Certainly he developed his gift for shocking conventional expectations, treating serious things lightly and frivolous things gravely. But he did even more than this. Stepping well beyond Postlethwaite's role as a 'poet' (a role that, after all, he had barely achieved himself), Wilde sought to become the very essence of Aestheticism – 'to embody', as one friend put it, 'in the eye of his fellow men a conception of life founded on the worship of beauty'. His own life, he seemed to declare, was 'a work of art'.[34] It was a vision for which he found an increasingly receptive audience.

His sayings – which imposed Aesthetic criteria upon every aspect of life – soon became part of the capital's social currency. He 'amused all London' with his assertion (adapted from another of his Oxford mots) that both Henry Irving's 'legs are distinctly precious, but his left leg is a poem'.[35] It was repeated that, when he saw a blossoming almond tree in the front garden of a London house, he exclaimed, 'I should like to be invited to this house simply to meet that almond-tree; I should even prefer it to a tenor voice.' An anecdote went the rounds about Wilde refusing to take some medicine on account of its being 'a dingy brown' colour. The chemist promptly replaced it with a bottle of beautiful 'rose-red' liquid and some pills that 'shone like gold', which Wilde was delighted to ingest. He recovered from

his illness, though not before confessing that he would *hate* to be really robust.[36] When he remarked imperturbably to a group of street urchins, who were making fun of him, 'I am glad to afford amusement to the lower classes', the press reported it.[37]

Other popular anecdotes included him coming down to breakfast, while staying at a country house, looking pale; asked if he were ill, he replied, 'No, not ill, only tired. The fact is, I picked a primrose in the wood yesterday, and it was so ill, I have been sitting up with it all night.'[38] His concern for primroses was also supposed to have led him into a Jermyn Street florists; he requested them to remove several bunches of the flower from the window. Asked how many bunches he wanted to have, he replied, 'Oh I don't *want* any, thank you. I only asked to have them removed from the window because they looked so tired.'[39] Much of this, of course, was apocryphal. The story that he paraded down Piccadilly with a lily in his hand – although it may have carried some memory to his floral gifts for Lillie Langtry – was essentially an invention. But, as he remarked, with mock pride: 'Anyone could have done that.' He had achieved 'the great and difficult thing' of making the 'world believe that [he] had done it'.[40] The world – encouraged by *Punch* and 'Postlethwaite' – was growing eager to believe. But although such stories spread Wilde's fame, it was not always clear whether the audience was being invited to laugh *with* Wilde for his wit, or laugh *at* him in his folly.

He, though, was not concerned. He chose to see a useful tension in the discrepancy. The gap between the calculated exaggerations of his public persona and the patent intelligence of his private self offered further scope to bemuse and confound. As one journalist was obliged to admit, 'if you light upon Postlethwaite [i.e. Wilde] alone, and take him off his guard, and discuss with him any subject which is not cognate to art, you may or you may not be astonished to find what a shrewd, sensible, practical fellow he is'.[41] On other occasions Wilde might abruptly abandon his affectations to achieve a sudden and disarming intimacy. Asked to take the Swedish opera diva Christine Nilsson in to dinner, he, making some graciously stilted compliment, drew the retort, 'Look here Mr. Wilde, Mme. Christine Nilsson will put up with no such stuff. This is all put on, and there is nothing in it but nonsense.' To which he deftly responded, 'Thank you. You are the first sensible woman and true friend that I've met.' After that, according to La Nilsson, they got on famously.[42]

There were other tensions, too, in Wilde's Postlethwaitian pose. In the

popular imagination and the pages of *Punch*, 'Aesthetes' were supposed to
be etiolated, weary, and consumed by the hopelessness of existence. Wilde,
over six feet tall and well built, retained conspicuous appetites for food,
life and, indeed, lawn tennis;* his utterances were invariably leavened with
humour and intermingled with 'happy phrases of native wit', and, though
his poems might flirt with despair, his general outlook on life was buoyed
with infectious optimism. But these discrepancies, enjoyed by some, were
ignored by most.[43] Only the earnest and kindly American Charles G.
Leland mistook Wilde's occasional poetic posturing for real 'pessimism',
and vowed to bounce him out of 'all morbid nonsense' and transform him
into 'a clear-headed, vigorous, healthy, manly writer'.[44]

Wilde – in his distinct Postlethwaitian persona – was becoming an
increasingly visible public figure, 'impossible to ignore' at fashionable
occasions, artistic and theatrical.[45] He lent his support to an all-male undergraduate production of Aeschylus' *Agamemnon* (in Greek) at Balliol that
June; his friend Walter Parratt composed the music, while Rennell Rodd
was one of the chorus.[46] Later in the year, when the company gave three
well-publicized performances in London, Wilde hosted a tea party for the
cast, inviting friends to meet 'Clytemnestra' (F. R. Benson) and 'Cassandra'
(George Lawrence) along with some of the 'Argive elders'.[47]

The party was held in a new setting. In the summer of 1880 Wilde and
Frank Miles moved into 1 Tite Street, the 'unpretentious' three-storey red-
brick 'studio house' designed for Miles by Godwin. It was a distillation of
up-to-date Aesthetic elements – light interiors, sparse furnishings, bare
boards, and 'balconies and other accessories to meet the taste of [Miles
as] a lover of flowers' – all set on the most distinctively artistic street in
London's most avowedly Bohemian suburb.[48] Godwin had now designed
four houses in Tite Street. Whistler's 'White House' stood on the other side
of the thoroughfare – even if Whistler no longer owned it.

Wilde relished his new abode. The house, he told Mrs Hunt, was 'very
pretty', even if the address was '*horrid*'. To improve the latter point, the
property was renamed 'Keats House'.[49] There was scope to continue the
entertaining traditions of Salisbury Street. Miles's new model, Sally Higgs,
an elfin teenage beauty 'of the Rossetti type', became a beguiling figure at

---

* In the summer of 1880 he was still cutting a dashing figure, playing tennis with Willie
and the spirited Davis sisters, on a 'lumpish lawn' in the public gardens behind the Davis
family home, dressed 'in a high hat with his frock-coat tails flying and his long hair
waving in the breeze'.

their elegant 'studio teas', robed in a kimono, a teapot in one hand, a lily in the other.[50] Living up to his creed of excess, Wilde decorated his own room with a determined disregard for economy. He overspent on a new desk, explaining to Norman Forbes-Robertson, 'I couldn't really have anything but Chippendale and satinwood – I shouldn't have been able to write.'[51]

Wilde was busy with literary schemes. His hopes of a parallel academic career, having met with little encouragement, seem gradually to have faded. The translation work for Macmillan was not followed up. And although he did announce plans to 'bring out... some essays on Greek Art' the only piece to come to fruition was an unsigned review for the *Athenaeum* of Professor Jebb's entries on Greek history and literature in the *Encyclopedia Britannica*.[52] Poetry remained Wilde's main concern, even if it was sometimes less obviously Aesthetic than might be expected. Following the example of Swinburne, he addressed not only the passions but politics too. 'Ave Imperatrix', a long, patriotic but questioning 'Poem on England,' which appeared in the *World*, attracted considerable attention.[53] The work, composed amid the setbacks of the Afghan War, gave an overview of the glorious achievements of the British empire framed as a narrative not of military triumph, but of Christ-like sacrifice; and beyond the sufferings of the moment it looked forward to a national resurrection as a republic. Wilde considered that the poem held a special place among his writings; he told one friend, 'I was never touched by anything not tangible and visible but once, and that was just before writing "Ave Imperatrix".'[54] He was justly proud of the work, sending a copy to the painter G. F. Watts.[55] Among the various tributes it received were a parody in *Truth* and a letter from a mess of British officers in Afghanistan, impressed by the 'truth and beauty' of its references to that country.[56] To build upon its success, Wilde reiterated his political preference for the 'State Republican' (provided it could be achieved without the violent 'kiss of anarchy') in another poem for the *World* – the sonnet '*Libertatis Sacra Fames*'.[57]

A more determinedly Aesthetic venture was *PAN*, a satirical weekly, of which he was 'installed as the poet'. It was printed on 'bilious' green paper, and Wilde's first contribution, a villanelle beginning, 'O Goat-foot God of Arcady... This northern isle hath need of thee!', provoked a parodic response (printed in the *Whitehall Review*) starting, 'Commissioner of Lunacee... Oscar Wilde hath need of thee.'[58]

Some of these modest literary achievements were mentioned in an article on Wilde that appeared in the August issue of *Biograph and Review*,

a popular monthly that profiled figures from the worlds of politics, religion and the arts. The entry on 'Mr. Oscar Wilde' – compiled by a friendly hand – gave a glowing account of his family background, university career and literary prospects, as well as quoting several of his sonnets, and getting the year of his birth wrong (either through journalistic incompetence or misinformation from the subject they gave it as 1856, rather than 1854).[59] Another fashionable paper – *Fact* – responded to the *Biograph* piece with a long article suggesting that Wilde, for all his talent and potential, scarcely merited such treatment, *yet*.[60] In the self-referential world of 1880s journalism, Wilde's very unworthiness of publicity could become a source of additional publicity.

3

Up to Snuff

'A most intense young man,
A soulful-eyed young man,
An ultra-poetical, super-aesthetical,
Out-of-the-way young man!'

W. S. GILBERT, PATIENCE

Among the claims of the *Biograph* article was the statement that Wilde was currently at work on a 'blank-verse tragedy in four acts'. This – like many of the specific details in the piece – was not quite accurate. Wilde had indeed been working hard on a play, but it was not a blank-verse tragedy. It was a prose melodrama set in contemporary Russia, entitled *Vera; or The Nihilists*. And he readily confessed that its 'literary merit' was 'very slight'.[1] Wilde's heroine, Vera Sabouroff, was a young Nihilist determined to overthrow the hated regime of 'Czar Ivan'. She falls in love with a fellow conspirator, Alexis, not realizing that he is in fact the youthful czarevitch (the czar's son and heir), who has disguised himself to join the plot against the cruel regime of his father. In the second half, following the czar's assassination by the Nihilists, Alexis, newly crowned in his stead, plans for a republican Russia. But the Nihilists, convinced that he has deserted them and their cause, conspire to assassinate him too. Lots are drawn, and Vera is chosen for the task. She steals into the royal bedchamber

ready to carry out the deed, only for Alexis to wake and declare his undying love for her. She reciprocates. But then, to save Alexis's life, she stabs herself, and flings the bloodied dagger out of the window to indicate to the waiting Nihilists below that the assassination has been accomplished. 'What have you done?' Alexis cries. 'I have saved Russia!' declares Vera, as she dies. 'Tableau'.

The subject, if it was not Aesthetic, was a topical: the autocracy of Czar Alexander II and the doings of the Nihilists were much in the news. In 1878 a young Nihilist called Vera Sussalich had been put on trial in St Petersburg for the attempted assassination of the city's governor. Her acquittal, greeted in the British press as a victory for liberty over oppression, unleashed a wave of further plots, assassinations and authoritarian reactions. As the *Era*, London's leading theatrical paper, remarked, 'On Russia's stage is... being played the most eventful and stirring drama of the century.' The same paper also carried an article entitled 'Modern History and Tragedy', urging the claims of contemporary history as a subject for modern drama. Whether this prompted or merely reflected Wilde's engagement with the Nihilists is uncertain. Although he had no personal ties to Russia, as both an Irish Nationalist and a Swinburnian, the themes of liberty and republicanism were close to his heart.[2]

The action of Wilde's play was dominated by the romantic idealism of its two principal characters – Vera and the czarevitch – but in Act II Wilde introduced the figure of 'Prince Paul', the czar's delightfully cynical prime minister, an aristocrat, autocrat and dandy who – according to his enemies – 'would stab his best friend for the sake of writing an epigram on his tombstone, or experiencing a new sensation'. His opening exchange, with a fellow government minister, sets the tone:

> PRINCE PAUL: For my own part, at least, I find these Cabinet Councils extremely exhausting.
> PRINCE PETROVITCH: Naturally; you are always speaking.
> PRINCE PAUL: No; I think it must be that I have to listen sometimes.[3]

Every remark of his lumbering colleagues – or of the impassioned young czarevitch – is skewered with an epigram, a paradox or an absurdity. To the czarevitch's desire for 'a change of air' he replies, 'A most revolutionary sentiment! Your Imperial father would highly disapprove of any reforms with the thermometer in Russia.' Challenged about a want of 'experience'

in some field, he observes, with a shrug of the shoulders, 'Experience is the name men give to their mistakes.'[4]

He is happy to be hated by the Nihilists, since 'indifference is the revenge they take on mediocrities' (not that he wastes time reading their 'violent proclamations' against him, because 'they are so badly spelt as a rule'). For himself the only immortality he desires is to invent a new sauce: 'I have never had time enough to think seriously about it, but I feel it is in me.' Politics he hopes may have prepared him for such gastronomic challenges. One of his aperçus runs: 'To make a good salad is to be a brilliant diplomatist – the problem is so entirely the same in both cases. To know exactly how much oil one must put with one's vinegar.' When a cabinet colleague complains that 'there seems to be nothing in life about which you would not jest', Prince Paul replies, 'Ah! My dear Count, life is much too important a thing ever to talk seriously about.'[5]

Prince Paul (who, having been sacked by the new czar, joins the Nihilists, and subjects them to his caustic asides) gave Wilde an opportunity to indulge his own wit. He was very pleased with the results.[6] Many of the character's mots Wilde had probably used already in his own conversation; certainly he would use them again.[7] Dramatically, though, he felt that humour served a real purpose; it would intensify, rather than undermine, the central tragedy.[8] And although Wilde was strongly in sympathy with the forces of 'democracy', Prince Paul allowed him to sound a note of caution about the violent demagogy of the Nihilists. And the character's statement that 'in a good democracy every man should be an aristocrat' may have been an echo of Wilde's own ever-shifting view.

The four-act play was finished over the summer. It was a substantial achievement, and Wilde had great hopes for it. He read the manuscript to his friends. He spent money on having a few copies printed up, and he dispatched them to the various theatrical contacts he had cultivated during the previous eighteen months – Henry Irving, Ellen Terry, Hermann Vezin, Genevieve Ward, Norman Forbes-Robertson, Dion Boucicault, and even E. F. S. Pigott, the examiner of plays for the Lord Chamberlain's office – seeking their approval and advice.[9] He invited Helena Modjeska to tea in the hope of soliciting her interest.[10]

The response was underwhelming. The actress Genevieve Ward did write to suggest a meeting so that she could tell him 'all I think about it'. But no one leapt forward with an offer to produce the play, or even a suggestion that it should be produced. Dion Boucicault – a hugely successful playwright

himself, and an old family friend – wrote a generous letter of practical advice, finding the 'spinal column' of the work – the relationship between Vera and the czarevitch – 'good, and dramatic', but pointing out that 'the ribs and the limbs do not proceed from the spinal column. Your other characters, your subjects of dialogue – which occupy 5/6th of the play – are not *action* but discussion… Your action stops for dialogue, whereas dialogue should be the necessary outcome of action exerting its influence on the characters.'[11]

After the gradually building achievements of his poetic appearances in the *World* and elsewhere, this was another rude check to set beside his earlier failure to find a publisher for a volume of his poems. Wilde, however, refused to be downhearted. The hated word 'failure' was not wholly applicable to the situation. The play was written; it existed, and would, he believed, find a producer in due course – even if the process was to take rather longer than expected or desired. In the meantime it could also be improved. Wilde was more than happy to 'take every actor's suggestion [he] could get'. Indeed he had had the play printed with interleaved blank pages to allow for the making of corrections and additions.

His immediate reaction, though, when confronted by the chorus of indifference, was to flee. He went for a late summer holiday to France, travelling again with his 'youthful disciple' Rennell Rodd – himself fresh from winning the Newdigate, and preparing for his final exams that December.[12] 'As we did not wish to be known,' Wilde explained with mock seriousness to George Lewis's twelve-year-old son, Rodd 'travelled under the name of Sir Smith, and I was Lord Robinson.' They visited Chartres and travelled down the Loire – 'one of the most wonderful rivers in the world, mirroring from sea to source a hundred cities and five hundred towers'.[13] They spent a charmed time at Amboise – 'that little village with its gray slate roofs and steep streets' – sketching, idling, and making 'plans *pour la gloire, et pour ennuyer les philistins*'.[14] Wilde then went on, alone, to Paris, where he enjoyed himself 'very much'.[15]*

Back in London at the end of October 1880, Wilde found that, despite the setback to his play-writing career, his profile as the exemplary Aesthete

---

* It was perhaps on this trip that Wilde displayed his Aesthetic outlook even in the midst of an altercation with a railway ticket collector. Rodd recalled in a letter of 1882 (now at Trinity College Dublin): 'Oscar, when the ticket collector would not let him pass the barrier *senza* ticket, in spite of his imposing appearance, and he protesting that it was really ridiculous. The collector extended him arms to press the poet back. Restrained but not subdued Oscar exclaimed, "Oh dear, What dreadful hands!"'

1. Lady Wilde, Oscar's mother, aged forty-three in 1864,
by the Dublin artist Bernard Mulrenin.

2. Oscar in a blue velvet dress,
aged about two.

3. Sir William Wilde towards the end
of his life, in the regalia of the Swedish
Order of the North Star.

4. A small sketch from Oscar's picture
album, possibly a drawing by him
of his beloved sister Isola.

5. Reverend Dr William Steele, the
inspirational headmaster at Portora.

6. J. P. Mahaffy, Professor of Ancient History at Trinity College Dublin; the scholar who showed Oscar 'how to love Greek things'.

7. John Ruskin, Slade Professor of Art at Oxford in the 1870s; Oscar thought him 'the Plato of England'.

8. Walter Pater, controversial Oxford don and author of *Studies in the History of the Renaissance*, one of Oscar's 'Golden Books'.

9. Drawing of a picnic at Blenheim from Florence Ward's diary, Oxford 'Commem', June 1876; Oscar is perhaps depicted as the third figure on the upper row, flirting with Florence's sister, Gertrude.

10. Oscar photographed having won the Newdigate Prize for his poem 'Ravenna' as well as a bust of Augustus Caesar left by a Magdalen fellow to the next undergraduate from the college to gain the prize. Oscar's brother, Willie, is seated on the right; Marian Willets is standing behind him.

11. 'Hosky' with his Oxford friends, Reggie 'Puss' Harding
and Willie 'Bouncer' Ward, 1876.

12. Frank Miles, the well-connected young artist and amateur gardener who introduced Oscar to London life.

13. Lord Ronald Gower by John Everett Millais; the portrait was exhibited at the inaugural exhibition of the Grosvenor Gallery in April 1877.

14. Guido Reni's *Saint Sebastian*, admired by Oscar at Genoa in 1877.

15. The 'exquisitely pretty' Florence Balcombe, drawn by Oscar, c.1876.

16. Lillie Langtry, first and greatest of the Professional Beauties; the 'New Helen' of Oscar's verses.

17. Ellen Terry, Irving's leading-lady at the Lyceum and the subject of several of Oscar's sonnets.

18. Sarah Bernhardt, photographed by Napoleon Sarony in New York, c.1880; Oscar said of the actress, 'There is absolutely no one like her'.

19. Helena Modjeska, the Polish-born actress; Oscar became her English champion.

20. George Lewis, the Society solicitor, featured, along with Oscar, as one of the 'Lights of London', in the Christmas Number of the *World* 1881.

21. H. Beerbohm Tree playing the Aesthetic poet Scott Ramsay in the manner of Oscar Wilde in the popular 1880 farce, *Where's the Cat?*.

22. George Du Maurier's cartoon introduces the Aesthetic poet 'Jellaby Postlethwaite' to the readers of *Punch*, 14 February 1880.

was continuing to rise – and rise steeply. Du Maurier's cartoons were maintaining his proxy presence in *Punch*. And there was more to come. On 20 November a new comedy opened at the Criterion Theatre, a ridiculous farce called *Where's the Cat?*. One of the principal characters, an Aesthetic poet named Scott Ramsay, was played by Herbert Beerbohm Tree as a broad caricature of Wilde. His colourful neckties, his 'putting himself into classical attitudes' and his 'sighing over a sunflower' were all accounted 'comical in the extreme'.[16] Beerbohm Tree claimed that he was reproducing 'not an individual, but a type', but few accepted this demurral. Beerbohm Tree, it was known, was acquainted with Wilde and had clearly 'studied his peculiarities' of dress and behaviour 'very closely'. According to the reviewer in the *Era*, 'there could be no mistaking' the impersonation of Wilde, 'the poet of society'.[17] It helped, too, that the twenty-seven-year-old actor shared Wilde's height and physique. On the night that Wilde's friend Lady Lonsdale attended the theatre, 'the name "Oscar Wilde" passed from lip to lip the moment... Beerbohm Tree set foot upon the stage, one trouser leg turned up at the bottom, after the manner of the poet.'[18]

Wilde went to the show.[19] And though he made no public comment upon it, the society paper *Life* did carry a paragraph reporting that, while 'one of the Aesthetic School has been absurd enough to write to Mr. Beerbohm Tree demanding an apology for having dared to imitate him', 'another of the School was, I am told, wise enough to write and congratulate Mr. Tree upon his felicitous performance'.[20] Given Wilde's cheerful attitude to du Maurier, and his 'happy facility for discovering compliments', it is difficult not to suppose that he was the second Aesthete.[21] Certainly the success of Beerbohm Tree's performance, and of the play (it ran into the following year, and toured the provinces), raised Wilde's celebrity another notch.

And the ratchet continued to turn. The new year saw two further hugely successful productions, each satirizing the excesses of the Aesthetic 'craze': *The Colonel* (a farce by F. C. Burnand, the new editor of *Punch*) opened at the Prince of Wales Theatre on 2 February 1881, and Gilbert and Sullivan's comic opera *Patience* premiered on 23 April at the Opera Comique, produced by Richard D'Oyly Carte.* Wilde attended the first nights of

---

* *Patience* ran for a then record 578 performances, initially at the Opera Comique, then at the newly completed Savoy Theatre. *The Colonel* ran for 550 performances. On 4 October 1881 there was even a command performance for Queen Victoria, at Abergeldie Castle, the Prince of Wales's retreat, near Balmoral, the first play the queen had seen since the death of Prince Albert, twenty years previously. She declared herself 'very much amused'.

both productions, conspicuous in the stalls. Taking his seat at the Opera Comique, looking 'unutterably utter', he was almost immediately 'spotted' by the 'denizens of the gallery', and 'had to bear a considerable amount of chaff'. He endured this with what one newspaper described as 'remarkable nonchalance' and 'much good nature'.[22] He ensured that he was part of the show. His enjoyment of the opera was noted, too, in several papers.[23] *The Colonel* was a less distinguished offering, hastily cobbled together. But although Wilde confessed privately to finding it 'dull' he took care to make no public pronouncement against it.[24]

Neither piece offered a direct caricature of Wilde. The comic villain of *The Colonel* – Lambert Streyke, 'professor' of Aestheticism, 'tone poet' and founder of the 'Aesthetic High Art Company' – was an elderly charlatan who merely used the fad to dupe the gullible female members of a well-to-do family out of large amounts of money so that he could fund his quite unaesthetic tastes. Gilbert and Sullivan's two 'Aesthetic' poets, Reginald Bunthorne and Archibald Grosvenor, were also 'shams' – posing as Aesthetes in the hope of winning the hand of the beautiful Patience. Nevertheless, many details of Lambert Streyke's creed – cribbed as they were from du Maurier's *Punch* cartoons – had a recognizably Postlethwaitian, and hence Wildean, tenor. Steyke claimed, for instance, that he 'could feed on a lily in a glass of water', and instructed one of his disciples to 'live up to' her teapot (provoking the response from the worldly Mrs Blyth, 'I understand living up to my income, but not up to my teapot').[25]

Gilbert, for his part, was praised by many critics for eschewing personal attacks on 'any particular representatives of aesthetic tastes'. He was adjudged to have presented, instead, a general satire upon their mannerisms and poses: the affected air of languorous melancholy, the self-absorption, the velvet jackets and china-mania, the love of things either Japanese or medieval, the delight in low tones, the reverence for the Grosvenor Gallery, the sentimental passion for flowers (which might extend even to 'an attachment à la Plato for a bashful young potato'). Many in his audience, however, were only too happy to make good such tactful omissions – even if they were in some dispute as to which personalities were being lampooned, and how.

The Times critic considered that Bunthorne, as played by the diminutive George Grossmith, had been modelled upon Swinburne. Others noted that the actor, with his eyeglass and a distinctive lock of white hair, was made up to look like Whistler. Most commentators, however, recognized a debt to

Wilde. Bunthorne's declaration that admission to the 'high aesthetic band' could be won 'if you walk down Piccadilly with a poppy or a lily in your mediaeval hand' seemed to carry a reference to Wilde's supposed actions; while Bunthorne's description of his own poem as 'a wild, weird, fleshly thing', appeared to be nothing short of a namecheck. Although some people ventured that it was, rather, the 'mild' self-regarding Archibald Grosvenor who derived from Wilde, the identification with Bunthorne very quickly prevailed.[26] Indeed, shortly after the opera's opening night, Wilde was introduced at a party where Grossmith had just performed Bunthorne's lament, with the line, 'this is the man'.[27]

After these three fusillades – Where's the Cat?, The Colonel and Patience – it was open season on the London stage for satires upon Aestheticism. By the middle of 1881 the Illustrated London News was reporting that the theatrical scene was 'thickly sown all over with a crop of lilies and sunflowers... There are aesthetes in every burlesque and comic opera produced.' And many of these stage Aesthetes made deliberate reference to Wilde: 'Even Mr. Toole' – the noted comedian-proprietor of the Folly Theatre – posing with a sunflower in one skit, as he emerged from a Margate bathing-machine, announced, 'it does make me so Wilde'.[28]

Fame seemed to nourish itself. References in the London papers were repeated across the provincial and metropolitan press. They were recycled in America, Australia, South Africa and New Zealand. Willie, and Oscar, fanned the flames. They had both learnt thoroughly 'the trick of advertisement' (as Willie called it), supplying the ever-proliferating 'society' papers with tidbits of news and personal information. One short-lived periodical, The London Cuckoo, even carried an interview with Willie about how he helped promote his brother.[29]

In May 1881 du Maurier tried to kill off Postlethwaite, producing a farewell cartoon – 'Frustrated Social Ambition' – depicting the distraught poet, weeping together with Maudle and Mrs Cimabue Brown, 'on reading in a widely circulated contemporary journal that they only exist in Mr Punch's vivid imagination. They had fondly flattered themselves that universal fame was theirs at last.'[30] Wilde, however, survived his alter-ego's demise. His own fame was, indeed, fast becoming 'universal'. Other caricaturists and sketchwriters, in other magazines, readily filled the breech left by du Maurier. And, indeed, Wilde continued to be parodied in Punch, appearing variously over the ensuing months as 'Oscuro Wildegoose', 'Drawit Milde' and 'the Wilde-eyed Poet'.[31] Linley Sambourne, the magazine's other leading artist,

depicted him – as *'Punch's* Fancy Portrait No. 37' – his head emerging from a sunflower.[32] Wilde was heralded everywhere as 'the "Poet" and self-constituted high priest of beauty and high art'.[33]

He cut so distinctive a figure, surrounded by adoring females, at the opening of that year's Royal Academy summer exhibition, that W. P. Frith felt he must include him – alongside such luminaries as Millais and Browning – in the large-scale painting he was composing of the private view. Wilde, of course, was delighted to sit for the painter.[34] His face was everywhere. Photographs of him began to appear 'in all the shop-windows' – 'long hair, close-shaved face, loose cravat, & velvet coat, with his hands clasped under one cheek, gazing into vacancy'.[35] One commentator considered that Wilde was now 'more talked about and paragraphed than any other male individual not being a murderer or a statesman'.[36]*

If Wilde had achieved a quite remarkable position, it was at a certain cost. The tide of parodies, satires and caricatures, although they had spread his name, had also reinforced the notion that he was, somehow, an absurd and comical figure. Attending the theatre one evening, he overheard a playgoer declare, 'There goes that bloody fool, Oscar Wilde.' At which he remarked brightly to his companion, 'It is extraordinary how soon one gets known in London.'[37] Wilde felt he could afford such equanimity. He knew that he was not a fool. He knew that in the private social sphere he could always rectify such an impression by the charm and intelligence of his talk. And he believed that, among the wider public, he could effect the same conversion through his art.

He had, however, perhaps underestimated how hard this would be. The lukewarm response to *Vera* gave him a first indication that popular fame might not translate directly into artistic advancement. He seems, though, to have been less aware that it could actually prove a hindrance. Wilde's great celebrity – and the way in which it had been achieved – produced huge resentment. In the literary world there might be few who considered him a fool, but there were many who thought him a buffoon. They found his self-advertising vulgar, and his affectations absurd. They resented too

---

* Wilde, drinking with a company of journalists at Romano's restaurant one day in 1881, remarked – 'in his ineffably superior way' – '"If I were not a poet, and could not be an artist, I should wish to be a murderer." "What!" exclaimed one [of the company], "and have your portrait-sketch in the *Daily Telegraph*?" "Better, that," cooed Wilde, "than to go down to the sunless grave unknown."' Extraordinarily this admission has not – thus far – encouraged anyone to suggest that Wilde was 'Jack the Ripper'.

that he had been able to attract such attention without having actually produced any substantial work. Fastidious spirits like Pater considered 'the whole panorama' of Wilde's fledgling career 'utterly distasteful'.[38]

Among some sections of the press there was resentment too at the social position Wilde had won. Wilde liked to present his eager engagement with society as an important part of his Aesthetic campaign: an attempt 'to sweep away all barriers and bring the artist in direct communication with his patrons'.[39] But many suspected less exalted motives. It was claimed that, like Lambert Streyke or Bunthorne, he must be 'an aesthetic sham', an upstart who had adopted his 'ridiculous' pose and his 'repulsive' long hair simply to impress fashionable hostesses and gain access to 'good society' – while all the time 'laughing in his sleeve'. Wilde had too much respect for society, and too much anxiety about his position in it, not to resent the imputation. One of the rare occasions on which he complained – albeit privately – to an editor, was over a piece in the *World* that charged him with such duplicity. Yates apologized, claiming not to have read the article before publication, having – he said – given 'distinct instructions' that nothing 'unpleasant' to Wilde was to be said in the piece.[40]

Another source of (male) resentment was Wilde's attractiveness. Already much admired by women, his fame only made him more alluring. He developed a reputation as a 'ladykiller'. It was noted that 'in many a London drawing room' young artistically inclined women could now be seen 'hovering around [him] with admiring eyes, and in attitudes suggestive of Grosvenor Gallery pictures'.[41] Willie fondly imagined that his brother would marry an heiress.[42] But Oscar gave little encouragement to the notion. Although he did provoke comment, at one informal dance, by monopolizing the 'very pretty' Lilian Major, pronouncing her 'a soothing gem' and even paying a visit to her family home at Sheen, the connection was not pursued further.[43] He continued to flirt mildly with Violet Hunt, calling on her parents almost every week. She, however, was not an heiress. Nor did she seem inclined to follow Wilde to the ends of the earth. When, discoursing on old maps, he described how vast tracts of Africa were often left blank except for the legend '*hic sunt leones*' – adding, excitedly, 'Miss Violet, let you and me go there' – she replied, 'And get eaten by lions?'[44]

More promising, perhaps, was a girl he met that summer. Constance Lloyd was the granddaughter of old Dublin friends, and the sister of Otho Lloyd, whom Wilde had known slightly at Oxford. She had come to live in London with her paternal grandfather and a maiden aunt at Lancaster Gate, while

her widowed mother (now remarried to a Mr Swinburne-King) lived nearby on Devonshire Terrace. Wilde was clearly struck by the beautiful blue-green-eyed twenty-two-year-old when they were introduced at a tea party hosted by Constance's mother. According to family legend, he announced to his own mother, as they left the reception, 'By the by, mamma, I think of marrying that girl.' Opportunities were soon engineered for them to meet again: an 'at home' given by Constance's aunt at Lancaster Gate; one of Lady Wilde's Saturday 'salons' – at which Wilde monopolized Constance 'nearly all the time'; an invitation to see Henry Irving's *Othello* at the Lyceum. Constance may have been shy. She confessed to 'shaking with fright' on first meeting Wilde. But she was attractive, with literary interests and artistic leanings, and also a ready intelligence. Her brother noted that she was 'surprisingly quick at detecting the flaw or weak point in any reasoning'. She could, he added, 'carry her own in any argument well, and always had the courage of her opinions' together with a 'quiet humour and a sense of the ridiculous'.[45]

Wilde would also have been aware that Constance had money, or the prospect of money. Her grandfather and *de facto* guardian, Horatio Lloyd, had made a great fortune as the inventor of a legal document 'familiar to investors in railway securities, known as a Lloyd's bond' – before an unfortunate scandal had led to him being temporarily disbarred (exhausted by overwork, he had run naked through the Temple Gardens, alarming a group of nursemaids). Constance, as one of Horatio Lloyd's grandchildren, might indeed be considered an heiress.[46] It was not a motive for romance, but it was a happy addition to the picture.

Wilde exerted himself to charm her – disarmingly dropping his more extravagant affectations. 'When he's talking to me alone,' Constance explained, 'he's never a bit affected and speaks naturally excepting that he uses better language than most people.'[47] He also took trouble with her grandfather, escorting him and Constance on a tour of the Pall Mall art galleries. The ploy was successful. 'Grand Papa I think likes Oscar,' Constance reported to her brother, though she was obliged to admit that the other Lloyd relations were inclined to laugh at him, 'because they don't choose to see anything but that he wears long hair and looks aesthetic'. She added, 'I like him awfully much but I suppose it is very bad taste.'[48] It is unclear at what level the intimacy established that June was kept up through the rest of 1881. But there is no doubt that Constance at least retained a romantic interest in the long-haired Aesthete, and even a hope that it might resolve itself into something more permanent.[49]

If Wilde was becoming a lion himself, he remained keenly aware that there were many older and greater lions at large. He used his newfound fame to get close to the heroic figures of the Aesthetic movement. Eager to build upon his acquaintanceship with Whistler, he sought the painter out, following up a general invitation to one of his celebrated 'breakfasts'. And although Whistler claimed to have been rather bounced into the friendship, he was impressed by Wilde's informed flattery, obvious intelligence and growing fame, as much as by his close associations with Lillie Langtry and Ellen Terry – both of whom the painter knew and adored.[50] When Whistler moved into a new studio in Tite Street over the summer, the friendship between the two men rapidly developed into a camaraderie. Whistler liked to work among company, and a small throng of supporters gathered regularly at his new address. Besides Wilde – and Frank Miles – there was Rennell Rodd, just down from Oxford, the painter Mrs Jopling, the American expatriate artists Harper Pennington and Waldo Story, the beautiful Lady Archibald Campbell, who was posing for a portrait, and a broken-down former pottery painter called Matthew Elden.[51]

For Wilde real glamour attached to the new association. The forty-seven-year-old Whistler, despite the setbacks of recent years, was undimmed in either vitality or self-belief. He retained all his audacious individuality and style, all the fabled sharpness of his wit and dress sense. He had returned to London as convinced as ever that he was the greatest artist of the age, and, notwithstanding much evidence to the contrary, he behaved as though everyone else was of the same opinion. His professional vanity was no less real for being tinged with deliberate absurdity. When an admirer flattered him with the remark, 'There are only two great painters – you and Velazquez', he replied, 'Oh, why drag in Velazquez?' Wilde accepted such judgements: whatever his own cheerful self-conceit he 'reckoned himself... a small figure' besides the 'Master'.[52] Though he did not forsake his established Pre-Raphaelite idols, he now maintained a parallel belief in the genius of Whistler. The painter became a new 'hero' – one to set beside Henry Irving.[53] The qualified approval of Wilde's earlier Grosvenor Gallery reviews gave way to fulsome praise. Whistler's 'Symphony in White' was accounted 'the most beautiful picture' Wilde had ever seen.[54]

Painting, though, was only ever part of Whistler's performance. He overflowed with bracing ideas and striking opinions about art. He championed the culture of Japan and the work of the French Impressionists. He 'reviled' Turner ('that old amateur') and disparaged the Pre-Raphaelites. His old

friend Rossetti was patronized as 'not a painter, but a gentleman and a poet'; while Burne-Jones (usually referred to as plain 'Jones') was dismissed as knowing 'nothing about painting'.[55]* From his years in Paris, Whistler knew many of the noted provocateurs, poets and painters of the French capital. He was friendly with Degas and Mallarmé, familiar with the ideas of Théophile Gautier and Baudelaire. He projected a cosmopolitan intellectual sophistication to which Wilde aspired. His work – Wilde came to realize – reflected all that was most daring and novel (and French) in contemporary thought. It was Gautier's doctrine of *l'art pour l'art* – with its insistence that art be free from all political, social and moral considerations, and concerned only with its own formal perfection, that stood behind Whistler's vague low-toned 'harmonies'. It was Gautier's idea that, with all motifs now available to the artist, there was a virtue in selecting the untried and the disparaged, that encouraged Whistler to paint fleeting impressions of the modern metropolis.

Although Wilde had already met Gautier's notions of 'art for art's sake' in the writings of Pater, it was another thing to encounter them in action, in an artist's studio. The effect was electric. Wilde hastened to pay his new friend a poetic homage, publishing in the *World* an avowedly Whistlerian verse, entitled – with a greater sense of French style than French grammar – 'Impression de Matin'.[56] The little vignette, beginning 'The Thames nocturn [*sic*] of blue and gold / Changed to a harmony of gray', sought to transpose the achievement of Whistler's impressionist art into verse. Aiming solely at formal perfection, it repudiated the idea that poetry should be either 'intellectual or emotional'.[57]

But if Wilde learnt something about art from Whistler, he learnt even more about self-advertisement. As one contemporary observed, 'Whistler taught him that men of genius stand apart and are laws unto themselves; showed him too that all qualities – singularity of appearance, wit, rudeness even, count doubly in a democracy.'[58] These were hugely important lessons that did much to mould Wilde's developing talent and developing style – although when it came to 'rudeness' for the sake of controversy, Wilde's good nature made him wary of accepting them fully. The two men, for all their enjoyment of each other's company, had very different temperaments. Wilde lacked Whistler's diabolical contempt for others and 'joy in conflict'.

---

*   One of Whistler's quips against Burne-Jones was, 'Well, you know, I don't go so far as to Burne-Jones, but really somebody ought to burn Jones' pictures!'

Indeed he often tried to restrain his hero's 'too brutal' campaigns.[59] Wilde's wit, too, was of a different stamp: abundant, inventive, generous, 'always brimming over', compared to Whistler's sharp, explosive, wounding ways.[60]

During the early part of their friendship, Wilde knew his place, and was kept in it. When he too eagerly approved Whistler's rebuke to the *Times* art critic about the limits of press criticism, with the aside 'I wish I had said that', Whistler shot back: 'You will, Oscar, you will.'[61] Nevertheless, despite such digs, Whistler remained a supportive presence. He sought Wilde's company, proposing trips to Paris and the Channel Islands ('Now Oscar you have simply to get on your disguise again and come off with me *tomorrow* to Jersey').[62] He involved him in schemes. They collaborated – along with Frank Miles – on plans for a house in Tite Street for Lillie Langtry, to be built by Godwin. Langtry recalled that her 'triumvirate of counsellors' got so carried away with ideas and suggestions that when their 'rough sketches' were inspected by the architect 'it was discovered that there was no possibility of a staircase'. The project was subsequently abandoned.[63] Together Whistler and Wilde visited the medievalist architect William Burges on his deathbed, and attended the opening of *Patience*; Whistler responded to George Grossmith's caricaturing of his appearance in the role of Bunthorne by writing an enthusiastic letter of praise to the actor – another example from which Wilde profited.[64]

This comradeship with Whistler was, however, never all-consuming. Wilde chose to ignore the rift that had opened up within the Aesthetic ranks after the Ruskin–Whistler trial. He continued to advance his connections with the great figures of the Pre-Raphaelite movement, becoming increasingly friendly with Burne-Jones. It was a mark of both his social confidence and tact that he was able to carry off this double game. Wilde was a welcome guest at The Grange, Burne-Jones's house in West Kensington. Burne-Jones's teenage niece, Alice Kipling (sister of Rudyard), encountering Wilde there at a family dinner, suspected that her uncle was slightly embarrassed by Wilde's worship – and 'winced, I think, when Oscar addressed him as "Master"'.[65] Burne-Jones' son, Phil, then an Oxford undergraduate, had – she noted, by contrast – an obvious 'adoration' for Wilde. But, in fact, a happy intimacy soon developed between the middle-aged painter and his young admirer. To the surprise of some, the two became really 'good friends'.[66] They shared many of the same loves in art and literature,[67] and Wilde made the kindly, melancholic Burne-Jones laugh. Indeed the painter considered 'Oscar the funniest of all men I ever knew' – with a rare ability 'to beguile

the merriment out of one'.[68] Wilde induced him to enjoy life: when Burne-Jones was dreading the 'martyrdom' of receiving an honorary doctorate from Oxford at the often rowdy Encaenia, it was Wilde who reconciled him to his fate: '[he] was very nice to me and came across the other day to say how pleased he was – and he looked so genuinely glad that I loved him'.[69] Burne-Jones seems to have repaid such kindnesses by giving Wilde several drawings.[70] Their friendship was fostered too by George Lewis and his wife, who – friends of both men – regularly brought them together, either at Portland Place or at their weekend retreat near Walton-on-Thames.[71]

Burne-Jones's endorsement perhaps encouraged William Morris to set aside his prejudices against Wilde. When they first met, in the spring of 1881, Morris confessed, 'I must admit that as the devil is painted blacker than he is, so it fares with O.W. Not but what he is an ass: but he certainly is clever too.'[72] At other meetings Wilde proved himself both 'a superb raconteur' and 'uncommon good company'.[73] He had, after all, a flattering enthusiasm for Morris's poetry and designs, as well as an openness to his political ideas. Wilde was already espousing 'socialism' – albeit partly perhaps for effect (when he first met Violet Hunt, he declared, 'I am a socialist. Have you been taught to dread them?').[74] In due course Morris came also to recognize Wilde's distinctive 'vein of good nature'. A friendship of sorts developed between them.[75]

Cosier, though, was the bond Wilde established with the ageing Ford Madox Brown. Wilde found the old painter's company restful, claiming that his was 'the only house in London where he did not have to stand on his head'. He would often call by for tea on Saturday afternoons. Madox Brown's grandson (the future novelist Ford Madox Ford) recalled Wilde on these visits as 'a quiet individual', who 'would sit in a high-backed arm-chair, stretching out one hand a little towards the blaze of the wood fire on the hearth and talking of the dullest things possible… the Home Rule for Ireland Bill or the Conversion of the Consolidated Debt', while 'on the other side of the fire in another high-backed chair and, stretching out towards the flames his other hand', sat Ford Madox Brown, usually dis-agreeing with his guest's views.[76]

Such easy intimacy, however, proved harder to achieve with Wilde's two greatest 'Pre-Raff' heroes. Swinburne was wary of his over-enthusiastic and self-promoting disciple. Indeed Wilde had become something of a *bête noir* for the poet. The two men did, though, come together at a reception chez Lord Houghton. Wilde, seizing the opportunity, persuaded a 'considerably

embarrassed' Watts Dunton (Swinburne's friend and companion), to effect an introduction. Swinburne consented to the meeting with the remark, 'Very well, introduce us. But I will not exchange a dozen words with him.' And he was true to his word. The encounter lasted barely three minutes. It would be their only meeting. Wilde, though, refused to acknowledge any sort of snub. He had done enough to claim a connection, even a friendship; Swinburne came away with the impression that Wilde was 'a harmless young nobody'.[77]

Rossetti, however, though he lived just round the corner from Tite Street, on Cheyne Walk, proved to be altogether out of reach. Prone to dark moods, he 'bitterly resented the way in which Oscar's name was linked with him and his circle', and refused to have anything to do with the upstart. He even berated Burne-Jones, his old friend, for 'taking up with the man who was posing as the leader of the new aesthetic movement' (Burne-Jones stoutly defended Wilde's talents).[78] Denied access, Wilde was reduced to constructing a sort of proxy relationship, eagerly gathering up anecdotes about Rossetti from his old intimates.[79]

The wider artistic world, less anxious about their supposed relationship to Wilde, proved more welcoming. William Blake Richmond, the new Slade Professor at Oxford, became a friend.[80] And Wilde was a frequent guest at the Aesthetic home of Laurence Alma-Tadema and his wife in St John's Wood.[81] He attended their regular Tuesdays, and was present at the 'brilliant' masked costume ball that they threw for fifty choice friends. Wilde, alone, insisted on coming unmasked. 'The Tademas think this most conceited of him,' Edmund Gosse reported, 'and beg that everyone will tease him as much as possible.'[82] Wilde also offered the painter advice about early Greek orthography for his picture of Sappho and her circle.[83]

But, of all Wilde's new connections, the grandest was the Prince of Wales. Wilde's friendships with Lillie Langtry and Frank Miles had always given him a sense of contiguity with royalty, but it had never crystallized into an actual meeting until now. Intrigued by Wilde's rising fame, the prince asked his friend Christopher Sykes to give a dinner to bring them together, fixing his request with the mot, 'I do not know Mr Wilde, and not to know Mr Wilde is not to be known.'[84] The dinner itself was not an unqualified success: one of the other guests, Bernal Osborne (the prince's licensed 'clown'), kept up such a barrage of crude witticisms that Wilde left the room. It was, however, some consolation that Osborne received a 'merited reproof' from the annoyed prince; and even more satisfactory

that news of the dinner became widely known. Indeed Edmund Yates celebrated the event with a poem – published in the *World* – under the title 'Ego up to Snuffibus Poeta'.[85]

There were other royal encounters too – duly advertised by Wilde, with Willie's enthusiastic co-operation.[86] Republican sentiments were trumped by social prestige. Wilde was thrilled to welcome the prince to Keats House, where he attended a 'startling' thought-reading demonstration given by W. Irving Bishop. Other guests included Whistler, Irving, the Lewises, Lady Archibald Campbell and Lillie Langtry.[87] At a Grosvenor Gallery reception the prince 'left the line' as he progressed through the crowded Long Gallery and, 'with extended hand', cordially greeted his new friend.[88] Wilde also attended a garden party at Marlborough House.[89]* He was certainly 'up to snuff'. Those irritated by his social success, became more irritated still.

---

*   The garden party gave Wilde a close-up view of Queen Victoria. He was entranced by her 'exquisite bearing'. She looked, he explained, 'like a ruby mounted in jet. She is very small... Everybody moved aside as she approached. By the rules of Court etiquette no one is allowed to look at her face in front, but only in profile. This makes it rather difficult, for you have to take care when her eye rests on you. Then you must bow and move towards her. She gives her hand... She has the most beautiful hands and the most beautiful wrists.'

4

An English Poet

''Tis a great advantage, I admit, to have done nothing, but
one must not abuse even that advantage.'

OSCAR WILDE, QUOTING ANTOINE DA RIVAROL

Wilde was determined to make practical use of his fame, and to fix his position as the new Aesthetic poet, by publishing a book of poems. After his previous frustrations on this front, the time now seemed ripe. Yet, for all his burgeoning celebrity, he still could not find a commercial publisher willing to support the venture. Impatient of further delay, he took matters into his own hands. That May (1881) he wrote to David Bogue – the publisher of *The Byron Birthday Book*, *Kenna's Kingdom* (a 'quaint' history of Kensington), and *A Cricketer's Notebook* – asking whether he might be able to bring out a volume of poems 'immediately'.[1] Wilde – as was not uncommon at the time – agreed to underwrite the costs of production. But Bogue does seem to have shown some confidence in the venture, amending his standard 'Memorandum of Agreement' at several places in Wilde's favour, and reducing his commission in acknowledgement of Wilde's financial contribution.[2]

Wilde conceived the book as a handsome Aesthetic production, a showcase for his taste. He lavished his resources upon it, and the project must have taken him further into debt. The forty-two poems – which included all

his periodical-published verses – were to be printed on 'hand-made Dutch paper' with generous margins, the top of the pages gilded, the whole bound in 'white parchment' decorated with panels stamped in gold with a japonesque design of stylized prunus blossoms.[3] The proposed retail price – a substantial 10s 6d (or half a guinea) – marked the book as a choice product for an exclusive readership.

Although Wilde wanted to bring out the book as quickly as possible, editorial concerns were not neglected. He grouped his poems into sections, each with its own running title. Eschewing flashier effects, he decided to title the volume *Poems*. He deployed his self-dramatizing sonnet 'Hélas'– printed in italics – as the book's opening statement, or 'Proem'. In the poem Wilde cast himself as one who had 'given away' the 'ancient wisdom and austere control' offered, perhaps, by religion or by academe, in order to embrace the sensual Paterian flux of momentary impressions and shifting passions – 'To drift with every passion' and make of his 'soul... a stringed lute on which all winds can play'. Although, characteristically, he wondered if – having thus touched 'the honey of romance' – he really 'must... lose a soul's inheritance'. The time for further changes of mind, he seemed to hint, might not be dead.

He pored over the printer's proofs. It was said that, asked at dinner how he had spent his day, he replied that it had been taken up with hard literary endeavour: 'I was working on the proof of one of my poems all morning and took out a comma.' Quizzed about his afternoon, he said, 'In the afternoon – well, I put it back again.'[4] By the middle of June 750 copies of the text had been printed. However, only 250 were bound up to make the 'First Edition'. This was another common practice among canny publishers: it reduced their initial outlay, and allowed them to stimulate excitement in the market by subsequently binding up fresh batches of the already printed folios as 'new editions'.

Displaying both ambition and commercial acumen, Wilde also looked to America, where he had a growing profile. His verses had, of course, been printed in the Boston *Pilot*, but, more than this, his position as the 'High Priest of Aesthetic Art' and 'the original of "Postlethwaite"' was being quite widely reported in the American press.[5] He arranged with the Boston firm of Roberts Brothers for them to bring out a simultaneous American edition of the book; identical as to text, but with an undecorated cloth cover, it was to be priced more modestly at $1.25, equivalent to 5s.[6]

By the end of June all was ready: advertisements began appearing in the press, and even on the walls of 'London-town'.[7] The *World* announced

'People who, hearing of Mr. Oscar Wilde, ask who he is and what he has ever done, will now be able to learn, as a volume of Mr. Wilde's collected poems will shortly be published.'[8] The book – with its emphatic title and handsome form – confirmed Wilde's long-assumed status as a 'Poet'. Justly proud of his achievement, he dispatched inscribed copies to a plethora of friends and luminaries, including Gladstone and Lillie Langtry, William Blake Richmond and Ellen Terry. Violet Fane and Margaret Burne-Jones were among those who received poetic dedications.[9] Now able, as he thought, to claim kinship with his literary heroes, he also sent books – with fulsome covering letters – to Swinburne, Rossetti, William Morris, Matthew Arnold, Robert Browning and John Addington Symonds. The response was gratifying.

Symonds – while privately considering Wilde's accompanying note almost 'a caricature of himself in *Punch*' – admired the book.[10] He wrote back a generous letter of considered praise, admitting the poems' inequalities, political contradictions and excessive 'Keatsian' sensuality – but recognizing 'the real poet's gift in them'.[11] Arnold replied, flatteringly acknowledging Wilde as a 'fellow worker', and thanking him for his 'too kind' note: 'I have but glanced at the poems as yet, but I perceive in them the true feeling for rhythm, which is at the bottom of all success in poetry; of all endeavour, indeed, which is not fictitious and vain, in that line of expression.'[12] Swinburne's response, if guarded, was not unwelcoming; he claimed to have enjoyed the impressionistic 'Les Silhouettes' in particular. Browning and William Morris sent 'complimentary letters'.[13] Only Rossetti, it seems, did not write back.*

In the press *Poems* created a decided stir. Wilde's notoriety ensured that the book was widely reviewed, both in Britain and the United States. It also ensured that – in Britain especially – it would not be treated altogether fairly. Wilde did what he could to counter the expected hostility, asking friends, including Oscar Browning and William Ward, to write reviews.[14] But he was largely at the mercy of critics, journalists and fellow writers who resented his fame, his 'vulgar' self-promotion, and his social success. *Punch* led the attack. Having trailed the book with the ditty 'Aesthete of Aesthetes! What's in a name? The poet is Wilde, But his poetry's tame', they

---

* Rossetti's personal assistant, Hall Cane, claimed that, on receiving a gold-inscribed copy of the book, Rossetti was quick to recognize 'the gifts that underlay a good deal of [the author's] amusing affectation'. But this account is undercut by the fact that the poet himself told Jane Morris, on 1 October 1881, 'I saw the wretched Oscar Wilde book, & glanced at it enough to see clearly what trash it is. Did Georgie [Burne-Jones] say Ned [Burne-Jones] really admires it? If so, he must be driveling.'

confirmed the verdict in a review that condemned the work as a volume of poetic 'echoes', or 'Swinburne and Water'.[15]

Wilde's rich literary culture was held against him. There was a general rush among the reviewers to point out that his poems were derivative, and not just of Swinburne. The critics showed off their knowledge by indicating debts to Milton, Rossetti, Morris, Elizabeth Barrett Browning, Keats, Wordsworth, Tennyson and Arnold. The only 'poet of the day' that Wilde was considered not to have imitated was Robert Browning – though, as one writer uncharitably suggested, 'His "imitations of Browning" are presumably kept for another volume.'[16]

While Wilde's 'cleverness' might be admitted, little else was.[17] The most insistent charges – besides imitation – were 'insincerity' and 'bad taste'. Wilde's emotions were deemed to be put on for effect. His ignorance of nature was gleefully exposed: 'He thinks that the meadowsweet and the wood-anemone bloom at the same time... and that owls are commonly met with in mid-ocean.'[18] His apparent ability to see 'equally the good and bad in everything' from Roman Catholicism to paganism, monarchy to republicanism, revolution to communism – was accounted confusion.[19] There were stern rebukes of 'the sensual and ignoble tone' of much of the work.[20] 'Charmides' – his tale of a Sicilian youth's erotic encounter with a statue of Athena – was considered the worst offender. In it he was adjudged to have 'greatly exceed[ed] the licence which even a past Pagan poet would have permitted himself' – with his references to 'grand cool flanks' and 'crescent thighs'.[21]

Meanwhile the comic paragraphists made sport of Wilde's line – in 'Silentium Amoris' – about 'the barren memory / Of unkissed kisses', wondering what on earth such kisses could be, and suggesting, among other things, that most of Wilde's poems seemed to be made of 'unthunk thoughts', or might provoke 'uncussed cusses'.[22]

Some judgements, though, were more generous. Wilde did have his supporters. One critic flatteringly suggested that 'a little fold of the mantle of Keats' had fallen upon him.[23] 'The Burden of Itys' received repeated commendation as the best poem in the collection.[24] The World (perhaps predictably) found much to admire both in the book's appearance ('a thing of beauty') and its contents ('well conceived and happily expressed').[25] And Oscar Browning, answering Wilde's call, contributed an approving – though not uncritical – review in the Academy, ending with the assertion that 'we lay down this book in the conviction that England is enriched with a new

poet'. American responses often echoed such positive sentiments. Across the Atlantic 'Ave Imperatrix' was particularly admired; the *New York Times* pronounced it 'an ode on England such as Tennyson has not [written] and cannot'.[26]

Though Wilde was delighted to receive such compliments, he remained frustrated by the prevailing tone of critical hostility in England.[27] It was becoming clear that his hard-won celebrity was not only a limited support but might actually be a positive hindrance to his artistic ambitions. His carefully projected pose, though it might appeal to some, provoked resentment, and encouraged derision among rather more. It irked many artists, and annoyed both the philistine press and the 'general public'. But, against this background, there was still room to manoeuvre. Publicity ensured that the book was known. It found its audience. The 'first edition' rapidly sold out, and a second 'edition' of a further 250 copies was at once bound up. By the beginning of October it was being announced that 'Mr Oscar Wilde has the best of the laugh with his critics. They have jeered his book into a third edition.'[28] And with the original 750 sets of sheets thus accounted for, plans were made for a new printing of 500 copies; a similar pattern obtained in America, where the book soon ran through two editions.[29]

Within the small world of literary London this could be accounted 'an extraordinary success'. And it was. Lady Wilde complacently told guests at one of her receptions: 'You know, they say there has been no such sensation since Byron... Everyone is talking about [Oscar's *Poems*].'[30] Certainly Wilde's friends were spreading the word. The book was 'taken up' by Ellen Terry.[31] Rennell Rodd advised one acquaintance that he 'ought to see Oscar Wilde's new volume, there's so much brilliant writing in it'.[32] Whistler hoped that a visiting American patron, and her travelling companions, had '*each* bought a copy of Oscar Wilde's poems – without which you *cannot* leave this land!'[33] Wilde himself could feel pleased with the overall result. If less than a total triumph the book was being discussed, written about and bought. And although the high production costs meant that he earned little more than 'pocket money' from the sales, it was still an achievement to have turned a profit on a first volume of poetry.[34]

At Oxford the book became the subject of heated debate. Wilde was still a figure at the university. He continued to visit regularly – finding not only friends there, but also imitators. Every college, it seems, now had its small group of Aesthetic 'extremists': 'they all wear their hair long,' explained a contemporary undergraduate, 'sport flame-coloured cravats, hang their

rooms with blue china and Botticelli, and read nobody but Swinburne and Rossetti.[35] And as these Wildean 'disciples' became more conspicuous, they became more resented. A proposal put forward by one of them (a Magdalen man), that the library of the Oxford Union should cancel its subscription to *Punch* because of that magazine's persistent ridiculing of Aestheticism, was summarily rejected. And when it became known that Wilde would be in Oxford at the end of the summer term (to attend a dance at University College and to visit his apostle at Magdalen) plans were laid by some members of the Magdalen boat club to seize him and his follower – and to put them both under the 'College pump'. Fortunately Wilde was tipped off by one of the conspirators and stayed away from Magdalen. His disciple, though, was ducked, and his rooms ransacked. The attack – and the threat of further assaults – rather diminished enthusiasm for Aestheticism at the university.[36]

It was against this background of mounting animosity that Wilde, upon request, had sent an inscribed copy of his *Poems* to the Oxford Union. When, at the close of the 11 July meeting, the librarian announced receipt of the book and proposed acceptance and a vote of thanks, Oliver Elton – the acknowledged leader of the university's 'Intellectuals' – took the unprecedented step of opposing the motion. Having prepared carefully (with the assistance the future poet Henry Newbolt) he delivered a comical 'mock-serious' speech denouncing the book:

> It is not that these poems are thin – and they *are* thin; it is not that they are immoral – and they *are* immoral: it is not that they are this or that – and they *are* all this and all that: it is that they are for the most part not by their putative father at all, but by a number of better-known and more deservedly reputed authors.

Claiming to have identified direct borrowings from over sixty writers – including Shakespeare, Philip Sidney, John Donne and William Morris – he proposed that the book should be rejected, as 'the Union Library already contains better and fuller editions of all these poets'. The suggestion was greeted with varied cheers and hisses. An impromptu debate followed, with several speakers on each side, and Elton's call for refusal was carried by 140 votes to 128. In an attempt to reverse the decision the librarian requested a poll of the membership. But this confirmed the verdict, by 188 to 180. And the book had to be returned, with the abject apologies of the Union secretary.[37] Wilde responded to this rebuff with an assumption of

lordly graciousness – his 'chief regret... being that there should still be at Oxford such a large number of young men who are ready to accept their own ignorance as an index, and their own conceit as a criterion of any imaginative and beautiful work'.[38]

The incident, though vexing, had one useful consequence. It attracted the attention, and secured the interest, of Henry Labouchère, founder of the 'society journal' *Truth* (as well as Liberal MP, theatre proprietor, wit, anti-semite, enemy of W. S. Gilbert and client of George Lewis). Up until this point *Truth* had either ignored or lampooned Wilde; now it came out in his support.[39] 'Labby' was a useful friend as well as an entertaining companion. Indeed Wilde acknowledged him as 'one of the most brilliant conversationalists and the most brilliant journalist in England'.[40] It was a fine thing to have this 'brilliant enemy' transformed into a no less brilliant ally. He was soon added to the select pantheon of Wilde's 'heroes'.[41]

But, if *Poems* gained Wilde a new supporter, it also cost him an old friend. Canon Miles, Frank's father, had always taken an interest not only in Wilde's work but also in his spiritual well-being. He read the book closely, and with increasing dismay. Although he found much that was 'pure and very beautiful' he was deeply disturbed by the 'antichristian' sentiments of some of the poems. One in particular – probably 'Charmides' – had so upset his wife that she had immediately excised it from the volume, convinced it would be extremely 'dangerous to the young of either sex'.[42] The canon wrote to Frank (twice) urging him to remonstrate with his friend. And although Frank did broach the subject in general terms, he hesitated actually to show Wilde his father's letters, obliging the canon to write directly to Wilde, setting out his anxieties, and asking Wilde to remove the offending verses from future editions so as not to 'mar... one of the most poetical volumes of modern times'.

Wilde defended his position, probably suggesting that art was separate from morality, just as 'subject' must be separate from 'treatment'. It was an idea that he was adumbrating just then: to the suggestion that his poetry was 'impure and immoral' Wilde informed another inquirer:

> A poem is well written or badly written. In art there should be no reference to a standard of good or evil. The presence of such a reference implies incompleteness of vision. The Greeks understood this principle, and with perfect serenity enjoyed works of art which, I suppose, some of my critics would never allow their families to look at.

The enjoyment of poetry does not come from the subject, but from the language and rhythm. It must be loved for its own sake, and not criticized by a standard of morality.[43]

The canon, however, was unmoved. He wrote back:

As to morality I can't help saying Frank ought to be clear – he has I believe often argued with you. If in sadness I advise a separation for a time it is not because we do not believe you in character to be very different to what you suggest in your poetry, but it is because you do not see the risk we see in a published poem, which makes all who read it say to themselves, 'this is outside the province of poetry', it is licentious and may do a great harm to any soul that reads it.[44]

The idea that Wilde might be banished from Keats House due to anxieties about his moral influence upon Frank Miles had a bitter irony to it. During their time as housemates Wilde had become increasingly aware of his friend's own, very real, moral deficiencies – the tendency for his interest in young girls to stray from the professional to the predatory. Beyond the suspicion that he was 'more than a mere friend' to the elfin Sally Higgs, there had been several incidents.[45] According to one (rather over-coloured) account, Wilde had once found Miles at Tite Street in a 'state of great distress and alarm, making hasty preparations as if for flight'. He confessed to an offence he had committed with 'a young girl', adding, 'I am sure the parents have laid an information and that I am liable to be arrested at any moment. I am trying to get away before the police come.' Wilde feared that it might already be too late, as he had noticed two figures, possibly detectives, in the street. Nevertheless he stemmed Miles's frantic talk of 'suicide, of throwing himself out of the window, of his disgrace and dishonour', and indicated a possible escape route over the rooftops. As Miles exited through the studio window, Wilde held the door against the knocking of the police. When he finally let them in, he pretended that he had thought their importunate demands for entry were 'some studio practical joke'. Miles, he told them, was away on the continent.[46]

Miles, too, must have been conscious of the injustice of the situation created by his father; nevertheless, dependent upon his parents, he felt unable to go against their wishes. Wilde was furious. There are few instances of him losing his temper, but this was one. According to Sally Higgs's account,

livid with rage, he demanded to know if Miles really intended to act upon 'so outrageous a breach of the ties of their long friendship', to 'part after years together just because your father's a fool?' Miles, distraught, protested that he had 'absolutely no alternative.'

'Very well, then,' said Wilde, 'I will leave you. I will go now and I will never speak to you again as long as I live.'

He tore upstairs, flung his few belongings into a great travelling trunk, and without waiting for the servant to carry it downstairs, tipped it over the bannisters, whence it crashed down upon a valuable antique table in the hall below, smashing it into splinters. Wilde swept out of the house, slamming the door behind him. He never returned.[47]

The rift gave Wilde a first bracing taste of British hypocrisy. For all his poetic allusions to kissing 'the mouth of sin', he himself still remained notably pure in his conduct. There was no trace of sexual deviancy, and little enough of sexual interest. Rennell Rodd recalled his sensitivity to 'the peril of undesirable associations' – and his remark about one seemingly impressive gentleman, met with at a studio exhibition, that, although 'most agreeable... he is not a man in whose company we could afford to be seen'.[48]

Thrust out of Tite Street, and banished from Miles's exalted social milieu, Wilde moved to Mayfair. He took a pair of furnished rooms on the third floor at 9 Charles Street (now Carlos Place), just off Grosvenor Square. The rooms were small but the address 'implied opulence' and indeed the house, kept by a retired butler and his wife, offered very good service. Its decor was anything but Aesthetic: the walls were panelled in oak and decorated with old engravings in heavy black frames.[49]

The move was a piece of defiant extravagance, but it did bring into even sharper focus Wilde's pressing need for money. Living alone, he now had to rely entirely on his own resources. The achievements of 1881 were gratifying: he had been parodied in *Punch* and *Patience*, had published *Poems* and been presented to the Prince of Wales; he could lay claim to 'fame', 'notoriety' and some measure of 'success'. Yet none of these things produced what he called 'the means for sustaining life'. If Wilde was reluctant to address the matter, his friends were more practical. George Lewis and his wife took a positive interest in him – as they also did in Lillie Langtry, who was similarly in need of a career. Discussions were held at Portland Place on 'schemes for Oscar's future'.[50]

Wilde continued to hope for a production of *Vera*. His expectations were perhaps encouraged by the success of another Russian-set melodrama,

Michael Strogoff, which had opened at the Adelphi in March. And the topicality of his own play seemed to have been enhanced that same month when Czar Alexander II was assassinated by Nihilists in St Petersburg. Nevertheless, in the absence of any immediate offers, he needed to explore different options – some more fanciful than others. Paragraphs appeared in the papers claiming that 'Mr Oscar Wilde intends to come before the public next season as a Shakespearian actor'.[51] Archibald Forbes – intrepid war correspondent for the *Daily News* and friend of the Lewises – unhelpfully suggested that, as 'an alternative to aestheticism and insolvency', Wilde should 'enlist in a cavalry regiment and try a year's soldiering as a private dragoon' (a notion received with 'a shudder of horror' by the penurious Aesthete).[52] There were even reports that Wilde might take up nursery gardening and grow 'acres of daffodils'.[53]★

Lewis, though, favoured lecturing in America.[54] Good money could be made on the circuit there. Indeed it was the path being followed, very successfully, by Archibald Forbes. The idea had been mooted earlier in the year by Dion Boucicault – and perhaps by Sarah Bernhardt even before that – but Wilde had been wary, doubtful of his ability to speak from a platform.[55] Now the moment seemed more propitious. He was becoming ever more self-assured. And growing transatlantic interest in both himself and his work, confirmed by the generous reception of *Poems,* suggested that he might find an audience.[56] The plan was enthusiastically endorsed by his friends and supporters.[57]

A promoter had to be found, and Lewis 'broached the matter' with the brilliant young impresario Richard D'Oyly Carte. The move was well made, and well timed. Carte had established his reputation as the producer for Gilbert and Sullivan's operas: he had just completed construction of the luxurious Savoy Theatre as a showcase for their work. International in outlook, he also managed productions and lecture tours across America and the Colonies; he was managing Forbes. He was certainly impressed by Wilde, finding him 'a clever young man' with 'lots to say'.[58] But, more than this, he recognized that Wilde offered an opportunity. An American

---

★ Discussions over Lillie Langtry's future followed a not dissimilar path. Frank Miles had suggested she set up a market garden for 'hardy flowers'; Wilde dismissed the idea, pointing out 'tragically' that it would 'compel the Lily to tramp the fields in muddy boots'. Whistler counselled her to become a painter; other friends suggested millinery and dressmaking. She was offered a generous contract to be a gossip columnist. Wilde, though, was convinced that 'the stage was the natural solution' to her future.

production of *Patience* had opened in New York in September 1881 and was doing well; others productions were being planned across the country. Although the satire of Aestheticism was greatly enjoyed, direct knowledge of the subject in America was limited. Wilde's name, however, had frequently been mentioned in the reporting on the opera, not just as the author of a much-discussed book of Aesthetic poems, but as 'the originator of the aesthetic idea'. Carte realized that if Wilde could be brought to the States 'with the view of illustrating in a public way his idea of the aesthetic... the general public would be interested in hearing from him'.[59] Wilde's social success in London might also secure him an entrée into American society, lending cachet to the venture and increasing the scope for publicity. More importantly, though, just as *Patience* had stimulated American interest in Wilde, so Wilde might stimulate American interest in *Patience*.

Carte's intuitions were confirmed by his business partner (and future wife) Helen Lenoir, who was over in New York. A well-connected 'lady' journalist there assured her, and Colonel W. F. Morse (the manager of Carte's New York office), that the American public would certainly be open to hearing Wilde lecture on Aestheticism – providing he did so in costume, with a sunflower in his buttonhole, and a lily in his hand.[60] Reassured, Carte acted decisively. A cable was dispatched to Wilde from New York: 'Responsible agent asks me to enquire if you will consider an offer he makes by letter for fifty readings, beginning November first. This is confidential. Answer.' Wilde cabled back the next day (1 October): 'Yes if offer good.'[61] It was a basis on which to begin negotiations.[62]

For Wilde it was exciting to be in demand. His initial thought was to present three talks: one 'devoted to a consideration of "The Beautiful" as seen in everyday life'; another 'illustrative of the poetical methods used by Shakespeare'; and the third, a reading of 'a Lyric Poem', most probably his favourite, 'Charmides'. The response, however, of the American booking agents, who were being solicited by Morse, encouraged him to reconsider. The Americans wanted their Aesthete to talk about Aestheticism – or, as Carte and Morse put it, the 'latest form of fashionable madness'.[63] The notion of a fifty-date tour was soon modified too. It was decided to open in New York, and then – depending on how matters went there – to visit some of the major eastern cities. The date, meanwhile, was pushed back into the new year. News of these arrangements was relayed in the press on both sides of the Atlantic.

The extent to which Wilde was going to be promoted as an embodiment

of the spirit of *Patience* became gradually more apparent. As Carte reported to Helen Lenoir, Wilde was 'slightly sensitive' on the point, 'although I don't think appalling[ly] so.' There was 'some awkwardness' after a couple of 'stupid paragraphs' appeared in the *Sporting Times*, one saying that Wilde was being sent out to America 'as a sandwich man for *Patience*', another claiming that the tour was off, because 'D'Oyly Carte found that he could get actual "sandwich men" in America with longer hair for half the money'. But Carte was able to smooth matters over, and push forward with his plans.[64]

He suggested to Wilde that, on arriving in New York, there would be a virtue in him going to the opera – in the 'private box' – 'and we were to let it be known beforehand' as 'he would probably be recognized'. Wilde 'quite took' to the idea, as did George Lewis, who was – as ever – on hand. Having gained this point Carte told Wilde that 'he must not mind my using a little bunkum to push him in America'.[65] Wilde was prepared to be persuaded: he had, after all, been using more than a little 'bunkum' to push himself in London. Carte stipulated that Wilde, in his lecture, should mention *Patience* at least once, and that he should appear on the platform dressed, like Bunthorne, in an 'Aesthetic' ensemble of black velvet jacket and knee-breeches[66] (Wilde already possessed the breeches from his old Masonic outfit, if not from his 'Prince Rupert' fancy-dress costume).

Terms, too, were under discussion. Wilde – guided by George Lewis – finally settled with Carte for half of net receipts, once expenses had been deducted.[67] There was much else for Wilde to do: he worked on his lecture, and considered his wardrobe. Besides his Bunthorne costume, he bought a 'befrogged and wonderfully befurred green overcoat' together with a Polish cap – provoking the amused indignation of Whistler: 'OSCAR, – How dare you! What means this disguise? Restore these things to Nathan's [the theatrical costumier], and never let me find you masquerading the streets of my Chelsea in the combined costumes of Kossuth and Mr. Mantalini.'[68]* Wilde also contacted numerous acquaintances – and friends – asking for letters of introduction. 'I know what a passport to all that is brilliant and intellectual in America your name is,' he told the American Minister in London, James Russell Lowell – as well as Lord Houghton and, doubtless, dozens more.[69]

In the midst of these preparations a scheme came to fruition for a staging of *Vera*. It was not to be a full-scale production but a promotional

---

*   Lajos Kossuth was a Hungarian (rather than Polish) political reformer; Mr Mantalini was the affected dandy in Dickens's *Nicholas Nickleby*.

performance – for one afternoon only – on the stage of the Adelphi (Charles Reade's *It's Never Too Late To Change* was running successfully in the evenings). The moving spirit behind the venture seems to have been the actress Mrs Bernard Beere, who was a protégée of Willie's. And, having launched her career supporting Modjeska, she had come to know Oscar too. She perhaps saw in *Vera* a chance to establish her credentials as a leading lady. The title role was a striking one; and the piece – coming as it did from 'Oscar Wilde' – was sure to attract publicity. 'Dot' Boucicault (Dion Boucicault's twenty-two-year-old son) also agreed to take a 'prominent part'.[70] It is unclear who was to fund the production. Even a one-off matinee involved considerable expense: the theatre had to be hired; staff had to be paid. Wilde put the cost at about £100.[71] Nevertheless, paragraphs trailing the play – to be staged 'about the 17th December' – were soon appearing in the press.[72]

Within days, however, they were contradicted. On 30 November the *World* announced: 'Considering the present state of political feeling in England, Mr. Oscar Wilde has decided on postponing, for a time, the production of his drama, *Vera*.' The suggestion – elaborated in further reports – was that the republican sentiments of the play and the several 'speeches of a very violent and revolutionary character' made the piece 'too risky for the "loyal English gallery and pit"'.[73] Indeed it was even claimed that 'so effusive has become the loyalty in theatrical circles since her Majesty witnessed *The Colonel*' (and allowed the leading actor to be presented to her) that Wilde had found it 'impossible to get actors, for love or money, to impersonate the Republicans in his play'.[74] Wilde himself hinted that he had been refused 'permission' to mount the piece – presumably by the inspector of plays – on account of its 'avowedly republican' tenor.[75] While, following the recent assassination of the czar, a diplomatic dimension was also suggested in some quarters: at least one paper reported that the foreign secretary had received a communication on the subject from the Russian ambassador.[76] But such reasons, though colourful, and not implausible, seem contrived. They served to divert the public. The postponement was more likely due to lack of funds.[77] Wilde consoled himself with the thought that he might find a taker for the play in republican America and – using Boucicault's name – he sent off copies to various New York producers, as well as to the American actress Clara Morris.[78]

The only theatrical debut that Wilde witnessed that winter was Lillie Langtry's. Having been swept up by Labouchère's actress-wife, Henriette (very probably through Wilde's influence), Langtry was bounced into

appearing in an amateur production of Tom Taylor's comic curtain-raiser *A Fair Encounter* at Twickenham Town Hall.[79] Wilde was prominent in the audience, sitting next to Mr Labouchère, 'the whiteness of [his] cravat, *plastron*, and waistcoat... relieved by a kerchief of sunflower hue, thrust with cunning carelessness into the last named garment'.[80] A few weeks later, he was once more in attendance when Langtry made her London bow – again as an amateur –in a charity production of *She Stoops to Conquer* at the Haymarket Theatre. The Prince and Princess of Wales were in the royal box, but Wilde still drew notice, sitting in the front row of the stalls, and conversing with Lady Lonsdale during the entr'actes.[81]

The event could be accounted a success. Despite Langtry's limitations as an actress, she had the aura of a star. The press was kind and the public enthusiastic. Wilde was able to praise her 'wonderfully musical and well-modulated voice', her 'delightfully joyous' manner, and her rich potential.[82] Squire Bancroft and his wife, Marie, who had the management of the Haymarket, were impressed: they promptly engaged her – at a pleasingly 'high salary' – to appear in their first production of the coming year. She had, it seemed, found 'salvation' upon the stage.[83] For Wilde, on the brink of his own new adventure, her success must have been both encouraging and daunting.

As the time of his departure approached, there was much to hearten him. He was saluted in the 1881 'Christmas Number' of the *World* as one of that year's illustrious 'Lights of London' (others included Gilbert and Sullivan, Swinburne, Labouchère, Dion Boucicault, Robert Browning and George Lewis).[84] Labouchère's *Truth* carried a generous paragraph about his forthcoming trip, prophesying success for his 'Republican play' and his lectures on 'modern life in its romantic aspect';[85] from the publishers of an American illustrated weekly called *Our Continent* he received a cabled request to 'write a poem, twenty lines, terms a guinea a line; subject – *sunflower or lily*, to be delivered on arrival'. It was a flattering confirmation of the interest in his work, and a first glimpse of the forthright transatlantic approach to both business and poetry.[86]

To send him on his way, Whistler, Rodd and the rest of the Tite Street gang gave him a dinner 'in a Bohemian tavern'. When Wilde remarked, 'I hope that I shall not be sea-sick crossing the Atlantic,' Whistler replied, 'Well, Oscar, if you are, throw up Burne-Jones.' On 24 December 1881, with this advice ringing in his ears, he boarded the SS *Arizona* at Liverpool, bound for New York.[87]

-PART IV-

THE REMARKABLE ROCKET

1882

AGE 27–28

Oscar Wilde by Napoleon Sarony, 1882.

1

The Best Place

'I am torn to bits by Society.'

OSCAR WILDE

The SS *Arizona* arrived off Staten Island on the evening of 2 January 1882. Unable to clear quarantine until the following morning, it anchored outside New York harbour. Wilde, full of the hope, anticipation and anxiety of arrival, had to endure the delay. Whatever his frustration, though, it was more than matched by that of the New York press.

Colonel Morse and Helen Lenoir had been working with great and effective energy to stimulate interest in Wilde's advent. They were happy to maintain a certain confusion as to whether Wilde was arriving in America as the comical 'too-too' embodiment of Bunthorne and Postlethwaite, or as a brilliant poet and scholar on a serious mission to explain the 'Aesthetic cult' to an interested public. And they added to both sides of the equation. Among their more 'serious' initiatives they had produced a small pamphlet, giving a brief account of 'the young English poet' – his distinguished parents, his glittering academic career at Trinity and Oxford (his time at Portora was reduced to a single year), his cultural influences (Ruskin, Italy and ancient Greece), his literary successes (the volume of *Poems* and his few reviews), his social distinction, and his deep knowledge of Aestheticism. But the glowing

portrait was subtly guyed in places. Without quite mentioning either *Patience* or *Punch*, the pamphlet acknowledged that Wilde's 'exaggerated expression' of Aesthetic ideas – the excusable 'enthusiasm and recklessness of youthful speech' – had led to him being ridiculed by some sections of the British media.[1] Much of that ridicule found its way into an anonymous illustrated pamphlet, entitled *Ye Soul Agonies in ye life of Oscar Wilde*, which offered an alternative introduction to the great Aesthete, running from the moment when, as an infant, he had first closed 'his mottled fist upon a sunflower' up to his becoming 'inseparable' from Ellen Terry, Sarah Bernhardt and the Prince of Wales.

The New York papers were eager to add their own touches to this picture; so eager, in fact, that several reporters hired a rowing boat to bring them out to the *Arizona* as it rode at anchor. Directed by Wilde's excited fellow passengers, they tracked 'the great English exponent of Aestheticism' to the captain's room. He came out to meet them, amused, but also slightly disconcerted by the jostle of notepads and fusillade of questions: How did he like America? How was the crossing? What was his mission here? What were his plans? Would he produce a play in New York? Would he get it copyrighted? Was he going to lecture? And, if so, how often? How long would he stay in America? Was Aestheticism a philosophy? Could he give a definition of it?

Such importunate 'interviewing' was entirely unknown in British journalism, and Wilde was taken aback. Nevertheless he maintained an admirable equanimity. The reporters were impressed by his easy grace, and his slow periods, with their peculiar emphasis on every fourth syllable. They were impressed, too, by his powerful physique (so very different from the popular image of the wilting aesthete), by his fur-trimmed Ulster, by his ultra 'Byronic' shirt collar; they even admired his teeth. And they enjoyed the ready laugh (a succession of broad 'haw, haw, haws') that punctuated his conversation.[2]

The whole interrogation lasted barely ten minutes; deadlines for the next day's editions allowed no more. Wilde's answers had been bald, vague and brief. But, as the newspapermen were returning to their boat, various other passengers offered their asides on Wilde's time on board. One mentioned that, after five days out at sea, Wilde had said to a gentleman with whom he was promenading the deck, 'I am not exactly pleased with the Atlantic. It is not so majestic as I expected. The roaring ocean does not roar. I would like to see a storm arrive and sweep the bridge from off the ship.' This was more like it.

The anecdote, appearing in several of the New York papers the following morning, captured the public imagination. 'Oscar Wilde Disappointed with the Atlantic' soon became a headline on both sides of that ocean, calling forth any number of satirical verses and sardonic commentaries over the coming weeks. 'What,' various papers wanted to know, 'did the Atlantic think of Oscar Wilde?'[3] The incident gave Wilde a first lesson in the workings of the American press, and its need for the quotable comment. It also served to portray him – at the moment of his arrival – as a humorous contrarian, rather than a sober scholar, a man calculated to amuse or annoy, depending on the taste of the listener.

The next morning when the *Arizona* docked at its North River pier, there were more reporters waiting on the quayside, along with Colonel Morse and a bevy of interested 'admirers'. While battling with the porter who was mishandling his luggage, Wilde gamely fielded further journalistic attempts to get him to 'define' and illustrate Aestheticism: 'Where,' asked one reporter, 'is the beauty in that striking grain elevator which is the chief object in New Jersey's landscape across the river there?' Wilde excused himself on the grounds that he was too near sighted to see it.[4]

From all this he was rescued by Morse, who whisked him off through the crowded streets of Manhattan to breakfast and the peace of a hotel suite.[5]* New York in scale and aspect was something entirely new to Wilde, with its broad grid-patterned streets, its towering buildings (some over ten stories high), its din and bustle. 'Everybody', Wilde later recalled, 'seems in a hurry to catch a train.' It appeared affluent, too, the people conspicuously well dressed, with an 'air of comfort' about them.[6]

From the moment of his arrival, Wilde was treated as a celebrity. It was a new and delightful experience – very different from what he was used to in London. His New York lecture was not until the following week, on 9 January; in the meantime Morse was concerned to manage his charge carefully, maintaining his profile in the press, and his mystery with the public. Wilde was instructed not to 'parade in the streets'. If he had shopping to do it should be done from a carriage that had been specially put at his disposal.

---

* There is, sadly, no evidence that Wilde told the New York customs officer, 'I have nothing to declare, except my genius.' This line – one of the most repeated of Wilde's sayings – was first recorded in Arthur Ransome's 1912 book, *Oscar Wilde: A Critical Study* (p. 64). It is probable that Ransome was told it by Robbie Ross, and it is possible that Wilde had told it to Ross – perhaps because he really did say it at the time or because he wished that he had said it.

'He should not make himself too common.'[7] One of the first calls Morse directed Wilde to make was on Mrs Frank Leslie, the handsome widowed proprietress of a string of American papers. She was ready to offer the support of her various publications. When Wilde complained to her of being swarmed by 'horrible reporters' before he had even disembarked, and told her that he had 'turned his back' on them, she reproached him: 'There you made a mistake, Mr. Wilde. If you come to America you must recognize the interviewer is a powerful institution. You represent to him so much capital. His business is to interview, the same as it is yours to lecture. If you don't speak to him, he must earn his money all the same, and will write something which is certainly not likely to be complimentary.'[8]

It was good advice and Wilde strove to follow it. But how should he present himself? He fully accepted that a certain amount of 'bunkum' might be necessary to promote his name in America, and to win him an audience. He was not averse to the double game being played by Carte, Morse and co. He had, after all, adopted the very ploy to establish his reputation in London, and he enjoyed many of its aspects. Nevertheless he chose to regard his 'mission' to America seriously, and he hoped others would do so too. His early interviews were full of earnest pronouncements about the nature of art. And there were plenty of them.

Wilde joked that during his first week in New York there had been 'about a hundred' interview requests 'a day'.[9] Morse sought to ease the burden by moving Wilde out of his hotel to the seclusion of a 'private apartment' on 28th Street. The address was supposed to be kept secret, but a journalist for the New York *Star* very 'shabbily' printed it in his paper – having received a letter of introduction from Wilde. Despite the 'great annoyance' caused by this (interviewers soon appeared on the doorstep) the place was calm enough to allow Wilde to put the finishing touches to his lecture.[10] He worked hard on the text. It was one thing to be the living embodiment of Aestheticism, another to try and define it. He was also able to fulfil his guinea-a-line commission for *Our Continent*, dispatching two twelve-line 'Impressions' in his best new Whistlerian manner: one ('Le Jardin') describing, as required, both the 'lily's withered chalice' and the 'gaudy leonine sunflower', the other ('La Mer') giving a vision of the sea at night.[11]

Ever since it had been announced that Wilde would be coming to America, photographers there had been vying for the right to take – and market – his photograph. Morse gave the commission to Napoleon Sarony.

It was an excellent choice. The diminutive artist – barely five feet tall, with his huge nose, impressive moustache and habitual fez – had a rare ability to create dramatically compelling images of celebrities. All the stage stars came to his studio. Two years previously he had taken a series of memorable publicity shots of Sarah Bernhardt at the start of her American tour.

A sitting was arranged for 5 January. The tiny photographer was delighted by his outsize sitter with his flowing hair, fur-trimmed coat and white walking-cane. 'Here,' he declared, 'is a picturesque subject indeed.'

Wilde had some experience of being photographed, and he had been adopting extravagant poses for much of his life. But in Sarony he found an artist ready to encourage him to new heights. The two men collaborated on an extraordinary series of images, fixing Wilde as the epitome of unconventional, self-assured, poetical genius – his long hair boldly parted in the middle, his eyes staring soulfully into the distance, glancing at the viewer, scanning the far horizon. There were several changes of costume, but in all save a handful of the pictures, Wilde was wearing his elegant and distinctive black knee-breeches.

At this first session some twenty-four exposures were made, Sarony taking 'extraordinary pains' over the postures: he danced about, keeping up a constant strain of small talk, while 'turning out the edges of [Wilde's] Ulster, turning back this corner, smoothing out a line here and a line there, turning the subject's hands this way and that way, putting him at side view, full face, three-quarters standing, sitting, his legs disposed so, and again so', as he strove for the best effect.[12]

Sarony had paid Bernhardt $1,500 for the privilege of taking her photograph, confident of recouping the amount against sales. And – with press interest rising – he was 'glad to pay as much for Wilde'.[13] Morse guaranteed Sarony exclusivity: the pictures he produced would be the only photographic representations of Wilde available during the period of his visit. They would fix Wilde's image for the American public, and fix it as something flamboyant, fine and very different. Sarony considered that 'he had never done such good photographic work before'.[14]

Photography sessions and interviews were not Wilde's only promotional obligations. There was also the stage-managed 'bunkum' of his attending a performance of *Patience* to be seen to. It was arranged for the evening of 5 January. Wilde caused a flurry of excitement, arriving in the private box together with a fashionable party, midway through the first act. Beneath his fur-trimmed Ulster he was in evening dress. Morse had ensured that

a reporter from the *New York Tribune* was also in the group. He was able
to record that, as Bunthorne came on stage, 'the whole audience turned
and looked at Mr. Wilde'. Wilde – seemingly unconcerned by the scrutiny
– was primed, with an epigrammatic line, borrowed from his lecture, at
the ready. Leaning, with a smile, towards one of the ladies in the party,
he said, in a voice loud enough for the *Tribune* man to hear, 'This is one
of the compliments mediocrity pays to those who are not mediocre.'[15] At
the interval Wilde drew more attention to himself by going backstage and
affably congratulating the company.[16] After the show the crowd lingering
to catch sight of him as he left the theatre was so great that he had to 'beat
a retreat through the back door'.[17]

Amid the succession of promotional duties there was also much social
distraction. New York society had a reputation of generosity towards, and
curiosity about, visiting celebrities. And Morse's press campaign ensured
that Wilde arrived as a celebrity. He came, moreover, with his myriad letters
of introduction, and even a few established American connections. From
the moment of his arrival invitations crowded in upon him: to an afternoon
tea given by Mrs Augustus Hayes (wife of a dilettante travel writer); to
dinner chez Mrs John Bigelow (wife of the former American ambassador to
London); to an evening party at the 5th Avenue apartment of the wealthy
Mrs Paran Stevens; to a literary reception hosted by the society journalist
Mrs D. G. Croly (aka 'Jennie June') in honour of Louisa M. Alcott – and
'Oscar Wilde'.

Even here the potential for publicity was not ignored. Morse understood
that Wilde's social cachet would be part of his appeal to the wider public:
his appearances in the salons and drawing rooms of Manhattan were
assiduously recorded by the press:

During the reception [given by Mrs Hayes] Mr. Wilde stood in the
middle parlor, and back of him was a gigantic Japanese umbrella,
covered with grotesque figures of gayly colored paper. The long, thick,
bamboo handle rested on the floor under a table at Mr. Wilde's left, and
protected him on that flank. On the other side was the partition dividing
the two parlors, and in the inclosure thus formed Mr. Wilde remained,
like a heathen idol, most of the time between three and six p.m...
His posture was full of grace, and strongly brought to mind the pictures
seen in *Punch*, with the element of caricature of course left out... At
one happy moment Mr. Wilde advanced a little from the seclusion

made by the rod of the Japanese umbrella and the partition, and was instantly surrounded by ladies, who stood grouped in the form of a horseshoe, with the heels of the shoe represented by Mrs. John Bigelow and the Marquise Lanza.[18]

It was claimed that Wilde's manager 'carefully scrutinized' the guest lists to ensure only the 'supremest cream of New York society' was invited to meet his protégé. There was some exaggeration in this: New York's grandest families, the Astors, Vanderbilts and their ilk, did not engage.[19] Nevertheless it was a bright and fashionable crowd that welcomed Wilde to New York. In London, he had won a place in society, but as an eccentric and minor element – a curiosity. Here, though still a curiosity, he was the star and guest of honour. It was a new experience, and a delicious one. He wrote elatedly to George Lewis's wife, 'I now understand why the Royal Boy [the Prince of Wales] is in good humour always: it is delightful to be a *petit roi*.'[20]

There remained, however, an anxiety. He had yet to deliver his lecture. Much depended upon his performance. Although Morse had already made provisional bookings for lectures in several other cities, definite plans would not be announced until after the test of his New York opening had been passed. As Wilde confided to Mrs Lewis: 'If I am not a success on Monday, I shall be very wretched.'[21]

The debut was scheduled for eight o'clock, at Chickering Hall on the corner of 5th Avenue and West 18th Street. The advertised title of the talk was, rather soberly, 'The English Renaissance'; the word 'Aestheticism' had been eschewed. Nevertheless Morse's marketing had been effective. The house was full, with over a thousand tickets sold at a dollar each. Most had been drawn by an 'amused curiosity' to see the much-talked-of young man. But, as the *New York Tribune* reported, there were also some devotees: 'aesthetic and pallid young men with banged hair… leaning in mediaeval attitudes' around the side walls of the stalls. The stage was dressed simply: an iron lecture-stand flanked by two chairs, set on a oriental rug, with a brown screen suspended from the ceiling, providing a plain backdrop.

Waiting backstage for the auditorium to fill, Colonel Morse was impressed by Wilde's air of calm (very different from many, more seasoned, performers). At around ten minutes past eight, the gaslights in the auditorium flared to full brightness, the audience broke into applause, and Wilde and Colonel Morse strode onto the stage. Wilde instantly drew all eyes, with his commanding height, his flowing hair, his black velvet 'claw

hammer coat' and, most extraordinary of all, his Bunthorne-esque knee-breeches. He seemed a vision of artistic unconventionality. He and Morse settled themselves on the two chairs. The applause – mingled with some 'tittering' – quieted. Wilde was seen to flush slightly. There was then an awkward pause while some late-comers had to be seated. Wilde became the focus for 'batteries of opera glasses' as the details of his 'picturesque' costume were scrutinized. The breeches commanded the most attention. But then there was the large white necktie; the white waistcoat (from the pocket of which hung a heavy gold seal); the large diamond shirt-stud; the black stockings; the low-sided shoes 'with bows'. The surprising absence of a buttonhole was noted. 'Open and frank curiosity', however, soon began to give way to 'whispered comments' and even some 'veiled sarcasms'. The awkward silence lengthened. 'Someone chuckled. This was followed by laughter from the rear of the hall.' Morse registered, with dismay, a critical – 'almost hostile' – edge to the audience.

The tittering increased, and was threatening to grow 'to the full strength of a general laugh', when Colonel Morse rose, stepped forward and announced to a suddenly silent house, 'I have the honour to introduce to you Oscar Wilde, the English poet, who will deliver his lecture upon the English Renaissance.' With a bow he then left the stage. Wilde, drawing out the dramatic moment, remained 'calmly seated' surveying the audience. Recognizing a lady in the stalls, he nodded to her. Then he rose and advanced to the lectern, rather dwarfing it with his size. Placing his manuscript upon the stand, he grasped the sides of the lectern, raised his eyes towards the ceiling, and began: 'Among the many debts we owe to the supreme aesthetic faculty of Goethe, is that he was the first to teach us to define beauty in terms the most concrete possible, to realize it, I mean, always in its special manifestations...'

His voice, as one newspaper reported, 'might have come from the tomb'. Wilde's diction – so compelling and musical in the drawing room – became oddly flat and monotone as he read from the platform. 'So in the lecture which I have the honour to deliver before you,' he ploughed on, 'I will not try to give you any abstract definition of beauty... but rather [try] to point out to you the general ideas which characterize the great English Renaissance of Art in this century, to discover their source, as far as that is possible, and to estimate their future, as far as that is possible.' He had chosen to call it 'our English Renaissance' because it was 'indeed a sort of new birth of the spirit of man, like the great Italian Renaissance of the

fifteenth century, in its desire to produce a type of general culture, its desire for a more gracious and comely way of life, its passion for physical beauty, its exclusive attention to form, its seeking for new subjects for poetry, new forms of art, new intellectual and imaginative enjoyments'.

This was not 'Bunthorne in the flesh'. The tenor was serious, the ideas abstract, the argument involved. He began to trace the genesis of the new artistic spirit, and new 'expression of beauty', from their origins in the ferment of the French Revolution up to time of the Pre-Raphaelites and their heirs. He sought to explain the movement's character as a combination of the two great 'forms of the human spirit': Hellenism and Romanticism, the one with its calm 'possession of beauty', the other with its 'intensified individualism'. The appeals to authority were many: Goethe was soon followed by Mazzini, Coleridge, Wordsworth, Ruskin, Rousseau, Shelley, Swinburne, Blake, Michelangelo, Dürer, Homer, Dante, Keats, William Morris, Chaucer, Theocritus, Cardinal Newman, Emerson, André Chenier, Byron, Napoleon and Pheidias.

The effect 'was fast becoming painful'. A 'grim silence' reigned over the crowd. But then, coming to the artists inspired by the poetry of Keats, Wilde paused and smiled, 'And these Pre-Raphaelites, what were they? If you ask nine-tenths of the British public what is the meaning of the word aesthetics, they will tell you it is the French for affectation or the German for a dado.' At this there was a great laugh. It was a laugh of relief as much as amusement, and the relief was shared by the lecturer. He was much 'gratified' at the reception of his joke. The mood was changed. From thereon, as Morse put it, Wilde 'found good sailing'. The sepulchral atmosphere was banished. The 'novel and picturesque' eloquence of Wilde's style began to take hold, as the lecture unfolded – and he mapped out a vision of art for art's sake, in which creative and imaginative work should be free from either political arguments or moral responsibilities.

The success of his first quip was followed by others. Wilde's claim that the early Pre-Raphaelites 'had on their side three things that the English public never forgives: youth, power and enthusiasm' provoked loud applause. His mot about 'satire being the homage which mediocrity pays to genius' (already delivered in the box at the Standard Theatre) was appreciated again. So too was his assertion that 'to disagree with three-fourths of the British public on all points is one of the first elements of sanity, one of the deepest consolations in all moments of spiritual doubt'. A burst of clapping, much of it said to come from the Irish element in the audience, attended

his observation that the 'commercial spirit of England' had destroyed the 'beautiful national life' of the country, thus reducing the possibilities for great drama, that 'meeting place of art and life'.

He caught attention with his bold declaration that 'one should never talk of a moral or an immoral poem: poems are either well written or badly written, that is all'; and he stimulated thought with the idea (borrowed, without acknowledgement, from Pater) that 'music' being the art in which form and subject were inseparable 'most completely realizes the artistic ideal, and is the condition to which all the other arts are constantly aspiring'. He fairly 'convulsed his hearers' by asking, 'with one of his peculiar smiles, as though letting the audience into his confidence', that as they had 'listened for a hundred nights to my friend Arthur Sullivan's charming opera Patience' they might 'listen to me for one night'. And his appeal for them not to 'judge Aestheticism by the satire of Mr Gilbert' – 'as little should you judge of the strength and splendour of sun or sea by the dust that dances in the beam, or the bubble that breaks on the wave' – was 'applauded to the echo'.

The audience 'heartily enjoyed' his remark, 'You have heard, I think, a few of you, of two flowers connected with the Aesthetic movement in England, and said (I assure you, erroneously) to be the food of some Aesthetic young men. Well, let me tell you that the reason we love the lily and the sunflower, in spite of what Mr. Gilbert may tell you, is not for any vegetable fashion at all.' The lecturer enjoyed it too, laughing with his audience. Solemnity briefly returned as he explained that the reason for the flowers' popularity with Aesthetes was their natural suitability for decorative art, 'the gaudy leonine beauty of the one and the precious loveliness of the other giving to the artist the most entire and perfect joy'. He urged his American listeners to look to the wonders of their own distinctive flora and fauna for motifs 'to make more precious the preciousness' of simple ornament, to achieve the 'treasure of [a] new beauty'. Then, drawing his themes together (rather abruptly), he ended with the declaration, 'We spend our days, each one of us, in looking for the secret of life. Well, the secret of life is in art.'

The close was greeted with vigorous applause. The decibels confirmed Wilde's triumph. He began to withdraw but, such was the clapping, he turned and bowed again. As he finally left the stage, 'he blushed like a school girl'.[22] Colonel Morse was deeply impressed. As he later recalled, in his long experience of handling lecturers, he could think of 'no instance... of so severe a trial' in front of a potentially hostile audience, nor 'of a more complete and convincing success'.[23] From the auditorium Wilde was

whisked along 5th Avenue to a grand, flower-bedecked reception given by Mrs John Mack, his arrival hailed by the band giving a patriotic rendition of 'God Save the Queen'. The *New York Herald* reported that 'scores upon scores of beautiful and elegantly dressed ladies crowded each other to grasp his hand'.[24]

Wilde had achieved a real success, a success confirmed by the following day's press. Despite some sniping and a few Bunthornian allusions – particularly from the *New York Tribune* – the prevailing tenor was admiring and respectful. Certainly, there was now no doubt that Wilde could lecture, and that his tour would proceed.[25] Carte, who arrived in New York on 11 January, was delighted to push forward arrangements. He was delighted, too, to note that box-office returns for the New York production of *Patience*, which had been declining, had 'taken a new lease of life'. The opera could now be kept on until the end of the season. He wrote to Arthur Sullivan, remarking 'inscrutable are the ways of the American public and absurd as it may appear, it seems that Oscar Wilde's advent here which has caused a regular "craze" ha[s] given the business a fillip up'. To the American press Carte announced that, in view of Wilde's success at Chickering Hall, he intended taking the Aesthete 'around the country' – probably for 'two or three months'.[26]

As the details of forthcoming dates – in Philadelphia, Washington, Baltimore, Albany, Boston and Chicago – were hastily confirmed, Wilde spent a happy week basking in his New York triumph. He was, as *Leslie's Illustrated Newspaper* reported, 'niched and pedestalled by Society'; together with invitations, 'letters, verses, flowers [and] petitions' flowed in upon him.[27] He had for his social guide and arbiter the irrepressible sixty-eight-year-old 'Uncle' Sam Ward, political lobbyist, occasional versifier, dedicated gourmet and inveterate anglophile. Ward assured Wilde the valuable interest and support of his friend, William Henry Hurlbert, editor of *New York World*; and, among other attentions, he organized a glittering lily-themed dinner at his own Clinton Place apartment, at which water-lilies floated in the gigantic punch-bowl, and all the guests sported lily-of-the-valley buttonholes.[28]

The largest party thrown for Wilde, though, was a great 'crush' hosted by Mrs Marion T. Fortescue (née Minnie O'Shea), the Dublin-born daughter of the editor of *Freeman's Journal*, and the mistress of Robert B. Roosevelt. It was there that Wilde was introduced to Joaquin Miller, the splendidly hirsute 'Poet of the Sierras', who urged him to seek out the 'natural

greatness and beauty' of the west. Everywhere he went Wilde was the centre of attention.[29] 'Loving virtuous obscurity as much as I do,' he joked to Mrs Lewis, 'you can judge how much I dislike this lionising.'[30] He was assured that there had been 'nothing like it' in New York since the visit of Charles Dickens. 'I stand at the top of the reception room when I go out,' he explained, 'and for two hours they defile past for introductions. I bow graciously and sometime honour them with a royal observation, which appears in all the newspapers the next day.'[31] At the Fortescue party, his unexceptional remark 'I like America – that is to say I like New York', was fixed on eagerly by the New York press.[32] To Norman Forbes-Robertson Wilde sketched the joys of his new life: 'Immense receptions, wonderful dinners, crowds wait for my carriage. I wave a gloved hand and an ivory cane and they cheer. Girls very lovely, men simple and intellectual. Rooms are hung with white lilies for me everywhere. I have "Boy" [champagne] at intervals... and generally behave as I always have behaved – "dreadfully".'[33]

Wilde's behaviour was, in fact, anything but dreadful. He may have showed off shamelessly, but he also impressed his hosts and fellow guests by his self-possession, his 'impromptu wheezes', his name-dropping, his intelligence, and his talk. He was soon being accounted 'the best *raconteur* since Lord Houghton's time'.[34] Something of his sweeping range was caught by *Punch* in its parodic account of 'the Poet's' New York conversation:

> He has been intimate with GLADSTONE, and considers him a meritorious politician, though he finds fault with his views on HOMER. He prattled glibly of his friend SIR WILLIAM HARCOURT, and expressed himself generally in harmony with the leaders of Continental nations... The Poet spoke in terms of general approval of Art, the Moon, Wine, and Republicanism, to which latter, it is no secret, that he has sought to convert English Royalty.[35]

A few who met him seem to have been overawed, or at least bemused, by the encounter; others strove to maintain a scientific detachment. Phoebe Pember (the redoubtable nursing pioneer) found herself quite unable to stop laughing when introduced to the young Aesthete. As she confessed to her nephew: 'I laughed all the time [he was talking].'[36] When John Bigelow took Wilde to dinner at the exclusive Century Association there was 'a great deal of interest', especially among the 'medical men', who were intrigued to inspect Wilde's distinctively 'effeminate features';[37]

while, at another gathering, the eminent oculist Dr Holcombe – a pupil of Sir William Wilde's, and founder of the New York genealogical and biographical society – announced himself 'particularly interested in the peculiarities of Wilde's eyes', and insisted that the company 'examine them through his magnifying glass'.[38]

Some New Yorkers did stand aloof. Among writers less generous spirited than Joaquin Miller, there were hints of resentment, professional anxiety and lofty distaste. The self-important poet and literary critic Edmund Clarence Stedman declined to meet Wilde, despite receiving *two* letters of introduction (much to his annoyance, several newspapers incorrectly listed him as having accompanied his wife to the reception given for Wilde at the Crolys). Stedman had been set against Wilde and his *Poems* by a letter from his friend Edmund Gosse, dismissing the 'atrocious book' as 'a malodorous parasitic growth' bumped into a third edition by the author's 'aristocratic friends'. And he was not inclined to relent.[39] In his estimation Wilde was a 'humbug' – albeit a clever one – and it was merely New York's wealthy 'Philistine' element that, from a mixture of 'snobbery and idiocy', was 'making a fool of itself' over him. He considered that the *'genuine'* writers and poets were keeping out of his way – and he did his best to encourage them.[40] The high-minded Emma Lazarus (whose 1883 sonnet 'The New Colossus' would provide the lines inscribed on the base of the Statue of Liberty) held off from meeting Wilde because – despite her admiration for his 'genuine imagination and talent' – she so disliked his 'bare faced courting of vulgar notoriety'.[41]

Wilde certainly kept his publicity obligations in view. Morse had provided the necessary support. As Wilde explained to Norman Forbes-Robertson, he had 'two secretaries, one to write my autograph and answer the hundreds of letters that come begging for it. Another, whose hair is brown, to send locks of his own hair to the young ladies who write asking for mine; he is rapidly becoming bald. Also a black servant, who is my slave – in a free country one cannot live without a slave – rather like a Christy minstrel, except he knows no riddles.'[42]

The Sarony photographs, printed on small cards, were already proving hugely popular, spreading Wilde's image across the States. Demand, Wilde boasted, 'far exceeds any possible supply'.[43] Morse also arranged for a young New York artist, James Edward Kelly, to make a portrait etching of Wilde, a simple line-drawn image that would be easier and cheaper to reproduce than any photograph. When Kelly called on Wilde to do the drawing, he

found him at home with 'a beautiful little boy with golden curly hair and blue eyes'. Wilde suggested the child pose in the picture, standing beside his chair. It made for a charming scene, although when Kelly came to etch the picture, he restricted the image to Wilde's head, viewed in profile.[44] The call for Wilde's picture was matched by calls for Wilde's book. Although his Aesthetic notions were shocked when he saw the 'commercial and common way' in which the American edition of his *Poems* was issued, Wilde was delighted that Roberts Brothers were reprinting the volume, to meet the great demand 'sung up' since his arrival.[45]

While in New York, Wilde also learnt more about America's engagement with Aesthetic ideas. He attended a select artistic lunch given by Kate Field at the offices of the Cooperative Dress Association – a pioneering venture dedicated to producing more healthful, better-designed and cheaper gowns for women.[46] And he paid a visit to the workshop of the 'Associated Artists', another collaborative feminist undertaking, set up to promote the decorative arts, especially needlework and fabric design. The firm's redecoration of President Chester Arthur's bedroom at the White House, undertaken the previous year, had been described in the American press as being suggestive of the 'super-aesthetical, ultra-poetical... Oscar Wilde school'.[47]

There was time, too, for Wilde to push his plans for an American production of *Vera*. His great hope was that he would be able to persuade the thirty-three-year-old actress Clara Morris to take the title role. Having already sent her a copy of the play, he now sought to follow it up in person. Sarah Bernhardt had whetted his appetite, telling him – as he informed one reporter – that 'there were two things in America worth seeing – one was Clara Morris's acting, and the other was some dreadful method of killing pigs in Chicago. She advised me to go and see both.'[48] He thought the hogs could wait (perhaps indefinitely), but he was eager to see Miss Morris as soon as possible, and to secure her interest in *Vera*.

At Wilde's prompting, Mrs Croly had invited the actress to her reception. She came glittering in white brocade, trimmed with pearl and crystal. Her mood, though, was less than sparkling. And, despite the *empressement* of Wilde's greeting (taking her hand in both of his, telling her how greatly pleased he was to meet her, and how much he had heard about her from Sarah Bernhardt) she remained out of sorts. One witness even noted that a 'haughty smile' seemed to curl her lip at the mention of La Bernhardt.[49] Wilde had more joy the following afternoon when they met again, at the

lunch hosted by Kate Field at the Dress Association. And if he did not get to her agree to take the part (as some papers reported), he did persuade her to consider the piece. Seeking to involve her further, he asked 'for her suggestions as to situations'. And he followed up his advantage the next day, when he went to see her act for the first time, in *The New Magdalen*.[50] She cannot but have been flattered by his enthusiasm: 'Miss Morris is the greatest actress I ever saw,' he told the *New York Herald*, 'if it be fair to form an opinion of her from her rendition of this one role. We have no such powerfully intense actress in England. She is a great artist, in my sense of he word, because all she does, all she says, in the manner of the doing and of the saying constantly evoke the imagination to supplement to it. That is what I mean by art... She is a veritable genius.'[51]

Later that week she allowed Wilde to accompany her and her husband to see Mary Anderson in W. S. Gilbert's *Pygmalion and Galatea*. It was a promising start. But, despite such interest, Morris put off making any definite commitment. This did not prevent Wilde exaggerating the situation; he boasted to Edgar Saltus over lunch at Delmonico's that he had been offered an advance of $5,000 for the play – 'mere starvation wages' as he put it. He did confess that the theatrical manager wanted him to make some changes to the text, before adding, 'But who am I to tamper with a masterpiece?'[52] When Wilde left New York on 16 January, heading for Philadelphia, he was full of optimism.[53]

2

Go Ahead

'Every thing is going brilliantly.'

OSCAR WILDE

The City of Brotherly Love seemed eager to welcome him. He had, already in place, several useful connections: literary, artistic and Irish. There was his old friend Charles Leland, recently returned to Philadelphia to establish a school of art and craft; Dr Samuel Gross, distinguished surgeon and sometime visitor at Merrion Square; and Mary Rebecca Darly-Smith, a poet who had dedicated a volume of verse to Lady Wilde. There was even a (second) cousin, Father Basil Maturin, an Anglican priest, who had come over from Dublin to be rector of one of the city's churches. And it was the Philadelphia-based publication *Our Continent* that had solicited the two poems from Wilde prior to his departure from England. Its co-proprietor, Robert S. Davis, had agreed to host a reception for the young lecturer. So too had both George W. Childs, proprietor of the *Public Ledger*, and J. M. Stoddart, another of the city's enterprising literary entrepreneurs.[1]

Public interest was huge. Wilde had been interviewed by one Philadelphia paper on the train down from New York, and by another shortly after checking into the Aldine Hotel. Indeed such was the stream of cards and callers arriving at the Aldine, that Wilde had his black valet stationed outside his room, informing visitors that 'Massa Wilde is too busy to recept today'.[2]

Wilde's lecture, scheduled for the evening of 17 January at the recently re-opened Horticultural Hall, was eagerly anticipated: 1,500 tickets had been sold.[3]

In the event it was something of an anti-climax. Notwithstanding the packed house – and the fact that many members of the audience carried sunflower-shaped fans distributed at the door by an 'enterprising tradesman' (who had also placed an advertisement on the reverse of each bloom) – neither the lecture nor the audience warmed up as they had in New York. The most vigorous applause was an ironic burst when Wilde took a sip of water. As he subsequently told a reporter, 'My hearers were so cold I several times thought of stopping and saying, "You don't like this, and there is no use my going on."'[4]

The failure was both a shock and a disappointment, softened slightly by the kind words of supportive friends, and a lone generous review in the *Public Ledger*.[5] It was, though, rather more effectively assuaged by a thrilling excursion that Wilde made on the following afternoon, to visit one of his great literary heroes: Walt Whitman. The sixty-two-year-old author of *Leaves of Grass* was living just across the river from Philadelphia in the little working-class town of Camden. Prematurely aged by a succession of small strokes, he had declined invitations to the lavish reception given by Davis on the evening of Wilde's arrival, and to a more intimate dinner Stoddart hosted after Wilde's lecture. But he sent word that he would be happy to meet the young poet, if he cared to call – between '2 and 3½' – on the afternoon of 18 January.[6]

Following a convivial breakfast hosted by Dr Gross, and a brief visit to the Philadelphia Women's School of Design, Stoddart escorted Wilde over the Delaware, and delivered him to the modest brick-built house where Whitman lived, cared for by his brother and sister-in-law. It was a happy meeting – between the 'old rough' (as Whitman called himself) and the eager young Aesthete. Whitman produced a bottle of homemade elder-flower wine to welcome his guests in the downstairs parlour. Stoddart recalled it as 'vile beyond description' and was amazed that Wilde was able to drink off several glasses 'with evident relish'. Taxed with this later, Wilde explained that 'if it had been vinegar' he would have drunk it just the same, such was his admiration for Whitman. Following these libations Stoddart tactfully withdrew, leaving the two poets together for the afternoon. They retreated upstairs to the cozy informality of Whitman's top-floor 'den', to talk of poetry and people.[7]

Wilde was charmed by the 'little bare whitewashed room' – with its big chair (for Whitman) and little stool (for himself), and its 'pine table' on which rested a copy of Shakespeare, a translation of Dante and 'a cruse of water'. Winter sunlight filled the chamber 'and over the roofs of the houses opposite were the masts of the ships that lay in the river'.[8] If its austere simplicity made the room a fine setting for artistic creation, Wilde did also notice the piles of 'newspaper cuttings' littering many of the surfaces.[9] Whitman, for all his vaunted naturalness, was an adept at courting the press. It was another bond between the two writers. They rapidly achieved an easy familiarity. When Whitman declared, 'I shall call you Oscar,' Wilde replied, 'I like that so much.'[10]

Wilde sat at the older man's feet (literally), and flattered him. 'I have come to you as to one with whom I have been acquainted almost from the cradle,' he declared, telling of how his mother had read to him from Whitman's work, and how he had taken Whitman's books with him on his Oxford 'rambles'. They talked of Tennyson and beauty and the practicalities of poetry. Whitman explained his own approach to 'versification' with 'Well, you know I was at one time of my life a compositor, and when a compositor gets to the end of his stick, he stops short and goes ahead on the next line' (Wilde subsequently introduced into his lecture the assertion that 'in order to be a successful poet a man should learn to set type').[11] Wilde spoke of Rossetti and Morris, and of Swinburne (Whitman's great champion in England), claiming a quite unfounded intimacy with the trio.[12] And, seeking to use one connection to reinforce another, he offered to write to Swinburne, conveying Whitman's compliments along with his photograph.*

Whitman found Wilde an engaging companion, later telling a reporter, 'He seemed to me like a great big, splendid boy… so frank and outspoken, and manly.' Moreover, as he confided to a friend, 'he had the good sense to take a great fancy to me'.[13] Wilde not only liked Whitman, he was awed by the natural grandeur of his spirit. Borrowing the estimate given by J. A. Symonds, he described him as 'one of those wonderful, large, entire men who might have lived in any age… Strong, true, and perfectly sane: the

---

*   The ploy proved a great success. Wilde received back a generous letter from Swinburne, detailing his admiration for Whitman – which Wilde duly transcribed, sending one copy to the American poet and another to the press. The exchange also prompted Swinburne to send Wilde an inscribed copy of one of his own books, a belated return for the presentation copy of Wilde's Poems.

closest approach to the Greek we have yet in modern times.'[14] He recognized, though, with surprise and admiration that there was also an element of 'poise' in all this.[15] The time raced by. Whitman made his guest a large glass of milk punch to soothe his thirst, and was impressed at the way he 'tossed it off'. It was growing dark when Stoddart returned to collect his charge. The two poets parted with much friendly feeling, Whitman calling out, 'Goodbye, Oscar, God bless you.'[16]

If the visit to Whitman was the highpoint, it was not the only interesting encounter of Wilde's Philadelphia sojourn. Stoddart took Wilde to call on Fr Maturin at St Clement's, his handsome neo-Romanesque church. The two Irish kinsmen enjoyed the meeting greatly, though Wilde declined his cousin's offer to 'put up' at the clergy house, having glimpsed the 'austere and somewhat meagre furnishings' of the accommodation.[17] There was a visit, too, to Florence Duncan, editor of the city's leading literary and social magazine, *Quiz*. Although her publication had – until then – taken rather a satirical line on Wilde's mission in America, Mrs Duncan was at once won over by the man, by his courtesy (in not referring to the magazine's earlier attacks on him) and by the bright intelligence of his conversation. 'He was at his best in talking of Keats,' she reported in the next issue of her periodical. 'A man who could talk about "The Ode to a Grecian Urn" as Mr. Wilde can, is a considerable distance from being a fool.'[18]

Having promised Rennell Rodd that he would try and find an American publisher for his volume of poems, *Songs of the South*, Wilde broached the topic with Stoddart. It was decided that the project could only work as an exercise in exclusivity. A plan was hatched to produce two choice – slightly amended – editions of the book, one 'de luxe' the other 'ordinary', but both aesthetically designed and graced with an 'introduction' by Wilde. Others, too, wanted Wilde to write for them. Robert Davis proposed a trio of articles from Wilde for *Our Continent*, touching on 'Modern Aestheticism [as] Applied to Real Life': one on 'the Home', one on 'Costume' and one on 'What makes a masterpiece'. Although Davis was offering $100 per piece, Wilde was wary: an article was only paid for once; a lecture could be delivered many times.[19]

As a result he was more inclined to follow up Davis's other suggestion, which was to use the same 'practical' template as the basis for a 'second lecture'. After the 'coldness' of the Philadelphia audience, and his early difficulties in New York, Wilde was already recognizing the need to amend his talk. 'The English Renaissance' was perhaps too erudite, 'too *abstract*'.

Lady Wilde, reading reports back in England, certainly thought so: 'Nothing to catch the attention,' she declared; 'give some personal descriptions' of 'modern celebrities... Ruskin, Mill, Carlyle.'[20] More than this, on 19 January George Munro, publisher of the popular 'Seaside Library' pamphlet series, brought out a pirated edition of Wilde's *Poems*, together with 'His Lecture of the English Renaissance'. Pieced together from shorthand transcripts and press reports, this provided an all-but-full text of Wilde's talk for just 10 cents.

In order to maintain an audience Wilde would certainly require a new lecture, and it would be well if it had a different slant. 'The American people are nothing if not practical,' Davis had explained:

> They care little for the abstract, the rhetorical, the remote. But they are extremely ready to recognize and applaud the immediate, the practically useful. They ardently want instruction and cheerfully receive it. As a rule the education of audiences is superficial and their opportunities of art culture have been scanty. This must be taken into account. Our people are also impatient to apply what they learn. Whatever art-theory is laid down should be copiously illustrated by applications to daily life. This would teach them its meaning without effort.[21]

It was sound advice. And even if he had, for the moment, to persist with 'The English Renaissance', Wilde at once began to amend and cut it. Over the coming weeks he pruned away much of the theoretical argument and historical background, he introduced more colloquial asides and practical suggestions, and reduced the running time from almost two hours to an hour and a half.

The work of revision was already underway when, on 19 January, Wilde caught the train south from Philadelphia, heading for Washington. Morse had been obliged to return to New York, so arrangements for the trip were entrusted to an 'office boy'. Wilde found himself sharing a Pullman coach with Archibald Forbes, who – coming to the end of his own American tour – had an engagement to lecture in Baltimore that evening. With their common attachment to the Carte Agency, and also to George Lewis, the two men greeted each other cordially.

Forbes, as a seasoned and able lecturer, was rather irritated at the fuss being made over Wilde. He had already written ungenerously to a friend back in England, that Wilde 'can't lecture worth a cent, but he draws crowds

wonderfully and fools them all to the top of their bent – which is quite clever'. Convinced that Wilde only excited interest as a curiosity, he claimed – in an attempt at humour – that the circus impresario P. T. Barnum had asked him to appear as an 'attraction'... along with 'a baby elephant', the king of the Zulus, and the body of Charles Guiteau (soon to be executed for assassinating President Garfield) – but only on condition that he always carried 'in one hand a lily and in the other a sunflower'.[22]* Forbes had also introduced into his own lecture facetious references to Wilde's knee-breeches and love of sunflowers. And although they were mild enough, done largely in the hope of getting a laugh, they did carry a hint of disparagement.

During the course of the train journey his resentment may have been further increased by the fact that Wilde made a conquest of one of the two young women with whom Forbes was travelling. Joseph Pennell, recently graduated from the Pennsylvania Academy of Fine Art, was also in the compartment, and – as he told his future wife, 'you should have seen how [Wilde] literally fascinated a beautiful Baltimore girl – she was gone in five minutes'. Pennell himself had been almost as fascinated by Wilde's conversation: 'For more than half-an-hour,' he reported,

I never heard a man talk as he did. There is no doubt of the fascination of his conversation, for unless he tells everyone the same things he told me it was simply wonderful, especially his descriptions of Whistler's paintings... He has a way of getting close to you and looking right into your eyes and with his face about six inches from yours keeps up a sort of musical sound which you soon find out is his ordinary way of speaking.[23]

Nevertheless, when they reached Baltimore, Forbes and Wilde parted as friends. There had, at one time, been a plan that Wilde – together with Morse or Carte – might stop over in Baltimore, and attend Forbes's lecture.

---

* Jokes about Barnum promoting Wilde as a novelty became commonplace, particularly when – later in the year – Barnum brought over from London zoo a huge, and elderly, elephant called 'Jumbo'. One syndicated paragraph ran: 'It is reported that Barnum has made an offer to Oscar Wilde for the latter to sit on top of Jumbo and ride in the street processions. If, says an American paper, instead of Wilde sitting on the elephant, Jumbo were to sit on Wilde, the result would be more satisfactory to the people, and it wouldn't hurt Jumbo much.'

But with Morse back in New York, and Carte having gone to Florida for his health, Wilde assumed the idea had been given up. He continued down to Washington. It was only that evening, having reached his hotel, that he learnt from a reporter that Baltimore had indeed been expecting him, and there was a rumour that his non-appearance had been caused by a disagreement with Forbes. Wilde scotched the idea, but was then surprised to receive a telegram from Morse urging him to return at once to Baltimore. It was, however, too late, and he was too tired.[24]

On the following day the reason for Morse's dispatch became clear. Wilde was aghast to learn that there had been a large party prepared in his honour by a Mrs Carroll. It had had to be cancelled at the last moment, due to his non-arrival. There was also a malicious report abroad that Wilde had demanded a fee to attend a reception given by a Baltimore arts club. The whole city, it was claimed, was upset and offended.

The press worked hard to build up their story of a 'miff' between Wilde and Forbes. They ascribed various 'sneering comments' to both parties in an effort to support the story, and provoke further strife. And although neither Wilde nor Forbes rose immediately to the bait, the seeds of discord were sown. Wilde was moved to write to Forbes, asking if he might remove the jesting allusions to Aestheticism from his lecture ('I feel bound to say quite frankly to you that I do not consider them to be either in good taste or appropriate to your subject'). Forbes took umbrage. His simmering irritation and 'foolish' jealousy came suddenly to the boil. In an 'ecstasy of rage' (as one observer put it) he lashed out at Wilde, refusing to 'trim' his lecture, and publicly denigrating Wilde's motives for coming to America. Wilde's understandable hope that he might earn money from his tour was twisted by Forbes into a supposed confession that he was only in America for 'utterly mercenary' reasons. Wilde attempted to defuse the situation, but it was too late. He was rudely rebuffed. Forbes then strove to lure his perceived rival into a newspaper controversy, and, failing that, resorted to making crude comments about him in the press. He only ceased on receiving a telegram (on 28 January) from George Lewis: 'Like a good fellow don't attack Wilde. I ask this as a personal favour to me.'[25] But even then he kept up a clandestine campaign, feeding negative paragraphs about Wilde to the English papers.[26]

Certainly the whole affair was an upsetting distraction for Wilde during his time in Washington. Thanks to the good offices of Sam Ward, the American capital had been primed to receive Wilde graciously. Wilde was

taken by the city, especially its 'beautiful new houses in red brick' with their 'charming woodwork and balconies'.[27] As in New York and Philadelphia, one splendid reception seemed to follow another: at the homes of Senator and Mrs George Pendleton, and Senator and Mrs Blaine, chez Edward G. Loring, at the exclusive Bachelors' Club (where Wilde – so the papers reported – declined to join the dancing with the line, 'I have dined, so I don't dawnce. Those who dawnce don't dine'). He attended a crowded meeting of the city's literary club in the elegantly bohemian, sunflower-bedecked house of Dr Swann Burnett and his wife, Frances Hodgson Burnett.[28]

The schedule was exhausting. Wilde, always 'on show' and expected to perform, was rapidly coming to recognize that he needed to conserve his energies. He took to hiding away for at least part of any evening in his host's study or 'den'. In company he began to ration his efforts. 'He says he never allows himself to be bored,' one of Wilde's admirers explained to a fellow party-guest. 'He never disguises his annoyance and that gives him ample protection.'[29] He needed it. At every gathering there were now those who resented Wilde's apparent success. Following the most negative estimate of the American press in viewing him as a mercenary fraud, they were determined to show that *they* at least had not been taken in by his 'vulgar' antics.

It was perhaps at Washington that he was asked pointedly by one woman whether he had come to America 'to amuse' them. At his reply that he had come 'rather to instruct', she had remarked, 'If that is your purpose, let me recommend that you wear your hair shorter and your trousers longer.'[30] Certainly during his time in the capital he had to face a succession of challenging old maids and pert young misses. Abigail Dodge, referring to his espousal of Aestheticism, demanded bluntly, 'How long is this joke going to last?' (Wilde, although rather 'staggered' by the directness of the assault, replied 'J-o-k-e? It is my life').[31] Caroline Healy Dall simply stared at him when they were introduced, and refused to offer her hand; while the pretty young Miss Nordhoff (daughter of the *New York Herald* correspondent) 'with the deliberate intention that she should make him ridiculous' asked, 'Pray tell me, Mr Wilde, were you born great?' Wilde replied, 'Little girl, you had better go and get some ice cream.'[32]

A few Washington figures exerted themselves to avoid Wilde altogether. Clover, the wife of Henry Adams, boasted that she had 'escaped his acquaintance'. She had told Henry James, who was also over from London and visiting Washington, '*not* to bring his friend Oscar Wilde [to her home]

when he comes' – adding 'I must keep out thieves and noodles'. Although whether she considered Wilde a thief – for borrowing the ideas of Ruskin, Morris and others – or a 'noodle' (a fool), for parading about in knee-breeches, is unclear.[33]

The thirty-nine-year-old Henry James was scarcely a 'friend' of Wilde's, though the chances of London's cultural life had brought them together. Their differences were unlikely to attract: James was diligent, diffident and discreet while Wilde was effusive, effeminate and attention seeking. Although James could not but be flattered by Wilde's admiration for his work (Wilde told an American reporter that 'no living Englishman' could be compared with the American-born James as a novelist) he seems to have found the younger man a disturbing presence, both personally and professionally. There was an odd savour of spite in his remark, to the art collector Isabella Stewart Gardner, that he had seen, at the Lorings', 'the repulsive and fatuous Oscar Wilde, whom, I am happy to say, no one was looking at'. The claim, apart from anything else, was completely false. The Lorings' daughter, Harriet, gave a vivid account of how Wilde had 'burst upon' the gathering – 'tights, yellow handkerchief and all'; and although he might have looked decidedly 'gruesome', it was at once clear that he was also 'very amusing': 'Full of Irish keenness and humour and really interesting' – and 'very unaffected'. Her father, she reported, as well as other guests, had thought so too. By contrast she had found Henry James – the other 'lion' of the evening – dull, 'very well meaning but very slow minded' and wanting altogether the 'divine spark'.[34]

James was too perceptive not to be aware that such comparisons could be made. He knew that he was no match for Wilde as a conversationalist – or as a draw. A huge crowd turned out to hear Wilde's Washington lecture at the Lincoln Hall on the evening of 23 January; and if some of the reviews carped at his poor delivery, they agreed that what he said was 'interesting' and how he said it 'decidedly eloquent'. They enjoyed his topical allusions, especially his remark that, although sculpture was the art for Washington, 'I think you have taken quite enough motives from war. You don't want any more bronze generals on horseback, I dare say.'[35]

Such successes left James confused, disapproving and perhaps even slightly envious. He continued his shrill disparagements, calling Wilde 'a fatuous fool and a tenth rate cad', even 'an unclean beast'. But he clearly relished Wilde's line about Washington's 'bronze generals': he later adopted it as his own.[36] And he took the trouble to call on Wilde at his hotel

on the day after his lecture. His motives remain unclear. Perhaps he was intrigued to discover the commercial realities of a new literary world in which a 'writer' with only one slim volume of poems to his credit could be launched on an international lecture tour.[37] Wilde, unaware, of James's animus, was overflowing with spirits. He irritated his guest with talk of 'Bosston'. And when James remarked that he was nostalgic for London, Wilde irritated the great traveller and expatriate even more, by replying, 'Really? You care for places? The world is my home.'[38]

The world certainly seemed to be opening up for Wilde. From Washington – piloted securely once more by Morse – he progressed to Baltimore, where he mollified the populace with his contrition and his enthusiasm for Edgar Allan Poe. From Maryland he went to Albany (state capital of New York), and on to Boston, before looping back to New York, with further lectures at New Haven, Hartford and Brooklyn.

Almost since the moment of his arrival in America people had been telling Wilde how much he would like Boston, and how much Boston would love him.[39] And they were not altogether wrong. Even as he arrived at the snow-girt Vendome Hotel in fashionable Back Bay, Wilde discovered an invitation from Oliver Wendell Holmes to lunch that very day with the 'Saturday Club' – the city's most illustrious, and jolliest, literary institution.[40] Hawthorne had been a member; Ralph Waldo Emerson and Longfellow still were – though both were now too infirm to attend the monthly lunches at the Parker House. The 'seventy-three years young'[41] Holmes – a favourite author of Wilde's student days – remained the club's presiding genius. And, swept into this 'bright party of men', Wilde passed a delightful and stimulating afternoon.[42]

From there (with only a short break, to be interviewed for the second time that day) Wilde was whisked up by John Boyle O'Reilly, the dashing editor of the *Pilot* – and, hence, publisher of several of Wilde's early verses – and taken to dine at another of Boston's intellectual sodalities, the Papyrus Club. Afterwards they took in a production – partly in Greek – of *Oedipus Tyrannus* at the Globe, before dropping in at the St Botolph Club on the way home to bed.[43] Wilde's social stamina was something phenomenal.

Throughout his time in the city Wilde was 'treated gloriously'. The grand receptions of New York were replaced with more intimate gatherings. Burne-Jones's great friend, the Harvard professor of the history of art, Charles Eliot Norton, was out of town (and, as he privately admitted, rather relieved to escape Wilde's 'affectations and maudlin sensualisms'), but his

son, Eliot, 'did honour in [his] stead'.[44] Wilde lunched with Wendell Phillips, the abolitionist and orator. And, following up the pleasures of the 'Saturday Club', he called on Oliver Wendell Holmes, admiring his daughter's needlework, and impressing his son (then on the verge of becoming a high court judge) with the 'extraordinary vividness' of his storytelling.[45] There was a welcome, too, at the home of Sam Ward's widowed sister, the impressive Julia Ward Howe – famed as the author of 'The Battle Hymn of the Republic'. She invited Wilde to an impromptu Sunday lunch party – just the family, along with Isabella Stewart Gardner and the mezzo-soprano Madam Braggiotti: 'Perhaps ten or twelve friends came after lunch,' she recorded in her diary. 'We had what I might call a "lovely toss-up," i.e., a social dish quickly compounded and tossed up like an omelet.'[46]

Sam Ward's influence also gained Wilde an interview with the aged, and fast-declining, Henry Wadsworth Longfellow, who had been part of Wilde's imaginary life since childhood.[47] Wilde greatly admired the poet's verse translation of Dante's *Divine Comedy*, even if Longfellow's other works had less enduring appeal (it became Wilde's line that 'Longfellow is a great poet only for those who never read poetry').[48] Nevertheless, he was the grand old man of American literature, and Wilde – always eager to associate with the great – was determined to meet him.

Overcoming some initial resistance, he secured an invitation to breakfast at Longfellow's home, near Harvard Square, and spent a happy afternoon there.[49] 'I went', Wilde said, 'in a snowstorm and returned in a hurricane, quite the right conditions for a visit to a poet.'[50] The encounter itself was an altogether milder affair – 'very pleasant', rather than cataclysmic.[51] Wilde was touched by the invalid writer (who would die barely a month later), and remembered him as 'himself a beautiful poem' – indeed, 'more beautiful than anything he ever wrote'.[52] He much enjoyed Longfellow's comment on Browning ('I like him well – what I can understand of him') and cherished his description of a visit to Windsor, when the queen had said some generous words about Longfellow's poetry; at Longfellow's expression of surprise that his verse was so well known at Windsor, she had replied, 'Oh, I assure you, Mr Longfellow, you are very well known. All my servants read you.' Longfellow confessed to still waking at night and wondering whether this was a 'deliberate slight'. Wilde – always prone to vainglory himself – suspected that it was her majesty's sly rebuke 'to the vanity of the poet'.[53]

Although hostile reports in the press later claimed that Longfellow had been 'forced to endure the infliction' of Wilde's visit, he seems to have

enjoyed the encounter – even if he was rather confused as to his visitor's attainments, beyond having written 'some good verses'.[54] 'A few days ago I had a visit from Oscar Wilde,' he informed a friend:

> Whatever he may be in public, in private he is a very agreeable young man; and, when we remember that he gained a first prize in mathematics at Cambridge, the mathematical university of England, we can perhaps pardon some eccentricities, otherwise unpardonable. Let us remember that Alcibiades cut off his dog's tail to make the Athenians talk, and that Petrarch was troubled because the maids of Avignon disordered his curls![55]*

Wilde gave his lecture at the Boston Music Hall on the evening of 31 January, to another full house of over a thousand people. For some days it had been known – and reported – that a body of Harvard students had bought up the front two rows of the stalls. Their intentions became clear when, shortly before the advertised starting time, with the rest of the house seated, they paraded into the auditorium – sixty youths, 'arrayed in all the "aesthetics" that ingenuity could devise':

> There were blond wigs and black wigs, wide-floating neckties of every hue and fashion... Knee breeches and black stockings of 'ye olden time,' and in every hand the 'precious loveliness' of the lily or the 'gaudy leonine' glare of the sunflower. As the youths entered they assumed all sorts of poses, and held aloft or looked languishingly down on the circling petals of flowers. Then they took their seats, utterly pleased with themselves.[56]

Wilde, however, had been apprised of the jape. With the audience in a state of expectation to witness his discomfiture, he made his way onto the stage with calm deliberation, arrayed not in his characteristic Aesthetic garb but in conventional evening wear: dress coat, white tie, black trousers. On reaching the lectern, and setting down his script, he allowed his eyes to travel over the ranks of 'fantastic masqueraders'. And then he smiled at

---

* Wilde's 'double first' – mentioned in Morse's publicity materials – had been misunderstood by some American commentators to comprise first-class degrees in classics *and* mathematics. The all-but innumerate Wilde would have relished the confusion – almost as much as being compared to Alcibiades and Petrarch.

them. The rest of the audience smiled too. Then laughed. Then broke into applause.

'As a college man I greet you,' Wilde suavely began, to the further delight of the audience. He subsequently brought home his advantage with the aside, 'As I look about me, I am impelled for the first time to breathe a fervent prayer, "Save me from my disciples."' The lightness of the rebuke made it the more effective. The lecture itself passed off well enough, but it was Wilde's chastening of the Harvard pranksters that drew most of the comment.[57] 'Mr Wilde achieved a real triumph,' reported the previously disparaging *Transcript*, 'and it was by right of conquest, by force of being a gentleman, in the truest sense of the word... Nothing could have been more gracious, more gentle and sweet, and yet more crushing, than the lecturer's whole demeanor to [the Harvard freshmen].'[58] Such was his success that some papers began to claim that the whole charade must have been stage-managed by Colonel Morse as a showcase for Wilde's ingenuity and wit.[59]

The incident marked another stage in Wilde's education as a public persona. He was, by and large, coping well with the demands of his rapidly increasing fame. He endured the intrusive attention of the public. At the hotels where he was staying, 'all sorts of strategic movements were indulged in' by fellow guests, 'in the hope of seeing Oscar at his evening meal'. He continued to deal with the demands of the autograph hunters. Having run through his stock of 'aesthetic green' paper slips he was now writing his name on large yellow-hued cards. It was tiring work, though. There had been twenty-seven letters asking for his autograph waiting for him when he arrived at his Washington hotel. In an effort to stem the flow he told one reporter that, in future, he would give his signature to 'beautiful ladies only'.[60]

Wilde strove to satisfy the insatiable press. He developed an effective formula for the never-ending succession of interviews, increasingly aware of what was wanted – a couple of quotable comments on American subjects, a suggestion of personal engagement, a touch of flattery, some serious name-dropping, and a suitably Aesthetic mise-en-scène. Recurrent props included a volume of verse (often his own), a vase of flowers, a lighted cigarette, the fur-trimmed overcoat and any number of coloured kerchiefs.[61] Every detail was considered. James Kelly recalled meeting Wilde off the train when he arrived in one new town, looking pale, tired and 'partly streaked'. Shortly afterwards, though, when Kelly brought a reporter to Wilde's hotel room, he found a very different figure. The stage had been set:

[Wilde] was sitting back in the arm-chair by the table, the sun streaking its brilliant light through on to the rose-coloured scarf [that Wilde had been wearing at the station], which was now taken off and replaced by one of bronze green. All this was apparently careless, but the effect was superb; the glow of the handkerchief cast a delicate reflection on his face, and gave him an usually fine effect.

The reporter was duly 'awed'.[62]

Wilde accepted with good grace some of the feeble bon mots which were foisted on him by imaginative paragraphists. It was told that, when asked by one Washington hostess, 'Where is your lily?', Wilde had replied, 'At home, madam, where you left your good manners.' Quizzed about this, he claimed – surely untruthfully – that the exchange was 'absolutely true', except that it had 'happened in London and that the lady was a duchess'. He deflected, though, the report that he had complained of there being 'no ruins or curiosities in America' (supposedly eliciting the barbed retort, 'Time will remedy the one, and as for curiosities, we import them'); the story, he pointed out, had first been told of Dickens, when he was in America fully forty years before.[63]

Not surprisingly, Wilde was stung by the personal attacks that appeared in the press. The New York Tribune remained unrelentingly hostile, keeping up their image of him as a mountebank on a mercenary exhibition tour. And it was a line that was taken up by others. Particularly galling had been the malicious and false reports filed in the wake of the Baltimore 'fiasco'. In the first flush of his anger Wilde did allow himself to complain about such treatment, telling a reporter from the New York Herald, 'If you expect English gentlemen to come to your country, you must improve the character of your journalism. I do not intend to come... again until this sort of thing is changed.'[64] And when he did finally reach Baltimore he sought out the reporter who had invented the story about him demanding money to attend a private reception. Wilde asked him how much he had been paid for his article. On learning that it was a meagre $6, he claimed to have replied, 'Well, the rate of lying is not very high in America. That's all I wished to ascertain. Good day.'[65] Soon, however, he recognized that anger and indignation were counterproductive. Behind the scenes, he might ask George Lewis to intervene with Whitelaw Reid, editor of the Tribune, in an effort to stem the flow of 'bad reports', but in public he strove to project an air of amused detachment about the press and its antics.[66]

Asked for his views on 'newspaper men' by a Boston reporter, Wilde replied:

> Yes, some of them have been very tedious, while some others have suc-
> ceeded in being very amusing. I was dressing one night [in Washington]
> when I received the card of a person: on the card was printed his name
> and also that he was correspondent for a lot of western papers. 'This
> must be an immense newspaper man,' I said; I cannot dream of keeping
> him waiting. So I put on my dressing gown and he was shown right up. A
> very young gentleman, or rather a boy, came into the room, and as I saw
> him I judged that he was nearly 16. I asked him if he had been to school.
> He said he had left school some time since. He asked my advice as to his
> course in journalism. I asked him if he knew French. He said no. I advised
> him to learn French and counseled him a little as to what books to read,
> and, in fact, I interviewed him. At last I gave him an orange and then sent
> him away... the meekness with which he took it all was very charming.[67]

He was cross with Morse for complaining to the *Washington Post* over its
crude juxtaposing of a portrait of Wilde holding a sunflower with a picture
of a 'Wild' man of Borneo, holding a tropical fruit, above the caption 'How
far from THIS to THIS?' 'I regard all caricature and satire as absolutely
beneath notice,' Wilde informed his manager grandly. 'I regret that you
took any notice.' Allying himself with the great Romantics, he told the
reporter from the *Boston Herald* that an artist should never take note of
'ridicule and abuse... Shelley was abused, but he did not heed it'.[68]

Nevertheless he was happy when people not connected to his management team rose in his defence. Julia Ward Howe and Joaquin Miller both
earned Wilde's gratitude for rebuking the puritanical and pompous Thomas
Wentworth Higginson over an intemperate piece he had written in *The
Woman's Journal* which had not only slated the 'immoral' and pagan nature
of Wilde's 'very mediocre verse', but also suggested his unfitness to be
received in society. Ward Howe, who had just entertained Wilde at Sunday
lunch, replied with a letter to the *Boston Globe*, concluding: 'If, as alleged, the
poison found in the ancient classics is seen to linger too deeply in [Wilde's]
veins, I should not prescribe for his case the coarse, jeering and intemperate
scolding so easily administered through the public prints, but a cordial and
kindly intercourse with that which is soundest, sweetest and purest in our
own society.'[69]

Wilde's growing celebrity in America was being echoed back in Britain. All the newspapers carried reports of his doings from US correspondents or wire services. Most of the comment was positive, although – as Lady Wilde reported – many papers (and 'especially *Vanity Fair*') were 'very angry with the knee *breeches*'. The *Pall Mall Gazette* was always apt to be 'sneering', while the *Daily News* – prompted by Forbes – kept up a succession of spiteful stories, such as the fable of a pun-loving member of New York's Century Club arriving on the evening that Wilde dined there, exclaiming, 'Where is she? Have you seen her? Well, why not say, "she"? I understand she's a Charlotte-Ann!'.[70] On the other side, Labouchère's *Truth* led the way with an enthusiastic round-up of Wilde's early achievements compiled from the American press.[71]

Rennell Rodd sent Wilde a copy, noting, 'you are indeed lucky to have both Yates and L[abby] on your side'. Mingling admiration and envy (and deploying Whistler's favoured adjective, 'amazing') he went on:

Well, you seem to be having amazing fun over there. We all feel a little jealous. And then your statements are amazing of course, but you must not assert yourself so pointedly when you come back, you see you've no one to contradict you! – Which is bad for you! We were surprised to read, that Mr Wilde declined to eat [in a report on the Davis reception in Philadelphia], on hearing the ladies were upstairs. It was never so known in Israel.[72]

Whistler, in whom envy was always prone to trump admiration, sent a bantering note to Wilde (and the New York papers) – with which, as Rodd reported, he was 'immensely pleased': 'Oscar! We of Tite Street and Beaufort Gardens joy in your triumphs, and delight in your success, but – we think that, with the exception of your epigrams, you talk like [new Slade Professor] Sidney Colvin in the Provinces, and that, with the exception of your knee-breeches, you dress like 'Arry Quilter [the despised *Times* art critic]. Signed J McNeill Whistler, Janey Campbell, Mat Elden, Rennell Rodd.' Wilde responded in the same vein, writing privately, 'My dear Jimmy, Your abominable attempt at literature has arrived: I don't believe that my lovely and *spirituelle* Lady Archie [Campbell] ever signed it at all. I was so enraged that I insisted in talking about you to a reporter. I send you the result.' For publication he also sent a telegram: 'I admit knee-breeches, and acknowledge epigrams, but reject Quilter and repudiate Colvin.'[73]

Wilde kept up a constant hymn of praise to Whistler throughout his time in America. The *New York World* reported him telling guests at one reception that Whistler was 'the first painter in England', before adding, '[but] it will take England three hundred years to find it out'.[74] And although Whistler had not been mentioned by name in the 'English Renaissance' lecture, Wilde – in conversation – gradually drew the artist into the picture. Wilde's championship was widely noted, even if he did rather overstep the mark when he claimed to Joseph Pennell that it was *he* who had really 'made Whistler's reputation'.[75]

Lady Wilde's jubilations at her younger son's successes knew few bounds. She delighted in Oscar's 'triumphs', and the stir they were causing in England. 'No news,' she told him in one of her almost weekly letters, 'except that nothing is talked of but you.'[76] A fair bit of that talking was done by Lady Wilde herself. Violet Hunt recorded a visit to a 'conversazione' at Lady Wilde's new Park Street home, at which the hostess had gone on at length 'about Oscar, his success in America, the "costume Oscar" which he has originated [i.e. knee-breeches], and which all young men of fashion are wearing there'; she also showed off one of the Sarony photographs, which Hunt thought 'looked very taking'.[77] Wilde's photograph was now everywhere in London. Americans staying at the Langham Hotel were buying it. Even Lady Wilde's milkman bought one.[78]

Wilde arrived back in New York (on 3 February) his star still in the ascendant. The interest generated by his first half-dozen lectures – and by his reception in society – was kept up. He remained a focus for constant press attention. He was also being accorded the twin tributes of musical homage and commercial exploitation. Music sellers were starting to offer such choice items as 'The Oscar Wilde Galop', 'Oscar Wilde, Forget Me Not (Waltz)', 'Oscar's Schottische', 'Wilde Oscar Wilde', and 'Oscar Dear!' (with its lively refrain, 'Oscar dear, Oscar dear, / How utterly, flutterly utter you are; / Oscar dear, Oscar dear, / I think you are awfully wild, ta-ta') – along with other, more general, 'Aesthetic' titles such as 'The Sunflower Waltz' and 'An Utterly Utter Young Man'.[79]

The 'windows of uptown fancy and dress goods establishments' were blooming with Aesthetic displays of sunflowers and lilies.[80] Indeed the 'leonine' sunflower became so ubiquitous that many florists struggled to maintain supplies.[81] Wilde's overcoat created a new vogue, with newspaper advertisements declaring that 'the ladies go "Wilde" over "Oscar's" Ulster'.[82] Gentlemen's outfitters (unsupported by either fact or probability) claimed

that their 'New and Stylish Goods' represented 'Oscar Wilde's Style'.[83] And although some companies did take a satirical line (a firm specializing in work-wear for railroad men offered a 'Hoss-Car Wilde' suit, and Willoughby, Hill & Co. of Chicago advertised an 'amusing' new tailcoat under an image of 'Wilde "Oscar"... the Ass-thete') for the most part he was taken seriously.[84]*

Over the course of 1882 his image – derived without permission, usually from the Sarony photographs – was more widely used on popular, mass-produced 'trade cards' than anybody else's. The name 'Oscar Wilde' was considered to lend distinction to a product. He was co-opted into promoting everything from cigars to kitchen stoves. Wilde's portrait was even used on a trade card for 'Mme Marie Fontaine's Bosom Beautifier' – a product that would 'in every instance, where the instructions are faithfully followed, enlarge and beautify the bosom, in both old and young ladies, [and where] the bosoms have become soft and flaccid, from whatever cause, its use will restore them, rendering them firm and hard'.[85]

Supported by this rising tide of publicity, the D'Oyly Carte office had been busy. Such was the interest in Wilde that Morse had been able to arrange a substantial lecture tour of the mid-west, fixed upon the major urban centres – Chicago, Cincinnati, Cleveland, Minneapolis and St Paul – but taking in many smaller towns as well. With twenty-seven dates in just six weeks, it was scheduled to run until the third week of March. After that there was demand from several cities in Canada, and requests for return visits to Philadelphia, Boston and New York. Wilde envisaged continuing into April, before returning to Europe in time for Paris Salons.[86]

---

* The term 'Ass-thete,' aside from its connotations of foolishness, derived from a 'conun-drum' then going the rounds: 'Who was the first Aesthete?' 'Balaam's ass, because the Lord made him to(o) utter.' In the Old Testament Book of Numbers, the story is told of how Balaam's ass is given the power of speech, so he can explain to the irate Balaam, that he – the ass – has stopped in his tracks because there is an angel barring the way.

3

This Wide Great World

*'Oh, some things he says are real sweet, but for the most part
I only get an idea of a smattering of something or other; but
I know it's about art.'*

FEMALE AUDIENCE-MEMBER

Wilde was excited by the challenge ahead, and by the opportunities it offered. He began also to conjure up visions of wealth. Dion Boucicault, whom he had seen in Boston, had urged him to 'throw over Carte', and arrange the tour himself, even offering to bankroll the venture, as this would provide far greater profits, and free Wilde from the circus-like aspects of Carte's promotion. But – as Boucicault explained to Mrs Lewis – Wilde was 'not a practical man of business' and the idea frightened him.[1] He preferred to continue with the existing arrangement. He nevertheless remained optimistic about his prospects, declaring that he hoped to return to England with £1,000.[2]

It was a wishful forecast, based, as it was, on a projected three months' lecturing, but it was encouraged by Wilde's shaky grasp of finance. He boasted – publicly and privately – that he had 'got' £200 (or $1,000) from his lecture in Boston. And Morse's accounts do indeed show receipts of $1,000 for the Boston talk. But from this amount were deducted $144.52 of business expenses and $89.15 of personal expenses, leaving a profit of $846.33.

This sum was then divided 50/50 between the Carte Agency and Wilde. So Wilde actually 'got' $423.16 (around £84 10s). It was still a substantial amount, but towns the size of Boston were few.[3]

The topic of Wilde's earnings was one that greatly engaged the press both in the US and in Britain. His own public overestimation of the lecture receipts, together with wildly exaggerated press projections (suggesting that he might net anything between £3,500 and £15,000) combined to breed resentment. Jibes were many. 'Oscar Wilde', it was claimed, 'was the first to discover that there are greenbacks to sunflowers.'[4] He responded with satire: 'I am extremely impressed by the entire disregard of Americans for money-making,' he told one reporter, causing the man to drop his pencil in surprise. 'They think it a strange and awful thing that I should want to make a few dollars by lecturing. Why, money-making is necessary for art. Money builds cities and makes them healthful. Money buys art and furnishes it an incentive. Is it strange that I should want to make money?'[5]

Wilde did recognize that the business and personal expenses of the project were rather 'heavy': first-class rail-travel; hotel accommodation for himself, his servant and his manager; meals in restaurants. But he loved the luxury of it all: sitting down to a light supper of oysters, flanked by three 'coloured waiters... to hand him his wine, and attend to his other wants'; having a suite of rooms at each hotel; settling into his Pullman seat on the train. These were new and delightful experiences.[6] 'I have a sort of triumphal progress,' he told Mrs Lewis, 'live like a young sybarite, travel like a young god.'[7] For the first time in his life he was actually earning money. He had always spent freely, and his new situation only encouraged him to spend more freely still. At every stop on his tour – beside the business and personal expenses incurred by Morse, Wilde also ran up substantial private expenses of his own (as they appear in Morse's account book): for wine, cigarettes, carriages, messengers, 'refreshments', newspapers, stamps, laundry, books, gloves and other 'sundries' – expenses that were then deducted from his share of the profits.

He made constant modifications and improvements to his dress, all in the direction of greater extravagance. He had no intention of wearing his trousers longer (or cutting his hair shorter): his public expected him to look as he did in the Sarony photographs. If some people regarded it as vulgar advertisement, Wilde knew that it was effective for that very reason. Before the end of February he had ordered – from a theatrical costumier, rather than a conventional tailor – two splendid new velvet coats, tight fitting but

with 'large flowered sleeves and little ruffs of cambric coming up from under the collar'. They would, he predicted, 'excite a great sensation'.[8] Later he would usher in 'a new departure in evening dress – black velvet with lace'.[9]

Boucicault wished he could make his young friend, 'less Sybarite – less Epicurean', urging Wilde to save his money and invest it in 'six-per-cent bonds'. But, as he reported ruefully to Mrs Lewis: 'He thinks I take "a painful view of life".'[10] Wilde did, in fact, show some signs of fiscal responsibility. With almost his first earnings he repaid his debt to Levy, and also sent the first of several cheques to his mother.[11]

Wilde set off on his mid-western adventure on 6 February. He travelled with 'two large tin trunks of the Saratoga pattern', his valet and a dedicated tour manager, the twenty-five-year-old J. Sydney Vale.[12]* Although he was still advertised as lecturing on 'The English Renaissance', he had been mapping out his new talk, evolved along the more practical lines suggested by Robert Davis. It came to be titled the 'Decorative Arts', and drew heavily on the ideas – and, indeed, the words – of Ruskin and Morris.[13] Although the 'English Renaissance' lecture had touched on the subject, its tenor had been largely abstract and descriptive; this new talk would be more concrete and prescriptive. It gave to Wilde's performance an additional sense of purpose. He was now a man on a mission not just to inform but to reform. He asserted the need for artistic handicraft in a machine age, for design to draw upon natural forms, for form to follow function. He stressed the benefits that accrued to society from good design, and the social conditions that were needed to support it.

He told the citizens of Utica (in the state of New York) – his first stop – that:

Great movements must originate with the workmen... We should have in our houses things that gave pleasure to the men who made them. The good in art is not what we directly learn from it but what we

---

*   The name of Wilde's black valet has proved elusive. Although not infrequently mentioned in press reports, and in Wilde's letters, his name is never given. In his *Oscar Wilde in Canada* (1982), Kevin O'Brien gives the valet's name as Stephen Davenport, but without citing a source. The identification is certainly plausible. The name 'Stephen' recurs several times among Wilde's private expenses in Morse's account book – for small amounts, ranging from 50 cents to $3.35. And the American 1910 census records do show a literate black man named 'Steven C. Davenport', born in 1856 in Virginia, but living in New York, and (then) working as a messenger in the Stock Exchange.

indirectly become through it. All the arts are fine arts and all the arts are decorative arts. By separating the handicraftsman from the artist you ruin both. Labor without art is merely barbarism. Decoration is the form of expression of the joy the handicraftsman has in his work. Design is the study and result of cumulative habit and observation. I believe in the elevation and education of the poorer classes. I want to see the homes of the humble beautiful.[14]

These were ideas that he developed and elaborated in his lectures at Rochester and Buffalo (both also in New York state) as he made his way towards Chicago; although at Rochester the crowd, dominated by sunflower-waving students from the local college, had been so rowdy that a large part of his talk was not heard; an incident that provoked an almost national outcry.[15]

After his lecture in Buffalo (a successful experiment with a matinee) Wilde visited Niagara Falls. Recalling the stir achieved by his 'disappointment' with the Atlantic, he affected a not dissimilar stance towards the mighty cataract. 'When I first saw Niagara Falls,' he told the *Buffalo Express*, 'I was disappointed in the outline. The design, it seemed to me, was wanting in grandeur and variety of line'; he did though allow the 'changing loveliness' of the colours, and went on to confess: 'It was not till I stood underneath the falls at Table Rock that I realized the majestic splendor and strength of the physical forces of nature here... It seems to me a sort of embodiment of pantheism. I thought of what Leonardo da Vinci said once, that "the two most beautiful things in the world are a woman's smile and the motion of mighty water".'[16] The only drawback was that, to take the view from Table Rock, it was necessary to don 'a yellow oil-skin, which is as ugly as a mackintosh'.[17] Wilde's position as 'a disappointed man' once more echoed noisily through the press.[18]*

About Chicago – or, rather, about Chicagoans – Wilde was almost unreservedly enthusiastic. He was welcomed by some of the great magnates

---

* Wilde later amplified his sense of disappointment. As the *New York Tribune* reported, he advised Lillie Langtry not to bother with Niagara: 'They told me that so many millions of gallons of water tumbled over the Falls in a minute I could see no beauty in that. There was bulk there, but no beauty... Niagara Falls seems to me to simply be a vast, unnecessary amount of water going the wrong way then falling over unnecessary rocks.' And in due course he developed the line, 'Every American bride is taken there, and the sight of the stupendous waterfall must be one of the earliest, if not the keenest, disappointments in American married life.'

of the thriving commercial city, America's food-processing capital. The city itself had been almost entirely rebuilt following the Great Fire of 1871, and Wilde was impressed by the new, wide, clean streets, even if, as he remarked, 'it is a little sad to think of all the millions of money spent on buildings and so little architecture'.[19]

Although the local press hailed him with good deal of satirical banter, the public turned out in force to hear his lecture – and to see his person. Some 2,500 people packed into the Central Music Hall. Wilde's talk on the 'Decorative Arts' was evolving; he delivered it from notes, with a certain amount of fluent improvisation, and frequent local allusions. The effect was winning. Wilde was delighted to find the audience listening with real interest and appreciation; surprised too, given the hostile 'tone of the press' beforehand.[20] His hearers thrilled with patriotic pride on learning that 'the grandest art of the world has always been the art of republics'. They took note that 'you can make as good a design out of an American turkey as a Japanese out of his native stork', and that 'no machine-made ornaments should be tolerated. They are all bad, worthless, ugly.' They enjoyed his comment that 'people should not mistake the means of civilization for the end. The steam engine and the telephone depend entirely for their value on the use to which they are put.'[21] And they were enthused by his belief that – as shown by the Italian Renaissance – the spirit of commerce could be an ally of great art.[22]

They were the best audience he had yet encountered. Wilde described them to George Curzon as 'delightful – a great sympathetic electric people, who cheered and applauded and gave me a sense of serene power that even being abused by the *Saturday Review* never gave me'.[23] Wilde had, though, stirred up one small outburst of dissent during his lecture. With his gift for provocation he had dared to denigrate the city's famous 154-ft mock-medieval Water Tower (one of very few structures to survive the Great Fire). Having praised the 'simple, grand, and natural' workings of its massive pumping engine he surprised his audience by condemning the tower's exterior as 'a castellated monstrosity with pepper boxes stuck all over it' – an amazing 'abuse' of 'Gothic art'. The remark prompted a few angry murmurings at the time, and many press inquisitions afterwards.[24] It also ensured that Wilde would always be remembered in Chicago.

Some criticisms the people of Chicago were prepared to accept. Wilde rebuked them for failing to recognize the rare 'artistic merit' of a young Chicago-born (and Paris-trained) sculptor, John Donoghue, who was

struggling to make a living in the city. Donoghue had secured Wilde's interest by presenting him with a small painted bronze *bas-relief* of a seated girl, illustrating Wilde's poem 'Requiescat'; the gift led to a studio visit, at which Wilde had been greatly impressed by the artist's beautifully modelled statuette of 'the young Sophocles', by his Celtic blood and by his bohemian poverty. Wilde's eloquent advocacy soon led to a flow of commissions from the chastened Chicagoans.

Using Chicago as his base, Wilde then set off on a succession of three great looping trips across the central states. Having left behind the sophisticated metropolitan centres of the eastern seaboard, he began to get a sense of the continent's scale and variety. 'America', he told more than one reporter, 'is not a country; it is a world.'[25] During his first twelve-day itinerary – which ran from Fort Wayne via Detroit, Cleveland, Louisville, Indianapolis, Cincinnati, St Louis and Springfield before returning to Chicago – he enjoyed (by his own estimation) two more 'great successes': at Cincinnati and St Louis.[26]

Cincinnati was unlovely in itself. Wilde even remarked to one reporter, 'I wonder no criminal has ever pleaded the ugliness of your city as an excuse for his crimes.' But it was filled with cultural institutions and art lovers. Wilde was impressed by the School of Design, if not by a 'No Smoking' sign displayed there – 'Great heaven,' he exclaimed, 'they speak of smoking as if it were a crime. I wonder they do not caution the students not to murder each other on the landings.' He called on art collectors. He toured the Art Museum. And he visited the Rookwood Pottery, a co-operative craft venture established only two years previously.

An audience concerned with artistic production was eager to listen to Wilde's ideas. And although in his lecture (a sell-out matinee at the Grand Opera House) he mentioned that one of the designs he saw on a Rookwood vase had been 'done by someone who, I should say, had only five minutes to catch a train', he also had words of praise. And he endeared himself to the Cincinnatians with his remark, 'I cannot express the delight it gives me that I stopped in your city and see the love you have for the beautiful art of decoration.'[27]

For his talk at St Louis Wilde had to contend with the poor acoustics of the hall and a small 'rowdy' element in the audience. He nevertheless felt that a real connection had been made with the substantial art-loving section of the community.[28] He had special praise for the city's 'School and Museum of Fine Arts', pronouncing it 'the finest museum of its kind in the

world.' He admitted that it did 'not contain very much' but all it did contain was 'excellently and brilliantly chosen, [so that] nothing in it could possibly lead a young student astray'.[29]

At Louisville, in northern Kentucky, Wilde enjoyed a success of a different kind. Following his well-attended lecture at the Masonic Temple, he was approached by a sweet gentle-mannered middle-aged woman called Mrs Emma Speed. She was, she explained, the niece of John Keats (her father was the poet's younger brother, George, who had emigrated to the States and prospered). Touched by Wilde's reference to Keats in his lecture, she invited him to her home to look over some of her relics of the poet. The following day Wilde spent several rapt hours pouring with 'tender reverence' over these literary treasures: letters from Keats to his brother in America, 'torn yellow leaves' of manuscript, a little edition of Dante in which Keats had made notes on Milton's *Paradise Lost*. The visit was a propitious one: Mrs Speed recognized Wilde as one 'consecrated to the Spirit of Beauty'. And not long afterwards she sent him the manuscript of Keats's sonnet beginning, 'Blue! 'Tis the life of Heaven…', in the hope that he – unlike Keats – might 'never know "the World's injustice and his pain"'.[30]

Wilde was overwhelmed to have this link with his hero – 'half enamoured of the paper' that had touched the poet's hand, 'and the ink that did his bidding, and… the sweet comeliness of his character'. 'What you have given me', he wrote back, 'is more golden than gold, more precious than any treasure this great country could yield me… It is a sonnet I have loved always, and indeed who but the supreme and perfect artist could have got from a mere colour a motive so full of marvel.'[31]

Wilde returned to Chicago on 28 February, but almost immediately set off again. His second mid-western itinerary – 'eleven consecutive nights in eleven different cities' – took him to Dubuque (Iowa), then through Illinois and Wisconsin to Rockford, Aurora, Racine, Milwaukee, Joliet, Jacksonville, Decatur, Peoria and Bloomington, before he headed back to Chicago. It was, though, a sad failure: a 'fiasco', Wilde called it. The towns were small, and the audiences smaller. In Joliet 'only 52 people… turned out'; at Peoria it was 78. Even Milwaukee, the largest city on the list, only produced a crowd of around 200, and 'probably one third of [them] left before the conclusion'.[32] He provoked neither outrage nor interest. The small and 'scattered' audience at Dubuque listened to him 'as though they were at the funeral of a friend'.[33] Although Wilde had been told by Wendell Phillips that the 'test of a true orator' was an ability 'to interest an audience of

twenty', he was not inclined to test himself in that way.[34] He was crushed, too, by the schedule. At Racine (4 March) he briefly broke down 'in the midst of his lecture, saying he was exhausted and could not read his lines'.[35] Morse, moreover, had failed to secure guaranteed returns from the various local promoters. At Aurora the receipts were a pitiful $7.35. There, and at Joliet, they failed to cover expenses. It was, Wilde complained, a 'depressing and useless' business wearing his 'voice and body to death' for such meagre reward.[36]

He was relieved to get back, once again, to Chicago. On 11 March Wilde made his second appearance at the city's Central Music Hall. He had written a new lecture for the occasion, even more practical and prescriptive than his talk on the 'Decorative Arts'. He now addressed how Aesthetic ideas might be applied to 'The Decoration of Houses'. Quizzed beforehand about the contents, he had explained, 'I shall begin with the door-knocker and go to the attic. Beyond that is Heaven, and I shall leave that to the Church.'[37] And he was true to his word, offering such useful, if mundane, advice as: 'the hall should not be papered, since the walls are exposed to the elements by the frequent opening and closing of the door; it should be wainscoted with beautiful wood... Don't carpet the floor: ordinary red brick tiles make a warm and beautiful floor... Don't paper [the ceiling of the drawing room]; that gives one the sensation of living in a paper box, which is not pleasant.' He recommended 'Queen Anne' furniture, small circular mirrors ('to concentrate light in a room'), brass fire-irons, and Albanian hatracks – 'Not, indeed, that in other matters the Albanians have shown much artistic taste, but in hatracks the Albanians have excelled every other nation. There are beautiful, nay, I may say artistic curves in their hatracks which we do not find elsewhere... Of course I need not mention to an audience of your intelligence that I do not refer to Albany, New York State, in America' (almost the only 'joke' in the lecture, this aside produced shrieks of merriment and applause).[38]

Wilde's final mid-western itinerary ran from the Twin Cities of Minneapolis and St Paul, via Sioux City to Omaha. His visit to St Paul coincided with St Patrick's Day (17 March). The Irish diaspora ensured that in many places across America Wilde received a special welcome, not so much as the 'Apostle of Aestheticism' but as 'Speranza's Gifted Son'. He was happy to accept the label, and to assert his position as a proud Irishman. At St Louis – which had a large Irish population – he had given a special interview to the *Globe-Democrat*, laying out some of his 'well-settled opinions on the

Irish Question'. He declared himself 'entirely at one with the position held by the Land League', urging a redistribution of ownership in favour of the long-impoverished 'peasantry', with 'the Government purchasing the land of Ireland from the landlords at a fair rate... and distributing [it] among the people'. Political change was needed too, although, as he remarked, 'Politics is a practical science. An unsuccessful revolution is merely treason; a successful one is a great era in the history of a country.' Drawing on a pamphlet about *The Irish Americans*, published by his mother, he noted that the modern spirit of *'practical* republicanism' alive in Irish politics was 'due entirely to the reflex influence of American thought' carried by emigrants returning to Ireland. Nevertheless he remained wary of too precipitous change. Ireland, he thought, was not yet ready to 'claim total separation' from the United Kingdom. Declaring himself, like his father before him, 'emphatically' a Home Ruler, he suggested that the 'first step... should be a local Parliament'.[39]

In St Paul, on the evening after his lecture, he attended a nationalistic St Patrick's Day event at the Opera House. Although not intending to speak, he was prevailed upon to make an impromptu address, encouraged in part by 'the generous response' the audience had given 'to the mention of the efforts of [Speranza] in Ireland's cause'. Linking politics to art, he described how the Irish race was 'once the most artistic in Europe', but with the coming of the English in the twelfth century that rich tradition was ended – 'for art could not live and flourish under a tyrant'. And it would take the restoration of Irish independence before the country's 'schools of art and other educational branches will be revived and Ireland will regain the proud position she once held among the nations of Europe'. It was a sentiment that drew 'generous applause'.[40]

As he travelled west Wilde came into contact with members of another oppressed race. He had long wanted to meet the American 'Indians' – 'to see men who spend all their life in the open air... to see how they carry themselves'.[41] He had been intrigued too to hear from one of his travelling companions about a tribe 'who used to subsist on a diet of sunflowers', only regretting that he could not go and dine with them.[42] The 'Indians' he did meet were rather less romantic: demoralized figures hawking goods on station platforms. As he wrote to Mrs Bernard Beere:

> Most of them are curiously like Joe Knight [an English theatre critic] in
> appearance, a few are like Alfred Thompson [the playwright] and when

on the war trail they look like a *procession of Salas*:* their conversation is most fascinating however as long as it unintelligible, but when interpreted is rather silly – like dear Dot [Boucicault]'s. There are also among them Burnands and Gilberts – in fact Burnand in a blanket and *quite* covered with scarlet feathers is now trying through the window to force me to buy a pair of bead slippers and making signs to a ruffianly looking Gilbert who is with him to tomahawk me if I refuse. It's most odd my meeting them so far. The squaws are poor imitations of Clara Jecks [an actress who had played an American Indian on the London stage] and the papooses – or babies – the images of Dot. Papoose is the word they are using for baby, but tomorrow it will mean river, or a maple tree, or something quite different.

Wilde contended that the Indians had 'such a strong objection to literature that they always use different words for the same object every day'.[43]

Even as Wilde made his way across the prairies his plans were changing. Morse had been approached by several rival promoters proposing to take Wilde even further west, past the Rockies and into California. By the time Wilde reached Omaha the details had been finalized. Rather than return east, as originally planned, Wilde and his party would push on to San Francisco. Although the press reported that the Californian promoter Charles E. Locke had contracted for twenty lectures over three weeks at a flat remuneration of $5,000 with all expenses paid, the final arrangement was slightly less daunting – and the remuneration rather less handsome. Wilde would give fifteen lectures over the three weeks, in California, Utah and Colorado, for a fee of $3,000.[44]

---

* George Augustus Sala, the flamboyant British journalist, who had also lectured in America, had – coincidentally – produced a 'Red Indian' themed comic skit for the 1881 Christmas Number of *The World*. It opened upon 'the Big Salt Lick Rolling Prairie' where the darkness of the night was deepened by 'the amalgamation of smoke, fog, and the Poetry of Obscurity specially supplied… by Oscar the Wild Boy'.

4

Bully Boy

'The further West one comes the more there is to like.'

OSCAR WILDE

The 1,867-mile train journey from Omaha to San Francisco took four days (and nights). Wilde described the shifting scene to Norman Forbes-Robertson as 'at first grey, gaunt desolate plains, as colourless as waste land by the sea, with now and then scampering herds of bright red antelopes, and heavy shambling buffaloes, rather like Joe Knight [again] in manner and appearance, and screaming vultures like gnats high up in the air, then up the Sierra Nevadas, the snow-capped mountains shining like shields of polished silver in that vault of blue flame we call the sky, and deep canyons full of pine trees'. It became Wilde's considered opinion that the Yosemite Valley, in the western Sierra Nevada, was one of the two most remarkable pieces of scenery in the States – the other being Delmonico's restaurant in New York.[1]

Although Wilde was travelling first class in one of the railroad's luxuriously appointed 'palace cars', the long journey was tedious – the pace slow, the stops frequent. With no dining car, meals had to be taken at station hotels and restaurants along the way. At several of these halts groups of locals gathered to cheer or gawp at the celebrated Aesthete. At Corinne (Utah) 'forty improvised aesthetes with sunflower accompaniment and a

dingdong brass band' even tried to 'invade' Wilde's car in their desire to serenade him. Such constant and intrusive attention soon became wearisome. Fortunately for Wilde, one of his fellow passengers was John Howson, an operatic tenor heading out to San Francisco to appear as Bunthorne in a D'Oyly Carte-approved production of *Patience*. The two men got on well, and on occasion Howson would relieve Wilde of his duties, by donning the Bunthorne costume and wig, and appearing at the carriage window as the poet.[2]

After four days of travel the train descended 'from the chill winter of the mountains down into the eternal summer' of the San Francisco bay, with its 'groves of orange trees in fruit and flower, green fields, and purple hills'. It was, Wilde declared, 'a very Italy, without its art'. Taken to San Francisco, he was installed in the opulent and recently constructed Palace Hotel, 'the largest hotel in the world' – and perhaps the ugliest.[3]

Locke had mapped out a full schedule of talks in the various cities around the bay: Oakland, Sacramento, San José, Stockton, and San Francisco itself – with repeat appearances and special matinees at several of the venues. Despite the animosity of Ambrose Bierce, who kept up a constant attack in his satirical paper the *Wasp*, Wilde was generally well received in California. His opening lecture, at a flower-bedecked Platt's Hall in San Francisco, drew, according to one paper, 'the most fashionable audience that any entertainment could attract'. The *Daily Report* estimated that: 30% chose to attend because they were determined NOT to be convinced by OW's 'tomfoolery' and wanted to experience his 'bunk' at first hand.

13% came because their 'wives insisted'.

10% were open-minded, and wanted to hear what OW had to say.

10% 'various other reasons'.

9% 'wanted to see and hear the Damphool on general principles'.

1% admitted to being 'honest admirers of Oscar'.

Wilde, however, was able to win over many of the doubters. As the *Examiner* reported, 'As soon as the first feeling of anxious wonder at the lecturer's appearance had passed away, [the audience] caught the infection of his enthusiasm in the subject and exhibited interest by marked attention and quite frequently applause and appreciative laughter.'[4]*

---

* Ambrose Bierce, in the *Wasp* (31 March 1882), reported rather less favourably on the occasion, with three paragraphs of vituperation, beginning: 'That sovereign of insufferables, Oscar Wilde, has ensued with his opulence of twaddle and his penury of sense. He has mounted his hind legs and blown crass vapidities through the bowel of

Although the original plan was for nine talks in California, crammed into just fourteen days, there was still scope for an additional lecture. At the special request of some of San Francisco's 'prominent citizens', on 5 April Wilde gave a fourth address at Platt's Hall, on 'Irish Poets and Poetry of the Nineteenth Century'. Refining upon (or contradicting) the remarks he had made at St Paul, he suggested that English oppression of the Irish had actually stimulated his nation's poetic urge, rather than crushing it. 'The poetry and music of Ireland are not merely the luxury of the rich, but the very bulwark of patriotism, the very seed and flower of liberty,' he declared. 'The Saxon took our lands from us and left them desolate. We took their language and added new beauties to it.' To illustrate his point, he read from the works of Thomas Davis, Gavin Duffy and other poets of his child-hood, as well as from John Boyle O'Reilly and, of course, Speranza. The performance drew an enthusiastic response from the fair-sized and partisan crowd. Indeed the *San Francisco Chronicle* adjudged it the most applauded of all Wilde's lectures in the city.[5]

Despite the almost daily lectures Wilde found ample time for pleasure. Indeed his fortnight on the west coast – between the bright sky and the sparkling ocean, amid peach blossom and greenery – seems to have been a charmed interlude during his American adventure. He always recalled San Francisco as a special place, 'a really beautiful city', the people 'warm and generous and... cultivated'. There was an exotic element too. Wilde had previously disparaged Chinese art, suggesting that it possessed 'no element of beauty, the horrible and grotesque appearing to be standards of perfection'; San Francisco made him change his mind. He was fascinated by the city's crowded and colourful Chinatown – 'the most artistic town I have ever come across' – where the inhabitants, despite their modest means, had 'nothing about them that [was] not beautiful'. Even a scribbled bill of charge, done on rice paper in Indian ink, was like a work of art; and a brothel might be touched with poetry (Wilde often repeated a 'Chinese distich' that he was told in 'a house of sin' at San Francisco: 'The moonlight touches the flowers / The flowers love the moon'.) He was particularly

---

his neck, to the capital edification of circumjacent fools and foolesses, fooling with their foolers. He has tossed off the top of his head and uttered himself in copious overflows of ghastly bosh. The insufferable dunce has nothing to say and says it – says it with a liberal embellishment of bad delivery, embroidering it with reasonless vulgarities of attitude, gesture and attire. There never was an impostor so hateful, a blockhead so stupid, a crank so variously and offensively daft.'

struck at the contrast between the little blue and white porcelain cups in the humblest Chinese tea house – 'cups as delicate as the petals of a rose-leaf' – and the brute ugliness of the teacups in his own 'gaudy' hotel, their rims fully 'an inch thick'.[6]

There were visits to libraries, art galleries and art schools. There were lunches and dinners, even a breakfast with the property tycoon Adolph Sutro. He was most anxious to have Wilde's opinion on his scheme for a new suburb, and led the somewhat 'indolent apostle over the sand dunes' as he mapped out his vision for 'Sutro Heights'. Wilde, always ready for the next meal, said he would be happy to give his advice – but 'after breakfast'. Wilde was entertained – twice – by San Francisco's rather inaptly named 'Bohemian Club' – an institution which, though established as a meeting place for 'gentlemen connected professionally' with the arts, had been invaded by the city's business and legal worthies. Wilde remarked, having lunched there, that he had never seen 'so many well-dressed, well-fed business-like Bohemians' in his life.[7]

At a dinner, given on April Fool's Day, the members – rather uncharitably – planned to show up their guest. 'Judge Hoffman and General Barnes were [detailed], after a good dinner and plenty of drink, to "attack" Wilde on the Classics and English Literature respectively.' But, despite being unprepared, and having drunk a considerable amount, Wilde outshone and defeated both his adversaries. The membership was impressed, and impressed too at the amount of liquor Wilde was able to put away. Several fellow diners were, apparently, asleep at the table or slumped beneath it, when Wilde finally rose at the end of the evening. For those who had considered the long-haired, breeches-wearing Aesthete something of a 'Miss Nancy' this was a stunning refutation. The 'Bohemians', as others before them, were obliged to acknowledge that Wilde 'was not such a fool as he looked'. A committee subsequently called at the Palace Hotel and secured Wilde's agreement to sit for a portrait, to be hung at the club among images of other notable guests.[8]

Wilde found a more genuinely bohemian milieu at an afternoon studio party hosted by the painters Joseph Dwight Strong and Jules Tavernier. The room had been artistically got up, its skylight painted with roses, while the Chinese studio hand, dressed in a gown of silk brocade, made tea for the assembled guests. 'This', Wilde declared, as he surveyed the scene, 'is where I belong! This is my atmosphere!' Strong's wife, Belle, recorded Wilde's infectious brilliancy that afternoon. 'He was charming. His enthusiasm, his

frank sincerity, dispelled at once any constraint… We were exhilarated by his talk, gay, quick, delightfully cordial and almost affectionately friendly.' In one corner of the studio there was a lay figure that had been dressed in women's clothing and perched on a chair; knocking up against this dummy, as he strolled about the room admiring the pictures and 'Indian' artefacts, Wilde momentarily took it for a fellow guest and apologized. Then, realizing at once his error, he went on 'without changing his voice [and] began a conversation' with the seated figure. 'He told her his opinion of San Francisco… replied to imaginary remarks of hers with surprise or approval.' It was 'a superb performance,' Mrs Strong recalled, 'a masterpiece of sparkling wit and gaiety… When he left we all felt we had met a truly great man.'[9]

San Francisco was also a city of romance. Almost from the moment of his arrival in America there had been speculation about Wilde's love life – and the possibility of him taking 'an American girl' back to England as his wife. Everywhere he went he was – like Bunthorne – surrounded by 'lovesick maidens'. Many were beautiful; some were interesting; a few were insistent. Helen Lenoir recalled one of them approaching him at a reception, with the ecstatic exclamation, 'Oh, Mr Wilde, this is what I have longed for.'[10] His mother hoped that he would return from America with a bride.[11] But his hectic travel plans and the constant scrutiny of the press were scarcely conducive to romance. Asked by one reporter about his 'private life', he replied wearily, 'I wish I had one.'[12] To another he lamented that any future Mrs Wilde remained 'a dream, a dream'.[13] He did admit, following his trip to Washington, that he had 'seen an original of Daisy Miller' (the alluring young heroine of Henry James's novel of the same name), but refused to give further details – as he hoped to see her again.[14]

To Sam Ward, however, he confessed that he had lost his heart in San Francisco.[15] The object of his adoration remains unknown, but the most likely candidate is Hattie Crocker, the twenty-three-year-old daughter of Charles Crocker, director of the Southern Pacific Railroad. She was bright, vivacious, beautiful and rich. She and her family were San Francisco nobility, living in a large mansion up on Nob Hill. They had an interest in the arts: her father was sponsoring an impressive new building on Post Street 'for a music hall and for art purposes'; her uncle – Edwin B. Crocker – had established an art gallery in Sacramento, which Wilde visited. Hattie's parents were listed as attending Wilde's first lecture at Platt's Hall, and – although it is surprising that her name was not given too – it is possible that she was with them. And perhaps Hattie was one of the 'young society girls'

who attended the Montgomery Street tea party. Certainly her cousin Amy Crocker was there.[16]

What is also certain is that, not long after he left San Francisco, Wilde wrote a fun-filled letter to a 'Dear Hattie,' lamenting their separation, and concluding, 'when I think of America I only remember someone whose lips are like the crimson petals of a summer rose, whose eyes are two brown agates, who has the fascination of a panther, the pluck of a tigress, and the grace of a bird. Darling Hattie, I now realise that I am absolutely in love with you, and for ever and ever, your affectionate and devoted friend, Oscar Wilde.'[17] Hattie Crocker would have been an impressive match for Wilde, such as his mother dreamed of. But the imperatives of his schedule gave him no opportunity to foster the connection.

Wilde was being whisked away across the plains of Utah. Still under Locke's direction, he lectured to the polygamous, homely and thoroughly 'unintellectual' Mormons at the Salt Lake City Opera House – 'an enormous affair', Wilde called it, 'about the size of Covent Garden', holding 'with ease fourteen families'.[18] He appeared twice at the opulent Tabor Grand Opera House in Denver, and once at the fashionable spa town of Colorado Springs. In between these engagements he also made an unexpected detour. Horace Tabor, Colorado's lieutenant-governor, had amassed his fortune from a silver mine high up in the Rockies, at Leadville; Wilde accepted his impromptu invitation to go and lecture there. The town was a place of legend: a sprawling miners' camp assembled around a broad main street, it was reputed to be both the richest and the most violent conurbation in the United States. Wilde had, since his arrival in America, wanted to see the town 'immensely': here was an opportunity.[19]

The visit was a memorable one. It had a hint of danger: Wilde acquired a revolver for the trip – though his claim to have practised with it by shooting sparrows off the telegraph wires seems doubtful. There was the long, slow-climbing narrow-gauge train journey, up over 10,000 feet, and the giddiness caused by the 'light air' on arrival. There was 'the silent and dignified reception from a well armed mob' as he made his way into the town. There was the unexpected charm of the eight-hundred-seat Tabor Opera House, filled with red-shirted, blond-bearded and attentive miners. Wilde considered them the best-dressed men he had seen in America. There was the delightful incongruity of the whole occasion; as Wilde fancifully put it, 'I described to them the pictures of Botticelli, and the name... seemed to them like a new drink... I approached modern art and had almost won them over to a real

reverence for what is beautiful when unluckily I described one of Jimmy Whistler's "nocturnes in blue and gold". Then they leapt to their feet and in their grand simple way swore that such things should not be.' The *Leadville Daily Herald*, though less eloquent, confirms the picture, reporting that Wilde's disquisition on the architectural splendours of Renaissance Pisa was interrupted by a cry from the audience, 'We live in adobes in this country!'[20]

Then, after the lecture, there was a guided tour of State Street's rowdy bars and bordellos, where Wilde was greatly impressed by a sign, hung up in Pap Wyman's saloon, reading 'Please Don't Shoot The Pianist. He Is Doing His Best'. It was, he declared, 'the only rational method of art criticism I have ever come across' – recognizing, as it did, 'the fact that bad art merits the penalty of death'.[21*] From State Street Wilde processed a couple of miles out of town, riding in a 'bullock cart' flanked by torch-bearing miners, for a late supper at Tabor's celebrated silver mine, 'The Matchless'. Having struggled into a protective rubber suit, he was lowered down the shaft in a large metal 'bucket'. Wilde claimed that, true to his principles, he remained 'graceful' throughout the operation, though the press reported him clinging anxiously to the bucket rope.

Accompanied by the mine manager, Wilde found a party of miners waiting to greet him, each armed with a bottle. A 'banquet' had been spread, though Wilde later said of the feast that 'the first course [was] whisky, the second whisky, and the third whisky'. The miners were certainly impressed by his capacity for drink. As he knocked back his first 'cocktail' without flinching they pronounced him 'a bully boy with no glass eye'; it was, he said, 'artless and spontaneous praise which touched me more than the pompous panegyrics of literary critics ever did or could'. Wilde's energy was unflagging. He 'chatted incessantly' during the several hours he spent underground.

Thinking that the miners might imagine that art was so 'bound up with respectability that there was no room for them', he strove to make clear that 'between art and respectability there was really no connection at all'. Considering them as 'men working in metals', he told them of the great

---

* Wilde was soon advocating capital punishment for a whole host of 'bad' artists. Commiserating with the Canadian watercolourist John C. Miles over the popularity of cheap chromolithgraphs, he declared that '[painting] will never by duly appreciated until one of those dreadful chromographers is hanged'. While, in discussing the antics of theatrical extras – or 'supers' – with the producer Steele Mackaye, he suggested that 'we will have no serious dramatic art until we hang a super'.

Renaissance goldsmith and 'most accomplished rough', Benvenuto Cellini, who had both killed a man and created a masterpiece. They wondered why Wilde had not brought this remarkable personage along, and – on learning that had been dead 'for some little time' – demanded, 'Who shot him?'[22] Wilde's one disappointment was that, having 'amidst unanimous applause' wielded a silver drill to open up a new vein (to be known as 'The Oscar'), he was not offered shares in the lode – only the drill.[23]

While Wilde had been exploring the world west of the Rockies, Colonel Morse was plotting his route back eastwards, securing fifteen further lecture dates across Missouri, Kansas, Nebraska, Iowa, Ohio and Pennsylvania. After the sunshine and glamour of California, it might have been something of a slog. The days, however, were enlivened by change, the advancing spring and Wilde's openness to his surroundings. 'Every day', he claimed, 'I see something curious and new.'[24] From St Joseph, Missouri, he wrote to Norman Forbes-Robertson:

Outside my window about a quarter of a mile to the west there stands a little yellow house, with a green paling, and a crowd of people pulling it all down. It is the house of the great train-robber and murderer, Jesse James, who was shot by his pal [Robert Ford] last week, and the people are relic hunters. They sold his dust-bin and foot-scraper yesterday at public auction, his door-knocker is to be offered for sale this afternoon, the reserve price being about the income of an English bishop... And his favourite chromo-lithograph was disposed of at a price which in Europe only an authentic Titian can command, or an undoubted Mantegna.

The Americans, he noted, 'are great hero-worshippers, and always take their heroes from the criminal classes'.[25]

At Lincoln, Nebraska, he spent an interesting day with George E. Woodberry, the young English professor at the university there. Together they visited the state penitentiary nearby. Wilde was oppressed by the 'poor, sad' prisoners, in their 'hideous' striped suits, making bricks in the sun, although relieved that, at least, they were all very 'mean-looking'. As he told Nellie Sickert, 'I should hate to see a criminal with a noble face'. In one of the 'tragically tidy' little whitewashed cells he noted a translation of Dante. 'Strange and beautiful it seemed to me,' he remarked, 'that the sorrow of a single Florentine in exile should, hundreds of years afterwards, lighten the sorrow of some common prisoner in a modern gaol.' He was

less impressed by the murderer who was spending the weeks before his execution 'reading novels'; a 'bad preparation,' he thought, 'for facing God or Nothing'.*

Amid the diversions and demands of travel, Wilde found time to carry forward the project for a new edition of Rodd's poems. He had composed his preface, or L'Envoi: 3,500 richly woven words that tested, as he put it, 'the rhythmical value of prose'[26] (he was, finally, taking up the challenge of prose-writing that Pater had thrown down at their first meeting). The matter of the piece looked not only to Pater, but also to Whistler, and to Gautier – whom Wilde had been reading during his travels. It was the proclamation of an 'important' and novel artistic creed, one that signified – as Wilde informed Stoddart – 'my new departure from Mr Ruskin and the Pre-Raphaelites'.[27]

Elements of the creed had, in fact, already found expression in his lecture on the English Renaissance, but Wilde now brought his ideas together with a new intensity. Emboldened perhaps by the time he had spent at Whistler's studio, he declared that he was casting aside the 'ethical' keystone of Ruskin's aesthetic system – the belief that one 'should judge a picture [or poem] by the amount of noble moral ideas it expresses'. In its stead he asserted 'the primary importance of the sensuous element in art, [the] love of art for art's sake'. Gautier was quoted, and Pater extensively paraphrased, as Wilde rejected 'all literary reminiscence and all metaphysical idea' from the province of art, in favour of the perfection of form and the expression of personality. The work of 'modern Romantic' poets such as Wilde (and Rodd) – men seeking to 'perfect the English Renaissance' – was described as 'essentially the poetry of impressions, being like that latest school of painting, the school of Whistler... in its choice of situation as opposed to subject; in its dealing with the exceptions rather than with the types of life; in its brief intensity, in what one might call its fiery-coloured momentariness, it being indeed the momentary situations of life, the momentary aspects of nature, which poetry and painting now seek to render for us'.

The true artist, Wilde claimed, guided by the 'principle of beauty', eschewed both 'facile orthodoxy' and 'sterile scepticism' for the fleeting impression, the changing mood – the search 'for experience itself' rather

---

*   The condemned man confessed that he was, just then, reading Charlotte M. Yonge's popular High Church romance, The Heir of Redclyffe, prompting Wilde to remark, later, to Woodberry, 'My heart was turned by the eyes of the doomed man, but if he reads The Heir of Redclyffe it's perhaps as well to let the law take its course.'

than 'the fruits of experience'.[28] This repudiation of Ruskin in the realms of poetry and painting did not extend to Wilde's views on the 'Decorative Arts'; his lectures on that subject continued to be dominated by Ruskinian notions about the virtues of handicraft and the uplifting effects of beauty in daily life.

Wilde also busied himself over the details of book production: choosing a typeface, discussing design, selecting papers, proposing decorations.* The title of the volume was changed to *Rose Leaf and Apple Leaf*. The original English edition of the book had been dedicated to Rodd's father, but Wilde substituted a fulsome tribute to himself: 'To / Oscar Wilde / "Heart's Brother" / These Few Songs And Many Songs To Come'.[29]

Preparing a book for the press was easier work than getting a play into production. Plans for *Vera* had become mired in difficulties. Wilde's initial optimism, after the meetings with Clara Morris, had been briefly buoyed by his success in persuading D'Oyly Carte to interest himself in the project. He had assured Wilde that 'something *ought* to come of it,' as the piece seemed 'a strong, affective and thoroughly artistic Drama'. He was prepared to offer the same terms as the lecture tour – a half-share of profits – with an advance of £200 once a New York production had been secured.[30] Like Wilde, he was 'aware how *difficile*' Clara Morris could be, 'and what practical dangers may attend the periling of [a production] on her', but he seems to have thought it worth persisting with efforts to secure the actress rather than approaching other lesser lights.[31]

Carte had urged Wilde to press ahead with writing a 'Prologue' to give a context to the drama, and while traversing the mid-west Wilde did complete a new opening scene, sketching a picture of czarist despotism and Siberian prison camps, and prefiguring some of the conflicts to be played out later in the drama.[32] The new text, however, arrived too late. Although Morris's husband had told Carte that her inability to commit to *Vera* was due to 'uncertain health', at the beginning of April it was announced that the actress would be taking the lead part in an adaptation of *Far From the Madding Crowd*, opening at the end of the month. By that time it was

---

*   Wilde told Alma Strettle (sister of Mrs J. Comyns Carr), when he met her in Denver, 'Printing is so dull... There is nothing exquisite about it at present. In my next publication I am hoping to give examples of something more satisfying in this way. The letters will be of a rarer design; the commas will be sunflowers, and the semi-colons pomegranates.' Floral punctuation, however, was one of the few innovations not attempted in *Rose Leaf and Apple Leaf*.

impossible for Carte to look elsewhere, at least for the current spring season. Morse sought to reassure Wilde that the autumn would prove better for 'heavy pieces' – such as *Vera* – but it was a disappointment, another setback in his efforts to bring the play to the stage.[33]

5

Different Aspects

'I have already civilized America – il reste seulement le ciel.'

OSCAR WILDE

Wilde got back to New York at the beginning of May, weeks after he had originally planned to finish his tour. Now, though, there was no thought of stopping. His exploits across the mid-west and beyond had enhanced his fame, and he was ready to seize the opportunity. New York, Philadelphia, Boston and Cincinnati were all anxious to hear him again. Canada expected him to visit. And there was a recently received proposal for a tour of 'the south'. Wilde was ready to push forward on all fronts – and to leave the disappointments of *Vera* behind, for the moment.

He returned to Philadelphia on 10 May, calling on the handicraft arts school run by his friend Leland and acquiring several items with which to illustrate his talks, impressing all observers with his Colorado-acquired 'cowboy' outfit, and visiting Whitman a second time.* On the following day

---

*   It was probably on this visit that Whitman touched obliquely on the subject of same-sex desire. Although he mentioned that he had 'resented' J. A. Symonds's too-direct 'curiosity' on the topic, Wilde came away with a clear understanding that Whitman was attracted to other men. They parted with an embrace, and ever afterwards Wilde was able to boast, 'I have the kiss of Walt Whitman still on my lips.'

he lectured at a packed Wallack's Theatre in New York. The great promoter and self-publicist P. T. Barnum was in the front row.[1]

The handful of Canadian dates originally fixed for March had been rescheduled by Morse and augmented into a two-and-a-half-week tour of Ontario and Quebec beginning on 14 May. Colonel Morse considered that this, for Wilde, was 'the most enjoyable part' of his whole transatlantic trip – the Canadian audiences 'more in sympathy with the man and his subjects' than their American neighbours. Wilde himself was more at ease, 'the constant work' of the preceding months having given him 'confidence and skill in delivery' as well as allowing him to refine his talk. The houses, in the major cities, were large. The press – with a few exceptions – was generous and respectful. And at every stop there were entertainments, dinners and receptions. He was lauded by writers, and feted by artists. The Torontonian sculptor Frederick Dunbar even persuaded Wilde to sit for a bust.[2]

In Toronto Wilde watched a lacrosse game between the 'Torontos' and the St Regis Indians (from a nearby reservation), and greatly enjoyed the spectacle. The *Toronto Globe* recorded him 'laughing heartily when any of the players went unceremoniously to grass, or clapping his hands when a good piece of work was done'. He told the reporter that he thought the game – then Canada's national sport – 'charming' and 'far ahead of cricket for physical development' as 'everyone seems to get an equal share of the play – or hard work', as Wilde considered it. From an Aesthetic point of view he particularly admired the play of the 'tall, finely built defense man' Ross Mackenzie, and was only disappointed that the 'Indians' were not wearing warpaint.[3]

Having returned to New York on 12 June, he then set off for his tour of the southern states – accompanied, as ever, by his valet, as well as by a new road manager, Frank Gray. Wilde was irritated to discover that the tour, under the direction of a Memphis promoter called Peter Tracy, had grown in length, if not in intensity. From a projected 'three weeks' it had extended to almost five. And yet there were only eighteen lectures to be given during this period, a ratio that Wilde considered 'quite ridiculous'.[4] Nevertheless he covered huge distances almost every other day, through Tennessee, Louisiana, Texas, Georgia, North Carolina and Virginia: Memphis, Vicksburg, New Orleans, Galveston, San Antonio, Houston, New Orleans (again), Mobile, Montgomery, Columbus, Macon, Atlanta, Savannah, Augusta, Charleston, Wilmington, Norfolk and Richmond. For all the 'excitement of lecturing', especially 'when one gets an interested audience', Wilde had grown to

loathe the travelling: 'I hate punctuality and I hate time tables,' he lamented. 'The railroads are all alike to me. One is simply intolerable; another is simply unbearable.'⁵ This journey, moreover, was made more stressful by the threat of yellow fever; though, as Wilde remarked, 'having survived [American] journalism one could always survive yellow fever'.⁶

Despite such irritations, Wilde was touched by the pathos of 'the beautiful, passionate ruined South', as he called it, in a letter to Julia Ward Howe: 'The land of magnolias and music, of roses and romance: picturesque too in her failure to keep pace with your keen northern pushing intellect; living chiefly on credit, and on the memory of some crushing defeats.'⁷ Nostalgia for the ante-bellum days pervaded everything. Wilde claimed that, once, on remarking to a Southern gentleman, 'How beautiful the moon is tonight,' he had received the reply, 'Yes, but you should have seen it before the war.'⁸ He felt an affinity for the place, seeing a bond between the Southern Confederacy and the Irish: both had risen in arms to achieve 'self-government', and both had been defeated.⁹

There was a family connection too. Wilde's uncle Judge John K. Elgee (Lady Wilde's older brother, who had emigrated to the US as a young man) had been a stalwart of the Confederate cause in Louisiana. He had died in 1864, but his memory was still revered. There were even excited reports that Wilde might have a claim to his old estate near Fort Adams. While admitting that it would be delightful to have 'proprietorship of groves of magnolia trees', Wilde dismissed the notion.¹⁰ He was content to come away from the south with only the honorary title of 'Colonel' – the preferred term of address in Texas.¹¹

Wilde made a special visit to Jefferson Davis, the defeated commander-in-chief of the Confederate States, on his plantation near Biloxi, Mississippi. Davis had extended an unlikely invitation, having been touched by Wilde's comments about his leadership in a newspaper interview. Wilde was greatly impressed by his host, 'a man of the keenest intellect'. The seventy-four-year-old Davis, however, seems to have found Wilde 'indefinably objectionable' – a harbinger, perhaps, of the new and uncongenial age. He excused himself early from the dinner.¹²

Among the many beauties of the south – the 'crystal sea' at Galveston, the old Spanish ruins of San Antonio, the alligators of Louisiana and the Georgia forests – Wilde was best pleased by 'the young negroes' he saw everywhere, disporting themselves in the sunshine, or dancing in the shade, 'their half-naked bodies gleaming like bronze'. Amidst the drab materialism

of so much American life, they seemed to offer a rare 'picturesqueness in human costume and habits'. He was astounded that American painters and poets did not use them more as a motif for art. Wilde, though he might exoticize them, seems to have engaged with their ways, and – at New Orleans – even attended one of their voodoo ceremonies.[13]

He became distressingly aware, though, of the racial animosities that still divided the south. Although newspaper reports that he had inadvertently witnessed a lynching when his train passed through the town of Bonfouca, Louisiana, were an invention, he did encounter other vivid examples of racial prejudice.[14] On the journey between Atlanta and Savannah, having boarded the first-class sleeping car together with his black valet, he was informed by a railroad official that it was 'against the rules of the company to sell sleeping-car tickets to colored persons' (the ticket had been bought in advance by Gray, the road manager). Wilde was incensed and refused to alter the arrangements, pointing out that he had never had trouble before. But one of the black porters explained directly to the valet that if passengers boarding the train at Jonesboro found a black man sitting in a whites-only car they might well lynch him. The valet agreed to move.[15]

The southern tour completed, Wilde returned to New York. It was the middle of July, and the city was in holiday mode. Morse, though, was still in the D'Oyly Carte office on Broadway. He rendered a full account of Wilde's earnings and expenses over the previous six and half months. Total receipts were $21,946.56; the associated costs of the tour (travel, accommodation, promotion, the services of Vale and co.) were $9,579.42. This left a net amount of $12,367.14. Wilde's half-share was an impressive $6,183.57 – about £1,100 – slightly more than the £1,000 with which he had hoped to return to England. But the matter was not quite so simple. Over the course of his travels Wilde had incurred private expenses (for wine, cigarettes, telegrams, newspapers, etc.) of $2,217.68. He had also already drawn $1,169.65 of the money owing to him: there had been sundry 'drafts' to Levy, Lady Wilde, to his American tailor, and other tradesmen. This left him with a rather more modest $3,344.07 (approximately £665) still due.

The amount was not negligible. It would be enough for some months of leisure, travel and literary endeavour in Paris or Rome. Or maybe even Asia. For several months Wilde had been scouting the idea of a trip to Japan – 'the most highly civilized country on the globe'. He mentioned it frequently in his interviews. He had half-hoped to persuade Whistler, or perhaps Walter Sickert, to accompany him, so that they might produce pictures for a book

on the country that he would write. He did have a commission from *Our Continent* for a series of articles on Japanese art, and had even begun to gather letters of introduction to potentially useful figures in the country. Nevertheless he hesitated to carry through his plan.[16]

He was becoming increasingly aware of other calls on his resources. Exaggerated reporting of his American successes, and American earnings, in the London papers had galvanized his many creditors. Lady Wilde's letters brought regular news of old bills being presented with demands for settlement. She urged him to pay while he could. She also added regular plaints about her own precarious financial condition and Willie's profligacies. Wilde felt that he needed to keep earning. He asked Morse to see if he could arrange some new lecture dates, and also to follow up the notion of a tour to Australia, where Forbes was now lecturing.[17] To the press Wilde suggested that his desire to go the Antipodes had been prompted by looking at the map: when he saw 'what an awfully ugly-looking country Australia is,' he felt that he must go there 'to see if it cannot be changed into a more beautiful form'.[18]

Despite such plans, after his months of hard travel and hard lecturing, Wilde felt in real need of a holiday. He had received several invitations to visit friends at their seaside homes on Long Island and elsewhere, and was eager to accept. Morse devised a happy solution: an informal 'summer tour' of fashionable east coast resort towns and Catskill mountain retreats. Wilde would holiday with friends in between engagements. Distances would be short, the schedule light (some twenty dates spread over six weeks) and the atmosphere relaxed. Morse, moreover, was hopeful that he might secure as much as $100 per engagement.[19] Summer lectures were a novelty, and Wilde remained a draw.

Morse, who accompanied Wilde as his tour manager, recalled this tour as a particularly happy interlude. In these summer lectures – given often in not very commodious hotel reception rooms – Wilde was 'at his best':

He had no longer to depend upon his manuscript, but varied his talks to suit the occasion, and often to suit the audience. Some of these addresses were far more interesting than the more formal affairs of the platform. The afternoon meetings, when his audiences were ladies, in charming toilettes, were a source of inspiration to the speaker, and responded to by the enthusiastic yet subdued applause of his hearers. They sparkled with wit, epigram and metaphor; the illustrations were drawn from his

own observations and later experiences; the higher intelligence of his audiences, appreciative of his best efforts, incited him to flights of fancy and oratory not reached before.

Unfortunately, as Morse lamented, none of these talks was adequately reported or preserved.[20]

There is a glimpse of Wilde lecturing in the Casino Theatre at Newport, Rhode Island, on 15 July, when he created 'quite a sensation' during his discussion of the enduring beauty of a well-designed dress, by remarking, 'I am now speaking to those who are not millionaires, if any such be present', at exactly the moment Mrs Vanderbilt made her entrance into the hall.[21] From Newport Morse steered Wilde along a meandering route to Long Branch, Babylon, Long Beach, Ballston Spa, Saratoga and beyond.[22]

The schedule allowed time for rest and recreation. Wilde accepted an invitation to stay for a few days with Julia Ward Howe at her farmhouse near Newport, although he threw the household 'into a flutter' with the announcement that he was bringing not only a 'Cyclopean' book-filled trunk ('I can't travel without Balzac and Gautier'), a hatbox and a portmanteau, but also his valet.[23] He had a delightful time there, dubbing Rhode Island that 'little island where idleness ranks among the virtues'.[24] He did test the Ward Howes and their guests with some of his affectations: for one walk into the wooded valley he wore his black velvet outfit, along with a slouch hat and a salmon-coloured scarf, while holding a rose, which he sniffed as he chatted.[25] But despite such stunts he was considered 'a rarely entertaining guest': he talked 'amazingly well... all that was best in the man [coming] to the surface'. He recited his 'noble poem' 'Ave Imperatrix' under the trees one afternoon, and 'told endless stories of Swinburne, Whistler, and other celebrities of the day'.[26] At one dinner he out-talked both the 'famous Boston wit' Tom Appleton and Oliver Wendell Holmes.

The visit fuelled press speculation that Wilde had become engaged to the youngest Ward Howe daughter, Maud. The rumour was entirely without foundation. Mrs Ward Howe scotched it at once, telling the press that 'if ever there were two people in the world who had no sympathy in common, those two were Miss Ward Howe and Oscar Wilde'. Nevertheless it was widely reported in the British papers; Lady Wilde was disappointed at having to deny the claim and turn aside the many 'notes of warm congratulations' that she received.[27]

There are numerous other sightings of Wilde in holiday mode that

season: resplendent in a bathing suit on the sands at Long Beach;[28] surprising the family of William Henderson (the New York theatre proprietor) with his tennis skills and unaffected charm;[29] cruising around the 'Great South Bay' together with the Fortescue family and 'Uncle Bob' Roosevelt in *Heartsease*, their new yacht (which he had earlier 'christened' with a bottle of champagne and 'a neat little speech');[30] attending the start of the Newport polo season with Sam Ward, and taking 'the deepest interest in the games';[31] dining *à trois* with Ward and Hurlbert at Long Beach with 'moonlight on the ocean, and the setting sun, and the loveliest sea breeze'.[32] Wilde had looked forward to talking 'nonsense to flowers and children' during his holidays, and there were opportunities for both. At the resort town of Babylon he entertained the young children at his hotel by inventing fairy stories, and recounting them in the ballroom before the music began.[33] He also delighted the five-year-old Natalie Barney with 'a wonderful tale', spun on the sands at Long Beach, after he had rescued her from a posse of rough-housing boys.[34]

Always ready to catch the reflected glory of a greater celebrity, he was pleased to be introduced to Ulysses S. Grant, former president of the United States, and commanding general of the Union forces in the Civil War.[35] He called on the naturalist John Burroughs, finding the disparity between the writer's rustic appearance and literary talk 'very oxymoronic, but very gracious too'. Burroughs found the disparity between his guest's 'splendid' eloquence and 'voluptuary' manner rather less appealing, noting the oddly 'disagreeable' motion of his 'hips and back' as he walked.[36] Wilde also made a well-publicized weekend visit to Julia Ward Howe's 'old crony', Henry Ward Beecher, at his 'beautiful villa on the Hudson'. Wilde thought the celebrated preacher and anti-slavery campaigner 'a splendid fellow'; they shared similar physiognomies, gifts of eloquence and disdain for public opprobrium.[37]*

The lecturing element of Wilde's summer – for all its pleasures – had not proved particularly remunerative, and he resolved to continue working into the autumn. Morse contracted with a promoter for Wilde to make a short tour of the industrial towns of northeast New England, and up into the 'maritime' provinces of Canada.[38] Using Boston as his base, Wilde lectured at Providence ('the Beehive of Industry'), Lynn ('City of Sin' and shoemaking),

---

*   In 1874 Beecher had been embroiled in a scandal over his supposed adulterous relationship with the wife of his protégé. But – having outfaced his accusers in the courtroom – he had re-established his position.

Pawtucket (a thriving mill town), North Attleboro (button capital of the US) and Bangor, Maine (New England's lumber hub). In several of these towns – with populations devoted to making things, and interested perhaps in how to make them beautiful – he got audiences of 'about 500'.[39] From Bangor he crossed over the border into Canada, lecturing at Fredericton (New Brunswick), before continuing on to the towns of Nova Scotia and Prince Edward Island.[40]

In Canada he was generally well received, though at Moncton (Nova Scotia) there was an unfortunate confusion when the local YMCA thought that they had secured Wilde to lecture under their auspices, only to find that he had, in fact, committed himself to a rival promoter. Incensed, they attempted to serve a writ preventing him from giving his talk. Fortunately the local sheriff was – as Wilde called him – 'a gentleman of some knowledge of the world' and 'declined to do anything so uncalled for and so impertinent'. The lecture went ahead 'very successfully'; the YMCA's subsequent demand to Wilde for $100 in compensation was dropped before it came to court when the facts became clear, leaving Wilde to comment that 'the whole thing shows the immorality of the most moral institutions'.[41]

After giving his final lecture – on the afternoon of 13 October at St John, New Brunswick – Wilde returned to New York, 'thoroughly exhausted'.[42] He had been on tour, almost without a break, for nine months. He had given some 140 lectures in some 130 places. He had travelled over 15,000 miles, and seen more of the North American continent than most Americans ever did. He had been more interviewed and more paragraphed than any other figure in the country. His name had become a legend and his features were almost universally recognized. And if he had not made his fortune, he had certainly made money.

He had also made an impression. Although his boast that he had 'civilized America' was the usual happy exaggeration, he had sounded a counterblast to the rampant materialism of the age.[43] He had made beauty a byword, and Aestheticism a known term. He had outfaced the hostility of some sections of the press. It came to be acknowledged that there was a point to his occasional 'grotesqueness and exaggeration': without them he would not have secured such a hearing.[44] Among the tens of thousands of people who had heard and seen him, on the lecture platform and off it, not a few had come away informed, encouraged or inspired. Some were fired to follow personal dreams, others to take up practical projects. F. Holland Day (the future publisher and photographer) regarded his youthful encounter

with Wilde on the platform of Boston's South Station as one of the turning points of his life. For years the autograph that he had solicited from 'the Sun God', together with the pencil used to write it, hung in his library as a relic.[45] Among the many letters of appreciation that Wilde received during the course of his tour was one from an admirer thanking him for his 'fructifying lecture' – which taught 'a gospel hitherto not heard here, and one which I believe will have a better effect than the foundation of a cotton factory'.[46] The New York-based artist-potter Charles Volkmar considered that Wilde's lectures, besides 'greatly benefit[ing]' his own work, bore 'an important share' in the 'art advancement' of the country. And it was a verdict that was echoed by others.[47]

6

The Dream of the Poet

'How long it seems to take one to get any business done!'

OSCAR WILDE

The tour finally over, Wilde was in no hurry to return to England. There were projects and pleasures to keep him a while longer in America. The imperatives of lecturing had not prevented him from maintaining an interest in his various literary schemes. Rodd's *Rose Leaf and Apple Leaf* had come out, and Wilde was delighted with the beauty of the finished volume (as – initially – was Rodd who wrote to compliment Stoddart on the sumptuous production).[1] Wilde now had hopes for a collected American edition of his mother's poems, with an introduction by John Boyle O'Reilly. But, sadly, nothing came of the project.[2] He himself did not take up the suggestion that he should start his own American periodical and bring his mother over to promote it.[3]

His real enthusiasm lay elsewhere. It was as a playwright that he still wished to succeed. To support this ambition he had asked Morse, at the end of the summer, to resume the search for an actress or a producer who might bring *Vera* to the stage. First, in order to establish US copyright for the piece, Wilde paid for a small edition of the new, amended, text (with 'Prologue'), to be printed and registered under Morse's name at the Library of Congress. Copies were then dispatched to the actress Rose Coghlan,

as well as to theatre managers in New York and Boston. After a month, though, he had received no very positive response.[4]

Impatient for success, Wilde also began work on a new theatrical project. He was keen to take up the idea of writing a Shakespearean verse-drama set during the Renaissance. He mapped out a scenario about 'The Cardinal of Avignon' – a prelate consumed with love for his beautiful young ward – and even produced some pages of dialogue. But then another notion took hold.[5] Over the summer Wilde had sought out the hugely popular twenty-two-year-old actress Mary Anderson, who had a holiday home at Long Branch. Wilde had met Anderson in New York, and seen her act. He had been impressed by her talent, reportedly characterizing her as 'pure and fearless as a mountain daisy; full of change as a river; tender fresh, sparkling, brilliant, superb, placid'.[6] He had also remarked in the press that she was 'a very beautiful woman' – ever a useful prelude to befriending an actress.[7] Wilde conceived the idea of writing a play as a showcase for her talents. It was to be a tragedy – with a commanding heroine – set in Renaissance Italy.[8]

The actual story – of the 'Duchess of Florence' (or 'The Duchess of Padua' as she was soon renamed) and her ill-fated love for a young courtier – existed only as a broad outline, and Wilde, seeking to bind Anderson to the project, insisted that he needed her collaborative input on the 'scenario'. 'All good plays', he told her, 'are a combination of the dream of the poet and that practical knowledge of the actor which gives concentration to action, which intensifies situation, and for poetic effect, which is description, substitutes dramatic effect, which is Life.'[9] There were meetings and discussions. With his distinctive blend of flattery and optimistic enthusiasm Wilde strove to sweep her along: 'I want you to rank with the great actresses of the earth [and] I doubt not for a moment that I can and will write for you a play which, created for you, and inspired by you, shall give you the glory of a Rachel [the celebrated early nineteenth-century French actress], and may yield me the fame of a [Victor] Hugo.'[10] Wilde hoped that Anderson would, at once, purchase the play from the elaborated scenario, and commit to appearing in it. But, though she was clearly engaged by the idea, her enthusiasm was held in check by the counsels of her stepfather and agent, Hamilton Griffin. He was not to be rushed.

Wilde kept up the attack throughout September, sending Anderson ideas and sketches for costumes and scenery. He had, too, the support of a newfound ally. During his time in New York Wilde had come to know the visionary and indefatigable Steele Mackaye (playwright, producer, teacher,

theatre manager, inventor and designer). They had met often in the bohemian setting of New York's Lambs Club. Although in his forties, Mackaye
had a youthful energy and a torrential eloquence to match even Wilde's. He
was an Aesthete too. He had studied painting in Paris, and was fascinated
by stage design. He was also an innovator: among his many theatrical
'inventions' were the safety curtain, tip-up seats, indirect lighting, moveable
stages, and the 'nebulator' – a machine for making onstage clouds. With more
sense of style than economy, his various business ventures rarely prospered.
In 1881 he had been ousted from his own extravagantly refurbished Madison
Square Theatre by exasperated business partners. When Wilde met him,
Mackaye was trying to raise funds for a new 'Dream Theatre' – a vast hotel-
theatre complex to be constructed on the corner of Broadway and 33rd
Street (neither the funds nor the theatre ever materialized).

A warm friendship was formed between the two men. Mackaye at once
recognized Wilde's talent – or potential – as a dramatist. He was greatly
excited by the idea of a verse tragedy set in the Italian Renaissance, with
Mary Anderson in the title role, and he proposed himself as designer-
director. Anderson, for her part, seems to have been excited at the prospect
of working with Mackaye. At a meeting with 'the lovely creature' and her
guard, 'the Griffin', Wilde sold them the idea. 'I told them [Wilde wrote
to Mackaye] that you *might be induced* to accept the superintendence and
management of the production... I explained that you must have absolute
control of everything and everybody. *They agreed.*' Anderson expressed a
desire to have the production ready for 22 January. She recognized the need
for lavish scenery and costumes. Mackaye estimated the costs of the production at $10,000; to Wilde's delight Anderson announced that she was
'ready to spend *any money on it*'.[11]

Despite this apparently satisfactory meeting, there were the further
inevitable delays to be encountered, before a definite agreement could be
reached with 'the Griffin'. He was 'a brute', Wilde complained, 'a padded
horror, with nothing but the showman's idea' – in contrast to the 'simple
and good and tractable' Mary Anderson.[12] Wilde tried to precipitate matters
by claiming – with what truth it is not known – that a rival actor, Lawrence
Barrett, had made 'a very large offer for the play'.[13] And perhaps the ploy
helped matters along. Anderson duly confirmed her commitment to the
piece, but suggested that the production should be put off until the following
September to give it more scope for 'a long run'.[14]

It was a minor frustration: 'Of course one is impatient in one's youth,'

Wilde wrote to her, 'but I am quite ready to wait a year in order to make our play the success it is entitled to be.'[15] It took, though, almost eight more weeks for Wilde and Griffin 'to come to terms'. A fee of $5,000 (giving Anderson outright ownership of the play 'for ever') was agreed, with Wilde to receive an advance of $1,000, and the rest once 'Miss Anderson' had received and accepted the work. A delivery date was set: Griffin's draft contract suggested 1 March 1883; Wilde put it back until the end of that month. The contract marked a huge step for Wilde towards achieving his great ambition to have a play produced upon the professional stage. It merely remained for him to write what the document called, 'a first class five-act tragedy'.[16]

Wilde's agreement with Anderson, and the schedule it committed him to, convinced him to set aside plans for lecturing in Australia, at least for the time being. The decision proved wise, as Wilde's first theatrical contract was soon followed by another. Mackaye, not content with working on plans for *The Duchess of Padua*, was also taking an interest in *Vera*. Wilde had given him a copy of the newly printed edition of the play, and though MacKaye thought the piece still needed some work, he was excited about its possibilities. He approached various actresses with a view to producing it.[17] The most encouraging response came from the controversy loving young star, Marie Prescott.

In early November the twenty-nine-year-old Prescott, together with her husband, William Perzel, met Wilde and Mackaye over breakfast at Delmonico's to discuss the project. She was impressed with the play – although, like everyone else, she thought some changes would be necessary. A New York production was mooted for the following year. The details of the contract needed to be ironed out, and Perzel proved an even less tractable negotiator than 'the Griffin', but it seems that Wilde received an 'oral assurance' from the actress 'that all would be well'.[18]

These theatrical schemes kept Wilde in America as the winter advanced. His mother wondered whether he was ever coming home; the American press wondered whether he was ever going to leave. They ensured he was in New York when Lillie Langtry arrived, on 23 October, to make her American stage debut. He greeted her with lilies and squired her about the city. He was on hand to console her when the Park Theatre burnt down on the eve of her opening there. Surveying the conflagration from the windows of Langtry's apartment, he remarked on its beauty.[19]

With Langtry's company hastily relocated to Wallack's Theatre, Wilde

was commissioned to write, for the *New York World*, not a review of the opening night but an Aesthetic appreciation of the leading lady. He produced some dozen paragraphs eulogizing the perfection of her 'pure Greek' face – 'the grave low forehead, the exquisitely arched brow; the noble chiseling of the mouth', and so on. And to those 'Philistines' who might contend that 'to be absolutely perfect is impossible', he countered, 'it is only the impossible things that are worth doing nowadays!'[20]

The two friends were delighted to see each other again. There was much laughter when they were together. J. E. Kelly recalled Langtry teasing Wilde about his 'wavy locks'.[21] When it was learnt that Wilde had been taking acting lessons from Steele Mackaye – studying *Hamlet* on the 'Delsartian system' (a method developed by the French actor François Delsarte, which used stylized gestures to communicate emotional experiences) – the press speculated excitedly that he was planning to appear as the Prince opposite Langtry's Ophelia. Or perhaps as Orlando to her Rosalind in *As You Like It*.[22] Lady Wilde was thrilled at the notion. '*You would* be a charming Orlando,' she told him. 'Try it. *£100 a night...* Orlando and Romeo – you and [Mrs Langtry] would make fabulous scenes.' The plan, however, was never taken up, and there is no evidence that Wilde ever entertained any real thespian ambitions.[23]

Langtry, moreover, was soon drawn off by those familiar masculine currents of power, money and sex that always swirled about her. The imbalance in her relationship with Wilde reasserted itself. Besieged by suitors from the 'fast set', she took up with the wealthy young broker and horseman, Freddie Gebhard, provoking comment in the press and a break with Henriette Labouchère, who had accompanied her to America. She was already moving out of Wilde's orbit before she left for Boston, at the beginning of December, to continue her theatrical tour.

Wilde, though, was able to console himself with his own advancing theatrical plans, and with the distractions of New York life. The grand receptions that had greeted his arrival were replaced with more intimate and bohemian gatherings: studio visits and convivial club dinners among poets, artists, actors and writers.[24] Sam Ward secured him guest privileges at the Manhattan Club. There were literary jaunts: with Theodore Tilton (Henry Ward Beecher's would-be nemesis) he visited 'the old room, overlooking the Hudson', where Poe had written 'The Raven'.[25]

If Wilde was no longer the novelty he had been, his appearance could still attract attention. As the temperature dropped he adopted a conspicuous

'high buttoned coat with rolling collar and big lapels', such as was worn by the eighteenth-century 'Incroyables'.[26] He was 'nearly mobbed' when he attended the Grand Opera one evening (the 'b'hoys' in the gallery 'hooted and yelled at him in the most disgraceful way'), and his visit to the stock exchange provoked such a display of 'good natured derision' that he had to escape by a back door.[27] He witnessed the 'contest of beauty' at Bunnell's Museum, but did not cast a vote for any of the beauties on view – perhaps because none of them was sufficiently 'Greek'.[28] He flirted with Marie Jansen, the pretty dark-haired actress who had just opened at the Standard Theatre in Gilbert and Sullivan's *Iolanthe*.* He made another visit to Philadelphia.[29] And, on 27 November, he even delivered a final New York lecture at the Parepa Hall.[30]

These last two commitments gave at least a notional fillip to his finances. Some thousand people attended his New York talk. And during his stay in Philadelphia he received, from the wealthy and artistic Mrs Bloomfield Moore, several shares in one of her pet projects: 'Keely's Perpetual Motion Company' (although Wilde lived in the hope that they might yield him a fortune, Keely's invention proved to be a hoax).[31] Money was needed. A regime of living in hotels or rented apartments, of dining out every day and attending the theatre most evenings, was expensive. And although Wilde's summer and autumn lecture tours had brought him perhaps over $1,000 – and Mary Anderson had paid him the same amount again – he was making substantial inroads into his earnings.[32] Always generous when in funds, he lent Mackaye $200 from the money advanced on the *Duchess*.[33] Matters, though, could have been very much worse.

On 14 December Wilde was duped into a rigged dice game by a young man posing as Tony Drexel (son of A. J. Drexel, the noted banker and partner of J. P. Morgan). After winning initially, Wilde began to lose – and in an attempt to recoup his losses, lost more. As the afternoon wore on his cash was soon exhausted and he was obliged to write three successive cheques – for $60, $100 and $1,000 – in order to cover his losses. As he was signing the last cheque it (finally!) dawned on him that he was being fleeced. Making his excuses, and shaking off 'Mr Drexel' – who tried to leave with him – he

---

* There is a charming letter from the actress, which reveals how Wilde's own sense of fun called forth the sense of fun in others: 'Dear Mr. Wilde, Upon hearing that murderers were the only people you conversed with – who did not bore you – I at once determined to make myself worthy of a chat or quarrel with you. All my leisure time has been employed in looking for a victim, but in vain – haven't found a good first class one yet. Words cannot express my regret at having to confess my failure.'

leapt into a cab and raced to the Madison Square Bank, where he stopped payment on the three cheques. He then went to the 30th Street police station, confessing to the sympathetic officer that he had made 'a *damned* fool' of himself. On being taken through the photographic 'rogues gallery' of noted criminals, Wilde at once pointed out 'Mr Drexel' – who was readily identified by the officer as the notorious conman, 'Hungry Joe' Sellick. Despite the urging of the policeman, Wilde declined to prosecute. He claimed he had been 'advertised enough, and didn't want the American public to know he had been taken in by a shark'. And, perhaps won by Wilde's frankness and contrition, the officer – uncharacteristically – did not release the story to the press.[34]

On top of this debacle Wilde's health gave way. He suffered from an attack of 'malaria', perhaps contracted during his tour of the south. He considered it 'an aesthetic disease', but confessed to a reporter that it was 'a deuced nuisance'.[35] The time had come to go home. He booked a passage for Liverpool on the SS *Bothnia*, departing on 27 December.

Rumours of Wilde's run-in with the 'Bunco' conmen had begun to leak out before he left the country. Approached at Delmonico's on Christmas Eve by a reporter wanting to know if it were true that he had been swindled out of $1,000, Wilde confounded the man by answering cryptically (after a long drag on his cigarette), 'I should object to losing $1,000, but I should not object to have it known if I had done so.'[36]

In a valedictory interview, the ever-disobliging *New York Tribune* claimed that Wilde had admitted that 'his mission to our barbaric shores had been substantially a failure' – and certain elements of the press were happy to support this notion.[37] But if Wilde had not exactly changed America, he had made his mark. And, no less importantly, America had changed him. He had enjoyed an extraordinary year: of travel, of independence, of new sights and new sensations. He had more than achieved his ambition of 'Fame'. He had made his ideas known across a continent. He had earned a substantial amount of money – and spent a large part of it. He had been feted and fussed over. He had met Whitman and Longfellow. And he had secured the interest of two leading actresses in his two dramatic projects.

-PART V-

THE DEVOTED
FRIEND

1883–1888

AGE 28–34

Oscar Wilde on the Isle of Wight, 1884.

1

Over the Seine

'I ought to be putting black upon white – black upon white.'

OSCAR WILDE

The return crossing was a rough one. Wilde was obliged to admit that his previous criticism of the Atlantic had been 'possibly somewhat harsh', and he was glad to reach England. Even as he landed he was overflowing with traveller's tales, rich in 'originality and graphic eccentricity'. In his own mind he was arriving home as a conquering hero, an estimate shared by his mother, with whom he stopped in London.[1] A consultation was arranged with Edwin Levy about his finances, which were not as healthy as everyone supposed. He had spent heavily during his last months in New York, and back in England old debts were still being called in.[2] But there was enough for his planned sojourn in Paris, and the prospect – once he had completed the script for Mary Anderson – of more to come.

During his few days in London he saw 'a great deal of Jimmy [Whistler]', perhaps wanting to be acknowledged for his tireless championing of the artist in America. Certainly he returned to Tite Street as a markedly bolder presence. And although he made a show of admiring Whistler's new Venice etchings ('such water-paintings as the gods never beheld'), he irritated some of the company that gathered at the studio with his newly assumed 'Olympian attitude' – as well as with his new and 'fantastic suit of red plush'.

Rennell Rodd was among the irritated. He had come to feel himself compromised by Wilde's handling of *Rose Leaf and Apple Leaf*. His initial enthusiasm for the exquisite volume had curdled into resentment. Wilde, it seemed to him, had hijacked the project – his too 'effusive' self-dedication, his too-too extravagant preface, 'the somewhat grotesque vignettes', all transforming the book into a sort of 'advertisement... to notoriety'. A letter from Rodd laying out these objections, and warning Wilde of the 'harm' he was doing himself 'by his extravagant performances' across America, had, unsurprisingly, caused 'profound offence'. To Wilde it seemed ingratitude combined with impertinence. Both parties had nursed their grievances, and they met again only to part in anger. It was the end of their friendship. Wilde affected not to regret it. He dismissed the letter with which Rodd closed the relationship as 'like a poor linnet's cry by the roadside along which my immeasurable ambition is sweeping forward'. Wilde would carry on his mission to 'perfect the English Renaissance' alone. In his commonplace book he inscribed the dictum, 'The only schools worth founding are schools without disciples.' Henceforth Rodd would be to him 'the true poet, and false friend'.[3]

By the end of January Wilde was in Paris. After a brief stop at the luxurious new Hôtel Continental, he installed himself at the more congenial Hôtel Voltaire on the Left Bank, just across from the Louvre; this was where he had stayed with his mother and brother in 1874.[4] There, in his 'little room over the Seine', he set to work on completing *The Duchess of Padua* and revising *Vera* – 'two plays', he declared to a friend of his mother's, '[it] sounds ambitious, but we live in an age of inordinate personal ambition, and I am determined that the world shall understand me'. To dramatize the moment further he acquired a white 'burnous' in which to work, a sort of cowled dressing gown such as Balzac had famously worn. The garment was, it seems, intended to inspire him to heights of Balzacian industry and production. It proved very effective.[5]

The *Duchess* advanced apace. Wilde elaborated the tale of 'sin and love' through five acts of stately blank verse, telling of the young Duchess's adulterous passion for the handsome Guido; her murder of the cruel Duke, her husband; her despair and anger when Guido rejects her on account of this horrific deed; her mingled relief and shame when he allows her to fix on him the blame for the crime; her belated decision to save him from the gallows and die in his stead – an act of self-sacrifice that prompts Guido also to take his own life, in final affirmation of their doomed love. The unfolding

melodrama chimed with echoes of Shakespeare and Fletcher, and the insistent note of Shelley's verse-play *The Cenci*.[6]

Despite the Italian Renaissance setting, Wilde was anxious to infuse the play with themes from 'modern life' ('the essence of art', as he described it, 'is to produce the modern idea under an antique form'). He made his Duchess into a would-be social reformer, concerned for the poor and destitute of the city. At a time of increasing social distress in England, and growing public sympathy, he felt that speeches about 'children dying in the lanes' or 'people sleeping under the arches of the bridges' could not 'fail to bring down the house'.[7] He also leavened the drama with touches of 'comedy'. The evil Duke – another dandified cynic, to rival Prince Paul in *Vera* – keeps up a flow of astringent epigrams: 'Conscience is but the name which cowardice / Fleeing from battle scrawls upon its shield'; 'Why, she [the Duchess] is worse than ugly, she is good'; 'the domestic virtues / Are often very beautiful in others'; and (perhaps with a nod to the author's own experience of the popular press) 'in this dull stupid age of ours / The most eccentric thing a man can do / Is to have brains, then the mob mocks at him'. Impatient for Anderson to accept the work, and Griffin to release the second part of his payment, Wilde even smuggled in a sly reference to 'the gold the Gryphon guards In rude Armenia'. The work was finished on 15 March, two weeks ahead of schedule, and dispatched at once to rude America.

In answer to an inquiry from the celebrated French actor Coquelin the elder, with whom he lunched soon after, Wilde declared, 'Mon drame? Du style seulment. Hugo et Shakespeare ont partagé tous les sujets: il est impossible d'être original, même dans le péché; ainsi il n'y a pas d'émotions, seulement des adjectifs extraordinaires. Le fin est assez tragique, mon héros au moment de son triomphe fait un épigramme que manque tout-à-fait d'effet, alors on le condamne a être académicien avec discours forcés.'[8]* But this was mere mystification. He had a high regard for his achievement.

Overflowing with nervous excitement and anxiety, he had followed up the manuscript with a long letter to Anderson, in which he described the play as 'the masterpiece of all my literary work, the *chef d'œuvre* of my

---

* 'My drama? It is of style only. Hugo and Shakespeare have used up all the subjects between them: it is impossible to be original – even in sin; thus there are no emotions, only extraordinary adjectives. The end of the play is quite tragic – my hero at the moment of his triumph makes an epigram that falls flat, so he is condemned to be an Academician with forced speeches.'

youth'. He had then set about explaining, in perhaps too much detail, the 'scientific' thinking behind his various authorial decisions – the admixture of 'comedy' and 'tragedy' ('the strain of emotion on the audience must be lightened: they will not weep if you have not made them laugh'); the setting of *intense emotion [against] a background of intellectual speculation*'; the deliberate introduction of 'modern' ideas into the 'antique form'. By the end of this 'Titan' epistle it was unclear whether he was trying to convince the actress or himself of the play's merits. He closed with a request that Anderson telegraph her decision to him at his mother's London address.[9]

Meanwhile he still had *Vera* to keep him busy. Marie Prescott was now proposing to produce the play in New York at the end of the summer. Although Wilde readily followed up many of her suggestions about the text, he was obliged to use similar arguments to the ones he had given Anderson in order to convince her not to cut out the 'comedy lines'. It was, he declared, 'one of the facts of physiology' that any 'intensified emotion' needed to be relieved by its opposite. 'Success is a science,' he went on; 'if you have the conditions, you get the result. Art is the mathematical result of the emotional desire for beauty. If it is not thought out, it is nothing.' Prescott, anxious to put all the 'conditions' in place, involved herself not only with the text but also with ideas for casting, costumes and scenery. She took on, too, the business negotiations from her husband, proposing to advance Wilde $1,000 for exclusive acting rights to the play, with a further $50 to be paid per performance (seven performances a week being guaranteed). It was an offer that Wilde was ready to accept.[10]

Things seemed to be falling into place. Wilde was working well: full of energy and overflowing with schemes. He completed some more of his poetic 'Impressions' (one about children carrying balloons in the Tuileries Garden), as well as a 'Symphonie en jaune', and dispatched them to the *World*. To his disappointment, however, Yates decided – 'on second thoughts' – against publishing them. 'Second thoughts are very dangerous,' Wilde declared, 'as they are usually good.'[11] Returning to the 'faery tales' he had spun during his summer in America, Wilde also sketched out 'a real children's story' and sent it to Dorothy Tennant – in the hope that she might provide illustrations. Her work, he considered, had the right admixture of 'fancy' and 'truth', 'delicacy' and 'directness' 'that faery tales require'. She was charmed by the story, but nothing came of the planned collaboration.[12]

Wilde's French, already good, improved. He began to compose epigrams in the language: 'La poésie c'est la grammaire idéalisée'; 'Artiste en poésie,

et poète; deux choses très différentes: c. q. Gautier et Hugo.'* His letters
to his mother, written in French, were, she at least declared, 'worthy of
Balzac' – 'so pure and eloquent'.[13] And indeed Wilde's engagement with
that author's novels, begun in America, was continued. It was an immersive
experience. 'After reading the *Comédie Humaine*,' Wilde later declared, 'one
begins to believe that the only real people are the people who never existed... A steady course of Balzac reduces our living friends to shadows, and
acquaintances to the shadows of shades.'[14] He developed a particular cult
for Lucien de Rubempbré, the beautiful would-be poet, who arrives in Paris
full of hopes for a literary career, is seduced by the criminal underworld,
betrays his friends and family, and, after a brief season of triumph, ends up
in prison, where he commits suicide. Wilde called Lucien's death 'one of
the greatest tragedies of my life' – 'a grief from which I have never been
able completely to rid myself. It haunts me in my moments of pleasure.
I remember it when I laugh.'[15]

The Balzacian dressing gown was not Wilde's only sartorial acquisition
that season. He began to model his dress on Lucien's 'elegancies', assuming
the costume and manner of an 1830s dandy – his trousers and sleeves so
tight as to draw comment on the boulevards. He even carried – as Balzac
had done – a turquoise-headed ivory cane. It was part of a complete
transformation in appearance that he effected while in Paris. Inspired by
a bust of Nero at the Louvre, he had his hair cut and curled in the same
manner. He let it be thought that he had taken his barber specially to inspect
the sculpture. The result was, he considered, a huge success: an outward
symbol of his new vision of himself – as Olympian lecturer, successful
playwright and Impressionist poet. 'The Oscar of the first period is dead,'
he declared. 'We are now concerned with the Oscar of the second period.'[16]

As the pressure of his dramatic deadlines eased, and spring advanced,
Wilde went out more into society. Having arrived in Paris with several
introductions – and several copies of *Poems* – he now began to make use
of them. He was taken up by Kate Moore, the formidable American socialite and hostess. He found himself invited to literary salons, exhibition

---

* 'Poetry is idealized grammar'; 'The artist in poetry, and the poet; two very different
things: c.f. Gautier [the former] et Hugo [the latter].' A further, more mysterious,
epigram ran, 'Il me faut des lions dans des cages dorées: c'est affreux, après la chair
humaine les lions aiment l'or, et on ne le leur donne jamais. (O.W.)' ['I need lions
in gilded cages: it's awful, after human flesh, lions love gold, and no one ever gives it
to them.']

openings and dinner parties. He received a gratifying invitation to visit the
great man of letters, Edmond de Goncourt. The way had been paved by the
art critic and friend of Whistler Théodore Duret, as well as by Wilde's own
gift of *Poems*, sent with a flattering letter to the infinitely admired 'auteur de
La Faustine'. Goncourt, an inveterate gossip, was amused by Wilde's tales of
literary London – recording in his diary: 'He described how Swinburne...
had done everything he could to convince his fellow citizens of his pederasty
and bestiality, without being in the slightest way either a pederast or a
bestialist.' Goncourt was intrigued by Wilde's own sexual identity, setting
him down as of 'doubtful sex' ('au sexe douteux').[17]

Wilde spent much time among painters and pictures. It may be that he
even planned to take up his idea of studying painting, although nothing
seems to have come of it. Whistler's name secured him an entré into the
Impressionist circles of the Paris art world. He attended a reception given
by Giuseppe de Nittis (a painter of exquisite metropolitan street scenes),
where he cut a distinctive figure, leaning against the tapestried wall, under
the flambeaux, talking of pictures to Camille Pissarro and Jean-Charles
Cazin. Even the famously gruff Degas was inclined to listen. And although
he considered that the newly dandified Wilde had the look of someone
playing Lord Byron in a provincial theatre, he was impressed enough to
invite him to his studio.[18]

Wilde saw a good deal of the expatriate American artist John Singer Sargent.
They dined together on the Left Bank at Lavenue, where Sargent made a
sketch of him – together with the writer Paul Bourget – in the restaurant's
'album'.[19] Wilde went round the galleries with Jacques-Emile Blanche; the
well-connected young painter, a friend of Walter Sickert, was, flatteringly,
exhibiting a picture of a woman reading a copy of Wilde's *Poems*.[20] Sickert
himself came over to Paris that spring, accompanying Whistler's picture
Arrangement in the Grey and Black (The Artist's Mother) on its way to the salon.
'Remember he travels no longer as Walter Sickert,' Whistler explained to
Wilde; he was now an ambassador: 'Of course he is amazing – for does
he not represent The Amazing One.' He stayed with Wilde at the Hôtel
Voltaire. In their talks about art, Sickert passed on a comment by Degas: 'Il
y a quelque chose plus terrible encore que le bourgeois – c'est l'homme qui
nous singe' ('There is one thing more terrible than the bourgeois – that is the
man who apes us'). Wilde noted it in his commonplace book.[21]

Among Wilde's useful contacts was Burne-Jones's one-time muse,
the beautiful and wealthy Maria Cassavetti Zambaco. Wilde, in his 1877

Grosvenor Gallery review, had described her – in her role as Vivien in Burne-Jones's *Beguiling of Merlin* – as 'tall, lithe... beautiful and subtle to look on, like a snake'. She was living in Paris, studying sculpture with Rodin. Young artists and writers – Sargent and Bourget among them – gathered at her table. At one of her dinners Wilde encountered a twenty-two-year-old Englishman called Robert Sherard. He was a striking figure, tall, blue-eyed with regular features, a broad brow and long blond hair. Wilde at first thought he was part of the entertainment: 'Herr Schultze on the violoncello'. He was soon disabused.

To Wilde's vivid account of how he would pass happy hours at the Louvre contemplating the beauties of the Venus de Milo, Sherard responded, with a blunt disavowal of all artistic interests: 'I have never been to the Louvre.' He claimed. 'When that name is mentioned, I always think of the Grands Magasins du Louvre, where I can get the cheapest ties in Paris.' Wilde was both intrigued and attracted. He recognized that the young man had 'scientifically' thought out a pose that might interest him.[22]*

Living amid the excitements of a foreign city, Wilde wanted a comrade. And Sherard, it seemed, had potential. The son (like Frank Miles) of a wealthy Anglican cleric, he had abandoned Oxford to come to Paris and write. Thus far his main claim to literary distinction was as the great-grand-son of William Wordsworth, but he had just finished a novel, was busy on a volume of poems, and contributed occasional articles to the press. Cut off by his disapproving father, he lived the bohemian life. But he was eager for literary connections. He counted Alphonse Daudet as a friend, and he could claim an acquaintance with Victor Hugo. On the evening after that first meeting Wilde invited Sherard to dinner amid the discreet opulence of Foyot's, in the rue de Tournon. Living in daily expectation of Mary Anderson's $4,000, Wilde announced that 'we dine with the duchess tonight'. It was the first of an almost daily round of meals and meetings over the coming six weeks.[23]

Sherard liked to present himself as a gloomy Calvinist, lit up by Wilde, the 'joyous Celt'. But, though there might be some truth in this picture, it fails to convey how attractive the young Sherard was as a person and a personality. One contemporary recalled him as 'astonishingly handsome', another as 'a

---

* Wilde was delighted by the remark of one of the guards at the Louvre: when asked for directions to the Old Masters, they had replied, 'Les maîtres anciens? C'est les momies, n'est-ce pas?' – directing the inquirer towards the Egyptian Mummies.

superb specimen of blond manhood'. His face and his story gave him an air
of romance. And if some people considered that he was like the doomed poet
Chatterton, he encouraged the idea. There was energy there too. He was
sometimes gauche and crass, but he could also be described as 'a wonderful
person... exceptionally well informed, and possessed of a tremendous flow
of conversation on any and every imaginable subject... a constant joy and
surprise to his intimates'.[24] Wilde certainly found him both 'lovable' and
stimulating; his descriptive powers were rare ('touched with colour, and
tinged with joy'), and they shared 'a desire for beauty in all things'.[25]

But if Sherard was to be a friend, he was obliged also to acknowledge
his position as a disciple. At their second meeting, when Sherard had called
for Wilde at his hotel and admired the view from his rooms, out across the
river, Wilde had asserted his position with the remark, 'Oh, that is altogether immaterial, except to the innkeeper, who, of course, charges it in
the bill. A gentleman never looks out of the window.'[26] Having established
his authority, Wilde carried Sherard off on a happy progress of Parisian
pleasures – dinners, lunches, theatres, excursions, suppers. He always paid;
Sherard assumed that he must be a very wealthy man. There were spontaneous gifts. When Sherard admired a print by Puvis de Chavannes propped above Wilde's desk – the strange image of a young, naked woman
seated on 'her unravelled shroud' in a verdant landscape – Wilde presented
it to him, inscribing the mount with Musset's line, 'Rien n'est vrai que le
beau', and advising that the image might look best in 'a slender, narrow
frame of vermilion streaked with a line of grey'.[27]

They called on Sarah Bernhardt in her dressing room at the Vaudeville
Theatre during the performance; she was delighted to see her old London
friend. And later they visited her home, on the avenue de Villiers, where
Sherard was impressed that an elderly playwright, who was also present,
addressed Wilde as 'cher maître'. Wilde found the old author 'tedious' – his
favourite adjective of disapprobation that season. They visited Wilde's barber
together. The new 'Neronian coiffure' required almost daily maintenance.
And Sherard was persuaded to have his 'honey-coloured' hair curled too,
for once.[28] As a return for all these favours, Sherard brought Wilde to a
reception chez Victor Hugo. Wilde impressed the assembled company with
his now well-rehearsed tales about Swinburne's peculiarities, although the
octogenarian Hugo failed even to register his scintillating guest; he was
dozing in his chair by the fireside.[29]

During those weeks, as Sherard recalled them, there was, for the two

companions, 'nothing outside literature'; it dominated all their thoughts and discussions. Wilde presented his new friend with a copy of *Rose Leaf and Apple Leaf*, hoping he would enjoy the poems and admire *L'Envoi*. He also sought out for him a small volume on the poet Gérard de Nerval. The French Romantic author, who had paraded through the Palais-Royal gardens with a lobster on a blue ribbon, was one of their shared passions.* They talked, too, of other poets, dead before their time; of Chatterton and Poe, and above all of Baudelaire, the poet of *Les Fleurs du mal*.[30]

Wilde – through his study of Swinburne – had already registered the attractions of Baudelaire, but now, back in Paris, he engaged anew with the poet: his verse, his life and his ideas. He enthused Sherard with an appreciation for the morbid horrors of 'The Carcase' and 'The Murderer's Wine', and the stately cadences of 'La Musique'.[31] He grappled again with the challenging idea that an artist could take subjects previously excluded from consideration as evil or ugly and make them beautiful through art.

Among the epigrams he composed that spring was: 'The Greeks discovered that "le beau était beau:" we, that "le laid est beau aussi."' He also recorded the following exchange from his meeting with Coquelin:

COQUELIN: Qu'est-ce que c'est la civilization, Monsieur Wilde?
EGO: L'amour du beau.
COQUELIN: Qu'est-ce que c'est le beau?
EGO: Ce que les bourgeois appellent le laid.
COQUELIN: Et ce que les bourgeois appellent le beau?
EGO: Cela n'existe pas.†[32]

These were notions that Sherard struggled to grasp. After their first dinner together, he had ostentatiously stubbed his cigar-end into his coffee-stained saucer, demanding where is the 'beauty' in that? There had been – he recalled – a rare 'glint of ill humour' behind Wilde's listless reply, 'Oh, yes.

---

*   Strange pets were a feature of Parisian literary life. Wilde was curious to learn of a gentleman, Count Robert de Montesquiou, who had a gilded tortoise, studded with emeralds, declaring that he, too, wanted 'des bibelots vivants'. And it was perhaps these examples that inspired Wilde later to acquire a pet snake; Mrs Jopling recalled opening her studio door one day to find him outside with it 'twisted around his neck'.

†   'What is civilization, Mr. Wilde?' / 'The love of beauty.' / 'What is beautiful?' / 'What bourgeois call the ugly.' / 'And what do the bourgeois call the beautiful?' / 'That does not exist.'

It makes quite an effective brown.' The beauty of ugliness was a paradox that Wilde wanted to explore, not explain.[33]

He was not alone. Bourget, with whom Wilde discoursed over the Left Bank café tables, had just published his *Essais de Psychologie Contemporain*, in which he identified Baudelaire as the dominant influence on the rising generation of Parisian poets and writers. He could lay out for Wilde the details of this new artistic tendency. A movement was becoming apparent, inspired by the dark tones and corrupted forms of *Les Fleurs du mal*, as well as by Gautier's celebrated introduction to the 1868 edition of the book (the only edition then in print). In his *notice* Gautier had described Baudelaire's poetic idiom as 'the style of decadence' – 'a style that is ingenious, complicated, learned, full of shades of meaning and research, always pushing further the limits of language' – a style perfectly adapted for expressing the shifting moods, over-subtle sensations and 'singular hallucinations' of the modern spirit. Gautier likened it to 'the language of the later Roman Empire, already mottled with the greenness of decomposition... the inevitable and fatal idiom of peoples and civilizations where factitious life has replaced the natural life, and developed in man unknown wants'.[34]

For the febrile Baudelaire-obsessed young poets who gathered at Le Chat Noir to drink absinthe and discuss their work, these were compelling ideas. 'Decadence' became their rallying call and their ideal. They adopted its distinctive taints of pessimism and nervous hypersensitivity, its stylistic complexity, and its fascination with depravity. They celebrated it in the novels of the Goncourts, and found it too in the poetry and person of Paul Verlaine. The thirty-nine-year-old Verlaine – balding, satyr-faced, alcoholic and homosexual – had recently returned to Paris after over a decade of self-imposed exile, to find that his three early volumes of Baudelarian verse, published in the 1860s, were rather less well remembered than his violent and doomed affair with the young Arthur Rimbaud. He was eagerly taken up by the young 'Decadents'. They encouraged his writing and published his poems.

Wilde and Sherard met Verlaine one evening, over his absinthe, at the café Françoise Première. Although Wilde held – and maintained – a huge reverence for the French poet, their first encounter was not a great success. Wilde's was distressed by the shabbiness of Verlaine's broken-down appearance, while the brilliant flow of his own talk was wasted on the childlike French poet. Verlaine, for his part, was irritated that Wilde failed to offer round his expensive-looking cigarettes.[35]

Less depressing, but even more alarming, was the poet Maurice Rollinat, author of the recently published *Les Névroses*. A fixture at the Chat Noir cabaret, he would sit – gaunt, pale, wreathed in his mop of black hair – and accompany himself on the piano while declaiming poems of murder, rape, theft, parricide, sex, sacrilege, disease and live burial. Some considered him superior even to Baudelaire. He was both a drug addict and a diabolist. Wilde read his verses with interest and admiration, and became fascinated by the poet's 'ravaged personality'.[36]

After they met, Wilde copied down several of his aperçus: 'Je ne crois pas au progress: mais je crois à la stagnation de la perversité humaine' ('I do not believe in progress: but I do believe in the stagnation of human perversity'); 'Il n'y a q'une forme pour le beau mais pour chaque chose chaque individu a un formule: ainsi on ne comprend pas les poètes' ('There is only one form for the beautiful, but for each thing every person has a formula: hence poets are not understood'); 'Il me faut les rêves, le fantastique; j'admire les chaises Japonais parce-que ils n'ont pas était faits pour s'asseoir' ('I need dreams, and the fantastic; I admire Japanese chairs because they were not made for sitting on'). He liked, too, Rollinat's notion of 'music continuing the beauty of the poetry without its idea'.[37]

Wilde invited Rollinat to dinner, together with Sherard, in his rooms at the Hôtel Voltaire; after the meal he persuaded him to recite his macabre 'Soliloque de Troppmann' – an imaginative recreation of the serial killer's thoughts as he carries out his crimes. The performance was lent additional horror by Rollinat's wild gestures and mounting nervous excitement. Wilde much enjoyed the occasion. Sherard was disturbed by what he considered to be Rollinat's wilful course of self-destruction. He could not understand why Wilde did not intervene. The next morning, as they were crossing the Pont des Arts, he asked, 'If you saw a man throw himself into the river here, would you go after him?' 'I should consider it an act of gross impertinence to do so,' Wilde replied.[38]*

Under the pervading influence of Baudelaire and *Les Décadents*, Wilde

---

* Rollinat's recitation was not the evening's only bizarre entertainment. Wilde, always interested in human dramas, had given some money to a male dancer from the Bal Bullier, who wanted to escape the 'depths of Parisian vice' and return to his native Brittany to join the navy; the young man appeared at the end of the dinner, anxious to show off the new suit that Wilde's funds had enabled him to buy for his journey home. And as an expression of thanks, he insisted on dancing, for the three dinner companions, a *pas seul* 'of amazing grace and agility'.

took up again his idea of writing a poem about the Sphinx (or 'Sphynx', as he spelled it). He had made a beginning during his previous visit to Paris and the Hôtel Voltaire, and went back to it now, refashioning it in a self-consciously decadent mode, rich in jewelled polysyllables, monstrous images, erotic suggestion and recondite reference.

Bourget, in his *Théorie de la décadence*, had suggested that 'a style of decadence' effected the disintegration of the whole into its parts 'the unity of… the page is decomposed to give place to the independence of the phrase, and the phrase to give place to the independence of the word'. Wilde embraced this idea. He had always loved words for their own sake, lingering over their sounds with sensual relish. Like Poe, he believed that their 'musical value' was greater than their 'intellectual value'. And 'The Sphinx' – like Poe's 'The Raven' – is a poem dominated by strange and sonorous words.

Wilde compiled lists of them – 'amenalk' 'chameleon' 'hippogryph' – and then sought to fix them into place. He laboured over the task, a craftsman of letters. Then, as he walked the boulevards, he would rehearse and refashion the ringing phrases. To Sherard's surprise, he announced that a rhyming dictionary was 'a very useful accessory to the lyre' – though he also expected his friend to contribute to the game. 'Why', he would demand, when they met, 'have you brought me no rhyme from Passy?' Sherard was made proud and happy when, for a wanting tri-syllable ending in 'ar,' he produced the word 'nenuphar.' It was duly installed at the end of the couplet:

Or did huge Apis from his car leap down and lay before your feet
Big blossoms of the honey-sweet and honey-coloured nenuphar?[39]

Still in decadent mode, but turning from the phantasmal realm to the sordid realities of the modern metropolis, Wilde also composed 'The Harlot's House' – in which the traffic of lust was reduced to a *danse macabre* performed by marionettes:

Like strange mechanical grotesques,
Making fantastic arabesques,
The shadows raced across the blind.

Paris was a city of sex and sin. But Wilde seems to have directed almost all of his erotic energies into his verse. Sherard was amazed that, during their six weeks together, Wilde appeared to have only a single sexual encounter

– picking up a *cocotte* at the Eden Music Hall one evening. The next day, when Sherard called at the Voltaire, Wilde's first words to him were, 'Robert, what animals we are.' For Wilde, sex – the secret of the Sphinx – seemed to be a destructive force: 'You wake in me each bestial sense, you make me what I would not be.'[40]★

Wilde had entertained Rollinat at the Hôtel Voltaire, rather than at a restaurant, because he was running short of ready money. By the end of April his American earnings were spent. There was nothing to be expected from his Keely's Perpetual Motion Co. shares.[41] And he had still not heard back from Mary Anderson about 'the Duchess of Bally-Padua' (as Willie referred to it). Seeking to force the issue, he sent the actress a telegram asking for her decision.[42]

Sherard was with him at the Hôtel Voltaire when he received the answer later that same day. A *petit bleu* cablegram was delivered as they sat smoking after lunch. Wilde read it without any show of emotion – only tearing a little piece off the form, rolling it into a pellet and putting it in his mouth, a little unconscious act that often accompanied his reading. He then passed the telegram over to Sherard, remarking, 'This, Robert, is rather tedious.' Anderson had rejected the manuscript. It was an awful reverse. He had founded so many hopes and expectations – both artistic and financial – upon the play, hopes that had been encouraged by Anderson and Griffin; he had worked so hard on the manuscript. But, if the blow to his pride was a heavy one, he absorbed it. He turned the conversation at once to other matters and did not mention the telegram again.[43]

They would not, though, be 'dining with the duchess' that evening. Wilde proposed instead a modest '*choucroute garnie* at Zimmer's'. But Sherard, feeling for his friend, insisted that Wilde must – for once – come as his guest to 'a little place on the other side of the water, where they don't do you too badly'. He then led Wilde through circuitous byways to the unpretentious side door of the Café de Paris. Only when they pushed through into the gilt-and-plush glory of the great *salle* did Wilde realize where they were. 'Quite a nice little place,' he observed. And they maintained the joke throughout the evening, considering the grand restaurant as a humble *marchand des*

★ The example of his brother would not have encouraged Wilde to visit prostitutes. Willie wrote to Wilde in Paris, asking him to 'Go and burn a candle for me at some saint's shrine who... knew remorse and *hated harlots*. Can't you find out some battered old Carmelite – some saintly swash-buckler that would teach me anodynes and sleeping-draughts and potions that would kill the past?'

vins. They went on to the Folies-Bergère, where Sherard had been given a box. But after not many minutes, Wilde suggested they leave. He had felt too many eyes upon him. 'There are occasions,' he remarked, 'on which a *loge* is a pillory.' It was the only indication that he was upset.[44]

A few days later a letter arrived from Anderson to confirm her verdict. She had returned the play to Wilde's London address. 'I could', she told him, 'under no circumstances produce your play at the time mentioned in the contract... The play in its present form, I fear, would no more please the public of today, than would *Venice Preserved* [by Thomas Otway] or [Victor Hugo's 1833 play] *Lucretia Borgia*. Neither of us can afford a failure now, and your Duchess in my hands would not succeed, as the part does not fit me. My admiration of your ability is as great as ever. I hope you will appreciate my feelings in the matter.'[45]

Having deliberately set out to achieve a 'modern idea' in 'an antique form', it was galling to be told the effect was akin only to the fusty unplayable works of Restoration tragedy and early Victor Hugo. The criticism was harsh. Wilde refused to acknowledge it. He had too much faith in his own play, and his own talent. He really did believe the *Duchess* was the *chef d'œuvre* of his youth.[46] Anderson's rejection might be a blow to his *amour propre*, but he would recover. A way forward was suggested by her claim that it was in *her* hands that the play would not succeed – as the part did not fit *her*. Wilde would have to find other, fitter, hands to take up the challenge. That, however, could not be achieved at once, and in the meantime there was the sudden, irretrievable 'loss' of an expected $4,000 (£800) to be faced. Wilde's literary life in Paris would have to come to an end.

Although he still had the prospect of *Vera* before him in August, he began to think of other practical schemes for earning money. Schemes for spending money remained always before him: with typical generosity he provided Sherard with the cash to return to England to face a family crisis. Wilde took up again the idea of lecturing. It was the field in which he had achieved his greatest success thus far. There was already the possibility of an Australian tour for later in the year, after *Vera* had opened in New York. But England, too, he recognized, might have potential.

As to subject matter, the notion of giving a talk based on his American experiences had been mooted even while Wilde was in the States, and it had followed him back across the Atlantic. During his time in Paris he began to work up his American anecdotes. He amused Goncourt, when they met again – chez de Nittis – with his 'tall stories' of life out west.[47] And at a

dinner hosted by the expatriate journalists and artists of the 'Pen and Pencil Club', Wilde set the company 'roaring' with an after-dinner speech about transatlantic life. The tale of the Leadville saloon, with its sign admonishing 'Please do not shoot the pianist; he is doing his best', was the hit of the evening.[48] Newspapers were soon reporting that Wilde was 'preparing a lecture for an English audience'.[49]

2

First Drama

'Never mind, Oscar, other great men have had their dramatic failures.'

WILLIE WILDE

Back in London by the middle of May, Wilde defied the imperatives of his unhappy financial situation and resumed his old rooms in Charles Street. In an effort to bring in some immediate funds, he did write to Steele Mackaye giving a glowing account of *The Duchess of Padua* – omitting to mention Mary Anderson's rejection of the piece – and asking for repayment of $200 he had loaned. It is uncertain, though, and perhaps unlikely, that the money was returned. As a more effective expedient he pawned, probably not for the first time, his Berkeley gold medal.[1]

Wilde was ready to invest in his own play. He paid to have twenty copies of *The Duchess* printed; the title page described him as 'Author of "Vera" etc.' – and the play as 'A Tragedy of the XVI Century, Written in Paris in the XIX Century'. In the left-hand top corner was the legend 'Op.II'. The scripts were sent out in the hope of securing interest in a production, but there were no immediate offers. If Lawrence Barrett really had expressed an interest in the play the previous year, he did not follow it up now. The one extant reply is from the painter Millais, who wrote, 'I read your play with great interest and I am sure it would be a success if put on the stage. The plot is admirable as are the delineations, but the dialogue might be improved in many parts.'[2]

Wilde refused to allow such setbacks to dent his pose of buoyant self-assurance. He plunged back into 'the splendid whirl and swirl' of London life. He had been away from the capital for almost a year and half, and was determined to catch up. There were 'at homes' and tea parties, receptions and dances. He attended breakfasts with Whistler, dinners chez George Lewis, and a banquet for Henry Irving.[3] 'I am hard at work being idle,' he informed Sherard, 'late midnights and famishing morrows follow one another.' Society, he declared, 'must be amazed and my Neronian coiffure has amazed it'.[4] Laura Troubridge kept her amazement in check: '[Wilde] is grown enormously fat,' she confided to her diary, 'with a huge face and tight curls all over his head – not at all the aesthetic he used to look.' She was no more impressed by his new manner: 'He was very amusing and talked cleverly, but it was all monologue and not conversation... He is vulgar, I think, and lolls about in, I suppose, poetic attitudes with crumpled shirt cuffs turned back over coat sleeves![5] A few people were prepared to interrupt the monologue. The writer Augustus Hare was amused to note, at one reception, when Wilde launched into a torrent of talk 'intended to be very startling', he was brought up short by the elderly Mrs Duncan Stewart saying quietly, 'You poor dear foolish boy! How can you talk such nonsense.'[6]

Amid the social swirl, Wilde sought out Constance Lloyd. During his absence in America, and then Paris, Lady Wilde had taken care to maintain the connection. Constance and her brother Otho had attended several of her 'at homes'. Otho found the occasions rather dizzyingly unconventional but he did note that his hostess had taken a fancy to his sister, and – 'despite all her oddities' – was 'a kind friend to girls... especially if [like Constance] they have brains'[7]. And it was at one of Lady Wilde's salons, in mid-May, that Oscar and Constance met again. The old rapport was immediately re-established. 'Oscar Wilde had a long talk with Constance,' Otho reported; 'it was of art, as usual, and of scenery.' Wilde greatly amused Otho by talking of 'that dreadful place, Switzerland, so vulgar with its ugly big mountains, all black and white, like an enormous photograph'.[8]

That meeting was rapidly followed up with others, at Park Street and chez Lloyd. There was even a joint outing to the 'Fisheries Exhibition', with Wilde in ebullient form. Constance, dining with an aunt that evening, remarked, 'How delightful it is to see you, Aunt Carrie, after spending three hours and a half with a clever man.'[9] Lady Wilde encouraged the growing intimacy, writing to 'Dear Constance' to confirm her attendance at a subsequent Saturday salon ('I like my rooms to be decorated'); although

she was occasionally vexed at the way Oscar ignored other guests to talk to decorative Miss Lloyd. When not talking to her, it was noted, his eyes followed her about the room.[10]

'If the man were anyone else but Oscar Wilde,' Otho remarked, 'one might conclude that he was in love with her.' There was little doubt that this was the way things were tending. But, with the special obtuseness of a brother, Otho failed to read the signs. 'I don't believe that he means anything; that is his way with all girls whom he finds interesting; and Constance told me afterwards that they had not agreed upon a single subject.'[11]

Although Wilde liked to claim that one of the things that had made him fall in love with Constance was that 'she scarcely ever speaks, [so] I am always wondering what her thoughts are like' – in fact she was forthright in her opinions, even if they were delivered in a low, grave voice. She was not impressed by Wilde's current Paris-inspired ideas, telling him, 'I am afraid you and I disagree in our opinion on art; for I hold that there is no perfect art without perfect morality, whilst you say they are distinct and separable things.'[12] But if they disagreed about the aims of art, they shared a sense of its great importance. Constance, like Oscar, had an intense 'delight in things artistic and beautiful'. That delight, together with her 'keen sense of form and colour', found expression in many aspects of her life, from her dress sense to the beautiful embroideries that she created.[13]

Wilde was particularly keen to discuss art just then. He had agreed to give a talk on the subject to the students' club of the Royal Academy Schools, where Norman Forbes-Robertson's younger brother, Eric, was secretary. It was to be an informal, undergraduate occasion and Wilde seems to have prepared for it by re-reading Pater and listening to Whistler.[14]

On the evening of 30 June he gave an 'audience of young brushes' (as one newspaper called them) his stimulating vision for 'Modern Art Training': 'What makes an artist and what does the artist make, what are the relations of the artist to his surroundings, what is the education an artist should get, and what is the quality of a good work of art.' The vision he elaborated was one of art created for art's sake.

'What you, as painters, have to paint,' he told his young listeners, 'is not things as they are but things as they seem to be; not things as they are but things as they are not.' 'The sign of a Philistine age', he told them, 'is the cry of immorality against art.' Cultural nationalism was exploded with the line, 'English art is a meaningless expression. One might just as well talk of English mathematics.' Specialisms of subject matter were decried

('all such divisions as animal painters, landscape painters, and painters of Scotch cattle in an English mist, painters of English cattle in a Scotch mist, racehorse painters, bull-terrier painters') along with 'all archaeological pictures that make you say, "How curious," all sentimental pictures that make you say, "How interesting," all pictures that do not immediately give you such artistic joy as to make you say, "How beautiful"'. Whistler was roundly declared 'the greatest artist of the day... a master of all time'.

Wilde launched himself into extemporized passages of Ruskinian word-painting when talking of how 'to the real artist nothing is beautiful or ugly in itself', since any scene or object might be transformed by the artist's vision and the effects of light:

> Even Gower Street, one of the most monotonously dull and colourless of formal London thoroughfares has periods when it is actually beautiful. I remember coming home from a party and passing through it when day was breaking when its aspect was most charming and I was forcibly struck by this fact. In the softening obscurity of the morning mist which had filled it with golden and purple hues, softening its outlines, and giving variety to its shadows, with the sunrays piercing it in long golden shafts, the roofs were shining like molten silver, and the vermilion pillar-[box] shone like a gem. It was a scene of almost fairy-like beauty.

He concluded with the Paterian assertion, 'A picture has no meaning but its beauty, no message but its joy. That is the first truth about art that you must never lose sight of. A picture is a purely decorative thing.'[15]

The talk, with its mix of epigram and humour, was hugely enjoyed by the students, even if the press noted that its 'brilliantly eccentric philosophy' was 'very heterodox from an Academic standpoint'.[16] It served also as both a preparation and an advertisement for a public lecture that Wilde was scheduled to deliver the following week.

On his return from Paris, Wilde had been delighted to discover that Colonel Morse, his American tour manager, had recently relocated to London. At an interview in Morse's offices, they discussed Wilde's idea for a lecture tour of Britain. It was decided that, to test the market, there should be an initial one-off London lecture, and not on art, but on his 'Personal Impressions of America'. The talk was scheduled for Thursday 10 July at half past eight in the evening, at Prince's Hall, Piccadilly. Wilde worked to

put all the conditions for success in place, rehearsing his material and his performance. Having been consistently criticized in America for his poor vocal delivery, he consulted Hermann Vezin about his diction, telling the actor, 'I want you to help me. I want a natural style, with a touch of affectation.' 'Well,' answered Vezin, 'and haven't you got that, Oscar?'[17]

Tickets for the event were expensive, at half a guinea. But even so the prospect of seeing Oscar Wilde in his first appearance upon a British lecture platform ensured a large crowd, close to the hall's 600-seat capacity. The audience was accounted 'very fashionable and decidedly aesthetic, especially in the female portion of it'. Whistler was conspicuous, jumping about 'like a cricket' as he 'put himself in evidence all over the hall'.[18] There was slight disappointment, in some sections of the crowd, when Wilde strode on to the platform – about twenty minutes late – not sporting Aesthetic knee-breeches, a velvet coat or long hair. Instead he was dressed in conventional evening attire, although the trousers were very tight, the shirtcuffs very long, and the buttonhole very fine. With his new curled hairstyle he was thought to look 'perfectly like the Prince Regent'.[19]

Wilde was now a completely assured performer, relaxed and spontane-ous; referring to notes but not reading them. Indeed his talk seemed less like a lecture and more 'a sort of subtle philosophical all-round chat, sometimes extravagantly coloured, sometimes fanciful, vague in structure, and full of a strong personal interest and an undercurrent of Irish fun'.[20] He recounted his experiences in New York and Chicago, among the Chinese of San Francisco and the Mormons of Salt Lake City. He repeated the old stories about the miners of Leadville and the old jokes about the disappointments of Niagara. He praised the beauty of American machinery and the intel-lectual power of American women. He lamented the tediousness of the landscape ('it seemed as if nature, alarmed at the extent of the country, gave up in despair, the job of decorating') and the national indifference to pomp and ceremony ('I saw only two processions during my whole visit, one was the Fire Brigade preceded by the Police, and the other was the Police preceded by the Fire Brigade'). He described American girls as the 'prettiest despots in the world... little oases of pretty unreasonableness in a vast desert of practical common sense' – and American men as being entirely given to business: 'Idleness is not with them, as it is with us, one of the fine arts.'

The laughs were constant: at his description of the ordinary American railway car, offering 'as much privacy as if one sat in an arm-chair in the

centre of Piccadilly'; at the little boy trying to sell him a bag of peanuts with the line 'You might buy some... I never sold peanuts to a poet yet'; at his refusal to lecture on the 'Beautiful' at a town called Griggsville because the 'name was so ugly' and 'the inhabitants would not change it'.[21] His views on American democracy were listened to with interest, and the occasional burst of applause. But even the sympathetic *World* considered that the talk was 'a little too long'. After almost two hours – and with the time approaching eleven o'clock – people began to leave. Wilde, quickly grasping the situation, hastened to his stirring conclusion: that America is 'a country which can teach us the beauty of the word "Freedom" and the value of the thing "Liberty"'.

Notwithstanding this slightly hurried end, the lecture was generally very well received. One characteristic review hailed it as 'very "Oscar Wildish"... paradoxical, audacious, epigrammatic, abounding in good stories well told, in picturesque descriptions, often humorously nonsensical, [and] with plenty of original information'.[22] Wilde, though, had retained the ability to polarize opinion. Some sections of the press insisted on casting the occasion in a negative light.[23] The most hostile review, however, came from a perhaps unexpected quarter: Labouchère's *Truth* printed a long spite-filled leader titled 'Exit Oscar'. After describing Wilde's 'lecturing to empty benches at the height of the season' as a most 'pathetic instance of collapse', it launched into a withering account of his career as an 'Epicene youth' and 'effeminate phrase-maker' at Oxford, as 'the temporary jest in London drawing rooms, the butt of American lecture halls, and a failure in Bohemian Paris'. The 'fiasco' of the Prince's Hall, it declared, must mark an end: 'The joke is played out; the soap bubble of prismatic hues blown from a clay pipe has burst.'[24]

Whether this attack by the previously supportive Labouchère was simply a manifestation of the new journalism's appetite for building people up only to knock them down, or reflected some rift between Mrs Labouchère and Wilde occasioned by Lillie Langtry's behaviour in America, is unknown. The article was certainly an annoyance to Wilde, although as he remarked, if it took Labouchère three columns to prove that he was forgotten, 'then there is no difference between fame and obscurity'.[25]

And, indeed, the general consensus prevailed that Wilde's lecture had been a success. It led – as Morse had predicted – to requests from across the country. The colonel was heartened by the initial response to a 'prospectus' he sent out to 'the Institutions', telling Wilde he could 'foresee a good season's work, and fair prices' – from 10 to 25 guineas per night. A handful

of talks was hastily arranged for later that month, while it was planned to build up a full schedule for an autumn/winter season, after Wilde had returned from assisting at the imminent premiere of *Vera* in America.[26]

At the start of August Wilde headed north to Liverpool. There he met Lillie Langtry, just returned from her own triumphant – and very lucrative – American tour. Wilde presented her with a bouquet of roses. He must have hoped that some of her theatrical success would adhere to him. The following day he embarked on the SS *Britannic* for New York.[27]

The crossing was a pleasant one. Among the passengers was a group of Oxford contemporaries, including Gussie Creswell and St John Brodrick. Brodrick, writing to George Curzon, described how Wilde had been 'the life and soul of the voyage. He has showered good stories and bons mots, paradoxes and epigrams upon me all the way, while he certainly has a never failing bonhomie which makes him roar with laughter at his own absurd theories and strange conceits... I don't know that I have ever laughed so much as with and at him all through the voyage.' In more serious mode, Wilde also gave a reading of his poem 'Ave Imperatrix' at the shipboard concert in aid of the Liverpool Orphans' Asylum.[28]

Arriving in New York on 11 August, Wilde was greeted by the inevitable interviewers when he checked in to the Brunswick Hotel. They were intrigued by his new, reformed, appearance – something 'like a rational being' as one termed it. His hair had undergone a further revision on the voyage over: no longer curled, it was now short, straight, thinned out and – as the American press termed it – 'banged' on his forehead. The velvet breeches, it was noted, had been replaced with 'regulation trousers'; and even the presence of 'a Byron collar, scarf, and diamond pin' could not quite dispel the prevailing effect of conventionality.[29]

Wilde at once set about pushing his play, which was set to open at the Union Square Theatre on 20 August. He exploded the notion that he had carried with him from England the actual scenery for the piece – '"corn field" and all'. He had, though, he admitted, brought 'some designs for the scenery and costumes' and some vermilion silk for Miss Prescott's dress. He claimed that he had been unable to mount the play in England because 'it touched on political subjects'; but since 'Americans are without prejudices' he had hopes of a fair reception in the States. Looking forwards, he mentioned that he had recently completed *The Duchess of Padua* – and had great expectations for its future production. He regretted that he would only be staying in America 'a few weeks' because of his lecture

commitments in England, but he hoped to visit Newport, and to see Henry Ward Beecher again at Peekskill.[30]

Wilde was anxious to 'superintend' the rehearsals for *Vera*. He recognized that changes might still have to be made. 'A good play is hardly ever finished,' he told the *New York World*. 'It must be fitted to the stage. It is not enough to make music; one must make music that the instruments can play.' Prescott had assembled a very serviceable collection of 'instruments': the imposing George C. Boniface as the Czar; Edward Lamb, a popular comic, as Prince Paul; and the dashing Jamaican-born Lewis Morrison as the romantic Czarevitch.[31]

Perzel (Marie Prescott's husband) claimed to have spent almost $10,000 on costumes and scenery, the greatest extravagance being the yellow-silk-lined council chamber for the second act.[32] Nor had promotion been neglected. The city 'was lithographed from one end to the other' with garish representations of 'the O'Wilde countenance', and images of Miss Prescott 'flying away' in an eight-horse sleigh while firing a Winchester repeating rifle.[33] Expensive typographical advertisements appeared in the papers; the play's title was now given as 'Vera – or the Nihilist' singular.[34] A long letter from Wilde to Prescott, in which he expressed his exalted vision for the piece, and the 'pride and pleasure' he had in her taking on the title role, was published in the *New York World*. Tickets were selling 'at a premium'.[35] Everything seemed set fair. That week was 'uncommonly cool' for mid-August New York, perfect for theatre-going. Many of Wilde's fashionable friends were returning to town for the show.[36]

But on the day of the opening the weather turned. The temperature soared to '95 degrees in the shade', and stayed there. It was into a sweltering theatre that the 'vast audience' crowded on the evening of Monday 20 August. Despite the stifling heat things began well. The opening prologue, in which Vera, working in her father's humble inn, sees her brother being led off in chains to the Siberian salt mines, and resolves to become a Nihilist, was accounted 'strong', with its touches of humour and its 'thrilling climax'. Wilde, seeing his work upon the stage for the first time, experienced some feelings of unease. There was a considerable 'gulf' between the characters as he had conceived them and as they appeared in the performances of Prescott and her company.[37] The audience, however, did not seem to share his disquiet. At the end of the first act (set in the den of the Nihilists) there were cries of 'Author!'. After the second act (with Prince Paul spouting epigrams in the yellow silk council chamber) the cries were renewed, and

Wilde came on stage to bow his thanks. The audience remained 'critical, but favourably disposed' until the fourth (and final) act. The staging of the passionate climax – in which Vera, arrayed in the 'flaming vermilion gown' stabs herself having declared her love for Alexis – was considered 'more than indelicate... and called forth the murmurings of the entire house'. Hisses were heard. But even so the incident seemed isolated. At the curtain Wilde came forward again, and 'made a speech which was well received'. He was able to leave the theatre that night feeling the play had been, overall, a success. Others, too, endorsed the sentiment.[38]

Among the notes of laudation he received was one from Lillie Langtry's sometime lover, Freddie Gebhard, who had come down from Newport for the show. 'My dear Oscar – Let me congratulate you on the great success of your play. I liked it so much that I cabled immediately over to our dear Lillie.'[39] This generous praise, however, arrived together with the morning papers. The press was not so kind: 'The play is unreal, long-winded, and wearisome' (*New York Times*); 'A foolish highly-peppered story of love, intrigue, and politics... little better than fizzle' (*New York Tribune*); 'long-drawn, dramatic rot, a series of disconnected essays and sickening rant, with a coarse and common kind of cleverness' (*New York Herald*); 'The play is absurd in plot, incongruous in costumes and scenery and utterly mean-ingless in its verbiage' (*New York Sun*).[40]

This was an appalling blow, and a fatal one. It was of no matter that the *New York World* thought that – despite the faults of the last act – 'the play opened well... and its distinctive merits are on the side of success'; or that the character of Prince Paul received a good deal of qualified approbation.[41] There was palpable hostility in the press chorus, and – as it seemed to Wilde – injustice too. The audience had enjoyed the play. The New York critics, however, were renowned for having 'no middle ground'; they would either praise a play 'up to the skies, or damn it to the bottomless pit of oblivion.' *Vera* had fallen on the wrong side of that divide. Rumours circulated that some critics had received orders from their proprietors to damn the play 'no matter what'. But the Boston *Pilot* thought it was the fault of Miss Prescott's 'inferior' acting; Mrs Frank Leslie blamed the vermilion dress.[42]

The artist James Kelly called at the Brunswick Hotel on the morning of 21 August, and found Wilde distraught amid the daily papers. 'I tried to say what I could in favor of [the play],' he recalled, 'but it was impossible to cheer him – he was cut too deep. Referring to the attacks, he said in a broken voice, "Kelly, Kelly, my first play!"'[43]

Although there was no appeal from the verdict, Wilde and Prescott did what they could to mitigate the damage. Wilde gave an interview saying 'he considered *Vera* a success, in spite of the critics' – while also admitting that it was overlong, and declaring that he would be pruning it 'at once'.[44] Prescott wrote to the *New York Times* citing 'a number of letters' she had received from 'prominent citizens' and literary men, expressing their 'indignation' at the treatment Wilde had received from the New York critics. Endorsements were sought: Lawrence Barrett pronounced the play 'a marvel'; Steele Mackaye was enthusiastic.[45] A friendly journalist was prevailed upon to write a piece in the *New York Mirror*, decrying the sneers of the newspapers, and insisting that the play was 'the noblest contribution to its literature the stage has received in many years'.[46]

These moves, though they served to irritate the New York press – which kept up a disparaging editorial commentary on the play and its tribulations – did not encourage the public. Audiences dwindled rapidly. By Saturday night the receipts were under $150, having been almost $900 on the opening night. Prescott and Perzel were losing money heavily. They had booked the theatre for a three-week run, but it was unclear whether they could continue. They consulted with Wilde on the Monday – after the playwright had returned from a visit to Coney Island – suggesting that they might be able to revive the fortunes of the piece if Wilde were to take some part in the proceedings – either appearing in one of the roles, or perhaps giving a lecture between the acts. He wisely declined the offer. The play did not go on that night.[47]

The withdrawal of the piece was reported in the New York press the following day, and promptly relayed back to London. The English papers had already printed extracts from some of the worst American reviews. Wilde was able to deflect the first journalist to seek his reaction: 'Ah,' he told them, 'but I am eating my breakfast, don't you see.' But the sangfroid was not easily maintained. The failure of the play was a bitter and very public humiliation.[48] Everything he had striven for since leaving Oxford had led up to this point. He had written a play, and it had failed – spectacularly and horribly.

Wilde stayed on in America for a month. He visited Newport and Saratoga. But the contrast with the excited optimism of the previous summer must have been painful. He had an invitation to holiday with friends in the wilds of Ontario – and perhaps he went.[49] Among the few incidents to distract Wilde from the anguish of *Vera*'s failure was a meeting with Thomas Edison.

When Wilde had been in America the previous year, he had told Morse that the great inventor was one of the two men he most wanted to meet – the other was Emerson. Emerson was now dead. James Kelly, however, was able to arrange an interview for Wilde at Edison's offices on 5th Avenue.

It was a cosy encounter, with the three men, and Edison's assistant, Samuel Insull, all crammed unceremoniously into a tiny back office. Kelly recalled how Edison – who had admired Wilde's poems – turned to the poet (squashed beside him on the sofa) and said, 'I've seen you before', and then began talking about Wilde's play:

> After discussing it a little, Wilde became more cheerful and said, 'Dion Boucicault told me, "Oscar, from the way you have written your play, it would take Edwin Booth, Henry Irving, Sarah Bernhardt, Ellen Terry and Ada Rehan to render it; you depend too much on the actors. Now when I write a play, if the leading man gets sick, or in any way fails me, I call up one of the ushers – and if he repeats my lines, the play will be a success."' Edison laughed heartily at this, winked at me, and jerking his head toward Wilde, said, 'He's laarnin – he's laarnin – he's laarnin!' Then after lots of bright talk by Wilde, cheerful talk by Edison and earnest remarks by Insull, we parted; as we went down the stoop, Wilde dropped into a moody silence, probably thinking over the contrast of his fortunes with those of Edison.

They walked on in silence, and separated at the Franklin Square station. Wilde was going on to Brooklyn. Kelly's last glimpse of him was sitting alone in the subway carriage: 'He was looking forward.' But to what?

3

Man of the Day

'The romance of life is that one can love so many people and marry but one.'

OSCAR WILDE

The *New York Sun* took particular delight in announcing that Wilde's 'doom' was now sealed in America. One satirical paper published a full-page cartoon to send the playwright on his way back across the Atlantic, juxtaposing the dashing young Aesthete who had arrived barely twenty months ago with the crushed and defeated figure now slinking out of the country, a battered copy of *Vera* under his arm. The British press was no less gleeful. *Punch* declared that his play had been 'Vera bad'; Alfred Bryan, who had caricatured Wilde as one of the men-of-the-year for the *World* in 1881, now depicted him for *Entr'acte*, collapsed in Willie's arms and being consoled with the fraternal observation, that other 'great men' had endured 'dramatic failures.'[1] There was, as one lone paper protested, 'a spirit of exultation', as if Wilde were 'a notorious criminal who had at last been convicted'.[2]

Wilde got back to England in late September 1883, at least able to bury himself in a very full season of lecturing. The work had none of the glamour and novelty that had enlivened his American lecture tour, but it gave him a sense of purpose. Almost sixty talks were scheduled before the end

of the year. Although Wilde started at Wandsworth Town Hall (on 24 September) most of the dates were well away from London – scattered from Exeter to Aberdeen, from Hastings to Birkenhead. Otho Lloyd, who saw Wilde that October, during one of his few days back in the capital, reported, 'He is lecturing still, going from town to town, but in the funniest way, one day he is at Brighton, the next he will be at Edinburgh, the next at Penzance in Cornwall, the next in Dublin; he laughed a good deal over it and said that he left it entirely to his manager.'[3] There was some customary exaggeration in Wilde's description – but the distances that he covered were prodigious, and a tribute to the extent of Victorian rail network.[4] Wilde filled the tedious hours of travel by setting himself to learn German with the aid of a small pocket dictionary and volume of Heine.[5]

Besides his 'Personal Impressions of America', Wilde was also offering, as an alternative, a lecture on 'The House Beautiful' – a variation on the practical guide to home decoration and dress that he had developed during his American tour. The failure of *Vera* – if it had dented his reputation in London – had not destroyed his appeal across the provincial cities of Britain: in most places he received good houses and positive notices. People may have gone out of curiosity 'to see what the much talked-of "Oscar" was like', but they almost invariably left impressed by his 'literary grace', his intelligence, his new haircut and his humour.[6] Remuneration depended on the size of the venues, and the deals struck by Morse: sometimes a flat fee, sometimes a percentage of the gross receipts. From his lecture at the Manchester Free Trade Hall (despite a difficult audience) Wilde took away a handsome £24 3s 9d; Weymouth produced a more modest £3. Nevertheless by mid-October Wilde had earned, after expenses, a very useful £91 9s.[7]

Back in London to receive this payment, Wilde was able to see something of Constance. She attended his mother's Saturday 'salon', and he called at her grandfather's house the following day. Although Constance was about to depart on an extended visit to her Atkinson and Hemphill relatives in Dublin, any separation would be brief. Wilde was scheduled to lecture in the Irish capital that November. They might meet there.[8]

Confiding to her his disappointment about *Vera*, he gave her one of the privately printed copies of the play, and asked for her verdict on it. From Dublin she sent a generous, well-measured, rather earnest letter of consolation, praising the play's 'good dramatic situations' and 'impassioned' calls for liberty – rather than its moments of wit. 'I cannot understand why you should have been so unfortunate in its reception unless either the

acting was very inferior or the audience was unsympathetic to the political opinion expressed in it.' Allying herself to his own defiant stance, she suggested, 'The world surely is unjust and bitter to most of us; I think we must either renounce our opinions and run with the general stream or else totally ignore the world and go on our own way regardless of all, there is not the slightest use in fighting against existing prejudices for we are only worsted in the struggle.'⁹

Constance had become important to Wilde. When he arrived in Dublin on 21 November he at once gravitated into her orbit. He found a note waiting at his hotel, inviting him round to the Atkinson home on Ely Place, and he went without delay. As Constance reported to her brother, he was 'decidedly extra affected, I suppose partly from nervousness' – but, nevertheless, he made himself 'very pleasant'. He continued to pay court over the following days, coming to tea, and securing a theatre box for the family. Constance and her cousins attended his two lectures (both matinees), much preferring the practical wisdom of 'The House Beautiful' to the discursive wit of his 'Personal Impressions of America'.* Although Constance might write disingenuously to Otho about how her cousin, Stanhope Hemphill, 'chaffs my life out of me about O.W., such stupid nonsense', it was clear to all that Wilde's attentions were those of a suitor.¹⁰

Wilde was due to lecture at Shrewsbury on 26 November, so time was limited. He made his declaration on Sunday 25 November, proposing in the drawing room at Ely Place. Constance accepted him at once. She was 'perfectly and insanely happy', as she told her brother, when she wrote to him with the 'astounding' news. The Dublin cousinage shared her pleasure. 'Mama Mary' considered her 'very lucky'. Constance had some anxieties about her own 'cold and practical' family, especially Aunt Emily, but hoped she could count on the support of Otho, and the approval of her grandfather – 'as he is always so pleased to see Oscar'.¹¹

Oscar was going to write to Horatio Lloyd, as well as to Otho and to Constance's mother, from Shrewsbury, and then come up to London, between lectures, at the end of the week, to seek personal interviews with the various family members.¹² His own mother was 'extremely pleased'

---

* The audience, initially, was not sympathetic. His opening remark, 'Let there be nothing in your houses which was not a joy to the man who made it', was received with 'ironical laughter'. He at once embarked on a eulogy of Ireland, gradually winning over the crowd. And it was with tearful enthusiasm that they greeted his line, 'When the heart of a nation is broken, it is broken with music.'

at the news, hopeful for the happiness of 'the two lovers', and excited at
the stability Constance's resources might bring: 'What lovely vistas of
speculation open out. What will you do in life? Where live?... I would like
you to have a small house in London and live the literary life and teach
Constance to correct proofs, and eventually go into Parliament.'[13] Willie
too was enthusiastic: 'My dear old Boz,' he wrote, 'This is indeed good
news, brave news, wise news, and altogether charming and amazing in the
highest and most artistic sense... She is lovely, and lovable, and all that is
sweet and right.'[14] Constance's mother, Mrs Swinburne-King, also approved,
writing back to tell Oscar how pleased she should be to have him as her
son-in-law.[15]

Passionate letters raced between the now separated lovers. Only two days
after the proposal Constance was writing:

> My own Darling Oscar, I have just got your letter, and your letters always
> make me mad for joy and yet more mad to see you and feel once again
> that you are mine and that it is not a dream but a living reality that you
> love me. How can I answer your letters, they are far too beautiful for
> any words of mine, I can only dream of you all day long and it seems as
> if everyone I meet must know my secret and see in my face how I love
> you, my own love.

She called Oscar her 'hero' and her 'god.'[16]

Amid the passion there were some complications to overcome. Constance's letter to her brother announcing the 'astounding news' of her
engagement had crossed with one from him, expressing his doubts about
Wilde as a suitor, and mentioning some tale he had heard against him. It
was unfortunate, and – as Constance told him – 'rather ill timed': 'I don't
wish to know the story but even if there were foundation for anything
against him it is too late to affect me now. I will not allow anything to come
between us... Please for my sake and because my happiness is dependent
upon this thing do not oppose it.'[17] He did not, writing generously to Wilde
to welcome him as 'a new brother'.[18]

Constance's grandfather, Horatio Lloyd, did indeed like Wilde, and – having received his letter – was minded to support the union, but on certain
conditions. Too ill to reply himself, he instructed Aunt Emily to pass on his
views. She informed Wilde, by return, that the old man had 'no objections
to you personally as a husband for Constance. He believes that you and she

are well suited to each other. He has confidence you will treat her kindly…
But he thinks it right as her guardian to put one or two questions to you…
He would like to know what your means are of keeping a wife… [and also]
if you had any debts.' Having been informed on these points, he would 'give
a considered consent'.[19]

Wilde interrupted his tour to come up to London (from Newcastle) for
the weekend of 1 and 2 December; Constance arrived back from Dublin at
the same time. Wilde was invited to dine on the Saturday evening at her
grandfather's house, along with Otho and Aunt Emily, and he returned
to Lancaster Gate the following day for further discussions about future
plans and hopes.[20] Wilde wrote subsequently, giving Horatio Lloyd a frank
account of his finances, and admitting to debts of around £1,500 (a very
substantial figure). His extravagance was certainly a cause for concern, but
it was matched by his industry and ambition. He had, he said, already paid
off £300, and he was able to point to his current earnings, and to a full
lecturing schedule, which was already extending into the following year.*
Perhaps, too, he spoke of his hopes for *The Duchess of Padua* – and even
for the American touring production of *Vera*. Horatio Lloyd was, in some
measure, reassured.[21]

He wanted to do what he could to help the young lovers. Constance's
happiness was his first consideration, and he felt she would be happy with
Wilde. At that time she was receiving an allowance from her grandfather
of £250 a year, though, on the event of his death, she was due to inherit a
portion of his estate. He proposed that this arrangement be brought forward, and £5,000 be settled in a trust fund, to provide Constance with an
immediate income of some £400 per annum. It was a generous provision.[22]
And to Wilde, beset with his debts and unsure of his earnings, it must have
registered as a huge relief. It appeared to offer the prospect of a life free
from immediate financial worry.

Not that Wilde was allowed to abandon his cares. A date for the wedding
had still to be set, and Constance's grandfather suggested it be delayed at
least until Wilde had paid off a further £300 of debt. Wilde, full of self-
confidence, thought this could be achieved by the coming April.[23]

Happy plans and reveries about Constance now dominated his thoughts

---

*   This £300 repayment had probably come, not from the proceeds of lecturing, but from
    the sale of the fishing lodge at Illaunroe. Wilde had received an offer for this amount on
    10 December 1883, and completed the sale in the new year.

as he travelled around the country, 'civilizing the provinces'. He devoted himself to doing 'all the foolish things which wise lovers do'. He wrote to her often and telegraphed her twice a day. He would race back to London to see her between lectures, sometimes even forgoing supper to snatch an evening with his beloved. He presented her with an engagement ring of his own design: two pearls enclosed in a heart formed of diamonds. The meetings were joyous; the partings brought sorrow. 'My darling love,' Constance wrote after one fleeting visit, 'I am sorry I was so silly: you take all my strength away. I have no power to do anything but just love you when you are with me, and I cannot fight against my dread of your going away... I know it is only for three days.'[24]

Wilde seems to have told Constance something of his past attachments – to Florence Balcombe, to Lillie Langtry, perhaps even to Violet Hunt and Hattie Crocker. He received a generous absolution. 'I don't think I shall ever be jealous, certainly not jealous now of anyone: I trust in you for the present. I am content to let the past be buried, it does not belong to me: for the future trust and faith will come, and when I have you for my husband, I will hold you fast with chains of love and devotion so that you shall never leave me, or love anyone as long as I can love and comfort [you].'[25]

The news that Wilde was to be married appeared first in the *World* at the beginning of December (placed there, no doubt, by Willie), and rapidly spread through the press.* His bride-to-be's name began to be reported in mid-December, before being formally announced later in the month. Wilde was used to being 'paragraphed', but for Constance it must have been a rude shock to find herself the object of so much coarse journalistic speculation – regarding the size of her dowry, her artistic tastes and her chances of happiness; one newspaper rated them low on the grounds that 'to please Oscar long will require more than human perfection'.[26]

Wilde's last lecture of the year was at the Crystal Palace. Constance attended with her aunt, Mary Napier. After that there was a break in the schedule over Christmas, and Wilde was able to spend the days in London, and with Constance. They went together to the theatre most evenings. At St James's the cast peeked through the curtains at the interval to glimpse 'Bunthorne' and his bride-to-be.[27]

---

* At the same period the papers were also reporting – rather less reliably – that Wilde was going to be touring the provinces in a play he had just completed; and that he was about to bring out a new book of poems, in which he had 'studied more what he calls the "conventionalities" of English morality than in the old one'.

Whistler entered enthusiastically into Wilde's happiness. He insisted on hosting one of his Sunday breakfasts in Constance's honour. There was some doubt, though, as to whether she would be able to attend, Aunt Emily deeming such bohemian gatherings unsuitable for a 'young unmarried lady'. But, after a plea from Wilde, the objections were waived on the condition that it should not establish 'a precedent for any more visiting of a like kind', and that Otho should accompany her as chaperone.[28]

Although Constance had speedily come to accept Whistler's great importance, Wilde did jokingly describe her to Waldo Story as 'quite perfect except that she does not think Jimmy the only painter that ever really existed: she would like to bring Titian or somebody in by the back door'. He went on: 'She knows I am the greatest poet, so in literature she is all right: and I have explained to her that you are the greatest sculptor: art instruction cannot go further.'[29] All who saw Wilde were struck by his happiness and excitement. Celebrating Boxing Day with the Sickerts, he inadvertently left two gold sovereigns behind on his chair. Mrs Sickert wrote, 'I feel inclined to scold you for being so careless but you are too happy to mind even a severe lecture so I will not waste one.'[30]

Wilde was due to restart his own lecturing in the new year with a two-and-a-half-week tour of Ireland. He left Constance with a pet marmoset to keep her company in his absence; it was – as a further homage to Whistler – christened 'Jimmy'.* Alas, he barely lasted a week: 'I am forlorn and miserable,' Constance wrote to Wilde on 4 January. 'Is it my fault that everything you give me has an untimely end? I don't think he suffered much as he looks so pretty.'[31] Wilde, though, remained fixed on the prettiness of his beloved. Towards the end of January 1884 he wrote to Lillie Langtry, who was back in America, to tell her – after a certain amount of tactful praise for her latest dramatic triumph – that he was 'to marry a grave, slight, violet-eyed little Artemis, with great coils of heavy brown hair which make her flower-like head droop like a flower, and wonderful ivory hands which draw music from the piano so sweet that the birds stop singing to listen to her'. Langtry was already aware of the attachment, but happy to hear it confirmed.[32]

With Wilde lecturing across the British Isles almost without a break from the second half of January to the end of March, the chances for seeing the

---

*   According to not entirely reliable press reports, Whistler repaid the compliment by naming a kitten that he had been given 'Oscar'. He was surprised, however, when 'Oscar' subsequently had kittens.

violet-eyed Artemis were few. He was obliged to console himself with the beauties of nature. In February he had a series of dates in the Lake District and its environs (lecturing at Carlisle, Workington, Cockermouth, Maryport and Ulverston). It was a landscape he knew from poetry, and also from the descriptions of Ruskin, who lived at Coniston. Between engagements Wilde visited Keswick, and, after being shown over the art school there, was taken by the principal for a walk along the banks of Derwentwater.

The local newspaper reported his enthusiastic response: 'This,' said he, 'is lovely'. He was delighted to spot Lodore, the gushing cataract about which Robert Southey had written his delightful onomatopoeic poem. The effect of the atmosphere was, he considered, 'just right for seeing a picture of this sort. The lake is just large enough for beauty. In America the lakes are like seas, where you lose sight of land, and there are cruel storms which wreck vessels.' He declared that 'open footpaths should exist through all beautiful places everywhere, and that it was a mistake to think the public were ruthless destroyers of property when admitted to private grounds. He inquired very closely into the subject of a railway being injurious to the effect of beautiful scenery, and said, without giving a direct opinion on the matter, "It must be a pleasant thing to look out of a first-class saloon carriage and see the beauties as you pass," and thought they would be better enjoyed when perfectly at one's ease.'[33]

Wilde's unceasing round of lectures did keep his name before the public. In the provinces at least he remained 'The Apostle of Aestheticism'. And his 'mission' – as he liked to call it – was not without effect. The design ideas of Aestheticism were gradually beginning to take hold and spread. After his lecture in Gainsborough, it was recalled, 'much Victorian furniture went out the back door'. He inspired some of the residents to become 'intrigued' by Liberty furniture and to start buying it for their homes.[34] The paint manufacturer Theodore Mander and his wife, having attended Wilde's Wolverhampton talk on 'The House Beautiful', began to transform his own house, Wightwick Manor, into an Aesthetic showcase of Morris fabrics and Arts and Crafts design.

In London, though, Wilde was coming to be regarded essentially as a society figure: an amusing 'sayer of smart things'. Although it was allowed that he was distinct, interesting and 'essentially modern', his approaching marriage and new dandified look seemed to suggest that he had given up the extravagances of his youth 'and accepted life'. This, at least, was the verdict when he appeared, that May, elegantly caricatured by 'Ape' in *Vanity Fair*'s

prestigious 'Men of the Day' series.[35] Besides a mention of his 'somewhat startling' 1881 volume of poems – and a fleeting allusion to his having 'produced a play' – the short accompanying article did little to suggest that Wilde was actually a writer.

And, indeed, against the background of constant provincial lecturing, it was a struggle to keep sight of his literary ambitions. He managed to produce one little love poem, which was published in the brochure for a charity event held at the Royal Albert Hall.[36] And he continued his search for someone to produce *The Duchess of Padua* – even drawing a positive, if self-deprecatory, response from the actress Ada Cavendish.[37] Her other commitments, however, and her uncertain health, meant that the plan could not be carried forward at once. Wilde himself received an interesting inquiry, from the young actor-manager Courtenay Thorpe, asking if he might provide a 'strong Play... modern dress – small cast', suitable for the coming summer season.[38] The notion of writing a modern-dress play had a definite appeal. Wilde had confided to a friend in New York that he would 'like to write a comedy', but 'did not think any manager would ever produce it'.[39] Here, it seemed, was a manager who might be interested in such a piece. But the pressures of Wilde's schedule left too little time for serious composition.

Wilde's few moments of leisure, moreover, were taken up with plans for the wedding. The date slipped back from April to the end of May. It was not to be rushed. The occasion was to be an Aesthetic event. Wilde, in his lectures on 'The House Beautiful', touched upon the subject of women's dress, urging 'more colour and brightness', greater simplicity of line, a ban on corsets and artificial flowers, and the absence of 'all useless and encumbering bows, flounces, knots, and other such meaningless things'. He cited as examples to follow: 'ancient Greek drapery', and the dresses of Renaissance Venice, Carolian England, or 'the period of Gainsborough'.[40] Anxious to see these ideals embodied, he involved himself in the design of Constance's wedding dress, and also the dresses for the six bridesmaids. It was a happy collaboration, as Constance had a great interest in fashion, and an able accomplice in her dressmaker, Adeline Nettleship, wife of the painter John Nettleship.[41]

The practicalities of their future married life had also to be addressed. Where were they to live? Wilde wanted to return to Chelsea, and by the end of March Constance could tell friends, 'We have been looking at a house in Tite Street, which I think we are likely to take.' Number 16 was part of new terraced development, just up from where Whistler had his studio (and

Frank Miles still had his house.) In due course, having paid a premium, they took a twenty-one-year lease on the property.[42]

Wilde asked Whistler to devise a decorative scheme for the new house, but was told, 'No, Oscar, you have been lecturing to us about the House Beautiful; now is our chance to show us one.'[43] Wilde certainly had ideas of his own, but he did enlist the assistance of Godwin to extend them and put them into practice. They evolved elaborate plans for built-in furniture, rare fabrics and interesting finishes. It soon became clear that more ready money would be needed. In the weeks before the wedding Wilde – rather than reducing his debts – was making arrangements to borrow £1,000 from Constance's trust fund, to be repaid with interest in due course.[44] It was probably over this transaction that Wilde told the Lloyd family solicitor, Mr Hargrove, that he was not sure when he could repay the amount, 'but I could write you a sonnet, if you think that *that* would be of any help'.[45]

The wedding took place on the afternoon of Thursday 29 May at St James's Church, Sussex Gardens, not far from Lancaster Gate.[46] The time and place had been kept out of the press to avoid the possibility of crowds gathering. Invited guests received special tickets. Horatio Lloyd was too ill to attend. 'There is only this much to be recorded about' the wedding cere-mony, reported the *World* with deliberate understatement: 'That the bride, accompanied by six pretty bridesmaids, looked charming, that Oscar bore himself with calm dignity; and that all most intimately concerned in the affair seemed thoroughly pleased. A happy little group of *intimes* saw them off at Charing Cross.'

This account failed to mention – as others did not – the arrival of a telegram from Whistler: 'Fear I may not be able to reach you in time for the ceremony. Don't wait.'[47] It did not list the presence of Burne-Jones and his family, George Lewis and his wife, or Mrs Bernard Beere, in the crowd of guests, nor the fifty or so local parishioners who insisted on being admitted to the event. The *World* gave no details of the various dresses on view: the bride's elegantly simple satin robe – of a pale 'cowslip tint'– with its high ruff and puffed 'Venetian' sleeves; the two youngest bridesmaids in 'some-what startling but aesthetic costumes of ripe gooseberry colour with yellow sashes' – 'after Joshua Reynolds'; the four older girls in 'faint red silk skirts over dresses of pale blue flowered *mousseline de laine*'. It did not describe the fine silver girdle – 'gift of the bridegroom' – around Constance's waist, nor the ingenious linked wedding ring that was placed on her finger. It was silent on the various allusions to classical antiquity: the saffron-coloured veil (such

as 'Greek maidens wore on their wedding day') arranged over a wreath of 'highly classical' myrtle ('a more poetical' adornment than the conventional orange blossom). It said nothing about Lady Wilde looking splendid in grey, or Oscar appearing 'in the ordinary and commonplace frock coat of the period'. It ignored Willie's role as best man and left unrecorded Wilde's plaintive aside to Margaret Burne-Jones: 'Miss Margaret, the clergyman was so dreadfully ugly that I have grave doubts whether the marriage is valid.'[48] They were doubts he intended to overcome.

4

∞∞∞∞∞

New Relations

'It is not easy to exhaust the message of Paris.'

OSCAR WILDE

The honeymoon began in Paris. It was a social and cultural whirl of dinners and lunches (attended and given), play going, exhibition visiting, reading and fun. Wilde was delighted to introduce his bride to Bourget and Sargent, his companions of the previous year; and also to the young Irish-American sculptor John Donoghue, whose work Wilde had praised in Chicago and who was exhibiting in the Salon that summer (Constance was impressed by his 'Irish blue eyes').* All who saw them together recognized that Wilde was 'ecstatically in love' with his bride.[1] When Sherard called on them at the Hôtel Wagram on the rue de Rivoli Wilde took him off, but paused almost immediately at a market stall to buy some flowers to send back to Constance, together with a note of 'impassioned adoration'. He seemed eager to discourse on the joys of matrimony, though

---

*   Sargent invited Wilde to visit his studio for a sneak preview of his own exhibition paint-ing for that year (the soon-to-be notorious 'Madame X'), telling him, 'You will find me still working on my portrait of Mme Gautreau which will go to the Salon on Thursday if it is finished and good. They will tell you I'm out but you must come and knock at the door: toc – toc-toc. You will see my sitter who looks like Phryné [the celebrated ancient Greek courtesan].'

Sherard (uncharacteristically) interrupted his opening – 'It's wonderful when a young virgin…' – and turned the talk to less intimate matters. Sherard, indeed, became so comically irritated by Wilde's superabundant happiness that he claimed – following an evening spent together with the joyful newlyweds – that he wanted to draw the blade from his swordstick and run it through his friend. Constance laughingly confiscated the stick, to prevent the tragedy.[2]

To a journalist from the *Morning News* who presented himself at the Hôtel Wagram, Wilde declared himself 'too happy to be interviewed' – though he then proceeded to give his views about novel reading ('I never read from the beginning… It is the only way to stimulate the curiosity that books, with their regular openings, always fail to rouse'), about dropping friends ('I would make it a positive satisfaction instead of a regret. Why should we not joyfully admit that there are some people we do not want to see again? It is not ingratitude, it is not indifference. They have simply given us all they have to give'), and about Sarah Bernhardt's Lady Macbeth ('There is nothing like it on our stage, and it is her finest creation. I say her creation deliberately, because to my mind it is utterly impertinent to talk of Shakespeare's *Macbeth*… Shakespeare is only one of the parties. The second is the artist through whose mind it passes. When the two together combine to give me an acceptable hero, that is all I ask').[3]

The wonders of married life outstripped those of Niagara Falls and the Atlantic Ocean: Wilde, as he wrote to a friend, was 'not disappointed'. His letter – reported in the press as 'thoroughly characteristic'– went on to say that he felt 'confident of his ability to sustain its labours and anxieties, and [saw] an opportunity in his new relation, of realizing a poetical conception which he has long entertained. He says that Lord Beaconsfield taught the peers of England a new style of oratory, and that he intends to set an example of the pervading influence of art on matrimony.'[4]

Constance was prepared to enter into this vision, certainly if it meant wearing nice frocks. Some voices in the press might snipe that she was merely 'a lay figure on whom Oscar may exhibit practical illustrations of his grotesque ideas of the beautiful and appropriate in feminine attire'. But she was delighted to tell her brother that her newest dress was creating a 'sensation' in Paris.[5] The *Lady's Pictorial* noted that the French ladies, despite their conventional tastes, were impressed by the 'picturesque becomingness' of Constance's outfits. And picturesque they were: 'Mrs Oscar Wilde, in her large white plumed hats, in her long dust cloaks of creamy alpaca richly

trimmed with ruches of coffee coloured lace, in her fresh and somewhat quaintly-made gowns of white muslin, usually relieved by touches of golden ribbon, or with yellow floss silk embroideries, is declared "charmante" and to be dressed with absolute good taste.'[6]

Amid the sun-filled pleasures of the honeymoon, Wilde continued his studies, begun the previous year, in the literature of French decadence. There was only one book to read: all Paris was talking of it. J.-K. Huysmans' À Rebours – published just a fortnight beforehand – had, in its author's words, fallen 'like a meteorite into the literary fairground, provoking anger and stupefaction' among the press, and awed wonder among the literary elect. It appeared as the very breviary of decadence: the strange tale of Duc Jean des Esseintes, a neurotic aristocrat, who, in flight from the materialism of the age, was devoting himself to a life of ultra-Aesthetic Paterian sensation-seeking in defiance of all conventional codes and moralities.

Grown weary of the obvious forms of hedonistic indulgence, he retreated to his country estate, and into the ever more refined realms of art and artificiality, memory and dream.[7] In a progression of ornately wrought chapters Huysmans delineated his protagonist's collection of poisonous plants and his store of hallucinatory perfumes, his fascination with late Latin prose, his delight in the paintings of Gustave Moreau and the poetry of Baudelaire, his love of the music of Wagner and the philosophy of Schopenhauer, while also mentioning his jewel-encrusted tortoise (an hommage to Robert de Montesquiou's fabled pet). The catalogue of des Esseintes' past excesses included a funereal banquet at which both the food and decor were black, and the guests were waited upon by naked 'negresses' in silver stockings. Among his past lovers were a strapping American trapeze artist, a lady ventriloquist (who would recite the dialogue between the Sphinx and Chimera from Flaubert's Temptation of St Antony as part of their foreplay) and – in a final abandonment of the female sex – a disconcerting young man, with a mincing walk, who picked him up in the street.

Wilde gave a richly coloured evocation of the book's 'poisonous' power: 'It seemed to [the reader] that in exquisite raiment, and to the delicate sound of flutes, the sins of the world were passing in dumb show before him. Things that he had dimly dreamed of were suddenly made real to him. Things of which he had never dreamed were gradually revealed.' To the reporter from the Morning News he remarked – rather more prosaically – that À Rebours was 'one of the best' books he had ever seen.[8] Although des Esseintes' project was doomed to ultimate failure, the details of his attempt were relayed with

such vividness as to seem almost convincing. Certainly Wilde was tempted to believe. At the very moment that he was embracing the happy conventions of married life, he found himself beguiled by an image of defiance – against convention, against nature, against morality, against the grain. But the poison of the book was slow-working. The honeymoon was still to be enjoyed. Paris was followed by a 'delightful week' at Dieppe.

Wilde and Constance returned to London on 24 June, only to find that they had nowhere to live; work at Tite Street was behind schedule. Wilde consulted with Godwin, anxious 'to press on the laggards'.[9] A familiar tale of building woe ensured. Exasperated by the poor quality of the work that *had* been done, Wilde sacked the contractor (Mr Green) who promptly seized some of the furniture and sued Wilde for non-payment of his bill. The case was only settled, after weeks of wrangling, on the eve of trial. Meanwhile a new builder, Mr Sharpe, engaged by Godwin, was soon exceeding his estimates, as he found that he had to re-do much of the 'imperfect work done by Green' (by the end of November his bill had reached £222 17s, and there was more to come).[10] Unable to move into their new home, the Wildes – after a very brief stay at Lancaster Gate – squeezed themselves into Oscar's lodgings at Charles Street. From there they launched themselves into the tail end of the London season. Oscar did not have to return to lecturing until the autumn.

They were a celebrity couple, the embodiment of married Aestheticism. The press engaged in much would-be funny speculation about the details of their new life. One skit had Constance at the dinner table asking, 'Which do you prefer, sunflower dried, or some toasted lily of the valley?' To her consternation, Oscar confesses that – in the seclusion of his own home – he would like 'some beef and potatoes and bread and a bottle of ale'.[11]

Wilde was noted – 'fat and merry' – at the Millais' summer ball. And if he was not wearing a lily in his buttonhole, 'to make up for it, his wife had her front covered in great water-lilies'.[12] As a couple they manned a stall at the fashionable charity fete held in the midst of the 'International Health Exhibition' at South Kensington. Good-naturedly Wilde had consented to sell the 'floral gifts' – which included 'an extensive assortment of sunflowers and lilies'.[13] At receptions and gallery openings the Wildes came to be objects of 'public interest' to rival even Lillie Langtry.[14] They attracted attention in the street, not all of it wanted. Walking down the King's Road, Oscar in a many-buttoned suit 'like a glorified page's costume', Constance in a 'large picture hat' decked with white feathers, they were hailed by a gang

of street urchins as, "Amlet and Ophelia out for a walk'. 'You are quite right,' Wilde replied, 'we are.'[15]

The drama of Constance's costumes, coupled with her shyness, meant that – in social settings – she was sometimes seen as being overwhelmed by both her clothes and her husband. At one tea party, she was – as Laura Troubridge put it –'dressed for the part' in 'drimp white muslin with absolutely no bustle, saffron-coloured silk swathed around her shoulders, a huge cartwheel Gainsborough hat, white, and bright yellow stockings and shoes'; while Oscar was being 'amusing, of course', she looked 'too hopeless'.[16] But this obscured her ready complicity in the project, and also her real excitement in being married. After a girlhood dominated by an uncaring mother and a disapproving aunt, she was thrilled at the possibilities of her new life. She found an ally and a friend, too, in Lady Wilde.

The round of post-honeymoon pleasure was interrupted (briefly) by Horatio Lloyd's death on 18 July. The event was not unexpected, and if it robbed Constance of one of her few supporters, it did bring her into her full inheritance. Her £5,000 trust fund was more than doubled, and her income along with it. With over £800 a year, there would be money for Tite Street and for dresses.[17] Financial planning, though, was almost as alien to Constance as it was to Oscar. They were a blithely improvident pair. A relative who had given them, as a wedding present, a generous cheque with which to buy something 'useful' was exasperated when they declared excitedly that they had spent the entire amount on a pair of Apostle spoons.[18]

Wilde did earn some money that summer, standing in as the *Vanity Fair* theatre critic while Willie was away on holiday.[19] It was, though, his own theatrical plans that continued to engage him most, with his hopes still fixed on *The Duchess of Padua*. Ada Cavendish had proved a broken reed, but – in between discussions about the Tite Street furnishings – he had enthused Godwin with the idea of producing the play. Godwin, a devotee of the theatre, with a particular interest in historically accurate costume and stage design, saw rich possibilities in Wilde's Italian tragedy. He began to map out plans for an elaborate production, suggesting – among other things – that the action be transferred from the sixteenth century to the fourteenth. He opened negotiations, too, with the actress Anna Conover (and her business manager, Philip Beck), who had recently taken over the Olympic Theatre, off the Strand. A contract was drawn up for a London opening early in 1885, followed by a provincial tour. Despite the scheme being well advanced, it faltered that November. There were rumours in the

press that Wilde's 'stout refusal' to alter 'a single line' may have contributed to the impasse. But given his eagerness to collaborate with actresses on previous occasions, this seems unlikely. The plan, however, was not revived. Wilde's hopes for the *Duchess* were again disappointed.[20]

The fraught negotiations over the play took place amid the demands of the autumn lecture season. Wilde had returned to the fray at the beginning of October, under the direction of a new young tour manager, George Appleton. He had prepared two new talks for the coming tour: one on 'Dress' (his leading item) and another on 'The Value of Art in Modern Life'.[21] The talk on 'Dress' – and the need to reform it – was first delivered at Ealing on 1 October 1884; it was a didactic affair, like 'The House Beautiful', part of Wilde's 'mission' to bring beauty into everyday life. And it built upon the Aesthetic ideas of his earlier lectures but with a new focus on the healthful effects of good clothing. This was a topical slant encouraged by that summer's 'International Health Exhibition'. Godwin had actually lectured at the exhibition on 'Dress and its Relation to Health and Climate', and Wilde borrowed freely from his ideas.[22]

Wilde's lecture sought to rescue 'dress' from the ephemeral folly of 'fashion', and restore it to the eternal laws of art – and good sense. 'After all,' he demanded, 'what is fashion, [but] a form of ugliness so absolutely unbearable that they have to alter it every six months.' In a bracing mix of prescription and proscription he launched into a succession of popular fads, decrying high-heeled boots, fancy French bonnets, unnecessary bows, 'spotted veils', corsets, the 'dress improver' (a sort of bustle), divided skirts, linen underclothes, and (for men) the 'monstrously ugly' top hat. There was a constant strain of humour, particularly on the subject of bonnets: 'If I told you the sum of money spent every year on bonnets alone, I am quite sure half of you would be filled with remorse, and the other half with desperation'; 'I have lately seen a very large picture [of a bonnet, accompanied by the note:] "With this kind of bonnet the mouth is worn slightly open"'. Among Wilde's most memorable asides was the observation that 'a Lancashire mill girl, with a shawl over her shoulders and wearing clogs, knows more about dress than a fashionable London lady recently returned from Paris, because in the former case there is comfort, while in the latter there is discomfort'.[23]

On the prescriptive side, Wilde suggested 'combining the German principle of science with the Greek principle of beauty' to create clothing that would ally 'health, comfort and Art' with the stamp of 'individuality'. He advocated finely spun woollen garments – as recommended by 'Dr Gustav

Jaeger of Stuttgart' – which should hang from the shoulder, rather than the waist or hip. There was to be no 'fancy dress' imitation of ancient Greek models, only a similar sense of simplicity and fitness, and a comparable understanding of colour and form. Addressing men's attire, he praised the clothes of peasants, 'fisher-folk', sportsmen, and seventeenth-century cavaliers – and suggested they could be usefully adapted for modern urban use, to produce a wardrobe of soft hats, double-breasted coats, warm cloaks and high-topped boots.[24]

The subject of dress was, for many, a fascinating one. When an appreciative account of the Ealing lecture appeared in the Pall Mall Gazette (a paper that had previously tended to disparage Wilde), it provoked an immediate flurry of correspondence. The opportunity was not to be missed. As Wilde explained to a friend, the surest way to fame and reputation was through self-advertisement: 'Every time I see my name is mentioned in the paper, I write at once to admit that I am the Messiah.'[25] Requesting 'an opportunity to indulge that most charming of all pleasures, the pleasure of answering one's critics', he sent a long letter to the paper, admitting that he was indeed the Messiah of dress reform, and re-affirming all his principal views.[26]

It helped that Wilde now had an entrée at the magazine through his old Oxford friend Alfred Milner. Milner, who was delaying the start of a political career by working as the paper's deputy editor, had invited Wilde to the Pall Mall Gazette's offices in May, to join a select band of 'worthies' attending a 'thought-reading' demonstration; Wilde had repaid the consideration by offering his views on the office decor, and by inviting Milner to his wedding.* And the connection had been maintained.[27] Wilde's letter to the paper stimulated further debate, and prompted a second – even longer – Wildean missive the following month, offering 'More Radical Ideas Upon Dress Reform'. By the end of the year even the 'dull crowd' was aware of Wilde's position as a leading 'dress reformer'. He was referred to, facetiously, by some as 'the dress-improver'.[28]

Wilde's 'Dress' lecture – as well as its more general companion piece about 'The Value of Art in Modern Life' – proved popular with the institutes

---

* As the Pall Mall Gazette itself reported, with a good humour to match Wilde's own: 'A lecture on art from one so distinguished and so eccentric as Mr. Oscar Wilde is worth hearing. And above all he is a candid critic. "Your decorations," he said, "are absurd. There is no system obeyed. One thought, like harmony in music, should pervade the whole. Does it? No. They show no soul. Can you exist without a soul? No soul, no harmony, and no…" "Sunflowers," suggested some one. "No, a flower is but an incident."'

and societies. Appleton was able to secure over sixty bookings, stretching from October 1884 into February 1885. Wilde was condemned to another winter of railway waiting rooms and provincial hotels. He read much on his travels. He saw old friends where he could – catching up with William Ward in Bristol and Hunter-Blair at Edinburgh. Often, though, he was lonely. From the Balmoral Hotel, Edinburgh, he wrote to Constance (the only one of his many letters to her to survive):

> DEAR AND BELOVED, Here am I, and you at the Antipodes. O execrable facts, that keep our lips from kissing, though our souls are one.
>
> What can I tell you by letter? Alas! nothing that I would tell you. The messages of the gods to each other travel not by pen and ink and indeed your bodily presence here would not make you more real: for I feel your fingers in my hair, and your cheek brushing mine. The air is full of the music of your voice, my soul and body seem no longer mine, but mingled in some exquisite ecstasy with yours. I feel incomplete without you.
>
> Ever and ever yours, OSCAR.

As in other aspects of his life, Wilde was ready to use exaggerated modes to express real feelings.

Separated from Constance and London, he was often at the mercy of his hosts. At almost every stopping place he had to endure a guided tour of the local art school, foundry or pottery works. There were invitations, too, to dine with local worthies. In some towns, though, sympathetic spirits would seek him out, and provide a brief respite. The Yorkshire artist William Howgate offered to show him 'the few places of interest that are to be seen in Leeds'. At Birmingham Wilde enjoyed a 'charming meeting' and some 'golden hours' with well-to-do young art lover called Philip Griffiths.[29] And after his Bradford lecture (3 December 1884) Wilde gratefully accepted an invitation to stay the night with the prosperous Shalders family at their Gothic villa in Manningham – even if he disconcerted his hostess the following morning by disdaining the hearty Yorkshire breakfast with the remark that it would be 'perfection' if he might have, instead, 'a handful of raspberries, pale yellow raspberries'.[30]

Such personal encounters – with interested people in Aesthetic settings – must have given some encouragement to Wilde and his hopes for his 'mission'. The size of his audiences too was, for the most part, heartening. At Glasgow (19 December) he lectured before a massive crowd of some 5,000

people; there was an 'excellent' turnout at Bristol (14 October), and a notably crowded house at the Harborne & Edgbaston Institute (4 November). If attendances were disappointing at Leeds and Sheffield, the appalling weather was held responsible.[31] Some sections of the press continued to carp, but most reports were positive. There was particular support for Wilde's campaign against that 'ugly, costly and comfortless abomination, the British top-hat'.[32] And if a note of disappointment was occasionally sounded, it was that Wilde did not 'practice what he preaches more extensively' in his own attire, and don 'doublet' and Hessian boots. Although, the following year, he did create a minor sensation with a curiously pleated red-bronze coat, fashioned – after his own design – to suggest the form of a violoncello,[33] in the winter of 1884 he did not 'seem induced to go beyond the cloak and broad-brimmed hat'.[34]

Whatever his successes on the road, there was no disguising a mounting sense of dissatisfaction – with the demands of constant touring, with the protracted delays over the Tite Street house (it was still not ready at Christmas 1884), and with the ephemeral nature of lecturing itself. Willie tried to console Constance, who shared these frustrations, with the remark, 'When you are settled in the fairest little nest in Tite Street, [Oscar] can and will I know sit down and write more lasting work than lectures, but for the passing "now" it is wise and right of him to keep "on the war path" – even if he has to leave his wife for a moment.' He considered that Oscar's punishing schedule was 'rais[ing] him up' and 'show[ing] people how earnest he is in the work he has taken up'.[35] Constance's longing for domestic calm was heightened by the fact that she was now pregnant. It was rather unkindly suggested by Violet Fane that Wilde's own steadily increasing girth might be in sympathy with his wife's condition.[36]

The newlyweds were finally able to move into their home at the end of the year, although almost immediately Wilde had to depart on tour again, leaving Constance to finalize the furnishing details alone. And although the New Year schedule was not quite as fraught as previous months, it still devoured his time and energy.

In the brief respites from touring, however, Wilde began to settle himself into 16 Tite Street, and to show it off. He, together with Godwin and Constance – who had frequently displayed a practicality wanting in her two male collaborators – had created something strikingly novel and distinctive. One of their first visitors, Douglas Ainslie (a young friend of the Lloyds, who, as a teenaged Etonian in the summer holidays of 1882, had developed

a tremendous crush on Constance) was quite bowled over. Constance reported to her brother that he thought 'our house the most charming he has ever
been in, and could hardly tear himself away'.[37]

The conventional red-brick terraced unit had been transformed into
an Aesthetic temple. The dominant themes of the interior were lightness
and simplicity, tempered with richer notes of exoticism and colour. But the
drama began at the front door. It was painted in gloss white, to look almost
like enamel. The effect was the more startling since all the other houses in
the terrace had doors stained or grained in shades of brown. When Wilde
received an anonymous note from a 'Disgusted Neighbour' that such a front
door was rank 'advertisement' intended only to make known that 'Mr Oscar
Wilde, the Titan of Tite Street is a being apart and not to be confused with
other common and garden residents' – he remarked, with a weary sigh,
'Symbolism not advertisement... the door of this house is painted white
because no one must bring an evil thought into the house which shelters the
whitest and purest soul in all the world, my beautiful and dearly loved wife.'[38]

The house abounded in such conceits. In Constance's elegantly fitted-
out bedroom – on the second floor, at the front – the lower part of the wall
was painted pink, the upper part green, with a narrow white line marking
the division. The idea was 'to symbolize a sea-shell' – an allusion to both
the natural world and the birth of Venus.[39]

Every detail of colour, form, texture and decoration had been considered.
Visitors were welcomed into a surprisingly 'ordinary' white painted hallway,
its side wall adorned with two large white-framed engravings – of 'Apollo
and the Muses' and 'Diana and Nymphs Bathing' – suggesting, perhaps,
the master and mistress of the house. A door on the right opened into the
library, a room that was still being fitted out during most of 1885. Beyond
this a white painted staircase with golden-yellow matting, set at right angles
to the hall, led up to the drawing rooms on the first floor. The larger front
drawing room was a light and airy space, its twin bow windows, framed
with off-white curtains, looking across the street towards the gardens of the
Royal Victoria Hospital. Both walls and mouldings were 'all white' and left
bare 'so as not to break the lines', but the ceiling was panelled in squares of
dull-gold 'Japanese leather-paper' – and from four pendants hung large blue
and white barrel-shaped Japanese paper lanterns. The fireplace, flanked by
low built-in 'three-cornered divans', was in the 'Queen Anne' style. Set into
the white painted moulding above the mantelpiece was the bronze plaque
given to Wilde by John Donoghue, with its lines from 'Requiescat', while on

the mantel shelf itself stood the bust of Augustus that Wilde had received for winning the Newdigate.

The furniture was sparse. One early visitor – Laura Troubridge's suitor, Adrian Hope – thought it looked as though the room had been 'cleared for a dance' for which 'the matting did not look too inviting'. There were only four chairs – two with arms, two without – all designed by Godwin, all 'white enamelled' and cane seated, and all appearing to Hope's eye as 'stiff,' 'uncomfy' and 'too slight and slender for Oscar's weight'. For those seeking more comfort there was 'an old settee in gold lacquer' (a present from Mrs Bloomfield Moore). Beside this sofa stood a little Louis Seize side table dotted with a few choice curios – including, it was claimed, Marie Antoinette's gold key to the Trianon. There were two other tables, both designed by Godwin; small 'Japanese' pieces, one octagonal on spindle-legs, the other oblong and made of bamboo. The only definite note of colour in the room was provided by the cushions (from Liberty), which were covered with a 'very quiet green' fabric of 'unobtrusive pattern'.*

By contrast the back drawing room, on the same floor, just across the curtained-off landing, was a glowing den of low tones and rich patterning. Adrian Hope described it as having 'a very distinct Turkish note'. There were no chairs at all – only a low divan running around two sides of the room with 'queer little Eastern inlaid tables' ranged about. The dado was painted some dark unspecified tint, the ceiling was 'gorgeous', and the floor matting was strewn with oriental rugs. The window (looking onto the 'slum' cottages of the inaptly named 'Paradise Walk' at the back of Tite Street) was obscured by a wooden lattice 'copied from a Cairo pattern'. A square wooden pillar, just inside the doorway, was set with plaques of coloured Italian marbles, while around the architrave ran an inscription, done in gilt, red and blue, from Wilde's 'Garden of Eros': 'Spirit of Beauty! tarry still awhile, / They are not dead, thine ancient votaries, / Some few there are to whom thy radiant smile / Is better than a thousand victories.' For many this was the most delightful room in the house. Adrian Hope fell in love with it at first sight.

---

*   Not long afterwards, to add more colour and interest, the lower section of the walls were painted 'a dull green', and hung with pictures: a full-length portrait of Oscar in his frock coat by Harper Pennington (a wedding present from the artist), and 'small white framed' prints and drawings by Whistler, Walter Crane, Mortimer Menpes and others; also the manuscript of Keats's sonnet 'On Blue'. The 'quiet green cushions' were augmented with pink satin ones.

Others favoured the dining room, which was on the ground floor at the far end of the hallway. It was a symphony in white: ivory white walls; brilliant white woodwork (including a convenient foot-wide shelf running around the whole room); curtains of creamy white 'African muslin'; a green-and-blue William Morris carpet with white patterning; white painted Chippendale chairs; and an oblong dining table covered with an unbleached linen tablecloth. Colour came from 'the rare glass and china', from the napkins and the carefully chosen flowers. In a period of dark-hued dining rooms the effect was startlingly original. And – as with Wilde's views on dress reform – it claimed to combine the Aesthetic with the hygienic. The prevailing whiteness allowed the room to be kept 'clean and fresh', while also providing, Wilde suggested, 'the only background against which a man looks picturesque in evening dress'.[40]

At the top of the house Wilde had his study, two small attic rooms knocked into one, with a little balcony looking down on to the street. It was a cosy book-lined garret, the exposed walls covered with matting, the woodwork painted his favourite vermilion. Lending their associative magic were a mahogany writing table said to have belonged to Carlyle, and a white plaster bust of the Hermes of Olympia.[41]

Although Wilde – and the world – may have considered the house a fit setting for the 'Apostle of Aestheticism', it was really far finer and more splendid than either his status or his own income warranted. Indeed the expense of completing the work seems to have taxed even Constance's resources, and they were obliged to borrow a further £500 from her brother Otho.[42] Wilde hoped, though, that his new vermilion study might inspire him not merely to more 'lasting' but to more remunerative work. It seems that, almost upon arrival at Tite Street, he may have commenced writing a new drama. Certainly at the beginning of February 1885 he sought a meeting with the successful comic dramatist B. C. Stephenson 'to talk about a play'.[43] Nothing, though, came of the project.*

Living in Chelsea brought the Wildes new neighbours and friends. They were taken up by a wealthy young polymath called Edward Heron-Allen,

---

* It is possible that a record of Wilde's play idea is preserved in the twenty-eight draft manuscript pages of 'The Wife's Tragedy' – an unfinished, unpublished and undated work now in the Clark Library. The play concerns the marital difficulties of a young English poet and his wife. Among its epigrams and witticisms are: '[Lord Merton has inherited] a lot of blue china... I hope he lives up to it'; and 'Women are not made to be believed in or disbelieved in – they're made to be loved.'

who, besides interests in science, literature, heraldry, violin making and 'asparagus culture', was an enthusiastic chiromancer. He lost no time in reading both Constance and Oscar's palms. Wilde inscribed his page in Heron-Allen's hand-reading album with the legend, 'rien n'est vrai que le Beau'; Constance embellished hers with the lines from Oscar's 'Garden of Eros' that ran round their back drawing room.[44]

5

In Black and White

'To the critic the work of art is simply a suggestion for a new work of his own.'

OSCAR WILDE

The move into 16 Tite Street might also have been expected to draw Wilde closer to Whistler, but it had the opposite effect. Always jealous of his own position and prestige, Whistler was becoming irritated by Wilde's continuing fame, by his gradually acknowledged role as an arbiter in matters of taste, and by the money he was earning on the lecture circuit. He convinced himself that Wilde's success derived entirely from ideas picked up in 'the Master's' studio. As early as March 1884 Alan Cole noted in his diary that Whistler was 'strong on Oscar Wilde's notions on Art, which he had derived from him (Jimmy)'.[1] In his mind Whistler kept returning to the help he had given in preparing Wilde for his address to the Royal Academy students.[2] Wilde's new lecture on 'The Value of Art in Modern Life' borrowed heavily from that talk. And despite – or, perhaps, because of – its extended paean in praise of Whistler it became a particular bugbear. Whistler developed a hatred of it that verged on paranoia.[3]

Although there was no direct confrontation, Wilde cannot have been unaware of his friend's simmering resentment. At one dinner, Whistler steered the conversation to Wilde's lecturing: 'Now, Oscar,' he demanded,

'tell us what you said to them?' Wilde was obliged to repeat all his points
in turn; at each phrase Whistler rose and made a solemn bow 'with his
hand across his breast, in mock acceptance of his guests' applause'.[4] To the
generous spirited Wilde, with his magpie instincts and broad understanding
of intellectual history, such petty point scoring must have seemed a complete
irrelevance. Certainly he refused to take offence. He retained his affection
for Whistler as a man, and his admiration for him as an artist.

Whistler's growing animus, however, found a further outlet early in 1885.
Anxious to assert his authority and reclaim his own Aesthetic theories, he
had determined to give a lecture himself. Enlisting the support of Archibald
Forbes, he even persuaded D'Oyly Carte to promote the venture: a single
London appearance at Prince's Hall on 20 February, at the improbable hour
of ten o'clock in the evening – an hour that allowed the fashionable audience
to dine beforehand.

Whistler had laboured long on his text. The talk was a sparkling declaration of his artistic creed, a creed almost identical to the one espoused
by Wilde in his recent lectures: that art was free from all moral and social
obligations, that it was 'occupied with [its] own perfection only', and that
such perfection could be achieved, not by direct imitation from nature,
but only by inspired selection and arrangement. Not a few of the phrase
echoed Wilde's dicta. 'Nature,' Whistler declared, 'contains the elements,
in colour and form, of all pictures, as the keyboard contains the notes of
all music. But the artist is born to pick and choose, and group with science,
these elements, that the result may be beautiful... To say to the painter,
that Nature is to be taken as she is, is to say to the player, that he may sit
on the piano.' The same metaphor – albeit without the closing joke – was
employed by Wilde in his talks.

Among the several objects of Whistler's contempt, the principal ones
may have been Ruskin and Harry Quilter – 'the Sage of the Universities' and
'the Art Critic'– but Wilde was not ignored. In discussing the contemporary
enthusiasm for trying to educate the public about art (a matter on which
they should have 'nothing to say'), Whistler lamented the rise of the self-
appointed expert: 'the Dilettante stalks abroad! – The Amateur is loosed –
the voice of the Aesthete is heard in the land – and catastrophe is upon us!'
And if all art experts were decried, special ridicule was reserved for the dress
reformer: 'Costume is not dress – and the wearers of wardrobes may not
be doctors of "taste"! – For by what authority shall these be pretty masters!
– Look well, and nothing have they invented! – nothing put together for

comeliness' sake... Haphazard from their shoulders hang the garments of the Hawker – combining in their person, the motely of many manners, with the medley of the mummers' closet.'

Wilde was, of course, in the audience (conspicuous in the sixth row).[5] He was not there, however, simply to listen. He had secured a commission to review the lecture from his friends at the *Pall Mall Gazette*. It was a task that he carried out with aplomb, turning the occasion deftly to his own account, without appearing to rise to Whistler's bait. Those of Whistler's friends who had supposed that Wilde had been riled by the lecture were disabused.[6]

Adopting an air of easy equality, he was gracious in his praises. He hailed the 'really marvellous eloquence' of the lecture – even if he promptly capped Whistler's own rather strained attempts at alliteration by describing the artist, memorably, as 'a miniature Mephistopheles, mocking the majority'. The opening note of genial approval sanctioned a succession of lightly phrased – and apt – caveats. Wilde pointed up the irony of Whistler lecturing an art-loving audience about how they did not, could not and should not know anything about art. For his own part, he cheerfully acknowledged that he was indeed a 'dress reformer' – '(*O mea culpa!*)' – but asserted the importance of the role. 'Of course,' he remarked, 'with regard to the value of beautiful surroundings I differ entirely from Mr. Whistler.' And just because true artists could 'find beauty in ugliness, *le beau dans l'horrible*', that was no excuse for condemning 'charming people' to live surrounded by the hideousness of 'magenta ottomans and Albert blue curtains'. He disputed too Whistler's 'dictum that only a painter is a judge of painting' – contending, instead, that 'only an artist is a judge of art' – and that all the arts were one – 'poem, picture, and Parthenon, sonnet and statue – all are in their essence the same, and he who knows one knows all'. He went on to claim that 'the poet' was 'the supreme artist, for he is master of colour and form, and the real musician besides, and is lord over all life, and all arts; and so to the poet beyond all others are these mysteries known, to Edgar Allan Poe and to Baudelaire, not to Benjamin West and Paul Delaroche [two unfashionable mid-nineteenth-century history painters]'.

The lecture, nevertheless, he declared 'a masterpiece' – to be remembered not only for its wit:

But for the pure and perfect beauty of many of its passages – passages delivered with an earnestness which seemed to amaze those who had looked on Mr. Whistler as a master of persiflage merely, and had not

known him as we do, as a master of painting also. For that he is indeed one of the very greatest masters of painting is my opinion. And I may add that in this opinion Mr. Whistler himself entirely concurs.

Wilde's article appeared prominently – under his name – on the front page of the *Pall Mall Gazette* the afternoon following the lecture. Despite its arch tone it was, in the general press reaction to the talk, among the more generous responses. The 'smartly-written critique' was soon being commented upon, and quoted from, in other papers. In such articles the reviewer was given equal weight with the reviewed; indeed one piece appeared under the headline 'Mr. Wilde and Mr. Whistler'.[7]

Although 'Mr. Wilde' must have been delighted by the attention – and by the ordering of their names – 'Mr. Whistler' was not. He responded to Wilde's review with the inevitable letter in the *World*: 'I have read your exquisite article in the *Pall Mall*. Nothing is more delicate, in the flattery of "the Poet" to "the Painter", than the *naiveté* of "the Poet", in the choice of his Painters – Benjamin West and Paul Delaroche! You have pointed out that "the Painter's" mission is to find *"le beau dans l'horrible"*, and have left to "the Poet" the discovery of *"l'horrible" dans "le beau"*!'

Wilde deftly turned away the thrust. 'Dear Butterfly,' he replied, 'By the aid of a biographical dictionary I made the discovery that there were once two painters, called Benjamin West and Paul Delaroche, who rashly lectured upon Art. As of their works nothing at all remains, I concluded that they explained themselves away. Be warned in time, James; and remain, as I do, incomprehensible: to be great is to be misunderstood. *Tout à vous*, Oscar.' This letter was published alongside Whistler's in the *World*; the correspondence also appeared in the *Pall Mall Gazette*.[8] In their previous exchanges, Whistler's egotism had always secured him a victory of sorts, and certainly the final word. But on this occasion he was bested.

Keeping the game going, the *Pall Mall Gazette* commissioned a second signed article from Wilde: 'The Relation of Dress to Art: A Note in Black and White on Mr. Whistler's Lecture.' It allowed Wilde – amid further praise for Whistler as an orator and an artist – to contrast the passionless 'wisdom' of Whistler's perfectly 'true' claim that art 'can never have any other aim but own perfection' with the 'noble unwisdom' of his own campaign for dress reform, which sought to make art 'the natural and national inheritance of all'. Indeed beauty in dress, Wilde suggested, might benefit not only society, but also art:

For Art is not to be taught in the Academies. It is what one looks at, not what one listens to, that makes the artist. The real schools should be the streets. There is not, for instance, a single delicate line, or delightful proportion, in the dress of the Greeks, which is not echoed exquisitely in their architecture. A nation arrayed in stove-pipe hats, and dress improvers, might have built the Pantechnicon [furniture bazaar], possibly, but the Parthenon, never.

If Whistler had hoped to obliterate Wilde with his 'Ten O'Clock', or precipitate a definite break with him, he failed on both counts. Wilde emerged from the confrontation with his reputation as an Aesthetic reformer and a wit enhanced. Nevertheless, though he maintained a tone of generous good humour in his published comments, and continued to encounter Whistler socially (Chelsea – and, indeed, London – were too small for him not to), it was clear that the warm camaraderie of previous years was irretrievably lost. This cooling of relations was given an outward form when, shortly after the Wildes moved into their new home, Whistler moved out of Tite Street, relocating his studio to the far end of the Fulham Road, and his home to The Vale, a picturesque cul-de-sac on the far side of the King's Road.

The contretemps precipitated another, rather happier, alteration in Wilde's circumstances: it opened up to him the world of journalism – or at least the world of reviewing. His several well-received contributions to the *Pall Mall Gazette* encouraged Milner to offer him a role as a regular book reviewer for the paper, starting in March.[9] The opportunity was welcome. The charms of lecturing had been waning for some time. The ceaseless travel, the endless repetition, the stress of the occasional mix-up, fluctuating audiences, uncertain returns, absence from London and from Constance: they all took their toll on Wilde's spirit. 'I am getting sick of the whole thing,' he had confessed to Appleton.[10] And though he held back from making an immediate break, he greatly reduced his commitments during the rest of the year. His role as the itinerant prophet of Aestheticism was gradually coming to an end.[11]*

To be reviewing for a London paper was, if not a significant professional

---

*   With barely more than a dozen dates during the autumn/winter season that ran from October 1885 into 1886, Wilde's concerted three-year campaign of lecturing across Britain quietly closed with a talk on 'Dress and the Mission of Art in the Nineteenth Century' at Penzance on Monday 25 January 1886. From then on he might address the occasional society or group, but the days of touring were over.

advance, at least both a change and a relief. The *Pall Mall Gazette* was, moreover, an appropriate berth. One of a new breed of 'Clubland' papers (costing, at 1*d*, twice as much as 'popular' titles such as the *Evening Standard*, the *Echo* and the *Star*), it had established a reputation, under the editorship of W. T. Stead, as 'the best evening paper London ever had': entertaining, liberal and courageous.[12] Although the paper's book reviews were unsigned, and only modestly rewarded (2 guineas per 1,000 words was the paper's usual rate), they could be accomplished from the comfort of the 'vermilion garret' at Tite Street, and accomplished quickly. Wilde's gift for speed-reading stood in his favour, even before he evolved the theory that it was both harmful and unnecessary for a reviewer to read the entire book: 'To know the vintage and quality of a wine one need not drink the whole cask. It must be perfectly easy in half an hour to say whether a book is worth anything or worth nothing. Ten minutes are really sufficient, if one has an instinct for form.'[13] He doubtless hoped that the new regime would allow him scope to pursue his own literary projects.

Wilde, initially, expected that he would review books about art, and one of his first acts was to ask Milner if he could be sent Comyns Carr's recently published *Papers on Art*. He received instead a cookery book called *Dinners and Dishes*. It was an early lesson in the promiscuous demands of book reviewing. Wilde, though, seems to have enjoyed the variety – and even the anonymity. Both were liberating. Certainly there is a happy holiday air about most of his *Pall Mall Gazette* reviews.[14] Over the next five years he contributed sprightly critiques of epic poems, Irish legends, etiquette manuals, verse anthologies, handbooks on oil painting, historical biographies, collected letters, popular novels and more besides. The pieces were usually generous and always droll – ideas were sported with and phrases turned.

In praising *Dinners and Dishes* he reported, 'it is brief, and concise, and makes no attempts at eloquence, which is extremely fortunate. For even on ortolans who could endure oratory? It also has the advantage of not being illustrated. The subject of a work of art has of course nothing to do with its beauty, but still there is always something depressing about the coloured lithograph of a leg of mutton.' The real wonder of the work, however, he suggested, was that there was 'actually a recipe for making Brussels sprouts eatable'.[15]

Kind-hearted by nature, and having suffered himself from spiteful notices, Wilde strove especially to be generous to minor poets. There was almost always a word of praise, however faint. Of one feeble but well-produced

volume he reported, 'if it is not quite worth reading, [it] is at least worth looking at'.[16] A steady course of popular novels (often reviewed three or four at a time) convinced him that, although 'the nineteenth century may be a prosaic age... it is not an age of prose'.[17] While he generously allowed that almost all of 'our ordinary English novelists' did have 'some story to tell' and most of them told it in 'an interesting manner', he considered that they nearly always failed 'in concentration of style'. Their characters were all 'far too eloquent, and talk themselves to tatters. What we want is a little more reality and a little less rhetoric.' Nevertheless, he conceded that 'one should not be too severe on English novels' since they were 'the only relaxation of the intellectually unemployed'.[18] And severe he was not, even if his lightly scattered compliments were often double-edged: 'It seems to be a novel with a high purpose and a noble meaning. Yet it is never dull'; 'The book can be read without any trouble, and was probably written without any trouble also. The style is pleasing and prattling.' '*Astray. A Tale of a Country Town* is a very serious volume. It has taken four people to write it, and even to read it requires assistance'. He drew the line, however, at Mr. E. O. Pleydell-Bouverie's *J.S.; or Trivialities*: 'The only point of interest presented by the book is the problem of how it ever came to be written.'[19]

He learnt to be careful in requesting specific titles for review, as the editors were 'much afraid of log-rolling' and would try to thwart any attempt of his simply to puff his friends.[20] It was probably chance that gave him the opportunity to say nice things about Mrs Alfred Hunt's three-volume novel, and to salute William Money Hardinge for his 'charming style'.[21] Design, though, must surely have been behind his reviewing *How To Be Happy Though Married*, a lightly humorous book written, pseudonymously, by the husband of his first cousin. Wilde hailed Rev. E. J. Hardy's work as 'a complete handbook to an earthly Paradise', calling the author 'the Murray of matrimony and the Baedeker of bliss'. This phrase – as much as his general endorsement – carried the book through five editions; Wilde always thought he should have received a royalty.[22]*

From behind his mask of anonymity Wilde criticized J. A. Symonds for his too-facile rhetoric and Edmund Gosse for his sciolism; he gently

---

* The book actually cited Wilde as an authority (on home decor rather than marriage): 'As regards one's relations when they are really decorative, even Mr Oscar Wilde can see no reason why their photographs should not be hung on the walls, though he hopes that, if called on to make a stand between principles of domestic affection and decorative art, the latter may have the first place.'

mocked the 'common sense' approach to art of his Tite Street neighbour John Collier, and less gently denigrated the philistinism of his old Oxford adversary Rhoda Broughton ('whatever harsh criticisms may be passed on the construction of her sentences, she at least possesses that one touch of vulgarity that make the whole world kin').[23] The mask, however, sometimes slipped. When Wilde wrote an anonymous attack on the pretensions of George Saintsbury, gleefully listing the writer's grammatical errors and infelicities, his authorship was guessed, and widely reported.[24] Not that Wilde seems to have minded. He certainly hoped that his responsibility for the delightfully disingenuous demolition of Harry Quilter would be recognized.[25] Nevertheless there was always scope for confusion: some of Wilde's more astringent reviews were credited by their hapless victims to George Bernard Shaw (who started writing for the *Pall Mall Gazette* at the same time as Wilde) or to William Archer, while their pieces were sometimes ascribed to him.[26] Well-connected writers, though, could usually discover the true authorship of any unsigned review, whether bad or good. It was probably inside information that led W. G. Wills to write, thanking Wilde for the generous praise of his epic poem *Melchior*.[27]

A review of George Sand's letters allowed Wilde to elucidate his ever-shifting ideas on art and its relation to life: 'Perhaps [Sand] valued good intentions in art a little too much, and she hardly understood that art for art's sake [to which she had voiced objections] is not meant to express the final cause of art but is merely a formula of creation.' He thought, though, that Sand was right to challenge Flaubert's attempts to obliterate his own personality in his work: 'Art without personality is impossible. And yet the aim of art is not to reveal personality but to please.'[28] The importance of pleasing was now a concern. Of another work he remarked, 'Seriousness, like property, has its duties as well as its rights, and the first duty of a novel is to please.'[29]

Seriousness, as well as pleasure, had, though, a certain attraction. Wilde had no desire to enter the coarse and bustling world of newspaper journalism that had laid claim to Willie, who was now a leader writer for the *Daily Telegraph* (an occupation that only too well suited his easy wit, fluent pen and indolent temperament).[30]* There was, though, the 'higher journalism' of informed

---

*   One of his fellow hacks left a vivid record of Willie's account of the working day: 'The journalistic life irksome? Dear me, not at all. Take my daily life as an example. I report at the office, let us say at twelve o'clock. To the Editor I say, "Good morning, my dear Le Sage," and he replies, "Good morning, my dear Wilde, have you an idea

critical comment and erudite discussion carried on in the monthly reviews: the forum in which Matthew Arnold and Swinburne (as a critic) had made their names. Wilde recognized that this might be a useful stage on which to appear. He followed up a suggestion from the editor of the *Fortnightly Review* that he should contribute an article – proposing 'Impressionism in Literature' – 'a subject I have been for some time studying'. But the idea languished.[31] More successful was an essay on 'Shakespeare and Stage Costume', which, combining his interests in literature and dress, appeared under his name in the May 1885 issue of the prestigious *Nineteenth Century*. It marked a small but gratifying debut in this elevated intellectual sphere.

---

to-day?" "Oh yes, Sir, indeed I have," I respond. "It is the anniversary of the penny postage stamp." "That is a delightful subject for a leader," cries my editor, beaming on me, "and would you be good enough, my dear Wilde, to write us a leader, then, on the anniversary of the penny postage stamp?" "Indeed I will that with pleasure," is my answer. "Ah! thank you, my dear boy," cries my editor, "and be sure to have your copy in early the earlier the better." That is the final, injunction, and I bow myself out. I may then eat a few oysters and drink half a bottle of Chablis at Sweeting's, or alternatively partake of a light lunch at this admirable club [the Spoofs], for as rare Ben Jonson says, "The first speech in my *Cataline*, spoken by Sylla's ghost, was writ after I had parted with my friends at the Devil Tavern. I had drank well and had brave notions." I then stroll towards the Park. I bow to the fashionables, I am seen along incomparable Piccadilly. It is grand. But meantime I am thinking only of that penny postage stamp. I try to recall all that I ever heard about penny postage stamps. Let me see? There is Mr. So-and-so the inventor, there is the early opposition, the first postal legislation, then the way stamps are made, putting the holes in the paper; the gum on the back; the printing – all these details come back to me; then a paragraph or two about present postal laws; a few examples of the crude drolleries of the official Postal Guide; perhaps as a conclusion, something about the crying need for cheaper letter rates. I think of all these circumstances as I stroll back along Pall Mall. I might go to the British Museum and grub up a lot of musty facts, but that would be unworthy of a great leader writer, you may well understand that. And then comes the writing. Ah! here is where I earn my money. I repair to my club. I order out my ink and paper. I go to my room. I close the door. I am undisturbed for an hour. My pen moves. Ideas flow. The leader on the penny postage stamp is being evolved. Three great meaty, solid paragraphs each one-third of a column – that is the consummation to be wished. My ideas flow fast and free. Suddenly some one knocks at the door. Two hours have fled. How time goes! It is an old friend. We are to eat a little dinner at the Cafe Royal and drop into the Alhambra for the new ballet. I touch the button; my messenger appears. The leader is despatched to 141, Fleet Street, in the Parish of St. Bride, and off we go arm in arm. After the shower the sunshine. Now for the enjoyment of that paradise of cigar ashes, bottles, corks, ballet, and those countless circumstances of gaiety and relaxation known only to those who are indwellers in the magic circles of London's Literary Bohemia.'

The article, an elegantly phrased endorsement of Godwin's views on the virtues of 'archaeologically' authentic stage design, was based on a shorter (but no less elegantly phrased) piece – 'Shakespeare on Stage Scenery' – that Wilde had published a few weeks earlier in a newly established weekly called the *Dramatic Review*. The line taken in both pieces was the direct opposite of the one that he usually adopted. He had told the Royal Academy students that 'archaeology' was 'merely the science of making excuses for bad art', while to a young painter who was working on a 'Viking picture' he remarked, 'Why so far back? You know, where archaeology begins, art ceases.'[32] It was yet another instance of his gift for holding, and enjoying, contrary positions.

If *Nineteenth Century* did not, at once, offer Wilde any more work, the *Dramatic Review* did. Under the energetic editorship of its founder, the Irish-born Edwin Palmer, the journal was committed to stimulating debate on cultural topics. William Archer was an early contributor. Shaw was taken on to write music criticism. Hermann Vezin had a regular column reminiscing about old actors. And during 1885 Godwin published a series of articles about 'Archaeology on the Stage'. It was not surprising that Wilde was drawn into the circle.[33] Following the success of his first article he began to provide occasional theatre reviews. They were no better paid than his pieces for the *Pall Mall Gazette*, but served to keep him close to the world of the stage – and his name before the public. Articles appeared above a facsimile of the author's signature.[34]

On 5 June 1885 Constance gave birth to a son. Wilde was thrilled with the arrival. 'The baby is wonderful,' he wrote to Norman Forbes-Robertson. 'Constance is doing capitally and is in excellent spirits... you must get married *at once!*'[35] Beyond the family circle, speculation was rife at how the child would fare. Laura Troubridge thought it 'much to be pitied', suspecting it would soon be 'swathed in artistic baby-clothes' of 'sage green' and 'peacock blue'.[36] The newspapers relished the gap between the Aesthetic ideal and the realities of parenthood: 'O wondrous cherub! Aesthete fair!', they imagined Wilde apostrophizing the infant. 'Style Renaissance, Greek and Doric; / Always howling, I declare! / Fetch me quick the paregoric.'[37] The boy was christened Cyril. As a further consideration, Edward Heron-Allen was asked to cast the child's horoscope (although both parents were anxious to know the child's 'fate', when Heron-Allen finally gave his report 'it grieved them very much).[38]

Wilde took to fatherhood with enthusiasm: within hours of the child's

birth he was boasting that the 'amazing boy... *already knows me quite well*'.[39] He was conscious, though, of new responsibilities, and of new expenses too. Money was needed. Constance's income had not been enough to support the household even before Cyril's arrival. And the nugatory amounts that Wilde received for reviewing, together with the falling returns from his few remaining lectures, were not enough to make up the shortfall. *The Duchess of Padua* was as far as ever from securing a production. And economy seemed out of the question. Constance lamented to her brother that neither she nor her husband had 'a notion how to live non-extravagantly'.[40] A different measure was attempted: Wilde tried to get a job.

Only weeks after Cyril's birth, he revived his idea of becoming 'one of her Majesty's Inspectors of Schools', asking his friend George Curzon (now a rising star in the Tory Party) to support the application. Not immediately successful, he continued his campaign over the coming months, badgering Curzon a second time, and enlisting the additional assistance of Mahaffy.[41] But even this was not enough to secure a post. Exploring other avenues, he applied to become the secretary of the Beaumont Trust Fund, a charity engaged in creating 'The People's Palace' in London's East End – an institute dedicated to promoting the arts and sciences among the urban poor. Wilde, in his letter of application, after citing his long experience as a lecturer on 'art-knowledge' and 'art-appreciation', called the Palace 'the realization of much that I have long hoped for.' Again, though, he was overlooked.[42]

These were real disappointments. Their implications were not merely practical, but artistic. Frustrated by his inability to write anything beyond reviews, Wilde had come to believe that 'leisure and freedom from sordid care' were necessary if he was to create 'pure literary work' of real worth. He hoped that a regular job might offer such freedom. As he explained to one young correspondent, if only he could 'make some profession... the basis and mainstay of [his] life', he would then be able 'to keep literature for [his] finest, rarest moments'.[43] He needed a proper job. Or so he thought. Shackled to the round of reviewing – and his ever-dwindling series of lectures – fine moments seemed rare indeed, and 'pure literary work' a dream.

6

L'Amour de l'Impossible

'Let us live like Spartans, but let us talk like Athenians.'

OSCAR WILDE

As Wilde reached his thirties, he began, increasingly, to look backwards. Youth, both the fact and the idea of it, took on for him a sort of magic. He sought it out, and made much of it. His work for the *Dramatic Review* took him back to Oxford. He reported on two student productions: *Henry IV, Part I* (with a prologue written by his friend Curzon) in May 1885 and *Twelfth Night* in February the following year. And though he greatly enjoyed the performances – saying so at length in his articles – he enjoyed even more being among undergraduates. It was six years since he had left the university, a span that sharpened the contrast between the pressing adult cares of his London life, and the infectious irresponsibility and optimism of studenthood. 'Young Oxonians are very delightful,' he enthused to Violet Fane, 'so Greek, and graceful and uneducated. They have profiles but no philosophy.'[1] He exerted himself to charm them. At a dinner following the performance of *Henry IV* he delivered an 'amazing speech'.[2] When he returned for *Twelfth Night* the actors treated him as their honoured guest.[3]

Wilde also received, in November 1885, an invitation to attend a performance of Aeschylus' *Eumenides* at Cambridge. It came from Harry

Marillier, the 'bright, enthusiastic' blue-coat boy whom Wilde had befriended at Salisbury Street during his early days in London; he was now a classical scholar at Peterhouse, Cambridge. Wilde was delighted to be in touch again with his young artistically inclined friend. They met briefly in London a few days later, and talked of poetry and pictures: 'Are you all Wordsworthians still at Cambridge,' Wilde had wanted to know, 'or do you love Keats, and Poe, and Baudelaire… what moods and modulations of art affect you most?' The encounter had, for Wilde, been full of 'keen curiosity, wonder, delight' – terminated too soon by the demands of his travel schedule.

'Harry,' he wrote from the Station Hotel, Newcastle on Tyne (where he had to lecture), 'why did you let me catch my train? I would have liked to have gone to the National Gallery with you, and looked at Velázquez's pale evil King, at Titian's Bacchus… and at that strange heaven of Angelico's.' Their hour together had, nevertheless, been 'intensely dramatic and intensely psychological' – rather like Browning. He looked forward to further meetings, and further talk: 'I have never learned anything except from people younger than myself, and you are infinitely young.'4

Although Wilde was unable to attend a performance of the *Eumenides*, he and Constance went up to Cambridge in the week beforehand, and passed a happy time with Marillier and his friends – and also with Oscar Browning.* 'Does it all seem a dream, Harry?' Wilde wrote afterwards. 'To me it is, in a fashion, a memory of music. I remember bright young faces, and grey misty quadrangles, Greek forms passing through Gothic cloisters, life playing among ruins and, what I love best in the world, Poetry and Paradox dancing together.'5

It was Wilde who led the dance. At a breakfast party in the rooms of Marillier's friend J. H. Badley, Wilde rhapsodized over the *œufs à l'aurore*, declaring that the dish looked like 'the standard of the Emperor of Japan'. He tried to lure his young host away from a conventional reverence for Shelley ('merely a boy's poet') to a proper admiration of the less-regarded Keats ('the greatest of them'). And when Badley excused himself for being a non-smoker with the observation that he was 'missing thereby what was, no doubt, good in moderation', Wilde rejoined, 'Ah Badley, nothing is good

---

* Wilde and Marillier lunched with Oscar Browning on one afternoon. Coming away, Wilde remarked, 'OB is a genial soul, but it is a *revolting* sight to watch him eat.' The next time Marillier saw 'OB', Browning commented, 'Your friend Oscar is very witty, but it is a pity he is such an ugly feeder.'

in moderation. You cannot know the good in anything till you have torn the heart out of it by excess.'[6]

On one evening Marillier invited a crowd of friends to his rooms to meet Wilde. The occasion nearly came to grief when – before the guests arrived, and with the room empty – a Chinese lantern caught fire and ignited the wooden panel above the mantelpiece; Marillier returned just in time to douse the flames. 'You are careless about playing with fire, Harry,' Wilde remarked, with a note of archness. Wilde talked 'brilliantly' that evening. Pressed for a story, he chose the fairy-tale form that he had first experimented with in America, and since toyed with in Paris. But, if previously he had conceived his stories as being for children, he now pitched the narrative for a more knowing adult audience.

Tempering pathos with the occasional touch of satire, he sketched out the touching tale of little bird who falls in love with the richly adorned statue of 'The Happy Prince'. From their vantage point, on a column, high above the town, they witness the travails of the poor and oppressed, and seek to relieve them by distributing pieces of the gold- and jewel-bedecked statue among the needy. Such charity costs the statue its splendour and the bird his life, as he misses the chance to fly south for the winter. Both are thrown on the rubbish heap. But when an angel is sent to fetch the two most valuable things in the city, he returns to heaven with the dead bird and the statue's leaden heart. If the story affected the listeners, it affected Wilde more. After the party disbanded, still feeling 'full of inspiration', he sat up through the night elaborating the tale and setting it down on paper.[7]

He was pleased with the result, and intrigued by its possibilities. The literary fairy tale was, after all, a rich Victorian tradition. Ruskin had done much to establish the genre with his 1841 story *The King of the Golden River*.[8] And many others, from Dickens and Thackeray to Andrew Lang and Mrs Molesworth, had followed his example, weaving apparently simple tales that, while touching the childish imagination, also reached beyond it. The old conventions, in time, had begun to be subverted and parodied. Lewis Carroll's *Alice* books were perhaps the most conspicuous instance of such playfulness, although Wilde had a particular admiration for the ingenious fables of the American Frank Stockton. And as a rival to Stockton's 'Floating Prince' he could now set his own 'Happy Prince'.[9]

The next morning half a dozen excited undergraduates escorted the Wildes to the railway station. As they clustered round the carriage window Oscar kept up a stream of epigrams, timed to culminate with the train's

departure. But the start proved to be a false one. The train backed into the station again, drawing Wilde's carriage alongside where the students were still standing. He knew better, though, than to revive the moment. He closed the window, and buried himself in his papers – the first draft of his fairy story among them.[10]

Wilde found Harry Marillier an oddly quickening presence. There were further meetings. Wilde visited the Marillier family home at Hampton. Marillier dined with the Wildes at Tite Street – a charmed occasion, at which Constance's young friend Douglas Ainslie was also present: they drank 'yellow wine' in green glasses to the memory of Keats, and Oscar wove fairy tales about the people who lived in Constance's beautiful moonstone jewellery.[11] There were letters too, continuing the dance of poetry and paradox. Wilde wrote from Glasgow – 'region of snow and horrible notepaper' – distilling a vision of the artistic life:

> You too have the love of things impossible – ερως των αδυνατων – *l'amour de l'impossible* (how do men name it?). Some day you will find, even as I have found, that there is no such thing as a romantic experience; there are romantic memories, and there is the desire of romance – that is all. Our most fiery moments of ecstasy are merely shadows of what somewhere else we have felt, or of what we long some day to feel. So at least it seems to me. And, strangely enough, what comes of all this is a curious mixture of ardour and of indifference. I myself would sacrifice everything for a new experience, and I know there is no such thing as a new experience at all. I think I would more readily die for what I do not believe in than for what I hold to be true. I would go to the stake for a sensation and be a sceptic to the last! Only one thing remains infinitely fascinating to me, the mystery of moods. To be master of these moods is exquisite, to be mastered by them more exquisite still. Sometimes I think that the artistic life is a long and lovely suicide, and am not sorry that it is so.
>
> And much of this I fancy you yourself have felt: much also remains for you to feel. There is an unknown land full of strange flowers and subtle perfumes, a land of which it is joy of all joys to dream, a land where all things are perfect and poisonous.

He then ended, with deliberate bathos, 'I have been reading Walter Scott for the last week: you too should read him, for there is nothing of all this in him.'[12]

With its elegantly poised paradoxes – reality and dream, ardour and indifference, martyrdom and scepticism, life and death, perfection and poison – this was a vision coloured by the wearied sensualism and the calculated inversions of Huysmans' des Esseintes. The letter's single French phrase, however, did not derive from *À Rebours*. *'L'amour de l'impossible'* was the title of an 1882 sonnet sequence by John Addington Symonds, charting the agonies of a tortured artistic soul, seeking an ever-elusive happiness in the 'mysteries of life' and in 'human affections'. One of the sonnets presented the 'artist' – happily married, 'strong and wise,' rocking 'the cradle where his firstborn lies' – being suddenly carried off by the bat-winged 'Chimaera': while his thoughts and senses rebel, he swoons, 'desiring things impossible'.[13]

Although Symonds publicly claimed that the sonnets were not autobiographical, privately he confided that the poems expressed his own desire for sexual relations with other men, and that the 'Chimaera' was the image of this forbidden but all-consuming lust – the desire for 'things impossible'.[14] And it seems more than likely that Wilde had divined, or learnt, this fact: that *'l'amour de l'impossible'* had become for him a coded phrase with a specific sexual meaning, not simply an expression of abstract yearning for fulfilment. His translating of the phrase into Greek might seem an attempt to connect it with the traditions of ancient Greek pederasty that had intrigued him since his student days. The subject of homosexual passion was certainly returning to the forefront of his mind. In his contemplation of *À Rebours* it was the passage about des Esseintes' relationship with the strange young man that came to fascinate him most.[15]

As so often in Wilde's life, a development in one direction stimulated a simultaneous and almost exactly contrary impulse. Happily married, apparently 'strong and wise' enough to consider a career as a school inspector, rocking 'the cradle where his first born [lay]', and with his wife already expecting another child, Wilde was suddenly carried away by that same *'amour de l'impossible'* which found its expression in an emotional and sexual yearning for young men. He later described it as being 'like a madness' which falls 'on many who think they live securely and out of reach of harm' making them 'sicken suddenly with the poison of unlimited desire', and leads them on to 'the infinite pursuit of what they may not obtain'.[16]

And it seems that he could not obtain Harry Marillier. Although the 'infinitely young', wonderfully sympathetic and very attractive Marillier provided both a focus and a stimulus for these feelings, there is no evidence that he either recognized or reciprocated them. Throughout their association

he maintained a certain detachment, addressing Oscar as 'Mr Wilde'. In June 1886 Wilde gave tentative expression to his desire in a letter to his young friend: 'There is at least this beautiful mystery in life, that at the moment it feels most complete it finds some secret sacred niche in its shrine empty and waiting. Then comes a time of exquisite expectancy.'[17] If this was an invitation, Marillier did not accept it. The letter is the last surviving one of their correspondence; there were no further meetings. For Wilde the moment of 'exquisite expectancy' was prolonged; the niche remained empty.[18]

Nevertheless, amid his various social cares and journalistic duties, Wilde took time to seek out the company of other artistically inclined young men. He was drawn into the idealistic world of the 'Century Guild', a group established in a house on Fitzroy Street by a trio of fervent Ruskin-ites: Arthur Mackmurdo, Selwyn Image and the twenty-two-year-old Herbert Horne. Dedicated to promoting a socially engaged vision of the arts and crafts, they had founded a small quarterly magazine, to which Wilde contributed an article about Keats.[19] Horne had poetic ambitions, and Wilde encouraged them. 'Your poems are most charming,' he declared. 'You combine very perfectly simplicity and strangeness.'[20]

Horne also shared Wilde's enthusiasm for the doomed Romantic poet Thomas Chatterton. And together they collaborated on a scheme to preserve and commemorate his birthplace – a little schoolhouse at Pile Street, Bristol.[21] In conjunction with this campaign Wilde planned to write an article on Chatterton for the *Hobby Horse*. The essay never appeared, but Wilde did deliver a lecture on the poet at the Birkbeck Literary and Scientific Institution, in London. Despite a night of 'dreadful' weather, Wilde to his amazement found 800 people in the hall, 'and they seemed really interested in the marvellous Boy'.[22]

Wilde characterized Chatterton as 'the father of the Romantic movement in literature', the precursor of Blake, Coleridge and Keats, of Tennyson, Morris and Rossetti.[23] Wilde, too, perhaps hoped to claim him as a parent, seeking in his life and work intimations of his own ideas about art and its relation to both morality and realism. Chatterton's brief career was certainly suggestive. He had been a literary forger. The main body of his work (completed before he took his own life at the age of just seventeen) consisted of poems that he claimed had been written by a fifteenth-century Bristol monk. It was a deception that, when revealed, had increased his romantic appeal and confused his critical standing. 'Was he', Wilde asked towards the end of his lecture, 'a mere forger with literary powers or a great artist?

The latter is the right view. Chatterton may not have had the moral conscience which is Truth to fact but he had the artistic conscience which is
truth to Beauty. He had the artist's yearning to represent and if perfect
representation seems to him to demand forgery he needs must forge. Still
this forgery came from the desire of artistic self-effacement. He was the pure
artist – that is to say his aim was not to reveal himself but to give pleasure.'
Chatterton – Wilde claimed – saw that 'the realm of the imagination differed
from the realm of fact' and understood that 'it is the ideal, not the realistic
artist who expresses his age'.[24]

Chatterton, though, was not the only 'marvellous Boy' occupying Wilde's
thoughts. It was during 1886 that Wilde came to know the seventeen-year-
old Robert (Robbie or Bobbie) Ross. Small, bright and snub-nosed, he had
the look and the liveliness of Puck. Exactly how he met Wilde remains
unclear, though there were many currents in London life that might have
drawn them together.[25] Ross was the youngest child of prominent Canadian
parents. His father, a lawyer and politician, had died when he was barely
two, prompting the family to move back to Europe. Ross had been brought
up – and privately educated – in England, and on the continent, developing
precocious interests in art and literature. He lived with his mother and
two sisters at Kensington, studying at a nearby crammer in preparation for
going to Cambridge. Wilde found him 'charming and as clever as can be,
with excellent taste and sound knowledge' too.[26]

Ross's precocity, however, extended beyond taste and knowledge to sex.
He had come to an early and untroubled acceptance of his homosexual
nature; at seventeen he was both experienced and curious. And, early in
their friendship, he seduced Wilde.[27] Wilde later formulated the theory
'that it [is] always the young who seduce the old'.[28] But he also suggested
that 'no one had any real influence on anyone else… Influence depends
almost entirely on the ground over which it is exercised.'[29] And in his own
case the ground had been well prepared. His intellectual fascination with
sexual inversion had been long, fuelled by his work with Mahaffy, his study
of Plato, his reading of Symonds and Pater, of Burton's *Arabian Nights* and
the novels of the French Decadents. And as the conventional constraints of
married life had tightened around him, the subject seems to have assumed
a new piquancy and an even greater attraction.

His sexual interest in Constance was waning, and perhaps hers in him
too. She was pregnant throughout much of the year, giving birth to a second
son, christened Vyvyan, on 3 November 1886.[30] And he later admitted to

a certain physical revulsion at his heavily pregnant wife.[31] If Wilde was slow to recognize that his own emotional and physical needs lay with men rather than women, he had become gradually aware of 'an impending fate' hanging over his sexual nature.[32] The exquisite expectancy that he had felt in his friendship with Harry Marillier had been a presage of what was to come. With Robbie Ross it finally found fulfilment.*

That first encounter came as a revelation to Wilde – of pleasure, excitement and liberation. It opened up new vistas of sexual activity and self-fulfilment. Wilde had always chosen to 'stand apart' – and now he stood apart in the matters of sex and passion. He described the 'joy, the delirium' that marked the discovering of his 'originality' and 'independence'.[33] And although to most Victorians, sex (of whatever description) was considered as something that people did – an individual act – rather than as the expression of a person's 'sexuality', there is no doubt that Wilde's new experiences gave him, in his own eyes, an enhanced and altered status.[34] It changed his relationship to the world around him, and to himself. Henceforth his actions would demand secrecy, and the elaboration of a double life. He was not only betraying Constance, he was breaking the law. The timing of Ross's seduction could scarcely have been more charged with significance. Although penetrative sex between men had been a felony in English secular law since the time of the Tudors, it was only in 1885 that *all* sexual contact between men became criminalized.† In that year, with the

---

* Exactly what was involved in that first homosexual encounter remains, not surprisingly, unknown. An account of another of Ross's seductions (of a younger boy rather than an older man) describes him inviting the boy into his bedroom, putting him on the bed, and placing his penis between the boy's thighs. Such 'intercrural sex' was the preferred mode of gratification in Greek paederastia and Victorian public schools. Sherard, however, who later took an enthusiastic – but highly speculative – interest in Ross's sex life, claimed that the most popular sexual activity among those in 'the Rossian orbit' was fellatio – or, as he neologistically termed it 'buccal onanism'.

† 'The detestable and abominable Vice of Buggery' – or sodomy, as it was also called – was not specifically defined in the 'Buggery Act' of 1533, although through the courts it came to mean not only penetrative anal sex between men, but also anal sex between a man and a woman, or any sort of penetrative sex between a person and an animal. It was a capital offence – and remained one even after the old act was replaced by the Offences Against the Person Act of 1828. The death penalty was not always enacted, but occasional executions in England for 'buggery' (almost invariably anal sex between men) continued up until 1835. In 1861 the revised Offences Against the Person Act abolished the death penalty for buggery, replacing it with penal servitude for anything between ten years and life. It remained a felony in England and Wales until 1967.

Criminal Law Amendment bill going through parliament to increase the age of sexual consent for women from thirteen to sixteen, and to suppress the worst excesses of female prostitution, Henry Labouchère proposed an 'amendment' to label any sexual act between males as 'gross indecency' and to make it illegal. His proposal, heard in a nearly empty House, was – after minimal debate – voted into law. Wilde, ever resistant to the conventions of society, could now count himself a criminal and an outlaw.

He could also count himself the heir to that rich – but largely hidden – tradition, running from Plato and the Greeks to Michelangelo and the great figures of the Renaissance, about which he had read. He was keen to embrace both its creative and its sexual possibilities. As he explained to one interested friend:

Plato, like all the Greeks, recognized two kinds of Love, sensual love, which delights in women – such love is intellectually sterile, for women are receptive only, they take everything, and give nothing, save in the way of nature. The Intellectual loves or romantic friendships of the Hellenes, which surprise us today, they considered spiritually fruitful, a stimulus to thought and virtue – I mean virtue as it was understood by the ancients and the Renaissance, not virtue in the English sense, which is only caution and hypocrisy.[35]

There was now a new colouring and a new urgency to Wilde's interest in young men. Relations could encompass both the intellectual and the sexual, though the line between the two might remain unfixed. He came to know the twenty-two-year-old Marc-André Raffalovich, son of a Russian banker from Paris, who held self-consciously artistic and theatrical gatherings at his elegant flat in Albert Hall Mansions. Wilde had generously praised *Tuberose and Meadowsweet*, Raffalovich's 'remarkable little volume' of 'strange and beautiful poems,' in the *Pall Mall Gazette*.[36] And although Raffalovich himself was anything but beautiful, he was strange – and interesting too, 'with the air of an exquisite, a slim waist, and a gardenia in is buttonhole' (one of his poems contained the arresting line, 'Our lives are wired like our gardenias').[37]

Wilde also befriended John Ehret Dickinson, the art-loving scion of a wealthy paper-manufacturing family, who had inherited Abbot's Hill, a mock-Gothic country house in Hertfordshire. Then there was W. Graham Robertson, a well-connected young painter, who lived with his socialite mother in Rutland Gate, and H. B. Irving, eldest son of the actor, on the verge

of going up to Cambridge; Bernard Berenson, a recent Harvard graduate and budding Aesthete, who had come over to study at Oxford, and the garrulous, dandified Harry Melvill; there was Arthur Clifton, a young solicitor with an interest in Liberal politics who also composed verse, and the twenty-five-year-old illustrator Bernard Partridge.

Wilde treated these young companions with a lordly flirtatiousness. 'What do you allow your friends to call you?' he asked Robertson, signing off one of his letters; '"W"? or "Graham"? I like my friends to call me – Oscar.'[38] 'What a charming time we had at Abbot's Hill,' he told 'dear Harry' Melvill, 'I have not enjoyed myself so much for a long time, and I hope that we will see much more of each other, and be together often.'[39] He over-praised their artistic efforts. Some lines by Raffalovich were compared to 'Herrick after the French Revolution'.[40] Clifton was commended on his 'delicate ear for music' in verse.[41] And John Ehret Dickinson received a fulsome dedicatory inscription 'in admiration of his incomparable art and incomparable personality' – although it is not known that he actually created anything, and the only surviving trace of a personality is that he had a dachshund called 'Oodles' who figured prominently in his will.[42]

But if there was a strong erotic current in all these friendships, it is uncertain how many of them actually resulted in sexual relations. The wonderfully good-looking Bernard Berenson, in later life, boasted that Wilde had made a pass at him; but he had resisted, drawing the retort that he must be 'completely without feeling' and 'made of stone'.[43] The rebuff, however, did nothing to break his growing friendship with Wilde. Harry Melvill, it seems, was more compliant. Wilde would later refer to having 'had' him.[44] W. Graham Robertson claimed that Wilde 'never once revealed' any sexual interest in him, and supposed he had been 'protected' by his own rather fastidious 'purity' of character.[45]

'Dear Sandy' Raffalovich was less pure and less protected. He was fascinated by the subject of same-sex desire. Several of his poems touched on it; he had even published an ode to 'Piers Gaveston', the lover of Edward II. 'You could give me a new thrill,' Wilde told him. 'You have the right measure of romance and cynicism.' The thrill was more likely to have been intellectual than physical; for, although Raffalovich's sexual instincts were directed towards men, he seems to have sublimated them into spiritual yearning and intellectual curiosity.[46] His eagerness for knowledge was stimulating. Certainly Wilde relished their long talks about 'the more dangerous affections'. (The nomenclature – and the classification – of same-sex desire

remained unfixed and debated: 'inversion', 'uranisim', 'unisexualité', and
'Greek love' were some of the terms employed by its devotees. 'Sodomy'
was preferred by its detractors. J. A. Symonds, in his privately printed pamphlet of 1883, *A Problem of Greek Ethics*, had called it 'homosexual passion'.)
No topics were taboo. Wilde gave over several happy hours to describing
the bizarre details of *Monsieur Venus*, a determinedly decadent French novel
in which a bored noblewoman (Raoul de Vénérande) seduces and corrupts a
young man; having schemed to have him killed in a duel, she then continues
her predatory sexual relationship with his embalmed and partly mechanized
corpse. Incest was touched on. But it was to des Esseintes' relationship with
the mysterious young man who had picked him up in the street that Wilde
returned most often.[47]

All these friendships contributed, in their different ways, to Wilde's growing engagement with homosexual desire and homosexual sex. But they
found their place within the framework of his domestic life. The young men
were invited to Tite Street and introduced to Constance; some became her
friends. Robbie Ross came to stay with the Wildes for two months in 1887
(while his mother was travelling), and although the arrangement almost
certainly allowed for more sex with Oscar, it also initiated a happy and
enduring friendship with Constance.[48]

For Wilde family life still retained many attractions. The physical side of
the relationship with Constance certainly altered and may have terminated,
but he continued, for the moment, to share with his wife all the old interests, affections, ambitions and anxieties. Indeed the enduring strength and
happiness of the Wildes' marriage was brought into sharper focus during
the summer of 1887 when Constance's brother, Otho, deserted his own
young wife and two small children, and ran off with another woman.[49] The
Wildes' own boys stood large in Oscar's thoughts, and he was distraught
when Vyvyan fell dangerously ill.[50]

Beyond the family circle Wilde's social life was still dominated by the
broader currents of fashionable London existence: private views and first
nights, receptions and dinner parties, if not dances (as Wilde confessed to
Graham Robertson, 'I am not sure whether we are too old or too young, but
[my wife and I] never tread any measures now').[51] Sundays would always see
him in Mrs Jeune's crowded drawing room. 'There are', he declared, 'three
inevitables: death, quarter-day and Mrs Jeune's parties'.[52] He and Constance
began to hold receptions of their own. The first, a crowded party on the
afternoon of 1 July 1886, gathered a notably 'modern' company of actors,

writers and relatives.[53] And from this developed the tradition of regular Tite Street 'at homes' on the first and third Thursday of each month (later changed to Wednesday).[54]

It was a stage on which Wilde loved to tread. His eloquence, honed by four years of lecturing, had grown even more assured. His wit – and his sense of joy – were undimmed; his pose as distinctive as ever. One contemporary has left a vivid sketch of his physical manner:

When standing and talking – [he] bent the head forward condescendingly to his listener (a trick inherited from his mother), was easily audible in any drawing-room through the buzz of conversation and filled and permeated a room with his presence… Attitude when seated and talking – Leant forward from his waist towards his listener; fixed his eyes full upon him; made much play with his right arm and hand, moving the arm freely from the shoulder, and letting the large hand with its full and fleshy palm move freely on the wrist. When he made a point… would throw himself back in the chair and look at his auditor as much as to say: 'What can you find to say to that?'[55]

The overall effect was that 'he might have stepped out of the Seventeenth Century or 'an aristocratic "salon" of the reign of Louis Quinze'.[56]

Conscious of his own gifts, Wilde was always ready to give place to others. He never monopolized the conversation. As another friend put it, he simply 'took the ball of talk wherever it happened to be at the moment and played with it so humorously that everyone was soon smiling delightedly… No subject came amiss to him; he saw everything from a humorous angle and dazzled one now with word wit, now with the very stuff of merriment.'[57] His laugh provided the punctuation: 'He would wait to see if you had caught his point, and suddenly burst into a peal of laughter of exquisite enjoyment at his own witticism or joke.'[58]

The young American author Edgar Saltus was rather disconcerted by the 'serenity' with which Wilde 'waded' in wit.[59] But most simply enjoyed it, carried along by the 'impressive levity' that was perhaps Wilde's great quality as a talker.[60] He retained all his old social tact and positive outlook, preferring to praise rather than to disparage. Dislike and disapproval were only ever hinted at.[61] He undercut his own brilliance with frequent notes of self-deprecation. Mary Costelloe, the young woman with whom Bernard Berenson was in love, recounted how Wilde, having met her 'five nights

in succession', announced, 'Now you have exhausted my repertory. I had only five subjects of conversation prepared and have run out. I shall have to give you one of the former ones. Which would you like?' (they settled on 'evolution').[62] But these were private performances, and the more private the jollier. Friends noted that, in his own home, his sense of humour (as distinct from his wit) became even more ebullient and contagious.[63]

In the public landscape Wilde's wit counted for less. It was generally noted that Oscar's star had been sinking gradually lower 'on the horizon since he cut his hair and became "Benedick the married man"'.[64] He seemed to have transformed, by degrees, into a complacent 'bourgeois'. His dress was now conventional – if always slightly too smart. He had grown plump. His new sexual interests remained unknown and unguessed. And although he might, occasionally, be mentioned in the press, the comments were fleeting.* As Edgar Saltus noted, 'He had been caricatured: the caricatures had ceased. People had turned to look: they looked no longer.' He was 'not only forgiven – but forgotten'.[65] In the five years since his return from America he had produced nothing of note and – despite a steady trickle of articles – seemed given over to 'the *dolce far niente*'.[66]

Although Wilde, beneath the plush exterior, retained his artistic ambitions, they vied with social ones. And on that score, at least, there were some gratifying marks of advance. He was seeing a great deal of his old friend Carlos Blacker, and through him had come to know 'Linny', the young Duke of Newcastle, as well as the duke's spendthrift younger brother, Lord Francis Hope. This connection secured the Wildes an occasional invitation to the ducal home at Clumber in Nottinghamshire.[67] For Oscar the visits marked an exciting new peak in his social climbing. They enormously gratified his romantic snobbery. Indeed the very name 'Clumber' seems to have had an actual magic for him. He introduced it whenever possible into his correspondence and his conversation, as confirmation of his new standing.[68]

Being among titled people stimulated Wilde's creative energies: he strove 'to surpass himself' in such company. After one of his visits to Clumber he missed his train, and was brought back to the house to wait for the next one.

---

*   Constance attracted rather more attention when, on 17 May 1886, she appeared as a non-speaking handmaiden wearing a sea-green gown edged with gold in a determinedly Aesthetic – or 'Neo-Hellenic' – matinee production of *Helena in Troas*, written by John Todhunter and mounted by Godwin. Herbert Beerbohm Tree played Paris, and Hermann Vezin Priam.

Having exhausted himself in his efforts to impress, he was, in his own recollection, an 'extinct volcano': he could no longer talk at all, he was 'played out', his powers of performance over.[69] There was, though, a virtue in all his chatter. It was through conversation that Wilde formed his ideas and mapped out his plans. 'Everything came to him in the excitement of talk,' recalled a contemporary; 'epigrams, paradoxes and stories.'[70] And it was storytelling that was playing an increasingly large part in his discourse.

From the time of his Cambridge visit to Harry Marillier he was, it seems almost constantly spinning tales. Towards the end of any social occasion, when the company shrank or the talk became general, he might make a start. Stories flowed from him: fantastical, historical, romantic, macabre, biblical – always alive with paradoxical humour, and often touched by unexpected profundity. These performances, according to one rapt listener, were 'so natural' that Wilde seemed to be speaking almost for his own benefit, yet so graceful that his audience had 'the flattering illusion' that they had indeed merited the 'expense of imagination and energy'.[71] No story, moreover, was ever fixed. Its details would be endlessly elaborated and refined, guyed with alternative endings, new jokes, and different emotional moods.

Having made a start with 'The Happy Prince', he had, though, been slow to commit himself again to paper, or to investigate the possibilities of print. His mother had been urging him towards fiction for some time. 'Suppose you lay the plot of your story... on the Isle of Wight,' she had suggested. 'Begin: the first sentence is everything.'[72] And gradually he came to accept the wisdom of her words. A short story, after all, might count as part of the 'more lasting work' that he so wanted to produce. And, in a market where almost every periodical regularly published short fiction, a story would be far easier to sell than a play. But, even so, he proceeded with caution. As a first step he sought to bolster his own position through association. Just as his first published poem had been a translation, so was his first published fiction – a short story by Turgenev, done from the French. He sent it to his old friend George Macmillan who, although initially doubtful of its appeal, did find a place for it in the May 1886 number of *Macmillan's Magazine*. It was a very modest debut, since Wilde was not even credited as the translator.[73]

Nevertheless it was something. And seeking to capitalize upon the achievement he sent off 'The Happy Prince' to another Macmillan periodical, the *English Illustrated Magazine*. The editor, Joe Comyns Carr, seems to have encouraged his hopes, and even commissioned from him a further piece – a humorous non-fiction essay on artists' models. Wilde delivered the article

promptly. But then a dismaying silence fell. Both manuscripts were left languishing in the editor's drawer.[74] Wilde, though, clearly believed that there should be a market for his fairy stories. He wrote up another one – 'The Selfish Giant' – which he showed to Laura Troubridge, in the hope that she might provide illustrations for it. But if he thought that pictures would be an additional inducement to a magazine editor, the ploy was not successful.[75]

Wilde finally achieved his breakthrough as a fiction writer not in a Macmillan-backed periodical, and not with a fairy tale. 'The Canterville Ghost', a humorous story of the supernatural, was published – with illustrations – in two numbers of the *Court and Society Review* at the beginning of 1887. The paper was a sympathetic one, a sophisticated (and short-lived) weekly that, under its editor Charles Gray Robertson and his young Balliol-educated assistant, Alsager Vian, covered such important topics as French '*Décadence*', contemporary opera, Godwin's theatrical productions, and 'ladies of the aristocracy'. Not only Oscar but also Constance and Lady Wilde were mentioned regularly in its social columns.[76] Robertson was delighted to add Wilde to his list of contributors.

Wilde's ghost story comically inverted the established tropes of the genre. The unfortunate ghost is terrorized by the boisterously philistine and materialist American family that takes a lease on the old English country house that is his home – before, in a romantically sentimental conclusion, he achieves a blessed release through the kindness of the family's teenage daughter. The American element in the story allowed Wilde to reuse and refine some of his transatlantic witticisms, such as the English having 'really everything in common with America nowadays, except, of course, language'. He even had the Ghost respond to a suggestion that he would not like America 'because we have no ruins and no curiosities', with the exclamation, 'No ruins! No curiosities! You have your navy and your manners.'*Although the Ghost might have not liked America, Wilde suspected that America would like the Ghost. He dispatched a copy of the typescript to Whitelaw Reid, editor of the New York *Tribune*, and the paper published the 'brilliant Anglo-American story' in their Sunday edition.[77]

Wilde hoped that the *Court and Society Review* would follow up the

---

* Wilde's decision to write a ghost story may have been, in part, an *hommage* to Godwin, who had died on 6 October 1886. According to the artist George Percy Jacomb-Hood, Godwin, during his last years, was cheerfully obsessed with 'ghost-lore', and would visit houses that had the reputation of being haunted, in the hope of seeing 'or even, by exceptional good luck, catching one'.

success of 'The Canterville Ghost' by publishing 'a short fairy tale' (perhaps 'The Selfish Giant').[78] But it seems that they wanted something more adult, more contemporary, more amusing, and perhaps more mysterious too. So Wilde set about writing up another of the stories he had been rehearsing over the previous months: the tale of the amiable young Lord Arthur Savile, who is told by a palmist that he is ineluctably fated to kill someone – and sets about trying fulfil his doom in the least offensive manner possible. In one brisk version Wilde recounted how Lord Arthur 'sent some poison by post to an uncle who had been ill for a long time, whose murder would be an act of humanity, and from whose will he expected to benefit. But what is one person's poison is another's cure, and a fortnight later his uncle gave a dinner party to celebrate his return to health.' Other well-meaning attempts are similarly foiled. Then: 'One night [Lord Arthur] was walking along the Thames Embankment in despair, and wondering whether suicide would count as murder, when he saw someone leaning over the parapet. No one was in sight, and the river was in flood. It was a heaven-sent-opportunity, the answer to his prayer. Leaning down quickly, he seized the unknown's legs; there was a splash in the dark swirling waters, and peace descended upon Lord Arthur. His duty done, he slept well.' Only on the following afternoon did he see in the paper a notice headed, 'Well-known Palmist drowned – Suicide of Mr. Ransom.' Lord Arthur sent to the funeral a wreath inscribed with the words, 'In Gratitude'.

Wilde spun numerous variations of the story, elaborating it with 'exquisite humour and fancy'. And although he might sometimes try to convince his listeners that he would not be publishing the tale – 'it's such a bore writing these things out' – no one was deceived.[79] 'Lord Arthur Savile's Crime' was duly published in the *Court and Society Review*, in three parts, in May 1887 (again with illustrations by the young artist F. H. Townsend). Although those who had heard the story might claim that Wilde's extemporized oral renditions had been far superior, there was still much to enjoy in the well-turned prose and crystallized wit of the print version. Lady Wilde wrote enthusiastically, calling the story 'most brilliant and attractive'. She thought the 'mystery' of the plot 'thrilling', and went on: 'All your epigrammatic style tells in this kind of work. You could be the Disraeli of fiction if you choose. And all your social knowledge comes in so well, especially your women.'[80]

Her verdict was very just. The story, even more than its predecessor, sounded a distinct and personal note – in the romantic glamour of its aristocratic settings (it opens at 'Lady Windermere's last reception before

Easter'), in the romantic unreality of its emotions, the playful absurdity of its plot, and the profligate scattering of its paradox. Wilde's own voice was clearly heard in such epigrams as: 'He had that rarest of all things, common sense'; 'Not being a genius, he had no enemies'; 'She had that inordinate passion for pleasure that is the secret of remaining young'; and 'Nothing looks so like innocence as an indiscretion'.

Wilde continued his happy connection with the *Court and Society Review* until shortly before its demise the following year, contributing occasional unsigned essays and reviews – and even a sonnet, just to remind the public that he was still a poet.[81] But his next two short stories were published in the *World*, which offered a higher profile and a wider readership. 'Lady Alroy' and 'The Model Millionaire' kept up the neat inversions, worldly comic tone and epigrammatic sparkle of the earlier pieces – while the second story (about a millionaire who poses for artists dressed as a beggar) also allowed him to redeploy some of the observations from his article about models that was still languishing in the manuscript chest at the *English Illustrated Magazine*.

It was pleasing to see his name regularly in print again. Bowered in his vermilion study, he could feel like a writer. Expanding into the role, he started to map out 'a story connected with Shakespeare's sonnets', as well as continuing to push his fairy tales.[82] Although he failed to find takers for them, he wrote up several more: 'The Nightingale and the Rose' (a poetical tale of love and self-sacrifice); 'The Devoted Friend' (a brutally comic story of exploitation); and 'The Remarkable Rocket', in which the supremely self-important firework of the title perhaps satirized the delusional vanity of Whistler. 'You should be thinking about others,' the Rocket informs a humble fire-cracker, at one moment, 'In fact you should be thinking about me. I am always thinking about myself, and I expect everybody else to do the same. That is what is called sympathy. It is a beautiful virtue, and I possess it in high degree.'

Not that any single interpretation of a story was ever allowed to hold sway. Wilde explained to one would-be expounder that he liked 'to fancy that there may be many meanings' in each tale: 'I did not start with an idea and clothe it in form, but began with a form and strove to make it beautiful enough to have many secrets, and many answers.'[83] Wilde called the stories 'studies in prose, put for Romance's sake into a fanciful form'. And if they were meant 'partly for children' they were intended more 'for those who have kept the childlike faculties of wonder and joy, and who find in simplicity

a subtle strangeness'[84] (he would sometimes describe the stories as being 'for Children from Eight to Eighty').[85] He read some of them to Theodore Watts, who was 'charmed' but suggested that they might be even better done in verse. Wilde, though, remained true to his conception of them as 'prose-cameos'.[86] They only wanted a publisher.

For all his activity, Wilde was still earning very little with his pen. Short stories, even when published, were scarcely more remunerative than book reviews. Financial worries continued to beset him. Interest payments on the money borrowed from Constance's marriage settlement and from Otho were not met.[87] When, in the rooms of Lord Francis Hope, the talk turned to finance, and it was reported that 'Money [was] very tight' in the City just then, Wilde cut in, 'Ah yes; and of a tightness that has been felt even in Tite Street.' Wilde claimed he had passed the morning 'at the British Museum looking at a gold-piece in a case'. To the young American author Edgar Saltus he cheerfully confided that the only thing he could now afford to pay was compliments.[88] In an effort at retrenchment there was even a plan to let Tite Street, the 'House Beautiful' upon which Constance and he had expended so much time, taste and money. But no tenant could be found, so they were obliged to live on there 'rather too extravagantly', as Constance put it, in the hope that 'after next year we shall be able to get on'.[89] And on this score there were some unexpected grounds for optimism.

7

Woman's World

*'It was a case of grammar versus mysticism, and the contest
is still raging. I fear I shall have to yield.'*

OSCAR WILDE

Oscar had been offered a job. In April 1887 he was approached by
Wemyss Reid, the general manager of Cassell's Publishing Company, with a view to editing 'and to some extent reconstructing' their
recently established up-market monthly, the *Lady's World*. Wilde's lingering
reputation as a dress reformer probably encouraged the approach, as well as
his profile as one half of a noted Aesthetic couple. The opportunity, with its
promise of an official title and a regular income, was both flattering and well
timed. Wilde agreed to take on the task.

He was full of ideas. Finding the magazine, in its existing state, 'too
feminine and not sufficiently womanly', he suggested a 'wider range' and a
'high[er] standpoint', less 'millinery and trimmings', fewer expensive fashion
plates, and more about what women 'think, and what they feel'. He wanted
women's thoughts on art and modern life, entertaining literary criticism ('if
a book is dull let us say nothing about it') along with a serial story ('exciting
but not tragic'). He imagined contributions from royalty (Princess Louise,
perhaps, or Princess Christian), from America (Julia Ward Howe), from Paris
(Madame Adam), from the universities (Mrs Humphrey Ward) and from the
occasional man.

Wilde was keen to disturb as well as exploit the conventional divisions between the sexes. In the realm of art, at least, he was ready to declare gender an irrelevance: 'artists have sex but art has none'. And he hoped that under his editorship the magazine would become one 'that men could read with pleasure, and consider it a privilege to contribute to'.[1] He advised a change of cover, and demanded a change of name.[2] The *Lady's World* seemed to him – and to all his women friends – to carry 'a certain taint of vulgarity'. A magazine that aimed to become 'the organ of women of intellect, culture and position' should be called *Woman's World*. The title, he claimed, had been suggested to him by Mrs Craik, the celebrated author of *John Halifax, Gentleman*.[3]

Terms were agreed, and Wilde began to draw a salary from 1 May. The exact amount is unknown, though one contemporary estimated it at £6 a week (over £300 a year); not huge, but very much more than he had been earning hitherto.[4] Although the first number for which Wilde was to be responsible was not due for over six months, he threw himself into preparations without a moment's delay: drawing up lists of potential contributors, aided by the indefatigable Mrs Jeune; arranging interviews 'with people of position and importance'; and writing 'innumerable letters' to solicit and suggest articles.

Women had been Wilde's great allies and supporters since the moment of his arrival in London. It was they who had welcomed him into their homes, delighted in his company and listened to his views on art. Now was a chance to repay them, through his enthusiasm, his engagement and his offer of 'a guinea a page' for all published articles (the same rate as the *Fortnightly Review* and *Nineteenth Century*). He wrote to established 'author-esses', literary ladies, social reformers, pioneering professionals, society hostesses and Oscar Browning. He sought contributions from Walter Pater's sister and the daughter of Matthew Arnold, from young Helena Sickert (freshly graduated from Girton) and from the scarcely older Violet Hunt. He swept up his friends Lady Archibald Campbell and Lady Dorothy Neville, and approached – more deferentially – the Countess of Jersey and the Marchioness of Salisbury. He commissioned his old companion Constance Fletcher ('George Fleming') to write the serial, and persuaded 'Violet Fane' (Mrs Singleton) to submit her poems.[5]

Perhaps his greatest coup was to secure the support of the popular novelist Ouida (or Maria Louisa Ramé). She was in London that season, over from Italy, and, having installed herself in a suite at the Langham Hotel, was entertaining with a lavish hand. Wilde went to pay court. There

was much to draw them together. The forty-eight-year-old Ouida was a literary phenomenon: her highly coloured novels of society life, with their independent-minded heroines and aristocratic heroes, may have been 'just beyond the high-water mark of books which could be safely admitted to the family library' but they were the bestsellers of the day. Born in modest circumstances in Bury St Edmunds, the young Miss Ramé had recast herself as a woman of mystery and allure. She possessed – as Mrs Jeune remarked – 'an insatiable love of notoriety' and a desire to know 'everyone worth knowing'. And despite her short, square figure, her eccentric dress sense and a voice like 'a carving knife', she had achieved the status of a 'Lionne' in London society, carried along by a mixture of romantic affectation and brazen self-assertion. 'Now that George Elliot [sic] is gone,' she is supposed to have declared, 'there is no one else [but me] who can write English.'

While most people of literary pretension looked down on her and her work, Wilde had been a champion of Ouida's books since his Oxford days. Although they might be overwritten, trivial and littered with solecisms, they had style. He claimed to find in them something of the same 'pictur-esqueness and loveliness of words' that he admired in Ruskin, Pater and Symonds (Ruskin, too, was an unlikely fan).[6]

Backed by his genuine enthusiasm Wilde soon became a privileged visitor at Ouida's Langham suite, attending not only the fashionable receptions but also her intimate dinners. He was an adept at flattering her and drawing her out. At one dinner party he told her, 'What I admire so much about your books is the wonderful vividness with which you portray scenery and environment. One but closes the eyes and finds oneself in the particular setting.' 'Ah, yes,' Ouida replied, 'all that is perfectly true, but that is not what is most wonderful about my books. What is most wonderful about my books is that I write as Duchesses talk.'[7] By the end of her stay (June 1887) Ouida was declaring that 'there was only one man in England... worth looking at or talking to, and he was Oscar Wilde'.[8] Wilde secured her commitment to write for his magazine – even though she, with charac-teristic contrariness, did not care for its new title.[9]

As news spread of his appointment, Wilde had also to field a deluge of unsolicited material. Among the old acquaintances who sought him out was the Irish artist and writer Edith Somerville. She gave an account of the editorial Wilde in action to her cousin and collaborator, Violet Martin: 'I went down to Oscar yesterday... He is a great fat oily beast... He pretended enormous interest... but it was all to no avail. He languidly took the sonnets

and is to return them by post. He talked great rot that "French subjects should be drawn by French artists" – I was near telling him, as Dr. Johnson said: "who drives fat oxen must himself be fat."'[10]

The inaugural number of *Woman's World* appeared at the beginning of November 1887, its handsome new decorative cover proclaiming the editorship of 'Oscar Wilde'. There were signed articles on E. W. Godwin's open-air theatricals at Coombe (illustrated with pictures of the author, 'Lady Archie' Campbell, cross-dressed as 'Orlando' in *As You Like It*), on 'Oxford Ladies' Colleges' and 'Alpine Scenery', on urban child poverty (by Mrs Jeune) and on Madame de Sevigny's grandmother (by Thackeray's daughter). One of Wilde's discoveries, Amy Levy ('a mere girl, but a girl of genius'), contributed a very short story. The Countess of Portsmouth provided a rather longer essay on 'The Position of Women' – ingeniously suggesting that the greater independence and growing power of women might be used 'to make men stronger'. Fashion was not neglected, but the eight well-illustrated pages on the latest modes from London and Paris were placed at the back of the magazine, rather than at the front, where such matter usually appeared.[11] Wilde contributed 'Literary and Other Notes', a round-up of books by female authors from Princess Christian to his old Oxford friend Margaret Bradley (now 'Margaret L. Woods') – whom he generously compared to Dostoyevsky. There was also a eulogistic paragraph on Mrs Craik, who had died shortly after sending her last story in to the new venture.

The debut of Wilde's magazine, eagerly anticipated, created a decided stir – at least in London. It was reported that on the evening after publication 'there was not one [copy] in the West End to be had for love or money'.[12] The reaction was favourable. The re-launch was pronounced a 'success' – a 'decided improvement' on *Lady's World*. Its 'excellent illustrations' received general notice, as did the 'distinguished' line-up of 'lady' contributors. There was praise for the 'wider scope' of the articles, the 'greater variety of subjects' and the 'higher' tone of discussion.[13] Wilde's literary notes were described variously as 'crisp', 'interesting' and 'well-written'. The *Spectator* remarked approvingly that he did not 'obtrude either his personality or his well-known views too much on his readers'.[14]

The future success of the magazine was prophesied, and set down to Wilde's role as editor – 'a circumstance which, no doubt, will carry its full weight with the gentle sex'.[15] Women had 'wooed his cause' before, and it was expected that they would do so again.[16] There was one dissenting voice: Lady Wilde was most put out that Oscar had failed to mention her

in his note about a recent anthology of women writers. And she hastened
to let him know it.

DEAR MR EDITOR,
   Why didn't you name *me* in the review of Mrs Sharp's book? Me,
who holds such an historic place in Irish literature? and you name Miss
Tynan and Miss Mulholland!
   The Hampshire Review gives me splendid notice – *you* – well, 'tis
strange. I have lent the *Woman's World* by O.W. to Mrs Fisher. Lady
Archie is the best of the women essayists. George Fleming begins inter-
esting – and is good – but women in general are a wretched lot.
   Did you read Willie on soda water – it is so brilliant – [Lewis] Arnold,
[editor of the *Daily Telegraph*] was delighted.
   Come for a talk on Sunday evening. I have so little time left now – for
I must certainly drown myself in a week or two. Life is quite too much
trouble.
   La tua
   LA MADRE DOLOROSA[17]

Wilde was able to assuage the maternal ire by placing Lady Wilde's 'Historic Women' as the opening piece for the January 1888 number. The 259-
line poem included some stirring words on Queen Victoria ('Supreme
above all women... blending with her royal majesty / The soft sweet music
of a woman's life').[18] And a copy was dispatched to Windsor, eliciting a
prompt response from a lady-in-waiting that the queen 'likes the poem very
much.'[19] Emboldened, Wilde inquired whether her majesty might care to
contribute to the magazine herself – perhaps 'some of the poetry written
by the Queen when young'. But the offer was not taken up.*
   Wilde's star was 'ascending once more'.[20] He relished his role as editor.
On three mornings a week he would set off from Tite Street, take the
underground from Sloane Square to Charing Cross (now Embankment
Station), stroll up the Strand and along Fleet Street, before turning through
an archway into 'La Belle Sauvage', the former coaching inn yard where
Cassell's had their premises. In this bustling establishment (which also

---

*   The queen wrote on the request, passed on by her private secretary: 'Really what will
     people not say and invent. Never could the Queen in her whole life write *one line of
     poetry* serious or comic or make a Rhyme even. This is therefore all *invention* and a *myth*.'

contained the firm's printing presses) Wilde stood out as an exotic bird.
Beautifully groomed and elegantly attired, he was, as one fellow employee
noted, 'easily the best-dressed man in the place'. His office was shared with
an editorial assistant. Wilde found the twenty-seven-year-old Arthur Fish
not only 'reliable and intelligent' but sympathetic also; he came to count
him as a 'real friend'.[21]

Fish later recalled those early days of editorial engagement: 'A smiling
entrance, letters would be answered with epigrammatic brightness, there
would be a cheery interval of talk when the work was accomplished, and
the dull room would brighten under the influence of [Wilde's] great personality.'[22] The magazine began to evolve a distinctive character: cultured,
high-minded, socially engaged, yet stylish too.

There seems to have been a deliberate editorial policy to give a balanced coverage of the great feminine topics of the day: 'The Fallacy of the Superiority
of Man' was matched by 'The Fallacy of the Equality of Women', 'Woman's
Suffrage' with 'Reasons for Opposing Woman's Suffrage'. But Fish had no
doubt that the 'keynote' of the periodical, under Wilde's guidance, was 'the
right of woman to equality of treatment with man'. Many of the articles on
political and social subjects were 'far in advance of the thought of the day'.
And Wilde encouraged this. Whenever Wemyss Reid called by to talk over
controversial articles, Wilde 'would always express his entire sympathy with
the views of the writers and reveal a liberality of thought in regard to the
political aspirations of women that was undoubtedly sincere'.[23]

Wilde had to endure some frustrations with the management. Reid protested against the 'too literary tendencies' of the first few numbers; and
also maintained a tight control on finances.[24] But such checks did little to
detract from the pleasures of the job. It was a novelty to hold an official
position. At least one friend considered that 'society' began to take Wilde
'seriously' for the first time when he became editor of Woman's World.[25]

Wilde's position at the helm of a respected monthly gave him a new standing in the literary sphere. He was now an acknowledged professional who
could meet with fellow professionals on more or less equal terms. He became
friendly with Frank Harris, the recently appointed editor of the Fortnightly
Review (the introduction was effected by Mrs Jeune). They lunched together
regularly. The brash, unscrupulous Harris, who had left school at thirteen,
was fascinated by Wilde's university-trained erudition and wit. Wilde found
Harris's energy and curiosity by turns bracing and exhausting.[26]

Another new, and equally combative, literary companion was W. E.

Henley, who until the year before had been the editor of Cassell's *Magazine of Art* and was now acting as consultant for its rival, the *Art Journal*. Five years Wilde's senior, Henley was a striking figure, tall and broad-shouldered, with unkempt red hair and beard. As a result of tuberculosis of the bone his left leg had been amputated below the knee. He walked with a crutch, and had, famously, served Stevenson as the model for Long John Silver in *Treasure Island*. Veering between rollicking joviality and furious indignation, he was both 'astoundingly clever' and astoundingly opinionated. In politics he was a rabid unionist and imperialist, while in art and literature he favoured 'realism'. It was said of him that he was affected by Pre-Raphaelitism 'as some people are affected by a cat in the room'.[27]

Given these prejudices it was unsurprising that, in the past, he had tended to regard Wilde with suspicion. Now, though, he was anxious to meet, and he persuaded a former Cassell's associate to arrange a dinner. According to legend, Henley attempted to rile Wilde with insults and contradictions throughout the meal, and although at first Wilde turned aside these thrusts, remarking blandly 'Yes,' 'No,' 'Is that so?', he eventually roused himself, and a long, impassioned argument ensued. Their host turned them out of the house in the early hours, still arguing. And when he saw Wilde the next day at the office and asked how matters had ended, Wilde replied, 'Oh, we finished the argument over a rasher just one hour ago.'[28]

The incident proved the basis for a sudden – and short-lived – friendship. W. B. Yeats recalled meeting Wilde for the first time at one of the regular 'Sunday evenings' that Henley hosted at his home in Chiswick. Wilde had been hugely impressive, talking brilliantly, and – to Yeats's amazement – in perfectly rounded sentences. It was on that evening that he described Pater's *Renaissance* as his 'golden book', claiming, 'I never travel without it; but it is the very flower of decadence; the last trumpet should have sounded the moment it was written.' To the dullard who asked, 'Would you not have given us time to read it?' he replied, 'Oh no – there would have been plenty of time afterwards – in either world.' Wilde had also impressed Henley with his account of how he kept the Cassell's management in its place by never answering their letters: 'I have known men come to London full of bright prospects and seen them complete wrecks in a few months through a habit of answering letters.'

Afterwards Henley had remarked approvingly of Wilde, 'No, he is not an aesthete [a term of abuse in Henley's book]; one soon finds that he is a scholar and a gentleman.' Wilde would have been pleased at the verdict.

He wanted to impress Henley. As he later confessed to Yeats, 'I had to strain every nerve to equal that man at all.'[29]

This tension created a stimulating energy to their relationship. The art-journalist C. Lewis Hind recalled one evening of 'wild, wilful' talk at Chiswick, when Henley and Wilde had discoursed on Shelley: it had been 'broadsword against rapier'.[30] The tension, however, was always likely to tip out of balance. Another contemporary remembered seeing the two men leaving the theatre in conversation; Wilde said something, and Henley threw his crutch at him.[31] Wilde described the basis of literary friendship as 'mixing the poison bowl', and the description would prove apt in the case of Henley. Wilde himself, though, was no poisoner. His instincts were all for human sympathy and professional generosity. When Henley's elderly mother fell ill, he wrote to condole: 'All poets love their mothers, and as I worship mine I can understand how you feel.'[32] And he wrote a very positive – if slightly arch – review of Henley's *Book of Verse*, praising 'the strong humane personality' revealed in the work.[33]

Associations such as these served to draw Wilde closer to the heart of the literary establishment. He became a member of the Society of Authors, which had been set up by Robbie Ross's older brother, Alec. He attended their banquet in recognition of the American authors who were working to achieve international copyright – although the evening proved something of a fiasco as he found himself sitting next to Lady Colin Campbell, with whom he had not been on speaking terms since she had referred to him as 'that Great White Caterpillar'.[34] He had a jollier time as the guest of honour at a bibliophiles' dinner given by the 'Sette of Odd Volumes', where he had delivered 'a most brilliant speech' in praise of Buffalo Bill, who had recently brought his Wild West show to London.[35] Henley offered to put him up for membership of the Savile Club, the leading literary club of the day. Wilde had thought that his appearing there even for lunch was akin to 'a poor lion' rashly intruding 'into a den of fierce Daniels', and that membership would be a step too far; so it proved. Despite the backing of Henry James, Edmund Gosse, Rider Haggard, Alec Ross, George Macmillan and some twenty-five others, Wilde's election was never secured.[36]

Nevertheless, despite such occasional rebuffs, Wilde was increasingly willing to involve himself in public life and public questions. He had become a figure at meetings, a member of committees. At one gathering to discuss a proposed 'British Association for the Advancement of Art and Industry' he good-humouredly denounced Edmund Gosse for quoting Board of Trade

statistics: 'Things,' Wilde declared, 'which we do not want to hear about at all.'[37] Much to Whistler's irritation he was also asked to join the committee of the National Art Exhibition that was being established by a group of Chelsea-based artists in opposition to the Royal Academy. Whistler promptly published a letter in the *World* condemning Wilde's involvement: 'What has Oscar in common with Art? except that he dines at our tables and picks from our platters the plums for the pudding he peddles in the provinces. Oscar – the amiable, irresponsible, esurient Oscar – with no more sense of a picture than the fit of a coat, has the courage of the opinions – of others!'[38] Wilde replied the following week, 'Atlas, this is very sad! With our James "vulgarity begins at home", and should be allowed to stay there.'[39]

He began to look beyond cultural issues to social and political ones. Although always, nominally, a Liberal voter, Wilde had previously stood aloof from party politics. Beyond espousing a firm belief in Irish Home Rule, a poetical Republicanism and a vague attachment to 'socialist' ideals, Wilde had concentrated his political creed into the statement that he was in favour of 'civilization' in its struggle against 'barbarism'.[40]

By the mid-1880s such splendid isolation was harder to maintain. In 1885, the seventy-five-year-old Gladstone, recently returned to office, 'converted' to the cause of Irish Home Rule and Land Reform, aligning himself and the Liberals with the eighty-six MPs of the Irish Parliamentary Party under their charismatic leader, Charles Stewart Parnell. Together with these new allies, Gladstone hoped to carry a Home Rule Bill. But the measure, brought before parliament in June 1886, was defeated when a large section of the Liberal Party rebelled and voted against it. The debacle split the Liberals between the 'Gladstonians' and the 'Unionists' and sharpened the divisions in British political life. Gladstone called an immediate election – effectively a referendum on the Home Rule question. He was soundly defeated, the Tories and 'Liberal Unionists' securing a large majority. Nevertheless the great hope of achieving political devolution for Ireland through the British parliamentary system had been kindled. Both Gladstone and Parnell were optimistic that victory was possible. And many people felt inspired to rally to the cause. Wilde was one of them.

In the summer of 1887 he became a member of the Eighty Club. It was a public proclamation of his political commitment. Founded in 1880 to promote 'the Liberal cause', the club was rapidly developing into the core ground for Gladstonian liberalism and a 'think tank' for Irish Home Rule policy. In the wake of the 1886 general election the club's 'Unionist'

members had been obliged to resign en masse; to replace them some eighty new members were elected at a meeting on 29 June 1887. Wilde was almost certainly part of this intake. He found himself among familiar faces. Others who joined at the same time included George Macmillan, Justin McCarthy and Lord Houghton; E. T. Cook (who edited the literary pages of the *Pall Mall Gazette*) and Charles Dilke were already members, and may have proposed Wilde for membership.

Whatever optimism was felt by the Eighty Club membership, it was tempered by concern and anger over the immediate political situation. In August 1887 Arthur Balfour, the Conservative chief secretary of Ireland, introduced his Coercion Act, assuming sweeping powers to 'restore order' in the face of widespread rural unrest. Aided by his implacable legal officer, Wilde's old Trinity contemporary Edward Carson, he secured summary convictions against prominent Home Rule campaigners working in Ireland. The English poet Wilfrid Scawen Blunt and the Irish politician William O'Brien were among those imprisoned.

Wilde deplored such measures, and worked – in his own way – to counter them. Besides attending official Eighty Club events, he also supported such occasions as Justin McCarthy's lecture at the Southwark Irish Literary Club on the revolutionary 'Literature of '48'. He even gave an impromptu address at the event, mentioning that his mother (whose work had been quoted in the lecture) was bringing out a volume on Irish Legends, and that he would 'present a copy of the work to every Irish club in London'.[41] He also began to salt his articles, and the occasional book reviews that he continued to contribute to the *Pall Mall Gazette*, with Home Rule sentiment and anti-Tory rhetoric. Old friends who espoused the wrong side of the debate were taken to task.

He penned a witty demolition of 'Mr Mahaffy's new book', an overview of 'Greek Life and Thought' that drew numerous parallels with the current Irish situation from a strong Unionist point of view – calling it an 'unworthy', 'biased' and 'provincial' attempt 'to treat the Hellenic world as "Tipperary writ large"... and to finish the battle of Chaeronea on the plains of Mitchelstown [where William O'Brien had been convicted]'.[42] When Wilfrid Blunt produced a volume of poems, *In Vinculis*, based on his Irish prison experiences, Wilde reviewed it enthusiastically, remarking on the 'admirable effect' that incarceration had had on his poetry. Literature, he suggested, may not be 'much indebted to Mr. Balfour for his sophistical *Defence of Philosophic Doubt*, which is one of the dullest books we know, but

it must be admitted that by sending Mr. Blunt to gaol he has converted a clever rhymer into an earnest and deep-thinking poet.'[43]

All the while Wilde introduced into *Woman's World* regular articles on Irish subjects, containing hints of the oppressive conditions of English rule and emphasizing the distinctiveness of Irish culture. Lady Wilde contributed a compendium of 'Irish Peasant Tales' to the November 1888 number, and only a few months later Wilde himself devoted his 'Literary Notes' to a discussion of Yeats's 'charming little book *Fairy and Folk Tales of the Irish Peasantry*'. Recalling his mother's earlier strictures, he included a long quotation from Yeats's book praising Lady Wilde's own works on the subject. He printed, too, Lady Sandhurst's ringing call to the pro-Irish Liberal cause, entitled 'A Woman's Work in Politics'.[44]

The specific concerns of Irish Home Rule also drew Wilde into the currents of political radicalism in general, and socialism in particular. As one contributor to *Woman's World* put it, the 'socialistic legislation' advocated by Gladstonian Liberals over Irish land reform meant that 'the Irish question is really a branch of socialism'. And this connection was dramatically reinforced in November 1887 when a mass rally in Trafalgar Square, organized by the Irish National League and the Social Democratic Federation to protest against Irish coercion and British unemployment, was brutally broken up by police and armed troops. 'Bloody Sunday', as it was soon dubbed, became a defining moment in the narratives of both Irish Home Rule and British socialism. Among those arrested were the Liberal MP Robert Cunninghame-Graham and the radical trade unionist John Burns.

The word 'socialism' had long had an attraction for Wilde. He had met it in the writings of William Morris. He had used it at the beginning of the 1880s to try and impress Violet Hunt. During the second half of the decade, however, he began to explore it more thoroughly. At the end of 1885 he took out a subscription to William Morris's socialist paper, *Commonweal*.[45] He also came to know his near coeval – and fellow *Pall Mall Gazette* reviewer – George Bernard Shaw. A Dubliner living in London and struggling to make a living with his pen, Shaw was an avowed radical. Together with his sister, Lucy, he attended a few of Lady Wilde's receptions, and he recalled Wilde's generous but ill-fated, attempts to be kind to him ('We put each other out frightfully'.) The lower-middle-class autodidact Shaw insisted on regarding the university-trained Wilde as a 'Dublin snob'. Yet, despite their differences of temper, outlook, education and background, they developed a certain mutual regard. Each recognised the other as 'a man of distinction', and one

unfairly judged by the popular estimate. If they did not quite become friends they shared an awkward, but real, admiration.

Shaw, an enthusiastic convert to socialism and a member of the Fabian Society, was always anxious to advance his views. Wilde was present at one small gathering, in the rooms of the Irish novelist Joseph Fitzgerald Molloy, when Shaw held forth at length on his plans for founding a magazine as an organ for his political thought. Wilde listened with interest; although when Shaw declared emphatically that the periodical was to be called 'Shaw's Magazine – Shaw! Shaw! Shaw!' – he did gently subvert the moment with the inquiry (punning on '*pshaw*'), 'And how would you spell it?'[46]

Despite this quip, Wilde 'thought highly' of Shaw as an original and challenging political thinker; indeed one mutual friend unkindly suggested that Wilde's whole admiration for socialism derived from the fact that 'it was odd and Shaw was Irish'. Although this was an exaggeration, the connection with Shaw certainly sharpened Wilde's interest in the subject. And Shaw, for his part, recognized that such interest was genuine. He was greatly impressed when Wilde – alone of all his literary contacts – signed his 1887 petition seeking clemency for six anarchists condemned to death after a bomb blast at a rally in Chicago.[47]

Wilde's growing engagement with social injustice – in his work and his life – was coloured by emotion as much as by thought. Although he hoped to 'mirror modern life' and 'deal with modern problems' in his fairy stories, the actions of the Happy Prince and the little swallow were perhaps examples more of Christian self-sacrifice than socialist engagement.[48] And although intellectually Wilde might espouse the socialist idea that charity degrades and demoralizes the poor by offering a temporary palliative rather than providing a permanent solution, in his own personal dealings he was always generous, if almost invariably quixotic. Edgar Saltus recalled arriving back at Tite Street with Wilde one winter's evening, and being approached by a poor thinly clad man, shivering against the bitter chill. Saltus gave the fellow a shilling. Wilde 'with entire simplicity took off his overcoat' and put it about the man's shoulders. The action was made more striking by the fact that Wilde – temporarily abandoning his socialist pose – had been holding forth earlier in the evening, declaring, 'If I were king I would sit in a great hall and paint on green ivory and when my ministers came and told me that the people were starving, I would continue to paint on green ivory and say: "Let them starve."' On another occasion, when approached by a beggar who lamented that he had 'no work' to do and 'no bread to eat', Wilde had

replied, 'Work! Why should you want to work? And bread! Why should you eat bread?' He had continued solemnly, 'Now, if you had come to me and said that you had work to do, but you couldn't dream of working, and that you had bread to eat, but couldn't think of eating bread – I would have given you half a crown.' Then, after a pause: 'As it is, I give you two shillings.'[49]

Nevertheless Wilde showed his commitment to the socialist cause in many direct ways. Although (unlike Shaw) he was not present at the 'Bloody Sunday' riot, he involved himself in its aftermath. He was at Bow Street police court on 14 November when Cunninghame-Graham and Burns were charged with assaulting the police.[50] He attended meetings promoting the various shades of socialist opinion, from moderate 'gradualism' to extreme 'anarchism'. He was seen – albeit an incongruous figure, beautifully dressed and decidedly fat – at the regular talks hosted by the Fabian Society and others at Willis's Rooms, off St James's. He was present at a 'crowded evening meeting in William Morris's Coach House' at Hammersmith – his buttonhole 'a very large dahlia, crimson, beautiful in its amplitude but not', according to one observer, 'what one would expect to find on a man's coat'.[51]

In his engagement with public and political life, Wilde was supported by Constance. She shared, and encouraged, his interests. She wrote to the papers on matters of dress reform, and became (in 1886) a member of the Rational Dress Society, even editing its journal from April 1888 to July 1889. She overcame her shyness to develop into an impressive platform speaker. She contributed two articles to Woman's World, both on dress.[52] She espoused Home Rule and the Liberal cause, signing up with the Women's Liberal Association, speaking at their events, and earning a reputation as a 'pretty little radical'. When Cunninghame-Graham came to trial, it was Constance rather than Oscar who was in the gallery.[53]

Politics drew the Wildes into the circles of the Liberal elite. They were present, along with Gladstone, at Lady Sandhurst's party on Portland Place, in aid of the Liberal Association of Marylebone.[54] They attended the crowded breakfast receptions hosted by T. P. O'Connor, the editor of the fervently radical Star newspaper. It was at one of these occasions that Wilde, in 'fairly scintillating' form, charmed his hostess with a characteristic spark of wit. With T. P. O'Connor talking intently to 'a radiant blonde', Wilde asked 'Mrs T. P.' if she wasn't jealous? She denied it, claiming that T. P. didn't know a pretty woman when he saw one. Harold Frederic (the London correspondent of the New York Times) cut in with, 'I beg leave to differ; what about yourself?' Mrs T. P. answered, 'Oh, I was an accident.' 'Rather,' Wilde corrected, 'a catastrophe!'[55]

8

A Study in Green

*'What we have to do, what at any rate it is our duty to do, is
to revive this old art of Lying.'*

OSCAR WILDE

In 1888 both Oscar and Constance, showing an impressive unanimity
of purpose, brought out volumes of fairy stories. *There Was Once* by
'Mrs Oscar Wilde' was a gathering of retold tales (Little Red Riding
Hood, Cinderella, etc.) recounted in both prose and verse, and illustrated
throughout. Oscar's book, his first published volume since the *Poems* of
1881, brought together five of his original fairy tales under the title *The
Happy Prince and Other Tales*. It had been a long struggle to get the stories into
print; repeated approaches to magazine editors had met without success.
He had then contacted George Macmillan with the idea of bringing them
out in book form, but the Macmillan's reader, having looked them over,
decided that, despite their 'point and cleverness', they were unlikely 'to
rush into marked popularity'.[1] In frustration Wilde turned to David Nutt
& Co., a smaller firm with a reputation for fine printing. They agreed to
produce the book, although whether Wilde contributed to the production
costs is not known.

While Constance's book was aimed squarely at the nursery, Oscar's tome
proclaimed a decidedly different intention. Like *Poems* it was – as Oscar put it

– very 'daintily got up', with illustrations from the prestigious pen of Walter Crane and 'decorations' by the young Impressionist George Jacomb-Hood. To appeal to the bibliophile a special edition of seventy-five copies was produced on hand-made paper, each copy signed by the author, and priced, steeply, at one guinea. The 'ordinary' edition was only slightly smaller in format and only slightly diminished in daintiness. It was published in a relatively modest first printing of 1,000 copies, priced at a still-substantial 5s. The book was dedicated to Carlos Blacker.[2]*

The Happy Prince and Other Tales appeared at the beginning of June and was well received, being widely noticed and generously reviewed.[3] Perhaps it was Wilde's choice of genre that had altered the critical perspective – and perhaps Wilde had guessed that this would be so.[4] Perhaps, too, Wilde's altered status played its part. He had changed from the bumptiously affected young Aesthete, who had so annoyed the critics at the beginning of the decade, into a seemly responsible public figure. Certainly none of the personal animus that greeted his *Poems* was evident in the press response: no cries of plagiarism, insincerity or affectation. He was frequently – and not unfavourably – compared to Hans Andersen. The *World* called the book 'the prettiest child's story-book we have had since *Alice in Wonderland*'.

There was general recognition that, although there was much for children to enjoy, the stories were likely to appeal rather more to adults, spiced as they were with 'a piquant touch of contemporary satire'. Wilde's recipe for friendship, given in 'The Devoted Friend', was much enjoyed: 'A true friend always says unpleasant things, and does not mind giving pain. Indeed if he is a really true friend he prefers it, for he knows that then he is doing good.'[5] The only doubt remained as to the pervading mood of the stories: the *Spectator* thought that beneath their 'subtle sarcasm' the defining 'note' was 'melancholy'; but Robbie Ross's brother, Alec, reviewing the book in the *Saturday Review*, suggested that, despite the spirit of 'bitter satire', the abiding mood was 'a very pleasant sensation of the humorous'.[6] Although one of the characters in the book remarks that 'to tell a story with a moral

---

*   As with *Poems* Wilde persuaded Roberts Bros of Boston to produce a simultaneous American edition, offering them 'the advance sheets and electros' from the English publishers. He was dismayed, though, when they trimmed down the pages to produce a very much smaller book: '*Why* oh! why did you not keep my large margin,' he lamented. 'I assure you that there are subtle scientific relations between margin and style, and my stories read quite differently in your edition.' Wilde to Thomas Niles, partner at Roberts Bros (Private Collection).

is always a very dangerous thing to do', it was noted approvingly that all the tales did seem to have 'a moral' even if it was never 'obtrusively pointed'. One reviewer described the underlying message as being 'that unselfishness is moral beauty, and that vain display is moral ugliness'.[7]

The book sold briskly, and Wilde was soon boasting of its 'success'.[8] He scattered presentation copies among friends and connections. Gladstone received one. So did Ruskin. Walter Pater wrote a gratifying thank-you note to say that he been 'consoling' himself with the 'delightful' book during an attack of gout. He praised some of the descriptions as 'little poems in prose' and hardly knew 'whether to admire more the wise wit of "The [Remarkable] Rocket," or the beauty and tenderness of "The Selfish Giant"'. Ellen Terry declared, 'I *think* I love "The Nightingale & the Rose" the best', and suggested that she might read it 'some day to some nice people – or even *not* nice people, and *make* 'em nice.' Wilde was delighted at this idea of a public recitation, but sadly nothing came of it.[9] The librarian at Toynbee Hall, to whom Wilde had likewise sent a copy, also loved 'The Nightingale and the Rose' best. He thought that 'every earnest man, woman and child (and that means all children)' should 'cry out a rich thanksgiving of delight' to the author of such a tale: 'To me it is nothing less than [a] miracle *to feel* the gorgeous flood-tide of human passion beneath the surface, and *to see* the delicate and steadfast simplicity of the language. You seem to have engaged with Human Love as the Eye with External Objects.'[10]*

Within six months the first edition was sold out. And although a new (and slightly cheaper at 3s 6d) – edition failed to maintain the momentum, there was no doubt that *The Happy Prince and Other Tales* had been, in its way, a minor triumph: one of the notable books of the season.[11]

The success encouraged Wilde to continue writing fairy stories, deploying the genre to extend the possibilities of his prose, his social commentary – and his subversion of sexual norms. He now found periodicals ready to publish them. His next tale concerned 'The Young King' – an extreme Aesthete, who, on the verge of his coronation, is confronted by the great social and moral cost of the worldly luxury he so adores, and – turning from it – embraces a Christ-like simplicity that, to the astonishment of his

---

* Wilde did have to endure some criticism from literal-minded ornithologists. A Mr J. R. Earl wrote to point out that Wilde's description of the nightingale making her nest 'in the holm-oak tree' was inaccurate, as 'the nightingale almost invariably builds her nest upon the ground'.

courtiers, his subjects and his clergy, yields him a far greater, miraculous, splendour. Despite the tale's emphatic spiritual and social message, Carlos Blacker seems to have disapproved of some elements in it – possibly the distinct homoerotic flavor of the young king's Aestheticism. He is described as worshipping an image of Adonis and kissing a statue of Antinous.

Certainly when the story was published in the *Lady's Pictorial* at the end of the year, Blacker wrote to the fervently Anglo-Catholic Duke of Newcastle, remarking: 'Our friend Oscar was impenetrable yesterday to my attacks on what "you wot of" & laughed it all away. It has now been however arranged that all his manuscripts are in future to be submitted to me for approval, & I shall make a wholesome slaughter of his humours and tempers, when the occasion deserves it. He had no excuses to offer & disarmed me by his extreme hilarity, saying he had foreseen and anticipated my strictures.'[12] Nevertheless, although one paper called the story a 'weird and wild' allegory, most commentators thought it possessed of both 'charm' and 'an admirable moral', besides being 'exquisitely expressed'.[13] Even Henley, it seems, was enthusiastic over its style. Claiming Flaubert as his master, Wilde told him 'to learn how to write English prose I have studied the prose of France. I am charmed that *you* recognize it: that shows I have succeeded. I am also charmed that no one else does: that shows I have succeeded also.'[14]

The return to story writing and book production gave Wilde a new sense of his own literary worth. It also began to draw him away from *Woman's World* and the chores of the editor's office. With his growing roster of commitments – literary, journalistic, political, social and domestic – he had come to feel himself 'overworked'. Something had to give. His three days a week at La Belle Sauvage soon dwindled to two. His assistant, Arthur Fish, became adept at telling 'by [Wilde's] footfalls along the corridor whether the day's work would be met cheerfully or postponed to a more convenient period'. In the latter case Wilde 'would sink with a sigh into his chair, carelessly glance at his letters, give a perfunctory look at the proofs or make-up, ask, "Is it necessary to settle anything to-day?" put on his hat with a sad "Good morning," and depart again'. The hours gradually shortened: his arrival became later and his departure earlier, 'until at times his visit was little more than a call'.

His 'Literary Notes' became cursory, then ceased altogether for seven months (between March and November 1888), before Wemyss Reid induced him to take them up again. Wilde's early industry meant that he had more than enough articles on hand, and instead of the pleasures of commissioning,

had to devote much of his time to rejecting work or explaining to contributors why their pieces had not yet appeared.[15]* And although it was nice to
have an income, he came to consider that it was not nearly large enough: he
took to writing verses and 'rude remarks' concerning it on the back of each
month's salary receipt form.[16]

He did, though, continue to enjoy the privileged position his job gave
him with women. He developed an enthusiasm for the elegantly mondaine
Bibidie Leonard. The daughter of an exiled Irish nationalist, she had been
brought up in Paris before moving to London, and something of the dangerous glamour of the French capital still attached to her. She had achieved
a reputation as both milliner and mistress to the fashionable. Wilde, who
seems to have met her through his mother's receptions, asked her to produce
an article on the celebrated *saloniste* 'Madame Adam'.[17] The piece was never
written, but Wilde became a frequent visitor to Leonard's house on Regent's
Park – fascinated by her sophisticated allure, and the hold that she exerted
over men. She became for him a model of the modern *femme fatale*. He
claimed that she taught him more than any other woman: 'She was not the
least immoral,' he explained to a friend. 'Immoral women are rarely attractive. What made her quite irresistible was that she was unmoral.'[18]

Constance – who was conscious of the drawing-away of Wilde's emotional and sexual interest, but misread its cause – became jealous at his fascination with Leonard. Wilde, it seems, was not entirely unhappy to break
off the connection, perhaps finding it rather too demanding. He brought it
to a definite end – although, to give suitable drama to the moment, he made
the break with 'three stanzas of passionate' verse. Leonard, however, was
not taken in. She suspected, probably correctly, that Wilde was re-using lines
from an already written poem.[19]

Among Wilde's other female protégées of the moment was the young
American actress Elizabeth Robins, who was passing through London in the
summer of 1888. Dark-eyed, beautiful and intense, she was already marked
by tragedy: only the year before, her husband, a minor actor in the same

---

*   OW did still engage with impressive thoroughness on many fronts. On 26 September
     1889, he wrote to Charlotte Stopes (mother of the more famous Marie) returning her
     article on frozen meat: 'With your contention that frozen meat ought to come into the
     scope of the Adulteration Act, I fully agree, and so I should think must everyone, but
     as to the prejudicial effects of the process of refrigeration on the flavour and nutritious
     properties of meat... I cannot help feeling that your views are somewhat exaggerated
     and should be glad if you could see your way to modify your expressions.'

Boston company, had committed suicide (by jumping into the Charles River in a full suit of stage armour), leaving her a widow at twenty-six. Wilde met her at a reception given by Lady Seton and encouraged her to think of staying in England and making a career on the London stage. 'You should give a matinee,' he suggested, as a first step. When, some weeks later, he learnt that she was on the verge of contracting to appear in a production of a 'questionable' play to be mounted by the 'penniless adventurer' Sir Randall Roberts, he advised her against the step.

Springing into action, he put Robins in touch with an agent. He insisted that she engage George Lewis as her solicitor, to look over any contracts (describing him as 'Brilliant. Formidable. A man of the world... he knows all about us – and forgives us all'). And he secured for her an interview with Herbert Beerbohm Tree, who was then enjoying his first great success as an actor-manager. Robins always remembered Wilde's energy and kindness. In her unpublished memoir, she wrote, 'I could do nothing for him; he could and did do everything in his power for me.' Her diaries of the time abound with notes of meetings, letters, practical suggestions, words of advice: one day concludes with the legend, 'A blessed man is Oscar Wilde.' In the end, Tree's half-promise to give her work convinced Robins to cash in her return ticket and remain in England.[20]

The whole affair allowed Wilde to engage with the theatrical world that he still longed to enter. But it was also an act of practical kindness and imaginative sympathy. The record of his life is littered with similarly generous deeds, often unglamorous and unsung. He interested himself, for instance, in the 'very poor friend' of a clergyman acquaintance, helping her sell a valuable 'Indian necklace'.[21] He was generous with his advice and, despite his own lack of funds, was always ready to lend what he had.[22] Although Wilde claimed to have no sympathy with sickness, Otho Lloyd was told that he had sat at the bedside of a friend who 'was in the height of smallpox'.[23] Bernard Berenson thought him 'the kindest man imaginable'.[24]

When Mrs Sickert's husband died unexpectedly she became almost 'mad with grief'. But, though she shut herself up, Wilde sought her out and insisted on seeing her. Nellie Sickert recalled how he took both her hands and drew her – still crying – to a chair, beside which he set his own:

> I left them alone. He stayed a long time, and before he went I heard my mother laughing. When he had gone she was a woman transformed. He had made her talk; had asked questions about my father's last illness

and allowed her to unburden her heart of those torturing memories. Gradually he had talked of my father, of his music, of the possibilities of a memorial exhibition of his pictures. Then, she didn't know how, he had begun to tell her all sorts of things which he contrived to make interesting and amusing. 'And then I laughed,' she said, 'I thought I should never laugh again.'[25]

In the autumn of 1888 Wilde was engaged in helping his own mother. The continuing unrest in rural Ireland meant that the rents of the Moytura estate were largely unpaid, and she was without an income. And although her books – *Driftwood from Scandinavia* (1884) and *Ancient Legends, Mystic Charms and Superstitions of Ireland* (1887) – and her occasional articles, brought in something, it was not enough. Willie, meanwhile, remained completely irresponsible; earning good money at the *Telegraph*, he spent it all on drink and late nights.* To reduce their expenses they moved from Park Street to Chelsea, taking a house at 146 Oakley Street, just round the corner from Oscar and Constance. More, however, needed to be done.

To improve his mother's position, Wilde revived the campaign to secure her a civil list pension, while at the same time also petitioning the Royal Literary Fund on her behalf for a one-off grant. His now impressive range of contacts – drawn from political and professional life – gave him a new assurance in dealing with officialdom. Both the applications proved successful: the RLF contributed £100; and (eventually, in May 1890) Lady Wilde was awarded a civil list pension of £70 a year. Her newfound enthusiasm for Queen Victoria perhaps helped tip the balance in her favour, expunging the memory of her insurrectionist battlecries of the 1840s.

All the while Wilde continued to add to his coterie of young male friends. He enjoyed the company of Jacomb-Hood (the decorator of *The Happy Prince*), even joining him and some of his fellow artists for a few days of Spartan summer fun in a cottage on Brownsea Island in Dorset. The time was spent sailing in small boats around Poole harbour. Wilde surprised his host by entering into the spirit of it all with enthusiasm, even joining 'like a schoolboy in the early-morning plunge' from the castle steps. His only plaint was the want of a cup of tea before getting up: 'My dear Jacomb,' he

---

*   A stalwart of numerous late-night establishments, such as the Fielding Club and the Spoofs, Willie was also a founder member of the Owl Club off St James's Square. Asked to compose a poetic motto for the club, he dashed off the couplet: 'We fly by night, and this resolve we make, / If the dawn must break, let the d-d thing break.'

explained, 'I positively cannot open my eyes without a cup of tea' (Jacomb-Hood generously rose early each day to provide him with one). Nevertheless, after one night spent wading up to his waist in the sea with a seine net, he did declare, 'Nature is so often very uncomfortable.'[26]

In London Wilde fostered his connection with the gauche but intelligent Yeats, whose Irish tales he had noticed so favourably. The Dublin-born poet was readily drawn in; he had known of the illustrious and eccentric Wilde family since childhood, and had first seen Oscar lecturing in Dublin in 1883. On the verge of bringing out his first book of poems, Yeats greatly valued the friendship, recalling how Wilde always 'flattered the intellect' of those he liked: how he encouraged Yeats to recount long Irish stories; how he suggested that he possessed 'genius' and compared his art to Homer; how he warned him against writing 'literary gossip' for the papers – it being 'no job for a gentleman'.[27]

Another budding poet was the intriguingly named Richard Le Gallienne, who wrote from Liverpool enclosing a privately printed volume of his verse, and shortly afterwards followed the book south. Like Yeats he had first encountered Wilde on the lecture platform. As an impressionable seventeen-year-old in Birkenhead in 1883, Le Gallienne had heard Wilde give his 'Impressions of America', and almost from that moment had determined to escape from his destined career as an accountant and become a poet. He had begun to write verse under the influence of the Pre-Raphaelites. The ungrammatical 'Le' was added to his name, to make it more memorable and more artistic. He evolved a determinedly Aesthetic look, his long hair 'fanning out' – as Wilde remarked – 'into a wonderful halo'. With his fine dark eyebrows and strongly chiselled features, Wilde thought he looked like Rossetti's Angel Gabriel; Swinburne called him 'Shelley with a chin'.[28] He arrived in London in 1888 bent on fostering his connection with Wilde. He attended a Tite Street 'at home' and secured an invitation to dinner. Other meetings followed. Wilde inscribed a copy of *Poems*: 'To Richard Le Gallienne, poet and lover, from Oscar Wilde. A Summer day in June '88'. Le Gallienne sought to fix the moment too, composing a poem, 'With Oscar Wilde: A Summer Day In June '88', which opened with the evocative couplet, 'With Oscar Wilde, a summer day / Passed like a yearning kiss away.' He sent Wilde a manuscript copy 'as a love-token, and in secret memory of a summer day in June '88'.[29] And Wilde reciprocated by offering him the manuscript of one of his fairy stories.[30] Yet, despite such heated exchanges, there is a strong suspicion that this was nothing more than poetical posturing by both

parties. Le Gallienne delighted in playing the role of the impassioned poet, and so did Wilde. For all the 'true-lover' talk, it was several years before they got properly on to first-name terms. Wilde recognized that Le Gallienne, charming though he might be, was a provincial careerist anxious to secure a footing in literary London; and with typical generosity he did what he could to help him.

Less poetic but more emphatically sexual was his relationship with the twenty-year-old Fred Althaus, which began towards the end of 1888. The pace of Wilde's clandestine affairs was quickening. The Greeks – according to J. A. Symonds – had counted homosexual desire as 'a mania', both 'more exciting' and 'more absorbent of the whole nature' than the love of women, and certainly Wilde was finding it so.[31] Althaus was the son of the distinguished German professor at University College London. A small cache of surviving letters from him to Wilde charts the course of their brief affair.[32] Wilde – it seems – swept the impressionable young man up, taking an interest in him, giving him concert tickets, exerting his charm. 'I hardly know a greater pleasure than being in your society,' Fred told him; 'and I am very grateful to you for the kindly interest you seem to take in me.'[33] They would meet at the receptions given by Ray Lankester, the eccentric, art-loving professor of zoology at University College, or else at the newly established Lyric Club, on Coventry Street, to which they both belonged. Althaus, conscious of his good looks, sent Wilde his photograph, 'an enlarged one of the one taken in flannels with my German friend – but he of course is not in it'.[34]

Although Althaus had a job in the City, his interest seems to have been the theatre, or at least dressing up. He was described as 'looking splendid' – together with Harry Melvill – in some 'Tableaux Vivants' staged for charity by Mrs Bancroft; his performance in *Jim the Penman*, with the St Swithin's Amateur Dramatics Club, however, was rated only 'fairly good'.[35] He and Wilde were soon arranging assignations and meetings out of town. 'I have heard from Barnes [where the Lyric Club had an annexe] that I can have a room there for 2 nights or more,' Althaus reported; he hoped 'very much' that Wilde would 'run down some time or other'. Over the holidays he suggested that they could 'perhaps go away together' for a few days.[36] If he was both vain and demanding, that seems to have been part of the attraction. He told Wilde of his hope that they could spend some summer days at the seaside, 'in heavenly sunlight in which I adore basking thinking that it was perhaps generous enough to lend some of its beauty to its admirers'.[37]

As Wilde juggled the different elements of his double life, his work

seemed to offer a commentary. Certainly the two projects on which he was engaged during the latter part of 1888 were both concerned, in their different ways, with deception. One was an unconventional biographical essay on the early nineteenth-century artist, critic and dandy Thomas Griffiths Wainewright (the friend of Charles Lamb and William Blake) who had forged bank drafts and murdered relations to pay his debts and support his lifestyle.

Wilde's essay – a brilliant *jeu d'esprit* – cast Wainewright as a decadent *avant le lettre*: 'Like Baudelaire he was extremely fond of cats'; he shared 'with Gautier' (and Swinburne) a fascination for 'that "sweet marble monster"' – the classical statue of the twin-sexed 'Hermaphrodite' in the Louvre; and his writings – touching on the Mona Lisa, the Italian Renaissance, the early French poets and the classical romance of *Cupid and Psyche* – seemed to anticipate the works of Walter Pater. He had, moreover, 'that curious love of green, which in individuals is always the sign of a subtle artistic temperament, and in nations is said to denote a laxity, if not decadence of morals'. Aside from the legend that Baudelaire had once claimed to have green hair, this supposed association between the colour and 'decadence' seems to have been a cheerful invention of Wilde's.[38]

Wainewright's varied careers – artistic, social and criminal – were then sketched from a determinedly Aesthetic point of view. This game had, of course, been played before, most memorably by Thomas De Quincey in his 1827 essay, 'On Murder Considered as One of the Fine Arts', but Wilde brought his own brio to proceedings, blithely recording (among other atrocities) how, when a friend reproached Wainewright with the murder of his sister-in-law, 'he shrugged his shoulders and said, "Yes; it was a dreadful thing to do, but she had very thick ankles."' Wilde went on:

> It may be partly admitted that, if we set aside [Wainewright's] achieve-ment in the sphere of poison, what he has actually left to us hardly justifies his reputation. But then it is only the Philistine who seeks to estimate a personality by the vulgar test of production. This young dandy sought to be somebody, rather than to do something. He recog-nized that life itself is an art, and has its modes of style no less than the arts that seek to express it.

Wilde seems to have fixed upon Wainewright as a subject, having abandoned his plans for writing on that other artist-forger, Chatterton.[39] Wainewright's

story had become part of Wilde's repertoire of spoken tales; a London gossip columnist reported how, at 'a social literary gathering' towards the end of 1888, 'Oscar Wilde gave such an interesting account' of the poisoner 'that some listeners lost their last train'. On that occasion Wilde was 'urged to put his story on paper' – and it is likely that he was already at work on his written essay, using the spoken performance to try out his ideas and test his effects. The article, entitled 'Pen, Pencil and Poison' (a phrase borrowed, with acknowledgement, from Swinburne), was finished by the end of the year, and accepted by Frank Harris for the Fortnightly Review.[40]

In tandem with this essay, Wilde was also composing a brilliantly playful 'Dialogue' on the nature of art for the Nineteenth Century. He called the piece 'The Decay of Lying'. The 'idea, title, treatment, mode, everything,' Wilde later recalled, was 'struck out' over a delightful dinner with Robbie Ross in a modest Soho restaurant.[41] Wilde had been wanting to write an overview of contemporary culture from an Aesthetic point of view for some time, but had perhaps been struggling to find the right form. His dinner with Ross suggested a solution, and suddenly brought his ideas into a new focus.[42]

A modern Socratic 'dialogue' – modelled on the example of Plato – would allow him to explore his ideas without having to come to anything so limiting as a conclusion, or to maintain anything so dull as consistency. Thought would take flight in conversation, winged with paradox, epigram, overstatement, humour and ambiguity. Talk – his own preferred mode of expression – could be honed and refined to become literature. And the whole would reflect, more closely than anything he had previously attempted, his own personality and his own voice. The result was a *tour de force*: he was able to achieve with the greatest success yet his vision of art as self-expression.[43]

Wilde created two cultured exquisites, calling them (like his sons) 'Cyril' and 'Vivian'; and he set them in 'the Library of a country house in Nottinghamshire', another thinly veiled allusion to his having been at Clumber.[44] Vivian is working on a paper – to be called 'The Decay of Lying: A Protest' – for the Retrospective Review, house journal of his club 'The Tired Hedonists' ('we are supposed to wear faded roses in our button-holes when we meet, and to have a sort of cult of Domitian'.) He reads extracts from this essay to the sometimes sceptical and dismissive Cyril. Vivian's article is concerned with the two great cultural debates of the day – the relationships between 'Art and Nature', and between 'Realism and Romance'. And it adopts the

most extreme views possible, extending the ideas of Baudelaire and Gautier, of Pater and Whistler, and of Huysmans' des Esseintes, to their very limits.[45]

Vivian, in his 'new Aesthetics', sets art entirely above both nature and life: 'All bad Art comes from returning to Life and Nature, and elevating them into ideals.' Advancing the claims of the imagination and 'romance' above the tedious 'realism' of facts, he declares that 'lying, the telling of beautiful untrue things, is the proper aim of Art'. He insists upon the absolute autonomy – and uselessness – of art: 'Art never expresses anything but itself.' It is really only concerned with it own perfection. But he does admit also art's power, claiming that it is artists – through their personal vision and style – who fashion our understanding of the world. 'No great artist ever sees things as they really are. If he did, he would cease to be an artist.' What we think of as the Middle Ages is the invention of medieval artists. The whole of Japan is the creation of Hokusai and his fellow 'native painters'. 'Life imitates Art far more than Art imitates Life.' Wilde had been rehearsing these ideas over the previous months, in his conversation, his book reviews and his notes. Now he brought them all together with a scintillating energy.

He refined and re-used many of his critical aperçus: 'There is such a thing as robbing a story of its reality by trying to make it too true, and [Mr Robert Louis Stevenson's] The Black Arrow is so inartistic as not to contain a single anachronism to boast of, while the transformation of Dr. Jekyll reads dangerously like an experiment out of the Lancet.' 'Mr. Henry James writes fiction as if it were a painful duty, and wastes upon mean motives and imperceptible "points of view" his neat literary style, his felicitous phrases, his swift and caustic satire.' 'M. Zola... is determined to show that, if he has not got genius, he can at least be dull. And how well he succeeds!' 'Ah! Meredith! Who can define him? His style is chaos illumined by flashes of lightning. As a writer he has mastered everything except language: as a novelist he can do everything, except tell a story: as an artist he is everything, except articulate.'

Whistler, also, was alluded to, if not by name. 'There may have been fogs for centuries in London. I dare say there were. But no one saw them, and so we do not know anything about them. They did not exist till Art had invented them. Now, it must be admitted, fogs are carried to excess. They have become the mere mannerism of a clique, and the exaggerated realism of their method gives dull people bronchitis. Where the cultured catch an effect, the uncultured catch cold.'

Wilde seems to have been particularly – and understandably – pleased with the piece. He read aloud from the proofs to his guests after Christmas

dinner. Yeats was at Tite Street that evening. Although he would later borrow from the dialogue's ideas about the power of art to create meaning in the world, at that first hearing he was swept up by the language and the wit of the piece: they seemed both 'an imitation and a record' of Wilde's 'matchless talk'.[46]

Yeats was impressed too by the domestic scene that he encountered at Tite Street: the restrained Aesthetic decor; the unexpected white dining room, its table decorated with 'a diamond-shaped red cloth' upon which stood a terracotta statuette illumined by a red shaded ceiling-light; the 'beautiful wife'; the two young children. There was also a kitten, a present from Robbie Ross. 'It does not *look* white,' Wilde reported in his thank-you letter, 'indeed it looks a sort of tortoise-shell colour, or a grey barred with velvety dark browns, but as you *said* it was white I have given orders that it is always to be spoken of as the "white kitten." The children are enchanted with it, and sit, one on each side of its basket, worshipping.'[47]

It was a charming scene. Indeed Yeats wondered if it was not almost 'too perfect'. He came away from the evening thinking that the 'perfect harmony of life' that he had witnessed 'suggested some deliberate artistic composition'. And perhaps he recalled too that the true aim of artistic composition was – according to Wilde's new Aesthetic – 'Lying, the telling of beautiful untrue things.'[48]

THE YOUNG KING

1889–1892

AGE 34–37

Oscar Wilde at Felbrigg near Cromer, 1892.

1

A Man in Hew

*'Make some sacrifice for your art and you will be repaid –
but ask of art to sacrifice herself for you and a bitter disappointment may come to you.'*

OSCAR WILDE

For the first four weeks of 1889 it was quite hard to pick up a British periodical that did *not* contain an article by Oscar Wilde. 'Pen, Pencil and Poison: A Study' filled fourteen pages in the *Fortnightly Review*, 'The Decay of Lying' was a prominent feature of the *Nineteenth Century*, 'London Models' (after Wilde had threatened to reclaim it) finally made its appearance in the *English Illustrated Magazine*, with pictures by Harper Pennington, while *Woman's World* was graced by the editor's 'Literary Notes'. It was a notable achievement.

'London Models' was accounted 'exceedingly entertaining' by the reviewers. Lady Wilde thought the piece 'capital – & *modest* too'; while Willie, she remarked, was also 'highly appreciative of it'.[1] In a 'very strong' literary number of the *Fortnightly Review*, including contributions by Swinburne, J. A. Symonds, Edmund Gosse and Henry Curzon, 'Pen, Pencil and Poison' was judged 'the most entertaining' piece, an 'original' and 'well-merited success'.[2] Even with *Woman's World* it was noted that Wilde had 'excelled himself', though less on account of his 'Literary Notes' than on his coup in securing an article by the queen of Romania.[3]

But in the general swell of praise 'The Decay of Lying' received the greatest approbation. If Wilde was pleased with the half-dazzled, half-bemused press comments upon it, he was more delighted by the private praise of friends. 'I am so very pleased that you like my article,' he wrote to Walter Pollock, editor of the *Saturday Review*; 'the public so soon vulgarize any artistic idea that one gives them that I was determined to put my new views on art, and particularly on the relations of art and history, in a form that they could not understand, but that would be understood by the few who, like yourself, have a quick artistic instinct.'[4]

It was a brilliant start to the year. 'I am so glad you have struck oil in Literature,' declared Lady Wilde with characteristic enthusiasm. 'I know of no writer at once so strong & so beautiful – except Ruskin.'[5] But Wilde was aware, too, that February would bring to the newsstands fresh issues of all the periodicals, and that (bar *Woman's World*) none of them would carry his name; in journalism – even the higher journalism of the *Fortnightly* and the *Nineteenth Century* – achievement was fleeting. Yeats recalled how Wilde, at this time, deprecated the 'general belief in his success' or even 'efficiency', and with sincerity too; he remained conscious of how little he had yet done. While he still wrote verse occasionally, he had come to realize that he would not be challenging the great poetic voices of the previous generation. His masters – Swinburne, Rossetti, Morris, Arnold, Tennyson, Browning – remained masters still. Perhaps seeking an explanation or an excuse, he told Yeats, 'We Irish are too poetical to be poets; we are a nation of brilliant failures, but we are the greatest talkers since the Greeks.'[6]

But he was making progress in prose; and it is hard not to connect the energy and invention of his work at this time, with the liberating effects of his new sexual life. His personality, as Ross noted, 'intensified' as he became 'an habitual devotee'.[7] There was a conspicuous buoyancy about him. Yeats, indeed, thought Wilde at his happiest during this period of his life.[8] His ambition remained undimmed. And even if the way forward was not immediately clear, he had a belief in the possibilities of his art, and a faith in his ability to explore them.

He continued to weave his elaborately cadenced fairy stories. 'The Birthday of the Princess' appeared in the innovative bilingual weekly *Paris Illustré*. 'In point of style it is my best story,' he told one friend. He was intrigued, though, that the tale of Spanish court life, which he described as 'black and silver' in its original, 'came out pink and blue' in the accompanying French translation.[9] He considered proclaiming the debt that his multi-coloured

prose owed to Flaubert by producing a translation of *La Tentation de St Antoine*.[10] But there were other energies at play. 'The Decay of Lying' had been such fun to write, he wanted to return to the dialogue form. And then there was also his long-mooted article on Shakespeare's sonnets – a daring play of fact and fiction, history and invention.

Wilde's vision was to connect Shakespeare to the Greek tradition of pederastic love as it had been rediscovered in the Renaissance. In the 'curious dedication' that Shakespeare had inscribed to 'Mr. W. H.' as the 'onlie Begetter' of his sonnets, Wilde detected the note of 'pure Platonism'. Shakespeare, he suggested, must have 'felt that his art had been created in him by the beauty' of this mysterious friend.[11] Conventional scholarship supposed that 'Mr W. H.' was simply an aristocratic patron: William Herbert, earl of Pembroke, or perhaps – through a transposition – the no less noble Henry Wriothesley, earl of Southampton. Wilde, however, proposed that the initials denoted the otherwise unknown 'Willie Hughes'. The idea had first been put forward by the eighteenth-century critic (and Chatterton scholar) Thomas Tyrwitt, who had detected recurrent puns on the words 'Will' and 'Hues' in several sonnets. But Wilde took the notion forward with typical elan. While Tyrwitt had suggested that Hughes – as the 'Fair Youth' addressed in many of the sonnets – might be a court musician, Wilde proposed that he was a boy actor who played the female roles in Shakespeare's company, a youth 'whose physical beauty was such that it became the very corner stone of Shakespeare's art'. Hughes, he suggested, was not merely the addressee of some poems, but the inspiration for all Shakespeare's plays, 'the very incarnation of Shakespeare's dreams'.

Rather than setting out his ideas as a mere essay, Wilde wrapped them up in a story. He did not want to be shackled to tedious facts or fixed positions. As he explained to a female writer friend, 'Fiction – not truth,' was his preferred mode; 'I could never have any dealings with truth. If truth were to come in to me, to my room he would say to me, "You are too wilful." And I should say to him, "You are too obvious." And I should throw him out the window.' When his friend queried, 'Is not Truth a woman?' Wilde allowed, 'Then I could not throw her out of the window; I should bow her to the door.'[12]

The fiction he devised was a tale of male friendship, artistic forgery and obsession, as the narrator learns from his friend 'Erskine' how another friend, the 'wonderfully handsome' and 'effeminate' 'Cyril Graham', had become fascinated by the 'Will Hughes' theory but, unable to find definitive proof, had forged an Elizabethan-style portrait of the young actor, his hand

resting upon an edition of the sonnets. Although the forgery was uncovered, and Cyril Graham committed suicide, first 'Erskine' and then the narrator finds himself beguiled by his theory, unable quite to dismiss it.

The story was a daringly sketched account of artistic creativity inspired by pederastic love, although the fictional form allowed Wilde to keep a certain distance from the topic. It absolved him, too, from having to declare any personal endorsement of the theory – although in private, he would playfully claim, 'Even I, who have tried not to believe – for the artist always questions his latest work in happy anticipation of the next – even I have been unable to doubt.'[13] It is very doubtful that Wilde had submitted the manuscript for the approval of Carlos Blacker, as he had, jokingly, promised he would.[14] Other influences were more apparent. As with 'The Decay of Lying', the idea for the piece had been evolved in discussion with Robbie Ross. Indeed Ross could almost lay claim to being the Willie Hughes to Wilde's Shakespeare. Wilde told him, 'indeed the story is half yours, and but for you would not have been written.'[15]

Wilde initially tried to place the story with the *Fortnightly Review*, but Frank Harris happened to be away from the office, and the piece was turned down by his deputy. It found a berth instead with the highly respectable *Blackwood's Magazine*; Wilde was able to persuade them to take it on the grounds that they had already published several interesting articles on the question of 'The Sonnets'.[16]

If 'The Portrait of Mr. W. H.' concerned itself with the ethics of forgery, the topic was engaging Wilde in other ways too at that moment. As part of the Tory efforts to discredit Parnell (and, with him, the Home Rule agenda), *The Times* had published the facsimile of a letter, purportedly from the Irish leader, condoning – if not inciting – violence in Ireland. Parnell had denounced the document as a forgery, and demanded an inquiry to clear his name. A special commission – directed by three unapologetic and hostile Unionists – was set up to investigate not just that charge but also numerous other accusations against the Home Rule leadership. It was a lengthy and contentious process. Parnell himself appeared before the commission in February, and Wilde was frequently in attendance during his testimony. He must have felt close to proceedings. George Lewis was acting for Parnell, and was largely responsible for uncovering the fact that the disputed letter had indeed been forged, by an Irish journalist called Richard Pigott. Willie was also a regular at the commission, showing an unwonted energy in his meticulous and partisan reports for the *Daily Chronicle*.[17]

The political tenor of life at Tite Street was further heightened by the fact that Constance was involved in her own cause célèbre during the early part of 1889, helping Lady Sandhurst's pioneering attempt to gain election to the inaugural London County Council (Lady Sandhurst won a majority, but a legal challenge prevented her from taking her seat). In the wake of these exertions, however, Constance's health collapsed. A trip to Brighton in March was only the first of series of rest-cures and holidays aimed at bracing her increasingly fragile constitution.[18]

Constance's absence allowed Wilde more time to pursue his friendships – both sexual and intellectual – with the various young men he gathered about himself. Fred Althaus was hoping that Wilde would be able to 'go away' with him over Easter. And perhaps Wilde went.[19] Richard Le Gallienne had established himself in London, and became a regular guest at Tite Street. Also in town over the spring and summer was the twenty-four-year-old American writer Clyde Fitch. He had met Wilde the previous year, when travelling in Europe with his mother. Now, though, he was on his own: 'slight, dark... very aesthetic and romantic looking... whimsical as a child, loving, loveable, gay, witty and gracious'; with lustrous black hair and a passion for fine tailoring, he had a huge admiration for Wilde.[20] And his surviving letters preserve the outline of a passionate, if brief, affair: 'You are my poetry – my painting – my music – you are my sight, and sound, and touch. Your love is the fragrance of a rose – the sky of a summer – the wing of an angel – the cymbal of a cherubim... Time – it stopped when you left – will, always, in every weather' – and so on.[21] Although Wilde seems to have found such levels of emotional intensity rather exhausting, he did reciprocate with a short, sexually suggestive lyric, beginning, 'Out of the mid-wood's twilight, / Into the meadow's dawn, / Ivory-limbed and brown-eyed / Flashes my faun.'[22]

While Wilde was embracing the body, Constance was becoming ever more interested in the spirit. The possibility of contact with the 'spirit world' was one of the great fashionable concerns of the late nineteenth century. And Constance, like her husband, was always up to date. Having been introduced to spiritualism soon after her marriage – probably by Lady Wilde's friend Anna Kingsford – she eagerly explored its more occult manifestations, becoming first an enthusiastic disciple of Madame Blavatsky's Theosophists, and subsequently (in November 1888) a founder member of the even more mystic and magical Order of the Golden Dawn. Wilde, it seems, encouraged her interest, content to learn something of

the movement and its mysteries at second hand, without having to commit himself to its discipline.[23]

He was, though, rather impressed by Madame Blavatsky herself. They spent a memorable afternoon of talk and tobacco smoke as the twin centres of attention at the opening of a philanthropical restaurant for working women on Oxford Street. Oblivious to the circle of listening guests, and the inquisitive crowd gathered at the window beyond, they sat deep in their wicker chairs, exchanging 'brilliant epigrams'. Even so, Wilde did not take up Blavatsky's invitation to join the Theosophical Society.[24]

A few days after the Oxford Street lunch 'The Portrait of Mr. W. H.' appeared in the July number of 'Maga' (as Blackwood's Magazine was generally known), having been trailed in selected papers. It was, on the whole, very favourably noticed in the press. And some of the private responses were effusive. 'Oh! Oscar!' wrote Clyde Fitch, having finished the piece in one late-night sitting, 'The story is *great* – and fine! *I* believe in Willie Hughes: I don't care if the whole thing is out of your amazing beautiful brain. I don't care for the laughter, I only know I *am* convinced and I *will*, I will believe in Willie H.'[25]

The article, however, was treated by the reviewers largely as an ingenious – if not wholly convincing – contribution to Shakespearean scholarship. Wilde's fictional framing narrative was almost completely ignored. And there was scarcely more comment upon the homoerotic and pederastic elements of his theory. The *World* (for so long Wilde's great supporter) proved a conspicuous exception; its paragraphist remarked that the 'subject' of Shakespeare's supposed passion for 'a boy actor' was 'a very unpleasant one', and that it was 'dilated upon in the article in a peculiarly offensive manner'. Its note of prudish disapproval was echoed, more faintly, by W. E. Henley, (now in Edinburgh, editing the *Scots Observer*); he referred to the article as 'out of place in *Maga* – or, indeed, any popular magazine'. Wilde felt able to ignore such barbs. 'To be exiled to Scotland to edit a Tory paper in the wilderness is bad enough,' he told Henley, 'but not to see the wonder and beauty of my discovery of the real Mr. W. H. is absolutely dreadful. I sympathize deeply with you... The Philistines in their vilest forms have seized on you. I am so disappointed.'[26]

Frank Harris's memory of the article was that it 'set everyone talking and arguing'. The mystery of 'Mr W. H.' became one of the topics in literary circles that season. Wilde enjoyed the success, and also the sense of subversion. He had managed to present, in a respected journal, a strikingly

frank exposition of pederastic love, and its artistic benefits, by framing them as a mystery story and connecting them to England's greatest poet. His self-confidence – both in relation to his writing and to his clandestine sexuality – advanced another step.[27]*

On the score of sex, however, rumours were beginning to circulate. The extreme discretion that he had advocated – and practised – during the first years of his new sexual life was beginning to fray.[28] Wilde's relations with young men were becoming a shared secret in some sections of London's artistic and theatrical world. Ellen Terry had provoked amused consternation amongst the few when, at the private view of the New Gallery's summer exhibition, she had innocently asked Wilde whether he had really meant it when he had told her friend, the now-grown-up Aimée Lowther, 'if only you were a boy I could adore you'. Henry Irving, who was present, tried to explain her inadvertent *faux pas* to her on the way home; but she was too innocent to understand.[29]

If Wilde was happy to flirt with indiscretion, others were not. The fastidious Raffalovich was not amused when Constance remarked (with an ingenuity to match Ellen Terry's), 'Oscar says he likes you so much – that you have such nice improper talks together.' After that Raffalovich claimed he never spoke with Wilde, except before 'witnesses'. He did not want to be tainted with Wilde's impropriety. Wilde responded to such priggishness with a series of increasingly ungenerous comments on Raffalovich's social position and physical appearance. 'As ugly as Raffalovich' became one of his habitual similes. And he repaid Raffalovich's lavish hospitality with the quip that 'Dear Andre' had come to London 'with the intention of opening a salon, and succeeded in opening a saloon.' Unsurprisingly the rift soon widened into barely concealed hostility. If they met it was only 'unwillingly and by accident'.[30]

Although Blackwood had suggested reprinting 'The Portrait of Mr W. H.' in their annual anthology, *Tales from Blackwood*, Wilde was anxious to expand the story and bring it out, on its own, in book form. After the success of *The Happy Prince* the previous year, he was keen to have another book to his name.[31] Wilde's sense that his professional stock was rising received further confirmation that summer, when, after a hiatus of almost five years,

---

* In another act of sly subversion, Wilde published a slightly amended version of his love lyric for Clyde Fitch, in the Christmas number of the *Lady's Pictorial*. It was retitled 'In the Forest'.

not one but two US producers approached him about the possibility of staging *The Duchess of Padua*. Anna Calhoun, an actress with whom he had come into contact through Elizabeth Robins, expressed a tentative interest in putting it on. And, at almost the same moment, he heard from the celebrated American tragedian Lawrence Barrett.

Barrett (so Wilde had told Mary Anderson in 1882) had been keen on the piece even before it was written. And it is likely that Wilde had sent him one of the privately printed copies of the play the following year. Perhaps the debacle of *Vera* had put Barrett off at the time; now, however, he took up the idea again with enthusiasm. Wilde was delighted – 'proud and pleased' that his work had not been 'forgotten' by such an eminent and 'artistic' producer. He hastened to assure Barrett that he would 'be very glad to make any alterations in it you can suggest', having 'no doubt that the play could be vastly improved'. In order to discuss these 'alterations' Wilde – despite being, as ever, short of funds – travelled to see the actor-manager at the German spa town of Kreuznach ('I thought it would be a superb opportunity for forgetting the language,' Wilde told Robbie Ross). He found Barrett in poor health, but on 'a delightful drive' through the hills above the Rhine, they discussed how best to 'condense' the play. It was also decided that to avoid any anti-Wilde sentiment that might still linger from the New York production of *Vera* it would be best to bring the play out anonymously, and under a different title. Even with these provisos it was thrilling for Wilde that the '*chef d'œuvre*' of his youth might yet achieve a professional staging. And although the production would take over a year to come to fruition, his confidence in the project remained strong.[32]

Not long after his return from Germany Wilde received an invitation from another old American contact. J. M. Stoddart (the Philadelphian publisher, with whom he had paid his memorable visit to Walt Whitman) was over in London on a visit, in his new role as editor of *Lippincott's Monthly Magazine*, and he invited Wilde to dinner at the Langham Hotel on 30 August. It was a select party: Stoddart, Wilde, the jovial Irish MP Henry Gill, and Arthur Conan Doyle. The thirty-year-old Conan Doyle always recalled it as 'a golden evening':

> Wilde to my surprise had read *Micah Clarke* [Conan Doyle's recent historical novel about the Monmouth Rebellion] and was enthusiastic about it, so that I did not feel a complete outsider... He towered above us all, and yet had the art of seeming to be interested in all that we

could say. He had the delicacy of feeling and tact, for the monologue man, however clever, can never be a gentleman at heart. He took as well as gave, but what he gave was unique. He had a curious precision of statement, a delicate flavour of humour, and a trick of small gestures to illustrate his meaning, which were peculiar to himself. The effect cannot be reproduced, but I remember how in discussing the wars of the future he said: 'A chemist on each side will approach the frontier with a bottle' – his upraised hand and precise face conjuring up a vivid and grotesque picture.

The dinner, however, was more than a social occasion. *Lippincott's Magazine* was already published simultaneously on both sides of the Atlantic but Stoddart wanted to enhance this Anglo-American flavour. Up until now the magazine had, as an editorial put it, 'confined itself to native American authors' when commissioning its most distinctive feature, the complete short novel printed entire in each monthly number. Stoddart had come to London to sign up some English writers. He asked both Wilde and Conan Doyle to contribute stories. With a suggested length of not less than 35,000 words, and a proposed 'honorarium' of £200, Wilde readily agreed.[33]*

The offer was not only flattering to Wilde but also welcome. For, despite the recent advances in his own literary reputation, his career as a magazine editor was drawing to a close. *Woman's World* may have garnered some excellent notices, but it had not prospered commercially. Cassell's announced that Wilde's tenure (and, indeed, the magazine itself) would come to an end in October. Wilde would miss the income, if not the work.[34]

The bright prospects of the *Lippincott's* commission, the proposed Laurence Barrett production of the *Duchess*, and the possible book version of 'Mr. W. H.' created a counter-current of optimism. And Wilde, enjoying the moment, set off on a late-summer holiday to Provence – with whom is unknown. He returned ready to work. His story for Stoddart would, he decided, be an elaborate fairy tale concerning a fisherman and a mermaid. He made a start, but progress was frustratingly slow. Wilde's energy was sapped by a debilitating illness (he called it 'malaria') contracted while in France. It dragged on for months. He toyed with his projects, but seemed

---

* Conan Doyle, five years younger than Wilde, was offered only £100 for a story of not less than 40,000 words. He produced 'The Sign of the Four' [*sic*], the second appearance of his fictional creation Sherlock Holmes. It was published in the February 1890 number of *Lippincott's Monthly Magazine*, and attracted only modest attention.

unable to bring them into focus. Eventually he wrote to Stoddart's agent in London suggesting that they would have put back the deadline for the fisherman story. 'I am unable to finish it,' he explained, 'and am not satisfied with it as far as it goes.'[35]

Progress was rather better on the expanded version of 'The Portrait of Mr. W. H.'. The subject, with its edge of sexual transgression, was perhaps more immediately exciting than the mystical tale of 'The Fisherman and his Soul'. Wilde, among his additions, made entirely explicit the connection between Shakespeare's love for 'Will Hughes' and the pederastic tradition that ran from of Plato's *Symposium* through to Marsilio Ficino and the Neo-platonists of the Renaissance, with 'its subtle suggestions of sex in soul, in the curious analogies it draws between intellectual enthusiasm and the physical passion of love, in its dream of the incarnation of the Idea in a beautiful and living [male] form'.

Over that autumn he read, or at least recounted, his revised story to friends and acquaintances, stirring up interest (as he hoped) for the book. Andrew Lang, he claimed, was 'not entirely hostile' and 'Balfour thinks he is convinced'. Wilde also submitted the expanded manuscript to a publisher, most probably *Blackwood's*. But the firm's reader took fright. 'This *gardien du sérail*,' Wilde reported, 'advises me not to print it, lest it should corrupt our English homes.'[36] The rebuff, it seems, only heightened his desire to bring out the book. The publication would, he thought, need a frontispiece – an image of the young 'Willie Hughes'; and Wilde began to consider who might be able to provide such a work.

He had recently been sent an interesting – and thoroughly Aesthetic – publication called *The Dial*. A collection of essay, stories, art notes and pictures, it had been privately produced by two young artists, Charles Ricketts and Charles Shannon. They lived very close to Tite Street, in a dilapidated Regency house (until recently inhabited by Whistler) set in a little rustic cul-de-sac off the King's Road. Wilde went to call on them.

He found an intriguing ménage: the lively twenty-three-year-old Ricketts, small, red-headed, bright-eyed, sharp-bearded, full of eager energy and inquiry; and the quieter, fairer, less hirsute, twenty-six-year-old Shannon. The house was bare, but touched with discriminating artistic details. There were Japanese prints pinned on the yellow walls. And the great mutual affection and dedication of the two artists was readily apparent too, although whether the relationship had a sexual dimension was less clear, and remains so. Many supposed that it did; others suspected that the two friends deliberately

sublimated their sexual energies into art. They were dubbed by one contemporary 'the Sisters of the Vale'.[37]

Ricketts later recalled the excitement of Wilde's visit: his over-generous praise of The Dial, and his admonition 'it is quite delightful but, do not bring out a second number, all perfect things should be unique'; his inspection of their own work; and then his unexpected request that Ricketts might paint for him 'a small Elizabethan picture – something in the manner of, shall we say, Clouet' – to adorn his proposed book about 'Mr W. H.'. A few days later Wilde read the new, enlarged, story to Ricketts, in his Tite Street study. And 'within a fortnight' Ricketts had produced the little portrait, framed in some 'worm-eaten moulding' pieced together by Shannon.[38]

Wilde was thrilled:

'My dear Ricketts,' he wrote, 'It is not a forgery at all – it an authentic Clouet of the highest *artistic* value. It is absurd of you and Shannon to try and take me in! As if I did not know the master's touch, or was no judge of frames!

Seriously, my dear fellow, it is quite wonderful, and your giving it to me is an act so charming that, in despair of showing you any return, I at once call upon the gods to shower gold and roses on the Vale, or on that part of the Vale where the De Morgans do not live. I am really most grateful (no! that is a horrid word: I am never grateful) I am flattered and fascinated, and I hope we shall always be friends and see each other often.[39]

Despite now possessing a perfect frontispiece for his story, Wilde still struggled to find a publisher for the book. The plan, carried forward so eagerly that autumn, was languishing by the end of the year. Whether publishers were reluctant to take up the project on moral or commercial grounds is not known. But there was, just then, a heightened public anxiety – almost an hysteria – about sexual relations between men. From the end of September London had been filled with 'prurient gossip' concerning the police discovery of a male brothel in Cleveland Street, near Tottenham Court Road. Most of the prostitutes working there were teenage telegraph boys from the Central Post Office, while their clientele was said to include several members of the nobility – and perhaps even royalty. Although the authorities initially strove to hush up the matter, the scandal erupted in the press at the end of the year, when the Earl of Euston felt himself obliged to sue the editor

of a north London newspaper for suggesting that he was an habitué of the place. Although there is no suggestion that Wilde ever visited 19 Cleveland Street, he would certainly have taken a keen interest in the case – and not just because George Lewis was acting as Lord Euston's solicitor.

The scandal, when it broke, provided generous scope for British hypocrisy. The press, while claiming to be shocked at the notion of 'noble lords' paying for sex with working-class telegraph boys, relayed the full details with gusto, sure of a ready readership. It was clear, too, that the authorities had been reluctant to act. The only two people actually prosecuted (both workers at the brothel) had been given light sentences; and their case had been barely reported. Meanwhile Lord Arthur Somerset, the most conspicuous of the society figures implicated in the scandal, had been allowed to escape abroad without a warrant being issued for his arrest.[40]

If Wilde followed the drama with interest, he had his own troubles – or minor irritations – to contend with. A young writer called Herbert Vivian, whom he had met and, in facetious mood, had encouraged to write his 'memoirs', began to publish extracts from these hastily penned *Reminiscences of a Short Life* in the *Sun* newspaper. He claimed Wilde as 'the fairy-godfather' of the work, and among the anecdotes he relayed were several relating to family life at Tite Street. Vivian reported Wilde's fanciful claim that he had adorned the walls of his children's nursery with 'texts about early rising and sluggishness and so forth, and I tell them that when they grow up, they must take their father as a warning, and occasionally have breakfast earlier than two in the afternoon'. He also gave an account of how the infant Cyril, when urged to say his prayers 'to make him good' had, 'after a prolonged altercation', announced as a 'compromise' that he 'wouldn't mind praying to God to make baby [Vyvyan] good' instead.[41] Wilde was dismayed at both the vulgarity and the intrusiveness of such details. 'Meeting you socially,' he reprimanded the bumptious young author, 'I, in a moment which I greatly regret, happened to tell you a story about a little boy. Without asking my permission you publish this in a vulgar newspaper and in a vulgar, inaccurate and offensive form, to the great pain of my wife, who naturally does not want to see her children paraded for the amusement of the uncouth.' In a heated correspondence, he insisted that his name should not be used to endorse the book.[42]

Herbert Vivian's ill-judged ramblings caused grief in other ways too. His comments about Wilde's supposed intellectual debt to Whistler opened up that old wound, and prompted the painter to fire off a stinging letter

to *Truth*, which was just then conducting a debate about the ethics of
plagiarism. Whistler denounced Wilde as being the 'fattest of offenders',
rehearsed all his old grievances, and pointed out (as Vivian had done) that
a phrase about 'having the courage of other people's opinions' – which
appeared in 'The Decay of Lying' – had been borrowed 'without a word
of comment' from an earlier 'well-remembered letter' that Whistler had
sent to Wilde.[43] The tenor of the attack was so deliberately offensive that
even the good-natured Wilde felt obliged to respond. He wrote to *Truth*,
regretting that it was necessary to take note of 'the lucubrations of so
ill-bred and ignorant person as Mr. Whistler' – nevertheless, he went on:
'The definition of a disciple as one who has the courage of the opinions
of his master is really too old even for [Whistler] to be allowed to claim it,
and as for borrowing Mr Whistler's ideas about art, the only thoroughly
original ideas I have ever heard him express have had reference to his own
superiority over painters greater than himself.'[44] The break was now open
and irrecoverable.

It was a sad ending. There were, however, enough new beginnings to
draw Wilde's attention onwards. The friendship with Ricketts and Shannon
was thriving. After that first visit to the Vale Wilde returned often. Soon he
was coming to 'jaw' three times a week. Happy evenings were spent talking
what Ricketts called 'inspired "rot"'.[45] Of the two 'Dialists' it was the lively,
erudite, abrasive Ricketts who engaged Wilde most. Half-French, he had a
Gallic delight in playing with ideas, trying out theories and revisiting old
opinions – often to the exasperation of his more literal partner. 'What's
the use of saying that?' Shannon would sometimes demand, 'You know
you don't think it.' Wilde, however, enjoyed such flights, and was ready to
match them. One regular visitor to the Vale – Charles Holmes, the future
director of the National Gallery – sketched the typical scene: 'Ricketts,
perched on the edge of the table, engaged Wilde in a long verbal combat.
So swiftly came parry and riposte, that my slow brain could only follow
the tongue-play several sentences behind, and cannot remember a word of
what passed, except "Oh! Nonsense, Oscar," from Ricketts, although it lives
in the memory as the most dazzling dialogue which I was ever privileged
to hear.'[46]

They vied with each other in showing off and sharing their literary interests and artistic enthusiasms. 'I viewed [Wilde],' Ricketts later recalled, 'as
a man who had known Swinburne, Burne-Jones, and who might have met
Rossetti. I think he made me read Pater and I made him read Villiers [de

Lisle Adam] and Verlaine; we had a common meeting ground in Baudelaire and Flaubert.' Ricketts had a knowledge of French literature and art that in many ways exceeded Wilde's own; he lent his new friend a copy of Verlaine's 1870 volume *Fêtes Galantes*, as well as introducing him to the works of some of Verlaine's followers.[47]

Wilde met another interesting young Francophile that February when he was in Oxford, visiting Pater and offering advice to a student production of Robert Browning's play *Strafford*. Prompted perhaps by Pater, he sought out an undergraduate poet called Lionel Johnson. 'On Saturday at midday,' Johnson reported to a friend, 'lying half asleep in bed, reading Green, I was roused by a pathetic and unexpected note from Oscar: he plaintively besought me to get up and see him. Which I did: and I found him as delightful as Green is not. He discoursed, with infinite flippancy, of everyone: lauded the *Dial*: laughed at Pater: and consumed all my cigarettes. I am in love with him.' Wilde, too, enjoyed the encounter, and hoped to see more of Johnson in London.[48]★

★   Wilde, for all his admiration for Pater as a prose stylist, was often amused and exasperated by his mentor's cautious and reticent manner. Something of Wilde's facetious attitude to his 'master' is suggested by his remark to Pater, after the latter's lecture at the London Institution on Prosper Mérimée on 24 November 1890. When Pater expressed a concern over whether audience had been able to hear him, Wilde remarked deftly, 'We overheard you.'

2

A Bad Case

*'The sphere of art and the sphere of ethics are absolutely
distinct and separate.'*

OSCAR WILDE

Meanwhile Wilde's plans for his *Lippincott's* story had begun to
shift. After toiling at 'The Fisherman and his Soul' for several
months, he abandoned the idea of sending it to the magazine.
At 15,000 words it was far too short. Besides, a new and 'better' idea had
occurred to him, for a tale about a mysterious portrait.[1] The initial seed for
the story had been sown a couple of years earlier when – in December 1887
– he had had his portrait painted by his friend, the Canadian artist Frances
Richards, who was over in London and staying with the Ross family in
Kensington. 'When the sitting was over,' Wilde recalled, 'and I had looked
at the portrait, I said in jest, "What a tragic thing it is. This portrait will
never grow older and I shall. If only it was the other way!" The moment
I had said this it occurred to me what a capital plot the idea would make
for a story.'[2]

He had subsequently gone on to evolve a Poe-like tale of a handsome
young man committed to a life of hedonistic dissipation who remains quite
unmarked by either age or debauchery, while his portrait gradually accumu-
lates all the terrible signs of both. It joined his repertoire of extemporized

fables to be spun out among friends and dining companions. Now, though, he determined to write it down – or write it up.* To achieve the 35,000-plus words required, the story needed some amplification. Wilde told Stoddart he could have the work done by the end of March. He also asked if he could have 'half the honorarium [£100] in advance', as he needed money after his months of illness-enforced idleness.[3]

Fired now with enthusiasm for the project, Wilde set about expanding the plot, and infusing it with his current concerns – the literature of the French Decadents, the relations between art and life, the creative force of peder-asty and the challenges of leading a 'double life'. He created the figures of Dorian Gray, the vain young man who wishes that his portrait might age so that he will not; Basil Hallward, the artist who – infatuated with Dorian – creates the magical picture; and Lord Henry Wotton, the worldly advocate of a 'New Hedonism', who leads Dorian along a fatal path of self-fulfilment through self-indulgence: 'The only way to get rid of a temptation,' he tells Dorian, 'is to yield to it.'

Dorian Gray's name carried not only an echo of Disraeli's first novel, *Vivian Grey*, but also a coded reference to the 'Dorians' of ancient Sparta, who were credited with introducing pederasty into Greek culture; while Dorian's relationship with Hallward – framed as an intense romantic friendship – is also that of the 'beloved', who through his beauty inspires his pederastic 'lover' to create an artistic masterpiece. Drawing on the genealogy mapped out in Pater's *Renaissance* and his own 'Portrait of Mr. W. H.', he characterized Basil's feelings for Dorian as a 'noble and intel-lectual' love – 'not that mere physical admiration of beauty that is born of the senses, and that dies when the senses tire. It was such love as Michael Angelo had known, and Montaigne, and Winckelmann, and Shakespeare himself.'[4]

To provide a blueprint and a guide for his career of pleasure, Lord Henry lends Dorian a fatal book – a French novel written in a 'curious jewelled

---

* Willie Maxwell was one of the several young companions to whom Wilde had told the 'portrait' story – among numerous other tales. He later recalled how, at around this time, 'I informed [Wilde] that I had taken an idea he had told us, and written a short story with it. For a few moments his face clouded, then it cleared, and he spoke with a mixture of approval and reproach. "Stealing my story was the act of gentleman, but not telling me you had stolen it was to ignore the claims of friendship." And again a cloud descended, and he became really serious. "You mustn't take a story that I told you of a man and a picture. No, absolutely, I want that for myself. I fully mean to write it, and I should be terribly upset if I were forestalled."'

style... without a plot, and with only one character, being indeed, simply a psychological study of a certain young Parisian, who spent his life trying to realize in the nineteenth century all the passions and modes of thought that belonged to every century except his own... loving for their mere artificiality those renunciations that men have unwisely called virtue, as much as those natural rebellions that wise men still call sin.' Although clearly inspired – as he privately admitted – by Huysmans' *À Rebours*, Wilde dubbed it *'Le Secret de Raoul'* by Catulle Sarrazin (in a rather congested allusion to the protagonist of Rachilde's novel, *Monsieur Vénus*; to the Decadent author Catulle Mendès; and to Wilde's friend Gabriel Sarrazin).[5] And although Wilde's vaguely sketched account of Dorian's pleasures and crimes was a model of reticence by contemporary French standards, he was well aware that its hints of drug abuse, sexual predation and 'unnatural' vice went far beyond the accepted limits of the contemporary English novel. He was to sound a new note in the fiction of the day.

He devised a low-life subplot in which Dorian falls in love with a young East End actress called Sybil Vane, enraptured by her performances as Shakespeare's romantic heroines, only to reject her when her all-too-real love for him undermines her artistic ability to simulate love convincingly in her acting. And he fashioned a climax in which Dorian, overcome with remorse after murdering Basil Hallward and marring the lives of countless others, finally attempts to obliterate the past by destroying the now-disfigured portrait, only to destroy himself.

The sometimes melodramatic aspects of the plot were countered by the sparkling play of epigrammatic wit among the three main characters, directed always by Lord Henry Wotton. Wilde's enjoyment in writing these parts sometimes threatened to unbalance the whole. Indeed, the story, he confessed to one friend, 'is rather like my own life – all conversation and no action. I can't describe action: my people sit in chairs and chatter.'[6] The chatter, though, enabled him to fix instances of his own spontaneous wit, and also to continue that successful blend of paradox and ideas that he had initiated with 'The Decay of Lying'. Frank Harris considered the 'first hundred pages' of the story to be 'the result of months and months of Oscar's talk', with Lord Henry being 'peculiarly Oscar's mouthpiece'.[7]

At almost 55,000 words, the story was his most sustained piece of writing to date. He had worked hard, even turning down luncheon engagements in his anxiety to meet his deadline.[8] He did take some short cuts: the descriptions of precious stones and church vestments were copied almost

verbatim from the 'art handbooks' of the South Kensington Museum.[9] But then other avenues were explored with more thoroughness. He took the trouble to quiz a young scientist acquaintance about the best way for Dorian to dispose of Basil Hallward's body. And, overall, his manuscript shows signs of meticulous care.[10]

Wilde had a finished typescript ready before the end of March. And although he might pretend to Bernard Berenson that he had knocked it off as a piece of magazine hack work, there is no doubt that he was proud and pleased at his creation. To another friend he described it, excitedly, as 'my best piece of work'.[11] As Basil Hallward had put much of himself into his portrait of Dorian, so Wilde had put much of himself into his story. As he later phrased it, 'Basil Hallward is what I think I am: Lord Henry is what the world thinks me: Dorian what I would like to be – in other ages, perhaps.'[12]

Wilde dispatched the typescript to Philadelphia, and, after a wait of almost a month, received a letter from Stoddart expressing his 'entire satisfaction with the story' – which he judged 'one of the most powerful works of the time'. It would appear in the July number of the magazine.[13] The letter, though, concealed quite as much as it revealed. Stoddart, on first reading the manuscript, while impressed by the strength of the story, had been alarmed to note 'a number of things which an innocent woman would take an exception to'. These 'objectionable passages' would, he told his employer, Craige Lippincott, 'undoubtedly have to be fixed' before the story could be published. And it was only after he had consulted with several of his literary associates (male and female) on how best to carry out this editorial task, that he wrote to Wilde accepting his story. In his letter, though, he made no mention of any of this; there would, after all, not be time to consult Wilde about changes to the text. Stoddart and one of his editors were already busy, excising over 500 words from the typescript. Some of the changes addressed – and toned down – the homoerotic nature of Basil Hallward's feelings for Dorian; others removed the decadent details of the fatal French novel presented to Dorian by Lord Henry Wotton (its fanciful title and author were among the things obliterated); the largest number, though, related to Dorian's promiscuous relations with women. All references to mistresses and prostitution were carefully removed.[14]

Back in London Wilde was unaware of these manoeuvres. His own excitement about the story was running on ahead. He was already looking beyond its imminent magazine life, and considering how to expand the tale for publication in book form, once the copyright reverted to him in

September. He thought that two extra chapters should be sufficient; and the result would 'make a sensation'. He approached at least two publishers in the hope that they would take it on. Macmillan & Co. was one of the firms. A 'sensation', however, was not what they wanted. Maurice Macmillan (the older brother of Wilde's friend George) wrote back at once, regretting that the story was not for them – 'We have done very little in the way of such strong situations; and I confess there is something in the power which Dorian Gray gets over the young nature scientist [whom he blackmails into helping him dispose of Basil Hallward's body], and one or two other things, which is rather repelling.' 'I dare say,' he added, 'you do not mean it to be.' And it seems that the other publishers were similarly wary. In the end Wilde came to an arrangement with Ward, Lock & Co., the firm that had recently taken on distribution of *Lippincott's Magazine* in Britain.[15]

The excitement of making plans for *Dorian Gray* seems to have stimulated the pace of Wilde's other literary productions. Building upon the success of 'The Decay of Lying' he produced a second, longer, 'Dialogue' for the *Nineteenth Century*: a discussion between the super-cultured 'Gilbert' and the rather earnest 'Ernest' on 'The True Function and Value of Criticism'. It was another celebration of Wilde's amoral and inutile Aesthetic, and an inversion of established hierarchies.

Overturning Matthew Arnold's resonant view, expressed in his famous 1864 essay 'The Function of Criticism in the Present Time', that the goal of criticism was 'to see the object as in itself it really is', Gilbert asserts that 'the primary aim of the critic is to see the object as in itself it really is not'. Criticism, he suggests, should be the purely subjective record of the critic's impressions. 'To the critic the work of art is simply a suggestion for a new work of his own, that need not necessarily bear any obvious resemblance to the thing it criticizes.' The critic does not seek to 'explain a work of art' but rather to respond to its beauty – to 'deepen its mystery, to raise round it, and round its maker, that mist of wonder which is dear to both gods and worshippers alike'. The work of the 'critic' is thus equal to that of the 'creative artist'; indeed superior, since the critic is engaging with refined 'art' rather than unrefined 'nature'. This – like much else in the dialogue – was well calculated to annoy Whistler.

To be fit for the task the critic must 'intensify' his own 'individualism' – not by limiting his sympathies, but expanding them. Wilde has Gilbert suggest that 'Sin' is one way to achieve this: 'By its curiosity Sin increases the experiences of the race. Through its intensified assertion of individualism,

it saves us from monotony of type.' But the critic must then adopt poses to express himself. 'Man,' Gilbert asserts, 'is least himself when he talks in his own person. Give him a mask, and he will tell you the truth... What people call insincerity is simply a method by which we can multiply our personalities.' The 'Dialogue' was to be published in two parts, in the periodical's July and September issues.

Added to his other recent essays, dialogues and stories – from 'Pen, Pencil and Poison' up to 'The Picture of Dorian Gray' – it confirmed Wilde's vision of himself as one of the thinkers of his age. He had, as he later declared, 'made art a philosophy, and philosophy an art', had 'summed up all systems in a phrase, and all existence in an epigram'.[16] His succession of publications had also confirmed his vision of himself as a purely literary figure. At last he felt able to abandon the mere 'journalism' of reviewing. The four book reviews that he contributed in early part of 1890 to the *Speaker* – a new weekly edited by his former Cassell's colleague Wemyss Reid – would be his last.[17] He had gained a place on a wider and more exalted stage.

By the third week in June the 'July number' of *Lippincott's Monthly Magazine* was on the London newsstands. Above its masthead ran the emblazoned legend: 'This Number Contains a Complete Novel, 'The Picture of Dorian Gray' By Oscar Wilde'. Wilde's name was enough to 'excite wide interest and curiosity' in the venture. And the curiosity was repaid. The story created an immediate sensation.[18] It was variously hailed and puffed as 'one of the most brilliant and remarkable productions of the year' – a story 'full of strong and sustained interest', 'attractively written, with an easy dialogue and good character studies'.[19] The plot was likened to Faust, the style to both Disraeli and Ouida. The 'magic motive' of the picture was compared to Poe and Hawthorne, and the essential idea to Stevenson's *Strange Case of Dr Jekyll and Mr Hyde*. It was very soon 'monopoliz[ing] the attention of Londoners that talk about books'.[20] There was no denying that it was the literary sensation of the moment. For the first time in his career, it seemed, Wilde had matched his notoriety with a comparably notorious achievement.

Lady Wilde was characteristically enthusiastic, confessing that she had 'nearly fainted at the last scene'. The story, she announced, was 'the most wonderful piece of writing in all the fiction of the day'.[21] Robbie Ross reported that 'even in the precincts of the Savile' there was 'nothing but praise of Dorian Gray though of course it is said to be very dangerous' (Ross had heard a clergyman tempering his admiration for the novel with

the regret that, 'some of the sentiments of Lord Henry [were] apt to lead people astray'). Eighty copies of the magazine had been sold in a single day from a Strand booksellers: 'the usual sale being about 3 a week'.[22]

There were over 200 reviews – an extraordinary response to a novella published in an Anglo-American periodical. Not all, of course, were favourable. Wilde, it transpired, retained all his old ability to annoy the critics. One complained at his 'uncertainty as to the use of "will" and "shall"', another at 'an amateurish lack of precision in the descriptive passages'.[23] The *Pall Mall Gazette*, in a long critique, suggested that 'Mr Oscar Wilde's new novelette is compounded of three elements in equal proportion. It is one part Stevenson, one part Huysmans, one part Wilde.' The distinctive Wildean strain ('the genuine Oscar – the Oscar *fin de siècle*, whom we know') was displayed in the 'copious stream of paradox' flowing through the dialogue. A generous selection of examples – both 'ingenious' and 'trite' – was provided (though it was left to the reader to judge which was which):

'Being natural is simply a pose, and the most irritating pose I know.' – 'I can believe anything provided it is incredible.' – 'A man can't be too careful in his choice of his enemies. I have not got one who is a fool.' – 'It is only shallow people who do not judge by appearances.' – 'The only difference between a caprice and a lifelong passion is that the caprice lasts a little longer.' – 'Sin is the only colour-element left in modern life.' – 'Nowadays people know the price of everything and the value of nothing.' – 'There are only five women in London worth talking to, and two of these can't be admitted into decent society.' – 'A cigarette is the type of a perfect pleasure. It is exquisite, and it leaves one unsatisfied.' – 'Lord Henry was always late on principle, his principle being that punctuality is the thief of time.' – 'I never approve, or disapprove, of anything now. It is an absurd attitude to take towards life.'

As for the Stevensonian portion, the reviewer considered that although Wilde's story could be 'classed with *Dr Jekyll* as a moral tale... its morality [was] only skin deep' – and not even logically coherent. The supposed moral served merely as 'a conventional garment... to secure Mr. Wilde's fantasy an entrance into decent Anglo-American society'. The 'dominant element' in Wilde's literary 'inspiration' – it was claimed – was, rather, 'the aesthetic paganism of the French "Decadents"' in general, and of *À Rebours* in particular:

It is the picturesque not the ethical aspects of virtue and vice that interest Mr. Wilde. Purity has its artistic value, if only as a contrast to its
opposite; corruption is scintillant, iridescent, full of alluring effects...
From the very outset [the author] plunges us in a sickly atmosphere.
The way in which Lord Henry Wotton and Basil Hallward talk of, and
to, Dorian Gray in the opening scene convinced us, for the moment,
that the beautiful Dorian must be a woman in male attire. We were
wrong; Dorian Gray with his 'finely-curved scarlet lips, his frank blue
eyes and his crisp gold hair' is of the same sex as his admirers; but that
does not make their worship of him, and the forms of its expression,
seem any the less nauseous. And the atmosphere does not freshen as the
story proceeds. The very vagueness of Mr. Wilde's allusions to his hero's
vices is exceedingly effective from the Baudelairian point of view. We
are conscious of a penetrating poison in the air, yet cannot see clearly
whence it proceeds.[24]

While some papers hailed the story's 'high spiritual import', the gathering
consensus chimed with the Pall Mall Gazette and the Savile Club membership
in considering Wilde's story somehow 'morbid', 'unhealthy', 'dangerous'
and tinged with 'poison'. The position was stated most emphatically in the
St James's Gazette, the Daily Chronicle and in W. E. Henley's Scots Observer
(where, ironically, Robbie Ross – after a single unhappy year at Cambridge
– had taken a job). Each of them focused, in their differently coded ways, on
the story's undercurrents of 'unnatural' homosexual desire. They condemned the cloying relationships of the novel's three main characters, the
hedonistic creed proposed by Lord Henry Wotton, and the descriptions –
vague though they might be – of Dorian's depravities coupled with Wilde's
apparent enjoyment in writing about them.

'Why go grubbing in muck heaps?' demanded Charles Whibley, writing
anonymously in the Scots Observer:

The world is fair, and the proportion of healthy-minded men and
honest women to those that are foul, fallen or unnatural is great. Mr.
Oscar Wilde has again been writing stuff that were better unwritten;
and while 'The Picture of Dorian Gary'... is ingenious, interesting, full
of cleverness, and plainly the work of a man of letters, it is false art, for
its interest is medico-legal; it is false to human nature – for its hero is
a devil; it is false to morality – for it is not made sufficiently clear that

the writer does not prefer a course of unnatural iniquity to a life of cleanliness, health and sanity.[25]

The *Daily Chronicle* called the story a 'poisonous' tale, 'spawned by the leprous literature of the French Décadents... heavy with the odours of moral and spiritual putrefaction'; the *St James's Gazette* wondered whether 'The Treasury or the Vigilance Society will think it worth while to prosecute Mr. Oscar Wilde' or his publishers, for producing such a 'corrupt' and offensive work; while the *Scots Observer* suggested that a story which 'dealt with matters only fitted for the Criminal Investigation Department or a hearing – in camera' would appeal to 'none but outlawed noblemen and perverted telegraph-boys'.[26] The allusions to 'telegraph boys' and 'outlawed noblemen' to 'medico-legal' interests and the 'Vigilance Committee' all reflected, and encouraged, the sexual anxieties about 'unnatural vice' stirred up by the Cleveland Street Scandal.

With (and even without) the insinuations of the press, many of those who read the book detected its 'dangerous' subtext. Violet Martin thought it 'the most daring beastliness ever'; while John Addington Symonds, to whom Wilde had sent a copy, suggested 'If the British public will stand this, they can stand anything.' Wilde could not have been surprised at such reactions. He had, after all, refused to let the innocent-minded Graham Robertson read the story, telling him, 'this book was not written for you'.[27] Pater declined to review the story on the grounds that it was 'too dangerous'; he was, he told Wilde, concerned that the 'veil of mystery' surrounding Dorian's 'sins' slipped in some places, revealing too clearly the sexual passion that Basil Hallward had for him. He may have been concerned, too, that Lord Henry's call to for a 'New Hedonism' seemed to echo the ideas, and even the phrases, of his controversial 'Conclusion' to *The Renaissance*, bending them to a new purpose. He himself had spent the intervening years seeking to qualify and mitigate his call to a life of seeking 'experience' for its own end. The hero of his own novel, *Marius the Epicurean* (published in 1885), advocated a more austere philosophy of life, very different from the 'New Hedonism' – an Epicureanism that recognized the importance of 'the moral sense' for the complete and 'harmonious development of man's entire organism'.[28]

In America there was general incomprehension about the furore. A *New York Times* editorial at the end of June reported that the story had 'excited vastly more interest' in Britain than it had in the States, 'simply because,

since last year's exposure of what are euphemistically styled the West End [i.e. Cleveland Street] scandals Englishmen have been abnormally sensitive to the faintest suggestion of pruriency in the direction of friendships'. Any such 'bestial suspicion' was unlikely to have crossed the mind of 'one American reader out of ten thousand'.[29]

Wilde professed to be delighted with the press attacks, on the grounds that, as the English public 'takes no interest in a work of art until it is told that the work in question is immoral', such reviews would 'largely increase the sale of the magazine'. He only regretted that, having been paid outright for the piece, he would not be benefiting from this. To keep the subject alive he entered into a bantering correspondence with the three papers – adopting a variety of different defences. 'I am quite incapable', he told the St James's Gazette, 'of understanding how any work of art can be criticized from a moral standpoint. The sphere of art and the sphere of ethics are absolutely distinct and separate; and it is to the confusion between the two that we owe the appearance of Mrs. Grundy, that amusing old lady who represents the only original form of humour that the middle classes of this country have been able to produce.'[30]

To the editor of the Daily Chronicle he confessed (with a deployment of one of his favourite alliterations) that the book 'is poisonous if you like; but you cannot deny that it is also perfect, and perfection is what we artists aim at'.[31] In a further letter to the St James's Gazette he ruefully admitted that – 'alas' – his story did indeed have a moral. 'And the moral is this: All excess, as well as all renunciation, brings its own punishment... Is this an artistic error? I fear it is. It is the only error in the book?'[32] He side-stepped Whibley's 'grossly unjust' insinuations, with the line that, although it had proved necessary for 'the dramatic development of the story' to 'surround Dorian Gray with an atmosphere of moral corruption' he had deliberately left the details to the imagination of each reader: 'Each man sees his own sin in Dorian Gray.'[33]*

Wilde's cheerful assertion that the rumoured immorality of the story

---

*   When Wilde was quizzed by his friend Mrs Walter Palmer about the exact nature of Dorian's sins, he replied 'Really, you know, I couldn't possibly tell about that at dinner. If you will come with me, alone, in to the conservatory, I will tell you all about it.' After dinner he took her into the conservatory, they returned a few minutes later, Mrs Palmer 'almost shrieking with laughter'. 'What do you think this wretch told me?' she announced. 'I had asked him to tell me the wickedest thing Dorian Gray did in Whitechapel. And he bent over and whispered in my ear, "He ate peas with a knife!"'

would be good for sales was not entirely borne out. Although things had begun well, on 10 July Ward, Lock & Co. received 'an intimation from W. H. Smith and Son, that "[Wilde's] story having been characterized in the press as a filthy one", they are compelled to withdraw *Lippincott's Magazine* from their bookstalls'. The publishers sought an immediate interview with Wilde, declaring that 'this is a serious matter for us'.[34] And it was. Over the previous two years the National Vigilance Society (a body established in 1885 'for the enforcement and improvement of the laws for the repression of criminal vice and public immorality') had twice successfully prosecuted the English publisher Henry Vizetelly for distributing the novels of Emile Zola in translation. He had been fined a total of £300 and imprisoned for three months.

It was perhaps Ward, Lock & Co.'s anxieties that prompted Wilde's visit to the offices of the *St James's Gazette*, where he sought an interview with Samuel Jeyes, the journalist who had penned the original hostile review, and was fuelling the ongoing controversy. Jeyes (who had been at Oxford the year behind Wilde) proved implacable. Though Wilde exerted 'all the resources of his persuasive manner and abounding wit', Jeyes refused to be mollified. 'What is the use of writing of, and hinting at, things you do not mean?' he asked. 'I assure you,' replied Oscar earnestly, 'I mean every word I have said, and everything at which I have hinted.' 'Then all I can say,' answered Jeyes grimly, 'is that if you *do* mean them, you are very likely to find yourself at Bow Street one of these days.' Wilde greeted this with a 'light laugh'.[35]

Jeyes's comment, however, carried a warning. There were many who were ready to read the hints about Dorian's 'disgusting sins and abominable crimes' as reflections of Wilde's own interests and deeds. As Whibley had suggested, the story left it unclear whether the writer himself 'does not prefer a course of unnatural iniquity to a life of cleanliness, health and sanity'. Certainly the American-born baritone David Bispham, who was on the fringe of Wilde's circle, regarded the story as little short of a reckless 'confession'.[36] The extraordinary interest and attention generated by the tale may have given Wilde a greatly enhanced literary standing, but it also hastened the insidious process of undermining his personal reputation. And although there was considerable exaggeration in Constance's comment that 'since Oscar wrote "Dorian Gray" no one will speak to us', the story's publication undoubtedly marked a further darkening of Wilde's reputation. From that summer, in London's cultured circles, it became harder to ignore the 'strange things' being whispered about him.[37]

On the surface, though, all continued swimmingly. Wilde was in fine form at a party given by Louise Chandler Moulton on 21 July, falling into conversation with the forty-three-year-old poet Katharine Bradley. Together with her niece and life-partner, Edith Cooper, Bradley made up one half of a collaborative dyad that wrote and published under the name 'Michael Field'. They talked of Pater's prose, French 'colour-words', English philistinism and the genius of Jane Austen: Wilde suggested that 'due to their imperfect education the only works we have had from women are works of genius'. Touching on celestial matters, Wilde sketched out his vision of heaven. He said that when he got there he 'would like to find a number of volumes [bound] in vellum that he would be told were his'.[38] It was a vision to be desired. Thus far – at the age of thirty-five – Wilde had still only produced two actual books, *Poems* and *The Happy Prince*. They offered meagre assurances of immortality, and he was anxious to augment the haul. And over the next sixteen months he would succeed in impressive fashion – not by writing a great deal more, but by repackaging between hard covers what he had already written.

Plans were already advancing with Ward, Lock & Co. for the expanded book version of *Dorian Gray*, though it was now thought that more than two additional chapters might be necessary to 'counteract the damage' of the 1s Lippincott version being so widely distributed. Carlos Blacker was dismayed at the news that Wilde's 'damned story' would be making 'a re-appearance... with additions but I fear no corrections'. 'Have you ever known such abominable "Cussedness"?', he remarked to the Duke of Newcastle. There was, however, some recognition that the moral message of the book might have to be emphasized and decadent details toned down.[39]*

Although Wilde remained frustrated in his hopes of finding a publisher for a book version of 'The Portrait of Mr. W. H.', he had more luck with his scheme for a volume of collected essays. In London that summer he met a young American publisher called Clarence McIlvaine, who was travelling together with two literary compatriots, Jonathan Sturges and Stuart Merrill.

---

*   George Lock, one of the partners in the firm, wrote to Wilde suggesting, 'Could you not make Dorian live longer with the face of the picture transformed to himself and depict the misery in which he ends his days by suicide or repents and becomes a better character? Lord Henry too goes off the scene very quickly. Could not he also live a little longer – and you could make an excellent contrast between the death of the two men. This is what has occurred to me. It is for you to decide if it is worth anything.' Wilde decided that it was not.

The twenty-four-year-old Bostonian was planning to establish a new Anglo-American publishing house, in partnership with the distinguished J. R. Osgood, and was in England looking for authors. Wilde set about wooing him and his two companions. 'In spite of his glory and our obscurity,' Merrill recalled, 'he was charming to us without displaying the least pose or arrogance.'[40] The charm had its effect: McIlvaine agreed to take on not only a collection of Wilde's essays (including the two dialogues) but also a compendium of his four published short stories from *Court and Society* and the *World*, and a second volume of fairy tales. All three volumes would be scheduled for the following year.

The phenomenal stir caused by 'The Picture of Dorian Gray' encouraged other offers of work. Norman Forbes-Robertson, who was taking on the lease of the Globe Theatre at the end of the year with an aim of producing 'good comedies well cast', approached Wilde with a request for a play. Unfortunately, though, he was unable to offer any advance. 'I am always in need of money,' Wilde explained, 'and have to work for certainties.'[41] More satisfactory was an inquiry from George Alexander. The thirty-two-year-old actor was also launching himself into management, and also wanted a play from Wilde. He had reason to respect Wilde's taste, since Wilde had written generously of his acting. And he had – as he put it – 'long been persuaded' that Wilde could write a good play. Reading *Dorian Gray* had confirmed his confidence in the author's 'dramatic faculty'. Alexander also wanted to gain some of the social cachet that he considered attached to Wilde's name, in order to bring to his new theatre (the St James's) 'the smart society circles in which Wilde himself already moved'. As an immediate response Wilde appears to have offered him *The Duchess of Padua*, which was scheduled for its New York production early in following year. But Alexander's vision was for a modern-dress 'society play'. And he – unlike Norman Forbes-Robertson – did have the resources to pay an advance of £100: £50 due upfront, £50 due on delivery of the script. Wilde readily agreed.[42]

Proving the rule of three, Wilde also received, that summer, a letter soliciting his support for a new independent theatre society, modelled on the Théatre de l'Art in Paris, which aimed to mount plays 'from the most prominent English men of letters' (Meredith, Hardy, Stevenson, Henry James) as well as 'certain masterpieces of foreign unconventionality' (Ibsen's *Ghosts*) – without the necessity of submitting the works to the lord chamberlain's office. The club's founders, two London-based Dutch writers, Alexander Teixeira de Mattos and J. T. Grein, hoped that Wilde might have

'a play of unconventional interest' which he would be prepared to 'lend...
for production'. Wilde did not; but the inquiry was flattering, and it perhaps suggested to him, for the first time, the idea of attempting something
in the line of 'experimental' drama.[43]

Any notion that the publication of *Dorian Gray* had led to the Wildes'
social ostracism was refuted by a summer holiday season spent staying
with a succession of Scottish baronets 'in the midst of purple heather and
silver mist'. It was, Wilde confessed, 'such a relief to me, Celt as I am, from
the wearisome green of England. I only like green in art. This is one of my
many heresies.'[44]

Back in London after this break, as part of his work on the forthcoming
book version of *Dorian Gray*, Wilde asked Ricketts to make some designs
for the volume's cover and title page. It was a happy collaborative project,
and would prove to be the first of many. It drew Wilde closer to the world
of the Vale. He became a regular at the little Friday-night gatherings,
sometimes bringing a friend with him to what he called 'the one house
in London where you will never be bored'.[45] He came to know the select
group of artists, craftsmen and writers that Ricketts and Shannon drew into
their orbit. Among them was an extraordinarily handsome, rather solemn,
young man called John Gray. A minor clerk in the civil service, and of
modest origins, he had taught himself French and was devoting himself to
literature. The first number of *The Dial* had contained an article by him on
'Les Goncourts' as well as a distinctly Wildean fairy story about 'The Great
Worm'. He also wrote verse. Wilde was impressed by the poetry (which
borrowed from the Parisian Decadents) quite as much as by the man, with
his quiet air of distinction and charming manners. Gray, like Ricketts, could
tell him things he did not know.[46]

It was exciting for Wilde to discover that so many of the rising generation
shared his fascination with contemporary French art and literature – 'the
one art now in Europe that is worth discussing,' as he told another new literary acquaintance, the self-consciously avant-garde critic and poet Arthur
Symons.[47] John Gray's own boyish good looks were, moreover, strangely
suggestive of the central motif in Wilde's novel. Indeed Wilde came to
consider Gray to be almost the image of 'Dorian'. 'I didn't find or see him
until after I described him in my book,' he later remarked: a wonderful
confirmation of the idea that art inspires and directs nature. 'This young
man,' he declared, 'would never have existed if I hadn't described Dorian.'[48]
The connection became a joke and a bond shared between them. Wilde

would allude 'laughingly to John Gray as his hero, "Dorian"'. And Gray even signed himself 'Dorian' in at least one letter to Wilde.[49]

The conceit was shared with Lionel Johnson and other members of the newly established 'Rhymers Club', an informal grouping of young poets, inaugurated by Yeats and some like-minded friends. Wilde – and Gray – occasionally attended the club's meetings at the Century Guild headquarters on Fitzroy Street. And Johnson, together with his fellow Rhymer Ernest Dowson was soon referring to Gray as '"Dorian" Gray', or 'the original of Dorian'; while Johnson elaborated the point in his description of Gray as 'a youth... aged thirty with the face of fifteen'. Gray was actually twenty-five; but the exaggeration enhanced the joke.[50]*Art and life were bound together.

---

* Lionel Johnson, himself, was – despite an ever-increasing enthusiasm for whisky drinking – quite as youthful looking as John Gray. Indeed Wilde once remarked, 'that any morning at eleven o'clock you might see him come out very drunk from the Café Royal, and hail the first passing perambulator'.

3

Suggestive Things

'An idea that is not dangerous is unworthy of being called an idea at all.'

OSCAR WILDE

During the first days of 1891, Wilde made a nostalgic visit to his former rooms in Charles Street for a small literary gathering hosted by Robert Sherard, who was over on a visit from Paris. Among the company was Sherard's old New College contemporary, the dashing and irascible John Barlas. Wilde was interested to meet him.

Barlas was both a poet and radical socialist. A sometime member of the Social Democratic Federation and a contributor to William Morris's *Commonweal*, he delighted in adopting extreme positions. At Sherard's party he had proclaimed his radical credentials by turning up with 'a weird young female, whom he introduced as his sister-soul and Muse'. To assert her own commitment to the revolutionary cause she wore – as she confided to the company – red flannel 'under things'. Despite the fact that Sherard considered her 'hardly a person to bring to a "respectable" house', Wilde treated her with great courtesy. But not enough for the ever-quarrelsome Barlas.

When the party broke up at the end of the afternoon, Wilde, Barlas and the 'Muse', together with Sherard and another poet (Barlas's friend and

fellow Scot, John Davidson) all left the house together. Walking through Grosvenor Square, Barlas suddenly hailed a hansom cab, bundled his lady friend into it, and then, turning on the others, rebuked them all – and Wilde in particular – for their 'want of respect to his sister soul'. It appears he thought that Wilde should have offered his arm to the lady when they left the house. The dramatic exit was rather spoiled when the cab driver, on hearing that Barlas lived in a Lambeth slum district, hesitated to accept the fare. Wilde stepped forward and good-humouredly reassured the cabman ('who knew him by sight, and addressed him as "my lord"') that all would be well.*

The incident amused, rather than offended, Wilde; and after a contrite Barlas apologized, a friendship developed between the two men. Wilde introduced him to John Gray and others of his circle.[1] Although Wilde appreciated Barlas's lush Swinburnian verse, his political views intrigued him more. Recent months had been taxing ones for Wilde's political allegiances. In November 1890, Parnell had found the details of his unconventional private life gleefully exposed, and picked over, in the British press, when the husband of Kitty O'Shea, his long-time mistress, finally sued his wife for divorce. The Unionist papers seized the opportunity to drag Parnell's name through the mud. In the face of much prudish public indignation, the Liberals threatened to break their ties with the Irish Parliamentary Party, while Parnell's refusal to stand down as leader split his own party into Parnellite and anti-Parnellite factions. In the welter of press-fuelled prurience and political infighting the hopes of achieving Irish Home Rule seemed, suddenly, to evaporate. It was a bitter moment.

Nevertheless, at the same time that Wilde's confidence in the ability of the British parliamentary system to deliver radical change was being frayed, his broader political ideas were taking on new colour. Towards the end of 1890 he had been approached by Archibald Grove, the editor of the recently established New Review, who hoped he might write a 'reply' to a forthcoming article on 'Socialism and Literature'. Grove wanted 'about 3500 words, from the point of view of individualism'.[2] Wilde did not take up the offer, deciding instead to write his own essay on the subject and place it with Frank Harris at the Fortnightly Review.

---

* Wilde had developed a penchant for taking hansom cabs that had become almost a dependency. Generous with his tips and his patronage (he would hail a cab for even the shortest trip, and often keep them on while he made calls and visits) he was revered among the drivers as 'the best rider in Chelsea'.

As Robbie Ross recalled it, Wilde wrote 'The Soul of Man Under Social-ism' 'in three consecutive mornings' in the library of the Ross family home at 85 Onslow Square, early in the New Year.[3] 'Socialism' was, of course, a topic that had interested Wilde for some time. His encounters with the witty and contrarian Shaw had both broadened his understanding and encouraged him to think that it was a subject on which he might write;[4] while his new friendship with Barlas – who was steeped in the writings of Proudhon, and tended more towards 'anarchism' in his views – offered a slightly different, and perhaps even more alluring, perspective.[5]

Abandoning his favourite dialogue form – though retaining much of its open-ended epigrammatic character – Wilde laid out a captivating and highly personal vision of socialism. He proclaimed the need to replace 'pri-vate property' with 'public wealth' – so that man might be freed from the tedious cares of ownership, and co-operation might supersede competition as the driving force of society. But he saw this only as a first step on the road towards the development of Individualism. 'The true perfection of man', he asserted, 'lies not in what man has, but in what man is.' In this Wilde was veering to the anarchist end of the socialist spectrum.

In support of his theory he held up the example of Jesus – not perhaps the divine figure of Christian orthodoxy, but the extraordinary human being, and great apostle of individualism, derived partly from Wilde's imagination and partly from Ernest Renan's determinedly secular 1861 book, *La Vie de Jésus* (Renan's volume was added to Wilde's select library of 'golden books'; he dubbed it 'the gospel according to St Thomas').[6] The message of Wilde's Jesus was 'Be thyself... You have a wonderful personality. Develop it... Don't imagine that your perfection lies in accumulating or possessing external things. Your perfection is inside yourself.'

In assisting towards this goal of self-development Wilde proclaimed the redundancy of all forms of government, and all conventional moralities. All authority was considered degrading: 'It degrades those who exercise it, and degrades those over whom it is exercised.' A society constituted on the lines he proposed would be a haven for all, but particularly for artists (and for Oscar Wilde), since 'art is the most intense mode of individualism that the world has known'.

Some of the large ideas adumbrated in the essay were given specific and topical point. In the wake of Parnell's fall, Wilde incorporated a damning indictment of the prurient intrusiveness of the British press, which would seek to 'drag before the eyes of the public some incident in the private life

of a great statesman… and invite the public to discuss the incident'. 'In old days,' Wilde remarked, 'men had the rack. Now they have the press.' It was scarcely an improvement. And taking a swipe at the critics who had condemned 'The Picture of Dorian Gray' as 'morbid', Wilde declared, 'What is morbidity but a mood of emotion or a mode of thought that one cannot express? The public are all morbid, because the public can never find expression for anything. The artist is never morbid. He expresses everything. He stands outside his subject.'

The essay appeared in the February issue of the *Fortnightly Review*. If, as one critic suggested, it had been written 'to startle and excite comment', it succeeded well. Press opinion might be divided, but there was considerable private enthusiasm for the piece. The young Roger Fry admired it greatly. The writer Grant Allen thanked Wilde for penning such a 'noble and beautiful essay'. And Barlas, writing to John Gray, hailed it as 'the most perfect revolutionary essay the world has yet seen, not only as a work of art, but for knowledge and insight'.[7] He had already saluted Wilde – and Gray – as fellow anarchists: 'All artists are so unconsciously from birth,' he had suggested.[8] And he was delighted to find his insight confirmed.

To give the text a visual – as well as a literary – distinction, Wilde had insisted on having many of his more apothegmatic statements set in italics: *'There is only one class in the community that thinks more about money than the rich, and that is the poor.' 'Art should never try to make itself popular. The public should try to make itself artistic'*, etc. And this conceit provoked almost as much as the political views expressed. At a fashionable lunch party the Liberal MP Herbert Asquith suggested to Wilde, with a slight edge of malice, that 'The man who uses italics is like the man who raises his voice in conversation and talks loudly in order make himself heard.' Wilde, however refused to rise to the bait. 'How delightful of you, Mr Asquith, to have noticed that!' he replied with smiling good humour. 'The brilliant phrase, like good wine, needs no bush. But just as the orator marks his good things by a dramatic pause, or by raising or lowering his voice, or by gesture, so the writer marks his epigrams with italics, setting the little gem, so to speak, like a jeweller – an excusable love of one's art, not all mere vanity, I like to think.'[9]

The stir caused in London by the essay was more than matched by exciting news from across the Atlantic. Wilde received a cable from Lawrence Barrett to say that *Guido Ferranti* (as *The Duchess of Padua* had been renamed) had opened at the Broadway Theatre in New York to very favourable reviews, and was running 'to crowded houses'. Although Wilde's authorship had

been kept off the playbills, it had been divined by the critic from the *New York Tribune*, and Barrett suggested that Wilde should cable the American press acknowledging that he was indeed the author, and expressing his thanks to the public for their reception of his play.[10]

Barrett had cut the piece down substantially; it now ran to just three hours. And, despite being fifty-three, he brought his customary vigour to the role of the youthful Guido; in the part of the Duchess, his regular leading lady, Minna Gale – for all her 'metallic infelicity of voice' and 'crudity of gesture' – was acclaimed, at least by some, as having achieved a new 'height of tragic power'. Wilde's 'blank verse' was hailed as 'scholarly and poetical' and, sometimes, 'full of the fire of eloquence'.[11]Although most of the reviewers qualified their praise – noting the play's literary debts, logical inconsistencies, tendency to 'melodrama', 'morbid' details and general 'improbability' – the consensus was favourable enough. Audiences were not discouraged from coming.

At least one press report suggested that Wilde had been taken by surprise at the play's production. Certainly there had been no suggestion that he travel to America for the opening night. His arrival would, in any case, have compromised the secret of his authorship. He was, nevertheless, delighted with the play's success (the 'immense success' as he termed it). He composed a paragraph about the production for the *Daily Telegraph*, and wrote promptly to Henry Irving, urging him to look again at the piece ('you are the one artist in England who can produce poetic blank-verse drama'). Irving, however, again demurred. Nor was the actor-manager Charles Cartwright, whom Wilde also approached, ready to take on the project.[12]* In New York the play ran for a creditable three weeks (until 14 February) at which point Barrett replaced it with another piece that he wished to try out. There was, though, a stated plan to revive it for the company's summer tour.[13]

The production of the *Duchess* reminded Wilde of his other theatrical commitment. He had hesitated to make a start on his play for George Alexander, and then found the task intractable. 'I can't get a grip on the play

---

* Wilde also wrote to the *New York Herald* (15 February 1891) correcting their 'interesting and inaccurate' article on his reasons for keeping his authorship a secret: 'When a work is anonymous, the public and the journalists can to a certain degree develop that temperament of receptivity to which alone are artistic effects revealed. When the author's name is affixed they are distracted by a desire to praise or to censure, according as they have principles or prejudices. This is bad for them.'

yet,' he confessed. 'The fact is I worked at it when I was not in the mood for work, and must first forget it, and then go back quite fresh to it.'[14] Not knowing when the mood might strike him, he offered – uncharacteristically – to repay Alexander the £50 advance, and terminate their agreement. To his alarm Alexander accepted the suggestion, leaving Wilde to backtrack, and explain that, actually, he was 'in a great mess about money' and would not have any until the *Duchess* had been on its tour.[15]

Wilde's immediate literary concern, though, was to put the finishing touches to the book version of *Dorian Gray*, adding six new chapters, enriching the melodrama of the plot, sharpening the social satire, polishing the text and amending some of the more contentiously homoerotic passages. A reference to Basil and Dorian walking back from the club 'arm in arm' was cut, along with another to Lord Henry placing his hand on Basil's shoulder. He also excised the gushing commentary given by Lady Brandon as she introduced her party guests to one another: 'Sir Humpty Dumpty – you know – Afghan Frontier – Russian intrigues: very successful man – wife killed by an elephant – quite inconsolable – wants to marry a beautiful American widow – everybody does nowadays.' It was, perhaps, too obviously a caricature of his own mother at one of her receptions. Lady Wilde had certainly thought that the story needed 'some alterations'.[16]

Among the passages added was a fuller account of the 'New Hedonism', Sir Henry's seductive theory of pleasure ('the only thing worth having a theory about'). According to his estimate, 'Pleasure is Nature's test, her sign of approval. When we are happy we are always good, but when we are good we are not always happy... To be good is to be in harmony with one's self... Discord it to be forced to be in harmony with others. One's own life – that is the important thing... Individualism has really the higher aim... no civilized man ever regrets a pleasure, and no uncivilized man ever knows what a pleasure is.'[17] It was a theory that Wilde was prepared to live by.

The editor at Ward, Lock & Co., a young writer called Coulson Kernahan, strove to keep Wilde within bounds. The task was taxing. When he criticized Wilde's line 'the sky was an inverted cup of blue metal' as an ineffective piece of 'Wardour Street artificiality' (on the grounds that the sky was soft not hard), Wilde interrupted, 'No! No!... Not Wardour Street – delete the "W", if you like, and say that with the "ardour" of the artist, and with my eyes all upon the picture, I have taken a brushful of colour from the wrong corner of my palette, for there is something in what you say of my use of the words "cup" and "metal". But such a phrase as "Wardour Street" which

I always associate with the painted harlots one sees parading there, makes me shudder.'* Kernahan thought he had managed to persuade Wilde to cut the 'Devil's doctrine' – as he termed it – of Lord Henry's advocacy of 'sin' as an element of self-fulfilment. But Wilde subsequently changed his mind, insisting the passage be reinstated. 'After all,' he claimed, 'it is merely Luther's "Pecca Fortiter" [Sin Boldly] put dramatically into the lips of a character.'[18]

The physical aspects of the book were, of course, addressed with care. Ricketts produced a series of small gold 'butterfly' designs to dot the cover, as well as a hand-lettered title page. As with Wilde's two previous publications it was decided to issue the title in two versions – a standard one (priced at 6s) and a 'de luxe' signed large-paper edition, limited to fifty copies, numbered and signed by the author, and priced at a guinea.

As a further refinement, Wilde composed a collection of twenty-three aphorisms about art and morality, to serve as a preface and to forestall the most obvious lines of critical attack. Among his assertions were: 'There is no such thing as a moral or an immoral book. Books are well written, or badly written. That is all.' 'It is the spectator, and not life, that art really mirrors.' 'When critics disagree the artist is in accord with himself.' And 'All art is quite useless.' Frank Harris, seeing the epigrams in the manuscript, begged to be allowed to publish them first in the *Fortnightly Review*. Wilde consented – and in what may have been a cheerful rebuke to the critics who had assailed the typography of 'The Soul of Man Under Socialism' he insisted they all be printed in italics.

For all the work to be done on the book there was still time for socializing. Wilde continued to see much of Dorian's namesake John Gray. They were together at a Rhymers' Club gathering chez Horne at the end of January, and a week later were both at the Vale.[19] Their constant companionship led some to suppose that there must be a sexual dimension to their relations. Rumours began to form. Barlas 'hinted, rather vaguely' to his friend Frank Liebich, of an '(alleged) intimacy' between the two. But Wilde himself, though he was surely attracted to Gray, and may have tried to seduce him, always characterized their friendship as a purely intellectual and artistic one; and Frank Harris supports the claim.[20]

---

*   Wardour Street, in Soho, was – during the late nineteenth century – a centre for the manufacture and sale of cheap over-ornate reproduction furniture. As a result it became a byword for tawdriness and a term of critical abuse.

Where Wilde's sexual interests lay just then is unknown, though a letter to the young actor Roland Atwood gives a flavour of the camp flirtatiousness that he sought out and enjoyed: 'I send you your necktie, in which I know you will look Greek and gracious. I don't think it is too dark for you... Has Gerald Gurney forgiven me yet for talking to no one but you that afternoon? I suppose not. But who else was there to talk to?'[21] The rate of his sexual encounters was, it seems, increasing. And although he lost none of his power to charm and inspire the young, he came to exercise it with a certain cynicism. He became – as he later recognized – 'reckless of young lives'. He would take a up a young man 'love him "passionately"' for a while, then 'grow bored' and cease even to notice him.[22]

Although Harris recognized that Gray 'of course found extraordinary stimulus in Oscar's talk', the stimulation was mutual. There was a keen 'intellectual sympathy' between the two men, and Gray's up-to-date knowledge of contemporary French culture made him specially interesting to Wilde. On a visit to Paris the previous year, Gray had sought out the avant-garde critic Félix Fénéon, and was corresponding with him. He had developed an understanding of how the established decadence espoused by many young French writers was now shading into a newly designated symbolism that sought to achieve its vague and allusive effects not by describing a thing directly but rather the effect that it produced. At the Rhymers' Club evening in Fitzroy Street, Gray read what Dowson described as, 'some very beautiful & obscure versicles in the latest manner of French Symbolism'; and he brought with him to the Vale the young Symbolist-inspired French artist Lucien Pissarro (son of the Impressionist painter Camille).[23] Such encounters seem to have ignited Wilde's interest. He introduced modish references to 'the symbol' among his aphorisms prefacing Dorian Gray: 'All art is at once surface and symbol.' 'Those who read the symbol do so at their peril.'

And with the editorial work on his book almost complete, he took himself off towards the end of February for a brief holiday in Paris. He had not spent time in the French capital since his honeymoon almost seven years before. Then he had been a young man with few achievements to his name, beyond charm, self-belief, a supposed intimacy with Swinburne, a slim volume of poems and an American lecture tour. Now he returned as a figure of some standing, and with the beginnings of a real connection to the French literary scene. One of his fairy stories had already appeared in French, and he had hopes that his two dialogues and The Picture of Dorian Gray might be translated too.[24]

The writer whom Wilde was most concerned to meet while in Paris was Stéphane Mallarmé, the acclaimed leader of the new Symbolist school, the author of *L'après-midi d'un faune*, and a man who – in Wilde's newly formed estimate – had taken French prose and poetry and made them into a single thing.[25] Mallarmé held a regular Tuesday evening gathering for writers and artists at his flat in the rue de Rome. Wilde attended the 'mardi' on 24 February.

He accounted it a 'really unforgettable' occasion. At the end of the evening Mallarmé presented him with a copy of his translation of *Les Poèmes d'Edgar Poe* inscribed 'A Oscar Wilde, en souvenir d'un premier soir'. And the following day Sherard asked Mallarmé to join him, Wilde and the poet Jean Moréas for lunch that Thursday (it was Moréas who had defined the Symbolist movement in a manifesto of 1886). There was some doubt as to whether the 'Cher et très-honoré Maître' would be turning up at the Café Riche, since his answer to Sherard's invitation was – like everything he wrote – worded in such an 'intricate and obscure manner' as to leave its meaning uncertain. But he did come, and a 'very cordial' time was had. In Sherard's recollection, Wilde succeeded in 'amazing' the two French poets.[26]

Although Wilde had intended to stay only a week in Paris, a sudden bout of illness, and the many diversions of the city, kept him there until the middle of March. He wrote to his five-and-a-half-year-old son, Cyril, hoping that he was 'taking great care of dear Mamma', and promising to bring back some chocolates. His extended visit allowed him to attend another Mallarmé *mardi*, and to broaden his acquaintance among the members of the Symbolist school. At Sunday lunch chez Jacques-Emile Blanche, he was introduced to Mallarmé's disciple Henri de Régnier; the twenty-six-year-old Régnier ranked Wilde as the first intelligent Englishman he had met (Wilde reported to John Gray that Régnier was 'bien gentile').[27] Carlos Blacker was in town, together with his beautiful mistress, '*la belle Kate*', and Wilde brought Régnier to dine with them one evening at the Maison Dorée.[28]

Accompanied by Blacker and Sherard, Wilde called on Emile Zola. The great Realist received the celebrated Aesthete graciously, claiming he was honoured by the visit. He talked of his current work, *La Débâcle*, describing his trawls through mounds of documents about the Franco-Prussian War, and visits to the battlefield at Sedan. Wilde – despite having disparaged Zola's 'unimaginative realism' – affected to agree with this research-based approach to novel writing, recalling that in writing *Dorian Gray* he himself had 'studied long lists of jewellery' and pored over the catalogues of horticultural firms:

'You cannot,' he told Zola, 'draw a novel from your brain as spider draws its web out of its belly.'[29]*

While in Paris Wilde was looking over the proofs of *Dorian Gray*. Back in London, Coulson Kernahan was startled to receive a telegram from his author: 'Terrible blunder in book. Coming back specially. Stop all proofs.' Wilde followed soon after, arriving in a hansom cab and a state of theatrical panic. 'It is not too late? For heaven's sake tell me it is not too late?' he affected to gasp. The cause of all this drama was that he had noticed the picture framer in his novel was named 'Ashton': 'Ashton', he declared in anguished tones, 'is a gentleman's name. And I've given it – God forgive me – to a tradesman! It must be changed to Hubbard. Hubbard positively smells of the tradesman!' As Kernahan remarked, having 'successfully worked off this wheeze on me', Wilde became his smiling self again.[30]

The book finally appeared in April. The storm of interest and controversy that had greeted the periodical publication the year before was not repeated. The 250 copies of the handsome large-paper, one-guinea, *edition de luxe* found a market among dedicated bibliophiles, but the modest 1,000-book run of the ordinary *6s* edition failed to sell out. The six new chapters were not enough to convince people that this was an entirely new work on which they should spend six times more than they had spent on *Lippincott's Magazine*. Wilde like to claim that in offering him a £125 (against royalties of 10 per cent) Ward, Lock & Co. had taken advantage of his naivety. But – given the poor sales – it was a very good deal for him.[31]

Reviews were scant. The most gratifying notice did not appear until November: Walter Pater, relieved at the excision of certain passages from the magazine version, felt able to pen some words of generous, though qualified, praise in the *Bookman*. While taking care to point out that 'Lord Henry Wotton' and 'Dorian Gray' had failed to grasp the 'moral' element in true 'Epicureanism' (as laid out by him in his novel, *Marius*), he saluted 'the skill, the real subtlety of art, the ease and fluidity withal' of Wilde's telling of an 'excellent story'.[32]

---

* Wilde appears to have given a rather more accurate account of their different approaches to research to another friend, explaining, 'whenever that man [Zola] writes a book he always takes his subjects directly from life. If he is going to write about dreadful people living in hovels he goes and lives in a hovel himself for months in case he shouldn't be accurate. It is strange. Take me for example. I have conceived the idea for the most exquisite tale that was ever written. The period is the eighteenth century. It would require a morning's reading in the British Museum. Therefore it will never be written.'

The appearance of Wilde's novel was followed swiftly by the publication, at the beginning of May, of his collected essays by Osgood & McIlvaine. Wilde had gathered together his two dialogues, 'Pen, Pencil and Poison' and his essay on Shakespearean costume under the title *Intentions*. All the pieces had been revised, and slightly expanded from their original forms. Nevertheless the last essay, with its plea for 'archaeological' accuracy in theatrical representations, sat rather awkwardly amid the calls to imagination and 'lying' in the other pieces – and Wilde felt obliged to tag it with an insouciant closing paragraph remarking, 'Not that I agree with everything I have said in this essay. There is much with which I disagree.'

If the re-appearance of Wilde's novel in a new guise produced a slightly underwhelming effect, the repackaging of his 'essays' was more enthusiastically received. Separated from the immediacy of topical journalistic debate, their distinctiveness, their originality and their brilliance became even more apparent. Frank Harris thought that 'Plato might have been proud to sign [several of the] pages'.[33] In Pater's view, Wilde was carrying on, 'more perhaps than any other writer, the brilliant critical work of Matthew Arnold'.[34] It was never going to be a popular a success, but it was admired and welcomed by the 'elect'. And the appearance, later that summer, of *Lord Arthur Savile's Crime and Other Stories* served usefully to keep Wilde's literary star in the ascendant.

4

The Best Society

*'A man who can dominate a London dinner table can
dominate the world.'*

OSCAR WILDE

One afternoon, towards the end of June, Lionel Johnson called
at Tite Street, bringing with him a friend: the twenty-year-old
Lord Alfred Douglas, third son of the celebrated Marquess of
Queensberry (renowned for codifying the rules of boxing). Douglas – a contemporary, and a bedfellow, of Johnson's at both Winchester and Oxford –
had sought the meeting, having been completely enraptured by *The Picture
of Dorian Gray*. He had read the novel straight through a dozen times, and
was anxious to meet the author. Wilde greeted his two undergraduate
admirers in the ground-floor 'library' and dazzled them with his talk. He,
for his part, though, was somewhat dazzled too – by the fair-haired, fair-
complexioned, youthful beauty of Lord Alfred. Beside his looks, Douglas
was also conspicuously charming: he had poetic ambitions; he admired
Wilde's work; he said amusing things; he made a good impression on
Constance when they went up to the drawing room to see her; and he had
a title. And, maybe, even at that first meeting, he hinted at his 'frank paganism' and enthusiasm for sex with other young men. Wilde was certainly
intrigued and excited.[1]

A friendship was immediately initiated, no different from the many other friendships that Wilde began with young, intelligent literary admirers. Douglas was invited to lunch at the Lyric Club a few days later, and presented with a copy of the deluxe edition of *Dorian Gray*, inscribed 'Alfred Douglas, from his friend who wrote this book, Oscar. July 91'. And there were perhaps a couple of other meetings over the summer. According to Douglas's later account, from the time of their second meeting, Wilde 'made "overtures" to me', but was rebuffed (Douglas's own sexual tastes were, as he put it, all towards youth and softness). Such refusals, however, did nothing to mar the burgeoning friendship.[2]

Lunching with a lord was not the height of Wilde's social success that summer. Indeed the season of 1891 had the aspect of a triumphal progress. Wilde's literary successes had opened new doors. He and Constance were invited to a succession of grand country house parties at Taplow Court, Wilton and Wrest. There were dinners in Carlton House Terrace and select group excursions to the London theatre.

Wilde owed all this to the interest of Ettie Grenfell, the wife of his Oxford contemporary Willie Grenfell, and the mistress of Taplow Court. Around the vivacious twenty-four-year-old society hostess there gravitated an extraordinary group of inter-connected friends and cousins, known – to themselves and others – as the 'Souls' (because, it was claimed, they spent all their time talking, not about politics, but about their 'souls'). In the conventional world of British society they were exceptional in being not only rich and aristocratic, but also intelligent and interesting. Among the leading lights were George Wyndham; his sister, Lady Elcho; her sometime lover, Arthur Balfour; the irrepressible young Margot Tennant; Harry Cust (renowned for his 'random flashes of wit');[3] the poet Wilfrid Blunt; St John Brodrick (whom Wilde had so amused when crossing the Atlantic in 1883); and George Curzon.

Wilde was thrilled to find himself drawn into this charmed and elevated circle. He had, it seemed, reached a new social empyrean, beyond even that inhabited by the sickly Duke of Newcastle and the reprobate Lord Francis Hope. And it was, as ever, the women who welcomed him. The men, jealous of their caste, were not entirely to be trusted. At the same moment that Ettie Grenfell was proposing outings and sending invites, Curzon – Wilde's supposed friend – was complaining of her 'pursuit of notoriety in any shape (if associated with cleverness)': it had, he regretted, already led to 'the decadence of our circle by the introduction of the "Osquiths"' – a term

he had coined by combining the Oscar Wildes and the Herbert Asquiths. He was furious that 'Ettie' had invited these 'new guns' – together with the (even less socially elevated) Beerbohm Trees – to a great Sunday party at Taplow. As Curzon lamented to the American diplomat Harry White, 'It means the dissolution of the fairest and strongest band of friends ever yet allied by ties of affection.' He urged White to capsize the interlopers during the days' punting, in the hope of drowning them.[4]

Wilde escaped undrowned from the Taplow party (on 31 May), although Ettie would later recall his 'stepping in mid-river' from one punt to another 'with heavy oscillations' and Mrs Beerbohm Tree hailing his arrival in her boat with the 'delicious greeting' 'Welcome, little stranger.'[5] He passed a delightful day, telling stories and showing off. Another guest remembered him, together with Balfour, Harry Cust and others, sitting on the Taplow lawn, talking over 'the most striking and impressive event' that each of them had witnessed; Wilde claimed that 'what had impressed him most in life was seeing a French widow in the heaviest crepe weeds fishing by the side of a canal!'.[6]

The undercurrent of animus was perhaps more detectable when Wilde spent a bachelor weekend at Crabbet Park – his introduction to Wilfrid Blunt's select but informal 'Crabbet Club'. The days of tennis and talk culminated in evenings of post-prandial oratory and competitive verse making.* As part of the process of Wilde's 'election' to the club, Curzon acted as devil's advocate, putting forward reasons why Wilde might be ineligible for membership. Drawing on their shared Oxford history, he argued that Wilde had been guilty of doing 'serious work' by reading the lessons in a surplice as a demy at Magdalen. Wilde countered this with the claim, 'I always read the lesson with an air of scepticism, and was invariably reproved by the Warden after Divine Service for "levity at the lectern"'.[7]

Curzon then began an assault 'bristling with innuendoes and sneering side-hits at strange sins'. Although the press coverage of *Dorian Gray* the previous year had created a tenuous link between the 'unhealthy' details of the story and the possible sympathies of the author, Curzon, and his circle, had – it seems – actual knowledge of Wilde's clandestine sexual interests and activities. Harry White, sympathizing with Curzon over the dilution of the Souls' circle, had remarked, 'I must say, I'm inclined to draw

* Wilde's prowess at lawn tennis had declined rather since his Oxford days. Blunt's daughter, Judith, recalled him on court, 'a great wobbly blancmange trying to serve underhand'.

the line at Oscar Wilde about whom everyone has known for years.' Blunt
felt Curzon's attack went too far, and was inclined to intervene. But Wilde
rose from his chair, and delivered 'an amusing and excellent speech'. Drawing on the arguments he had mapped out for his extended version of 'The
Portrait of Mr. W. H.', he made an impassioned defence of the ideal friendship – both creative and romantic – that can exist between a man and a
youth. The debate continued long, and though the 'Curzon–Wilde duel'
was remembered as being brilliant, its 'ferocity' was noted too. The other
club members looked on with a mixture of 'hilarity and disquiet' as Wilde
indicted Curzon's intellectual mediocrity and his toiling hard for a second-
class degree as a prelude to a second-class career. Blunt was relieved that
both antagonists kept their temper. But he recognized that the occasion had
been an uncomfortable one for Wilde (despite urgings from Blunt, Wilde
never returned to Crabbet).[8]

The house party at Wilton, with Blunt's great friend the Earl of Pembroke,
was less charged with hostile undercurrents, but Wilde was expected to play
up to the role of court jester. The composer Hubert Parry, a fellow guest,
recalled him as 'the centre of attraction' throughout the stay. During a week
full of 'the clatter of society' – he 'talked incessantly', devoting himself to
'tête-à-têtes' with the various ladies during the day, or entertaining groups
of 'entranced listeners' with his stories and paradoxes. In the evening, after
dinner, when 'a sort of symposium' would form in the smoking room, George
Wyndham (a fellow Crabbet Club member) would direct the discussion to
make Wilde talk more generally. Parry thought Wilde sometimes 'amusing,
once or twice, brilliant, often fatuous… at his best about art and literature,
and thoroughly idiotic about politics and social questions'.

He considered that Wilde's 'great gift is perfect assurance – truly brazen
when he is talking nonsense. For when he is quite tired out he trusts to his
deliberate manner of slow enunciation to carry off perfectly commonplace
remarks. One evening when he was quite exhausted with successive tête-
à-têtes, the smoking-room symposium formed itself as usual with George
Wyndham as leader. G.W. really did all the talking, and all O.W. could do was
to reiterate very slowly, when reference was made to somebody, or another,
"How old is he?" at which the assembly looked uncommonly interested.'[9]

Wilde does not seem to have made any effort to charm Parry – who, by
the end of week, 'thoroughly detested him'. The composer did, however,
make friends with Constance, who, seemingly unsettled by the gathering
momentum of her husband's successes – both literary and social – as much

as by his divergent sexual interests, was increasingly left trailing in his wake. Parry found her 'a very strange person, who ha[d] abnegated all balance of mind and all self-control, but [was] at the same time kind, natural and willing to serve her friends at any moment'.[10]

A week later at Wrest Park, the Bedfordshire home of Lord and Lady Cowper, in another Souls-dominated throng, the pattern was repeated, with Wilde once again the centre of attention. One fellow visitor recalled him sitting on the lawn 'surrounded by a large audience of ladies' telling them stories. Among his improbable conceits was that there should be 'a Form of Prayer used for a Baronet'.[11] And perhaps it was at Wrest, over tea, that he astounded the company by suddenly tearing off the petals from a magnificent rose that his hostess was passing round for everyone to admire. As a 'tremor of indignation' rose against this sacrilege, he quelled it with the explanation that, 'it would have been too sad to see such a rose wither'.[12] Wilde's confidence in his powers, and sense of his own success, was made manifest when he came to sign the visitors' book. Rather than inscribing his name on the same page as the rest of the party, he took a fresh leaf, writing his name towards the top and then executing an immense flourish so that no other name could be written below.[13]

He celebrated his new social prestige in other ways too. Preparing his second collection of fairy tales, *The House of Pomegranates*, for the press, he elected to dedicate each of the four stories to a different and distinguished woman – to 'Mrs William H. Grenfell', 'Miss Margot Tennant', 'H. S. H. Alice, Princess of Monaco' (whom he had met in Paris), and 'Margaret, Lady Brooke', the ranee of Sarawak and a London literary hostess. The volume itself – a choice creation designed by Ricketts and illustrated by Shannon – was dedicated to 'Constance Mary Wilde'.

More significantly, the social excitements of the summer seem to have inspired him, finally, to write his play for George Alexander. Telling Frank Harris that he had come up with an idea he 'rather' liked, he announced, 'Tomorrow I am going to shut myself up in my room, and stay there until it is written... I wonder can I do it in a week, or will it take three? It ought not to take long to beat the Pineros and the Joneses.'* The idea was for a comic

---

* Arthur Wing Pinero (1855–1934) and Henry Arthur Jones (1851–1929) were two of the most popular dramatists of the period. While Wilde described one of Pinero's plays as 'the best play I ever slept through', it became his theatrical axiom that 'There are three rules for writing plays. The first rule is not to write like Arthur Henry Jones; the second and third rules are the same.'

drama set in the convention-bound world of contemporary society, and it appears to have been written within a month.[14]

A Good Woman, as Wilde provisionally titled his play, told the story of young Lady Windermere, who suspects her husband of having an affair with the worldly and mysterious Mrs Erlynne, to whom he has made several large, and secret, payments. When confronted on the topic, Lord Windermere refuses to explain the true nature of their relationship, only insisting on its innocence. Lady Windermere is not convinced and, in a moment of rash despair, decides to leave her own birthday ball and run away with the witty and irresponsible Lord Darlington, who has declared his love for her. Mrs Erlynne, however, discovers her plan, follows her to Lord Darlington's house and persuades her to change her mind before it is too late. At that moment the two women hear the voices of Lord Darlington, Lord Windermere and other friends about to enter the room where they are conversing. They hide, to avoid discovery, but Lady Windermere leaves her distinctive fan – a birthday gift from her husband – on the table. The men enter. The fan is spotted. Lord Windermere suspects his wife of being on the premises. But before he can initiate a search, Mrs Erlynne steps forward from her hiding place, thus compromising her own reputation; she claims that she must have picked up Lady Windermere's fan by mistake when she left the ball. Disaster for Lady Windermere is averted, as she makes her escape. It is revealed to the audience – though not to Lady Windermere – that Mrs Erlynne is in fact Lady Windermere's mother, who had herself run off, deserting the marital home and her infant daughter, some twenty years previously, and was now seeking to regain a place in society under an assumed name (and by blackmailing Lord Windermere for funds). Nevertheless her self-sacrifice, to save her daughter from a similar fate, ensures that she herself earns the right to be called 'a good woman'.

The outward details of the plot were conventional enough. There were distinct echoes of Dumas. And Wilde's friend, the Australian-born dramatist Haddon Chambers, had enjoyed a success in the previous year with a play in which the married heroine – in trying to save her husband from blackmail – had nearly compromised herself by leaving her fan behind in the blackmailer's room.[15] What gave Wilde's play distinction was not just its scintillating dialogue but also its blithe dissection (and acceptance) of society's convenient hypocrisies and double standards.

The paradoxical wit that Wilde had honed in his own conversation, in his dialogues and essays, and in the pages of Dorian Gray, now found dramatic

expression. Lord Darlington was the most assured and accomplished of Wilde's epigrammatic dandies so far; the duchess of Berwick his finest comic creation. Wilde cheerfully plundered his own earlier works for choice lines and epigrams.* The action conformed to Vivian's dictum – in 'The Decay of Lying' – that what is interesting about people in good society is the mask that each one wears, not the reality that lies behind the mask. No conventional moral was pointed. Lord Windermere remained in ignorance of his wife's near-elopement, Lady Windermere is kept unaware of her true relationship to Mrs Erlynne. And Mrs Erlynne, having briefly experienced the terrible passions of motherhood, escapes back into the world of pleasure. Earlier in the year Wilde had been a serial attendee when Elizabeth Robins premiered Ibsen's controversial *Hedda Gabler* at the Vaudeville Theatre; and his own play's challenge to the established values of middle-class morality proclaimed an allegiance to the new spirit of dramatic Realism ushered in by the great Norwegian dramatist.[16]

Alexander – according to his own later recollection – never forgot the delight he experienced in hearing Wilde read the play script to him. When Wilde asked whether he liked it, he replied, 'Like is not the word. It is simply wonderful.' He supported his wonderment with an offer of £1,000 to buy the piece outright. Wilde, however, countered, 'I have so much confidence in your excellent judgment, my dear Alec, that I cannot but refuse your generous offer – I will take a percentage.'[17] Contemporary evidence, how-ever, suggests that Alexander may have been marginally less bowled over by the play's merits. Although glad to have the piece, and to pay Wilde the second part of his advance, he did not want to be bound to any specific time for its production, recognizing that it would take 'a world of labour' to get 'right'.[18] Wilde himself was full of mingled hope, excitement and anxiety about the play's prospects. He immediately sent a copy of the script to the American impresario Augustin Daly (who was over in London) in the hope that he might buy the American rights. But no immediate deal was reached.[19]

The only transatlantic production on the horizon was the splendidly improbable marriage of Willie Wilde to the American magazine owner and editor Mrs Frank Leslie who, at fifty-five, was twelve years his senior.

---

* For example, Lord Henry Wotton's observation – in *Dorian Gray* – that 'nowadays people know the price of everything and the value of nothing' – was refined to Lord Darlington's definition of a 'cynic' as, 'a man who knows the price of everything and the value of nothing'.

The formidable and dynamic Mrs Leslie had been coming over to England regularly during the previous seven years, and had become friendly with the Wilde family, developing a particularly 'strong affection' and admiration for Lady Wilde. Willie seems to have recognized that her wealth might offer him a haven. She, for her part, was amused by his wit, and half-persuaded by his apparent ardour. She also considered that his fluent writing style might be an asset to her various American publications. Ignoring the fact that he spent little of his time working and most of his money on drink, she carried him away to New York, married him (on 4 October 1891) and – after the inevitable honeymoon at Niagara – installed him in her luxurious apartment in the Gerlach building on West 27th Street. Constance (perhaps echoing Oscar) reported to her friend Lady Mount Temple, 'The news has much the same effect upon me socially that poor Mr Parnell's [recent] death has upon me politically – that is, that it is the best solution to a difficulty, and that things in both cases will now right themselves.'[20] Her optimism on both fronts would prove misplaced.

Wilde himself was exhausted by his efforts in writing A Good Woman. His nerves, moreover, had been additionally frayed when the Tite Street house was burgled one night while he and the children slept. Much of Constance's jewellery had been stolen, along with the children's christening cups and other silver. If no money was taken, it was – as malicious gossip pointed out – because 'there was no money to steal'.[21]

And there were other strains too. On 16 October the young publisher William Heinemann (together with the French writer Gérard Harry) called at Tite Street to try and interest Wilde in writing an introduction for an English-language edition of Maeterlinck's symbolist drama Princess Maleine. They found their host dressed in deep mourning. Wilde explained, 'This day happens to be my birthday [his thirty-seventh], and I am mourning the flight of one year of my youth into nothingness, the growing blight upon my summer.'[22] For all these accumulating cares, Wilde's doctor recommended a six-week rest cure. Wilde decided to take it in Paris, that least restful of cities.

23. Constance Lloyd around 1883, shortly before she became engaged to Oscar.

24. James McNeil Whistler, variously Oscar's 'hero', friend, teacher and enemy.

25. Henry Labouchère, the magazine publisher and MP, another sometime friend and enemy to Oscar.

26. E.W. Godwin, the innovative architect and designer, who helped Oscar and Constance create their 'House Beautiful' on Tite Street.

27. Mary Anderson for whom Oscar wrote *The Duchess of Padua*.

28. Marie Prescott who played the title role in the ill-fated New York premier *Vera*.

29. Walt Whitman in 1880, old before his time; Oscar thought him 'the closest approach to the Greek we have yet in modern times'.

30. Clara Morris as Camille by Sarony: although the American actress was known to be '*difficile*', she was Oscar's first choice to play the part of Vera.

31. Robert H. Sherard, the friend Oscar made in Paris in 1883; he was considered 'astonishingly handsome', well-informed and 'lovable'.

32. Carlos Blacker (*left*) and Norman Forbes Robertson: two of Oscar's oldest friends. Blacker was the dedicatee of *The Happy Prince*, although they fell out later, during Oscar's exile in Paris.

33. Raffalovich (*right*), Oscar's *bête noire*, together with John Gray and unknown woman friend.

34. Frank Harris, a tireless but sometimes exhausting supporter.

35. Cyril, aged seven, in the garden at Felbrigg, near Cromer, 1892.

36. Vyvyan in his sailor-suit; although Constance wondered about a naval career for him, Lady Wilde insisted that he was 'a born writer'.

37. Robbie Ross, Oscar's first male lover and most enduring friend.

38. John Gray, the poet admired
by Oscar for his verse as much
as his profile.

39. Charles Ricketts and Charles
Shannon drawn by William
Rothenstein; their home in Chelsea
was, Oscar claimed, 'the one house in
London where you will never be bored'.

40. John Barlas, the poet and anarchist
for whom Oscar stood bail.

41. Ada Leverson, Oscar's beloved
'Sphinx', the 'wittiest woman in London'.

42. Max Beerbohm's 'Some Persons of "the Nineties"' (1925); *from left to right*: Arthur Symons, Henry Harland, Charles Conder, William Rothenstein, Max Beerbohm, Aubrey Beardsley. *Back*: Richard Le Gallienne, Walter Sickert, George Moore, John Davidson, Oscar Wilde, W. B. Yeats and (barely visible) 'Enoch Soames'.

43. Pierre Louÿs, the dedicatee of the French edition of *Salomé*; Oscar was disappointed by his response to this honour.

44. André Gide, who was awed by Oscar's talk, his storytelling and his sexual freedom.

45. A scene from the original production of *Lady Windermere's Fan*, Oscar's first theatrical triumph; George Alexander is at the far right.

5

The Dance of the Seven Veils

'A Paris on montre tout, ici on cache tout: – même l'esprit!
C'est là la différence entre l'Angleterre et la France.'

OSCAR WILDE

The French capital, nevertheless, had a tonic effect. Wilde was delighted to be back on the boulevards. As he explained to one friend, 'I am not really myself except in the midst of elegant crowds, in the intoxication of capitals, at the heart of rich districts or amidst the sumptuous ornamentations of palace hotels, surrounded by desirable objects and with an army of servants, and the warm caress of plush carpets beneath my feet.' There was the usual spice of exaggeration in all this; after a brief stint at the passably grand Hôtel Normandie, he removed to a low-ceilinged room on the Boulevard des Capucines.[1]

The friendships and associations with French writers that he had initiated at the beginning of the year were taken up again, and reinforced. Indeed Wilde had come to feel such a kinship with France and its literature that he conceived the notion of hiring a translator to have *The Good Woman* turned into French and premiered not in London but at the Comédie-Française. To make his debut as a modern dramatist in Paris, and in French, would certainly leave the English critics wrong-footed. The piece – like many other French productions of the period – might then be transferred to London as

an established success. He announced this bold plan at breakfast one morn-
ing to Wilfrid Blunt, George Curzon and Willy Peel, who were all over in
Paris. Indulging the fantasy, they agreed to attend the opening night, 'George
Curzon as Prime Minister.'[2]

Wilde, as ever, had travelled with a stock of presents. He sent an inscribed copy of *Intentions* to Lord Lytton, the British ambassador and a cousin
of Blunt's (Wilde had come to know Lytton, who was a poet as well as the
former viceroy of India, at Ouida's Langham Hotel receptions, and a literary friendship had developed). Lytton, already a great admirer of the book,
was delighted to receive the gift from his 'brilliant Confrere', but apologized that he was too ill to see guests. He hoped, nevertheless, that Wilde
would lunch at the embassy with the rest of the Lytton family. Lytton's
seventeen-year-old daughter, Emily, reported of the occasion that 'we all
thought him [Wilde] very amusing and not so odious as we expected,
though he is evidently fearfully conceited. He talked chiefly about his own
health and his books [and his plans for his French play], but he was certainly
amusing.'[3]*

To Mallarmé Wilde sent an inscribed copy of *The Picture of Dorian Gray*,
as a prelude to attending the poet's *mardi* on 3 November. The mood of
that evening was slightly coloured by the presence – on the sideboard –
of a telegram from Whistler, announcing in shrill capitals: 'PREFACE
PROPOSITIONS PREVENIR DISCIPLES PRECAUTION FAMILIARITE
FATALE SERRER LES PERLES BONNES SOIREE' ('Preface Propositions
– Forewarn Disciples – Precaution – Familiarity Fatal – Hide the Pearls –
Have a Good Evening). The painter, who was now living in Paris and was an
old friend of Mallarmé's, had worked himself up into an almost hysterical
state about the fact that Wilde was being admitted into the poet's circle.
He kept up a steady stream of letters denouncing Wilde as a 'farceur' –
who had purloined Whistler's ideas (for, among other things, the preface to
Dorian Gray), and would steal 'the pearls' from Mallarmé and his disciples
given half a chance. Mallarmé, with a fine appreciation of artistic rivalries,
soothed Whistler's anxieties while welcoming Wilde to his table. And
Wilde, too, rose above the pettiness of Whistler's jibes. When Whistler's

---

*   Lord Lytton did not recover from his sudden illness; he died on 24 November. Wilde
     attended his funeral service at the English church in rue d'Aguesseau, opposite the
     embassy – impressed by 'the purple-covered bier with its one laurel wreath', a lone
     'solemn note of colour and sadness in the midst of the gorgeous uniforms of the
     Ambassadors'.

name was introduced by Mallarmé into the general discussion, he readily echoed the admiration expressed by the rest of the company.[4]

Mallarmé wrote a densely phrased letter of thanks for The Picture of Dorian Gray, praising the inner reverie and strange 'perfumes of the soul' that it stirred up, and saluting it as a true work of art. 'It was the portrait that had done everything,' he concluded. 'Ce portrait en pied, inquiétant, d'un Dorian Gray, hantera, mais écrit, étant devenu livre lui-même' ('This disquieting full-length portrait of a Dorian Gray will haunt, but being written, has itself become a book'). It was a flattering recognition. Yet Wilde, it seems, attended only few more of the Maître's gatherings.[5]

He was swept up by other commitments, drawn excitedly into the literary stream. He sought an entrée to Madam Adam's celebrated salon, sending her a copy of Dorian Gray and a flattering letter. He called on the princess of Monaco and received from her a photograph graciously inscribed 'Au vrai Art – à Oscar Wilde'. He secured an introduction to Count Robert de Montesquiou, the supposed model for Huysmans' des Esseintes.[6]

Both Sherard and Stuart Merrill were on hand to pilot him among the cafés of the Latin Quarter. His old Oxford friend Bodley was also in Paris, having settled there the previous year to pursue a journalistic career. Already well connected, he hosted a small 'banquet' to introduce Wilde to 'some of the writers of France'. Perhaps it was there that Wilde came to know Marcel Schwob, who assisted Catulle Mendès in editing the literary pages of the Parisian daily L'Echo de Paris. The twenty-four-year-old Schwob, already the author of a volume of Symbolist fairy tales, shared Wilde's enthusiasms for the medieval criminal-poet François Villon, and for the slang of the urban underclass. It proved a happy basis for a friendship, and Schwob became another of Wilde's guides over the coming weeks – his 'cornac', or elephant-driver, as Jean Lorrain called him.[7]*

The days and nights were filled with an almost ceaseless round of talk – in cafés, in restaurants, strolling along the boulevards, driving in the Bois, at fashionable salons and intimate dinners, around Mallarmé's exalted board in the rue de Rome, or with the reprobate vagabond Bibi la Purée, among the crowded tables of the Café Harcourt on the Boulevard St Michel. Wilde

---

* The Decadent novelist Jean Lorrain, though both a fellow homosexual and a fellow dandy, was one of the few Parisian writers with whom Wilde failed to achieve a rapport. Having been introduced to each other, Wilde was asked what he made of Lorrain. He replied, 'Lorrain is a poseur'. Lorrain, asked what he thought of Wilde, declared, 'He is a faker.'

became the 'great event' of the season. Stuart Merrill recalled Wilde's presiding presence during those weeks, 'smooth and rosy, like the High Priest of the Moon in the time of Heliogabulus' talking, listening, smiling.[8] De Régnier remembered the enchantment that Wilde cast over all who heard him: everyone was seduced by the 'sumptuous inventions created by the storyteller in his slow, even, melodious voice'. He enjoyed a legendary status.[9] Tales were told that he was 'a millionaire' that 'publishers snatched up his slightest literary efforts, their hand filled with banknotes', that he was the darling of the English aristocracy.[10] He gathered new friends and disciples. First among them was the handsome dandified figure of Pierre Louÿs. A devoted Hellenist and poet, he had replaced the conventional 'i' in his surname with a 'y' – or 'i-grec' – in homage to his literary heroes.

In Louÿs's wake came André Gide. The twenty-two-year-old writer, who had recently published a treatise on Narcissus, found himself almost swept away by Wilde's commanding personality, his amazing flow of talk, his fables and stories, his praise of hedonism, his contempt for accepted moralities. Among Wilde's topics of the moment was the life of Christ. Having suggested in 'The Soul of Man' that Christ's message was really about the development of personality, he was anxious to take the idea further. To Coulson Kernahan he claimed that, more than anything else, he wanted to write 'the Iliad of Christianity'. His vision of 'Christianity as taught by Christ' would, however, be a novel and idiosyncratic one, stripped of both metaphysics and morality. As he explained to Gide, there was nothing that Christ had said 'that could not be transferred immediately into the sphere of Art, and there find its complete fulfilment'.[11]

Gide filled his diary with notes of their meetings – the 'three hour' dinners, with Louÿs, Merrill, Schwob, Henri de Régnier and others. On these occasions, when Wilde was in full flow, elaborating an almost endless succession of stories, Gide – as Merrill noted – would stare distractedly at his plate. It seemed to some that he must be in love with the older writer. He had Wilde's photograph prominently displayed on his mantelpiece. In the immediate aftermath of these intense few weeks of association, Gide declared that Wilde's effect on him had been almost entirely 'evil' – 'with him I had unlearned how to think. My emotions were more and more diverse, but I didn't know how to organize them; above all I could no longer follow other people's deductions.' He excised many pages from his diary, perhaps relating to Wilde. But the fascination and attraction remained.[12]

Wilde always sought out the young. He took up the engaging eighteen-

year-old Enrique Gómez Carrillo, recently arrived in Paris on a literary scholarship from his native Guatemala. He called on the English students studying at the Académie Julian, befriending the gifted Will Rothenstein and the amiable Charles Conder. Rothenstein was amazed and enchanted by Wilde's conversation, and his extraordinary knowledge of people and books, but even more taken by his generosity of spirit. 'I had met no one', he later recalled, 'who made me so aware of the possibilities latent in myself.' Wilde insisted on regarding his nineteen-year-old friend as 'a sort of youthful prodigy': he enthused about Rothenstein's pastels, and introduced him to the literary life of Paris. Together with Sherard and Merrill they made a memorable pilgrimage one evening to the Château Rouge, a notorious inn-cum-doss-house, frequented by thieves and prostitutes. 'The criminal classes have always had a wonderful attraction for me,' Wilde declared delightedly. He had, though, to dissuade Sherard from vociferously warning off the various low characters who approached them. 'Robert,' he declared, 'you are defending us at the risk of our lives.'[13]*

Perhaps it was the following day that Schwob called for Wilde at his rooms; as they were about to head out, Wilde declared that he could not find his walking stick: 'My gold-headed cane has disappeared. Last night I was with the most terrible creatures, bandits, murderers, thieves – such company as Villon kept. They stole my gold-headed cane. There was a youth with beautiful sad eyes who had slain his mistress that morning because she was unfaithful. I feel sure it was he who stole my gold-headed cane.' Enjoying the romance of it all, he concluded, 'My gold-headed cane is now between the hands that slew the frail girl who had the grace of a spent rose-bush in the rain.' 'But, Mr Wilde,' interjected Schwob, 'there is your gold-headed cane in the corner.' 'Ah, yes,' said Wilde, rather put out. 'So it is. There is my gold-headed cane. How clever of you to find it.'[14]

The dramas and conflicts of Parisian low-life were certainly matched in the literary sphere. It was a world, Wilde soon discovered, rent with divisions. In poetry Mallarmé and the Symbolists stood opposed to José-Maria de

---

* Although Wilde met the twenty-year-old Marcel Proust through Jacques-Emile Blanche and was impressed by his knowledge of Ruskin and George Eliot, no friendship developed between them. Nevertheless the account, first recorded in Philippe Jullian's *Oscar Wilde* (1976), of an aborted dinner chez Proust, when Wilde, not finding his host there to greet him, retreated to the lavatory (after looking in on Proust's parents in the drawing room and declaring 'How ugly your house is') before eventually fleeing into the night, is not perhaps to be trusted.

Heredia's technically exacting Parnassian school (Wilde visited Heredia, whose younger daughter would later marry Pierre Louÿs). Merrill took Wilde to dine with Jean Moréas and his disciples, who had broken away from the Symbolists to found the École Romane as a re-assertion of classical purity against allusive vagueness. According to Merill's account Wilde was half-diverted, half-appalled, when, after dinner (and a general dismissal of all French literature from Hugo onwards), the white-faced, black-moustachioed Moréas commanded his disciples to recite their verses. 'Sonnet to Jean Moréas' was followed by 'Ode to Jean Moréas'; at the announcement of the 'Tomb of Jean Moréas', Wilde made his excuses and left. [15]

He found more amusement in listening to the caustic Catulle Mendès who, having denigrated Baudelaire, Rimbaud and Verlaine, launched into Mallarmé and his disciples: 'the symbolists make us laugh', he declared. 'They've invented nothing. The symbol is as old as the world.' Mallarmé was dismissed as 'a broken Baudelaire whose fragments have never come together.' Henri de Régnier was all contained in Banville and Hugo. Paul Fort had adopted 'the Belgian aesthetic' and there appeared to be nothing at all in Vielé-Griffin. [16] Adolphe Retté, meanwhile, could offer a similar denunciation of Jean Moréas and his school. Only Verlaine, amiably innocent and usually drunk, seemed to stand above – or below – the strife.

The House of Pomegranates was published in mid-November, while Wilde was still in Paris. He ensured that Constance, the volume's main dedicatee, received the first copy off the press. He also wrote to excuse the appearance of those other names attached to the separate stories. 'To you the Cathedral is dedicated,' he told her. 'The individual side chapels are to other saints. This is in accordance with the highest ecclesiastical custom! So accept the book as your own, made for you. The candles that burn at the side altars are not so bright or beautiful as the great lamp of the shrine which is of gold and has a wonderful heart of restless flame.' Constance was thrilled by this apparent affirmation of her continuing place at the centre of Wilde's life and affections. Although it might be tempting to doubt Wilde's sincerity, the statement did probably reflect some aspect of his feeling, and, as with so many of his statements, the mere fact of uttering it made him believe it... almost. [17]

The book looked sumptuous with its richly decorated cover, and was heftily priced – like Wilde's other collectors' items – at one guinea. But the rich effect was rather undercut by the fact that Shannon's four full-page illustrations were almost invisible; the new 'improved' process used to reproduce them had gone badly awry. It was a sad blow. And most of the

few reviews dwelt ungenerously on the invisibility of the pictures. The rest fussed tediously over whether the tales were really intended for children. Wilde was moved to write to both the *Speaker* and the *Pall Mall Gazette* to explain that 'in building the House of Pomegranates' he had had 'about as much intention of pleasing the British child as [he] had of pleasing the British public'. The stories had been written to please himself. If Wilde had hoped that the book would establish him as a *conteur* to rival Flaubert, he was disappointed; of the three volumes that Wilde brought out with Osgood & McIlvaine during the course of 1891 it was the least successful.[18] Its main use was as a literary calling card. A copy was presented to Louÿs, inscribed 'au jeune homme qui adore la beauté, au jeune homme que la beauté adore, au jeune homme que j'adore, Oscar Wilde'.[19]

Through such gifts Wilde strove to make his work better known in France. *The Picture of Dorian Gray* existed as a name, but few (beyond those like Mallarmé who had been given copies) had actually read the book. There was no sign of the mooted French edition of the novel, nor of Wilde's dialogues. Extracts from his 'Soul of Man Under Socialism' had, however, been published that summer in the anarchist journal *La Révolte*. They had enhanced Wilde's reputation among the younger Symbolists, even if the Parisian correspondent for the *Pall Mall Gazette* exaggerated in claiming that these writers now regarded Wilde as 'a kind of Messiah'.[20] As a small but gratifying next step Schwob had undertaken to make a translation of 'The Selfish Giant' for publication in *L'Echo de Paris*.[21]

As part of his pose, though, Wilde deflected inquiries about his work – at least during the early part of his stay. When Ernest Raynaud, one of Moréas's disciples, tried to draw him about his writings, he remarked, 'I do them to relax and to prove myself, as your Baudelaire used to with more genius, that I am not inferior to my contemporaries whom I hold in low esteem. My ambitions do not stop with composing poems. I want to make my life itself a work of art.' And one afternoon at the Café Harcourt – together with Gómez Carrillo, Verlaine and the impressively named Yvanhoe Rambosson – Wilde confessed, 'I have put only my talent into my works. I have put all my genius into my life' (it would be a line he would use again). Verlaine, suddenly attentive, remarked to Rambosson, in an approving aside, 'This man is a true pagan. He possesses the insouciance which is half of happiness, for he does not know penitence.'[22]

The young French writers were dazzled by Wilde's performance, almost literally. Gide recalled that at a dinner hosted by the Princess Ouroussof, the

princess suddenly gave a loud shriek and declared she had seen a halo around Wilde's head.[23] And Wilde, though he might conceal it, was equally impressed by the young French writers. For all his affected indifference to literary production, he found great stimulation in their energy and commitment, their concerted desire to achieve 'a richer Romanticism, with subtleties of new colour and strange music and extended subject matter'. The 'transformation of the French language, in the hands of the leaders of the new schools' was, Wilde considered, 'one of the most interesting and attractive things to watch and wonder at'.[24] Despite the rather irritating character of Moréas, Wilde saw attractions in the École Romane, but it was the Symbolism of Mallarmé and de Régnier that continued to attracted him most. And although, initially, he seems not to have been confident enough of his own French to do more than 'watch and wonder', the weeks spent immersed in the language, in telling and retelling his fables in French, encouraged him to reconsider.

Certainly many of his new friends were impressed by his command of their language, by his ability not only to express his ideas but also to dress them in what Adolphe Retté called 'an irresistible softness'. 'He knew French admirably,' Gide recalled, 'but he pretended to hunt about a bit for the words which he wanted to keep waiting.' He had, moreover, almost no accent, or 'only such as it pleased him to retain and which might give the words a sometimes new and strange aspect'.[25]

Among Wilde's repertoire of spoken tales, one story recurred with greater frequency than the others: the story of Salome, daughter of Queen Herodias, who danced for her stepfather, Herod, and demanded in return the severed head of his prisoner, John the Baptist. The biblical accounts were so terse as to invite invention, and three of Wilde's favourite French writers had embroidered the narrative. Flaubert had recounted the story as one of his *Trois Contes*; in *À Rebours* des Esseintes spends much of Chapter V in ecstatic contemplation of Gustave Moreau's jewelled dreamlike image of Salome dancing before Herod, and the same artist's yet more disturbing 'Apparition', in which the severed head of the saint hovers in an auriole of light before the now-horrified dancer. Wilde had the passages of lush description by heart, and loved to recite them.[26] And Mallarmé was known to be engaged with the subject too, in an ongoing poetic work that took the figure of Herodias as the starting point for an investigation into the nature of language and beauty (the work was begun when Mallarmé was twenty-two, but remained incomplete at his death). Wilde was stimulated rather than daunted by these illustrious precursors.

His interest in the story, after all, predated his trip to Paris. Edgar Saltus recalled an afternoon, some years before, when he and Wilde had seen, in the rooms of Lord Francis Hope, an engraving of Salome dancing 'on her hands, her heels in the air', just as Flaubert describes her in his story. Confronted with the image, Wilde exclaimed 'La bella donna della mia mente' ('the fair lady of my dreams').[27] The dream stayed with him, and in Paris came gradually into sharper focus.

As was his usual practice, he remoulded the story over many tellings, trying variations and testing effects upon his listeners. He imagined Salome shameless and cruel ('her lust must be an abyss, her corruptness, like an ocean'). He imagined her almost chaste, a 'sad princess' dancing 'as though under divine command so that the impostor and enemy of Jehovah might be punished'.[28] In one version he had Salome, banished to the desert by a remorse-stricken Herod, living like a hermit, until one day she sees Jesus pass by and recognizes him as the Messiah. She then sets out to spread the word. Years later, crossing a frozen lake, she falls through the ice, her head being cut from her body as she drops, her mouth uttering the names of Jesus and John with its final breath. Travellers coming after see her head, resting on the ice, a golden halo shining around it. She had become a saint.[29] In another variant (told one evening chez Jean Lorrain) Salome only wants the head of John the Baptist because she is in love with a 'young philosopher', and he has expressed a desire to possess it. But when she presents the trophy to him, he remarks, 'What I really want, beloved, is your head.' In despair she goes off and has herself decapitated. When they bring her head to the philosopher, he asks, 'Why are you bringing this bloody thing to me?' before turning back to his Plato.[30] Wilde was not at all impressed when Rémy de Gourmont, citing the ancient historian Josephus, pointed out that Wilde, in all his tales, was confusing two separate people both called 'Salome' – one the daughter of Herod, the other the fatal dancer. 'Poor Gourmont,' Wilde remarked to Gómez Carrillo. 'What he told us was the truth of a professor of the Institute. I prefer the other truth, my own which is that of the dream. Between two truths, the falser is truer.'[31] In the end, from among the shifting dreamlike truths, Wilde settled upon a succinct yet macabre narrative line in which Salome, overcome with unrequited lust for the imprisoned John the Baptist, seeks to gain his severed head so that – at last – she is able to kiss his lips.

Wilde had wondered at first whether to fix his tale as a short story, or perhaps a poem.[32] But then he had the inspiration to make it a drama, and

a drama in French. He had been 'thinking much' about Maeterlinck, in preparation for the introduction (that he never quite got around to writing) to *Princess Maleine*. The preparation, however, proved fruitful. Maeterlinck's play was the evangel of a new Symbolist drama – spare, anti-naturalistic, written in incantatory, repetitive, deliberately stilted, prose. Indeed Wilde thought that 'a great deal of the curious effect that Maeterlinck produces' was due to the fact French was not his first language. And he began to perceive that he might be able to achieve something similar. Freed from the demands of realistic dialogue, there was no reason why his own French should not be sufficient for the task. Oddities of expression would 'give a certain relief or colour' to the piece.[33]

According to his own account the work was begun one afternoon after he had lunched with a group of young writers. He had told them – as he had told others – the story of Salome, but, on returning to his room, he had noticed a blank notebook on the table and had decided to write the story down. 'If the blank book had not been there on the table,' Wilde claimed, 'I should never have dreamed of doing it.' He wrote without break deep into the evening. At ten o'clock he went out to sup at a nearby café. He told the leader of the gypsy orchestra that he was 'writing a play about a woman dancing with her bare feet in the blood of a man she has craved for and slain. I want you to play something in harmony with my thoughts.' The band struck up 'such wild and terrible music' that soon the whole café fell into an awed and shocked silence. 'Then,' Wilde claimed, 'I went back and finished *Salomé.*' Although the details are certainly embellished, there does exist a notebook, purchased from a stationer's in the Boulevard des Capucines, and containing an early draft of the play, to confirm the outline of the story.[34]

That first session of furious activity was, though, only the prelude to a more concerted campaign. Wilde worked hard at the manuscript, revising and improving. Salome dominated his conversation and his thoughts. His new Parisian friends were excited by the project. They were keenly aware of the possibilities of Symbolist drama: Maeterlinck's play *L'Intruse* (*The Intruder*) had been successfully premiered at Paul Fort's experimental Théâtre d'Art that May.[35]

Wilde was encouraged by such tales, and his thoughts were soon running ahead to details of staging and design. He wondered whether Salome should dance clothed or naked, or simply covered in jewels. He lingered outside the boutiques in the rue de la Paix, pondering which ornaments or fabrics might best suit his heroine. He steeped himself in images of the

fatal dancer. He wished he could accompany Gómez Carrillo to Madrid to see the painting of her by Titian in the Prado with its 'quivering flesh'. In his obsession to find the perfect representation of the dancer-princess he declared himself, 'mad, like Des Esseintes'. And, like the hero of *À Rebours*, he returned always to the erotically charged jewel-encrusted image created by Gustave Moreau. It was, he announced, 'one of the wonders of the world'. Fired by the picture, he looked for Salome's ideal representative in the women he passed on the boulevards; he imagined Sarah Bernhardt in the role; although when he saw a Romanian acrobat at the Moulin Rouge dancing on her hands, he sent round his card, in the hope that he could interest her in the part. He paid a visit to the morgue, to see the body of a recently executed criminal, so that he might feel the weight of a severed head. He was 'astonished' by how heavy it was.[36]

Pierre Louÿs affected an introduction to Paul Fort, and it was arranged that Wilde should give a reading of the play script under the auspices of the Théâtre d'Art.[37] The occasion (in mid-December) was, according to Wilde, a great success: the 'young poets' who made up the audience admired the work-in-progress 'immensely'. One friend recalled Wilde's great satisfaction in 'chanting' the sonorous yet simple phrases of the play. Plans began to be laid for a production the following year.[38] Wilde could account himself a figure on the Parisian literary scene: it became his semi-humorous boast that he was now 'a famous French author!'[39]

His position was confirmed in the press. There were lengthy articles on him in *Le Figaro* and *Le Gaulois*, and an interview in *L'Echo de Paris* (Lady Wilde noted approvingly that the interviewer seemed to approach her son with 'a kind of awe'). The *Echo de Paris* also printed Wilde's adroit open letter to Edmond de Goncourt, correcting a passage from Goncourt's recently serialized diary entry for 21 April 1883, which suggested that Wilde had described Swinburne as 'a braggart of vice' ('un fanfaron du vice'). Wilde began with the neat paradox that, since the intellectual basis of his aesthetic was the philosophy of unreality, he should be allowed to make a small rectification of a mis-statement doubtless caused by his limitations as a French speaker. 'French by sympathy,' he declared (in French), 'I am Irish by race, and the English have condemned me to speak the language of Shakespeare.' Goncourt showed his regard for Wilde by removing the offending passage when his diary was published in book form; he also – though Wilde had not complained of the phrase – excised the reference to the Irish writer being of 'sexe douteux'.[40]

6

Charming Ball

'We are all in the gutter, but some of us are looking at the stars.'

OSCAR WILDE

Wilde returned to England in time for Christmas. Constance and the children were delighted to have him back. He revised and completed *Salomé* at Torquay over the festive season, before going to stay for a few days at Glyn-y-Garth, a 'princely mansion' by the Menai Bridge belonging to Mrs Salis Schwabe, the widow of a wealthy cotton magnate. It was a brief interlude of rest and pleasure.[1]

Back in London there were projects demanding his attention. He had been approached by a new publishing company, recently established by Elkin Mathews and John Lane at 'the sign of the Bodley Head'. The firm was developing a reputation for producing handsomely designed, and handsomely priced, volumes of contemporary verse and *belles lettres* in small editions. It was a ploy calculated to appeal to the growing market of Aesthetically inclined bibliophiles, and it was proving surprisingly successful. Wanting to add Wilde, the arch-Aesthete, to their list, they had proposed buying up the remaining 220 copies of Bogue's edition of his *Poems*, and repackaging them as an exclusive collector's item. Wilde was delighted at the idea (the unbound sheets had been languishing in a warehouse ever

since Bogue's bankruptcy in August 1882). Ricketts was commissioned to design a new decorative title page and cover for the book. Wilde proposed signing each copy, to further enhance 'the special character' of the edition.[2]

He also found himself drawn into an unexpected drama, when John Barlas was arrested on 31 January for firing a revolver at the Palace of Westminster in an anarchist protest; to show, as he put it, his 'contempt for the House of Commons'. Together with Gray and John Davidson, and several family members, Wilde attended Barlas's arraignment at Westminster Magistrates' Court on 7 January. There was some anxiety that the authorities would declare Barlas insane, but this was averted. And Wilde returned the following week, together with the socialist publisher H. H. Champion, when Barlas was released by the magistrate, 'bound over' to keep the peace for the next two months, on a surety of £200. Wilde and Champion agreed to stand bail. Wilde seems to have enjoyed his brief appearance in the role of responsible member of society; in the crowded courtroom, he was invited to sit beside the magistrate. And, at the end of the hearing, the 'beak' remarked to him, in an attempt at legal humour, 'I think, Mr Wilde, that this is clearly a case for [a calming dose of] bromide of potassium.'[3]*

When Champion had called at Tite Street with news of Barlas's impending court appearance, he had found Wilde on the point of heading out of the house to see George Alexander, to discuss plans for his forthcoming play. In the confusion of the moment, Wilde dropped the furled typescript he was carrying. It did not – he was pleased to note – 'fall flat'. The omen seemed propitious.[4]

Alexander's plans were in flux. His first production of the new year (Joe Comyns Carr's *Forgiveness*) was failing. He had hoped that he might be able to replace it with R. C. Carton's *Liberty Hall*, but Carton had fallen ill with the piece still unfinished. It was in the face of these difficulties that he summoned Wilde and proposed putting *A Good Woman* into production for the following month. For Wilde it was an opportunity to be seized. He was invited to read the script to the assembled company at the St James's Theatre. One of those present recalled how he arrived, his silk hat 'ruffled', and stumbled as he stepped on to the stage. But then his self-assurance

---

* Despite Wilde's continued help and friendship, Barlas's mental health problems persisted. He was committed to a mental institution briefly in 1892, and permanently in 1894. When Wilde was told that Barlas's insanity had been partly 'a result of reading the Bible', he remarked, 'When I think of all the harm that book has done I despair of ever writing anything the equal of it.'

asserted itself. 'He put a large box of cigarettes on the table in front of him, and saying, "May I smoke?" lit one and began to read.' The company was prepared to be unimpressed, but 'after the first sentence all listened in breathless silence to the close'.⁵ Ricketts was told 'that no one surpassed' Wilde as a reader of his plays and, 'where dialogue was concerned, diction and expression were alike varied and vivid'.⁶

It was agreed that the play's name should be changed to *Lady Winder-mere's Fan*. Lady Wilde, among others, had disliked the original title: 'It is mawkish,' she declared. 'No one cares for a good woman.' Rehearsals began in early February, on the now empty stage of the St James's. Wilde attended regularly, fussing over details of set design, stage business, dialogue and even make-up. Alexander was subjected to reams of notes after almost every session: 'I want you to arrange Mrs Erlynne on a sofa more in the centre of the stage and towards the left side.' 'Hopper had better have either his own hair or a quiet wig. His face last night was far too white, and his appearance far too ridiculous.' 'The Duchess left out some essential words in her first speech. It should run, "[Australia. It must be so pretty with all the dear little] kangaroos flying about. Agatha has found Australia on the map. What a curious shape it is! However, it's a very young country, isn't it?" The words left out are those I have underlined. They give the point to the remark about the young country.' 'I think that [Cecil] Graham should not take his aunt into the ballroom – young dandies dislike their aged relatives – at least rarely pay them attention.' 'Pray give your serious attention to all these points.'⁷

To add to Wilde's cares, a problem with the drains at 16 Tite Street necessitated the family moving out. While Constance and the children decamped to the country, he took up residence at the Hotel Albemarle, just off Piccadilly. It was only a few hundred yards from the theatre, and allowed him to keep an even closer eye on proceedings. He was proving a nervous and difficult author. There was a prolonged struggle over the closing line of Act 2. Alexander finally prevailed (having cursed the playwright's 'damned Irish obstinacy') and Wilde, 'rather to his [own] annoyance', was obliged to recognize that the revised and lighter ending was a great improvement on his more obviously 'dramatic' original.

He refused, however, to accept Alexander's main point: that it was drama-tically essential for Mrs Erlynne's identity as Lady Windermere's mother to be revealed early in the play, rather than held back until the final act. The change could be very easily made, requiring only a couple of lines in Act 2. But Wilde was 'inexorable', ignoring all arguments and pleas. Alexander, in

his exasperation, started referring to Wilde as 'this conceited, arrogant and ungrateful man'. The dispute increased the stress of rehearsals.[8] Wilde also had to 'submit to a good deal of well-deserved banter' from the cast, on account of some impromptu remarks he had made at a meeting of the Play-goers' Club. The newspapers had reported him as dismissing actors as no more than 'a set of puppets' – and the stage as merely 'the frame to the picture'. It was not a view likely to be well received by the acting profession.[9]

Wilde wrote a long letter to the *Daily Telegraph* explaining that he had been misquoted: 'What I really said was that the frame we call the stage was "peopled with either living actors or moving puppets."' Nevertheless an extended paragraph about how the intrusive 'personality of an actor is often a source of danger in the perfect presentation of a work of art' can only have increased the irritation of Alexander and the other cast members.[10] Wilde's letter had also corrected another point. The paper had described John Gray, whose lecture had been main feature of the evening, as Wilde's 'protégé'. Gray, it appears, had been upset by the designation. And Wilde wrote to disavow it. 'Allow me to state,' he declared with less than complete accuracy, 'that my acquaintance with Mr John Gray is, I regret to say, extremely recent, and that I sought it because he had already a perfected mode of expression in both prose and verse.' Armed with his 'high indifference of temper' and his love of art, 'he needs no other protection, nor indeed, would he accept it'. Another article, in the *Star* (perhaps written by Le Gallienne), had described Gray as 'the original Dorian of the same name'. The poet, supported by Wilde, threatened to sue, and secured a retraction. Whether Gray's anxieties were artistic or social is unclear. But he was certainly aware of Wilde's dangerous sexual relationships with other young men, and may well have been concerned to distance himself from them.[11]

Wilde's sexual interests, just then, were fixed elsewhere. Being at the Albemarle placed him close to the Bodley Head premises on Vigo Street, where he was able to go over the production details for the new edition of his *Poems*. On his visits he took note of a tall 'distinguished looking' sales assistant called Edward Shelley, often stopping to chat with him for a few moments. The young man – eighteen years old – despite his modest background (his father was a blacksmith) had both literary and social aspirations; he spoke and dressed well, and Wilde described his face as 'intellectual'. His rather nervous and needy disposition was partially obscured by his eagerness to learn, and his great admiration for Wilde's work. Wilde encouraged these latter traits with gifts of books, including an inscribed copy of *The Picture*

of Dorian Gray. According to Shelley's own account, at the end of one day, Wilde invited him to come and dine at the Albemarle. He was thrilled to accept. If he did not recognize that this might be a prelude to seduction, he soon discovered it. Wilde ordered champagne. They talked of books, and about Shelley's own literary aspirations. Then, after dinner, they sat in Wilde's rooms, where they continued the conversation over whisky and soda and cigarettes. The evening ended with Wilde taking him to bed.[12]

The affair was carried on with Wilde's now habitual recklessness, and in the face of Shelley's shifting anxieties and demands. It may well have been Shelley that Wilde brought to a party in Frank Harris's rooms in Jermyn Street that year. After dinner Harris noticed that the young man 'was angry with Oscar and would scarcely speak to him, and that Oscar was making up to him. I heard snatches of pleading from Oscar – "I beg of you... It is not true... You have no cause"... All the while Oscar was standing apart from the rest of us with an arm on the young man's shoulder; but his coaxing him was in vain, the youth turned away with petulant, sullen ill-temper.' It was, Harris recalled, a troubling 'snap-shot'.[13]

Nevertheless Shelley was one of those to whom Wilde distributed tickets for the opening night of his play on Saturday 20 February. Wilde arranged for another young friend to sit beside him in the dress circle, and keep him company.[14] Others to receive seats, from what Wilde regarded as his too modest allocation, included Frances Forbes-Robertson and Coulson Kernahan. Wilde sent Richard Le Gallienne a pair, urging 'bring your poem [i.e. wife] to sit beside you'. And he asked Arthur Clifton to look after Constance, and her aunt, in Box D: '[Constance] will be very nervous probably, and it would be nice for her to have an old friend with her.'[15]

In the midst of these arrangements Wilde was struck with 'a new idea'. Encountering Graham Robertson (another of his invitees) on the eve of the premiere, he instructed him to go to a certain fashionable florist and order 'a green carnation' buttonhole for the following night. The carnations were ingeniously coloured, by having their stems placed in a solution of blue-green aniline dye. 'I want a good many men to wear them tomorrow,' Wilde explained. 'It will annoy the public.' To Robertson's query, 'But why annoy the public?', he replied, 'It likes to be annoyed.' The actor playing the young dandy Cecil Graham would also be wearing the strangely tinted flower: 'People will stare at it and wonder. Then they will look round the house and see every here and there more and more little specks of mystic green. "This must be some secret symbol," they will say. "What on earth can

it mean?"' 'And what does it mean?' Robertson asked. 'Nothing whatever,' Wilde said, 'but that is just what nobody will guess.' Wilde was delighted at the thought.[16]*

Frank Harris's memory of the first night was that the house was not only brilliant and fashionable but also intellectually distinguished. To the social columnist from the *Pall Mall Gazette* it was a distinctively 'Oscar Wilde audience' – the playwright's many modes and moods reflected in the gathering of 'painters and lawyers, actors and managers, pretty women' (none prettier than Lillie Langtry, prominent in a box), and the 'score of faultless young dandies' scattered through the stalls, many of them sporting green carnations. The audience loved the play from the very first exchanges. Mrs Jopling's recollection was that she had never enjoyed a first night so much.[17]

The critics, however, were less tractable. There remained much professional resentment of Wilde in literary and theatrical circles. During the first interval Harris went down to the foyer, where he found the newspaper reviewers quite untouched by the delightful 'freshness' and 'unexpected humour' of Wilde's treatment. 'The humour is mechanical, unreal,' pronounced Joe Knight, the lumbering critic for the *Athenaeum* (a man whom Wilde had consistently mocked during his book-reviewing career). It was an opinion supported by several other pressmen. Harris was astounded and said so. Even less than halfway through, he thought the play might be 'the best' and most 'brilliant' comedy in the English language; worthy to rank alongside Congreve. The dialogue – with its 'stream of whimsical, elusive flippancies' – might be far more artificial than even the most ponderous stage talk, but to many in the audience it seemed 'natural' because of its novelty. As Graham Robertson recalled, 'it amused and amazed'.[18]

Wilde had the huge pleasure of witnessing the amusement and the amazement. His witticisms were laughed at. Almost every scene was greeted with 'enthusiastic applause' – and from all parts of the house. Henry James noted that the 'pit and the gallery' felt pleased with themselves at being 'clever enough' to 'catch on' to at least some of the ingenious and daring mots;

---

* There was, certainly, a clandestine sexual element in the equation. Wilde had borrowed the name 'Cecil Graham' from the cross-dressing Ernest Boulton (aka 'Stella') who, together with his friend Frederick Park (aka 'Fanny'), had been the subject of a celebrated court case in 1870, when they faced charges of conspiracy to commit sodomy. When arrested – in female attire – at the Strand Theatre, Boulton had given his name as 'Cecil Graham'. Boulton and Park had been represented by George Lewis; he helped secure their acquittal.

while their belief that the dialogue faithfully represented 'the talk of the *grand monde*' made them feel 'privileged and modern'.[19] Wilde, for all his socially subversive touches of Ibsenism, also shared with Ouida that special gift for convincing the middle classes that he wrote 'as Duchesses talk'.

At the final curtain, after the cast had been saluted three times, there were calls for the author. Wilde appeared before the footlights, sporting a large green carnation in his buttonhole, bowed, and then retired. When the calls were redoubled, he re-appeared, now smoking a cigarette. At the cries of 'Speech' he seemed to hesitate, but then, placing his right hand in his trouser pocket, he began: 'I believe it is the privilege of an author to allow his works to be reproduced by others while he himself remains silent. But as you seem to wish to hear me speak, I accept the honour you are kind enough to confer upon me.' Pausing only to puff on his cigarette (out of nervousness, according to Mrs Jopling), he went on to thank George Alexander for the 'admirable completeness' of the production, and to praise the entire company for the 'infinite care' they had taken in turning his 'sketch' into a 'finished picture.' He concluded neatly, by telling the audience: 'I think that you have enjoyed the performance as much as I have, and I am pleased to believe that you like the piece almost as much as I do myself.' This audacious piece of self-assertion was 'received with hearty laughter and applause', as Wilde, still smoking, left the stage.

The curtain call, however, incensed the literal-minded critics almost more than the play itself. Patronizing, impertinent and attention seeking were some of the epithets used of Wilde, his speech, his cigarette, and his 'electric green boutonnière'. Only *The Sunday Times* thought his closing remark 'clever', and only the *Era* had the grace to admit that he was merely uttering aloud what all 'successful dramatic authors invariably think of their works'.[20]

As for the play itself, despite a handful of good reviews – and a general recognition that, if 'daring' and 'cynical', it was 'very clever' and amusing – most critics lined up ungenerously to point out Wilde's theatrical borrowings (from Dumas, Sardou, Haddon Chambers, et al.). Faults were found with the 'construction'. Doubts were cast about the moral tone. Some considered the behaviour of Lord Windermere improbable; others thought the actions of his wife absurd.[21]

Wilde, though, could afford to be disdainful. He recognized that the pettiness of the critical response had been trumped by the enthusiasm of the audience. Even the meanest reviews had to concede that the play had been much enjoyed The novelist and magazine editor Oswald Crawfurd

wrote spontaneously to the *Pall Mall Gazette*, redressing the balance of their
official coverage with an encomium of the play: 'an epoch in the history of
the drama', marking the overthrow of 'dull' and 'unreal' melodrama, by a
concentration of 'deliberate wit and finished epigram' not heard 'since the
days of Sheridan's *School for Scandal*'.[22]

Word of mouth ran ahead of the newspaper reports. There could be no
denying – or stopping – the play's success. The *London Standard* was soon
condoling that Wilde would have to surrender his reputation for originality
and eccentricity and 'submit to the humiliation of being stigmatized as the
author of a brilliantly successful play. It is even to be feared that it will have
a long run and return a great deal of mere vulgar profit.'[23]

Wilde had thought that he would escape to the South of France immediately after the opening night. But with success achieved, he relaxed instead
in the glow of euphoria. Coulson Kernahan recalled a visit from the excited
playwright the morning after the premiere when Wilde 'hugged himself
with delight' as they talked over the events of the evening.[24] Wilde – no
longer in a frenzy of nerves – relented over the important matter of when
to disclose Mrs Erlynne's true identity to the audience. Alexander had conspired with Clement Scott, getting the critic to point out, in his review,
the need for such a change. The conspiracy, as it turned out, was hardly
necessary since the fault was noted by almost all the critics, and most of the
audience. Wilde sent 'a graceful telegram' to Alexander acknowledging that
the actor had been 'right all through', and amended the text accordingly
in time for the second performance on the Monday evening. He insisted,
though – in a letter to the press – that his decision had not been prompted by
the strictures of any 'journalists'; he had acted on the advice of some young
friends with whom he had supped after the performance: 'The opinions of
the old on matters of Art are, of course, of no value whatsoever. The artistic
instincts of the young are invariably fascinating.'[25]

Wilde was thrilled with his triumph, as was his mother. Both of them set
such store by success, and they were now able to enjoy it to the full. There
were gratifying letters from Ettie Grenfell and Wilfrid Blunt. Curzon invited
Wilde to dinner. Lady Elcho had to be dissuaded from taking a walk-on part
in the ball scene. The 'best lines' were repeated 'all over town': 'I can resist
everything except temptation.' 'In this world there are only two tragedies.
One is not getting what one wants, and the other is getting it.' 'Scandal is
gossip made tedious by morality.' 'A cynic is a man who knows the price
of everything and the value of nothing.' 'We are all in the gutter, but some

of us are looking at the stars.' When asked how the play was going, Wilde boasted, 'Capitally. I am told Royalty is turned away nightly.' To Alexander's observation that the cheap seats seemed to be as crowded as the stalls and boxes, Wilde replied complacently, 'My dear Alexander, the answer is easy. Servants listen to conversations in drawing rooms and dining rooms. They hear people discussing my play, their curiosity is aroused, and so they fill your theatre. I can see they are servants by their perfect manners.'[26]

The green carnation, following its appearance on the opening night, became the fashionable flower of the moment. It 'bloomed profusely in the stalls' when John Gray's verse translation of de Banville's *Le Baiser* was staged by the Independent Theatre that March.[27] André Raffalovich published a sonnet 'against' it, in some 'weekly rag', counting the poem as his 'public rejection' of the whole Oscar Wilde 'set'.[28]

From the beginning the play drew 'exceptionally large' audiences. Wilde's arrangement with Alexander was for 5 per cent of the gross receipts (until he had earned £600) and 7.5 per cent thereafter, and he was soon earning more than £40 per week. For only the second time in his life he was confronted with the delightful prospect of making money. To improve matters still further Constance received a legacy of £3,000 on the death of her aunt Emily. Although the immediate call on their resources was to repay debts built up over several years, it seemed as though the pervading sense of financial worry might be lifting. There was even a thought that they might move to a larger house in Tite Street.[29]

Among the new friends that the play brought into Wilde's orbit was Ada Leverson. It was she perhaps who wrote the good-natured skit, 'A Wilde "Tag" to a Tame Play', that appeared in *Punch*. She was certainly a contributor to Oswald Crawfurd's magazine, *Black and White*, and it was at the Crawfurds' house that Wilde met her. Leverson was then twenty-nine, clever, amusing and literary, but shackled to a conventional and much older husband. She and Wilde fell into an easy and intimate friendship, Leverson's intellect and humour stimulating Wilde's own. He was soon calling her 'the wittiest woman in London'.[30]

The play's success was something to be built upon, and Wilde now perceived that writing modern society comedies was his métier. 'I always knew that play-writing was my province,' he told Frank Harris. His mistake had been to write 'plays in verse' or dramas about the Russian politics. 'Now I know better,' he announced. 'I'm sure of myself, and of success.'[31] But if he was confident that he would be able to repeat the trick, he did not

want to limit himself. His other literary projects might be carried up on the thermal of *Lady Windermere*'s success. He began to imagine a whole range of dramatic possibilities. He was keen to follow up on the excitement of composing *Salomé*: bringing out a Symbolist drama would give him literary prestige. And – despite his reservations about 'plays in verse' – he remained ever hopeful of finding an English producer for *The Duchess of Padua*.

Having abandoned his idea of a restorative trip to the South of France, Wilde instead went over to Paris for a few weeks at the end of March. Beside the pleasures of Paris in the springtime, it seems he wanted to consult with his friends there on plans to have *Salomé* published in France. Merrill was asked to look over the manuscript and to remove any egregious grammatical errors. He did manage to dissuade Wilde from beginning most of the principal speeches with the idiomatic expletive, 'Enfin', but his other suggestions were ignored, Wilde loftily declaring that the American-born (but Paris-raised and bilingual) Merrill was 'a foreigner and did not know French'. Merrill, much amused at this, passed Wilde on to Retté – who culled a few more Anglicisms and cut down a very long list of precious stones recited by Herod – before he too was superseded. Pierre Louÿs was brought in as a third arbiter, putting forward some final suggestions (which were largely ignored) and making some final corrections, mainly relating to the use of the subjunctive (which were largely accepted). The manuscript was then handed over to the printers.[32]

Back in England, Wilde discovered that the success of his play had called forth the tribute of parody. The actor Charles Brookfield – together with the composer Jimmy Glover (an old Dublin friend) – had put together a skit on Wilde and *Lady Windermere's Fan*. It was titled the *The Poet and the Puppets*, in allusion to Wilde's now infamous comments about 'puppets' being preferable to actors. Wilde, having embraced the satires of *Punch* and *Patience* for the sake of notoriety in the early 1880s, had come to doubt the benefits of such advertisement. He knew, though, that it was both futile and fatal to complain. He also knew that the censorship laws, in theory, forbade the representation of living people on the stage. Actors might impersonate individuals, but the play text itself was supposed to be free of direct portraiture. Wilde looked to the licenser of plays, E. F. S. Pigott, for protection. He also requested that he might review the script himself.

A reading was arranged at Tite Street. Glover recalled how, 'while cigars burned' Wilde 'punctuated each page as it was read with such praises as "Delightful!" "Charming, my old friends!… It's exquisite!" etc., etc.' Wilde

was clearly recognizable as the effete Oxford-educated 'Poet' of the piece. The dialogue borrowed many of his mots, including 'the greatest pleasure in life is to be misunderstood'. But there was nothing in the way of personal attack, and no sly allusions to sexual relations with young men. Nevertheless, to make his point, Wilde did raise an objection to having his name specifically mentioned in the opening song (not wanting to cross the censor, Brookfield agreed to alter the line). As Wilde showed the collaborators to the door he gave them a 'parting shot: "I feel, however, that I have been, well, Brookfield, what is the word? What is the thing you call it in your delightfully epigrammatic Stage English. Eh? Oh yes! delightfully spoofed!"'[33]*

Wilde's lordly refusal to be offended by the satire sharpened Brookfield's existing animus against him. The Eton-educated actor, with his own small reputation as a wit, had long been jealous of Wilde's preeminence. It was said, too, that he harboured a resentment at having once been corrected by Wilde over some solecism in his dress. And the increasingly insistent rumours about Wilde's sexual proclivities allowed him to colour his enmity with a sense of moral outrage. Wilde was too perceptive not to detect such antipathy, but too certain of his own powers to care.[34]

Brookfield's 'travestie' (which opened on 19 May) achieved its own minor triumph without compromising Wilde's play or Wilde's name. Charles Hawtrey gave an 'exquisitely comic' impersonation of Wilde – exact in every gesture and cadence. One of the few not to be impressed was the actor Hermann Vezin; he thought Wilde should write his own 'burlesque' ('I believe it would be a great success'). Wilde, though, confined his comments upon *Lady Windermere's Fan* to a speech delivered at the Royal General Theatrical Fund dinner. In response to a toast from a well-meaning Alderman, which had praised him for having written a play that 'lashed vice as it was supposed to exist', and revealing himself as an author prepared to 'call a spade a spade', Wilde demurred. 'I would like to protest against the statement that I ever called a spade a spade,' he began. 'The man who did so should be condemned to use one.' As to 'lashing vice', he could assure the company that nothing was further from his intentions. 'Those who have

---

*   The actor Arthur Roberts, who had recently coined the term 'spoof', recalled that Wilde and Beerbohm Tree once took him to supper at the Carlton Grill to quiz him about the phenomenon. When Roberts had explained that 'spoofing' was 'the knack of persuading people that something wildly improbable is gospel truth,' Wilde remarked, 'I am afraid, my dear Roberts, that some of us have been playing "spoof" all our lives without knowing the name of the game.'

seen *Lady Windermere's Fan* will see that if there is one particular doctrine contained in it, it is one of sheer individualism. It is not for anyone to censure what anyone else does, and everyone should go his own way, to whatever place he chooses, in exactly the way that he chooses.'[35]

7

White and Gold

*'All charming people, I fancy, are spoiled. It is the secret of
their attraction.'*

OSCAR WILDE

The great success of *Lady Windermere's Fan* gave Wilde the confidence – and the resources – to follow his own doctrine of individualism. He was able to re-assert that vision of self-realization that he had held since his university days, with a new force and a new focus. He declared his own life 'a work of art'. It seemed to one friend that 'what he desired was no less than to embody in the eyes of his fellow men a conception of life founded on the worship of beauty and pleasure'. Even the minor details of existence were addressed. Pierre Louÿs was impressed at the way that Wilde and his disciples 'envelop everything in poetry'. Instead of simply offering a cigarette to a friend, they would – in an 'exquisite' refinement – light it, and not hand it over until they had taken the first drag. If the new focus on 'pleasure' tended to find expression in luxurious living – expensive dinners and more expensive cigarettes – he was delighted to indulge himself, content to carry out the realization of his vision 'with contempt for any objections raised by the excesses of his hedonism'.[1]

Success touched all aspects of Wilde's life. He blossomed under the bright light of attention. He was in conspicuously 'good form' at a dinner

given by Violet Fane (and her future husband), sitting up into the early hours with Wilfrid Blunt and a few others. And he added to the conviviality of a dinner with the 'Sette of Odd Volumes', to which he had been invited by Heron-Allen. There were some, though, who detected a new taint of snobbery in his manner. Edith Cooper (one half of 'Michael Field') was most put out by him not speaking to her at one reception: 'We do not belong to the fashionable world, so Oscar rolls his shoulders towards us.' His play, meanwhile, was taking on a life of its own. Although he seems to have abandoned his own plans for a French-language production, there was interest from Italy, Germany and Austria. Wilde sold the American per-forming rights to Charles Frohman who was over from New York, and also secured the services of the splendidly effective Elisabeth Marbury to act as his agent in the States.[2]

Another transatlantic visitor that summer was Mrs Frank Leslie, who arrived with the unfortunate Willie. Before leaving New York she had informed her friends, 'I'm taking Willie over, but I'll not bring Willie back.' The marriage had proved a disaster. Willie refused to work. In his view there was far too much work being done in America already: 'What New York needs,' he declared, 'is a leisure class, and I am determined to introduce one.' He refused to go to the office. Dividing his days between the luxurious Gerlach and the convivial Lotos Club, he spent his time – and his wife's money – on drink and idleness. He would entertain his fellow club members with 'simply killing' imitations of Oscar, striking Aesthetic attitudes, and extemporizing parodies of Aesthetic verse in a 'fat, potato-choked sort of voice'. His wife very soon wearied of settling his bar bills, enduring his boorishness and urging him to work. Willie had, in her estimate, 'more laziness to the square inch than any man of his size in Christendom'. She ruefully came to the conclusion that he was no use to her 'by day or night', and would have to be got rid of. Oscar – and Lady Wilde – were scarcely thrilled to have Willie back in London, more a liability than an asset. Although he hoped to resume his connection with the *Telegraph*, he found the paper did not want him. He continued on his downward spiral, 'doing drama criticism for unimportant papers and writing general articles in which he would mention tradespeople and get perquisites'.[3]

Oscar tried not to engage; his own thoughts were directed more towards how he might spend the money he was earning. One scheme was to pay for the publication – by Mathews and Lane – of John Gray's poems. Wilde admired Gray's French-influenced decadent verses immensely, and relished

the idea of promoting them, with the help of Ricketts, in a beautifully-crafted volume. He had hoped, also, to celebrate the success of *Lady Winder-mere's Fan* by having it published in book form, but Mathews and Lane, after the success of their edition of Wilde's *Poems* (which had sold out in a matter of days), really wanted another poetical work. So Wilde arranged for them to bring out his *Sphinx*; the poem's 174 lines might be disposed elegantly over enough pages to make up a book, which could be handsomely decorated by the ever-inventive Ricketts.[4]

In the midst of these various plans, Wilde was surprised to receive 'a most pathetic and charming letter' from Lord Alfred Douglas, up at Oxford. Douglas was 'in terrible trouble with people who were blackmailing him'. The details of this 'unfortunate Oxford mishap' remain obscure: a compromising letter fallen into the wrong hands, perhaps; an outraged parent or guardian. Wilde (who, by his own estimate, 'hardly knew' Douglas at this point, and had not seen him for some time) was both 'touched' and flattered by the appeal. He offered his assistance, putting Douglas in contact with George Lewis, the great expert on evading scandal. Edwin Levy was brought in, and together with Wilde he arranged for the blackmailers to be paid off with £100. Levy recognized the signs of danger in the debacle, and in Douglas's refusal to take responsibility for it (Wilde, it seems, provided the money). He devoted an hour to warning Wilde against continuing the friendship. His efforts, though, were wasted.[5]

The incident, with its freight of danger, sex, conspiracy and crime, was exciting in its way – for Wilde. For Douglas it provoked relief and gratitude; Wilde had saved him from disaster. The varied elements worked a strange alchemy: Wilde's friendship with Douglas was transformed, shelving quickly into, first, a mutual and all-consuming infatuation, and then an enduring, but always turbulent, love. Wilde, already drawn to Douglas's youthful loveliness and ancient name, was now snared by all his traits of character: his aristocratic contempt for convention, his 'pagan' guilt-free enjoyment of sex, his extraordinary disregard for consequences; his willingness to depend upon others; if he was selfish, spoilt, vain, intemperate, needy and demanding, that only added to his attractiveness. Lust, as ever, was mixed with idealism. There was a glamour about Douglas that readily allowed Wilde to view him as that ideal and inspiring Platonic 'beloved' – a 'Willie Hughes' to his Shakespeare, a 'Dorian Gray' to whom he might play both Basil Hallward and Lord Henry Wotton.

Douglas matched his devotion. 'I was fascinated by Wilde,' he later told

Frank Harris, 'adored him and was "crazy" about him.' All Wilde's gifts for inspiring youthful adulation came into play. Douglas acknowledged how Wilde 'quickened' him, transporting him 'out of this tedious world into a fairy land of fancy, conceit, paradox and beauty by the power of his golden speech'. And his great delight in Wilde's brilliance was perhaps heightened by an unconscious delight in his power to command it.[6]

In the aftermath of the blackmail payoff, Wilde overwhelmed Douglas with attentions, among them a copy of his *Poems* (in the recent Bodley Head edition) inscribed 'From Oscar, To the gilt-mailed Boy. At Oxford, in the heart of June.' There was sex too. Douglas recalled (some thirty years later, when his attitude to homosexuality had altered completely) how Wilde took him to bed at an empty Tite Street after a night on the town: there, in the spare bedroom, 'he succeeded in doing what he had wanted to do ever since the first moment he saw me'. Douglas claimed that Wilde treated him 'as an older boy treats a younger one at school and added what was new to me... He "sucked" me.' The tone of detached surprise is not to be trusted. Douglas – promiscuous since his Winchester days and notorious at Oxford – was certainly the more experienced party.[7] And the true tenor of their sexual relationship is perhaps better conveyed by his letter to Wilde signed 'your own loving darling boy to do what you like with'.[8]*

The great excitement of this new passion was matched by another. Sarah Bernhardt was in town. Wilde met her at Henry Irving's. According to reports, she asked whether he (now the author of a West End hit) might write a play for her; he replied in jest that – with *Salomé* – he had already done so. The quip seems to have been enough to whet her interest. Wilde gave her a reading of the piece, and to his amazed delight found her 'charmed and fascinated' by it. She wanted to act the title role. And not at some unspecified future date, but right away, as part of her current London season, which was being extended into July. For Wilde the prospect of having the 'Divine Sarah' – 'undoubtedly the greatest artist on any stage' (as he thought her) – premiering his work in a London theatre was a dizzying coup. It offered the prospect of an 'artistic' triumph to match the commercial success of *Lady Windermere's Fan*.[9]

---

* Douglas, in later life, after he converted to Roman Catholicism and renounced his homosexual past, became almost frantic in his insistence that he had never been sodomized by Wilde. And perhaps this was true, even if Douglas's letters to Maurice Schwabe (see below) seem to indicate that he was happy to take the passive role during penetrative sex.

Rehearsals were begun at once. Bernhardt recognized that the play was not 'religious' but dealt, rather, with 'love, passion, nature, the stars' (Wilde told her that 'the moon played the principal role'). In her conception the piece was 'héraldique' – with the stateliness of a 'fresco'. Ricketts recalled that, for days, she and Wilde 'discussed the pitch of voice' required for the performance. Bernhardt's notion was that each word should fall like 'une perle sur une disque de cristal'. There should be no rapid movements, only stylized gestures.[10] If Wilde harboured any doubts about the forty-seven-year-old actress taking the part of the young princess, they were soon dispelled. To hear his words 'spoken by the most beautiful voice in the world' was, he considered, 'the greatest joy that is possible to experience'. He came to recognize that Bernhardt was, indeed, 'the only person' who could act the part; age was immaterial.[11] Wilde's own estimate of his play seems to have shifted at this time. Ricketts suspected that he had initially regarded it as little more than a '*jeu d'esprit*', crafted to 'interest the French and charm his friends'. But now, illuminated by Bernhardt's brightness, he came to see it as a minor masterpiece – one that could enlarge the 'artistic horizon' of the stage.[12]

Wilde enlisted Graham Robertson to help with the staging and costumes, though he himself had long been mulling over ideas. Robertson recalled Wilde wanting 'everyone on the stage to be in yellow'. He also suggested, in place of an orchestra, 'braziers of perfume'. His excited vision, however, of 'scented clouds rising and partly veiling the stage from time to time – a new perfume for each new emotion!', was dispelled by Robertson's objection that it would be impossible to 'air the theatre between each emotion, and the perfumes would get mixed and smell perfectly beastly'. Besides, there was scarcely time (or money) for such extravagant conceits. Bernhardt considered that her scenery and costumes from *Cleopatra* could be adapted for the occasion.[13]

Matters were advancing well, to Wilde's 'intense pleasure.' His copy of the rehearsal script is dotted with amendments and notes – including the arresting stage direction for Salome, 'Elle danse la danse des sept voiles'. Then disaster struck. The script had been submitted as a matter of course to the lord chamberlain's office in order to receive a performance licence. Mr Pigott, however, ruled that no licence could be granted. The censorship laws (drafted in the seventeenth century) forbade the representation of biblical characters on the stage, and this seems to have been the reason given for Pigott's decision. But even without such legislation, the sexual

perversity of the drama – with its themes of incest and necrophilia – would probably have placed it beyond acceptable bounds. Certainly the production could not go ahead.*

To Wilde it seemed both incredible and 'ridiculous'. In a series of interviews and letters, and in a speech to the Authors' Club, he bewailed the inequalities of a system that allowed painters, sculptors and poets to depict or describe biblical figures, but denied the same right to dramatists and actors. 'The insult in the suppression of *Salomé*,' he declared, 'is an insult to the stage as a form of art and not to me.' Although Wilde surely knew that getting a licence for the play might be problematic (and he was perhaps remiss in leaving the matter so late), he would also have been aware that the rules were never applied consistently. His recent experience of *The Poet and the Puppets* had shown how regulations might be ignored. And there was, besides, a tradition of considerable extra latitude being given to plays in French. Pigott's irrevocable judgement fell as a terrible blow. It was a blow, too, that so few artists and critics came forward to support him. William Archer and Bernard Shaw were the rare exceptions.[14]

Wilde tried to salvage something from the wreckage by proposing an 'invitation performance' – perhaps along the lines of the Independent Theatre – but Bernhardt declared that such a ploy was not her 'style'. She would, instead, give the 'admirable' play its premiere in Paris, where it would be 'un immense succès'. She was unsure just when this would happen, but, as she informed a reporter, 'The role is mine. Mr Oscar Wilde has given it me, and nobody else can perform it. No, no, no.'[15]

In the fury of the moment Wilde announced that he too would be transferring himself to the French capital – 'the abode of artists, nay... la ville artiste' – and have himself 'naturalised as a Frenchman'. He was stung both by the official disapproval of his work, and the glee taken in his discomfiture. He could not consent to call himself a citizen 'of a country that shows such narrowness in its artistic judgement'. The philistine press at

---

* Pigott seems to have regarded the work – and the idea of producing it – as little more than a joke in very poor taste. He wrote confidentially to his colleague Spencer Ponsonby on 27 June 1892, sending him the MS for his '*private* edification and amusement': 'It is a miracle of impudence; and I am bound to say that when Mr Abbey, [OW's] Acting Manager, called on me, in answer to my summons, he lifted up his eyes with a holy shudder of surprise, when I described the piece to him, & recommended him (as Uncle Toby advised the father of the juvenile Poet [in Sterne's *Tristram Shandy*]) to "wipe it up & say no more about it"... The piece is written in French – half Biblical, half pornographic – by Oscar Wilde himself. Imagine the average British public's reception of it.'

once started speculating that he would be expected to do French military service; *Punch* produced a cartoon of him in uniform.[16]

But instead of taking up residence in France he went to Germany. He needed to recuperate from the stress and disappointment of the *Salomé* debacle, and perhaps also from the over-excitement of the great success of *Lady Windermere's Fan*. July found him at the fashionable spa town Bad Homburg, in a handsome guest house overlooking the beautiful 'English' park. Constance reported to her brother that Oscar was 'under a regime: getting up at 7:30, going to bed at 10:30, smoking hardly any cigarettes and being massaged, and of course drinking waters: I only wish I was there to see it.' Wilde hoped that Carlos Blacker might join him, claiming he was 'very miserable'. But, in fact, he soon found congenial friends. A 'charming day' was spent with Pierre Louÿs, who was passing through town on his way to Bayreuth. Rider Haggard was taking the waters. The young Douglas Ainslie, now serving as an unpaid diplomatic attaché, arrived at a neighbouring guest house and promptly borrowed money from the always generous – and now seemingly wealthy – Wilde. Alexander had written, transferring £1,000 to Wilde's account, and relaying news of the continued success of *Lady Windermere's Fan*, which was then about to set off on a summer tour of the provinces. The ban on smoking seems to have been double edged in its effect: 'Je me porte très bien,' Wilde reported to Louÿs, 'et je suis horriblement triste'. Rider Haggard, though he found Wilde 'amusing' company, was surprised to discover how keenly he had felt the recent 'sneers and attacks' on him and his work; he had supposed 'they were the breath of his nostrils'.[17]

After a month of recuperation Wilde returned to London. His stay there was brief; Constance had rented a farmhouse at Felbrigg, near Cromer, in Norfolk, as a place for a summer holiday (George Alexander had recommended the locale to Wilde). Constance's anxiety that 'Oscar will get bored to death' by country life was offset by the fact that there was 'heaps of room' and they would be able to 'ask people down to cheer him up'. At first, though, Wilde was happy with rural calm, and 'sweet' country air. There were afternoon walks with Constance into Cromer, where they 'would generally come across some friend to have tea with'; the Liberal politician Cyril Flower and his wife, Constance de Rothschild, had a beautiful Aesthetic holiday home nearby at Overstrand. And in the mornings and evenings Wilde could work.

At Homburg he had allowed his mind to turn on ideas for a new play –

a comedy to build upon the triumph of *Lady Windermere's Fan*. Now he began to write. The piece, provisionally entitled *Mrs Arbuthnot*, was to be another elegantly subversive variation on the 'fallen woman' theme, playing upon the 'double standard' that pervaded society with regard to the pre-marital (mis)behaviour of men and women.[18]

The Mrs Arbuthnot of the title, having been seduced as a young woman by the 'wicked' Lord Illingworth, has been left alone to raise their illegitimate son, Gerald. Keeping him in ignorance of his shameful parenthood, and her shameful past, she has launched him into the world, only to learn that he has – by chance – been taken up by Lord Illingworth, who wishes to appoint him as his private secretary. The inevitable revelations, recriminations and reconciliations ensue, as Gerald discovers the secret of his parentage, forgives his mother, secures the hand of Hester Worsley, a wealthy but high-minded American heiress, and joins in the general condemnation of the thoroughly unrepentant Lord Illingworth.

It was Wilde's conceit – and one readily enough believed by the public – that 'the art of play-writing... consisted of writing a series of epigrams, and then finding characters to fit them, with a tag of incident thrown in'.[19] Certainly his new piece, set during twenty-four hours at a country house party, allowed for a welter of wit and paradox: 'A well-tied tie is the first serious step in life'; 'The Peerage... is the best thing in Fiction the English have done'; 'One must have some occupation nowadays. If I hadn't my debts I shouldn't have anything to think about'; 'I adore simple pleasures, they are the last refuge of the complex'; 'The English country gentleman galloping after a fox – the unspeakable in full pursuit of the uneatable.' Indeed Wilde described the opening scene as his rebuke to the critics who had complained at the lack of action in *Lady Windermere's Fan*. Amid a great deal of amusing talk about love, marriage and society, there was 'absolutely no action at all'; it was, Wilde claimed, 'a perfect act'.[20]

There were many fine female characters in the play (the worldly Mrs Allonby, the formidable but foolish Lady Hunstanton, the passionate Hester Worsley, Mrs Arbuthnot herself) but most of the witticisms fall to the cynical Lord Illingworth. He was the next in line of Wilde's brilliant epigrammatic dandies, following on from Prince Paul, Lord Henry Wotton and Lord Darlington, though Wilde – with his usual relish for exaggeration – claimed, that he was 'like no one who has existed before'. Indeed, immediately contradicting this assertion, he went on: 'He is certainly not natural. He is a figure of art. Indeed, if you can bear the truth, he is MYSELF.'[21] And doubtless

much of the character's wit did borrow from Wilde's own conversation. Certainly it borrowed from his writings: numerous lines were taken from *The Picture of Dorian Gray*. Wilde also used the play to comment slyly upon his own position as a man leading a precarious and illicit double life in the midst of society. To those who knew – or suspected – his secret, there would be a keen double edge to such comments as, 'It is perfectly monstrous the way people go about, nowadays, saying things against one behind one's back that are absolutely and entirely true.' This was self-concealment through self-revelation.

The theatrical world was eager for news of the play. Wilde was now in demand. And, after the stressful production process of *Lady Windermere's Fan*, Wilde was ready to look beyond George Alexander. Beerbohm Tree had for some time been jockeying for the right to produce his next piece. Wilde – who thought Tree best suited to historical roles – had initially tried to interest him in *The Duchess of Padua*; but the suggestion had been deflected. Tree wanted something modern and comic. And Wilde, having been brought together with the actor-manager by the illustrious Ettie Grenfell, was perhaps inclined to look upon his wishes with particular favour. Certainly he consented to give Tree 'first refusal' of his new script.[22]

He retained, though, some doubts about the actor's ability to play the aristocratic and dandified Lord Illingworth (he would be far better suited, Wilde thought, as Herod in *Salomé*). To Tree's assertion that his recent performance as the Duke of Guisbury in A. H. Jones's *The Dancing Girl* had been highly praised, Wilde remarked, 'Ah! That just it. Before you can successfully impersonate the character I have in mind, you must forget that you ever played Hamlet; you must forget that you ever played Falstaff; above all you must forget that you ever played a duke in a melodrama by Henry Arthur Jones.'[23]

Progress on the script was good during those first weeks in Norfolk, although there were distractions. 'I'm afraid Oscar is going to become bitten by golf mania,' Constance reported to her friend Lady Mount Temple. 'He played his first game on the links here yesterday and has joined for a fortnight.'[24] Cyril was collected from friends in Cambridgeshire, though his younger brother remained behind, suffering from whooping cough. Wilde invited Edward Shelley down, but he did not come. Arthur Clifton and his new wife did arrive, in the midst of their honeymoon (Wilde had given them £160 to enable them to get married).[25] And then, on the last day of August, a telegram came from Lord Alfred Douglas 'asking to be put up

for a night'. Constance was happy to accommodate him. The single 'night', however, seems to have been no more than a formula; Douglas installed himself for the duration. He joined Wilde for his daily round on the links (Constance lamented, laughingly, that she was becoming 'a golf widow'). He appeared in some of the photographs that Constance arranged to be taken before the party broke up on 10 September.

It had been planned that Wilde would stay on for another week, on his own, to finish the play. Douglas, however, also contrived to remain behind. There seems to have been a fiction that he had fallen ill (Constance wrote from Babbacombe, where she had gone, to ask whether she should return 'to look after him'). Douglas's own memory, though, was of days playing golf, and of trips in a 'pony cart' that 'Oscar used to drive himself – to the great danger of the traffic'. There were also regular visits to the Flowers at Overstrand. At one lunch Wilde declared that 'if he had to work for his living he would like to be a shepherd'. When Mrs Flower suggested that he might 'find looking after a lot of sheep rather trying' he replied, 'Oh, I should not like to have more than one sheep.' Amid the general laughter, Mrs Flower countered with the remark, 'Well you've got one lamb already with a golden-fleece.' Wilde was delighted with this allusion to the fair-haired Douglas; and Douglas was delighted too. The comment was ingenuous: Mrs Flower regarded 'Bosie' as little more than a child, and indeed, later, even asked him to a children's party at her house in London.[26]*

But she was deceived by his boyish looks. The week together at Felbrigg was certainly an opportunity for Douglas and Wilde to have sex, but it was also a chance for Wilde to learn something of Douglas's voracious promiscuity. How much Bosie disclosed about the sexual bond he shared with his friend and exact contemporary, Maurice 'Pretty Boy' Schwabe, is not known. Douglas's surviving letters to Schwabe, in which he declares undying love, and proclaims himself 'your loving boy-wife, or your "little bitch" if you prefer it', make clear the intensity, and the dynamic, of the relationship; as does a photograph – taken at Oxford – of Bosie sitting on Schwabe's knee. What Douglas did talk about was the London subculture of male prostitution that he and Schwabe were busy exploring together. Wilde remembered it as Douglas's sole topic of conversation. The Cleveland

---

* Cyril Flower was unlikely to have regarded the relationship between Wilde and Douglas in such an innocent light. He too was a lover of men – and (as Douglas later reported) in 1902 'got into serious trouble for activities on the O.W. lines & had to leave the country hurriedly'.

Street brothel may have been closed down, but there were plenty of other places where gentlemen could meet working-class youths and pay them for sex. The Knightsbridge roller-skating rink was a rich cruising ground, as was the bar at the St James's restaurant. Douglas and Schwabe's guide to this clandestine sex-fuelled world was Alfred Taylor. A feckless but well-educated young man, just turned thirty, who was reputed to have squandered an inheritance of £45,000, Taylor acted as an informal procurer, picking up interested youths and introducing them to clients with money. Douglas and Schwabe were eager for such charged encounters, with their mix of power, abasement, depravity and danger. Blackmail, as Bosie had already discovered, was a constant risk.

This was an erotic world beyond Wilde's ken, and – always seeking new experiences – he was both intrigued and excited to learn of it, and even more intrigued and excited to experience it. 'Danger', as Mrs Allonby in his new play was made to remark, 'is so rare in modern life.' And something of Wilde's attitude towards it was conveyed by her further observation: 'The one advantage of playing with fire, is that one never gets even singed. It is the people who don't know how to play with it who get burned.'

-PART VII-

The Selfish Giant

1892–1894

AGE 37–40

Oscar Wilde and Lord Alfred Douglas, Oxford, 1893.

1

The Eternal Quest for Beauty

*'Any preoccupation with ideas of what is right or wrong in
conduct shows an arrested intellectual development.'*

OSCAR WILDE

Wilde's initiation into the fire seems to have occurred shortly
after he returned to London, at a small dinner laid on by
Schwabe and Douglas in a private room at Kettner's. Alfred
Taylor arrived bringing with him a 'modest and nice' young man called
Sydney Mavor, a twenty-year-old clerk at a lamp-wick manufactory in the
City, who lived with his widowed mother. He had been specially chosen
to appeal to Wilde. 'I am glad you've made yourself pretty,' Taylor had
told Mavor before they arrived at the restaurant. 'Mr Wilde likes nice clean
boys.' Wilde certainly did like Mavor. 'Our little lad has pleasing manners,'
he declared complacently towards the end of the evening. 'We must see
more of him.' According to Mavor they had sex that night in Wilde's room
at the Hotel Albemarle. Whatever the commercial elements of the transaction, Wilde insisted on giving the encounter a human aspect – even a
romantic one: a few days afterwards Mavor received an expensive silver
cigarette case inscribed inside, 'Sidney from O.W. October 1892.' The gift
was, he said, 'quite a surprise'.[1]

It was the first of many such assignations – and many such cigarette

cases ('I have a great fancy for giving cigarette cases,' Wilde later admitted). It marked, too, a shift in Wilde's relationship with Bosie. Their mutual infatuation continued, coloured by poems and passionate letters and occasional sex, but it was now fired by a shared and predatory enthusiasm for sex with others; 'the eternal quest for beauty', as Douglas termed it. Wilde became a regular visitor at the all-male tea parties that Alfred Taylor hosted at his flat above an empty baker's shop in Little College Street, Westminster. Taylor's rooms, shuttered and curtained against the daylight, were a bower of cut-price Aestheticism, decked with fans and artificial flowers, draped with oriental textiles and theatrical costumes. A 'really noble crucifix' added a distinctive touch. Scented pastilles clouded the air. And there was piano which, Wilde claimed, Taylor could play 'very charmingly'.[2]

In the same month as his meeting with Sidney Mavor, Wilde and Constance were invited down to Bracknell to call on Douglas's mother, Lady Queensberry – a needy yet supercilious woman who, having obtained a divorce from the marquess in 1887, had devoted herself to fretting over and spoiling her children. She had been concerned about her third son's growing friendship with Wilde, even writing to Dr Warren, the President of Magdalen (and an old friend of Wilde's), to ask whether it was a suitable association. Warren had informed her that Bosie was indeed fortunate to have obtained the notice of so able and eminent a man.[3] Reassured, Lady Queensberry now sought Wilde's advice over her errant child, and his various travails at Oxford. As Wilde 'sat in the Bracknell woods' listening to Lady Queensberry list her concerns, he must have felt the absurdity and awkwardness of his position, as well as enjoying the experience of having a marchioness confide in him. 'Bosie' was, she said, vain and 'all wrong about money'. When Wilde queried why she did not tackle him on these points, she mentioned her son's terrible temper. It was not something that Wilde had encountered. Yet.

The visit to Bracknell drew Wilde for the first time into the web of Douglas family relations. He would find it hard to escape. The encounter with Lady Queensberry was soon followed by a meeting with her former husband. The 'Mad Marquess' was a man of fierce opinions and combative temper. Beside his contributions to the world of pugilism and racing, he was a committed secularist and a frustrated politician, with the rare ability (as one paper described it) 'to attract public attention to himself'. Even in a family of noted eccentrics, he was conspicuous. In 1882 he had famously

interrupted a performance of Tennyson's *The Promise of May* to protest against the treatment of atheism in the piece.*

As Bosie's relationship with Wilde developed, and the two friends began to be seen often about town together, he grew uneasy. Aware of rumours circulating about Wilde's sexual interests, he disapproved of the connection. With an uncharacteristic attempt at paternal tact, he 'light-heartedly' suggested to his son that he should give up the friendship. Douglas, however, was not to be dictated to or advised – and certainly not by a parent who, he felt, had always neglected him. Although he wrote back respectfully, his letter provoked the marquess's easily roused ire: Bosie was called a 'fool' and a 'baby'; there were threats to cut off his allowance.

But, before matters could worsen, the marquess chanced upon Wilde and Douglas lunching together at the Café Royal. Douglas insisted his father join them. Wilde exerted himself to please, and soon had the marquess not only engaged but actually laughing. When he steered the talk on to the iniquities of Christianity (Queensberry's favourite topic) Bosie 'got bored' and left them to it. Wilde later reported that they had continued the lunch till after four. Following the encounter Queensberry wrote to Bosie praising Wilde as a 'charming fellow' and 'very clever'. Having experienced his conversation, he could well understand why his son should be so fond of him. He was heartened too to hear that Lord and Lady de Grey considered him 'perfectly all right' in every way. It seemed as though a danger had been averted.[4]

These new emotional currents coursing through Wilde's life had to accommodate themselves alongside the plans for his new play. Shortly after his return from Norfolk, Wilde paid a visit to his friends the Palmers at Reading, where Walter Palmer was head of the biscuit-making firm Huntley and Palmer. The sixty-four-year-old novelist George Meredith was also of the party. This was a source of considerable excitement. Meredith had a

---

* 'The 'refreshingly original' doings of the Douglas family were a frequent feature of the newspaper social columns. One of Queensberry's sisters, Lady Gertrude, had married a baker, and lived with him above his 'little shop in Shepherd's Bush'; the other, Lady Florence Dixie, kept a pet jaguar, a souvenir of her travels across Patagonia; she claimed that it had saved her from attack by Fenians in Windsor Great Park. Of the Marquess's brothers, Lord John (before his suicide in 1891) had often found himself in court – on one occasion for having described his wife, on the census return, as a 'cross sweep' and a 'lunatic'. The other brother, Lord Archibald, in reaction to the marquess's secularism, had converted to Catholicism and become a priest, running a boys' home on the Harrow Road.

reputation as 'the most brilliant talker of his day', his conversation overflowing – as one contemporary recalled – with 'expressions of the comic spirit,
ranging from the playful antics of boyish "larkishness" up to the mature and
artfully adjusted attack of wit and irony'. Theodore Watts considered him
the one conversationalist who could be put in the same bracket as Wilde.
Meredith, he thought, was the better when he could 'choose his topic'; Wilde
excelled him when it came to turning 'any chance remark to happy and
apt use'. To have both men under one roof was a great coup. Mrs Jopling,
a fellow guest, noted 'how the two writers thoroughly enjoyed their first
meeting'. Unfortunately she noted little more. 'The talk at the dinner table
was most interesting. I wish I could remember it, if only a sentence or two.'
After the encounter Meredith, who had previously expressed reservations
about *Dorian Gray*, declared that Wilde was 'good company'.[5]

Eager to test his new play, Wilde read the last act aloud to the assembled
guests one afternoon. He would have been pleased to note that some of
them were moved to tears at the scene when the wronged Mrs Arbuthnot
strikes her seducer, Lord Illingworth, in the face with her glove, though –
typically – Wilde defused the moment, declaring that 'I took that situation
from the *Family Herald*.'[6] Wilde re-used this line (with variations), when
shortly afterwards he met up with Beerbohm Tree and his company in
Glasgow – where they were on tour – and read the script to them. To the
actor-manager's fulsome praise of the plot, he replied:

> Plots are tedious. Anyone can invent them. Life is full of them. Indeed
> one has to elbow one's way through them as they crowd across one's
> path. I took the plot of this play from the *Family Herald*, which took it
> – wisely, I feel – from my novel *The Picture of Dorian Gray*. People love
> a wicked aristocrat who seduces a virtuous maiden, and they love a
> virtuous maiden for being seduced by a wicked aristocrat. I have given
> them what they like, so that they may learn to appreciate what I like to
> give them.[7]

Tree certainly thought the public would like it. A contract was drawn up,
and it was arranged that the play would open at the Haymarket the following spring. Meanwhile *Lady Windermere's Fan* continued to draw the crowds.
It returned to the St James's Theatre from its provincial tour on the last day
of October, and finally closed at the end of November. The ten-month run
had earned Wilde perhaps as much as £3,000. Blacker, who saw Wilde soon

afterwards, reported him as 'beaming with the inebriation of success', and delighted at having produced so apparently 'excellent' a new play with such 'remarkable rapidity'.[8]

Some of the money he received from Tree was spent on renting Babbacombe Cliff, Lady Mount Temple's beautiful house outside Torquay, for three months (from mid-November to mid-February). Constance had been wanting to buy a country house; this was a more manageable option. Babbacombe would be a place of retreat for the family. Wilde told Lady Mount Temple that he was looking forward to the 'peace and beauty' of her home, where he would be able to do imaginative work – 'to hear things the ear cannot hear, and see invisible things'. Babbacombe would also be good for Wilde's health. The constant regime of drinking, smoking and dining out, of late nights and little exercise, of professional stresses and private worries, took its toll. He was becoming increasingly prone to attacks of nervous and physical exhaustion. But he did also use his 'health' as an excuse, and means of escape.[9]

Even as he was making arrangements over Babbacombe, Wilde ran off, for a few days, to the Royal Bath Hotel in Bournemouth – ostensibly because he was 'not very well'. In fact he was accompanying Douglas, who had been sent there by his own doctor, but 'hated being alone'. Already the pattern of Bosie's demands and Wilde's acquiescence was being established. But there was encouragement and patronage too. Douglas had just taken on the editorship of an Oxford undergraduate magazine, The Spirit Lamp, and Wilde agreed to contribute a poem to the next number. The trip also, it seems, gave Wilde a first taste of Bosie's terrible temper. Wilde was unsettled by it, and unsettled too by other cares. It seems possible that already his dealings with male prostitutes had opened him up to threats of blackmail and extortion. Constance's brother, Otho, recalled meeting Wilde just after he had returned from Bournemouth. 'An important note or letter... he said, had been either mislaid or mis-delivered by the porter of the hotel in which he was staying, and he seemed to me to be worried, as if some trouble were haunting him.'* And to Douglas (now back at Oxford) he referred obliquely to 'strange and troubling personalities walking in painted pageants' through his London life.[10]

---

* Otho Lloyd was himself in difficulties: he had lost money in a financial speculation and was being pursued by creditors. He soon afterwards retreated to Switzerland and adopted his own middle name, Holland, as an alias.

Such anxieties, however, did nothing to deflect him from his course. His fascination with the sexual underworld increased. It became his consuming passion. As he later recalled (and explained) it: 'Tired of being on the heights I deliberately went to the depths in the search for new sensations. What the paradox was to me in the sphere of thought, perversity became to me in the sphere of passion.'[11] If there were perils, Wilde accepted them as part of the game: 'It was like feasting with panthers; the danger was half the excitement.'[12] Schwabe introduced him to a teenage bookmaker's clerk, a would-be music hall comedian (and accomplished blackmailer) called Freddie Atkins. There was another bacchanalian dinner in a private room of a Soho restaurant, during which – according to Atkins – Wilde kissed the waiter. If he did not sleep with Atkins that night, he seems to have done so later. Shortly afterwards Wilde had to go over to Paris for a few days to oversee details of the publication of *Salomé* (Mathews and Lane wanted to have their names added to the title page to create a simultaneous edition for the British market). Atkins and Schwabe accompanied Wilde on the jaunt. They shared three adjoining rooms at Wilde's old hotel on the Boulevard des Capucines, which was convenient for bed-hopping: Atkins claimed that he returned from a night at the Moulin Rouge to find Wilde in bed with Schwabe. At the end of the trip Atkins received his silver cigarette case.[13]

Constance and the boys had been installed at Babbacombe since the middle of November, living in daily expectation of Oscar's arrival. He finally came down on 3 December, bringing tin soldiers for the children.* They were thrilled to see him. Within days, however, his health collapsed, and he took to his bed for over a week. The doctor declared that 'he must not live in London'. It was not a piece of advice he was likely to follow.[14]

Babbacombe Cliff was a Pre-Raphaelite dream house, described by one visitor as 'full of surprises and curious rooms, with suggestions of Rossetti at every turn'. There was a Burne-Jones window. All the bedrooms had been given names: Wilde was installed in 'Wonderland' – Lady Mount Temple's boudoir, and 'the most artistic' of all the chambers. Constance

---

* Wilde had strong views on toys. He was overheard in 'a well-known toy-shop in Regent Street', asking for 'a Noah's Ark... not one of your modern Noah's Arks, but a good old-fashioned one, one in which Noah is the same size as the dove, and the dove the same size as the elephant.' When something along those lines was produced, he asked whether he might check its suitability by sucking the painted figure of Noah, to see whether it tasted like the toy of his own childhood.

reported that he was busy feeding the 'cheeky' pigeons that came to his window, or sat prettily 'in rows along the branches of the fir trees' outside. He was absorbed, too, in reading a book of 'supernatural stories' full of intimations from beyond the grave. It was an interest that drew him closer to Constance. Her own attention was increasingly absorbed with spiritual and religious questions. Some of these she shared also with Robbie Ross, who came down to stay. A Dante enthusiast with Catholic leanings, he was ready to engage with her about religion and the *Divine Comedy*. He even presented her with a rosary, and a guide to how to use it.[15]

For Wilde, though, the pull of London, of Bosie, and of promiscuous commercial sex, remained dangerously strong. He was drawn up to town before the end of the year. He had learnt from Bosie of Taylor's latest discovery: a handsome, thick-set, fair-haired working-class youth of seventeen called Alfred Wood. Douglas had already had sex with him, but was eager for Wilde to share the experience. There was the inevitable champagne supper in a private room, Wilde with his hand inside Wood's trousers by the end of the meal. And then, the house being empty, they were able to return to Tite Street for sex.

Several other assignations followed, before Wilde had to go over to Paris to consult on the final details of his *Salomé* book, which Marcel Schwob had been seeing towards completion. While in the French capital, Wilde had a fleeting glimpse of Constance; a 'delightful peep' she called it. She was on her way to Italy, together with her aunt, Mary Napier, and two cousins. She would be away for almost two months.[16]

Wilde returned to Babbacombe, to the children, and to work. He had high hopes. With *A Woman of No Importance* – as it was now called – completed, he had already committed himself to a new project. Ignoring, it seems, a verbal agreement to write something for Alexander, he contracted to produce a society comedy for John Hare, the ambitious actor-manager of the newly built Garrick Theatre. And, for himself, he planned also to compose a piece 'in blank verse' – though whether it was to build upon the achievement of *Salomé* or of *The Duchess of Padua* is unclear.[17] But the prospect of productive calm was shattered, almost at once, by the arrival of Lord Alfred Douglas. He came with his fox terrier and his tutor, a recently graduated Oxford scholar (and friend of Lionel Johnson's), called Campbell Dodgson. Douglas had been rusticated from Magdalen for the spring term, after neglecting his studies, and was supposed to be making good his deficiencies with a course of reading ahead of the final examinations in June.

Wilde had suggested that he might come to Babbacombe whenever he liked, and he had wasted little time in arriving.[18]*

To Lady Mount Temple Wilde described a scene of studious endeavour: 'Babbacombe Cliff has become a kind of college or school, for Cyril studies French in the nursery, and I write my new play in Wonderland, and in the drawing room Lord Alfred Douglas – one of Lady Queensberry's sons – studies Plato with his tutor for his degree at Oxford in June. He and his tutor are staying with me for a few days, so I am not lonely in the evenings.' But a letter written to Dodgson – after he had departed – gives perhaps a truer flavour of a regime that Wilde claimed succeeded 'in combining the advantages of a public school with those of a private lunatic asylum'. He provided a full prospectus:

BABBACOMBE SCHOOL

HEADMASTER – MR OSCAR WILDE

SECOND MASTER – MR CAMPBELL DODGSON

BOYS – LORD ALFRED DOUGLAS

RULES.

Tea for masters and boys at 9.30 a.m.

Breakfast at 10.30.

Work	11.30–12.30.
At 12.30.	Sherry and biscuits for headmaster and boys (the second master objects to this).
12.40–1.30.	Work.
1.30.	Lunch.
2.30–4.30.	Compulsory hide-and-seek for headmaster.
5.	Tea for headmaster and second master, brandy and sodas (not to exceed seven) for boys.

---

* Campbell Dodgson, in a letter to Lionel Johnson, gave a vivid account of their flight from Douglas's mother's house at Salisbury: 'Our departure was dramatic; Bosie was as usual in a whirl: he had no boots, no money, no cigarettes, and had omitted to send many telegrams of the first importance. Then, with a minimum of minutes in which to catch our train, we were required to overload a small pony chaise with a vast amount of trunks, while I was charged with a fox terrier and a scarlet morocco dispatch box, a gorgeous and beautiful gift from Oscar. After hurried farewells to the ladies, we started on a wild career, Bosie driving. I expected only to drag my shattered limbs to the Salisbury Infirmary, but we arrived at the station. When we had been gone an hour or so it occurred to Bosie that he never told Oscar we were coming, so a vast telegram was dispatched from Exeter.'

6–7.	Work.
7.30.	Dinner, with compulsory champagne.
8.30–12.	Ecarté, limited to five-guinea points.
12–1.30.	Compulsory reading in bed. Any boy found disobeying this rule will be immediately woken up.

At the conclusion of the term the headmaster will be presented with a silver inkstand, the second master with a pencil-case, as a token of esteem, by the boys.[19]

Dodgson's own memory of the visit was of 'lazy and luxurious' days more given over to playing 'with pigeons and children', driving by the sea and talking than to serious study. He found Wilde's command of language 'extraordinary'. 'We argue for hours in favour of different interpretations of Platonism,' he reported to Lionel Johnson. 'Oscar implores me, with outspread arms and tears in his eyes, to let my soul alone and cultivate my body for six weeks... Bosie is beautiful and fascinating, but quite wicked. He is enchanted by Plato's sketch of democratic man, and no arguments of mine will induce him to believe in any absolute standards of ethics or of anything else.'[20]

Douglas was also distracted with his editorial duties for *The Spirit Lamp*, conducting a copious correspondence by telegram. The periodical, abandoning all absolute ethical standards, had been developing an increasingly homosexual – or 'Uranian' – tone over its recent issues. Douglas had solicited contributions from both John Addington Symonds and Lord Arthur Somerset. It declared itself as a magazine dedicated to 'the new culture' – a coded phrase referring to the promotion of same-sex relations between men.[21] Wilde certainly approved of the venture, and Bosie's part in it. He provided one of his quasi-biblical prose poems – 'The House of Judgment' – for the forthcoming issue, and he also encouraged Douglas's own poetic ambitions. Of one love sonnet that Douglas had sent prior to his arrival, Wilde had written with customary exuberance, 'My Own Boy, Your sonnet is quite lovely, and it is a marvel that those red rose-leaf lips of yours should have been made no less for music of song than for madness of kisses. Your slim gilt soul walks between passion and poetry. I know Hyacinthus, whom Apollo loved so madly, was you in Greek days.'[22]

Wilde, for his own part, had the pleasure of receiving, from Paris, the first copies of *Salomé*. He considered that its binding of 'Tyrian purple' looked particularly well against the 'gilt-haired' Douglas. Swinburne, Pater,

Bernard Shaw, William Archer, Edmund Gosse, Florence Stoker and Frankie Forbes-Robertson were among those to whom he sent copies. Although Douglas ensured that *The Spirit Lamp* hailed the play as both 'a daring experiment and a complete success', the public prints were less generous. Having been denied a sight of the play on stage, they stirred themselves to 'stern and indignant condemnation' of the book. *The Times* called it 'an arrangement in blood and ferocity, morbid, *bizarre*, repulsive, and very offensive in its adaptation of scriptural phraseology to situations the reverse of sacred'. Wilde was becoming inured to the 'philistine' hostility of the critics; more distressing was that Pierre Louÿs, to whom he had dedicated the book, sent only a facetious telegram of acknowledgement. 'A drop of froth without wine. How you disappoint me,' Wilde declared. 'It is new to me to think that friendship is more brittle than love is.' Louÿs hastened to repair the fault by composing an elegant sonnet of appreciation. [23]

The regime at Babbacombe broke up towards the end of February in the face of one of Douglas's sudden and hysterical rages – even more ferocious than the one at Bournemouth. What provoked it remains unknown, and was probably insignificant. But it left Wilde shaken and upset. It was a shocking sight to see the boy he loved – and liked to regard as a 'sunbeam' – suddenly transformed, distorted in 'mind and body', 'a thing terrible to look at'. Dodgson, who seems to have returned in time to witness the scene, explained that he – and 'most of the men at Magdalen' – considered Douglas was 'at times... quite irresponsible for what he said and did'. Douglas left the next morning, and Wilde determined that it must mark the end of the relationship. He never (so he claimed later) wished to see or speak to Douglas again.[24]

The sudden calm that descended upon the house must have been striking. Wilde's mind could turn to thoughts of Constance. They had been in daily communication during her travels through Italy. He had been enjoying – at one remove – her discovery (a volume of Ruskin in hand) of the beauties of Tuscan art and Roman splendour. In his own daily letters he encouraged her notion that they might spend the coming autumn together in Florence. But the vision struggled to take form.[25] Douglas only got as far as Bristol before he 'wrote and telegraphed' pleading for a reconciliation. It would become a familiar trope. Once his rages had passed, Bosie seemed to forget them completely. For Wilde, whose world was made of words, the furious insults lived on in the memory. But even so his resolve weakened. As André Gide noted, in the wake of another of Bosie's outbursts, for all Wilde's distress

at such 'terrible' scenes, there was 'a kind of lover's infatuated pleasure in being mastered'.[26] In this instance he relented at once. They met and, on their way up to town, Douglas begged to be taken to the Savoy.[27]

The hotel, the most luxurious in London, stood just off the Strand, close to where Wilde had first lodged when he came down from Oxford. The acme of comfort and modernity, it had opened in 1889, built by Richard D'Oyly Carte from the profits of Gilbert and Sullivan's operas – and of Wilde's American lecture tour too. Carte had installed electric lighting and electric lifts. The bathrooms were numerous and well appointed. César Ritz was the manager, Escoffier the chef. Douglas, it seems, was already an habitué; he and Maurice Schwabe had slept together there on several occasions. And he had a connection with the place through D'Oyly Carte's son, Lucas, a contemporary at both Winchester and Oxford, and another of his regular bedfellows. It was expensive. But Wilde now had money coming in from the US production of *Lady Windermere's Fan*, and hopes that *A Woman of No Importance* would soon be going into rehearsal.[28]

They took adjoining rooms, and embarked on a spree of sybaritic abandon. Though Wilde needed little encouragement when it came to extravagance, Douglas encouraged him. They ran up huge bills in the restaurant. Wilde recalled the 'clear turtle soup – the luscious ortolans wrapped in their crinkled Sicilian vine leaves' and 'the heavy amber-coloured, indeed almost amber-scented champagne'. With Bosie in tow, he found it quite possible to spend as much as £20 simply on 'the ordinary expenses' of an 'ordinary' London day – 'luncheon, dinner, supper, amusements, hansoms and the rest of it'. Originally intending to stay for a couple of nights, Wilde installed himself for a month, in a suite with a sitting room overlooking the river. Douglas came and went, and so did a succession of rent boys. Taylor introduced Wilde to two more young lads, brothers Charlie and William Parker. Charlie, Wilde supposedly declared, 'is the boy for me'. And there were others. Douglas, on his regular visits, would recklessly allow these youths to spend the night in his room, at the risk of the hotel servants seeing them still abed in the morning. Wilde, though, did nothing to diminish the air of licentious abandon. He insisted on kissing the hotel page boys when they delivered him messages, much to their alarm; though, as one remarked, 'he always tips me 2/6'.[29]

The pageant of pleasure was interrupted, but not halted, when Wilde found himself being blackmailed – or 'rented' – by Alfred Wood. It was Douglas's fault, though he refused to acknowledge any responsibility. He had

taken Wood up to Oxford for a few days, and while there Wood had stolen several letters – some written by Wilde, others from Lucas D'Oyly Carte. Wood later claimed that he had found them in the pocket of a suit that had been given to him by Douglas. It was a serious alarm. Wilde was uncertain what letters Wood held. The one describing Bosie's 'rose-leaf lips' as made for the 'madness of kisses' would certainly be compromising. He felt he had no other recourse than to call in George Lewis. It was the second time he had had to consult him on such a matter – and although he may have tried to dress it up as another commission for a 'friend' in trouble, Lewis would have suspected the truth. Nevertheless he undertook to 'settle' Wood 'at once' – and dispatched a solicitor's letter to Wood's lodgings. In fact, though, it was Alfred Taylor, distraught at having been the person to have introduced Wood to Wilde, who negotiated the settlement. He brought the two men together at Little College Street. Wood explained that he only asked for money as he wanted to go to America in order to escape from 'a certain class of person' – a pair of notorious blackmailers – who were seeking to draw him into their schemes. Wilde accepted the story and gave Wood some £30 in return for the three stolen letters. The 'madness of kisses' letter, he noted, was not among them. He was not sure whether to be relieved or perturbed. The experience of being 'rented' was a new and unsettling one. Although he appeared to have 'got through all right' (as Douglas put it), the incident marked another significant downward step. He was, he recognized, beginning to lose Lewis's 'esteem and friendship' – a friendship that stretched back almost fifteen years, and had sustained and directed much of his London life.[30]

There were other ruptures. Gray broke with him, after a period of mounting emotional turmoil and distress. The young poet had – shortly before he met Wilde – converted to Roman Catholicism, but then, in the wake of that step, had immediately embarked on what he described as a deliberate 'course of sin', immersing himself in the world and its pleasures. His time as Wilde's devoted disciple had marked that course. 'Michael Field', to whom, many years later, Gray confided something of his past life, understood that his indulgence in 'exotic habits' had been limited enough – 'not so much sinning' as 'conversing with sin'. But, even so, it had provoked its reaction. The death of his father perhaps heightened Gray's sense of remorse. And Wilde's growing absorption by Lord Alfred Douglas almost certainly played its part too. Gray seems to have suffered some sort of breakdown at the end of 1892. To Sherard he confessed fears of 'death, madness, epilepsy and

other horrors'. Wilde was not on hand to offer support or assistance. His place was readily taken by André Raffalovich; he became Gray's devoted friend and protector. Although there was real generosity in his actions, Raffalovich perhaps enjoyed too the idea of drawing away one of Wilde's most conspicuous protégés. The old ties were soon broken. The *Silverpoints* contract was redrafted, with Wilde's contribution no longer required. Although one of the poems in the volume remained dedicated 'to Oscar Wilde', it was valedictory gesture. On 16 March Gray wrote to Pierre Louÿs confirming that his 'falling out with Oscar' was 'absolute'.[31]

Edward Shelley was another casualty. He turned up at the Savoy lamenting that he had lost his place at the Bodley Head. Rumours of his relationship with Wilde – while provoking the ribald amusement of his fellow clerks, who took to calling him 'Miss Oscar' and 'Mrs Wilde' – had scandalized Elkin Mathews, and provoked his dismissal. He, too, was now determined to make a break with the past. But his visit to the Savoy did not go well. He quarrelled with Wilde – perhaps because Wilde made a pass at him. But then, only days later, when his father threw him out of the house (again over his friendship with Wilde), he wrote pleadingly to Wilde for money and help. Within the small world of literary London Wilde's activities were a matter of common rumour, if not common knowledge. Both Le Gallienne and Lane – though they maintained their own apparently friendly relations with Wilde – urged Shelley to break with him.[32]

One other figure removed from the equation was Maurice Schwabe. He had been sent to Australia by his despairing parents at the beginning of March, in the hope that he would make a fresh start there. He had ideas of joining the church. Douglas was distraught to lose his 'darling Pretty', and sent several impassioned letters after him – along with a bangle ('Please darling never take [it] off'). He was, though, soon consoled by a new and close friendship with Robbie Ross. Wilde brought them together and they at once established a bond based – it seems – on their shared predilection for handsome public school boys.[33]

Wilde now made scant effort to hide his own tastes or proclivities. He was growing rapidly reckless. One observer noted him at the Empire Music Hall, with Bosie 'pressed against him' in a most 'improper' fashion. Frank Harris was appalled to come across him one evening at the Café Royal, throned in a corner seat between two 'quite common' youths ('in fact they looked like grooms'). He was informing them – 'if you please!' – about the ancient Olympic games. It was a bravura display of impassioned eloquence

that made the sun-baked palestra shimmer into life – at least until one of the youths asked: 'Did you sy they was nikid?'

'Of course,' Oscar replied. 'Nude: clothed only in sunshine and beauty.'

As the lad giggled 'Oh my', Harris and his companion fled. It was no surprise that the Marquess of Queensberry had come to revise his good opinion of Wilde, and was once more demanding that Bosie break off the friendship. It was a demand that Bosie ignored.[34]

Wilde stayed on at the Savoy – to the growing dismay of the management – until 29 March.[35] He was not back at Tite Street to welcome Constance when she returned from her Italian trip on 21 March. And, on leaving the Savoy, instead of going home, he moved to the Hotel Albemarle, to be on hand when rehearsals of his play began at the Haymarket the following week. Douglas came with him.[36] Pierre Louÿs, over in London, was distressed by the scene one morning when Constance arrived in tears at Wilde's rooms, bringing the post from Tite Street.[37] To the suggestion that he might return home, he replied that he had been away so long that he had forgotten the number of the house.[38]

2

Feasting with Panthers

Mrs Allonby: 'Have you tried a good reputation?'
Lord Illingworth: 'It is one of the many annoyances to which
I have never been subjected.'

OSCAR WILDE, *A WOMAN OF NO IMPORTANCE*

Wilde buried his own heartlessness amid the preparations for *A Woman of No Importance*. He was a constant presence at the theatre over the next three weeks. When Tree was asked if the play was being rehearsed 'with the assistance of Wilde', he replied, 'with the interference of Wilde'. There certainly were moments of tension. But there was also much useful collaboration. Wilde consented to numerous suggested cuts, and made several telling additions to the text. Tree was amazed at the way he would retire 'into a corner of the theatre and shortly emerg[e] with a completely new scene bristling with wit and epigram'. He also added to the fun. When, one morning, the rehearsal was interrupted by a terrific crash, Wilde responded to the moment by announcing that the crash was merely some of H. A. Jones's dialogue that 'had fallen flat'.

It was a convivial time. Wilde often joined the generous-spirited Tree and the other actors for lunch at the Continental Hotel on Lower Regent Street. Among his friends in the cast was 'Bernie' Beere, who was playing Mrs Arbuthnot. Tree was relishing his role as Lord Illingworth. Having

begun his career imitating Wilde in *Where's the Cat?* he could now give
an even richer account of Wilde's manner, as the witty and cynical peer.
His performance was inclined to extend beyond the stage. He would jot
down Wilde's impromptu witticisms in his notebook for later use, and even
began coining his own variations upon them. 'Ah,' Wilde declared, 'every
day dear Herbert becomes *de plus en plus Oscarisé*; it is a wonderful case of
Nature imitating Art.'

Perhaps the imitation needed to go further. When the actor-manager
Squire Bancroft inquired whether Tree would be good in the part, Wilde
disloyally replied: 'Good? No.' 'Surely not bad?' Bancroft countered. 'Bad?
No.' 'Indifferent, then?' 'No, not indifferent.' 'Then what on earth will he
be?' 'In the strictest confidence... but you will not repeat this?' 'Not a word.'
'Then I will whisper in your deaf ear. Tree will be... we must face it manfully... he will be Tree.'[1]

The opening night on 19 April quite matched the glamour of *Lady Windermere's Fan*. As it was a Wednesday parliament was not sitting, so many leading
political 'notabilities' were able to be there. Setting aside all differences on
the Irish question, Balfour was in Wilde's own box, together with George
Wyndham and the Countess of Grosvenor. Cyril Flower – recently ennobled
as Lord Battersea – sat opposite. George Lewis, Burne-Jones, Alma-Tadema,
Mrs Jopling, Conan Doyle, Le Gallienne and even Swinburne swelled the
ranks of talent. Willie, too, was in attendance.

The audience, it was clear, loved the play. At the end there were calls for
the author – although when Wilde appeared to take his bow, some 'hoots
and hisses' mingled with the cheers. The reasons for this were not given:
it has been suggested that Hester Worsley's line about 'English society'
lying 'like a leper in purple... a dead thing smeared with gold', might have
offended the patriotic sensibilities of the pit. There were calls from the
'gods' for Wilde to return and speak. But, mindful of his 'mixed reception,'
he declined. It was left to Tree – having declared his own pride in being
connected with 'such a work of art' – to report that Wilde had already
departed the auditorium.[2]

Backstage Wilde congratulated the cast, and they congratulated him. He
enthused to Tree, 'I shall always regard you as the best critic of my plays.'
'But,' Tree said, 'I have never criticized your plays.' 'That's why,' Oscar
answered complacently. The press response was, again, wilfully ungenerous. As one friend noted, 'How the critics attack gentle Oscar.' With the
exceptions of William Archer in the *World* and A. B. Walkley in the *Speaker*

'the rest have scarcely tried to write about the play at all. They have simply abused Oscar.' But even hostile critics had to allow that the play would prove popular. And its prospects were further enhanced when the Prince of Wales attended the second night. He was reported to have told Wilde not to alter 'a single line', drawing the reply, 'Sire, your wish is my command' – and the later observation: 'What a splendid country where princes understand poets.'[3] Wilde, it was clear, had been able to repeat the magic of *Lady Windermere's Fan*. With full houses and an advantageous royalty arrangement, Wilde could look forward to earning as much as £200 a week – substantially more than he had taken even from his first success.[4]

But the euphoria of the moment was immediately punctured. On the day after the opening night, Tree passed Wilde a piece of paper. It had been handed to him in the street – headed, 'Kindly give this letter to Mr Oscar Wilde and oblige yours [signature illegible].' Tree noted that the sentiments expressed might be open to misconstruction. The missive was a copy of Wilde's 'madness of kisses' letter. To Tree's suggestion that it could be 'dangerous', Wilde affected a laughing unconcern, claiming that the letter was a 'prose poem' and 'if put into verse might be printed in such a respectable anthology as the *Golden Treasury*'. 'Yes,' Tree replied, 'But it is not in verse.' 'That no doubt explains why it is not in the *Golden Treasury*,' Wilde replied. Such insouciance, however, was put on. A demand for money, Wilde knew, was sure to follow. And soon enough he was approached in the street by a man who said he wanted to speak about a letter in his possession. Wilde claimed he was too busy with the play to be bothered with such matters. He needed time.[5]

Following the line that he had taken with Tree, he and Douglas devised a plan. The letter – with its references to Hyacinthus and Apollo – was indeed so effusive as to be more like a work of literature than a regular communication. Its artistic excess could be turned to advantage. Pierre Louÿs was asked to transform the text into a sonnet – a French poetic version of Wilde's 'prose poem'. It could then be published, if not in the *Golden Treasury*, in *The Spirit Lamp*. By making the letter public, they sought to destroy its power. No one had been blackmailed over a published poem. Louÿs – despite his growing misgivings about Wilde's relationship with Douglas – agreed to undertake the task. His translation would appear, barely two weeks later, in *The Spirit Lamp*'s May number, under the heading, 'A letter written in prose poetry by Mr Oscar Wilde to a friend and translated in the rhymed poetry by a poet of no importance.'

Wilde was so far prepared when, some days later, he received a caller at
Tite Street (to which he had finally returned). At about quarter to eight in the
evening, shortly before dinner, Wilde's servant announced that a Mr Allen
was in the hall, wishing to see him 'on particular business'. Wilde went down
to meet the caller. As he later told Frank Harris, something in the man's
manner told him that here was 'the real enemy'. Mr Allen informed him that
he was in possession of a letter of Wilde's that he might want to have back.
'I suppose you mean my beautiful letter to Lord Alfred Douglas,' Wilde said.
'If you had not been so foolish as to send a copy of it to Mr Beerbohm Tree,
I should have been glad to have paid you a large sum for it, as I consider it
to be a work of art.' The bravado was impressive; as Wilde later admitted,
throughout the encounter, 'my body seemed empty with fear'. 'A very
curious construction could be put on that letter,' Allen said. 'No doubt, no
doubt,' Wilde replied lightly, 'Art is rarely intelligible to the criminal classes.'
'A man has offered me £60 for it,' Allen countered defiantly. 'You should take
the offer,' Wilde said. '£60 is a great price. I myself have never received such
a large sum for any prose work of that length. But I am glad to find that
there is someone in England who will pay such a large sum for a letter of
mine.' Allen replied weakly that the man was 'out of town'. Pressing home
what seemed to be his advantage, Wilde said, 'He will no doubt return, and
I don't care for the letter at all.' As Wilde sought to terminate the interview,
Allen changed tack, and began to plead that he was very poor, and had been
put to considerable expense in trying to track Wilde down. Wilde presented
Allen with half a sovereign to relieve his 'distress', while assuring him that he
really had no interest in the letter – which was, indeed, soon to be published
in 'a delightful magazine'. 'I will,' he added, 'send you a copy.'

Despite this brave parting shot, the encounter left Wilde shaken and
crowded with 'vague apprehensions'. And his nerves were further unsettled,
when, five minutes later, there was another knock on the door. It was a
youth named Cliburn. He had come about 'a letter of Allen's'. 'I cannot be
bothered any more about that letter,' Wilde told him. 'I don't care tuppence
about it.' To Wilde's great surprise, Cliburn then produced the letter from
his pocket, saying, 'Allen has asked me to give it back to you.' 'Why does he
give it back to me?' Wilde asked carelessly. 'He says you were kind to him
and that it's no use trying to "rent" you; you only laugh at us.' Wilde made
a show of inspecting the much-creased and soiled document, remarking,
'I think it quite unpardonable that better care was not taken of an original
manuscript of mine.' Accepting Cliburn's apologies, he presented him too

with half a sovereign, saying, 'I am afraid you are leading a wonderfully wicked life.' 'There is good and bad in every one of us, Mr Wilde,' Cliburn stated. 'You are a born philosopher,' replied Wilde.[6]

The incident had been alarming, but Wilde seemed to have survived. And as it receded, he drew from it a sense of power, and even an erotic excitement: he had outfaced 'the bold scheming enchanting' panthers. Details of the encounter, however, began to leak out, fuelling the fire of gossip. The rumours about Wilde's sexual tastes and sexual adventures were becoming increasingly widespread.[7] There remained, though, always an element of doubt. There were many – both 'friends and the friends of friends' – who dismissed the tales, assuming they were merely part of his pose: that 'It was only Oscar... He talks about it, but he does not do it.' For others – rather more worldly – his sexual tastes were a matter for amused discussion, but no more. What he did in private was his own affair.[8]

If some old friends did begin to detach themselves, new ones hurried to replace them. There were young actors and recent graduates who surrounded Wilde with a chorus of approval and even adoration. But there were also artists and writers of the rising generation, who – besides admiration – offered something more challenging. William Rothenstein had returned to England, and to London. At rehearsals for *A Woman of No Importance*, Wilde came to know Tree's diminutive half-brother, Max Beerbohm, then an undergraduate at Oxford. Beerbohm, an extraordinarily precocious talent as both a writer and caricaturist, had a sort of cult of Wilde, borrowing aspects of his style, his wit and his pose. But this admiration was always tinged with a subversive gloss. 'Did I tell you about Oscar at the Restaurant?' he asked his friend Reggie Turner:

> He ordered a watercress sandwich: which in due course was brought to him: not a thin, diaphanous green thing such as he had meant but a very stout satisfying article of food. This he ate with assumed disgust (but evident relish) and when he payed [*sic*] the waiter, he said, 'Tell the cook of this restaurant with the compliments of Mr Oscar Wilde that these are the very worst sandwiches in the whole world and that, when I ask for a watercress sandwich, I do not mean a loaf of bread with a field in the middle of it.'

And it was not only food in which Wilde overindulged. 'I am sorry to say that Oscar drinks far more than he ought,' Beerbohm also reported. 'Indeed

the first time I saw him, after all that long period of distant adoration and reverence, he was in a hopeless sate of intoxication... I think he will die of apoplexy on the first night of the play.' Something of this tone of ironic appraisal informed a spoof essay – 'Oscar Wilde by An American' – that Beerbohm produced for the *Anglo-American Times*. Wilde pronounced it 'incomparably brilliant' – even if he was stung by its lightly satiric touch.[9]

No less precocious, and no less prone to ironic appraisal, was the twenty-one-year-old artist Aubrey Beardsley, a recent 'discovery' of Robbie Ross's. Beardsley, then at the outset of his career, had produced an extraordinary drawing in pen and ink depicting the climax of *Salomé*. Wilde was impressed by the highly stylized 'japonesque' image of the princess preparing to kiss the severed head of John the Baptist. He was impressed too by the angular, consumptive, yet poised figure of the artist. In acknowledgement of both he presented Beardsley with a copy of the French edition of the play, inscribed, 'March 93. For Aubrey: for the only artist who, besides myself, knows what the dance of the seven veils is, and can see that invisible dance. Oscar.'[10]

Wilde at once began to consider Beardsley's potential as an illustrator of his own work. When Gray's *Silverpoints* was published that month, with its elegant Ricketts cover, its modishly sparse text and its modishly wide margins, Ada Leverson suggested that Wilde should go a step further and produce 'a book *all* margin; full of beautiful unwritten thoughts'. Wilde approved, telling her, 'It shall be dedicated to you, and the unwritten text illustrated by Aubrey Beardsley. There must be five hundred signed copies for particular friends, six for the general public, and one for America.' Soon afterwards, when Wilde convinced Mathews and Lane to bring out an English-language edition of *Salome*, it was arranged that Beardsley would provide ten pen-and-ink illustrations and a cover design.[11]

The commission did not mark a desertion of Ricketts and Shannon by Wilde. They remained involved in his other publishing projects of the moment. Despite certain irritations over late payments and advertising budgets, Wilde had been impressed by Lane and Mathews' handling of his books, and negotiations were entered into for the Bodley Head to produce his entire oeuvre. Besides the English version of *Salome*, there was to be a uniform edition of Wilde's plays – *Lady Windermere's Fan*, *A Woman of No Importance* and *The Duchess of Padua* (*Vera* seems to have been consigned to obscurity) – with bindings designed by Shannon. *The Duchess of Padua*, having not yet been performed in Britain, would have an introduction by Wilde's friend, the American poet Edgar Fawcett. It was also envisaged

that Ricketts, once he had finished work on 'The Sphinx', would design a cover and initial letters for an edition of 'The Incomparable History of Mr. W. H.'. The scheme – if it could be achieved – seemed to offer Wilde an impressive literary permanence.[12]

Douglas, however, took precedence. Wilde spent a succession of week-ends at Oxford, staying at the rooms on the High Street that Douglas shared with his friend Lord Encombe. There were almost nightly dinners in his honour, given by members of *The Spirit Lamp* coterie. Wilde was delighted to be back at his alma mater, surrounded by eager young listeners. He regaled them with ironic tales of self-sacrifice: of Lydia and Metellus, patrician lovers and converts to the early church, who were condemned to death as Christians, but, despite each having lost their faith in prison, felt they could not save themselves by renouncing their religion, as they believed it would break the other's heart. 'And so when the appointed day came, in their turn Lydia and Metellus were thrown to the wild beasts in the Circus – and thus they both died for a Faith in which they did not believe.' He told of Pope John XXII, who, on his way to meet his mistress, stops at a little church where, sitting in the confessional, he hears the confession of a man who has undertaken to assassinate him. Having assured the would-be killer that God will forgive him even for this great crime, the pope then proceeds to his tryst. As he embraces his mistress, the assassin steps from the shadows and stabs him. 'With a groan he fell to the ground – a dying man. Then with a supreme effort he raised his hand, and, looking at his assailant, said in the last words of the Absolution: "*Quod ego possum et tu eges, absolve te.*"'

Wilde's presence in Oxford provoked a satirical attack in an undergraduate periodical, the *Ephemeral*, produced on successive days during Eights Week. One of the two editors (Arthur Cunliffe) contributed a parodic account of 'Ossian Savage's New Play' ('[it] was progressing fast and well as usual, though it had not yet got a plot. The plot came afterwards in Ossian's plays with the "finishing touches",' etc.). The skit, though gentle enough, described the playwright as 'a man of coarse habit of body and of coarser habits of mind', a 'spiteful' jibe that provoked Douglas into a 'full blooded correspondence' over the paper's subsequent issues. And although both editors offered qualified apologies, Cunliffe defended his use of the adjective 'coarse' in relation to Wilde's 'mental tendencies' as revealed in his published works.

Nevertheless Hamilton Grant (Cunliffe's co-editor) agreed to meet Wilde at dinner in Douglas's rooms; like so many others, he was soon won over.

Wilde greeted him winningly with, 'I hear that you are called "Gragger."
But this is dreadful. It must not go on. We must find a new name for you,
something beautiful and worthy and Scottish.' And when, at the end of the
meal, Grant produced a cigar (to distinguish himself from the 'perfectly
dressed effeminate types' who had been smoking gold-tipped cigarettes
throughout the proceedings), Wilde stilled the cries of protest, saying,
'How too terrible of you! But we shall call it a nut-brown cigarette – and
you shall smoke it.' After another dinner, held in rooms on St Giles', when
Wilde's presence on the first-floor balcony had attracted a small but rowdy
crowd of townspeople, shouting 'Hoscar – let's 'ave a speech, Hauthor,
Hauthor, Hoscar, Hoscar!', Grant and a friend had sallied forth to disperse
them. Wilde hailed their triumphant return with, 'You are magnificent –
you are giants – giants with souls.'[13]

Soulful Scottish giants were not the only attractions of Oxford. At
Douglas's lodgings there was a seventeen-year-old servant boy called Walter
Grainger. It is hard to suppose that Douglas had not already had sex with
him; Wilde certainly did so during his regular weekend visits. Grainger later
recounted how, over successive days, when he took a morning cup of tea
to Wilde's bedroom, Wilde first kissed him, then played with his 'private
parts', and finally induced him to lie on the bed where 'he placed his penis
between my legs and satisfied himself'. On giving Grainger ten shillings
after one of these encounters, Wilde stressed the need for discretion. His
own behaviour, though, was anything but discreet.[14]

Pierre Louÿs had been upset by what he had seen in London. He had not
cared at all for Douglas, and disapproved of his relationship with Wilde. The
shared (or adjoining) bedrooms at the Albemarle left no room for doubt
about its nature, even before Wilde's boast that he had been 'married three
times in [his] life, once to a woman and twice to men'. Worse, though,
than this reckless flaunting of convention, was the thoughtless cruelty to
Constance that Louÿs witnessed. He confided these misgivings to Henri
de Régnier, who wasted little time in sharing them with others. Goncourt
delightedly recorded in his journal on 30 April: 'Ah you don't know?' (said de
Régnier, when Oscar Wilde's name was mentioned), 'Well, he's not hiding
it himself. Yes, he admits that he is a pederast... following the success of his
play in London, he left his wife and three [sic] children and set himself up in
a hotel, where he is living conjugally with a young English lord.'

In a city dedicated to gossip, Wilde's sexual proclivities became, henceforth, an abiding theme. Goncourt suspected that his pederasty was an

hommage to – if not a plagiarism of – Verlaine (of whom Wilde often spoke eulogistically); or perhaps a tribute to the perverted English nobleman 'Lord Annandale' in Goncourt's own novel *La Faustin*. There was much debate as to whether Wilde was 'actif' or 'passif' in his sexual relations with men – the majority supposing the former; though one commentator declared that he must be 'passif' as only then does a man 'encounter a pleasure that he does not enjoy with a woman'.[15]

For Louÿs, though, Wilde's behaviour was the cause of real anguish. When Wilde was over in France at the end of May, Louÿs called on him at his hotel and urged him to break the connection with Douglas. It was a futile interview. Forced to choose between Louÿs and Bosie, Wilde – as he later put it – 'chose at once the meaner nature and the baser mind'. 'Adieu, Pierre Louÿs,' Wilde said sorrowfully at the close of the encounter, 'Je voulais avoir un ami; je n'aurai plus que des amants' ('I had hoped for a friend; from now on I will have only lovers').[16]

3

Brief Summer Months

'Live for the present and the future.'

OSCAR WILDE

Wilde soon returned to England and to the demands of his ever-exacting lover. Douglas, claiming illness, failed to take his degree that June. His parents and the college authorities were disappointed, though Wilde congratulated him on choosing – like Swinburne – to remain an undergraduate all his life. Distractions nevertheless were called for. At Douglas's prompting Wilde took a lease on The Cottage, a picturesque house on the Thames at Goring. There was a suggestion that Wilde would be able to work there: his play for Hare was not progressing as well as the *Ephemeral* had suggested. But the overriding concerns were, it seemed, to ensure comfort and luxury. Wilde allowed Douglas to oversee the ordering of the supplies and the hiring of the (eight) servants; the former involved copious amounts of champagne, the latter included the Queensberrys' old family butler, and young Walter Grainger from Oxford.[1]

That summer was extremely hot, and it was pleasant to be out on the river. Wilde ensured that punts, skiffs and a canoe were available; although tennis was deemed too exhausting, croquet offered a diversion. Constance brought Cyril down, together with a governess. There was a

constant stream of visitors from London and Oxford. Arthur Clifton and his wife came. The young would-be poet Theodore Wratislaw enjoyed a memorable weekend visit. Bosie's college fellows arrived in relay, while Willie – and his friend, 'the fascinating Dan' – had to be put off, so full was the house. Oscar, with typical generosity, compensated by affecting horror at the news that Willie had taken to smoking American cigarettes: 'I am greatly distressed... You really must not do anything so horrid. Charming people should smoke gold-tipped cigarettes or die, so I enclose you a small piece of paper, for which reckless bankers may give you gold, as I don't want you to die.' George Grossmith and his wife had a house nearby, and regularly joined the croquet parties and evening 'theatricals'. The Henley Regatta at the beginning of July provided 'fireworks of surpassing beauty'.[2]

But, for all this, the atmosphere was oppressive – sometimes literally so. Apocalyptic thunderstorms provided regular interruptions to the brooding heat. The servants, besides making inroads into the champagne (much to Wilde's amusement), could not get on together. Scenes were frequent. After the cosy domesticity of Cromer the previous year, Constance felt excluded in an atmosphere dominated by Douglas, his wants, his friends, his demands. Oscar, she complained, 'so nice to others' was 'so cold' to her. She eventually fled, leaving Cyril and his governess behind.[3]*

A bacchanalian spirit prevailed in her absence. The vicar called one day to find Wilde sitting wrapped in a bath towel, and Bosie lying naked on the lawn; they had been dousing each other with the hosepipe to cool off. At the sight of this 'perfectly Greek scene', the poor clergyman turned very red and left. Wilde was sleeping regularly with Walter Grainger, a fact that was soon known by the other servants, and became the gossip below stairs. The governess, Gertrude Simmonds, was very much surprised to notice Wilde, on the night of the regatta, with his arm on the shoulder the house boat-boy. The locals, too, were disapproving of the goings on at The Cottage. There was hostility in the village: the local publican recalled that there were those who wanted to punch Wilde. Back in London 'weird stories' of the life at Goring began to circulate.[4]

Wilde tried to work, but not very hard. Nothing got done. To Ricketts he confessed 'the river-gods have lured me to devote myself to a Canadian

---

* Constance's growing irritation with Wilde led to him humorously dubbing her 'Mrs Cantankeray', in *hommage* to the title character of A. W. Pinero's sensational drama *The Second Mrs Tanqueray*, which opened at the St James's Theatre on 27 May 1893.

canoe, in which I paddle about. It is curved like a flower.' He claimed to
Lady Randolph Churchill that his progress was hampered because he had
'no pen!'. Bosie offered a constant distraction. There were the now familiar
outbursts of temper. Wilde later reminded Douglas how – after one 'dreadful' scene – 'we stood on the level croquet-ground with the pretty lawn
all round us, [me] pointing out to you that we were spoiling each other's
lives, that you were absolutely ruining mine and that I evidently was not
making you really happy, and that an irrevocable parting, a complete
separation was the one wise philosophic thing to do. You went sullenly
after luncheon, leaving one of your most offensive letters behind with the
butler to be handed to me after your departure.' But then, of course, before
'three days had elapsed', Bosie was telegraphing from London begging to
be forgiven. And, of course, Wilde forgave him.[5] To encourage Douglas
into some sort of productivity, and to link their names in a single artistic
endeavour, Wilde suggested that Bosie should provide the translation for
the planned English-language edition of *Salome*. It gave him a task, even if
he was slow to take it up.

The high life at Goring – which Wilde estimated was costing some £445
a month – appeared to be sustained by the continuing success of *A Woman of
No Importance*. Wilde travelled to Birmingham on 14 August for the opening
night of the play's provincial summer tour, with Lewis Waller taking the role
of Lord Illingworth. And two nights later Wilde went up to London with
Bosie for the closing night of the Haymarket run. They supped afterwards
with Ross, Beerbohm and Beardsley. Beerbohm reported to Turner that
Wilde was both inebriated and 'fatuous': 'He called Mrs Beere "Juno-like"
and Kemble "Olympian quite" and waved a cigarette round and round his
head. Of course I would rather see Oscar free than sober, but still... I felt
quite repelled.'[6]

But if Beerbohm considered that Wilde was in a bad state, so too did
Wilde. His health was causing him concern. It may have been at this
moment that he consulted Sir William Dalby, an eminent London ear
specialist. Although Wilde seems to have been suffering from an infection
of the middle ear and a degree of hearing impairment, Danby reassured
him that 'with proper care there was no reason at all why he should lose
his hearing'.[7]

At the end of August, encouraged by his doctor, Wilde went to Dinard,
on the Brittany coast, for a fortnight. He travelled alone, needing – as he
later put it – a relief from the 'terrible strain' of Douglas's company. His

hopes of 'seclusion and rest', however, were not entirely fulfilled. He found himself swept up into a 'round of gaiety' and was soon complaining of the late hours. Among the diversions he attended was a drawing-room performance given by his adored Aimée Lowther. Nevertheless change and sea-air created a sense of new hopes and possibilities. He told a journalist who accosted him on the beach, 'I am thinking of publishing a book of maxims called *Oscariana*, which may or may not be acceptable to the thinking world. My idea is that every day should begin [with] a new thought, a fresh idea, and that "yesterday" should be a thing of the past. Forget everything unpleasant in the past and live for the present and future.'[8]

Wilde strove to embody his own philosophy. A young barrister, Chartres Biron, recorded his encounter with Wilde at Dinard that summer at a modest and conventional family dinner. 'There were then unpleasant rumours about Wilde,' Biron recalled, 'and I was strongly prejudiced against him. His appearance was not in his favour, heavy and sensual; but directly he spoke his whole face lit up, the aspect of the man changed and he seemed a different personality.' The past was obliterated by the present. Though Wilde held the company 'spellbound,' he did not monopolize: his wit, and also his 'wisdom', arose from the 'general conversation'. He impressed with his comments on Browning's supposed 'obscurity', explaining, 'You must remember, every great truth is unintelligible. Then the master wants an audience and waters it down to the level of a disciple; then it becomes popular and is lost.' He amused with his advice that, in life, instead of beginning at the bottom of the ladder and working one's way up, it was better to 'begin at the top and sit upon it'.[9]

Wilde returned to England via Jersey, where the touring production of *A Woman of No Importance* was being played. During his absence Douglas had completed the translation of *Salomé*: unfortunately, though, Wilde was unimpressed. The work was full of 'schoolboy faults' ('On ne doit regarder que dans les miroirs' had, for instance, been rendered, 'One must not look at mirrors' rather than 'One should look only in mirrors'). Douglas – who had been 'rather proud' of his effort – did not take criticism well. The usual violent letters of resentment and abuse followed. In one of them Douglas asserted that he was under 'no intellectual obligation of any kind' to Wilde. He refused to accept Wilde's corrections. To John Lane he wrote, washing his hands of the project, declaring, 'I cannot consent to have my work altered and edited, and thus to become a mere machine for doing the rough work of translation... My private opinion is that unless Oscar translates

it himself, he will not be satisfied.' It seems, though, that Beardsley then put himself forward as a possible translator, and Wilde consented to let him try.[10]

Wilde had his own literary project to focus on. He had still not written his comedy for Hare, although the initial deadline was now passed, and news of the play had been leaked in the press. In an effort to precipitate himself into action he took rooms at a private hotel in St James's Place, as a space where he could work each day away from home. It proved a productive setting; within a week he had completed the first act of what would be *An Ideal Husband*. But the sanctum was soon invaded. His initial ire over the *Salomé* translation having abated, Bosie would turn up daily at noon, and stay 'smoking cigarettes and chattering till 1.30'. Then – as Wilde later reminded him – 'I had to take you out to luncheon at the Café Royal or the Berkeley. Luncheon with its liqueurs lasted usually till 3.30. For an hour you retired to White's. At tea-time you appeared again, and stayed till it was time to dress for dinner. You dined with me either at the Savoy or at Tite Street. We did not separate as a rule till after midnight, as supper at Willis's had to wind up the entrancing day.'[11]

Of course Wilde consented to such distractions, and enjoyed them too. He always found it easy not to work. The good resolutions of Dinard were soon forgotten in the pursuit of pleasure. Charles Parker came to St James's Place for regular assignations. New friendships were nurtured, too. Wilde – together with Douglas – saw much of the wealthy would-be novelist George Ives. A cricket-loving Hellenist and a convinced lover of men, Ives was set on establishing a secret society to promote his idealized vision of the Uranian 'new culture' – or 'the Cause' – as he dubbed it. The society was to be named 'The Order of Chaeronea' after a celebrated battle of 338 BC in which a military company of Theban male lovers had been annihilated by the Macedonians. As a first step – 'having obtained leave from M[other]' – Ives had shaved off his moustache, on the grounds that it was so 'anti-Hellenic'. Ives hoped to enlist Wilde and Douglas for his new order, though he found both of them hard to fathom.[12]

Wilde's determined un-seriousness bemused him. After a small dinner party at the Savoy he fretted in his diary: '[O.W.] is such a puzzle to me, born it would seem, a teacher, he either cannot or will not give the key to his philosophy, and till I get it I can't understand him. He seems to have no purpose and I am all purpose. Apparently of an elegant refined nature, and talented as few men are, brilliant as a shining jewel, yet he teaches

many things which cannot be held, and which are so false as not even to be dangerous.' Nevertheless he considered that Wilde's 'influence will be considerable'.

Douglas would have been able to support the notion. He told Ives's friend Charles Kains Jackson that 'nobody knows as I do' what Wilde has done for 'the "new culture", the people he has pulled out of the fire, and "seen through" things, not only with money, but by sticking to them when other people wouldn't speak to them. He is the most chivalrous friend in the world, he is the only man I know who would have the courage to put his arm on the shoulder of an ex-convict and walk down Piccadilly with him, and combine with that the wit and the personality to carry it off so well that nobody would mind.' Douglas himself Ives found fascinating. But he thought him set on a course of wilful self-destruction – and even warned him that he 'was indulging in homosexuality to a reckless and highly dangerous degree'. There seemed every chance that he would get himself 'arrested one day'.[13]

Certainly Douglas's latest piece of 'foolishness' had brought him close to disaster. It involved a seventeen-year-old schoolboy 'with wonderful eyes', whom Ross had recently taken up. The boy, Claude Dansey, was on his way back to the 'English College' in Bruges, a school run by a friend of the Ross family, when Douglas 'stole' him from Ross, and installed him at the Hotel Albemarle, sleeping with him over the weekend, and paying for him to sleep with a woman on the Monday night. Dansey returned to Bruges three days late. His tardy arrival provoked an inquiry by the headmaster, which uncovered Dansey's 'indecent' relations with both Douglas and Ross – as well as Ross's earlier seduction of the headmaster's eldest son. Scandal threatened. Ross and Douglas travelled to Bruges in an attempt to negotiate a settlement. Dansey's father, a colonel in the Guards, wanted to prosecute, and was only dissuaded when George Lewis (acting, it seems, for Ross) pointed out that although the perpetrators would 'doubtless get two years' his son would 'get six months' as a willing accomplice. In the end, after various incriminating letters were returned and destroyed, the affair was hushed up. But it had been a very near thing.[14]*

* Claude Dansey (10 September 1876 – 11 June 1947), after a varied military career, went on to become a senior figure in British intelligence, and – as 'Agent Z' – was assistant chief of MI6 during the Second World War. He was knighted in 1943. His later enthusiasm for secretiveness perhaps dated from the experience of having his letters intercepted and read.

The drama, played out during that October, placed a further strain on Wilde's relations with Douglas. Wilde had been obliged to miss a Lloyd family wedding to go over to Calais to 'fetch' Bosie back from the continent. There were fierce rows, and fresh recriminations. Wilde, though, seems to have recognized in the debacle a possible means of breaking the emotionally exhausting and self-destructive cycle: he convinced Douglas that he must go abroad for a while. Ross had been banished, by his despairing family, to Davos in Switzerland, supposedly for two years, in order to avoid what Beerbohm called 'a social relapse'. Wilde wrote to Douglas's mother, suggesting that Bosie had rather lost his way since coming down from Oxford, and urging her to send him out of England – to stay with Lord Cromer, the British Consul-General in Egypt, for several months 'if that could be managed'.[15]

Lady Queensberry leapt at the idea. Her attitude to Wilde had altered. She no longer saw him as a benign mentor, and was only too keen to break up the friendship between him and her son. Conscious that her always-difficult child was becoming yet more difficult, she put it down to Wilde's influence. She had perhaps heard rumours of their life together in London – and, ignorant of Bosie's already established commitment to a course of 'pagan' amorality, suspected that Wilde had played 'the part of Lord Henry Wotton' to her son's 'Dorian'. He was, in her opinion, the 'murderer' of Bosie's 'soul'. Indeed she told Bosie that she would almost like to murder Wilde for what he had done. To Wilde, though, she wrote more temperately, merely seeking an assurance that, if Douglas went abroad, Wilde would not try to visit him there. Piqued at this implied rebuke, Wilde hastened to give her some details of the recent scandal that Douglas had precipitated, and that was the real reason why he needed to be sent away. He asserted that he had no desire ever to see her son again.[16]

It was to be a season of separations. Willie's divorce was finalized that autumn, but in its wake came reports from the American press about his behaviour in New York: his 'simply killing' impersonations of Oscar at the Lotos Club, and his stated plan 'to buy a second-hand copy of Rochefoucauld's *Maxims*' and 'set up a play foundry' of his own, in opposition to his brother. These were new betrayals, and Oscar felt unable to forgive them. The brothers, much to Lady Wilde's distress, were estranged.[17]

Wilde seems to have felt only relief in the face of these breaks. Certainly the imminent prospect of being parted from Bosie acted as tonic. He re-engaged with family life, taking Constance to the theatre three times in one

November week (they particularly enjoyed Sheridan's *School for Scandal*), dining with her at the Albemarle Club, attending a lecture by William Morris on printing, and hosting a small dinner party at Tite Street, a now rare event. Wilde was delighted with the appearance of *Lady Windermere's Fan* in book form that month. Among the letters he received was one from Adela Schuster – a particular favourite among his young women friends – thanking him for 'some hours of the keenest enjoyment I have ever experienced'. Although still ignoring the pressing claims of his new comedy, Wilde did begin work on a 'mystery play' (almost certainly *La Sainte Courtisane*, a Symbolist drama about a beautiful courtesan converted to the religious life by an ascetic hermit – who, himself, is then drawn to the world of sensual pleasure on account of her beauty). Constance and other friends were delighted – and bemused – at this sudden turn of events. Wilde confided to his wife that supernatural forces were involved: he had received a communication from his father's spirit – through 'raps' – at a séance.[18]

With an American production of *A Woman of No Importance* about to begin in New York, Wilde's US agent, Elisabeth Marbury, was urging him to come over for the opening night. It would, she suggested, greatly 'advance the success' of the production. And Wilde might combine his visit with a short lecture tour and gain 'a very large amount of money'. Indeed she put forward so many 'convincing and compelling' reasons that Wilde felt he could not possibly do anything so 'reasonable'. He declined to sail.[19]

Besides he needed to be in London to oversee the troubled gestation of the English edition of *Salome*. The publisher was proposing a 'coarse', 'common' and 'quite impossible' cloth binding for the 'ordinary' edition of the book, and had to be dissuaded. There were other problems too. Wilde found Beardsley's attempted translation of the play even less satisfactory than Bosie's. According to Douglas, he declared it 'utterly hopeless' – and decided that 'he would on second thoughts rather have mine'. It was a decision encouraged by Ross, who had been urging Wilde not to demoralize Douglas at the outset of his literary career. The reversal drew Wilde back into close contact with Bosie. All textual changes still had to be negotiated, Douglas insisting that, if his work were altered, his name should not appear on the title page. In the end Wilde devised an elegant solution, omitting Douglas from the title page, but dedicating the book to 'To My Friend Lord Alfred Bruce Douglas, The Translator Of My Play'. Douglas, in a rare moment of acquiescence, allowed himself to be persuaded that this

arrangement was of 'infinitely greater artistic and literary value' – being 'the difference between the tribute of admiration from an artist and a receipt from a tradesman'.[20]

Beardsley's illustrations were proving scarcely less contentious. Ever subversive, he had smuggled lewd details into many of the pictures. There were phallic candlesticks and garments distorted by obvious erections. Wilde complained that 'dear Aubrey's designs are like the naughty scribbles that a precocious schoolboy makes on the margins of his copy books'. In a couple of instances the too-conspicuous genitalia of the male characters had to be edited out, to ensure that the book could be displayed openly in bookshops. Lane rejected three other drawings outright, leading Beardsley to replace them with three others, which he described to Ross as 'simply beautiful and quite irrelevant'. The illustrator's satiric campaign extended beyond indecencies to caricaturing Wilde: the playwright appeared as King Herod, as a mage heralding the entrance of Herodias, and – more contentiously – as the 'Woman in the Moon' (described in the text as 'mad', 'drunken' and 'seeking everywhere for lovers'). Tensions over both the pictures and the translation led to much feverish debate as the book was readied for the press. 'I can tell you I had a warm time of it between Lane and Oscar and Co.,' Beardsley reported archly to Ross. 'For one week the numbers of telegraph and messenger boys who came to the door was simply scandalous.'[21]

As so often a stressful situation was rendered more stressful by Bosie's vanity and temper. After one 'more than usually revolting' scene – at the end of November – Wilde fled to Paris, giving Constance an 'absurd' excuse and leaving a false address, simply to relieve the torture. In the French capital he was able 'to pour out his soul' to Carlos Blacker, who reported to his fiancée, 'poor fellow... [Oscar] has much to make him unhappy but his grand spirit of optimism will ultimately I am sure carry everything before it'.[22] Wilde's 'grand spirit' had, though, to contend with Douglas's implacable will. Although Wilde felt able to ignore the 'usual telegrams of entreaty and remorse', Bosie's threat not to proceed to Egypt prompted a rapprochement. Wilde agreed to a meeting, and 'under the influence of great emotion' consented to forgive the past (while saying 'nothing at all about the future'). It was enough to secure Bosie's departure for Cairo.[23]

For Wilde the thumbscrew had been removed. For neither the first nor the last time he resolved never to see Douglas again. Queensberry, it

seems, was mollified by the separation.* The pace of life could right itself. He resumed work on his comedy for John Hare; although he had 'grave doubts' that he would be able to convince the actor-manager that it was 'a masterpiece', he was desperate to get it finished. After the extravagances of Goring over the summer he was in sore need of money: 'vulture creditors' were circling. On one humiliating occasion the butcher refused to send round a joint to Tite Street until the bill was settled.

Even after Douglas's departure he continued to see something of George Ives – and, apparently, kissed him on at least one occasion. He had shown, in his own way, a commitment to Ives's 'cause' that November, proudly taking Verlaine around with him, when the poet (pederast and ex-convict) came over to England to give a series of readings. Wilde introduced him at a reception hosted by Lady de Grey and encouraged him to recite his poem 'D'un Prison': the performance, poignant and tragic in its simplicity, had reduced the sophisticated society audience to tears.[24] Old connections were also maintained. Robbie Ross sneaked back to town briefly in December 'lame and bearded!' and ready for dinner at Kettner's. It was perhaps at this juncture that – in order to assist Wilde in his efforts to complete *An Ideal Husband* – he gave him a sheaf of epigrams that he had copied down from Wilde's conversation during his stay at Tite Street back in 1887.[25] Wilde also exerted himself to assist Carlos Blacker, who had fallen out badly with the Duke of Newcastle. The duke had accused him of cheating at cards, and Blacker felt obliged to sue. Wilde consulted with Blacker's solicitor (unfortunately Newcastle had engaged George Lewis), and also sought an interview with Newcastle in an effort to resolve the matter.[26]

Such was Wilde's sense of returning equilibrium that by the end of December he even felt able to write to Bosie, who had been bombarding him

---

* The marquess had been enduring other troubles. That summer he had fallen out with his oldest son, Lord Drumlanrig, an assistant private secretary to Lord Rosebery, the secretary of state for foreign affairs in Gladstone's government. As part of a scheme to increase the Liberal representation in the House of Lords, the twenty-six-year-old Drumlanrig had been raised to the peerage, taking the title Baron Kelhead. Queensberry, still smarting at his own exclusion from the Upper House by his fellow Scottish peers., had come to resent this. His increasingly angry letters on the point, to Gladstone, the Queen and Lord Rosebery, were ignored, convincing him that the whole thing was a plot against him. His rage grew. In August he had travelled to Bad Homburg in the hope of picking a fight in public with the 'Jew pimp' 'liar' and 'Bloody Bugger' Lord Rosebery. It was only due to the intervention of George Lewis and the Prince of Wales that a confrontation was averted.

from Egypt with the inevitable letters of contrition and pleas for attention:
'My dearest Boy,' he declared with a lightly measured affection, 'I am happy
in the knowledge that we are friends again, and that our love has passed
through the shadow and the night of estrangement and sorrow and come
out rose-crowned as of old. Let us always be infinitely dear to each other,
as indeed we have been always.' It seemed safe to make such declarations
with Douglas over 2,000 miles away.* Back in London Wilde threw himself
into the pleasures of the family Christmas. Gertrude Simmonds recalled
him in the Tite Street dining room that year, 'happy as a boy', doling out the
Christmas pudding and pulling crackers.[27]

---

*   Douglas was enjoying himself in Cairo. Among various sexual adventures, he had (so
     he later claimed) a 'romantic meeting' with the forty-four-year-old Herbert Kitchener –
     then a brigadier with the Egyptian army. And to Robbie Ross he wrote describing the
     attractions, and ready accessibility, of the 'beautiful and bright-eyed' local boys. He also
     started work on a 'burlesque (unpublishable of course)' but containing a variation on
     the music hall hit 'Daddy wouldn't buy me a bow-wow' – apropos 'Labby's clause in the
     Criminal Law Amendment Act' – which he thought would be a good song and dance
     number 'for Oscar (in Coster Costume)':

        Labby wouldn't let me have a boy-woy
        Labby wouldn't *etc, etc.*
        I've got a dear old Dutch
        And I like her very much
        But I'd rather have a boy-woy-woy.

4

∞∞∞∞∞∞

Enemies of Romance

'It is not wise to show one's heart to the world.'

OSCAR WILDE

A t the start of 1894 it was reported that Wilde had received an invitation from the superstition-defying Thirteen Club, inviting him to attend a dinner of thirteen courses, to be held on 13 January in Room Number 13 of the Holborn restaurant. He had written back promptly, regretting that he would be unable to attend: 'I love superstitions,' he explained. 'They are the colour element of thought and imagination. They are the opponents of common sense. Common sense is the enemy of romance. The aim of your society seems to be dreadful. Leave us some unreality. Don't make us too offensively sane.'[1]

For Wilde work was the current 'unreality' of choice. As he wrote to Henley, in a letter of condolence following the tragic death of Henley's six-year-old-daughter: 'To work, to work... that is what remains for natures like ours. Work never seems to me a reality, but a way of getting rid of reality.'[2] For the first time in many months he was without distractions: he was able to concentrate, and engage his imagination. *An Ideal Husband* continued to advance; he hoped to have it finished by the end of January.[3]

He regarded the play as something of a departure. Certainly it had more plot than his previous pieces – unfolding a complex and many-sided intrigue in which a British cabinet minister, Sir Robert Chiltern – the supposedly

'Ideal Husband' of the title – stands in danger of having the shady financial dealings of his youth exposed by the scheming adventuress Mrs Cheveley, unless he falls in with her own nefarious money-making plans. Although the character of Lord Goring – Sir Robert's great friend (and Mrs Cheveley's former fiancé) – might be another epigrammatic dandy, Wilde regretted that, unlike his previous plays, 'there is no one like myself' in the piece. In some of his moods he condemned all the characters as 'horrid objective creations of serious folk' and feared that the critics would rush to declare, 'Ah, here is Oscar unlike himself!' But, at other moments, he was ready to admit that he had become 'engrossed' in writing the piece, and that – beneath all the conventions of the well-made melodrama – 'it contain[ed] a great deal of the real Oscar'.[4]

The conventional aspects of the play perhaps stimulated a desire to try out other, less orthodox, forms and effects. Although Constance had described his 'mystery play' as 'not for acting, but to be read' – Wilde seems to have evolved other ideas. He thought *La Sainte Courtisane* could form part of a 'triple bill' of experimental one-act pieces. It was a notion he proposed to the young actor-manager Lewis Waller, who was negotiating with George Alexander for the British touring rights to *Lady Windermere's Fan*, and was looking for additional works for the tour repertory. Wilde already had a possible second piece well in hand – a short Renaissance-set drama in blank verse entitled *The Florentine Tragedy*. Having almost finished both this piece and the *Sainte Courtisane*, Wilde was confident that he could complete the whole triple bill by the end of March.[5]

Overflowing with schemes, he also thought of writing another full-length historical verse tragedy, to build upon the New York 'success' of *The Duchess of Padua*. He approached the American Shakespearean actor Richard Mansfield with a proposal that he should commission *The Cardinal of Avignon*, the Renaissance drama that he had first mooted back in 1882. The play remained unwritten, but Wilde redrafted the scenario, mapping out a tale of thwarted loves and vaulting ambitions, deliberate falsehoods and impassioned suicides.* It was, Wilde considered, the sort of piece that Mansfield could do 'splendidly'.[6]

---

* Among the convolutions of the plot the Cardinal, secretly in love with his beautiful young ward, seeks to break her engagement to a handsome youth in his own retinue by *falsely* informing the boy that the girl is in fact his own long-lost sister. This same plot device occurs in – if it was not borrowed from – *Melmoth the Wanderer*, the novel by Wilde's illustrious relative Charles Maturin.

There was in all this slightly hectic activity – besides the excitement of creation – a pressing need for funds. Money, once more, was tight in Tite Street, and bills were overdue: £13 was still owing from the summer at Goring. There were several threats of legal action. 'London is very dangerous,' Wilde complained; 'writters come out at night and writ one, the roaring of creditors towards dawn is frightful, and solicitors are getting rabies and biting people.' Matters were not helped by the newspapers reporting that Wilde had made £2,000 out of royalties from *Lady Windermere's Fan* in the two years since it opened. That money was long since spent.[7]

Some semblance of literary productivity was maintained with the appearance in February of the English edition of *Salome*. The volume appeared to the press and public as the very distillation of *fin de siècle* decadence. But Wilde was uncomfortably aware that the project had been unbalanced – if not hijacked – by Beardsley's extraordinary illustrations. It was a point made by many of the critics. To Ricketts Wilde might admit 'I admire, [but] I do not like Aubrey's illustrations. They are too Japanese, while my play is Byzantine.' And privately he might even confess to loathing them. To the public, though, he projected an informed enthusiasm. Taking Beardsley to see *The Second Mrs Tanqueray*, he wrote a note Mrs Patrick Campbell, who was playing the title role, asking whether he could bring the artist round to her dressing room so that he might lay a copy of the *édition de luxe* of *Salome* at her feet. 'His drawings,' Wilde declared, 'are quite wonderful.'[8]

Wilde continued to see much of Beardsley (and Beardsley presented the drawing that he subsequently made of Mrs Patrick Campbell to Wilde). But there was a certain tension in the relationship. Wilde was disposed to patronize his precocious protégé. 'Aubrey is too Parisian,' he declared on one occasion; 'he cannot forget that he has been to Dieppe – once.' 'Don't sit on the same chair as Aubrey. It's not compromising' was another of his lines. He even likened him to a 'monstrous orchid'. The effect, however, was strained. Beardsley might borrow something of Wilde's dandified manner and wit (he declared he had caught a chill having left the tassel off his cane), but his powers of assimilation were such that he never appeared to be a mere echo of the 'master'. Indeed Frank Harris, who saw the two men together often, considered that Wilde was more influenced by Beardsley than vice versa. He took from the younger – and much abused – artist a reinforced sense of 'artistic boldness and self-assertion', of 'contempt' for critics and public alike.[9]

Beardsley's 'contempt', it sometimes seemed, might extend even to Wilde

himself. Certainly Wilde was conscious of the artist's sly satirical attitude: the caricatures that had littered *Salome* were followed by others. When a reviewer complained of Beardsley's poor taste in introducing a recognizable likeness of Wilde (wreathed in vine leaves) among the fantastical figures in his frontispiece to John Davidson's *Plays*, the artist had written to the paper suggesting that Wilde was 'surely beautiful enough to stand the test even of portraiture'. Such flourishes, though seemingly playful, contrived to irritate Wilde. At one lunch he declared that, when Beardsley was present, he would henceforth only drink absinthe: 'Absinthe is to all other drinks what Aubrey's drawing are to other pictures; it stands alone; it is like nothing else; it shimmers like southern twilight in opalescent colouring; it has about it the seduction of strange sins... It is just like your drawings, Aubrey; it gets on one's nerves and is cruel.'[10]

There were similar undercurrents in Wilde's friendship with the young Max Beerbohm. Indeed Beerbohm was busy working on a new satirical article about Wilde during the first months of 1894. Entitled 'A Peep into the Past', it professed to be an interview with the half-forgotten 'old gentleman, Oscar Wilde', who had 'at one time' amused the readers of *Punch*. It was shot through with knowing allusions: 'As I was ushered into [his] little study, I fancied that I heard the quickly receding frou-frou of tweed trousers, but my host I found reclining, hale and hearty, though a little dishevelled, upon the sofa.' Despite such dangerous asides, Beerbohm was actually considering the piece for a new periodical – to be called *The Yellow Book* – that John Lane was planning to launch that spring, with Beardsley as art editor and the American novelist Henry Harland as editor. In another small but wounding cut, by the agreement of all concerned, Wilde was to be excluded from the venture.

Ada Leverson, too, sometimes parodied Wilde in her pieces for *Punch*, despite Burnand's determination not to revive a 'cult' of 'the Great Aesthete' in the magazine. Her tone, though, was gentler, chiming with Wilde's notion that successful parody 'requires a light touch... and, oddly enough, a love of the poet whom one caricatures. One's disciples can parody one – nobody else.' And Wilde certainly enjoyed the 'brilliant' sketches that Leverson produced. Nevertheless such pieces contributed in their small way to the re-gathering sense of Wilde as a figure who might be laughed at by the public, and even disparaged.[11]

His position was further compromised by the return of Lord Alfred Douglas that March. If Wilde had felt relief at their separation, Bosie had

been overcome with remorse and longing. He had begun a campaign of letter writing, pleading for a full reconciliation. When Wilde refused to engage, Douglas had persuaded his mother to intercede on his behalf, having striven to convince her that his relationship with Wilde, far from being destructive to his soul, was necessary to his artistic development. And when that failed he turned to Constance. Despite her personal dislike of Douglas, and her awareness of his ill effect on Wilde's character, she took the extraordinary step of urging her husband to write back. Steeped in Christian notions of forgiveness, she could not bear to see him being 'unkind' to a 'friend'. Even so Wilde hesitated. It was only when Douglas hastened to Paris, and from there sent a long and desperate telegram that seemed to hint at suicide, that he relented. They met in the French capital, and over a dinner of mingled tears and champagne the old passion was renewed with all its old force – and with all its the old extravagance too. Wilde calculated that their eight days together in Paris cost him nearly £150. Constance understood too late what she had done. Wilde's failure to write from Paris, or to let her know of his plans, suggested the decisive realignment in his affections.[12]

Wilde and Douglas returned to London for what was supposed to be a brief continuation of their season of pleasure and love. Douglas, while in Cairo, had received the offer of an unpaid diplomatic position from Lord Currie at the embassy in Constantinople, and intended to take it up in June. On their second day back in London, though, Wilde and Bosie were spotted lunching together at the Café Royal by Lord Queensberry. He was shocked to see his son back in England, and in such company. And although he made no comment – and even joined their table – he immediately afterwards wrote to Bosie, expressing his disapproval, first, at his idle way of life and, secondly, at his 'intimacy with this man Wilde'. He demanded that it cease:

Or I will disown you and stop all money supplies. I am not going to try and analyse this intimacy, and I make no charge; but to my mind to pose as thing is as bad as to be it. With my own eyes I saw you both in the most loathsome and disgusting relationship as expressed by your manner and expression... No wonder people are talking as they are. Also I now hear on good authority, but this may false, that his wife is petitioning to divorce him for sodomy and other crimes. Is this true, or do you not know of it? If I thought the actual thing was true, and it became public property, I should be quite justified in shooting him at sight.

These Christian English cowards and men, as they call themselves, want waking up. Your disgusted so-called father, Queensberry.[13]

Douglas did not recognize his father's right to dictate terms to him. Without consulting Wilde he replied by telegram: 'WHAT A FUNNY LITTLE MAN YOU ARE.' He was immensely pleased with this riposte: the line was borrowed from a music hall song of the moment – 'Oh Kicklebury-Brown of Camden Town, What a funny little man you are.' It provoked the expected reaction. 'You impertinent young jacknapes,' Queensberry fired back:

If you send me any more such telegrams, or come with any impertin-ence... I will give you the thrashing you deserve... If I catch you again with that man I will make a public scandal in a way you little dream of; it is already a suppressed one. I prefer an open one, and at any rate I shall not be blamed for allowing such a state of things to go on. Unless this acquaintance ceases I shall carry out my threat and stop all supplies... So you know what to expect.[14]

Wilde found himself in the midst of a conflict between two reckless and intemperate foes, over whom he could exert little influence and no con-trol.* Douglas relished the thought of confrontation; Wilde did not. And he was spared for the moment when Lady Queensberry dispatched Bosie to Florence. While Wilde was envying him the sight of 'Giotto's tower' and Cellini's 'green and gold god', Douglas was asking his friend Kains Jackson for the address of the notorious Lord Arthur Somerset – still in exile after the Cleveland Street Scandal – as well as for other tips regarding 'the eternal quest for beauty to which I am bound!'[15]

Wilde remained in town, lost 'in the purple valleys of despair' about his want of 'gold coins' – although, typically, when approached by the impe-cunious Edward Shelley, he responded generously. 'As he betrayed me

---

*   Queensberry's general rage against the world had been increased by his own personal travails. The previous November he had married a young woman called Ethel Weeden. The marriage had proved a disaster, apparently due to the marquess's inability to con-summate the union. Having been served with divorce papers by his wife (on 9 March) he had filed a counter suit, claiming that the marriage had indeed been consummated, and that he was neither impotent nor frigid. On 10 April, the week after his exchange with Bosie, he had to endure a humiliating medical examination to determine the truth of his statement. His wife had to go through a no less harrowing examination, to establish whether she was a virgin, on 20 April.

grossly I, of course, gave him money and was kind to him,' he explained to Douglas. 'I find that forgiving one's enemies is a most curious morbid pleasure; perhaps I should check it.' There were other irritations. He had to endure the appearance of the first *Yellow Book*: 'It is dull and loathsome,' he told Douglas, 'a great failure. I'm so glad.' The magazine – with its distinctive yellow and black cover by Beardsley – in fact created a sensation and, despite many hostile reviews, sold well. Beerbohm's essay on Wilde did not appear. In its stead he provided a paradoxical 'Defence of Cosmetics'. Wilde thought it 'wonderful… quite delightfully wrong and fascinating'. Despite Wilde's absence from the magazine as either contributor or subject, his association in the public mind with Beardsley and decadence ensured that many assumed he *was* involved. Indeed one review even described *The Yellow Book* as 'the Oscar Wilde of periodicals'.[16]

About *An Ideal Husband* there was frustrating news from Hare: although he seems to have liked the play well enough, it had arrived so late that his forthcoming season at the Garrick had already been scheduled, and it was uncertain when the play could be put on. Hare offered to return the manuscript if they could not agree on a satisfactory way forward. Wilde seized the opportunity to offer the play instead to Lewis Waller, and his partner Harry Morrell: not for their tour, but for a London run. They agreed to pay a handsome advance of £500, undertaking to perform the play before 1 February 1895, in a theatre to be decided upon. This coup was followed by the pleasing news that Miss Marbury had also negotiated a handsome advance for the play's American performing rights from Daniel Frohman.[17]

These arrangements allowed Wilde – at the beginning of May – to travel to Italy. Constance had hoped, the previous year, to be in Florence with her husband; instead Wilde would be there with Douglas. The visit, though, was clandestine. Perhaps to obscure his real destination, he went via Paris, where he spent a few days. Henri de Régnier saw him on the boulevards flanked by two young men. By an unspoken mutual agreement they did not greet each other.[18]

In Florence Wilde saw much of Bernard Berenson and his mistress (later wife) Mary Costelloe, who were now living in the city. Mary took him to call on his old acquaintance, Violet Paget (who now wrote under the name Vernon Lee), and her brother, the invalid poet Eugene Lee Hamilton. 'It was a great success,' she reported to her sister. 'Oscar talked like an angel, and they all fell in love with him – even Vernon, who had hated him almost as bitterly as he had hated her.' He, on his part, was charmed with her,

finding her less 'restless and self-assertive' than when he had known her in London. 'Oscar,' as Costello explained, 'likes people without souls, or else with great peace in their souls.'[19]

Bosie – as so often before – proved an agent of division. Mary Costello sensed, beneath Wilde's charm and brilliance, the corrupting influence of the younger man; Douglas's appetite and indulgence were 'somehow' transforming him into 'a loathsome beast'. Berenson – who back in London had already expressed to Wilde his dislike of Douglas ('that dreadful man') – was distressed to find them still together. He tried to intervene, telling Wilde that he was courting destruction, but his efforts were turned aside with 'elegant insolence'. Wilde terminated their interview – if not quite their friendship – with the remark: 'Bernard, you forget that in every way I want to imitate my Maker, and like him I want nothing but praise.'[20]

Wilde needed to return to London at the end of May. He had received news that Richard Mansfield considered the scenario of The Cardinal of Avignon 'very fine', and might be interested in producing the play not only in America but also in London. He was due to arrive in England on 1 June, and was anxious for a meeting.[21] Douglas would be accompanying Wilde back to town under a cloud. Lord Currie, furious at Douglas's delay in coming to Constantinople, had withdrawn the job offer. On their last day in Florence they bumped into André Gide and were able to offer him their flat overlooking the Arno, which they had taken for a month but were leaving after two weeks. Although Wilde was, initially, rather taken aback at the encounter – concerned as he was to preserve the secret of his Florentine visit – he was soon pouring out a succession of 'delicious stories' over the café table while Gide sipped a vermouth in 'imbecilic' silence.[22]

The meeting with Mansfield did not produce any definite commitment or advance. More immediately satisfactory was the appearance, on 11 June, of Wilde's poem 'The Sphinx'. It was a masterpiece of fin de siècle production: beautifully bound in 'vellum and gold', printed in three colours (red, black and green), 'decorated throughout' by Ricketts, and dedicated to Marcel Schwob. The meagre text, widely spaced and set in small capitals, was elegantly disposed over some forty pages. Wilde liked to claim that his first idea had been 'to print only three copies: one for myself, one for the British Museum, and one for Heaven' – though he admitted he 'had some doubt about the British Museum'. Commercial considerations pushed by John Lane and the American publishers Copeland & Day resulted in an only slightly expanded edition of 250 copies plus twenty-five large-paper 'specials'

priced at a massive 5 guineas. It was generally acknowledged that, as a piece of clever marketing, it must be 'an immediate and complete success'. About the poem itself the reviewers were more grudging, remarking on its debt to Poe, its 'cynical' use of the meter from *In Memoriam*, and the 'daring eccentricity' of its erotic imagery.[23]

For unqualified approval the thirty-nine-year-old Wilde relied on Bosie and his other young friends. He was now often to be found sitting in the upstairs room the Café Royal, surrounded by adoring young disciples, 'men newly down from the Universities', who regarded him as 'sort of god'. Among the new additions to the circle were two young men whom Douglas had met, and travelled with, during his brief sojourn in Egypt: the comical gnome-like Reggie Turner (Max Beerbohm's great Oxford friend), and Robert Hichens, a music-loving journalist with literary ambitions. There was much real talent and wit in the group, though Willie Wilde considered them no more than 'a gang of parasites' who offered up a continual hymn of praise in return for Oscar's generosity.[24]*

Society still opened its doors to Wilde. Indeed, to some, he seemed at 'the height of his social glory' that season. He was conspicuous as one of 'six poets' at the fashionable Knightsbridge wedding of Violet Maxse to Lord Edward Cecil (the Marquess of Salisbury's third son). Together with Constance he attended Countess Spencer's grand reception at the Admiralty. And Wilfrid Blunt recorded his presence at 'a brilliant luncheon' given by Margot Tennant (as was) and her new husband, the home secretary, Herbert Asquith. Asquith had married Margot earlier that year, following the death of his first wife. With all the guests 'immensely talkative,' it was – Blunt recalled – 'almost like a breakfast in France'; only Asquith seemed 'rather out of it'. When the company dispersed, Wilde remained 'telling stories' to Margot and Blunt late into the afternoon.[25]

But, behind the scenes, Queensberry was moving against him. Frank Harris recalled hearing the marquess coming out of one of his clubs, bragging that he would stop Wilde going about with his son. As a first step Bosie's money supplies were cut off, provoking a flurry of furious telegrams. Queensberry also began to make inquiries about Wilde's friends

---

* Willie had remarried, at the beginning of the year, a sweet-natured but penniless Irish girl called Lily Lees. She had joined the ménage at Oakley Street. Lady Wilde continued to plead for a reconciliation between her estranged sons: 'otherwise *I shall* die of utter despair.' But Oscar, in this one instance, was prepared to overlook 'the curious morbid pleasure' of forgiving his enemies.

and connections. A private detective named Cook, who had been used to track down Bosie's younger brother, Sholto, when he had disappeared on a drinking-spree the previous year, was able to furnish some interesting information.[26]

5

Scarlet Marquess

> 'It is perfectly monstrous the way people go about nowadays
> saying things against one that are absolutely and perfectly
> true.'
>
> OSCAR WILDE

On 30 June 1894, at four o'clock in the afternoon, Wilde returned home, en route as he thought for a weekend away with some 'young Domitian' of poetic aspirations, only to be told that Lord Queensberry and another gentleman were waiting for him in the downstairs library. Queensberry was standing by the window; the other 'gentleman' was his friend Edward Pape. Wilde was not to be cowed, and a heated confrontation ensued. Wilde – at least in his telling of the incident – seized the initiative, demanding to know whether Queensberry had come to apologize for the libellous allegations he had made in his letter to Bosie – about Constance planning to divorce him for sodomy. Queensberry back-tracked, claiming that the letter was privileged as it was written to his son. At Wilde's direct challenge – 'Do you seriously accuse your son and me of sodomy?' – he countered, 'I don't say you are it, but you look it, and you pose as it, which is just as bad.' Nevertheless the marquess's wild scattering of accusations displayed a worrying knowledge of Wilde's recent movements; he suggested that Wilde and Douglas had been 'kicked out of the Savoy for [their]

disgusting conduct', and crowed that Wilde had been 'thoroughly well black-mailed' over 'a disgusting sodomitic letter' he had written. His rage through-out the interview was alarming, Wilde later recalled, his small hands waving in the air 'in an epileptic fury' as he uttered 'every foul word his mind could think of' before screaming 'If I catch you and my son together in any public restaurant, I will thrash you!' It was a loathsome spectacle and a frightening one. Wilde claimed to have replied, 'I don't know what the Queensberry Rules are, but the Oscar Wilde rule is to shoot at sight', before demanding that Queensberry leave his house, and instructing the servant (his startled young 'butler') that the marquess was never to be admitted again. In Queensberry's estimation, though, Wilde had 'plainly shown the white feather'.[1]

Douglas, when he learnt of the encounter, was incensed, and more deter-mined than ever to continue the feud with his father. His family, though, were less keen on provoking a scandal which would bring down upon them yet more embarrassment. Lady Queensberry's father, Alfred Montgomery, sought to calm the marquess's ire, but was rudely dismissed: 'Your daughter is the person who is supporting my son to defy me... I have made out a case against Oscar Wilde and have to his face accused him of it. If I was quite certain of the thing I would shoot the fellow on sight, but I can only accuse him of posing.'[2] Lady Queensberry was, in fact, doing her best to defuse the situation, but it was little enough. She sent her cousin, 'plausible George Wyndham' (as Wilde called him), to see Wilde and convince him to 'gradually drop' Bosie. Breaking the connection, however, was not really in Wilde's power. Bosie was enjoying the mounting tension. Lady Queens-berry – knowing her former husband's litigious nature – wrote, pleading with Wilde not to involve solicitors in the dispute.[3]

But Wilde could see no other recourse. He wrote to George Lewis seek-ing his advice. Lewis, however – the great expert on evading confrontations and keeping matters out of the courts, the friend who had guided Wilde's career almost from its outset – could not help him. He had been retained by Queensberry in relation to the marquess's ongoing divorce proceedings. He was able to write only a formal note of reply: 'Under these circumstances you will at once see that it is impossible for me to offer any opinion about any proceedings you intend to take against him. Although I cannot act against him, I should not act against you. Believe me, Yours faithfully, George Lewis.'[4]

Instead Wilde turned, on Robbie Ross's advice, to the firm of C. O. Humph-reys, Son and Kershaw. Mr Charles Humphreys (senior) dispatched a stern letter to Queensberry giving him an opportunity, as he put it, of retracting

– in writing – the 'assertions and insinuations' contained in 'certain letters' that the marquess had written to his son, which 'most foully and infamously libelled' both Wilde and Lord Alfred. He demanded a written apology to both Wilde and Douglas and hinted that, should it not be forthcoming, it might be necessary to publish the offending letters, which, besides their libellous claims, mentioned certain 'exalted personages' (almost certainly Queensberry's usual bugbears from the Liberal establishment, Gladstone and Rosebery) who might be wounded by such a disclosure.[5]

The response was not encouraging: 'I have received your letter with considerable astonishment,' Queensberry wrote back, 'I shall certainly not tender to Mr. Oscar Wilde any apology for letters I have written to my son.' The marquess disavowed all knowledge of having referred to 'exalted personages' and claimed that, such was 'Mr Wilde's horrible reputation, I can afford to publish any private letters I have written'. His resolve to provoke a 'public row' with Wilde hardened. He took to patrolling his favoured haunts – the Berkeley, Willis's Rooms and the Café Royal – in the hope of catching him and Bosie dining together.[6]

Douglas, meanwhile, stoked the fire. When Queensberry returned his letters unopened, Bosie sent a postcard, informing his father that he treated his 'absurd threats with absolute indifference', flaunting the fact that he and Wilde often dined together in restaurants, and would continue to do so. 'I am of age and my own master.' Placing others in the firing line, he claimed that Wilde could certainly prosecute Queensberry for his 'outrageous libels' and have him sent to prison. As to threats of violence, he boasted that he now carried a loaded revolver – 'and if I shoot you, or if [Wilde] shoots you, we should be completely justified as we should be acting in self-defence against a violent and dangerous rough, and I think if you were dead not many people would miss you.'[7]

The revolver proved a mistake. It went off by accident in the Berkeley. Fortunately no one was hurt, but the scandal had to be hushed up. And Queensberry recognized it as an opportunity. He made a personal call on Wilde's solicitors, informing them that unless Bosie ceased carrying the gun, he would report him to the police. This was followed up by a letter in the afternoon stating that – although he had now 'heard that the revolver has been given up'– the police would still be informed of the shooting incident, should Wilde and Bosie continue to defy him by any 'further scandals in public places'.[8]

And for Queensberry the very idea of Wilde and his son being together

was a scandal. It became his obsession. He went from restaurant to restaurant 'spreading vile scandals' and announcing that the next time he saw Wilde together with his son, he 'was going to hit [him] across the face with a cane'.[9] In the sporting club circles to which he belonged, he found many to support his resolution, and to repeat his 'vile scandals'. Wilde's flamboyant otherness had always provoked conventional male antipathy. But, as his reputation and demeanour became tinged with something more sinister, such hostility grew. The journalist Frank M. Boyd, when approached at the Café Royal by one of Wilde's 'young men admirers' with a suggestion that Wilde would like to meet him, replied, 'You can tell your friend to go to the devil as far as I am concerned... and you can add that I am a friend of "Q[ueensberry]".' John Boon, another journalist and Queensberry acquaintance, took it upon himself to warn the sons of two friends against associating with Wilde. And Frank Harris recalled hosting a lunch 'to meet Oscar Wilde and hear a new story' (the event perhaps coincided with the publication of six of Wilde's 'prose poems' in the July issue of Harris's *Fortnightly Review*). Out of the dozen invitations sent to men, seven or eight were declined, three or four of the men specifically telling Harris that 'they would rather not meet Oscar Wilde'. Wilde could not wholly ignore such slights. There were incidents, too, in clubs with members pointedly walking out when he entered the room.[10]

Queensberry's campaign was producing a sense of mounting disquiet. It seemed to Wilde that nowhere in London was safe from possible invasion. And to be 'dogged by a maniac' was 'intolerable'. Moreover, he was becoming increasingly aware that his position in the unfolding drama, though central, was secondary. He was merely providing a focus for old-established family antipathies and resentments.[11] Yet he would be the main victim of any confrontation. Although Queensberry might fulminate against his ingrate son – doubting his legitimacy and cursing his name – some family sense remained. His motive in wanting to break up the friendship between Bosie and Wilde – never easy to estimate, and perhaps never completely fixed – resolved itself into a determination to 'smash' Wilde, and Wilde alone.[12]*

---

*   It seems that George Lewis attempted, in some measure, to correct Queensberry's estimate of the relationship between Wilde and his son. Certainly he told Queensberry of the 'Oxford incident', when Bosie had been blackmailed, and Wilde (though not involved in the matter in any way) had come to his assistance. But Queensberry, while accepting the truth of Lewis's account, failed to make any adjustment in his attitude towards Wilde. [Lord Queensberry to Minnie Douglas, 26 February 1895; and Lord Queensberry to Percy Douglas, 27 March 1895]

Wilde could see no obvious way of escape. He regretted that he had not instructed Humphreys to have Queensberry bound over to keep the peace. When Harris joined the chorus in suggesting that, in order to avoid any confrontation, he should 'drop' Bosie, Wilde had demanded, 'Why should I cringe to this madman?' 'Because,' replied Harris, 'he is a madman.'[13] Such a break, though, was unthinkable. Douglas would not countenance it. And nor would Wilde. 'I can't live without you,' he declared, when Douglas was out of town for a few days. 'You are so dear, so wonderful. I think of you all day long, and miss your grace, your boyish beauty, the bright sword-play of your wit, the delicate fancy of your genius, so surprising always in its sudden swallow flights towards north or south, towards sun or moon, and above all, you yourself.'[14]

Despite his misgivings Wilde found himself carried along by Bosie's delight at the gathering storm. Douglas had never been in 'higher spirits', and his only disappointment was that no confrontation came. He tried to enlist his family's support, but – as he complained to his brother Percy (away in Australia) – 'with the exception of course of darling Mamma' they all 'simply backed out of it: & Francy [Drumlanrig] absolutely refused to even stick up for me to the small extent of dining in public with me & OW to show that he did not believe what my father said, though I implored him to do it'.[15]

Indeed the family worked to keep Bosie out of London. They were assisted by the coming summer, which was drawing everyone away from the capital. Douglas, it seems, was in Sussex for the Goodwood Festival at the beginning of August; and Wilfrid Blunt (another 'cousin') took him on a riding holiday to Stratford-upon-Avon, where they read Shakespeare's sonnets besides the playwright's tomb 'as an appropriate form of prayer'. Queensberry himself was away in Scotland.[16]

Although Wilde felt bereft during the weeks of separation from Bosie, he was consoled by a visit to the palmist Mrs Robinson. The 'Sibyl of Mortimer Street' made him 'very happy' by her vision of his future. 'I see a very brilliant life for you up to a certain point,' she declared. 'Then I see a wall. Beyond the wall I see nothing.' Wilde, with his optimistic outlook, was inclined to focus on the brilliant life before the 'wall'. He was delighted too at her prediction that early in the coming January he would 'go away' together with Bosie 'for a long voyage', and that their lives would walk 'always hand in hand' together.[17]

It was a bright prospect at a moment when darker thoughts were crowding in. At the end of July Walter Pater died, aged just fifty-four. Wilde

reported to Bosie that, on one evening, he went and sat with his now-ageing mother: 'Death and Love seem to walk on either hand as I go through life: they are the only things I think of, their wings shadow me.'[18] Lady Wilde now rarely left the house. She found walking difficult, and bright sunlight painful. Besides the occasional visitor, and the yet more occasional 'salon', what she really liked was a good fire and a good book. 'Who is there,' she asked, 'that can speak as Ralph Waldo Emerson speaks to you?' Apart from her younger son there was no one. Her financial situation remained precarious. The collapse of Willie's first marriage had brought to an end a yearly allowance from Mrs Leslie of £100 – a 'very dreadful' loss. She regularly called on Oscar for 'advances' of £10 or £20. He was always ready to oblige, even if he sometimes had to rely upon his wife's money to provide the necessary sums.[19] His own resources remained frustratingly low. The substantial sums received for An Ideal Husband seem to have been consumed already. He was £41 overdrawn at the bank and, as ever, 'pressed for money'. Plans for both The Cardinal of Avignon and the 'triple bill' had apparently stalled. He would need to look elsewhere.

6

A Capacity for Being Amused

'Remember my epigrams then, dear boy, and repeat them to me tomorrow.'

ESMÉ AMARINTH TO LORD REGGIE, *THE GREEN CARNATION*

As the summer advanced Wilde's thoughts turned to writing a new play. George Alexander, he knew, was interested in taking his next work. He conceived the idea of producing something different: not a comic 'drama', like his previous pieces, but an outright comedy, even a farce. After his recent exposure to *A School for Scandal*, he considered attempting something 'eighteenth-century'. But he soon settled, instead, upon transposing Sheridan's comic spirit into a modern setting.[1]

He mapped out a rough idea of the plot for Alexander:

ACT I. EVENING PARTY. 10 PM.

Lord Alfred Rufford's rooms in Mayfair. Arrives from the country Bertram Ashton his friend: a man of 25 or 30 years of age: his great friend. Rufford asks him about his life. He tells him that he has a ward, etc. very young and pretty. That in the country he has to be serious, etc. that he comes to town to enjoy himself, and has invented a fictitious younger brother of the name of George – to whom all his misdeeds are put down. Rufford is deeply interested about the ward.

Guests arrive: the Duchess of Selby and her daughter, Lady Maud Rufford, with whom the guardian [Bertram] is in love – Fin-de-Siècle talk, a lot of guests – the guardian proposes to Maud on his knees – enter Duchess – Lady Maud: 'Mamma, this is no place for you.'

Scene: Duchess enquires for her son Lord Alfred Rufford: servant comes in with note to say that Lord Alfred has been suddenly called away to the country. Lady Maud vows eternal fidelity to the guardian whom she only knows under the name of George Ashton. (P.S. The disclosure of the guardian of his double life is occasioned by Lord Alfred saying to him 'You left your handkerchief here the last time you were up' (or cigarette case). The guardian takes it – the Lord A. says 'but why, dear George, is it marked Bertram – who *is* Bertram Ashton?' Guardian discloses plot.)

ACT II. THE GUARDIAN'S HOME – PRETTY COTTAGE.

Mabel Harford, his ward, and her governess, Miss Prism. Governess of course dragon of propriety. Talk about the profligate George; maid comes in to say 'Mr George Ashton'. Governess protests against his admission. Mabel insists. Enter Lord Alfred. Falls in love with ward at once. He is reproached with his bad life, etc. Expresses great repentance. They go to garden.

Enter guardian. Mabel comes in: 'I have a great surprise for you – your brother is here.' Guardian, of course, denies having a brother. Mabel says 'You cannot disown you own brother, whatever he has done.' – and brings in Lord Alfred. Scene: also scene between [the] two men alone. Finally Lord Alfred arrested for debts contracted by guardian: guardian delighted: Mabel, however, make him forgive his brother and pay up. Guardian looks over bills and scold Lord Alfred for profligacy.

Miss Prism backs the guardian up. Guardian then orders his brother out of the house. Mabel intercedes, and brother remains. Miss Prism has designs on the guardian – matrimonial – she is 40 at least – she believes he is proposing to her and accepts him – his consternation.

ACT III. MABEL AND THE FALSE BROTHER.

He proposes and is accepted. When Mabel is alone, Lady Maud, who only knows the guardian under the name of George, arrives alone. She tells Mabel she is engaged to 'George' – scene naturally. Mabel retires: enter George, he kisses his sister naturally. Enter Mabel and sees them.

Explanations, of course. Mabel breaks off the match on the grounds that there is nothing to reform in George: she only consented to marry him because she thought he was bad and wanted guidance. He promises to be a bad husband – so as to give her an opportunity of making him a better man; she is a little mollified.

Enter the guardian: he is reproached also by Lady Maud for his respectable way of life in the country: a JP: a county-councillor: a churchwarden: a philanthropist: a good example. He appeals to his life in London: she is mollified, on condition that he never lives in the country: the country is demoralizing: it makes you respectable. 'The simple fare at the Savoy: the quiet life in Piccadilly: the solitude of Mayfair is what you need etc.'

Enter Duchess in pursuit of her daughter – objects to both matches. Miss Prism, who had in early days been governess to the Duchess, sets it all right, without intending to do so – everything ends happily.

Result

Curtain

Author called

Cigarette called

Manager called

Royalties for a year for author

Manager credited with writing play. He consoles himself for the slander with bags of red gold.

Fireworks.

The 'scenario' was, of course, just a first sketch; the 'real charm of the play', Wilde suggested, would be in the dialogue. He hoped, though, that the idea would appeal enough for Alexander to advance him £150 to secure the first refusal – the money to be returned should he not care for the finished script. He suggested that – if he were able 'to go away and write' – it could be done by October.[2]

Wilde *was* able to get away and write. After the excesses of Goring the year before, Constance – working to a budget of 10 guineas a week – had taken a more modest place for the last month of the summer. The Haven was a terraced house belonging to a friend of hers, on the Esplanade at Worthing, on the south coast. She and the boys (now aged nine and seven) – with their governess, and two of the Tite Street servants – went down at the beginning of the second week in August. Wilde arrived three days later

and claimed the top-floor room with a balcony as his 'writing room'.[3] It was to be a season of seaside fun and literary endeavour, and not just for Wilde. He had passed on his 'Oscariana' idea to Constance. She was to compile an anthology of his epigrams, taken from his plays and other works; and the little book was to be privately printed by Arthur Humphreys, the young manager of Hatchard's bookshop.

A special rapport had grown up between Constance and the twenty-nine-year-old (married) Humphreys during their collaboration. The recent months of neglect by Oscar had made Constance susceptible to kindness and attention. In one letter to Humphreys she confessed that she considered him 'an ideal husband, indeed... you are not far short of being an ideal man!' When he came down to Worthing for the day, to work on the project, she took a moment to write 'darling Arthur' (as she now called him) a note, while he was out smoking his cigarette, a note – 'to tell you how much I love you, and how dear and delightful you have been today'. Whether this romantic friendship evolved into an affair is uncertain, and perhaps unlikely, but it did, perhaps, show Wilde that his wife was desirable to others, and desiring of them too.[4]

Wilde threw himself into his play, and was only partially deflected by the arrival of Lord Alfred Douglas on 14 August. Although, before coming down to Worthing, Wilde had suggested Douglas might visit, he had then tried to put him off with tales of the boringness of family life (the children's governess was 'horrid, ugly... quite impossible,' and Swiss; 'also, children at meals are tedious'). Bosie, however, was not to be gainsaid. Despite Wilde's warnings, he curtailed his travels with Wilfrid Blunt to join the fun at the seaside. Although he seems to have put up at a hotel, he was a regular presence at The Haven, much to Constance's dismay. He soon became aware that he was a 'bone of contention between Oscar and Mrs Oscar', but – with characteristic selfishness – ignored their discomfort and set about enjoying himself. In his own recollection, he greatly contributed to the composition of Wilde's play, sitting alongside the playwright, approving the jokes as they were read out to him, and suggesting many of his own.[5]

Douglas's presence could not entirely dispel the air of the family seaside holiday. Indeed Wilde's son Vyvyan later remembered that summer as a charmed one, with Oscar 'at his best', taking his boys swimming, fishing and sailing – 'when it was not too breezy'. They established two aquaria in which the day's rock-pool discoveries could be deposited. Wilde threw himself into sandcastle building, 'an art in which he excelled', devising 'long,

rambling castles... with moats and tunnels and towers and battlements'. There were other treats: the Worthing Annual Regatta provided a fine spectacle (marred only for Wilde by the presence of sailing boat, bearing 'a huge advertisement for a patent pill'). At the lifeboat demonstration the Wilde party was conspicuous in the flotilla, 'flitting about' in a small rowing boat. Wilde also took Cyril to at least one concert, in the very full programme laid on at the Assembly Rooms.[6] The special bond between Wilde and his older son was reinforced that summer. Indeed Wilde would refer to the 'beautiful, loving, loveable' Cyril as 'my friend of all friends, my companion of all companions'.[7]

Nevertheless, for at least some of the time Wilde allowed himself to be monopolized by Douglas. They would go off sailing together, often accompanied by a trio of local lads who they had picked up on the beach: the sixteen-year-old Alphonse Conway and his friends Stephen and Percy. The boys would swim naked off the boat, diving for prawns and lobsters. Wilde characterized Alphonse – or 'Alphonso', as he dubbed him – as a 'bright, happy, boy' without any obvious occupation, and his brightness added to the attractions of the holiday. He and his friends became part of the summer scene. After one outing Wilde and Douglas took Alphonse and Stephen to lunch at the Marine Hotel. The boys would also join in the family activities, taking Wilde's sons out 'prawning' in the boat. Alphonse even attended a children's tea party for Cyril at the Esplanade.[8]

Wilde developed a particular fondness for 'Alphonso', who lived with his widowed mother close to the seafront. He encouraged his ambition to go to sea, and stimulated his imagination with gifts of *Treasure Island* and a book called *The Wreck of the Grosvenor*. He also bought him a blue serge suit and a straw hat with a red and blue ribbon, so that he need not be ashamed of his 'shabby' clothes during the summer festivities. But, although there seems to have been a certain affection in all this, there was also a definite sexual element.[9] According to Conway, shortly after they became acquainted, Wilde suggested that they meet on the parade at about nine in the evening. They walked out of the town together on the little coastal road towards Lancing. In a quiet place Wilde suddenly 'took hold' of 'Alphonso', and, putting his hand inside his trousers, masturbated him until he 'spent'. He did not ask Alphonse to 'do anything'. The incident did not seem to perturb the boy, and was repeated a few nights later. Whether Douglas also had sex with Alphonso, or with either of his friends, is unknown, but it is certainly possible.[10]

There was a heightened sense of sexual danger that summer. News arrived from London of a police raid on a house in Fitzroy Street (just round the corner from Cleveland Street), during which eighteen men had been arrested, two of them in 'fantastic female garb'. Among those taken into custody were Wilde's friends Charlie Parker and Alfred Taylor. Although, in the end, no charges were brought due to lack of evidence, the court reports indicated that the premises had been under surveillance for some time, and that many of those arrested were 'known' to the police. Although there is no suggestion that Wilde had ever visited the house, it was worrying to learn that the police were taking an active interest in such places. Certainly Wilde was distressed at the news: 'a dreadful piece of bad luck', he called it, that spelt 'real trouble' for 'poor Alfred Taylor'. But, as the incident resolved itself, he adopted a lighter tone. 'Do tell me all about Alfred,' he asked a mutual friend, 'Was he angry or amused? What is he going to do?' (Taylor went back to doing what he always did: not very much. Charlie Parker, though, reacted to the scare by enlisting in the Royal Artillery).[11]

Bosie left Worthing at the beginning of September, allowing Wilde to re-devote himself to his play, with regular breaks for bathing. He had not heard back from George Alexander about the project, and suspected that the scenario had been 'too farcical' for his tastes and his theatre. It turned out, though, that Alexander's letter expressing interest had simply got lost in the post. This was revealed when Alexander wrote again, anxious for news of the piece, and concerned to know whether he would be able to have American – as well as British – rights, as he was planning to tour the States for the first time the following year.[12]

Though Wilde pleaded that he was too poor to come to London to discuss the project, Alexander lured him up for lunch at the Garrick. It was a satisfactory meeting: Wilde was able to get some money out of Alexander in exchange for allowing him the 'first refusal' of the finished script. But he dissuaded him from his idea of taking the play to America, where, rather than being given a proper premiere and run in the major cities, it would serve simply as an occasional repertory item on Alexander's tour. Wilde envisaged selling the American rights separately to an American producer for perhaps as much as £3,000.[13]

On returning to Worthing Wilde dashed off a scenario for another play that he thought might be more suitable for Alexander to take on tour to the States: a 'comedy-drama' with more drama than comedy. The scenario neatly reversed the dynamics of *Lady Windermere's Fan*: an unfaithful

husband is rescued from a compromising situation by the smart action of his 'simple sweet' wife. But she then deserts him to run off with the husband's friend, to whom she has become passionately attached. 'You have made me love you,' she tells him. 'All this self-sacrifice is wrong, we are meant to live. This is the meaning of life.' Compared to the cheerfully convoluted absurdities of his farce, this was to be a drama of real power and passion, and – as such – much better attuned to Alexander's 'romantic' acting style. 'I see great things in it,' Wilde told the actor-manager, 'and, if you like it when done, you can have it for America.'[14]

In the meantime, though, he returned to his farcical comedy. He was 'quite delighted' with the piece. It was imbued with his own deliciously subversive philosophy: 'That we should treat all the trivial things of life very seriously, and the serious things of life with sincere and studied triviality.'[15] The original scenario had been enriched over the summer: now both the male characters were engaged in living 'double lives'. Just as the 'guardian' (renamed Jack Worthing in honour of the seaside resort) had invented his imaginary reprobate brother (now renamed Ernest) to provide an excuse for coming up to town, so his friend (transformed from Lord Alfred Rufford to plain Algernon Moncrieff, perhaps to lessen his resemblance to Lord Alfred Douglas) had invented an imaginary invalid friend called Bunbury to give him a pretext for avoiding tedious social obligations. In a further elaboration, parodying the involved coincidences of popular romantic fiction, Jack became Algernon's long-lost brother (actually called Ernest), having been abandoned as an infant by his nurse (the young Miss Prism) and raised by a kindly old gentleman in ignorance of his true identity.

Wilde doubtless enjoyed the echoes that the plot provided with his own increasingly involved 'double life' as respectable husband and clandestine lover of young men. Indeed the whole piece was shot through with subversive intimations of Wilde's sexual interests and connections. The renaming of Jack's imaginary brother as 'Ernest' did, of course, provide a satirical comment upon conventional Victorian notions about the virtues of 'earnestness', and allowed for the play to be called *The Importance of Being Earnest*, but it also offered a coded reference to a recently published volume of 'Uranian' verse, entitled *Love in Earnest*, in which the author, John Gambril Nicholson, had proclaimed his love for a schoolboy named Ernest. 'Ernest Worthing', moreover, is described as living at E4, the Albany – the very rooms inhabited by George Ives.[16]

But not all of Wilde's sly allusions were to his secret sex life. He renamed

Jack's pretty young ward 'Cecily Cardew' as a tribute to the infant niece of an old Oxford friend.[17] To honour Max Beerbohm he inserted into a list of British generals beginning with 'M', the improbable 'General Maxbohm'. He named the play's two butlers 'Lane' and 'Mathews' to vent his annoyance at his publishers (though he later relented and changed 'Mathews' to 'Merriman'). The imaginary invalid 'Bunbury' was perhaps a disparaging allusion to Charles Brookfield, who had played a character of that name in his recent comedy, *Godpapa*.[18]

Throughout everything, though, there was a sense of Wilde's pleasure in the work. The dialogue – absurd, light and paradoxical – was, he thought, the best he had ever written. Nevertheless the play itself still needed shaping. 'It lies in Sibylline leaves about the room,' he told Douglas. Arthur, the young 'butler' who they had brought with them from Tite Street, had 'twice made a chaos of "tidying up"' – though Wilde claimed to detect dramatic possibilities in this random re-ordering: 'I am inclined to think that Chaos is a stronger evidence for an Intelligent Creator than Kosmos is.'[19]

Constance left Worthing on 12 September to prepare the boys for school. Cyril was being sent away to Bedales, the progressive boarding school recently established by Harry Marillier's Cambridge friend J. H. Badley, while Vyvyan was going to a prep school in Broadstairs (the money from Alexander arrived just in time to allow Wilde to pay the fees).[20] Wilde remained at The Haven to work. There were, of course, some distractions. Wilde had, during his weeks of residence, achieved the position of a local celebrity, and was asked to give out the prizes at the 'Venetian Fete' that ended the town's season of waterborne festivities.

His speech, dilating upon the charms of Worthing, was enthusiastically received. He praised the town's amenities – its beautiful surroundings and many 'lovely long walks, which he recommended to other people, but did not take himself'. It is unclear whether the be-suited Alphonse Conway was present in the Pier Pavilion to hear this partial untruth. Wilde concluded his remarks by saying that 'he was delighted to observe in Worthing one of the most important things... the faculty of offering pleasure'.[21]

Constance's departure seems to have been a signal for Bosie to re-appear. He and Wilde even made a fleeting visit across the Channel to Dieppe ('very amusing and bright' during the summer season).[22] They returned, however, to find themselves illuminated in the glare of an unwanted new notoriety. During their absence there had appeared, anonymously, a book entitled *The Green Carnation*. Published by Heinemann, it was creating a

sensation with its thinly veiled, and very funny, depiction of Wilde and Lord Alfred Douglas – as the epigrammatic 'Esmé Amarinth' and his gilt-haired disciple 'Lord Reggie Hastings' – a young man who 'worshipped the abnormal with all the passion of his impure and subtle youth'.

The book was less a caricature than a photograph. It showed a quite startling familiarity with the details of Wilde and Bosie's life. On receiving a fulminating letter from his irate and bewhiskered father, the insouciant Lord Reggie replies by telegram, 'What a funny little man you are'. Although the plot – such as it was – centred on Lord Reggie's unsuccessful courtship of 'Lady Locke', there were broad hints about the heroes' real sexual interests. Both men follow 'the higher philosophy' elaborated by Amarinth: 'To be afraid of nothing, to dare to live as one wishes to live, not as the middle classes wish one to live; to have the courage of one's desires, instead of only the cowardice of other people's.' And, as Amarinth made clear, while the middle classes celebrated what was 'natural', he favoured the 'unnatural' in all aspects of life. Wilde was more amused than alarmed at it all. He considered the book 'very clever', even 'brilliant' in many places.[23]

There was much discussion – both in the press and down at Worthing – as to who could have written it. Wilde suspected Ada Leverson, who had parodied him so nimbly in *Punch*, but she assured him of her innocence.[24] They had discovered by then that the culprit was Robert Hichens. He had absorbed all that Douglas had told him during their trip down the Nile, and embellished it with what he had learnt since returning to England, both from meeting Wilde and from listening to Beerbohm. Wilde called him 'the doubting disciple who has written the false gospel'; Douglas complained that 'all the best jokes in the book were really [his]' and had been stolen 'without acknowledgment'. They both sent off comic telegrams, Wilde to tell Hichens that the secret was discovered, Bosie advising him to flee from their righteous wrath.[25]

Wilde also sent a humorous letter to the *Pall Mall Gazette* dispelling a suggestion, made by the paper, that he himself was the author of *The Green Carnation*. 'I invented that magnificent flower,' he declared, with a slight amplification of the truth. 'But with the middle-class and mediocre book that usurps its strangely beautiful name I have, I need hardly say, nothing whatsoever to do. The flower is a work of art. The book is not.' And to the manuscript of his play he added a line in which Lady Brancaster mentions having received a copy of the book, before dismissing it as 'a morbid and middle-class affair' seemingly about 'the culture of exotics'.[26]

Wilde's levity was misplaced. The book, which romped through three editions before the end of the year, greatly increased the awareness of, and prejudice against, his friendship with Douglas. '*The Green Carnation* ruined Oscar Wilde's character with the general public,' Frank Harris recalled. 'On all sides [it] was referred to as confirming the worst suspicions.' Certainly it 'inflamed' the Marquess of Queensberry.[27]

Douglas returned to town on 22 September, allowing Wilde a week of uninterrupted work at The Haven. Or almost uninterrupted: he had Alphonse Conway to dinner at the house on two, perhaps three, occasions. Afterwards, as Alphonse recalled, Wilde 'took me to his bedroom and we both undressed and got into bed'.[28] Wilde also fulfilled a promise of taking Alphonse on an overnight trip, 'as a reward for being a pleasant companion' to Wilde and his children over the summer. They went to Brighton, and put up at the Albion Hotel. Wilde ensured they had connecting rooms, and that night – after dinner in the hotel restaurant – he took Alphonse to bed. 'He acted as before', Alphonse said, although on this occasion he also 'used his mouth'. It was perhaps on the following day that Wilde presented Alphonse with a signed photograph, a fancy walking stick and a cigarette case inscribed 'Alfonso from his friend Oscar Wilde'.[29]

Before September was quite over, Douglas was back once again at Worthing, on another fleeting visit. He arrived with a 'companion' so unsuitable that Wilde refused to allow them to stay, preferring to put them up at a hotel. Only the following day, after the companion (presumably a London 'renter') had 'returned to the duties of his trade' did Douglas move into The Haven. The holiday season, however, was over, and the little town was emptying. Douglas soon became bored with the limited domestic routine. He insisted that they relocate to the brighter lights of Brighton.[30]

It was not a happy interlude. Soon after they arrived at the Hotel Metropole, Douglas fell ill with influenza. Wilde nursed him diligently, filling the room with flowers and sending for exotic fruits from London, since Bosie did not care for the grapes at the hotel. 'I sit by his side and read him passages from his own life,' Wilde reported to Ada Leverson. 'They fill him with surprise.' After four days of expensive hotel life, and with Bosie recovered, they moved into lodgings. Wilde hoped the setting might allow him to finish his play. But, instead, he himself succumbed to the flu. Douglas was not inclined to nurse him; he went off to London for a couple of days, leaving Wilde 'entirely alone without care, without attendance, without anything' (as Wilde bitterly recalled it). When he did return, he amused

himself in the town until the early hours. At Wilde's mild remonstration he flew into a fury, accusing Wilde of incredible 'selfishness' in expecting him to give up his pleasures to sit in a sick room. And the following morning he appeared in Wilde's bedroom, not to apologize, but to renew this attack. Wilde, alarmed at the almost hysterical fury, felt in actual physical danger and, scrambling out of bed, fled downstairs to the common sitting room. Bosie then departed, although not before 'silently' gathering up what money he could find in Wilde's rooms.

Even in a relationship regularly vexed by Douglas's temper, this was an exceptional row. Wilde was left badly shaken. Perhaps 'the ultimate moment' really had arrived. Wilde recalled that the thought came as 'a great relief... I knew that for the future my Art and Life would be freer and better and more beautiful in every possible way... Ill as I was, I felt at ease. The fact that the separation was irrevocable gave me peace.' He had, of course, made such resolutions before. But this time his determination was strengthened a few days later, when, on his fortieth birthday, amid the various messages of goodwill, he received a letter from Douglas, rehearsing once more all his bitter ire: taunting Wilde with 'common jests', bragging at how he had run up Wilde's tab at the Metropole, 'congratulating him on his panicked "flight" from his sick bed, and concluding, 'When you are not on your pedestal you are not interesting. The next time you are ill I will go away at once.' In the face of such 'revolting... coarseness and crudity' Wilde settled 'with himself' to see George Lewis immediately on his return to London that Friday (19 October); he would get him to write to the Marquess of Queensberry, stating that he was breaking off all relations and communications with Douglas.[31]*

On the Friday morning, though, he opened his morning paper to discover the shocking news that Bosie's eldest brother, Lord Drumlanrig ('the real head of the family, the heir to the title, the pillar of the house') had been killed in an 'accident' during a day's shoot down at Quantock in Somerset. He had been found, by other members of the party, in a ditch, with his gun beside him, half his face blown away. Wilde's resolve evaporated in the instant. He cabled to Bosie, full of sympathy for his terrible loss. They

---

* Douglas had taken himself off to Oxford, putting up at the Clarendon together with Beerbohm and Reggie Turner. 'Bosie is still in the hotel, and is very amusing,' Beerbohm reported to Ada Leverson. 'It appears that he has had a very serious quarrel with Oscar. Oscar fell ill at Brighton. Bosie went to a music-hall in the evening and, returning at 2 in the morning, sang loudly. Oscar was furious and called him inconsiderate. Bosie left the next morning – and Oscar does not answer Bosie's telegrams.'

met a few days later at Tite Street. No allusion was made to Bosie's terrible behaviour at Brighton, nor to his yet more terrible letter. Everything was washed away by the tragedy of Drumlanrig's death. 'Your grief,' Wilde later reminded Bosie, 'seemed to me to bring you nearer to me than you had ever been. The flowers you took from me to put on your brother's grave were to be a symbol not merely of the beauty of [Drumlanrig's] life, but of the beauty that in all lives lies dormant and may be brought to light.' All thoughts of terminating the friendship were swept aside in the face of this new intimacy.[32]

Although at the inquest, held in Somerset on 20 October, a verdict of accidental death had been returned, many of those connected with events suspected suicide. Only the motive remained mysterious. Drumlanrig had been on the verge of announcing his engagement to the young niece of his host. Had something perhaps gone wrong? Queensberry wrote with typical intemperance to Alfred Montgomery on the subject, blaming him and his daughter, along with the 'The Snob Queers like Rosebery & canting Christian hypocrite Gladstone', for making 'bad blood' between him and his eldest son over his peerage. Otherwise things might have turned out differently:

> I smell a Tragedy behind [Drumlanrig's death] and have already got wind of a more ghastly one if it is what I am led to believe, I of all people could & would have helped him, had he come to me with a confidence, but that was all stopped by you people – we had not met or spoken hardly for more than a year & a half. I am on the right track to find out what happened. *Cherchez la femme*, when these things happen. I have already heard something that quite accounts *for it all*.[33]

Sadly there is no further record of Queensberry's suspicions and discoveries. Was the *'femme'* behind the tragedy Drumlanrig's fiancée Alix Ellis? Or another? And what role did she play? Queensberry's assertion that he 'of all people' would have been able to help his son is intriguing, but hard to fathom. Did it perhaps relate to his own recent and ill-fated marriage, which was ended on the 24 October at a hearing held in camera – annulled 'by reason of the frigidity impotency and malformation of the parts of generation of the said Respondent'?[34] It is impossible to know. Then (as now) the mystery of Drumlanrig's death encouraged speculation. There were persistent rumours that the forty-six-year-old Rosebery (a widower since the death of his

wife in 1890) was sexually interested in young men. His tendency to take on good-looking private secretaries was noted, and inclined some to 'believe the worst'. His habits of opening his own letters, and of going on holiday to Naples, also counted against him. Queensberry certainly relished such gossip: 'Bloody Bugger' to 'Snob Queer' were among his rich arsenal of Rosebery insults. Although there is little in Queensberry's initial reaction to suggest that he connected Rosebery's supposed proclivities with the 'catastrophe' of Drumlanrig's death, others certainly did make such a link. And it may be that, in time, he came to share their suspicions.[35]*

Certainly the tragedy did nothing to deflect the marquess from his pursuit of Wilde. He talked of the matter – and the distress it was causing him – to his son Percy, now returned from Australia. Percy counselled bringing the 'miserable business... to a head'. Time seemed pressing. For anyone, like Queensberry, who suspected that the upper reaches of British society were being corrupted by a secret network of sodomites there had recently been a number of disturbing signs. The 'new culture' seemed to be asserting itself with increasing boldness. In response to debate in the press about Victorian social conventions regarding marriage, several articles had appeared suggesting that complete personal liberty should extend to same-sex relations. In April Charles Kains Jackson was sacked as editor of *The Artist* after making this point in an outspoken essay on what he termed the 'New Chivalry'. In October, George Ives penned a similar piece in the *Humanitarian* (after his article was savaged in the *Review of Reviews*, Wilde congratulated him: 'When the prurient and the impotent attack you, be sure you are right').[36]

At Oxford, although *The Spirit Lamp* had not survived Douglas's departure, plans were being laid for a new periodical that would continue to promote

---

* Although definite information about Rosebery's supposed homosexual relations remains elusive, it is clear that the rumour of them was well established in the period. André Gide reported a conversation he had with Reggie Turner on the beach at Dieppe in August 1902: moving on from a discussion of Wilde, they touched on others (some unexpected) who had shared his sexual tastes:

> Lui [Turner]: 'Balfour... Kitchener... Rosebery.'
> Moi [Gide]: 'Kipling.'
> . Lui: 'Non.'
> Moi: 'Je vous assure.'
> Lui: 'C'est la première fois que je l'entends dire.'
> *Silence*

the 'new culture' at the university. At Ives's rooms in the Albany Wilde met the young editor, 'an undergraduate of strange beauty' called John Bloxam. They discussed possible names for the magazine, eventually fixing upon *The Chameleon*. Pressed to provide something for the inaugural number, Wilde offered a page of 'aphorisms'. Douglas offered a pair of sexually charged sonnets, one of them, 'Two Loves', with the memorable last line, 'I am the Love that dare not speak its name.' Wilde's contribution – 'Phrases and Philosophies for the Use of the Young' – was less obviously contentious. Many of the maxims were borrowed from *An Ideal Husband*, and framed a vision of intellectual, rather than sexual, inversion, but a few did carry more dangerous suggestions. 'Wickedness', Wilde asserted, 'is a myth invented by good people to account for the curious attractiveness of others.'[37]

Wilde may have been inclined to include these aphorisms in *Oscariana*, along with those from another gathering published in the *Saturday Review* under the title 'A Few Maxims for the Instruction of the Over-Educated'. He had been disappointed with the initial selection put together by Constance: 'The plays are particularly badly done,' he complained to Humphreys. 'Long passages are quoted, where a single aphorism should have been extracted.' He was now busy amending and augmenting the text himself. As he tried to impress upon Humphreys, the book needed to be 'a really brilliant thing'.[38]

For Wilde, though, the most pressing concern was *The Importance of Being Earnest*. At the end of October he sent the finished typescript – under the disguised title of *Lady Lancing* – to George Alexander. He did so with reservations. 'Of course, the play is not suitable to you at all,' he told him: 'you are a romantic actor'; here was a farcical comedy, well outside 'the definite artistic line' usually followed at the St James's Theatre. Wilde suggested that the piece really wanted comic actors like Charles Wyndham or Charles Hawtrey. And it is possible that Wilde had already sounded out both these men about the play. Certainly when Alexander failed to commit at once to the piece Wilde took the play to Wyndham, securing his commitment to put it on at the Criterion Theatre in the new year. With this agreement he seems also to have received an advance of £300 – although, from this, he probably had repay whatever he had already received from Alexander.[39]

It was good news at last. After more than twelve months without a new production, Wilde now had two plays in prospect for the coming year. Rehearsals for *An Ideal Husband* began in the second week of December; the play was to open on 3 January at the Haymarket. Wilde was a constant

presence at the theatre. Julia Nielson, the actress playing Lady Chiltern, recalled him there, always accompanied by three young men, who stood beside him in descending height 'like the Three Bears' (where the 5ft 9in Bosie ranked in this line-up is not recorded). Wilde remained doubtful of the play's prospects. Constance reported him as very 'depressed about it'.[40] After the conviviality of Beerbohm Tree's company the previous year, he found the cast less sympathetic. There was an unfortunate dispute with Waller's wife, Florence, who insisted on playing the part of Mrs Cheveley, in the face of Wilde's reservations. Charles Hawtrey (who had lampooned him in *The Poet and the Puppets*) was playing Lord Goring; and although Wilde admired Hawtrey's comic talent, the actor had retained an unspoken resentment against him. When an interviewer – seeking a general answer – asked Wilde, 'What are the exact relations between the actor and the dramatist?' Wilde replied, with a smile, 'Usually a little strained.' And to the follow-up question, 'But surely you regard the actor as a creative artist?' Wilde answered, with a touch of pathos, 'Yes, terribly creative – terribly creative!'[41]

The tension between actors and playwright was heightened by the presence in the cast of Charles Brookfield. The author of *The Poet and the Puppets* had taken the minor role of Goring's valet – because, as he ungraciously explained, he did not want to learn too many of Wilde's lines. By not rising to such provocations, Wilde of course antagonized the actor further. He was adept at such ploys. When Brookfield, furious at having to rehearse over the Christmas holiday, asked, 'Don't you keep Christmas, Oscar?', Wilde replied, 'No, Brookfield, the only festival of the Church I keep is Septuagesima. Do you keep Septuagesima, Brookfield?' 'Not since I was a boy,' Brookfield replied. 'Ah,' said Wilde, 'be a boy again.'[42]

THE HOUSE OF JUDGEMENT

1895

AGE 40

Oscar Wilde in the dock, by 'Yorick' (Ralph Hodgson), 1895.

1

The Last First Nights

'The truth is rarely pure and never simple.'

OSCAR WILDE

'Remember to what a point your Puritanism in England has brought you,' declares the dangerous Mrs Cheveley in Act 1 of *An Ideal Husband*:

In old days nobody pretended to be a bit better than his neighbours. In fact, to be a bit better than one's neighbour was considered excessively vulgar and middle-class. Nowadays, with our modern mania for moral- ity, every one has to pose as a paragon of purity, incorruptibility, and all the other seven deadly virtues – and what is the result? You all go over like ninepins – one after the other. Not a year passes in England without somebody disappearing. Scandals used to lend charm, or at least interest, to a man – now they crush him.

The speech was just one of the jewels of sparkling perspicacity that glit- tered on the play's opening night. Wilde's anxieties about the piece proved unfounded. It was welcomed enthusiastically, bar a few growls from 'the pittites'. To most in the crowded theatre it seemed to display 'a distinct advance in dramatic power'. There was much laughter, real enjoyment

and real engagement. Wilde, 'faultlessly groomed' and dressed in the 'last note of fashion' was conspicuous in a stage box, surrounded by a flattering crowed of 'most distinguished persons' whose praise he received with a 'semi-royal graciousness'. Called before the curtain, he gave his now expected turn of insouciant self-assertion (or 'studied insolence'), declaring – 'I have enjoyed myself very much.'[1]*

The reviewers might still carp at Wilde's supposedly formulaic witticisms and second-hand plot devices but their ungenerous comments were neatly skewered by Bernard Shaw in the *Saturday Review*: 'As far as I can ascertain,' he wrote, 'I am the only person in London who cannot sit down and write an Oscar Wilde play at will. The fact that his plays, though apparently lucrative, remain unique under these circumstances, says much for the self-denial of our scribes. In a certain sense Mr. Wilde is to me our only thorough playwright. He plays with everything: with wit, with philosophy, with drama, with actor and audience, with the whole theatre.'[2]

Wilde had achieved an almost unprecedented feat: his first three plays 'all successes'.[3] If this was a rare attainment, it was also a great relief. He would be earning money again, and in large amounts. Success, however, did not make him humble; it made him insufferable. Taxed as to whether he considered *An Ideal Husband* his best play, he replied that 'only mediocrities improve'; his three comedies, he suggested, 'form a perfect cycle, and in their delicate sphere complete both life and art'. 'Humility,' he explained to the same interviewer, 'is for the hypocrite, modesty for the incompetent. Assertion is at once the duty and the privilege of the artist.'[4] Not everyone was impressed by the pose. Arthur Conan Doyle thought Wilde must have become 'mad' when the playwright solemnly urged him to see his new play with the line, 'Ah, you must go. It is wonderful. It is genius!'[5]

---

*   In the audience that night was Henry James. Sick with nerves, he had come as a means of avoiding having to witness the first night of his own play – *Guy Domville* – which was opening that evening at the St James's Theatre, under the direction of George Alexander. James subsequently wrote to his brother, William: 'I sat through [*An Ideal Husband*] and saw it played with every appearance (so far as the crowded house was an appearance) of complete success... The thing seemed to me so helpless, so crude, so bad, so clumsy, feeble and vulgar, that as I walked away across St James's Square to learn my own fate, the prosperity of what I had seen seemed to me to constitute a dreadful presumption of the shipwreck of *Guy Domville*... "How *can* my piece do anything with a public with whom *that* is a success?"' His presumption proved only too correct. His play was not a success. And, when called before the curtain at the end, James was greeted by a volley of boos from some sections of the audience.

In a series of statements to the press Wilde re-affirmed his current views on the relative positions of the playwright, the public and the critic. 'I write to please myself,' he explained. The critics 'have always propounded the degrading dogma that the duty of the dramatist is to please the public', but the 'aim of the artist is no more to give pleasure than to give pain. The aim of art is to be art.' Such 'art' should be an expression of the artist's personality. 'We shall never have a real drama in England until it is recognized that a play is as personal and individual a form of self-expression as a poem or a picture.' 'The public makes a success when it realizes that a play is a work of art.' As a result it was the artist who was 'the munificent patron of the public', rather than the other way round. 'I am very fond of the public,' Wilde declared; 'and, personally, I always patronize them very much.'[6]

He pointed out that the critics had missed the 'entire psychology' of the piece: 'the difference in the way in which a man loves a woman from that in which a woman loves a man'. Lady Chiltern, he suggested, displays a female 'weakness' in making an 'ideal' of her husband, while Sir Robert displays his masculine shortcoming by not daring to 'show his imperfections to the thing he loves'. When quizzed about the so-called 'double standard' of the contemporary moral code, Wilde asserted that it was 'indeed a burning shame that there should be one law for men and another law for women', before adding 'I think that there should be no law for anybody.'[7]

Constance was not at the first night. Over the Christmas holidays she had suffered a health crisis, perhaps exacerbated by a fall downstairs. Her ailment remained a mystery, but she found it difficult to walk. To aid her recuperation she went down to Babbacombe to stay with Lady Mount Temple. Oscar was left – installed at the Hotel Albemarle – to enjoy his success, along with Douglas and his other friends.[8] There was a lessening of anxiety, since the Marquess of Queensberry was away from London, arranging the sale of his Scottish estates.

Amid the pleasures of the moment there was also a fresh professional excitement. Henry James's play *Guy Domville* was failing badly at St James's Theatre, leaving George Alexander in dire and unexpected need of a replacement piece. Not having anything immediately to hand, he approached Wilde about the possibility of putting on *The Importance of Being Earnest*. The play (which Alexander had initially turned down) was scheduled for production by Charles Wyndham at the Criterion later in the year. Nevertheless Wilde, ready to help his first producer, and perhaps also keen to see the production date of the piece brought forward, asked Wyndham whether he might

consider surrendering the rights to Alexander. Wyndham (almost certainly encouraged by the promise of first refusal of Wilde's next piece) generously agreed to the arrangement – asking neither a premium from Alexander, nor a return of Wilde's advance.[9]

The play had to go into rehearsal almost at once. But, as with *Lady Windermere's Fan*, Alexander was not convinced by Wilde's structuring of the drama. It seemed too long and too diffuse; four-act farces were almost unknown. Alexander proposed the radical solution of combining Acts 2 and 3, editing much of the dialogue, and cutting completely the episode in which a solicitor called Grigsby arrives to arrest 'Ernest Worthing' for debts that he has run up at the Savoy.[10] Wilde acquiesced. According to one account, when Alexander told him the Grigsby scene made the play twenty minutes too long, he replied, 'You may be right, my dear Alec. I can only tell you that it took just five minutes to compose.'[11]

The play's reduced running time encouraged Wilde to propose *The Florentine Tragedy* as a curtain-raiser. Alexander was open to the idea, but Wilde – away from Tite Street and his study – failed to produce the manuscript.[12] He busied himself instead with attending rehearsals for *The Importance of Being Earnest* and, although his presence sometimes created tensions, and Alexander was even reported to have once ordered him out of a rehearsal, he remained anxious to assist.[13] He would write the occasional extra line on request, for example when it was found that there was not enough time for an actor 'to get across the stage' or someone 'wanted a better exit'.[14]

Douglas, however, was – as always – impatient for pleasure. The palmist Mrs Robinson had predicted that he and Wilde would make a trip together in January, and he was eager to fulfil the prophecy. He insisted on being taken on a trip to Algeria, and they departed on the 15th.[15] Alexander was not sorry to see them go. For Wilde the escape from an English winter into the light, lassitude and sexual licence of North Africa was delightful. 'There is great beauty here,' Wilde reported to Ross. 'The Kabyle boys are quite lovely.' Even the beggars, he noted, had 'profiles, so the problem of poverty is easily solved'. Wilde and Douglas took to smoking hashish: 'It is quite exquisite: three puffs of smoke and then peace and love.'[16]

During their second week, in the beautiful walled city of Blidah, 30 miles south of Algiers, they again ran into André Gide. At Gide's inquiry as to what he was doing so far from London, Wilde replied, 'I am running away from art. I want to worship only the sun. Have you noticed how the sun despises all thought, makes it retreat, take refuge in the shadows. Once

thought lived in Egypt; the sun conquered Egypt. It lived for long in Greece; the sun conquered Greece. Then Italy, and then France. Today all thought is pushed back to Norway and Russia, where the sun never comes. The sun is jealous of art.' The brilliance of this flight was only slightly undercut by the fact that the weather was deteriorating, and rain – if not snow – was forecast.

For all Wilde's friendliness, there appeared to Gide a new coarseness in his manner – 'less softness in his look... something raucous in his laughter, and a wild madness in his joy. He seemed at the same time more sure of pleasing and less ambitious to succeed in doing so.' He was becoming reckless, hardened and conceited. When they met up again in Algiers soon afterwards, Wilde announced, 'I have a duty to myself to amuse myself frightfully.' But it was not happiness he sought: 'Above all not happiness. Pleasure! You must always aim at the most tragic.' Wilde was on his own. There had been another terrible row with Bosie, who had stormed off in pursuit of a beautiful 'sugar-lipped' fourteen-year-old, with whom he planned to 'elope' to Biskra.

Gide found himself swept up in Wilde's wake, and they spent several happy days together. Gide recalled how, as they walked the streets, Wilde would be followed by a throng of young 'ragamuffins'; he chatted with each one; he regarded them with joy and tossed his money to them haphazardly. 'I hope,' he remarked, 'to have quite demoralized the city.'[17]

Certainly he succeeded in 'demoralizing' Gide, or – rather – in liberating him. Wilde perceived that his young friend was in a state of tortured sexual confusion, unable to acknowledge or embrace his own homosexual yearnings. On one of their evenings in the old quarter, Wilde arranged for the choked and nervous young Frenchman to spend a night of sexual passion with a beautiful dark-eyed flute player whom he had been admiring in one of the cafés. It marked the great climacteric of Gide's life. Gide recalled how, at dawn the following morning, he had run through the empty streets of Algiers, overcome by a joyful lightness of body and spirit. Nevertheless, despite this great event, Gide remained perturbed by Wilde; by the recklessness with which he treated both his own life and his own art. 'Wilde!' he wrote to his mother, 'What more tragic life is there than his! If only he were more careful – if he were capable of being careful – he would be a genius, a great genius.' Never having seen any of Wilde's plays, Gide was prepared to accept the writer's self-deprecatory verdict upon them: 'Oh, but [they] are not at all good; and I don't put any stock in them... although if you only knew the amusement they give!'[18] Wilde – reiterating

a favoured line – had then confided, 'the great tragedy' of his life: 'I have put my genius into my life, I have only put my talent into my works.'[19]

Wilde's life, though, seemed to be veering close to the precipice. His flaunting of his homosexual liaisons made him an increasingly compromising companion. Gide confessed that, should they meet in London or Paris, he would not be able to acknowledge him. 'If Wilde's plays in London did not run for three hundred performances,' Gide suggested, 'and if the Prince of Wales did not attend his first nights, he would be in prison, and Lord Douglas as well.'[20]

For all the 'bold joy' of Wilde's pose, there lurked beneath it – as Gide noted – a strain of 'dark anxiety'. Indeed Wilde confessed something of his fears about Queensberry's campaign against him. When asked about the risks involved in returning to London, he replied, 'One should never know that... my friends advise prudence. Prudence! But can I have any? That would be going backwards. I must go as far as possible... I can not go further. Something must happen... something else.'[21]

Wilde left Algiers on 31 January, and returned alone to London. With Constance still down at Babbacombe, he took rooms at the luxurious but 'loathsome' Hotel Avondale on Piccadilly. He was unable to return to his preferred Albermarle, as his bill there remained unpaid. *The Importance of Being Earnest* was set to open on 14 February.

If the public were excited at the prospect, so too was the Marquess of Queensberry. He was now back in London, and more determined than ever to bring matters to a head. Wilde's new play seemed to offer a perfect opportunity. Fortunately Lady Queensberry learnt of his plans to cause a disruption on the opening night, and passed the information on to Wilde. The whole Douglas family was united in deploring the marquess's campaign of harassment; not out of any concern for Wilde, but because they saw it as damaging to Bosie. Even Percy Douglas concurred, having been convinced by his younger brother that there were no grounds for the marquess's suspicions.[22]

Prompted by Wilde, George Alexander wrote to the marquess cancelling the ticket that he had acquired for the opening night.[23] Even so, Wilde remained anxious. He alerted the police to the possibilities of an incident.

There was an increased presence outside the theatre on the evening of the premiere. Inside the theatre, though, as the fashionable crowd thronged the foyers, glad to have escaped the swirling snowstorm outside, Wilde remained unsure of what the marquess was planning, and whether or not

he would succeed. He strove to bury his anxieties beneath the glitter of the occasion. Bosie remained in Algeria, but Constance (though still in poor health) had returned from Babbacombe to attend the opening.[24]

The play took from the first. 'What brings you up to town?' 'Oh, pleasure, pleasure. What else should bring one anywhere?' As Irene Vanbrugh, the young actress playing Gwendolen, recalled, the performance 'went with a delightful ripple of laughter from start to finish'.[25] Ada Leverson (there, in a box, with Aubrey and Mabel Beardsley) thought the auditorium suffused with a 'strange almost hysterical joy' as the inspired 'nonsense' of the play unfolded. Alexander's deft editorial interventions ensured that the pace never let up. To a friend who had suggested that a farce should be like a mosaic, Wilde had countered, 'No, it must be like a pistol shot.' And there was no doubt that Wilde's 'trivial comedy for serious people' had hit the target. The author was 'loudly cheered' when he was called before the curtain to take his bow. He declined, though, to make a speech.[26]

It was clear, even before the near-unanimous clamour of press approbation, that, in his procession of theatrical successes, this marked a new high.* The play was considered both delightfully 'modern' and quintessentially Wilde. Well might he boast (as he did later) that he had taken 'the drama, the most objective form known to art, and made it as personal a mode of expression as the lyric or the sonnet'.[27] Although, even in the euphoria of the first-night triumph, he did obliquely acknowledge Alexander's contribution to the piece, remarking, 'My dear Aleck, it was charming, quite charming. And, do you know, from time to time I was reminded of a play I once wrote myself called *The Importance of Being Earnest*.'[28]

But, despite the thrill of success, Wilde did not join Ada Leverson and her party for supper at Willis's, as was expected. He had been perturbed at news of Queensberry's antics. The 'Scarlet Marquess', he discovered, had arrived, together with a prizefighter bearing 'a grotesque bouquet of vegetables'. Unable to gain entry to the theatre, he had 'prowled about for three hours', then – leaving his 'bouquet' for Wilde at the box office – had departed 'chattering like a monstrous ape'.[29]

If Wilde felt hounded by Queensberry, he also felt that the marquess had perhaps over-reached himself with this latest pantomime. His threatening behaviour had been witnessed by many of the staff at the St James's. The

---

* Among the few negative assessments of the piece was one by Bernard Shaw in the *Saturday Review*. Ever the contrarian, Shaw claimed to find the play 'heartless'.

bunch of vegetables remained at the box office. There was the memory, too, of the marquess's disruption of Tennyson's play thirteen years earlier, to suggest what he was capable of. Wilde had regretted in the past not going to the law to restrain Queensberry. Here, it appeared, was something to act upon. The following day, having consulted with Percy Douglas, he instructed Humphreys to investigate the possibility of prosecuting the marquess 'for his threats and insulting conduct'.

Bosie returned from Algiers soon after, delighted to learn of the plan. He wanted, as he said (repeatedly), to see his father 'in the dock'.[30] He stayed with Wilde at the Avondale, happy to share in the luxuries of the place, and to abuse them too. When Wilde remonstrated with him for bringing a young rent boy to stay in his room, he flew into a rage and moved – together with the boy – to another hotel; as ever, Wilde was obliged to pay the bill.[31]

With two money-making plays now running in the West End (and a successful revival of Lady Windermere's Fan just opened at Camberwell's Metropole Theatre), Wilde wanted to be able to enjoy himself. London, however, seemed over-full of cares. Queensberry remained a constant threat. Bosie's behaviour was tiring. Creditors, alive to rumours of his new prosperity, were clamouring for payment; within days of the opening of Earnest Wilde had been served with writs for £400.[32] He planned to escape to Paris, where Sarah Bernhardt had – very excitingly – revived her scheme for a production of Salomé.[33] But even here Wilde was thwarted. His bill at the Avondale was now £148; he did not yet have the money to pay it, and the management would not let him remove his luggage until the account was settled.[34]

This frustration was followed by another. On 28 February Humphreys wrote to say that the firm would be unable to prosecute Queensberry for his threatening antics at the St James's Theatre, as neither George Alexander nor the theatre staff were prepared to give witness statements. They were anxious to stay out of the conflict. The 'only consolation' Humphreys could offer was that 'such a persistent persecutor as Lord Queensberry will probably give you another opportunity sooner or later of seeking the protection of the Law' – at which moment the firm would be delighted to assist in bringing him to justice.[35] It seemed a rather bleak comfort.

2

Hideous Words

'My whole life seems ruined by this man.'

OSCAR WILDE

L ate on that winter afternoon, of 28 February 1895, Wilde visited Ricketts and Shannon's new home on Beaufort Street in Chelsea. He found Ricketts, alone, working at a woodblock. They talked of plans for 'Mr W. H.' and of Wilde's Symbolist dramas.* Coming away from the house, Wilde bumped into Shannon. They stood chatting for a while in the street. Looking in at the lighted windows of a baker's shop at the display of sausage rolls, Wilde remarked 'What extraordinary things people eat, I suppose they are hungry.' He then hailed a cab, and headed for the Albemarle Club.[1]

He had not been there for several weeks. Going in, the porter stopped

---

* Wilde consulted Ricketts about set designs for *Salomé* – probably apropos Bernhardt's planned Parisian production. Ricketts recalled: 'I proposed a black floor, upon which Salomé's feet could move like white doves; this was said to capture the author. The sky was to be a rich turquoise green, cut by the perpendicular fall of gilded strips of Japanese matting forming an aerial tint above the terraces.' It was Wilde, perhaps, who suggested the division of the actors into separate masses of colour: 'The Jews were to be in yellow, John in white, Herod and Herodias in blood-red. Over Salome the discussions were endless; should she be clothed in black – like the night, in silver like the moon – or, the suggestion was Wilde's – green like a curious poisonous lizard?'

him, and handed him an envelope, saying that the enclosed had been left for him some ten days earlier. Inside the envelope was the Marquess of Queensberry's card. Across the top were scrawled five, or six, words; the first three were easily legible as 'For Oscar Wilde' the last was, no less, clearly 'Somdomite [sic]'. The squiggle in between might be interpreted as 'ponce and'. Despite the mis-spelling of the final word the intent seemed unmistakable: Queensberry was accusing Wilde of being a sodomite. This, it seemed, was Queensberry's long-threatened attempt to make a public scandal. The card had been left openly at the club, where anyone (and the club had female, as well as male, members) might have read it. It was only through the discretion of the porter, Mr Wright, that it had been placed inside an envelope.

But if it was a public scandal, it was also a public libel. Queensberry may have been anxious to 'bring matters to a head', but Wilde now shared his desire. The stress caused by the marquess's campaign had become intolerable. It was blighting what should have been his season of triumph. This seemed to be the 'opportunity' of which Humphreys had spoken in his letter of that very morning, and Wilde was eager to seize it. He returned to the Avondale, and wrote at once to Robbie Ross, sending the note by messenger: 'Since I saw you last something has happened. Bosie's father has left a card at my club with hideous words on it. I don't see anything now but a criminal prosecution. My whole life is ruined by this man. The tower of ivory is assailed by a foul thing. On the sand my life is spilt. I don't know what to do. If you could come here at 11.30 do so tonight.'[2]

He wrote too, it seems, to Constance at Tite Street, announcing that he must see her. Whatever steps he decided to take, he would need her support – if not her understanding.[3] According to her brother, she remained, despite the ever-widening gulf in their marital relationship, entirely ignorant about Oscar's homosexual relations, either with Bosie or with others. There are possible hints of anxiety on the subject; after a visit to a medium in 1893 she announced the need to 'pray for my boys and when they are older teach them to pray & to struggle'. But such doubts as she had do not seem to have resolved themselves into any real acknowledgement of the situation. She was ready to accept whatever Oscar told her.[4]

When Ross arrived at the Avondale late that evening, he found Douglas already there. Wilde had hoped to consult with Ross alone first, but Douglas had turned up by chance, and was eager to involve himself in the deliberations.[5] All three players were enthusiastic about taking legal action.

It was the chance they had been waiting for. To all of them it seemed that the accusation had been made in the context of Queensberry's hostility to Wilde's friendship with Bosie. And it was in that context that they imagined taking action. There appeared to be every prospect of success. To defend a charge of criminal libel, the marquess would have to prove not only that the offending statement (that Wilde was a 'sodomite') was true, but also that it had been made 'in the public interest'. How could Queensberry possibly do either? Wilde and Douglas were only too ready to defend their relationship as something exalted and Platonic. And when it came to the question of their sexual relations with each other, they could simply deny them. If Queensberry was planning to suggest that Wilde had corrupted his son, and might corrupt others, Bosie himself could surely refute the charge. Douglas began to look forward to having his father incarcerated, or sent to a lunatic asylum.[6]

The following day Wilde went – together with Ross and Douglas – to see Humphreys. They found the old solicitor encouraging. There was an awkward moment when he asked if there was any truth at all in Queensberry's allegation. Wilde emphatically denied it. 'If you are innocent,' the lawyer replied, 'you should succeed.'[7] The question of money remained. Mounting a prosecution would be expensive, whatever fruitful results it might yield. Here Wilde hesitated. The money he might expect from his plays was yet to come. Douglas, however, insisted that his family would pay whatever was 'required', so anxious were they to see the marquess held to account. Supported by this promise, Wilde signalled for the inexorable legal process to begin.[8]

It moved quickly. A warrant was obtained that afternoon, and the following morning Queensberry was arrested in his room at Carter's Hotel (a few doors down from the Albemarle Club). He was brought to Marlborough Street Magistrates' Court and charged with publishing a criminal libel. George Lewis, who had been summoned at short notice to represent Queensberry, at once asked for the case to be adjourned for seven days, and his client to be released on bail. The magistrate agreed, but first allowed the club porter to give his evidence as to Queensberry having written the offensive card. When Mr Wright asserted that the inscribed words ran, 'For Oscar Wilde ponce and somdomite', the marquess interjected that the phrase was, in fact, '*posing as* sodomite'.[9] The correction was small but telling: as an accusation it was more nebulous, less serious, and perhaps rather easier to defend. Queensberry was quite uncowed by proceedings,

insisting that he was delighted to have 'succeeded' in 'bringing matters to a head'.[10]

This, however, did nothing to dim the mood in the Wilde camp. During that week Wilde was heartened to learn that George Lewis had withdrawn from the case, citing his friendship with Wilde and Constance, and passing on his instructions to the thirty-two-year-old Charles Russell. Less encouraging was the news that Russell – on the advice of his father, the lord chief justice – had secured the services of Wilde's old Trinity contemporary, Edward Carson, as his lead counsel. Humphreys, on Reggie Turner's advice, had been hoping to engage Carson for Wilde's team. Wilde, however, refused to be unduly concerned, ignoring Carson's ever-growing reputation, and recalling instead his career as a plodding second-class student at Trinity.[11]

The huge cost of the venture was becoming clear. Humphreys required an advance of £150 just to institute proceedings. Neither Lady Queensberry nor Percy were on hand. And although Wilde raised some £800 in advances from George Alexander and others, much of this was 'swallowed up' in paying his impatient creditors. Douglas – according to his own not very reliable testimony – also emptied his own bank account to contribute to the immediate legal expenses.[12]

Wilde's arrival at the committal hearing on Saturday 9 March was made in grand style. He came – accompanied by both Bosie and Percy Douglas – in a coach and pair. Despite arriving ten minutes early, they found the cramped Marlborough Street courtroom already packed. There were some thirty journalists there. Wilde, resplendent in a dark blue velvet-trimmed overcoat, a white flower in his buttonhole, took a seat at his solicitor's table. Bosie and his brother were, however, both ordered to leave the court when the magistrate entered. Carson was there to represent the marquess.

The hearing was a preliminary procedure to ascertain whether there was sufficient evidence against the defendant to warrant a criminal trial. Although largely taken up with legal niceties, it still had its telling moments. Wilde, when examined briefly by Humphreys, at once showed himself to be a less than ideal witness. Asked, 'Are you a dramatist and author?' he replied, loftily, 'I believe I am well-known as a dramatist and author.' The magistrate – 'nipping the play of Oscarism in the bud' (as the *Pall Mall Gazette* put it) – told him sharply to confine himself to answering the questions. Humphreys also sought to introduce some of the letters that Queensberry had written to Bosie and other family members, in which he appeared to libel Wilde. Piquing the interest of the press, he declined to read them out in court, on

the grounds that they made reference to 'exalted personages'. Carson, for his part, while indicating that Queensberry would be pleading 'justification', confirmed the notion that – in attacking Wilde – the marquess had been motivated solely by a desire to 'save' his son. The magistrate duly committed Queensberry for trial at the next sessions of the Central Criminal Court at the beginning of April. Wilde was bound over in the sum of £40 to attend and prosecute.[13]

Matters appeared to be going to plan. Humphreys was very positive. To aggravate Queensberry's offence, and increase the seriousness of the case, he framed the indictment in two parts to claim that the insult 'posing as somdomite' might mean not merely that Wilde was 'posing', but that he had actually 'committed and was in the habit of committing the abominable crime of buggery with mankind'.[14] Having seen the lawyer on the Monday after the committal hearing, Bosie informed his brother that 'everything is splendid and we are going to walk over'.[15] Others, too, were optimistic. Arthur Humphreys (just completing work on the revised text of *Oscariana*) wrote on the same day to Wilde, enthusing, 'I am confident of your success, as is everyone.'[16]

Although it might have seemed like a moment for taking counsel and making plans, Wilde allowed himself to be persuaded by Douglas – and the general air of optimism – that what was needed was another holiday. Pawning some jewellery to raise funds, they left for a week in Monte Carlo. While Bosie lost money at the casino, Wilde struggled to escape his anxieties about the approaching case.[17]

Back in London, Wilde found waiting for him new and massive legal bills (as well as several old domestic ones). He had to raise £500 to secure the services of Sir Edward Clarke as his lead counsel, together with Willie Mathews and Travers Humphreys as juniors. With Lady Queensberry still away in Florence, and Percy out of town, he was obliged to seek the assistance of friends. At very short notice Ada Leverson's husband, Ernest, provided the required sum, supposedly as a loan until the money could be got from the Douglas family in 'a week or ten days at most'.[18] Wilde – accompanied, as ever, by Bosie (who was now referring to the action as 'our case') – met with Sir Edward in his chambers. The former solicitor general, a man of the greatest probity, asked (as Humphreys had done) whether there was any truth behind Queensberry's charges, and was given the solemn assurance that they were absolutely false. Douglas came away from the interview under the impression that Clarke would be wanting to

call him and his brother Percy as witnesses to testify against their father's character. He was delighted at the prospect.[19]

It appeared that Queensberry's plea would rest largely on the supposed 'immorality' – and 'sodomitic' character – of Wilde's published writings, most notably *The Picture of Dorian Gray*. It was thin stuff. The arguments made against Wilde's story at the time of its first appearance were familiar and Wilde felt well equipped to counter them. There seemed even less to fear from the news that Queensberry was planning to produce a copy of *The Chameleon* in the belief that it would 'substantiate what I said of this fellow Oscar Wilde'. The marquess was initially under the mistaken impression that Wilde was the author of an anonymous 'story of sodomy' about a young priest who enters into a suicide pact with the teenage acolyte for whom he has developed a consuming passion. Although when he subsequently discovered that the story had, in fact, been written by the magazine's editor, J. F. Bloxam, he felt it 'did not much matter' since Wilde's 'name is in the magazine signed to a lot of his filthy principles'. The publication, he noted, also contained two 'filthy' 'so-called poems' by his son, 'In Praise of Shame' and 'Two Loves' – the latter 'ending up with these words, "I am the love that dare not breathe [*sic*] its name" – meaning Sodomy'.[20]

Beyond literature, though, it was unclear what the marquess could produce. He had boasted to Percy's wife that the detective, Cook, had incriminating information about Wilde. But the threat was left vague.[21] From his own memory of the Tite Street visit (as well as from Queensberry's various letters to Bosie) Wilde was aware of some of the marquess's suspicions. He seemed to know that Wilde had been blackmailed over his 'madness of kisses' letter, and had heard rumours regarding his time at the Savoy. But this was little enough. Wilde was able to pre-empt the blackmail story, spinning Humphreys and Clarke the tale that the letter was an artistic effusion, almost a 'prose poem', and that it had, indeed, been translated into French verse and published in a magazine. The original letter, moreover, he was able to point out, had been returned to him without the payment of any blackmail.

Wilde's sense of optimism received a check, however, when he approached Frank Harris to ask whether he would be prepared to give evidence that *Dorian Gray* was not an immoral book. Although Harris readily agreed, he remonstrated with Wilde against the absolute folly of going to court – where (whatever his solicitors might tell him) outcomes were never certain, and where an English jury would be most unlikely to give a verdict against

a father who claimed to be 'trying to protect his son'. Harris's conviction was reinforced when, over that weekend, he began to make inquiries among his legal connections, and found all 'people of importance' agreed that Wilde would lose the case, and not just because of Queensberry's pose as a concerned parent; Wilde's actual guilt was generally assumed. Harris urged Wilde to desist – to go abroad with his wife, and leave Queensberry and Douglas to pursue their feud alone. It sounded a first, and disturbing, note of danger.

Wilde met Harris again the next afternoon (Monday 25 March) at the Café Royal to discuss the matter further. Bernard Shaw, who was lunching with Harris, also counselled Wilde to drop the case and leave the country. Harris suggested Wilde might write a plausible letter to the *The Times* giving reasons for his decision. The plan had a real attraction, at least on the surface, and Wilde seemed, for a moment, tempted to adopt it. There would be financial consequences: besides having to pay the £40 surety for abandoning his prosecution, Wilde would be liable for Queensberry's legal costs to date. It is unlikely, though, that the impractical Wilde had calculated this side of the equation. And before he could, Douglas joined the party. He dismissed the scheme at once. 'Such advice shows you are no friend of Oscar's,' he fumed at Harris, before storming out. Wilde followed meekly after, telling Harris, 'It is not friendly of you, Frank. It really is not friendly.' It was clear that his course was set, and that Douglas would hold him to it.[22] Wilde drowned out the suggestions of Harris and Shaw with other voices. The 'wonderful' Mrs Robinson, Wilde reported to Ada Leverson, prophesied 'complete triumph'.[23]

There was no let-up. Counsel on both sides were anxious that the case should be 'speedily dealt with'. Although Queensberry's lawyers claimed not to be able to deliver the plea of justification until Saturday 30 March, Wilde's side decided against 'adopting the customary course of asking for an adjournment' in order to investigate its assertions, and the trial date was set for Wednesday 3 April.[24] In the meantime yet more money was required. Wilde asked Walter Palmer for the loan of £400, though it seems doubtful that he received it.[25] Constance raised £50 from her cousin Eliza Napier, and £100 from Eliza's mother, as well as supplying £50 from her own funds.[26]

When, on the Saturday morning, the plea of justification was delivered, Wilde's returning confidence vanished. Although the document cited both *The Picture of Dorian Gray* and *The Chameleon* as works 'calculated to subvert morality and encourage unnatural vice', these expected literary charges

were preceded by a long, and unexpected, list of human ones. In paragraph after paragraph it was asserted that Wilde had solicited and incited young men 'to commit sodomy and other acts of gross indecency', although in each instance it was claimed that Wilde had succeeded only in committing 'the said acts of gross indecency' rather than sodomy itself. The wording nimbly relieved the defence from the difficult business of proving that 'sodomy' had actually occurred, and (as Sir Edward Clarke noted) relieved their witnesses from having to admit that 'they themselves have been guilty of the gravest of offences'. At the same time it forcibly suggested that Wilde had done considerably more than merely 'pose' as a sodomite. Names, dates and places were given: Edward Shelley and Sidney Mavor at the Albemarle Hotel; Fred Atkins and Maurice Schwabe in Paris; Alfred Wood at Tite Street; Charles Parker at the Savoy; Walter Grainger at Oxford and Goring; Alphonse Conway at Worthing and Brighton. The catalogue ran back over three years. It was, as Reggie Turner recalled, 'a knock down blow'. It was difficult to comprehend how such information could have been assembled.

Although Wilde remained in ignorance of the fact, the making of the case against him had been an oddly fortuitous business. At the outset of proceedings, Queensberry had little to back up his plea of justification besides hearsay, the tenor of Wilde's published writings and one fulsomely phrased letter to Bosie that had come into his hands. Indeed Carson was, initially, reluctant to accept the brief, in part because he disliked the idea of appearing against his erstwhile classmate, but principally because he considered the case too weak. Queensberry's solicitor, Russell, however, had encouraged him with news that his investigators (ex-Scotland Yard detectives Littlechild and Kearley) deployed on Queensberry's instructions, were following several promising leads. And his mentor, Lord Halsbury, had further convinced him to take the case.

Even so Carson had, apparently, been inclined to advise Queensberry to plead guilty until only moments before the committal hearing at Marlborough Street. It was then that he learned that, following up a lead from the Savoy Hotel, Russell's investigators had tracked down Charles Parker to his Royal Artillery barracks, and put pressure on him to make a statement about his sexual relations with Wilde. It was a difficult business as Russell was not acting for the Crown, so could not offer Parker immunity from prosecution for evidence that must necessarily be self-incriminating. Both legal threats and financial inducements played their part.

Following that first discovery other incidents were brought to light. Charles Brookfield, obsessed with his animus against Wilde, had begun his own investigation into Wilde's sexual habits and clandestine contacts. Having elicited from an unsuspecting commissionaire at a London theatre the name of Alfred Taylor as one of Wilde's associates, he passed it on to Littlechild and Kearley. At one of Taylor's former addresses – 3 Chapel Street – Kearley discovered a 'hatbox full of papers' that Taylor had left behind. It contained much incriminating information. From various of Taylor's letters and notes Russell was able to identify, track down and get statements from Sidney Mavor, Alfred Wood, Fred Atkins, Robert Cliburn and William Allen. Wilde's past movements were tracked: at Oxford and Goring and Worthing; at the Savoy Hotel and the Albemarle. Former servants were interviewed and suborned. Walter Grainger, Alphonse Conway and Edward Shelley found themselves caught in Russell's net.[27]

Looking over the plea of justification Wilde may have noted that some of the precise details were incorrect. And he might have perceived that none of the charges was easy to prove in law. But he did recognize their essential truth. And it was blindingly clear that their discussion in open court could only mean complete social ruin. If they could be substantiated at all they must result not only in Queensberry's acquittal, but also – very probably – in his own arrest. A vertiginous chasm had opened at his feet. From this time on, as Turner put it, he had 'death in his heart'.[28]

A withdrawal must have looked even more attractive now. But it was too late. Indeed it had probably been too late even when Harris and Shaw had suggested it at the start of the week. If Wilde abandoned his prosecution it was most unlikely that Queensberry would allow the matter to rest. He would be entitled to bring an action against Wilde for having falsely accused him of libel. Or, as it now appeared, he could pass on a mass of damaging information about Wilde's sexual liaisons to the director of public prosecutions. If Wilde went abroad (as Harris had urged) it would be construed as an admission of guilt. Wilde began to perceive that he had blundered into a 'booby trap'.[29] There was no option but to go forward. Wilde found himself – accompanied as ever by Douglas – back in the 'ghastly glare' of Humphreys' bleak room, going through the plea of justification line by line, denying its veracity and 'with a serious face telling serious lies to a bald man'.[30]

On the Monday evening, in a public show of defiance, Wilde attended *The Importance of Being Earnest* together with Constance and Bosie. Though

he affected to enjoy the evening, Constance was – understandably – 'very much agitated' throughout. Douglas noted that she had 'tears in her eyes' when they parted at the end of the evening. Alexander was agitated too. When Wilde went round between the acts, the actor-manager joined the chorus of those urging him to leave the country. 'Everyone wants me to go abroad,' Wilde replied. 'I have just been abroad. And now I have come home again. One can't keep on going abroad, unless one is a missionary, or, what comes to the same thing, a commercial traveller.'[31]

Wilde's one slender hope was that Queensberry's lawyers did not actually have the witnesses or the hard evidence to back up the bold claims of their plea of justification (there was no obligation for the defence to disclose such matters). In an effort to discover how things stood, Wilde sent word to Alfred Taylor. He also tried to contact Sidney Mavor, the most 'respectable' of the young men listed in the plea. Taylor came to see him at Tite Street on the day before the trial began. He seems to have been as mystified as Wilde by the apparent flood of revelations, and undertook to investigate. His findings were chilling. He wrote to Wilde shortly afterwards to say that he was being watched by a private investigator (an ex-inspector named Littlechild), and that he, or another, had gained access to his old rooms in Chapel Street – rooms that might have yielded much incriminating evidence.[32] It was ominous news.

3

The Prosecutor

*'We have been to the Sibyl Robinson. She prophesied com-
plete triumph, and was most wonderful.'*

OSCAR WILDE

The case of 'Regina (Wilde) versus the Marquess of Queensberry'
began in the Central Criminal Court at the Old Bailey at half past
ten on Wednesday 3 April 1895. It was eagerly anticipated. The details
of Queensberry's plea of justification, though not published, had become
partly known. Wilde arrived to find the small panelled courtroom thronged
with bewigged barristers, anxious to witness the drama. They filled the
seats and benches, and stood, 'a serried mass of voluble, grey wigged, black-
gowned humanity, in the gangways and approaches of the court'. The few
places they had not secured were taken by the press; while, up above, the
narrow public gallery was crammed with lookers-on, all of them male.
Wilde, pushing through the crowd to reach his legal team, had to pass close
to where the Marquess of Queensberry stood – thin and drawn, but still
pugnacious – sporting a Cambridge-blue hunting stock instead of a collar
and tie. His red-tinged side whiskers bristled. Wilde himself was dressed
with studied sobriety, even gravity, in a black morning coat, his black tie
fastened with a diamond and sapphire pin. He wore – it was noted – no
buttonhole.[1] The judge, Justice Henn Collins, took his place on the bench.

Queensberry entered the dock, where, refusing a chair, he stood with his arms folded. The jury (of a dozen north London shopkeepers) was sworn. And the case began.[2]

Sir Edward Clarke referred briefly to the allegations of 'indecency' made in Queensberry's plea of justification, but sought to make light of them: it would be up to the defence to provide 'credible witnesses', he suggested pointedly, and actual evidence to support such serious charges. There followed an outline of Wilde's career, his family life and his literary achievements; his friendship with Lord Alfred Douglas, and his dealings with an increasingly intemperate Queensberry. Sir Edward touched on *Dorian Gray* and *The Chameleon*. And, in an attempt to forestall one possible line of the defence, he laid out the story of Wilde's 'extravagant' madness-of-kisses letter to Douglas, telling of how it had fallen into the hands of Alfred Wood, of how Wilde had refused to be blackmailed over it by Allen and Cliburn, and of how it had been transformed from a 'prose poem' into a French sonnet. He then proceeded to take Wilde over the same ground.

Posed easily in the witness box, with his arms resting on the rail, Wilde gave an assured performance. Clear and succinct for the most part, his well-honed accounts of the confrontations at Tite Street, first with Allen and Cliburn, and then with Queensberry, provoked frequent laughter. The line 'I don't know what the Queensberry Rules are, but the Oscar Wilde rule is to shoot at sight' was especially enjoyed. From the dock, only a few feet away, Queensberry looked on with undisguised contempt, his lower lip working ceaselessly.[3]

The examination-in-chief lasted just over an hour. Then Carson rose to commence his cross-examination. In anticipation of the confrontation, Wilde had remarked to his junior counsel, 'No doubt he will perform his task with all the added bitterness of an old friend.'[4] And he was right. Wilde faced his adversary with a smile. 'A man', remarked the *Daily Chronicle*, 'might as well have smiled at the rack'. Carson may have been suffering from a bad cold, but he pursued his task with his wonted remorseless zeal. His first move was to establish that Wilde was not thirty-nine, as he had claimed to Sir Edward Clarke, but 'something over forty'. The point was small enough (a matter of six months) but it revealed Wilde's casual attitude to the truth, and also emphasized the disparity in age between him and the twenty-four-year-old Lord Alfred Douglas. Carson, however, did not press home the point at once. Instead Wilde found himself led on to the surer ground of literature: here he defended Douglas's two poems in

the *The Chameleon* as 'exceedingly beautiful' and refused to be drawn upon the tale of 'The Priest and the Acolyte'. Asked whether he did not consider the story 'immoral', he provoked laughter by replying, 'Worse, it is badly written.' About his own contributions to the magazine he was playful:

CARSON: Listen sir. Here is one of your 'Phrases and Philosophies for the Use of the Young': 'Wickedness is a myth invented by good people to account for the curious attractiveness of others.' (*Laughter*) ... Do you think that is true?

WILDE: I rarely think that anything I write is true. (*Laughter*) ... Not true in the sense of correspondence to fact; to represent wilful moods of paradox, of fun, nonsense, of anything at all – but not true in the actual sense of correspondence to actual facts of life, certainly not; I should be very sorry to think it.

As to whether such axioms as 'Religions die when they are proved to be true' or 'If one tells the truth one is sure sooner or later to be found out' were suitable 'for the Use of the Young', Wilde suggested to his former college mate, 'Anything that stimulates thought in people of any age is good for them.'

He continued to assert his belief in the absolute division between art and morality as Carson drew him into discussions of *Dorian Gray* and Huysmans' *À Rebours*. He was obliged to admit that, in revising his own original magazine story for publication in book form, he had altered one passage to avoid conveying the unintended 'impression that the sin of Dorian Gray was sodomy'. But this, he claimed, had been done, not to assuage any moral clamour in the popular press, but on the advice of the great literary critic Walter Pater. It had been an artistic judgement.

Wilde turned aside Carson's repeated attempts to draw connections between the story of *Dorian Gray* and Wilde's own friendship with Lord Alfred Douglas. When Carson quoted – from what he called the 'purged' passage – Basil Hallward's description of how he had 'adored [Dorian] madly, extravagantly, absurdly', and demanded, 'Have you ever felt that feeling of adoring madly a beautiful male person many years younger than yourself?' Wilde replied, 'I have never given adoration to anybody except myself.' It called forth another burst of laughter, as did his assertion that he had 'borrowed' the idea of such an infatuation from Shakespeare. Wilde proudly declared his 'love' for Douglas, but described him as his great

'friend'. He defended his extravagantly phrased letters as 'beautiful' works of art.[5]*

Carson remained implacable. It seemed to many of those present in the courtroom that they were witnessing 'a contest of giants'. Wilde maintained his poise, and won his laughs, but Carson refused to be deflected. His 'white, thin, clever' face stood out in sharp relief beneath his wig. He deployed his arsenal of mannerisms – of pregnant pauses, quizzical looks and grim smiles. His 'self-possession is absolute', reported the *Daily Chronicle*. 'Against him a witness, however good his case, is, while the cross-examination lasts, as lath against iron.'[6]

On and on the questions went, throughout the long afternoon session, as they moved from literature to life – and to Wilde's friendships with a succession of young men. Who was Alfred Wood? What was his occupation? What was his age? How had they met? Had Wilde taken him to supper and given him money? How had he come to know Edward Shelley? When and where had he met Alphonse Conway? Had Wilde bought him a new suit of clothes, or given him a cigarette case? Did Conway call him Oscar?' At every juncture Carson pointed up the disparities in age, in class, in intellectual attainment between 'Oscar' and these 'boys': Wood, the 'twenty-four-year-old' unemployed 'clerk', Shelley, the Bodley Head 'office boy' aged 'eighteen'; Conway, the similarly aged 'loafer' on the Worthing seafront.[7]

But Carson's questions also swooped into darker places: 'Did you ask [Wood] to your house at Tite Street?' 'Was your wife away at that time at Torquay?' 'Did you ever have immoral practices with Wood?' 'Did you ever open his trousers?' 'Put your hand upon his person?' 'Did you ever put your own person between his legs?' 'Did [Shelley] stay all night [at the Albemarle Hotel] and leave the next morning at eight o'clock?' 'Each of you having taken off all your clothes, did you take his person in your hand in bed?'; 'Did you kiss [Conway] on the [Lancing] road?' 'Did you put your hands in his trousers?' To this barrage of questions, Wilde could only put up a succession

---

*   In discussing Wilde's correspondence, Carson was delighted to reveal that he had been totally unaware of 'the madness of kisses' letter before it was brought up in court and elaborately explained away. Nevertheless Wilde had been right to suspect that Queensberry's side had got hold of one of his letters: it was a marginally less compromising missive that he had sent to the 'Dearest of all boys' from the Savoy, regretting Bosie's tendency to 'make scenes': 'They wreck the loveliness of life. I cannot see you, so Greek and gracious, distorted by passion – I cannot listen to your curved lips saying hideous things to me. Don't do it. You break my heart. I had sooner be rented all day than have you bitter, unjust, horrid.'

of stout denials, but the questions were damaging enough. And they revealed to Wilde for the first time the extent of the information that the defence had managed to secure. It was clear that they had detailed first-hand statements from the various witnesses.[8] When the court rose at quarter to five, Wilde must have been exhausted. It had been a punishing day, the successes of the morning undermined by the revelations of the afternoon.

There was much for a prurient press to cover and a prurient public to discuss. The case was hailed as 'about the most "tasty" thing that the masculine barbarians of the West End have enjoyed for many a day'. Its combination of illicit sex and Wildean wit proved irresistible to a newspaper-buying public.[9] Even as Wilde left the court the newsboys were hawking evening papers with accounts of the morning's proceedings. 'Scandal', 'Sensation', 'Extraordinary Revelations', ran the headlines. Many of the papers carried verbatim reports, transcribing large portions of the cross-examination – only obscuring references to 'sodomitical' habits with allusions to 'nameless' crimes, or with rows of ellipses. In the frenzy of press coverage, the *St James's Gazette* distinguished itself by refusing to mention the case at all – a move that won it rather more publicity than sales.

The grim circus began again the following morning. Wilde, considerably subdued, was obliged by Carson to describe his 'intimacy' with Alfred Taylor, and tell of the all-male tea parties held at his 'strongly perfumed' candlelit rooms in Little College Street.[10] Carson then embarked on a roll call of working-class, and usually unemployed, young men whom Wilde – he suggested – had met and entertained, through Taylor: Fred Atkins, Charles Parker and his brother William, Sidney Mavor, Ernest Scarfe (a one-time valet 'about twenty years of age'). Had Wilde engaged in 'intimacies' with them? He denied it. Had he given them cigarette cases? He confessed that he was fond of giving people cigarette cases. Asked what he could possibly have in common with such people, he replied, 'Well, I will tell you Mr Carson. I delight in the society of people much younger than myself. I like those who may be called idle and careless. I recognize no social distinctions at all of any kind and to me youth – the mere fact of youth – is so wonderful that I would sooner talk to a young man for half an hour than even be, well, cross-examined in court.'

It was one of several sallies. Taxed as to whether 'iced champagne' was a favourite drink of his, Wilde replied, 'Yes, strongly against my doctor's orders.' 'Never mind the doctor's orders,' cut in Carson, allowing Wilde the riposte: 'I don't. It has all the more flavour if you discard the doctor's orders.'

Such facetiousness might win a laugh, but Carson knew that it would not sway a jury. He moved implacably on to Walter Grainger, the teenage servant from Douglas's lodgings at Oxford: 'Did you have him to dine with you?' 'Never in my life'; 'Did you ever kiss him?' 'Oh no, never in my life; he was a peculiarly plain boy.' The qualification was lightly given, but Carson pounced upon it, rapping out question after question:

CARSON: He was what?

WILDE: I said I thought him unfortunately – his appearance was so very unfortunately – very ugly – I mean – I pitied him for it.

CARSON: Very ugly?

WILDE: Yes.

CARSON: Do you say that in support of your statement that you never kissed him?

WILDE: No, I don't; it is like asking me if I kissed a doorpost; it is childish.

CARSON: Didn't you give me as the reason that you never kissed him that he was too ugly?

WILDE (*warmly*): No, I did not say that.

CARSON: Why did you mention his ugliness?

WILDE: No, I said the question seemed to me like – your asking me whether I ever had him to dinner, and then whether I had kissed him – seemed to me merely an intentional insult on your part, which I have been going through the whole of this morning.

CARSON: Because he was ugly?

WILDE: No.

CARSON: Why did you mention his ugliness? I have to ask these questions.

WILDE: I say it is ridiculous to imagine that any such thing could have occurred under any circumstances.

CARSON: Why did you mention his ugliness?

WILDE: For that reason. If you asked me if I had ever kissed a doorpost, I should say, 'No! Ridiculous! I shouldn't like to kiss a doorpost?' The questions are grotesque.

CARSON: Why did you mention the boy's ugliness?

WILDE: I mentioned it perhaps because you stung me by an insolent question.

CARSON: Because I stung you by an insolent question?

WILDE: Yes, you stung with by an insolent question; you make me irritable.

CARSON: Did you say the boy was ugly, because I stung you with an insolent question?

(*Here the witness began several answers almost inarticulately, and none of them
finished. His efforts to collect his ideas were not aided by Mr Carson's sharp staccato
repletion, 'Why? Why? Why did you add that?' At last the witness answered...*)

WILDE: Pardon me, you sting me, insult me and try to unnerve me in every
way. At times one says things flippantly when one should speak more
seriously, I admit it, I admit it – I cannot help it. That is what you are
doing to me.

CARSON: You said it flippantly? You mention this ugliness flippantly; that
is what you wish to convey now?

WILDE: Oh don't say what I wish to convey. I have given you my answer.

CARSON: Is that it, that that was a flippant answer?

WILDE: Oh, it was a flippant answer, yes; I will say it was certainly a flippant answer.

CARSON: Did ever any indecencies take place between you and Grainger?

WILDE: No, sir, none, none at all.[11]

For many in the court it seemed a climactic moment, with Wilde rattled
and retreating, having inadvertently and indirectly admitted that he would
have considered kissing a less 'unfortunate-looking' boy.[12]

When Carson concluded his cross-examination soon afterwards, Sir
Edward Clarke tried to wrest the initiative back by re-examining Wilde, getting him to cast his various associations in a better light: to emphasize the
respectability of Alfred Taylor (a cultured piano-playing Old Marlburian)
and of the deliberately unnamed Maurice Schwabe ('a gentleman of high
position, good birth and good repute'); to show the real engagement and
generosity in his dealings with Shelley and Conway. To capture attention he
introduced as evidence Queensberry's intemperate letters to Lord Alfred
Douglas and Alfred Montgomery. Certainly the reference to Wilde as a
'damned cur and coward of the Rosebery type' created a momentary stir
when it was read out, but the rest of the letter made clear that Queensberry's ire against Rosebery was over the political slight that he and
Gladstone and the queen had delivered in raising Viscount Drumlanrig to
the peerage. There was sympathy, too, for the marquess, as he stood in the
dock throughout the interminable reading, 'gazing alternately' at Wilde in
the witness box, and at his son, who was sitting at the opposite end of the
court. 'Every now and then', the *Sun* reported, 'he turned to the man in

the witness-box and ground his teeth together and shook his head at the witness in the most violent manner. Then when the more pathetic parts of the letter came [relating to Drumlanrig's death], the poor old nobleman had the greatest difficulty in restraining the tears which welled into his eyes, and forced him to bite his lips to keep them back.'[13] As evidence it did nothing to advance Wilde's case. It did, though, allow Rosebery's enemies, both political and personal, to claim that he had been 'mentioned' in the case – or to suggest rather more.*

The introduction of new evidence opened up the option for Carson to re-cross-examine. It was not a prospect that Wilde relished. At the lunch break he asked his counsel whether he could be examined 'on anything they choose'. Pressed as to what his anxiety was, he confessed that 'some time ago I was turned out of the Albemarle Hotel in the middle of the night and a boy was with me. It might be awkward if they found out about it.' Sir Edward Clarke cannot have been encouraged by the revelation.[14] When Wilde failed to resume his place in the witness box after lunch, it was whispered in the courtroom that he must have fled, rather than face Carson again. But the rumour proved false. He appeared at quarter past two, apologizing that the clock in the restaurant where he had lunched was running slow.

In the event Carson did not seek to cross-examine on the new evidence. Nor did Clarke, as some expected, at this stage call Alfred Douglas as a witness. He preferred to close his case 'for the present'. Wilde took the opportunity to leave the witness box and the courtroom. He missed the opening of Carson's assured and devastating address, but had certainly returned in time to hear that Alfred Wood, whom Wilde supposed to be in America, was back in London and would be giving evidence: '[He] will describe to you – I am not going to anticipate to you – how time after time Mr Oscar Wilde, almost from the commencement of their acquaintance, adopted filthy and immoral practices with him.' A 'gasp of amazement' went round

---

*   Rosebery, just then, was beset with cares. On 19 February he had tried to resign as prime minister, feeling that he lacked the support of his cabinet colleagues. He had been dissuaded. But his health had then collapsed. He was left almost incapacitated by an unspecified nervous affliction that affected his digestion and destroyed his sleep. His illness continued throughout March and April (and into May). Given the rumours about Rosebery's sexual interest in young men, there were those who were ready to draw damaging connections. On 21 April 1895 Lord Durham informed Reginald Esher that 'the Newmarket scum [the racing set] say that R[osebery] never had the influenza, and that his insomnia was caused by terror of being in the Wilde scandal. Very charitable.'

the courtroom at this announcement. But it was only one among many. Carson had already indicated that Charles Parker would also be appearing, and that witnesses from the Savoy would prove 'up to hilt' the allegations about Wilde's 'immoralities' at that hotel. When the court rose, Carson was not yet halfway through his remarks.[15]

Wilde retired to the nearby Holborn Viaduct Hotel, where he was staying for convenience. He – together with Bosie – telegraphed to Ada Leverson, crying off dinner that evening: 'We have a lot of very important business to do,' they explained. 'Everything is very satisfactory.'[16] But 'satisfactory' it was not. Although they could perhaps convince themselves that most of the witnesses Carson was threatening to produce were accomplices and self-confessed criminals, whose testimony might be discredited, to fight on such ground was extremely dangerous and uncertain.

Sir Edward Clarke sought a conference with Wilde the following morning. He had considered the matter overnight, and thought that, on what they had already heard, the jury would be bound to acquit Queensberry, and that the only sane course of action was for Wilde to withdraw from the prosecution, and to allow Clarke to consent to a verdict of 'not guilty' as regards the lesser charge of 'posing' as a sodomite on the basis of his literary works. Otherwise, there was a real risk that, if the case ran to its end, with the full parade of evidence being given, and the jury found for the defendant, the judge would order Wilde's arrest in open court. The junior counsel, Willie Mathews, did offer a counter-view: he thought that the credibility of Queensberry's witnesses could be impugned and the case might still be won. But Wilde had grown doubtful on the point.[17] He was, apparently, moved by Clarke's opinion that the case might run for another three or four days; the expense would be more than he could afford. It seems, too, that Clarke thought he had secured a private agreement with Carson that if the case were dropped now 'nothing more would be heard of the matter'.[18] At all events Wilde accepted Clarke's advice.

He was relieved to learn that his own further presence in court would not be necessary. While his counsel entered the courtroom, where Carson had already picked up the thread of his remorseless opening address, Wilde left the building by a side entrance and drove the short distance to the Holborn Viaduct Hotel. There he was soon joined in conference by Alfred Douglas and his brother, Percy, as well as by Robbie Ross and (most probably) Reggie Turner.[19]

His case had failed. This great shock was soon followed by others.

Wilde was informed that Clarke had been unable to limit Queensberry's victory merely to the 'posing' element of the charge, that the marquess had been awarded costs, and that no indication had been given that 'matters' would now be dropped. When a reporter from the *Sun* arrived, seeking an interview, Percy came out to answer his questions, asserting that Bosie had been eager to go into the witness box, but Wilde had forbade it. He stressed, however, that he – 'and every member of our family, excepting my father' – refused to believe the allegations against Wilde made by the defence, and claimed that 'with Mr Wilde's full authority he could state that Mr Wilde had no thoughts of immediately leaving London, and would stay to face whatever might be the result of the proceedings'. Wilde dispatched a letter along the same lines to the London *Evening News*.

4

Regina Versus Wilde

'All trials are trials for one's life.'

It was not the only letter written that afternoon. Wilde, it seems, scribbled a note to Constance, urging her to let no one enter his 'bedroom or sitting-room'. Queensberry's solicitor, Charles Russell, meanwhile, wasted no time in writing to the Crown's director of prosecutions, Hamilton Cuffe, enclosing 'a copy of all our witnesses' statements' together with the trial transcript, in order that 'justice' might be done.[1] Cuffe, besides seeking an immediate interview with Russell, also sent the particulars round to the House of Commons for the attention of Asquith, the home secretary, and the law officers Sir Robert Reid (attorney general) and Sir Frank Lockwood (solicitor general).

This high-level consultation is certainly suggestive: the case had acquired a political dimension. Clarke's decision to read out Queensberry's letters had had unintended consequences. The fact that the names of Rosebery and Gladstone had been mentioned (however obliquely) in court placed the Liberal establishment in an awkward position. They needed to be seen to be acting without fear or favour in their dealings with Wilde, lest it be claimed that they were involved in some sort of cover-up. Wilde's three erstwhile Eighty Club colleagues – Asquith, Reid and Lockwood – swiftly

agreed that a warrant should be applied for, and Asquith gave instructions that Wilde should be stopped 'wherever he might be found'.[2]

The marquess, for his part, had stepped out of the Old Bailey to be greeted as a conquering hero by cheering bystanders and supporters. It was reported that he had sent a message to Wilde, declaring, 'If the country allows you to leave, all the better for the country, but if you take my son with you I will follow you wherever you go and shoot you.'[3] To the reporters who gathered at Carter's Hotel that afternoon he suggested, however, that, rather than being allowed to flee, Wilde 'ought to be placed where he can ruin no more young men'.[4]

If Wilde had decided to leave England for the continent that afternoon, it is probable that he would have been allowed to go, despite the stated hopes of Asquith and Queensberry that he be apprehended.[5] But, as Percy's statement – and his own letter – made clear, Wilde had resolved to stay. Quite why is less obvious. Ross had urged him to go to France. There was perhaps a touch of defiance in his refusal, but inertia probably played a greater part. Wilde was stunned by his reversal; 'With what a crash this fell!', he later lamented to Ada Leverson. 'Why did the Sibyl [Mrs Robinson] say fair things?'[6] Disappointed by fortune tellers, he seems to have surrendered himself to his fate, and become almost an observer of his own catastrophe.[7]

He did make one last small effort to face the crisis, calling at the offices of Messrs Lewis & Lewis, in nearby Ely Place. But his old friend Sir George was unable to help. 'What is the good of coming to me now,' the lawyer exclaimed. 'I am powerless to do anything. If you had had the sense to bring Lord Queensberry's card to me in the first place, I would have torn it up and thrown it in the fire, and told you not to make a fool of yourself.'[8] Wilde had made more than a fool of himself.

Uncertain what to do next, he took his brougham and, having called at his bank in St James's, went on to the Cadogan Hotel, where Bosie had been staying for the past week. His progress across town was tracked by a troop of journalists and by Queensberry's hired detectives. As Wilde drove through St James's he may have noticed his name being removed from the playbills outside the Haymarket and the St James's Theatres. Over the three days of the trial it had been remarked that attendances at both theatres has 'fallen off'.[9]*

---

*   Of the performances on 5 April it was noted (by the *Glasgow Herald*) that at neither theatre 'was there any hostile demonstration', although at the St James's the audience

Installed in Bosie's rooms at the hotel by the middle of the afternoon, Wilde sat and waited with his trio of friends. He drank hock-and-seltzer with a steady determination. Already the evening papers were predicting his arrest. Ross was dispatched to take the news of Queensberry's victory to Constance, who was staying with her aunt in Lower Seymour Street. She had Vyvyan with her; Cyril had been taken out of Bedales and sent to relatives in Ireland. Through her tears, she pleaded with Robbie to encourage Wilde to go 'away abroad'.[10] Wilde, however, remained unmoved and immovable. He deflected all suggestions of flight, with the assertion – quite untrue – that 'the train has gone... it is too late'. There were, in fact, regular boat-trains from Victoria until quarter to ten in the evening. Bosie, unable to bear the strain of waiting, took himself off to the House of Commons to consult his cousin, George Wyndham, about the government's plans to prosecute. While he was absent, a reporter from the *Star* arrived and informed Ross that he had seen confirmation on the news 'tape' that a warrant for Wilde's arrest had indeed been issued. The authorities had acted with almost unexampled speed. When Ross relayed the news, Wilde's face turned 'very grey'.[11]

At around half past six came the knock on the door. Two plainclothes policemen entered. 'Mr Wilde, I believe?' Wilde rose to his feet. He would give no trouble. Pausing only to put on his overcoat, gather his gloves, and pick up a copy of Pierre Louÿs's latest novel, he was led down to the waiting 'growler'. He was driven first to Scotland Yard, where the arrest warrant was read, charging him under Section 11 of the 1885 Criminal Law Amendment Act with 'committing acts of gross indecency with other male persons'. From there he was taken to Bow Street police station, where he was booked and taken down to a cell for the night. Neither Douglas nor Ross was allowed to see him.

At ten o'clock the following day the committal proceedings began, heard before the magistrate, Sir John Bridge, in the small – and crammed – 'upper' courtroom at Bow Street Police Court. Wilde found himself joined in the dock by Alfred Taylor, who had been arrested that morning at his lodgings in Pimlico. They greeted each other with a bow. Charles Gill – Carson's junior in the Queensberry trial – acted as the prosecutor for the

---

'was much smaller than usual'. And 'in one or two places slightly discordant remarks were made' – chiefly from the gallery – 'especially when reference was made to the town of Worthing' – which was now associated with Wilde's seduction of Alphonse Conway.

Crown. He began to lay out the case against Wilde and Taylor with slow deliberation. The witnesses mentioned by Carson began to be produced: the Parker brothers, Alfred Wood, Fred Atkins, Sidney Mavor and – in due course – Edward Shelley. The dangers and difficulties facing Wilde became horribly vivid. Ready to implicate themselves, it was apparent that the witnesses had been granted immunity from prosecution in exchange for their testimony. It became clear, too, that they had received – or were receiving – financial support from Queensberry's solicitors. Edward Shelley had, it was said, received 20 guineas for his two days' attendance during the libel trial, despite the fact that his weekly wage, when at the Bodley Head, was a modest 15s. Charles Parker appeared resplendent in a new suit paid for by the prosecution.[12]

Wilde had to listen as they detailed their various encounters with him: the dinners at Kettner's, the nights at the Savoy, the parties in Taylor's rooms, the assignations in rented lodgings, the clandestine visits to Tite Street and St James's Place – and the sex. William Parker claimed that Taylor had told him and his brother that Wilde would like them to behave 'the same as women'. Charles Parker described how he and Wilde had undressed and got into bed naked at the Savoy (before Gill interposed with 'I don't propose to take this further, in any detail' – for the present). Alfred Wood's account of what occurred between him and Wilde at Tite Street was so graphic as to be 'unreportable', even by the downmarket *Reynolds's Newspaper*.[13] After them came the first of a succession of hotel employees, lodging-house keepers, waiters and servants who had seen Wilde in more or less compromising circumstances. There was the masseur and the chambermaid at the Savoy who had noticed a 'common' boy in Wilde's bed; the same maid had also been shocked by the 'peculiar' staining of Wilde's bed sheets and night shirt, apparently smeared with Vaseline, semen and 'soil'.[14]

Wilde was supported by the same legal team that had handled his unfortunate prosecution of Queensberry. Sir Edward Clarke – regretting, it seems, having advised Wilde to withdraw from that case – insisted that he and his juniors would give their services without charge.[15] Humphreys, too, ceased to send in his bills (Taylor was represented by his own barrister, J. P. Grain). At the first hearing at Bow Street, one small victory was achieved. When Sidney Mavor was called to give evidence, he provided a full account of his visit to Wilde at the Albemarle Hotel but then – to the surprise of the prosecution (who had his very full statement to the contrary) – he flatly denied that any improprieties had occurred. The credit for this unexpected

coup was claimed by Douglas; he had encountered Mavor in the corridors of the police court and told him, 'For God's sake, remember you are a gentleman and a public school boy. Don't put yourself on a level with scum like Wood and Parker. When counsel asks you the questions, deny the whole thing, and say you made the statement because you were frightened by the police. They can't do anything to you.'[16] Mavor's volte-face left the prosecution without its most outwardly 'respectable' witness, and also the one who linked Wilde most closely to Taylor.

The defence still faced many obstacles. The prosecution had determined that Wilde and Taylor should be tried together, an arrangement likely to be detrimental to Wilde's chances. One day was not enough for the Crown to produce all its witnesses; two further hearings would be required, on 11 and 19 April. In the meantime an application for bail was denied, owing – it was stated – to the 'gravity of the case'. Sir John Bridge, going considerably beyond his judicial discretion, suggested that 'there is no worse crime than that with which the prisoners are charged' – this, in spite of the fact, that 'gross indecency' was, technically, not a crime at all, but a misdemeanour.

The prejudice was typical. Queensberry's victory and Wilde's arrest had called forth an extraordinary outpouring of self-righteous vituperation from press and public alike. Among the sheaf of telegrams that the victorious Queensberry had received was one stating, 'Every man in the City is with you. Kill the bugger!'[17] George Wyndham noted that such hostility was common to 'all classes'.[18] Frank Harris thought it fiercest among the 'puritan middle class, who had always distrusted Wilde as an artist, an intellectual and "a mere parasite of the aristocracy"'.[19] Many old friends turned their backs.* In all quarters Wilde's guilt was generally assumed. The *Echo* was living up to its name in announcing that 'Mr Oscar Wilde is "damned and done for".' It was expected – and hoped – that more arrests might follow. Hooting mobs gathered outside Bow Street to greet Wilde's arrival at his subsequent hearings. The more salacious details revealed by the witnesses were circulated in hastily produced pamphlets.[20] Street songs of 'questionable, if not infamous character' relating to the case were sung 'in many of the public thoroughfares, particularly in South London'.[21]

---

* Ettie Grenfell would recall how her husband, Willie, had taken Wilde's side during the early stages of the libel trial, protesting that the claims made against him were 'impossible'. But, as the case proceeded, his innocence was shocked. He said, even before Wilde's arrest, 'We can never have him to Taplow again.'

Condemnation, however, was not only personal but also artistic. Lucien Pissarro, writing to his father, described the hatred unleashed against Wilde, as less an attack on '*sodomisme*' than an assault upon the artist and the human spirit. Wilde's fall would mark the end of the Aesthetic movement in England, just at the moment when the rest of Europe was coming to admire it. '*L'Anglais*,' Pissarro declared, '*déteste l'Art.*'[22] The 'English' press certainly did now detest Wilde's artistic vision. The *National Observer*, though no longer edited by Henley, announced, 'There is no man or woman in the English-speaking world possessed of the treasure of a wholesome mind who is not under a deep debt of gratitude to the Marquess of Queensberry for destroying the High Priest of the Decadents.' He looked forward to the 'legal and social sequels' of Queensberry's victory: 'There must be another trial at the Old Bailey, or a coroner's inquest – the latter for choice; and of the Decadents of their hideous conceptions of the meaning of Art, of their worse than Eleusinian mysteries, there must be an absolute end.'[23]

If Wilde had pulled down the temple of art upon himself, it was clear that others were to be injured in its fall. All modern artistic expression stood condemned, 'lumped' together as part of a perceived 'Oscar Wilde' tendency.[24] Six prominent Bodley Head authors cabled John Lane, away in America, stating that unless he at once removed Wilde's name from the Bodley Head catalogue and suppressed Beardsley's work in the forthcoming volume of *The Yellow Book* they would withdraw their books. Lane hastened to comply.[25]*

Having been denied bail, Wilde was moved from the police cells at Bow Street to Holloway to await his further committal hearings. Although he might be in gaol, as a prisoner on remand he was allowed to wear his own clothes. By paying a small supplement he received a large, fully furnished 'special' cell. He could have food sent in from a local restaurant. He was permitted to read books, write letters and see visitors. Despite such amenities, incarceration still took its toll. Smoking was not permitted. At his subsequent committal hearings, the press noted – with evident satisfaction – Wilde's rapid physical decline. By the end of fortnight it was

---

* Lane, already greatly distressed by the fact that his publishing house had been mentioned in the Queensberry trial, as the place where Wilde had met Edward Shelley, was even more perturbed by press reports that Wilde had left the Cadogan Hotel after his arrest with *The Yellow Book* under his arm. The volume was in fact Pierre Louÿs's *Aphrodite*, bound – like all French novels – in yellow wrappers.

reported that his face was 'grey', his cheeks 'fallen in', his hair 'unkept' and his mien one of 'general depression and sudden age'.[26]

He had few allies to hand. Both Ross and Reggie Turner found it advisable to leave the country and go over to France. Ross's flight was, it seems, precipitated not by fear of arrest but by the fact that had been subpoenaed by the Crown to give evidence against Wilde.[27] The Leversons remained wonderfully loyal and attentive. Sherard wrote a cheering letter from Paris to say that Wilde had the sympathy and support of Bernhardt, Goncourt, Pierre Louÿs, Stuart Merrill and other 'artists'. Slightly less welcome was a letter from Willie saying that he was 'defending' him 'all over London'. 'My poor brother', Wilde remarked; 'he could compromise a steam-engine.'[28]

Wilde's one constant visitor at Holloway, besides his lawyers, was Bosie. He had remained in London. He came daily but the interviews – held amid a cacophony of other prison visitors, across a divide patrolled by a warder – were distressing. Wilde, following his ear infection, found it increasingly hard to hear. Nevertheless the mere sight of Bosie brought comfort. 'A slim thing, gold-haired like an angel, stands always at my side,' Wilde wrote to the Leversons. 'His presence overshadows me. He moves in the gloom like a white flower.'[29] Wilde had come to dramatize his predicament as the climax of a doomed romantic passion. He had, so he now claimed, been motivated in his legal action solely by a desire to defend Bosie from his father.[30] And now, in his misery, he was sustained by 'the beautiful and noble love' that he and Douglas shared:[31]

What wisdom is to the philosopher, what God is to his saints, you are to me. To keep you in my soul, such is the goal of this pain which men call life. O my love, you whom I cherish above all things, white narcissus in an unmown field, think of the burden which falls to you, a burden which love alone can make light. But be not saddened by that, rather be happy to have filled with an immortal love the soul of a man who now weeps in hell, and yet carries heaven in his heart. I love you. I love you, my heart is a rose which your love has brought to bloom, my life is a desert fanned by the delicious breeze of your breath, and whose cool springs are your eyes; the imprint of your little feet makes valleys of shade for me, the odour of your hair is like myrrh, and wherever you go you exhale the perfume of the cassia tree. Love me always, love me always. You have been the supreme, the perfect love of my life; there can be no other.[32]

It was a notion that Douglas readily endorsed. He announced that, should Wilde be convicted, he would buy a house next to the prison, and live there until his release. That Douglas might be himself arrested, and charged along with Wilde and Taylor, was a prospect eagerly anticipated in many quarters. But Bosie's relatives were aware, from early on, that there would be 'no case' against him;[33] the authorities had convinced themselves that not only was there insufficient evidence to secure a conviction, but that Douglas's 'moral guilt' in the matter '(assuming his guilt)' was 'less', since he had been corrupted and led astray 'when a boy at Oxford' by the 'great influence' that Wilde had exerted over him.[34]

Constance, having rescued her personal effects from Tite Street, had retreated again to Babbacombe, taking Vyvyan with her. She was now being advised and assisted by George Lewis, and also by Burne-Jones's son, Philip. Both men counselled that she must abandon her husband to his troubles, his debts and his fate. Tite Street, too, should be given up. 'If the landlord means to distrain for rent – let him,' counselled Lewis; 'Simply leave it – for the landlord to enter and distrain if he wishes.'[35]

Trapped at Holloway, Wilde struggled to attend to the details of his disintegrating life. He was distraught at not being on hand to help his mother with the regular doles that he 'provided for her subsistence'.[36] He had little time to prepare his defence. Despite the efforts of his counsel to delay the case, it was set for trial on 26 April. Meanwhile his many creditors were anxious to recover their debts (even before Queensberry could add his legal costs to the equation). Wilde, though, had little money to hand; his plays might continue to run, but to ever-dwindling houses.* And there was no hope from America. *An Ideal Husband*, which had opened to good reviews in New York on 12 March, had already been taken off; *The Importance of Being Earnest*, which opened on 22 April, lasted barely a week.[37] Sarah Bernhardt's plans for a Parisian production of *Salomé* were abandoned. Wilde's hope that the actress might buy the rights to the play (for £400) was not fulfilled. Bernhardt sent messages of sympathy and made promises of help. But, in the event, the time was inconvenient. She had nothing to give.[38]

Three tradesmen succeeded in getting a judgement against Wilde for

---

* *An Ideal Husband*, having transferred from the Haymarket to the Criterion (on 13 April), where Wilde's name was actually restored on the programme, did not close until 27 April; although on the night following the verdict in the Queensberry trial, 'the house dropped to £11'. *The Importance of Being Earnest* continued to play at the St James's until 8 May, a run of eighty-three performances.

their outstanding bills – totalling 'about £400' – 'principally for cigarettes and cigarette cases'. The bailiffs were put into Tite Street. And in a chaotic 'sheriff's auction' held on the premises, on 24 April, there was a general sale of Wilde's effects – his books, his pictures, his papers, his furniture, his clothes, even the toys from his children's nursery.* Some of Wilde's friends attended, in an effort to salvage something from the ruins. The Leversons, ever ready to assist, bought the Harper Pennington full-length portrait, among other pieces (they got it for £14, the same amount as was paid for 'Carlyle's writing desk'). Although a few items fetched 'fancy prices' – notably the inscribed copies of Wilde's own books – many pieces, especially towards the end of the sale, went for absurdly low amounts. Will Rothenstein got a Monticelli for £8; Joseph Pennell picked up a Whistler etching for a shilling. The total realized was slightly under £300.[39]

On the same day as the auction Douglas, yielding to the pleas of his family and Wilde's legal team, finally left London for France, joining Ross and Turner at Calais. The afternoon before his departure he had seen Wilde at Newgate, where the prisoner had been brought while the grand jury made their ruling that the trial could go ahead. Wilde kissed the end of Douglas's finger through the iron grating, and begged him to remain true to their love.[40] They could, at least, continue to correspond. Over the coming days Wilde reported to Ada Leverson of his regular letters from 'Jonquil' or 'Fleur de Lys', and told of the joy they brought him. To Bosie he wrote: 'Your love has broad wings and is strong, your love comes to me through my prison bars and comforts me, your love is the light of all my hours... I stretch out my hands towards you. Oh! may I live to touch your hair and your hands. I think your love will watch over my life.'[41]

In *An Ideal Husband* Sir Robert Chiltern remarks, 'when the gods wish to punish us they answer our prayers'. As a schoolboy Wilde had hoped that he might be the hero of a cause célèbre – the defendant in such a case as 'Regina versus Wilde'. Now that moment had come. On the morning of Friday 26 April 1895, he found himself in the dock at the Old Bailey, together with Alfred Taylor. Justice [Arthur] Charles was presiding. The two men were charged under a single indictment. There were twenty-five counts alleging acts of gross indecency by both men, as well as conspiracy to procure the

---

*   Ross, prior to his departure for France, had retrieved from Tite Street – at Wilde's request – several unpublished manuscripts, including *The Florentine Tragedy* and *La Sainte Courtisane*. These he entrusted to Ada Leverson.

commission of such acts. Taylor was also charged with having acted as the procurer for Wilde. The charges against Wilde concerned his 'misconduct' with Charles Parker, Fred Atkins, Sidney Mavor, Alfred Wood, with unknown 'male persons' at the Savoy, and with Edward Shelley.

After three weeks on remand, Wilde looked 'haggard and worn', his long hair no longer carefully arranged. Taylor appeared dapper beside him, as the long list of charges was read and legal arguments were entertained. Clarke tried, unsuccessfully, to have the conspiracy charges removed, as being different in kind to the charges of gross indecency. Charles Gill then opened for the prosecution, outlining – at some length – the circumstances of the case, and his proposed plan of procedure. It was a tedious recital and the spectators in the crowded courtroom grew restless. Wilde appeared bored. His boredom, however, soon passed when the witnesses began to be called.

Charles Parker came first. The reticence of the police court proceedings was abandoned. Gill encouraged the witness to give graphic accounts of his assignations with Wilde. However, it was perhaps to the surprise of his own counsel that Parker – going beyond the charges on the indictment – declared that, on their first night together at the Savoy, Wilde 'committed the act of sodomy with me'. He went on to describe Wilde asking him 'to imagine that I was a woman and that he was my lover. I had to keep up this illusion. I used to sit on his knees and he used to play with my privates as a man might amuse himself with a girl.' Although Parker readily admitted to 'tossing [Wilde] off', and being tossed off by him in return, he claimed that he had resisted Wilde's several attempts 'to insert "it" in my mouth'.

And so it went on and on for five gruelling days (with the Sunday off): William Parker telling of how, over dinner at Kettner's, his brother had repeatedly accepted preserved cherries from Wilde's own mouth; Alfred Wood recounting how, during dinner in a private room at the Florence restaurant, Wilde had put his hand inside Wood's trousers, and persuaded Wood to do the same to him; Fred Atkins describing how he had come back from the Moulin Rouge to find Wilde in bed with Maurice Schwabe; Edward Shelley reluctantly confessing that Wilde had 'kissed' and 'embraced' him after supper at the Albemarle Hotel; most of them telling of how they had slept with Taylor in the low double bed at his draped and scented lodgings. And, in between, came a succession of landladies, hotel servants and others, all willing to link Wilde to Taylor and both men to the key witnesses. Mary Applegate, the landlady at Atkins's lodgings in Osnaburgh Street, like the

chambermaid at the Savoy, reported finding horribly stained bed sheets following Wilde's several visits to her tenant.

On the third day Gill read out the full transcript of Wilde's cross-examination from the Queensberry trial, adding its revelations and arguments to the record. At the beginning of the fourth day Gill announced that the conspiracy charges would, after all, be withdrawn. If this had been done at the start of the trial – Clarke pointed out – there would have been a strong argument for the cases against the two prisoners being heard separately. Now it was too late. As Gill remarked of Wilde's chances, 'only a miracle can save him'.[42]

Clarke did his best to discredit the main witnesses, pointing out that the young men (except for Mavor and Shelley) were self-confessed blackmailers, thieves and liars. Atkins, indeed, was ordered from the witness box by the judge after it was proved that he had perjured himself in denying that he had ever been taken to Rochester Row police station in connection with an attempt to blackmail a gentleman that he had picked up at the Alhambra Music Hall. Clarke was able to show that Shelley, besides being mentally unstable, had continued to see, and to write to, Wilde as a friend for many months after the supposedly distressing incidents at the Albemarle had taken place. As to the 'disgusting' state of Wilde's bed sheets at the Savoy and Osnaburgh Street, he suggested they might have been the result of nothing worse than diarrhoea.[43*]

In Wilde's defence Clarke suggested that no man would have instituted proceedings against Queensberry if he were guilty of any wrongdoing; and that it was even less possible to believe a guilty man would have stayed in the country having seen Queensberry's plea of justification. 'Insane would hardly be the word for it, if Mr Wilde really had been guilty [of the deeds listed in the plea] and yet faced the investigation.'[44]

Wilde then stepped from the dock into the witness box. While admitting his 'association' with the various witnesses, and the various presents bestowed and dinners given, he denied that any of the 'alleged improper behaviour'

---

* The evidence of the Savoy masseur and chambermaid – about having seen a 'boy' in Wilde's bed, though forceful, was incorrect. They had confused Wilde's room with the adjoining one belonging to Lord Alfred Douglas. Wilde, anxious to defend Bosie, had not mentioned this fact. Douglas, away in France, did – it seems – wire to Wilde's lawyers, eager to point out the error. He was informed that his intervention was 'most improper' and that any further attempts at interference 'can only have the effect of rendering Sir Edward [Clarke]'s task still harder than it is already'.

had taken place. He gave his evidence with quiet deliberation. Although Clarke had sought to dismiss all discussion of Wilde's works – such as had occupied Carson during the libel trial – Gill insisted on addressing 'the literary part of the case'. Ignoring *The Picture of Dorian Gray*, though, he turned his attention to *The Chameleon* – and not to Wilde's own contribution, but rather to Douglas's two sonnets 'In Praise of Shame' and 'Two Loves'. Both were read out. At the close of the second, Gill demanded to know, 'What is the "Love that dare not speak its name"?' – was it 'unnatural love'?

Wilde replied:

The 'Love that dare not speak its name' in this century is such a great affection of an elder for a younger man as there was between David and Jonathan, such as Plato made the very basis of his philosophy, and such as you find in the sonnets of Michelangelo and Shakespeare. It is that deep, spiritual affection that is as pure as it is perfect. It dictates and pervades great works of art like those of Shakespeare and Michelangelo, and those two letters of mine, such as they are. It is in this century misunderstood, so much misunderstood that it may be described as the 'Love that dare not speak its name,' and on account of it I am placed where I am now. It is beautiful, it is fine, it is the noblest form of affection. There is nothing unnatural about it. It is intellectual, and it repeatedly exists between an elder and a younger man, when the elder man has intellect, and the younger man has all the joy, hope and glamour of life before him. That it should be so the world does not understand. The world mocks at it and sometimes puts one in the pillory for it.

Wilde's words created a sensation in court, and there was an outburst of clapping from the public gallery – mingled with some hisses. These were ideas, and even phrases, that Wilde had been rehearsing for many years: they informed 'The Portrait of Mr W. H.'; they echoed the defence of his own behaviour that he had made to the Crabbet Club. But to deliver them, unprepared, in court, with such wonderful fluency and assurance, was something exceptional. The writer Robert Buchanan considered it nothing short of 'marvellous'. By some it was declared to be 'the finest speech of an accused man since that of St Paul before Agrippa'.[45]

Max Beerbohm (back from America, and in the court that day) wrote to Reggie Turner:

Oscar has been quite superb. His speech about the Love that dares not
tell his name [*sic*] was simply wonderful, and carried the whole court
right away, quite a tremendous burst of applause. Here was this man,
who had been for a month in prison and loaded with insults and crushed
and buffeted, perfectly self-possessed, dominating the Old Bailey with
his fine presence and musical voice. He has never had so great a triumph,
I am sure, as when the gallery burst into applause – I am sure it affected
the gallery.[46]

How much it affected the jury was another matter. While it may have
reflected Wilde's idealized vision of his love for Lord Alfred Douglas, it was
scarcely germane to his fleeting encounters with Parker, Wood and co. The
social and intellectual imbalance in these relationships was certainly dwelt
on by Gill in his cross-examination:

GILL: Why did you take up with these youths?
WILDE: I am a lover of youth!
GILL: You exalt it as a sort of god?
WILDE: I like to study the young in everything. There is something fasci-
   nating in youthfulness.
GILL: So you would prefer puppies to dogs and kittens to cats?
WILDE: I think so. I should enjoy, for instance, the society of a beardless,
   briefless barrister quite as much as the most accomplished QC.

Gill added to the laughter in court with the rejoinder: 'I hope the former,
whom I represent in large numbers, will appreciate the compliment.' He
then went on: 'These youths were much inferior to you in station?'
   'I never inquired, nor did I care, what station they occupied. I found
them, for the most part, bright and entertaining. I found their conversation
a change. It acted as a kind of mental tonic.'[47]★
   At the end of that fourth day, after Wilde and Taylor had given evidence,

---

★ Wilde might have done better to suggest that he associated with these youths for *their*
benefit, rather than his own. A benign interest in corrupted working-class youth was
one of the accepted forms of late Victorian philanthropy. Gladstone gave tea parties
for 'reformed' prostitutes. And such interest could be used to justify more dubious
behaviour. In 1895 Wilde's friends Professor Ray Lankester and George Alexander were
both cleared of charges of consorting with (female) streetwalkers by claiming that they
were seeking to assist them.

counsel made their closing speeches. Sir Edward Clarke argued that Wilde's openness – in his association with the various witnesses, in his dealings with staff at the Savoy, in his appearing in the witness box, in his initiation of the libel action against Queensberry – was the 'best proof of his innocence'. His behaviour throughout had shown none of 'the cowardice of guilt'. 'Mr Wilde,' he admitted, 'is not an ordinary man'. His writings might be 'inflated, exaggerated, absurd' – but that should not condemn him. In his generous association with the young Atkins, Wood and Parker he had found himself sadly 'taken in' by an unscrupulous gang of practised blackmailers. 'I do not defend Mr Wilde for this,' he intoned; 'he has unquestionably shown imprudence, but a man of his temperament cannot be judged by the standards of the average individual'. If these 'tainted witnesses' now came forward 'in a conspiracy to ruin' his client, their evidence should not be credited. Urging the jury to put from their minds all the 'bias' occasioned by the prejudicial reporting and discussion of the case, he trusted that 'the result of your deliberations will be to gratify those thousands of hopes which are hanging upon your decision, and will clear from this fearful imputation one of our most renowned and accomplished men of letters of to-day, and, in clearing him, will clear society of stain'. His final ringing words were greeted with applause. Wilde was visibly affected by the oration, and scribbled a note of appreciation and gratitude. It was handed down to Clarke, who returned a nod of thanks to the prisoner in the dock.[48]

Grain, in his address (on behalf of Taylor), reiterated the idea that the uncorroborated evidence of known blackmailers such as the Parkers could not be accepted. Gill, however, in the final speech of the day, asked, 'Why should any of the witnesses have sought to give false evidence? What end could they serve? What good could they get by it?' Corroboration was never likely to be possible concerning incidents that were almost invariably private. But the many gifts that Wilde had given these 'lads' – invariably made after he had been alone with them 'at some rooms or other' – told their own tale. 'In these circumstances even a cigarette case is corroboration.' Though Clarke might 'protest against any evil construction' being put on Wilde's gifts and dinners for these 'vulgar, ill-bred' youths, 'in the name of commonsense what other construction is possible?'

However impressed Wilde had been with Clarke's advocacy, he held little hope for the outcome of the trial. That evening he wrote, from his cell at Holloway, a long letter to Bosie, beginning, 'My dearest boy. This is to assure you of my immortal, my eternal love for you. Tomorrow all will be over.

If prison and dishonor be my destiny, think that my love for you and this idea, this still more divine belief, that you love me in return will sustain me in my unhappiness and will make me capable, I hope, of bearing my grief most patiently.'[49]

The proceedings next morning (Wednesday 1 May) began with the judge's summing up. Over the course of three hours, in an exceptionally crowded court, he went over the evidence, listened to in 'breathless silence'.[50] It was a measured performance, leaning, perhaps, wherever doubt existed, towards the defendants. He approved the removal of the conspiracy charges from the indictment; he found that there was nothing to answer in relation to the counts involving Sidney Mavor, since Mavor had insisted that no improprieties took place; and they too were struck out. On the literary part of the case, he thought it 'absurd' to hold Wilde responsible for things that he had not written in *The Chameleon*. He remarked of Wilde's actual contribution, 'Phrases and Philosophies for the Use of the Young', that 'some are amusing, some cynical, and some of them – if I may be allowed to criticize them myself – silly; but wicked, no.' He questioned whether it was right to regard Wilde's extravagantly phrased letters to Lord Alfred Douglas as 'horrible and indecent', not least because Wilde himself appeared to be proud of them. He mentioned Shelley's 'very excited state' in the witness box, and the inconsistencies in his behaviour. He drew attention to Atkins's extraordinary piece of perjury – 'a falsehood so gross that you would be justified, if you think fit, in declining to act on any of his evidence'. He admitted that, to him, it seemed 'strange' that, if what the Savoy servants alleged with regard to seeing a boy in Wilde's bed were true, 'there were so little attempt at concealment'. He mentioned, too, that Wilde had 'the right to ask you to remember that he is a man of highly intellectual gifts, a person whom people would suppose incapable of such acts as are alleged' – and Taylor, too, 'though nothing has been said about his abilities', was 'well brought up'.

The jury went out shortly after half past one. It was generally expected that their deliberations would be brief, and that the guilt of the prisoners would be confirmed. But those in the court who had witnessed Justice Charles's summing-up were less certain. And their doubts seemed confirmed as the time lengthened, the hours passed. At three o'clock lunch was called for. Rumours began to circulate that there might be disagreement. It was not until quarter past five that the jury filed back into court.[51]

Wilde and Taylor were brought back into the dock; Beerbohm reported that 'Hoscar stood very upright', looking 'most leonine and sphinx like'.

Taylor seemed insignificant beside him.[52] The suspicions in the courtroom were confirmed: the jury had been unable to reach an agreement, except on 'the minor question' relating to Atkins, where they found the defendants 'not guilty'. Formal 'not guilty' verdicts were also returned on the conspiracy charges, and the charges relating to Mavor. Wilde received the news 'without any show of feeling'.[53]

Gill at once announced that the case would 'certainly be tried again' and probably 'at the next sessions' (in three weeks' time). An application for bail was again refused, and Wilde was returned to the tedium of Holloway.[54]

5

The Torrent of Prejudice

'Do keep up your spirits, my dearest darling.'

ALFRED DOUGLAS TO OSCAR WILDE

Despite Gill's assertion, there was some disquiet about the prospect of a retrial, with the 'raking up anew' of all the 'loathsome details'. Some hoped that a second trial – if it had to happen – 'could be heard in private'. But the pressures for action were great. When the Irish nationalist MP T. M. Healy begged Lockwood not to put Wilde 'on his country' again – to spare his 'venerated' mother 'further agony', the solicitor general replied, 'Ah, I would not but for the abominable rumours against [Rosebery].'* Carson, it seems, made a similar appeal, and received a similar answer. Rosebery himself (so George Ives heard) considered doing something to aid Wilde, but was told by his home secretary, Asquith, 'If you do, you will lose the election.'[1]

---

* Lockwood's personal feelings in the matter may well have been conflicted – or sharpened – by the fact, that, like Asquith, he had been on friendly terms with Wilde both socially and politically. He was a vice-president of the Eighty Club. Wilde even owned a sketch of Pigott (the Parnellite forger) done by Lockwood. As a further complication, Lockwood's nephew (by marriage) was Maurice Schwabe, whose name – though kept out of the original libel trial – had been mentioned in subsequent proceedings as the man who had introduced Wilde to Taylor.

The case had become a lightning rod for conspiracy theories. There was 'a wide-felt impression' that the judge had been '*got at*, in order to shield others of a higher status in life'. Some suspected that 'the Government were trying to hush up the case' for the same reason. The newspapers were bombarded with letters clamouring for further prosecutions, and suggesting that 'the police in their action against immoral practices are paralysed by orders from above to see that nothing is done'. It was claimed that there were 'hundreds of members of parliament, judges, artists, actors and others guilty of such offences'. Douglas, on the other hand, believed that the government was relentlessly driving the case forward under pressure from Queensberry and 'a body of private persons' who threatened to produce evidence against 'important and exalted persons' unless Wilde's conviction was secured.[2]

There was much reporting – and much disagreement – about the division within the jury. Some put it down to a single 'cantankerous juryman'; *L'Echo de Paris* suggested it was ten to two in favour of conviction; Beerbohm understood 'nine out of the twelve jurors was for [Oscar]'. One newspaper printed a supposed breakdown of the voting on the various charges, showing splits ranging from 10/2 (in favour of convicting Wilde for having had sex with Edward Shelley) to 2/10 (in favour of convicting Taylor of having had sex with the Parker brothers). But, overall, a 'strong suspicion' remained that the 'hopeless disagreement... was not entirely free from the taint of corruption'. Queensberry was only too ready to believe that 'individuals' had been bribed. He even suspected his son Percy – 'the great Lord Hawick and Shitters' – of putting up the money. In such a climate, continued prosecution became inevitable.[3]

Bail was eventually granted on 3 May, but the amount was set at £5,000. Several further days were needed to arrange the money. £2,500 was allowed on Wilde's own cognizance; Percy Douglas put up £1,250 to oblige his brother and to vex their father. The final £1,250 – after some frantic searching – was provided by Rev. Stuart Headlam, an independently wealthy and independently minded Anglican clergyman of socialist sympathies. Although he barely knew Wilde, he was a friend of Ross's great friend, flatmate and occasional literary collaborator, More Adey. To those who expressed surprise – or horror – at his action, Headlam explained that he had come forward on 'public grounds', believing that the press coverage had been calculated to prejudice the case. He was not, he pointed out, a 'surety' for Wilde's 'character'; only for his appearance in court – and, on this score, he felt confident of the writer's 'honour and manliness'.[4] After

the formal bail hearing at Bow Street on 7 May, Wilde was finally released. He had been in Holloway for over a month.

Freedom, however, brought its own problems. Accompanied by Percy and Headlam, Wilde went to the Midland Hotel, St Pancras. He was consulting there with some of his legal team when the Marquess of Queensberry arrived, accompanied by his friend Sir Claude de Crespigny. Queensberry was convinced that Bosie was back in London, and he was determined to prevent his joining Wilde. Confronted by the marquess, Wilde hastily decamped across the road to the Great Northern Hotel, by King's Cross. But Queensberry followed him there. And, it seems, this performance was repeated at several other hotels across London during the course of the evening. 'There was no occasion for [Wilde] to bolt as he did, if the wretched [Bosie] was not with him,' Queensberry wrote to Percy's solicitor. 'The display of the white feather was delicious all round.'[5]

Eventually, towards midnight, Wilde – harassed and desperate – sought refuge at his mother's house in Oakley Street. Willie lived there too, together with his new wife, Lily. Oscar – according to his brother – collapsed over the threshold, 'like a wounded stag'. 'Willie, give me shelter,' he pleaded; 'or I shall die in the streets.' Oscar was put up on a camp bed in the bare spare room. He at once succumbed to nervous – and physical – 'prostration'. There is no record of his reception by his mother. Oscar's travails had left her 'very poorly and utterly miserable'.* According to some accounts she had taken to her bed, and was dosing herself with gin.[6]

Alcohol was certainly a ready resource at Oakley Street. Willie was a dedicated inebriate. And when Sherard came over from France to see what could be done, he found a flushed and worn Oscar lying on his narrow bed, smelling strongly of drink. But oblivion was hard to come by. 'Oh, why have you brought me no poison from Paris?' Wilde demanded in a broken voice.

There was widespread expectation, even hope, that Wilde might kill himself. George Ives believed that it would have been for the best. Robert Cunningham Graham claimed that during an encounter in Hyde Park, Wilde – after telling 'his tale of woe' – had asked, 'What am I to do?' Without thinking, Cunningham Graham raised his arm and, pointing to his

---

* Adding to her misery was the thought that Constance (on the advice of Philip Burne-Jones) was planning to change her name and that of the children. It would, she suggested, 'bring them much confusion'. She urged Constance to wait 'until the trial is quite over': 'Neither', she went on, 'do I approve of the Navy [as a future career] for [nine-year-old] Vyvyan. I think it quite unfit as he is a born *writer*, made for literature alone.'

temple with his index finger, 'made a noise similising a revolver shot, by flicking the middle finger over the thumb'. He felt terrible when – at once – he realized what he done. Wilde apparently broke down, sobbing, 'I know it's the only way out, but I haven't the courage.' The notion that Wilde was funking the option was reiterated by Henley in a stupendously tasteless letter to Charles Whibley: 'They say, he has lost all nerve, all pose, all every-thing; and is just now so much the Ordinary Drunkard that he hasn't even the energy to kill himself.'[7]

The atmosphere at Oakely Street was depressing. The forced rapproche-ment with Willie brought little consolation. 'Willie makes such a merit of giving me shelter,' Oscar complained. 'He means well, I suppose, but it is all dreadful.' Among his many insensitivities was the comment, 'Thank God my vices were decent.' Sherard noted, however, that Wilde did not attach 'any idea of criminality' to his own behaviour. It was the men who did not like 'bestowing sexual caresses' on boys whom he now considered 'abnormal'. He earnestly asked the writer Alexander Teixeira de Mattos, who had called at Oakley Street, whether 'truly and honestly he could declare that he had never liked young men, never wished to fondle and caress them' and he 'seemed almost to doubt Tex's sincerity when he emphatically repudiated the very conception of such a thing'.[8]

A trickle of callers came to offer their support. Wilde was roused from his depression by a pleasant hour of talk with the poet Ernest Dowson. A tall veiled lady (possibly Ellen Terry) came to the door one evening and delivered a horseshoe with a bunch of violets, 'For Luck'. The Leversons had him to dine.[9]

Sherard had arrived, determined to persuade Wilde to flee abroad. It was an idea that many supported. Frank Harris took Wilde out to lunch and urged the same course. He even claimed to have a steam yacht waiting in the Thames, ready to bear them across the Channel. Douglas, meanwhile, was expecting him daily in France. Wilde, however, had determined to stay. As Willie constantly reiterated to visitors, 'Oscar is an Irish gentleman, and will face the music.' Beside his commitment to his bailsmen, he had given his word to his mother. 'If you stay,' she had declared, 'even if you go to prison, you will always be my son. It will make no difference to my affection. But if you go, I will never speak to you again.'[10]

Although Harris set down Wilde's refusal to flee as 'weakness' – or 'extra-ordinary softness of nature' – combined with 'a certain magnanimity' (in not letting down his bailsmen), in his own mind Wilde framed it as bold

defiance. He would rather be a martyr than a fugitive. He would suffer for his great love for Bosie. 'A false name,' he wrote to Douglas, 'a disguise, a hunted life, all that is not for me, to whom you have been revealed on that high hill where beautiful things are transfigured.'[11] In his resolve there was, too, besides love, a sense of the dramatic. Harris certainly considered that Wilde's fascination (and identification) with Jesus played its part: 'He felt vaguely that the life-journey of genius would be incomplete and farcical without the final tragedy: whoever lives for the highest must be crucified.'[12]

From the discomforts and irritations of Oakley Street Wilde was rescued by the Leversons, who invited him to come and stay with them at Courtfield Gardens. Before he arrived they canvassed their servants, giving them the opportunity to leave if they wished. All elected to stay, and assist 'poor Mr Wilde'. He was installed in the two adjoining rooms of the nursery usually occupied by the Leversons' young daughter, Violet. It was a refuge of comfort and calm. He would come down each evening at six, exquisitely dressed, and spend an evening of talk with 'the Sphinx' and other friends. Though he might arrive muted and depressed, the atmosphere of wit and loving friendship – as well as the good cigarettes – soon roused him. He discoursed on the joys of absinthe and the effects of opium. He told tales and talked of books. It was to Ada that he remarked, concerning *The Old Curiosity Shop*, that 'one must have a heart of stone to read the death of Little Nell without laughing.' The trial was never alluded to.

During the day, though, Wilde would remain on the nursery floor, and it was there – 'in the presence of a rocking horse, golliwogs, and a blue and white nursery dado with rabbits and other animals on it' – that he consulted with his lawyers over the forthcoming trial. By special arrangement his case, and that of Taylor, was to be called on the opening days of the sessions. And, in an extraordinary move, the prosecution would be led by the solicitor general, Frank Lockwood, supported by Charles Gill and Horace Avory. The determination of the Crown to secure a conviction was clear.

Wilde also received a visit from Constance. She had come up from Babbacombe 'with an urgent message from her lawyer [presumably George Lewis] imploring him to go away'. Even this was to no avail. She left in tears. Her distress prompted Ada to send up a note to the nursery begging Wilde to do as his wife had asked. She received no answer. But that evening, when Wilde came down, he returned the note with the comment, 'That is not like you, Sphinx.'[13]

In his resolve he was heartened by some messages of support and

sympathy. Yeats had called at Oakley Street after his departure with a sheaf of letters gathered from 'Dublin literary men'.[14] Frederick York Powell even relayed the unexpected news that Whistler was touched by his plight, and had 'expressed himself very kindly and gently' on the subject.[15]

Wilde remained at Courtfield Gardens until Monday 20 May, the date on which he had to surrender to his bail at the Old Bailey. The case was to be heard before the sixty-six-year-old Justice Wills, a noted Alpinist, and also – by chance – a neighbour of the Wildes in Tite Street.[16] Proceedings, however, were delayed when Sir Edward Clarke made a successful application for the cases of Wilde and Taylor to be tried separately. And then – to his dismay, and despite his protestations – the prosecution elected to take Taylor's case first. It was another reverse: if Taylor were convicted, Wilde's already slim chances would be further reduced.

Taylor's case was quickly heard. Beginning at noon on Monday 20 May, by the following afternoon the jury had declared him guilty of gross indecency with both Parker brothers. They were unable to decide on the question of whether Taylor had procured the Parkers for Wilde, but the judge felt it was sufficient to have come to a verdict on the principal charges. Sentencing was postponed until Wilde's case had been heard.

During the course of 21 May, Wilde was present at the Old Bailey, ready if his case were called. While in the building he was approached by the ex-police inspector Kearley and handed the Marquess of Queensberry's formal demand for payment of his £677 3s 8d legal costs. Failure to pay within seven days would constitute a statutory 'act of bankruptcy'.[17] It was a new misery to contemplate, piled upon his own legal expenses, his outstanding trade debts, his borrowing from friends and relations, his advances from theatrical producers.

Almost at the moment of this crisis, though, he received a communication from his friend Adela Schuster. She wished to place £1,000 at his disposal. In the note accompanying the gift she wrote, 'I desire this money to be employed for your own personal use and that of your children as you may direct.' Wilde chose to call the money a 'trust' or 'deposit fund'. Rather than using it to repay immediate debts it would be used to provide for emergencies and necessities, depending upon the outcome of the case. He handed the sum over to Ernest Leverson to administer: £120 was converted immediately into banknotes, and handed to Wilde to distribute; £150 was used to pay Humphreys.[18]

Wilde's own trial commenced – before a new jury – on the morning

after his encounter with Kearley. It continued for four days, during which he stayed again at his mother's house in Oakley Street, being collected and returned each day by Headlam, sometimes together with Percy Douglas. Wilde now had to face only the eight counts of gross indecency: with Charles Parker, Alfred Wood, Edward Shelley and the unknown boys at the Savoy. But it was enough.

The evidence and the arguments rehearsed at the previous trials and court hearings were gone over once again. But the appetite of the public – and even of the press – seems almost to have been sated. The reporting of the case began to slacken. Wilde, too, seemed a notably diminished and wearied figure. He was allowed to sit, even when giving evidence. He declared that he found it difficult to hear.[19] 'Most of the time he seemed in a daze, and now and then, when consciousness of his position returned to him, he swayed backwards and forwards as if overwrought with mental distress. The evidence that was being given made no impression on him.' During much of the time he doodled on a piece of foolscap that lay on the ledge of the dock, gradually turning it black with ink.[20]

The only people whose energy appeared undimmed were the two leading counsels and the Marquess of Queensberry. From the beginning of proceedings Queensberry had been a conspicuous presence in the crowded courtroom. He greeted the news of Taylor's conviction with a crowing telegram to Percy's wife, ending, 'Wilde's turn tomorrow'. And, when confronted by Percy that evening on Piccadilly, he succeeded in giving his son a black eye (the fist-fight was broken up and both men were arrested, and bound over the next day to keep the peace).[21]

In the courtroom the 'stubbornness' with which the case was fought on both sides was considered 'most remarkable', and 'the personal encounters' between Lockwood and Clarke would – it was suggested – be long 'remembered as the fiercest scenes of the kind which have ever been witnessed in court'.[22] Clarke (as a former long-serving solicitor general) reminded Lockwood that he was a public 'minister of justice' and was 'not here to try to get a verdict of guilty by any means'.[23] He portrayed Wilde as the victim of a conspiracy of 'all the blackmailers in London', his name besmirched by men who, in 'testifying on behalf of the Crown... have secured immunity for past rogueries and indecencies'.[24]

Justice Wills was certainly sceptical about the admissibility of much of the evidence against Wilde. To Lockwood's fury, he agreed with Clarke that Edward Shelley (the Crown's one witness not tainted by allegations of

blackmail) must be regarded as an accomplice, whose evidence could not be accepted without corroboration. As there was no such corroboration, he ordered that the count be removed from the consideration of the jury, and a formal verdict of 'not guilty' recorded. The ruling – at the end of the Thursday sitting – created a great buzz of excitement. That evening Lockwood fulminated against the judge around the clubs of London, calling Wills 'an incompetent old fool'.[25] Clarke secured another telling point, eliciting that Jane Cotter, the chambermaid at the Savoy who claimed to have seen a boy in Wilde's bed, was severely short-sighted yet never wore 'eye-glasses' at work.[26]

Although, in the public mind, there was (apparently) 'not a shadow of doubt' as to Wilde's guilt, 'somehow the feeling spread abroad that in view of all the circumstances' there would almost 'certainly be another disagreement' of the jury, and perhaps even an acquittal.[27] Wilde, perhaps, dared not hope so much.

Coming away from court on the afternoon of Friday 24 May, he was accompanied back to Oakley Street in the carriage by Ernest Leverson. There were financial matters to discuss. Leverson gave assurances that, should Wilde be convicted, his mother would be provided for from Adela Schuster's 'trust fund'. Leverson also asked, though, whether he might repay himself – from the same source – the £250 still owing from his emergency loan of £500. And, it seems, that Wilde readily agreed.[28]

That night Wilde took farewell of his friends. All would be over on the morrow. Lockwood would conclude his closing address, and the judge would make his charge to the jury. Wilde informed each of those gathered at Oakley Street of 'a little gift, from the poor trinkets which remained to him' – a souvenir in case he did not return home the next day. After his bouts of depression and apathy, he seemed to have achieved an impressive serenity. On retiring he kissed – with 'stately courtliness' – the hand of Willie's wife. He had been touched by her kindness and sympathy.* He then spent a 'long hour' with his beloved mother.[29] And, almost certainly, he wrote, yet again, to Bosie.

'Every great love has its tragedy,' Wilde declared, 'and now ours has too, but to have known and loved you with such profound devotion, to have had you for a part of my life, the only part I now consider beautiful, is enough

---

*   Lily Wilde was then heavily pregnant. On 11 July 1895 she would give birth to a daughter, christened Dorothy Irene Wilde – to be known as Dolly.

for me... Our souls were made for one another, and by knowing yours through love, mine has transcended many evils, understood perfection, and entered into the divine essence of things.'[30]

In court the next morning, Lockwood continued his closing address. He seemed determined to make good any deficiencies in the evidence through the vehemence of his rhetoric. Wilde would later recall the strange sensation of sitting in the dock listening to this 'appalling denunciation' and being sickened by what he heard. And then it had suddenly occurred to him: 'How splendid it would be if I was saying all this about myself?' He saw then that 'what is said of a man is nothing. The point is, who says it.' Now, unfortunately, it was being said by the solicitor general.[31]

The summing up of Justice Wills, though moderate, was – when compared to that of Justice Charles – markedly less disposed towards the defendant. He made no allusions to the prejudicial reporting of the newspapers. He was not inclined to accept an artistic interpretation of Wilde's passionate letters to Lord Alfred Douglas. He suggested there was 'some truth in the aphorism that a man must be judged by the company he keeps' – adding, 'Gentlemen, you have seen the Parkers, as you have seen Wood... Are these the kind of young men with whom you yourselves would care to sit down to dine?'

The jury retired at half past three, and Wilde was taken down to the cells to wait upon their return. Despite Lockwood's powerful performance, and Justice Wills's closing remarks, there still existed in the courtroom a suspicion that there might again be a hung jury. If that were to occur, there was a strong possibility that the Crown would abandon the prosecution, and Wilde would be allowed to go free – doubtless in the hope that he would depart into self-imposed exile. As the minutes extended, and the first hour passed, this began to seem an ever more likely outcome. 'You'll dine your man in Paris, tomorrow,' Lockwood is supposed to have remarked to Clarke. Wilde's counsel, however, was less sanguine. The jury re-appeared shortly after half past five. But it was only to inquire about a piece of evidence, and – following the judge's elucidation of the point – they retired again. A few minutes later they returned. It was clear they had reached a decision.

Wilde was brought back into the dock. He stood, ashen-faced, to hear the verdicts. To the first count: Guilty. Wilde was seen to slump forward and clutch the rail. Guilty. Guilty, guilty, guilty, guilty, guilty. Only on the charge relating to Shelley was he found, formally, not guilty.

Taylor was brought up into the dock to hear sentence pronounced.

Justice Wills was scathing in his comments. He had not 'the shadow of a doubt' that the jury had come to the correct decision. 'It is no use for me to address you,' he informed the prisoners:

> People who can do these things must be dead to all sense of shame, and one cannot hope to produce any effect upon them. It is the worst case I have ever tried. That you, Taylor, kept a kind of male brothel it is impossible to doubt. And that you, Wilde, have been the centre of a circle of extensive corruption of the most hideous kind among young men, it is equally impossible to doubt.

He passed the severest sentence that the law allowed: two years' imprisonment, with hard labour. 'In my judgement,' he added, 'it is totally inadequate for such a case as this.'[32]

The harshness of the sentence caused 'considerable sensation' in court. There were cries of 'Oh! Oh!' and 'Shame!'. Taylor appeared to hear the sentence with calm indifference. But Wilde seemed stunned. He made a movement as if he wished to address the judge. He struggled to articulate a phrase (perhaps, 'And I? May I say nothing, my Lord?') The words, however, were lost. The warders hurried him out of sight.[33]

PART IX

In Carcere Et Vinculis

1895–1897

AGE 40–42

'Oscar Wilde in Prison', as imagined by U.S. magazine The Standard, 1895.

1

The Head of Medusa

'Don't ask me to speak of it please.'

OSCAR WILDE

The nightmare then began in earnest. Wilde was now a prisoner of the Crown, and the full weight of the unreformed Victorian penal system crashed down up him. He lost, at a stroke, all choice in his own movements and actions. Taken briefly to a cell in Newgate, adjoining the Old Bailey, while the warrant was signed for his detention, he was then loaded into a closed police carriage (or 'Black Maria') – together with Alfred Taylor and two warders – and transferred across north London to Pentonville.[1]

In the bare reception ward the details of his age, religion and education were taken down. He was subjected to a medical examination. His weight was recorded as 190lbs; he had lost more than half a stone during his time on remand in Holloway, and had not regained it over the course of his second trial. Although he had been sentenced to hard labour, the Pentonville medical officer deemed the out-of-shape forty-year-old prisoner quite unequal to its rigours. Wilde was passed fit only for 'light labour' – the sewing of mailbags and the picking of oakum.[2] He was little aware of his good fortune.

Next he was made to undress before the prison staff, and immerse himself

in a tub of 'filthy water'. He dried himself with a damp, brown rag and then donned the prison uniform: the drab coarse trousers, the loose jacket and vest, the blue worsted stockings, the heavy boots, and the grey-and-red Scotch cap, all printed over with the infamous 'crow's foot' arrow. His hair was cropped. He received his first daily dose of bromide of potassium – or 'prison medicine', as the libido-quelling sedative was called. He was assigned a cell, and its number became his new 'name'.[3]

He heard the iron-clad door clang shut on his new home – a 13ft × 7ft box of bare whitewashed walls, dimly lit by a barred window of opaque glass. He felt the hardness of his narrow plank bed, and the thinness of the regulation blanket. He confronted his first dish of prison food (the sight and smell of it turned his stomach; he could not eat). Time slowed to a crawl.

Pentonville, built in the 1840s, housed some thousand inmates, but Wilde felt entirely alone. The prison operated on the 'separate system', which aimed to keep inmates completely isolated from each other, confined to their cells for all but a couple of hours each day. Although they might be brought together in the exercise yard and the chapel, at such moments they were not allowed to converse, or even to look at each other. Only during the 1860s did prisoners cease having to wear hoods – or 'peak' caps – when out of their cells.[4] Some prisoners might be allowed to work with others 'in association', but at such moments, too, silence had to be maintained. Punishments for talking to fellow inmates were harsh; they included loss of food, loss of work, loss of privileges, and even solitary confinement. The great concern of the authorities was to prevent the contamination of first-time offenders by hardened criminals, to stop prisons becoming 'seminaries of sin'. Prison presented a wasteland of 'endless silence' punctuated only by the slam of metal-framed doors, the clank of chains, the echo of footsteps, the bark of orders and reprimands, and by obscure cries of pain, distress and despair. Wilde who had lived for conversation, for social intercourse, for intellectual stimulation, for beauty, for comfort, for good food and ease, had lost them all, absolutely and at a stroke. The horror of it overwhelmed him.

Although the novelty of his first day had been appalling, more appalling still was the uniformity of every other day – and night. Wilde found himself oppressed by the 'three permanent punishments authorized by law in English prisons: Hunger, Insomnia, Disease'. The diet was deliberately inadequate. And the pace of Wilde's weight loss was soon increased by frequent bouts of diarrhoea. The condition was one of the miseries of prison life, made even worse by the wholly inadequate sanitary arrangements.

Prisoners, confined to their ill-ventilated cells from five in the afternoon until eight the following morning, had only one too-small pot for 'the purposes of nature'. The stench was brutal.[5]

Wilde's mental condition declined along with his physical state. Regular doses of bromide were apt to produce feelings of mental prostration and melancholy among new prisoners,[6] but it was the 'endless silence' and 'eternal solitude' of existence that oppressed him most.[7] Alone in his cell for hours upon end his thoughts turned inward: regret gnawed at his soul; he was tortured incessantly with 'self-reproaches'.[8] His daily allocation of oakum picking was carried out alone in his cell. And though designated as 'light labour', the work of unplucking the twisted strands of old tarred rope was hard on both the fingers and the spirit.*

And behind the tedium there lay always the dread of punishment. Wilde, who had always considered himself made for exceptions rather than rules, struggled to comprehend his new world of regulation, or to make sense of its inhumanity. When, in the exercise yard, the man walking in front him whispered how sorry he was for him and how he hoped he would 'bear up', Wilde – forgetting the edict against all conversation – stretched out his hands, and cried, 'Oh, thank you, thank you.' He was, of course, punished, for the response. Wilde was at a disadvantage: at 6 feet tall he was – as one warder recorded – 'considerably taller than the majority' and always a conspicuous figure in the exercise yard. Indeed he often served the officers as a 'landmark' as they counted the prisoners walking the ring. His 'very long stride', moreover, was always bringing him close on the heels of the man in front, prompting calls of 'keep your distance'. He developed a dread of the daily cell inspection. Each of his small collection of containers and utensils had its set place, and if this was neglected in the smallest degree he was liable to be punished. 'The punishment was so horrible,' he recalled, 'that I often started up in my sleep to feel if each thing was where the regulations would have it, and not an inch either to right or left.'[9]

---

* Public interest in Wilde's imprisonment was great during the first weeks. Among many entirely spurious, but imaginative, reports was one that described how he was put directly on to the treadmill upon his arrival, but after four days of such punishing labour (roughly equivalent to climbing Ben Nevis twice over each day), he collapsed and had to be taken to the infirmary ('Oscar Wilde in Prison', *Western Mail*, 7 June 1895). Other equally fanciful reports declared that Wilde was 'as full of quaint and epigrammatic expressions as of old' and, in telling one visitor of his cell, had remarked, 'I always thought I was born to be a monk. Now, since my confinement here, I am convinced of it' (*Evening News* (Sydney, NSW) Friday 15 November 1895).

There was no hope of relief. Wilde refused to engage with the prison chaplain. He could find no consolation in the Bible, and even less in *Pilgrim's Progress*, the one non-liturgical text permitted him.[10] Contact with the outside world was impossible. According to the regulations, only at the end of three months would he be permitted to send – and receive – one letter, and to receive two visitors. After that, communication might then be continued at the same rate, each quarter, during the rest of his sentence. In the meantime, though, he was alone, hungry, sleepless and miserable.

He knew nothing of the world outside, which at least spared him something. The press – which had, over the course of Wilde's three long trials, almost exhausted its capacity for prurient gloating and moral indignation – had roused itself for one final bout of scorn, before consigning Wilde to an ignominious obscurity that it was hoped would extend well beyond the two years of his 'well-merited' but sadly 'inadequate' sentence. 'Oscar Wilde will never again be anything but a memory,' declared the leader writer of the *Western Mail*; 'a beacon light set up to warn youth from the dangers that lurk in a life of ease and pleasure. His personality has been wiped out from the haunts of men, and his name has become a bye-word and a reproach.'[11]

Privately there might be some sympathy: Wilde's fall had been so spectacular, his sentence so harsh. The writer Hall Caine told Coulson Kernahan he thought it 'the most awful tragedy in the whole history of literature'. But little made it into the print. *Reynolds's Newspaper* published an unsigned letter from Wilde's future bibliographer C. S. Millard, disputing the law's right to pronounce on matters of private passion. And this view was echoed by the Dutch anarchist Alexander Cohen, in *The Torch* – a tiny magazine produced by Dante Gabriel Rossetti's two nieces. Public expressions of disapproval, though, were widespread: at Portora Wilde's name was erased from the 'Honours Board'; he was blotted from the 'Golden Book' of the Churchill Masonic Lodge at Oxford; W. P. Frith even offered to paint out the portrait of Wilde from his picture 'A Private View at the Royal Academy, 1881'.[12]

Into Wilde's darkness, however, some light unexpectedly fell. On 12 June, barely two weeks into his sentence, he received an unscheduled visit from the enlightened Liberal MP Robert Haldane. Haldane (two years younger than Wilde) had been a fellow member of the Eighty Club. He was able to arrange the visit, having just served on a departmental committee charged with investigating the deficiencies of the prison system. The meeting took place in a special visiting room. At first Wilde refused to speak. 'I put my

hand on his prison-dress-clad shoulder,' Haldane recalled, 'and said that I used to know him and that I had come to say something about himself.' Haldane – an impressive intellect who had translated Schopenhauer into English – suggested that Wilde had not fully used his great literary gift, because he had allowed himself to live too much for pleasure, and had not made any great subject his own. His current misfortune might, though, give him a great theme, and carry his work to new heights. Although, under standard regulations, prisoners were not allowed access to books – other than devotional texts – until they had served three months (and then only at the rate of one a week), Haldane suggested that he would try to get some more stimulating reading matter for Wilde at once, as well as pen and ink. And then, when his sentence was complete, Wilde might be ready to produce something truly great. At this peroration Wilde burst into tears. Nevertheless he promised to try.

Certainly he was eager for books. He began to talk about possible titles. Haldane was obliged to turn aside the suggestion that these might include some of Flaubert's novels, pointing out that an author who had been prosecuted for indecency was unlikely to be sanctioned by the prison authorities. Wilde laughed in recognition of this truth, and became almost cheerful. Their talk opened up into a discussion of literature, and they settled on a list of fifteen non-fiction titles that included St Augustine's *Confessions*, Mommsen's five-volume *History of Rome*, Cardinal Newman's *Apologia* and Walter Pater's *Renaissance*. Despite the objections of the Pentonville governor, the books – but not the writing materials – were sanctioned by the home secretary, and, in due course, were delivered to the prison library.[13]

There were elements of personal concern and common humanity in Haldane's visit. But his intervention also revealed that the authorities were taking an interest in Wilde's case. At the beginning of June fanciful press reports had announced that Wilde was 'going insane' and had been 'confined to a padded cell'. Although the governor had acted quickly to deny such claims, Asquith (the home secretary, at whose table Wilde had dined barely eleven months earlier) asked the prison commissioners to inquire into the truth of the allegations.[14]

The Pentonville medical officer reassured the commissioners (and the government) that Wilde, whatever minor setbacks he had endured, was neither insane nor dying: indeed, apart from a 'little relaxed throat', he was giving 'no anxiety to any of the officials' at the prison. Haldane's visit followed upon this report, and his own findings seem to have been relayed

to Lord Rosebery. Subsequently, Haldane maintained a watchful eye over Wilde's condition. In his concern, he was joined by the newly appointed head of the prison commission, Evelyn Ruggles-Brise. A man of imagination and humanity, Ruggles-Brise had both an admiration for Wilde and an understanding that his experience of prison must be 'much more severe [than] it would be to an ordinary criminal'. Although he and Haldane did not always share the same priorities, they were two powerful allies to Wilde's cause. But they had to act with discretion. As Haldane explained to one of Wilde's friends, 'they must not be thought to be giving [Wilde] differential treatment further than his Condition requires'.[15]

Wilde himself seems to have been too crushed by his new circumstances to register even a hint of this concern. He felt abandoned to the hell of prison life. His misery was compounded by a visit, on 2 July, from ex-police inspector Kearley, who had come to serve Wilde with a copy of Queensberry's petition for a receiving order in bankruptcy. The proceedings had been initiated on 21 June, as the marquess sought to reclaim his legal costs, and would now continue along their prescribed path through the bankruptcy court. To the grinding horror of the prison regime was now added an anxiety about his financial affairs – an anxiety that he could do nothing to assuage. With Ross, Turner and Douglas all abroad, the overseeing of Wilde's affairs fell to Ross's friend, More Adey. Although he had never been an intimate of Wilde's, he now found himself drawn into the heart of things; it was he who had to liaise with Humphreys.[16]

Two days after Kearley's visit Wilde was moved from Pentonville and transported across London to Wandsworth. Although Haldane may have had a hand in the choice of destination, the move itself had been prompted by 'suspicions that the Officers at Pentonville Prison were being tampered with by O. Wilde's friends'. Manning, the Pentonville governor, was glad to see Wilde go. The keen public interest in the prisoner, and the leaked information about his well-being, were a nuisance and an embarrassment.[17]*

---

* Several weeks after Wilde had left Pentonville, Manning received an extraordinary coded communication from 'a few American friends' asking whether, for £100,000, he might co-operate in a plot to have Wilde sprung from prison: 'All you have to do is pay some people in the prison to look the other way.' They asked him to take this risk out of respect for Wilde's 'respectable father and mother and the position [he] has lost by his heinous unnatural crimes, which we have no wish to excuse'. Their motive was to prevent him becoming 'tainted with the abominations of prison life'. They looked forward to receiving his answer via the personal columns of the *New York Herald*.

Wandsworth was designed and run along the same lines as Pentonville, but Wilde seemed unsettled by the move. The prison chaplain, W. D. Morrison, noted that he arrived in 'an excited flurried condition'. The flurry, however, soon passed, along with any determination 'to face his punishment without flinching'. Wilde's 'fortitude' gave way beneath the regime. The food, disgusting at Pentonville, was even worse at Wandsworth. Some of the warders were 'brutes'. His books, although they were supposed to be transferred with him, did not arrive until 17 August. Hunger and lack of sleep took their toll; he began to have 'wild delusions' and thought he might be going mad. He wanted to kill himself. Haldane, when he visited Wilde at his new prison, was 'painfully struck' by his 'depressed' state.' Morrison considered the prisoner 'quite crushed and broken'. The doctor was concerned by his physical decline; he had lost 22lbs – over 10 per cent of his body weight – since his reception at Pentonville. Some of the more experienced prison officers openly doubted that he would be 'able to go through the two years'.[18]

And new cares arrived from outside the prison walls. On 29 July Wilde received a visit from an official of the bankruptcy court. Following a meeting of Queensberry and the other creditors, a Mr Wildy had been appointed as the official receiver of Wilde's estate. In an interview at Wandsworth, he led Wilde 'step by step... over every item of [his] life', enumerating his assets, detailing his extravagances and confirming his debts. 'It was horrible,' Wilde recalled. Despite having earned some £4,000 in the two years since mid-1893, Wilde found himself with outstanding debts of £3,591 9s 9d. Besides the £677 3s 8d due to Queensberry, he owed: £1,557 16s 1d to the trustees of Constance Wilde's marriage settlement (having borrowed £1,000 from the trust on the eve of their marriage, and failed to pay back either the principal or any interest); £500 to Otho Lloyd for another loan, made in 1885; £414 19s 11d to George Alexander for advances against royalties on *The Importance of Being Earnest*; £70 16s 11d to the Savoy for board and residence between 1893 and March 1894; and over £230 'for tobacco, wine, jewellery and flowers'.[19]

Wilde's assets were minimal. More Adey drew up a list of them. His possessions had been dispersed for a fraction of their true value at the disgraceful sheriff's sale at Tite Street. There remained his various copyrights, along with his unpublished (and, indeed, unfinished) manuscripts *The Florentine Tragedy*, *La Sainte Courtisane* and *The Cardinal of Avignon*. There was a mystery as to the whereabouts of the extended 'Portrait of Mr W. H.'.

Lane claimed that he had returned the manuscript to Tite Street, though Wilde knew nothing of it. But, as Adey noted, 'I don't fancy much can be got out of it. Difficulties as to publication now enhanced.' His one other asset was his 'life interest' in Constance's marriage settlement – although, given that she was younger than he was, and, as a woman, had a greater life expectancy, its actuarial value was considered small.[20]*

As his mind turned obsessively over the events that had brought him to ruin, incarceration, disgrace and humiliation, Wilde came to see that everything led back to Douglas. It was he who had antagonized Queensberry; it was he who driven forward the fatal legal action; it was he who (together with his family) had promised to pay Wilde's legal costs, and failed to do so. In brooding incessantly on these points, the great love that had carried him through the previous months curdled into hate. The change was abrupt and total. From now on every action that Douglas made (and had made) seemed to confirm, in Wilde's eyes, his shallowness and unworthiness. The impassioned phrases of his recent love letters were forgotten. When a solicitor's clerk who had come to take a deposition relating to his bankruptcy leant across the table and said in a low voice, 'Prince Fleur-de-Lys wishes to be remembered to you,' Wilde stared at him blankly. Only after the phrase had been repeated, with the qualification 'the gentleman is abroad at present', did Wilde grasp that the message must have come from Douglas. The name 'Fleur-de-Lys', borrowed from one of Douglas's ballads, had only weeks before been a sacred currency between them. Now, in the hideous setting of Wandsworth prison, it struck Wilde with horror. A bitter laugh escaped him. 'In that laugh,' he later recalled, 'was all the scorn of the world.'[21]

The repudiation of Douglas was accompanied by a dawning recognition of Constance's great love for him, and his own love for her and his children – affections that he had abused and damaged through his 'mad' infatuation with Douglas. And it was against this background that Wilde received his first scheduled visit, on Monday 26 August, from Robert Sherard. While so many of Wilde's close companions remained on the continent, Sherard had travelled in the other direction, feeling unable to stay in Paris while his friend suffered in England.

---

* The 'life interest' entitled Wilde to the income from Constance's marriage settlement (roughly £800 a year) for the duration of his own life, should she predecease him. After his death, it would revert to Constance's heirs.

The twenty-minute encounter took place beneath a loudly ticking clock, in a bare vaulted room divided by two rows of iron bars. In the passage between the bars patrolled a warder, poised to intervene should the conversation stray on to forbidden topics. As they stood facing each other – each clinging to the bars 'for support' – Sherard was shocked to see his friend's sorry condition: his hands disfigured, the nails broken and bleeding from the oakum picking; his face 'untidy' with stubble. Wilde's depression was obvious, even before tears welled in his eyes. Sherard strove to affect a cheerfulness he did not feel, and was thrilled to have drawn a laugh before their twenty minutes were up.[22]

He was perhaps able to tell Wilde something of the French reaction to his imprisonment. A succession of writers had sprung into print to denounce, variously, the barbarity, the stupidity and the hypocrisy of English 'justice' in its treatment of Wilde. There were rousing and supportive articles by Henri Bauer in *L'Echo de Paris*, by Octave Mirbeau in *Le Journal*, by Paul Adam in the *Revue Blanche* and by Louis Lormel, Laurent de Tailhade and Henri de Régnier. Indeed it was asserted in some quarters that, if Wilde could only be got to Paris, 'he would be cheered in the streets'.[23]

Sherard was heartened to learn of Wilde's changing attitudes to Douglas and to Constance. He determined to do what he could to foster a possible reconciliation between husband and wife. It was, he believed, the best hope for Wilde's salvation. Constance, in a quest for anonymity, had left London, taking the children to Switzerland, and adopting – like her brother – the family name of 'Holland'. On the advice of her family solicitor, Mr Hargrove, and also of George Lewis, she was planning to divorce her 'poor misguided husband'. It was not that she no longer cared for him – indeed, her love and solicitude seem almost to have been quickened by his fall – but it was a practical necessity. If she should die, Oscar, having the life interest in her marriage settlement, would receive all the income from the fund, leaving the children technically penniless. Although he might very well want to provide for his sons, his debts and, above all, the 'way he has behaved about money affairs' convinced everyone concerned that this must not happen. And the easiest way to ensure that was by a divorce.[24]

Sherard wrote to her, urging her to reconsider; and he perhaps encouraged Wilde to do likewise. Certainly when Wilde was permitted, at the end of August, to send a letter, he wrote – full of humility and contrition – to Constance. Her solicitor, to whose care he addressed the missive,

considered it 'one of the most touching and pathetic letters that had ever come under his eye'.[25]

That it might find a receptive audience was confirmed when, only days after it had been dispatched, Wilde received his first letter. It was from Otho Holland in Switzerland. Although it had clearly crossed with his own, it suggested that Constance was prepared to reconsider her decision about the divorce. And then, barely a week after that, on 21 September, Wilde had a visit, by special dispensation, from Constance herself. She had travelled from Switzerland, having received his letter, to tell him that 'there was forgiveness for him' and the hope of a future together – in another country, under an assumed name, but with their children. Cyril, she reported, 'never forgets him'. From her account, it seems that she may have had to talk to her husband from behind a screen. She informed Sherard that the whole experience had been more awful than she could have believed: 'I could not see him and I could not touch him, and I scarcely spoke.' Nevertheless for Wilde it provided a small chance of relief. He told her that 'he had been mad the last three years' and that, if he saw Lord Alfred Douglas, 'he would kill him'. Constance sincerely hoped he never would see Douglas again.[26]

Sherard found Wilde 'greatly cheered' by the interview when, two days later, he paid his own specially sanctioned visit. He had claimed that he was about to depart for Madagascar and had urgent business matters to discuss with the prisoner. And, because it was nominally a business interview, they met, without a fixed time limit, in the prison offices, rather than in the barred visiting room. At the end of the meeting Sherard seized the opportunity to embrace his old friend. Having seen Constance shortly after her visit, he was able to reassure Wilde that his wife's 'heart was altogether still with him' and that there was the real possibility of a life together 'once his punishment was over'.[27]

He also brought news from Paris. Through his contacts there he had learnt that Douglas, in his desire to strike a blow for his friend, had written a long polemic for the *Mercure de France*, detailing the background to the Wilde trials, proclaiming the virtues of 'Greek love', and quoting extensively from the passionate letters that Wilde had sent him from Holloway. Wilde, in his new mood, was appalled. Publication of such 'foolish' expressions of 'misplaced, ill-requited, affection for one of crude and callous nature, of coarse greed, and common appetites' would only add to his shame. 'The gibbet on which I swing in history now is high enough,' he declared. 'There is no need that [Douglas] of all men should for his own vanity make it more

hideous.' He urged Sherard to prevent publication. And Sherard – who had never cared for Douglas – was only too happy to oblige.[28]*

The excitements of the week were not over. On the following day Wilde was taken out of prison to attend the bankruptcy court. He was dressed in his old clothes, but they hung about him now. It had been expected that he would have to face his 'public examination' in court that day, but he was not called. His counsel successfully asked for an adjournment. Falling in with Constance's desire to avoid a divorce, Mr Hargrove had come up with an ingenious plan that might annul the bankruptcy and obviate the need for Wilde to be examined at all, while also addressing the question of his 'life interest' in the marriage settlement. According to this scheme, the trustees of Constance's marriage settlement would withdraw their claims to both the £557 16s 1d interest and the £1,000 loan, in exchange for Wilde surrendering his 'life interest' for a nominal £5, and allowing a charge on all his existing literary and dramatic rights. His remaining debts of £2,033 13s 11d might then be met by a subscription from among his friends and sympathizers. More Adey had already got promises for £1,500, and was confident that the rest could be raised before the court reconvened on 12 November.[29]

While all this was being laid out in the courtroom, Wilde waited with his two warders in an adjacent office. Arthur Clifton, in his capacity as one of the trustees of the marriage settlement, was – unexpectedly – allowed to see him there. Clifton was 'very much shocked' at his friend's appearance, and at his distressed state. '[He] cried a good deal,' Clifton reported; 'he seemed quite broken-hearted and kept on describing his punishment as savage.' Clifton tried to cheer him up with news of friends and talk of books: Wilde had been reading his volumes of Pater and Newman at the permitted rate of one a week. But it was a hard task. Wilde remained 'terribly despondent and said several times that he did not think he would be able to last the punishment out'. When Clifton tried to explain Hargrove's proposed scheme, Wilde expressed no particular opinion but suggested that 'he ought to be left something out of the settlement if possible'. Clifton, as

---

* Douglas, as part of his energetic but ill-conceived campaign of protest, had also written to Henry Labouchère (still editor of *Truth*) and W. T. Stead (now editor of the *Review of Reviews*) extolling the virtues of homosexual love. He had also dispatched a letter to Queen Victoria [25 June 1895] asking her to exercise her power of pardon on Wilde's behalf. He received no reply from the Queen. Labouchère printed an extract from his letter, with the comment that 'it is to be regretted that he is not afforded an opportunity to meditate upon [his opinions] in the seclusion of Pentonville'.

a qualified lawyer, should have explained that this was not really possible – that the life interest, as an asset, needed to be sold in full. Instead he casually embraced the idea, telling Wilde he thought it 'a very good plan... that he should retain about a third of his life interest'. He mentioned this to Constance shortly afterwards, and she too, with her ignorance of the law, thought that it sounded very reasonable. It was, though, an idea that would lead to endless complications and strife.[30]

The small scraps of comfort offered by these interviews with Clifton, Sherard and Constance were not enough to raise Wilde's spirits, and his physical and mental condition remained precarious. The prison chaplain (a passionate advocate of penal reform) was convinced that – with his 'morbid disposition' – Wilde had succumbed to 'perverse sexual practices' and was masturbating compulsively. 'This is a common occurrence among prisoners of his class,' Rev. Morrison wrote to Haldane, 'and is of course favoured by constant cellular isolation. The odour of [Wilde's] cell is now so bad that the officer in care of him has to use carbolic acid in it every day.' The charge was not insignificant: many Victorians authorities regarded masturbation as a symptom, if not the cause, of insanity. There were regular instances of prisoners being certified on the grounds of their indulgence in 'self-abuse'. Wilde, happily, avoided this fate.[31]

An inquiry was launched by Ruggles-Brise; it concluded there was no evidence to support the chaplain's rather overheated suspicions. The medical inspector to prisons, Dr R. M. Gover, dismissed Morrison's 'extraordinary allegation' as 'a vile and malignant misrepresentation'. And even Ruggles-Brise (writing to the Home Office) regretted that the chaplain was probably 'a dangerous man who is trying to make Wilde a peg whereon to hang his theories of the brutality of our prison system'. The curious smell in Wilde's cell was put down to his use of 'Jeyes' purifying fluid' in cleaning his utensils.[32]

Dr Gover (veering in the opposite direction from the chaplain) reported that Wilde was, in fact, perfectly fine – with 'an excellent appetite' and 'in good mental and bodily health'. He did concede that – to lessen the prisoner's apparent sense of isolation – it might be advisable to start him working 'in association', perhaps at rebinding the prison hymn books, an idea that had been mooted by Haldane. But, to achieve this, some 'special arrangement' would be necessary, to avoid placing the prisoner 'in association with the London thieves and other low criminals who form the bulk of the population of Wandsworth prison'. This concern to prevent Wilde

consorting with 'London thieves' seems to have prompted plans to 'advise the Secretary of State to transfer Wilde to a country prison'.[33]

In the midst of these deliberations – and despite Dr Gover's optimistic assessment – Wilde's physical health broke down completely. The crisis came towards the middle of October. Weak from a bout of 'dysentery', he collapsed on the floor of the prison chapel during the Sunday service and was taken to the prison infirmary. As he later told Frank Harris, he thought that he had died and been reborn 'in heaven'. 'My hand rested on a clean white sheet... it was so smooth and cool and clean.' The nurse gave him some thin white bread and butter – it was 'so delicious' he burst into tears.[34] His sense of rebirth was not, however, immediately apparent to either Sherard or Willie's wife, Lily, both of whom received permission to visit him in the infirmary. They found the patient pitifully weak and still 'very unhappy'. Sherard pronounced him 'a perfect wreck'.[35]

Hoping to cheer the invalid, Sherard suggested that something might be done towards improving his living arrangements by agitation in the *Daily Chronicle*, a paper committed to prison reform. This remark, however, led to Sherard being reported by the warder for 'subversion' (he had already disclosed details of Wilde's daily routine to the *Chronicle* after his previous visits). The governor of Wandsworth, like his colleague at Pentonville, was beginning to find Wilde a rather too taxing charge with his overactive friends and supporters. He hastened to put forward the recommendation that Wilde be removed 'to a country Prison where he would be less accessible to such influences'.[36]

The idea found general support, and Haldane thought it necessary for Wilde's mental well-being. While he accepted that Rev. Morrison might have rather overstepped the mark with his allegations, he had been unconvinced by Dr Gover's rosy report. And his reservations had persuaded the Home Office to sanction a fuller assessment of Wilde's mental state.[37] Whatever the continuing popular animus against Wilde, there was a clear recognition in official circles that it would be a bad thing (even a 'loss to English literature') should the prison system totally destroy him. 'If [Wilde] were to go off his head under cellular discipline,' Morrison had written, 'it is almost certain to arouse a good deal of indignation in the public mind and the authorities will no doubt be blamed for allowing such a thing to happen.'[38]

Two doctors, experts in criminal lunacy (one the governor of Broadmoor), examined Wilde in the Wandsworth infirmary on 22 October. They were heartened to discover him 'smiling and conversing' in a 'cheerful way'

with the other ward inmates. And this positive impression (as to his mental state) was largely confirmed by their subsequent interview:

> He entered freely in to the circumstances of his past history, more especially as they had relation to his present position which he appeared to feel acutely, and upon which he dilated with great fervour and some amount of emotional depression, occasionally accompanied by tears. This display of feeling was no doubt referable, as he himself gave us to understand, to remorseful and bitter thoughts of the blasting of his future by the abominable follies of the past, and we do not regard this as being either unnatural or as indicating moral derangement.[39]

Aware of the evolving plans for Wilde's transfer, they considered that 'with careful treatment and, shortly removal to a Prison in the country, with different work and a greater range of reading there is nothing to indicate that prison will prejudicially affect him'. They also recognized that it would be beneficial if he were allowed more 'association with other prisoners' – although their concerns about bad influences ran in the opposite direction. Given Wilde's 'proclivities' and 'avowed love for the society of males', they stipulated that such interaction should only be allowed 'under the continuous supervision of a warden'.[40] In the wake of Doctors Nicolson and Bryan's report, it was decided that Wilde should be transferred to Reading Prison in Berkshire as soon as possible.[41]

There would be a short delay, as Wilde needed to remain in London until the bankruptcy court proceedings were concluded. The optimism that followed from the first court hearing in September had not been sustained. Percy Douglas – who had promised £500 to Adey's fund – had failed to come through, claiming, improbably, that rather than giving money that would go to pay his hated father's legal costs, he would reserve the sum to give to Wilde after he came out of prison. On the eve of the second hearing the fund being assembled by Adey was still some £400 short.[42] Hargrove's plan had to be abandoned, and the bankruptcy had to proceed.

Wilde was brought from the infirmary to the bankruptcy court, in Lincoln's Inn Fields, on the morning of 12 November. He looked 'very unwell and broken down' swathed in his 'long blue overcoat'. He wore the same silk hat that he had worn to the Old Bailey, but it had lost its sheen. Much to Wilde's distress a crowd of 'loafers and sightseers' had gathered, hoping to glimpse him. But, as he was escorted by two uniformed warders

down the long corridor towards the courtroom, he was heartened by the sight of Robbie Ross (now back in England), standing to one side. As Wilde passed, Ross 'gravely' raised his hat in greeting. Wilde regarded it as the act of a saint. He never forgot it. The examination itself was brief (barely half an hour) and Wilde, leaning against the witness box for support, confined himself to answering the questions 'yes' or 'no'.[43]

After the examination both Clifton and Ross were allowed to see him for half an hour each in a private room. Ross, who had not seen Wilde since his arrest, was shocked. 'Indeed I really should not have known him at all,' he reported to Oscar Browning. 'This I know is an ordinary figure of speech, but it exactly described what I experienced. His clothes hung about him in loose folds and his hands are like those of a skeleton. The colour of his face is completely changed, but this cannot be altogether attributed to his slight beard. The latter only hides the appalling sunken cheeks.' Mentally, Ross considered Wilde's condition 'better than I had dared hope', but acknowledged that his mind was 'considerably impaired'. Wilde was still in the infirmary, but told Ross he wanted to leave 'as he hoped to die very soon. Indeed he only spoke calmly about death, every other subject caused him to break down.'[44]

The following week Wilde was taken back to Lincoln's Inn Fields to sign the transcript of his statement. The formalities were complete. The next day, 20 November, he was transferred to Reading. The move was supposed to mark an improvement in his circumstances, but it began in traumatic fashion. He was transported – handcuffed and in his prison clothes – not in a prison van, but by rail, and in the middle of the day. Brought to Clapham Junction station, he was forced to stand, between his warders, for half an hour (from two o'clock to half past) on the central platform, attracting the attention and the contempt of the public. A laughing crowd gathered. He was recognized, and one man spat at him. 'For a year after that was done to me,' Wilde wrote later, 'I wept every day at the same hour and for the same space of time.'[45]

2

The System

'To those who are in prison, tears are a part of every day's experience.'

OSCAR WILDE

Reading Gaol had been selected specially by Ruggles-Brise. The prison governor, Lieutenant-Colonel H. B. Isaacson (an ex-marine) was conscious of the honour, and informed his staff that 'a certain prisoner' was due to be transferred, 'and you should be proud to think the Prison Commissioners have chosen Reading gaol as the most suitable for this man to serve the remainder of his sentence in'. No name was mentioned but Wilde's identity was divined at once upon his arrival. His distress at having his hair cut seemed characteristic to the warder charged with the task. '"Must it be cut," he cried piteously to me. "You don't know what it means to me," and the tears rolled down his cheeks.' For Wilde, part of the 'horror of prison life' was 'the contrast between the grotesqueness of one's aspect, and the tragedy of one's soul'.[1]

Wilde served out the remaining eighteen months of his sentence at Reading. Although the gaol was very much smaller than Pentonville and Wandsworth (with a shifting population of about 150 inmates) it was built to the same standard Victorian design, with a central core and four radiating wings. Wilde – as prisoner C.3.3. – was assigned cell 3 on the third

landing of Gallery C. He was an exceptional figure in this new world: the only educated middle-class convict among dozens of young labourers and squaddies, most of them serving short sentences for drunkenness or petty theft.[2]

Some aspects of his existence improved at once. The air was cleaner. He was put on to a better diet. He was given coal sacks to sew in his cell, rather than oakum to pick. But these were tiny ameliorations. The regime was quite as strict as at Wandsworth. And Wilde frequently fell foul of its petty regulations. 'The worst of it is I am perpetually being punished for nothing,' he lamented. Lieutenant-Colonel Isaacson, he claimed, 'loves to punish'. Certainly the governor, with his military background, was a stickler for discipline. Wilde called him a 'mulberry faced dictator' – a man with 'the eyes of a ferret, the body of an ape, and the soul of a rat'; but he also recognized that the real reason for Isaacson's harshness was that 'he was entirely lacking in imagination'. It became Isaacson's boast that he was 'knocking the nonsense out of Wilde'. Of all the punishments he imposed, the one Wilde dreaded most was being denied access to his books (his personal library followed him from Wandsworth); they alone made life endurable. Without them the mind was left to 'grind itself away between the upper and nether millstones of regret and remorse without respite'.[3]

Wilde found no relief from the prison doctor. As a class he considered such officials as 'brutes and excessively cruel'. But Dr Oliver Maurice seems to have exceeded the norm. Described by Ross as resembling – with his 'greasy white beard' – a 'bullying director of a sham city company', he was consistently 'unkind' and uncaring to Wilde.[4]

Nevertheless, on a visit to Reading at the end of November, More Adey was pleased to detect some small improvement in Wilde's mental condition, after the horrors of Wandsworth. 'I think that he is conscious that he must make efforts to prevent his mind suffering more,' Adey reported, 'because he was so very anxious to get some rather drudging mental work to do, in order to occupy and, in a sort of way, discipline his mind.' By the new year Wilde was set to rebinding the prison hymn books, as well as working in the prison garden.[5]

Adey had been busying himself on Wilde's behalf but with little effect. He had tried to raise a petition to the home secretary seeking Wilde's early release, but – beyond the two self-designated 'cranks', Bernard Shaw and Stewart Headlam – he could find few people to sign it. York Powell, Regius Professor of History at Oxford, was an honourable exception. The literary

and artistic establishments turned their backs.* Adey was, though, able to put together a further collection of books for Wilde, and – through the intervention of Haldane and Ruggles-Brise – have them sent directly to the ill-stocked prison library at Reading. They included Dante and selections from the Greek and Latin poets.[6]

In drafting his ill-fated petition Adey had listed, among the several indications of Wilde's pitifully diminished mental state, the fact that having, in the past, 'always showed the tenderest solicitude for his mother, charging himself with the larger part of her maintenance, and commending her specially to his friends during the most harassing days of his two trials, he now seems quite indifferent to her'. In fact she came to his mind often. On the night of 3 February she appeared to him in a vision, dressed in her outdoor clothes. When he asked her to take off her hat and cloak and sit down, she shook her head sadly, and vanished. It seemed like an intimation of death.[7]

Some two weeks later he was informed that he had a special visitor. It was Constance. Although weak with illness (following an operation just before Christmas) she had travelled from Italy, where she was living, to bring him the news that his mother had indeed died on 3 February. Constance had been unable to bear the thought 'that such a terrible thing' might otherwise be told to him 'roughly'. The news – even if it confirmed his premonition – still stunned him. 'Her death was so terrible to me,' he wrote afterwards, 'that I, once a lord of language, have no words in which to express my anguish and my shame.' She – along with Sir William – had bequeathed him 'a name made noble and honoured, not merely in Literature, Art, Archaeology, and Science, but in the public history of our country in its

---

*   In Paris, despite the apparent support for Wilde, Stuart Merrill had fared scarcely better with another proposed petition by French writers in December of 1895. There was no great rush from Wilde's old literary friends. Although Bourget, Bauer and Maurice Barrès agreed to sign, Zola refused. Alphonse Daudet and Sardou begged to be excused. Jean Lorrain – although known to share Wilde's homosexual tastes – claimed that his employers at Le Courrier Français had threatened to sack him if he lent his name. The playwright François Coppée wrote an article in Le Journal calling Wilde 'un insupportable poseur' but offering to sign the petition 'as a member of the Society for Prevention of Cruelty to Animals'. Goncourt disingenuously claimed that, following an article by Bauer in L'Echo de Paris castigating Maurice Donnay and Lucien Descaves for their 'pharisee-ism' in not signing, it was now impossible for him to do so, as it would look like he has been intimidated into it. Even Marcel Schwob (so helpful to Wilde during the composition of Salomé) made the cheap jest that he had agreed to sign the petition 'only on the condition that [Wilde] should never again... write'. In the face of such responses the petition was abandoned.

evolution as a nation'. And he had 'disgraced that name eternally... made it a low byword among low people... dragged it through the mire'.[8]

He was consoled, though, for the moment by Constance. In view of the exceptional circumstances they met 'in a room other than the ordinary visiting room'. She was 'gentle and good' to him. And even in his own distress he recognized that her suffering quite equalled his own. 'My soul and the soul of my wife met in the valley of the shadow of death,' he later told Ross; 'she kissed me; she comforted me: she behaved as no woman in history, except my own mother perhaps, could have behaved.' They talked of the future, and 'arranged everything' privately between themselves. Constance was desirous 'to have nothing done in a public court'. Her plan (sanctioned by Hargrove) was that Wilde, on his release, was to have an allowance from her of £200 a year, and – should she predecease him – one third of the life interest in her marriage settlement. The idea of an immediate and complete reconciliation upon Wilde's release seems to have been put on hold; it would be something to work towards. Constance, meanwhile, would assume custody of the children. Wilde acquiesced, while imploring her not to spoil Cyril. He suggested that if she were daunted at the prospect of bringing the boys up alone she should 'get a guardian to help her'.[9]

Constance touched also on the difficulties that More Adey was creating over the life interest. He was insisting that he and Wilde's 'friends' should buy a third of it on Wilde's behalf, rather than having to rely on Constance's goodwill in the matter. Wilde, though, had 'full trust' in his wife, and at once undertook to use his next permitted letter to write to Ross and tell him to let Constance purchase the life interest unopposed.[10]

Besides the tidings of his mother's death, there was the happier news that his play *Salomé* had been given its premiere in Paris. It had been mounted not by Sarah Bernhardt, but by the young actor-manager Aurélien Lugné-Poe, whose Théâtre de l'Œuvre had picked up the torch of Symbolist drama from the defunct Théâtre d'Art. This was the fulfilment of a dream; Wilde only wished he could take more pleasure in it. But he felt 'dead to all emotions except those of anguish and despair'. Even literature, for the moment, seemed to hold no charm for him. He suffered from headaches when he tried to read his Greek and Roman poets.[11]

Constance was greatly distressed by Wilde's condition. 'They say he is quite well,' she told Otho, 'but he is an absolute wreck compared to what he was.' The news of his mother's death undermined him further. And Constance's sad assessment of his health was confirmed by Ross at the end

of May when, together with Sherard, he paid Wilde his quarterly visit. In a long and vivid letter to Adey, he catalogued the marks of decline: not only was Wilde even thinner, but 'he had lost a great deal of his hair (this when he turned round and stood in the light). He always had great quantities of thick hair, but there is now a bald patch on the crown. It is also streaked with white and grey.'[12]

More distressing, though, was the vacant look in his eyes. He hardly spoke and cried much of the time. Literary and artistic news failed to interest him. He complained that he could not concentrate on his reading, and was still not allowed writing materials. His pressing fear was that he might be losing his mind. Ross shared the anxiety: he reported to Adey that imprisonment seemed to have made Wilde 'temporarily *silly*'. He would not – he said – be surprised if Wilde died within the coming months, not from any specific ailment, but because, 'he is simply wasting and pining away... sinking under a broken heart'. Sherard's verdict was scarcely less dire. 'I thought Oscar very bad indeed,' he told Adey. 'All elasticity and resistance seem to have gone out of him, and his state under the circumstances is really alarming. It was very terrible.'[13]

That Wilde's deterioration had taken place against the supposedly 'improved' conditions of Reading made it perhaps even more shocking. May 1896 marked the first anniversary of Wilde's incarceration. He was only halfway through his sentence. And if one year's imprisonment had wrought such an appalling change upon his health and well-being it was frightening to contemplate what a second year might do. Ross's fears for Wilde's life did not seem an exaggeration. Certainly that May visit provoked a resolve among Wilde's friends that something must be done, either to ameliorate his circumstances further, or secure his early release.

But how to proceed? Ross and Adey solicited the help of Frank Harris who, as the editor of the *Saturday Review*, was deemed to carry influence with the authorities. Harris (recently returned from South Africa) swung into action. He secured from Ruggles-Brise permission for a special 'interview of one hour's duration with the prisoner Oscar Wilde in the sight but not within the hearing of an officer'.[14]

At the meeting, which took place on 16 June, Harris confirmed the sorry changes in Wilde's appearance and manner. Even if the loss of weight gave him a superficially trimmer look, it could not disguise his worn and depressed state. Wilde regaled Harris with his woes: his want of writing materials; the harshness of the regime; and, particularly, a persistent pain,

and occasional bleeding, in his right ear. Although Wilde traced this debility back to his fall in the Wandsworth chapel, its seems more likely that it was a recurrence of his chronic middle-ear disease, the bleeding caused by a perforation of the eardrum.[15]

Nevertheless Harris's presence would have reassured him of the interest being taken in his case by the prison commissioners. And, being out of the warder's hearing, Harris was able to suggest plans for using this interest. He could explain to Wilde that the only allowable reason for a prisoner's early release was on medical grounds – whether physical or mental. And this understanding, doubtless, lay behind the tenor and detail of the long self-dramatizing 'petition' that Wilde addressed to the home secretary shortly after Harris's visit.

He opened his appeal with a frank admission of 'the terrible offences' of which he had been 'rightly found guilty' – offences that he characterized as 'forms of sexual madness'. He suggested, indeed, that in many European countries such 'horrid' and 'revolting' forms of 'erotomania' as he had indulged in were now considered to be more properly the concern of the medical rather than the judicial powers. Continued incarceration, however, he suggested, would only exacerbate his disturbed mental state: the extended periods of solitude, without books, left him prey to morbid thoughts and sexual imaginings, and in constant 'apprehension lest this insanity… may now extend to his entire nature'. At the same time his 'bodily health' was failing: he had 'almost entirely lost the hearing of his right ear through an abscess that has caused a perforation of the drum', while his eyesight – so important to a 'man of letters' – was strained by 'the enforced living in a whitewashed cell with a flaring gas-jet at night'.[16]

Although Isaacson forwarded the petition together with a terse report from Dr Maurice pointing out that 'prisoner Wylde' [sic] had in fact put on 'flesh' since arriving at Reading, and that the very cogency of his letter 'gave clear evidence of his present sanity', the Home Office did decide to institute further inquiries. Ruggles-Brise, having been briefed by Frank Harris, arranged for the prison's five-man 'visiting committee' to interview Wilde. Sherard and Ross, on their visit (speaking in French to avoid detection by the guard), had tried to explain that, should he be interviewed by the authorities, Wilde must try to appear as ill as possible. They, like all his friends, recognized that Wilde's natural 'vanity' would probably lead him 'to conceal any signs of weakness, whether mental or physical, from medical men' sent to find evidence of either. And this, it seems, is what happened.

Certainly the committee members found nothing obviously wrong with the prisoner.

Not quite trusting their own judgement, however, they did suggest that 'an expert medical enquiry' should be made into Wilde's physical and mental condition. As a lesser measure Wilde's 'remarkable petition' was, instead, sent to Dr Nicolson, one of the two Broadmoor doctors who had interviewed Wilde at Wandsworth. Nicolson, who was now the 'visitor in lunacy' attached to the Home Office, saw 'no indication of insanity or approaching insanity' in the document, but did think that 'it would be well to give [Wilde] increased and exceptional facilities as to books and writing materials'. At the end of July a set of instructions to this effect was issued by Ruggles-Brise.[17]

These developments were played out against the background of two significant events in the life of Reading gaol. On 7 July one of Wilde's fellow inmates – a young soldier, Charles Thomas Wooldridge – was hanged on the gallows erected in a shed in the prison exercise yard. The event was exceptional: it was only the second execution at Reading in eighteen years. Trooper Wooldridge had been convicted, as the local paper described it, of cutting 'his wife's throat in a very determined manner, she having excited his jealousy and (so far as the evidence went) greatly annoyed him'. The sight of the now-remorseful young man at exercise in the days before his execution had a profound effect on Wilde, as did the awful atmosphere of foreboding that hung over the whole prison throughout that time. The morning when the prison bell tolled to announce Wooldridge's impending death made 'a terrible impression' on Wilde's mind, as his imagination 'conjured up' the awful scene. Of all the hateful incidents of his two years in prison, this – Wilde averred – was the one that affected him most: 'It was horrible, horrible!'[18]

Overseeing the execution was almost the last act at Reading carried out by Lieutenant-Colonel Isaacson; shortly afterwards he was promoted to a new job at Lewes Prison in Sussex. His place was taken by the thirty-seven-year-old Major James O. Nelson. It was a piece of extraordinary good fortune for Wilde: very possibly it saved his life, and certainly it restored his spirit.[19]

3

From the Depths

'There is a luxury in self-reproach. When we blame ourselves we feel that no one else has a right to blame us.'

OSCAR WILDE

Major Nelson was a man of entirely different stamp to his predecessor. Imaginative, gentle and humane, Wilde characterized him as 'the most Christ-like man I ever met', and although he could not alter the rules of the prison system, he could alter the spirit in which they were carried out. Under Nelson the whole 'tone' of prison life altered completely, and for the better. He achieved a rapport with both the warders and the prisoners. Recognizing that here was an exceptional case, he went out of his way to befriend and help Wilde, administering the new instructions for the prisoner's treatment with sympathetic intelligence. He ensured that Wilde received spectacles for his eyesight, and daily treatment for his ear (the unsympathetic, if not incompetent, Dr Maurice, having previously declared Wilde's ear infection untreatable, was obliged to alter his views). Wilde's diet was increased and improved. He was allowed the 'luxury' of white bread. He was also given more exercise, sometimes being taken out of his cell four times in a day. And although he continued with his gardening work, he was not expected to do any other 'manual labour whatever' beyond keeping his cell clean.[1]

Instead he was to have greater access to books. Nelson encouraged him to draw up a list of volumes that might be added to the prison library. The twenty or so titles included a Greek Testament, Keats's poems, the works of Chaucer, and Renan's *Vie de Jésus*, which the chaplain was prepared to allow so long as it was 'in the original French'. Even more importantly, Nelson applied for Wilde to be allowed not only a daily allowance of foolscap paper but also a 'strong, coarsely bound manuscript book for his use'. Wilde was thrilled to have regular access to writing materials: 'The mere handling of pen and ink helps me,' he told Adey. 'I cling to my note-book.' He felt his mind and spirit reviving. It was wonderful to be treated once again as a human being. Regulations permitted prisoners a short daily interview with the governor, and Nelson ensured that Wilde availed himself of this privilege every day. It gave him a chance to converse, and to be appreciated. As Nelson later recalled, 'I looked forward to those morning talks. I always allowed Wilde to stay the full quarter of an hour to which a prisoner is entitled – or, rather, I kept him the full time. For it was a pleasure to me. Wilde was certainly the most interesting and brilliant talker I have ever met.'[2]*

Wilde's health began to improve almost immediately. Adey, having visited Wilde at the end of July, saw him again on 4 September and reported that he seemed 'wonderfully better in appearance and in spirits'. And the amelioration was maintained. After a third visit (on 28 January 1897), Adey informed Adela Schuster that Wilde was not only 'in excellent spirits' but actually 'playful'. Wilde's upward curve even survived the formal refusal (towards the end of the year) of his petition for early release. He would console himself by reading Dante. And he proposed to take up German again, telling Ross that 'indeed this seems to be the proper place for such a study'. Freed from his other duties, he was able to spend most of his time in reading and writing. Rather than the regulation weekly allowance of two books, he was permitted 'quite a library' in his cell.[3]

Nelson's benign regime encouraged the warders to behave with greater humanity towards their charges. Wilde began to make friends. As one warder noted, 'no one I think could have had daily intercourse with Oscar

---

* According to report, at one of these interviews Nelson, giving Wilde news of the outside world, mentioned the recent death of one of his relatives, as well as informing him that Edward Poynter had been elected president of the Royal Academy. Wilde solemnly thanked Nelson for telling him about his poor aunt, but suggested that he might perhaps have broken the news about Poynter more gently.

Wilde without growing to like him. He was as simple as a child in many things, but he was always the gentleman.' Although extended conversation with inmates was forbidden, ways were found to snatch moments of talk during the daily round. The constant challenge was keeping Wilde's enthusiasm in check. One of his gaolers recalled, 'I had often considerable difficulty to prevent him from raising his voice above a whisper. He would at times forget that he was in a prison cell... and would... commence to declaim on some subject that I would have given anything to hear, had I dared. But it was too risky and so I had to put up a warning hand.' This particular warder was an autodidact, always eager to consult Wilde about 'knotty problems' in his studies. He had a keen interest in literature, and Wilde cherished the memory of some of their exchanges.[4]

'Excuse me, sir, but Charles Dickens, sir,' the warder asked on one occasion, 'would he be considered a great writer now, sir?'

'Oh, yes, a great writer indeed. You see he is no longer alive.'

'Yes, I understand, sir. Being dead he would be a great writer, sir.'

On another occasion, the popular novelist of army life, John Strange Winter, was mentioned.

'Would you tell me what you think of him, sir?'

'A charming person,' Wilde replied, 'but a lady you know. Not a man. Not a great stylist, perhaps, but a good simple storyteller.'

'Thank you, sir. I did not know he was a lady, sir.'

The warder later touched on another popular woman novelist.

'Excuse me, sir, but Marie Corelli. Would she be considered a great writer, sir?'

This, Wilde later recalled, was more than he could bear. Putting his hand on the warder's shoulder, he answered gravely, 'Now don't think that I have anything against her moral character, but from the way she writes she ought to be here.'[5]

When unable to converse, Wilde would provide his student with extensive written answers on sheets of foolscap passed under his cell door each morning.[6]

Other warders would consult Wilde over newspaper prize competitions that required witty or ingenious responses. Wilde told Ross that during his time at Reading he had 'won a silver tea-service and a grand piano' as well as several guinea and half-guinea prizes.[7] The tea set had been secured for a recently married warder with a list of punning 'reasons' as to why the man and his new wife needed such an item: '(1) Because evidently spoons

are required, and my girl and I are two. (2) Because it would suit us to a T. (3) Because we have good "grounds" for wanting a coffee pot. (4) Because marriage is a game that should begin with a love set. (5) Because one cannot get legally married without a proper wedding service.'[8]

In this new atmosphere Wilde's whole attitude to his incarceration started to shift. His all-consuming 'loathing' for the prison 'and every official in it' began to abate. Bitterness and hatred ceased to dominate – and poison – his spirit.[9] He perceived that there might actually be a transformative power in imprisonment. Having held that incarceration 'turns a man's heart to stone' he came to recognize that, in fact, it could teach one pity – 'the greatest and most beautiful thing in the world'. Before his sentence he had, so he claimed, thought only of himself; now he was developing sympathy for the sufferings of others. To a man in the exercise yard who whispered to him, 'I pity you, for you are suffering more than me,' he replied simply, 'No, my friend; we all suffer alike.'[10]

Once awakened, Wilde's sense of pity certainly found much to occupy it. He expended his meagre resources in acts of kindness. On one occasion he asked a sympathetic warder to pass on 'half his bread' to the prisoner in the next cell, as he was 'very hungry, and doesn't get nearly so much food as I do'. As the warder remarked, 'the giving of half a loaf in prison requires a bigger heart than the giving of half a sovereign outside'. Through such deeds, and by the general tenor of his being, Wilde won a real popularity among the other inmates. By the end of his time at Reading there was 'a lot of competition' about 'who should get beside him on the exercise ring or in the prison chapel'.[11]

Wilde enjoyed the idea of making friendships across social divides, and he wrote to Reggie Turner mentioning his particular 'pals' among the 'many good nice fellows' inside. Despite the restrictions imposed by the separate system, he claimed to have 'seven or eight friends': 'they are capital chaps: of course we can't speak to each other, except a word now and then at exercise, but are great friends'. Although all were young men in their twenties – and one of them, Harry Elvin, was praised as 'very handsome' – Wilde's interest in these youths seems not to have been overtly sexual. Even before his release he was plotting ways in which to assist them with small sums of money.[12]

Among the glaring injustices of prison life the most distressing, for Wilde, were the routine imprisonment of young children and the brutal treatment of the 'half-witted'. The latter, often condemned for 'shamming' or

malingering when they unwittingly infringed minor rules, were continually being punished. One unfortunate young 'lunatic' – whose condition was clearly proclaimed by his 'silly grin and idiotic laughter', his sudden, silent, tears and his 'fantastic gestures'– was subjected to a brutal flogging 'by order of the visiting justices on the report of the doctor'. Wilde cried all night after the 'horror' of the incident, unable to get the sound of the man's shrieks out of his head: 'At first I thought some animal like a bull or a cow was being unskilfully slaughtered.'[13] He determined to try and reform these horrors on his release.

There were cares, too, from outside the prison. He had been upset when Ross informed him (during his May visit) that Lord Alfred Douglas was planning to bring out, in Paris, a volume of poetry dedicated to him. Wilde wrote subsequently to Ross urging him to prevent it: 'The proposal is revolting and grotesque.' He also asked that Ross retrieve all Wilde's letters to Douglas, so that they might be destroyed. He even wanted to get back all the presents he had given – books and jewellery. 'The idea that he is wearing or in possession of anything I gave him is peculiarly repugnant to me. I cannot of course get rid of the revolting memories of the two years I was unlucky enough to have him with me, or of the mode by which he thrust me into the abyss of ruin and disgrace to gratify his hatred of his father and other ignoble passions. But I will not have him in possession of my letters and gifts.'[14]

Although the still-exiled Douglas – distraught and bemused by Wilde's 'terrible' tergiversation – did withdraw the book, he refused to part with the letters. He told Ross that 'possession of these letters and the recollections they may give me, even if they can give me no hope, will perhaps prevent me from putting an end to a life which has now no *raison d'être*. If Oscar asks me to kill myself I will do so, and he shall have back the letters when I am dead.'[15] For the future, Douglas resolved to regard anything that Wilde might say while in prison as 'non-existent'.[16] And, in the meantime, as a record of his 'undying love,' he went ahead and published – in the *Revue Blanche* – a rambling and indiscreet defence of his relationship with Wilde, who, in his estimate, was 'suffering' in prison simply for being 'a uranian', even though a quarter of all men shared the same tastes. The article – which provoked considerable criticism from French writers – only strengthened Wilde's animus against his former beloved.[17] Ross, Adey and Reggie Turner all strove to plead Douglas's case; but 'the deep bitterness' of Wilde's feelings was not to be assuaged.[18]

Wilde was also distressed to receive at the beginning of November 'a violent and insulting letter' from Mr Hargrove, announcing that Constance – vexed by the continued attempts of Wilde's friends to purchase the life interest in the marriage settlement – now wanted complete legal control of the children. She was also threatening to stop any proposed allowance.[19] The news fell upon him like a 'thunderbolt'. He had been under the impression that all had been settled to allow Constance to acquire the life interest, and it was shocking to learn that this had not been done, and that Adey and Ross, ignoring his clear instructions on the point, had continued with their plans to buy the life interest from the official receiver.[20] They were motivated by a desire to protect Wilde from having to depend upon the goodwill of Constance's less-than-friendly 'advisors' and family, in the event of her predeceasing him, but the plan was misguided. It shattered the growing accord between Wilde and his wife: unable to believe that he was not party to the scheme, she too wrote a 'violent' and bitter letter. Moreover the action was entirely futile.[21]

The existing marriage settlement, and the attendant life interest, would be rendered obsolete in the event of a divorce. And in the face of Adey's continued intransigence, Constance and her solicitors resolved to begin proceedings. These would bring Wilde into fresh danger. There would be a new trial. Although the law allowed a husband to divorce his wife for adultery alone, a wife could divorce her husband for adultery only if he were also guilty of incest, bigamy, bestiality, rape, cruelty, desertion (for two years), or sodomy. Constance's lawyers – Wilde learnt, to his alarm – seemed to have got a statement from Walter Grainger, Douglas's young Oxford servant, admitting that, among various intimacies, Wilde had sodomized him. If this were brought out in a divorce court, Wilde might – potentially – find himself re-arrested and charged anew in the criminal court. Sodomy could carry a much longer sentence than the two years attendant upon mere acts of 'gross indecency'. Here was a fresh horror to contemplate.[22]

Once he perceived the precariousness of his position, Wilde strove to draw back from the precipice. Dispensing with the services of the ineffectual Mr Humphreys, he engaged a new solicitor, Arthur D. Hansell, to try to resolve the debacle without the need for a divorce. As a first step (and with great sadness) he agreed to surrender his guardianship of the children to Constance and her cousin, Adrian Hope.[23]

Wilde was trying to put the pieces of his life back together again. During the first three months of 1897 he worked daily on what began, at least, as

a long letter to Lord Alfred Douglas. In some 50,000 words he sought to explain to his former lover – and to himself – what had brought him to his current position, and then to draw some spiritual lesson from his situation.[24]* In unsparing detail he chronicled the history of his relationship with Bosie, through all its worst phases: the 'reckless' extravagances; the coarse debaucheries; the 'loathsome' and petty rows. And everything was laid to Douglas's account. The tenor of their affair had – Wilde asserted – been set by the 'shallowness' of his character; a character dominated by vanity and a sexual fascination with the 'gutter'. These were things that should have rendered him an unfit companion for an artist of Wilde's stature and stamp, 'one, that is to say, the quality of whose work depends on the intensification of personality... the companionship of ideas... quiet, peace, and solitude'. Certainly Wilde's indulgence of his friend had led to the 'absolute ruin' of his art. Anything he had managed to create had been despite, not because of, their friendship.

There was almost no trace of Wilde's great love for Bosie. And though Wilde admitted that Douglas had, after a fashion, loved him, that love, he suggested, had been 'entirely outstripped' by the hatred that Douglas had for his father. It was Douglas's insistence on drawing Wilde into his own hate-fuelled family conflict that had brought Wilde to the narrow confines of cell C.3.3. 'I am here,' Wilde declared, 'for having tried to put your father into prison.' But for his ill-fated libel case, Wilde insisted (with some truth), neither 'the Government' nor 'Society' would have taken any interest in his sexual peccadillos.

For all this Wilde – with dramatic magnanimity – 'forgave' Douglas. He accepted that he himself must bear responsibility for his own downfall, if only because he had – through his amiable nature – allowed himself to fall in with Douglas's base desires and mean designs: 'It was the triumph of the small over the bigger nature,' he declared; the 'tyranny of the weak over the strong'. Wilde blamed himself terribly for it. Nevertheless the utter despair that he had felt on entering prison had now passed away and, as he explained, he had begun to perceive the positive aspects of his predicament. He boasted of his newfound 'humility', as he called it. 'To reject one's own

---

* According to the prison regulations Wilde should have received only one sheet of paper per day, which had to be handed in upon its completion. And although the internal evidence of the manuscript (now in the British Library) suggests that this rule was not always enforced, the letter, as a whole, was composed without the benefit of Wilde being able to refer back to what he had written previously.

experiences,' he declared, 'is to arrest one's own development.' He had been awakened by prison life to a 'new world' of pity and sorrow, and he wanted to explore it. 'I now see that sorrow, being the supreme emotion of which man capable, is at once the type and test of all great Art. What the artist is always looking for is that mode of existence in which soul and body are one and indivisible: in which the outward is expressive of the inward: in which Form reveals.' And although there were several such modes – 'youth and the arts preoccupied with youth', 'modern landscape art', 'music', 'a flower or a child' – 'Sorrow is the ultimate type both in life and Art.' While pleasure might produce 'the beautiful body', it was 'pain' that produced 'the beautiful Soul'. And in this perception Wilde aligned himself with Christ.

Wilde's new vision of his prison existence – coupled with his daily reading of the Greek gospels – had drawn him back to the contemplation of Jesus. Formal religion continued to hold no interest for him. He passed the daily chapel service sitting 'in a listless attitude with his elbow resting on the back of his chair, his legs crossed', as he 'gazed dreamily' about himself with an air of exaggerated ennui.[25] Nevertheless he considered the chaplain, Rev. M. T. Friend, a perfectly 'nice fellow'.[26] There had been one unfortunate incident when the clergyman had responded to Wilde's complaint that his cell window gave no view of the sky with the pious observation, 'Let your mind dwell [not] on the clouds, but on Him who is above the clouds'; at which Wilde, losing his temper, had pushed him towards the door, shouting 'get out you damned fool'.[27] But for the most part they got on well enough. Friend was certainly impressed by the 'spiritual side' of Wilde's nature, and recalled how during their regular interviews his eye would sometimes light up as he talked, 'his body would straighten, and he would pull himself together and seem… almost to endeavour to project himself physically back into his old intellectual life'.[28]

And it seems to have been in discussion with Friend that Wilde elaborated his idea of Jesus as 'the supreme Artist'. Wilde admitted that he did not, 'of course', believe in 'the divinity of Christ, in its generally accepted sense', but he had 'no difficulty in believing that [Jesus] was as far above the people around him as though he had been an angel sitting on the clouds'. In Wilde's personal creed, Christ was fashioned in his own image: 'a supreme Individualist', 'an artist in words'; 'it was by the voice he found expression – that's what the voice is for, but few can find it by that medium, and none in the manner born of Christ'. He was a teller of beautiful tales, a master

of paradox, a genius of imaginative sympathy to equal Shakespeare, a poet who had made of his own life the most wonderful of poems.[29]

Initially Wilde was reluctant to proselytize his 'unique creed' – insisting that 'the moment I discovered that anyone else shared my belief I would flee from it'. But he had come to think that it was a subject on which he might write, perhaps after his release.[30] The fact of composing his letter to Douglas gave him a more immediate opportunity, and he interrupted his gazetteer of Douglas's failings to devote several pages to an imaginative panegyric to this vision of Christ as the 'precursor of the romantic movement in life' through his 'union of personality and perfection'.

The letter was an exercise in catharsis. It gave Wilde an outlet for his resentment against Douglas and his disappointment in himself. It offered him a means of comprehending his own imprisonment, and finding a way past it. It also allowed him to feel again the joy of literary creation. The glorious flow of language, and of thought, confirmed that neither his mind nor his spirit had been impaired by two years on a plank bed. The rhetorical effects of his prose, the obvious relish 'of sound and syllable', might seem to overwhelm the looked-for sincerity of his sentiments, but Wilde had always donned a mask to express a truth.

For all the bitterness of its early passages, the letter (addressed to 'Dear Bosie' and signed 'your affectionate friend, Oscar Wilde') both expected an answer and assumed a rapprochement of sorts following Wilde's release. 'At the end of a month, when the June roses are in all their wanton opulence, I will, if I feel able, arrange through Robbie to meet you in some quiet foreign town like Bruges, whose grey houses and green canals and cool still ways had a charm for me, years ago.' But if the mood of the letter had shifted over the course of its composition, so too had Wilde's vision of his creation. He had come to regard the epistle as a piece of literature, to take its place among his other works. (Although his own thought was that the text might be called 'Epistola: in Carcere e Vinculis', it would come to be known to posterity as *De Profundis*.)[31]

Rather than dispatch the manuscript directly to Douglas, he planned to send it to Ross as his 'literary executor', that he might have two typed copies made, one for Ross and one for himself, with a view to its eventual publication – 'not necessarily in my lifetime or in Douglas's'. He also hoped that additional copies of those passages relating to his spiritual development might be made and sent to such special friends as 'the Lady of Wimbledon' (Adela Schuster) and Frankie Forbes-Robertson. But these plans had to be

put on hold, when, at the beginning of April, the prison commissioners
declined Major Nelson's request for permission to send out the letter. It was
stipulated, instead, that the document should be handed to Wilde on his
release the following month.[32]

The end of Wilde's sentence no longer seemed impossibly distant. From
the beginning of the year they had ceased to crop his hair in preparation
for his release; much to his delight he felt it growing back over his ears[33] (he
amused the warders by insisting that his hair – very slightly tinged with grey
– was now 'perfectly white').[34] There was a further lightening of the mood
with the arrival at this time of a sympathetic new warder, Thomas Martin.
Belfast-born, he had a great admiration for Wilde, and took considerable
risks to improve his lot, smuggling him newspapers and additional food.
Wilde was introduced to 'Scotch scones, meat pies, and sausage rolls' –
those improbable delicacies which he had wondered at in the King's Road
only two years before.[35] 'My dear friend,' Wilde scribbled in one clandestine
note, 'What have I to write about except that if you had been an officer in
Reading Prison a year ago my life would have been much happier. Everyone
tells me I am looking better – and happier. That is because I have a good
friend who gives me the [Daily] Chronicle, and promises me ginger biscuits.'
To which Warder Martin added the superscription, 'Your ungrateful I done
more than promise.'

Wilde's mind turned increasingly on what he might do after his release.
The prospect filled him with both excitement and apprehension. He realized
that he would be leaving one prison to enter another, returning 'an unwel-
come visitant to that world that does not want me... Horrible as are the
dead when they rise from their tombs, the living who come out from tombs
are more horrible still.'[36] Neither England nor society could have any place
for him. He planned to go abroad quietly, and under an assumed name.
Donning the mantle of the damned and wandering hero of his 'Uncle'
Maturin's novel, he resolved to call himself 'Mr Melmoth'.[37] To this he
appended the Christian name Sebastian, taken from the beautiful martyr,
whose image, by Guido Reni, he had so admired in Genoa, all those years
ago. He had a vision of taking a little flat in Brussels.[38] Or perhaps he might
go to the remote coast of Brittany, where he could enjoy the twin benefits
of 'really bracing air' and 'freedom from English people'.[39] He had no plans,
he assured Adey jestingly, of taking up Ricketts's 'kind offer' to join him in
a Trappist monastery.[40]

He thought that if he could have 'at least eighteen months of free life to

collect [him]self', he might be able to work again.[41] He had been heartened to learn that imprisonment had not quite obliterated his artistic reputation; that in England, as in France, his books were still being read and his plays produced.* He chose to believe that the improvement in his circumstances should be traced back to the Parisian production of *Salomé*, which had obliged the 'Government' to accept that he was an artist of enduring and inter-national repute.[42] It was a base upon which to build. Frank Harris had assured him that he might find a regular outlet for his prose in the *Saturday Review*.[43] There were projects he wanted to attempt. Comedy might have to be given up. 'I have sworn solemnly to dedicate my life to Tragedy,' he informed Warder Martin. 'If I write any more books, it will be to form a library of lamentations.'[44] He hoped to return to the subject of 'Christ as the precursor of the Romantic Movement', as well as addressing 'the Artistic life consid-ered in relation Conduct' – taking Verlaine and the Russian anarchist Prince Kropotkin as exemplars.[45] He saw possibilities in making more 'beautiful coloured musical things' in the biblical-Symbolist manner of *Salomé*.[46] And although prison was, he considered, 'too terrible and ugly to make a work of art of', he wanted to write about it 'to try and change it for others'.[47]

First, though, he must recuperate, and for that he needed to buy time. Although he was still uncertain about his wife's plans for his allowance, Ross and Adey assured him that they had gathered from among his friends and supporters enough money to give a 'breathing space' for 'eighteen months or two years'.[48] The exact details were left vague, but Wilde understood that the sum was 'not small', and he looked forward to being able to repay some of his 'debts of honour' to friends and relations.[49] There was also what remained of the £1,000 that Adela Schuster had given him at the time of his trials and which Ernest Leverson had been looking after. Even if there had been some disbursements from it – for his mother's rent, her funeral costs, the expenses of Lily Wilde's confinement – the remainder, Wilde imagined, must still be a fair amount.[50] And beyond this there was the prospect of

---

* Ada Leverson had reported to More Adey the previous year of a 'really beautifully played and staged' touring production of *An Ideal Husband*, in which 'Cossie' Gordon Lennox was playing the part of Lord Goring. It had been 'splendidly received' at Brighton (where she had caught it). She had seen Cossie, who had told her of a 'very curious incident' that had occurred in Newcastle, when a man had called on him at the theatre: '[He] was like a shadow of Oscar, an exact imitation and great likeness. He adores Oscar and always has his photograph in a silver frame covered with forget-me-nots. He kissed Cossie, once for Oscar's sake, once for Lord Goring's and once for his own.'

£500 or £600 from Percy Douglas – the contribution promised towards Wilde's legal costs and supposedly 'set aside' at the time of his bankruptcy to await his release.[51]

These glowing financial expectations grew even brighter when, on 7 April, Wilde received another 'special' visit from Frank Harris. Harris, flush from a successful speculation in South Africa (which, he claimed, had made him some £23,000) insisted that he would set Wilde free from all 'money anxieties' with a cheque for £500. He also proposed whisking Wilde away, immediately upon his release, for a month's driving holiday in the Pyrenees. Wilde, overcome with emotion, accepted both offers.[52]

He was greatly touched by the solicitude of friends as he contemplated the various practicalities of his life 'outside'. He asked Ross to put together a collection of books for him: gifts solicited from his literary confreres, either their own recent works or enduring classics: 'You know the sort of books I want: Flaubert, Stevenson, Baudelaire, Maeterlinck, Dumas *père*, Keats, Marlowe, Chatterton, Coleridge, Anatole France, Gautier, Dante and all Dante literature: Goethe and ditto and so on.'[53] He was delighted to learn of several items – pictures, manuscripts, trinkets – which had been salvaged by friends from the sale at Tite Street and were to be returned to him.[54] And then there was a new wardrobe to be thought of. Robbie had got him a blue serge suit at Doré, but there was much else to be done. Wilde delighted in specifying the details of handkerchief borders, tie designs and collar shapes. He requested 'two or three sets' of mother-of-pearl shirt studs, announcing, 'I want to make "nacred" an English word'.[55]

Adey was sent a long list of toiletries to be bought: 'some nice French soap' (either 'Peau d'Espagne' or 'Sac de Laitue' would do); 'Canterbury Wood Violet' scent and 'Eau de Lubin' toilet water ('a large bottle'); Pritchard's tooth powder; and, as a tonic for his greying hair, a 'wonderful thing called Koko Marikopas, to be got at 233 Regent's Street... the name alone seems worth the money'. Wilde explained that, 'trivial as they may sound', these items were of 'really great importance', as 'for psychological reasons' he needed 'to feel entirely physically cleansed of the stain and soil of prison life'.[56] He learnt with pleasure that Reggie Turner was giving him a beautiful 'dressing bag' in which to keep his things (it was to be monogrammed with his new initials: 'S.M.').[57] The one annoyance, amid all these preparations, was the disappearance of his fine fur coat, which had been left at Oakley Street and pawned by the indigent Willie and his wife.[58] Otherwise all seemed set fair.

Then, in the week before his release, things began to unravel. Prior to

a meeting on Tuesday 11 May with Ross and Adey, Wilde had pressed for precise details about his financial position: they finally admitted that there was no great fund. There was only £50 – all that remained of the £150 that Adey had raised from well-wishers in 1895 and then spent on securing the life interest. Wilde was stunned. There was worse to come. On their visit to Reading, Adey and Ross relayed a verbal message from Frank Harris that he was 'very sorry' but he was unable to contribute anything at the moment. Neither could Percy Douglas help.[59]

On top of these blows Wilde learnt that there was barely £100 left of the money given him by Adela Schuster. Over £300 had gone to paying his former solicitor Humphreys. But Wilde's real shock was 'discovering' that Ernest Leverson had, back in 1895, taken £250 from the fund to redeem his outstanding debt. This, of course, was exactly what Wilde had insisted he should do. But he had forgotten it. And now, in his fragile and anxious state, it struck him as a betrayal. He insisted on regarding Leverson's action as an 'outrageous' piece of financial dishonesty akin to 'fraud'.[60]

It suddenly seemed to Wilde that he might have no money at all when he came out prison, not even enough to escape to the continent. It was an appalling thought. He wrote tersely to Leverson asking for a full statement of account, and the immediate handover of all monies,[61] while to Ross and Adey he fired off a succession of intemperate letters accusing them of gross incompetence and stupidity in all business matters. Poor Adey was castigated as a 'solemn donkey' who would be 'quite incapable of managing the domestic affairs of a tom-tit in a hedge for a single afternoon'.[62] Whatever 'mistakes' had been made, this was a poor return on so much selfless work. Reggie Turner felt obliged to write, telling Wilde he was being unjust to two 'dear and devoted friends'; and, as far as Ross was concerned, 'I fear, dear Oscar, that you have gone very near to breaking his heart.' Reggie was confident, though, that 'in a day or two crooked things will be put straight'.[63]

Amid all these distressing developments there had been one great relief: the troubled question of the marriage settlement was finally resolved.[64] Hansell had been able to report that a divorce, with the attendant scandal of court proceedings, could be avoided if both parties agreed to a voluntary 'mutual separation'. Such an arrangement, while legally binding, had the additional benefit of being reversible. It allowed the possibility of a future reconciliation. Wilde readily acquiesced to the plan, and on whatever conditions Constance desired. A 'deed of separation' was duly drawn up by

Hargrove and Hansell and acceded to by Adey's solicitor, Mr Holman. Under its terms Adey and Ross were obliged to assign to Constance the 'life interest' (which they had bought for £75); and in return Wilde was to receive a yearly allowance of £150 from his wife. There was an assurance that this arrangement would be maintained in the event of her predeceasing him. The quarterly payment of the allowance, however, was to be dependent upon Wilde's good behaviour: he was not to approach Constance or the children without her permission, nor could he 'be guilty of any moral misconduct or notoriously consort with evil or disreputable companions'.

Wilde balked rather at such conditions. As he remarked, since 'good people, as they are grotesquely termed, *will* not know me, and I am not to be *allowed* to know wicked people, my future life, as far as I can see at present, will be passed in comparative solitude'.[65] What constituted an infringement was to be left to the discretion of Mr Hansell – an arrangement that Adey thought most inadvisable. But it was allowed to stand. The solicitor, when he brought the 'deed of separation' down to Reading for Wilde to sign on 17 May, explained that 'moral misconduct' would certainly include any resumption of Wilde's relationship with the thoroughly 'disreputable' Lord Alfred Douglas. Wilde did not imagine that this would be a problem.[66]

Constance accompanied Hansell on his visit to Reading, though Wilde was unaware of the fact. She remained outside the 'consultation room' where Wilde 'sat at a table with his head in his hands' going through the details of the deed with his solicitor. She did, however, ask the warder at the door if she might have 'one glimpse' of her husband. He silently stepped aside, allowing her a lingering – and unobserved – look at the sad scene. Then, 'apparently labouring under deep emotion', she drew back. The warder considered it perhaps the 'saddest' incident of Wilde's prison life.[67] With typical thoughtfulness Constance ensured that the first quarterly instalment of Wilde's allowance – £37 10s – should be available to him when he came out of prison.[68] Amid the collapse of all his other financial hopes, it was a real comfort, although he did remark with some wonderment that he would now have 'to live for a year on what I used to spend in one week'.[69]

Things were not quite as bad as that. He heard the following day from Ernest Leverson, who – while defending his right to have repaid himself the £250 – was happy to make a 'fresh loan' of the same amount. But not all at once. As a first 'instalment' he had given £80, in bank notes, to Adey, along with a cheque for £111 11s 6d (the amount remaining from Adela Schuster's fund).[70] Miss Schuster had also sent Adey a further cheque, for

£25, anxious that Wilde should have something 'actually in his pocket – directly he comes out'.[71]

With even these modest sums in prospect, Wilde's thoughts turned at once to others. On the same afternoon that he signed the deed of separation he had been greatly distressed by the sight of three very small children who had just been brought into the prison for stealing rabbits. The following day Wilde managed to pass a note to Warder Martin asking him to find out the details of their case; he wanted to pay their fine and 'get them out'. 'Please, dear friend, do this for me. I must get them out. Think what a thing for me it would be to be able to help three little children. I would be delighted beyond words. If I can do this by paying the fine, tell the children that they are to be released tomorrow by a friend, and ask them to be happy, and not to tell anyone.' (Wilde did, in due course, secure their release.)[72]

As Wilde's time in prison approached its end there had been a growing anxiety among his friends about unwanted attention from the press or the public. Despite several requests to have his sentence shortened, if only by a few days, so that he could be got discreetly out of the country, the authorities were adamant that he would have to serve his two-year term in full. Nevertheless they did accept that it would be a good thing if his release on 19 May were handled without the glare of publicity. Reading, it was known, was filling up with journalists. Major Nelson had already received at least one letter, from an American reporter, 'offering any sum' for an interview with Wilde over breakfast on the morning of his release.[73] So, at almost the last moment (17 May), Wilde was informed that on the following day he would be taken from Reading to Pentonville, and released from there the next morning. The indignities of his earlier transfer were not to be repeated. Wilde would travel 'under humane conditions as regards dress and not being handcuffed'.[74] He had wanted to avoid London; instead he would be plunged into its midst. Nevertheless, from there he hoped to be spirited – by Adey or Turner – over to France. After his disappointment over the £500 he could no longer face the thought of travelling with, or even seeing, Frank Harris.

On the same day that he learnt about the plans for his return to liberty, he received a visit from Rev. James Adderley, a high church clergyman and devotee of the stage. An acquaintance of Wilde's, he was also a close associate of Stewart Headlam, and may have been making arrangements for Wilde to find a temporary refuge at Headlam's London home in the immediate aftermath of his release. Wilde would need a place to wash and

change and breakfast before setting off for the continent. Adderley recalled that, when he confessed that he had never visited a prisoner before – despite Jesus's admonitions on the subject – Wilde remarked, 'Then, bad as I am, I have done one good thing. I have made you obey your Master.' Adderley was also amused at Wilde declaring that, during his time in prison, he had learnt 'a wonderful thing called "humility"', immediately before describing his own prose as 'the finest prose in the English language – with the exception of Pater's'.[75]

On the evening of 18 May, having employed an element of deception to put off the journalists waiting at the gate, Wilde left Reading prison in a closed carriage, accompanied by the deputy governor and Warder Harrison.[76] Despite all the stresses of his final few days, Major Nelson recalled that he 'went out full of hope' and even 'grateful for his terrible punishment'.[77] And he took with him his long letter to Lord Alfred Douglas. Wilde's physical condition seemed to have improved alongside his mental powers during the ten months he had passed under Nelson's care, and he had regained some of his stoutness. One friend even described him as, apparently, 'radiant with health'.[78]

Wilde and his companions headed for Twyford station, where (exceptionally) the express train was to stop and pick them up. Waiting on the platform, Wilde nearly blew his cover by throwing open his arms at the sight of a budding tree, and exclaiming, 'Oh beautiful world! Oh beautiful world.' 'Now, Mr Wilde,' interjected Warder Harrison, 'you mustn't give yourself away like that. You're the only man in England who would talk like that in a railway station.'[79] On the journey to London, Wilde, though still not officially allowed to read a newspaper, was permitted to squint at an upside-down copy of the *Morning Chronicle* ('I never enjoyed it so much,' he claimed. 'It's really the only way to read newspapers').[80] Avoiding the terminus at Paddington, they alighted at Westbourne Park, and took a cab to Pentonville, the site of Wilde's first unhappy weeks of incarceration.

THE FISHERMAN
AND HIS SOUL

1897–1898

AGE *42–44*

Oscar Wilde and Lord Alfred Douglas, Naples, 1897.

1

Asylum

*'I think [Oscar's] fate is rather like Humpty Dumpty's, quite
as tragic and quite as impossible to put right.'*

CONSTANCE WILDE TO OTHO LLOYD

The press had been successfully put off the trail. Wilde was released at
quarter past six the following morning, into the brightness of a cold
spring day. More Adey and Stewart Headlam were there to meet
him, having received special permission to drive their curtained brougham
into the prison courtyard. They brought him back to Headlam's house in
Bloomsbury. As they drove down the Euston Road they saw a newspaper
placard announcing 'Release of Oscar Wilde'. At Upper Bedford Place, with
its tasteful decor of Pre-Raphaelite pictures and Morris wallpapers, Wilde
bathed and changed into his new clothes. After two years of prison cocoa,
he relished his first cup of coffee.[1]

Ada and Ernest Leverson arrived together with several other friends,
including Arthur Clifton and his wife. Ada recalled how Wilde at once
dispelled the awkwardness of the moment. 'He came in with the dignity
of a king returning from exile. He came in talking, laughing, smoking a
cigarette, with waved hair and a flower in his button-hole.' He looked,
she thought, not only 'markedly better, slighter, and younger' than he had
before his incarceration, but somehow, 'transformed and spiritualized'. His

first words were, 'Sphinx, how marvellous of you to know exactly the right hat to wear at seven o'clock in the morning to meet a friend who has been away! You can't have got up, you must have sat up.'[2] Everyone was put at ease. Wilde's irritation with More Adey and his anger at Ernest Leverson were forgotten. He was eager to talk of books and ideas. He discoursed on Dante, insisting on writing down for Headlam the best authorities to read on the poet.[3]

There was some discussion of immediate plans. Although all had been made ready for him to go over to Dieppe, where Ross and Turner were waiting, he seems to have been assailed by doubts (he would be too well known in Dieppe; he had too little money). According to Ada Leverson, his thoughts turned to the possibility of going on a religious retreat – if not actually entering a Trappist monastery. He had been talking about religion, telling Headlam that he looked on all the different religions of the world as 'colleges in a great university', with Roman Catholicism as 'the greatest and most romantic' of these colleges. And, prompted perhaps by this idea, he broke off to send a short letter by special messenger to one of the Catholic priests at either Farm Street or the Brompton Oratory, asking whether they might be able to provide him with a refuge.[4]

While waiting for a reply, Wilde talked gaily on, walking up and down the drawing room. One of his conceits was that 'the dear Governor' at Reading – 'such a delightful man, and his wife is charming' – having noticed him working in their garden, and supposing him to be the gardener, had invited him to spend the summer with them. 'Unusual, I think? But I don't feel I can,' he declared. 'I feel I want a change of scene.' His flow of humorous chat was broken by the return of the messenger. As Wilde read the letter he brought, his face assumed a sudden seriousness. Then he broke down and sobbed bitterly. The priests had replied that they could not accept him at a retreat on the impulse of the moment; such a step must be thought over for at least a year. It was the first rejection of his new life.[5]

It had been intended that Adey and Wilde should go down to Newhaven and take the morning boat to Dieppe. But Wilde's sudden interest in a Catholic retreat, as well as his general excitement at seeing so many old friends again, meant that the train was missed. Arrangements had to be altered, and Wilde and Adey crossed instead by the night boat.[6] Wilde telegraphed ahead to let Ross know that he 'must not mind all foolish unkind letters'.[7]

When the steamer docked at half past four the following morning, Ross and Turner were there, on the landing stage. Wilde lit up at the sight of them.

'His face,' Ross recalled, 'had lost all its coarseness, and he looked as he must have looked at Oxford in the early days.' After the usual 'irritating delay' Wilde stalked off the boat, a conspicuous figure, with his 'odd elephantine gait' and imposing height. He was holding a large sealed envelope, containing his long letter to Douglas. 'This, my dear Bobbie, is the great manuscript about which you know.' He went on, 'More has behaved very badly about my luggage and was anxious to deprive me of the blessed bag which Reggie gave me.' At this he gave out a great 'Rabelasian' laugh. The remark set the tone for much more high-spirited banter over the next couple of hours, as Ross and Turner piloted him through the customs formalities, and brought him back to the modest Hôtel Sandwich in the rue de la Halle au Blé, where they had arranged for an array of sandwiches to be set out, together with a bottle of red and a bottle of white wine. Perhaps it was the pathos of this modest but carefully ordered spread that caused Wilde's determined euphoria to falter: he 'broke down' and wept.[8]

The tears, however, were short-lived. Wilde's spirit was unfurling with each new hour of freedom. He relished the beautiful spring weather, the sea breeze, the apple blossom in the Normandy orchards, the sights and sounds of life. He was touched by the solicitude of his companions. He found his little room at the hotel filled with flowers. Ranged on the mantelpiece were all the books that Ross and Turner had collected; towards the centre, placed to 'catch his eye', were two volumes by Max Beerbohm: his collected essays and *The Happy Hypocrite*.[9] There were letters from 'Bernie' Beere and other friends. He also discovered two suits sent by Frank Harris, together with a cheque for £50. Although not the promised £500, it was still a generous gesture, and Wilde wrote at once to thank him. He wrote also to Ada Leverson, anxious, on his 'first day of real liberty', to acknowledge her sweetness and goodness in being 'the very first to greet [him]'. Other letters followed over the coming days, as Wilde hastened to thank his friends for their kindness and support.[10]

Adey returned almost immediately to London, but Ross and Turner stayed on for the week. It was all they could manage: both of them faced the disapproval of their families, and the possible loss of their allowances if it became known that they were consorting with Wilde. Nevertheless during their time together the three friends made a happy trio. There were endless jokes about Reggie's gift of the monogrammed dressing case, and Ross's unfailing kindness (Wilde insisted on canonizing him as 'St Robert of Phillimore', after his mother's new Kensington address). All Wilde's

great love and admiration for Ross returned: 'No other friend have I now in this beautiful world,' he declared. 'I want no other.'[11] It was intoxicating to be back in the world of talk. Ross recalled that Reading was Wilde's abiding subject during those first days of freedom. The prison became – in his more fantastical moods – 'a sort of enchanted castle of which Major Nelson was the presiding fairy. The hideous machicolated turrets were already turned into minarets, [and] the very warders into benevolent Marmelukes'.[12]

Not that the realities of the place were forgotten. When Wilde learnt, from an article in the *Daily Chronicle*, that Warder Martin had been dismissed for giving biscuits to a young child who had been brought into the prison, he wrote a long, impassioned, letter to the paper, defending Martin's action, and discoursing on the iniquities of locking up both children and 'imbeciles' under a regime so oblivious to their needs. 'People nowadays do not understand what cruelty is,' Wilde contended:

> It is the entire want of imagination. It is the result in our days of stereotyped systems of hard-and-fast rules, and of stupidity. What is inhuman in modern life is officialism. Authority is as destructive to those who exercise it as it is to those on whom it is exercised. It is the Prison Board, and the system that it carries out, that is the primary source of the cruelty... The people who uphold the system have excellent intentions. Those who carry it out are humane in intention also. Responsibility is shifted on to the disciplinary regulations. It is supposed that because a thing is a rule it is right.

He urged a change to the rules, to acknowledge the specific needs and conditions of the very young and the mentally impaired.[13]

Ross and Turner had tried to discourage him from making a public statement on the matter, anxious that he should not draw attention to himself. But Wilde was not to be deflected, and much to his gratification the letter (which was printed above his own name) provoked extensive comment and prompted questions in parliament.[14] As a piece of writing – cogent, humane, rich in allusion and language – it also gave public notice that his literary power was still intact. Wilde felt ready to be drawn back into the life of letters. He enjoyed a stimulating *déjeuner* with Aurélien Lugné-Poe, who was passing through Dieppe. 'I was quite charmed with him,' Wilde informed Adey. 'I had no idea he was so young, and so handsome.'[15] The actor-director, having mounted the premiere of *Salomé*, was anxious to

produce a new piece from Wilde's pen, and this was an idea that Wilde readily embraced. He was keen that his 'artistic re-appearance' after prison should be in Paris, not in London. It was 'a homage and a debt' that he felt he owed to the 'great city of art' that had preserved his reputation even during the dark days of his imprisonment.[16]

Peace and quiet, however, were needed for work. Dieppe, with its distractions, was unsuitable. He was too conspicuous in the little tourist-filled town to escape notice. There was also the question of economy. Ross was growing alarmed at Wilde's capacity for expenditure. With typical generosity he was insisting on sending small sums of money – from £1 to £3 10s – to many of his Reading 'pals' – as well as to Warders Martin and Grove. The Dieppe markets, too, were a temptation. As Wilde facetiously related to Turner, 'Robbie' had found him among 'the sellers of perfumes, spending all my money on orris-root and the tears of the narcissus and the dust of red roses' to fill the vials in the fabled dressing case. 'He was very stern and led me away. I have already spent my entire income for two years.'[17]

After a week Wilde moved 5 miles along the coast to the little village of Berneval-sur-Mer. There were no English visitors to recognize him, and very few French ones. When Ross left him, installed in the modest but salubrious Hôtel de la Plage, he endured a momentary pang of bitterness, as he grasped his 'terrible position of isolation', but the mood soon passed. The place had its charms, and the mere fact of freedom was delicious.[18] Only days after the move he was writing to Ross (back in London):

I am going tomorrow on a pilgrimage. I always wanted to be a pilgrim, and I have decided to start early tomorrow to the shrine of Notre Dame de Liesse. Do you know what Liesse is? It is an old word for joy... I just heard of the shrine, or chapel, tonight, *by chance*, as you would say, from the sweet woman of the *auberge*, a perfect dear, who wants me to live always at Berneval! She says Notre Dame de Liesse is wonderful, and helps everyone to the secret of joy. I do not know how long it will take me to get to the shrine, as I must walk. But, from what she tells me, it will take at least six or seven minutes to get there, and as many to come back. In fact the chapel of Notre Dame de Liesse is just fifty yards from the hotel! Isn't it extraordinary? I intend to start after I have had my coffee, and then to bathe. Need I say that this is a miracle? I wanted to go on a pilgrimage, and I find the little grey stone chapel of Our Lady of Joy is brought to me. It has probably been waiting for me

all these purple years of pleasure, and now it comes to meet me with
Liesse as its message.

The old buoyancy, merriment and invention were evident in every line.
Frank Harris, when Ross showed him the letter, considered it 'the most
characteristic thing' Wilde ever wrote; 'more characteristic even than *The
Importance of Being Earnest*'. And if Wilde missed Ross and Turner, he continued 'talking' to them – as well as to other old English friends – in a ceaseless flow of scarcely less characteristic missives. Not that he was bereft of real
company. There were the simple but charming denizens of Berneval, from
the local customs-house officers to whom he lent Dumas novels to the local
Catholic priest with whom he discussed religion and stained glass. He also
found friends at Dieppe. Of course many of the expatriate holiday crowd
were embarrassed by his presence, and sought to avoid him, but others
were bolder. The unflappable Norwegian painter Frits Thaulow ('a giant
with the temperament of Corot') and his engaging wife welcomed Wilde
into their happy family home, even hosting a reception for him, to which
they optimistically invited both the mayor of Dieppe and the president
of the town's chamber of commerce.[19] Mrs Stannard (the 'John Strange
Winter' about whom Wilde had discoursed with the Reading warder) was
similarly generous; she and her husband regularly invited Wilde to meals
at their apartment.[20] He was greatly touched by these marks of kindness,
and the small flavour they afforded him of family life. He came to set a
special store by female company, both for itself and for the 'respectability'
that it bestowed upon him. He was delighted, too, to find himself among
children again, entertaining the Stannards' three daughters and one son
with a stream of improvised tales and jokes.[21]

There was also a more bohemian element around the town. Ernest
Dowson, who was staying for the summer at nearby Arques-la-Bataille,
came over to Berneval for an extremely jolly visit, with Charles Conder
and a young composer called Dalhousie Young. Young, though previously
unknown to Wilde, had not only published a polemical pamphlet in his
defence, but had also contributed £50 to the fund put together by Adey
for his support.[22] They all stayed up until three in the morning, and that
charmed night was followed by others. Wilde was much taken by the generous 'Dal' Young, and also by his sympathetic wife, though he felt unable to
accept their too generous offer to put up the money for him to build a little
villa at Berneval.[23] He was pleased to see Conder again, relishing how the

delicate vagueness of his art was matched by the delicate vagueness of his personality. He was amused, too, at his wonderful lack of business acumen: 'Dear Conder,' he declared, 'With what exquisite subtlety he goes about persuading someone to give him a hundred francs for a [painted] fan, for which he was fully prepared to pay three hundred.'[24]

But it was with the bibulous and tubercular Dowson that he forged the closest bond. Wilde admired his work and was stimulated by his company. It was necessary, as he declared, 'to have a poet to talk to'. He approved of Dowson's 'dark hyacinth locks', his green suit and his blue tie. 'Why are you so persistently and perversely wonderful?' he asked after one of their absinthe-fuelled meetings. 'There is a fatality about our being together that is astounding – or rather quite probable.'[25]

William Rothenstein was another of those who made a 'pilgrimage to the Sinner' at Berneval. He arrived together with Edward Strangman, 'a charming sweet fellow' who, to Wilde's delight, had plans for translating *Lady Windermere's Fan* into French. And André Gide, having been the last of Wilde's French friends to see him before his fall, came up from Paris specially, in order to be the first to greet him after his release. They talked late into the night of prison life and literature. 'Russian writers are extraordinary,' Wilde declared. 'What makes their books so great is the pity they put into them. You know how fond I used to be of *Madame Bovary*, but Flaubert would not admit pity into his work, and that is why it has a petty and restrained character about it.' Wilde also invited Arthur Cruttenden, one of his recently released Reading 'pals', over for a short visit. Cruttenden, a former soldier, had been imprisoned after getting drunk and 'making hay' in the regimental stables: 'the sort of thing,' Wilde declared, 'one was "gated" for at Oxford'.[26]

Although Wilde claimed that he neither dreamed of – nor wanted – 'social rehabilitation', the modest lines of his new life made it clear how much he had lost. That grand social world of fashionable dinners and aristocratic receptions, of first nights and private views, that he had both enjoyed and adorned, was lost forever. He had to face a new reality. As part of his post-prison pose, Wilde wore two conspicuous rings: one he claimed brought good fortune, the other ill luck, and he insisted that he was presently under the influence of the 'evil ring'; that having been, for so many years, the happiest of men, he was now (very deservedly) the most unhappy.[27]

There was, however, a general consensus among his friends that he was in remarkably good shape and even better spirits. Gide found him like the

'sweet Wilde' of the early 1890s, rather than the arrogant sensualist of more recent years.[28] Dowson reported to Henry Davray that the most noticeable change from Wilde's 'old' self was 'the extreme joy he [now] takes in the country and simple things'.[29] To Rothenstein Wilde listed among his principal blessings 'the sun and the sea of the beautiful world'.[30] He relished his regular morning swim, having rented a bathing hut on the Berneval *plage*.[31] He even began to quote Wordsworth.[32]As he cautiously admitted to one correspondent, 'I suppose I am getting happy again. I hope so.'[33]

He had embraced contrition, after his own self-dramatizing fashion. 'I drank the sweet, I drank the bitter,' he declared, 'and I found bitterness in the sweet and sweetness in the bitter.'[34] Prison, he claimed, had taught him both 'pity' and 'gratitude'. He kept up a regular attendance at the village church. 'I am seated in the Choir!' he told Ross. 'I suppose sinners should have the high places near Christ's altar.'[35] The old *curé* was hopeful for his conversion, and though Wilde was tempted, he declared himself still unworthy.[36] Nevertheless he chose to regard St Francis of Assisi as his new model for life.[37] It became his line that, whatever the tragedy of his fall, he had 'no bitterness' in his heart against anyone: 'I accept everything,' he would tell his friends. 'I really am not ashamed of having been in prison. I am thoroughly ashamed of having led a life quite unworthy of an artist... sensual pleasures wreck the soul: but all my profligacy, extravagance, and worldly life of fashion and senseless ease, were wrong for an artist. If I have good health, and good friends, and can wake the creative instinct in me again, I may do something more in art yet.'[38]

But beneath the apparent peace and contentment of Wilde's new life tensions remained. Wilde had written to Constance immediately upon his arrival in France, hopeful of a swift reconciliation. In a 'very beautiful' letter, 'full of penitence' and touched with an 'almost spiritual enthusiasm', he had suggested that they might meet. The gentle-hearted Constance – who, only days before her husband's release, had asserted that it would be 'impossible' for her 'to go back to Oscar' – was inclined to relent. Her brother, Otho, however, counselled caution. He thought the mood of Wilde's letter 'too overwrought and high pitched to last'.[39] Certainly it should be tested by a delay. Constance temporized. She replied to Oscar's letter enclosing photographs of the boys ('such lovely little fellows in Eton collars', Wilde thought them), and promising that she, at least, would meet him in due course. Further letters followed (at the rate of one a week), but no immediate plan for a visit. Wilde was disappointed: 'She says *she* will see

me, twice a year,' he informed Ross, 'but makes no promise to allow me to see [the children].' This was a blow. 'I want my boys,' he lamented. 'It is a terrible punishment, dear Robbie, and oh! how well I deserve it.'[40]

Others, meanwhile, were only too eager to see him. At almost the same moment that Wilde heard from Constance, he received a letter from Douglas (then in Paris). He acknowledged Wilde's supposed hatred of him, but proclaimed his own unwavering love and pleaded for a meeting. Wilde was unsettled by the communication. There had not yet been time to have the long prison letter copied and sent to Douglas, so much ground remained uncovered. Wilde offered a measured response, assuring Douglas that he did not 'hate' him, but enumerating some criticisms of his past behaviour, and insisting that any meeting must be deferred indefinitely. This was not at all what Douglas wanted to hear. Sure of his own devotion, and riled by what he considered the 'somewhat priggish, if not canting tone' of Wilde's letter, he replied 'vigorously', pointing out that Wilde's attitude towards him was 'unfair and ungrateful' and appeared only 'to reflect the psychological results of imprisonment in a way which he would probably soon grow out of when he got back the full use of his brains and intellect'. After receiving this fusillade, Wilde spent a sleepless night. As he explained to Ross, 'Bosie's revolting letter was in the room, and foolishly I had read it again and left it by my bedside.'

Further, similarly 'infamous,' missives followed, together with a 'love-lyric', which Wilde considered 'absurd'. Wilde's attempted remonstrations were returned unread.[41] It was clear that Douglas was not to be easily set aside. Wilde began to feel 'a real terror' of him. In practical terms, as he acknowledged to Adey, 'Bosie' could 'almost ruin' him.[42] Wilde's income from Constance depended upon him avoiding any public contact with the 'notoriously disreputable' Douglas. Adey's solicitor had, moreover, passed on news that Lord Queensberry 'has made arrangements for being informed if his son joins Mr. Wilde and has expressed his intention of shooting one or both' should he do so. As Mr Holman remarked, 'a threat of this kind from most people could be more or less disregarded, but there is no doubt that Lord Queensberry, as he has shown before, will carry out any threat that he makes to the best of his ability'.[43]

But Wilde's fear of Douglas perhaps masked a fear of himself. The selfish and insensitive Bosie might be recognized as 'an evil influence' but he remained a dangerously attractive one. His declarations of undimmed adoration had a certain force, and Wilde soon found himself drawn towards

the flame. He was heartened when Douglas wrote – 'for him nicely' – about his own, and Wilde's, artistic plans. It seemed safer 'to meet on the double peak of Parnassus'.[44] He read 'with great pleasure and interest' the volume of Douglas's *Poems* which had been published in 1896, without the dedication to Wilde.[45] Soon they were in almost daily communication, and Wilde was declaring, 'My dear Boy… Don't think I don't love you. Of course I love you more than anyone else… and every day I think of you, and I know you are as poet, and that makes you doubly dear and wonderful.'[46]

Even the acceptance that they must not meet was soon eroded. Wilde sought to enlist Lady Queensberry's support for the idea of a rapprochement – although she declined to involve herself in the matter.[47] Nevertheless by the middle of June he was arranging for Douglas to come to Berneval, under the conspicuous alias of 'Jonquil de Vallon'. But, on the eve of the visit, Wilde received a letter from his solicitor, warning him that the plan was known (perhaps through Queensberry's informers) and, if carried through, would result in serious consequences to Wilde's income and maybe even to his safety. Although Douglas would have been delighted to defy his father (once again), Wilde was more circumspect and more easily shaken. He forbade Douglas from coming, at least for the moment.[48]

Douglas took the delay badly, unreasonably blaming Ross for agreeing to the legal constraints that had been put upon Wilde seeing him. But although Wilde defended Ross from Douglas's intemperate and ill-mannered attacks, the rift between Wilde's two young friends added a new tension to his life. He wove his sense of divided loyalties and affections into an elegant couplet: 'Two loves have I: the one of comfort; the other of despair. The one has black; the other golden hair.'[49]

2

∞∞∞∞∞∞

Artistic Work

*'I hope to get back the concentration of will-power that con-
ditions and governs art, and to produce something good again.'*

OSCAR WILDE

W ilde was able to find some solace in work. He was full of schemes,
as he sought to maintain the creative momentum built up
during his last months at Reading. After the success of his letter
to the *Daily Chronicle* he had considered writing a three-part article for the
paper on his 'Prison Life', from a 'psychological and introspective' angle. He
would be able to draw on his long letter to Douglas, to provide a section on
'the lovely subject' of 'Christ as the Precursor of the Romantic Movement
in Life'. Certainly Wilde felt the need to address his prison experiences in
literary form. But – perhaps recalling the hopes of both Viscount Haldane
and Warder Martin on this score – he began to wonder whether his approach
might, after all, be artistic, rather than merely polemical. Leaving the article
unstarted, he took off in a new direction. On 1 June he informed Ross, 'as
you, the poem of my days, are away, [I] am forced to write poetry. I have
begun something that I think will be very good.'[1]

It was a 'ballad', recounting, in a heightened but barely fictionalized
form, the story of the execution of Trooper Wooldridge for the murder of
his wife. Wilde's approach was, initially, personal. His narrator – a thinly-

veiled self-portrait – allies himself with the condemned man as he walks
in the exercise yard each day looking wistfully 'upon that little tent of blue
which prisoners call the sky'. The man 'had killed the thing he loved / And
so he had to die.' But, as the narrator noted, it was the punishment rather
than the crime that was exceptional. He himself – along with all the other
prisoners – shared the trooper's guilt: for 'each man kills the thing he loves',
some with a sword, some by a kiss:

> Some do the deed with many tears,
> And some without a sigh:
> For each man kills the thing he loves,
> Yet each man does not die.

From a literary point of view Wilde relished the ballad form. He commended it to Douglas. It had the ability to be dramatic, Romantic and popular all
at the same time. It had been employed by Lady Wilde for one of her most
successful works, and had a rich tradition in English literature: Wilde cited
both Coleridge's *Rime of the Ancient Mariner* and Thomas Hood's *Dream of
Eugene Aram* as models. It had echoes, too, of rhythms and cadences found
in A. E. Housman's recently published *A Shropshire Lad*, which Wilde was
reading just then with great enjoyment. Section IX of Housman's poem
even dealt with the execution of a man in Shrewsbury gaol.[*2]

Progress was good, aided by the fact that, towards the end June, Wilde
moved from the increasingly crowded and noisy Hôtel de la Plage into
the nearby Chalet Bourgeat. He did, however, worry about using such
obviously personal subject matter. The poem, he told Laurence Housman
(A. E.'s younger brother), is 'terribly realistic for me, and drawn from actual
experience, a sort of denial of my own philosophy of art in many ways.

---

*   In the poetry of Wilde's childhood it reached back not only to his mother's ballad *The
     Brothers*, but also to Denis Florence MacCarthy's *New Year Song* with its ringing lines:

> There's not a man of all our land
> Our country now can spare,
> The strong man with his sinewy hand,
> The weak man with his prayer!
> No whining tone of mere regret,
> Young Irish bards, for you;
> But let you songs teach Ireland yet
> What Irish man should do.

I hope it is good, but every night I hear cocks crowing in Berneval, so I am afraid I may have denied myself, and would weep bitterly, if I had not wept away all my tears'.[3] Realism, however, might have its virtues. Wilde thought the topicality of the poem would ensure a ready market. He had – so he claimed – been offered £1,000 by an American newspaper for an account about his prison experiences. And while he was not tempted to accept such a sensation-hunting journalistic proposal, he supposed that an artistic treatment of the same subject might command an only slightly lesser interest. He envisaged publication of his poem in the *Daily Chronicle* and one of the New York papers for anything between £100 and £300.[4]

In tandem with his work on the 'ballad' Wilde kept in view the possibilities of play-writing. He was toying with several schemes. Although disappointed to learn that Lugné-Poe would not be able to pay anything upfront for a new play, Wilde remained keen to follow up the success of *Salomé* with another Parisian premiere, even if it had to be with a different producer. He had two ideas for further biblical-Symbolist pieces, to be written (apparently) in French: the first was his story of Pharaoh and Moses, the second a fantastic variation on the tale of Ahab and Jezabel, in which he imagined Bernhardt might take the female lead. Either piece could serve to launch him back into literary world of Paris.[5] As an aid to his research, Wilde asked Ross to find him a copy of Adolf Erman's magisterial *Life in Ancient Egypt* so that he might know 'how Pharaoh said to his chief butler, "Pass the cucumbers"'.[6] Wilde's commitment to France and French culture was strengthened by flattering reports that, if it were decided to include foreign authors in the new Académie Goncourt (set up in the wake of Edmond de Goncourt's death the previous year), the names likely to be put forward were Count Tolstoy, Henrik Ibsen and 'Mr Oscar Wilde'.[7]

Although England was offering no such distinctions, it was not forgotten. Wilde was very conscious that he remained in financial and moral debt to George Alexander and Charles Wyndham, and he was anxious to atone by writing plays for both men as soon as possible.[8] Any work for the London stage would have to appear – in the first instance at least – anonymously. Wilde doubted that the English public was ready to welcome him back quite yet.[9] But anonymity need not preclude success. And a popular English-language drama would give Wilde a chance to refill his own coffers. He needed to start making money, and quickly. His existing resources would, he calculated, only last out the summer. And unless Percy Douglas came through with the long-promised £500 'debt of honour', he must rely on his own endeavours.[10]

As a first step, he planned to complete *The Florentine Tragedy*. Although Wilde, rather fancifully, suggested that the one-act blank-verse historical drama might command an advance of £500, he seems to have recognized that something with a more obvious commercial appeal would probably also be needed.[11] His thoughts appear to have turned to the scenario of the unfaithful husband and less faithful wife that he had first mapped out for George Alexander in the summer of 1894 (as a possible alternative to *The Importance of Being Earnest*). And although he hesitated to make a start on the script – provisionally entitled 'Love is Law' – he did begin gathering aphorisms that might enliven the dialogue. Besides his own quip about everyone nowadays being 'jealous of everyone else, except, of course, husband and wife', he also wanted to borrow Reggie Turner's riposte to the remark that someone had been 'born with a silver spoon in his mouth': 'Yes! But there was somebody else's crest on it.'[12]

Charles Wyndham, though, had ideas of his own. On 23 July the actor-manager crossed over to Berneval for the day, with a proposal that Wilde should adapt Scribe's drama, *Le Verre d'eau*, a comic intrigue set at the court of Queen Anne. The plan had its attractions for Wilde, not only because it would spare him the trouble of inventing a plot, but also because he hoped that Ross would help him with the task. He urged Robbie to come over, and bring with him a Queen Anne chair 'just for the style'. 'If *you* work hard,' he joked, 'I shall have a great success.'[13]

Wyndham, even on his fleeting visit, must have been encouraged by Wilde's readiness to embark on such flights of fancy. The comic sense had clearly not deserted him. Indeed it informed most of his letters and many of his actions over the summer. Wilde, always an admirer of Queen Victoria, embraced her approaching Diamond Jubilee with enthusiasm. He stuck up, in pride of place, a reproduction of William Nicholson's 'wonderful' woodcut of her ('Every poet should gaze at the portrait of his Queen, all day long,' he declared). And he proudly told visitors that the three women he most admired were Queen Victoria, Sarah Bernhardt and Lillie Langtry, adding for effect, 'I would have married any one of them with pleasure.'[14]* On the day of the Jubilee itself (22 June) he had amazed the inhabitants of Berneval by hosting a splendid tea party in the garden of his villa, for a

---

*   As a variation on this line, he told the French poet Jean Joseph-Renaud that 'the Nineteenth Century has had three great men: Napoleon the First, Victor Hugo, and Queen Victoria'.

dozen of the local schoolboys along with their form master. The company was regaled with strawberries and cream, apricots, chocolates, *sirop de grenadine* and a huge iced cake with *'Jubilé de la Reine Victoria'* in pink sugar, rosetted with green, and a great wreath of red roses round it all. Each of the children was presented with a musical instrument (selected by lot). 'They sang the Marseillaise and other songs,' Wilde reported to Douglas, 'and danced a *ronde*, and also played "God save the Queen": they said it was "God save the Queen," and I did not like to differ from them. They also all had flags which I gave them. They were most gay and sweet. I gave the health of *La Reine d'Angleterre*, and they cried, *"Vive la Reine d'Angleterre"*!!!! Then I gave *"La France, mère de tous les artistes,"* and finally I gave *Le Président de la République.* I thought I had better do so. They cried out with one accord *"Vivent le Président de la République et Monsieur Melmoth"*!!!'[15]

Although Wilde's wit could animate a letter, he found it hard to sustain any more concerted literary endeavour. He could only work for an hour at a time.[16] But if this made play-writing difficult, it suited well enough the composition of *The Ballad of Reading Gaol* (as Ross had dubbed his poem.) Throughout the summer Wilde went on adding stanzas to the work in an almost piecemeal fashion. He also took on other short tasks. For a new book of Rothenstein's clever portrait drawings he composed a barbed but brilliant paragraph on W. E. Henley, ending with the observation, 'He has fought the good fight, and has had to face every difficulty except popularity.'[17] Alas the paragraph was too barbed – or too brilliant – and Rothenstein's cautious young publisher thought better of using it.[18]

As the summer season advanced, and Dieppe filled with visitors, there were more distractions. Wilde was at the centre of a riotous gathering of young French writers at the Café Tribunaux in Dieppe, which drew the attention of the town's *sous-préfet*.[19] He was introduced, by Dowson, to the irrepressible Leonard Smithers – a publisher, book dealer and sometime pornographer, who, during the years of Wilde's imprisonment, had emerged as significant figure on the fringes of London's literary scene.[20] While John Lane had joined the general rush to disavow anything remotely connected with decadence, artistic experiment, and 'the Oscar Wilde tendency', Smithers had moved in the opposite direction. He offered a haven to the more daring writers and artists of the younger generation. It was his boast that he would 'publish anything the others were afraid of'. When *The Yellow Book* 'turned grey overnight' with the sacking of Aubrey Beardsley in the wake of Wilde's arrest, Smithers hastened to set up the *Savoy* as a rival

publication, with Beardsley installed as art editor. He also began publishing volumes of self-consciously decadent verse – by Ernest Dowson, Arthur Symons and Theodore Wratislaw – as well as an edition of Pope's *Rape of the Lock* with elaborate illustrations by Beardsley.

Smithers was delighted to meet Wilde. Back in 1888 he had written a 'charming' letter of appreciation to the author of *The Happy Prince*, and received a gracious reply.[21] Wilde, for his part, was richly amused by the thirty-five-year-old Yorkshire-born *bon viveur*, with whom he was soon passing many a bibulous hour in the cafés of Dieppe. 'I do not know if you know Smithers,' he asked Turner:

> He is usually in a large straw hat, has a blue tie delicately fastened with a diamond brooch of the impurest water – or perhaps wine, as he never touches water: it goes to his head at once. His face, clean-shaven as befits a priest who serves at the altar whose God is Literature, is wasted and pale – not with poetry, but with poets, who, he says, have wrecked his life by insisting on publishing with him. He loves first editions, especially of women: little girls are his passion. He is the most learned erotomaniac in Europe. He is also a delightful companion, and a dear fellow, very kind to me.[22]

Ernest Dowson was not the only Smithers author in Dieppe that summer. Wilde came to know and (eventually) to like the young American short-story writer Vincent O'Sullivan.[23] Beardsley, too, arrived in the town, seeking a healthful climate for his consumptive lungs. Wilde shared an enjoyable lunch with him and Smithers, finding him 'in good spirits' and looking surprisingly well.[24] Sitting side by side on the casino terrace they discoursed on the 'incredible history' of Dieppe – which Beardsley described as running 'from Brennus to Oscar Wilde'.[25] On another occasion Wilde made 'Aubrey buy a hat more silver than silver', telling Turner that 'he is quite wonderful in it'.[26] Such meetings, however, were complicated – for Beardsley – by the fact that he was now under the patronage of Wilde's bête noir, André Raffalovich. By associating with Wilde, Beardsley risked upsetting his patron, and losing his stipend.

Although Wilde constantly looked for the return of either Ross or Turner, neither of them was able to come during the long days of July and early August. Arrangements were made, and then deferred. He received, instead, a visit from their young friend John Fothergill. The twenty-one-year-old

dilettante (who, having embarked on a course at the London College of Architecture, was dubbed 'the architect of the moon') arrived, bringing with him Erman's *Life in Ancient Egypt*. A 'sextette of suns' was passed in talk – and drinking. Fothergill was slightly alarmed by Wilde's insistence that it was the accepted thing, when leaving a French country inn, to kiss the servant.[27] Behind the almost ceaseless flow of sparkling chat, Fothergill thought that he detected a sadness and loneliness in his host. But he was also touched by Wilde's humanity. On one evening they went to a 'three-penny show' in the village schoolroom; as the 'poor little reciter shouted and screamed and squealed and sweated at his work' Fothergill noted Wilde, 'rapt and absorbed' in the performance, his face alive with 'pity, pathos, care, patience and understanding' and 'on his big cheek a tear ran'.[28]

Smithers was a frequent visitor during the days of Fothergill's stay. And the impecunious Dowson was actually installed at the Chalet Bourgeat, having been 'rescued' by Wilde 'from a position of great embarrassment at the inn at Arques'.[29] The presence of both men encouraged Wilde's absinthe drinking; Fothergill described Smithers as having turned 'green' through his devotion to the spirit. At a dinner chez Thaulow Wilde defended the absent Dowson from the charge – made by one of the other guests – that he drank too much. 'If he didn't drink,' Wilde replied, 'he would be somebody else. *Il faut accepter la personalité comme elle est. Il ne faut jamais regretter qu'un poète est soûl, il faut regretter que les soûls ne soient pas toujours poètes.'** Wilde went on to claim (in jest) that he was at work on an essay entitled 'A Defence of Drunkenness', claiming that 'the soul is never liberated except by drunkenness in one form or another'. At Dieppe, beside the sea, one might become intoxicated with nature: the soul could 'listen to the words and harmonies and behold the colours of the Great Silence'. But elsewhere it might be necessary to resort to absinthe: 'A waiter with a tray will always find [the Great Silence] for you. Knock; and the door will always open, the door of *le paradis artificiel.'*

Amid the drinking and the summer fun, there were not infrequent snubs. On at least one occasion Wilde was discreetly asked to leave a Dieppe restaurant following objections to his presence from fellow diners.[30] On another afternoon he was rescued by Mrs Stannard, who, seeing him being snubbed by a group of English visitors, heroically crossed the road, took

---

* 'One must accept a personality as it is. One must never regret that a poet is drunk, one must regret that drunkards are not always poets.'

his arm, and declared loudly, 'Oscar, take me to tea.'[31] Even at Berneval there was a shift in mood, as the true identity of 'Monsieur Melmoth' became more widely known to the villagers. And if there was no open hostility, there was a new note of guarded suspicion.[32] In Dieppe he became conscious of being avoided by old friends such as Jacques-Emile Blanche and Walter Sickert.[33] And when Beardsley failed to turn up for a proposed dinner, he was hurt. 'It was *lâche* of Aubrey,' he later remarked. 'If it had been one of my own class I might perhaps have understood… But a boy like that, whom I made! No, it was too *lâche* of Aubrey.'[34] The jibe at Beardsley's 'class' was as inappropriate as the claim that Wilde had 'made' the artist. Both assertions, though, revealed the real hurt caused by such rebuffs. Every social encounter had become tinged with uncertainty: Wilde could not be sure how – or if – his presence would be received. And while it was uncomfortable to be 'cut', any hint of condescending sympathy was equally irksome. Ross registered that it 'galled' Wilde 'to have to appear grateful to those whom he did not, or would not have regarded [either intellectually or socially] before his downfall'.[35]

He had been hoping that Constance and the children could be persuaded to come to Dieppe. His position in the town would certainly have been improved by their presence. At the end of July, however, he was 'terribly distressed' to receive a letter from Carlos Blacker informing him that Constance's health worries had returned. Her creeping spinal paralysis had left her all but unable to walk. It was heartbreaking news.* 'Nemesis,' Wilde declared, 'seems endless.' He proposed going to his wife in Switzerland.[36] Blacker, however, put him off, suggesting he should wait until Constance was settled back at Nervi, outside Genoa.[37] It was another frustrating delay. And as August advanced, Wilde's resolve ebbed and his anxieties grew.

He had come out of prison determined to escape the sexual 'madness' of his past. And according to Dowson, after one of their evenings together, they repaired to a Dieppe brothel in order that Wilde might acquire 'a more wholesome taste' in sexual matters. After the visit Wilde was said to have remarked, 'The first these ten years, and it will be the last. It was like cold mutton!', before adding, 'But tell it in England, for it will entirely restore my character.'[38] The escapade, however (if it really did take place) appears

---

*   The nature of Constance's illness was debated at the time by her doctors, and since by scholars. In 2015 her grandson Merlin Holland, drawing on family letters, plausibly suggested that she was suffering from multiple sclerosis.

to have been something of a diversion. Wilde had come to the conclusion that it was not 'Uranian love' itself that he needed to renounce so much as the wilful excesses of promiscuous sex with London rent boys. The love of men, rather than of women, was, he declared, simply 'a matter of temperament'. And in this regard his temperament was unchanged.[39]

Although he had felt obliged to assure Turner that his prison 'pal' Arthur Cruttenden was not 'a beautiful boy' but a quite unfanciable fellow of twenty-nine with prematurely greying hair and a 'slight, but still *real* moustache', the protest revealed the direction of his thoughts.[40] And when – in the middle of August – Robbie Ross finally came over to stay at Berneval, he and Wilde slept together. Sherard, who was also staying, reported that, to his 'absolute knowledge', Ross 'dragged Oscar back into the delights of homosexuality' at this time.[41] The incident marked another alteration in the possibilities and expectations of Wilde's post-prison life. Certainly the commitment to Franciscan abstinence was faltering.

Wilde's hopes of being able to produce artistic work again were receiving some encouragement. The ballad continued to develop. It took on a polemical tone, to match the personal one, as Wilde sought to point up not only the cruelties of prison life, but also the guilt of society in imposing them.

> [For] every prison that men build
> Is built with bricks of shame,
> And bound with bars lest Christ should see
> How men their brothers maim.

And as the poem grew, so did Wilde's hopes for it. He began to think that it might be substantial enough to publish in book form. Smithers was the obvious choice of publisher. After their first meeting Wilde had written to him expressing the hope that 'some day I shall have something that you will like well enough to publish'.[42] The day had arrived sooner than expected. They discussed the matter over dinner at the Café des Tribunaux. Smithers quixotically suggested that Wilde should have the 'entire profits of the book'. Wilde, however, demurred, proposing that a more businesslike arrangement would be to share the profits 50/50.[43] As an initial practical step he sent the publisher his first draft to be typed up. 'It is not finished,' he explained, 'but I want to see it type-written. I am sick of my manuscript.' Smithers showed the poem to Beardsley who 'seemed to be much struck by it'. Although Beardsley 'promised at once to do a frontispiece' for the

book, Smithers had seen too many of the artist's recent plans and promises change, or evaporate, to believe that it would ever be done.[44] Nevertheless preparations for the publication advanced.

But, aside from the ballad, Wilde's literary plans showed few signs of progress. His various plays remained stubbornly unstarted. 'The shock of alien freedom', as he put it, was still upon him.[45] He hoped that in due course, he would 'get back the concentration of will-power that conditions and governs art'.[46] He had acquired a red tie in the belief that it might give him inspiration – but to no effect.[47] He came to accept that he would not be able adapt Le Verre d'eau for Wyndham. Even with the assistance of Ross, and the example of Congreve, it was beyond him. As he lamented to Carlos Blacker, 'I simply have no heart to write a clever comedy.'[48] He continued to hope that he might be able to do something with The Florentine Tragedy or his other theatrical projects. But even so he hesitated to begin.

A change in the weather depressed him. But what he really missed was the stimulation of daily companionship, and the support of domestic struc-ture. Dowson and Smithers had returned to England, and Wilde by now realized that he could not rely on Ross or Turner for more than the brief and occasional stay. Dieppe's summer crowds were beginning to depart. A planned visit by Ricketts and Shannon failed to materialize.[49] Fothergill wrote a priggish letter to say that he found it was not 'politic' for him to continue his friendship.[50] Constance and the children seemed as distant as ever. Long vistas of rain-swept autumnal loneliness began to open up, beyond the fading days of summer.

In this mood of gathering ennui Wilde turned to Bosie, who remained near at hand at Nogent-sur-Marne, enduring his own sad and continuing exile. Plans for a clandestine meeting had stuttered on during the summer, but with limited commitment on either side. At the end of July Douglas had written suggesting that Wilde come and stay with him in Paris. Wilde, however, felt he 'could not face Paris yet'. To his own proposal that they should meet, instead, at Rouen, Douglas had replied that he did not have the 'forty francs' necessary to make the journey. After that matters had lan-guished. Until now. With the prospect of autumn and winter before them, they resolved to act.[51]

Their meeting took place at Rouen (almost certainly on 28 August) and was, in Douglas's words, 'a great success'. They spent a day, and a night, together. Wilde cried when they met at the station. It had been two years and four months, since their last sight of each through the prison grating at

Newgate. The wastes of pain and acrimony were obliterated in the glow of remembered love, of shared experience and mutual need. There were no recriminations.* If they were two outcast men, strapped for cash, shunned by society and a burden upon their friends, they had each other. Bosie, as Wilde recorded, 'was on his best behaviour, and very sweet'.[52] They walked about all day, 'arm in arm, or hand in hand, and were perfectly happy'.[53] It seemed that the past could be recaptured and revived, that from the ashes of their old love something might yet arise.[54]

During their charmed day together they began to form a plan of escaping to Naples for the winter. There – amid 'the sunlight and *joie de vivre*' of the south – they could be together and work. Douglas was hopeful that he might raise money from his family to support the venture.[55] He wanted, as he said, to give Wilde a 'home' – a refuge from his cares, a place where he should 'never want for anything', and would be able to write again.[56] It was a vision that Wilde dared to believe possible. 'If I cannot write in Italy,' he asked rhetorically, 'where can I write?'[57] To Bosie he declared, shortly after they parted: 'My own Darling Boy... I feel that my only hope of again doing beautiful work in art is being with you. It was not so in old days, but now it is different, and you can really recreate in me that energy and sense of joyous power on which art depends.'[58]

The meeting at Rouen was supposed to have been secret, although Wilde had been greatly disappointed that, since Douglas was well known at the hotel where they stayed, there was no opportunity for him to use his romantic pseudonym.[59] Ross, however, came to know of the encounter from Turner who, being in Rouen, had bumped into 'Sebastian and the "Infant Samuel"' by chance.[60] Neither he nor Turner was delighted at the rapprochement, recognizing the practical troubles that might follow in its wake. Wilde, however, assumed an air of defiance, telling Ross, 'Yes: I saw Bosie, and of course I love him as I always did, with a sense of tragedy and ruin.'[61] He avoided, though, mentioning their planned flight to Naples.

Back at Berneval, Wilde devoted himself to raising the money necessary for the trip. 'It costs £10 to go to Naples,' he lamented. 'This is awful.'[62] After three months of heedless expenditure and serial generosity he was

---

* Wilde was under the impression that Douglas had by now received a copy of the long letter that he had written from prison. And he was glad that he seemed able to move beyond it. Douglas's equanimity, however, was due to the fact that he had not read the long indictment. He had, it seems, destroyed the copy he received after merely glancing at the first few disobliging paragraphs.

'penniless' and beset with bills. Conder and Dowson had departed owing him money. He reported to Smithers that he had 'just lent a French poet forty francs to take him back to Paris', adding, 'He is very grateful, and says he will send me a sonnet in three days!'.[63] Wilde's hope that the publisher could advance him £20 *'at once'* for the ballad was not realized, but he found relief in other quarters: the second instalment of his allowance from Constance arrived (several days late) at the beginning of September; he also received a cheque for £15 from Rothenstein who had managed to sell the Monticelli painting that he had bought at the Tite Street sale; and Dalhousie Young generously proposed commissioning a libretto for an opera of *Daphnis and Chloe* ('£100 down, and £50 on production').[64] Despite this, Wilde still 'borrowed' 100 francs from one of his Berneval neighbours to help get himself to Paris, and once there touched Vincent O'Sullivan for the price of his ticket to Naples.[65] As a prelude to his departure Wilde visited a Parisian fortune teller. 'I am puzzled,' she told him. 'By your line of life you died two years ago. I cannot explain the fact except by supposing that since then you have been living on your line of imagination.'[66]

Wilde also wrote disingenuously to Carlos Blacker describing the decision to head south as necessary for his work and his sanity, only adding that he was 'greatly disappointed' that Constance had still not asked him 'to come and see the children'.[67] He of course omitted to mention that he would be travelling with Douglas. And in fact there was some last-minute doubt about Bosie's plans. After the eager scheme-making at Rouen he had gone off on holiday with his mother and sister to the spa town of Aix-les-Bains, and seemed in no hurry to leave. He was even considering going on from there to Venice. Wilde knew better than to chide: 'Do just as you will,' he wrote, 'but the sooner you come to Naples the happier I shall be.'[68] The assumed nonchalance had its effect. Douglas met him as the train passed through Aix, and they journeyed on together to Naples. There, Wilde hoped, with Bosie's help, he might 'remake' his 'ruined life'.[69]

3

Outcast Men

'My existence is a scandal.'

OSCAR WILDE

N aples in mid-September was still quiet. The fashionable winter season had not yet started, and the big hotels were only just stirring back into life. Wilde and Douglas installed themselves in one of the biggest: the Hôtel Royal des Étrangers, on the waterfront, close to the Castello dell'Ovo, its glorious view across the bay framed by Vesuvius to the left and Capri on the right.[1] For Wilde it was thrilling to have escaped loneliness and the drear north, to be together with Bosie, and to be in Naples – a place 'full of Ionian and Dorian airs'.[2] 'Pleasure,' as he remarked, 'walks all around'.[3] Wilde felt that in this new environment he would be able to write again. They might take a little villa or an apartment together for the winter, perhaps even for longer.[4]

In holiday mood, during those first days, they embarked on a campaign of carefree extravagance. Douglas's plans for raising money from his family had not been fulfilled, or even pursued. His title, however, was good for credit. To an Italian hotel proprietor of the late nineteenth century any English 'milord' needs must be also a millionaire. Within a little over a week Douglas and Wilde ran up a bill for £68.[5] Even in a hotel of 'absurd prices' this was an impressive performance, carrying with it, perhaps, an echo of those lavish days at the Savoy.[6]

But the elation of the moment could not shut out the concerns of the world beyond. Among the letters forwarded to Wilde from Paris was one from Constance, offering the longed-for meeting, urging him to come to her at the Villa Elvira. She confessed that the children would be away at school, but she enclosed photographs of – and remembrances from – them. It was too late. Wilde had, as he later told Smithers, 'waited four months in vain' for just such a letter. But now it arrived after he had committed his hopes and himself to Douglas and to Naples: 'In questions of the emotions and their romantic qualities, unpunctuality is fatal.'[7]

He sought some additional justification for his change of attitude from the fact that Constance seemed to have deliberately waited until the children were back at school before sending for him. It was their love that he wanted, or so he claimed. And now he feared it was 'irretrievable'.[8] He told Blacker (a letter from whom had also been forwarded to Naples) that 'had Constance allowed me to see my boys' things would have been 'quite different' – adding, disingenuously, 'I don't in any way venture to blame her for her action, but every action has its consequence.'[9]

He wrote back to Constance, nevertheless, suggesting that he would come and see her, though not until the following month. The note of urgency and yearning that had dominated his communications over the summer had quite evaporated. Constance, full of happy preparations for what she supposed would be Wilde's imminent arrival, was completely 'ballottée' by this brief and noncommittal reply.[10] Vyvyan, on the eve of his departure for school, always recalled how her expectant joy turned to misery when she found that Oscar 'had other claims upon his time'.[11] She wrote at once to Blacker to vent her unhappiness. And although Wilde had carefully avoided mentioning that he was in Naples with anyone, least of all with Lord Alfred Douglas, her suspicions were piqued. 'Question: has he seen the dreadful person [Douglas] at Capri? No-one goes to Naples at this time of year, so I see no other reason for his going, and I am unhappy.'[12]

To Wilde she wrote back at once (as she subsequently explained) 'saying that I required an immediate answer to my question whether he had been to Capri or whether he had met anywhere that appalling individual. I also said that he evidently did not care much for his boys since he neither acknowledged their photos which I sent him nor the remembrances that *they* sent him.'[13] To these blows others were added: Ross and Turner *did* know that Wilde was with Douglas, and both of them wrote to express

their concern at a reunion which they knew must damage Wilde's chances of rehabilitation – and which might well affect his right to an income.

Wilde countered with a mixture of grand statement and self-pity: 'My going back to Bosie,' he told Ross, 'was psychologically inevitable: and setting aside the interior life of the soul with its passion for self-realization at all costs, the world forced it on me. I cannot live without the atmosphere of Love: I must love and be loved, whatever price I pay for it… Of course I shall often be unhappy, but still I love him: the mere fact that he wrecked my life makes me love him.'[14] While to Turner he claimed that going back to Bosie – who 'is himself a poet' – would be good for his work, 'and that, after all, whatever my life may have been ethically, it has always been *romantic*, and Bosie is my romance. My romance is a tragedy of course, but it is none the less a romance, and he loves me very dearly, more than he loves or can love anyone else, and without him my life was dreary.'[15]

Turner was urged to 'stick up' for them.[16] He would have been kept busy. News of the elopement, as it spread round Wilde's circle of friends, was greeted with dismay: W. R. Paton (an Oxford contemporary) was 'physically & actually sick' when he learnt of it;[17] Blacker felt that Wilde was now 'beyond redemption'.[18] Sherard, probably 'in his cups' at the Authors' Club one afternoon, declared blunderingly that it was 'an unfortunate mistake' and that Wilde's 'actions would everywhere be misconstrued; that his traducers and enemies would be justified in the eyes of the world, and many sympathies would be alienated'.[19] Others wrote 'long tedious letters' informing Wilde that he had 'wrecked [his] life for the second time'.[20] Even Ross continued to 'bombard' him with admonitory epistles – 'an unfair thing,' Wilde complained, 'as unfortified places are usually respected in civilized war.[21]

Ross's reprimands were endured in silence.[22] But when the report reached Naples of Sherard's ill-considered outburst, Wilde wrote a sharp note of reprimand, charging his old friend with playing the moralizing hypocrite 'Tartuffe'– always one of the strongest terms of contempt in his personal lexicon.[23] It marked a sad end to their intimacy, if not quite their friendship. Douglas's family were no more pleased with the arrangement than were Wilde's friends. Lady Queensberry had hoped that her son's attachment to Wilde had dwindled away over the years of enforced separation. But for the moment she forbore from challenging him – perhaps aware of how intransigent he became when crossed.[24]

Constance, of course, very soon discovered from Blacker that Wilde and

Douglas were together. She at once fired off what Wilde described as a 'terrible' letter, full of prohibitions: 'I *forbid* you to see Lord Alfred Douglas. I forbid you to return to your filthy, insane life. I forbid you to live in Naples. I will not allow you to come to Genoa.'[25] Wilde chose to regard such demands as 'foolish'.[26] He refused to apologize, to explain, or to yield to her demands. 'I wrote to her,' he told More Adey, 'to say that I would never dream of coming to see her against her will, that the only reason that would induce me to come to see her was the prospect of a greeting of sympathy with me in my misfortunes, and affection and pity. That for the rest, I only desired peace, and to live my own life as best I could. That I could not live in London, or, as yet, in Paris, and that I certainly hoped to winter at Naples.'[27] Wrapped up in his own drama, he refused to acknowledge the feelings of others.[28]

To Constance his reply came as a final blow. 'Had I received this letter a year ago,' she told Blacker, 'I should have minded, but now I look upon it as the letter of a madman who has not even enough imagination to see how trifles affect children, or unselfishness enough to care for the welfare of his wife. It rouses all my bitterest feeling, and I am stubbornly bitter when my feelings are roused. I think the letter had better remain unanswered and each of us make our own lives independently. I have latterly (God forgive me) an absolute repulsion of him.'[29] Her bitterness would soon find a practical expression.

Wilde realised that her silence was ominous, and that he might expect 'a thunderbolt' from her solicitor. 'I suppose she will now try to deprive me of my wretched £3 a week,' he wrote bitterly to Ross. 'Women are so petty, and Constance has no imagination.'[30] Money was certainly on his mind. It was needed to fulfil the dream of self-realization, and, more pressingly, so that he and Douglas could escape from the expensive hotel and into a rented villa. Douglas received 'about £8 a week' from his mother but was, Wilde claimed, 'of course... penniless as usual'.[31] It was left to Wilde to take up the burden. There was the promised £100 from Dalhousie Young for the *Daphnis and Chloe* libretto, a work that Wilde now conceived as a collaboration with Douglas. And, after various irritating minor delays, the money arrived.[32] There were several loans that Wilde had made to friends – notably the £18 or £20 to Ernest Dowson – which might be recalled.[33] Wilde also retained his conviction that Leonard Smithers should pay him an advance of £20 for *The Ballad of Reading Gaol*, and he diligently set about convincing Smithers of the fact too.[34] And, beyond that, Wilde had dreams

of a large US serial rights sale for his poem: 'I really think £500 should be *asked*, and £300 taken.'[35]

On the strength of these sums, actual and wished for, he and Douglas took a 'gracious apartment' in a charming villa in Posillipo on the northern edge of the town, paying four months' rent in advance at the beginning of October.[36] Framed by shaded tree-lined alleys and well-kept flower-beds, it had a view over the bay, a terrace, and marble steps leading down to the sea.[37] There was even a piano (which Douglas could play).[38] It seemed a haven from the chorus of disapproval from across the Alps. Some of the rooms might be adorned with ill-omened peacock feathers, but such things could be (and were) removed.[39] There were four servants, who cost little more than their keep: a cook, Carmine; a maid; and two boys, Peppino and Michele. Douglas estimated that the immediate daily outgoings should be less than 10s a day.[40]

The idyll was slightly undercut when, on moving in, they discovered that the villa was infested with rats. And Douglas, having sat up in bed for two nights 'frozen with terror',[41] insisted that they must move to a nearby hotel to sleep.[42] The villa's proprietor undertook to poison the pests, but – as Douglas reported – 'apparently they live on poison. The more they eat the more active they become. They seem to treat it as a sort of aphrodisiac.'[43] Wilde felt that a surer measure would be to call on the services of a local witch – who 'with two flutes' would be able to charm the rats off the premises.[44] Michele produced a gratifyingly hideous old sorceress, bent double and with a distinct beard, who, he claimed, was 'infallible'. And certainly Wilde chose to believe that it was her 'burned odours' and muttered incantations, rather than the conventional arsenic, that were chiefly responsible for seeing off the vermin.[45] The witch also told their fortunes, but it is not recorded what she foresaw.[46]

Life at the Villa Giudice began in an aura of productive harmony. 'Oscar and I are getting on capitally,' Douglas reported to Adey.[47] Wilde strove to believe that 'his old power' was coming back to him now that he was 'happy' and in the south. He felt 'the bruised leaves' of his spirit begin to unfold in the light and warmth of the Neapolitan sun and Douglas's affection. 'I can write as well, I think, as I used to write,' he told Smithers. 'Half as well would satisfy me.'[48] His various play plans were all jostling for attention. He was preparing himself for *Daphnis and Chloe* by reading the libretto of *'Tristan'*.[49] Douglas, meanwhile, was setting a good example, producing a 'lovely' lyric for the opera,[50] as well as three sonnets which Wilde chose to

consider 'quite wonderful': he dubbed them the 'Triad of the Moon'. They were sent to Henley at the *New Review* – though whether as a provocation, a joke or a serious proposition, it is hard to know. They were not published. Another Douglas sonnet, on Mozart, was sent to Robin Grey, the editor of the *Musician*, but with the same lack of success.[51]

For Wilde the most pressing task was completing *The Ballad of Reading Gaol* and arranging the details of its publication. Having been working on the typed-up draft that he had received back from Smithers, he was able to produce, and send off, a much-amended version at the beginning of October. Within days, however, he was dispatching a sheaf of further additional verses ('*four* more... of great power and romantic-realistic suggestion').[52] And others followed at regular intervals throughout the month. There was a need to bulk up the poem to book length, and also to balance its various artistic aims.[53] He worked hard.[54] The task was not an easy one: 'I find it difficult,' he confessed, 'to recapture the mood and manner of [the poem's] inception. It seems alien to me now – real passions so soon become unreal – and the actual facts of one's life take different shape and remould themselves strangely.'[55] He later pretended that the additional material added during these weeks reflected his life in Naples rather more than his time at Reading.[56]

He sought – as so often before – Ross's literary and critical advice on the text, receiving from him 'a lot of suggestions', and accepting 'half of them'. He retained, though, his use of such charged adjectives as 'dreadful' and 'fearful' for the commonplace incidents and objects of prison life, defending it as being 'psychologically' apt: they described not the thing itself, but 'its effect on the soul'.[57] And Douglas – whose poetry Wilde so much admired, and who had himself been working in the ballad form – was also on hand, to act both as a sounding board and as a slightly rivalrous counterbalance to Ross's editorial ideas. Wilde even paid him the poetic tribute of borrowing one of his couplets to fashion the phrase, 'That night the empty corridors / Were full of forms of Fear, / And up and down the iron town / Stole feet we could not hear'.[58]

On the whole Wilde was pleased with his efforts:[59] in places he had – as he put it – been able to 'out-Kipling Henley'.[60] Of course there were reservations: 'Much,' he told Turner, 'is, I feel, for a harsher instrument than the languorous flute *I* love.'[61] But this, he acknowledged, was probably inevitable: 'The poem suffers under the difficulty of a divided aim in style. Some is realistic, some is romantic: some poetry, some propaganda. I feel it

keenly but as a whole I think the production interesting: that it is interesting from more points of view than one is artistically to be regretted.'[62]

Although Wilde was travelling incognito as Sebastian Melmoth, rumours of his, and Douglas's, presence in Naples soon began to circulate. The first Italian paper to announce the fact managed, however, to confuse Lord Alfred Douglas with the young writer Norman Douglas who, retiring from a brief diplomatic career at the age of thirty, had recently moved to a villa also in Posillipo. *Norman* Douglas had staying with him an aged and infirm Spanish count (who was duly confused with Wilde) and as a result it was reported that Wilde was in Naples very much broken down in health. The British consul in Naples, Eustace Neville-Rolfe (who was a aware of Wilde's presence) wrote to the *Corriere di Napoli* to point out the error of their account, and a brief correction duly appeared.[63] The false report of Wilde's decrepit state had, however, already been taken up by numerous British and foreign newspapers, and was much recycled – though without any mention of an accompanying Douglas, whether 'Norman' or 'Lord Alfred'.[64]

Other articles in the Neapolitan press soon followed.[65] Some papers dismissed Wilde with a few slighting references to 'the English *décadent*' and his trial.[66] Others, though, sensed a story. Journalists began to 'dog his heels'.[67] A reporter from one of the city's evening papers tricked his way into the villa in the hope of an interview. Wilde dismissed him, irritated by the intrusion. A report of the brief non-encounter duly appeared.[68] Wilde, who had once delighted in playing on the press, no longer desired to play. He was annoyed by the unwanted attention, and by the ungenerous assessments of some of the articles; *Il Mattino* referred to him as 'the most insufferable kind of bore that contemporary chronicles have inflicted upon the patient public'.[69] 'I don't want to be written about,' he complained 'I want peace – that is all.'[70] When he learnt that there were no newspapers on Capri, he half-jokingly suggested moving to the island.[71]

The fashionable expatriate community, increasing as the autumn advanced, chose to ignore him. 'It is very curious,' he told Ross with mock innocence, 'that none of the English colony here have left cards on us.'[72] There was, however, always the danger that indifference might shade into hostility. Wilde was made uncomfortably aware of this when he and Douglas (using the £10 received from Smithers) took the short trip across the bay to Capri in mid-October. They planned to stay three days: 'I want,' Oscar explained, 'to lay a few simple flowers on the tomb of Tiberius. As the tomb is of someone else really, I shall do so with the deeper emotion.'[73] The exact

details of the expedition are unclear, but it seems they intended to stop at the Hotel Quisisana, and were just settling down to dinner there, when the proprietor appeared and 'with perfect ceremony' asked if they might leave. Some British guests, recognizing Wilde, had complained of his presence. They moved on to a second establishment only for the same awful charade to be repeated. Rather than risk a third rebuff they contemplated the tedium of sitting up all night, without dinner, waiting for the dawn steamer to take them back to Naples.[74]

From this sorry vigil they were, it seems, rescued by the island's Swedish-born doctor, Axel Munthe. Chancing upon the two 'lost souls' wandering in the piazza, Munthe hailed Douglas, whom he had come to know the previous year. He had no objection to being introduced to Wilde, indeed was shocked that Douglas could suppose him 'so ignorant and so brutal as to be unkind to anyone who has suffered so much or been so shamefully treated'. The conviction of Wilde had always seemed to him 'utterly absurd'.[75] He insisted that both men accompany him home to dinner and rest.[76] Wilde was delighted with the art-filled villa at Anacapri, and with Munthe himself, finding him 'a wonderful personality' and 'a great connoisseur of Greek things'.[77] Douglas stayed on at Capri the next day, to dine with the American socialite Mrs Snow, but Wilde, chastened perhaps by the experience at the Quisisana, returned at once to the greater anonymity of Naples. He chose not to mention the distressing incident to Ross.[78]

There were, though, a few English friends and acquaintances who, on passing through Naples, did not shun them. John Knapp, an Oxford contemporary of Douglas's, spent some happy hours in their company,[79] while the campaigning journalist Harry de Windt (who wrote – approvingly – about Russian prison camps) hailed Wilde when he came across him 'seated in solitary state, with a *Bock* before him, outside the Café Gambrinus'; and there was a subsequent dinner together with Douglas one evening.[80] Both these visitors, however, noted the slightly claustrophobic devotion of the two exiles, isolated as they were from the wider social scene. Knapp remembered Douglas as being 'quite infatuated with Oscar', while to de Windt Wilde delivered a 'long eulogy' on Douglas, saying how he had 'stuck to him through thick and thin and was his best and most faithful friend'.[81]

But if English companionship was often limited, other diversions were to hand. Wilde, to his great gratification, was taken up by a coterie of young Neapolitan writers. Of these the most enthusiastic was a twenty-five-year-

old poet and sometime magazine editor G. G. Rocco (the initials stood for 'Giuseppe Garibaldi'), who had sought Wilde out within days of his arrival. An excellent English speaker, he undertook to teach Wilde Italian, coming three times a week for sessions of 'Italian conversation'.[82]

Although Wilde's trials had been widely reported in Italy, knowledge of his actual work remained very limited. There had – extraordinarily – been a production of *Vera* at the Teatro Diana in Milan in 1890, which closed after three performances; and a few passages from 'The Soul of Man Under Socialism' had appeared, in translation, in 1892, as a supplement to a Sicilian anarchist magazine.[83] Rocco suggested that he might translate *Salomé* into Italian. Wilde was delighted. He wanted to be recognized in Naples not merely as a notorious celebrity but also 'as *an artist*'.[84] He did not, however, have a copy of the play with him, and had to write to London in the hope of borrowing one. Ada Leverson, with typical generosity, lent hers.[85]

Rocco was also convinced that, once the play was translated, it would be possible to mount a production in Naples.[86] This was an exciting idea. 'It would help me greatly to have it done,' Wilde informed Turner.[87] His only concerns were practical; it would be necessary to find 'an actress of troubling beauty and flute-like voice' for the title role, and (as he explained to Stanley Markower) 'unfortunately most of the tragic actresses of Italy – with the exception of Duse – are stout ladies, and I don't think I could bear a stout Salome.'[88] The religious objections that had stymied the London production did not hold in Italy. Indeed Rocco was friendly with Giovanni Bovio, a Neapolitan writer and MP, whose own biblical drama, *Cristo alla festa di Purim*, had already enjoyed a nationwide success.[89] And when Rocco completed his first draft of the translation, under supervision from Wilde, he organized a reading of it at Bovio's home. The play was enthusiastically received by the assembled crowd of writers, poets, students and journalists – and most especially by Signora Bovio, who, according to Rocco, was unstinting in her praises.[90] It was an auspicious start. And another of the guests, Luigi Conforti, impressed by the vigour of Wilde's writing, suggested a rather more public second reading at the Circolo Filologico di Napoli; sadly, though, nothing came of the plan.[91]

Conforti, a poet and historian, was also the secretary of the Museo Nazionale at Naples, and had just published a guide to its collections. Wilde was a frequent visitor to the museum, delighting in its incomparable gathering of antiquities from Pompeii and Herculaneum, Stabiae, Cumae and Rome. He was drawn particularly to the gallery of 'lovely Greek bronzes'.[92] There,

among the emperors, dancers and philosophers, he could ponder the lithe and naked *Wrestlers*, the so-called *Narcissus*, and *Mercury Reposing* (described by *Baedeker* as 'a beautiful picture of elastic youth').[93] These were wonderful things. 'The only bother,' as Wilde reported archly to Dowson, 'is that they all walk about the town at night.' But, as he added, 'one gets delicately accustomed to that – and there are compensations.'[94]

If that solitary night with Ross at Berneval had re-introduced Wilde to 'the delights of homosexuality', Naples offered something more. Although celebrated as a place of fashionable resort, it had also a darker reputation as a land of sexual opportunity. The old pagan morality of the Greeks seemed to persist in its shaded alleys and sunlit streets. Young men were readily available for sex. As one foreign visitor recorded, it was only necessary 'to show an interest in a half-grown youth, to remark on his curly hair or his almond-shaped eyes, and the young man begins to flirt... and with unmistakable intentions'.[95] And as long as public decency was not offended, the law did not concern itself with such encounters. Douglas had confirmed the truth of all this during his visit the previous year, and was now eager to introduce Wilde to the city's sexual underworld. Wilde's assertions, made in the weeks after his release, about how his former promiscuous life among the London renters had been 'unworthy of an artist', were soon modified, and then forgotten. Over the coming months he – in Ross's phrase – 'reverted to homosexual excesses'.[96] The pleasure of bought casual sex was as piquant as ever. If Wilde noted that, with age, 'one is more difficult to please' in sensual matters, he also found that 'the sting of pleasure [was] even keener than in youth and far more egotistic'.[97]

Rocco seems to have joined Wilde and Douglas in these sexual adventures, along with a new English friend, I. D. W. ('Sir John') Ashton – described by Wilde as 'a most charming and delightful fellow', astounding 'in his capacity for pleasure, grand in his cups, and with a heart of gold'.[98] Having sex with Neapolitan youths was stimulating for Wilde's language skills: he talked to them about the aesthetics of attraction, and they taught him the idiom of the streets. 'I am getting rather astonishing in my Italian conversation,' he boasted to Adey. 'I believe I talk a mixture of Dante and the worst modern slang.'[99]

The press began to take note of Wilde's assignations. There were knowing references to his 'nocturnal walks... in search of adventure'.[100] One scandal sheet carried a fanciful account of Wilde passing the night at a hotel with five young soldiers, each from a different regiment (the hotel porter

was concerned that, with Wilde seducing so many of the military, there might be a danger to national security).[101]

In the wake of such stories and 'all sorts of unpleasant gossip', Douglas's 'people' – his mother and brother – increased their efforts to break up the ménage. At their prompting Denis Browne, an attaché from the embassy and an Oxford friend of Douglas's, came down from Rome. After an apparently jolly luncheon at the villa, he took Douglas aside and urged him to abandon Wilde and leave Naples. Douglas, characteristically, bridled at this interference. Browne called him 'a quixotic fool', and they 'parted in anger'.[102]

In truth, though, life at Posillipo was beginning to show signs of strain. The bright start could not be maintained. The lack of money was a constant source of stress and division. They lived in a wearying state of 'daily financial crisis'.[103] Douglas's modest allowance was – as Wilde announced more than once – 'not enough for his own wants', let alone for both of them.[104] The 'hand to mouth struggle' was only 'kept up by desperate telegrams to [Douglas's] reluctant relations, and pawning of pins and studs'.[105] When they were totally without cash they had to dine back at the Hôtel Royal des Étrangers, where they could at least eat on credit.[106]

Dowson did send Wilde £10 of what he owed;[107] an unexpected £9 arrived as a gift from Ross ('a miracle of a very wonderful kind');[108] and Turner, if he did not send money, paid for a £2 10s postal order to be left, in Wilde's name, for the handsome Harry Elvin on his release from Reading.[109] But the £20 advance due from the always cash-strapped Smithers only arrived in piecemeal fashion, and only after numerous (expensive) telegrams and many fruitless visits to Cook's. 'I calculate the expenses incurred by waiting for [your] £20 at £34 up to the present,' Wilde told his publisher at the beginning of November, when half of it was still owing. 'The mental anxiety cannot be calculated. I suppose you think that mental anxiety is good for poets. It is not the case, when pecuniary worries are concerned.' In desperation Wilde even wrote to Ernest Leverson, reviving his claim to the money he felt was due to him. He received no reply.[110]

Adding to the sense of anxiety and frustration was the lack of progress in selling the rights to The Ballad of Reading Gaol in America. 'I keep on building castles of fairy gold in the air,' Wilde told Dowson. 'We Celts always do.'[111] But the golden castles, as is so often the case, were slow to materialize. No offers arrived, and all the feedback was discouraging. It was both a shock and surprise. 'I had no idea that there were such barriers between me and publication in America,' Wilde lamented to Ross. 'I thought I would romp

in, and secure a good lump sum. It is curious how vanity helps the successful man, and wrecks the failure. In the old days half of my strength was my vanity.'[112] As a final ploy he suggested contacting his wonderfully efficient American play agent, Elisabeth Marbury, in the hope that she would be able to do something.[113]

The silence from across the Atlantic – and the ever-pressing need for money – persuaded Wilde to revisit his decision about British serial rights. Having assured Smithers that he would let the publisher have 'the perfect virginity of my poem for the satyrs of the British public to ravish',[114] he now suggested a simultaneous publication in a newspaper. He claimed to have been offered £50 by Robin Grey at the *Musician*, and he told Ross that he would, indeed, be prepared to 'accept *any* English paper' – the *Sunday Sun*, the *Saturday Review* or even *Reynolds's Newspaper* – 'it circulates widely amongst the criminal classes, to which I now belong, so I shall be read by my peers – a new experience for me'.[115]

Smithers was horrified by the notion and, supported by Ross, issued an ultimatum, threatening to abandon plans for the book's publication if any such arrangement were made.[116] Wilde backed down: 'I dare say you will think me very unpractical and all that,' he told Smithers, 'but I candidly confess that if I have to choose between *Reynolds* and Smithers, I choose Smithers.'[117] And, although he sought to excuse himself to Ross by claiming that Smithers had written to him 'several times' saying 'he did not mind the thing appearing elsewhere' he was obliged to abandon the plan: 'I quite see that it would spoil the book.'[118]

And Wilde did want a book. He kept up a close correspondence with Smithers about the physical form of the volume. The challenge was to make something distinct and distinguished: 'The public is largely influenced by the *look* of a book,' Wilde declared. 'It is the only artistic thing about the public.'[119] His initial idea was for a 'very artistic' production – with a wonderful cover (paper of course), frontispiece, initial letters, *culs-de-lampe* etc. But his hopes of a frontispiece – something 'sombre, troubled and *macabre*' by Paul Herrmann, an 'interesting genius' he had met in Paris – gradually dwindled as no drawing arrived. He accepted that the first edition at least would have to be without illustration.[120]

The sense of distinction would be created by the choice of materials and the use of typography. In order to give the book 'thickness and solidity' and prevent it looking too like 'a sixpenny pamphlet', it was decided to print the text on alternate pages.[121] This, together with the thick Dutch hand-made

paper chosen by Smithers, gave sufficient bulk to warrant a cloth binding. And – on Wilde's recommendation – a 'cinnamon' colour was chosen, with white cloth (and gold lettering) for the spine. The proposed format, rather taller and thinner than the standard, also 'delighted' the author.[122]

On receiving the first set of proofs, Wilde approved of Smithers' choice of typeface, though he considered the question marks 'lacking in style, and the stops, especially the full-stops, characterless'.[123] Much additional care, though, had to be expended upon the wording and layout of the title page. It was agreed that Wilde's name was not to appear, but rather the author should be designated solely by his prison number, C.3.3. The public, Wilde remarked, 'like an open secret'.[124]

Although there was to be an epigraph commemorating Trooper Woold-ridge as the subject of the poem, Wilde wanted to add also a personal dedi-cation to Ross: 'When I came out of prison / some met me with garments and spices, / and others with wise counsel. / You met me with love.'[125] Ross, however, demurred, partly because he thought the wording both 'unsuitable' and untrue – he *had* met Wilde with garments and spices, to say nothing of wise counsel – but also because, as he pointed out to Smithers, since his name was not mentioned (nor even indicated by initials), 'every-one will believe rightly or wrongly that Bosie Douglas is intended. This will *damage the reputation* of the poem everywhere and immediately prejudice everyone against it directly they open the book.' Indeed Ross half suspected that Wilde had worded the dedication so he could 'tell me and Douglas and two or three other people that each was intended'.[126]

What sort of market the book might have remained unclear. The size and pricing of the first edition was much debated between author and publisher, with the former tending towards optimism, and the latter coun-selling caution. Wilde dismissed Smithers' early suggestion of 'an edition of 600 copies at 2/6!': 'If the thing goes at all it should certainly sell 1500 copies, at that price. If on the other hand 500 is the probable sale, it should be 5 shillings.'[127] Money dominated Wilde's thoughts.

As the autumn drew on, the daily anxiety about 'ways and means' was tak-ing its slow toll on the mood at Villa Giudice. Douglas felt sure that Wilde could earn good money from writing plays, as he had in the past, and could not understand why progress was so slow. He became sullen and resentful at Wilde's failure to produce a commercial drama. He was not accustomed to want. And when the local tradesmen began to turn up demanding pay-ment for small debts, Douglas's temper 'went to pieces'.[128] The hoped-for

idyll of domestic happiness and creative productivity receded with every day. Both Wilde and Douglas grew increasingly unhappy with their predicament, yet neither was prepared to confess it to the other. Having fought so hard, and sacrificed so much, to achieve their reunion, any admission that it was not ideal was too painful to contemplate. Nevertheless the great emotional fact was unignorable, even if it remained unspoken: their old love could not be rekindled.

Douglas did at least admit to himself: 'I had lost that supreme desire for [Wilde's] society which I had before, and which made a sort of aching void when he was not with me.'[129] But this knowledge merely made him feel even less able to abandon Wilde. It could not be done without a loss of honour: an excuse was needed. He sought to provoke a crisis. There were – as he put it – 'several quarrels'.[130] Crockery was thrown.[131] Wilde recalled the horror of one row, when Douglas, smarting from having been 'dunned' for an unpaid laundry bill, raged and 'whipped' Wilde with his acerbic tongue: 'It was appalling.'[132] But Wilde – without other options, worn down in spirit, and naturally non-confrontational – had neither the energy nor the inclination to rise to the bait. 'I could only stand and see love turned to hate,' he later told Frank Harris; 'the strength of love's wine making the bitter more venomous.' Only once, it seems, did he snap. When Bosie asked him what he had meant by the line, 'Each man kills the thing he loves' he answered, without emotion, 'You should know.'[133]

Wilde's room to manoeuvre was further reduced when, on 16 November, the long-dreaded 'thunderbolt' finally struck: a letter arrived from Hansell informing him that he was to be deprived of his allowance from Constance because he was living with Douglas. He railed against the decision: 'I do not think it fair to say that I have created a "public scandal" by being with him… my existence is a public scandal. But I do not think I should be charged with creating a scandal by continuing to live: though I am conscious that I do so.' He railed against Hansell – who was, after all, his own solicitor, rather than Constance's – for accepting the definition of Douglas as a 'disreputable person'; he had, after all, never been convicted of any crime. He railed against Ross and Adey for not opposing Hansell's view: 'I do not deny that Alfred Douglas is a gilded pillar of infamy, but do deny that he can be properly described in a *legal* document as a disreputable person.'[134] He railed against the world: 'I wish you would start a Society for the Defence of Oppressed Personalities', he told Smithers. 'At present there is a gross European concert headed by brutes and solicitors against us.'[135]

There was, though, little that could be done. Forces were massing against them. Douglas received a letter from his brother urging him to separate from Wilde ('You have gained your point and proved you are not to be interfered with').[136] And this was followed up by letter from Lady Queensberry announcing that she would be stopping Douglas's own allowance if he continued to live with Wilde.[137] Wilde wondered whether, if Douglas moved out of the Villa Giudice, and they no longer shared a roof, that might satisfy the powers, and restore their respective allowances: 'To say that I would never see [Bosie] or speak to him again would of course be childish – out of the question.'[138] But there was no support for this idea. It was clear that they would 'be forced to compromise the matter… and separate at least for the present'.[139] There was perhaps a sense of relief in this for both Wilde and Douglas: a termination for which neither of them would have to take responsibility.

Certainly Douglas claimed that he finally 'felt and saw' that Wilde did not really wish him to stay 'and that it would really be a relief to him if I went away'. Even so he felt unable to abandon the now allowance-less Wilde without some provision. He persuaded his mother that he would leave Naples only if she arranged payment of at least some of the £500 'debt of honour' that the Douglas family owed Wilde for the costs of his case against Queensberry. She promised £200 on receipt of written declarations from both Wilde and Bosie that they would never live together under the same roof – declarations that were duly made.[140] She sent also an immediate £68 to pay the bill at the Hôtel Royal. This account having been settled, Bosie departed for Rome in the first week of December with – as he put it – 'a clear conscience'.

He insisted to his mother that he still loved and admired Wilde: 'I look on him as a martyr to progress. I associate myself with him in everything. I long to hear of his success and artistic rehabilitation… at the very summit of English literature.' He declared his intention of writing to him occasionally and seeing him 'from time to time in Paris and elsewhere'. But he confirmed that the experience of Naples had been both chastening and 'lucky': 'If I hadn't rejoined him and lived with him for two months, I should *never* have got over the longing for him. It was spoiling my life and spoiling my art and spoiling everything. Now I am free.'[141]

Wilde too was free, left alone at Posillipo to 'try to get to literary work'.[142] There was, at least, a small flurry of last-minute editorial problems to occupy his attention, as *The Ballad of Reading Gaol* advanced towards the

press. The printers (the 'idiotic' Chiswick Press) became anxious that the descriptions of the prison doctor, chaplain and governor – variously designated in the poem as coarse-mouthed, shivering and yellow-faced – might be libellous. They needed to be reassured that the figures were generic, not specific.[143] And Wilde himself had a sudden doubt about the resonant opening description of Trooper Wooldridge: 'He did not wear his scarlet coat, / For blood and wine are red.' Wooldridge's regiment was the Royal Horse Guards – famously known as the 'Blues'. Did they, Wilde wondered, actually wear blue uniforms? 'I cannot alter my poem if they do,' he told Smithers; 'to *me* his uniform was red.'[144] He conceded also that it would be best to wait until the new year before bringing out the book: as he remarked, 'I am hardly a Christmas present.'[145]

In these deliberations and decisions Wilde no longer had the informed support of Robbie Ross. There had been an unfortunate falling-out (provoked by Douglas) over what was deemed to be Ross's unsupportive attitude to the sale of serial rights in the poem.[146] Ross had written to Smithers declaring that he felt he no longer had Wilde's 'confidence in business matters' and so did not wish to be connected with his affairs any more. Wilde was at once contrite, begging Ross for forgiveness – and telling Smithers that if Ross 'will kindly send me a pair of his oldest boots I will blacken them with pleasure, and send them back to him with a sonnet'.[147] Ross, however, was not to be wooed back at once.

4

Bitter Experience

'I have made an important discovery... that alcohol, taken in sufficient quantities, produces all the effects of intoxication.'

OSCAR WILDE

The sonnet of contrition was never written, and in this it was sadly like Wilde's other literary projects. Alone in the villa at Posillipo, he struggled to bring his energies into focus. The hopeful vision of 'turning to the Drama' once work on the ballad was completed proved vain. The proposed collaboration with Douglas on the *Daphnis and Chloe* libretto had been foundering even before Douglas's departure; with him gone the project faded completely from view. There were several attempts to begin his 'modern social comedy'. And perhaps hoping to prompt himself into action, he even asked Smithers to re-approach Augustin Daly with a view to securing the American rights.[1]

But Wilde recognized that there was something wilfully paradoxical in the undertaking. Two years of prison and six months of exile had crushed his comic sense. 'I suppose it is all in me somewhere,' he told Turner, 'but I don't seem to feel it. My sense of humour is now concentrated on the grotesqueness of tragedy.'[2] He did not put himself to the test. It is uncertain whether Daly ever received his proposal; certainly he never replied to it. And Wilde, sticking to the tragic, instead tried to take up *Pharaoh* and *The*

Florentine Tragedy. But these more modest projects proved equally beyond him. 'I find the architecture of art difficult now,' he admitted.[3] Even his newly invented recipe for stimulating literary composition – 'reading a dozen pages' of Flaubert's *Temptation of St Anthony* and taking 'two or three haschich pills' – failed to work its magic.[4]

Under less formal constraints he did retain many of his old gifts of imaginative invention. His letters and conversation were full of fantastical conceits. He conjured up visions of writing a life of Heliogabalus for Smithers, having inspected a bust of the dissolute emperor in the Museo Nazionale – 'rather like a young Oxonian of a very charming kind, the expression a mixture of pride and *ennui*.' The incident of the emperor's 'marriage to the moon' touched on in *The Picture of Dorian Gray* would – he thought – make an excellent chapter of jewelled words. But the sustained effort necessary to bring such ideas to the page was, for the moment at least, more than he could manage.[5]

In the absence of new work Wilde looked to his existing oeuvre. He continued to foster schemes for promoting his name in Italy. When one of the young poets in Rocco's circle, the teenage Biagio Chiara, expressed a desire to translate *The Picture of Dorian Gray*, Wilde hastened to arrange for him to be sent a copy.[6] He strove, too, to re-ignite interest in *Salomé*, sending the Italian text to Cesare Rossi, the actor-manager who had taken the Teatro dei Fiorentini for the autumn season. Rossi was 'astounded' by the script, but regretted there was in his company 'no actress who could possibly touch the part'.[7] Only Eleonora Duse would do. She arrived in Naples in early December, and Wilde attended every evening of her brief season.[8] He considered her 'a fascinating artist', even if 'nothing to Sarah [Bernhardt]'.[9] Through friends he sent her a copy of the play, begging her to consider it.[10] She was certainly intrigued, and might indeed have taken on the role if only 'the bad reputation of the author' did not, in her opinion, make it impossible. In this sadly conventional view she was supported by some of her fellow actors.[11] Duse left Naples on 14 December, and with her went all immediate prospects for *Salomé*'s Italian production.[12]

As the hopes of artistic advancement dwindled, Wilde sought consolation in the more immediate pleasures of self-pity. 'My life cannot be patched up,' he told Smithers. 'There is a doom on it. Neither to myself, nor to others, am I any longer a joy. I am now simply an ordinary pauper of a rather low order: the fact that I am also a pathological problem in the eyes of German scientists is only interesting to German scientists: and even in

their works I am tabulated, and come under the law of *averages*! *Quantum mutates!*[13] A sense of grievance against Douglas – not for deserting him (that had been inescapable) – but on account of his behaviour while he had been in Naples, began to grow as the days past, and the bitter incidents were recalled and rehashed. Everything seemed to have gone against him.

In his desire to dramatize the moment and – as he put it – drain the chalice of his misery to the dregs, he even took himself one evening to the public gardens favoured by Neapolitan suicides. Sitting alone in the darkness, however, he became aware of the rustling and sighing of 'misty cloud like things' coming about him; the souls, he decided, of those who had killed themselves, and – rather than finding rest – were condemned to linger in the place for eternity. It was enough to make him dismiss the idea of suicide. Apart from everything else, the notion of spending the entire afterlife in Naples was more than he could bear: the cooking, as he remarked, was really too bad.[14]

There were, of course, other reasons to choose life. 'Vanity, that great impulse' was still driving him 'to think of a possible future of self-assertion': he wanted to see *The Ballad of Reading Gaol* safely published. Inertia, too, stood against taking any decisive step. And there was also the prospect of £200 from Lady Queensberry. Vincent O'Sullivan, when he passed through Naples in mid-December, found Wilde living in daily expectation of the money. O'Sullivan suspected that there was a strong dramatizing element in his friend's litany of complaint.[15] He was more amused than alarmed when, dining together in a restaurant, Wilde became suddenly perturbed by a local 'witch' (quite possibly the one who had got rid of the rats) pausing to look in at them through the window; 'Did you see that?' Wilde asked. 'Some great misfortune is going to happen to us.'[16]

Nevertheless O'Sullivan was unhappily aware that something of Wilde's essential elasticity of spirit had been lost. This was made clear to him on another evening, when they had been sitting late in a restaurant, and Wilde became uncharacteristically disturbed at a party of theatre-goers who, coming away from a first night, pointed him out. Although their action seemed prompted more by curiosity than malice, Wilde bolted from the restaurant in distress. 'We went a little way in silence,' O'Sullivan recalled. 'Then one of those tragic beggars of Naples arose in a doorway where he had been crouching and held out his hand. Wilde gave him some money, and I heard him murmur in English: "You wretched man, why do you beg when pity is dead?"'[17]

The first instalment of £100 from Lady Queensberry, when it did arrive

(via More Adey), might not have been able to alter Wilde's dejected mood, but it could offer the possibility of new distractions – of madder music and stronger wine. Robbie Ross certainly claimed that it was in Naples, and probably during this period, that Wilde started drinking with a new and steady determination.[18] He may not have shown obvious signs of inebriation, but the edge of unhappiness was blunted. Sex, too, was a ready diversion; it was cheap to buy.

A young acquaintance, Wilfrid Blaydes (a friend of the Berensons), found Wilde in a sorry state that December: 'At present under the feeling that every man's hand is against him, he is utterly demoralized and going as straight as he can to the devil. He is provided with money for the present (which he uses chiefly to that end).'[19] Perhaps unaware that the funds came from Lady Queensberry, and entertained by Wilde's tales of Heliogabalus, Blaydes suspected – without, it seems, foundation – that Wilde was 'mak[ing] money writing obscenities for Smithers'.[20] Although Wilde expressed a desire to 'to pull himself round', Blaydes feared that he was 'mixed up with rascally people' and would 'find great difficulty' in doing so.[21] Moral support was needed. The Berensons were urged to write to Wilde, and to get other former friends to do likewise, since – Blaydes believed – Wilde would prove 'very susceptible to personal influence'.[22] It is not clear whether Berenson, or any other friends, did write. And it is far from certain that their letters would have reached him anyway.

Rather than face a sad Christmas alone at Naples, Wilde took off on what Blaydes described as 'a foolish trip to Taormina' in Sicily.[23] He went as the guest of an elderly and 'very cultivated' Russian, quite possibly one of his 'rascally' new associates.[24] In Taormina Wilde lodged at the Hotel Victoria on Corso Umberto, and visited the gardens created by Florence Trevelyan, one of several exiles from British prudery living in the town (she had been obliged to leave England, and her post as lady-in-waiting, following rumours of an affair with the Prince of Wales).[25] Wilde also came to know the young Russophile Albert Stopford, who had fled London in 1894 to avoid arrest on a charge of gross indecency.[26] But the principal draw of the place seems to have been the studio of Count Wilhelm von Gloeden. The Count, a forty-one-year-old German long settled at Taormina, had established a reputation for his mock-classical photographs of Sicilian youths, posing (usually nude) as fauns and shepherd boys. Wilde acquired at least two of these arrestingly homoerotic images and, according to one source, even helped with arranging the poses of the 'marvellous boys'.[27]

Despite the congenial company – and sexual opportunities – in Sicily, Wilde returned to Naples early in the new year. He arrived to find that all his clothes, and some of his possessions, had been stolen by the servant who had been left in charge at the villa. This misfortune was then compounded by a bout of influenza. It was a sad start to 1898. Bruised by ill health, loneliness and 'general *ennui* with a tragi-comedy of an existence', he decided to leave the Villa Giudice (even though the rent was paid until the end of the month) and move back into town. He took lodgings at 31 via S. Lucia, close to fashionable heart of things.

There was disappointing news about *The Ballad of Reading Gaol* from America, Miss Marbury reporting that 'nobody here seems to feel any interest in the poem'. She had, nevertheless, managed to secure a modest offer of $100 (around £20) from the *New York Journal*. It was the best that could be managed.[28] Against this setback there was the actual excitement of receiving from Smithers the first advance copy of the book. Wilde was 'really charmed' by its elegant appearance. The title page was, he declared, 'a masterpiece – one of the best I have ever seen'.[29] Smithers, too, was excited. Having initially ordered a first printing of just 400 copies, he had – perhaps at the prompting of Ross – then doubled the run. And in addition to these 800 copies (priced at 2*s* 6*d*) he also produced thirty special copies on Japanese vellum, priced at a guinea. Wilde set about drawing up a list of those who should receive presentation copies: besides his various literary and artistic friends (Dowson, Beerbohm, Vincent O'Sullivan, Ada Leverson, etc.) it included both Major Nelson and Warder Groves.[30]

The task, although congenial, must have pointed up his loneliness – his separation from the intellectual and social camaraderie that he so relished. Although he had taken up with a new and 'beautiful love', he had to admit to himself (and to Leonard Smithers) that he was growing 'tired of Greek bronzes'.[31] What he craved was company and conversation. In Naples he had to find it where he could. Among the various unsuspecting tourists upon whom he genially imposed himself were two English schoolmasters (one of them the father of Graham Greene): joining their café table, Wilde delighted them with his talk for more than an hour, before departing, leaving them to pay for his drink. As Greene senior would remark in later life, it was a indication of how lonely Wilde must have been, that he was ready to expend so much time and wit on a couple of holidaying schoolteachers.[32]

It was clear that Wilde could not work, isolated and alone, in Naples. 'My life has gone to great ruin here,' he told Smithers, 'and I have no brain now,

or energy.'[33] By early February he had resolved to go to Paris. It would, as Blaydes suggested, be a far 'better' place for him. He would be closer to his English friends, and there would be intellectual stimulation and companionship, and the chance of working. 'I hope,' Wilde declared, on the eve of departure, 'to make an effort in Paris.'[34]

THE TEACHER OF WISDOM

1898–1900

AGE 44–46

Oscar Wilde in Rome, 1900.

1

The Parisian Temple
of Pleasure

*'The only place on earth where you will find absolute tolera-
tion for all human frailties, with passionate admirations for
all human virtues and capacities.'*

OSCAR WILDE

Wilde reached Paris towards the middle of February 1898, and installed himself in the modest Hôtel de Nice in the rue des Beaux-Arts on the Left Bank. The moment seemed propitious. His arrival coincided with the publication in London of *The Ballad of Reading Gaol*. The book proved an instant success. Smithers had presaged its appearance with a well-placed advertisement in the *Athenaeum*,[1] and on Sunday 13 February – the official publication date – *Reynolds's Newspaper* welcomed the volume with a long and appreciative notice, including lengthy quotations. Using their inside knowledge gleaned from negotiations over the serial rights, they were able to blow the supposed anonymity of 'C.3.3' at the outset. Heading their piece, 'A New Poem by Oscar Wilde', they suggested that the highly 'dramatic' poem 'will be read with the greatest interest, not only for its artistic merits, but for the touches of self-revelation of a remarkable man; one who, whatever his offence, has borne the retribution with dignity and self-restraint'.[2] Another paper, the *Sunday*

Special, declared that 'not since the first publication of "The Ancient Mariner" have the English public been proffered such a weird, enthralling and masterly ballad-narration'.[3]

On the Monday morning business was brisk. One bookshop was reported as having sold fifty copies. Within days the whole print run was sold out, and a second edition of 1,000 copies was in preparation, to be 'ready next week'. In its 'strikingly vivid and realistic description of prison life' the poem offered something arresting and new. It demanded engagement: the novelist Mrs Lynn Linton considered Wilde's treatment of the subject 'as perverted as ever... all excuse for crime, and pity for the criminal, but not for the victim';[4] while 'Michael Field', writing in their diary, saluted 'the immortal outrageous Paradox' at the heart of the poem – 'We needs must kill the thing we love'; they thought 'Oscar was sent into the world to generate this stimulating monster'.[5]

If the book was not universally noticed, there were reviews in the *Daily Chronicle* and the *Telegraph*, as well as in lesser publications such as *Echo* and *War Cry*. Ross, back on good terms with Wilde, sent over a sheaf of cuttings.[6] The *Pall Mall Gazette* hailed the book as 'the most remarkable poem that has appeared this year' – though, admittedly, it was only February. Arthur Symons provided a perceptive and generous critique in the *Saturday Review*, and W. E. Henley (perhaps stung by Symons' comparing the ballad to Henley's own recently published free-verse volume, *In Hospital*) contributed a less generous, and less perceptive, assessment in *Outlook*.[7] For Wilde *The Ballad of Reading Gaol* marked a triumphant artistic return. Although slightly disappointed that the *Daily Chronicle* seemed to regard the poem as merely 'a pamphlet on prison-reform', he was both impressed and 'greatly touched' by Symons' review.[8] Henley he chose to ignore, telling Smithers '[he] is simply jealous. He made his scrofula into *vers libre*, and is furious because I have made a sonnet out of "skilly".'[9]

He enjoyed, too, the generous praise of friends, such as Rothenstein and Laurence Housman.[10] He received 'a charming letter' from Cunninghame-Graham and another from Bernard Berenson (which gave him, so he said, 'more pleasure [and] more pride than anything has done since the poem appeared').[11] From Ross he doubtless heard that Edmund Gosse admired the poem, and that Major Nelson judged parts to be 'very fine' indeed; and perhaps, too, he learnt that Constance had found it 'exquisite', and Burne-Jones 'thinks it wonderful'.[12] It was reported that Sir Edward Clarke had bought 'a dozen copies'.[13] Wilde, in his excitement, drew up almost daily

lists of those who should receive complimentary copies – 'people who have been kind to me and about me'.[14]

The book's momentum had to be maintained. And although Wilde joked that Smithers was so used to selling suppressed books that he was apt to suppress his own, in fact the publisher responded well to the challenge. At Wilde's prompting he issued, at the beginning of March, a special 'Author's Edition', with a cover decoration by Ricketts; each of the ninety-nine copies was numbered and signed, and the volume was priced at half a guinea. There were also three further printings of the ordinary edition, bringing the total number of copies, by the end of May, to 5,000. This was a singular achievement for a volume of poetry.[15] *The Ballad* was easily the most successful of Wilde's books.

To enhance the topicality of the poem, Wilde, signing himself 'The Author of *The Ballad of Reading Gaol*', sent a long, passionately argued letter about the need for penal reform to the *Daily Chronicle*. It was published – on the eve of the second reading of the government's Prison Bill. And, gratifyingly, *The Ballad* itself was also quoted by at least two MPs during the course of the debate.[16] In the wake of these successes, Wilde and Smithers hatched excited plans for getting W. H. Smith to take a cheap 'sixpenny' edition, with Wilde suggesting that, as he wanted 'the poem to reach the poorer classes', it might be an idea to give away a cake of 'Maypole soap' with each copy: 'I hear it dyes people the most lovely colours, and is also cleansing.' The scheme, however, sadly came to nothing.[17] Wilde was also disappointed in his hopes that a small book edition might be possible in the States.[18]

Paris, though, was receptive. A poem, Wilde announced complacently, 'gives one *droit de cité*'. He distributed copies among those who had defended him during his imprisonment: Henri Bauër, Octave Mirabeau and others.[19] But the landscape of literary Paris had altered during the years of Wilde's imprisonment. Goncourt and Verlaine were dead. Mallarmé was ailing; he had given up his *mardis* and would die that September. The young writers who had gathered so eagerly around Wilde at the beginning of the 1890s were not keen to renew the association. Although Paul Valéry might write enthusiastically about *The Ballad* to Pierre Louÿs (declaring that prison was clearly '*excellent aux poètes*') there was no suggestion of a rapprochement with their former friend.[20] Schwob and Retté also stood aloof. Henri de Régnier declined to engage, although when they passed in the street it was Wilde who turned away. De Régnier was left to note – disapprovingly – Wilde's too-conspicuous yellow check suit and his 'varnished' shoes.[21]

Others were more welcoming. Stuart Merrill sought him out. *The Ballad* was generously received by the progressive journals. There was 'a capital notice' in the *Revue Blanche*, along with an invitation from its editor, Félix Fénéon, to meet the paper's staff. Wilde dined also with the editor of 'that artistic *revue*' *L'Ermitage*;[22] while the young poet Henry Davray, who had sent Wilde both books and messages of sympathy on his release from prison, proposed writing a French prose translation. Wilde was charmed at the idea – offering his assistance, since, as he pointed out, Davray had not had the advantage of imprisonment, and was likely to be puzzled by some of the vocabulary. They collaborated on the project over the ensuing weeks. Initially Wilde hoped that Smithers might publish the work in a dual-language book edition from London, but in the event the translation appeared that May in the pages of the *Mercure de France*.[23] Its publication further enhanced Wilde's Parisian standing. Ross thought it 'charming', the French 'so unlike the original that one has all the sensation of reading a new poem'.[24] Later in the year the translation was re-issued in book form – under the *Mercure de France* imprint – with the English text in parallel.

There were other marks of esteem: a recitation was arranged of some of Wilde's 'poems in prose' (in French translation) as part of a literary matinee at the Odéon.[25] Memories of the successful production of *Salomé* prompted interest in Wilde's future dramatic projects. He attended at least one performance at the experimental Théâtre Libre as the guest of its director, and was invited to dine by Maeterlinck and his mistress, the opera singer Georgette Leblanc.[26]

Despite these flattering attentions, Wilde could not but be conscious that the real interest of the French capital had shifted away from the concerns of art and literature. At the beginning of 1898 the city – and, indeed, the whole country – was riven by the unfolding drama of the Dreyfus '*affaire*'. Captain Alfred Dreyfus, a Jewish officer serving with French military intelligence, had been convicted in December 1894 of spying for the Germans, and sentenced to life imprisonment on Devil's Island, the penal colony in French Guiana. But doubts had persisted about his guilt. And an army investigator scrutinizing the handwriting on the key piece of evidence – an intercepted inventory, or *bordereau*, passing on sensitive military information – became convinced (quite correctly) that it had been written not by Dreyfus at all, but by another disaffected French officer, Major Ferdinand Esterhazy. Although the military establishment was not inclined to accept (or share) these findings, the information was made public towards the end

1897, provoking a storm of controversy and protest. The guilt or innocence of Dreyfus might be the ostensible matter of dispute, but it also provided a focus for long-standing political and religious animosities. The anti-Dreyfusards, besides their respect for established institutions, were also fuelled by anti-Semitism. Their pro-Dreyfus opponents tended to be anti-clerical, anti-militarist intellectuals. Among those who weighed in on the Dreyfusard side was Emile Zola. When in January 1898 a closed military tribunal summarily exonerated Esterhazy of having written the *bordereau*, the novelist published a furious denunciation at this travesty of justice. His article – headlined '*J'accuse*' – raised the temperature a few more degrees. It also landed Zola in court, charged with defamation of a public authority.

Wilde, though he arrived in Paris with no particular interest in the affair, found himself drawn unexpectedly close to its heart. Among his expatriate friends in the city was the journalist Rowland Strong, who acted as correspondent for the *Observer, Morning Post* and *New York Times*. Strong, a louche, red-haired alcoholic who claimed to be descended from Chateaubriand, was a vehement anti-Dreyfusard (and anti-Semite), and used his journalistic position to promote both prejudices. He had recently made the acquaintance of Esterhazy, electing himself his friend and champion. And at a bibulous gathering in a bar on the rue St Honoré he introduced Wilde to 'Le Commandant'. Strong's secretary, a young Irish 'poet' called Chris Healy, who was present, recalled that Wilde regaled the company 'with a flow of his gayest witticisms' in perfect French, both bemusing and impressing the bitter, duplicitous, black-moustachioed Esterhazy.[27]

On the other side of the divide stood Carlos Blacker, who had arrived in Paris only shortly before Wilde, together with his wife Carrie. Blacker had been greatly relieved to learn that Wilde had broken with Douglas, and – prompted by Constance – he sought out his old companion. At an emotional meeting in Wilde's modest hotel room (at four o'clock on the afternoon of 13 March) they rekindled their friendship. During an afternoon of excited talk Blacker confided that since his arrival in Paris he had become obsessed with the Dreyfus affair, and convinced of Dreyfus's innocence. He was, by chance, an old intimate of Alessandro Panizzardi, the Italian military attaché in Paris, and from him had gained unique access to the full, and secret, details of the case. There were two arresting points: that Esterhazy was indeed the traitor who had sold sensitive material (some 200 documents) to the German military attaché, Colonel von Schwartzkoppen; and that, as part of a cover-up operation, a French intelligence officer

(Lieutenant-Colonel Henry) had forged a letter, purporting to be from Panizzardi to Schwartzkoppen, and appearing to implicate Dreyfus. Blacker, carried away by the moment, revealed much of this to Wilde, along with the fact that Panizzardi had in his possession facsimiles of some of Esterhazy's letters to Schwartzkoppen, which he was planning to send, anonymously, to the British press.

Wilde enjoyed the story. It added an additional frisson of excitement when he found himself dining in company with Esterhazy a few days later. 'The Commandant was astonishing,' Wilde reported to Blacker. 'I will tell you all he said some day. Of course he talked of nothing but Dreyfus *et Cie.*'[28] Wilde, however, always the soul of indiscretion, could not resist passing on the inside information he had gained from Blacker to his regular drinking companions, Strong and Healy. They were electrified by the news, and put it to use – albeit in very different ways. Healy, who was secretly sympathetic to the Dreyfusard cause, went straight to Emile Zola. He and his associates used the information as the basis for an unsigned article that appeared in *Le Siècle* on 4 April, re-affirming Esterhazy's treachery and asserting that the military had forged documents in their efforts to confirm Dreyfus's guilt. Strong, meanwhile, attempted to diffuse the power of Blacker's revelations in advance, writing an article for the *New York Times* reporting that Esterhazy would denounce any supposedly compromising facsimiles as forgeries.[29]

In the fraught era of the Dreyfus affair no claims were ever uncontested, no victories were ever assured and nothing was ever achieved quickly, but the information that Wilde had blithely passed on (via Healy) to Zola came to be seen as marking a decisive shift. It gave the initiative to the Dreyfusards and set them on the way to ultimate victory.[30] In the short term, though, it brought down a tide of anti-Dreyfusard anger upon poor Carlos Blacker. Strong, in his article, had named him as the source of the revelations; many supposed him to be the author of the article in *Le Siècle*. 'Then commenced my troubles,' Blacker recorded. He was attacked in the partisan press, and insulted in the street. He was even placed under police surveillance.[31] Understandably he felt considerable irritation with Wilde who had put him in this uncomfortable position – as well as spoiling his and Panizzardi's plans for breaking the story in a more controlled way.[32]

Wilde, however, was unconcerned by Blacker's travails. He also declined an invitation from Zola to talk over the case – now dismissing the writer as 'a third-rate Flaubert' who 'is never artistic, and often disgusting' (he was

perhaps aware that Zola had refused to sign the petition circulated among French writers at the time of his imprisonment).[33] Over the following weeks Wilde did, though, continue to meet with the increasingly harassed and paranoid Esterhazy. He took a certain relish in the company of the damned. At one of their dinners Esterhazy had declared, 'We are the two greatest martyrs in all humanity,' before adding, after a pause, 'but I have suffered more.'[34] Wilde rejoined, without hesitation, 'No, I have.'[35] When Henry Davray remonstrated with Wilde for keeping such company, he replied that since coming out of prison he was obliged to make his society among 'thieves and assassins.' Besides, the guilty were more interesting than the innocent: innocence required only being wronged; it needed imagination and courage to be a criminal. If Esterhazy were innocent, Wilde claimed, 'I should have had nothing to do with him.'[36]

Although Wilde (according to Sherard) was essentially sympathetic to Dreyfus, with the great injustice at the heart of the *affaire* he simply refused to engage. When quizzed about his understanding of the case he retreated into glibness, declaring, 'Zola wrote the *bordereau* at the dictation of Dreyfus, and Esterhazy took it round to the German Embassy, and sold it for fifteen francs.'[37] Uninterested in politics, his own thoughts, when not touching on literature, were directed more towards the eternal questions of sex, love, money and death.

For the disappointments of the moment 'Love, or Passion with the mask of Love' became his 'only consolation'. Wilde returned to the French capital as a proselytizing advocate of 'Uranian love'. The notion that he might have been 'cured' of a 'madness' by his time in prison had been set aside in Naples, and was not taken up again. He now defiantly proclaimed – and indulged – his homosexual tastes. His line was that 'A patriot put into prison for loving his country loves his country, and a poet in prison for loving boys loves boys.' To have altered his life, he told Ross, 'would have been to have admitted that Uranian love is ignoble. I hold it to be noble – more noble than other forms.' He aligned himself with George Ives's vision of the 'Cause': 'I have no doubt we shall win,' he assured Ives, 'but the road is long, and red with monstrous martyrdoms.'[38]

Wilde's sexual preferences, however, were rather different from the exalted intellectual ideal held up by Ives and the 'Order of Chaeronea'. The sort of 'Uranian love' that he wanted was casual – and commercial – sex with young working-class men. 'How evil it is to buy Love,' he exclaimed, 'and how evil to sell it! And yet what purple hours one can snatch from that grey

slow-moving thing we call Time!'[39] For Wilde 'change' had become 'the
essence of passion'.[40] And in a Paris unburdened by the intrusive writ of the
Criminal Law Amendment Act the opportunities for change were many.
The names of young pick-ups dot Wilde's correspondence with Ross and
Turner: Leon, whom he encountered 'wandering in the moonlit chasm of
my little street'; Marius (who was susceptible to colds) or Giorgio, 'a most
passionate faun' who worked at the Restaurant Jouffroy.[41]

Wilde developed, though, a particular *tendresse* for a young marine infan-
tryman called Maurice Gilbert, whom he picked up in the street having
been struck by his beautiful eyes, and his fine profile ('He looked like
Napoleon when he was first Consul, only less imperious, more beautiful').
Their friendship was sealed by the gift of a bicycle. It was what he 'desired
most in the world', Wilde told Frank Harris; 'he talked of nickel-plated
handle bars, and chains'.[42] Much time was passed in playing bezique. Wilde
lost his heart at the card table. 'Maurice has won twenty-five games... and I
twenty-four,' he reported to Smithers; 'however, as he has youth, and I have
only genius, it is only natural that he should beat me.' Although driven,
initially, by passion, the relationship had its intellectual aspect. Wilde was
soon lending books to Maurice, delighting to see how his mind 'opened
from week to week like a flower'.[43]

Wooing Maurice Gilbert was an additional call of Wilde's resources.
Although it is hard to believe that he had already spent all of the £200
received from Lady Queensberry, he seems to have arrived in Paris in want
of money. Despite the relative success of *The Ballad of Reading Gaol*, there
was no immediate rush of royalties. He was, after all, only due '3d a copy',
according to his own estimate, and had already received a £30 advance.[44]
He turned instead to his friends. No sooner had they reconnected than
he began requesting small loans from Carlos Blacker, to meet pressing
necessities.[45]

Wilde, though, as Blacker soon found out, was not as bereft as he claimed.
Constance, on hearing that he had separated from Douglas, had restored
his allowance, sending the money via Ross so that it might be passed on
at the modest rate of £10 a month. 'If [Oscar] had plenty of money,' she
explained to the Blackers, 'he would drink himself to death and do no
work.'[46] Wilde complained bitterly both at the reduced monthly amount,
and at the fact that Constance was not intending to pay 'the arrears' due
for the three months when his allowance had been stopped. In an effort at
economy he moved from the Hôtel de Nice into the neighbouring Hôtel

d'Alsace – 'Much better, and half the price.'[47] To Ross he lamented, 'I must try and invent some scheme of poverty, and have found a restaurant where for 80 francs a month one can get nothing fit to eat – two chances a day – so shall *abonner* myself there.'[48] Constance, however, was not impressed by such demonstrations. She warned Blacker against having anything more to do with Wilde's financial affairs, remarking tartly, 'Oscar is so pathetic and such a born actor.'[49] What he really needed, she suggested, was 'a person of strong will to live with him and look after him'.[50]

It was one of her last comments upon her husband. On 7 April, at a Genoese clinic, five days after undergoing a further operation to address her creeping paralysis, Constance died. Medical opinion was divided upon the exact cause of death; her son Vyvyan always believed she died of a broken heart.[51] Wilde, when he heard the news, was distraught. Although he claimed to have been troubled by unsettling dreams of Constance on the night of her death, the information arrived as a shock.[52] He fired off telegrams to Ross and Blacker proclaiming his 'great grief' and begging to see them. Blacker came at once. And Ross hastened over from England, although, by the time he arrived, Wilde seemed to have recovered his equanimity. 'He is in very good spirits and does not consume too many,' Ross reported to Smithers. Although Wilde might enjoy the grief of the bereavement (and even return to it in his thoughts) he remained quite incapable of understanding how 'cruel' he had been to wife. His immediate anxiety seemed to be that his allowance might cease with Constance's death. But on this point he was soon reassured.[53]

Her death closed a chapter in his life. It removed all possibility of him seeing his children for the foreseeable future. They were now under the guardianship of Constance's cousin Adrian Hope. Wilde felt the deprivation keenly, at least in certain moods and moments. When a young French boy who dined, together with his mother, at the same modest restaurant where Wilde ate, asked him whether he had any sons of his own, tears sprang to his eyes. 'I have two,' he replied, in French, but 'they don't come here with me because they are too far away'. Then drawing the child towards him, he kissed him on both cheeks, murmuring (in English), 'Oh, my poor dear boys.'[54]

Constance's death was not the only intimation of mortality that spring. Three weeks earlier Beardsley had died at Menton, aged just twenty-five. Despite their very different characters, Wilde had been greatly impressed by the young artist. As he wrote to Smithers, 'There were great possibilities

always in the cavern of his soul, and there is something macabre and tragic in the fact that one who added another terror to life should have died at the age of a flower.'[55] Wilde's own health had been causing him concern. At the beginning of May he had a minor operation on his throat for quinsy (peritonsillar abscess): the operation itself was 'all right', as he was 'drenched with cocaine', but afterwards his throat was 'very painful'.[56]

Paris in the springtime had, however, its distractions. English visitors were numerous. Wilde dined frequently with the Harlands, and Frank Harris entertained him handsomely.[57] He made no attempt to hide himself. Either from 'bravado or genuine inclination', he would chose – whenever he had the chance – to be entertained in 'expensive and much-frequented places'. Stares were to be outfaced, and rebuffs ignored.[58] He remained an 'imposing' figure, conspicuous in any setting; and although his wardrobe was sadly reduced, he was always 'well dressed' and 'well shaved'.[59]

He attended the *vernissage* of the New Salon ('Rodin's statue of Balzac is superb – just what a *romancier* is, or should be').[60] He went to the Folies-Bergères with the poet Robert Scheffer, and to a 'Miracle Play' with Stuart Merrill: they supped afterwards with the student cast, 'and the whole Quartier Latin was bright with beauty and wine'.[61] He met the wild-haired young playwright Alfred Jarry, author of *Ubu Roi*.[62] Out for dinner with the Thaulows, on another evening, he came face to face with Whistler. They did not speak. 'How old and weird he looks!' Wilde reported gaily to Ross. 'Like Meg Merrilies.'[63] More distressing were the encounters with Sherard. He had returned to Paris to cover the Dreyfus affair, but his anti-Dreyfusard monomania, as well as his drunkenness, made him a tedious companion. And Wilde continued to nurse a resentment over his comments about Naples and Bosie. They did meet occasionally but, as Sherard later recalled, Wilde 'became more and more distant'; encountering each other on the boulevards, they would often pass 'in silence, with only a faint wave of the hand'.[64]

Bosie, too, was back in Paris, installed in a small but 'charming flat' on the avenue Kléber. And although the shadow of Naples now lay between them, he and Wilde met as friends, and as the spring advanced they saw each other with gradually increasing regularity. Wilde helped Douglas choose the furniture for his flat, and dined there regularly.[65] But the all-consuming intimacy of the past was not recovered. And without the distorting lens of love, Bosie's selfishness became all too apparent. As Ross reported to Smithers, after a visit to Paris, Douglas 'is less interested in other people than ever before, especially Oscar, so I really think that alliance will die a

natural death'.[66] He was spending most of his time and all of his money at the races. 'He has a faculty for spotting a loser,' Wilde declared; 'which considering he knows nothing at all about horses, is perfectly astounding.'[67] It was really their shared and enduring interest in having sex with the gamin 'renters' of the *quartier* that drew them together. Bosie was obsessed with a 'dreadful little ruffian aged fourteen' dubbed 'Florifer' because, Wilde explained, 'in the scanty intervals he can steal from an arduous criminal profession, he sells bunches of purple violets in front of the Café de la Paix'. The fact that the Florifer regularly attempted to blackmail Bosie only seems to have increased his attractiveness.[68]

Douglas – along with Ross and Reggie Turner – also developed a passion for Wilde's friend Maurice Gilbert. Indeed the beautiful young man rapidly became the shared darling of the group. That May Ross confessed to having spent a whole quarter's allowance on a single Parisian week of 'selfish and notorious living with Maurice' (he was, as Ross explained to Smithers, 'a costly courtesan for those who adore him').[69] In due course the 'golden Maurice' also took on an additional role as Rowland Strong's not very efficient 'secretary'.[70]

Over the summer he was often part of the shifting group – together with Wilde, Douglas, Strong and Strong's dog Snatcher – that escaped periodically to *L'Idée*, a quaint country inn at Nogent-sur-Marne, just outside Paris. It was a charmed spot. 'Oh, the joys of the little riverside *pavilion*, or cottage,' Strong enthused, 'with its big garden filled with flowers and vegetables and fruit-trees, *en plein rapport*, with laden branches. It was but a cab drive to get there! No need for railways. Boating, fishing, and bathing, were the day-long amusements.'[71] Perhaps even more importantly, the landlord offered credit. Wilde found a nostalgic solace in the surroundings. Taking one visitor for a stroll along the river, he declared, 'Might not this be a bit of the Thames?' Then, peering through the iron gate of one of the large villas that stood along the bank, he remarked: 'This is what I like, just to stand and peep through the bars. It would be better than being in paradise to stand like this, catch a glimpse as now, and want to go in. The reality would sure to be disappointing.'[72]

At the beginning of June, Carlos Blacker came down from Paris to see Wilde. The meeting, though it ended with 'protestations of devotion', was not quite satisfactory. The friendship had been faltering for some months. Blacker was under pressure from his wife to break off all connection with Wilde. He was also aware that Wilde was seeing Bosie again, and he

disapproved. But, worse than this, he suspected that Wilde was the source of embarrassing information about his dispute with the Duke of Newcastle that was appearing in the French press, and causing him much distress. When Blacker followed up the Nogent visit with 'a Nonconformist conscience letter' reiterating these points, Wilde chose to take offence. He sent 'a very strong' reply, asserting his innocence, accusing Blacker of hypocrisy, and putting an end to their long and rewarding friendship. 'So,' Wilde commented to Ross, 'Tartuffe goes out of my life.'[73]

Although Wilde might affect (and even feel) a callous indifference, the rupture with Blacker had implications for his standing in Paris. It was seen by Blacker's many Dreyfusard friends as a rank betrayal. Henry Bauër, the critic to whom Wilde had sent a copy of The Ballad of Reading Gaol, wrote of the 'contempt' that he now felt for Wilde, a man whom he had 'defended so ardently' up until then. 'He betrays his friends who have stood by and supported him. I turn away from this foul odour. He no longer exists for me.'[74] The view was shared by others. But if Wilde broke with Blacker, he continued to meet, and dine, with the embattled Esterharzy. The net was closing in upon the traitor following the exposure of Colonel Henry's forgeries; and on 2 September, encouraged by Strong, he slipped away from Paris and fled to England. In the British press at least it was supposed that Wilde was in some way involved in this sensational development.[75]

Wilde wanted to flee from Paris himself. The city was in the grip of a terrible heatwave. 'I walk in streets of brass', he complained to Frank Harris. There was no one around except 'perspiring English families'. And though at night it could be charming, by day it was 'a tiger's mouth'.[76] From this discomfort he was rescued by an invitation to stay with Charles Conder at Chantemesle, a little village near La Roche-Guyon, on the Seine, west of Paris. Wilde joined a happy party including Will Rothenstein and his soon-to-be-wife, Alice. Conder reported to Mrs Dalhousie Young: 'I think some people were rather annoyed at my bringing [Oscar] – but he turned Chantemesle into a charming little state, made himself king and possessed himself of [Arthur] Blunt's boat – for his barge – and got little boys to row him from Chantemesle to La Roche every day; there he took his aperitif and returned laden with duck-ham and wine usually which served as extras to the frugal dinners we get here.'[77]

Despite such jollities, Conder reported that Wilde was 'much more serious' than he had been at Dieppe the previous summer – even 'very depressed at times, poor fellow'.[78] The limitations of his Parisian life seemed already

to be grating on him. Conder asked why he did not take a flat: 'Everybody would be happy to come and see you. You would have all the *littérateurs* and artists.' To this Wilde had replied mournfully, 'My dear fellow, that is just it: I do not care about *littérateurs*. The only people I like are the Great. I want duchesses.'[79] Duchesses, however, he had come to realize – with 'much sorrow' – were now out of reach. He would 'never get into society again'. Instead he must strive to embrace 'a Bohemian existence' – a mode of living (Ross claimed) that was 'entirely out of note with his genius and temperament'. To Conder he admitted that he was beginning to feel 'rather old for the volatile poets of the *"quartier"*'.[80]

2

Going South

'There is only one class in the community that thinks more about money than the rich, and that is the poor.'

OSCAR WILDE

Wilde's own poetic inspiration remained in abeyance. His belief that the 'stimulating' intellectual atmosphere of Paris might restore his creative energy was proving as vain as his previous hope that sunshine and Naples would effect the change. The early assurances that he would soon be starting on 'a new play' were not followed through.[1] Instead he began referring to *The Ballad* as his *'chant de cygne'* – the dying swan's final lament.[2] Nevertheless he refused to abandon all hope. As he reminded Ross, he had 'done a good year's work' since coming out of prison: 'Now I want to do work again, for the next year,' even if it was 'not easy to recapture the artistic mood of detachment from the accidents of life.'[3]

In the meantime a semblance of literary endeavour could be kept up. To follow on the success of *The Ballad*, Smithers was advancing plans to bring out editions of both *An Ideal Husband* and *The Importance of Being Earnest*, done in the same elegant format that had been used by John Lane for Wilde's two earlier society comedies. It was decided to publish *The Importance of Being Earnest* first, since – as Ross pointed out – it was not

only 'far the best', and most critically acclaimed, of Wilde's plays, but also the least known: 'It ran for so short a time that many people would buy it who could not have seen the play.'[4]

Wilde devoted much of the year to revising the typescript. His ear for comedy remained as sure as ever. He made dozens of small textual changes, improving adjectives and refining speeches. To Lady Bracknell's pronounce- ment – 'Fortunately, in England, at any rate, education produces no effect whatsoever. If it did, it would prove a serious danger to the upper classes, and probably lead to acts of violence' – he added the resonant closing words, 'in Grosvenor Square'. The book was to be dedicated to Ross. Wilde had chaffed him over his great enthusiasm for the play with the (patently untrue) remark, 'There are two ways of disliking my plays. One is to dislike them, the other is to like *Earnest* best.'[5] Wilde's own name would not be appearing on the title page. It was still, he thought, too soon. He suggested, instead, the formula 'By the author of *Lady Windermere's Fan*'.[6]

Musing on his past successes brought mingled pain and pleasure. On the future, though, he refused to dwell. He might tell the young English novelist Wilfrid Chesson, who visited him at Nogent, 'I do not doubt that there are as wonderful things in my future as my past'; but such a claim can only have been made for his own encouragement.[7] When Healy asked him about his plans, he replied, 'I cannot say what I am going to do with my life; I am wondering what my life is going to do with me. I would like to retire to some monastery, some grey stoned cell where I could have my books, write verses, and reverently smoke my cigarettes.'[8] He was content, for the most part, to live in the present. The discovery of a stray franc for another *cannette* of beer was all he asked of the passing moment. 'You worry too much,' he admonished Chesson; 'never worry.'[9]

He strove to follow his own advice, and for the most part succeeded. Drink helped. The level of consumption begun in Naples was continued, and increased. Beer, wine, champagne, brandy, whisky and soda, advocaat, were all imbibed in quantity. But absinthe now became his drink of choice.[10] At Berneval he had discoursed to John Fothergill upon the three stages of absinthe intoxication. 'The first stage' he described as being 'like ordinary drinking'; during the 'second' you began to see 'monstrous and cruel things'; but if you were able to persevere and enter upon the third stage you would 'see things that you *want* to see, wonderful and curious things'. He described how, after one long evening of solitary absinthe drinking, he achieved this third stage, just as the waiter came in with his green apron and began to close

up the café, piling the chairs on the tables. When he brought in a watering can and began to water the sawdust on the floor, 'the most wonderful flowers, tulips, lilies and roses, sprang up' all around. They remained invisible to the waiter, Wilde recalled, but 'as I got up and passed out into the street I felt the heavy tulip-heads brushing against my shins'.[11]

Reality, however, could not always be kept in check. Vincent O'Sullivan noted that sometimes, during the course of a conversation, Wilde's 'face would be swept with poignant anguish and regret' or with 'the apprehension of the future'. At such moments he would 'pass his large hand with a trembling gesture over his face and stretch out his arm' as though to ward off the thought.[12]

He refused, though, to make any provision for the morrow. His monthly allowance was dedicated more to rent boys than to rent. He consoled himself with small extravagances. To the amazement of a group of poets, with whom he was drinking, he sent out a page boy with a 20-franc piece to fetch a packet of gold-tipped cigarettes. The brand proved disappointing when he lit the first one. But, as the boy handed him the change – about 15 francs – Wilde announced, 'No, keep it. That will give me the illusion that these cigarettes are good.'[13] He could run up an impressive bill of over 27 francs for 'Eau de Cologne' and other toiletries in just a couple of visits to Jules & Roger in the rue Scribe.[14]

Always generous when he was in funds, he expected his friends to provide for him when he was without them. An inability to budget meant that he ended almost every month in want. Ross received regular pleas for early payment of the allowance. After one particularly urgent appeal – in which Wilde described himself as both penniless and 'dinnerless' – Ross sold a Beardsley drawing that he owned for £5, and had Smithers send the money anonymously to Wilde.[15] Ross did, though, soon become wise to Wilde's habits of exaggeration and, indeed, deception. Wilde was obliged to apologize, having been caught out in a lie about desperately needing funds to retrieve his impounded luggage from the innkeeper at Nogent: 'I am so sorry about my excuse,' he wrote. 'I had forgotten I had used Nogent before. It shows the utter collapse of my imagination, and rather distresses me.' And Frank Harris recalled a tragi-comic dinner at Durand's when – at the beginning of the evening – he had given Wilde a generous cheque with which to pay off his current debts. As they parted (at three in the morning), Wilde – having forgotten the earlier gift – asked Harris whether he might have 'a few pounds' as he was very 'hard up'.[16] Wilde, though, in matters of

money, had moved beyond either embarrassment or shame. Poverty might be 'dreadful', but it was principally a periodic inconvenience.*

He retained hopes for a brighter financial future, if not from the book edition of *The Importance of Being Earnest*, then from his modern play scenario 'Love is Law'. Properly developed, it had the potential to earn him thousands. Although nothing had come of Smithers' approach to Augustin Daly, in October Wilde arranged to sell the British performing rights for the unwritten play to a London theatre producer called Horace Sedger, who was then enjoying a successful run with an adaptation of *Alice's Adventures in Wonderland*.[17] But if Wilde hoped that signing a contract might stimulate his ability to work, he was disappointed. The advance simply allowed him to indulge himself more.

Paris, though, seemed empty that autumn. He did see a few old friends, even if Ross and Turner – who were making a three-month tour of Italy – bypassed Paris on their way south. Ada Leverson came over for a visit. She had lost none of her bracing wit: when Wilde regaled her with the tale of a devoted young apache who accompanied him everywhere with a knife in his hand, she remarked, 'I'm sure he had a fork in the other.'[18] But Wilde's regular companions were away. Strong was over in London trying to sell Esterhazy's story to the British press. Bosie, too, after almost three and a half years in exile, had returned to England, his mother having received assurances from the public prosecutor that he would not face arrest. He remained in London for several months, arranging publication of two slim volumes, one a collection of his poems (not including 'In Praise of Shame' or 'Two Loves') and the other a gathering of nonsense verse for children; both books were to appear without his name upon the title page. While in England he also attempted a reconciliation with his father. The meeting, in the smoking room of Bailey's Hotel, went well, with Queensberry embracing him, calling him his 'darling boy' and promising to restore his allowance. But when the marquess followed this up with a letter demanding to know what exactly were his son's relations with 'that beast Wilde', Bosie sent back a bitter and intemperate reply, ending all possibility of a rapprochement.[19]

In the absence of his English cronies, Wilde devoted time to flirtatious

---

* Poverty had, too, its paradoxical side. Wilde liked to tell of the occasion when he had been forced to get out of an omnibus because he did not have the few *sous* for the fare, and – instead – hail a cab, because this could be paid for by the doorman at the apartment building to which he was heading.

correspondence with some of the young men of artistic and/or Uranian inclination, who wrote enthusiastically to him from England: there was Louis Wilkinson, a seventeen-year-old Radley schoolboy who claimed that he was planning to dramatize *The Picture of Dorian Gray*; and Jerome Pollitt, a wealthy cross-dressing Aesthete who sent photographs with every post.[20] Wilde, though, hated being alone in his unlovely and 'too yellow' hotel room. He might read for a while in the little back yard of the Hôtel d'Alsace, but he soon sought the sociability of the streets. He would wander through the Latin Quarter. He knew the wares of all the local antique dealers. He was often to be seen in the Luxembourg Gardens. If he walked slowly, with short paces, it was thought – by those who knew him – that he did so in order to allow himself better to enjoy his memories of 'what he had once been'.[21]

Although Wilde remained cut off from the currents of ordinary social life, it was sometimes by his own choice. When invited home by his old Oxford contemporary J. E. C. Bodley, he fled at the door on learning that Bodley's family was there.[22] He gravitated instead to French literary circles. The Calisaya American Bar on the Boulevard des Italiens (close to the Opera) became – as he told Turner – his chief 'literary resort'; at five o'clock he would gather there with is 'friends' Moréas, Ernest La Jeunesse, 'and all the young poets.'[23] The ritual of the five o'clock aperitif gave a structure to the day, and a starting point to the evening. And if the excellent champagne cocktails, for which the bar was renowned, were stimulating, so too was the discourse.[24] Literary disputes were not infrequent, but there was much fun as well. The science fiction writer Gustave Le Rouge, who first encountered Wilde at the Calisaya, recalled being impressed by his 'sincere good spirits and by his laughter which rang true, revealing his teeth which were nearly all capped with gold and which gave him a vague semblance of an idol'.[25]

The crowd at the Calisaya provided Wilde with an audience, and he poured forth an endless succession of parables and stories.[26] Though he delighted in entertaining, La Jeunesse suspected that he was also improvising 'for himself', to assure himself that 'he still *could*, still *would*, still *knew*'.[27] The heroes of Wilde's tales were almost 'invariably' kings and gods – although one story concerned a king and a beggar. At the close of it Wilde remarked, 'I have been king; now I will be a beggar.' The self-dramatization was typical, as was the exaggeration. Whatever Wilde's periodic financial embarrassments, he remained (as La Jeunesse noted) always the perfect, well-groomed Englishman – 'and [he] did not beg'.[28]

In another exercise of self-mythologizing Wilde elaborated a tale of how,

in his former life, he had reached such a level of success and happiness that he was suddenly seized by 'a secret feeling of terror, that in reality [he] was too happy, that such improbable bliss could only be a trap set by [his] evil genius'. Recalling the example of the tyrant Polycrates, he determined to make a sacrifice to the gods to assuage their jealousy, and like that Greek king he 'flung a valuable ring into the sea.' But, as happened with Polycrates, the ring was brought back to him by a fisherman who had discovered it in the belly of a fish: 'The unfortunate thing about it,' Wilde added with a 'strange smile', was that the 'little fisherman' who returned the ring was 'far too handsome a fellow...'[29]

The suggestive allusion to the fisher-boy's good looks marked a new auto-biographical note in Wilde's storytelling, a hint of his now defiant sexual boldness. He made no attempt to hide his proclivities. Indeed he seems to have introduced some of his pick-ups at the Calisaya. He mentioned to Turner a 'beautiful boy of bad character' who was sometimes present, explaining that 'he is so like Antinous, and so smart, that he is allowed to talk to poets'.[30] Such doubtful company, however, unsettled the more priggish of the young Parisian writers. Vincent O'Sullivan recalled how Stuart Merrill and others 'were constantly begging me to get Wilde's English friends to make him realize that he was ruining what sympathy was left for him' among former friends, by appearing at the Calisaya 'with sodomist outcasts, who were sometimes dangerous in other ways [too]'.[31]

As a result of such attitudes Wilde found it impossible to build upon, or even sustain, some of the connections and much of the goodwill occasioned by the publication of The Ballad of Reading Gaol. He did continue to dine with Merrill, but not often.[32] Gide he saw again only twice: both rather awkward chance encounters upon the boulevards, at which Wilde strained to recapture the gaiety of former years, and Gide felt a great sadness lurking behind the attempt.[33] Nevertheless there were many who did enjoy his company. He took up with a young American writer called Charles Sibleigh, who was engaged in translating The Rubaiyat of Omar Khayyam from English into French.[34] He saw something of Henri de Toulouse-Lautrec; the diminutive artist found him a 'most sympathetic companion since he didn't always stare at him as if he were a monster or a miracle'.[35] But it was the twenty-four-year-old critic and novelist Ernest La Jeunesse who became Wilde's 'great friend'. A fantastical figure, bushy-haired and eccentrically attired, his face patched with eczema, and in his hand 'an empire cane', he and Wilde made a striking pair when patrolling the boulevards.[36] Wilde

was amused by La Jeunesse's piercing falsetto voice and his malicious wit.*
He was impressed too by his energy. La Jeunesse was forever starting short-
lived literary reviews. Wilde promised to contribute 'a poem in prose' to
one of them. But the 'great effort' involved in setting even a very short
story down on paper seems to have been beyond him.[37]

Away from the relative chic of the Calisaya, Wilde – embracing his new
bohemianism – also explored the low dives of the Latin Quarter: the student cafés, the 'wine cellars', 'the dens of ill-repute'. There was, of course,
a sexual element in these expeditions. But there were artistic rewards too.
Wilde's generosity in buying drinks for – and bestowing praise on – the
unknown songwriters, would-be artists and 'unpublished poets' that he
met along the way gave him an enjoyable status and popularity. He found
friends and listeners among the shifting population of American expatriate
art students, young Scandinavian painters and popular versifiers. When
he attended a poetry recital in a Montmartre café, he was 'received with
great honour' – and even the waiter, 'a lad of singular beauty' asked for his
autograph.[38]

In London, also, Wilde was not completely forgotten. The wider literary
establishment, dismayed at the news that he had 'returned to Paris and to
his dog's vomit', continued to shun him.[39] But some old friends remained
true. Among them it was Frank Harris who took the most active interest
in his well-being. Flush with funds, having sold the *Saturday Review* and
pursuing ambitious plans to buy a hotel in Monaco, he offered to take
Wilde with him to spend winter in the South of France – hoping that the
change of scene, and the absence of material care, might enable him to
write. It was a very generous offer, and Wilde accepted, despite a certain
trepidation about the exhaustion of being in Harris's company for three
whole months.

In the event his worries proved unfounded. Having installed Wilde at
the Hôtel des Bains in the picturesque fishing village of Napoule, just outside Cannes, Harris disappeared along the coast to Monaco to pursue his
business plans. They met up only occasionally, for bracing evenings of

---

* Wilde liked to recount how, when La Jeunesse discovered that a noted publisher had
suggested that his high-pitched voice was an indication that he was 'completely impotent', he had plotted revenge. After a long campaign, La Jeunesse had succeeded in
seducing the publisher's wife. In due course she had a child by him. And the publisher
was perturbed to find himself bringing up a child with a very distinctive and very high-
pitched wail. Wilde called it 'the greatest repartee in history'.

literary talk, philosophical discourse and debate about sexual attraction.*
After these encounters, Wilde told Turner, 'I stagger to my room, bathed in
perspiration; I believe [Harris] talks the Rugby game.' Wilde was perspiring
again when Harris dragged him on a not-very-long walk to visit a nearby
monastery. The old abbé, impressed by Wilde's manner and bearing, asked
Harris if he were a not a 'great man'. 'Yes,' Harris replied, 'a great man
– incognito.'[40]

For much of the time, though, Wilde was left to his own devices. But
still he wrote nothing except the occasional letter. The days were passed in
happy idleness, enjoying the aromatic air of the pine trees, 'the high sapphire wall of the sea' and 'the gold dust of the sun'. He read much. Henry
James's The Turn of the Screw impressed him particularly: he thought it 'a
most wonderful, lurid, poisonous little tale, like an Elizabethan tragedy'.[41]
His evenings were spent picking up young men. He would go into Cannes
or Nice, where 'romance' was 'a profession plied beneath the moon'.[42] But
even at Napoule he found that the fisher-lads had 'the same freedom from
morals as the Neapolitans have'.[43] By the beginning of the new year he
was boasting to Ross that he was 'practically engaged to a fisherman of
extraordinary beauty, age eighteen'.[44] And when Harris chivvied him about
his writing, he suggested that he might undertake The Ballad of a Fisher
Boy as a sort of joyful companion to The Ballad of Reading Gaol; it would
'sing of liberty instead of prison, joy instead of sorrow, a kiss instead of an
execution'. The poem, however, never got beyond a few verses, and even
these were not consigned to paper.[45]

There were many British visitors to the Riviera, and Wilde's days were
marked by the occasional unexpected encounter. George Alexander passed
by on a bicycle but did not stop, giving only 'a crooked sickly smile'. Wilde
thought it 'absurd and mean of him'.[46] The Prince of Wales did better:
having driven past Wilde in his carriage, he turned and raised his hat.[47]
Wilde befriended a wealthy young Swiss-domiciled Englishman called
Harold Mellor, who was staying at Cannes together with his handsome

---

*   Harris was working on a series of articles about Shakespeare, and had embraced the
notion of the playwright's homosexuality. While holding forth on the subject one
afternoon in the Café Royal dining room, he had boomed to the Duc de Richelieu,
'No my dear duke, I know nothing of the joys of homosexuality. You must speak to
my friend Oscar about that.' A profound silence descended upon the room. 'And yet',
Harris mused, in a more subdued but still reverberating tone, 'if Shakespeare had asked
me, I would have had to submit.'

young Italian servant. Mellor, though depressive and often depressing, provided welcome companionship and the occasional champagne supper. It was Mellor who took Wilde to Nice to see Bernhardt in *Tosca*. 'I went round afterwards to see Sarah,' Wilde told Ross, 'and she embraced me and wept, and I wept, and the whole evening was wonderful.'[48]

As the new year advanced, however, Wilde grew restless. He presumed increasingly upon Harris's generosity, moving from Napoule to Nice to Monte Carlo and back again, each relocation occasioning importunate demands that his hotel bill be paid at once. Harris might not have minded but for Wilde's failure to work. When Harris finally pointed out that 'everyone grows tired of holding up an empty sack', Wilde took umbrage. As an escape he accepted an invitation to spend March with Mellor at his villa in Gland on the shores of Lake Geneva. Mellor, at least, did not expect him to work.[49]

Before departing for Switzerland, however, Wilde crossed the Italian border and travelled to Genoa. There, in the gleaming cemetery outside the town, he visited Constance's grave. 'It is very pretty,' he told Ross, 'a marble cross with dark ivy-leaves inlaid in a good pattern... It was very tragic seeing her name carved on a tomb – her surname, my name, not mentioned of course – just "Constance Mary, daughter of Horace Lloyd, QC" and a verse from *Revelations*. I brought some flowers. I was deeply affected – with a sense, also, of the uselessness of all regrets. Nothing could have been otherwise, and Life is a very terrible thing.'[50]

At Gland, soon afterwards, Wilde received news of another loss: the death of his brother Willie, aged forty-six. He left a widow and an infant daughter. The 'wide chasms' that had existed between the brothers could now be closed. By Willie's death Wilde inherited the 'absurd' and much impoverished family property at Moytura; but the meagre asset was almost immediately claimed by that 'octopus of the law', the official receiver.[51]

If this was a disappointment, there were more telling ones to hand. The publication of *The Importance of Being Earnest* in February had been greeted by a resounding silence in the press and meagre interest from the public. Its failure did not come as a surprise to the author. Wilde had suggested to Harris that the play was 'so trivial, so irresponsible a comedy: and while the public like to hear of my pain – curiosity and the autobiographical form being the elements of interest – I am not sure that they will welcome me again in airy mood and spirit, mocking at morals, and defiant of social rules'. In confirmation of his view, *The Ballad of Reading Gaol* continued

to sell so well that Smithers was arranging for a large (2,000-copy) printing of a new edition, bearing Wilde's name, in brackets, on the title page.[52] But, while it now seemed commercially astute to acknowledge authorship of his prison poem, Wilde thought it best to maintain his anonymity on all other fronts.* He was furious at Horace Sedger for announcing in the press that he would be producing 'a new comedy by Oscar Wilde' on the London stage. As he explained to Ross: 'My only chance is a play produced anonymously. Otherwise the First Night would be a horror, and people would find meanings in every phrase.'[53]

Despite the minimal sales of *The Importance of Being Earnest* Smithers courageously continued with plans for an edition of *An Ideal Husband*; Wilde spent some of his time at Gland amending and correcting the typescript of the play, and fussing over the details of publication. He planned to dedicate the volume to Frank Harris – as 'A Slight Tribute to his Power and Distinction as an Artist, his Chivalry and Nobility as a Friend'. The editorial work proved a diversion from the tedium of Swiss life. A month chez Mellor was altogether too long. By the beginning of the third week Wilde was ungraciously complaining that 'Mellor is tedious, and lacks conversation: also he gives me Swiss wine to drink: it is horrid: he occupies himself with small economies, and mean domestic interests. So I suffer very much.' The vaunted beauty of the Swiss landscape was 'obvious' and 'old fashioned', the Swiss themselves 'so ugly to look at' as to 'convey melancholy' into the soul, and a terrible 'chastity' into the body.[54]

At the beginning of April Wilde fled back to the Italian Riviera, in search of sunshine, beauty, cheap lodgings and convenient sex. 'I am going to try and find a place near Genoa,' he informed Smithers, 'where I can live for ten francs a day (boy *compris*).'[55] This modest ideal was achieved in the 'quite delightful' little port village of Santa Margherita, just a mile out of Genoa, where Wilde took rooms above the Ristorante Christofero Colombo. But, whatever the charms of the place, it was not stimulating. Boredom and loneliness soon set in. Even 'the lad' Wilde was in love with proved a

---

* Wilde still registered at his hotels as 'M. Sebastian Melmoth'. When, in Italy, a local newspaper announced his presence as 'Oscar Wilde', stirring up a great deal of interest and excitement, Wilde refused to drop his incognito with the students who flocked to his café 'to talk – or rather to listen'. As he explained to Ross: 'To their great delight I always denied my identity. On being asked my name, I said every man has only one name. They asked me what name that was. "Io" [the Italian for "I"] was my answer. This was regarded as a wonderful reply, containing in it all philosophy.'

disappointment.[56] Only a lack of money for the rail fare back to Paris kept him tethered there.

A diversion, and the chance of escape, was provided by the arrival of Leonard Smithers. There had been developments concerning Wilde's proposed play. Sedger, impatient at Wilde's failure to deliver a script, and in financial difficulties himself, had transferred his rights in the project to a fellow producer called Roberts. New terms were discussed. Roberts agreed to pay Wilde £100 on the delivery of each act, besides defraying his expenses.[57] It was an excellent deal, and it seems that Roberts, together with Smithers, came out to Italy to finalize the plan. There was a dinner at the Café Concordia in Genoa, but it appears not to have been entirely satisfactory. Roberts returned 'home in utter disgust and offered to transfer his contract' to Smithers at a price that 'tempted' the publisher.

Smithers duly succumbed to the temptation. He wrote to Wilde proposing to take over the project. He would 'square' Wilde's hotel bill at Santa Margheritia, pay his return fare to Paris and provide a weekly stipend, allowing Wilde to work free from daily financial care – at least until 'I find that you are not serious in promising to write'.[58] Wilde readily accepted, but then almost immediately fell ill. Ross – summoned by a series of plaintive telegrams – came, once again, to the rescue. Taking charge of the situation he managed to convince Wilde that many of his health problems related to his ever-increasing intake of alcohol. With dire warnings he was able to scare Wilde off drinking – at least for the present.[59] He then piloted the patient back to Paris.[60]

Having overcome a short-lived misunderstanding with Smithers about the business arrangements, Wilde was soon at work on the play. By the beginning of June he claimed to have written 'more than half of the Fourth Act'.[61] He had started with the play's 'serious' and 'tragic' denouement since he found it difficult 'to laugh at life' as he used to, and 'the comedy of Acts I and II' frightened him 'a little'.[62] Nevertheless he was in optimistic mood when he ran across the American producer Augustin Daly, together with his wife and also his star actress, Ada Rehan, in a Paris restaurant. The encounter was a happy one. Wilde joined their table, and 'talked so charmingly' – Rehan later recalled – 'it was just like old times'.[63] Theatrical plans were discussed. Daly was ready to make a 'large offer for the American rights' to 'Love is Law', the play on which Wilde was working, but he and Rehan also wanted him 'do something' new for them too.[64] Unfortunately Daly died almost the next day before any arrangements could be made. Wilde

with typical generosity put himself at the service of Mrs Daly and Ada Rehan, helping them to deal with the French authorities. He 'was more good and helpful than I can tell you', Rehan related, 'just like a very kind brother'.[65]

If Wilde was shocked and disappointed by Daly's death, he did have other projects to contemplate. On his return to Paris he had found a letter from an old London friend, the actor Kyrle Bellew, who wanted him to collaborate on a play about Beau Brummell, possibly to be put on by the wealthy society actress Mrs Brown-Potter.[66] Wilde, who had always been stimulated by working concurrently on multiple projects, encouraged the idea. And, having received a draft typescript at the beginning of July, he accepted Bellew's proposal that they meet at Boulogne, or one of the other Normandy summer resorts, to discuss the undertaking.[67]

The meeting led to a slight amendment of plans over the course of the summer. Wilde – who passed most of the season just outside Paris at Chennevières-sur-Marne – became gradually disillusioned with Smithers' ability to produce any play by him. The publisher, after all, had no experience of the London theatre. As an alternative Wilde persuaded Bellew that, rather than proceeding with the Beau Brummell project, he should buy out Smithers' interest in 'Love is Law', and that he – and Mrs Brown-Potter – should produce the piece. Smithers apparently agreed to this plan on one of his visits to Paris. Wilde offered to repay him the £160 he had thus far received, but not immediately; the money would come 'out of the proceeds of the play'. In the meantime Wilde was already getting £5 a week from Bellew to continue work on the piece, an arrangement that was superseded after five weeks when Mrs Brown-Potter paid an initial advance of £100 for the play, with more due on completion.[68]

Although all this could be construed as progress of a sort, there was no doubt that Wilde's second year of freedom had not been as productive as his first. His literary output from Chennevières-sur-Marne consisted largely of begging letters to friends and acquaintances about his Parisian living arrangements. He was anxious to move back to the Left Bank, but his bill at the Hôtel Marsollier – where he was installed – remained unpaid, and his luggage was impounded.[69] Nevertheless he did have one new publication to celebrate. *An Ideal Husband* ('By the Author of *Lady Windermere's Fan*') was issued that July. If it received no reviews, Wilde could bestow complimentary copies on his friends in England and in Paris. Major Nelson and Toulouse-Lautrec were among those to be sent copies.[70]

At the end of the summer Wilde returned to Paris, effecting his escape from the Hôtel Marsollier, and moving back across the river to rooms at the congenial Hôtel d'Alsace, where the proprietor, M. Dupoirier, was sympathetic, provided breakfast and extended credit.[71]* He re-established his Parisian daily round of late rising and light reading, of the five o'clock aperitif and the long evening of talk and drink. Often he was lonely, sometimes he was sad. Although never drunk, he was not always sober.[72] He could present a sorry figure. One French writer recalled the sight of him sitting alone outside a café late one evening as the waiters cleared up around him, and the rain poured down.[73]

Certainly he had his moments of depression, and even despair. But it was 'part of his pose to luxuriate a little in his tragic circumstances'. The cries of woe that dotted his letters and his conversation had a rhetorical flourish: 'I am going under,' he told Frank Harris: 'the morgue yawns for me.'[74] Douglas, who saw him often, considered that throughout his time in Paris Wilde was 'on the whole, fairly happy'. His buoyant temperament remained largely unimpaired; his sense of humour and 'unrivalled faculty for enjoyment of the present' continued to sustain him.[75] The young Augustus John recalled two weeks he spent in Paris that autumn (together with Conder and the Rothensteins) when he saw Wilde regularly. He was impressed that, for all he had endured, Wilde was so untouched by 'bitterness, resentment or remorse'.[76] Surrounded by attentive listeners, there was 'nothing lugubrious or sinister about him. He fancied himself a kind of Happy Prince, or, admitting a touch of vulgarity, the genial although permanently overdrawn millionaire'. Although he kept up an easy – and impressive – 'flow of practical wit and wisdom' there was nothing middle-aged about him. He had, instead, 'the frank, open, friendly, humorous face' of a young man; for – as John noted – 'he had too much sense to grow old'.[77]

Laurence Housman – also in Paris that autumn – left a vivid record of Wilde's talk, as he entertained the young disciples who gathered around his café table. He amused them with his conceits (that he had chosen a particular *boîte* because the decor complimented his complexion) and he fascinated them with his tales: of the 'Man who sold his Soul' only to find – to his great disappointment – that he could no longer sin; or of a hell in

---

*   Wilde liked a boiled egg for breakfast: 'An egg is always an adventure,' he declared; 'it may be different... there are a few things – like the Nocturnes of Chopin – which can repeat themselves with-out repetition.'

46. Lord Alfred Douglas at Oxford in 1891, around the time he first met Oscar.

47. Lord Alfred Douglas sitting on the lap of Maurice Schwabe. In 1930 Douglas recalled that the picture was 'taken in my second year at Oxford' [1890–1]... rather by way of being a joke, though really I forget what the idea was now.'

48. John Sholto Douglas, the intemperate 9th Marquess of Queensberry, and Oscar's nemesis.

49. Robbie Ross with Reggie Turner (*right*), the legally-trained friend, whom Oscar jokingly dubbed 'the boy-snatcher of Clement's Inn'.

50. (*Above*) A house party at the home of Mr and Mrs Walter Palmer, September 1892. *Front from left*: David Bispham, George Meredith, Jean 'Moonbeam' Palmer, H. B. Irving. *Back*: Mrs Jopling, Oscar Wilde, unknown, Marie Meredith, Johnston Forbes-Robertson, Walter Palmer.

51. (*Right*) One of Aubrey Beardsley's illustrations for *Salome*. Oscar appears at the front as the mage-like author. Although Beardsley was obliged to add a fig-leaf to the naked page, he left unaltered the phallic candlesticks and erection-distorted robe of the fetus-like attendant.

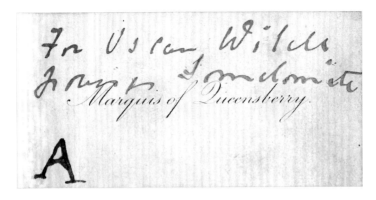

52. The offensive card left by Queensberry at the Albemarle Club. He claimed
that it read, 'For Oscar Wilde, posing as sodomite'. It became 'Exhibit A'
in Oscar's subsequent libel action against Queensberry.

53. Edward Carson, the barrister and
politician, as drawn by Spy, *Vanity
Fair*, 1893. He carried out his cross-
examination of Oscar with 'all the
added bitterness of an old friend'.

54. Sir Edward Clarke, from *Vanity
Fair*, 1903; Oscar's counsel in all
of his three trials.

THE
ILLUSTRATED
Police News
LAW COURTS AND WEEKLY RECORD
ESTABLISHED 1864.

No. 1627. [REGISTERED FOR CIRCULATION IN THE UNITED KINGDOM AND ABROAD.]   SATURDAY, APRIL 20, 1895.   Price One Penny.

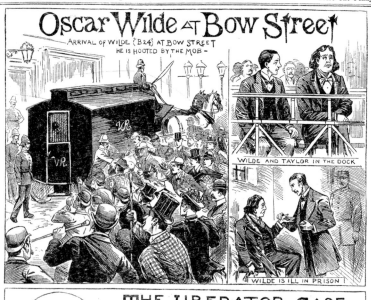

Oscar Wilde at Bow Street
ARRIVAL OF WILDE (B 24) AT BOW STREET
HE IS HOOTED BY THE MOB —

WILDE AND TAYLOR IN THE DOCK

WILDE IS ILL IN PRISON

THE LIBERATOR CASE
JABEZ AT LAST SAILS FOR ENGLAND

JABEZ SPENCER BALFOUR

— SAFE ON BOARD THE TARTAR PRINCE —

IMPROVED AND ENLARGED.

55. The reporting of Wilde's trials was lurid and sensational.

Alfred Taylor

Edward Shelley

Fred Atkins

Alfred Wood

Charles Parker

William Parker

56. Press drawings of Oscar's co-defendant Alfred Taylor,
and some of the witnesses brought against them.

57. Henry Bushnell, one of Oscar's 'pals' amongst the inmates at Reading Prison. Oscar arranged for the habitual thief to be sent £2 10s on his release.

58. Ernest Dowson, the 'persistently and perversely wonderful' poet, who saw much of Oscar during the early days of his exile.

59. Leonard Smithers, the ever generous but cash-strapped publisher who sought to resurrect Oscar's career after his release from prison.

60. Major Ferdinand Esterhazy, the real traitor in the Dreyfus Affair. Oscar professed to enjoy his company, claiming 'the guilty' were more interesting than 'the innocent'.

61. The modest Hôtel
D'Alsace in the rue des
Beaux Arts, Paris, where
Oscar lived, and died.

62. Oscar on his deathbed photographed by his friend Maurice Gilbert; clearly
visible is the wallpaper with which he declared he was 'fighting a duel to the death'.

which a poet, by the power of his verse, was able to convince his former muse that she was, in fact, in heaven.[78]

The wit and invention remained; only the ability to write any of it down was missing. It was almost two years since he had completed *The Ballad of Reading Gaol*, and he had composed nothing – neither a Symbolist drama nor a social comedy; neither a poem nor a parable. He had also turned down, or failed to honour, several lucrative journalistic commissions as either too vulgar or too tedious.[79] There had been practical setbacks. The notebook containing his draft of *La Sainte Courtisane* – which had been in the safekeeping of Ada Leverson, and which might have provided a ready-made template for a short Symbolist play – was brought over to Paris, and promptly mislaid in a cab (Wilde laughingly told Ross that he thought 'a cab was a very proper place for it').[80] But the real failure was one of will. The mainspring seemed broken. When Housman quizzed Wilde about his literary plans, he replied, 'I told you that I was going to write something: I tell everybody that. It is a thing one can repeat each day, meaning to do it the next. But in my heart – that chamber of leaden echoes – I know that I never shall. It is enough that the stories have been invented, that they actually exist: that I have been able, in my own mind, to give them the form which they demand.'[81]

He ascribed his continuing incapacity to the fact that, when he took up his pen, his past life sprang up too vividly before him, and 'made him miserable and upset his spirits'. Douglas, though, suspected that the real reason for his 'literary sterility' was that his great gift was as 'an interpreter of life', and that his bohemian existence in Paris was simply 'too narrow and too limited to stir him to creation'. It was not worth reflecting in the 'magic mirror' of his genius. He needed the stimulus of 'a gay season in London'. Indeed Wilde often told Douglas that what he missed most in his Parisian exile was 'the smart and pretty women' who in the old days had sat at his feet and listened to his words.[82]

Faced with his inability to produce new work, Wilde began to elaborate a philosophy of failure. He claimed that artists might be successful 'incidentally' but 'never intentionally':

If they are, they remain incomplete. The artist's mission is to live the complete life: success, as an episode (which is all it can be); failure, as the real, the final end. Death, analysed to its resultant atoms — what is it but the vindication of failure: the getting rid for ever of powers, desires, appetites, which have been a lifelong embarrassment? The poet's noblest

verse, the dramatist's greatest scene deal always with death; because the
higher function of the artist is to make perceived the beauty of failure.[83]

Such a theory might entertain a dinner table but it was poor company during
the long days and weeks of an often solitary existence. As winter drew on
and visitors became less frequent, Wilde's spirits sank. He was diagnosed
as suffering from 'neurasthenia', the catch-all medical term of the period,
designating nervous exhaustion and depression. He found himself 'quite
unable to get out of bed till the afternoon, quite unable to write letters of
any kind – beyond the occasional flirtatious missive to Louis Wilkinson'.
Even his begging letters to Smithers were 'reduced to postcards'.[84] Drink,
which seemed to offer a release, merely exacerbated the condition.[85]

Working on the 'Love is Law' script was entirely beyond him. He was
alarmed, though, to discover that the American-based producer Louis
Nethersole – brother of the actress Olga Nethersole – considered that he,
too, had bought the 'scenario of the play' and was anxious to see the script.[86]
Nethersole had acquired his 'stolen' copy of the plot outline from Sedger's
former partner, 'a scoundrel' called Arthur Eliot.[87] It was a fresh and unwel-
come difficulty. The stress did nothing to improve Wilde's health. At the
beginning of 1900 his neurasthenia was compounded by an uncomfortable
and mysterious skin rash that itched terribly and made him look 'like a
leopard'. Wilde considered that it was due to mussel poisoning.[88] In February,
as a further blow, he developed a serious infection that attacked 'the throat
and the soul'. And it seems to have been accompanied by 'a sort of blood-
poisoning' (current medical scholarship suggests that Wilde was suffering
with 'septicaemia from a streptococcal sore throat').[89] To recover from this
low ebb he was obliged to spend ten expensive days in a private hospital.[90]

His own condition, though, was put into perspective by the news from
London of Ernest Dowson's death (on 23 February), aged just 32. The poet
had been in Paris only that summer. Wilde asked Smithers to put some
flowers on the grave of the 'poor wounded wonderful fellow'.[91] Dowson
had been nursed during his final days in Catford by Sherard. And when
Sherard was next in Paris, he made a point of calling on Wilde to let him
know some of the details of the poet's end. Wilde, though still in his dressing
gown, received his old friend. He was saddened by Dowson's death but
confident that 'much of what he has written will remain'. To Sherard's
inquiry about the progress of his own 'work' – which lay in a litter upon
the table – he replied, 'One has to do something. I have no taste for it now.

It is a penance to me, but, as was said of torture, it always helps one to pass an hour or two.' He was cheered by Sherard's quick assertion (echoing his own verdict on Dowson) that, even if he never wrote another line, he had done enough to ensure 'immortality'.[92]

The new year had also carried off the Marquess of Queensberry, who died in London on 31 January, aged 55. On his deathbed he effected an improbable return to the Christian faith of his childhood, receiving 'conditional absolution' from his brother Archibald, a Catholic priest. There had been, though, no such rapprochement with either Bosie or Percy. Indeed the marquess had roused himself from his pillow to spit in Percy's face, when the heir to the title had appeared at his bedside. Nevertheless, neither son was cut out of the will. Even as a younger son Bosie inherited some £15,000 (£8,000 came to him immediately, the rest was to follow); Percy received considerably more.[93]

For Wilde this was excellent news. There was now a real chance that he would get the remaining money owing to him from the Douglas family, for the legal expenses he had incurred at the time of his ill-fated court case. Bosie and Percy came over to Paris briefly at the end of February. 'They are in deep mourning and the highest spirits,' Wilde reported. 'The English are like that.'[94] Bosie promptly paid Wilde £125, as his share of the 'debt of honour'(together with an additional £20). Percy, however, dragged his heels.[95]

Wilde, meanwhile, was increasing his resources in other ways. At the beginning of February he had agreed terms with Ada Rehan for 'a new and original comedy, in three or four acts' – a different play, it seems, from 'Love is Law'. He was to receive an advance of £100, with a further £200 due on delivery of the manuscript, on or before 1 July.[96] He had hopes that the playwright Maurice Donnay might adapt one of his plays for the French stage.[97] He was also in contact with Herbert Beerbohm Tree, hopeful of receiving some royalty payments for a touring production of *A Woman of No Importance* that had recently been mounted. Tree regretted that the play had only been given once, and that any monies would have to be sent to 'the Trustees in Bankruptcy'. He did, though, mention that George Alexander held some 'fees' that he would be 'glad to settle'.[98]

Having bought the performing rights to both *Lady Windermere's Fan* and *The Importance of Being Earnest* from the official receiver, Alexander offered to make some discretionary payments to Wilde. Both plays, though rarely performed in London, had become fixtures of the touring repertoire.[99] It

was a generous gesture, and one that Wilde readily appreciated. The unfortunate bicycling encounter outside Napoule was forgotten. Alexander also
pushed forward plans to produce cheap acting editions of the both plays,
to encourage amateur productions.[100] Nor were these Wilde's only ties to
the London theatrical world. Charles Wyndham continued to solicit work.
Wilde was flattered by his persistence, and though he turned aside a suggestion that he adapt Dumas's *La Dame de Monsoreau*, he did promise to
try and think of an alternative.[101] Thought, however, seems to have been
almost as difficult as serious application for the ailing Wilde.

Perhaps to spur his recuperation, Wilde accepted an invitation from
Harold Mellor to make an Italian tour of Sicily, Naples and Rome. Although
Mellor's company was less than stimulating, Wilde had lost none of his
power of enjoyment, and was able to draw great pleasure from the spring
sunshine, the dark eyes of young men and the wonders of art. 'Sicily was
beautiful', he told More Adey; the mosaic-covered Cappella Palatina at
Palermo was a 'marvel of marvels: when one was in it one felt as if one was
in a precious shrine, consecrated almost in a tabernacle'. Naples was 'evil
and luxurious'.[102] Among other diversions Wilde 'fell in love with a Sea-
God, who for some extraordinary reason [was] at the Regia Marina School
instead of being with Triton'.[103]

Rome, though, was 'the one city of the soul'.[104] They arrived there just
before Easter, recalling the visit of Wilde's student days. While Mellor
returned to Switzerland, Wilde immersed himself in the ceremonies and
pageantry of the Catholic Church. He was blessed by the pope, not once
but seven times.[105] One happy effect of the papal benediction was that he
was 'completely cured' of his 'mussel-poisoning'. The miracle he thought
deserved a 'votive' picture: 'The only difficulty,' he mused, 'is the treatment
of the mussels. They are not decorative, except the shells, and I didn't eat
the shells.'[106] Wilde was also amused at the sight of John Gray, who was
now studying for the priesthood in Rome: 'mockery dangled' in the air, as
the new seminarian passed by without speaking.[107]

The pleasures of the Roman holiday were increased by the fact that
Ross was also in the Eternal City, wintering with his mother. He and Wilde
spent much time together, picking up young men and looking at classical
statues. Despite the miraculous rash cure, Ross was struck by the 'great
change' for the worse that had come over his friend's general health in the
previous six months. Nevertheless he found Wilde 'in very good spirits'.
Amid the round of fun Wilde asked Ross to introduce him to a priest with

a view to being 'received into the Church'. Ross demurred. He was still not convinced that Wilde was serious – though, as he admitted, Wilde himself was never quite sure when he was serious either. His refusal allowed Wilde to joke that 'whenever he wanted to become a Catholic [Ross] stood at the door with a flaming sword' barring the way.[108]*

After Ross's departure Wilde idled on in Rome for a couple of weeks, diverting himself with his latest hobby. Having acquired a camera he took innumerable photographs 'with a most childlike enthusiasm'. He was particularly thrilled with a picture of some cows in the Borghese Gardens, telling Ross that 'cows are very fond of being photographed, and, unlike architecture, don't move'.[109]

---

* Adela Schuster thought that Wilde's 'one chance of redemption' – if he were unable to resume writing – would be to convert. 'He would make a splendid preacher,' she told More Adey. 'This is not meant flippantly,' she added, 'though I fear it may sound so.'

3

All Over

Jack Worthing: 'He seems to have expressed a desire to be buried in Paris.'
Miss Prism: 'I fear that hardly points to any very serious state of mind at the last.'

OSCAR WILDE

Wilde returned to Paris towards the end of May, breaking his journey north with a ten-day visit to Mellor at Gland. His stay was made memorable by the fact that Mellor had just acquired an 'automobile'. Wilde thought the new contraption 'delightful' – although, as he explained to Ross, 'of course, it broke down: they, like all machines, are more wilful than animals – nervous, irritable, strange things: I am going to write an article on "nerves in the inorganic world"'.[1]

He would have found good material for such a piece back in Paris. Nervous new machines were everywhere: diesel engines, moving-film projectors, escalators, a giant Ferris wheel, the 'telegraphone' sound recorder. The city was *en fête* for a vast Exposition Universelle to celebrate the achievements of the past century and look forward to the possibilities of next one. There was excitement in all this – the national pavilions, the bustling crowds, the curving art nouveau outlines of the Grand Palais and Petit Palais – but it provided, too, a reminder of how little Wilde himself had achieved over the past year. June had now arrived and he had written nothing.

The habitual optimism that allowed him to think that, perhaps, 'tomorrow' he might be able to begin, seems to have faltered. On 1 July he wrote to Ada Rehan's business manager regretting that he had been unable to write her comedy, and admitting there was no possibility of his doing so in the near future. He promised to repay the £100 advance, asking only a 'little time' to gather the money.[2]

Ross hoped that the newly wealthy Bosie might help with Wilde's financial position – perhaps by supplying him a regular income, or else by paying off his creditors and giving him the chance of earning money again from his existing copyrights; Douglas, however, declined.[3] He was ready to be generous to Wilde, but on his own terms, and at his own rate. Having come into money for the first time in his life, he was anxious to set about spending it – for the most part on racehorses, 'boys, brandy and betting'.[4] Wilde could look forward to occasional cheques and more frequent banknotes. But when, after one dinner, he suggested that he might warrant some more formal consideration, Bosie went into 'paroxysms of rage, followed by satirical laughter, and then said it was the most monstrous suggestion he had ever heard'.[5] When Wilde pressed his point, Douglas told him he was behaving like 'an old fat prostitute'.[6]

The meanness of Douglas's vision was thrown into relief by the generosity of George Alexander. The actor-manager came over to Paris with his wife that summer. Their meeting with Wilde was a happy one. Discussing the discretionary payments that Alexander wished to make, Wilde suggested that it would be a 'great boon' if – via Ross – he sent '£20 on the first of every month'. With the assurance of such regular money Wilde even held out the hope that, perhaps, some day, he might 'do something [Alexander] would like'.[7] The vain struggle to write continued. In an effort finally to get to grips with 'Love is Law' for Mrs Brown-Potter (who was growing understandably impatient), Wilde agreed to collaborate with Frank Harris on writing the piece. This arrangement at least offered a possibility of progress. Wilde was supposed to undertake only the first act. But even so he failed to make a start on the work.[8]

He had, since his return to Paris, abandoned himself to the distractions of the Exposition. It was as if, recalling the memories of his 1867 visit, he felt himself a boy again. He ignored his ailments. Nature had 'gathered all her glories together for him' and he was determined to enjoy the show. Ernest La Jeunesse reported how he loved it, drinking it 'in large measures, greedily, as one drinks blood on the battlefield. In every palace of it he

built again his own palace of fame, riches and immortality'.[9] He watched the wanton flamenco dancers in the Spanish pavilion, and drank at the Café d'Egypte, served by a 'slim brown Egyptian, rather like a handsome bamboo walking stick'.[10] Everything interested him.[11] Among the exotic imports, new inventions and old artworks he 'amused himself' – as Stuart Merrill noted – 'like a big child'.[12]

Wilde was greatly impressed by the dedicated Rodin pavilion, out beyond the Porte de L'Alma. Because of its location it was a rather under-visited exhibit, but as Rodin boasted to Jean Lorrain, 'I don't attract quantity but I do get quality' – and he cited the recent visits of Countess Potocka 'and the poet Oscar Wilde'.[13] Rodin showed Wilde 'anew all his great dreams in marble' and plaster – including 'The Gates of Hell'. And Wilde pronounced the sculptor 'by far the greatest poet in France'.[14]

It was a sociable time. Wilde went round the exhibits with the still adored and still promiscuous Maurice Gilbert (who was just then involved in a *ménage à trois* with a rose-like girl and her lightly moustachioed lover). He also saw much of Paul Fort: they attended wrestling matches together, following the fortunes of the impressively named 'Raoul le Boucher'.[15] The Exposition brought English visitors to Paris in their thousands. For Wilde there were a few uncomfortable encounters, and many disapproving glances. It may have been at this time that he and Edward Carson met, exchanging only a look.[16] There was an awkward moment, too, when he ran into the Rothensteins. They had not mentioned that they were in Paris, and they registered the pained look in Wilde's eyes as he deduced that they were perhaps planning to avoid him. The suspicion was correct: Will was still irritated that, on their previous visit, Wilde had led them to a restaurant, claiming that he liked the music there, only for it to become clear, during the dinner, that 'he was less interested in the music than in one of the players'. Will thought that Wilde looked ill and slightly 'down at heel', and – over the course of a dinner together – suspected that he was now depending on drink 'to sustain his wit'.[17] Other meetings were happier. Smithers and Vincent O'Sullivan came over. Harold Mellor paid a visit.[18] Wilde was spotted by Aimée Lowther and Ellen Terry staring into the window of a pastry shop; they invited him to dine with them and he 'sparkled just as of old'.[19] He also greeted his old friend Anna, comtesse de Brémont, and talked with her of past times, when they met on a bateau-mouche heading towards St Cloud.[20]

Wilde enjoyed such excursions as a relief from the summer heat of the city. He would go sometimes to Fontainebleau. It was there, sitting outside

a café, that he was spotted by Peters Chalmers Mitchell, the young zoologist who – years before – had advised him about the best way for Dorian Gray 'to get rid of a body'. They passed a stimulating couple of hours, talking of crimes and punishments, poetry and science. Mitchell was impressed by the breadth of Wilde's knowledge, and also his tact. Wilde turned down an invitation to dine that evening, suspecting that Mitchell's two rather conventional travelling companions would not approve.[21]

In August Douglas took a shoot, together with Percy, at Strathpeffer in the Scottish Highlands. Before departing, though, he gave Wilde a splendid dinner at the Grand Café. All resentments were set aside. Wilde was in the 'highest spirits', amused by Bosie's anxiety to reach Scotland in time for the 'Glorious Twelfth'. But at the end of the meal he became suddenly depressed. He told Douglas that he did not think he would live out the year. He had had 'a presentiment'. 'If another century began,' he remarked gravely, 'and I was still alive, it would really be more than the English could stand.' Douglas brushed this aside as characteristic exaggeration. He promised to send a cheque from Scotland and did so – for £15.[22]

The money allowed Wilde to visit Mellor again. Having struggled all year to free himself from the persistent sense of ill health and melancholia, Wilde was pleased to report that the 'Mellor cure' – though 'dull' – had been effective.[23] Back in Paris his spirits flared briefly. At the Calisaya one evening he ran through almost his whole repertoire of fables for Ernest La Jeunesse.[24] He even told Aimée Lowther that his story of 'The Poet' in hell would be appearing in a French magazine, although there is no sign that it ever did.[25]

His ever-deferred plans for writing 'Love is Law' were forestalled, when – towards the middle of September – Harris arrived in Paris with a completed script (retitled *Mr and Mrs Daventry*). Having grown tired of waiting for Wilde's version of the first act, he had written it himself. Wilde professed to be annoyed, but rapidly accepted the fait accompli. His suggested terms were that Harris buy the 'plot and scenario' for '£200 down', £500-worth of shares in Harris's hotel venture, and a quarter-share of Harris's profits from the play.[26] Harris accepted, anxious to get the play into production.

This should have been exciting news. But Wilde's pleasure in it was rather undercut by a recurrence of his chronic ear trouble. He had been suffering from increasingly painful headaches over the summer as part of his general malaise.[27] Now the problem asserted itself with a concerted force. On 24 September Wilde was examined by a new doctor, Maurice

A'Court Tucker, a thirty-two-year-old physician with a growing practice among the expatriate British colony.[28] Although a 'kind, excellent man' with a real admiration for Wilde's literary gifts, Tucker was – in Robbie Ross's estimate – also rather 'silly'.[29] His initial diagnosis seems not to have recognized the true nature of Wilde's condition.[30] And certainly whatever course of treatment he prescribed produced no ameliorating effect. The ear continued to suppurate. In the second week of October Tucker felt it necessary to call in 'a well-known' otologist for an expert opinion.[31]

The specialist was alarmed at his findings. The infection in Wilde's middle ear appeared to have extended into the surrounding mastoid (the hard honeycomb-like structure around the ear), and there was a danger that it might spread further. As Wilde reported, 'the surgeon felt it his duty to inform me that unless I was operated on immediately it would be too late, and that the consequence of delay would probably be fatal'. It seems probable that the procedure proposed was a radical mastoidectomy, to eradicate the diseased tissue and prevent any extension of the disease to the brain and its enveloping meninges.[32]

The operation was carried out under anaesthetic in Wilde's hotel room on 10 October. Wilde described the ordeal – which almost certainly involved the exteriorizing of the middle ear and the mastoid cavity – as 'most terrible'.[33] Part of the horror, though, was the expense. The surgeon initially presented a bill for 1,500 francs (£60), although this was eventually halved at the prompting of Dr Tucker. Nevertheless the surgery appeared to have been successful. And Wilde was well looked after; the extensive post-operative regime of dressings and pain relief involved the daily attendance of both 'a hospital male nurse' and Dr Tucker, as well as the nightly presence of another doctor. Wilde's chemist's bill was soon 'about £20'.[34] Wanting support and companionship, he telegraphed to Ross, begging him to come 'as soon as possible'.[35] He felt suddenly overwhelmed with cares.

Adding to the stress of the moment was the arrival in Paris of Louis Nethersole. Perhaps hearing news of Harris's planned play production, he 'intruded' himself 'almost daily' at the Hôtel d'Alsace in the days before Wilde's operation, insisting that he held the rights to the 'Love is Law' scenario.[36] Wilde, despite his debilitated state, managed to get Nethersole 'to see that he had no right to use or produce [the] scenario'. The victory, however, was only partial. Nethersole subsequently approached Frank Harris, claiming that he had the right to use the play script in New York.[37] Nor was this the only issue that Harris was having to face. From the outset

of their 'collaboration' Wilde had pointed out that Mrs Brown-Potter (with Kyrle Bellew) owned the rights to the scenario, and that Harris would have to come to some arrangement with them. Harris, having taken legal counsel, thought that he might get away without making any such deal, there being 'no copyright in a plot'.[38] But it seems that he found it hard to maintain this position, and he subsequently paid £125 to Bellew and Brown-Potter.[39] But even this was not all.

As the play went into production in early October, Harris was also approached by the recently bankrupted Leonard Smithers, who had still received nothing of the £160 that Wilde had promised to pay back to him. Ignoring Wilde's vigorous objections, Harris felt obliged to buy Smithers off too for a further £100.[40] These were large and unlooked-for expenses. And, having paid them, Harris was only able – or only willing – to send Wilde £25 rather than the £175 stipulated in their letter of agreement. Wilde, weak and vexed by doctors' bills, was incensed. From his sickbed he dispatched a long letter filled with self-justification and reiterated demands for his missing money.

He was seething upon the subject when Ross, having made haste, arrived in Paris on 17 October, the day after Wilde's forty-sixth birthday. Ross rather sympathized with Harris, pointing out that Wilde was now in 'a much better position' than he had been, because Harris, by producing the play, would not only pay off all the people who had advanced money to Wilde, but would be able to remit Wilde a share of any resulting royalties. To this Wilde replied in his 'characteristic way' that Harris had deprived him of his 'only source of income by taking a play on which I could always have raised £100'.[41] The humour was comforting. Indeed Ross had been heartened to find Wilde in remarkably 'good spirits'. As he reported to More Adey, 'though he assured me his sufferings were dreadful, at the same time he shouted with laughter and told many stories against the doctors and himself'. He was entertaining a steady succession of friends.[42]

Although the nurse who was in daily attendance was concerned that Dr Tucker did not fully realize the seriousness of Wilde's condition, the immediate signs of recovery were promising.[43] Wilde was cheered by the arrival of Reggie Turner; he and Ross called every day, sometimes twice. Often they lunched or dined together with Wilde in his room. Food was brought in from a neighbouring restaurant, and 'too much champagne' was invariable drunk. Wilde, though he looked ill, remained 'always very talkative' and full of fun. When his irritating skin rash returned, and Ross

arrived to find him scratching himself, Wilde remarked: 'Really, I'm more like a great ape than ever, but I hope you'll give me a lunch, Bobbie, and not a nut.'[44]

There was a particularly jolly gathering on 25 October when Ross's brother, Aleck, also called, along with Willie's widow and her new husband, Alexander Teixeira de Mattos.[45] Wilde, in sparkling form, repeated his line about the English not being able to stand it if he outlived the century. He also claimed that the French would not stand it either, as they held him personally 'responsible for the failure of the Exhibition', the English having deserted it 'when they saw him there so well-dressed and happy'. And, alluding to his mounting medical bills, or his taste for champagne, he remarked that he was 'dying above his means'.[46]

The witticism obscured Wilde's real anxiety about his debts, the large amounts that he owed – to his doctors, to Ada Rehan, to Dal Young, and, especially, to Dupoirier, the ever-patient and ever-generous patron of the Hôtel d'Alsace. Wilde calculated the total at 'something over more than £400' – of which almost a quarter was his hotel bill. So often insouciant on the subject, he was now suffering 'remorse about some of his creditors'.[47] Indeed Dr Tucker thought anxiety on the score of his hotel bill might be impeding Wilde's recovery. Ross and Turner, with very limited resources of their own, were unable to offer assistance. Ross, though, wrote to Douglas alerting him to Wilde's condition, and emphasizing the concern that he felt over his debts.[48]* Harris's failure to send the outstanding £150 continued to rankle. It became an *idée fixe*. Wilde, though he wrote nothing else, produced a weekly letter of prolix recrimination, always ending with a plea for Harris to send the money 'that you owe'.[49]†

Despite the promptings of Dr Tucker, Wilde had been reluctant to rise from his bed since the operation. On 29 October, however, he not only got up but actually proposed going out. Ross took him for an evening stroll to a nearby café. Although Wilde walked with 'some difficulty' he seemed 'fairly

---

*   Unknown to Ross (and Wilde), Douglas had, only two weeks before, made a brief, clandestine visit to Paris, in pursuit of a young rent boy with whom he was infatuated. The visit ended badly, with Douglas being attacked and robbed by the youth's two protectors.

†   It is not recorded whether Wilde was encouraged or irritated by news that the play had opened at the Royalty Theatre on 25 October to an enthusiastic reception. The play's cleverness was widely acknowledged, along with its daring. Although some in the audience were aware that the piece derived from an idea by Wilde, no mention of this connection was made in the press.

well'. Ignoring the doctor's command to avoid strong liquor, he 'insisted on drinking absinthe'.[50] Perhaps unsurprisingly he was confined to bed the following day. But only the day after that, wanting to enjoy the autumn sunshine, he felt up to going for a drive in the Bois du Boulogne.[51] The expedition, made with Ross, was punctuated by several café stops, during which Wilde again ordered absinthe. When Ross remonstrated with him, he replied gravely, 'And what have I to live for, Robbie?'[52]

'Death' was joining 'Frank Harris' as one of Wilde's recurrent topics. He dreamed one night that he had been 'supping with the dead'. On hearing this, Turner – much to Wilde's delight – commented, 'My dear Oscar, you were probably the life and soul of the party.'[53] When Ross returned from an expedition to the Père Lachaise cemetery, Wilde asked whether he had selected a place for his tomb, and then began discussing – 'in a perfectly light-hearted way' – what his epitaph should be.[54] He hoped that Ross might be buried nearby: and 'When the last trumpet sounds and we are couched in our porphyry tombs, I will turn and say, "Robbie, Robbie, let us pretend we do not hear!"'[55]

More orthodox ideas flitted, too, across his mind. To a journalist from the *Daily Chronicle* who tracked him to his sickroom, Wilde (having unburdened himself about the perfidy of Frank Harris) discoursed on the consolations of religion. 'Much of my moral obliquity,' he declared, 'is due to the fact that my father would not allow me to become a Catholic. There is an artistic side to the church, and the fragrance of its teaching would have curbed my degeneracies. I intend to be received into it before long.'[56] Ross remained unconvinced, though he promised to fetch a priest if Wilde were really dying.[57] That moment, however, seemed not yet to have arrived.

Although Wilde himself might proclaim that he was advancing rapidly towards his end, there was – as ever – much self-dramatization in the pose. There were times when he very probably did feel that he had 'only a short time to live'.[58] But at other moments he began to make schemes for the future.[59] Dr Tucker remained optimistic. It was his belief that even if Wilde did not 'pull himself up' – and renounce drink altogether – he would still live for at least another 'five years'.[60]

Heartened by this prognosis, Ross continued with his own plans to meet up with his mother in Nice for the winter. Wilde, similarly encouraged, hoped to follow them south in due course. But in the second week of November – a few days before Ross was due to leave – the pain in Wilde's ear increased sharply. There had been a relapse of the infection. When Ross called, on the

eve of his departure, he found Wilde slurring his words, although whether
this was due to his illness, to the injections of morphine, or to the intake of
champagne, was uncertain.[61] They had a distressing interview. Wilde sent
Turner and the attending nurse out of the room, and begged Ross to remain
in Paris; 'a great change', he insisted, had come over him in 'the last few
days'. Breaking down in tears, he said that he feared he would never see Ross
again. Ross, however, considered all this as no more than histrionics. He
refused to be moved. And, indeed, Wilde presently retrieved his equilibrium.
They talked of other things. His parting shot was that Ross should 'look out
for some little cup in the hills near Nice' where he could go when he was
'better' – and 'where you can come and see me often'.[62]

In Ross's absence Turner took on the duties of care, aided by a succession
of nurses, by Dupoirier, and occasionally by Maurice Gilbert. Dr Tucker
attended daily. Wilde was moved from his ground-floor room by the courtyard to room 13 on the first floor.[63] He was a reluctant patient – often 'very
difficult and rude'. He refused to let the nurse put mustard plasters on his
legs.[64] But the regular morphine injections – often administered by Dupoirier
– assuaged the pain, and he was able to get up occasionally. Turner even
took him out for several drives.[65]

Friends continued to call; poets from the *quartier* and the Calisaya. There
were bouts of talk and laughter. It was to the writer Claire de Pratz that
Wilde remarked, 'My wallpaper and I are fighting a duel to the death. One
of us has to go.'[66] Plans for travelling to the South of France remained a
constant topic. But Wilde now grew easily tired. He slept more and more.[67]
When the exiled Romanian poet Hélène Vacaresco called, she found him
lying in bed, his face to the wall. Leaving a bottle of champagne and some
other 'comforts' on the table, she slipped away. 'Merci, inconnue,' Wilde
murmured without turning.[68]

A fragile equilibrium was maintained for over a week. But on the night
of 24 November Wilde's condition deteriorated. He became 'suddenly light
headed' and delirious. He was unable to rise from his bed the following day.
Tucker, alarmed at the turn of events, sought a second opinion from the
'brain specialist' Dr Paul Claisse. It was clear that the suppurating middle-
ear infection was now affecting Wilde's brain. This was the dreaded development. There was now very little hope of recovery. Turner wrote at once to
Ross informing him of Wilde's parlous state.[69]

On 27 November Tucker and Claisse, noting a worsening of the symptoms,
issued a joint medical certificate. The diagnosis of 'meningoencephalitis'

could be made without doubt. With both his brain and the surrounding meninges inflamed, no surgical intervention was possible. The patient's condition could only be alleviated by drugs and other palliative treatments.[70]

Wilde drifted in and out of sleep. Ice packs were held to his head to ease the pressure.[71] Often delirious, he seemed to be talking 'nonsense the *whole* while in English and French'. But there were abrupt flashes of lucidity. He announced that Turner ought to have been a doctor because he 'always wanted people to do what they didn't want' (this was after Turner had begged him not to smoke).[72] On another occasion, after Turner had been holding an ice bag to his head for three-quarters of an hour, Wilde remarked, 'You dear little Jew, don't you think that's enough?'[73] He had previously observed, 'Jews have no broad philosophy of life, but they are *sympathique*.'[74] Words sometimes eluded him. He asked for a 'paraphine' – when he wanted to see a copy of the *Patrie*,[75] and requested that Turner get a 'Munster to cook for him?' – adding 'one steamboat [is] very like another'. The chain of association may have been drawing him back Ireland and his youth: the SS *Munster* was one of the packet boats that ran from Kingstown to Holyhead.[76]

On the morning of Thursday 29 November Ross arrived back in Paris. After receiving Turner's letter he had set off at once, taking the overnight train. He was distressed to find Wilde lying gaunt and thin, his flesh livid, his breathing heavy. The hair on his head had been partially shaved so that leeches might be applied. Though he seemed conscious of Ross's presence he was unable to speak. Tucker and Claisse were in attendance. They confirmed that Wilde could not live for more than two days. Recalling his promise, Ross asked if he should fetch a priest. Wilde raised his hand in mute acquiescence.[77]

Ross returned at about four in the afternoon with Fr Cuthbert Dunne, a young Passionist priest attached to St Joseph's Church on the avenue Hoche (close to the Arc de Triomphe). On their arrival Wilde, drifting into consciousness, tried to speak, but was unable to articulate a word. Nevertheless when Fr Dunne explained that he had come to receive Wilde into the Catholic Church and administer the sacrament of the sick, Wilde's 'signs' and 'attempted words' were sufficient to convince the priest that he gave his consent. Wilde was duly baptized, Fr Dunne ignoring two leeches attached above the candidate's forehead. Leaning close, the priest spoke into Wilde's good ear 'the Acts of Faith, Hope, Charity and Contrition' together with 'the words to express resignation to the Divine Will'. And Wilde – it seemed – attempted to repeat the phrases.[78]

Having assisted in this performance, Ross went off to send telegrams to Douglas and Frank Harris, letting them know that Wilde was dying. He also wired the solicitor Holman, in order that he might inform Adrian Hope, the guardian of Wilde's children. Dr Tucker called again in the evening. He thought the patient could linger on 'for a few days'.

Throughout that night a vigil was maintained at the bedside. A dedicated *garde-malade* was requisitioned, as the regular nurse was worn out. Ross and Turner slept at the hotel in a room on the floor above. 'We were called twice by the nurse, who thought Oscar was actually dying,' Ross reported to More Adey:

> About 5.30 in the morning a complete change came over him, the lines of the face altered, and I believe what is called the death rattle began, but I had never heard anything like it before. It sounded like the horrible turning of a crank, and it never ceased until the end. His eyes did not respond to the light test any longer. Foam and blood came from his mouth, and had to be wiped away by someone standing by him all the time.[79]

At some moment during the morning Fr Dunne, summoned by telegram, returned and administered the sacrament of extreme unction.[80] At noon Ross and Turner went out briefly, in turn, to find some lunch. By one o'clock they were both back at the bedside. The strange noise from Wilde's throat became louder and louder. Dupoirier came in to relieve the two nurses who were also in attendance. At quarter to two Wilde's breathing altered. Ross went to the bedside and held his hand. Wilde heaved a deep sigh, and his limbs seemed to stretch involuntarily. The breathing became fainter. He died at ten minutes to two exactly.[81]

After the days of 'awful struggle', Ross and Turner felt a surge of relief at seeing their friend 'quiet' at last.[82] But beyond the immediate concerns of physical suffering, there was also sense that an intractable problem had been solved. During the course of the previous three years it had become harder and harder to see how Wilde's life might develop in happy and productive ways. And although there was, of course, much to regret in the loss of so great and rare a spirit, it did seem as though in this case 'the terrible commonplace' really were true: 'It was for the best.'[83]

Wilde's passing drew no great outpouring of interest and attention from either the public or the press. The funeral, on the morning of 3 November,

was a modest affair. Some fifty people gathered in the chapel behind the high altar at St-Germain-des-Prés for the simple service: a handful of minor French writers, the staff from the Hôtel d'Alsace, a few journalists, and fewer old friends. Ross and Turner followed the coffin, together with Maurice Gilbert. Douglas was there, as 'chief mourner', having arrived from England the previous day, but Frank Harris – ill in bed – had been unable to travel.

There were perfunctory notices in the French and English papers. Ross thought that, on the whole, silence was preferable to cheap moralizing.[84] And there was some of that. Prevailing notions of 'poetic justice' demanded that Wilde's last years should have been unhappy.[85] The obituary in *The Times* closed its brief outline of Wilde's career with the observation that death had brought an end to 'what must have been a life of wretchedness and unavailing regret'.[86] *The Sunday Times* claimed that 'the dregs of sympathy' left for Wilde at the time of his release 'were flung away by his conduct and pernicious surroundings in his latter days'. The notice ended: 'No sadder record of a life wilfully blighted can be found... The only epitaph for the unfortunate man is, "Oh, the pity of it!".'[87]

Ross was confident that 'later on' people would come to recognize Wilde's real achievements, and that his works would last, but the few immediate verdicts on his literary output (rather than his person) suggested that the wait might be a long one. The *Pall Mall Gazette* claimed that, for all his 'wonderful cleverness' he had 'no substantiality': his plays, though filled with 'bright moments' of wit, lacked 'constructive capacity' as drama. Even *The Ballad of Reading Gaol* could be dismissed as no more than 'an adroit pastiche'. And while he might perhaps have been a useful 'corrective to British stolidity' during the days of his Aesthetic 'absurdities', 'nothing he ever wrote had strength to endure'. According to their considered estimate, Wilde's most abiding contribution to the cultural record would remain his 'disappointment' with the Atlantic Ocean.[88]

L'Envoi

Robert Ross's hope that, in time, Wilde's literary reputation would revive might have seemed fanciful in the winter of 1900. But some measure of redemption was actually achieved with surprising speed.

The popular notion that Wilde's plays remained unperformed in Britain for a generation is not borne out by the facts. As Michael Seeney has shown in his theatrical history, *From Bow Street to the Ritz*, Wilde's comedies continued to be played successfully – albeit on the provincial touring circuit – throughout the decade following his fall. The pleasure that they gave could not be denied.

Ross, as Wilde's recognized literary executor, diligently nurtured the few copyrights that still belonged to the estate. Of these the most immediately profitable was *Salomé*. Although the play remained banned in Britain, it found an audience in Europe, and particularly in Germany. A celebrated production by Max Reinhardt in Berlin in 1902 was witnessed by Richard Strauss, and inspired him to treat the story operatically. Foreign recognition brought enhanced status at home. Strauss's opera *Salome* was premiered

– triumphantly – in Dresden in 1905, and was one of the elements that encouraged the British censor to reconsider his ban on the play (it was lifted in 1907).

As part of a project to establish a definitive edition of Wilde's various works, Ross brought out in 1905 a much-edited version of Wilde's great prison letter. It was entitled *De Profundis*. Shorn of all the bitter personal recrimination (and indeed of all reference to Douglas) it offered a philosophical meditation on punishment and repentance. The book proved hugely, and perhaps unexpectedly, popular. By presenting a vision of chastened suffering it served to redeem Wilde in the eyes of the public. He had paid for his sins.

By the beginning of 1906 Ross could celebrate releasing Wilde's estate from bankruptcy. In 1909 Wilde's body was moved from the suburban obscurity of Bagneux to Père Lachaise – where, in due course, a splendid funerary monument, designed by Jacob Epstein, was erected over it.

The growing appreciation of Wilde's work was matched by a growing interest in his life. In 'The Critic as Artist' Wilde had written, 'Every great man nowadays has his disciples, and it is always Judas who writes the biography.' It would perhaps be harsh to cast the well-meaning Sherard as the Judas among Wilde's many disciples; he was, though, the first to hasten into print, producing *Oscar Wilde: The Story of an Unhappy Friendship* (1902) and then *The Life of Oscar Wilde* (1906); the following year saw the publication of *Oscar Wilde*, an opportunist scissors-and-paste job by 'Leonard Creswell Ingleby', one of the pseudonyms of Leonard Smithers' former crony Ranger Gull. Although none of the books was worthy of its subject, they began to fix the compelling story of Wilde's heady rise and tragic fall. They began, too, to fix the vision of Wilde as the archetypal homosexual man – flamboyant, witty, defiant and tinged with effeminacy. It was an arresting combination.

When Christopher Millard (under the name 'Stuart Mason') produced his magisterial *Bibliography* of Wilde's work in 1912, Ross could write in the introduction that its appearance confirmed the truth of his prophecy that Wilde's writings would come to 'excite wider interest than those of almost any of his contemporaries. Indeed, with the possible exception of Dickens and Byron,' he added, 'I doubt if any British author of the nineteenth century is better known over a more extensive geographical area.'

The gathering momentum had been complicated though, when, two years previously, under Ross's guidance, the young Arthur Ransome

produced *Oscar Wilde: A Critical Study*. Although largely concerned with Wilde's work, the biographical portion of the book (composed with information gleaned from Ross and the unpublished part of *De Profundis*) contained veiled references to Wilde's animus against Douglas for the role he had played in his downfall and its aftermath. Douglas – who by then had married, converted to Roman Catholicism and developed an abhorrence of his homosexual past – launched a libel action against Ransome and the publishers. Having destroyed, unread, the copy of the *De Profundis* letter that had been sent to him in 1897, he was unaware of the source of Ransome's comments. He had to endure the ignominy of listening to the whole text of Wilde's letter (preserved and produced by Ross) being read aloud in court, with all its denunciations of his meanness and want of talent. The experience was shattering.

Springing to his own defence he dashed off (with the assistance of his combative associate, T. W. H. Crosland) *Oscar Wilde and Myself*, a withering and unbalanced account of Wilde as a talentless and corrupt charlatan. It was the beginning of long campaign against the memory of Wilde. In another court appearance Douglas would describe him as the 'greatest force for evil that has appeared in Europe in the last three hundred and fifty years'. And although Douglas did eventually relent, and come to a more balanced view of his relationship with Wilde, it was his threats of further legal action that prevented the publication in Britain of Frank Harris's 1916 biography of Oscar Wilde. That book, for all its moments of invention, presented a vivid portrait. It became a bestseller in America, where interest in Wilde had grown at an almost faster rate than in Europe. Although Harris's book remained unpublished in Britain until 1938, its suppression did little to dent Wilde's ever-growing prestige.

In 1927 the art critic Roger Fry could write to his friend Helen Anrep that he was 'rather staggered and ashamed' – on re-reading Wilde's essays – 'to see how little I did him justice'. Although Fry recognized that Wilde was 'an exhibitionist', he still managed to come 'infinitely nearer to some kind of truth than all the noble rhetoricians, the Carlyles, Ruskins, etc, of the day. He has a way of being right, which is astonishing at that time, or any for that matter.'

The verdict has been echoed in different forms and cadences down the years since then. It has adapted to different circumstances and adopted different emphases. Wilde's shimmering wit creates an open-ended discourse that encourages all heresies. And, in his posthumous existence, he has

assumed quite as many masks as he did during his own life, and with the same élan. He has appeared as the counter-cultural rebel, the gay martyr, the victim of British colonial oppression, the proto-modernist, the proto-postmodernist, the precursor of 'Cool'. And the list will continue. Wilde retains all his fabled ability to communicate. And he still has 'a way of being right' which is both 'astonishing' and delightful.

Abbreviations used
in the Notes

People

CMW	Constance Mary Wilde, née Lloyd, later Holland
ES	Edward Sullivan
JFW	Jane F. (Lady) Wilde, née Elgee, aka 'Speranza'
JMW	James McNeill Whistler
LAD	Lord Alfred Douglas
LVK	Lotten von Kraemer
MQ	Marquess of Queensberry
OW	Oscar Wilde
RR	Robert Ross
WCKW	Willie Wilde
WRWW	Sir William Robert Wills Wilde

Works by Oscar Wilde

AIH	*An Ideal Husband*
BRG	*The Ballad of Reading Gaol*
LWF	*Lady Windermere's Fan*
IBE	*The Importance of Being Earnest*
PDG	*The Picture of Dorian Gray*
WNI	*A Woman of No Importance*

The Oxford English Text series,
comprising the complete works of Oscar Wilde

OET I	*Poems*, eds Bobby Fong and Karl Beckson (2001)
OET II	*De Profundis*, ed. Ian Small (2005)
OET III	*The Picture of Dorian Gray*, ed. Joseph Bristow (2005)
OET IV	*Criticism*, ed. Josephine M. Guy (2007)
OET V	*Plays I*, ed. Joseph Donohue (2013)
OET VI	*Journalism I*, eds John Stokes and Mark Turner (2013)
OET VII	*Journalism II*, eds John Stokes and Mark Turner (2013)

Libraries and institutions

Austin	Harry Ransom Center, University of Texas at Austin
Berg	The Berg Collection, New York Public Library
BL	British Library
Clark	William Andrews Clark Memorial Library, UCLA, Los Angeles
GUL	Glasgow University Library
Fales	Fales Library, New York University
Houghton	Houghton Library, Harvard
TCD	Trinity College Dublin
Yale	Beinecke Library, Yale

Other works

Blackwood's	[Macmillan, George A.] 'A Ride Across the Peloponnese', *Blackwood's Magazine*, 123, no. 751, May 1878
Beckson	Karl Beckson, ed., *Oscar Wilde: The Critical Heritage* (1970)
CL	Hart-Davis, Rupert and Merlin Holland, eds, *Complete Letters of Oscar Wilde* (2000)
Coakley	Coakley, Davis, *Oscar Wilde: The Importance of Being Irish* (1994)
Croft-Cooke	Croft-Cooke, Rupert, *The Unrecorded Life of Oscar Wilde* (1972)
Dibb	Dibb, Geoff, *Oscar Wilde: A Vagabond with a Mission* (2013)

DNB   *Oxford Dictionary of National Biography* (2004)

Dulau   A. Dulau & Co., *A Collection of Original Manuscripts, Letters and Books of Oscar Wilde* (1929)

Ellmann   Ellmann, Richard, *Oscar Wilde* (1987)

Friedman   Friedman, David M., *Wilde in America* (2014)

Guy & Small   Guy, Josephine M. and Ian Small, *Oscar Wilde's Profession: Writing and the Culture Industry in the Late Nineteenth Century* (2000)

Harris   Harris, Frank, *Oscar Wilde, His Life and Confessions* (1916)

Hofer & Scharnhorst   Hofer, Matthew and Gary Scharnhorst, eds, *Oscar Wilde in America: The Interviews* (2010)

Holland   Holland, Merlin, *Irish Peacock, Scarlet Marquess* (2003)

Hunter-Blair   Hunter-Blair, Sir David, 'Oscar Wilde As I knew Him', In *Victorian Days and Other Papers* (1939), 115–43

Hyde, *Aftermath*   Hyde, H. Montgomery, *Oscar Wilde: The Aftermath* (1963)

Hyde, *LAD*   Hyde, H. Montgomery, *Lord Alfred Douglas: A Biography* (1984)

Hyde, *Oscar*   Hyde, H. Montgomery, *Oscar Wilde: A Biography* (1974)

Hyde, *Trials*   Hyde, H. Montgomery, *The Trials of Oscar Wilde* (1948)

Lewis & Smith   Lewis, Lloyd and Henry J. Smith, *Oscar Wilde Discovers America* (1936)

Maguire   Maguire, J. Robert, *Ceremonies of Bravery: Oscar Wilde, Carlos Blacker, and the Dreyfus Affair* (2013)

Mason   Mason, Stuart, *Bibliography of Oscar Wilde* (1914)

McKenna   McKenna, Neil, *The Secret Life of Oscar Wilde* (2003)

Melville   Melville, Joy, *Mother of Oscar: The Life of Jane Francesca Wilde* (1994)

Mikhail   Mikhail, E. H., ed. *Oscar Wilde: Interviews and Recollections* (1979)

Morse   Morse, W. F., 'American Lectures', in *The Works of Oscar Wilde* (1907)

Moyle   Moyle, Franny, *Constance: The Tragic and Scandalous Life of Mrs Oscar Wilde* (2011)

NYT   *New York Times*

O'Sullivan	O'Sullivan, Vincent, *Aspects of Wilde* (1936)
OWIA	Oscar Wilde in America website, www.oscarwildein-america.org
Pearson	Pearson, Hesketh, *The Life of Oscar Wilde* (1946)
PMB	*Pall Mall Budget*
PMG	*Pall Mall Gazette*
Raffalovich/Michaelson	'Alexander Michaelson' [André Raffalovich], 'Oscar Wilde', *Blackfriars* VII, no. 92 (1927), reprinted in Sewell, Brocard, *Footnote to the Nineties* (1968)
Ransome	Ransome, Arthur, *Oscar Wilde: A Critical Study* (1912)
Ricketts	Raymond, Paul and Charles Ricketts, *Recollections of Oscar Wilde* (1932)
Robins	Robins, Ashley H., *Oscar Wilde: The Great Drama of His Life* (2011)
Schroeder	Schroeder, Horst, *Additions and Corrections to Richard Ellmann's* Oscar Wilde (2002)
Sherard, *Life*	Sherard, Robert H., *The Life of Oscar Wilde* (1907)
Sherard, *Real*	Sherard, Robert H., *The Real Oscar Wilde* (1916)
Sherard, *SUF*	Sherard, Robert H., *Oscar Wilde, The Story of an Unhappy Friendship* (1902)
Smith & Helfand	Smith, Philip E. and Michael S. Helfand, eds, *Oscar Wilde's Oxford Notebooks* (1989)
Tipper, *Hilson*	Tipper, Karen Sasha Anthony, ed., *Lady Jane Wilde's Letters to Mr John Hilson, 1847–1876* (2010)
Tipper, *Kraemer*	Tipper, Karen Sasha Anthony, ed., *Lady Jane Wilde's Letters to Froken Lotten von Kraemer, 1857–1885* (2014)
Tipper, *Oscar*	Tipper, Karen Sasha Anthony, ed., *Lady Jane Wilde's Letters to Oscar Wilde* (2011)
White	White, Heather, *Forgotten Schooldays: Oscar Wilde at Portora* (2002)
Wright	Wright, Thomas, *Oscar's Books* (2008)
WW	*Woman's World* magazine

Other works

| ts | Typescript |

Endnotes

Proem

1   *The Times*, 19 December 1864, 6.

2   *Saunders's News-Letter*, 29 April 1864, quoted in Melville, 96–7.

3   *Belfast News-Letter*, 19 December 1864; Miss Travers, it was said, had refused the offer of £1,000 from the Wildes to settle the case before it came to court, and had also declared her intention not to accept for her own benefit any damages that might be given to her.

4   'Extraordinary "High Life" Revelations in Ireland', *Caledonian Mercury* (Edinburgh), 15 December 1864.

5   *The Sunday Times*, 25 December 1864, 2: 'Notes of the Week'.

6   *The Times*, 19 December 1864, 6.

7   *Belfast News-Letter*, 19 December 1864. The costs have been conventionally cited as £2,000. Horace Wyndham, *Speranza: A Biography of Lady Wilde* (1951), 97; Terence de Vere White, *The Parents of Oscar Wilde* (1967), 200; Melville, 102; Ellmann, 14; Coakley, 91. The only source for this figure, however, seems to be Harris, 12, where he claims Sir William had to pay 'a couple of thousands of pounds in costs'. And the figure should perhaps be treated with caution. £2,000, it should also be noted, was the amount that Mary Travers had claimed as damages.

8   *The Times*, 20 December 1864, 6.

Part I: *The Star Child*
Chapter 1: A Small Unruly Boy

1   Robert Perceval Graves, *Life of Sir William Rowan Hamilton*, vol. III (Dublin, 1889), 497.

2   The station, the terminus of the Dublin & Kingstown commuter line, was renamed the Pearse Station in 1966; St Mark's church is in Pearse Street. OW was christened on 26 April 1855 at the Church of St Mark, Dublin. On the certificate his names are given as 'Oscar Fingal O'Flahertie'. 'Wills' was an informal addition. The service was performed by WRWW's older brother, Ralph. There is a copy of the certificate at Clark.

3   Gerard Hanberry, 'Discovering Oscar Wilde in the Heart of Galway', *Wildean*, 44 (2014), 99.

4   Lotten von Kraemer diary, quoted in Elisabeth Mansén, 'A Splendid New Pic-

ture of Jan Francesca Wilde?', *Wildean*, 40 (2012), 113.

5   Melville, 71.

6   J. S. Blackie even described WRWW as 'tall'; *The Letters of John Stuart Blackie to his Wife*, ed. Archibald Stodart Walker (1909), 227–9; Melville, 70.

7   Melville, 54; Sir William Rowan Hamilton, letter quoted in *DNB*.

8   Gerard Hanberry, 'Discovering Oscar Wilde in the Heart of Galway', *Wildean*, 44 (2014); WRWW's mother's name is also sometimes given as 'Amalia Fynne', or 'Emily Fynn' (as on the family gravestone at Mt Jerome).

9   WRWW, 'Address to the Anthropological Section of the British Association, Belfast, 1874' in Lady Wilde, ed., *Legends, Charms and Superstitions of Ireland* (1919), 346.

10 Iain Ross, *Oscar Wilde and Ancient Greece* (2013), 9–18.

11 T. G. Wilson, *Victorian Doctor: Being the Life of Sir William Wilde* (1942), 78; Terence de Vere White, *The Parents of Oscar Wilde* (1967), 65.

12 He had been initiated in 1838 while still a student; on his return to Dublin he served a term as master of the lodge.

13 M. Hone, ed. *Jack Butler Yeats Letters: Letters to his Son, W. B. Yeats and Others* (1944), 277.

14 Ransome, 22; G. B. Shaw to Frank Harris, as quoted in Stanley Weintraub, ed. *The Playwright and the Pirate* (1986).

15 Melville, 26.

16 Melville, 271–3.

17 JFW to [John Hilson], 13 December 1847.

18 JFW to [John Hilson], December 1850, Tipper, *Hilson*, 46.

19 Melville, 37–9.

20 Ellmann, 13.

21 J. B. Yeats to W. B. Yeats, May 1921;

William M. Murphy, *Prodigal Father: The Life of John Butler Yeats (1839–1922)* (1978), 551 n.75.

22 Lotten von Kraemer diary, quoted in Elisabeth Mansén, 'A Splendid New Picture', 113.

23 JFW to [John Hilson], 1852, Tipper, *Hilson*, 56–7.

24 *DNB*.

25 JFW to John Hilson, 1852.

26 JFW to John Hilson, 17 June 1855.

27 Melville, 70.

28 Barbara Belford, *Oscar Wilde, A Certain Genius* (2000), 3.

29 It has been suggested that this outfit was, in some way, the guise of an Ossianic hero. See Owen Dudley Edwards, 'Impressions of an Irish Sphinx', in *Wilde the Irishman*, ed. J. McCormack (1998), 50.

30 Elisabeth Mansén, 'A Splendid New Picture', 112–25, provides the best and fullest account of LVK's various descriptions of the Wildes.

31 JFW to LVK, 17 February 1858, in Tipper, *Kramer*, 13.

32 JW to [John Hilson], 18 May 1858, in Tipper, *Hilson*, 69.

33 Karen Sasha Anthony Tipper, *A Critical Biography of Lady Jane Wilde* (2002), 360.

34 Wright, 31.

35 Melville, 70; Mansén, 'A Splendid New Picture', 114.

36 JFW to John Hilson, 18 May 1858, in Tipper, *Hilson*, 69.

37 Melville 71–9; they were there in 1858, 1859 and 1861.

38 JFW to LVK, 1860, in Tipper, *Kraemer*, 21.

39 Tipper, *Kraemer*, 35, 37.

40 Oblates of Mary Immaculate, *Register of Personnel 1862–1863*.

41 Melville, 80–1; JFW began work on *Eritis Sicut Deus* in 1860 according to Tipper, *Kraemer*, 25.

42 *CL*, 25.

43 Coakley, 112–13.
44 Rev. Lawrence Charles Prideaux Fox,
    'People I Have Met', *Donahoe's Maga-
    zine*; April 1905, quoted in Mason, 118.
    Fr Fox says he baptized 'two of [Mrs
    Wilde's] children'; he mentions Oscar
    by name and I have assumed that the
    other must be Willie; Isola would have
    been too young.
45 Mason, 118. The date of the supposed
    incident is unknown. Mason suggests
    1862 or 1863, but by this time the Wil-
    des had acquired their holiday home
    in Bray, just a couple of miles east of
    Enniskerry, so it seems likely to have
    been earlier. Their one securely recor-
    ded visit to Enniskerry was in 1858,
    the year the reformatory opened, but
    Fr Fox suggests that they took lodgings
    in a farmhouse at Enniskerry several
    years in succession. Fr Fox did not be-
    come the superior and manager at the
    reformatory until 1867, though he was
    serving in Dublin, at Inchicore, from
    1854, and could perhaps have been
    a visiting priest during the holidays.
    After that summer he never met any of
    the family again; this was probably be-
    cause the Wildes subsequently spent
    their time at Bray. Fr Fox remained
    at Glencree until 1874. OW had later
    contact with Glencree Reformatory;
    see *CL*, 53. Intriguingly the inventory

of William Wilde's library (when it
was sold in 1879) lists, among various
works of religious history, Item 816:
Rev. Patrick Power's *Catechism* (2nd
ed., 1864), the approved work for the
instruction of Irish Catholics.
46 O Sullivan, 63.
47 Sherard, *SUF*, 78.
48 Sherard, *SUF*, 78; also variant at She-
    rard, *Life*, 89-90
49 Pearson, 21.
50 Reggie Turner to A. J. A. Symons, 26
    August 1935, in Clark.
51 Tipper, *Kraemer*, 15, 17, 32, 35, 37.
52 Melville, 76.
53 'Oscar Wilde', *Biograph & Review*, IV,
    no. 20 (August 1880), 131.
54 Oscar Wilde, 'Irish Poets of the Nine-
    teenth Century', lecture notes, ed.
    Michael J. O'Neill, *University Review*,
    1 no. 4 (1955), quoted in Melville, 73.
    O'Brien returned to Dublin in 1856
    and died in 1864 when OW was ten.
55 Melville, 78–9.
56 LVK, diary, in E. Mansén, 'A Splendid
    New Picture', 113–14.
57 Davis Coakley, 'The Neglected Years:
    Wilde in Dublin', in C. George Sandu-
    lescu, ed., *Rediscovering Oscar Wilde*
    (1994), 55–6.
58 Melville, 76.
59 'Oscar Wilde', *Biograph and Review*,
    131.

Chapter 2: A Fair Scholar

1 Melville, 87; White, 10. The Christmas
   holidays ended that year on 29 January. Melville states that OW began
   school in February. White speculates
   that – as the Wilde children are the last
   two names on the roll of twenty-three
   new entries – they may have arrived at
   the beginning of February, but offers
   no evidence for this. And, indeed, the

school prospectus was very insistent
about prompt returns from holidays.
In May of the previous year, WCKW
had been sent to St Columba's School
in Dublin, but the experiment was
short-lived.
2 Dublin – since the completion of
   the line to Enniskillen in 1859 – was
   barely three hours away; the journey

involved a change at Drogheda, from the Dublin & Drogheda Railway, to the INW's line to Enniskillen.

3   The basic fees for boarders were 60 guineas a year, with additional charges for music (pianoforte), drawing, and the 'drill-sergeant' (as per the 1864 prospectus). Drawing and music, which both Wilde children took, cost 1 guinea a quarter, the drill-sergeant 5s. There was also a 2 guinea entrance fee (White, 38); a reduction in fees for siblings was only given in cases where three or more brothers were at the school (1866 prospectus).

4   Herbert Beatty, quoted in White, 34.

5   Steele to William Cotter Kyle, September 1864, quoted in White, 5.

6   John Sullivan, quoted in White, 33.

7   L. Purser, quoted in White, 34.

8   John Sullivan, quoted in White, 33.

9   Steele's speech, and Mr Christian's reply at 1867 dinner, in White, 93–4; see also Purser on Steele in White, 34.

10 Press report of Steele's 1867 prize-day address; White, 92.

11 John Sullivan, quoted in White, 112.

12 1867 prospectus; special 'medals' were awarded each year to the three pupils from the head class who came top in the Easter examinations in classics, mathematics and modern literature (English, French, German) respectively. Prizes were given to all pupils who – in the Easter, midsummer, or November examinations – achieved 'answering averages of Sixty per cent in Classics; Fifty per cent in Mathematics; Seventy per cent in Modern Literature' (1867 prospectus).

13 White, 36. Between 1859 and 1869 Steele spent £4,420 19s 4d of his own money on 'enlargements and improvements' to the school, according to his 'Statement of Facts' to the commissioners of endowed schools.

14 August 1865 notice in the *Impartial Reporter*, in White, 63.

15 OW, in Harris, 18.

16 Harris, 16; Sherard, *Life*, 103.

17 Coakley, 77; White, 23–4.

18 JFW, quoted in Melville, 104.

19 Tipper, *A Critical Biography of Lady Jane Wilde*, 587; White, 23.

20 Melville, 103.

21 R. Y. Tyrrell, quoted in Harris, 13. Sherard and others have doubted whether the quotation really does derive from Tyrrell, who remained a friend of the Wildes, and a regular guest at Merrion Square.

22 Lord Rathcreedan, *Memories of a Long Life* (1931), 52.

23 For example, they were both present at a talk given by John Butler Yeats in the lecture hall at King's Inn on 21 November 1865 (Murphy, *Prodigal Father*, 45–6; *Freeman's Journal*, 7 December 1869, records WRWW and Isaac Butt among the 'distinguished' attendees of the law students' debating society; they were both among the fifty members elected to act on the council of the Home Rule League in February 1874.

24 Melville, 103.

25 Sherard, *Life*, 103.

26 Harris, 19.

27 'Our New York Letter', *Philadelphia Inquirer*, 4 January 1882, Hofer & Scharnhorst, 18.

28 Vyvyan Holland, *Son of Oscar Wilde* (1954), 45.

29 Joseph Hone, *George Moore* (1936), 24.

30 *CL*, 85.

31 'Oscar Wilde', *Biograph and Review*, 131.

32 Ross, *Oscar Wilde and Ancient Greece*, 15.

33 WRWW's *Lough Corrib its shores and islands*, 258–9. The structure is now considered to have been an early ex-

ample of a 'sweat house'. WCKW also featured in the book: he contributed a drawing of Hag Castle.

34 'E.R.F', *New York Herald*, 22 August 1881.

35 WRWW to LVK, in Mansén, 'A Splendid New Picture', 114.

36 JFW to LVK, 16 April 1867, Tipper, *Kraemer*, 46.

37 We can acknowledge this without going so far as Melissa Knox, who, in her *Oscar Wilde: A Long and Lovely Suicide* (1994) posited an incestuous attraction, if not relationship, between the two.

38 Harris, 210; 'E.R.F', *New York Herald*, 22 August 1881. None of these verses survives. His graveside poem 'Requiescat', although he came to view it as a memorial to his sister – with its opening stanza 'Tread lightly, she is near / Under the snow, / Speak gently, she can hear / The daisies grow' – was written many years later. It is dated from Avignon, which Wilde probably visited in the summer of 1875. Variant versions in the MS 'Poems' notebook (Philadelphia Public Library) indicate that he was working on it close to the time of the publication of *Poems* in 1881; they also suggest that he initially conceived it as an elegy to a dead lover, rather than to a dead sister.

39 White, 91–2.

40 Harris, 18.

41 James Glover, *Jimmy Glover His Book* (1911), 34; the friend was George Henry, father of the novelist George Moore. Sherard, *Life*, 90, also gives a version, dated to 1864, which appears to derive from George Moore. 'Willy is all right, but Oscar is wonderful, wonderful. He can do anything.' These accounts should be set against the less reliable claim – recorded by Arthur Ransome, 30, and echoed by Sherard

in a letter to LAD, 7 March 1937 – 'that his mother always thought that Oscar was less brilliant than her elder son'.

42 'Oscar Wilde', *Biograph and Review*, 132.

43 JFW to LVK, 16 November 1867, in Tipper, *Kramer*, 49.

44 OW won Mr Robert Christian's classical prize (shared with Herbert Beatty); the Rev. A. D. J. Robinson prize in classics (also with Beatty, along with Leslie Creery and William Lendrum), and a general lower school classics prize for his results in the preceding year's examinations. For OW's modest attainments in schoolboy French, see Sherard, *Life*, 111, and OW's annotated copy of Voltaire's *Histoire de Charles XII*; Thomas Wright, 'Wilde the Doodle Dandy: a Scholarly Doodle', *Wildean*, 47 (2015), 72–3. Sherard, *Life*, 92, quotes a very unreliable 'biographical sketch' from 1891, claiming that OW's 'passion' for French literature began immediately after this childhood visit to Paris. But it is not convincing, nor corroborated by the other sources.

45 *Poems by Speranza (Lady Wilde)* (1870); the *National Review*, edited by James Godkin, started as a monthly in June 1868, and became a weekly in September 1868. No 1, vol. 3 (1 August 1868) included 'To Ireland' – 'A New Poem by Speranza' on page 60; No. 1, vol. 4, was indeed published on 5 September, though it is hard to think that OW would have been thrilled by its contents, which included articles on 'The Last Irish Land Tragedy', 'Dr Pusey's Appeal to the Wesleyans' and the Mountains of Mourne, as well as poem by William M'Comb in memory of the Marquis of Downshire.

46 Harris, 210.

47 Sherard, *Real*, 177.

48 Purser to A. J. A. Symons, 28 January 1932, in Clark.

49   Purser to A. J. A. Symons, 28 January 1932, in Clark; OW, in Harris, 12.

50   Purser to A. J. A. Symons, 28 January 1932, in Clark; also ES, in Harris, 15. 'Willie was perhaps in those days even better than [OW] was at telling a story'; Sherard, *Life*, 109–10; R. H. Johnstone to A. J. A. Symons, 26 July 1932, in Clark.

51   Sherard, *Life*, 108.

52   ES, in Harris, 16.

53   Sherard, *Life*, 109, quotes a contemporary: 'He was very superior in his manner towards Willy [*sic*].'

54   OW, in Harris, 19, 17; the one area where OW perhaps did admit his brother's superiority was music. Though he took music lessons throughout his school career, OW remained 'poor' at it.

55   Harris, 260–1.

56   For OW's juvenile scruffiness, see R. H. Johnstone to A. J. A. Symons, 26 July 1932, in Clark: 'He was most untidy in his person, in fact kept himself dirty'; also W. H. Drennan, another Portora contemporary: 'Oscar Wilde was most slovenly in dress and appearance; both hands and face seemed to want a washing and his nails were always in mourning', quoted in White, 119. There is also a fleeting vision of how OW 'sat in soiled white ducks and elbowless jacket, in the dingy Merrion Square dining-room, and picked crab-claws in his schoolboy fingers', quoted from *Life* in 'Society Gossip', *Wrexham Advertiser*, 28 January 1882, 7.

57   Purser, in Harris, 17; see also Purser, *Notes on Portora* (1932), in Clark: 'He paid rather more attention to his dress than did the other boys.'

58   Sherard, *Life*, 109.

59   ES, in Harris, 15.

60   Sherard, *Life*, 109.

61   Purser, in Harris, 17; his book bill (Clark) lists book costs of £7 18s 6d to 1 February 1871; £1 15s 4d to August 1871; and £1 12s to the end of the school year.

62   Harris, 260–1.

63   OW in Harris, 18.

64   Sherard, *Life*, 110–11. He certainly knew these authors, and it is most likely that he read them in childhood. When he was in Holloway Prison in 1895, and in need of comfort, he asked for Stevenson's *Kidnapped* and *Master of Ballantrae* (*CL*, 647). And when suggesting works for the prison library at Reading, he cited Scott, Austen and Thackeray, along with Dickens and Stevenson; Wright, 172.

65   ES, in Harris, 17.

66   Wright, 54–5.

67   OW, 'Some Literary Ladies' *Woman's World*, January 1889

68   *CL*, 249; OW knew of Poe from early childhood: see Tipper, *A Critical Biography of Lady Jane Wilde*, 360; he considered he should have been included in any list of 'The Best Hundred Books', *CL*, 277.

69   *CL*, 26.

70   Mikhail, 47. OW claimed, with characteristic exaggeration, to have known Whitman's work 'almost from the cradle'; For Lady Wilde's purchase of Whitman's poem in 1868, see Tipper, *A Critical Biography of Lady Jane Wilde*, 360.

71   Purser, in Clark, but see also R. H. Johnstone to A. J. A. Symons, 26 July 1932, in Clark: 'He [OW] was decidedly unpopular... and made no friends in the School. He did not join in games, which is a bad tray [*sic*] in boy's character.'

72   ES, in Harris, 16; Purser, in Clark.

73   ES, in Harris, 16; Purser, in Clark, says 'He had rather a quick temper, but it was not very marked.'

74 ES, in Harris, 15.

75 ES, in Harris, 16; Sherard, *Real*, 163, mistakenly claims that this occurred in 'the nursery', rather than at school.

76 Sherard, *Real*, 163.

77 G. B. Shaw to Frank Harris, 24 June 1930, in Dan H. Laurence, ed. *Collected Letters of Bernard Shaw 1926–1950* (1988), 191; OW, in Harris, 18.

78 Harris, 18.

79 Harris, 19.

80 ES, in Harris, 15.

81 Slason Thompson, *Eugene Field, a Study in Heredity and Contradiction* (1901), vol. I, 213.

82 ES, in Harris, 15: 'Even as a schoolboy he was an excellent talker'; and OW, in Harris, 28: 'I was a great talker at school.'

83 ES, in Harris, 15.

84 ES, in Harris, 16.

85 ES, in Harris, 15. The case – because of appeals – was heard three times: on 30 April 1869; 18 November 1869 and 20 July 1870. Only the two 1869 hearings would have been in term time. For a full discussion of the case, see Dominic Janes, *Visions of Queer Martyrdom* (2015), chapter 2.

86 ES, in Harris, 17; Sherard, *Life*, 104.

87 ES, in Harris, 17.

88 Sherard, *Life*, 110.

89 Purser, in Harris, 17; Purser, *Notes on Portora*, in Clark.

90 ES, in Harris, 15–16; Sherard, *Life*, 104; OW claimed that he remained 'a mere boy till I was over sixteen' (i.e. c. 1870); see Harris, 18.

91 ES, in Harris, 15. In letter from OW and six classmates to the Portora assistant master, Rev. Benjamin Moffett, OW is the only boy to sign with his Christian name (and surname) rather than with his initials. *CL*, 5.

92 ES, in Harris, 16. OW was presented with a seven-volume edition of Gibbon's *Decline and Fall of the Roman Empire*; see Wright, 60.

93 Although Sullivan was sixteen, over a year older than Wilde, he was actually placed in the year below him. As he proved a very able student, it must be supposed that something had interrupted his early schooling.

94 Purser, in W. Steele, *Portora Royal School* (1891), 13.

95 Purser, *Notes on Portora*, in Clark.

96 He also won prizes for classics and drawing; WCKW won a drawing prize. For the general excellence of biblical knowledge at Portora, see White, 65, 77.

97 Purser, *Notes on Portora*, in Clark.

98 OW, in Harris, 18.

99 OW, in Harris, 19.

100 William Smith, *A Smaller History of Greece* (1873), 112; White, 72, lists the textbooks used at Portora.

101 OW, in Harris, 19.

102 OW, in Harris, 18; Purser, in Harris, 17; Sherard, *Life*, 111.

103 OW, in Harris, 18.

104 Purser, *Notes on Portora*, in Clark.

105 ES, in Harris, 17.

106 OW, in Harris, 19.

107 Conor Maguire, quoted in T. de Vere White, 220; see also *Freeman's Journal*, 8 July 1870, 'Fashion & Varieties', 'Lady Wilde, Mr Wilde, and Mr Oscar Wilde have left Merrion Square for Moytura House, Co. Mayo.'

108 Purser, in Harris, 17.

109 Sherard, *Life*.

110 Purser, *Notes on Portora*, in Clark.

111 White, 123.

112 OW, in Harris, 19.

113 JFW to LVK, 3 April 1870, Tipper, *Kraemer*; Louis C. Purser to A. J A. Symons, 28 Jan 1932, in Clark; in April 1870, Purser recalled him being as 'pleasant and lively' as ever, though 'a little more florid perhaps and with

more of the manner of a man of the world'.

114 Harris, 19–21.

Chapter 3: Foundation Scholarship

1   His entrance exam marks were: Greek, two papers: 8, 8; Latin, two papers: 8, 7; Latin composition: 4; English composition: 5; history: 8; arithmetic: 2 (Sherard, *Life*). There were two principal matriculations or entrance examinations each year – one at the commencement of the Michaelmas term (early October), the other in the Trinity term (April) – together with five supplementary ones. In 1871 forty-four new students matriculated on 10 October 1871, followed by a supplementary twenty-three on 21 October. There was another substantial intake in November.

2   The exam took place on 26 October: Trinity College Dublin, *Calendar* for 1871; Mason, 99, states that there were six other royal scholarships awarded at that time (the other 'royal schools of Ulster' eligible for such awards were Armagh, Cavan and Dungannon). The special exam was also sat by pupils from schools of the Erasmus Smith foundation. Portora royal scholarships were worth either £50 or £30; *Portora: The School on the Hill* (2008), 133. There is no indication which amount OW received, though his being listed after Purser and McDowell on the honours board might suggest the lesser amount. The costs of attending TCD included a £15 charge at entrance, followed by £8 8s each half year. This covered tuition, but not 'rooms and commons'; *Calendar*, 1871.

3   WRWW received his honorary degree in 1863; he is regularly listed as being 'on the platform' at the meetings of the TCD Historical Society.

4   Harris, 26.

5   Harris, 24; Coakley, 136, estimates the number of students at Trinity in 1871 as 'some 1,100'.

6   Pearson, 23; this may have occurred when Willie proposed thanks for an essay about the surplus of unmarried women in society – entitled 'Daughterfull houses. For What?' – at a meeting of the Philosophical Society on 5 June 1873.

7   ES, in Harris, 23.

8   Horace Wilkins, in Mikhail, 2.

9   Mason, 99, and *Freeman's Journal*, 2 December 1871: OW won the composition prize for Greek verse (worth £2) in the entrance prize exams at the end of his first term, as well as a 'premium for composition at the term lectures'.

10   Harris, 24.

11   'Death of Dr. R. Y. Tyrrell'; *The Times*, 21 September 1914, 10.

12   'Obituary: Robert Yelverton Tyrrell', *Hermathena*, 18 (1940), xi; *The Times*, 21 September 1914.

13   W. B. Stanford, 'Robert Yelverton Tyrrell', *Hermathena*, 125 (1978), 16–17.

14   *The Times*, 21 September 1914.

15   Stanford, 'Robert Yelverton Tyrrell', 13.

16   *The Times*, 21 September 1914.

17   Stanford, 'Robert Yelverton Tyrrell', 10.

18   Stanford, 'Robert Yelverton Tyrrell', 16.

19   'Obituary: Robert Yelverton Tyrrell', x; Tyrrell married Ada Shaw, the daughter of the senior fellow at TCD, on 1 August 1874.

20 'The Provost of Trinity' (obituary), *The Times*, 1 May 1919, 10.

21 Ross, *Oscar Wilde and Ancient Greece*, 26–8.

22 'John Pentland Mahaffy', *Hermathena*, 19 (1920), vii.

23 Harris, 24.

24 See register and *Calendar* for the role of 'tutor'.

25 Quoted in W. B. Stanford & R. B. McDowell, *Mahaffy: A Biography of an Anglo-Irishman* (1971), 75.

26 Harris, 28.

27 *CL*, 562; JFW to OW, Tipper, *Oscar*, 92–3, dated 1882, but should be 1881. JFW reminded OW that Mahaffy gave 'the first noble impulse to your intellect'.

28 Mahaffy, 'Life of Trinity College Dublin', *The Dark Blue*, i, 487–93, quoted in Coakley, 136; Mahaffy, *Principles of the Art of Conversation*, 1.

29 Stanford, 'Robert Yelverton Tyrrell', 16–17.

30 Stanford, 'Robert Yelverton Tyrrell', 17.

31 U. O'Connor, *Oliver St John Gogarty* (1981), 18.

32 W. B. Stanford & R. B. McDowell, *Mahaffy: A Biography of an Anglo-Irishman* (1971), 79.

33 Oliver St John Gogarty, 'A Picture of Oscar Wilde', *Intimations* (1950), 33.

34 Stanford, 'Robert Yelverton Tyrrell', 11–12.

35 Harris, 24.

36 Harris, 28.

37 JFW to OW [1881]; Tipper, *Oscar*, 92–3. Mahaffy 'kept you out of the toils of meaner men and pleasures'.

38 Harris, 207; Stanford, 'Robert Yelverton Tyrrell', 16.

39 Louis Purser to A. J. A. Symons, 1932, in Clark.

40 Pearson, 22.

41 Croft-Cooke, 33. During the Michael-

mas term 1871 OW attended twenty-one out of twenty-eight of Professor Abbot's 'science' lectures; in Hilary term 1872 he attended two out of seventeen English literature lectures by Professor Dowden (Coakley, 137).

42 ES, in Harris, 23.

43 OW was put forward for membership on 23 November 1871 at the opening meeting of the 1871–2 session, proposed by the president and seconded by the secretary. At the same meeting WCKW was awarded the society's second silver medal for his essay on Molière during the previous session.

44 Walter Starkie, *Scholars and Gypsies* (1963), 98.

45 OW, 'Mental Photograph' lists lawn tennis – and snipe – as his 'favourite game'.

46 ES, in Harris, 22–3.

47 ES, in Harris, 23.

48 Hofer & Scharnhorst, 85.

49 Wilfrid Hugh Chesson, 'A Reminiscence of 1898', *Bookman* (1911), in Mikhail, 379.

50 OW's copy dated Michaelmas 1872; see Ellmann, 31.

51 Hofer & Scharnhorst, 85.

52 OET VII, 231.

53 LAD, *Oscar Wilde and Myself* (1914), 209.

54 Thomas Maitland [Robert Buchanan], 'The Fleshly School of Poetry: Mr. D. G. Rossetti', *Contemporary Review*, October 1871.

55 William John Courthope, 'The Latest Development in Poetry: Swinburne – Rossetti – Morris', *Quarterly Review*, 132 (1872) 61ff.

56 *CL*, 13; OW bought a copy of Morris's verse morality play *Love is Enough* during the Michaelmas term 1872, as soon as it appeared; Ellmann, 31, from G. F. Sims catalogue no. 79.

57 Quoted in Wright, 34; 'Draft review of Rossetti's Poems (1881)' in Clark.

58   Hofer & Scharnhorst, 52; Stella Bottai, 'Keats and the Victorians', www.victorianweb.org.

59   *CL*, 157.

60   The 'Pre-Raphaelite Brotherhood' had been founded in 1848 by Dante Gabriel Rossetti, John Everett Millais and William Holman Hunt, but the artistic impulse that it embodied had, by the 1860s, become focused upon Rossetti, his friends and followers; the epithet 'Pre-Raphaelite' was used generally to describe their work.

61   Frederic William Burton, the one Irish painter associated with the Pre-Raphaelites, and a connection of WRWW's, had moved to London in 1874 to become director of the National Gallery.

62   Algernon C. Swinburne and William Michael Rossetti, *Notes on the Royal Academy Exhibition, 1868* (1868), 44–5.

63   'The Theories of a Poet', *New York Daily Tribune*, 8 January 1882, 7.

64   ES, in Harris, 23.

65   J. A. Symonds, *Studies of the Greek Poets* (1873), 414.

66   Symonds, *Studies of the Greek Poets*, 415.

67   Symonds, *Studies of the Greek Poets*, 309; Crabbe, Wordsworth and Goethe are also seen as inheriting from the naturalistic tradition of Theocritus; OW, 'Mental Photograph'.

68   Symonds, *Studies of the Greek Poets*, 422n.

69   Mahaffy, *Social Life in Greece from Homer to Menander* (1874), 100.

70   Harris, 24.

71   Harris, 22; OW added a Whistlerian butterfly to his picture.

72   OW ms notebook (Berg), see OET I, 1; the poem is almost certainly unfinished. The additional stanza may have been intended for it: 'What shall we give thee? lies of men / Enough thou hast – enough to spare; / For men wax sick and faint with pain / Because thy face and form are fair, / Because thy form is fair to see, And lithe limbs, fashioned amourously.' Swinburne's *Rosamond* was published together with *The Queen Mother*. His last published play was the similarly named *Rosamund, Queen of the Lombards* (1899). It is interesting that the title of OW's poem 'Ye Shall Be Gods' provides an echo of *Eritis Sicut Deus* ('You Shall Be As God), the novel that JFW had translated as *The First Temptation*.

73   Philosophical Society minute book, re. meetings on 10 December 1870 and 1 Feb 1872. Other indications of the vitality of literary culture at the 'Phil' are Charles Frizzell's paper on Chatterton (2 February 1871) and Professor Dowden's paper on Walt Whitman (4 May 1871).

74   Harris, 2.

75   Poems by WCKW in *Kottabos*: 'Per Amica Silentia Lunae', (Hilary 1872), 261; 'Le Voile' (Trinity 1872), 292–3; 'Nil restat ni quale decorum puellae (from Victor Hugo)' (Michaelmas 1872) 312; 'Saith the Poet' and 'Riposta' (Trinity 1873), 4–5; 'Italia (from Vincenzo da Filicaia' (Hilary 1874), 80–1; 'Love's Axioms' (Michaelmas 1874), 124; 'Les Lendemains' (Michaelmas 1874), 134–5; 'Ad Amicam Meam (from the French of Victor Hugo)' (Hilary 1875), 161; 'Schubert' (Hilary 1876), 245.

76   Mahaffy, 'Life of Trinity College Dublin', in Coakley, 136.

77   Harris, 25.

78   Horace Wilkins, 'Memories of Trinity Days', in Mikhail, 2.

79   Ellmann, 557 n.61: 'Letter to the editor of the *Irish Times* 28 Aug 1954, from Murroe Fitzgerald. In 1919, he says, he prepared a claim for a woman who had been nannie for both the Wilde children and Edward Carson at

Dangarvan when she was fifteen years old, in 1859'; Hyde, *Oscar*, 15; Sherard, *Life*, 115. Carson never rose out of the second rank while at TCD.

80 ALS Reggie Turner to A. J. A. Symons, 26 August 1935 (Clark). OW probably overstated in telling Turner that he and Carson went about 'arm in arm'; Mahaffy, quoted in Coakley, 143. Edward Marjoribanks, *The Life of Lord Carson* (1932), 13, states that Carson, even at this period, disapproved of OW's 'flippant approach to life', but is a very unreliable source for the relations between Carson and Wilde.

81 Hyde, *Oscar*, 15.

82 Harris, 26; Sullivan matriculated in June 1872, aged nineteen (TCD Register).

83 JFW to LVK, 3 April 1870, Tipper, *Kraemer*, 51–2. Although in this letter JFW says the receptions ran 'from 3 to 6', an invitation card at the BL is printed: 'At Home, Saturday, 4 pm to 7 pm. *Conversazione.*'

84 'Oscar Wilde', *Taranaki Herald* (NZ), 13 April 1895, 2.

85 Melville, 115 n.24.

86 'Oscar Wilde', *Taranaki Herald*, 2.

87 'Oscar Wilde', *Taranaki Herald*, 2.

88 Melville, 116.

89 Melville, 116.

90 Harris, 23; OW and WRWW attended the 'Vice-regal Reception' given by Lord Lieutenant and Countess Spencer; *Freeman's Journal*, 25 February 1874.

91 Harris, 28.

92 Sherard, *Life*, 115. Each term began with term exams, followed, later, by exams for honours and prizes.

93 Purser, *Notes on Portora*.

94 Mahaffy, 'Life of Trinity College Dublin', in Coakley, 136.

95 Sherard, *Life*, 119, lists all OW's marks.

96 Purser, *Notes on Portora*. This achievement dispelled the idea, apparently

held by some of his contemporaries, that OW was – academically – only 'an average sort of man'. Sherard, *Life*, 116–17.

97 Hyde, *Oscar*, 13; the room was 'believed to have been on the first floor of [staircase] No. 18'. He also states that he 'shared [the] rooms' with WCKW.

98 Harris, 23.

99 Sile O'Shea (Assistant Librarian at the King's Inns) to M. Sturgis, 10 November 2015. At that time students for the Irish Bar were obliged also to 'keep terms' at one of the English Inns of Court; it was, though, only necessary for them to eat three dinners at the Inn per term in order to fulfil this requirement. WCKW kept the following terms at the King's Inns: Hilary and Easter 1872; Hilary, Easter, Trinity and Michaelmas 1873; Hilary 1874; Hilary and Easter 1875; and at the Middle Temple Inn: Michaelmas 1872; Hilary and Easter 1873; Hilary 1875. He does not appear to have kept term at either Inn during Easter, Trinity and Michaelmas 1874.

100 *Freeman's Journal*, 21 January 1874. It was the same motion on which WCKW had spoken two years earlier, on 17 January and 7 February 1872. It is not recorded whether OW's side carried the motion.

101 Harris, 23.

102 Harris, 25.

103 Mikhail, 2.

104 Ellmann, 29, suggests OW was caricatured in the Philosophical Society 'Suggestions Book' (TCD MS 2058), but the image of two figures contemplating a poster advertising a 'Midnight Meeting' [such as were regularly held for the reform of prostitutes], and captioned 'The Benevolent Bobby' (Crozier), 'That Prig of a Policeman' (Wilde) is very hard to

decipher. It is possible that the taller clean-shaven figure, with his hair falling over his collar, is supposed to be OW, although it does not look very like him. It may, perhaps more probably, be WCKW. The smaller bearded figure (whom Ellmann supposed to be OW) bears a passable resemblance to later photographs of John B. Crozier, OW's TCD contemporary and the future archbishop of Armagh. But why is 'Wilde' (whether OW or WCKW) wearing a policeman's hat, and why is he captioned as (or shown remarking) 'That prig of a policeman'? These are mysteries that await elucidation.

105 TCD contemporary, quoted in Hyde, *Oscar*, 14.

106 Horace Wilkins, in Mikhail, 2; Hyde, 14; ES, in Harris, 23.

107 Hyde, *Oscar*, 16, quoting ES; Harris, 23, refers to the don as John Townsend Mills, but in the TCD registers, and other sources, he appears merely as Townsend Mills. He took his degree in 1864, and his MA in 1867.

108 Sherard, *Life*, 96.

109 O'Sullivan, 189.

110 Harris, 23; Whistler began using his stylized butterfly signature at the beginning of the 1870s. Several of the Nocturnes that he exhibited at Dudley Gallery in 1872 were signed in this way.

111 Fr Dunne to the secretary of the Catholic Truth Society of Ireland [n.d.] (Clark): 'Even in his early years while still in his Father's house in Dublin he was moving towards the Catholic Church under Jesuit influence, I believe'; Hunter-Blair; Katharine Tynan, *Twenty-five Years* (1913), 130.

112 OW, quoted in the *Chicago Tribune*, 3 December 1900 (reproduced in *Intentions*, October 2010); Alice ffrench recalled talking to OW on 'religious matters' when he was at Trinity and noting that he 'seemed to hold decidedly... High Church views', though she (erroneously) assumed they were 'advanced Anglican' rather than Catholic. W. E. Redway to Robert Ross, 17 July 1924 (Ross Memorial Collection, University College, Oxford).

113 Croft-Cooke, 33; the TCD chapel 'communion book' has no record of Wilde taking the sacrament during his time at college.

114 *CL*, 1226; OW, quoted in the *Chicago Tribune*, 3 December 1900; Tynan, *Twenty-five Years*, 130; Fr Dunne to the secretary of the Catholic Truth Society of Ireland [n.d.] (Clark).

115 William Dillon, *The Life of John Mitchell* (1888), 2:285, refers to 'a pleasant dinner' chez Wilde, in September 1874, at which 'Father Thomas Burke, the celebrated Dominican', was present.

116 *CL*, 1226; Stanford, 'Robert Yelverton Tyrrell', 9; in 1893 when CMW was considering becoming a Catholic, OW discouraged her, saying 'it would be the ruin to the boys [their sons]... No Catholic boy is allowed to go to Eton or to take a scholarship at the University.' Moyle, 229.

117 Another able Trinity classicist, of the half-generation before, Henry B. Leech, had moved on from Dublin to take his degree at Cambridge, subsequently becoming a fellow at Gonville and Caius; William Ridgeway would follow a similar path (*The Times*, 26 March 1921).

118 Typescript of Robert Ross's introduction to the German edition of OW's works (Clark). 'It was Sir Henry Dyke Acland and Professor Mahaffy who persuaded Sir William Wilde to allow his son to go to Oxford.' WRWW was relieved that OW would be escaping from his Jesuit connections by going

to Oxford (Hunter-Blair), so this may have been one of the arguments used by Mahaffy to persuade him.

119 Hyde, *Oscar*, 15.

120 Louis Perrin, of 12 Merrion Square, matriculated October 1873; Peter Vernier, 'Oscar at Magdalen', *Wildean*, 19 (2001), 24.

121 Oxford Handbook; Vernier, 'Oscar at Magdalen', 19, 26; G. T. Atkinson, Cornhill, in Mikhail, 16; the examination was held jointly with candidates for scholarships to Worcester College.

122 JFW to [John Hilson], 5 May [1875], Tipper, *Hilson*, 75, where the letter is [mis]dated '1876'; JFW to Rosalie Olivecrona, Melville, 122; Ellmann, 34.

123 Ellmann, 34; Schroeder, 14; Carlyle made two visits to Ireland, in 1846 and 1849; JFW had a copy of Tennyson's poems inscribed by Carlyle. It is unclear whether this was also the volume in which Carlyle had written the lines of Goethe.

124 Wilfrid Hugh Chesson, 'A Reminiscence of the 1898', *Bookman*, 34 (1911), 389–94, in Mikhail, 378.

125 For OW's place at the head of the list, see Vernier, 'Oscar at Magdalen', 26; for the Wildes' travels see JFW to Rosalie Olivecrona, 'late July' 1874, quoted in Melville, 122; for Sphinx see Isobel Murray, ed., *Oscar Wilde: Complete Poetry* (1997), 199.

126 Mahaffy, *Social Life in Ancient Greece from Homer to Menander* (1874), viii, dated '4 November 1874'; Ross, *Oscar Wilde and Ancient Greece*, 24.

127 Hyde, *Oscar*, 17, follows Mahaffy's biographers, in suggesting that this passage might have been one of Wilde's 'additions' to the text, given that it embodies the 'Art's for art's sake' creed that he later espoused. But it seems more likely that, at this stage, the current of influence was still running the other way.

128 Plato, *Symposium*, 202–12. Linda Dowling, *Hellenism and Homosexuality in Victorian Oxford* (1996), xiv–xv.

129 Mahaffy, *Social Life in Ancient Greece from Homer to Menander* (1874), 306–12.

130 Oliver St John Gogarty, *As I was going down Sackville Street* (1937), 239.

Part II: *The Nightingale and the Rose*
Chapter 1: Young Oxford

1 Margaret L. Woods, 'Oxford in the Seventies', *Fortnightly Review*, 150 (1941), 276.

2 Harris, 26; OW called Oxford 'the most beautiful city I had ever been in', Hofer & Scharnhorst, 19; 'The Theories of a Poet', *New York Tribune*, 8 January 1882.

3 Peter Vernier, 'Poem-sites at Magdalen: Oscar Wilde', *Wildean*, 23 (2003), 38. The rooms, 'Chaplain's I, 2[nd floor] Pair Right' are still undergraduate accommodation.

4 Harris, 26.

5 Atkinson, in Mikhail, 16.

6 Atkinson, in Mikhail, 16.

7 Arthur Shadwell to A. J. A. Symons, 7 July 1931 (Clark).

8 [Bodley], 'Oscar Wilde At Oxford', *NYT*, 4 February 1882.

9 [Bodley], 'Oscar Wilde At Oxford'.

10 Bodley diary, 25 October 1874. They met again in the Pembroke Junior Common Room after a dinner; [Bodley], 'Oscar Wilde At Oxford'.

11 Dr Bulley's notebook (Magdalen College archive), lists ninety-nine undergraduates at the 1874 terminal

examination; some thirty are listed as in lodgings.

12 Besides OW's fellow demy, G. T. Atkinson, there was only Arthur Edmund Street, the oldest son of G. E. Street, the Oxford architect to whom William Morris had been apprenticed. There is, however, no evidence of any friendship between Street and OW.

13 [Bodley], 'Oscar Wilde At Oxford'.

14 Hunter-Blair, 117.

15 Atkinson, in Mikhail, 17; Harold Hartley, *Eighty-Eight Not Out* (1939), 269. Hartley was told by an Oxford contemporary that when OW first came up he was keen to take part in games, but 'physically he was quite unfitted. Yet he showed great courage in persisting.' While others laughed at him, Hartley's friend 'backed him up and endeavoured to help him'; OW was always grateful for this kindness.

16 Oliver St John Gogarty, 'A Picture of Oscar Wilde', 50.

17 Atkinson, in Mikhail 17.

18 B. De Sales La Terrière, *Days that Are Gone, being the Recollections of some Seventy Years of the Life of a very ordinary Gentleman and his Friends in Three Reigns* (1924), 75; even in Dr Bulley's notebook he is listed as having been only two years at TCD.

19 Atkinson, in Mikhail, 17.

20 Dowling, *Hellenism and Homosexuality*, xiii.

21 Smith & Helfand, 77–8, 108; Wright, 85: OW bought the five volumes of the 1875 edition of Jowett's translations of Plato's *Dialogues*. 'Max Müller loves him,' JFW reported proudly of her son's achievements; JWF to [John Hilson], 5 May [1875], Tipper, *Hilson*. For OW's knowledge of Green's ideas at a slightly later date, see Ross, *Oscar Wilde and Ancient Greece*, 155–6.

22 John Ruskin to JFW, 5 December 1879 (TCD), thanking her 'for having taught your son to care for me'.

23 Atkinson, in Mikhail, 19.

24 OW, 'English Poetesses', *The Queen*, 8 December 1888, OET VII, 124; Harris, 28, says that Ruskin 'was an inspiration when he sang'.

25 Harris, 28.

26 OW, in Harris, 28.

27 Hofer & Scharnhorst, 19; 'The Theories of a Poet', *New York Tribune*, 8 January 1882.

28 OW quotes from this passage in his 'Oxford Commonplace Book', Smith & Helfand, 145, 197; and, more fully, in his lecture 'The English Renaissance in Art'.

29 Hofer & Scharnhorst, 22–3; 'The Science of the Beautiful', *New York World*, 8 January 1882.

30 'University and City Intelligence', *Jackson's Oxford Journal*, 7 November 1874; *Berrow's Worcester Journal*, 7 November 1874, 6.

31 [Bodley], 'Oscar Wilde At Oxford', makes it clear that OW did *not* join the road-makers in November 1874. OW gave various fanciful accounts of his connection with the road-making scheme; e.g. Hofer & Scharnhorst 19; 'The Theories of a Poet', *New York Tribune*, 8 January 1882. The fullest and most inventive is in his 1882 lecture 'Art and the Handicraftsman': 'Well, we were coming down the [High] street – a troop of young men, some of them like myself only nineteen, going to river or tennis-court or cricket-field – when Ruskin going up to lecture in cap and gown met us. He seemed troubled and prayed us to go back with him to his lecture, which a few of us did, and there he spoke to us not on art this time but on life, saying that it seemed to him to be wrong that all the best physique and strength of the young men in

England should be spent aimlessly on cricket ground or river, without any result at all except that if one rowed well one got a pewter-pot, and if one made a good score, a cane-handled bat. He thought, he said, that we should be working at something that would do good to other people, at something by which we might show that in all labour there was something noble. Well, we were a good deal moved, and said we would do anything he wished. So he went out round Oxford and found two villages, Upper and Lower Hinksey, and between them there lay a great swamp, so that the villagers could not pass from one to the other without many miles of a round. And when we came back in winter he asked us to help him to make a road across this morass for these village people to use. So out we went, day after day, and learned how to lay levels and to break stones, and to wheel barrows along a plank – a very difficult thing to do. And Ruskin worked with us in the mist and rain and mud of an Oxford winter, and our friends and our enemies came out and mocked us from the bank. We did not mind it much then, and we did not mind it afterwards at all, but worked away for two months at our road. And what became of the road? Well, like a bad lecture it ended abruptly – in the middle of the swamp. Ruskin going away to Venice, when we came back for the next term there was no leader, and the "diggers", as they called us, fell asunder.'

32 Dr Bulley's notebook. Vernier, 'Oscar at Magdalen', 26, points out that during OW's five years at Magdalen, only ten students – including OW – were placed in this category.

33 Dr Bulley's notebook; Vernier, 'Oscar at Magdalen', 26.

34 [Bodley], 'Oscar Wilde At Oxford'.

35 De Sales La Terrière, *Days that Are Gone*, 74.

36 Spiers and Sons' bill for Oscar O'Flahertie Wilde Esq, 'Ross Collection' Univ; reproduced in *Wildean*, 44 (2014), 45. OW's first purchase, '2 china jugs', made on 19 January 1875, is misdated by Ellmann, 44, to Wilde's 'first term', Michaelmas 1874, and misdescribed as 'two blue mugs'.

37 Harris, 27; WRWW to OW, Dublin, 1874, re. some money which he expects from 'Maturin' and proposes to divide; he will credit OW with his share, £315 (Dulau); Anne Clark Amor, 'Heading for Disaster: Oscar's Finances', *Wildean*, 44 (2014), 37, suggests WRWW gave OW an allowance of £300 p.a., but gives no reference. The amount seems unlikely.

38 Bodley, 'Diary'; [Bodley], 'Oscar Wilde At Oxford'.

39 Walter Hamilton, *The Aesthetic Movement in England* (1882), 99; *CL*, 42, and OW's 'scrapbook' (National Library of Congress, Washington).

40 Bodley, 'Diary'.

41 [Bodley], 'Oscar Wilde At Oxford'.

42 Bodley 'Diary', 8 May 1875; Bodley also refers to OW's 'chaffable innocence'; R. Childers to J. E. C. Bodley, 13 March [1875], regretting he had missed OW's initiation to the Apollo Lodge, 'Wilde must have been great sport' (Bodleian Library).

43 [Bodley], 'Oscar Wilde At Oxford'.

44 [Bodley], 'Oscar Wilde At Oxford'.

45 Bodley, 'Diary'.

46 [Bodley], 'Oscar Wilde At Oxford'; Y. Bereisner, 'Oscar Wilde: A University Mason', www.Freemasons-Freemasonry.com.

47 Bodley, 'Diary', 21 February 1875.

48 Bereisner, 'Oscar Wilde: A University Mason'; although WRWW had been a

mason since 1838, there is no evidence that WCKW ever became one.

49 De Sales La Terrière, *Days that Are Gone*, 77.

50 [Bodley], 'Oscar Wilde At Oxford'.

51 Bodley, 'Diary'; Bereisner, 'Oscar Wilde: A University Mason'.

52 Bodley 'Diary', 6 May 1875.

53 Atkinson, in Mikhail 19.

54 Even the stern critic A. E. Housman was impressed. When Alfred Pollard included the poem in his anthology *Odes from the Greek Dramatists* (1890), Housman wrote that is was 'not bad at all'.

55 'Oscar Wilde', *Biograph and Review*, 132; OW, 'Art and the Handicraftsman', *Miscellanies: Vol. XIV of The Complete Works of Oscar Wilde*, [ed. Robert Ross] (1908); OW in both these accounts (and in other references made in 1882) refers to his work being done on 'November mornings' (i.e. during his first term), but many of the other specific details he gives are demonstrably untrue, and Bodley's account in the *NYT* suggests that any actual engagement with the road-builders came after OW's first term.

56 Atkinson, in Mikhail, 20; JFW to LVK, 6 May 1875, in Tipper, *Kraemer*, 57; JFW to [John Hilson], 5 May [1875], Tipper, *Hilson*, 74–5: 'Oscar is now a scholar at Oxford and resides there in a very focus of intellect. Ruskin had him to breakfast.'

57 The first mention of OW and Miles together occurs in Bodley's 'Diary' entry for 7 May 1875: 'Met Wilde with Frank Miles "the Gardener's daughter" [the name of one of Miles's pictures]'.

58 *Nottinghamshire Guardian*, 26 September 1873; Molly Whittington-Egan, *Frank Miles and Oscar Wilde* (2008), 28–31.

59 Advertisement, *Graphic*, 25 December 1875.

60 *Graphic*, 18 September 1875. Among those publishing Miles's work were George Rees, Mrs Agnes Russell and Mansell & Co.

61 OW to Ward, *CL*, 22.

62 Bodley, 'Diary', 16 December 1875. Bodley's contemporary accounts disproves the anecdote – recorded by G. P. Jacomb-Hood, *With Brush and Pencil* (1925), 114 – that Miles had sent some of drawings to Ruskin asking 'what he thought of them', and received the answer, 'Dear Sir, I think nothing of them.'

63 Bodley, 'Diary', 8 May 1875.

64 Harris, 23; his Oxford tailor's bill from Joseph A. Muir lists on 18 May 1875 the purchase of some 'super Angola trousers' for £1 12s 6d.

65 'Sonnet on Approaching Italy', written in 1877, on his return to Italy.

66 OW to WRWW, *CL*, 8–9. Wilde's full itinerary is unknown. The first surviving letter clearly belongs to a sequence. From the evidence of his 1877 review of the Grosvenor Gallery he seems perhaps to have visited both Parma and Perugia. Perugia is close to Lake Trasimene.

67 'The Theories of A Poet', *New York Tribune*, 8 January 1882, in Hofer & Scharnost, 19.

68 *CL*, 10–13.

69 *CL*, 11–13; Ruskin, in a letter to Dean Liddell (12 October 1844) listed Giotto, Fra Angelico, 'John Bellini' and Titian as the four Italian artists most needed by the new National Gallery in London.

70 'San Minato' ms version, quoted in Mason, 64; the 'Angelic Monk' is a reference to the painter – and monk – Fra Angelico, not that he ever painted in the church of San Miniato.

71 'Oscar Wilde's Visit to America', prospectus published 24 January 1882,

Boston, 3; 'Oscar Wilde', *Biograph and Review*.

72 'Oscar Wilde', *Biograph and Review*; OW's poem 'Rome Unvisited' is dated 'Arona', though it seems to have been finished after he had left. OET I, 223.

73 [Unknown] to OW, Bray, 29 July [1875?] (Clark); Miles's picture is dated 12 August 1875. Ellmann, 55, says it was done in Dublin, but does not give a source.

74 JFW to OW [July/August 1875], Tipper, *Oscar*, 32–3. Tipper dates the letter August 1876, but the 1875 date seems more probable on account of the reference to the 'ode' having just been finished and sent of 'at once for there was not a day to spare'. JFW's ode on O'Connell was published in the Boston *Pilot* on 6 August 1875, and perhaps also in Ireland. There is a letter from J. D. Sullivan, editor of the *Nation*, to Lady Wilde, dated 31 August 1875 (Clark) praising her for the ode on O'Connell, 'You, whose poetry has the range and swell of a great organ.' The *Pilot*, America's oldest Catholic paper, was edited by John Boyle O'Reilly (1844–90), a one-time member of the Irish Republican Brotherhood, who had made his way to Boston, having been transported to Australia and then effected a daring escape. He had begun publishing JFW's poems in 1874. WRWW and JFW were both in Dublin on 6 August 1875, the day of the 'The Grand Centenary Banquet' in O'Connell's honour.

75 OET I, 226, list the echoes of Swinburne, Rossetti and Morris; Wilde's scrapbook notes that the poem was 'Written going over from Kingston to Holyhead October 22nd 1875'.

76 Cloisters VIII, Ground Floor Right (the rooms are currently the JCR dining room); Hunter-Blair, 116.

77 Hunter-Blair, 118.

78 Atkinson, in Mikhail, 16; De Sales La Terrière, *Days that Are Gone*, 75.

79 Hunter-Blair, 118. Hunter-Blair says the vases were acquired from Spiers, but they do not appear on Wilde's Spiers account. So either Hunter-Blair misremembered where they were acquired, or OW paid cash for them.

80 OW's Spiers bill lists these purchases in October 1875.

81 Hunter-Blair, 117–18. Hunter-Blair records these parties as beginning in OW's 'first year'; but from his narrative, and the description of the room's location, it is clear that he is describing OW's second year (1875–6). Indeed the chronology throughout Hunter-Blair's account is awry.

82 John Sproule to JFW, 3 November 1875 (Clark); Kenningdale Cook, sometimes referred to as the 'editor' of the *Dublin University Magazine*, was the 'proprietor'; he sent Lady Wilde a 'cordial note of congratulation' on her son's debut, along with four copies of the magazine.

83 WCKW's contributions to *Kottabos* up to Michaelmas 1875: 'First Series', 261, 292–3, 312; 'Second Series', 4–5, 6–7, 80–1,124, 134–5, 161.

84 Kenningdale Cook to OW, 21 July 1877, in Mason, 67.

85 JFW to LVK, 6 May 1875, in Tipper, *Kraemer*, 56–7.

86 JFW to [Hilson], [May 1875], in Ellmann, 33.

87 JFW to OW [July/August 1875] in Tipper, *Oscar*, 32–3; JFW to OW [January 1876] 'of course he [WCKW] *must* marry Katy'. Tipper, *Oscar*, 19–20.

88 Bodley 'Diary', 31 October 1875: 'White knows Armstrong by repute, he says old Wilde is a damned compromising acquaintance.' Although the phrase has often been attached to

OW (e.g. McKenna, 9), Bodley uses the term 'old Wilde' consistently in his diary to refer to WCKW. In one instance he even adds 'old' with a caret to make the distinction clear: 6 December 1875, 'Went later in the evening to the Churchill where Wilde was elected... I sang for the first time old Wilde's "Song of the Glass".'

89   Catalogued as [Unknown Person] to James R. Thursfield, 1 November 1875 (Clark). The letter, addressed from Oriel College, is signed 'Lt' i.e. Lancelot [Shadwell]; Shadwell and Thursfield were the two university proctors for 1875, see *Historical Register of the University of Oxford* (1900). Ellmann, 64, misdates the incident to 1876. The other undergraduates were Arnold Fitzgerald, Foster Harter and Baillie Peyton Ward.

90   [Bodley] 'Oscar Wilde At Oxford', mentions that 'an especially painful interview with a proctor at a college consecrated to the education of youths from the Welsh mountain-wilds reminded Oscar that moderations were at hand.' It also led to him getting a First. Jesus is the Oxford college with strong Welsh connections, and Thursfield the only proctor from Jesus during Wilde's time at Oxford.

Chapter 2: Heart's Yearnings

1   De Sales La Terrière, *Days that Are Gone*, 75.

2   *CL*, 40.

3   Florence Ward, 'Diary', 23 June [1876] (Magdalen).

4   Bereisner, 'Oscar Wilde: A University Mason'; OW was not present at the meeting when his membership was announced, though he does seem to have attended the following meeting, on 6 December 1875, when Bodley (as he records in his diary) 'sang for the first time old Wilde's "Song of the Glass" [from Offenbach's *La Grande Duchesse*].'

5   For nicknames see Florence Ward's diary; De Sales La Terrière, *Days that Are Gone*; and *CL*, 14n, 15n.

6   Hunter-Blair, 119–20.

7   Hunter-Blair, 124–5; for the name of the 'old Catholic chapel' – St Ignatius's – I am indebted to Brendan Walsh.

8   Hunter-Blair, 125–8; St Aloysius was opened on 23 November 1875; Mass was celebrated by Dr Ullathorne, bishop of Birmingham, and the sermon preached by Cardinal Manning. Hunter-

Blair's account is slightly garbled.

9   Lord Ronald Sutherland Gower, *My Reminiscences* (1883) 2:133–4; [Bodley], 'Oscar Wilde At Oxford'.

10   'Oscar Wilde', *Biograph and Review*, 134.

11   OET I, 6; 7–9; the lines for the early version, regarding the nightingale, were converted into a separate piece, 'By the Arno'.

12   Hunter-Blair, 128–9.

13   The lectures were held twice weekly from 2 to 27 November 1875.

14   E. T. Cook, *The Life of John Ruskin* (1911) 2:26; M. L. Woods, 'Oxford in the Seventies', 281.

15   Walter Pater, 'Conclusion', *Studies in the History of the Renaissance* (1873), 231; the passage originally appeared in Pater's review 'Poems by William Morris', *Westminster Review*, 34 (1868). Pater had dedicated his book to 'C. L. S.' – [Charles] Lancelot Shadwell, the proctor and Oriel don to whom OW had behaved so insultingly at the Clarendon Hotel in November 1875.

16 Pater, 'Conclusion'.

17 'Mr Pater's Last Volume', OET VII, 243; OW, writing in 1897, claimed to have read the book in his 'first term' at Oxford (*CL*, 735); and it is certainly possible, although he frequently misremembered such details in his desire to appear precocious, or to obscure his intellectual debts. There are surprisingly few traces of Pater in OW's early Oxford writings. He is not mentioned in OW's letters before 1877. The revised version of OW's poem 'San Minato', probably worked on in late 1875, contains an echo of Pater's phraseology from the chapter on Winckelmann (OET I, 222), and OW's essay 'The Women of Homer' – which may date from the summer of 1876 – refers approvingly to Pater's prose style. It was not, however, until 1877, at the beginning of his fourth year, that OW met Pater. OW's copy of *The Renaissance* has not been traced. WCKW's copy of the 1873 edition – with marginalia possibly by OW – is at the Gleeson Library at the University of San Francisco; it is inscribed 'WCK Wilde, 1877' (thanks to Thomas Wright for this information). From 1875 up until Trinity term 1876 Pater gave a course of lectures on 'Republic of Plato – Book I' for students from Brasenose, Magdalen, Oriel and five other colleges taking 'final school of *Literae Humaniores*' ('Greats'). OW – still in his second year – did not attend; Mason, 101. But it is likely that Ward, who was in the year above, did go to these lectures. By the time OW was reading for 'Greats' the lectures on Plato were being given by a 'Mr Henderson' of Wadham.

18 Harris, 28.

19 OW, 'The Grosvenor Gallery', OET VI, 11.

20 Ross, *Oscar Wilde and Ancient Greece*, 128. Ross also notes Pater's admiration for archaic Greek culture.

21 'Preface' and 'Leonardo da Vinci', in Pater, *Studies in the History of the Renaissance*.

22 'The modern student most often meets Plato on that side which seems to pass beyond Plato into a world no longer pagan, based upon the conception of a spiritual life. But the element of affinity which he presents to Winckelmann is that which is wholly Greek, and alien from the Christian world, represented by that group of brilliant youths in the Lysis, still uninfected by any spiritual sickness, finding the end of all endeavour in the aspects of the human form, the continual stir and motion of a comely human life.' From Pater, 'Winckelmann', *Studies in the History of the Renaissance*.

23 *The Memoirs of John Addington Symonds*, ed. Phyllis Groskurth, 101–2; Ellmann, 58.

24 Billie Andrew Inman, 'Estrangement and Connection: Walter Pater, Benjamin Jowett, and William M. Hardinge', in *Pater in the 1990s*, eds Laurel Brake and Ian Small (1991), 1–20, gives a full account of the scandal and its aftermath, quoting letters from Milner (and Arnold Toynbee) to Philip Gell, as well as A. C. Benson's *Diary* on the interview between Jowett and Pater.

25 Bodley, 'Diary', 8 December 1875.

26 JFW to OW, [Jan 1876], re. Sir William's talk 'of letting No. 1 furnished – Amen. I am content – A great change might do us good – Sir W to Moytura. Willie to Chambers, you in Oxford. I – Lord knows where. Tipper, *Oscar*, 18, 21,

27 R. J. Le Poer Trench to OW, 'Sunday' [1875], in Clark (catalogued as 'French, R. J. to OW).

28 OET I, 330–1; OW, 'Scrapbook', refers to the poem as being written partly

at Clonfin (December 1875), partly at Oxford. Published May 1876.

29 JFW to OW, in Tipper, *Oscar*, 24–5.

30 JFW to OW, in Tipper, *Oscar*, 25–6.

31 Lewis R. Farnell, *An Oxonian Looks Back* (1934), 57: 'We only knew of him as a... "freak", who wrote poetry'; Gower, *My Reminiscences*, 2:133–4, refers to OW's 'long-haired head'.

32 JFW to OW, in Tipper, *Oscar*, 20.

33 *CL*, 32; 'Rome Unvisited' – as it appeared in *Poems* (1881) – was first published in the *Month* (September 1876) as 'Graffiti d'Italia – Arona. Lago Maggiore'.

34 *CL*, 16n, 32.

35 JFW to OW, 'Monday Night' [March 1876], in Tipper, *Oscar*, 22–3.

36 'Oscar Wilde', *Biograph and Review*; OET I, 330; the poem is entitled 'To the Author of "Graffiti d'Italia"'; OW has marked the cutting optimistically 'perhaps by Newman'.

37 JFW to OW, in Tipper, *Oscar*, 25–6; Tipper suggests that it was the 'worldliness' rather than the Catholicism that Mahaffy objected to.

38 De Sales La Terrière, *Days that Are Gone*, 75.

39 Hunter-Blair, 122.

40 Atkinson, in Mikhail, 16.

41 JFW to Sir Thomas Larcom, in Melville, 128.

42 Sherard, *Life*, 27–8.

43 T. G. Wilson, *Victorian Doctor – Being the Life of Sir William Wilde* (1942), 311.

44 *Belfast News-Letter*, 24 April 1876, mentions on the funeral at Mount Jerome Cemetery 'the coffin, on which one of the sons of the deceased placed several handsome wreaths of immortelles and camellias'; J. E. C Bodley to OW, 20 April 1876, in Clark; *World*, 26 April 1876.

45 JFW to Thomas Larcom, in Melville, 131.

46 *CL*, 20; in his poem 'O Loved one lying far away', OW refers to his father's 'helping hand'; OET I, 29.

47 'O Loved One Living Far Away'; 'The True Knowledge' and 'Lotus Leaves' also seem to refer to WRWW's death. OET I, 29, 19–20, 26–8.

48 Melville, 132; WRWW's will was lost in 1922 when the Four Courts building in Dublin, including the Irish Public Record Office, was destroyed during the civil war.

49 JFW to Sir T. Larcom, in Melville, 132.

50 JFW to Sir T. Larcom, in Melville 132–3, says both loans were dated '5 June last' (i.e. 1875); JFW to OW [1876], in Tipper, *Oscar*, 31–2, gives the date of 'the last £1,000' loan as '1874'; Amor, 'Heading for Disaster: Oscar's Finances', *Wildean* 44, 38, gives the date 'November 1874' for the Moytura loan, and the amount as £1,260.

51 JFW to OW [1876], in Tipper, *Oscar*, 31–2; Ellmann suggests that WRWW might have given it to his former mistress.

52 JFW to Sir T. Larcom, in Melville, 132–3.

53 JFW to OW, in Tipper, *Oscar*, 26–7.

54 Inland Revenue to JFW, 7 August 1884 (Clark), the re. WRWW's will: legacy and succession duty still due 'in respect of leasehold property in Bray and Clonfeacle to Mr Oscar F. O. F. Wilde for which you and your co-executor are responsible'. Other papers in Clark show that OW held the Clonfeacle property in conjunction with various members of the Maturin family.

55 JWF to Sir T. Larcom, in Melville, 133.

56 'In the Midnight', *Dublin University Magazine*, January 1877; JFW to OW, in Tipper, *Oscar*, 46.

57 Melville, 133; JFW to OW, in Tipper, *Oscar*, 36–7.

58 JFW to OW, in Tipper, *Oscar*, 43.

59 Sherard, *Life*, 30–32.

60 Ross, *Oscar Wilde and Ancient Greece*, 36.

61 *CL*, 19, 17.

62 *CL*, 17; Florence Ward ms diary (Magdalen); Marion Fowler, *Blenheim* (1998), 68.

63 Florence Ward, ms diary.

64 Florence Ward, ms diary.

65 Atkinson, in Mikhail, 16–17.

66 De Sales La Terrière, *Days that Are Gone*, 75.

67 Gower, *My Reminiscences*, 2:133–4.

68 Hunter-Blair, 129.

69 *Private and Public Galleries of Holland and Belgium* (1875); OW's copy is in Clark. *Three Hundred French Portraits representing Personages of the Courts of Francis I., Henry II., and Francis II., by Clouet. Autolithographed from the originals ... by Lord Ronald Gower* (1875); *Some passages of the life and death of the Right Honourable John, Earl of Rochester / reprinted in facsimile from the edition of 1680; with an introductory preface by Lord Ronald Gower* (1875).

70 Hunter-Blair, 130.

71 OW to R. Harding, *CL*, 19; the beautiful but 'flighty' Maria 'Minnie' Preston had married the 4th Earl of Desart in 1871; they divorced in 1878 on account of her affair with the actor Charles Sugden, whom she subsequently married, and – in 1891 – divorced.

72 *CL*, 18.

73 *CL*, 18.

74 *CL*, 20; D. Inman, *The Making of Modern English Theology: God and the Academy at Oxford, 1833–1945* (2014), 175.

75 *CL*, 20.

76 Shane Leslie, *Memoir of John Edward Courtenay Bodley* (1931), 17.

77 *CL*, 20; Hunter-Blair, 123; there were 23 Firsts among the 118 examinees. Wilde's fellow Magdalen demy, Atkinson, also got a First.

78 *CL*, 20; *The Times*, 6 July 1876.

79 *CL*, 20.

80 OW's Spiers bill lists the purchase, for £3 15s, on 8 July 1876; *CL*, 28.

81 *CL*, 23.

82 *CL*, 21–3.

83 *CL*, 22.

84 *CL*, 25.

85 *CL*, 39, 41.

86 *CL*, 25.

87 *CL*, 27; O'Sullivan, 66.

88 *CL*, 27–8.

89 Cathcart & Hemple & Co [Solicitors] to Oscar OF F. [*sic*] Wilde, 1 May 1876 (Clark); advertisements appeared in *Freeman's Journal* on 24 August, 29 August and 4 September 1876, listing the houses as 'Property of Oscar Fingal O'Flahertie Wilde, Esq'.

90 *CL*, 30.

91 *CL*, 30, 31.

92 JFW to OW, [August 1876], in Tipper, *Oscar*, 34–5.

93 Arthur Llewelyn Roberts to OW [5 July 1876], (Clark); Roberts was a Magdalen contemporary, and later secretary of the Royal Literary Fund.

94 Edith J. Kingsford to OW, 11 October 1876 (Clark).

95 OW to Reginald Harding, *CL*, 29, although OW does not mention her name, and gives her age as 'seventeen' the letter almost certainly refers to Florence. Her birthday was on 17 July.

96 Merlin Holland, *The Wilde Album* (1997), 16–17, 53; *CL*, 29; *CL*, 71–3.

97 OET I, 17; OW ms at Morgan Library (New York) opening: 'I saw her thick locks like a mass / of honey dripping from the pin, / Each separate hair was like the thin / gold thread within a Venice glass.'

98 OW notebook at Beinecke Library, Yale. The first fifty-six pages contain notes on Roman history; two pages at the back of the notebook contain

scrawled aphorisms. It also contains –
reversed – a pencil draft of his play *Vera*.

99   Ethel Smyth, *Impressions that Remained*
(1919), 116; Smyth was being chaper-
oned by Mrs Evelyn Wood. *Freeman's
Journal*, 7 September 1876, lists both
'W. C. K Wilde' and 'The Hon Mrs
Wood, family, and suite' as having 'left
Kingstown for England'.

100 *CL*, 32.

101 *Freeman's Journal*, 9 August 1878, 'Law
Intelligence' gives the un-met 'reserve
price'; ms 'Estimate', 25 October 1876
(Clark). Although hard to make out,
the total seems to be £67; *Freeman's*

Journal, 20 November 1876.

102 JFW to OW [October 1876], in Tipper,
Oscar, 42–3.

103 The ceremony took place on 27
November 1876; Bereisner, 'Oscar
Wilde: A University Mason'; OW's ac-
count with G. H. Osmond, St Aldate's,
Oxford, reproduced in *Wildean*, 44
(2014), 43.

104 *CL*, 36; Hunter-Blair, 120–1.

105 *CL*, 35–6. The ring was preserved at
Magdalen College but was stolen in
2002; the inscription, in Greek, ran
round the outside with, on the inside,
'OFFW & RRH to WWW, 1876'.

Chapter 3: Hellas!

1   *CL*, 34–6; Harris, 31.

2   *CL*, 34–5; Arthur Dampier May, painter,
b. 1857.

3   'Gower Lodge', acquired that year;
see Gower, Lord Ronald, *Bric-a-Brac*
(1888).

4   'Mr. Punch's Select Committees', 'No.
I: On Drawing-Room Decoration',
Punch, 12 May 1877, 216.

5   Mary Ward (Mrs Humphrey Ward),
quoted in L. W. B. Brockliss, *The University of Oxford: A History* (2016), 472.
The Wards moved into Bradmore
Road, North Oxford, in 1872.

6   Harry Quilter, 'The New Renaissance
or the Gospel of Intensity', *Macmillan's
Magazine*, September 1880, 392–3.

7   George Macmillan to Alexander Macmillan, 28 March 1877; *CL*, 43–4.

8   *CL*, 40, 42; OW's Spiers bill, purchase
made in January 1877, together with
'six coffee cups and saucers'.

9   *CL*, 38–40.

10 *CL*, 389; WCKW had been experimenting with the form too. He seems to
have considered poetry writing as a
useful weapon in his amatory arsenal.

He had one sonnet (on Schubert) published in *London Society*, and several
more in *Kottabos*.

11 Symonds, *Studies of the Greek Poets*,
408.

12 G. T. Atkinson, in Mikhail, 19.

13 *CL*, 42.

14 *CL*, 42. JFW to OW [Feb 1876], in
Tipper, *Oscar*, 20–1, describes Lady
Westmeath approvingly as 'young,
Greek head, ivy wreath'.

15 *CL*, 28–9; the chorister Eric Richard
Ward was born in 1863 at Bedmin-
ster, Somerset. Charles John Todd had
been one of the guests at OW's dinner
at the 1876 Commem. He became a
vicar.

16 OET I, 10, 42; 'Choir Boy' is an almost
Betjeman-esque fragment, beginning:

Every day in the chapel choir
Praises to God I sing,
And they say that my voice mounts
     higher,
Than even a bird can sing –

Though the organ be loudly pealing,
It reaches the heavens blue,

Up through the vaulted ceiling
To where God sits out of view.

17　CL, 39.

18　*Exhibition of Works by the Old Masters and by Deceased Masters of the British School*, Royal Academy, 1876; the exhibition opened in December 1876.

19　CL, 42.

20　CL, 41.

21　Although OW's own desire for success was quite enough to ensure that he would work hard, on 7 March 1878 J. A. Symonds sent him a letter – and a photograph – admonishing, 'Get a good degree if you can. It is worth something in after life.' (The Oscar Wilde collection of John B. Stetson, cat. item 407).

22　Atkinson, in Mikhail, 17; Vernier, 'Oscar at Magdalen'.

23　Atkinson, in Mikhail, 18; Mr Bulley's 'President's Notebook' (Magdalen), 30 May 1875, records that Prince Leopold, together with Princess Alice and Prince Louis of Hesse 'attended Chapel Service this day, at 5 o'clock… They are on a visit to the Dean of Christ Church'; Vernier, 'Oscar at Magdalen', 28–9.

24　CL, 39.

25　Hunter-Blair, 31–2, where he misdates the incident to 'early in 1876'; CL, 41, 43.

26　G. Macmillan to A. Macmillan, CL, 44.

27　G. Macmillan to A. Macmillan, CL, 44; G. Macmillan to Margaret Macmillan, quoted in Ellmann, 68.

28　OW, 'Tomb of Keats', OET VI, 11–12; Ruskin, *Modern Painters*, II.

29　OW, 'Mental Photograph', 44–5; OW, 'The Grosvenor Gallery', OET VI, 5.

30　OW later (1881) changed the phrase 'honied hours' to 'Hellenic hours'; OET I, 33, 234.

31　Letter from Mahaffy to his wife [2 April, 1877], quoted in Starkie, *Scholars and Gypsies*, 100–1.

32　G. Macmillan to Margaret Macmillan, 29 March 1877, in Ellmann, 68.

33　G. Macmillan to A. Macmillan, CL, 44.

34　OW, ms notes on Greece (Berg).

35　CL, 45.

36　John Mahaffy, *Rambles and Studies in Greece* (1878), 48; [George A. Macmillan], 'A Ride Across the Peloponnese', *Blackwood's Magazine*, 123, no. 751 (May 1878), 550; OW ms notes on Greece (Berg).

37　G. Macmillan to Malcolm Macmillan, 14 April 1877 (Hellenic Society); OW, Grosvenor Gallery review, 1877, OET VI, 1–11.

38　OW, OET I, 'Santa Decca', 44.

39　*Blackwood's*, 551.

40　*Blackwood's*, 552, 554–6.

41　Mahaffy, *Rambles and Studies in Greece*, 290.

42　Ross, *Oscar Wilde and Ancient Greece*, 53: OW made this remark to Ricketts apropos the Hermes of Praxiteles, which was unearthed at Olympia the week after OW's visit, and which he never saw at first hand.

43　OET I, 34–5.

44　[Otho Lloyd], 'Stray Recollections' by his 'brother in law', *The Soil*, 1, no. 4 (1914), 155–6.

45　Mahaffy, *Rambles and Studies in Greece*, 404; G. Macmillan to Malcolm Macmillan (Hellenic Society); *Blackwood's*, 558, 561; Starkie, *Scholars and Gypsies*, 100–1.

46　G. Macmillan to Malcolm Macmillan, 14 April 1877 (Hellenic Society).

47　G. Macmillan to Malcolm Macmillan (Hellenic Society); *Blackwood's*, 563–4. It is worth recapping OW's full Peloponnesian itinerary (derived from G. Macmillan's 'A Ride Across the Peloponnese' article and his letters) as it is incorrectly given in Ellmann: 1 April (Easter Sunday), leave Brindisi by steamer at 8.30 pm; 2 April, morning,

arrive at Corfu; 3 April, depart Corfu at 5 pm by steamer; 4 April, arrive Zante, pick up a lift on a sailing boat 'through the kindness of an American merchant', arrive Katakolo 5.30 pm, spend night at Pyrgos; 5 April, ride to Olympia and look over site, spend night at Druva; 6 April, ride to Andritzena; 7 April, visit Bassae, spend second night at Andritzena; 8 April (Greek Orthodox Easter), attend Easter Service in the early hours of the morning, then ride to Megalopolis, arriving in the early evening; 9 April, ride to Tripoliza; 10 April, visit Tegea, then take carriage to Argos, spend night at Argos; 11 April, visit Argos in the morning, then visit Mycenae in the afternoon, return to Argos before setting off to Nauplia; 12 April, ride from Nauplia to Epidaurus, take sailing boat from Epidaurus to Piraeus.

48   G. Macmillan to Malcolm Macmillan (Hellenic Society).

49   G. Macmillan to Olive Macmillan, 17 April 1877 (Hellenic Society).

50   'George Fleming' [J. C. Fletcher], *Mirage*, 3 vols (1877), 2:94.

51   Mahaffy, *Rambles and Studies in Greece*, 55.

52   G. Macmillan to Olive Macmillan (Hellenic Society).

53   *CL*, 66.

54   G. Macmillan to Olive Macmillan (Hellenic Society).

55   [Otho Lloyd], 'Stray Recollections', 155–6.

56   [Otho Lloyd], 'Stray Recollections', 155–6. Otho Lloyd to A. J. A. Symons, 22 May 1937 (Clark).

57   It is not known which sonnet he wrote in the immediate aftermath of his audience. The two likely candidates are 'Urbs Sacra Aeterna' and 'Easter Day', which both mention pilgrims kneeling before the 'Holy' Lord of Rome, OET I, 35, 37.

58   OW 'Tomb of Keats', OET VI, 11; OW to Lord Houghton, *CL*, 49–50.

59   Hunter-Blair, 133; *CL*, 57.

60   'Mental Photograph' lists 'Cardinal' as ambition, and 'Renaissance' as time he would have liked to live; and the 'Apoxymenos' as favourite sculpture. J. A. Symonds on the Apoxymenos; [unknown] to OW, 26 October 1878 (Clark) re. WCKW wanting to be an MP, and OW wishing to be a cardinal; Harris, 31.

61   Denis Gwynn, *Edward Martyn and the Irish Revival* (1930), 61; OW's 'Mental Photograph' lists Correggio as one of his favourite painters; Ruskin condemned the artist in *Modern Painters*. OW also knew and admired Correggio's work at Parma. Although the details of his visit there are unrecorded, the city was a major railway hub, and it is possible that OW called there, together with Mahaffy and co., on the train journey from Genoa to Ravenna.

62   Ward, in Mikhail, 14; *CL*, 58, 61; Fleming/Fletcher's first book was *A Nile Novel* (1877).

63   *CL*, 58; J. C. Fletcher to OW, 19 August 1877 (Clark).

64   President's notebook, 26 April 1877 (Magdalen), *CL* 47n.

65   Ricketts, 35; *CL*, 47.

66   President's notebook, 4 May 1877 (Magdalen).

67   *CL*, 47.

68   OET VI, 197: OW probably attended Rubinstein's concert on the afternoon of 9 May 1877, at which Beethoven's 'Sonata in F Minor' (the '*Appassionata*') was played.

69   'Grosvenor Gallery', *Morning Post*, 1 May 1899; 'London Notes', *Ipswich Journal*, 1 May 1877; OW, 'The Grosvenor Gallery', OET VI, 1.

70 'Variorum Notes', *Examiner*, 5 May 1877.

71 *CL*, 33; OET VI, 11 and *CL*, 52 suggest OW's acquaintanceship with Whistler.

72 OW, 'Mrs Langtry', OET VI, 23.

73 Laura Beatty, *Lillie Langtry: Manners, Masks and Morals* (1999), 38; 'Interview with the Jersey Lillie', *Daily Telegraph*, 3 October 1882.

74 Beatty, *Lillie Langtry: Manners, Masks and Morals*, 38.

75 Shane Leslie, *Memoir of John Edward Courtenay Bodley* (1931), 68: Bodley, talking of Langtry, recalled how 'one night, when an undergraduate' (he graduated in 1877) he was leaving the Vaudeville Theatre with OW, who said he 'had to hurry away, explaining enthusiastically that he was going to meet the loveliest woman Europe in the ... studio of Frank Miles'.

76 Gower, *My Reminiscences*, 2:153; 'Laura' was the muse of Petrarch's sonnets.

77 There is a possibility that he retitled his mock-medieval 'Chanson' (published in *Kottabos* the previous year) in Lillie Langtry's honour. A manuscript of the poem (Austin, Texas) is titled 'Lily-Flower'. OW's list of sonnets, written and planned, compiled c. July 1877 (OET I, 322) has none obviously relating to Mrs Langtry, although the titles 23 'Bournemouth', 24 'Picture', and 25 'Friendship' are vague enough to allow the possibility.

Chapter 4: Specially Commended

1 *CL*, 48.

2 *CL*, 48; Mahaffy's lectures *On Primitive Civilizations and Their Physical Conditions* were published in 1869. There is no record of when, or even if, OW delivered his lectures; two unpublished manuscripts, 'Hellenism' and 'Women of Homer', may perhaps be drafts for these lectures. See Thomas Wright, 'Oscar Wilde: Hellenism', *Wildean*, 41 (2012), 2–50.

3 Mason, 75–6.

4 *Irish Times*, 25 May 1877; Thomas Wright and Paul Kinsella, 'Oscar Wilde, A Parnellite Home Ruler and Gladstonian Liberal: Wilde's career at the Eighty Club (1887–1895)', https://oscholars-oscholars.com/.

5 *CL*, 36.

6 *CL*, 46.

7 *CL*, 48.

8 Lord Houghton to OW, 20 May 1877 (Austin); W. M. Rossetti to OW, 3 August 1877 (Austin) thought Shelley more deserving of a statue than Keats.

9 OW to Keningale Cook, *CL*, 51.

10 OW, 'The Grosvenor Gallery', *Dublin University Magazine*, July 1877; OET VI, 1–11.

11 *CL*, 58.

12 Walter Pater to OW, 14 July [1877] (Austin).

13 *CL*, 58–9.

14 Florence Balcombe to OW, 'Thursday' [June 1877] (Clark).

15 D. Hunter-Blair to OW, 1 June 1877 (Clark).

16 He died at 'midnight' on Tuesday 12 June, so his death was registered as 13 June. *Freeman's Journal*, 15 June 1877. His address is mistakenly given as '2 Merrion Square'.

17 *CL*, 54.

18 *CL*, 54; in due course he consulted a lawyer, and paid WCKW £10 to renounce his claims on Illaunroe. 3 August 1877: 'Draft Assignment & Release' from J. A. Rynd, a Dublin solicitor (Clark).

19 JFW to OW [1879], in Tipper, *Oscar*, 54.

20 Mason, 67, quoting a letter from editor of the *Dublin University Magazine* to OW, 21 July 1877, 'I shall be glad to see your Greek paper when ready' but suggesting that he should also try it with 'Allingham of *Fraser's Magazine*'.

21 *CL*, 60; Mason, 243–5; *Freeman's Journal*, 15 February 1879.

22 The thirty-five-line opening section of the poem runs from 'A year ago I breathed the Italian air' to 'I stood within Ravenna's walls at last'. In the published version the poem is prefaced by a date-line – 'Ravenna, March 1877. Oxford March 1878' – but it is not clear that this would have been in the ms submitted to the judges. In OET I, Fong and Beckson list over twenty-five self-borrowings from pre-existing poems, both published and unpublished (247–51); Hunter-Blair, 137, re. King and Pope.

23 Holland, *Wilde Album*, 44–5; Peter Vernier, 'A "Mental Photograph" of Oscar Wilde', *Wildean*, 13 (1998), 29–51.

24 The details of the transaction are recorded in the reports of case 'Wilde v Watson', *Freeman's Journal*, 8 July, 9 July, 12 July, 13 July, 18 July 1878; the sale memorial was dated 4 October. The friendship between the Quains and the Wildes is confirmed by JFW's letters to OW, in Tipper, *Oscar*, 49; Tipper, *Oscar*, 52 suggests that Mr Quain hoped OW would have access to the money he had offered.

25 President's notebook, 15 October 1877 (Magdalen).

26 *CL*, 62.

27 Shane Leslie, *Memoir of John Edward Courtenay Bodley* (1930), 17–18.

28 Walter Pater to OW (six letters 1877–8) (Clark); also The Oscar Wilde collection of John B. Stetson, cat. item 392:

Walter Pater to OW, 'I look forward to seeing you at dinner at my room in B.N.C [Brasenose College] on Wednesday, 6. to 6.30.' etc.

29 Leslie, *Memoir of John Edward Courtenay Bodley*, 17.

30 H. E. Wortham, *Oscar Browning* (1927), 186.

31 'Mr Pater's Last Volume', OET VII, 243.

32 Harris, 28.

33 *CL*, 349.

34 G. T. Atkinson, 'Oscar Wilde at Oxford', in Mikhail, 19 (where he misdates the lectures to 1874); 'Housman on Ruskin, Oxford 1877', www.victorianweb.org.

35 H. W. Nevinson, *Changes & Chances* (1923), 55. Nevinson matriculated at Christ Church in May 1875.

36 *CL*, 349; Atkinson, in Mikhail, 18.

37 Smith & Helfand, 145, 196–7. The phrase 'Rien n'est vrai que le beau' comes from Alfred de Musset's poem 'Après une lecture', and is an inversion of the phrase 'rien n'est beau que le vrai' from an earlier poem, of that title, by Nicolas Boileau.

38 *CL*, 61; [Otho Lloyd], 'Stray Recollections', 155; Atkinson, in Mikhail, 16.

39 OW to JFW, in Tipper, *Oscar*, 48–9.

40 Mrs Ernest Stuart Roberts (née May Harper), *Sherborne, Oxford and Cambridge* (1934), 66, recalls talking to OW after dinner in 1878; he told her of his blue and white china experience. 'He told me, too, that he was having his rooms decorated, and didn't know what to do about the ceiling, but was thinking of having it gilt.' For Burne-Jones's reproductions see Ellmann, 66, 560 n.560; and *CL*, 68.

41 'The Science of the Beautiful', *New York World*, 8 January 1882, in Hofer & Scharnhorst, 23; members of the clique included Leonard Montefiore and Harold Boulton.

42 Woods, 'Oxford in the Seventies', 281; CL, 67–68; Roberts, *Sherborne, Oxford and Cambridge*, 68; although the heads of colleges had long been permitted to marry, the ancient requirement for teaching fellows to be celibate was only just beginning to be relaxed in the late 1860s and early 1870s, each college following its own line in the matter. The trend was encouraged by the Oxford and Cambridge Universities Act of 1877.

43 Roberts, *Sherborne, Oxford and Cambridge*, 68.

44 Sherard, *Life*, 137–8; 'Oscar Wilde', *Biograph and Review*, 134.

45 Cf. 'Ravenna', 'Magdalen Walks' (published in the *Irish Monthly*, April 1878) and 'The Burden of Itys'; Sir James Rennell Rodd, *Social and Diplomatic Memories* (1922), 22.

46 Lady Poore, *An Admiral's Wife in the Making* (1917), 58. Lady Poore, née Ida Margaret Graves, with her sister Lily, attended the 1878 Commem. Lily thought OW's views 'silly and affected'; Ida came to realize that they were, in fact, rather sensible.

47 CL, 65.

48 Hofer & Scharnhorst, 27; Woods, 'Oxford in the Seventies', 282; Douglas Sladen, *Twenty Years of My Life* (1914), 109. Neither account appears to be first hand.

49 Roberts, *Sherborne, Oxford and Cambridge*, 60.

50 CL, 41.

51 Smith & Helfand, 141, 154, 159.

52 Woods, 'Oxford in the Seventies', 281.

53 Hofer & Scharnhorst, 23.

54 G. T. Atkinson, in Mikhail, 18.

55 A. T. D., 'Familiarum Sermones, II: O'Flighty', *Oxford and Cambridge Undergraduate's Journal*, 27 February 1879, 249, mentions it as 'a favourite remark' of 'O'Flighty's [Wilde's]'.

56 'The Theories of a Poet,' *New York Tribune*, 8 January 1882, 7, in Hofer & Scharnhorst, 20; OW was approximating the quotation from memory. Hunter-Blair, 118, records that the sermon was preached by Dean Burgon. The *Historical Register of the University of Oxford* (1900) lists John William Burgon (BD, Oriel) as one of the 'Select Preachers' for the academic year beginning Michaelmas 1877 (i.e. OW's last year). And it seems likely that the 'blue china' mot was made in 1878 during OW's final year, when he was becoming more exaggerated in his aestheticism. Ellmann, 44, however, dates the saying to 1876 based on an assertion by Oscar Browning. In a letter written in October 1912 to the periodical *Everyman*, Browning wrote: 'When I went to Oxford, in 1876, to stay with my old pupils, George Barnes and W. R. Paton, Barnes said to me, "There's a man at Magdalen named Wilde, who is very anxious to make your acquaintance. He says that he has heard you so much abused that he is sure you must be a most excellent person." He then added, "He's the man who said he wished that he could live up to his Blue China." So that M. Mazel's story is older than he imagines. The friendship thus begun continued to Wilde's death.' There are, however, reasons for supposing that the date given by Browning – recalled over thirty years after the event by a man of seventy-five – is not quite correct, and should be put back a couple of years. Although Browning is known to have visited Oxford in the spring of 1876 (H. E. Wortham, *Oscar Browning* (1927), 150), neither William Roget Paton nor George Stapylton Barnes were there at that time; they did not matriculate at University Col-

lege until October 1876. And although it is possible that Browning made an unrecorded return visit to Oxford at the end of 1876, there is nothing to suggest that Wilde knew Paton and/or Barnes at this early date. They were in different colleges, studying different subjects; they came from different backgrounds, and neither Paton nor Barnes was a Freemason. Moreover, Oscar Browning's biography, written by his nephew and friend H. E. Wortham, records (186) what was clearly an established family tradition, that Browning first met Wilde at Oxford when he was staying with Walter Pater. Pater did indeed become a friend of both Paton and Barnes, and of Wilde too. But Pater's connection with Wilde did not begin until 1877. And it would seem much more likely that Browning's introduction to Wilde, and his awareness of the 'blue china' mot dates from after 1877 – perhaps even to the time of his visit to Oxford in May 1878. (Lene Ostermark-Johansen, "'Don't forget your promise to come here soon": Seven Unpublished Letters from Walter Pater to Oscar Browning', *The Pater Newsletter*, 59/60 (2011), 17–28). The earliest direct evidence of Browning's friendship with OW is a letter at Austin, dated 29 May 1879, and beginning, 'My dear Wylde' [*sic*], which suggests a fairly recent connection. As does OW's reply – CL, *80* – beginning 'Dear Mr. Browning'.

57　W. Ward, in Mikhail, 13; Woods, 'Oxford in the Seventies', 281 (on OW's unpopularity); G. T. Atkinson, in Mikhail, 17, states that he had no knowledge of OW being ragged. There are, however, three accounts of such an incident but each of them is highly suspect. Sherard, *Life*, 138–9,

claims that OW was set upon by some 'healthy young Philistines' who 'bound him with cords and dragged him to the top of a hill. "Yes," said he when released, flicking the dust from his coat... "the view from this hill is really very charming."' As Atkinson remarks, 'It sounds strange', and would seem to be an elaborate misremembering of the occasions when Bodley and his friends rolled OW down the bank at Blenheim. Sladen, *Twenty Years of My Life*, 108–9, describes how 'another gang of sportsmen... broke into his rooms, smashed his blue china, and held his head under the college pump for an appreciable period'. This was the treatment meted out to Aesthetic undergraduates in the years after OW left – see 'From our London Correspondent', *Newcastle Courant*, 17 March 1882, where it is specifically said that OW did not suffer such indignities. And Sir Frank Benson, *My Memoirs* (1930), 136–9, gives a highly coloured account of OW thwarting an attempt on his rooms made by 'three or four inebriated intruders' from the Magdalen JCR, in which he hurls them down the stairs one by one. But – as Horst Schroeder points out – Benson did not matriculate until after OW left Oxford, and his story (in the words of one critic) 'betrays the tritest kind of anecdote-making'.

58　Dinner on 16 March 1878. P. Vernier, 'Oscar Toasts the Boat Club', *Magdalen College Record*, 2001.

59　CL, 64.

60　Fr Bowden to OW, 15 April 1878 (Clark).

61　Raffalovich/Michaelson, 111.

62　[Bodley] 'Oscar Wilde At Oxford'.

63　William Ward, in Mikhail, 13.

64　CL, 39.

65　OW, *PDG*, re. Dorian's flirtation with Roman Catholicism; see Ellmann, 91.

66　O'Sullivan, 65.

67　Roberts, *Sherborne, Oxford and Cambridge*, 60.

68　OW, in Harris, 26.

69　Harris, 26.

70　Woods, 'Oxford in the Seventies', 281; she refers to it as a 'hired suit of plum coloured velvet'.

71　G. T. Atkinson, in Mikhail, 18; Sladen, *Twenty Years of My Life*, 10–11. The incident occurred in 1878 (not, as Ellmann suggests, in 1876); the *Oxford University Gazette* shows that W. A. Spooner was one of the examiners in 1878, but not in 1876. Also Sladen matriculated at Trinity College, Oxford in 1875; he took 'Rudiments' in May 1878, and received his BA in 1879.

72　Robert Forman Horton, *An Autobiography* (1917), 44.

73　Tipper, *Oscar*, 51.

74　Tipper, *Oscar*, 52.

75　Dulau records letters to OW from Leonard Montefiore and S. Fletcher.

76　*Irish Monthly*, November 1878, 610; reproduced in Mason, 246. The same issue of the *Irish Monthly* also contained an article entitled 'An Irish Winner of the Newdigate', 630–3.

77　Hunter-Blair, 136–7; *Irish Monthly*, November 1878, 'An Irish Winner of the Newdigate', 630–3: 'Whatever halo the sun of Hellas may throw around [Byron's] early death, it is, alas, an amiable extravagance to speak of his "perfect name" or to imply that pitying Truth has not almost as bad a story to tell of him as venomed Slander.'

78　Stuart Mason, *A Bibliography of the Poems of Oscar Wilde* (1907), 3. OW's account in the Shrimpton's ledger, reproduced in Mason, 245, confirms OW bought at least 168 copies.

79　Walter Pater to OW, 10 June [1878] (Clark).

80　Reproduction of a sketch of OW, signed

'Yours Oscar Wilde, Magdalen 1878' (Yale).

81　Lady Poore, *An Admiral's Wife*, 58.

82　*Oxford and Cambridge Undergraduate Journal; Jackson's Oxford Journal*, 29 June 1878; Harris, 26; Thomas F. Plowman, *In the Days of Victoria* (1918) 270; JFW to OW, [28 June 1878], in Tipper, *Oscar*, 52.

83　*CL*, 69.

84　*CL*, 69; the letter dated 'Thursday' could be 18 July, with Wilde concerned about recovering the costs.

85　*Freeman's Journal*, 18 July 1878; Watson and Pym seem to have been considering an action against Messers Battersby, which might have held up any payment.

86　Hunter-Blair, 123

87　*The Times*, 20 July 1878, 8. OW was one of eighteen Firsts from a field of ninety-five candidates; G. T. Atkinson, the other Magdalen demy, got a Third.

88　*CL*, 103.

89　*CL*, 70.

90　*CL*, 70.

91　Hunter-Blair, 122.

92　*World*, 21 August 1878, 11; *Freeman's Journal*, 19 August 1878.

93　[Otho Lloyd], 'Stray Recollections'; almost certainly Marian Huxley (1859–87), artist, studying at the Slade.

94　*World*, 2 October 1878.

95　Tipper, *Oscar*, 52.

96　JFW to OW, 'Friday night' [1878], in Tipper, *Oscar*, 56–7.

97　Tipper, *Oscar*, 55–57; Tipper dates these two letters to early 1879, but the reference to the Ashford [Castle] photograph suggests a late 1878 date.

98　Tipper, *Oscar*, 53.

99　Harris, 210.

100　Tipper, *Oscar*, 52–3.

101　*CL*, 71–2.

102　'Apologia' ll. 29–36. The four poems in the sequence are 'Apologia', 'Quia

Multum Amavi' (Because I Have Loved Much), 'Silentium Amoris' (The Silence of Love) and 'A Farewell'. 'A Farewell' appeared in *Poems* (1881) divided into two poems, 'Her Voice' and 'My Voice'. The poems are hard to date exactly as no manuscripts exist. It has been suggested that they could refer not to Florence Balcombe but to Lillie Langtry. This, however, seems unlikely to me. OET I, 122–6, 279–81.

103 *World*, 8 October 1879, 9; Lewis R. Farnell, *An Oxonian Looks Back* (1934), 70.

104 Smith & Helfand, 37ff; Ross, *Oscar Wilde and Ancient Greece*, 59–62.

105 28 November 1878.

106 Peter Vernier, 'Oscar at Magdalen', 32.

Part III: *The Happy Prince*
Chapter 1: A Dream of Fair Women

1   'Mental Photograph', 44.

2   W. Ward, in Mikhail, 14.

3   Hunter-Blair, 120–1.

4   *CL*, 739.

5   The arrangement was made when OW, together with WCKW, returned briefly to Dublin at the beginning of 1879. Both brothers were in want of ready money. Repairs needed to be undertaken at Merrion Square before it could be sold, and OW wanted to arrange the rental of Illaunroe for the coming summer (he took out an advert in the *Field*). OW was able to raise £250 from a Miss Catherine Knox by mortgaging his share of the property at Clonfeacle; William C. Hogan & Sons to OW, 20 October 1882 (Clark).

6   L. Langtry, *The Days I Knew* (1925), 60; H. C. Marillier memoirs quoted in Jonathan Fryer, 'Harry Marillier and the Love of the Impossible', *Wildean*, 28 (2006), 2. General Sir John Bisset had his London pied-à-terre on the ground floor; an ancient Dr Turner lived in the attic.

7   *CL*, 85.

8   Fryer, 'Harry Marillier and the Love of the Impossible', 3; Mrs Claude Beddington, *All That I Have Met* (1929), 34.

9   'A Chat with Oscar Wilde', *Quiz* (Philadelphia), 25 January 1882, 4; Tom Taylor to Mrs Boughton, Monday, 19 May [1879] (Austin).

10 Pearson, 49, has a (surely garbled) anecdote in which OW calls unannounced on Spottiswoode in London, saying 'I have come to dine with you; I thought you would like to have me.' L. B. Walford, *Memories of a Victorian Lady* (1912), 147; Desmond Hillary to M. Sturgis, 19 June 2013, quoting Gordon Raybould's 1967 pamphlet on Combe Park and its environs; *CL*, 78 n.; Walter Crane, *An Artist's Reminiscences* (1907), 191–4.

11 'Exit Oscar', *Truth*, 11 July 1883; JFW to OW, [13 May 1879], in Tipper, *Oscar*, 60: 'If you like call on Mrs Cashel Hoey [the Irish short-story writer]. She is in the Literary Set – & would be delighted to see you.' Mrs T. P. O'Connor, *I Myself* (1910), 158.

12 'Fashion and Varieties', *Freeman's Journal*, 18 July 1879. Among OW's fellow guests were 'the Hon De La Poer Trench', 'the Hon. David Plunkett, M.P.' and 'Mr A. Moore'.

13 *CL*, 87, Melville, 159. Melville, 149 describes 1 Ovington Square as 'lodgings', but the 1881 census suggests that

JFW and WCKW, together with one servant, were the sole occupants of the house. Reginald Auberon [Horace C. Wyndham], *The Nineteen Hundreds* (1922), 75.

14 Mrs Clement Scott, in her memoir of her late husband, *Old Days in Bohemian London* (1919), 238, records that '[OW] had almost a reverence for the art of acting even then [when still dividing his time between Oxford and London], and several of his college-day essays on plays and players were printed by Clement Scott in the *Theatre* Magazine… They appeared under the pseudonym, if it can be called one, of "A Young Oxonian".' The statement is something of a mystery. Clement Scott only took over the editorship of *The Theatre* magazine in 1880, after OW had moved permanently to London. And I have been unable to trace any articles in *The Theatre* by 'A Young Oxonian' – or any very suggestive of OW's style. The early numbers of the magazine (1878–80) contain unsigned compendium reviews of London theatre productions, and it may be that OW contributed material anonymously to these.

15 *CL*, 154.

16 He had made his stage debut at seventeen, and had already appeared with Ellen Terry before following her to the Lyceum for the 1879 productions of *The Iron Chest* and *The Merchant of Venice*.

17 Obituaries in *The Times*, 30 September 1932, 7; 1 October 1932, 6. In later life Norman Forbes-Robertson had a part interest in a Bond Street gallery and was instrumental in identifying Vermeer's *Christ in the House of Martha and Mary*, now in the National Gallery of Scotland.

18 *CL*, 89. The letter is dated by Hart-Davies and Holland to March 1880, but a letter at Austin from Norman Forbes-Robertson to OW, dated '20 March 1879', indicates that it belongs to March 1879. Forbes-Robertson's letter runs: 'Dear Wild [*sic*] – I am very sorry I could not call on you yesterday more especially so as I should have had you all to myself. But I had an engagement to dine with a friend which I couldn't very well get off. Perhaps I may call some other day as I want to learn about your poems. Yours very truly, Norman Forbes-Robertson.'

19 E. W. Godwin, 'Diary 1879' (V&A). Godwin attended almost every Forbes-Robertson 'at home' between 9 May and 1 August, listing OW among those also present.

20 Langtry, *The Days I Knew*, 87.

21 Langtry, *The Days I Knew*, 86. Ellmann, 89, suggests that his teeth were discoloured due to a course of 'mercury treatment' for syphilis contracted while he was at Oxford (mercury could turn the teeth black). There is, however, no contemporary evidence that OW contracted the disease, or took mercury. And nothing in his behaviour makes it likely. The discolouring was more likely due to smoking, or a dead front tooth. For further discussion of OW's supposed syphilis see Part XI, chapter 3, n. 70.

22 Langtry, *The Days I Knew*, 86; Augusta Fane, *Chit Chat* (1926), 103.

23 Thomas Hake and Arthur Compton-Rickett, *The Life and Letters of Theodore Watts-Dunton* (1916), 1:172.

24 Harry Marillier, quoted in Fryer, 'Harry Marillier and the Love of the Impossible', 2.

25 Julian Hawthorne's diary, 18 Feb 1880, quoted in Ellmann, 57; and 'We had several acquaintances in common, and I saw him frequently. I was impressed,

like others, with the brilliance of his mental quality... something in him repelled and something attracted me to him.' J. Hawthorne, 'Oscar Wilde and What He Wrote', *Philadelphia North American*, 3 Dec 1900, 8.

26 Harris, 36; Langtry, *The Days I Knew*, 87.

27 Langtry, *The Days I Knew*, 86–7.

28 Violet Hunt, 'My Oscar' (ms Cornell), quoted in Robert Secor, 'Aesthetes and Pre-Raphaelites: Oscar Wilde and the Sweetest Violet in England', *Texas Studies in Literature and Language*, 21 (1979), 402–3; *Topeka Daily Capital*, 16 January 1882.

29 'Wilde's Personal Appearance' by his 'sister-in-law' (Mrs Frank Leslie?), *The Soil*, 1, no. 4 (1914), 150.

30 Harris, 36.

31 Langtry, *The Days I Knew*, 87.

32 Harris, 36.

33 Langtry, *The Days I Knew*, 96.

34 Walter Sickert to Alfred Pollard, 27 August 1879 (private collection).

35 'Oscar Wilde', *Pasadena Star-News*, 17 July 1924, 8, quoted in Gary Scharnhorst, *Julian Hawthorne: The Life of a Prodigal Son*.

36 Tom Taylor to Mrs Boughton, Monday, 19 May [1879] (Clark); Frank Harris, in his biography of Wilde, stated that OW arrived in London describing himself as a 'Professor of Aesthetics and a Critic of Art' – a piece of presumption that he castigates as 'at once infinitely ludicrous and pathetic'. But the description (as Harris acknowledges) was taken from Foster's *Alumni Oxonienses*, a volume not published until 1886. The epithets (given either by OW or the editor) date from that time, not 1879.

37 Godwin, 'Diary'; Walter Crane, *An Artist's Reminiscences* (1907), 191–4. Whistler was declared bankrupt on 8 May 1879. He left for Venice in September

1879 and did not return until November 1880. The White House was sold, on 18 September 1879, to the art critic Harry Quilter.

38 The Sickerts were also friends of the Forbes-Robertsons, and of Godwin. See Godwin, 'Diary 1879' (V&A).

39 *CL*, 77.

40 *CL*, 88.

41 Harris, 37; Maureen Borland, *D. S. MacColl* (1995), 25.

42 The date of their first meeting is unknown, but OW knew – and admired – James when they met again in Washington in 1882.

43 Ann Thwaite, *Edmund Gosse: A Literary Landscape* (1984), 211.

44 'Violet Fane' to OW [mid May 1879] (Austin), thanking him for an inscribed copy of *Ravenna*, saying that she had already read the poem, having been given a copy, by 'Mrs Lacy – our mutual friend', adding, 'the beauties I found in it prepared me in some measure for the more mature perfection of 'The Triumph of Time' which I admire *very very much*.' She looks forward to seeing OW and his brother at her reception on 28 May 'between 5 and 7'. The letter is mis-catalogued at Austin as from 'Violet Lane'.

45 C. G. Leland to OW, 4 October 1879 (Austin); see also JFW to C. G. Leland (TCD), 1 Ovington Square, hoping to see him 'again on Saturday afternoon'.

46 Frank Harris, *My Life and Loves* (1964), 456.

47 Langtry, *The Days I Knew*, 86–7.

48 These points are well drawn out in Beatty, *Lillie Langtry: Manners, Masks and Morals*, 3–4.

49 'Exit Oscar', *Truth*, 11 July 1883.

50 The two Newdigate prizewinners before OW – Mallock and Hardinge – both turned to novel writing, as did George Moore.

51 Quoted in R. B. Glaenzer, ed., *Decorative Art in America: A Lecture by Oscar Wilde* (1906), 32; *CL*, 98.

52 OW, 'Grosvenor Gallery', *Irish Daily News*, 5 May 1879, OET VI, 18.

53 'Oscar Wilde', *Biograph and Review*, 134.

54 WCKW to Miss Campbell, Thursday [30 January 1879] (Clark); the stories referred to in the letter had appeared in the *World*, 29 January 1879, 12; Harris, 32. WCKW to Ellen Terry, 19 November 1879 (Leeds) refers to editing the 'Christmas Number' of *Vanity Fair*, and ends, 'I hope you got my notice of the Merchant [of Venice] in the Irish Daily News.' It is possible that WCKW was writing for other papers as well.

55 OET VI, 16–18; *CL*, 79; OW's only other foray into criticism during 1879 was an unsigned review for the *Athenaeum* of J. A. Symonds' new volume *Sketches & Studies in Italy*, in which he praised the author's keen appreciation of beauty and lamented his occasional want of linguistic restraint.

56 Edmund Yates to WCKW, 30 January 1879 (Houghton); Yates seems to have had a belief in the cachet of the Newdigate Prize. William Money Hardinge, winner in 1876, contributed verse to the *World*: see W. M. Hardinge, 'A Benediction', *World*, 19 March 1879, 14; 'A Chance Meeting', *World*, 27 August 1879, 13.

57 W. L. Courtenay, *The Passing Hour* (1925), 118. Courtenay lists Yates and Harry Cust as the only two people he heard who, at their best, came 'somewhere near' OW as a conversationalist.

58 'The Conqueror of Time'; see OET I, 104–16. When the poem appeared in OW's 1881 volume, *Poems*, it was retitled 'Athanasia'.

59 *World*, 4 June 1879, 9: the ball took place on the evening of Thursday 29 May 1879. Charles Dilke described Mrs Douglass-Murray as 'agreeable but rather superfine'. Stephen Gwynn, *The Life of the Rt. Hon. Sir Charles W. Dilke* (1917).

60 Harris, 32.

61 The prize was not awarded that year. A very full – but not finished – manuscript of OW's essay is preserved at Clark. OW's correspondence makes no reference either to his submitting the work, or failing to win the prize. See OET IV, xxii.

62 *CL*, 78; Ross, *Oscar Wilde and Ancient Greece*, 100–1.

63 *CL*, 79.

64 *CL*, 78n. OW's application for a reader's ticket at the British Museum gave as his 'Purpose': 'Study of Greek and Latin literature with ref. to University career.'

65 Harris, 29.

66 He published two poems in *Waifs and Strays*, vols 1 and 3: 'Easter Day' and 'Impression de Voyage'; Mason, 216–18; R. Rodd, *Social and Diplomatic Memories* (1922), 10.

67 Gower, *My Reminiscences*, 2:320. The visit was in December 1879.

68 *CL*, 80–1, 84; Oscar Browning, *Memories of Sixty Years* (1910), 281–2, mentions a visit in October 1879 when he and OW 'went together to the A.D.C. Some of the actors came to supper with me afterwards.' H. E. Wortham, *Oscar Browning* (1927), 185.

69 *CL*, 86; Francis Adams, 'Frank Miles', *Boomerang*, 5 May 1888, 9, quoted in Meg Tasker, *Struggle and Storm, the Life and Death of Francis Adams* (2001).

70 Marillier, quoted in Fryer, 'Harry Marillier and the Love of the Impossible', 3; diary entry 'July 1879' in Laura Troubridge, *Life Amongst the Troubridges* (1999), 152.

71 OW, quoted in Harris, *My Life and Loves*, 457.

72 William Shepard, ed., *Pen Pictures of Modern Authors* (1882), 210, quoting 'An English Aesthete' from the *Boston Herald*. This article (with other early American press reports) claims that OW's afternoon receptions were held by candlelight with the blinds down, but this seems to be a confusion with Lady Wilde's parties, and is not supported by the contemporary accounts of known visitors, such as Lillie Langtry or Laura Troubridge.

73 Troubridge, *Life Amongst the Troubridges*, 152.

74 *CL*, 86 and n; *Vanity Fair*, 13 December 1879, gives the picture's theme as 'An Ocean Wave'.

75 Marillier, quoted in Fryer, 'Harry Marillier and the Love of the Impossible', 3.

76 'The New Helen' was to have appeared in the June 1879 number of *Time*, but was held over for the July edition, 400–2. Edmund Yates to OW, 20 May 1879 (Austin); the delay was due to Yates having committed to two long topical poems by Violet Fane and 'Mr Scudamore'. Violet Fane to OW [May 1879] (Austin), re. the delay in publication: 'I don't see "The New Helen" in the advertisement of the contents of *Time* – perhaps our fat Editor [Yates] put it by for next time, thinking that, like the beauty of the original it would keep.'

77 'The Apostle of Beauty in Nova Scotia', *Halifax Morning Herald*, 10 October 1882, in Hofer & Scharnhorst, 170; *CL*, 65, n.3.

78 Sarah Bernhardt, *My Double Life* (1907), 297–8. The crowd was not huge; indeed there are references to 'the scanty, but not the less eager contingent of sightseers', 'Arrival of Comédie Français', *Daily News*, 2 June 1879.

79 *CL*, 80; in a mixed programme, including two plays by Molière (*Le Misanthrope* and *Les Précieuses Ridicules*) Bernhard played Act 2 of *Phèdre*.

80 WCKW to Miss Campbell [June 1879] (Clark).

81 'Queen Henrietta Maria', *World*, 16 July 1879, 18; 'Portia', *World*, 14 January 1880, 13.

82 *CL*, 81.

83 Shepard, ed., *Pen Pictures of Modern Authors*, 211, quoting 'An English Aesthete' from the *Boston Herald*.

84 Ward, in Mikhail, 14: 'She had tried to see how high she could jump and write her name with a charcoal on the wall. From the scrawl on the side of the room and not much below the ceiling it seemed that she had attained a considerable success in the attempt.' H. Marillier, memoirs, 'Sarah Bernhard had scrawled [her name] in large letters with a carpenter's pencil right across one panel.' Quoted in Fryer, 'Harry Marillier and the Love of the Impossible', 3.

85 Quoted in Arthur Gold and Robert Fizdale, *The Divine Sarah* (1992), 151; Christian Krogh, 'Fitz Thaulow and Oscar Wilde at Dieppe, 1897', *New Age*, 10 December 1908, in Mikhail, 349.

86 'Humanitad', OET I, 96; *CL*, 107, indicates that OW had confided to Ellen Terry at least his former devotion to Florence.

87 *CL*, 107.

88 OW to Henry Irving, 13 Salisbury Street [on St Stephen's Club letterhead] [1979], requesting seats for Mrs Langtry for *Hamlet*. Ref 8497 in Henry Irving Correspondence online in HI Foundation Centenary Project; *CL*, 91.

89 Lillie Langtry to OW [1879], quoted in Beatty, *Lillie Langtry: Manners, Masks and Morals*, 138: 'I called at Salisbury

Street... I wanted to ask you how I should go to a fancy ball here.' W. Graham Robertson, *Time Was* (1931), 70.

90 Langtry, *The Days I Knew*, 95; Langtry describes the lectures as occurring at King's College London, and during her 'first season' – i.e. 1877. But the course of lectures, by C. T. Newton, keeper of classical antiquities at the British Museum (and president of the Hellenic Society), was given at University College, in May/June 1880; see 'Literary Miscellany', *Leeds Mercury*, 29 May 1880. Langtry and OW's presence made the lectures 'fashionable' and ensured that 'the aesthetic world was... strongly represented'. 'London Gossip', *Hampshire Telegraph*, 16 October 1880.

91 Langtry, *The Days I Knew*, 150–1; Violet Hunt, 'My Oscar', quoted in Secor, 'Aesthetes and Pre-Raphaelites', 402. Ellmann, 109, recounts that Ruskin 'drove [Langtry] out of the room in tears with one of his diatribes against Jezebels. "Beautiful women like you hold the fortunes of the world in your hands to make or mar," he called after her retreating form.' But Hunt's terse account does not allow for this gloss. Langtry could just as well have been moved to tears of awe by the tribute paid to her beauty by the great man.

92 Ricketts, 29; The 'Jersey lily' (*amaryllis belladonna*) had been associated with Lillie Langtry ever since Millais had exhibited her portrait entitled 'A Jersey Lily' at the Royal Academy in 1878, depicting the Jersey-born Langtry holding a single bloom of *amaryllis belladonna*. 'The Jersey Lily' became her nickname.

93 Langtry, *The Days I Knew*, 93.

94 Langtry, *The Days I Knew*, 96.

95 OET I, 118–21, 278; although the inscription 'To L. L.' certainly suggests a connection to Lillie Langtry, she is not very recognizable in the shy, flitting grey-green-eyed creature in the poem. Moreover, it should be noted that OW was not above writing poems to one person and then dedicating them to another. He adapted his sonnet 'Helena' – written for Modjeska – into 'Camma', a sonnet celebrating Ellen Terry. See OET I, 290.

96 Langtry, *The Days I Knew*, 96; Vincent O'Sullivan to A. J. A. Symons, 26 May 1937 (Clark): 'I think that Wilde was certainly in love with Langtry during his first years in London... She was not in love with him at all, and I feel sure that she never gave him anything.'

97 Beatty, *Lillie Langtry: Manners, Masks and Morals*, 160–6.

98 Beatty, *Lillie Langtry: Manners, Masks and Morals*, 140.

99 Langtry, *The Days I Knew*, 96; Gerson, *Lillie Langtry*, 54.

100 Lillie Langtry to OW, Shipley, Derby, 'Monday' [1879–81] (Austin); she was '*so* disgusted' with herself 'for forgetting till this moment all about the brougham'.

101 'London Gossip', *Hampshire Telegraph*, 16 October 1880.

102 Frederick Locker Lampson, *My Confidences* (1896), 309–10; *World*, 3 December 1879, 9: 'Here is a correct copy of some lines that were written by a well-known society versifier, and handed about at Mrs Millais' on Friday night [a party at which OW was present]:

For MRS LANGTRY

When youth and wit and beauty call,
I never walk away;
When Mrs. Langtry leaves the ball
I never care to stay.

I cannot rhyme like Oscar Wylde

Or Hayward (gifted pair!) [Abraham
  Hayward, 1801–84]
Or sing how Mrs. Langtry smiled,
Or how she wore her hair.

And yet I want to play my part,
Like any other swain;
To fracture Mrs. Langtry's heart –
And patch it up again

103 For OW's copy of Lord Ronald Gow-
  er's *A Pocket Guide to the Public and
  Private Galleries of Holland and Belgium*
  (1875) at Clark see Thomas Wright,
  'Tite Street Books at Clark Library',
  Wildean 48, 88–90

104 OW '*L'Envoi*', preface to Rodd's *Rose
  Leaf and Apple Leaf* (1882); in which
  Rodd's sonnet 'Une heure viendra qui
  tout paiera' appears. In Rodd's own
  annotated copy of the book, the poem
  is marked 'Tournai, 1879', W. Schrikx,
  'Oscar Wilde in Belgium', *Revue des
  Langues Vivantes*, 37 (1971), 122.

105 OW lecture, 'The Renaissance of English Art', 1882.

106 Paul de Reul, quoted in Schrikx, 'Oscar
  Wilde in Belgium', 119–20.

107 Schrikx, 'Oscar Wilde in Belgium',
  126–7; the lines are from Peck's poem,
  'A Monsieur de Reul', dated 'Diekirch
  25 Juillet, Dans un café'; Mathilde
  Thomas confirmed that the young
  Englishman referred to was OW
  rather than Rodd. Jacques Peck died
  in 1882, acclaimed as a harbinger of
  the Aesthetic 'Eighties generation' in
  Dutch literature. Xavier de Reul's art
  historical studies focused particularly
  on Rubens; he – like OW – was a great
  admirer of the artist's *Christ Bearing
  the Cross* at Brussels.

108 Walter Sickert to Alfred Pollard, 27
  August 1879 (private collection);
  Helena Swanwick, *I Have Been Young*
  (1935), 65–6.

109 Swanwick, *I Have Been Young*, 64–5;
  Oswald V. Sickert to Edward Marsh,
  30 August 1895 (Berg).

110 *CL*, 82.

111 Harris, 39.

112 Harris, 36, 38.

113 *CL*, 84.

114 Harris, 39; *CL*, 156.

115 The examination, held at Trinity, commenced on 23 September 1879, at
  9.30 am. 'The subjects of examination
  will be such as are recognized in the
  Classical Schools', *Oxford University
  Gazette*, 17 July 1879, 487.

116 Lewis R. Farnell, *An Oxonian Looks
  Back* (1934), 70–1.

117 *CL*, 87. The Trinity fellowship was
  awarded to Mr James Saumarez Mann
  MA, late of Exeter College (*Oxford
  University Gazette*, 10 October 1879,
  17). The examination for two classical
  fellowships at Merton was announced
  on 4 November 1879. On the day of
  the exam (23 December) OW was in
  London; *CL*, 85.

118 *CL*, 85.

119 *CL*, 87–8.

120 Marillier, quoted in Fryer, 'Harry Marillier and the Love of the Impossible', 3.

121 OW to 'Mr Silter', [n.d], 13 Salisbury
  Street; OW claimed to be in demand
  ('As I have one other offer I should be
  glad to hear from you soon what you
  intend to do about matters this summer') but this may have been a ploy to
  help close the arrangement. Bloomsbury Auctions, 20 August 2015, lot
  402.

122 Constance Westminster to OW, 4 January [1880] (Austin).

123 Rodd, *Social and Diplomatic Memories*,
  23; flooding was not infrequent in
  London at this period. *Morning Post*,
  28 August 1879, mentions flooding in
  Lambeth and 'the damage inflicted…
  upon the inhabitants of the poorer

districts' being of 'a most serious character'.

124 George E. Woodberry to C. Eliot
Norton, 25 April 1882 (Houghton), in
Ellmann, 192.

125 CL, 85.

126 J. Ruskin to OW, 'Thursday' [Decem-
ber 1879] (Berg): 'My dear Oscar, I
can manage nicely (I find) to be at
Ovington Sq by 4 tomorrow; and very
happy in being there I shall be – as you
made me all through Sunday.'

127 The visit occurred on a 'Sunday Morning' in December 1879; David Waller,
The Magnificent Mrs Tennant (2009),
238.

128 J. Ruskin to OW, 'Thursday' (Berg).

129 This was the verdict Ruskin passed on
to OW after the visit; Waller, The Magnificent Mrs Tennant, 238.

130 CL, 84.

131 L. B. Walford, Memories of Victorian
London (1912), 147–8; much of the
material in the book is based on contemporary letters and diary entries
written by Lucy Bethia Walford's
friend and 'sister' (identified by John
Cooper of Oscar Wilde in America
(OWIA), as Mrs Humphrey Ward);
Walford, though, misdates the above
incident to 1874, most likely a misreading of '1879'.

Chapter 2: The Jester and the Joke

1   Hake and Compton-Rickett, The Life
and Letters of Theodore Watts-Dunton,
1:172–3.

2   Lady St Helier, Memories of Fifty Years
(1909), 180.

3   'Postlethwaite from a new point of
view', World, 16 February 1881, 7–8.

4   Sherard, Life, 168.

5   Hugh and Mirabel Guinness, Imperial Marriage (2002), 34; OW to Mrs
Maxse, Salisbury Street [1879?] (BL),
inviting her and Violet to tea.

6   Troubridge, Life Amongst the Troubridges, 152, entry for 30 June 1879, at
a tea party given by Charles 'Tardy'
Orde, a cousin of the Troubridges and
Creswells.

7   Adrian Hope, Letters of Engagement
(2002), 6. Another of the Troubridges'
cousins, Charlie Orde, took a different
line, refusing to allow OW to introduce him to Ellen Terry, as it might
'destroy the illusion and he preferred
to imagine [actresses] to be really the
beautiful beings they appeared to be
on the stage', 91.

8   Fletcher had become engaged to Lord
Wentworth (Byron's grandson) in
October 1879, after meeting him in
Venice. Plans for the wedding, to be held
in Rome, were well advanced when,
on Christmas Day 1879, the engagement was dramatically broken off by
Lord Wentworth. Although the reason
was not made public, Wentworth had
discovered that Fletcher's mother had
divorced (or separated) from her father,
before taking up with Mr Benson.
Fletcher, devastated by the blow,
became dangerously ill in Rome. She
recovered, and revisited London later
that year, but never married. Lord
Wentworth married Mary Stuart-Wortley on 30 December 1880; CL, 82 n2.

9   C. Hamilton Aidé to OW (Austin),
asking OW to call on the Count Bon-
zenta, 'to whom I introduced you &
make the acquaintance of his charming wife – it is possible you or your
brother might be of some service to
them. She is to appear on the London
boards in May. She seems to be a very

gifted and sympathetic woman – her name under which she is well known in America is "Modjeska". The address is no. 6 Half Moon Street.'

10 CL, 90, 99; OET I, 152, 290. An early ms version of OW's poem 'Camma' (Clark) is titled 'Helena' and was composed for Modjeska; see M. Sturgis, 'From Cleopatra to Camma', *Wildean*, 50 (2017), 97–100. *Sheffield & Rotherham Independent*, 18 June 1881, 12, re. report in 'Figaro' of 'the faithful Mr. Oscar Wilde' at Modjeska's new production. Modjeska to Frank Miles, 18 February 1881 (Clark), re. studio. *World*, May 1881, re. the charity bazaar in aid of the National Hospital for the paralysed and epileptic, at the Duke of Wellington's riding school. CL, 95, re. 'The Artist's Dream' by 'Madame Helena Modjeska. Translated from the Polish by Oscar Wilde', in *The Green Room*; Helena Modjeska, *Memories and Impressions* (1910), 396.

11 Atkinson, in Mikhail, 20.

12 OW to Mrs Maxse, 13 Salisbury Street [1879] (BL), 'I have been so busy with my play that I have had no time to come and see you and arrange for our art pilgrimage to the National Gallery'; also William Powell Frith's painting *A Private View at the Royal Academy, 1881*; *The Hampshire Advertiser*, 8 January 1881, 'Notes on Current Events', re. the Grosvenor Gallery opening.

13 William Powell Frith, quoted in Christopher Wood, *William Powell Frith* (2006), 211.

14 John Coleman, *Charles Reade – As I Knew Him* (1903), 266.

15 William King Richardson to Dudley [Lincoln], 29 May 1881 (Houghton).

16 Violet Hunt, 'My Oscar', quoted in Secor, 'Aesthetes and Pre-Raphaelites', 402–4.

17 CL, 88, 93, 94, 101, 102, 108, 114.

18 Violet Hunt, 'My Oscar', quoted in Secor, 'Aesthetes and Pre-Raphaelites', 403; Ellmann, 221.

19 C. Hale-White, 'A Tribute to Mark Rutherford', ts, Bedford Public Library, Mark Rutherford Resource, MS. JHW7, 25–29 (I am grateful to Thomas Wright for alerting me to this source). Arthur Hughes's second daughter, Agnes, married John-Henry [Hale-]White in 1891, and her recollections are reported in the manuscript. Other guests at Wandlebank included Theophil Marzials, the Macdonalds, Huxleys, Darwins, Burne-Joneses and Rossettis – but there is no evidence that OW met any of them there.

20 Hale-White, 'A Tribute to Mark Rutherford'. The manuscript gives a full account of OW's ghost story, involving a haunted piano that would play mysteriously during the night.

21 The origins and date of OW's friendship with Burne-Jones are impossible to fix exactly. There were, of course, other mutual friends, including Ruskin, who might have brought them together. David Waller, in *The Magnificent Mrs Tennant*, 195, records a curious entry in Mrs Tennant's diary apparently for 27 December 1876: 'Had to labour to amuse Mr Burne-Jones and Mr Oscar Wilde. Oh how bored. Vexed.' It is curious, because OW was certainly in Ireland in late December 1876. Harold Hartley (*Eighty-Eight Not Out*, 269) claims that he was told by Miss Holiday (sister of the artist Henry Holiday) that OW simply arrived chez Burne-Jones, one day, in a velvet jacket, holding a lily in one hand and letter of introduction in the other. But the account seems fanciful, even if Burne-Jones did hold an open studio on afternoons which might have allowed OW to call in this way.

22   Edward Burne-Jones to OW, [1880] (Morgan Library), re. Burne-Jones's desire to give 'Mlle Sara Bernhardt' a picture 'as homage and remembrance of an interview I had long looked for' and ending 'thank you for having helped me to such an opportunity'; Edward Burne-Jones to OW, [1880] (Austin), re. a visit to 35 Grosvenor Place, with 'Mr Bastien Lepage'; Bastien-Lepage and Sarah Bernhardt had been entertained at a supper party at the Lyceum, hosted by Henry Irving and Ellen Terry, on 3 July 1880. It seems very possible that OW was also present at the dinner. Certainly he acted as interpreter between Bastien-Lepage and Irving when the artist worked on a portrait of the actor following the dinner. Shepard, ed., *Pen Pictures of Modern Authors*, 211, quoting 'An English Aesthete' from the *Boston Herald*.

23   DNB, 'Sir George Lewis'.

24   *New York Tribune*, 23 October 1881, 5; Eve Adam, ed., *Mrs J. Comyns Carr's Reminiscences* (1926), 84. *PMG*, 20 August 1880, 'Some Recent Verse': 'The world was never so full of poets – especially minor poets – as now.'

25   'Postlethwaite' appeared in *Punch* during 1880 in 'Mutual Admiration Society', 14 February 1880; 'The Mutual Admirationists', 22 May 1880; 'A Love-Agony', 5 June 1880; 'Affiliating An Aesthete', 19 June 1880; 'An Aesthetic Midday Meal', and 'Fleur des Alpes; or, Postlethwaite's Last Love', 25 December 1880.

26   'Distinguished Esthetes', *Argus* (Melbourne), 27 August 1881.

27   Henri de Régnier, *Les Annales Politiques et Littéraires*, in Mikhail, 465.

28   'The Theories of A Poet', *New York Tribune*, 8 January 1882, in Hofer & Scharnhorst, 20. In this interview OW, or the journalist, confuses Postlethwaite (the poet) and Maudle (the painter), whether deliberately or accidentally it is impossible to say. T. Martin Wood, *George Du Maurier: The Satirist of the Victorians* (1913) 20–1; Shepard, ed., *Pen Pictures of Modern Authors*, 212, quoting 'An English Aesthete' from the *Boston Herald*.

29   Certainly the idea – following its appearance in *Punch* – became rapidly identified with Wilde: see *Providence Journal*, July 1881 (reprinted *Intentions*, April 2012). A *London Cuckoo* (1881) interview with WCKW asks 'Is your brother really so fond of lilies... as Mr Du Maurier represents him to be?'

30   'The Six-Mark Tea-Pot', *Punch*, 30 October 1880. The *Hampshire Advertiser*, 8 January 1881, described OW as 'reputed to be the original of many of Du Maurier's aesthetic young men in *Punch*' and 'the central figure of that now well-known satire which makes him suggest to an aesthetic maiden that they should "live up to their blue china"'. Shepard, ed., *Pen Pictures of Modern Authors*, 212, quoting 'An English Aesthete' from the *Boston Herald*, also mentions that OW was behind Du Maurier's 15 January 1881 drawing of Postlethwaite, 'supplemented by the caption that he never bathed, because he disliked seeing himself foreshortened in the water'.

31   J. M. Whistler, *The Gentle Art of Making Enemies* (1890), 241; J. and E. J. Pennell, *The Life of James McNeil Whistler* (1911); Julian Hawthorne, *Shapes that Pass* (1928), 158, sets the scene for this encounter at a Grosvenor Gallery reception, but Whistler's own account (not contradicted by Du Maurier), placing it at the Fine Art Society exhibition of 'Venice Etchings' in December 1880, is to be preferred. Although OW became generally recognized as 'the original of

Postelthwaite', some commentators, confusing Du Maurier's two artistic creations, would mistakenly refer to him as model for 'Maudle'; and indeed perhaps the closest 'likeness' between one of Du Maurier's drawings and OW's actual appearance was the portrayal of Maudle in 'Maudle on the Choice of Profession' (*Punch*, 12 February 1881).

32 Langtry, *The Days I Knew*, 87–8; Harris, 38. The relationship between OW and Postlethwaite was well summed up in the *Leeds Mercury*, 5 January 1882: 'It may be that the curious personal resemblance which exists between Mr. Oscar Wilde and the immortal but unrecognised "Mr Postelthwaite" of *Punch* is the real reason of his [OW's] sudden leap into fame. But if that be so, many of us would like information upon one material point; that is, as to whether "Postelthwaite" is a representative of Wilde, or Wilde merely an imitator of "Postlethwaite".'

33 Henri de Régnier, *Les Annales Politiques et Littéraires*, in Mikhail, 465.

34 De Régnier, *Les Annales Politiques et Littéraires*, in Mikhail, 465.

35 William Mackay, *Bohemian Days in Fleet Street* (1913), 16; The earliest version of this remark (that I have found) is in *Life*, 24 July 1880, 586: 'Two of the [Aesthetic] School were discussing the appearance of an eminent actor, one admired, the other did not. Said the non-admirer, "you can't admire his legs;" to which the admirer replied, "yes, I think they are very poetic legs. I am not sure which is the most poetic. I think the left leg is thinner.' Shepard, ed., *Pen Pictures of Modern Authors*, 211, quoting 'An English Aesthete' from the *Boston Herald*, has OW as 'the author of the now well-known line, "Don't you think that Irving's left

leg is very expressive?" and, perhaps, even the reply, "Yes, and his left leg is so much more expressive than the right."' Richard Le Gallienne, gives the mot – which 'amused all London' – as 'One [of Irving's legs] is a poem and the other is a symphony.' *The Writings of Oscar Wilde* (1907), vol. 15, Richard Le Gallienne, 'His Life – a Critical Estimate of his Writings', 54; William King Richardson to Dudley Lincoln, 6 March 1881, Balliol College, Oxford (Houghton), 'He [OW] it is who, when asked what he thought of Irving's legs, answered "Both are consummate, but I think the right is the purer poem".'

36 Walford, *Memories of Victorian London*, 148–9.

37 *Bucks Co. Gazette* (Pennsylvania), 13 October 1881, 1.

38 Augustus Hare, *The Story of My Life* (1900), 5:386.

39 Pearson, 50.

40 W. B. Maxwell, *Time Gathered* (1937), 96.

41 'Postlethwaite from a new point of view', *World*, 16 February 1881, 7–8.

42 *Los Angeles Herald*, 20 December 1882. Christine (aka Cristina) Nilsson (1843–1921) had her final London seasons in 1880 and 1881. OW achieved the same effect with Mrs J. E. Panton (a poet and sometime contributor to the *World*); she recalled that 'when I met [OW] in a London drawing-room he came up and talked to me in his most affected style; but I soon showed him I did not care for either symphonies or neurotics, and when I mentioned casually he was casting pearls before swine and wasting jewels many others would be glad of, he gave a good humoured laugh and talked delightfully until retrieved by his mother'. *Leaves from a Life* (1908), 287.

43 'The Poet's Day', *Punch*, 4 Feb 1882;

'Mr Oscar Wilde's Poems', *World*, 3 August 1881, 17.

44   C. G. Leland to OW, 4 October 1879 (Austin).

45   Langtry, *The Days I Knew*, 87–8.

46   *New York Telegram*, 13 January 1882, in Ellmann,101;*MorningPost*,4 June1880; Rodd, *Social and Diplomatic Memories*, 10. Neither OW's involvement in the production, nor even his attendance of the performance on 3 June 1880, is specifically confirmed by the press reports. The actors did thank 'Mr Burne-Jones, Professor Richmond... and others'; and the newspapers reported the audience was made up of 'the *elite* of the University' including 'many of its most distinguished scholars' (*Jackson's Oxford Journal*, 5 June 1880); the *Daily News*, 5 June 1880, mentioned the presence of 'Mr Newton and Robert Browning' among 'the large audience'. OW and/ or WCKW may have been responsible for the arch paragraph on the play that appeared in the *World*, 9 June 1880, expressing surprise at the improper nature of the piece, with its discussion of 'the frank amours of the Trojan priestess [Cassandra] and the Argive queen [Clytemnestra]' but suggesting that nobody minded because it was in Greek. 'Agamemnon's death cry was amusingly tragic; and the final triumph of vice in the closing scene was received with as much enthusiasm as the more ordinary triumph of virtue in a London theatre.'

47   The London performances took place on 16, 17, 18 December 1880; *CL*, 103–4. Sadly Madame Modjeska was unable to attend the tea party, as her husband was unwell and she felt that it would be unwise – even for 'an old woman' like herself (she was forty) to 'pay visits to young men' unaccompanied. see

H. Modjeska to OW, 'Saturday' [1880] (Austin).

48   Devon Cox, *The Street of Wonderful Possibilities* (2015), 61–5.

49   *CL*, 94; the homage to Keats may also have been a play upon the fact that a Miss Elizabeth Skeats had lived in a house nearby in the early years of the century. Perhaps too there was a nod to Sir Percy Shelley (son of the poet) who lived literally round the corner on the newly formed Chelsea Embankment.

50   Jacomb-Hood, *With Brush and Pencil*, 115; Fane, *Chit Chat*, 103.

51   *CL*, 99.

52   'Oscar Wilde', *Biograph and Review*; OET VI, 21–3.

53   *World*, 25 August 1880; E. Yates to OW, 11 August 1880, in Mason, 232.

54   John Sloan, *Oscar Wilde* (2009), 101–2; George E. Woodberry to C. Eliot Norton, in Ellmann, 192.

55   *CL*, 95.

56   Shepard, ed., *Pen Pictures of Modern Authors*, 213, quoting 'An English Aesthete' from the *Boston Herald*; Sherard, *Life*, 165.

57   *World*, 10 November 1880, 15.

58   Mason, 168–70; 'Our London Correspondence', *Liverpool Mercury*, 25 September 1880; the parody was the first published work of Julia Frankau – or Julia Davis, as she was then. Her brother, James, was the founder and editor of *PAN*. The poem secured Julia the interest of Edmund Yates. *Lloyd's Weekly Newspaper*, 10 October 1880, mentions the October issue of *Kensington* 'is principally remarkable for a sonnet by Oscar Wilde'. But that issue of the magazine is untraced.

59   'Oscar Wilde', *Biograph and Review*, 130–5.

60   'Slate and Puff', *Fact*, 21 August 1880, 8–9.

Chapter 3: Up to Snuff

1   *CL*, 98.

2   Francis Miriam Reed, ed., *Oscar Wilde's 'Vera; or, The Nihilist'*, Studies in British Literature, Vol. 4 (1989), xvii–xxvi; in an interview in the *New York World*, 12 August 1883, OW claimed he had begun *Vera* in 1876, but this seems most unlikely. Quoted in R. B. Glaenzer, ed., *Decorative Art in America: A Lecture by Oscar Wilde* (1906), 195.

3   OW, *Vera; or, The Nihilists* (1880), 19, 16. These page references are to the rare 1880 edition, *A Drama in Four Acts*, printed by Ranken & Co., Printers, Drury House, St Mary-le-Strand, W.C. London. The copy inscribed to 'Miss Genevieve Ward from her sincere friend and admirer, the author. Sept 1880' is in the Eccles Collection at the BL.

4   OW, *Vera; or, The Nihilists*, 17, 16.

5   OW, *Vera; or, The Nihilists*, 19, 17.

6   *CL*, 98: having deprecated the literary worth of the play to E. F. S. Pigott, OW confessed 'I think the second act is good writing.'

7   'Experience is the name we give to our mistakes' – for example – would make a re-appearance in *LWF* (1892).

8   *CL*, 204.

9   H. Irving to OW (Austin); D. Boucicault to OW (Clark), G. Ward to OW (Clark); *CL*, 96, 98, 99.

10 Jopling, in Mikhail, 204. Jopling mistakenly suggests that the play OW was hoping to interest Modjeska in was *Salomé*.

11 G. Ward to OW (Clark); D. Boucicault to OW (Clark).

12 *CL*, 101; *World*, 16 June 1880, 12, paragraph on Rodd's reading of his Newdigate poem, described him as 'a youthful disciple of Mr Oscar Wilde'.

13 *CL*, 101. That OW and Rodd visited Chartres is suggested by OW's references to Chartres in 'Envoi' and 'The English Renaissance', and Rodd's poem on Chartres.

14 OW, 'Envoi'.

15 *CL*, 101.

16 *Era*, 28 November 1880; *Where's the Cat?* was adapted from the German by James Albery.

17 Shepard, ed., *Pen Pictures of Modern Authors*, 213, quoting 'An English Aesthete' from the *Boston Herald*. *Era*, 28 November 1880. *Morning Post*, 22 November 1880 concurred: 'Mr. Beerbohm Tree... made up as a ludicrous caricature of a well-known "society poet" is highly comic.'

18 Shepard, ed., *Pen Pictures of Modern Authors*, 213; *Harper's Weekly*, 23 July 1881, 491, reported that 'All who saw the character in the play exclaimed "Oscar Wilde!"'

19 Ellen Terry to OW, 18 February 1881 (Austin), inviting OW to share her box for '*The Cat*' next Thursday'; it seems likely, though, that he would also have seen it earlier in its run (see paragraph from *Life* in n.20 immediately below). Ellmann, 128, says OW thought the play 'poor', but gives no reference.

20 *Life*, 25 December 1880, 1037.

21 *World*, 2 November 1881, 11; Shepard, ed., *Pen Pictures of Modern Authors*, 212: the hostile, and only partially informed, author of the *Boston Herald* article quoted suggests that OW must have 'objected' to Tree's performance, and claims that he did write 'an indignant letter, in which he protested against [Tree's] having taken advantage of "the accident" of their acquaintance'. His account, however, is highly suspect.

22 *World*, 27 April, 1881, 12. 'DISTINGUISHED AESTHETES', *Argus* (Mel-

bourne), 27 August 1881. Although OW wrote to George Grossmith hoping to get a 'three-guinea box' for the opening night (*CL*, 109), press reports indicate that he was seated in the stalls.

23 *Era*, 30 April 1881, noted the spectacle of 'Postlethwaite [i.e. Wilde] grinning at his counterfeit presentment [i.e. Bunthorne] in the opera'. *Freeman's Journal*, 25 April 1881, reported, 'One of the most interesting features of the performance on Saturday night was the fact that it was listened to throughout with stolid earnestness by the gentleman who is generally supposed to have supplied Du Maurier with his character of Postlethwaite, and also by several others of the best known disciples [of] Æstheticism.'

24 *CL*, 109; 'Mr Oscar Wilde's Poems', *World*, 3 August 1881, 15: 'He treated the [satirical] attacks upon him with the cheeriest good humour; he never replied to them.'

25 Anne Anderson, 'The Colonel: Shams, Charlatans and Oscar Wilde', *Wildean*, 25 (2004), 34–53; F. C. Burnand, *The Colonel*, at www.xix-e.pierre-mateau.com/ed/colonel.html.

26 *Era*, 30 April 1881; Ian C. Bradley, ed., *The Complete Annotated Gilbert and Sullivan* (2016), 360; 'Interview with a Theatrical Manageress' (Helen Lenoir), *South Australian Weekly Chronicle* (Adelaide), 8 August 1885; Walter Hamilton, *The Aesthetic Movement*, 63; Millard to W. A. Clark, 9 October 1922 (Clark); the part of Grosvenor was played by Rutland Barrington.

27 Shepard, ed., *Pen Pictures of Modern Authors*, 213.

28 *Illustrated London News*, 18 June 1881, 598.

29 'An Interview with Oscar Wilde's Brother', *New Zealand Herald*, 8 April

1882, 2, reprinting an article from *The London Cuckoo* (1881).

30 *Punch*, 21 May 1881, 229.

31 For a full list of *Punch* satires on OW see Mikhail, 227–9.

32 'Punch's Fancy Portraits No. 37: "O.W."', *Punch*, 25 Jun 1881, 298.

33 'The High Priest of Aesthetic Art, Postlethwaite', *Bristol Mercury and Daily Post*, 14 May 1881

34 *World*, 7 December 1881, 11. Although OW was flattered by the request, Frith privately confessed that his reason for including 'the well-known apostle of the beautiful' and his 'eager worshippers' in the picture was a desire to 'hit the folly of listening to self-elected critics' in matters of art.

35 William King Richardson to 'Dudley [Lincoln]', 17 April 1881 (Houghton); the photo alluded to has not been traced, but for others of this date see Holland, *The Wilde Album*, 54, 77, 94–5.

36 'Our London Letter', *Sheffield & Rotherham Independent*, 1 December 1881.

37 Frank Benson, *My Memories* (1939), 138.

38 V. O'Sullivan to A. J. A. Symons, 8 June 1931 (Clark).

39 'The Science of the Beautiful', *New York World*, 8 January 1882, in Hofer & Scharnhorst, 23.

40 'Postlethwaite from a new point of view', *World*, 16 February 1881, 7–8; Edmund Yates to OW, 28 February 1881 (Houghton), reproduced in Mason, 234.

41 Verily Anderson, *The Last of the Eccentrics: Life of Rosslyn Bruce* (1972), 45; 'A Jackdaw's Flight', *Leeds Mercury*, 22 July 1882.

42 *London Cuckoo* (1881).

43 W. B. Maxwell, *Time Gathered* (1937), 95.

44 Ellmann, 221.

45 'Unknown Wives of Well-Known Men:

Mrs Oscar Wilde', *Ladies Home Journal* (Philadelphia), October 1892, reprinted in *Intentions*, 42 (2006), 21–5; Moyle, 45–7, 33.

46 Moyle, 17.

47 CMW to Otho Lloyd, 7 June 1881, quoted in Moyle, 46.

48 CMW to Otho Lloyd, 10 June 1881, quoted in Moyle, 46.

49 Moyle, 54–5.

50 Hake and Compton-Rickett, *The Life and Letters of Theodore Watts-Dunton*, 1:172–4, gives an account of OW's first appearance at one of Whistler's breakfasts, when Whistler professed not to know who he was. Watts-Dunton, who was also present, suggested, 'You have met him at some "outside" dinner where the "etchings" were being bought, and he jumped down your throat... and you gave him a general invitation to come to your breakfasts, and he has at once taken you at your word.' Whistler agreed that that was exactly what had happened. Nevertheless, within a few weeks OW had made a 'conquest' of him.

51 Pennell and Pennell, *The Life of James McNeill Whistler*, 212, 224; Rodd, *Social and Diplomatic Memories*, 16; *CL*, 148 n.1.

52 William Rothenstein, *Since Fifty* (1939), 76.

53 *CL*, 154.

54 'Aesthetic: An Interesting Interview with Oscar Wilde', *Dayton Daily Democrat*, 3 May 1882, 4, quoted in Hofer & Scharnhorst, 145.

55 Pennell and Pennell, *The Life of James McNeill Whistler*, 336; William Rothenstein, *Men and Memories I* (1931), 114; E. R. and J. Pennell, *The Whistler Journal* (1921), 34, quoted in Ellmann, 126.

56 *World*, 2 March 1881, 15; OW, when re-issuing the poem in book form, corrected the title to 'Impression du Matin'.

57 George E. Woodberry to C. Eliot Norton, 25 April 1882 (Houghton), in Ellmann, 192.

58 Harris, 38.

59 Harris, 47; JMW to S. W. Paddon, 22 March 1882 (Library of Congress), re. OW calling JMW's attacks on Howell 'really too brutal'; also JMW to T. Waldo Story (Morgan Library), 'Oscar, too, always says, "Jimmy, you are a devil."'

60 William Rothenstein, quoted in Count Harry Kessler, *Journey to the Abyss* (2011), 293. Rothenstein called OW 'much the richer character' and said JMW only 'made a witticism from time to time'.

61 Harris, 38. Whistler had told the critic Humphrey Ward that 'you must never say that this painting's good or that bad... Good and bad are not terms to be used by you; but say, I like this, and I dislike that, and you'll be within your right.'

62 JMW to Fox [April/May 1881] proposing 'next time [to] bring Oscar Wilde with me'; JMW to OW [9 October 1881]; there is no evidence that OW made either trip.

63 Langtry, *The Days I Knew*, 60.

64 J. Mordaunt Crook, *William Burges and the High Victorian Dream* (1981), 328; Robert Garthorne-Hardy, ed., *Ottoline* (1964), 82; JMW to George Grossmith (GUL).

65 Alice Kipling to Rudyard Kipling, 18 March 1881, quoted Ian Taylor, *Victorian Sisters* (1987), 136–7, where the letter is misdated 1882.

66 Mrs J. Comyns Carr, *Reminiscences* (1926), 85.

67 E. Burne-Jones to Charles Eliot Norton, 12 December 1881, *CL*, 132: '[OW] really loves the things you and I love.'

68 Edward Burne-Jones to Mrs George Lewis, 'Friday' [July 1883]; Edward

Burne-Jones to Mrs George Lewis, 27 June 1881 (Bodleian); it seems to have been OW's joke to dub the church of St Peter, Vere Street, for which Burne-Jones was designing a stained glass window, 'the church of SS Marshall & Snelgrove' – after the department store next door.

69 Edward Burne-Jones to Mrs George Lewis, 20 Jun 1881 (Bodleian).

70 Violent Hunt to OW, July 1881, in Ellmann, 221, 'you quite deserve your four Burne-Jones drawings'; it is not directly stated that they were a gift from Burne-Jones, but it seems likely.

71 Comyns Carr, *Reminiscences*, 85–6; George Lewis, ms notebook, 'Parties 79–80' (in fact covering 1879 to 1884) (Bodleian) lists guests chez Lewis, including: 19 May 1881, 'Mr & Mrs Langtry, Mr & Mrs [Comyns] Carr, Mr Burne-Jones, Mr [Alexander] Wedderburn, Oscar Wilde, Frank Miles'; 27 October 1881, 'Mr & Mrs Burne-Jones, Mrs Langtry, Oscar Wilde'. Wilde's only other appearance at dinner chez Lewis in 1881 was on 8 March with 'Mrs Phillips, Mr & Mrs Perugini, Mr O[scar] Clayton, [and] Brill.'

72 Norman Kelvin, ed., *The Collected Letters of William Morris*, 2:38, William Morris to Jane Morris, 31 March [1881].

73 George Bernard Shaw to Robert Ross, 13 September 1916, in Dan H. Lawrence, ed., *Collected Letters of Bernard Shaw 1911–1925* (1985), 414.

74 Violet Hunt, 'My Oscar', quoted in 'Aesthetes and Pre-Raphaelites', 402.

75 Hake and Compton-Rickett, *The Life and Letters of Theodore Watts-Dunton*, 180; Edmund Yates to OW, 8 July 1881 (Houghton), refers to Morris among 'other of your friends'.

76 Ford Madox Ford, *Memories of Oscar Wilde* (1939); Sondra Stang, ed., *The Ford Madox Ford Reader* (1986), 139.

77 Hake and Compton-Rickett, *The Life and Letters of Theodore Watts-Dunton*, 175; Lord Houghton to Theodore Watts[-Dunton] (Houghton); the letter is marked 'Whistler – 9 July 1881 – meeting between ACS and Wilde'. A. C. Swinburne to E. C. Stedman, 4 April 1882, in Cecil Y. Lang, *The Swinburne Letters (1959–62)*, 4:226.

78 Hake and Compton-Rickett, *The Life and Letters of Theodore Watts-Dunton*, 175–6.

79 O'Sullivan, 209–11. OW enjoyed William Morris's account of how, when telling Rossetti about his plans for a poem involving a medieval knight who had a dragon for a brother, Rossetti kept expostulating, 'A dragon for a brother!'; until, losing patience, Morris had retorted, 'Well, Gabriel, it is better than having a fool for a brother.' To which Rossetti had said, thoughtfully, after a pause, 'Ah yes. There's not much to be said for William Michael.'

80 It was at his house that William Morris met OW; see above.

81 'Distinguished Esthetes', *Argus* (Melbourne), 27 August 1881.

82 'Feminine Fashion and Fancies', *Newcastle Courant*, 11 March 1881; other guests included Edmund Gosse, brother-in-law of the hostess; Mr and Mrs George Lewis, Mr and Mrs John Collier, Mr and Mrs Comyns Carr, Edmund Yates, Frederick Macmillan, Sydney Colvin and Johnston Forbes Robertson. George Lewis to OW (Austin), 25 January 1882, mentions '[Mrs Tadema's] Tuesdays go on as usual'. Edmund Gosse to Hamo Thornycroft, in Thwaite, *Edmund Gosse*, 211.

83 *CL*, 105–6; Laurence Alma-Tadema's letter to OW, asking for his assistance, dated 18 March 1881, is at Austin, where it is catalogued as from 'unidentified'.

84 Shane Leslie, *Memoir of John Edward Courtenay Bodley* (1930), 74; Mrs Julian Hawthorne, *Harper's Bazaar*, quoted in Ellmann, 123.

85 Leslie, *Memoir of John Edward Courtenay Bodley*, 74; *World*, 21 December 1881; reproduced in Mason, 233: 'Albeit nurtured in democracy / And liking best that state Bohemian / Where each man borrows sixpence and no man / Has aught but paper collars; yet I see / Exactly where to take a liberty. / Better to be thought one, whom most abuse / For speech of donkey and for look of goose, / Than that the world should pass in silence by. / Wherefore I wear a sunflower in my coat, / Cover my shoulders with my flowing hair, / Tie verdant satin round my open throat, / Culture and love I cry, and ladies smile, / And seedy critics overflow with bile, / While with my Prince long Sykes's meal I share.'

86 Shepard, ed., *Pen Pictures of Modern Authors*, 213–4 refers to a dinner with OW, the Prince of Wales, Arthur Sul-

livan, George Grossmith and others; 'An Interview with Oscar Wilde's Brother', *New Zealand Herald*, 8 April 1882, 2, reprinting an article from the *London Cuckoo* (1881). Willie told the interviewer: 'I had a letter from dear Oscar, this morning to say that the Prince has been to tea with him.' Asked whether the prince really had, he replied, 'Ah, that I cannot say – but he says he has and whether he has or not people will believe it... I would show you the letter, only I have just sent it to Lady Wilde.'

87 *The Times*, 4 June 1881, 7; *World*, 8 June 1881, 14; *Dundee Courier & Argus*, 6 June 1881.

88 Edwin Ward, *Recollections of a Savage* (1923), 50.

89 The *Hampshire Telegraph and Sussex Chronicle*, 23 July 1881, quoting *Life*, says that the crowd that gathered to watch the departing guests 'seemed specially interested in the picturesque appearance of Mr Oscar Wilde'.

Chapter 4: An English Poet

1 *CL*, 110; Harris, 39. It is not known who, or what, led OW to David Bogue, but several of his friends had brought out books with the publisher, including Welbore Saint Clair Baddeley, *Legend of the Death of Antar and Other Poems* (1881) and Zadel Barnes Gustafson, *Genevieve Ward: A Biographical Sketch from Original Material Derived from Herself and Friends* (1881), which included two letters by OW. The firm also produced an English edition of Walt Whitman's *Leaves of Grass* (1881).

2 George Moore, Wilde's near contemporary, contributed £25 towards the costs of producing his *Pagan Poems*

early in 1881. OW's expenses were likely to have been rather more. He presented a copy of the book, 'To Oscar Wilde, with the author's compliments' (Adrian Frazier, *George Moore* (2000), 77). It is even possible that Wilde was stirred by rivalry to secure a publisher for his own poems on receipt of the gift. He held the literary abilities of his old Connemara neighbour in sovereign contempt: see Josephine M. Guy and Ian Small, *Oscar Wilde's Profession* (2000), 84–8. The manuscript of the memorandum is in the Clark. The amended Clause IV states: 'That the said David Bogue

shall account for all the copies he may dispose of at ~~half the published price~~ *the trade sale price and thirteen as twelve deducting a commission of ten per cent.*' The expression 'thirteen as twelve' denoted a discount given to booksellers; they received thirteen copies for the price of twelve. William Hale White, *The Autobiography of Mark Rutherford* (1881), 150. Hostile critics claimed that David Bogue accepted the poems without reading them, simply impressed by OW's notoriety. Leonard Cresswell Ingleby, *Oscar Wilde* (1907), 18–19.

3 Mason, 281–3; Although the book was advertised as 'Handsomely Bound in Parchment' (i.e. animal skin) it was, in fact, covered with 'Japanese vellum', a treated paper.

4 Sherard, *SUF*, 72; see also OWIA for early (1884) variants of the anecdote in the press.

5 'Personalities', *National Republican*, 25 January 1881, 2; 'Literary Notes', *New York Tribune*, 2 March 1881, 6; *Worthington Advance* (Minnesota), 3 March 1881, 4.

6 Mason, 324–5. An advert in the *New York Tribune*, 25 July 1881, 6, describes the book as 'Ready July 26'. That OW had been striving for some time to get his poems published (in both Britain and the US) is suggested by an article in the *New York Tribune*, 2 March 1881, 6, quoting the *Boston Courier*: it mentions that OW, 'being about to publish a volume of poems in England wrote to a Boston house proposing that the volume be issued here at the same time. The house wrote back that they should be pleased to examine the work with a view to deciding upon Mr. Wilde's proposal, but the poet-aesthete was so disgusted with the impertinent presumption of an American... that he broke off negotiations at once.'

7 *World*, 6 July 1881, 20; Shepard, ed., *Pen Pictures of Modern Authors*, 214.

8 *World*, 6 July 1881, 13. The exact date of publication is unknown; Mason gives it as 30 June 1881 (see *CL*, 111); *PMG*, 25 June 1881, announced OW had a book of poems in the press 'which will be published next week by Mr. David Bogue'.

9 *CL*, 113, 65n; Harris, 44; W. B. Richmond to OW (Austin); OET I, 157. Gladstone, in his diary for 26 July, records that he wrote to OW on receipt of the book, and also that met OW at Burne-Jones's studio shortly afterwards (3 August). H. C. G. Matthew, ed., *The Gladstone Diaries* (1990), 10:98, 10:104.

10 J. A. Symonds to Horatio F. Brown, 31 July 1881, in Horatio F. Brown, ed., *Letters and Papers of John Addington Symonds* (1923), 120.

11 OW to J. A. Symonds, quoted in Ellmann, 138–9; Symonds endorsed these judgements in private, telling his friend Horatio Brown, 'There are good things in the book, and he [OW] is a poet – undoubtedly, I think.' He considered ΓΛΥΚΥΠΙΚΡΟΣ ΕΡΩΣ 'one of the best'. Brown, ed., *Letters and Papers of John Addington Symonds*, 120, 132.

12 Matthew Arnold to OW, 9 July 1881 (Austin).

13 'Literary Notes', *New York Tribune*, 20 August 1881, 6: 'It is said that the author received complimentary letters, after the appearance of his book, from William Morris, Mr. Swinburne, Robert Browning, Matthew Arnold, Mr. Gladstone and others.'

14 *CL*, 111, 112.

15 *Punch*, 23 July 1881, 26.

16 *Punch*, 23 July 1881, 26; *Athenaeum*, 23

July 1881, 103–4; *Saturday Review*, 23 July 1881, lii, 118; 'Our London Correspondence', *Liverpool Mercury*, 13 July 1881.

17 Variants of the word 'clever' appear in almost every review: *Saturday Review*, 23 July 1881, lii, 118; *Spectator*, 13 August 1881, liv, 1050; 'Recent Poetry and Verse', *Graphic*, 23 July 1881.

18 *Saturday Review*; see also *Spectator* on the 'very curious medley of inconsistent flowers'; and *Morning Post*, 8 August 1881, 6: 'Before closing this necessarily brief notice we must draw the author's attention to a few phases of nature which he has misunderstood, *e.g.* the traveller's joy (*clematis vitalba*), is not yellow but white; sops-in-wine, *i.e.* the clove gillyflower, does not bloom till long after the daffodil; the corncrake is mute when the almond-tree blossoms; and "boy's love," by which he probably means "lad's love" the old North-country name for Southernwood, is not pale. By the by, what flower is meant by "bellamour" – we really ask for information, and in no carping spirit, as the implied association has its interest.'

19 *World*, 3 August 1881, 15–16

20 *Saturday Review*, 23 July 1881, lii, 118

21 'Current Literature', *Daily News*, 23 July 1881; 'Current Literature', *Argus* (Melbourne), 19 November 1881.

22 *Leicester Chronicle and the Leicestershire Mercury*, 3 September 1881; *New North-West* (Montana), 26 August 1881, 1; *The Daily Cairo Bulletin* (Cairo, Illinois) 7 September 1881. *World*, 21 September 1881, 14, selected a passage from 'Panthea' for satirical treatment: suggesting that in it 'the secrets of the great hereafter' which 'vex and trouble the mind of man' have been revealed by 'the recognized genius of the day': 'Mr Oscar Wilde informs

us not merely that "we shall know / Who paints the diapered fritillaries" whatever they may be – but that "the joyous sea / Shall be our raiment, and the bearded star / Shoot arrows at our pleasure." This will leave the Toxophilite Society far behind. Also "we shall be / Part of the mighty universal whole, / And through all aeons mix and mingle with the Kosmic Soul!" That will be nice!'

23 *Daily News*. W. E. Henley to Sydney Colvin [1881], quoted in E. V. Lucas, *The Colvins and their Friends* (1928), 130: 'Oscar's book has come out at last. The "Atheneum" wigged it horrid. A writer in the D[aily].N[ews]. whom I suspect to be Lang, was more kindly, but scoffed at it too. It seems, by the extracts I've seen, to be tolerably putrid.' In another letter Henley says the *Athenaeum* was written by Joe Knight. Damian Atkinson, *Letters of W. E. Henley to Robert Louis Stevenson* (2008), 168.

24 'Mr Oscar Wilde's Poems', *Morning Post*, 8 August 1881, 6: 'Incomparably the best of the poems is "The Burden of Itys". It is full of melody, and contains some fresh and pleasant imagery'. 'Current Literature', *Daily News*, 23 July 1881: 'Of the longer poems the "Burden of Itys" is the most charming and flawless'. 'Recent Poetry and Verse', *Graphic*, 23 July 1881: 'Perhaps the best of the pieces is "The Burden of Itys"'. 'Our London Correspondence', *Liverpool Mercury*, 13 July 1881 hailed Wilde's 'positive genius for musical metre'.

25 *World*. From the internal evidence of the piece it is clear that the review was not by WCKW.

26 *Dial* (Chicago), August 1881, ii, 82–5; *Providence Journal*, July 1881; *NYT*, 14 August 1881, 10; *Century* (New York),

November 1881, xxiii, 153, echoed the praise for 'Ave Imperatrix' and the dissatisfaction with *Punch*. The *New York Tribune*, 31 July 1881, 6, while admitting that 'Mr. Oscar Wilde is not an idiot' and finding some merit in the verses, was rather less generous.

27   Harris, 42.

28   Mason, 282–3; the cover design on the 'second' and subsequent 'editions' was reproduced at a slightly larger scale (Mason, 287). 'Our London Letter', *Northern Echo* (Darlington), 4 Oct 1881; the new 'title page' – for the third edition – was printed on 26 September 1881 (Mason, 283).

29   *New York Tribune*, 20 August 1881, 6: 'A third edition of Mr. Oscar Wilde's poems has already been called for in London, and Roberts Brothers are preparing a second edition for this country.' The second US edition is dated 1882, though there may have been more than one 'impression' of the first edition – see Mason, 324.

30   Harris, 49.

31   Harris, 44.

32   J. R. Rodd to unknown [1881] (Clark).

33   JMW to Louisine Waldron Elder, 21 September 1881 (GUL).

34   Harris, 42.

35   William King Richardson to Dudley Lincoln, Balliol College, 6 March 1881 (Houghton).

36   Francis Gribble, *The Romance of the Oxford Colleges* (1910), 164–70. *World*, 8 June 1881, 12, reported the incident: 'And so these naughty Magdalen youths pumped on their only appreciator of the fine arts and *belles lettres* amid shouts of "No more aesthetes in Magdalen!"'. The culprits were gated. William King Richardson to Dudley Lincoln, 29 May 1881 (Houghton) confirms OW's presence in Oxford on 'Monday last'.

37   Henry Newbolt, *My World As In My Time* (1923), 96–7. Newbolt confesses that Elton's speech was 'no doubt better than my recollection'. Sandra F. Siegel, 'Wilde's Gift and Oxford's "Coarse Impertinence"', in T. Foley and S. Ryder, eds, *Ideology and Ireland in the Nineteenth Century* (1998) 7; Ellmann, 140; Schroeder, 55. The copy of *Poems* inscribed 'To the Library of the Oxford Union, my first volume of poems, Oscar Wilde' is in the Eccles Collection at the BL. Curiously it is dated 'Oct 27 '81.' Was this, perhaps, the date on which the book was returned?

38   *CL*, 116.

39   Shepard, ed., *Pen Pictures of Modern Authors*, 214. Labouchère had been associated with Edmund Yates in establishing the *World* in 1874, before leaving two years later to set up the very similar *Truth*, which may account for his magazine's initial reluctance to write about OW. A parody of OW's 'Ave Imperatrix' did, however, appear in the magazine in 1880.

40   'Philosophical Oscar', *Chicago Times*, 1 March 1882, 7, in Hofer & Scharnhorst, 94.

41   *CL*, 154.

42   Canon Miles to OW, 21 August 1881 (Clark).

43   'Oscar Wilde: An Interview with the Apostle of Aestheticism', *San Francisco Examiner*, 27 March 1882, in Hofer & Scharnhorst, 103; Henry Cole, in his diary, 26 August 1881, mentions meeting OW at Whistler's studio: 'He informed me that in literature a dull thing is dull on account of the writer's fault and not on account of the subject treated by him' (GUL).

44   Canon Miles to OW (fragment) [1881] (Clark).

45   Frank Harris, *My Life and Loves* (1966 edition), 457; there is a hint of Frank

Miles's questionable reputation in Rodd's comment (to an unknown friend): 'A little lady with dark eyes, called Daisy turned up at [Whistler's] studio today… Frank, she told us, was an immense favourite – he had such a taking way. – only one and the same old way I suppose.' R. Rodd to [Unknown], 15 August 1882 (TCD).

46   Sherard, *Real*, 110–12. The incident is also described, more briefly, in Sherard, *Life*, 139. In neither instance is Frank Miles mentioned as the artist friend, nor is the fact that his victim was a 'young girl'. These pieces of information are supplied in a letter from Sherard to A. J. A. Symons, 18 August 1935 (Clark): 'The artist whom Oscar helped to escape from the police at Keats House, Tite Street, Chelsea, was Frank Miles who was wanted for some minor offence towards a young girl. The story is quite authentic. Oscar avoided any recriminations from the invading myrmidons on the accepted plea that he had fancied that a rag was projected from fellow lodgers.' Another friend of Wilde's recalled a separate incident, when Frank Miles was being blackmailed by a woman who had induced him to 'commit an act of extreme folly'; Wilde again saved the day, insisting on an interview with the woman, tricking her into giving him the one incriminating document, and then throwing it into the fire. He then saw off the 'bully' who had accompanied the woman and had been 'waiting below'. Anon., *The Great Reign* (1922), 94–9, in Mikhail, 275. Whether this incident also involved an underage girl is hard to determine. Sherard certainly told Hesketh Pearson, 'Miles had a predilection for Exhibition natural enough in a struggling artist but reprehensible, *paraît-il*, where only small

girls in single spies are invited to contemplation.' Pearson, 55–6. Despite such instances it is sometimes claimed that Frank Miles was homosexual: Croft-Cooke, 40; Hyde, *Oscar*, 23; McKenna, 14. There seems, however, no evidence to support this claim.

47   Ward, *Recollections of a Savage*, 108; Harris, 457.

48   Rodd, *Social and Diplomatic Memories*, 23. It is possible that this 'gentleman' was Lord Ronald Gower. Although Gower's clandestine sexual relationships with young men had long been a matter of rumour, Wilde may have chosen to disbelieve them at first. In 1878 a scurrilous newspaper, *The Man of the World*, had implicated Gower in 'a loathsome scandal' involving 'immorality of the most revolting character'. But, on threatening to sue the paper, Gower had secured a full retraction without the case coming to court; see *PMG*, 1 January 1879. If Wilde initially took this victory at face value, he may have later changed his view. Certainly his friendship with Gower, close in the late 1870s, seems to have all but ended after Wilde moved to London. Perhaps he had come to recognize him as an 'undesirable' associate.

49   Sherard, *SUF*, 86–7; Sherard, *Life*, 144, describes the rooms as 'small'.

50   Archibald Forbes, 'London Jottings', syndicated to *South Australian Advertiser* (Adelaide), 9 July 1884: 'I remember some three yeas ago assisting at a conference in which were discussed schemes for Oscar's future.'

51   *Daily Globe* (Minnesota), 30 October 1881, 5.

52   Forbes, 'London Jottings'.

53   'What the World Says', *Bristol Mercury and Daily Post*, 4 August 1881.

54   'London Letter', *Leicester Chronicle*, 12 November 1881, 5.

55 The possibility of a lecture tour was first mentioned in the press in June 1881, in 'Our London Letter', *Northern Echo* (Darlington), 27 June 1881; it was described as being promoted by Boucicault. *PMG*, 4 January 1882 (quoting an interview with Boucicault in the *New York Herald*) says that OW had originally told Boucicault that 'whatever effect he could make would only be appreciated by a drawing-room audience'. For Bernhardt's possible involvement, suggested by Louis Fréchette, 'Oscar Wilde', *La Patrie* (Montreal), 20 April 1895, see Schroeder, 56.

56 OW told Blanche Roosevelt that 'he thought of coming to America to see what we are like, and referred with apparent pleasure to the flattering manner in which some of his poems had been received by a portion of the American press'. *Memphis Daily Appeal* (Tennessee), 14 October 1881, 2, reprinted in the *New York Tribune*.

57 *Public Ledger* (Tennessee), 9 September 1881, 4.

58 D'Oyly Carte interview, from the *New York Tribune*, quoted in *Freeman's Journal*, 25 January 1882.

59 Richard D'Oyly Carte to T. B. Pugh, 8 November 1881 (Morgan); the letter is in the hand of Carte's American agent, W. F. Morse. Pugh was a leading promoter in Philadelphia.

60 The unnamed American's conversation with Helen Lenoir, quoted in Nathan Haskell Dole 'Biographical Introduction' to *Poetical Works of Oscar Wilde* (1913); Morse refers to the advice having been given by 'a lady well known in English and American newspaper circles as a writer upon the current society topics of the day'. W. F. Morse, 'American Lectures', in *The Works of Oscar Wilde* (1907). Some have

suggested the 'lady' may have been Mrs Frank Leslie, but this seems doubtful – see Lewis & Smith, 24. Blanche Roosevelt is another possibility.

61 Morse, 73. Hyde, *Oscar*, 60, and Ellmann, 145, assume the cable was sent from Carte's New York office, but Morse's terse account does not state this, and it seems more likely that the cable was sent by the 'lady' journalist, the 'responsible agent' being W. F. Morse. The cable was addressed to OW at his mother's address, 1 Ovington Square.

62 'Reports that Mr. Wilde has been engaged for the United States are premature. More than one offer has, we learn, been made him to give some "aesthetic" lectures in New York this winter, and negotiations are now in progress as to terms.' *Graphic* (London), 26 November 1881.

63 Richard D'Oyly Carte to T. B. Pugh, 8 November 1881 (Morgan).

64 Richard D'Oyly Carte to Helen Lenoir (copy), 17 December 1881, quoted in Regina B. Oost, *Gilbert and Sullivan: Class and the Savoy Tradition* (2009), 57–8.

65 Richard D'Oyly Carte to Helen Lenoir (copy), 17 December 1881, quoted in Oost, *Gilbert and Sullivan: Class and the Savoy Tradition*, 57–8. Oost suggests that this relates to OW attending a performance in London, but the context implies that Carte is referring to OW attending the show in New York.

66 Friedman, 70. Aside from fancy-dress appearances and Masonic meetings there is no evidence to suggest that Wilde had ever sported such a costume before this date, though elements of the outfit had been lampooned regularly in Du Maurier's various 'Aesthetic' cartoons since 1877.

67 *CL*, 118; Hart-Davis and Holland (*CL*,

123) state that the arrangement was for one-third of net receipts, but 'W. F. Morse's Statement of Accounts, 1882' (Arents Collection, New York Public Library) makes clear the division was 50/50.

68 J. Lewis Hind, *Naphtali* (1926), 235; Whistler, *The Gentle Art of Making Enemies*, 243; Hind says JMW's comment was published in the *World*, but that was not the case. It appears to have been a private communication.

69 *CL*, 118.

70 Mrs Bernard Beere, after her husband's early death, 'turned her attention to the stage, finding a histrionic master in Hermann Vezin, and an intellectual guide in Willie Wilde (Oscar's elder brother). Under the direction of these two men she became a woman of superior intellectual attainments, but not at first of any great histrionic facility.' 'Social Gossip from Home', *Argus* (Melbourne), 24 March 1888. For 'Dot' Boucicault's involvement, see 'The Theatres', *Daily News*, 21 November 1881. His participation seems to have led to the erroneous report that his father Dion Boucicault was involved – and was even the producer of the piece. 'From our London Correspondents', *Newcastle Courant*, 2 December 1881. The error has been often repeated since: Ellmann, 146. Dion Boucicault's non-involvement is confirmed by the fact that he was busy with work commitments in Dublin in November 1881, and in New York in December: see George Rowell, 'The Truth about Vera', *Nineteenth Century Theatre Research*, vol. 21 (1993).

71 Elizabeth Robins, *Both Sides of the Curtain* (1940), 18; OW told Robins that the cost of mounting a single matinee performance in a London theatre would be £100.

72 The first hint was in the *World*, 9 November 1881, 10: in a paragraph on OW's forthcoming American lecture tour, 'I hear that Mr. Wilde is also making arrangements for bringing out an original play before he leaves London'. This was followed by the *Daily News*, 21 November 1881; *World*, 23 November 1881; *Freeman's Journal*, 28 November 1881, etc.

73 'Private Correspondence', *Birmingham Daily Post*, 5 December 1881.

74 'London Gossip', *York Herald*, 15 December 1881, 8.

75 *CL*, 97.

76 *NYT*, 26 December 1881.

77 Rowell, 'The Truth about Vera', 99. The lack of funds may be alluded to in an oblique comment on the cancellation from the *Birmingham Daily Post*, 5 December 1881: 'As regards the theatrical arrangements, the essential preliminary to which, in the eyes of those who have plays to dispose of, [had not] been even seriously approached.'

78 *CL*, 97; in 1883 the copy of OW's play sent to Arthur Wallack, the New York theatre producer, was discovered in a drawer. When asked why he had not produced Wilde's drama, Wallack's assistant, Mr Moss, remarked, 'I guess it needed cutting, like his hair.' *Evening News* (Sydney), 21 April 1883.

79 Beatty, *Lillie Langtry: Manners, Masks and Morals*, 212–14.

80 Langtry, *The Days I Knew*, 163–5; *World*, 23 November 1881, 15; *Burra Record* (South Australia), 20 June 1882.

81 *Dundee Courier & Argus* (Dundee), 17 December 1881.

82 'Philosophical Oscar,' *Chicago Times*, 1 March 1882, 7, in Hofer & Scharnhorst, 93–4. OW is (mis)quoted as praising Langtry's 'delightfully joyousness of manner'.

83 Beatty, *Lillie Langtry: Manners, Masks and Morals*, 220.

84 *World*, 'Christmas Number', 21 December 1881, 19. 'Ego Upto Snuffibus Poeta' (by Edmund Yates), illustrated by Alfred Bryant. The verse relating to Swinburne includes references to Wilde, Hardinge and Mallock.

85 *Truth*, 22 December 1881, 813.

86 *World*, 4 January 1882, 14.

87 Rodd, *Social and Diplomatic Memories*, 25.

Part IV: *The Remarkable Rocket*
Chapter 1: The Best Place

1 *Oscar Wilde's Visit to America* (1882), eight-page prospectus (Toronto University Library).

2 'Ten Minutes With A Poet', *NYT*, 3 January 1882; *Sun* (New York), 3 January 1882; *World* (New York), Lewis & Smith, 31.

3 The anecdote was reported as being passed on by a fellow passenger in the *World* (New York), the *New York Herald* and the *NYT*. The *Sun* (New York), 3 January 1883, put the lines into OW's own mouth: 'By the by, do you know, I was very disappointed in the Atlantic Ocean. It was very tame.' But the accounts – very similar though not identical – from the other three papers are to be preferred. For the spread of the anecdote across America and the UK see Morse, 76; *Daily News*, 4 January 1882; *PMG*, 4 January 1882; *Freeman's Journal*, 5 January 1882; *London Daily Herald*, 9 January 1882; for satirical verses see 'Disappointed', in *Reynolds's Newspaper*, 8 January 1882, 2; Lewis & Smith, 33; Ellmann, 151, mentions 'The Disappointed Deep' in *PMG* – though it is not to be found in the publication; *Leeds Mercury*, 5 January 1882.

4 *New York Evening Post*, in Hofer & Scharnhorst, 15–16.

5 It is not known for certain to which hotel OW was first taken. The two most likely possibilities are the Grand Hotel or the Brunswick. See OWIA, and Lewis & Smith, 35.

6 OW, 'Impressions of America', 22.

7 *CL*, 127; typescript of Dan O'Connell, 'Bohemian Experiences of Oscar Wilde and Sir Samuel Barker', originally published in *The Chronicle* (San Francisco) (Clark).

8 Quoted in Dick Weindling and Marianne Colloms, *The Marquis de Leuville: A Victorian Fraud?* (2012).

9 *Boston Globe*, 29 January 1882, in Hofer & Scharnhorst, 48.

10 Morse, 76; *Boston Globe*, 29 January 1882, 5; *NYT*, 8 January 1882, 7; 'Wilde's Experience,' *Topeka Daily Capital*, 16 January 1882.

11 Mason, 124–6.

12 'Art's Apostle' (from the NY correspondent of the *Boston Herald*); *Evening Star* (Washington, DC), 21 January 1882. John Cooper has pointed out that of the twenty-seven numbered images of OW (reproduced in *The Wilde Album*, 65–91), the first twenty-three belong to one sitting; the final four to a second sitting (OW's hair is appreciably longer). The *Topeka Daily Capital*, 16 January 1882, refers to OW having 'thirty sittings' (i.e. thirty photographs) with Sarony, and this was perhaps the number stipulated in the contract – with some of the exposures not being printed up.

13 *Topeka Daily Capital*, 16 January 1882;
    Lewis & Smith, 39, state that Morse
    'was so eager for Sarony to shoot his
    star that he waived the customary
    charge'. And this is repeated in most
    biographies. But the suggestion is con-
    tradicted by the *Topeka Daily Capital* and
    other papers, e.g. 'Miscellaneous' in
    Northern Argus (Clare, South Australia),
    30 January 1885. It may be that Morse
    waived an advance payment, having
    settled with Sarony for a percentage of
    the sales.

14 *Topeka Daily Capital*, 16 January 1882.

15 'The English Renaissance', *Miscellanies*,
    121; *New York Tribune*, 6 January 1882,
    5.

16 *New York Tribune*, 6 January 1882, 5.

17 *Era*, 21 January, 1882.

18 'Vanity Fair', *The Argonaut* (San Fran-
    cisco), 10, no. 1, 7 January 1882.

19 Lewis & Smith, 57.

20 *CL*, 124.

21 *CL*, 124.

22 Morse account; *NYT*, *New York Tribune*,
    10 January, 1882, 2; *CL*, 126; versions
    of the speech from *NYT*, *Miscellanies*,
    Seaside Edition. 'Oscar the Aesthete'
    (US newspaper cutting), 29 January
    1882 (Clark).

23 Morse, 78–9.

24 'Living Up to Beauty', *New York Herald*,
    10 January 1882.

25 *New York Herald*, *New York World*,
    NYT, in Friedman, 77. 'Wilde's Experi-
    ence', *Topeka Daily Capital*, 16 January
    1882 lists Mr Connery of the *Herald*,
    Whitelaw Reid, *Tribune*, George Jones,
    NYT, William H. Hurlburt, *World*, Mr
    Fiske, *Star*.

26 'The Drama in America', *Era*, 21 Janu-
    ary 1882; Richard D'Oyly Carte to
    Arthur Sullivan, [January 1882] (Clark);
    D'Oyly Carte interview, from the *New
    York Tribune*, 12 January 1882, reprinted
    in *Freeman's Journal*, 25 Jan 1882.

27 Quoted in Lewis & Smith, 55.

28 Friedman, 77–8; *Argonaut*. Hurlbert
    also organized a 'charming' dinner for
    OW (on the evening of 10 January);
    see *New York Tribune*, 10 January 1882,
    2; *Topeka Daily Capital*, 16 January
    1882.

29 *Argonaut*.

30 *CL*, 126.

31 *CL*, 127.

32 *Argonaut*.

33 *CL*, 127.

34 Friedman, 76; 'Our London Corres-
    pondence', *Liverpool Mercury*, 24 Janu-
    ary 1882.

35 'The Poet's Day', *Punch*, 4 February
    1882.

36 Phoebe Pember to 'Clavius', 16 January
    1882, New York (Southern Historical
    Collection, Wilson Library, University
    of North Carolina at Chapel Hill).

37 Jervis McEntee, 'Diaries', 14 January
    1882 (Archives of American Art, Smith-
    sonian Institution); diary of James Her-
    bert Morse, quoted in Friedman, 79.

38 J. E. Kelly, 'Memoirs' (Archives of
    American Art, Smithsonian Institu-
    tion).

39 Edmund Gosse to E. C. Stedman, quot-
    ed in Thwaite, *Edmund Gosse*, 211.

40 Laura Stedman and George M. Gould,
    *Life and Letters of Edmund Clarence Sted-
    man* (1910), 2:31.

41 Quoted in Bette Roth Young, ed.,
    Emma Lazarus in Her World (1995), 189.

42 *CL*, 127.

43 *Manchester Times*, 27 May 1882.

44 Kelly, 'Memoirs'. Kelly states that he
    went to meet OW 'two or three days'
    after his New York lecture, and made
    the drawing the following day. It is
    often suggested that the small child in
    the drawing was Kelly's son. But Kelly
    had no son. His memoirs make clear
    that the boy was a friend of Wilde's.
    Perhaps he was the 'little Ganymede'

referred to in *CL*, 124, maybe one of the several children of Robert B. Roosevelt and Mrs Fortescue. In 1907, the original etching plate having been lost, a new print – a wood engraving – was made from Kelly's original drawing. Shortly afterwards Kelly also modelled a relief of Wilde's head from the same study, which was cast in bronze.

45 'Wilde's Experience', *Topeka Daily Capital*, 16 January 1882; Mason, 324–5.

46 Gary Scharnhorst, 'Kate Field Meets Oscar Wilde', *Wildean*, 28 (2006), gives a full account of the lunch.

47 Mary Warner Blanchard, 'Oscar Wilde's America: Counterculture in the Gilded Age', 46; a letter from Posie Emmet to 'Billy', 17 January [1882] (Archives of American Art, Smithsonian Institution), mentions Oscar Wilde's visit to the studio of Dora Wheeler (daughter of Candace Wheeler); *Bismark Tribune* (North Dakota), 23 December 1881, 4.

48 'Oscar Wilde', *Chicago Tribune*, 1 March 1882, 7, in Hofer & Scharnhorst, 91.

49 *Argonaut.*

50 *Argonaut.*

51 'Is this Aesthetic Taffy', *New York Herald*, 13 January 1882.

52 Edgar Saltus, *Oscar Wilde; An Idler's Impression* (1917), in Mikhail, 427.

53 *CL*, 128.

Chapter 2: Go Ahead

1 Margaret Stetz, 'Everything is going brilliantly' (lecture, University College London, 2016).

2 Pearson, 62.

3 *CL*, 128.

4 *Philadelphia Press*, in Lewis & Smith, 73.

5 Lewis & Smith, 73.

6 Stoddart to W. Whitman, 11 January 1882 (Library of Congress); Lewis & Smith, 71.

7 Horace Traubel, Jeanne Chapman and Robert Macisaac, eds, *With Walt Whitman In Camden* (1992), 7:366: 'Years back [Stoddart] came over with Oscar Wilde, when Wilde was here in America and the noise over him was at its height. They came in great style – with a flunkey and all that. And what struck me then, instantly, in Stoddart was his eminent tact. He said to me, "If you are willing – will excuse me – I will go off for an hour or so – come back again – leaving you together." etc. I told him, "We would be glad to have you stay – but do not feel to come back in an hour. Don't come for two or three" – and he did not – I think did not come till nightfall.' *Kansas City Journal*, 12 November 1899, 12, at OWIA.

8 'With Mr. Oscar Wilde', *Cincinnati Gazette*, 21 February 1882, in Hofer & Scharnhorst, 69.

9 Sherard, *Life*, 214.

10 Lewis & Smith, 75.

11 *Philadelphia Press*, quoted in Lewis & Smith, 75–7; Morse, 118. 'Wilde's Buncombe', *National Republican* (Washington, DC), 24 January 1882, 1.

12 Hofer & Scharnhorst, 29.

13 Lewis & Smith 75; Walt Whitman to Harry Stafford, 25 January 1882, at OWIA.

14 *Boston Herald*, 29 January 1882, in Hofer & Scharnhorst 43.

15 Traubel, Chapman and Macisaac, eds, *With Walt Whitman In Camden*, 4:79: 'When Wilde was here, after our talk, he expressed some surprise; he

said, "You are not exactly as I pictured you." I asked him: "Worse or better?" He said, "Better – and different." He told Donaldson afterwards what he referred to. Tom asked him. He said: "His poise that was what surprised me."'

16 Lewis & Smith, 75, 77.

17 Morse, 136.

18 Alan Grey and Joane Whitmore, eds, *Florence* (privately printed, 2008) 1:162–3, quotes fragments of a letter from OW, received 17 January 1882, 'Dear Mrs Florence Duncan, I thank you for your very courteous letter & as I should not like to leave Philadelphia without seeing its most...'; 'A Chat with Oscar Wilde', *Quiz*, 25 January 1882, 4; [Unknown] to OW, 10 February 1882 (Clark), '[Mrs Duncan] is very bright, asking me if I had told you of *her* criticism of your writings. "Oh, no, the *Quiz* is seen by him in London," said I. She looked aghast, and said – "how could he overlook it and be so good as to come to see me!" I replied, "Because he is a *Gentleman*." Was a good reply?'

19 R. Davis to OW (Clark). George Lewis urged OW to keep his eye 'open for an engagement as Correspondent to some paper, or some other engagement which may bring with it pecuniary advantage'. George Lewis to OW, 25 January 1882 (Austin); even so, OW turned down the chance to write an article for the *Sunday Star* (Wilmington, Delaware) giving his 'impressions of American life'. J. C. Farra to OW, 21 January 1882 (Clark).

20 JFW to OW, 19 February 1882, in Tipper, *Oscar*, 69.

21 Robert S. Davis to OW, 20 January 1882 (Clark).

22 Archibald Forbes to Flossie [Boughton], 15 January 1882 (Clark).

23 J. Pennell to Elizabeth Robins [Pennell], 19 January 1882, in Elizabeth Robins Pennell, *The Life and Letters of Joseph Pennell* (1930), 51.

24 'What Oscar Has To Say', *Baltimore American*, 20 January 1882, in Hofer & Scharnhorst, 34–5; 'Wilde and Forbes', *New York Herald*, 21 January 1882, in Hofer & Scharnhorst, 35–8.

25 *CL*, 133n, 134; Morse, 79–80.

26 *CL*, 148, 159.

27 Hofer & Scharnhorst, 45.

28 Lewis & Smith, 82ff; *Argonaut*; Caroline Healey Dall, 'Diary' (Massachusetts Historical Society).

29 Healy Dall, 'Diary'.

30 'The United States', 'New York, Feb 4 [1882]', *Argus* (Melbourne) 21 March 1882; also 'Oscar the Aesthete' [newspaper cutting], 29 January 1882 (Clark) where the incident is placed in Philadelphia.

31 *Argonaut*.

32 Healy Dall, 'Diary'.

33 Ward Thoron, ed. *Letters of Mrs Henry Adams* (1936), 328–9.

34 Harriet Loring to John Hay, 23 February 1882; quoted in George Monteiro, 'A Contemporary View of Henry James and Oscar Wilde, 1882', *American Literature*, 35 (1964), 529–30.

35 'Wilde's Buncome', *National Republican* (Washington, DC), 24 January 1882; *Evening Star* (Washington, DC) 24 January, 1882.

36 Henry James, *The American Scene* (1907), 335.

37 Friedman, 122–3.

38 *Letters of Mrs Henry Adams*, 113, Clover Adams to her father, 31 January 1882.

39 Lewis & Smith, 114.

40 *CL*, 132.

41 Holmes used the phrase '70 years young' about himself in a letter to Julia Ward Howe, 27 May 1879; *CL*, 131; J. R. Lowell, too, had been a member,

and it was his letter of introduction that secured OW's invitation.

42 Hofer & Scharnhorst, 70. Hofer & Scharnhorst 47, list two of the other guests at the lunch – James Freeman Clarke and Phillips Brooks, both of them ministers and writers.

43 Lewis & Smith, 116; Hofer & Scharnhorst, 50; OW presented O'Reilly with a letter of introduction from Florence Duncan, though his own name would have been enough to secure him an entrée. See Grey and Whitmore, eds, *Florence*, 1:165.

44 CL, 137; C. E. Norton to Mr Simon, 6 February 1882, in Kermit Vanderbilt, *Charles Eliot Norton* (1959), 178; C. E. Norton to J. R. Lowell, 22 February 1882, in Sarah Norton and M. A. de Wolfe Howe, eds, *The Letters of Charles Eliot Norton* (1913).

45 CL, 137, 132, Mark De Wolfe Howe, *Justice Oliver Wendell Holmes: The Proving Years 1870–1882* (1963), 255n.

46 Laura E. Richards, Maud Howe Elliott and Florence Howe Hall, *Julia Ward Howe* (1916), 70. The colourful first-hand account of the occasion in Alice Cary Williams's memoir, *Thru The Turnstile* (1976) does not seem credible – not least because Williams was not born until 1892. A letter from F. Marion Crawford to OW, 'Monday morning' [1882] (Austin), suggests OW went to call on the eldest Ward Howe daughter, the poetically inclined Mrs Angauos, the following afternoon.

47 Two letters from JFW to Henry Longfellow – 30 November 1875 and 11 May 1878 (Clark).

48 Mikhail, 379, 384.

49 Lewis & Smith 115–6; Hofer & Scharnhorst, 84.

50 Hofer & Scharnhorst, 70.

51 Hofer & Scharnhorst, 49.

52 Hofer & Scharnhorst, 129.

53 Lewis & Smith, 116; O'Sullivan, 215

54 *Boston Evening Traveller*, 30 January 1882, in Ellmann, 172.

55 Lewis & Smith, 116; H. W. Longfellow to Mrs Bean, 5 February 1882 (Morgan).

56 *Journal*, in Lewis & Smith, 125.

57 Lewis & Smith, 125–6, Kelly, 'Memoirs'.

58 Transcript in Lewis & Smith, 128.

59 *Detroit Saturday Night*, in Lewis & Smith, 128.

60 *Washington Star*, January 1882, quoted in Lewis & Smith, 88; ibid., 90; 'Wilde's Experience', *Topeka Daily Capital*, 16 January 1882: initially when OW's 'green' paper ran out, 'he was obliged to his chagrin to write his name on common cream tint'.

61 Friedman, 136–8; OW confessed to being disappointed in American cigarettes. Having used up the supply of Turkish cigarettes he had brought with him from England he settled on 'Old Judge' as his favoured American brand.

62 Kelly, 'Memoirs'.

63 'A Man of Culture Rare', *Rochester Democrat and Chronicle*, 8 February 1882, in Hofer & Scharnhorst, 55.

64 'Wilde and Forbes', *New York Herald*, 21 January 1882, in Hofer & Scharnhorst, 36.

65 *St Louis Globe-Democrat*, 26 February 1882, in Lewis & Smith, 82.

66 CL, 136.

67 'Oscar Wilde', *Boston Herald*, 29 January 1882, in Hofer & Scharnhorst, 40; OW gave other versions of this story, including to the *St Louis Globe-Democrat*, 26 February 1882, in Lewis & Smith, 88–9.

68 CL, 141; Lewis & Smith, 101; 'Oscar Wilde', *Boston Herald*, 29 January 1882, in Hofer & Scharnhorst, 44.

69 Higginson and Ward Howe, quoted

in Lewis & Smith, 119–21; see also Schroeder, 62; for Joaquin Miller's open letter to OW, published in the *New York World* (10 February 1882), apologizing for 'the coarse comments of the Philistine press' – and OW's reply – see *CL*, 141–3.

70 JFW to OW, 19 February 1882, in Tipper, *Oscar*, 70; 'Mr Oscar Wilde in America', *Daily News*, 2 March 1882 ('by our New York correspondent'), 6; *CL*, 148n. WCKW wrote, on 10 March 1882, to T. G. Bowles, editor of *Vanity Fair* (of which WCKW was the drama critic): 'I have held my tongue on one special matter which is very painful indeed to me and mine – why is it that whenever you get an opening you "go for" my brother Oscar so wickedly? Chaff, satire, wit, fun, honest criticism are all fair enough, but such stories as your "Chief" [in the magazine's 'Notes' section] tells of his being "utterly out of English Society" – neither received nor recognized – (about two numbers ago) are nasty and, as a matter of fact, false… [and] the apocryphal American anecdotes are surely attacking a young man from ambush – not after the wonted honest fashion of the paper. I have said my say, cost what costs.'

71 'The Aesthete and His Travels', *Truth*, 2 February 1882, 175–7.

72 Rennell Rodd to OW, [February 1882], (Austin).

73 Rennell Rodd to OW, [February 1882], (Austin); *CL*, 147, 148n.

74 Quoted in *Argonaut* (San Francisco), 10, no. 1, 7 January 1882.

75 William [Merritt] Chase to OW, 21 November 1882 (Clark), 'I am much stimulated by your enthusiasm for

Whistler.' 'Aesthetic: An Interesting Interview with Oscar Wilde', *Dayton Daily Democrat*, 3 May 1882, in Hofer & Scharnhorst, 144–5; Joseph Pennell to Elizabeth Robins [Pennell], 19 January 1882, in Pennell, *The Life and Letters of Joseph Pennell*, 51.

76 LFW to OW, 19 March 1882, Tipper, op. cit. 73.

77 Violet Hunt diary for 27 May 1882, quoted in 'Aesthetes and Pre-Raphaelites', 399. Lady Wilde reported Violet Hunt's presence at the party: 'Pretty Violet all eager to see you.' LFW Letters to OW, 28 May 1882. Tipper, *op. cit.*, 78.

78 JFW to OW, 25 February 1882, in Tipper, *Oscar*, 70; JFW to OW, 18 September 1882, in Tipper, *Oscar*, 88.

79 *Intentions*, 14 (2001), 9; CD available; Hofer & Scharnhorst,162.

80 'American Letter – New York, 13th Jan. 1882', *Belfast News-Letter*, 26 January 1882.

81 Lois Foster Rodecape, 'Gilding the Sunflower: A Study of Oscar Wilde's Visit to San Francisco', *California Historical Society Quarterly*, 19 (1940), 104.

82 *Freeman's Journal*, 9 February 1882.

83 H. C. Weiner's clothing store advert in the *L.A. Times*, 12 April 1882.

84 Lewis & Smith, 157; OWIA, 'Ephemera'.

85 Friedman, 96–7; Kit Barry, of the 'Ephemera Archive for American Studies' has traced 'nearly a hundred' different products advertised with Wilde's image; more than for any other figure during 1882.

86 'Speranza's Gifted Son', *St Louis Globe-Democrat*, 26 February 1882, in Hofer & Scharnhorst, 81.

Chapter 3: This Wide Great World

1   D. Boucicault to Mrs Lewis, 29 January 1882, *CL*, 135n.

2   *CL*, 136.

3   *CL*, 136; Hofer & Scharnhorst, 63; Morse, Accounts book (New York Public Library).

4   'London Gossip', *Royal Cornwall Gazette* (Truro), 9 June 1882; 'London Gossip', *York Herald*, 10 June 1882; *Aberdeen Weekly Journal*, 8 July 1882.

5   *Chicago Inter-Ocean*, 13 February 1882; Hofer & Scharnhorst, 64.

6   Hofer & Scharnhorst, 36.

7   *CL*, 136.

8   *CL*, 141.

9   *CL*, 163.

10 *CL*, 135n.

11 Morse, Accounts book: 5 February, draft to Levy $343.00 (c. £68 12*s*); JFW to OW, 25 February 1882, in Tipper, *Oscar*, 70; OW sent JFW £15, from which WCKW was to receive £5.

12 For trunks see *St Louis Daily Globe Democrat*, 26 February 1882. The 1880 US census lists J. Sydney Vale (born 1856, England) as 'President of Literary Bureau'. Morse gave his name as 'J. H. Vail'; Lewis & Smith as 'J. H. Vale' and Ellmann as 'J. S. Vail'. Lewis & Smith, 204, 211, claim that the valet was called 'John' (quoting, it seems, a report in the *St Louis Post-Dispatch*). Ellmann, 177, apparently misreading the reference in Lewis & Smith, 204, where 'John, the "liver-coloured" valet' is mentioned in the same sentence as the St Louis theatrical manager W. M. Traguier, dubs OW's valet 'W. M. Traquair'.

13 Kevin O'Brien, *Oscar Wilde in Canada* (1982), 150.

14 *Utica Daily Observer*, 7 February 1882.

15 Lewis & Smith, 156–8.

16 *Buffalo Express*, c. 9 February 1882; Hofer & Scharnhorst, 57.

17 OW, 'Impressions of America'.

18 'The United States', *Standard*, 11 February 1882; 'Politics and Society', *Leeds Mercury*, 13 February 1882: 'Poor Mr. Oscar Wilde is once more a disappointed man. It was first the Atlantic Ocean which failed to rise to the occasion when he crossed it, and now the Falls of Niagara have been guilty of the same grievous offence.' *Fun*, 8 March 1882, 103, in Friedman, 157–8.

19 *Chicago Inter-Ocean*, 13 February 1882, 2; Hofer & Scharnhorst, 61.

20 Hofer & Scharnhorst, 132, 147.

21 Lewis & Smith, 178.

22 Friedman, 160.

23 *CL*, 139.

24 'Oscar Wilde, The Aesthetic Apostle,' *Chicago Tribune*, 14 February 1882.

25 'Wilde', *Cleveland Leader*, 20 February 1882, 'Speranza's Gifted Son', *St Louis Globe-Democrat*, 26 February 1882, in Hofer & Scharnhorst, 66, 80.

26 *CL*, 143, and *St Louis Globe-Democrat*, 26 February 1882.

27 Lewis & Smith, 188–91, 199–201; 'With Mr Oscar Wilde', *Cincinnati Gazette*, 21 February 1882, in Hofer & Scharnhorst, 70; 'Oscar Wilde', *Chicago Tribune*, 1 March 1882, in Hofer & Scharnhorst, 89.

28 John Wyse Jackson, *Oscar Wilde in St. Louis* (2012) 52, 54; Hofer & Scharnhorst, 132, 161. According to the *St Louis Globe-Democrat*, which maintained a hostile attitude towards him, Wilde, as he stepped off the stage, declared the St Louis audience 'villainous', and pronounced it the worst he had experienced since coming to America. But all his other known pronouncements about his St Louis lecture were positive.

29 'Oscar Wilde', *Chicago Tribune*, 1 March 1882, in Hofer & Scharnhorst, 89.

30 OW, 'Keats' Sonnet on Blue', OET VI, 84; Emma Keats Speed to OW, 12 March [1882] (Austin).

31 *CL*, 157.

32 *CL*, 146; OWIA; *Milwaukee Sentinel*, 6 March 1882, 5.

33 *Dubuque Herald*, 3 March 1882, at OWIA.

34 Hofer & Scharnhorst, 63.

35 *Chicago Tribune*, 7 March 1882, 4, at OWIA.

36 OWIA; *CL*, 146, 147; Morse, Account book: Aurora: Receipts: $7.35 against expenses (personal, business, and private) of $15.32; Joliet: Receipts $18.75 against expenses of $27.64.

37 'Oscar Wilde', *Chicago Tribune*, 1 March 1882, 7; Hofer & Scharnhorst, 91–2.

38 'The House Beautiful', in O'Brien, *Oscar Wilde in Canada*, 165–81; O'Connell, 'Bohemian Experiences of Oscar Wilde'.

39 'A Home Ruler', *St Louis Globe-Democrat*, 26 February 1882, in Wyse Jackson, *Oscar Wilde in St. Louis*, 75–7; *CL*, 115–16.

40 *Daily Globe* (St Paul, Minnesota), 18 March 1882, 1; OWIA.

41 Hofer & Scharnhorst, 45.

42 Hofer & Scharnhorst, 45; Phil Robinson, *Sinners and Saints, A Tour Across the States* (1892), 39.

43 *CL*, 152–3 and n.

44 *Alta California*, 17 March 1882, in Rodecape, 'Gilding the Sunflower', 98; W. F. Morse to OW, 11 March 1882 (Clark) shows Morse negotiating with two other promoters – Seager of Lincoln and Fulton of Kansas City – for 'this California trip' – suggesting terms of '60% of the gross and a guarantee of $200 per night' in advance, plus three return fares. *CL*, 155; Morse's account book (New York Public Library) gives the actual figures: 'Receipts: $3,000.00' minus 'personal' expenses: $212.50 and 'business: $547.90'. The net – $2,239.60 – was divided 50/50 with the Carte Agency. During his time in the far west OW also ran up $267.90 of 'private' expenses.

Chapter 4: Bully Boy

1 *CL*, 158; 'Dinners and Dishes', *PMG*, 7 March 1885; OET VI, 40.

2 *San Francisco Chronicle*, 27 March 1882; *Record-Union* (Sacramento, California), 27 March 1882; OWIA.

3 Rodecape, 'Gilding the Sunflower', 100; 'Oscar Wilde At Home', *San Francisco Examiner*, 9 April 1882, in Hofer & Scharnhorst, 123–4.

4 *San Francisco Chronicle*, 28 March 1882, OWIA; *Examiner*, 28 March 1882, in Rodecape, 'Gilding the Sunflower', 102. *Daily Report*, 28 March 1882, in *Wildean*, 30, 82. Having been booked to give three lectures in San Francisco, Wilde had revived his talk on 'The English Renaissance' for this occasion, delivering it from memory; *Alta California*, 28 March 1882, in Rodecape, 'Gilding the Sunflower', 102. The full schedule of OW's Californian lectures (established by John Cooper at OWIA) is: 27 March, San Francisco: 'English Renaissance'; 28 March, Oakland, 'English Renaissance'; 29 March, San Francisco, 'Decorative Arts'; 30 March, Oakland, 'Art Decoration'; 31 March, Sacramento, 'Decorative Arts'; 1 April, San Francisco (matinee), 'House Beautiful'; 3 April, San José, 'Decorative Arts'; 4 April, Stockton, 'Decorative Arts', 5 April, San Francisco (an

5 Robert D. Pepper, *Oscar Wilde, Irish Poets and Poetry of the Nineteenth Century* (1972); OWIA; The *Livermore Herald*, 6 April 1882, had noted that OW on his train journey to Sacramento was 'absorbed in stealing the matter for his next lecture… from a weighty volume on the poets and prose of Ireland'.

unscheduled addition), 'Irish Poets and Poetry of the Nineteenth Century'; 8 April, Sacramento (matinee), 'House Beautiful'.

6 Hofer & Scharnhorst, 104, 146, 133; OW, 'Impressions of America', 28–9 (here OW increases the thickness of the hotel teacup to 'an inch and a half').

7 O'Connell, 'Bohemian Experiences of Oscar Wilde', in Rodecape, 'Gilding the Sunflower', 105.

8 O'Connell, 'Bohemian Experiences of Oscar Wilde'; Lewis & Smith, 255–6; the portrait, by Bohemian Club member Theodore Wores (1859–1939) was destroyed in the San Francisco earthquake of 1906.

9 Isobel Field, *The Life I've Loved* (1937), 143–9. Isobel 'Belle' Field, née Osbourne, was the stepdaughter, and sometime amanuensis, of Robert Louis Stevenson.

10 'Interview with a Theatrical Manageress' (Helen Lenoir), *South Australian Weekly Chronicle* (Adelaide) 8 August 1885; *Freeman's Journal*, 3 August 1882.

11 JFW to OW, 25 April 1882, in Tipper, *Oscar*, 75.

12 Hofer & Scharnhorst, 2.

13 *Peoria Evening Review*, 11 March 1882.

14 *Topeka Daily Capital*, 16 January 1882.

15 M. H. Elliott, 'This Was My Newport'; 'Andrew's American Queen', 17 June, 15 and 29 July 1882, in Ellmann, 193.

16 *San Francisco Chronicle*, 'Local Art Notes', 30 April 1882; 'Oscar Wilde', *Argonaut*, vol. 10, no. 13, 1 April 1882, 4; Field, *The Life I've Loved*, 147. Aimée [Amy] Crocker, in her 1936 autobiography *And I'd Do It Again* (286) mentions a dinner chez Crocker at which the guests tried to drink OW under the table, and failed. But the story rings false, and is probably an adaptation of the Bohemian Club anecdote.

17 CL, 19 April 1882. The letter (at Clark) was written from 'St Joseph, Missouri'; Wilde had visited Kansas City, Denver, Colorado Springs, Leadville and Salt Lake City in the ten days before, but had never stayed more than a day in any of them, so it is hard to imagine him developing attachments during that time. His fortnight based in San Francisco seems the likely moment for a romance to have sprung up. The 1880 Census lists 'Hattie Crocker' as the only 'Hattie' in San Francisco, together with three less socially plausible 'Harriets' of similar age. A 'Hattie Rice' also appears occasionally in the San Francisco social pages during 1882.

18 CL, 161; Hofer & Scharnhorst, 147.

19 *Chicago Inter-Ocean*, 13 February 1882, 2; in Hofer & Scharnhorst, 63.

20 CL, 161–2; *Leadville Daily Herald*, 14 April 1882; 'Mr. Oscar Wilde on America', *Freeman's Journal*, 11 July 1883.

21 OW, 'Impressions of America', 31; Sherard, *Life*, 226.

22 CL, 165–6; OW, 'Impressions of America'; 'Mr. Oscar Wilde on America', *Freeman's Journal*, 11 July 1883; these sources suggest that OW mentioned Cellini in his lecture, and although this is not confirmed in any of the press reports it is possible. OW's answer to the question about Cellini's whereabouts, however, suggests a less formal setting for the discussion about the artist.

23 CL, 162.

24 CL, 166.

25 CL, 164.

786 OSCAR: A LIFE

26 CL, 205.

27 CL, 140, 175.

28 OW, L'Envoi; see also 'Aesthetic: An Interesting Interview with Oscar Wilde', Dayton Daily Democrat, 3 May 1882, in Hofer & Scharnhorst 144: here OW claims to be no longer a 'Pre-Raphaelite' and disciple of Ruskin, but, rather, 'the Champion' of Whistler's 'new school'.

29 Martin Birnbaum, Oscar Wilde: Fragments and Memories (1914), 18; Mason, 182–6.

30 R. D'Oyly Carte to OW [fragment] (Clark); CL, 150.

31 CL, 150n.

32 CL, 151.

33 [Unknown employee of Carte Agency in NYC] to OW, 21 March 1882 (Clark), 'As Mr Carte wrote you, Mr Harriott [Morris's husband], in his last communication seemed disposed to throw cold water on the matter rather – at any rate for this season, owing to Mrs Harriott's uncertain health.' Morse to OW, CL, 156n.

Chapter 5: Different Aspects

1 CL, 169.

2 Morse, 84–5. Receipts from first lecture at Montreal (15 May) were $300, from first lecture at Toronto (25 May) $403.55, from Quebec City (18 May) $158.50; Frederick Dunbar to Richard Glaezner, 28 July 1911 (Clark). Dunbar recalled that when the bust was exhibited at the Art Institute, 'in true Hellenic style' the pedestal was daily decorated with flowers by adoring maidens.

3 Toronto Globe, in O'Brien, Oscar Wilde in Canada, 98–9.

4 Friedman, 216–17; CL, 174.

5 'Oscar Wilde in Brooklyn' (newspaper cutting), George Lewis archive (Bodleian).

6 'Mr Oscar Wilde in America', Freeman's Journal, 11 July 1883.

7 CL, 175.

8 OW, 'Impressions of America'.

9 New Orleans Picayune, 25 June 1882, in Hofer & Scharnhorst, 157; Saratoga Weekly Journal, 20 July 1882, in Ellmann, 187.

10 Richard III programme notes, Carll's Opera House, New Haven, 30 January 1882, reprinted in Intentions, June 2010, 25; Lewis & Smith, 362.

11 Hofer & Scharnhorst, 157. OW later claimed that 'When I went to Texas I was called "Captain"; when I got to the centre of the country I was addressed as "Colonel," and, on arriving at the borders of Mexico, as "General"' ('Impressions of America').

12 Friedman, 223–4; see E. P. Alexander to Jefferson Davis, 12 June 1882, Louisville, Kentucky, introducing OW, item 372 in the Oscar Wilde collection of John B. Stetson.

13 Hofer & Scharnhorst, 156–7; CL, 176; Hofer & Scharnhorst, 362.

14 'New Notes', Sedalia Weekly Bazoo, 27 June 1882, in Friedman, 218, but see Michèle Mendelssohn, Making Oscar Wilde (2018), 193ff.

15 'Oscar Wilde and His Negro Valet', NYT, 9 July 1882, in Friedman, 227.

16 Hofer & Scharnhorst, 166, 161; Manchester Times, 27 May 1882; CL, 174, 166. H. W. B. Howard to Oscar Wilde, 2 September 1882 (Clark), offering OW $500 for four articles of 3,500 words each on Japanese art and handicraft 'to be written while you are in Japan or immediately after starting your return', and suggesting that he

could then publish the articles in book form; *CL*, 177; there are three letters of introduction to Japanese officials and academics at Clark.

17 Morse; Hofer & Scharnhorst, 147.

18 *CL*, 183; W. F. Morse to OW, 20 November 1882 (Fales), re. 'I have got track of the Australian man Lyons and have written him'; Lewis & Smith, 420.

19 Morse to 'Dear Sir', 5 August 1882, MSL collection, Delaware.

20 Morse, 91. *Sun* (New York), 20 August 1882, quotes OW: 'Of course there are many disadvantages in lecturing in summer hotels. The lectures are apt to be badly managed, the rooms are often difficult to speak in, and there is an inevitable bustle and confusion, which nobody can help, and for which nobody is to blame.'

21 'From the *Ladies Pictorial*', *Hampshire Telegraph and Sussex Chronicle*, 9 August 1882. OW introduced the line about 'millionaires' at the time of his Californian tour; *San Francisco Chronicle*, 30 March 1882. 'Oscar Wilde at Newport', *Sun*, 16 July 1882, does give an outline of his talk there: 'He made a stir among the ladies when he spoke of the ugliness of their bonnets, which is only equaled, he said, by the extreme ugliness of the artificial flowers, which he hoped none of them wore.'

22 Other dates included: Sharon Springs, Cooperstown, Richfield Springs, the Catskills, Cornwall, Saratoga Springs, Seabright, Spring Lake, Asbury Park, Ocean Beach and Cape May.

23 *CL*, 175; Richards, Howe and Howe Hall, *Julia Ward Howe*, 2:72.

24 *CL*, 177.

25 'Guide to the Oscar Wilde Invitation', catalogue of Newport Historical Society, MS 2012.3.

26 Richards, Howe and Howe Hall, *Julia Ward Howe*, 2:72. Julia Ward Howe

refers to OW's poem as 'The Ode to Albion'.

27 *Democrat and Chronicle* (Rochester, New York), 11 July 1882, 2; 'London Gossip,' *Freeman's Journal*, 17 July 1882; JFW to OW, 6 August 1882 and 16 August 1882, in Tipper, *Oscar*, 82, 83.

28 *Frank Leslie's Illustrated Newspaper*, v. 54, 12 August 1882, 389; OWIA.

29 James L. Ford, *Forty-odd Years in the Literary Shop* (1921), 143.

30 *New York Mirror*, 'The World of Society', August 1882, 8. Stops mentioned included Babylon, Jesse Conkling's, the Surf Hotel (aka 'Sammis'), Fire Island, Bay Shore, and Wa Wa Yanda Club.

31 'Polo at Newport', *Sun* (New York), 16 July 1882.

32 Sam Ward to Maud Howe, 31 July 1882, in Maud Howe Elliott, *Uncle Sam Ward and his Circle* (1938).

33 *CL*, 175; Lily Morgan Morrill, *A Builder of the New South: Notes in the Career of Thomas M. Logan* (2011), 142.

34 Natalie Barney, *Aventures de l'esprit* (1929), at OWIA.

35 Lewis & Smith, 391.

36 Edward J. Renehan Jr., *John Burroughs: An American Naturalist* (1998), 148; Ellmann, 154.

37 *Sun* (New York), 30 July 1882; 'From the *Ladies Pictorial*'; Sam Ward to F. Marion Crawford, 3[0] July 1882, in Maud Howe Elliott, *My Cousin, F. Marion Crawford* (1934), 134; Hofer & Scharnhorst, 78. Kerr & Co. advertised their 'spool cotton' with a cartoon trade card depicting Wilde and Beecher (see *Intentions*, 64 (October 2009), 27).

38 OW received $623.96 from his Summer Lecture Tour (Morse, 'Receipts,' BL). *CL*, 183, 182. It was hoped that Moore could guarantee '700 [dollars] a week' for two weeks that autumn. Initial returns, however, were disappointing.

39 'Gleanings', *Birmingham Daily Post*, 13 October 1882.

40 His itinerary ran from St John, to Amherst, Truro, Halifax, Charlottetown, Moncton and St John (again).

41 'Oscar Wilde Explains', *Moncton Daily Transcript*, 18 October 1882.

42 'Oscar Wilde Thoroughly Exhausted', *New York Tribune*, 27 November 1882, in Hofer & Scharnhorst, 172–3.

43 Ellmann, 195.

44 'By a Correspondent of the Manches-

ter Examiner', *Manchester Times*, 27 May 1882.

45 Estelle Jussim, *Slave to Beauty* (1981), 77.

46 E. Brainerd to OW [1882] (Clark).

47 Charles Volkmar to OW, 29 August 1883 (Clark); Charles G. Leland to OW, 11 May 1882, in John B. Stetson, cat. item 385: 'I can never thank you as you deserve for the good you have done the Great Cause of Art Education – and to me as one of its humble teachers.'

Chapter 6: The Dream of the Poet

1   *CL*, 178, Ellmann, 189.

2   *CL*, 182.

3   Unknown to OW, 10 February 1882 [Clark].

4   *CL*, 183n; Morse's accounts show the sum of $69.00 'for Printing Play'.

5   There are c. 1882 manuscripts of the scenario of *The Cardinal of Avignon*, and some pages of dialogue, at Dartmouth College and Princeton.

6   'Literary Notes', *PMG*, 1 November 1883; OW made these remarks to Whistler at the Hogarth Club 'Conversazione'.

7   Lewis & Smith, 47; *Topeka Daily Capital*, 16 January 1882, re. Anderson at Croly reception.

8   OET V, 3–5.

9   *CL*, 178–9.

10 *CL*, 178–9; 'Rachel' was the stage name of Elisa Felix (1821–58).

11 OW to S. Mackaye, [26 September 1882], Providence, RI, in *Epoch*, 446; *CL*, 181.

12 OW to S. Mackaye, [26 September 1882], in *Epoch*, 446; *CL*, 181.

13 *CL*, 181. The editors date the letter [September 1882], but I think it more probable that it dates from around 2 October, and follows on from OW's letter to Mackaye, *CL*, 184.

14 S. Mackaye to OW, 4 October 1882 (Clark).

15 *CL*, 185.

16 H. Griffin to OW, 1 Dec 1882 (Clark); Mason, 327; Schroeder, 71–2; *CL*, 191.

17 *CL*, 186, 187; Mary Anderson to OW (Morgan); her handwriting is not very legible but the letter seems to read, '*Vera* charms me; it is very powerful. I think I would like to play the part – for me it is stranger [stronger?] than the *Duchess*'. OW, however, felt it important that she tackle the 'Duchess' first. As he explained to Mackaye – in his letter of 26 September – 'to begin with the *Nihilists* would be very foolish; as it affords no opportunity for artistic and beautiful setting'.

18 Mason, 258: the meeting took place on Sunday 12 November 1882; Lewis & Smith, 442.

19 *Standard* (London), 31 October 1882; this led to a poetic parody – 'The Too-Too Fire' in *PMG*, 2 November 1882: 'He dwelt on its chords of intense white and yellow, / Of umber and chrome he impassionedly spoke, / He remarked how the crudest of reds became mellow / In softening effects of harmonious smoke.'

20 'Mrs Langtry', *New York World*, 7 November 1882, 5; in OET VI, 23–5.

21 Lewis & Smith, 420; Birnbaum, *Oscar Wilde: Fragments and Memories*, 19.

22 Ellmann 197; 'London Gossip', *Hampshire Telegraph and Sussex Chronicle*, 11 October 1882; 'Literature & Art', *Nottinghamshire Guardian*, 20 October 1882, 3; *Liverpool Mercury*, 21 October 1882.

23 JFW to OW, 22 December 1882, in Tipper, *Oscar*, 95–6; although there is no evidence that OW ever seriously considered taking to the stage, he did, while in New York, apparently visit a clairvoyant who predicted – among other things – that he would 'play Hamlet'. He was delighted, declaring that it had been 'the dream of his life' to play the part and that 'if he went to Australia he would'. 'The Trifler' [James Huneker], *Musical Courier* (New York), 26 July 1893.

24 Lewis & Smith, 420. *Illustrated Police News*, 14 October 1882, on dinner at Brown's Chop House with John Howson, Harrison Gray Fiske and others; Edgar Fawcet to OW, 10 November [1882] (Austin) re. dinner at the Union Club with 'Tal, Martin van Buren, Frankie Riggs & Myself'. Desmond Hawkins, ed., *The Grove Diaries* (1995), 785, notes that on 18 November 1882 Agnes Grove was at 'Mrs Botta's party. Mr [Waldo] Story the sculptor read his poems. Oscar Wilde was there'. William Merritt Chase to OW, 21 November 1882, 'Hoping again I may have the pleasure to see you at my studio.'

25 *CL*, 190n.

26 *Evening News* (Sydney), 20 January 1883.

27 *Standard* (London), 20 September 1882, 5; *Era* (London) 30 September 1882.

28 'Oscar Wilde See the Beauties', *Sun* (New York), 20 November 1882, 3.

29 'Oscar Wilde's Legs', *National Police Gazette* (New York) 30 December 1882, in *Intentions*, 35 (December 2004), 34–5.

30 Robert Marland and John Cooper, 'Wilde's Final Farewell Lecture in New York', *Wildean*, 42 (2013), 57–61.

31 Sherard, *Life*, 172.

32 W. F. Morse to OW, 20 November 1882 (Fales): 'I enclose a cheque for $500. The whole amount due now is $550 – without a return from Moncton which has not yet come to hand, and exclusive of our Petty Cash a/c which is still open.' Morse's account book (Berg) indicates that – for the second part of the year – OW was owed $1010.50, although by 21 December – after the deduction of various private expenses and cash advances – there was only $44.12 outstanding. OW had moved to rooms in Greenwich Village, at 48 West 11th Street.

33 *CL*, 209 transcribes the figure as '£200' (i.e. $1,000), but $200 seems more likely.

34 Morse, 132–3; Lewis & Smith, 439–40; 'The United States', *South Australian Register* (Adelaide), 16 February 1883.

35 'Andrew's American Queen', 23 November 1882, in Ellmann, 195; Theodore Tilton to OW, 13 December [1882] (Clark), having just heard OW was ill.

36 Lewis & Smith, 440.

37 *New York Tribune*, 10 January 1883; Lewis & Smith, 442–3.

Part V: *The Devoted Friend*
Chapter 1: Over the Seine

1 *World*, 10 January 1883.

2 E. Levy to OW, 26 January 1883 (Clark); JFW to OW, 9 [Feb? 1883], in Tipper, *Oscar*, 100, re. 'the creditors are dreadful'.

3 *CL*, 195; Rodd, *Social and Diplomatic Memories*, 25; Walter Ledger to Thomas Bird Mosher, 2 April 1906 (Houghton); Sherard, *SUF*, 40; OW, *L'Envoi*; *CL*, 205. Schroeder, 74, notes that there is 'no evidence' linking the epigram in OW's commonplace book to Rodd; but the entry can be confidently dated to OW's time in Paris in 1883, immediately after the break; and Rodd had been described in print as OW's 'disciple'. So the connection seems plausible.

4 The Hôtel Continental is now the Westin Paris – Vendôme, rue Castiglione; the Hôtel Voltaire is now called the Hôtel Quai Voltaire.

5 Sherard, *SUF*, 26.

6 OET V, 34–42.

7 *CL*, 197.

8 OW notes (Berg).

9 *CL*, 196–203.

10 Mason, 259–65; *CL*, 203–4 (where OW's letter to Marie Prescott is re-dated from 'December 1882' to '[March–April, 1883]'; There is a 'contract' at Clark between Prescott and Wilde, drawn up by a New York solicitor, dated 7 February 1883, and signed by Prescott (but not Wilde). It gives the same terms as Prescott gives in her letter to OW (Mason). OW seems to have expressed some anxiety about being able to countersign the document (not being in New York). There are two letters from George Lewis to OW at Clark, which seem to address this issue: the first, 27 February 1883, about drawing up an 'agreement' for 'the Play' ('I hope it may turn out as well as you anticipate'); the second (15 March 1883) apologizing for his clerk's failure to draft the agreement, and recommending R. O. Maugham (father of Somerset Maugham) at 54 rue Faubourg St Honoré, for the task.

11 *CL*, 206.

12 OW to Dorothy Tennant [1883], in Waller, *The Magnificent Mrs Tennant*, 216–17; Dorothy Tennant to OW, Richmond Terrace, 9 April [1883] (Austin). Mrs Tennant, an ardent Francophile, was a friend of Coquelin the elder.

13 Harris, 48; OW notes (Berg); JFW to OW, [1883], in Melville, 174.

14 OW, 'Balzac in English', *PMG*, 13 September 1886, in OET VI, 89.

15 OW, 'Decay of Lying'.

16 Sherard, *SUF*, 21, *Real*, 200; JFW to OW, in Melville, 174.

17 Kate Moore to [OW] 'Mr Wylde', [1883] (Clark); *CL*, 207; *Goncourt Journal*, 2:1002, Saturday, 2 April 1883.

18 *CL*, 204, OW to Clarisse Moore, 'I will now, along with my art work, devote to the drama a great deal of my time.'; Sherard, *SUF*, 18; Anna Gruetzner Robins, ed., *Walter Sickert: The Complete Writings on Art* (2000), 520; Sherard, *Real*, 243.

19 Sherard, *SUF*, 66 – the picture is now lost; the Oscar Wilde collection of John B. Stetson, cat. item 404; J. S. Sargent to OW, [1883], 'I hope you will be able to come to-morrow morning and see my portrait. If you cannot please send me an answer about Sunday at once, for I should like to ask a Frenchman to meet you, Bourget, a clever writer and Poet.'

20 *CL*, 206, J. E. Blanche, *Portraits of a Lifetime* (1937), 98.

21 JMW to OW, [1883], 'The Correspondence of James McNeill Whistler' at GUL; for Degas' comments see OW notes [1883] (Berg) 'Degas to Walter [Sickert])' (10).

22 Sherard, *SUF*, 23–4.

23 Sherard, *Real*, 235; *SUF*, 33–6.

24 Sherard, *SUF*, 36; Edgar Jepson, *Memories of a Victorian* (1933), 261; Augustus John, *Chiaroscuro* (1954), 35; CMW to Otho Lloyd, *CL*, 228; Reginald Auberon [Horace C. Wyndham], *The Nineteen Hundreds* (1922), 78–9.

25 *CL*, 210; 211.

26 Sherard, *SUF*, 26.

27 Sherard, *SUF*, 29–30; R. H. Sherard to OW, [26 May 1883] (Clark).

28 Sherard *SUF*, 67–9; *Life*, 233.

29 Sherard, *SUF*, 17–18.

30 *CL*, 205; Sherard, *SUF*, 32, 43–6.

31 Sherard, *SUF*, 46.

32 OW notes (Berg).

33 Sherard, *SUF*, 33–4.

34 Théophile Gautier, 'Notice' preceding Charles Baudelaire, *Les Fleurs du mal* (1868) quoted in Matthew Sturgis, *Passionate Attitudes* (2011), 22–3.

35 Sherard, *SUF*, 56.

36 *CL*, 207–8; Sherard, *SUF*, 48.

37 OW notes (Berg).

38 Sherard *SUF*, 48–50.

39 Sherard, *Real*, 274–6; *SUF*, 31–2; 'I believe the musical value of a word is greater than its intellectual value and nowhere is this better exemplified than in that supreme imaginative work of the young American who wrote "The Raven"'. 'Wilde in Utica', *Utica Daily Observer*, 7 February 1882.

40 Sherard, *Real*, 155; R. H. Sherard to A. J. A. Symons, 3 June [1937] (Clark). The cocotte's name was Marie Aguétant; she achieved an unwanted fame three years later when she was murdered by a petty thief. Sherard found it necessary to visit a prostitute once a week for what he termed an 'evacuation.'

41 Sherard, *Life*, 243; Sherard to A. J. A. Symons, 13 May (Clark).

42 Sherard, *SUF*, 85; *Real*, 236.

43 Sherard, *SUF*, 85; *Real*, 236–7.

44 Sherard, *Real*, 237–8.

45 Mary Anderson to OW, Friday, Victoria [1883]; Oscar Wilde collection of John B. Stetson, cat. item 374; Ellmann, 212. Anderson later told a reporter that she had found the play 'unsuitable, as it dealt almost entirely with crime, so I was compelled to return it'. 'Literary Notes', *PMG*, 7 September 1883.

46 Sherard, *Real*, 238.

47 Edmond and Jules de Goncourt, 'Journal', ed. by Robert Ricatte (1989), *Goncourt Journal* 2:1005. Goncourt mistakenly refers to the stories as relating to a town in 'Texas'.

48 20 April 1883, *Daily Advocate* (Newark, Ohio); *Liverpool Mercury*, 15 March 1883 in Dibb, 17.

49 'The European Mail', *Brisbane Courier*, 6 June 1883.

Chapter 2: First Drama

1 *CL*, 209; Sherard, *Real*, 148; OW lost the pawn ticket and had to swear an affidavit at Marlborough Street Police Court to secure a replacement ticket.

2 J. E. Millais to OW, 7 July 1883; the Oscar Wilde collection of John B. Stetson, cat. item 390.

3 JMW to OW, 26 May 1883 (GUL). OW dined chez Lewis on 22 June 1883; Mr & Mrs Comyns Carr and Burne-Jones were also present, along with five others; *CL*, 213.

4   CL, 211.

5   Laura Troubridge, diary, July 1883, *Life Amongst the Troubridges*, 164–5.

6   Hare, *The Story of My Life*, 5:386, re. a reception on 21 June 1883 at Madame du Quaire's; Mrs Duncan Stewart (1804–84) had been born Harriet Everlinda Gore in Donegal.

7   Otho Lloyd to Nellie Hutchinson, in Melville, 176.

8   Otho Lloyd to Nellie Hutchinson, in Melville, 177.

9   Melville, 178.

10 Melville, 178; JFW to CMW, 25 May 188,3 in Moyle, 67; Otho Lloyd to Nellie Hutchinson, in Melville, 179.

11 Otho Lloyd to Nellie Hutchison, in Melville, 178, 179.

12 Jopling, in Mikhail, 204; CMW to OW, 11 November 1883 (BL).

13 Marie Belloc Lowndes, 'Something About Our Lady Contributors', *Answers*, 13, no. 315 (9 June 1894); 'Men, Manners and Moods', *Collier's Weekly*, 26 August 1897, reprinted in *Intentions*, August 2007, 11–15.

14 CL, 212–13; Dibb, 22–3 on his borrowings from Pater's 'Preface'; JMW letter to *Truth*, 2 January 1890 in Ronald Anderson and Anne Koval, *James NcNeill Whistler* (1994), 316.

15 OW, 'Modern Art Training', 224–32.

16 Newspaper cutting, 4 July 1883, quoted in Dibb, 28.

17 Sherard, *Real*, 288.

18 *Freeman's Journal*, 11 July 1883; *World*, 18 July 1883; cheaper seats were also available at 7s 6d at the back of the stalls, and 5s in the balcony.

19 *North Eastern Daily Gazette*, 11 July 1883; *Leicester Chronicle*, 21 July 1883, in Dibb, 30–1.

20 *World*, 18 July 1883; OW's manuscript notes for the lecture were sold at Christie's, Vander Poel sale, 3 March 2004.

21 'Mr. Oscar Wilde on America', *Freeman's Journal*, 11 July 1883; the shorthand account of the lecture indicates '(laughter)' at frequent intervals.

22 *Queen*, 14 July 1883, in Dibb, 33; W. F. Morse, 'Lectures in Great Britain'.

23 *Tatler*, 14 July 1883, in Dibb, 33; 'Theatrical Gossip', *Era*, 14 July 1883.

24 'Exit Oscar', *Truth*, 19 July 1883, 86–7.

25 *New York Herald*, 12 August 1883, in Ellmann, 226.

26 W. F. Morse to OW, 18 August 1883 (Clark). The letter was sent to OW in New York.

27 Don Mead, 'Personal Impressions of America – Oscar Wilde in Southport', *Wildean*, 16 (2000), 18–32.

28 Kenneth Rose, *Superior Person* (1969) 72; *NYT*, 12 August 1883: the other members of the group were Sir Savile Crossley and Mr Hanbury.

29 *NYT*, 12 August 1883; 'Oscar Wilde's Return', *Fort Worth Daily Gazette*, 18 August 1883.

30 *NYT*, 12 August 1883; 'Oscar Wilde's Return', *Fort Worth Daily Gazette*, 18 August 1883.

31 *NYT*, 12 August, 1883; *Wheeling Daily Intelligencer*, 14 August 1883; *New York World*, 12 August, 1883, quoted in R. B. Glaenzer, ed., *Decorative Art in America: A Lecture by Oscar Wilde* (1906), 32.

32 R. B. Glaenzer, ed., *Decorative Art in America: A Lecture by Oscar Wilde* (1906), 196; 'Losing Money on Vera'; *NYT*, 27 August 1883.

33 *Argonaut*.

34 Mason, 271.

35 Mason, 265–6; *Argonaut*.

36 'Flaneur,' *Argonaut*, 1 September 1883; CL, 218.

37 *Morning News*, 10 June 1884 (Clark): OW added, 'I shall never forget the two hours and a half I passed in the playhouse in New York on the first night of my piece.'

38 Mason, 272–3; Birnbaum, *Oscar Wilde: Fragments and Memories*, 19; *Argonaut*, 1 September 1883.

39 F. Gebhard to OW, 21 August 1883, Union Club, New York (Fales). The *Argonaut* noted that Gebhard had taken a box with 'Lord Manderville and three other Englishmen'.

40 Mason, 273; *Sun*, 23 August 1883.

41 *New York World*, quoted in *Freeman's Journal*, 23 August 1883; *Sun*, 23 August 1883. *Argonaut*: 'Mr. Wilde in this scene attempts to be witty, but is a signal failure. He puts a number of commonplace and aged jokes in the mouths of the few comedians that the piece asks for, and they roll them off unintelligibly one after the other. Ed. Lamb was the principal comedian. He is an actor of undoubted excellence, and the small hit that he made was due to his own mannerisms rather than to the brightness of the lines. It is likely that after the play has been running a little while this act will be touched up so as to be the brightest of the piece.'

42 *Argonaut*; *Era*, 8 September 1883; Mason, 273; Ellmann, 228.

43 James Kelly, 'Memoirs'.

44 Quoted in the *Standard*, 22 August 1883.

45 'The Play and the Public,' *NYT*, 28 August 1883.

46 *New York Daily Mirror*, 25 August 1883; Mason, 273.

47 *NYT*, 27 and 28 August 1883. Although the play's 'withdrawal' was reported in the press on 28 August, the decision was made on 27 August; and the last performance of the play was on 25 August. The *Pilot* commended OW for not appearing in the piece – 'A young man can outlive even a bad play; but there are limits which may not be passed.'

48 *NYT*, 28 August 1883.

49 Ellmann, 228; Jessica Sykes to OW [1883] (Clark), inviting him to join a party at St Leonard's Island, Lake Rosdean, Ontario, at the end of August, ends, 'I am sure that your play will be successful, but if it should not be it would simply make no difference in my gladness to see you.' Jessica Cavendish-Bentinck had married Sir Tatton Sykes in 1874.

Chapter 3: Man of the Day

1 *Entr'acte*, 1 September 1883.

2 *Birmingham Daily Post*, 29 September, 1883, in Dibb, 47.

3 Otho Lloyd, quoted in Ellmann, 229.

4 For the best and fullest itineraries of OW's lecture tour see Dibb.

5 Sherard, *Life*, 30–1.

6 Dibb, 59–90.

7 'Mr Oscar Wilde in a/c with W. F. Morse' (Clark); OW's share of commission on his first thirteen lectures, beginning with Margate and Ramsgate (before the visit to America) and ending with Erdington on 10 October, came to £145 2s 3d, from which was subtracted £58 13s 4d in business expenses. The balance – £91 9s – was paid to OW on 12 October 1883. See Dibb, 58–9, for the Manchester audience.

8 Melville, 180.

9 CMW to OW, 11 November 1883, in Ellmann, 229–30.

10 *CL*, 221; the lectures were at the Gaiety Theatre, 3 pm, 22 and 23 November.

11 CMW to Otho Holland Lloyd, 26 November 1883, *CL*, 222.

12 Moyle, 74.

13 JFW to OW, [Nov 1883], in Tipper, *Oscar*, 105.

14 WCKW to OW, 29 November 1883 (Clark).

15 Ada Swinburne-King to JFW, 30 November 1883 (Clark).

16 CMW to OW, [27 November 1883] (BL).

17 CMW to Otho Lloyd, 27 November 1883, in Moyle, 75.

18 *CL*, 222n.

19 Emily Lloyd to OW, 30 November 1883 (Clark).

20 Moyle, 76.

21 Emily Lloyd to OW, 6 December 1883 (Clark).

22 Schoeder, 81–2.

23 Emily Lloyd to OW, 6 December 1883; Emily Lloyd to OW, 14 December 1883 (Clark).

24 *CL*, 224, 225; Moyle, 73; CMW to OW (BL).

25 CMW to OW (BL).

26 *World*, quoted in *York Herald*, 5 December 1883; *Dundee Courier and Argus*, 5 December 1883; *Belfast News-Letter*, 12 December 1883; *Freeman's Newsletter*, 20 December 1883; 'Our London Letter', *Dundee Courier and Argus*, 20 December 1883.

27 Moyle, 82.

28 Emily Lloyd to OW, 14 December 1883 (Clark). Whistler had been supporting OW in other ways too, e.g. taking his side after he was attacked in print by Augustus Moore. See A. Moore to JMW, 16 October 1883 (GUL) and R. H. Sherard to OW, 13 October 1883 (Clark).

29 *CL*, 225.

30 Eleanor Sickert to OW, 26 December 1883 (Clark).

31 CMW to OW, 4 January 1884 (BL).

32 *CL*, 224; Langtry, *The Days I Knew*, 94.

33 *Cumberland and Westmorland Advertiser*, 26 February 1884, in Dibb, 95–6.

Dibb, 112–13 lists seventy-six lectures given by OW between 1 January and 26 April 1884.

34 Russell Thorndike, *Sybil Thorndike* (1929), 43–4; after the Gainsborough lecture (28 January 1884) OW praised Sybil Thorndike's mother, Agnes, as 'a witty young woman'; she was inspired by his ideas, becoming a local arbiter of taste, and leading the trips up to town.

35 *Vanity Fair*, 24 May 1884; see [Carlo Pellegrini / 'Ape'] 'Unidentified' to OW, 28 April [1884] (Austin): 'My dear Oscar, On Thursday next at 5 o'clock exact you will find me here [53 Mortimer Street]... P.S. Bring with you a couple of your latest photographs.'

36 OW, 'Under the Balcony', appeared in the *Shakespearean Show Book* (1884); see Mason, 196–9.

37 Ada Cavendish to OW, 13 March 1884 (Clark): 'I have... read your Play,' she told him, 'and think it is very *fine* and I sincerely trust that I may be able to produce it, if you cannot find a better exponent.'

38 Courtenay Thorpe to [OW], 17 April 1884 (Clark).

39 'The Trifler' [James Huneker], *Musical Courier* (New York), 26 July 1893.

40 'The House Beautiful', in O'Brien, *Oscar Wilde in Canada*, 178.

41 Moyle, 85–6.

42 Moyle, 86, mentions the need for down payment. The lease was terminable at seven or fourteen years by either party. The rent was '£130 for the first 7 years, £140 for the 2nd 7 years, and £150 for the 3rd 7 years, payable quarterly, the first payment to be made on 29 September [1884] and to be £22.10.0 for the period ending that day' (Hargrove & Co. to OW, 13 May 1884).

43 Johnston Forbes-Robertson, *A Player Under Three Reigns* (1925), 110.

44 Schroeder, 82, quoting information from Merlin Holland (also see Maguire, 54); this corrects Ellmann, 234, which suggested that OW borrowed '£1,000 on what remained of his father's estate' on 15 May 1884. A letter from George Lewis to OW, 15 May 1884 (Clark), enclosed a copy of a letter from Hargrove & Co. regarding a covenant by OW to repay to the trustees *on demand* the sum of £1,000 and in the meantime to pay them interest at the rate of 5 per cent p.a. by half yearly payments. Lewis asks if OW would like him to insert a clause saying that while the interest will be paid 'the principal sum should not be called up for a certain number of years'.

45 Otho Lloyd to A. J. A. Symons, 27 May 1937 (Clark).

46 The Church of St James has been the parish church of Paddington since 1845.

The building was remodelled in the Gothic style in 1881 by G. E. Street, the work being completed under the direction of his son, A. E. Street (who had read classics at Magdalen with OW).

47 Pennell and Pennell, *The Life of James McNeill Whistler*, 228.

48 'London Jottings', by Archibald Forbes, London, 30 May 1884, syndicated to the *South Australian Advertiser* (Adelaide), 9 July 1884; OW and many of the guests must have been rather light-headed as, on the evening before the wedding, the Lewises had hosted a big dance at Portland Place. OW (though he did not dance) had stayed till 4 am, taking down 'a succession of aesthetic ladies to successive suppers'. One of them, Mrs Jopling, had given him advice on 'how a young husband should treat his wife'.

Chapter 4: New Relations

1 Marie Belloc Lownes to Hesketh Pearson, 10 Dec 1943 (Austin): 'He was ecstatically [or 'extremely'?] in love with her when they married. During their honeymoon in Paris that seemed quite clear to the people who saw them. Both French and English people.'

2 Sherard *SUF*, 93–4; *Life*, 158.

3 *Morning News*, 20 June 1884 (Clark).

4 Quoted in the *Queensland Figaro* (Brisbane), 17 January 1885.

5 'London Jottings [by Archibald Forbes] London 8 August 1884', in *South Australian Weekly Chronicle* (Adelaide) 11 October 1884; *CL*, 229.

6 *Lady's Pictorial*, quoted in the *Derby Mercury*, 3 September 1884, in Moyle, 93.

7 J.-K. Huysmans, *À Rebours* (1959), trans-

lated and with an introduction by Robert Baldick.

8 *PDG*; *Morning News*, 20 June 1884 (Clark).

9 *CL*, 231; they arrived back in London on 24 June.

10 *CL*, 236–7, 242; 'Final bill for works and materials by Sharpe' [up to 22 November 1884] and two certificates from Godwin re. work done by 'Mr George Sharpe' (Clark).

11 'Echoes of Society', *North Wales Chronicle*, 12 July 1884, 6.

12 Leslie Linder, ed., *The Journal of Beatrix Potter 1881–1897* (1966), 97; it was Potter's parents who had been to the ball: 'an extraordinary mixture of actors, rich Jews, nobility, literary etc'.

13 *The Ladies Treasury: A Household Magazine*, 1 September 1884, quoted in

Dibb, 134; the fete took place on 23 July 1884.

14 'Society Gossip', *Hampshire Telegraph and Sussex Chronicle*, 2 May 1885.

15 Mrs Jopling, in Mikhail, 205.

16 Adrian Hope, *Letters of Engagement* (2002), 6; Laura Troubridge's diary entry for 8 July.

17 Horatio Lloyd's estate was valued at £92,392, of which some £23,000 was divided equally between Otho and CMW. Moyle, 100.

18 Walford, *Memories of Victorian London*, 152; among other financial pressures, OW was being pursued by the Inland Revenue for 'Legacy and Succession Duty' still due on the Bray houses and the property at Clonfeacle. Inland Revenue to OW, 23 April 1884 (Clark).

19 *CL*, 232.

20 OET V, 8; 'Theatrical Mems', *Bristol Mercury and Daily Post*, 25 November 1884; 'Dramatic Musical', *Derby Mercury*, 26 November 1884.

21 *Yorkshire Gazette*, 12 July 1884; Dibb, 138; Morse, 'Lectures in Great Britain', 166–7; OW also claimed to have prepared a lecture on Benvenuto Cellini, but there is no evidence that he ever delivered it.

22 Godwin published his lecture as 'Dress and its Relation to Health and Climate' (Handbook of the International Health Exhibition, 1884).

23 Dibb, 262–75. See also 'Gleam of Common Sense'; *Argus* (Melbourne), 21 December 1885; 'Lancashire Mill Girls', *Lancaster Gazette and General Advertiser*, 27 December 1884.

24 Dibb, 262–75.

25 Harris, 69–70.

26 *CL*, 233–4.

27 A. Milner to OW, 22 May [1884], the Oscar Wilde collection of John B. Stetson, cat. item 391; Terence H. O'Brien, *Milner* (1979), 63; 'Muscle-Reading by

Mr Stuart Cumberland', *PMG*, 24 May 1884, 2; OW to A. Milner, [1885], Bloomsbury Book Auctions (London) 19 May 2014, lot 49, where the putative date in the letter is given as 1882; an obvious impossibility.

28 *PMG*, 14 October 1884; *PMG*, 11 November 1884; Hope, *Letters of Engagement*, 91.

29 W. Howgate to OW [1884] (Clark); *CL*, 239.

30 Bryan Connors, *Beverley Nichols: A Life* (1991), 20–21; Dibb, 153–5. Alfred and Rebecca Shalders, Beverley Nichols' maternal grandparents, lived at 7 Oak Villas, Manningham, Bradford. They were keen gardeners, and later had extensive hot-houses, so OW's request may not have been totally capricious.

31 Dibb, 160–2.

32 *Isle of Wight Observer*, 4 October 1884; Dibb, 147–8.

33 W. Partington, ed., *Echoes of the 'Eighties* (1921), 220–1; John Cooper, 'Oscar Wilde's Cello Coat', and 'Cello Encore', OWIA.

34 *Bath Chronicle and Weekly Gazette*, 23 October 1884; Dibb, 160.

35 WCKW to 'My dear Little Sister' (CMW), [Oct/Nov, 1884] (Clark).

36 Violet Fane [Mrs Singleton] to J. M. Whistler, 23 February 1885 (GUL): 'How very large, everywhere, – [OW] has grown since marriage!... Is there any real reason for this?... or can it be that he is merely following the custom of those [Red] Indians of whom I have read, who, in certain circumstances, simulate the uncomfortable & unbecoming condition of their "Squaws", & are there other Oscars & Oscaresses lurking in the Womb of the Future, to be let loose amongst us in due time?'

37 CMW to Otho Lloyd, 15 January 1885; Moyle, 118.

38 Coulson Kernahan, 'Oscar Wilde: Some Recollections', ts (Clark).

39 [Otho Lloyd], 'Stray Recollections', 155. Ellmann, 241, erroneously ascribes authorship to Alexander Teixeira de Mattos (the second husband of WCKW's second wife). Accounts of the house indicate that some details of decor and design altered over time. The earliest account is provided by Adrian Hope (in a letter to Laura Troubridge on 15 March 1885), and the fullest by Otho Lloyd (in 'Stray Recollections'). I have combined them here to give a picture of the house as it was in 1885.

40 Louise Chandler Moulton's enthusiasm for the dining room was reported in the *Oakleigh Leader and District Record* (Brighton, Victoria) Saturday 14 January 1888; 'How to Decorate a House by Mrs Oscar Wilde', *Young Woman*, January 1895 (reprinted in *Intentions*, 10 February 2009, 6–10);

Petersburg Times (South Australia), 15 June 1888.

41 Marylin Hill, 'A Tale of a Table', *Carlyle Studies Annual*, 29 (2013), suggests that the table which OW owned was not Carlyle's actual 'writing-table', although it may well have come from Carlyle's house.

42 Bankruptcy no. 724 of 1895, High Court of Bankruptcy, PRO – Chancery Lane, London B9/428–9, in Maguire, 54.

43 B. Charles Stephenson [aka 'Bolton Rowe'] to OW, 2 February 1885 (Clark).

44 *CL*, 245n; CMW to Edward Heron-Allen, 12 December 1884 (Clark); Edward Heron-Allen, 'Chyromantia' [hand-reading album] (Houghton): CMW's palm was read on 9 December 1884. OW's was read on 2 January 1885. W. S. Gilbert has his hand read on the same day.

Chapter 5: In Black and White

1 A. S. Cole 'Diary', 26 March 1884 (online at GUL).

2 *Truth*, 2 January 1890.

3 Anderson and Koval, *James NcNeill Whistler*, 263.

4 Herbert Vivian, quoted in Pennell and Pennell, *Life of Whistler*, 227.

5 Daniel E. Sutherland, *Whistler: A Life for Art's Sake* (2014), 206.

6 Alan Cole to JMW, 21 February 1885 (GUL). 'Wilde's face was a picture when you talked of aesthetic costumes'; Violet Fane to JMW, 22 February 1885 (GUL).

7 'Mr Whistler's Ten O'Clock', *PMG*, 21 February 1885; 'Our London Letter', *Belfast News-Letter*, 23 February 1885; *York Herald*, 23 February, 1885; 'Our London Correspondence', *Liverpool*

Mercury, 23 February 1885; 'Mr. Wilde and Mr. Whistler,' *Western Mail*, 24 February 1885.

8 *CL*, 250n; the exchange of letters although engineered for the weekly *World* (25 February 1885) in fact appeared first in the daily *PMG* (24 February 1885) under the heading, 'Tenderness in Tite Street'.

9 OW to A. Milner, [1885], Bloomsbury Book Auctions (London), 19 May 2014, lot 49; the letter, sent from 16 Tite Street, runs 'I want Comyns Carr's Essays on Art, Macmillan, to review: it and Machin should have a column between them. Essays on Art are naturally what I like to write about – Ever Yours, Oscar Wilde'. Joseph Comyns Carr's *Papers on Art*

(not *Essays on Art*) was published by Macmillan in February 1885.

10   *CL*, 227; Dibb, 173, convincingly re-dates the letter to 11 February 1885 (rather than February 1884).

11   Dibb, 214–15.

12   Ernest Rhys, *Everyman Remembers* (1931), 53.

13   OET VI, xlvii; OW 'The Critic as Art-ist'.

14   Not to be confused with a vulgar 'bank holiday atmosphere' – the epithet OW uses of Harry Quilter's *Sententiae Artis* in 'A "Jolly" Art Critic', *PMG*, 18 November 1886.

15   'Dinners and Dishes', *PMG*, 7 March 1885, in OET VI, 39–40.

16   OET VI, 96.

17   OET VI, 61.

18   OET VI, 87–8.

19   OET JVI, 50, 87, 101, 70.

20   W. B. Yeats to John O'Leary, in OET VI, xxviii.

21   OET VI, 102, 166.

22   'A Handbook to Marriage', *PMG*, 18 November 1885, OET VI, 60; W. H. Chesson, 'A Reminiscence of 1898', *Bookman*, 34 (1911), in Mikhail, 380. Edward John Hardy (1849–1920) had married the daughter of WRWW's sister, Margaret (wife of Rev. William Noble of Mostrim, Edgeworthstown); he was an assistant master at Portora (Mason, 136).

23   OET VI, 95, 114–17, 117–19, 101.

24   Mason, 137.

25   OW sought the right of reply to Quil-ter's outraged letter of objection on the grounds that, as he told the editor, 'my style is recognizable, at least by my friends'; quoted in OET VI, xxv.

26   George Bernard Shaw to David J. O'Donaghue, 9 May 1889 (Berg); Shaw to Tighe Hopkins, 31 Aug 1889, Dan H. Laurence, ed., *Bernard Shaw Collected Letters*, Vol. 1, *1874–1897* (1965), 222.

27   Mason, 135; Wills misspells OW's name 'Wylde'.

28   'The Letters Of A Great Woman', *PMG*, 6 March 1886. OET VI, 64–6.

29   OET VI, 102.

30   OW turned down an offer to 'do an interview' of 'some notable person' for the *Age* for 2½ guineas. Joseph Hatton to OW, 8 April 1885 (TCD).

31   *CL*, 253; T. H. S. Escott, the editor of the *Fortnightly Review*, was also the deputy editor of the *World* until 1886.

32   Trevor Blackmore, *The Art of Herbert Schmalz* (1911), 35.

33   John Stokes, 'Wilde's World: Oscar Wilde and Theatrical Journalism in the 1880s', in *Wilde Writings: Contextual Conditions*, ed. Joseph Bristow (2003), 41–58; The first issue of the *Dramatic Review* was 1 February 1885; the first of Godwin's seven articles appeared in the second issue (8 February 1885); OW's article appeared in the seventh issue (14 March 1885).

34   OW received 2 guineas for 'Shakespeare of Stage Scenery'; *CL*, 256. Stokes, 'Wilde's World'.

35   *CL*, 262.

36   Hope, *Letters of Engagement*, 134; Laura Troubridge to Adrian Hope, 9 June 1885.

37   'Facetiae', *Illustrated Sydney News*, 15 April 1886.

38   *CL*, 262.

39   *CL*, 261.

40   Moyle, 124; CMW to Otho Lloyd, 29 July 1887.

41   *CL*, 264, 266, 280.

42   *CL*, 278, 279.

43   *CL*, 264–5.

Chapter 6: *L'Amour de L'Impossible*

1   *CL*, 278.

2   'Ignotus' [Edwin Palmer], *Dramatic Review*, 23 May 1885, 267, in Stokes, 'Wilde's World', 54.

3   Arthur Bourchier to OW, Christ Church, Oxford, 'Wednesday' [1887] (Austin).

4   *CL*, 266–7.

5   *CL*, 269.

6   J. H. Badley, *Memories and Reflections* (1955), 78–9. *Eumenides* ran at Theatre Royal, Cambridge, from 30 November to 5 December 1885; see www.cambridgegreekplay.

7   Marillier memoirs, quoted in Fryer, 'Harry Marillier and the Love of the Impossible', 5–6; the fire damage was hastily patched up by the young American painter Harper Pennington, who happened to be present; with a few brush strokes he 'turned the charred panel into a lurid vision of Venice by night'. Beddington, *All That I Have Met*, 35; *CL*, 296.

8   OW was very aware of Ruskin's engagement with the fairy story. On 5 June 1883 OW, with his mother, attended a private lecture by Ruskin on the subject of 'Fairyland'. *Morning Post*, 7 June 1883.

9   OW to Mr. [Frank R.] Stockton [c. 1889], typed copy (Clark): 'It was a great pleasure meeting you – your work has charmed and delighted me for a long time'; Stockton's *Floating Prince* was published in 1881, and his most famous story, 'The Lady, or the Tiger' in 1882.

10 Badley, *Memories and Reflections*, 79.

11 *CL*, 273, 274; 281; Marillier memoirs, in Fryer, 'Harry Marillier and the Love of the Impossible', 7; Beddington, *All That I Have Met*, 39–40; H. L. Marillier to A. J. A. Symons, 4 May (Clark);

Marillier, responding to OW's creativity, composed his own poem about 'the moonstone people'.

12 *CL*, 272.

13 J. A. Symonds, *Animi Figura* (1882); for contemporary reviews, see 'Mr. Symonds' New Poems', *PMG*, 25 July 1882; 'Literary Notes', *Liverpool Mercury*, 14 June 1882.

14 Phyllis Grosskurth, ed., *The Memoirs of John Addington Symonds* (1984), 240, 267, 272.

15 Raffalovich, in Ellmann, 238.

16 OW, 'The Critic as Artist'.

17 *CL*, 282; Badley, *Memories and Reflections* describes Marillier as the most sympathetically attractive person he had known; his Norwegian landlady nicknamed him the 'Thief of Hearts'.

18 Fryer, 'Harry Marillier and the Love of the Impossible', 7; Marillier did see OW once more, in November 1886, at the Shelley Society's production of the verse drama *Hellas* at St James's Hall, London (H. Marillier to A. J. A. Symons, 4 May [1937?] (Clark).

19 *Century Guild Hobby Horse*, 1 July 1886.

20 *CL*, 283.

21 *CL*, 284, 285, 289–90.

22 *CL*, 290.

23 'Chatterton' (Clark), in Dibb, 297, 327. The epithet was borrowed from Theodore Watts's essay on Chatterton, in T. H. Ward, ed., *The English Poets, Selections with Critical Introductions*, Volume 3 (1880); see also Joseph Bristow and Rebecca N. Mitchell, *Oscar Wilde's Chatterton: Literary History, Romanticism, and the Art of Forgery* (2015).

24 'Chatterton' (Clark), in Dibb, 326–7; the opening passage echoes in places the phraseology of Theodore Watts's essay on Chatterton; see Dibb, 209.

25 Margery Ross, in her edited compen-

dium of her uncle's correspondence, *Robert Ross – Friend of Friends* (1952), 9, states that 'his first meeting with Oscar Wilde was at Oxford in 1886'. This has often been dismissed on the grounds that Ross did not go to Oxford University but to Cambridge (and even then not until 1888) but it could, of course, be a mere statement of geographical fact, accurately reporting established family knowledge. OW was in Oxford at least twice during 1886, for the performance of *Twelfth Night* in February, and to hear Henry Irving lecture on acting on 26 June ('English Gossip, London July 1 [1886]', *Sydney Morning Herald*, 14 August 1886; 'The Commemoration', *Jackson's Oxford Journal*, 26 June 1886). There were probably other visits too. He wrote, for example, to Douglas Ainslie (then an undergraduate at Exeter College, Oxford) promising to visit him and his friends (*CL*, 281). And it is certainly possible that, if Ross were also visiting friends in Oxford on one of these occasions, he could have been introduced to Wilde. Other potential connections were through Frances Richards (1852–1934), a Canadian painter, whom Wilde had met in Ottawa in 1882. She was a friend of Ross's sister, Mary (Maureen Borland, *Wilde's Devoted Friend: A Life of Robert Ross, 1869–1918* (1990), 19). She had relocated to England by 1887 (the *Ottawa Citizen*, quoted in *Intentions*, April 2006, suggests that she may have introduced OW to Robbie Ross). Ross's elder brother, Alec (1860–1927), was a figure on London's literary scene. He was the founder and secretary of the Society of Authors, an organization that OW joined in 1887 (*CL*, 291, 294–5). Frank Harris claimed to have been told that OW had met Ross when the younger man had propositioned him in a public lavatory (Moyle, 121, citing BL Eccles 81731) The story, however, seems unlikely.

26   *CL*, 360.

27   That Wilde's first homosexual encounter was with Robbie Ross in 1886 is remarkably well supported – given that the incident was private, covert and illegal. It was attested, independently, by both parties. In 1935 Reggie Turner, writing to A. J. A. Symons, declared, 'As to his [OW's] abnormal inclinations and practices I don't think he ever developed them till much later [than his university days]. He certainly never hinted at any such early relationships or episodes. Indeed he asked me – not long before he died – to guess who it was who had seduced him.' Turner was coy of writing down the seducer's name in a letter – 'even though they are dead'. And he also declared that the unnamed person, when taxed on the subject, has claimed it was an 'invention of Oscar's'. (Reginald Turner to A. J. A. Symons, 26 August 1935 (Clark)). Symons replied saying that he supposed that Turner was referring to Ross. He explained that Ross had told Christopher Millard '(according to the latter) that it was because *he* [Ross] had first led O.W. "astray" that he felt responsible for Cyril's and Vyvyan's welfare'. Millard also pointed out the statement in Arthur Ransome's 1912 study of Wilde: 'In 1886 he [OW] began that course of conduct that was to lead to his downfall in 1895.' Ransome got most of his biographical information from Ross – and it was because of Ross's involvement in the matter that he was thus able to date OW's 'change of nature' so accurately (A. J. A. Symons to Reggie Turner, 29 August 1935 (Clark)). This information confirmed

Turner in his conviction that OW had been telling the truth. Ross's denial, he suspected, had been on account of the fact that he was just then having to defend himself in the courts against charges of homosexual activity levelled by Lord Alfred Douglas. Turner had been impressed by OW's 'seriousness' in making the claim, while at the same time noting, 'Oscar himself did not set much importance by it but told it to me as a matter of interest & not in any way of fixing any blame on anybody. He was far too wise for that' (Reginald Turner to A. J. A. Symons, 4 September 1935 (Clark)). Despite this body of evidence, there have been periodic attempts to suggest – or claim – that OW must have had earlier homosexual experiences with Frank Miles, Reggie Harding, Rennell Rodd, Harry Marillier and/or others. See Croft-Cooke and McKenna. There is no direct evidence to support such claims, although Croft-Cooke, 42, reported that 'it was only during a sentimental visit of return [by OW] to Oxford with Bosie Douglas in 1892 that Douglas learned the bare fact that Frank Miles has been his predecessor in Oscar's affections, and thereafter Wilde could not be induced to speak of Miles, perhaps because of his tragic end, from which Oscar would naturally have averted his memory'. Croft-Cooke did know Douglas (1870–1945) during the latter part of Douglas's life. But the account of OW's visit to Oxford and his reference to Frank Miles does not appear in any of Croft-Cooke's earlier works relating to OW, *Bosie: The Story of Lord Alfred Douglas* (1963) or *Feasting With Panthers* (1967) nor indeed in any other printed source, and must – I think – be treated with some caution.

28　Reginald Turner to A. J. A. Symons, 28 August 1935 (Clark).

29　Reginald Turner to A. J. A. Symons, 26 August 1935 (Clark).

30　Before settling on the name, OW had suggested to Adrian Hope that he was thinking of calling his new son, 'Nothing' – as then 'it can be said he is nothing Wild(e)'. The spelling of Vyvyan's name was variable. Although christened 'Vyvyan', he was usually referred to by his parents, in their letters, as 'Vivian'. Nevertheless, since he became known in adult life as 'Vyvyan', that spelling is preferred.

31　Harris, 284–5; although the coarseness of Harris's account seems wholly unconvincing, there is no reason to doubt that it did record some aspect of OW's feeling.

32　Reginald Turner to A. J. A. Symons, 26 August 1935 (Clark); the passage is hard to decipher. Turner is describing how OW had told him about Ross being the first to seduce him: 'Though he said he was conscious of impending fate [or 'taste'] before that.'

33　M. A. Raffalovich, *L'Affaire Oscar Wilde* (1895), 5: where OW's comment is apropos all 'the unisexuals of the world'.

34　For Victorian understanding of same-sex relations see Joseph Bristow, 'A Complex Multiform Creature', in Peter Raby, ed., *The Cambridge Companion to Oscar Wilde* (1997), 198.

35　Ricketts, 31.

36　'A Bevy of Poets', *PMG*, 27 March 1885; exactly where and how OW met Raffalovich is unknown. Raffalovich, in his 1927 memoir of OW (written for *Blackfriars* and reprinted in Brocard Sewell, *Footnote to the Nineties* (1968)), thinks it may have been through Whistler. He also mentions, as another point of contact, a leading society hostess; Raffalovich disguised her under the name 'Egeria Stevenson (not yet Lady Keats)'; and she may

well have been the indefatigable Mrs Jeune (later Lady St Helier). Raffalovich was also a friend of George Lewis and his wife, dining twice chez Lewis, on 7 July 1883 and 8 March 1884. Mrs Lewis became 'Lady Lewis' in 1893 when her husband was knighted.

37 Jacomb-Hood, *With Brush and Pencil*, 42.

38 *CL*, 347.

39 *CL*, 352.

40 Raffalovich/Michaelson, 109.

41 *CL*, 374.

42 OW presented copies of *Poems* and *The Happy Prince* to Dickinson in 1888 (see 1910 US Book Auction Records) simply inscribed to 'John Ehret Dickinson, Esq. from his friend the author'; the fulsome inscription – done on a sheet of paper – is dated 1894, and was probably for insertion into a copy of *The Sphinx*. Regarding his will, see *Morning Post*, 31 December 1896.

43 Merle Secrest, *Being Bernard Berenson* (1980), 126; Ernest Samuels, *Bernard Berenson, The Making of a Connoisseur* (1979), 63, quoting Mary Berenson's unpublished 'Life of BB'. Secrest reports that Berenson had told at least two friends (Kenneth Clark and Frances Francis) that OW had never made a pass at him. It was to the Philadelphia collector Henry P. McIlhenny that he confessed the attempted seduction.

44 *CL*, 1095.

45 Kerrison Preston, ed., *Letters from Graham Robertson* (1953), xvi. McKenna, 129, claims that 'Robertson was proud of having been a favoured lover of Oscar, even boasting of it in later life' – but gives no reference.

46 Brocard Sewell, *Footnote to the Nineties: a memoir of John Gray and André Raffalovich* (1968); Lord Alfred Douglas, in his unpublished 1896 article for the *Revue Blanche* (Austin) claimed that Raffalovich had, in London, 'the reputation of a confirmed sodomite', but Douglas's extreme hostility towards Raffalovich makes the accuracy of the statement suspect.

47 Raffalovich/Michaelson, 109–10.

48 *CL*, 1229.

49 Moyle, 123–4.

50 *CL*, 330–1.

51 *CL*, 337.

52 Sir George Turner, *Unorthodox Reminiscences* (1931), 152; Lady St Helier (Mrs Jeune), *Memories of Fifty Years* (1909), 183.

53 'A Lady's London Gossip, July 5th', *West Australian*, 31 August 1886; among material relating to his reception is an invitation card from CMW to Herbert Horne: 'At Home. July 1st 4–7' (Fales); Frederic Leighton to Mrs Oscar Wilde, regretting he cannot come on 1 July due to a 'previous engagement' (Yale); Laura Troubridge to Adrian Hope, 1 July 1886, *Letters of Engagement*, 247; copy of Leconte de Lisle, *Poèmes Tragiques* (1886) inscribed by Edgar Saltus to 'The poet of the Sphinx' – London – '1 July '86'.

54 *CL*, 301, 352.

55 'Wilde's Personal Appearance' by his 'sister-in-law', 150.

56 'Wilde's Personal Appearance' by his 'sister-in-law', 150.

57 Harris, 79.

58 'Wilde's Personal Appearance' by his 'sister-in-law', 150.

59 Edgar Saltus, *Oscar Wilde: An Idler's Impression* (1917), 13–26, in Mikhail, 427.

60 George Bernard Shaw to Robbie Ross, 10 Sept 1916, in Laurence, ed., *Collected Letters of Bernard Shaw 1911–1925*, 413.

61 Harris, 76.

62 Harold Nicolson, *Diaries and Letters 1930–1939* (1966), 274.

63 'Wilde's Personal Appearance' by his 'sister-in-law', 150.

64 *PMG*, 16 September 1887.

65 Saltus, *Oscar Wilde: An Idler's Impression*, 13–26, in Mikhail, 428; in June 1887 OW attended the press view for an exhibition of Gerald Du Maurier's latest cartoons at the Fine Art Society. There were none of him (*Northern Echo*, 11 June 1887).

66 *PMG*, 16 September 1887.

67 Maguire, 19, *CL*, 287, 356/9.

68 *CL*, 256, 259; Harris, 100, though Harris gives the wrong date.

69 Laurence Housman to Hesketh Pearson, 4 April 1944 (Austin). Housman reversed the dynamic of the anecdote when he used it in *Echo de Paris*.

70 Harris, 67.

71 Henri de Régnier, *Les Annales Politiques et Littéraires*, 29 November 1925, in Mikhail, 463.

72 JFW to OW, 21 September, in Tipper, *Oscar*, 103. Tipper dates the letter to 1883, but 1884, around the time of OW's visit to the Isle of Wight, might be more likely.

73 Guy & Small, 68; Anya Clayworth has speculated that OW's initial approach to G. Macmillan had been for a book of Turgenev short stories, and that Macmillan, having turned down that idea, passed on the single story to the editor of *Macmillan's Magazine*.

74 *CL*, 385.

75 Laura Troubridge to Adrian Hope, 1 July 1886.

76 OET VI, xxx–xxxi.

77 *New York Tribune*, 28 March 1887; *CL*, 295; OW later received a welcome cheque 'for £8 odd' from Reid, *CL*, 325. The amount of the cheque OW received from Robertson of the *Court and Society Review* around 2 March 1887 is unknown; BL RP3752 (i). There is a curious undated letter from OW, on *Court and Society Review* letterhead, offering 'my ghost story' to 'Dear Robinson' (BL RP 4301). Phil Robinson was the editor of *The Sunday Times*, but it is hard to believe that OW offered the story to *The Sunday Times* before he had offered it to the *Court and Society Review* on *Court and Society Review* letterhead.

78 OW to Robertson (BL).

79 Bernard Partridge to Hesketh Pearson, 30 September, 1943 (Austin).

80 JFW to OW, [13 May 1887], in Tipper, *Oscar*, 110–11.

81 'Un Amant de Nos Jours', which appeared on 13 December 1887, opens with the lines, 'The sin was mine, I did not understand; / So now is music prisoned in her cave'. It is unknown, though, when the poem was written, so it is hard to gauge whether it reflected some real pang of remorse at lost love – for Florence Balcombe perhaps, or Lillie Langtry, or Constance – or whether it was just some literary exercise. It has echoes of George Meredith's 1862 sonnet sequence, *Modern Love*.

82 *CL*, 325.

83 *CL*, 354; modern critics have found OW's fairy tales rich ground for differing interpretations – personal, political, sexual and spiritual; see Jarlath Killeen, *The Fairy Tales of Oscar Wilde* (2007), for an excellent overview of the topic.

84 *CL*, 352.

85 Coulson Kernahan, *In Good Company: Some Personal Recollections* (1917), 195. Although he told Gladstone that his stories were 'really meant for children' (*CL*, 350) neither the stories themselves, nor his other statements, make this credible. In *CL*, 388, OW refers to his stories as being written 'for childlike people from eighteen to eighty'.

86 Theodore Watts to OW, 7 June 1887 (Austin); OW to Roberts Bros, (rec. 26 March 1888) (Columbia).

87 Moyle, 124.
88 Saltus, *Oscar Wilde: An Idler's Impression*, 13–26, in Mikhail, 428.

89 CMW to Otho Lloyd, 17 July 1887, in Moyle, 124.

Chapter 7: *Woman's World*

1 *CL*, 297.
2 *CL*, 317.
3 *CL*, 317; *WW*, vol. 1, 40.
4 *CL*, 299; RR to Frank Harris, 17 May 1914 (Austin).
5 *CL*, 297–301.
6 OW, 'Homer's Women' essay (Morgan). E. Fitzsimmons, *Wilde's Women* (2015), 193.
7 Arthur Lambton, *The Salad Bowl* (1927), 57. For another dinner party see Moreton Frewen, *Melton Mowbray and Other Memories* (1924), 105; for one of Ouida's 'receptions' at the Langham – 5 pm, c. 30 people – see Lady Paget, *Embassies of Other Days* Vol. II (1923), 418: guests included OW, Violet Fane, Lady Boo Lennox, Lady Dorothy Nevill, Robert Browning, Lord Lytton and Lord Ronald Gower.
8 'Some Famous Living Women', *Brisbane Courier*, 19 November 1889.
9 Note: she published four articles in *WW* between March 1888 and May 1889: 'Apropos of a Dinner', 'The Streets of London', 'War' and 'Field-Work for Women'. Although initially very enthusiastic (calling the magazine 'so good'), by March 1889 her tone had altered slightly. She told Lady Constance Leslie, 'Look out for an article of mine on war in Oscar Wilde's Review. I write in it now and then out of camaraderie. He is a clever fellow though too vain and not always I fear sincere.' Eileen Bigland, *Ouida: The Passionate Victorian* (1950), 202–3.
10 Gifford Lewis, *The Selected Letters of Somerville and Ross* (1989), 67–8.

11 *Spectator*, 5 November 1887.
12 *Irish Times*, 5 November 1887. Fitzsimmons, *Wilde's Women*, 58.
13 *Hampshire Advertiser*, 3 November 1887; *Spectator*, 5 November 1887.
14 *Morning Post*, 2 November 1887; *Bury and Norwich Post*, 22 November 1887; *Spectator*, 5 November 1887.
15 *Bury and Norwich Post*, 22 November 1887.
16 *PMG*, 16 September 1887.
17 JFW to OW, 'Friday Night' [November, 1887], in Tipper, *Oscar*, 111–12.
18 *WW*, vol. 1, 98.
19 Lady Churchill to OW, 6 January 1888 (Austin).
20 *PMG*, 16 September 1887.
21 Arthur Fish, 'Memories of Oscar Wilde', *Cassell's Weekly*, 2 May 1923, 215; A. J. A. Symons notes, (Clark); *CL*, 413, 455.
22 Arthur Fish, 'Oscar Wilde as Editor', *Harper's Weekly*, 58 [1913], 18.
23 Fish, 'Oscar Wilde as Editor', 18; the daring of OW's editorial policy is suggested by a letter from Marie Bancroft to OW (Austin), 9 November [1888 or 1889]: 'I will think over your suggestion. The subject is a very *delicate* one, and there is always a fear of scalding our toes! How long should the article be? I will try but I may fail.' It seems she did fail, as no article appeared by her, after her piece on Switzerland in the first number.
24 *CL*, 337, 338.
25 Anna, comtesse de Brémont, *Oscar Wilde and his Mother* (1911), 73.
26 Harris, 53, 67; *CL*, 1121. Frank

Harris describes himself as meeting 'Oscar Wilde continually' from 1884 onwards; but their friendship seems to have begun later in the decade.

27 W. B. Yeats, *The Trembling of the Veil* (1922), 15.

28 Newman Flower, in *Cassell's Weekly*, 1923, quoted in *The Register* (Adelaide) 30 June 1923.

29 Yeats, *The Trembling of the Veil*, 20.

30 C. Lewis Hind, *Naphtali* (1926), 54.

31 J. M. Barrie, quoted in Alfred Noyes, *Two Worlds for Memory* (1953), 55.

32 *CL*, 367.

33 'A Note on Some Modern Poets', *WW*, December 1888; OET VII, 108–13.

34 *CL*, 294; 356; G. B. Shaw, 'My Memories of Oscar Wilde', in Harris, 334.

35 J. Lewis May, *John Lane and the Nineties* (1936), 31; Walter Crane, *An Artist's Reminiscences* (1907), 310. OW took Walter Crane's children backstage to meet the Colonel 'in his tent' after the show.

36 *CL*, 362n; OW's official proposer was not Henley, but Rev. W. J. Loftie, formerly of Trinity College Dublin. At the Savile Club candidates were not 'blackballed', but if members expressed opposition to a candidate, his name was left in the candidate's book but his election was postponed indefinitely.

37 *PMG*, 9 June 1888; *Leeds Mercury*, 9 June 1888; Crane, *An Artist's Reminiscences*, 324; E. R. Pennel, *Life and Letters of Joseph Pennel* (1930), 1:202.

38 *World*, 17 November 1886.

39 *CL*, 288; Crane, *An Artist's Reminiscences*, 295, recalled OW being present – and speaking – at one meeting.

40 The discussion, below, of OW's engagement with Liberal politics and Home Rule, draws on Wright and Kinsella, 'Oscar Wilde, A Parnellite Home Ruler and Gladstonian Liberal'.

41 *Freeman's Journal*, 23 September 1887. Wright and Kinsella, 'Oscar Wilde, A Parnellite Home Ruler and Gladstonian Liberal', record OW attending an Eighty Club dinner at Willis's rooms on 13 December 1887.

42 OET VII, 12ff. OW was only slightly more generous to Mahaffy's *The Principles of the Art of Conversation*, 'Aristotle at Afternoon Tea', *PMG*, 16 December 1887, OET VII, 35–7: 'it pleases in spite of its pedantry' and 'the arid and jejune character of the style'.

43 'Poetry and Prison', *PMG*, 3 January 1889.

44 *WW*, January 1889.

45 Jane Morris to Henry Sparling [Autumn 1885], in Frank C. Sharp and Jan Marsh, eds, *Collected Letters of Jane Morris* (2012), 143.

46 Bernard Partridge to Hesketh Pearson, 30 September 1943 (Austin); George Bernard Shaw's diary mentions the meeting on 14 September 1886.

47 LAD, *Oscar Wilde and Myself*, 60–1; see from George Bernard Shaw's diaries: 15 December 1887 OW and Shaw meet at H. Horne's house in Fitzroy Street. The talk was stimulating and Shaw did not leave until one in the morning; [Sunday], June 1888, OW and Shaw both at an afternoon reception chez Miss Charlotte Roche, in Cadogan Gardens. 'The conversation was on art and how socialism would metamorphose it.' July 1888, Fabian Society meeting at Willis's rooms, Walter Crane on 'The Prospects of Art Under Socialism' – reported in the *Star*, 7 July 1888 – both OW and Shaw speak from the floor. Shaw to Frank Harris, 7 Oct 1908, in Dan H. Laurence, ed., *Bernard Shaw Collected Letters*, Vol. 2, *1898–1910* (1972), 813.

48 *CL*, 388; Killeen, *The Fairy Tales of Oscar Wilde*, 37–8.

49 Saltus, *Oscar Wilde: An Idler's Impression*, 13–26, in Mikhail, 428; Richard Le Gallienne, *The Romantic '90s* (1926), in Mikhail, 394.

50 *PMG*, 15 November 1887. Shaw would have been able to give OW details of the riot when they met four days later at the wedding reception for Shaw's sister, Lucy. Shaw diary, 17 November 1887.

51 C. K. Shorter, *An Autobiography* (1927),

59; Stanley Weintraub, 'The Hibernian School: Oscar Wilde and Bernard Shaw', in J. A. Bertolini, ed., *Shaw and Other Playwrights*, 30; Georgina Sime, *Brave Spirits* (1952), 14.

52 'Children's Dress in this Century', *WW*, July 1888; 'Muffs', *WW*, February 1889.

53 Moyle, 148.

54 *PMG*, 7 March 1888.

55 Mrs T. P. O'Connor, *I Myself* (1910), 238.

Chapter 8: A Study in Green

1 Macmillan Reader's Report, 16 February 1888, quoted in Guy & Small, 69.

2 Mason, 331–4; OW to Roberts Bros, (rec. 26 March 1888) (Columbia), gives an idea of the initial production plans: 'The book will be very daintily got up, and will appear in May....There will be a first edition probably at 10/- limited in number and a popular edition to follow.'

3 Millard's annotated copy of his own bibliography at the Clark lists: *Athenaeum, Universal Review, Christian Leader, Dublin Evening Mail, Glasgow Herald, World, Morning Post, Liverpool Daily Post, Manchester Guardian, Wit and Wisdom, PMG, PMB* (with a cartoon by F. C. G[ould], 7 June), *Literary World, Lady's Pictorial, St James's Gazette, Star, Scotsman, Daily Express* (Dublin). To these can be added the *Saturday Review* (20 October 1888) and *Spectator* (2 March 1889). The only carping review was in *Graphic* (30 June 1888); but even it admits that the stories – though 'somewhat insipid' – were 'well written', and the book itself 'admirable'.

4 OW consistently referred to the book self-deprecatingly as 'my little book'; *CL*, 350, 352.

5 *PMG*.

6 *Spectator, Saturday Review*.

7 *Morning Post*, 20 June 1888; *Spectator*.

8 Walter Crane to OW, 1 July 1888: 'I am glad to hear the book has been so successful'. OW to Thomas Niles [1888], 'Here it has been a great success.'

9 Ellen Terry to OW, 9 June 1888, in Don Mead, 'An Unpublished Letter from Ellen Terry to Oscar Wilde', *Wildean*, 8 (1996); *CL*, 350.

10 Samuel Hales to OW, 16 June 1888 (Clark). Justin Huntly McCarthy was another who liked 'The Nightingale and the Rose'; see his poem 'The Happy Prince – To Oscar Wilde', in Mason, 335.

11 The second edition had still not sold out in September 1894, when OW wrote to John Lane, complaining that Nutt's 'average yearly sale of *The Happy Prince* is about 150!' He called the figure 'really absurd'.

12 Carlos Blacker to the Duke of Newcastle, 5 December 1888, in Maguire, 24.

13 *Isle of Man Times*, 29 December 1888. 'Christmas Magazines', *Hampshire Telegraph*, 8 December 1888: 'In the front by merit is Mr Oscar Wilde's charming allegory "The Young King", original, vivid, exquisitely expressed'.

'Christmas Leaves', *Penny Illustrated Paper*, 1 December 1888: 'There is an admirable moral in Oscar Wilde's excellent fairy story.' See also *Liverpool Mercury*, 28 November 1888; *Jackson's Oxford Journal*, 24 November 1888; *Morning Post*, 5 December 1888.

14 *CL*, 372.

15 See 3 letters from OW (written by a secretary) to Annie Schletter, re. her 'extremely interesting' article, and the delay over publishing it: 28 February 1888, 19 March 1888, 23 April 1889 (Yale).

16 Newman Flower, in *Cassell's Weekly*, quoted in *Register* (Adelaide), 30 June 1923.

17 See JFW to OW [1887], 'Miss Leonard wrote to me to say that she can supply an article on French matters if you wish, as her father sends all the latest news.' OW to 'Miss Leonard', 28 February 1888 (Washington) asking for 'a *short* article (about 2500 words) on Madame Adam – giving an account of her receptions and literary career.' The article never appeared.

18 Pearson, 262.

19 Pearson, 262; [Anon], *East and West – Confessions of a Princess* (1922), 176; the poem used may have been 'Remorse (A Study in Saffron)'. *OET* I, 169; Fitzsimmons, *Wilde's Women*, 233–4.

20 Elizabeth Robins, *Both Sides of the Curtain* (1940), 9–10, 14–28 (Sir Randall Roberts is called 'Sir Mervyn Owen' in the book); *CL*, 357–8; Elizabeth Robins ms memoir quoted in *CL*, 357; Diaries (Fales).

21 Rev. F. B. D. Bickerstaffe-Drew to OW, 5 May 1890 (Clark).

22 C. Dyett to OW, 28 April 1891 (Clark): 'Had it not been for you we should have had to part with our home... I shall always remember your kindness in our time of trouble.'

23 [Otho Lloyd], 'Stray Recollections', 156.

24 Secrest, *Being Bernard Berenson*, 125.

25 Swanwick, *I Have Been Young*, 68–9; Oswald A. Sickert died on 11 November 1885.

26 Jacomb-Hood, *With Brush and Pencil*, 115.

27 Yeats, *The Trembling of the Veil*, 24, 25.

28 Coulson Kernahan, '*Oscar Wilde As I Knew Him*', ts 22 (Clark)

29 *CL*, 367.

30 R. Le Gallienne to OW, 11 November 1888 (Clark); Le Gallienne chose 'The Nightingale and the Rose' as it had 'a beauty so much your own'.

31 J. A. Symonds, *A Problem in Greek Ethics* (1883).

32 The eight letters from Frederick C. Althaus to OW are at the Clark. McKenna, 131–6, gives an excellent reading of their emotional content, though he mis-transcribes their text in several places, failing to register the references to the Lyric Club, and suggesting that a word beginning with 'C' refers to the Cock Tavern, a bohemian pub on the Charing Cross Road. This leads him to suppose (wrongly) that Althaus was socially 'different from the usual run of young men that Oscar mixed with at this time'.

33 Frederick C. Althaus to OW, 12 November 1888 (Clark).

34 Frederick C. Althaus to OW, 12 November 1888 (Clark).

35 Frederick C. Althaus to OW, 12 November 1888, is sent from 'New Court, E.C.' (where Leopold Rothschild had his offices), and regrets that 'I shall not be able to get away from the City' that day. *PMG*, 26 February 1891; *Era*, 18 March, 1893. Frederick C. Althaus to OW, 19 March 1889, mentions 'my brother and I are going to the *Femmes Nerveuses*', a French play then running at the Royalty Theatre.

36 Frederick C. Althaus to OW, 'Wednesday'; Frederick C. Althaus to OW, 19 March 1889; see 'The Remarkable Story of the Lyric Club', *The Press* (New Zealand), 4 November 1892.

37 Frederick C. Althaus to OW, June [1889].

38 Horst Schroeder, 'Volume IV of the OET Edition of *The Complete Works of Oscar Wilde*: III "Pen, Pencil and Poison,"' *Wildean*, 36 (2010), 32; Josephine Guy, 'Introduction', in Josephine Guy, ed., *Criticism* (OET IV), xxxi–xxxiii.

39 Ellmann, 283; Lawrence Danson, *Wilde's Intentions* (Oxford, 1996), 89–92; Bristow and Mitchell, *Oscar Wilde's Chatterton*, 215–29. OW's attraction to criminal figures had also led him to 'collect many particulars of the social career' and crimes of Henry Fauntleroy, a banker hanged in 1824 for forgery. But he felt that the case was not quite 'fascinating' enough for an article. 'Our London Letter', *Sheffield & Rotherham Independent*, 10 January 1889.

40 'Anglo-Colonial Gossip', 'London, Jan 4th', *South Australian Register*, 7 February 1889: the journalist dates OW's performance to 'a few weeks back' – so, perhaps, November/December 1888. The January number of the *Fortnightly Review*, in which the essay appeared, was being reviewed by 2 January – and was indeed described (*Derby Mercury*) as being 'early afield', so OW's contribution must have been submitted and accepted by early / mid-December 1888. That the article could have been completed quickly is suggested by the fact that on 10 February 1890 Frank Harris wrote to OW, after a lunch together, asking if he 'would write an article for the March Fortnightly [Review]. Can you do this within 8 days? An article on Literature or any social subject as paradoxical as you please' (Austin). Swinburne, 'William Blake' (1868) had referred to Wainewright's use of 'pen... palette... or poison'.

41 *CL*, 688.

42 *CL*, 253; some early ms pages relating to 'The Decay of Lying' are not written as dialogue, leading Lawrence Danson (*Wilde's Intentions*, 37) to suggest that the adoption of the dialogue form was a 'happy afterthought' to the dinner with Ross. But that was not Wilde's memory of the event. And Josephine Guy ('Introduction', OET IV, xl) argues persuasively against the suggestion. The dinner with Ross could have occurred in November 1888, shortly after the Cambridge term ended.

43 Hilda Schiff, 'Nature and Art in Oscar Wilde's "The Decay of Lying"', *Essay and Studies*, 18 (1965), 100ff, in Schroeder, 19–20.

44 Schroeder, 22.

45 Schroeder, 17–19; Whistler's 'Ten O'Clock' had been the most conspicuous contribution to the debate on 'Art and Nature'; among articles on 'Realism and Romance' Schroeder lists: R. L. Stevenson, 'A Gossip on Romance' (November 1882) and 'A Note on Realism' (January 1884); Rider Haggard, 'About Fiction' (February 1887); J. A. Symonds, 'Realism and Idealism' (September 1887) and Andrew Lang, 'Realism and Romance' (November 1887).

46 Yeats, *The Trembling of the Veil*, 28; Ellmann, 285.

47 Yeats, *The Trembling of the Veil*, 24; CL, 377.

48 Yeats, *The Trembling of the Veil*, 24.

Part VI: *The Young King*
Chapter 1: A Man in Hew

1   'Literature', *Derby Mercury*, 2 January 1889; also called 'a really good article' in *PMG*, 24 December 1888; 'a racy contribution', *Ipswich Journal*, 28 December 1888; JFW to OW, in Tipper, *Oscar*, 116.

2   'Magazines for January', *Morning Post*, 3 January 1889; 'The Reviews for January', *PMG*, 2 January 1889; 'Our London Letter', *Sheffield & Rotherham Independent*, 10 January 1889.

3   'Literature', *Derby Mercury*, 2 January 1889.

4   OW to Henry Lucy, who had praised 'Pen, Pencil and Poison' – the Decay of Lying 'is so much the better of the two', *CL*, 384. On press comments: *CL*, 392, 394; OW to W. Pollack, *CL*, 387; see also OW to Mrs George Lewis, *CL*, 389.

5   JFW to OW, [late December 1888/ early 1889], in Tipper, *Oscar*, 116.

6   Yeats, *The Trembling of the Veil*, 25, 24.

7   Ransome, 100.

8   Yeats, *The Trembling of the Veil*, 25.

9   Mason, 174; see also *CL*, 409; 'Michael Field', Journal (BL), 21 July 1890, refers to the French version of the story coming out 'Pink and Blue'; in Mason, 174, it is described as 'Pink and Silver'.

10 *CL*, 372+n; W. Pater to OW, 15 November [1877?] (Clark).

11 Ricketts, 31.

12 'Michael Field', Journal (BL), 21 July 1890.

13 Ricketts, 33.

14 Carlos Blacker to the Duke of Newcastle, 5 December 1888, in Maguire, 24.

15 *CL*, 407–8.

16 Harris, 69; *CL*, 398; submitted in April, the story was finally accepted on 20 May 1889. H. Schroeder, *Oscar Wilde:*

THE PORTRAIT OF MR W.H. – *Its Composition, Publication and Reception* [1984], 12.

17 Wright and Kinsella, 'Oscar Wilde, A Parnellite Home Ruler and Gladstonian Liberal'; Bridget Hourican, 'A Veritable Tragedy of Family Likeness', *History Ireland*, issue 5, vol. 14 (2006).

18 Moyle, 148, 151.

19 F. C. Althaus to OW, 19 March 1889 (Clark); *CL*, 397.

20 Quoted in McKenna, 149.

21 Clyde Fitch to OW (Clark).

22 McKenna, 154; McKenna suggests that Clyde Fitch's letter to OW – at the Clark – referring to himself as a 'brown eyed Faun [lying] on his grass green bed' – inspired the poem. But it seems more probable that the poem was the basis for the references in the letter. An earlier letter in the sequence (beginning 'Perfect, *Perfect*, **Perfect** – It is the most delicate, the most exquisite, the most complete idyll I have ever read') – was perhaps an acknowledgement of the poem.

23 Moyle, 174.

24 The lunch at 'Dorothy's Restaurant' was on Friday, 21 June 1889. Gertrude M. Williams, *The Passionate Pilgrim: A Life of Annie Besant* (1931), 200; Anne Taylor, *Annie Besant: A Biography* (1992), 283; Marion Meade, *Madame Blavatsky: The Woman Behind the Myth* (2014).

25 Schroeder, *Oscar Wilde*, THE PORTRAIT OF MR W.H., 14–21; Clyde Fitch to OW (Clark).

26 Schroeder, *Oscar Wilde*, THE PORTRAIT OF MR W.H., 14; *CL*, 409.

27 Harris, 69.

28 Ransome, 100, OW 'became an habitual devotee' of homosexual sex in 1889. Raffalovich/Michaelson, 108–9,

says that he was warned against knowing OW.

29 Marguerite Steen, *A Pride of Terrys: A
    Family Saga* (1962), 206.

30 Raffalovich/   Michaelson,   110;
    Ellmann, 369; O'Sullivan, 104. Alan
    Aynsworth's account – quoted at H.
    Pearson, 244, of OW arriving at Raf-
    falovich's flat, with five other men,
    and saying to the butler, 'a table for six'
    seems improbable.

31 *CL*, 407; OW had previously consid-
    ered the idea of gathering the story
    together with 'Pen, Pencil and Poison'
    and the 'Decay of Lying' in a single
    volume. *CL*, 405.

32 *CL*, 406, 456; *PMG*, 6 February 1891.

33 Sir Arthur Conan Doyle, *Memories and
    Adventures* (1924), 78–9; *CL*, 413, 416;
    'Current Notes', *Lippincott's Monthly
    Magazine*, 44 (1889), 743, in *PDG*, OET
    III, xvii.

34 *CL*, 411; 'Current Notes', *PMG*, 5
    October 1889 announced that a 'Mr
    Williams' would be taking over as edi-
    tor, in an effort to make the magazine
    more 'practical'; but a month later
    (*PMG*, 7 November 1889) reported
    that 'it died a natural death with the
    October number'.

35 *CL*, 413, 414, 416.

36 Ricketts, 29–30. OW also added: 'It

seems he [the reader] and his wife
have sometimes asked poor Thomas
Hardy to alter his stories!' Although
in the 1880s Hardy's main publisher
was Smith, Elder, he did publish some
of the stories that appeared in *Wessex
Tales* (1888) in *Blackwood's Magazine*.

37 J. G. P. Delaney, *Charles Ricketts: a biog-
    raphy* (1990), 24–5.

38 Ricketts, 28–35.

39 *CL*, 412.

40 A warrant was finally issued against
    Lord Arthur Somerset on 12 Novem-
    ber 1889. He never returned to
    England. H. M. Hyde, *The Cleveland
    Street Scandal* (1976); Theo Aronson,
    *Prince Eddy and the Homosexual Under-
    world* (1994).

41 Herbert Vivian, 'The Reminiscences of
    a Short Life', *Sun*, 17 November 1889,
    4, in Mikhail, 154–8.

42 *CL*, 426, 427, 415.

43 *CL*, 418.

44 *CL*, 420.

45 'Michael Field' Journal, in Delaney,
    Charles Ricketts, 45.

46 C. J. Holmes, *Self and Partners* (1936)
    168.

47 C. Ricketts to G. Bottomley, 20 July
    1918, in Delaney, *Charles Ricketts*, 56–
    7.

48 *CL*, 423n.

Chapter 2: A Bad Case

1   *CL*, 416.

2   *PMG*, 23 September 1890; the article
    refers to 'a Canadian artist who was
    staying with some friends of hers and
    mine and South Kensington'. For the
    identification with Frances Richards
    see *The Beaver: Exploring Canada's His-
    tory*, 86 (2006); the Ross family lived in
    South Kensington.

3   *CL*, 416.

4   Nicholas Frankel, ed., *The Uncensored
    Picture of Dorian Gray* (2011), 150.

5   *CL*, 524; Frankel, ed. *The Uncensored
    Picture of Dorian Gray*, 156; Isobel
    Murray, ed., *Oscar Wilde* (1989), 582,
    suggests a character from Pater's *Gas-
    ton de Latour* as a possible source for
    the name 'Raoul'.

6   *CL*, 425.

7   Harris, 70–1.

8 *CL*, 424–5; *PDG*, OET III, emphasizes the care OW had taken with the manuscript.

9 *PDG*, OET III, xliii.

10 Sir Peter Chalmers Mitchell, *My Fill of Days* (1937), 183–4; *PDG*, OET III, xxxv.

11 Bernard Berenson, *Sunset & Twilight* (1964), 10; *CL*, 443.

12 *CL*, 585.

13 J. M. Stoddart to OW, 22 April 1890, in Frankel, ed., *The Uncensored Picture of Dorian Gray*, 44.

14 Frankel, ed., *The Uncensored Picture of Dorian Gray*, 43–8, 232–4. Frankel's introduction and notes contain much new information from the J. B. Lippincott Co. records at the Pennsylvania Historical Society (Stoddart received the typescript in Philadelphia on 7 April 1890).

15 *CL*, 425; Maurice Macmillan to OW, 16 June 1890 (Austin); George Lock to OW, 7 July 1890 (Clark). In June 1890 Ward, Lock & Co. published 'in volume form' *A Dead Man's Diary* by Coulson Kernahan, which had also been serialized in *Lippincott's Magazine*.

16 *CL*, 729.

17 Stokes and Turner, in the 'Dubia' section of OET VII, list five possible OW contributions to *PMG* in 1890, the last on 3 April.

18 'Literary Intelligence', *Liverpool Mercury*, 25 June 1890.

19 'Literature', *Derby Mercury*, 25 June 1890; 'Magazines and Reviews', *Leeds Mercury*, 24 June 1890.

20 'England and the Nations', *NYT*, 29 June 1890, quoted in *PDG*, OET III, l.

21 JFW to OW, in Tipper, *Oscar*, 119.

22 R. Ross to OW [July, 1890], in Ross, ed., *Robbie Ross – Friend of Friends*, 20–1.

23 'Magazines', *Graphic*, 12 July 1890; *Speaker*, 5 July 1890.

24 'Mr. Oscar Wilde's "Dorian Gray"', *PMG*, 26 June 1890; *À Rebours*, although not named, is quoted in the review.

25 *Scots Observer*, 5 July 1890.

26 *Daily Chronicle*, 30 June 1890; 'A Study in Puppydom,' *St James's Gazette*, 24 June 1890; *Scots Observer*, 5 July 1890.

27 Gifford Lewis, *The Selected Letters of Somerville and Ross* (1989), 222; Elizabeth Lee, *Ouida: A Memoir* (1914), 157; J. A. Symonds to H. F. Brown, 22 July 1890, Brown, ed., *Letters and Papers of John Addington Symonds*, 240; Preston, ed., *Letters from Graham Robertson*, xvi.

28 Holland, 78, 219–20; 312; Walter Pater, 'A Novel by Mr. Oscar Wilde', *Bookman*, November 1891, in Beckson, 84.

29 'England and the Nations', *NYT*, 29 June 1890, quoted in *PDG*, OET III, l.

30 *CL*, 428–9.

31 *CL*, 435–6.

32 *CL*, 429–31.

33 *CL*, 438–9.

34 Ward Locke and Co. to OW, 10 July 1890, quoted in McKenna, 185–6.

35 Sidney Low, *Samuel Henry Jeyes* (1915), 42.

36 David Bispham, *A Quaker Singer's Recollections* (1920), 150.

37 Bispham, *A Quaker Singer's Recollections*, 150; Harris, 72.

38 'Michael Field', Journal, 21 July 1890 (BL: available online via 'The Victorian Lives and Letters Consortium', tundra.csd.sc.edu).

39 Carlos Blacker to the Duke of Newcastle, [28 July 1890], in Maguire, 26.

40 Stuart Merrill, 'Oscar Wilde' ms (Clark), translated by H. M. Hyde. Stuart Merrill, though American-born, had been brought up in Paris, where his father had a diplomatic posting. The poet Stéphane Mallarmé was one of his schoolmasters. After a brief interlude in America, he was – in 1890 – returning to live in France. It was the bilingual Merrill who had produced the 'pink

and blue' French translation of Wilde's 'Birthday of the Princess' story.

41 CL, 454, 451; 'The Theatres', Daily News, 25 August 1890.

42 Pearson, 220; OW praised GA's 'brilliant performance of Laertes' in his review of Irving's Hamlet for the Dramatic Review (9 May, 1885); G. Alexander, quoted in Evening World (New York), 30 September 1892; J. Kaplan, 'A Puppet's Power', Theatre Notebook, 46 (1991), 62. Frank M. Boyd's A Pelican's Tale (1919), 298, refers to OW first offering GA 'a play in blank verse'; CL, 421, although in CL, 421 OW's letter to GA is provisionally dated '[?Late January 1890]' because it also contains a reference to Alexander's production of 'Dr. Bill' by Hamilton Aidé, which opened at the Avenue Theatre on 1 February 1890. But Aidé's play proved a huge success and ran through most of the year. Letters from Alexander to Clement Scott written in January 1892, referred to in Guy & Small, 94n, place the initial arrangement between Alexander and Wilde to 'eighteen months' earlier – i.e. July 1890 – and this date seems to be confirmed by Alexander's comment in the Evening World that it was reading PDG that encouraged him to think OW could write a play. The sum received by OW in July 1890 was £50, but G. Alexander gave the total agreed advance as £100 in a letter to R. Ross (Ross, ed., Robbie Ross – Friend of Friends, 152). The notion that this sum was divided into two separate payments is my conjecture, but based on a similar arrangement that OW proposed to Norman Forbes-Robertson, CL, 454.

43 Alexander Teixeira de Mattos to OW, 19 July 1890 (Mark Samuels Lasner collection, Delaware).

44 CL, 452.

45 T. Sturge Moore, ed., Self-Portrait – taken from the Letters & Journals of Charles Ricketts, R. A. (1939), 16.

46 Harris, 73. OW's first meeting with Gray has traditionally been placed rather earlier – and before the writing of PDG. But this seems unlikely. It is not mentioned in any contemporary record. The one source for this early date is the typed copy of a 1910 manuscript by Frank Liebich (1860–1922) at the Clark, which describes a dinner with OW, John Barlas, John Davidson and John Gray in a private room of a Soho restaurant in 'the early summer of 1889' – and suggests that, even at that date, Gray and Wilde were intimate friends. John Sloan's 1995 biography of John Davidson, however, makes it clear that Davidson was not in London during the early summer of 1889 – and was only very briefly, and unhappily, in town later that year. He did not return, and settle in London, until 1890. And it was during 1891 that he came to know OW and John Gray well. Philip Cohen's 2012 biography of John Barlas also indicates that Barlas's friendship with Wilde did not develop until the beginning of 1891. It seems much more likely that the convivial dinner described by Liebich occurred in the 'early summer' of that year.

47 CL, 455–6.

48 Louis Latourette, quoted in Ellmann, 540; although the passage, referring to a meeting with an unnamed 'young Englishman' in Rome in 1900, does not refer explicitly to John Gray, the connection seems highly probable. OW certainly encountered John Gray in Rome in April 1900. And he certainly did come to regard him as the type of 'Dorian Gray'.

49 J. H. McCormack, John Gray: Poet, Dandy and Priest (1991), 55, 49; Harris, 73.

50   Lionel Johnson to Campbell Dodgson, 5 February 1891; Ernest Dowson to Arthur Moore, [2 February 1891], in H. Flower and D. Mass, eds, *The Letters of Ernest Dowson* (1967), 182; the letter is postmarked 9 January 1891.

Chapter 3: Suggestive Things

1   R. H. Sherard to J. Barlas, 29 January 1891: 'Glad you have made it all [square] with Oscar Wilde. Don't neglect him as he may be able to help you to a good publisher & anyway he is worth cultivating if only as a friend.' In Philip K. Cohen, *John Evelyn Barlas: A Critical Biography* (2012), 105.

2   Archibald Grove to OW, [December 1891] (Washington, Library of Congress), the letter enclosed 'proofs of a symposium which will appear in the January number'. The article on 'Socialism and Literature' was written by Henry S. Salt.

3   Robert Ross to Mrs Colefax, 20 June 1912, reproduced in *Intentions*, February 2011, 22.

4   George Bernard Shaw recalled: 'I delivered an address on Socialism, at which Oscar turned up and spoke. Robert Ross surprised me greatly by telling me, long after Oscar's death, that it was this address of mine that moved Oscar to try his hand at a similar feat by writing "The Soul of Man Under Socialism"' (Harris, 331). It is hard to fix the details of this story, although the various encounters between the two men, noted in Shaw's diary (see Stanley Weintraub, 'The Hibernian School' in J. A. Bertolini, *Shaw and Other Playwrights* [1993]), provide a suggestive context. On 18 July 1890 Shaw had delivered a lecture to the Fabian Society, at the St James's restaurant, on 'Socialism in Contemporary Literature' under the title 'The Quintessence of Ibsenism',

but it is not known if OW attended.

5   For Barlas's contribution to 'The Soul of Man Under Socialism' see Cohen, *John Evelyn Barlas*, 106–16; he quotes a letter from Sherard to Barlas [March 1891], 'Wilde speaks highly of you and your service.'

6   *CL*, 743; In 'The Soul of Man Under Socialism' Renan himself is cited, along with Darwin, Keats and Flaubert as among the few figures in the nineteenth century to have been able to realize their own perfection.

7   Denys Sutton, ed., *Letters of Roger Fry* (1972), 601; J. Barlas to J. Gray, [February 1891], in Cohen, *John Evelyn Barlas*, 105; see also OW to J. S. Little, *CL*, 475.

8   J. Barlas to J. Gray, 29 January 1891, in Cohen, *John Evelyn Barlas*, 105.

9   Harris, 100; Schroeder, 146–7.

10   OET V, 11; *CL*, 467–8; the play opened on Monday 29 January 1891.

11   *CL*, 468; 'The Drama in America', *Era*, 21 February 1891; 'Lawrence Barrett in a New Play', *New York Tribune*, 27 January 1891, in OET V, 14; *NYT*, 27 January 1891, in Beckson, 87.

12   *PMG*, 6 February 1891, quoting the 'London correspondent' of the *Glasgow Herald*, says that OW had received an 'indefinite' reply to an inquiry about when Barrett planned to put on the play, 'but two or three days ago, there came to Mr. Wilde, a cablegram from New York – "Guido Ferranti" produced; a great success"'. *CL*, 464; Guy & Small, 105; 467–8.

13   OET V, 15.

14   Rodney Shewan, 'A Wife's Tragedy',

Theatre Research International, 7 (1982), 94, suggests that this early abortive effort referred to by OW may be the ms of 'The Wife's Tragedy'.

15 *CL*, 463, 486; arrangements for the tour were complicated when Lawrence Barrett, long in failing health, died on 20 March. Minna Gale, however, determined to keep the show on the road. There is a signed receipt dated 20 June 1891 (on Lyric Club letterhead): 'Received from Minna K. Gale of New York City the sum of £200 – two hundred pounds sterling – for the Sole Right for the United States of America and Canada of my play the Duchess of Padua as per agreement – Oscar Wilde.' (Clark).

16 *PDG*, OET III, li–lvi. Guy & Small, 234–7. Besides the six new chapters – 3, 5, 15, 16, 17 and 18 – OW also divided chapter 13 in two, creating chapters 19 and 20 in the book version. JFW to OW [June 1890], in Tipper, *Oscar*, 130.

17 *PDG*, Chapter 6.

18 Coulson Kernahan, 'Oscar Wilde: Some Recollections', ts 12–13, (Clark); Coulson Kernahan, 'Oscar Wilde As I Knew Him', ts 52, (Clark).

19 Ernest Dowson to Arthur Moore, [2 February 1891], in Flower and Mass, eds, *The Letters of Ernest Dowson*, 182, re. meeting chez Horne on 29 January; Lucien Pissarro to Camille Pissarro, 10 February 1891, in Anne Thorold ed., *The Letters of Lucien to Camille Pissarro 1883–1905* (1993), 179; J. Barlas to J. Gray, 29 January 1891, in Cohen, *John Evelyn Barlas*, 105: 'I am glad that you [OW and JG] are both anarchists'.

20 Frank Liebich, 'Oscar Wilde', ts (Clark); *CL*, 686; Harris, 73.

21 *CL*, 482.

22 CL905.

23 Harris, 73; McCormack, *John Gray*, 27–9; Ernest Dowson to Arthur Moore, [2 February 1891], in Flower and Mass, eds, *The Letters of Ernest Dowson*, 182; Lucien Pissarro to Camille Pissarro, 10 February 1891, in Thorold, ed., *The Letters of Lucien to Camille Pissarro*, 179.

24 OW to Arthur Symons, [pm 1 October 1890]: 'Your friend has my full authority to translate my essay on Criticism – I think that on "The Decay of Lying" has been already done, and I am making arrangements for a translation of Dorian Gray' (Christie's, 19 May 2000). Although not specified, it is to be supposed that the translations were to be in French. No such translations, however, appeared.

25 *CL*, 471.

26 Horst Schroeder, 'Oscar Wilde and Stéphane Mallarmé', *Wildean*, 41 (2012), 75–81; also *CL*, 471; Sherard, *SUF*, 114–16.

27 D. J. Niederauer and F. Broche, eds, *Henri de Régnier, Les Cahiers inédits 1887–1936* (2002), 244, 464; John Gray to Félix Fénéon, 14 April 1891, in M. Imbert, ed., *Félix Fénéon & John Gray: Correspondance* (2010), 40.

28 *CL*, 472; Maguire, 24; OW to Henri de Régnier, 2 March 1891 (Paris); Niederauer and Broche, eds, *Henri de Régnier*, 244.

29 OET VI, 88; Robert Sherard, 'Aesthete and Realist', *Morning Journal*, 22 March 1891, in Ellmann, 304; see also Horace G. Hutchinson, ed., *Private Diaries of Rt. Hon. Sir Algernon West* (1922), 63.

30 Coulson Kernahan, *In Good Company* (1917), in Mikhail, 310–11.

31 *CL*, 295; Guy & Small, 57–61; Mason, 341–5.

32 *Athenaeum*, 27 June 1891; Walter Pater, 'A Novel by Mr Oscar Wilde', *Bookman*, November 1891, I, 59–60.

33 Schroeder, 111.

34 Pater, 'A Novel by Mr. Oscar Wilde', 59–60.

Chapter 4: The Best Society

1   LAD, *Autobiography* (1929), 59.

2   LAD to F. Harris, 20 March 1925, Texas; LAD to A. J. A. Symons, 14 March and 16 March, 1939 (Clark); the inscribed *PDG* is at the Clark.

3   W. L. Courtenay, *The Passing Hour* (1925), 118, says that only Cust or 'perhaps Edmund Yates, at his best, came somewhere near Oscar Wilde's random flashes of wit'.

4   R. Davenport-Hines, *Ettie* (2008), 57–8; OW's host, Willie Grenfell, 'a model English athlete gifted with peculiar intellectual fairness' was not party to this disparagement. He considered OW to be 'most surprising, most charming, a wonderful talker'. Harris, 85.

5   Lady Tree, 'Herbert & I', in *Herbert Beerbohm Tree, Some Memories of Him and of His Art Collected by Max Beerbohm* (1918), 87.

6   CL, 484; Lionel Earle, *Turn Over the Page* (1935), 77.

7   Douglas Ainslie, *Adventures Social and Literary* (1922), 92–3.

8   Harris, 258–9; Harry White to G. Curzon, in R. Davenport-Hines, *Ettie*, 58; Elizabeth Longford, *A Pilgrimage of Passion: The Life of Wilfrid Scawen Blunt* (1979), 289–90. OW had visited Crabbet Park before, in July 1889, for the annual garden party and horse show, known as the 'sale of the Arabs'. Tynan, *Twenty-five Years*, 303.

9   Charles L. Graves, *Hubert Parry: His Life and Works* (1921), 1:343; Parry records that 'When G. W. went away one of the Peels [sons of the Speaker, and fellow Crabbet Club members] played up to O. W. in the same way and made him talk even greater bunkum.'

10 Graves, *Hubert Parry*, 1:344.

11 A. G. G. Liddell, *Notes from the Life of an Ordinary Mortal* (1911), 283 (from diary entry, 1 August 1891); Arthur Balfour in a letter to Lady Elcho, dated 5 August 1891, records seeing OW and CMW at Wrest that Sunday, along with Mrs E. Grenfell, H. Cust, Lord Northampton, the Alwynne Comptons, Bobby Spencer, the L. Drummonds and the Earl of Dudley. Jane Ridley and Percy Clayre, eds, *The Letters of Arthur Balfour to Lady Elcho 1885–1917* (1992), 77.

12 René Gimpel, *Diary of an Art Dealer* (1963), reporting an incident told him by Albert Clerk-Jeannotte, who had witnessed it as a young boy (Jeannotte was born in 1881 in Montreal).

13 Liddell, *Notes from the Life of an Ordinary Mortal*, 283.

14 Harris, 81–2. I have been unable to find any corroborative evidence for the story that OW wrote the play on a visit to a friend's 'cottage' in the Lake District (hence his use of the name 'Lady Windermere') and his return from there via the North Yorkshire town of Selby (hence the mention of Selby in the final act of the play). This story was apparently mentioned by Robert Ross to Hesketh Pearson; see Pearson to Rupert Croft-Cooke (Texas). But OW had already used the name 'Lady Windermere' in his story 'Lord Arthur Savile's Crime', and had used 'Selby' as one of Dorian Gray's estates.

15 *The Oscar Wilde Encyclopedia*, 179; Chambers' *The Idler* was turned down by Herbert Beerbohm Tree, but taken up by Elisabeth Marbury, and put on in New York in November 1890.

16 OW to Elisabeth Robins [1891] (Fales), OW to Marion Lea [1891] (Fales); for OW's affinity with Ibsen see George Bernard Shaw to LAD, in Mary Hyde, ed., *Bernard Shaw and Alfred Douglas: A Correspondence* (1982), 128–9.

17 *Evening Standard*, 29 November 1913, quoted in Ellmann, 315; Boyd, *A Pelican's Tale*, 298.

18 Kaplan, 'A Puppet's Power', 62.

19 CMW to Lady Mount Temple, 22 October 1891, in Moyle, 195; *CL*, 488,489. OW originally sent the script to Daly's London agent, Joe Anderson, but then asked to have it back 'as I would like to touch it up a little before Daly sees it'.

20 Weindling and Colloms, *The Marquis de Leuville* for an account of WCKW's relationship with Mrs Frank Leslie; Moyle, 194.

21 *PMG*, 28 September 1891, refers to the break-in, 'through a skylight', occurring on 'Friday night', i.e. 25 September 1891; John Davidson to McCormick, quoted in John Sloan, *John Davidson: First of the Moderns* (1995), 67.

22 Frederic Whyte, *William Heinemann: A Memoir* (1928), 82–4.

Chapter 5: The Dance of the Seven Veils

1   Ernest Raynaud, *La Mêlée Symboliste (1890–1900) Portraits et Souvenirs II* (1920), 133, translation in Ellmann, 328 and Schroeder, 119.

2   Wilfrid Scawen Blunt, *My Diaries – Part One* (1919), 72: diary entry for 27 October 1891. It is sometimes supposed that the 'play' referred to is OW's *Salomé* (see for example *CL*, 491n). But OW to HSH Princess of Monaco (*CL*, 491, 495) clearly suggests that it is *The Good Woman* about which he is talking; as does Emily Lytton to Rev. Whitwell Elwin, 3 November 1891 (quoted in Lady Emily Lutyens, *A Blessed Girl* (1953), 68): '[OW] has just written a play which he wants to have translated into French and acted at the [Comédie] Français, nothing less would be good enough for him.' Her comments indicate that the 'just written play' had been composed in English, and was to be translated into French, by OW or another. *Salomé* was written directly in French.

3   The copy of *Intentions* inscribed 'To Robert, Earl of Lytton, with best wishes, and in sincere admiration, from the author, Paris '91' is in the Mark Samuels Lasner Collection, University of Delaware; Lord Lytton to OW 'Saturday' [31 October 1891] (Austin); Emily Lytton to Rev. Whitwell Elwin, 3 November 1891 (quoted in Lutyens, *A Blessed Girl*, 68.

4   *CL*, 492; the copy of *PDG* is inscribed 'A Stéphane Mallarmé, Hommage d'Oscar Wilde, Paris '91'. Telegram JMW to Mallarmé, 3 November 1891; JMW to Mallarmé, 2 November 1891, quoted in Ellmann, 317–19.

5   *CL*, 492n; S. Mallarmé to JMW, 11 November 1891; 24 November 1891; 23 December 1891 (GUL).

6   *CL*, 500; *CL*, 495; Sherard, *SUF*, 109; Margaret Talbot to Robert de Montesquiou-Fézensac, 7 November [1891] (GUL).

7   Leslie, *Memoir of John Edward Courtenay Bodley*, 18; Arthur Kingsland Griggs, ed., *The Memoirs of Léon Daudet* (1926), 200; Jean Lorrain, *Sensations et souvenirs* (1895), in Bernard Gauthier, 'Marcel Schwob et Oscar Wilde', in Bruno Fabre et al., *Marcel Schwob. L'homme au masque d'or* (2006), 59.

8   Stuart Merrill, 'La Jeune littérateur anglaise', *La Plume*, 15 March 1893.

9   Henri de Régnier, *Les Annales Politiques*, in Mikhail, 464–5.

10 Gustave Le Rouge, 'Oscar Wilde' [3 November 1928], in Mikhail, 459.

11 Coulson Kernahan, 'Oscar Wilde As I Knew Him', ts 50 (Clark); CL, 741.

12 André Gide, Journal I, 1887–1925, ed. Eric Marty (1996), 138ff; the first meeting occurred on 26 November chez Henri de Régnier, at least a dozen meetings between then and 15 December. Robert Mallet, ed., André Gide and Paul Valéry Correspondance 1890–1942 (1955), 139; Jules Renard, Journal Inédit 1887–1895 (1925), 131. Gide, Journal I, 1887–1925, 148: 'Wilde ne m'a fait, je crois, que du mal. Avec lui j'avais d'appris de penser. J'avais des émotions plus diverses mais je ne savais plus les ordonner; je ne pouvais surtout plus suivre les déductions des autres.'

13 William Rothenstein, Men and Memories I, 86–93; Sherard SUF, 95, fails to grasp the humour of Wilde's comment, recording it as, 'Robert was splendid and defended me at the risk of his life.'

14 O'Sullivan, 75–6.

15 Gide, Journal I, 1887–1925, 138; Stuart Merrill, Prose et vers: Oeuvres posthumes (1925), 142–5, in Ellmann, 328; Rothenstein, Men and Memories I, 92.

16 Raynaud, La Mêlée Symboliste, 136–7, translation in Ellmann, 330.

17 Moyle, 200.

18 Glasgow Herald, 26 November 1891; JFW to OW, in Tipper, Oscar, 130; Liverpool Mercury, 23 December 1891; Mason, 365–9; Moyle, 200.

19 Intentions, 62 (2009), 26.

20 PMG, 21 August 1891. It is unclear from the report whether the article was published in translation or in the original English; David Goodway, Anarchist Seeds Beneath the Snow (2011), 78, records that Mallarmé also subscribed to La Révolté.

21 L'Echo de Paris, 27 December 1891.

22 Raynaud, La Mêlée Symboliste, 134; Yvanhoe Rambosson, 'Oscar Wilde et Verlaine', in Comedia, 7 June 1923, in Ellmann, 322.

23 A. Gide, If It Die (1951), 249.

24 CL, 499.

25 A. Retté, Le Symbolisme: Anecdotes et Souvenirs (1903), in OET V, 329; A. Gide, Oscar Wilde: A Study (1949), 26.

26 E. Gómez Carrillo, 'Comment Oscar Wilde rêva Salomé', La Plume (1902), in Mikhail 195.

27 Edgar Saltus, 'On the origins of Salome', ts (Clark).

28 Gómez Carrillo, in Mikhail, 195.

29 Guillot de Saix, 'Oscar Wilde chez Maeterlinck', Les Nouvelle Littéraires, 25 October 1945, in Ellmann, 325.

30 Jean Lorrain, 'Salomé et les Poètes', La Journal, 11 February 1896; Pierre Léon-Gauthier, Jean Lorrain (1962), 370–1, in Ellmann, 324.

31 E. Gómez Carrillo, Treinta Años De Mi Vida (1974 edition), 295, translation in Ellmann, 323–4.

32 H. Gómez Carrillo, in Mikhail 194: 'Wilde began a short story [about Salome] entitled "The Double Beheading". Not long after he tore up what he had written and considered writing a poem.'

33 OW to W. Heinemann, 29 Boulevard des Capucines [November/December 1891] (BL, RP 3753), apologizing for not having got the 'preface' done: 'Somehow, I have not been in the mood for it, and to be in the mood is everything in art.' OW in PMB, 30 June 1892, 947, in Mikhail, 188.

34 O'Sullivan, 32–3; OET V, 337, re. the notebook at in the Bodmer collection, Geneva.

35 A. Lugné-Poe Le Sot du Tremplin, Souvenirs et Impressions de Théâtre (1931), in OET V, 332; L'Intruse was given its UK premiere at a matinee at the Haymarket Theatre on 27 January 1892, with Herbert Beerbohm Tree as the

Grandfather. It is to be supposed that OW was in the audience.

36 Gómez Carrillo, *Treinta Años De Mi Vida*, 296, in Ellmann, 323; Gomez Carrillo, 'Comment Oscar Wilde rêva Salomé', *La Plume* (1902), in Mikhail 195; Louise Thomas, *L'Esprit d'Oscar Wilde* (1920), in Ellmann, 324; O'Sullivan, 216. O'Sullivan claims the executed man was the anarchist Ravachol, but he was executed, and buried, at Montbrison on the Loire.

37 *CL*, 506; see OET V, 337–9, which plausibly suggests that OW's requests to Merrill, Retté and Louÿs to correct the manuscript did not occur till later.

38 OW quoted in *PMB*, 30 June 1892, 947, in Mikhail, 188; *Gil Blas*, 27 December 1891: 'M. Oscar Wilde, le poète anglais, vient de lire au Théâtre d'Art: *Salomé*, pièce au une acte, en prose, qu'il a écrit en française. Cette pièce sera au mois d'hiver prochain'. See also OET V, 342–3 for other references to OW reading. Robertson, *Time Was*, 136, on OW's diction, re. a private reading of the script.

39 Ricketts, 52–3.

40 Huges Le Roux, 'Oscar Wilde', *Le Figaro*, 2 December 1891; [interview by Jacques Daurelle] *L'Echo de Paris*, 6 December 1891, in Stefano Evangelista, ed., *The Reception of Oscar Wilde in Europe* (2010), 69; R. H. Sherard, *Le Gaulois*, 17 December 1891, reprinted in *SUF*, 258–70; *L'Echo de Paris*, 19 December 1891; JWF to OW, December 1891, in Tipper, *Oscar*, 133; *CL*, 504n.

Chapter 6: Charming Ball

1 R. Ross, 'A Note on "Salome"'; 'Latest News', *Liverpool Mercury*, 5 January 1892. OW's visit to Glyn-y-Garth is a tantalizing new discovery. Mrs Schwabe was the grandmother of Maurice Salis Schwabe, whom OW came to know during the course of 1892, but there is no evidence to suggest that they met during (or before) this visit.

2 James G. Nelson, *The Early Nineties: A View from the Bodley Head* (1971), 79; Mason, 319–23; *CL*, 490, 494.

3 Cohen, *John Evelyn Barlas*, 111–16.

4 H. H. Champion, 'Wilde As I Saw Him', *Booklover* (Melbourne), 1 December 1914.

5 Guy & Small, 106; Sherard, *Real*, 295; the source says OW had 'just crossed from Ireland', but this seems unlikely.

6 Ricketts, 35.

7 JFW to OW, in Tipper, *Oscar*, 134; *CL*, 513–15.

8 *CL*, 518; Pearson, 222; Kaplan, 'A Puppet's Power', 72.

9 'Music and Drama', *Glasgow Herald*, 15 February 1892.

10 *CL*, 518–20.

11 *CL*, 520; James G. Nelson, *The Early Nineties* (1971), 199; Ernest Poole (editor of the *Star*) to OW, 16 February 1892 (Mark Samuels Lasner/Delaware); the original article in the *Star* appeared on 6 February 1892, the retraction on 15 February.

12 Holland, 133–43; Hyde, *Trials*, 212–16, 296. Although, at his trial, OW was eventually found 'not guilty' in relation to this supposed incident, on technical grounds, the probability of a sexual relationship between the two men seems very strong. It was certainly assumed (or known) by John Lane, Richard Le Gallienne, John Gray and others. The suggested date of this incident – on OW's indictment

– was 20 February 1892. But, as this was the night of the premiere of *LWF*, it is clearly impossible. Wilde's own memory was that he first had 'supper' with Shelley about 'the beginning of March'.

13 Harris, 77.

14 Holland, 231+n; the 'friend' was designated as 'Mr B' in a letter from Shelley to OW read out in court. Holland suggests that he may have been the young actor Sydney Barraclough. But OW mentioned 'being on terms of the most intimate friendship' with the family of the 'cultivated' Mr B. There is no evidence that OW knew Sydney Barraclough's family. They came from Yorkshire. A more plausible candidate might be Aubrey Boucicault, the twenty-two-year-old son of Dion Boucicault, who was just starting on a theatrical career. Dion Boucicault (senior) had died in 1890.

15 *CL*, 517–21.

16 Robertson, *Time Was*, 135–6; Schroeder, 122, on the identification of the florist as Goodyear in the Royal Arcade, and the character wearing the flower being 'Cecil Graham'. The 'dyeing' of flowers had been pioneered in the late 1880s by British chemist Alfred Nesbit (elder brother of the author and sometime contributor to *WW*, Edith Nesbit). According to contemporary reports, during 1891, the supporters of one of the French political parties had designated themselves by wearing 'green carnations'. And it was supposed by some that Wilde had become familiar with the blooms while in the French capital. Charles Nelson, 'Beautiful Untrue Things', *Wildean*, 48 (2016), 96–103.

17 'By our Special "First Nighter", *PMG*, 22 February 1892; 'Society Gossip', *Preston Guardian*, 27 February 1892.

Louise Jopling, *Twenty Years of My Life* (1925), 81.

18 Harris, 82–3; Robertson, *Time Was*, 135.

19 H. James to Mrs Hugh Bell, [23 Feb 1892], in Leon Edel, ed., *Henry James Letters* (1981), 3:372–3.

20 George Alexander's account – given years later to Hesketh Pearson (and relayed by Hyde, *Oscar*, 174, and Ellmann, 346) presented the speech as a short and studied paradox – quite possibly prepared in advance. But the contemporary press accounts attest to its impromptu nature, and slightly rambling form, brought to a smart conclusion. See: *Morning Post*, 22 February 1892; *Era*, 27 February 1892; 'Our London Letter', *Dundee Courier & Argus*, 22 February 1892; *The Sunday Times*, 21 February 1892; 'Last Night's Theatricals', *Lloyd's Weekly Newspaper*, 21 Feb 1891; 'By our Special "First Nighter"', *PMG*, 22 February 1892; *Glasgow Herald*, 22 February 1892.

21 *Manchester Guardian*, 22 February 1892.

22 Oswald Crawford, 'A Contributor's Opinion', *PMG*, 22 February 1892.

23 *Standard*, 22 February 1892.

24 Coulson Kernahan, '*Oscar Wilde As I Knew Him*', ts 21 (Clark).

25 Kaplan, 'A Puppet's Power', 59–73. See: *PMG*, 22 February, 1892; *Birmingham Daily Post*, 22 February 1892; *Glasgow Herald*, 22 February 1892, etc. *CL*, 521–2; The decision to alter the scene seems to have been made on, or soon after, the opening night. See *Era*, 27 February 1892: 'On the fall of curtain Mr Wilde acknowledged that from the point of view of holding the attention of the audience riveted on the characters and exciting sympathy, Mr Alexander's view had been entirely the right one.'

26 JFW to OW, [26 February 1892], in

Tipper, *Oscar*, 138; although JFW was not at the first night she certainly saw the play, going – probably not for the first time – in a party with OW's old friend Julia Ward Howe, who came over to London that summer. L. E. Richards, M. H. Elliott and F. H. Hall, *Julia Ward Howe* (1916), 2:168; *CL*, 524–7; Longford, *A Pilgrimage of Passion*, 295; Harris, 83; Pearson, 225; Ellmann, 347.

27   *PMG*, 25 February 1892; 'Our London Correspondence', *Glasgow Herald*, 9 March 1892.

28   Raffalovich/Michaelson, 111.

29   *Standard*, 22 February 1892; *PMG*, 23 February 1892; Guy & Small, 107–8. Some of OW's receipts are preserved at the Clark: for the weeks ending 11 March 1892: £43 15s 1d; 25 March 1892: £46 12s 5d; 13 April 1892: £36 17s 11d; and 8 June 1892: £48 1s 11d. Moyle, 210; CMW to Mrs Fitch, 14 September 1892 (Clark).

30   Harris, 83, records Ada Leverson writing in praise of *LWF* in *Punch* 'of all places in the world'. The anonymous 'A Wilde "Tag" to a Tame Play', accompanied by a caricature by Bernard Partridge, was the magazine's only comment on the play (besides a short poem and an even shorter paragraph about 'Mr George Alexander running Wilde at the St James's Theatre'). Leverson later told Osbert Sitwell that she had met Wilde because he had been amused by an anonymous skit on Dorian Gray that she had written in *Punch* – and, on seeking a meeting, he had been amazed to discover that the author of the piece was a woman. But this would seem to be a false memory, as Leverson's first parody mentioning Dorian Gray ('New Year's

Eve at Latterday Hall') did not appear in *Punch* until December 1893, by which time her friendship with Wilde was well established. Perhaps it was an anonymous skit on *LWF* that had piqued Wilde's curiosity. And perhaps 'A Wilde "Tag" to a Tame Play' was that skit. Julie Speedie, *Wonderful Sphinx* (1993), 33–4.

31   Harris, 100.

32   O'Sullivan, 169; H. M. Hyde, 'Prefatory Note' to Stuart Merrill, ts 'Oscar Wilde' (Clark); Wilde's March/April visit to Paris (attested by a several entries in Pierre Louÿs' diary, and a letter to Paul Valéry, 14 April 1892 in Peter Fawcett and Pascal Mercier, eds, *Correspondances A Trois Voix* (Paris, 2004), 581–2) is previously unrecorded. Interestingly, Joseph Donohue posited the possibility of such a visit in his excellent account of the complex relationship of the various surviving *Salomé* manuscripts, and their corrections, given at OET V, 337–8; P. Louÿs to OW, 22 May 1892 (Austin).

33   Jimmy Glover, *His Book* (1911), 37. Glover had initially been collaborating with Chance Newton on a skit to be called 'Lady Windowblind *Fin-de-Siécle*' (*PMG*, 8 March 1892) but then joined forces with Hawtrey and Brookfield; Charles Brookfield, *The Poet and the Puppets: A Travestie Suggested by Lady Windermere's Fan* (1892).

34   Pearson, 246–7.

35   *The Artist and Journal of Home Culture*, 1 June 1892; *Standard*, 20 May 1892; Hermann Vezin to OW, 24 June 1892 (Clark); *Proceedings at the Forty-Seventh Anniversary Festival of the Royal General Theatrical Fund* (1892) (Berg). I have converted the reported text from the past to the present tense.

Chapter 7: White and Gold

1   Henri de Régnier, *Les Annales Politiques et Littéraires*, in Mikhail, 465; P. Louÿs to A. Gide, June 1892, quoted in Mc-Cormack, *John Gray*, 91.

2   Blunt, *My Diaries – Part One*, 81; Anne Anderson, 'There is Divinity in Odd Numbers', *Wildean*, 43 (2013), 77–86; 'Michael Field', Diary, 25 May 1892. Teodoro Serrao to OW, 21 July 1892, Rome: 'Please send me the manuscript of the "Fan" [*LWF*] as soon as you can, so that I might be able to have it ready for the winter' (Clark); J. T. Grein to OW, 5 September 1892, re. a contract with Dr O. Blumenthal for the rights to produce *LWF* in Austria and Germany (Dulau cat. no. 161; item 122); 'Theatrical Gossip', *Era*, 18 June 1892; *Evening World* (NY), 23 June 1892.

3   Tynan, *Twenty-five Years*, 130; 'Dropped from the Lotos', *NYT*, 18 September 1893; Weindling and Colloms, *The Marquis de Leuville*; S. N. Behrman, *Conversations with Max* (1960), 239–40.

4   *CL*, 527–8. OW first approached McIlvaine about publishing *LWF*, but without success; see 'Unknown Publisher' [C. McIlvaine] to Jonathan Sturges, 18 March 1892 (GUL); Guy & Small, 70–1; *CL*, 533–4.

5   *CL*, 701–2; 725, 795. McKenna, 241ff, suggests that it was LAD's brother, Lord Drumlanrig, who approached OW, but this seems to be a misreading of *CL*, 795.

6   LAD to F. Harris, 1925 (Austin); R. Croft-Cooke, *Bosie* (1964), 91.

7   The Oscar Wilde collection of John B. Stetson, cat. item 11; LAD to F. Harris, 1925 (Austin).

8   Gertrude Simmons, 'Witness statement', quoted in *Guardian*, 6 May 2001.

9   R. Ross, 'A Note on *Salomé*', in *Salomé* (1912); 'The Censure and *Salomé*', *PMB*, 29 June 1892. The notion that Bernhardt should play the role had been mooted earlier. On 2 February 1892 *L'Echo de Paris* had even announced that she and her company would be putting on the play in London, with Bernhardt in the title role. But this seems to have been a piece of wishful – if prophetic – journalistic invention (OET V, 341).

10 'The Censorship and *Salomé*', *PMG*, 6 July 1892; 'The Censure and *Salomé*', *PMG*, 29 June 1892; Ricketts, 53.

11 In Paris OW had told Gómez Carrillo that he wanted to see 'Sarah Bernhardt, by some miracle a young woman again, dancing naked before Herod' (in Mikhail, 194); *CL*, 1196.

12 Ricketts, 52; *CL*, 874.

13 Robertson, *Time Was*, 126–7.

14 *PMG*, 29 June 1892; OW's annotated typescript of *Salomé* is at the Free Library of Philadelphia (and can be viewed online); Kerry Powell, *Oscar Wilde and the Theatre of the 1890s* (2009), 34.

15 *PMG*, 6 July 1892; Bernhardt wrote in CMW's autograph album: 'Je vous promets, Madame, d'avoir un immense success dans Salomé et je vous affirme que le public français sera très fier d'avoir la première de cette admirable pièce' (BL).

16 *PMG*, 29 June 1892; 'Mr Oscar Wilde', *Standard*, 30 June, 1892, quoting *Le Gaulois* (Paris), 29 June 1892; *Punch*, 9 July 1892.

17 OW, after a brief sojourn at the Royal Victoria Hotel, moved to 51 Kaiser-Friedrichs-Promenade; see the 'Zugangs-Liste' in *Amtliche Homburger Fremden-listen*; CMW to Otho Lloyd, 7 July 1892, *CL*, 530n; Maguire, 27; *CL*, 530; Ross, ed., *Robbie Ross – Friend of Friends*, 358. It is often stated (Hyde, *Oscar*,

189; Ellmann, 356; McKenna, 253; Moyle, 204) that LAD accompanied, or met with, OW at Bad Homburg but Schroeder, 130–2, makes clear that he did not.

18 It is perhaps suggestive that amongst OW's fellow guests listed at 51 Kaiser-Friedrichs-Promenade, in Bad Homburg, was 'Alex. Arbuttnot' – very probably Sir Alexander Arbuthnot, the former Indian administrator.

19 Chris Healy, *Confessions of a Journalist* (1904), 255.

20 OW in *Sketch*, 9 January 1895, in Mikhail, 241.

21 H. Pearson, *Beerbohm Tree* (1956), 65.

22 H. Beerbohm Tree to OW, 12 December 1891 (Austin), returning, and

criticizing, OW's play (*The Duchess of Padua*), and praising his 'brilliantly written' essays 'The Decay of Lying' and 'Pen, Pencil and Poison'. *Liverpool Mercury*, 26 October 1892, mentions that John Hare had also wanted OW's new play for the Garrick, but Beebohm Tree had 'first refusal'; *CL*, 535–6.

23 H. Pearson, *Beerbohm Tree*, 65.

24 Moyle, 205.

25 Ada Leverson, *Letters to the Sphinx* (1930), 47.

26 Moyle, 206–7; LAD to A. J. A. Symons, 16 March 1939 (Clark). LAD's interest in golf seems to have been heightened by the presence at the links of a young lad called 'Jack'; Laura Lee, *Oscar's Ghost* (2017), 39–40.

Part VII: *The Selfish Giant*
Chapter 1: The Eternal Quest for Beauty

1   Hyde, *Trials*, 211–12; Sidney Mavor witness statement, quoted in McKenna, 281. In court Mavor stated that Schwabe was the nominal host of the dinner. He also suggested that Wilde and Alfred Taylor were meeting for the first time on the occasion. This corroborates OW's statement that Schwabe introduced him to Taylor in October 1892. LAD later claimed that it was Ross – rather than himself – who had introduced Wilde to 'the male prostitution of the streets' (LAD to Frank Harris, 22 March 1925 (Austin)). But, as Harris remarked, LAD told so many lies it was hard to know and difficult to believe (F. Harris to Henry Davray, 1 March 1926 (Clark)). There is no evidence to suggest that Ross was responsible.

2   Holland, 225; W. B. Yeats to Olivia Shakespear, 30 June 1932, in Allan Wade, ed., *The Letters of W. B. Yeats*

(1954), 798.

3   Hyde, *LAD*, 25–6.

4   LAD, *Autobiography*, 99. The incident occurred in November 1892; see Schroeder, 149.

5   James Sully, *My Life & Friends* (1918), 326; J. Dobson and C. Wakeley, *Sir George Buckstone Browne* (1957), 79; Jopling, *Twenty Years of My Life*, 81. Horst Schroeder, 'The OET Edition of the "The Critic As Artist. Part I"', *Wildean*, 38 (2011), 69–70. Wilde met Meredith again soon afterwards, at a dinner hosted by W. S. Blunt at Brown's Hotel (W. S. Blunt to Sir H. B. Loch, 25 October 1892, at National Records of Scotland).

6   Jopling, *Twenty Years of My Life*, 81.

7   Pearson, *Beerbohm Tree*, 67; critics, and the time and since, have also noted the plot's similarities to Dumas's *Le Fils naturel* (1858); during his visit to Scotland, OW also spent a night with

Margot Tennant's family at The Glen, their house in the Scottish Borders. Horace G. Hutchinson, ed., *Private Diaries of Rt. Hon. Sir Algernon West* (1922), 63 (entry 5 October 1892).

8   *CL*, 536; Guy & Small, 110f, refute the figure of £7,000 given in Ward, *Recollections of a Savage*, 51 and used by Ellmann (315) and others; Maguire, *Ceremonies of Bravery*, 27.

9   Moyle, 212–14; *CL*, 538.

10 *CL*, 538, 763, 156.

11 *CL*, 730.

12 *CL*, 758.

13 Hyde, *Trials*, 206–7; Holland, 182–91; *CL*, 546–7.

14 Moyle, 214.

15 Campbell Dodgson to Lionel Johnson, 8 February 1893 (BL); CMW to Lady Mount Temple, 12 December 1892, in Moyle, 215; CMW to RR, 4 December 1892 (Austin); CMW to RR, 16 April 1893 (Clark).

16 McKenna, 284–5; OET V, 347–51. CMW to Lady Mount Temple, 2 February 1893, in Moyle, 217.

17 *CL*, 538; CMW to Lady Mount Temple, 2 February, 1893, in Moyle, 218; *CL*, 582. Hare had wanted *WNI* but had been pipped by Beerbohm Tree. *Liverpool Mercury*, 26 October 1892.

18 *CL*, 544.

19 *CL*, 547; *CL*, 555–6.

20 Campbell Dodgson to Lionel Johnson, 8 February 1893.

21 McKenna, 266.

22 *The Spirit Lamp*, 3, no. 2 (17 February 1893); *CL*, 544; the sonnet was 'In Sarum Close'.

23 *CL*, 552–6; *The Times*, 'Books of the Week' Column, 23 February 1893; *PMG*, 27 February 1893; *CL*, 552; *Black and White*, 11 May 1893; *Spirit Lamp*, 4, 21–7; *CL*, 557; Mason, 375.

24 *CL*, 689, 691.

25 Moyle, 219, 221.

26 *CL*, 691; André Gide, *If It Die* (1915), 300.

27 *CL*, 691.

28 *CL*, 549–50.

29 *CL*, 688; see Bills at BL (Hyde); *CL*, 774–5. LAD to Maurice Schwabe, 5 March 1893, from Salisbury: 'I went to the Savoy with Oscar for two nights; and I was sentimental enough to go down to the old room 123 next to the restaurant where we used to sleep together, the valet enquired after you as "votre cousin"'. OW said that Douglas stayed at the Savoy with him 'three times' that spring (*Yorkshire Herald*, 25 May 1895); C. Parker witness statement, in McKenna, 293; *CL*, 714; Harris, 166; Herbert Tankard witness statement, in McKenna, 298.

30 McKenna, 305–6; LAD to M. Schwabe, 9 March 1893; LAD to M. Schwabe, 17 March 1893; *CL*, 701–2.

31 McCormack, *John Gray*, 39–40; R. H. Sherard to Pierre Louÿs [November 1892] (Austin); Ellmann, 369; John Gray to Pierre Louÿs, 16 March 1893, in McCormack, *John Gray*, 105.

32 Hyde, *Trials*, 215, McKenna, 297; Holland, 233.

33 Mary J. Schwabe to Maurice Schwabe, 25 October 1894 (Library of NSW); LAD to Maurice Schwabe, 5 March 1893 (Library of NSW); McKenna, 354–64.

34 Memoirs of Charles Hirsch, quoted in Caspar Wintermans, *Alfred Douglas* (2007) 32; Harris, 90; LAD, *Autobiography*, 99.

35 Anon., *Oscar Wilde: Three Times Tried* (1915), 143.

36 McKenna, 301; Moyle, 222; *Era*, 23 March 1893; 'Theatrical Mems.', *Bristol Mercury*, 28 March 1893.

37 *Goncourt Journal*, 30 April 1893.

38 Jacomb-Hood, *With Brush and Pencil*, 115.

Chapter 2: Feasting with Panthers

1   Pearson, *Beerbohm Tree*, 69–71; Pearson, 233–4; OW further acknowledged Tree's rare distinctiveness in his remark that 'imitations of Tree are all alike – except Tree's'.

2   Ellmann, 360; Schroeder, 134; Julia Neilson, *This For Remembrance* (1940), 139–40 thought the hissing may have been occasioned by the scandalous rumours already circulating about OW, but this seems unlikely at this date; 'Theatrical Gossip', *Era*, 21 April 1893; *Freeman's Journal*, 20 April 1893; 'Mr Oscar Wilde's New Play', *Birmingham Daily Post*, 20 April 1893; *Morning Post*, 20 April 1893. The anecdote (in Pearson, *Beerbohm Tree*, 71) that OW himself announced from his box, 'Ladies and Gentlemen, I regret to inform you that Mr Oscar Wilde is not in the house' – is not supported by any of the contemporary accounts.

3   Pearson, 237; Max Beerbohm to Reggie Turner, [30 April 1893], in Rupert Hart-Davis, ed., *Max Beerbohm's Letters to Reggie Turner* (1964), 38; quoted in Ellmann, 360.

4   Guy & Small, 116; Schroeder, 135; even towards the end of the run, when audiences had begun to dwindle, OW was still earning *c*. £70 a week.

5   *Oscar Wilde: Three Times Tried* (1906), 57; Pearson, 274.

6   Harris, 94–6; Holland, 32, 52–4.

7   George Ives Diary, 23 December 1893; Harris, 94; 'London Correspondence', *Freeman's Journal*, 27 May 1895.

8   Raffalovich, *L'Affaire Oscar Wilde*, 5.

9   Hart-Davis, ed., *Max Beerbohm's Letters to Reggie Turner*, 36, 35, 34.

10 Beardsley's copy of *Salomé* is at the Sterling Library, University of London. It is often stated – e.g. Ellmann, 290 – that Beardsley had met OW at Burne-Jones's studio in July 1891, but, although Beardsley did refer to meeting 'the Oscar Wildes' on that occasion, it was only Constance and the children that he encountered. See Matthew Sturgis, *Aubrey Beardsley* (1998), 73–4.

11 Leverson, *Letters to the Sphinx*, 19–20; John Lane to OW, 8 June 1893 (Austin): 'I have this day seen Beardsley and arranged for 10 plates and a cover for 50 guineas!'

12 J. G. Nelson, *The Early Nineties*, 244–245; Guy & Small, 160–4. The agreement, drafted in May, was finalized – and signed by Wilde – on 3 August 1893.

13 A[lfred] Hamilton Grant, 'The Ephemeral: Some Memories of Oxford in the 'Nineties', *Cornhill Magazine* (December 1931), 641–53, in Mikhail, 220–7.

14 McKenna, 320–1; Although McKenna states that Grainger was sixteen, he was born in late 1875 (and christened on 9 January 1876) so would have been seventeen and a half in May 1893.

15 *Goncourt Journal*, 30 April 1893, 7 April 1895, 14 April 1894.

16 H. P. Clive, *Pierre Louÿs* (1978), 92–3, quoting OW's account given to A. Gide. Louÿs memory of Wilde's parting lines had been 'Vous pensiez que j'avais des amis. Je n'ai que des amants' ('You thought I had friends. I have only lovers'). When OW gave an account of the conversation to Léon Daudet, word of it got back to Louÿs, who wrote a final indignant note of farewell, ending the friendship on 25 May 1893. Both Marcel Schwob and Paul Valéry attempted to heal the breach, but it was not to be done.

Chapter 3: Brief Summer Months

1 Hyde, *LAD*, 1984; McKenna, 321; Moyle, 208–9, 224–5.

2 Gertrude Pearce (née Simmonds) letter (1906), in Ellmann 389–90; Moyle, 210; Theodore Wratislaw, 'Memoir of Wilde' (Clark); *CL*, 569.

3 Moyle 210, 224–5; Gertrude Pearce, in Ellmann, 390.

4 Harris, 104–5; witness statements of Gertrude Simmonds and Ernest Mitchelmore (landlord of Miller of Mansfield inn, Goring), in McKenna, 323–4.

5 *CL*, 566, 567; 692.

6 *CL*, 688; *The Sunday Times*, 20 August 1893; *Birmingham Daily Post*, 15 August 1893; Max Beerbohm to R. Turner, 19 August 1893, in Hart-Davis, ed., *Max Beerbohm's Letters to Reggie Turner*, 53.

7 *CL*, 659; Robins, 101–2; the date of OW's consultation with Danby remains conjectural.

8 'Oscar Wilde's Philosophy', *Weekly Standard and Express* (Blackburn), 16 September 1893; *Le Gaulois*, 9 September 1893, says that Aimée Lowther put on the one-act play *5 O'Clock*.

9 Sir Chartres Biron, *Without Prejudice; Impressions of Life and Law* (1936), 211–12, in Mikhail, 339.

10 *CL*, 692; Ellmann, 379; LAD to John Lane, 30 September 1893; LAD ms copy (at BL, RP 1802), later included as a note in *Autobiography* (1931 edition), 160n. The exact sequence of events is hard to fathom. LAD wrote to Lane on 30 August, saying he had completed the translation and sent it to Wilde at Dinard. OW wrote to LAD on 9 September, following his return from France, saying that LAD should expect proofs soon. There is no hint of a dispute – suggesting that either OW had not yet read the translation, or (perhaps) that he had read it, correct-

ed it, passed on to Lane, and was hoping that Douglas would simply accept any corrections that he had made. See OET V, 662ff. Donohue (OET V, 672–3) feels that LAD's claim that Beardsley attempted a translation is 'questionable' given some of the other – patently untrue – statements he made in the same note (i.e. that OW had originally written the play in English, and then translated it into French with the assistance of Louÿs and Gide). But the idea of a Beardsley translation seems to me very plausible, given Beardsley's literary ambitions and linguistic ability. And there is no obvious motive for LAD to have invented it.

11 *CL*, 686; *The Sunday Times*, 6 August 1893, carried news of the play. OW's letter to George Alexander at *CL*, 582 (dated January 1894) should be re-dated accordingly.

12 McKenna, 269–70; George Ives Diary (Austin) 14 October 1893; OW had made the acquaintance of Ives the previous year (30 June 1892) at the meeting of the Authors' Club when he denounced the Censor's treatment of *Salomé*.

13 George Ives, Diary, 15 October 1893, 26 October 1893 (Austin); LAD to Charles Kains Jackson, 10 September 1893 (Clark).

14 McKenna, 354ff; twenty-five years after the event, Oscar Browning claimed that 'on Sunday [the boy] slept with Oscar'. And while this scenario is possible, it seems more likely that Wilde was not involved. Certainly he later reproached Douglas over the whole business in a manner that suggested he had no share in it. And Max Beerbohm's contemporaneous account of the affair does not implicate OW in the incident,

only in its aftermath. Oscar Browning to Frank Harris, 3 November 1919; *CL*, 694; Hart-Davis, ed., *Max Beerbohm's Letters to Reggie Turner*, 84.

15 *CL*, 575; McKenna, 362.

16 Lady Queensberry to LAD, in Ellmann 390–1; *CL*, 694; LAD to A. J. A. Symons, 24 August 1937 (Clark).

17 *NYT*, 18 September 1893; JFW to OW, 29 March 1894, in Tipper, *Oscar*; WCKW wrote two plays after his return from America. Nicoll's *History of English Drama 1660–1900* lists *The Dumb Princess*, a two-act piece performed on 17 January 1894 at Baskcome House, West Kensington, and *French Polish* (1895). Neither received any critical attention.

18 *CL*, 574, 576; Adela Schuster to OW, 26 November 1893 (Clark); Moyle 233–6.

19 Elisabeth Marbury to OW, 10 November [1893] (Clark); Elisabeth Marbury, *My Crystal Ball* (1923), 97–103, in Mikhail, 437–8.

20 *CL*, 574, 576, 578–9; LAD, *Autobiography* (1931 edition), 160n; LAD to John Lane, 16 November 1893 (Rosenbach Library, Philadelphia). Joseph Donohue (OET V, 674–5) points out that in the absence of the manuscript sent to the printers (T. and A. Constable) it is impossible to know how much of the published work was OW's and how much LAD's. Although LAD's pronouncements are often unreliable, on 6 July 1906 he did write to John Lane, who was planning to re-issue the play,

saying, 'I should think [my name] had better be omitted. I only translated it, as you will remember, to oblige Oscar Wilde, & he himself revised the translation to the extent of taking out from it most of the elements of original work on my part' (John Lane archive).

21 Frances Winwar, *Oscar Wilde and the Yellow Nineties* (1940), 214; H. Maas, J. L. Duncan & W. G. Good, *The Letters of Aubrey Beardsley*, 52, 58; Sturgis, *Aubrey Beardsley*, 158–61.

22 Carlos Blacker to Carrie Frost, 1 December 1893, quoted in Maguire, 33.

23 *CL*, 693–4. If OW's account is correct, it seems likely that the meeting between LAD and OW took place in Paris, with LAD en route to Egypt. Blacker's letters – at Maguire, 34 – make clear that OW remained in Paris until 4 December, while LAD's letter to Charles Kains Jackson, 29 November 1893 (Clark), ends 'I am very unhappy… I start Friday [1 December] at 11 in the morning. My address will be c/o Lord Cromer, British Agency, Cairo.'

24 *CL*, 578; Gertrude Pearce letter [906], in Ellmann, 389–90; George Ives Diary records meals and meetings on 8, 13, 17, 22 December; Emma Calvé, *My Life* (1922), 96–7.

25 RR to Adela Schuster, *CL*, 1229.

26 Maguire, 34.

27 *CL*, 578; Gertrude Pearce, in Ellmann, 389–90.

Chapter 4: Enemies of Romance

1 *CL*, 581; J. D. Murphy (Facebook) makes a convincing case that OW's original letter – though quoted by Harry Furniss in January 1894 – and reported in *Today* 13 January 1894, had been written in 1890.

See *St James's Gazette*, 14 May 1890.

2 *CL*, 585.

3 *CL*, 581.

4 *CL*, 625; Sturge Moore, ed., *Self-Portrait*, 124.

5　CL, 581–2; OW's plan for the final play in his 'triple bill' is unknown, but it may have been another quasi-biblical drama about Pharaoh and Moses. Ricketts recalled a conversation with OW (in 1895) about La Sainte Courtisane, which then leads to a discussion of Pharaoh, perhaps suggesting that, in his mind at least, the two were linked (Ricketts, 40). Guy & Small, 121, suggest that LWF was intended to be part of OW's triple bill – assuming the three plays were to played on separate nights, but this seems unlikely. Triple bills of short plays – all played as part of single evening programme – were a popular feature of the late Victorian theatre. One of the most successful had been launched in 1891 by Brandon Thomas, comprising his own Lancashire Sailor, Weedon Grossmith's A Commission and Cecil Clay's A Pantomime Rehearsal.

6　The scenario (Clark) is printed in Mason, 383–5; CL, 589. OW had been nurturing a connection with Mansfield for some time; see Richard Mansfield to OW, 10 August 1888 (Austin), thanking him for his 'kind letter'.

7　CL, 588; Among those threatening legal action were Rooper & Whately, of 17 Lincoln's Inn Fields, who wrote to OW on 17 February 1894 regarding his overdue account with Powell Turner & Co. – for £14 4s 10d – requesting settlement by Wednesday or proceedings will be started (Clark); writ dated 30 May 1894 for Peter Robinson (of 216 Oxford Street) against Oscar Wilde, for £30 3s 7d, for drapery, hosiery and millinery goods (plus £3 3s costs) (Washington). OW to 'Dear Sir' [26 April 1894] (BL, RP 6688) re. Goring: 'I don't really knw what I owe you – as I have lost yr account... I enclose a chque for £13 which I think is what

I owe you.' 'Theatrical Mems', Bristol Mercury and Daily Post, 27 March 1894.

8　Saturday Review, 24 March 1894, 317–18; S. Weintraub, Aubrey Beardsley (1976), 56; R. Ross, quoted in Sutton, ed., Letters of Roger Fry, 21: '[OW] loathed the drawings to Salomé but dared not say so'; CL, 587.

9　Sturgis, Aubrey Beardsley, 160; Ada Leverson, 'The Last First Night', Criterion, January 1926, in Mikhail, 270; LAD, Oscar Wilde and Myself, 60: Harris, 76.

10　A. Beardsley to the editor of the Daily Chronicle, 1 March 1894, in H. Maas, J. L. Duncan and W. G. Good, The Letters of Aubrey Beardsley (1970), 65; Harris, 75.

11　CL, 390; 577; F. C. Burnand to Ada Leverson, 2 April 1894 (Clark); Speedie, Wonderful Sphinx, 63.

12　CL, 695–6; Hyde, LAD, 51–2; CL, 621.

13　LAD to Charles Kains Jackson, 30 March 1894 (Clark), ends 'I am going to Constantinople this June for many months'; CL, 696; MQ to LAD, 1 April 1894, in Ellmann, 394; Moyle, 236–7.

14　Croft-Cooke, Bosie, 97–8; James Wallis to H. M. Hyde, 10 August 1948; the song had been written by OW's friend Corney Grain.

15　Linda Stratmann, The Marquess of Queensberry (2013), 178: the examination took place on 10 April 1894. CL, 588–9; LAD to Charles Kains Jackson 9 April 1894 (Clark). LAD departed on Saturday (14 April).

16　CL, 588, 589; see also Ricketts, 52, for further comments by OW; The Critic (US), quoted in Karl Beckson, Aesthetes and Decadents (2005), i.

17　Some twelve months later the Era printed a paragraph saying 'It has come out that Mr Hare refused An Ideal Husband after reading the piece, and paid Mr Oscar Wilde £100 for so doing' ('Theatrical Gossip', Era, 30 March 1895). This may be the root of the oft-

repeated claim that Hare turned down the play because he disliked the last act (see *CL*, 578). But, as Guy & Small, 123, point out, this is not supported by Hare's letter to OW, in which the only problem indicated seems to be about scheduling the play. And the notion that Hare's reservations were technical and contingent – rather than aesthetic and absolute – is also suggested by a letter from OW to 'Harry' [Morrell] on Albemarle Club letterhead: 'Will you *wire* to Waller at Brighton to say that Hare's definite decision cannot be obtained till Thursday at 12 o'clock. Therefore he need not come up Tomorrow as I can do nothing' (TCD). Contract for *AIH* between OW and Waller and Morrell, 20 April 1894, for 'sole English and Australian rights' (Clark); it specified that OW was to be consulted about the cast, and that OW 'would object' to the play being put on at the Avenue Theatre, but not the Trafalgar, the Shaftesbury or the Court. The financial arrangement involved with Hare is unknown. OW had had a 'contract' with Hare to write the play (*CL*, 686) which would certainly have included an advance against royalties, and maybe – as indicated in the *Era* – OW was able to retain at least some of the money. But it is likely he would have had to repay something when he took back his manuscript. There is a letter from a Mr Matthews to OW, 7 June 1894 (Clark), on Garrick Theatre letterhead, thanking him for his 'cheque' and wishing his play 'every success'. OW would have been able to write such a cheque having received monies from Waller and Morrell. The new arrangement, though not officially announced, was common theatrical gossip that May. See William

Archer to OW, 29 May 1894 (Austin). Elisabeth Marbury to OW, 9 July 1894 (Clark), mentions OW having already received £300 from Frohman for the US performing rights and being due to receive a further £300 after he has made 'changes and improvements in the MS… to his satisfaction'.

18 Niederauer and Broche, eds, *Henri de Régnier*, 386.

19 Barbara Strachey and Jayne Samuels, eds, *Mary Berenson: A Self-Portrait from her Diaries and Letters* (1983), 55–6.

20 Samuels, *Bernard Berenson*, 218; Bernard Berenson, *Sunset & Twilight* (1964), 320; this also corrects Ugo Ojetti's mis-quoting of OW's remark in his diary ('I am a Christian, and like Christ will speak evil of no one'). Freya Stark (a friend of Berenson's) gives another variant: 'I am like God in every way and must have constant praise.' *Freya Stark: Selected Letters* (1988), 283.

21 Felix Mansfield to OW, 22 May 1894 (Clark).

22 André Gide to H. de Régnier, [30 May 1894], in D. J. Niederauer and H. Franklyn, *Correspondance (1891–1911) André Gide, Henri de Régnier* (1997), 139–141; LAD, *Autobiography*, 87–9.

23 Mason, 392–4; O'Sullivan, 217; 'Mr Oscar Wilde and Edgar Poe', *Daily News*, 11 June 1894; *PMB*, 21 June 1894; *Athenaeum*, 25 August 1894; *PMG*, 9 July 1894; *Punch*, 21 July 1894. *CL*, 593.

24 John Boon, *Victorians, Edwardians and Georgians* (1929), 1:200–1; Harris, 108; Melville, 243.

25 Hugh and Mirabel Cecil, *Imperial Marriage* (2002), 74; *Morning Post*, 26 July 1894; Blunt, *My Diaries, Part One*, 177–9.

26 Stratmann, *Marquess of Queensberry*, 182–4; *CL*, 708, Harris, 101; MQ to Lady Douglas [Minnie], 18 February [1895] (BL).

Chapter 5: Scarlet Marquess

1 Holland, 56–9; The second 'gentleman' has often been referred to as a 'boxer' or 'rough'; in the press reports of OW's trial he is referred to as 'Mr Pip' – suggesting perhaps a reference to Dickens's *Great Expectations*. But the full trial transcript (in Holland, 57) records OW saying, '[the gentleman] was introduced to me by Lord Queensberry as a Mr Pape, as well as I remember that is the name'. Edward James Pape, a property dealer of Portland Place (Stratmann, *Marquess of Queensberry*, 162), was one of Queensberry's confidants. MQ to Alfred Montgomery, in Hyde, *Trials*, 154–5.

2 *CL*, 708; Hyde, *Trials*, 154–5.

3 *CL*, 763, McKenna, 387–8.

4 George Lewis to OW, 7 July 1894 (Austin).

5 C. O. Humphreys to MQ, 11 July 1894, in Hyde, *Trials*, 162.

6 MQ to H. O. Humphreys, 13 July 1894, in Hyde, *Trials*, 162–3; MQ witness statement 1895, in McKenna, 388.

7 Hyde, *Trials*, 162.

8 MQ to H. O. Humphreys, 18 July [1894], in Hyde, *Trials*, 163: *CL*, 708.

9 LAD to Percy Douglas, 19 August 1894, in Stratmann, *Marquess of Queensberry*, 190.

10 Harris, 101; not the Pelican Club, which closed in 1891, re-emerging as the National Sporting Club. Boyd, *A Pelican's Tale*, 95; Boon, *Victorians, Edwardians and Georgians*, 1:200–1; Harris, 99.

11 *CL*, 598, 708.

12 Hyde, *Trials*, 154.

13 *CL*, 589; Harris, 101–2.

14 *CL*, 594.

15 *CL*, 708; LAD to Percy Douglas, 19 August 1894, in Stratmann, *Marquess of Queensberry*, 190.

16 *CL*, 594–5; Longford, *A Pilgrimage of Passion*, 307. The visit was in mid-August.

17 *CL*, 594; O'Sullivan, 35.

18 *CL*, 594.

19 Melville, 246–9; Moyle, 212.

Chapter 6: A Capacity for Being Amused

1 *CL*, 598; LAD to James Agate, 18 November 1940, quoted in James Agate, *The Selective Ego* (1976), 54: LAD gives himself the credit, saying, '[OW] originally planned [it] to be an eighteenth-century play... Oscar told me the idea of the play two or three times before he wrote it. I suggested that it would be much better to make it modern, and he said, "I believe you are perfectly right," and he adopted my suggestion.' Interestingly, Charles Frohman, in a letter to OW (2 March 1893) at Clark, asked for 'a modern *School for Scandal* style of play'.

2 *CL*, 595–7.

3 Moyle, 243; Antony Edmonds, 'Alphonse Conway – the "Bright Happy Boy" of 1894', *Wildean*, 38 (2011), 20–3; LAD to A. J. A. Symons, 8 October 1935 (Clark). Edmonds integrated and expanded his articles on OW at Worthing in his book, *Oscar Wilde's Scandalous Summer* (2014).

4 CMW to Arthur Humphreys, 1 June 1894 (BL); CMW to Arthur Humphreys, 11 August 1894 (BL); CMW to Arthur Humphreys, 22 October 1894 (Clark). See also Antony Edmonds, 'Constance Wilde at Worthing',

Wildean 42 (2013), 18ff.

5   CL, 598–9; Ellmann, 241; Agate, The
    Selective Ego, 54; R. Mangan, ed.,
    Gielgud's Letters (2004), 53; Antony
    Edmonds, 'Chronology of Oscar Wilde
    in Worthing in 1894', Wildean, 43
    (2013), 108–9.

6   V. Holland, Son of Oscar Wilde,
    43; Moyle, 246; quoted in Antony
    Edmonds, Oscar Wilde's Scandalous Sum-
    mer (2014), 170, 13.

7   CL, 715.

8   Edmonds, 'Alphonse Conway', 30–4.
    Conway was born on 10 July 1878, so
    was just sixteen when OW met him,
    not 'fifteen' as in McKenna, 402, nor
    'about eighteen', as OW claimed in
    court. CMW to Otho Lloyd, 31 August
    1894, in Moyle, 247.

9   Edmonds, 'Alphonse Conway', 27.

10 Alphonse Conway witness statement,
    quoted in McKenna, 402; the 'witness
    statements' were intended to focus on
    OW, and to exclude references to LAD.

11 CL, 603; McKenna 410.

12 CL, 610. The chronology of OW's let-
    ters to G. Alexander and LAD from
    Worthing (CL, 598–610) is certainly
    incorrect. They should, I think, be re-
    ordered: (1) OW to G. Alexander, CL,
    610; (2) OW to LAD [8 September],
    CL, 607–8; (3) OW to LAD (not 13
    August, but 10 September, as convinc-
    ingly re-dated by Antony Edmonds,
    in 'Bosie's Visits to Worthing 1894',
    Wildean, 39 (2011), 26ff); (4) OW to G.
    Alexander, CL, 599–600. I have based
    the narrative of the following para-
    graphs on that re-ordering.

13 CL, 607, OW had first made these
    points about America in his letter at CL,
    610; and surely reiterated them up in
    London.

14 CL, 599–600.

15 CL, 602, 'Mr Oscar Wilde on Mr Oscar
    Wilde', St James's Gazette, 18 January
    1895, in Mikhail, 250.

16 John Gambril Nicholson, Love in Earnest
    (1892); the sonnet 'Of Boy's Names'
    contains the line 'Tis Ernest sets my
    heart aflame.' The notion, however,
    that 'Earnest' was a contemporary
    code-word for homosexual is not
    supported by any evidence, and was
    emphatically rejected by John Gielgud,
    who – as he said – 'would have known'
    (The Times, 2 February 2001, 19); in the
    printed version of the play the address
    was changed to 'B.4.'

17 Geoff Dibb, 'Oscar Wilde and the
    Cardew Family', Wildean, 33 (2008),
    2–12: both Arthur and Herbert Cardew
    were contemporaries of OW at Mag-
    dalen. Their elder brother, Philip, had
    a daughter Cicely (not Cecily) Cardew,
    born on 2 May 1893. OW was charmed
    by the sound of her name.

18 There was a well-connected Bunbury
    family from Ireland, who were known
    to the Wildes (Henry S. Bunbury wrote
    to OW to congratulate him on win-
    ning the Newdigate). But there seems
    to be little to connect them with the
    character in OW's play. The writer and
    occultist Aleister Crowley claimed in
    1913 that the name was a portmanteau
    of Banbury and Sunbury, concocted by
    OW after he had met a good-looking
    schoolboy on a train going to the for-
    mer place, and then arranged an as-
    signation with him at the latter. But,
    although, Crowley did meet OW, he
    is a notoriously unreliable witness. T.
    d'Arch Smith, Bunbury: Two Notes on Os-
    car Wilde (1998).

19 CL, 602, 610; as a process in the com-
    position OW had a first draft of the
    play typed up around the middle of
    the month. The draft is stamped 19
    September, most probably the date
    the work was completed, rather than
    when the ms was handed in. Edmonds,
    'Chronology of Oscar Wilde in Worth-
    ing', 110.

20 A. Edmonds 'Constance Wilde at Worthing', *Wildean* 43 (2013), 46; *CL*, 607; Moyle, 239; J. H. Badley to OW, 15 September 1894 (Clark), thanking him for the cheque, agreeing with OW about 'the power of reading and writing English well being of far more importance than the acquirement of information', and approving OW's proposal to let Cyril bring OW's 'Canadian canoe' to school.

21 The 'Venetian Fete' was held on the evening of Thursday, 13 September. *Worthing Gazette*, 19 September 1894, in Antony Edmonds, 'Wilde and the Worthing "Festivals"', *Wildean*, 40 (2012), 28–9.

22 *CL*, 607.

23 *CL*, 615.

24 *CL*, 615.

25 LAD to Hesketh Pearson, 13 Nov 1944 (Austin); *CL*, 615; John St John, *William Heinemann: A Century of Publishing* (1990).

26 *CL*, 617; Beckson, 124.

27 Harris, 107; LAD to Hesketh Pearson, 13 Nov 1944 (Austin).

28 *CL*, 607. Edmonds, 'Chronology of Oscar Wilde in Worthing', 110–11; A. Conway witness statement, in McKenna, 402.

29 Holland, 146–51; A. Conway witness statement, in McKenna, 403.

30 *CL*, 697.

31 *CL*, 618, 696–8.

32 *CL*, 710.

33 MQ to Alfred Montgomery, 1 November 1894, quoted (in slightly different transcriptions), in Stratmann, *Marquess of Queensberry*, 201–2, and Ellmann, 402.

34 National Archives J77/532/16267/1, quoted in Stratmann, *Marquess of Queensberry*, 184.

35 James Lees-Milne, *The Enigmatic Edwardian* (1986), 99; McKenna, 334–5, 426.

36 MQ to Lady Douglas (Percy's wife), 12 May 1895 (BL); Matt Cook, *London and the Culture of Homosexuality* (2003), 191; *CL*, 618; the debate was occasioned by Grant Allen's article in the *Fortnightly Review* on 'The New Hedonism', calling for personal liberty in heterosexual relationships.

37 *CL*, 625; Jack Bloxam to Kains Jackson, 19 November 1894. Bloxam credited Ives with suggesting the 'very good' title. It related, perhaps, to a passage in *The Green Carnation* in which Lord Reggie is described as 'one of the most utterly vicious young men of the day… because, like the chameleon, he takes his colour from whatever he rests upon, or is put near. And he has been put near scarlet instead of white.'

38 *CL*, 623.

39 Guy & Small, 129–30.

40 Julia Neilson, *This For Remembrance* (1940), 139–40, in Mikhail, 243–4; CMW to Lady Mount Temple, 8 December 1894, in Moyle 252.

41 Florence Waller to OW, 11 December 1894 (Clark); Pearson, 246; Gilbert Burgess, 'An Ideal Husband at the Haymarket Theatre: A Talk with Mr. Oscar Wilde', *Sketch*, 9 January 1895, in Mikhail, 242.

42 Pearson, 246–7.

Part VIII: *The House of Judgement*
Chapter 1: The Last First Nights

1 'London Correspondence', *Freeman's Journal*, 27 May 1895; G. B. Shaw to Golding Bright, 30 January 1895, in Laurence, ed., *Bernard Shaw Collected*

Letters, Vol. 1, *1874–1897*, 480. Shaw excused OW's words with the suggestion that it was 'an Irishman's way of giving all credit to the actors and effacing his own claims as author'.

2   *Saturday Review*, 12 January 1895.

3   Ian [Forbes] Robertson to OW, 13 January 1895 (Clark).

4   'Mr. Oscar Wilde on Mr. Oscar Wilde', *St James's Gazette*, 18 January 1895, in Mikhail, 246–50.

5   Conan Doyle, *Memories and Adventures*, 79. Conan Doyle describes the incident as happening 'many years' after his first meeting with OW in 1889.

6   Burgess, 'An Ideal Husband at the Haymarket Theatre', in Mikhail, 239–44; 'Mr. Oscar Wilde on Mr. Oscar Wilde', *St James's Gazette*, 18 January 1895, in Mikhail, 246–50.

7   Burgess, 'An Ideal Husband at the Haymarket Theatre', in Mikhail, 241.

8   Moyle, 253. CMW seems to have gone to Babbacombe in the first week of February 1895.

9   Guy & Small, 130.

10 Guy & Small, 256.

11 Val Gielgud, *Years in a Mirror* (1965), 178.

12 G. Alexander to C. O. Humphreys, Son & Kershaw, 12 September 1895.

13 Guy & Small, 255 *CL*, 629.

14 Donald Sinden, 'Diversions and Digressions', *Wildean*, 16 (2000), 13–14, quoting Joan Benham, daughter of the stage manager at the St James's Theatre.

15 *CL*, 629.

16 *CL*, 629.

17 A. Gide, 'Oscar Wilde: In Memoriam', in Mikhail, 296.

18 Mikhail, 297 4n.

19 André Gide to his mother, in Jonathan Fryer, *André & Oscar* (1997), 115.

20 André Gide to his mother, in Jonathan Fryer, *André & Oscar* (1997), 115.

21 Gide, 'Oscar Wilde: in Memoriam', in Mikhail, 296.

22 *CL*, 632; Francis Douglas, *Oscar Wilde and the Black Douglas* (1949), 41. It was Algy Bourke, a 'cousin' of the Douglases, who had got wind of Queensberry's planned outrage; the news was passed on to Wilde by Percy Douglas.

23 *CL*, 631.

24 Leverson, 'The Last First Night', in Mikhail, 267, mentions OW arriving 'with his pretty wife'; others present included the recently knighted Sir George Lewis, Lord Hothfield, Mr and Mrs Bancroft, Mr Stuart Ogilvie, Mr Inderwick QC, Judge Baon and Mrs Bernard Beere. *Leeds Mercury*, 15 February 1895.

25 Irene Vanbrugh, *To Tell My Story* (1948), 33–5, in Mikhail, 265.

26 Leverson, 'The Last First Night', in Mikhail, 267–70; 'The Drama', *Daily News*, 15 February 1895.

27 *CL*, 729.

28 A. E. W. Mason, *Sir George Alexander & the St James' Theatre* (1935), 79.

29 *CL*, 632.

30 *CL*, 709.

31 *CL*, 795–6.

32 *CL*, 633; the first week's receipts for *IBE* came to £903 14s; OW, due 10 per cent of the weekly gross (up to £1,000, and 15 per cent thereafter) would receive £90 7s 6d.

33 Holland, 46: OW, when asked on 3 April whether the play was 'in rehearsal now', replied: 'I don't know that it is actually in rehearsal, Madame Sarah Bernhardt promised to produce it before the middle of May.' Although Holland (307 n94) doubts the truth of OW's statement, it is confirmed by a letter from Mrs Enid Lambart (née Spencer-Brunton) to A. J. A. Symons, 11 July 1931 (Clark) in which

she mentions that she possesses a letter from OW written from Holloway (i.e. 5 April – 7 May 1895) mentioning an aborted production of *Salomé* with Sarah Bernhardt. Bernhardt's plans were perhaps prompted by a successful dance version of the story performed by Loie Fuller, which had opened at the Comédie Parisienne on 4 March.

34 *CL*, 796.

35 C. O. Humphreys & Co. to OW, 28 February 1895 (Clark).

Chapter 2: Hideous Words

1 Ricketts, 39–43.

2 *CL*, 634.

3 *CL*, 633. OW's letter to CMW is undated, but – like the letter to Ross – was written in pencil on Hotel Avondale paper. And it has been plausibly assumed to relate to this crisis. It proposes a meeting 'at nine' – although whether this was nine in the evening (as is generally assumed), or in the morning, is not made clear.

4 Moyle, 229. Moyle suggests that CMW's comments about praying for her boys does indicate knowledge of OW's relationship with Douglas. But against this must be set her readiness to allow her relatives to lend money to OW to support his libel action – which must have been based on a belief in his innocence.

5 *CL*, 634, 796.

6 *CL*, 634, 796; Ross – in his 1914 'Statement', prepared for his libel case v. Crosland (Clark) – when he was anxious to blame Douglas for encouraging the ill-fated action, suggested that he counselled caution; but there is nothing in the contemporary record to suggest this.

7 Hyde, *Oscar*, 253.

8 *CL*, 796, 635; LAD to Percy Douglas [25 March 1895] (BL) confirms that Percy had offered only to pay 'half' the probable expenses, estimated at 'about £500'.

9 Holland, 4; it seems that, even here,

Queensberry may have been misquoting himself. Although his handwriting is barely legibly it can, more credibly, be read as 'For Oscar Wilde / posing somdomite' – rather than 'posing as somdomite'.

10 Holland, 22; *New York Herald*, 3 March 1895, in McKenna, 343.

11 Marjoribanks, *Life of Lord Carson*, 202.

12 LAD to F. Harris, 30 April 1925 (Austin); *CL*, 633; LAD to Percy Douglas 25 [March 1895] (BL), mentions OW raising £800 'by sacrificing property worth about £3,000'.

13 Holland, 9–22, xxiii; A. H. Robins, *Oscar Wilde: The Great Drama of His Life* (2011), 17; *PMG*, 9 March 1895; MQ to Lady Douglas, 11 March [1895] (BL). The magistrate's decision was formally confirmed when a grand jury returned a True Bill against Queensberry on 25 March; see *PMG*, 25 March 1895.

14 Holland, 285.

15 LAD to Percy Douglas, 11 March 1895 (BL).

16 Arthur Humphreys to OW, 11 March [1895] (MSL/Delaware).

17 Maguire, 65; on 1 March OW raised £10 2s 6d; *CL*, 690–1.

18 *CL*, 635; LAD to Percy Douglas, 25 March 1895 (BL).

19 Hyde, *Trials*, 346–51.

20 MQ to Minnie Douglas, 11 March 1895 (BL); MQ, enraged at Percy publicly siding with OW and LAD, began

bombarding first him, then his wife, and finally their solicitor, with letters outlining his suspicions and findings, in the hope that he might change Percy's position. And it seems probable that Percy would have passed on this information to OW and LAD. It is likely that MQ's attention had been drawn to *The Chameleon* by an article in Jerome K. Jerome's magazine, *To-Day*, which demanded its withdrawal from circulation. OW (as represented in *The Green Carnation*) was supposed to have offended Jerome by describing his writings as 'vulgar without being funny'. Anon., *Oscar Wilde: Three Times Tried*, 175.

21   MQ to Minnie Douglas, 26 February 1895 (BL).

22   Robins, *Oscar Wilde: The Great Drama of His Life*, 17, makes the telling observation about the costs involved; Harris, 113–17; the date of the lunch is conjectural. It was on a Monday shortly before the trial, and it was certainly not Monday 1 April, as Harris, 119, suggests that news of Queensberry's plea of justification followed some days after the encounter.

23   *CL*, 636.

24   *Northern Echo*, 26 March 1895; *PMG*, 28 March 1895.

25   Gladys Brooke (née Palmer), *Relations and Complications* (1929), 3–4: she recalled, as a child, hearing OW asking her father in a voice 'full of anguish', 'Oh, Walter, Walter! I ask you as man to man to lend me four hundred pounds for my trial.' It seems unlikely that he did. Nevertheless Gladys states that her parents helped OW 'both financially and morally during his trial'.

26   Moyle, 262.

27   Hyde, *Trials*, 33–4; Marjoribanks, *Life of Lord Carson*, 201; OW's letter had, apparently, come into Queensberry's hands via a blackmailing solicitor called Bernard Abrahams. [I. Playfair, *Some Gentle Criticisms of British Justice*, (1895); McKenna, 468–70.

28   Reginald Turner to G. F. Renier, 22 March 1933 (Clark).

29   Robins, 18.

30   *CL*, 759.

31   Pearson, 288; that afternoon CMW had hosted an 'at home' at Tite Street. Only a handful of people had called. It was noticed that she seemed 'depressed and distracted', Moyle, 261.

32   Holland, 251; Hyde, *Trials*, 61.

Chapter 3: The Prosecutor

1   Holland, xxvii; *PMG*, 3 May 1895. In the 1890s there were four courtrooms in the Central Criminal Court (the old building has since been demolished and replaced). It does not seem to be recorded which courtroom Wilde appeared in.

2   *PMG*, 3 April 1895.

3   Holland, 52ff; *Western Mail*, 4 April, 1895.

4   Travers Humphreys, Foreword to Hyde, *Trials*, 8.

5   Holland, 104–5.

6   'Silk and Stuff', *PMG*, 4 April 1895; *Daily Chronicle*, 4 April 1895, in Holland, xxviii.

7   Holland, 115; 134; 144.

8   Holland, 134, 138–9, 146, 116–18.

9   'Our London Letter', *Dundee Courier & Argus*, 4 April 1895.

10   Hyde, *Trials*, 51; Holland 152–6.

11   Holland, 207–9, 321; Hyde, *Trials*, 150.

12   Sherard, *Life*, 115–16.

13   *Sun*, 4 April, 1895, quoted in Holland, 322.

14 Hyde, *Trials*, 53.

15 Holland, 271; Hyde, *Trials*, 55; 178, 269.

16 *CL*, 636, dates the telegram to '3 April 1895', but the original – at the Houghton Library at Harvard – while imperfectly stamped, shows a date of '4 April' and a time of '4.21 p.m.'; the court rose at 4.20 on the afternoon of Thursday 4 April, so it may be that the telegram was dispatched by Bosie (or another) on OW's instructions.

17 Hyde, *Trials*, 55–6.

18 C. H. Norman, quoted in Holland, xxxix; George Bernard Shaw to LAD, 12 August 1938, in Mary Hyde, ed., *Bernard Shaw and Alfred Douglas: A Correspondence* (1982), 87.

19 *Northern Echo*, 6 April 1895, describes (quoting the first-hand observation of the *Star* reporter), how OW left the Old Bailey just after the verdict had been delivered. 'His brougham was waiting, and he stepped rapidly into it, calling to the coachman to drive to the Holborn Viaduct Hotel. Before the carriage had stopped at the door of the hotel he thrust his arm and a gold-headed cane out of the window, and signaling to a man who stood there, apparently waiting, hoarsely cried, "The verdict is not guilty!" they entered the hotel together, and shortly afterwards Lord Alfred Douglas was also seen to go into the hotel.' 'Within half an hour' of OW's arrival at the hotel, several gentlemen arrived hurriedly, and were conducted at once to the rooms which have been reserved for Mr Wilde since Thursday.' ('Arrest of Oscar Wilde', *Western Mail*, 6 April 1895). The *Leeds Mercury*, 6 April 1895, reported that 'the party remained in earnest conference in a private room until one o'clock, when they partook of luncheon, at which much wine was drunk'. The paper described one of the men as 'a lawyer': Turner was a qualified barrister.

Chapter 4: Regina Versus Wilde

1 Hyde, *Trials*; the letter was sent at two o'clock that afternoon.

2 Anon., *Oscar Wilde: Three Times Tried*, 129.

3 'A Society Scandal', *Northern Echo*, 6 April 1895; MQ later clarified that his message, sent before the end of the trial, had not said he 'would shoot Mr. Wilde', only that, if OW 'persuaded his misguided son to go with him he would feel quite justified in following him (Wilde) and shooting him, did he feel inclined to do so, and were he worth the trouble'.

4 *New York Herald*, 6 April, 1895, in McKenna, 507.

5 Although it was reported in the press that, after leaving the court, 'He appears... to have been so carefully shadowed by detectives that he had no chance of flight', most of those shadowing him seem to have been newspaper reporters ('London Letter,' *Western Mail*, 6 April 1895; Borland, *Wilde's Devoted Friend*, 45). A police source later claimed that they had been reluctant to act: 'We couldn't help ourselves. Scotland Yard knew all that Lord Queensberry could tell long before, but we never move in such cases unless obliged.' 'Why?' 'Well, experience has taught us prosecutions of a certain character do far more harm than good. They are in effect suggestive instead of deterrent.' *Evening News* (Sydney), 12 February 1896.

6   CL, 642.

7   Ransome, 18.

8   Hyde, Trials, 58.

9   Northern Echo, 6 April 1895; 'Our Lon-
    don Letter', Belfast News-Letter, 6 April
    1895.

10 Moyle, 266; Hyde, Trials, 59–60; Hyde
    mentions 'hock-and-seltzer'; the acc-
    ount in To-day refers to 'a spirit decanter
    on the table', from which OW helped
    himself, and an empty 'soda-water
    bottle' (quoted in the Broadford Courier
    and Reedy Creek Times (Broadford,
    Victoria), 7 June 1895).

11 Hyde, Trials, 60; Holland, xxxi.

12 Anon., Oscar Wilde: Three Times Tried,
    167; More Adey to [Unknown], June
    1895, draft letter (Clark) mentions wit-
    ness payments; Ellmann, 447.

13 Reynolds's Newspaper, 7 April 1895.

14 Hyde, Trials, 63–4; Jane Cotta [sic]
    witness statement, quoted in McKenna,
    295. In the trial transcripts the cham-
    bermaid's name is given as Jane Cotter.

15 Holland, xxxix; LAD to George
    Bernard Shaw, 22 August 1938 (BL),
    states Clarke's 'conscience reproached
    him' over the advice he had given OW;
    contemporary press opinion seems to
    support the notion: 'no counsel ever
    committed a grosser or more inex-
    plicable error of judgement, from
    his client's point of view, than did Sir
    Edward Clarke when he accepted a ver-
    dict in the Queensberry trial. There was
    nothing to gain and everything to lose
    – as has been proved – by Sir Edward
    Clarke's action. In all probability Lord
    Queensberry would have got a verdict
    anyhow, but a verdict secured in face of
    the unbroken denials of Wilde would
    have been a different matter for a
    verdict obtained on his own admission
    of the truth of Lord Queensberry's
    charge. That fatal admission made on
    the astounding advice of Sir Edward

Clarke dogged his wretched client
through all the subsequent proceedings and minimized to the last degree
his chance of escape. Sir Edward
Clarke tied a millstone round his
unfortunate client's neck.' 'London
Correspondence', Freeman's Journal, 27
May 1895.

16 LAD, Autobiography, 119–20; Anon.,
    Oscar Wilde: Three Times Tried, 156.

17 New York Herald, in Hyde, Oscar, 292.

18 George Wyndham to Percy Wynd-
    ham, 7 April 1895, in Hyde, Oscar, 296.

19 Harris, 218.

20 Illustrated Police News, 20 April 1895.

21 'The Oscar Wilde Case', Western Mail
    (Cardiff), 2 May 1895.

22 Lucien Pissarro to Camille Pissarro, 16
    April 1895, in Thorold, ed., The Letters
    of Lucien to Camille Pissarro, 421.

23 National Observer, 6 April 1895; Henley
    was no longer editor of the paper; he
    had been replaced by James Edmund
    Vincent in 1894.

24 John Stokes, In the Nineties (1989), 14.

25 J. Lewis May, John Lane and the Nineties
    (1936), 89.

26 Anon., Oscar Wilde: Three Times Tried,
    178.

27 W. E. Henley to C. Whibley, 19 April,
    1895: 'Bobbie [Ross] has been sub-
    poenaed: with a view to obliging him
    to clear. But he is impudent – and
    quixotic – enough for anything.' In
    John Connell, W. E. Henley (1949), 300.
    Ross, in his 1914 'Statement' (Clark)
    says he was subpoenaed in connection
    with the Queensberry libel trial, but
    Henley's contemporaneous letter
    indicates that it was in relation to
    OW's first criminal trial.

28 W. B. Yeats, Autobiographies (1938), 226.

29 CL, 641.

30 CL, 642.

31 CL, 646.

32 CL, 651–2.

33 George Wyndham to Percy Wyndham, 7 April 1895, in Hyde, *Oscar*, 295–6: 'I know on the authority of Arthur Balfour, who has been told the case by lawyers who had all the papers, that W[ilde] is certain to be condemned... There is no case against Bosie.'

34 Charles Gill to Hamilton Cuffe, 19 April 1895; Hamilton Cuffe to C. S. Murdoch, 20 April 1895, in Holland, 294–6.

35 Philip Burne-Jones to CMW, 11 April 1895, in Moyle, 271. P. Burne-Jones was passing on advice from George Lewis. CMW went down to Babbacombe on 19 April.

36 *CL*, 646.

37 Elisabeth Marbury to OW, 15 March 1895 (Clark), 'the outlook is encouraging' (for *AIH*); *Leeds Mercury*, 8 April 1895: 'The directors of the Lyceum Theatre [New York] have decided to discontinue the performance of Oscar Wilde's play, *An Ideal Husband*, after this week'; Beckson, *Oscar Wilde Encyclopedia*, 154.

38 *CL*, 643, Mrs Enid Lambart (née Spencer-Brunton) to A. J. A. Symons, 11 July 1931 (Clark).

39 Donald Mead, 'The Pillage of the House Beautiful', *Wildean*, 47 (2015), 38–55; 'Oscar Wilde's Goods', *Weekly Standard and Express* (Blackburn), 27 April 1895; *PMG*, 25 April 1895; 'Sale of Oscar Wilde's Effects', *Newcastle Morning Herald* (New South Wales), 4 June 1895. The price of Carlyle's writing desk is variously given by the different papers as £14, 14 guineas, and 'fourteen and half guineas'.

40 Hyde, *LAD*, 85; LAD to More Adey, 27 September 1896 (Clark).

41 *CL*, 647.

42 Hyde, *Oscar*, 323.

43 Hyde, *Oscar*, 321–2, 339.

44 Hyde, *Oscar*, 325.

45 Anon., *Oscar Wilde: Three Times Tried*, 272.

46 Max Beerbohm to R. Turner, 3 May 1895, in Hart-Davis, ed., *Max Beerbohm's Letters to Reggie Turner*, 102.

47 Hyde, *Trials*, 239.

48 Anon., *Oscar Wilde: Three Times Tried*, 291; Hyde, *Oscar*, 336.

49 *CL*, 646.

50 'The Oscar Wilde Case', *Hampshire Telegraph*, 4 May 1895.

51 William Archer to Charles Archer, 1 May 1895: 'This infernal Oscar Wilde business, which by the way will be over today. I'm afraid Oscar hasn't the ghost of a chance' (Charles Archer, *William Archer* (1931), 215); *Freeman's Journal*, 2 May 1895: 'Those who had heard the judge's charge were not unprepared for such an unsatisfactory result of a highly unsavoury case.' 'The Oscar Wilde Case', *Western Mail*, 2 May 1895.

52 Max Beerbohm to R. Turner, 3 May 1895, in Hart-Davis, ed., *Max Beerbohm's Letters to Reggie Turner*, 102–3.

53 *Belfast News-Letter*, 2 May 1895.

54 Hyde, *Trials*, 268–9; Hyde, *Oscar*, 343.

Chapter 5: The Torrent of Prejudice

1 *Freeman's Journal*, 2 May 1895; *Hampshire Advertiser*, 4 May 1895; T. M. Healy, *Letters and Leaders of My Day* (1928), 2: 416–17; H. M. Hyde, *The Life of Sir Edward Carson* (1953), 143; Schroeder, 169.

2 Sir Edward Hamilton (assistant financial secretary) diary, 21 May 1895, and 25 May 1895, in Michael S. Foldy, *The Trials of Oscar Wilde* (1997), 27; 'London Letter', *Western Mail*, 3 May 1895;

Reynolds's Newspaper, 5 May 1895; More Adey to [unknown], draft letter, from Rouen, June 1895 (Clark).

3   Sir Edward Hamilton (assistant financial secretary) diary, 21 May 1895, in Foldy, *The Trials of Oscar Wilde*, 27; Ellmann, 437; Max Beerbohm to R. Turner, 3 May 1895, in Hart-Davis, ed., *Max Beerbohm's Letters to Reggie Turner*, 102; McKenna, 529; *Freeman's Journal*, 27 May 1895; MQ to Minnie Douglas, 14 May 1895 (BL).

4   F. G. Bettany, *Stewart Headlam: A Biography* (1926), 130. Headlam told Bettany 'he consented to act because "a third party came to Selwyn Image, who was unable to take on the responsibility, and so I agreed to do so." Selwyn Images confirms this – and says the third party was a member of a City business firm [Ernest Leverson] who was debarred by the articles of his firm from going bail for anybody.' Image had no money, so asked Headlam, who consented. Leverson, however, gave the assurance that – in the event of a default – any liabilities would be covered by himself and other businessmen.

5   MQ to Stoneham, 9 May 1895; a telegram from MQ to Stoneham, 8 May 1895, runs: 'Unless I can get some assurance that Alfred is away and does not intend joining this fellow [OW] – shall keep hunting him and seeking from every Hotel as I did last night.' Stoneham, in his letter to MQ, 8 May 1895, refers to 'avoiding a repetition of the scene of last evening' (BL). Quite what the 'scene' involved is uncertain. But the colourful account, provided in Sherard, *Life*, of OW being pursued across town by a gang of Queensberry's hired thugs – who threatened to wreck any establishment that gave the poet shelter – is not supported by the contemporary reports. See Stratmann, *Marquess of Queensberry*, 243.

6   Sherard, *Life*, 358; *CL*, 649; *Goncourt Journal*, vol. 3, 1136. The information about JFW came from Sherard, via Léon Daudet.

7   George Ives Diary, 1895 (Austin): in a 'p.s. many years later' he recalled 'I hoped he would kill himself in the interval when he had the chance'; A. F. Tschiffely, *Don Roberto* (1937), 349; Connell, *W. E. Henley*, 301–2.

8   Harris, 168; Yeats, *Autobiographies*, 227; the 'rumour', reported by Yeats, that WCKW refused to 'sit at the same table' as his brother, and dined, instead, at a nearby restaurant – at Oscar's expense – are not supported by the first-hand accounts of Sherard and Frank Harris. R. H. Sherard to A. J. A. Symons, 8 June 1937 (Clark).

9   Sherard, *SUF*, 168–9; *CL*, 649–50.

10   Harris, 168; Yeats, *Autobiographies*, 227; LAD to OW, 15 May 1895, Hôtel des Deux Mondes, Paris: 'I hope you will join me next week' (Clark). Sherard, *Life*, 366; Ada Leverson, *Letters to the Sphinx.*, 41, Bettany, *Stewart Headlam*, 130: 'More than once [OW] said to me, "I have given my word to you and to my mother, and that is enough."'

11   *CL*, 652

12   Harris, 168; *CL*, 652; Harris, 81.

13   Leverson, *Letters to the Sphinx*, 41; George Lewis was acting as CMW's legal advisor, though her old family solicitor was Mr Hargrove.

14   W. B. Yeats to Professor Dowden, 19 May [1895] (Austin).

15   Frederick York Powell to More Adey, 29 April 1895 (Clark). Elizabeth Pennell to A. J. A. Symons, 26 August 1935 (Clark): JMW 'had no sympathy whatever with that [homosexual] side of Wilde – *indeed* I used to think he had a puritanical trait in him... Inher-

ited from his mother. But, though he spoke frankly to us, I never heard him say an unkind word on the subject to anyone else.'

16 Hyde, *Oscar*, 348, gives his age as seventy-seven (and this is often repeated); but Alfred Wills was born on 1 December 1828.

17 Maguire, 52.

18 *CL*, 827; *CL*, 814; Percy Douglas promised to repay half of this £150.

19 Anon., *Oscar Wilde: Three Times Tried*, 415.

20 'London Correspondence', *Freeman's Journal*, 27 May 1895.

21 Anon., *Oscar Wilde: Three Times Tried*, 373–7.

22 *Westminster Gazette*, quoted in *Yorkshire Herald*, 28 May 1895.

23 Anon., *Oscar Wilde: Three Times Tried*, 413.

24 Anon., *Oscar Wilde: Three Times Tried*, 433.

25 More Adey, to [unknown], draft letter, June 1895, Hôtel de la Poste, Rouen (Clark).

26 Anon., *Oscar Wilde: Three Times Tried*, 398.

27 'London Correspondence', *Freeman's Journal*, 27 May 1895.

28 *CL*, 872–8; although OW (*CL*, 814) denied this arrangement, Leverson's account seems the more reliable.

29 Sherard, *Life*, 367–8.

30 *CL*, 650; McKenna, 532, plausibly suggests that this letter was written on the night before the verdict in OW's second trial.

31 *CL*, 769.

32 Justice Charles, the judge in the first trial, declared privately that, if his jury had returned a verdict of guilty, he would have sentenced OW to only two months' imprisonment. Ricketts, 22.

33 Anon., *Oscar Wilde: Three Times Tried*, 463–4; Hyde, *Trials*, 339.

Part IX: *In Carcere et Vinculis*
Chapter 1: The Head of Medusa

1 *Reynolds's Newspaper*, 26 May 1895; *Belfast News-Letter*, 27 May 1895. Anon., *Oscar Wilde: Three Times Tried*, 466, states that OW was not transferred to Pentonville until the Monday, but the contemporary press reports all appear to confirm that the transfer happened on the Saturday evening.

2 Hyde, *Oscar*, 378; Hyde describes having seen these entries in the register at Pentonville. The current whereabouts of the register are unknown. It is at neither the National Archives (Kew) nor at the London Metropolitan Archives.

3 Harris, 194, *Reynolds's Newspaper*, 26 May 1895; 'Oscar Wilde in Prison', *Western Mail*, 7 June 1895.

4 Michelle Higgs, *Prison Life in Victorian England* (2007), 45: at Pentonville 'masks were abandoned in 1853'.

5 George Ives Diary, 12 March 1898, quoted in McKenna, 538.

6 'Oscar Wilde in Prison', *Western Mail*, 7 June 1895, claimed that OW had succumbed to just such 'Prison Head'.

7 *CL*, 1080.

8 Harris, 196.

9 *CL*, 1045, 1080; Harris, 194; Anon warder, 'Wilde's Prison Life' (Clark); Hyde, *Oscar*, 380.

10 R. B. Haldane, in Mikhail, 323.

11 'Editorial Comments', *Western Mail*, 27 May 1895.

12 Coulson Kernahan, '*Oscar Wilde As I Knew Him*', ts 37–8 (Clark); other

expressions of sympathy and regret can be found from John Davidson (Sloan, *John Davidson: First of the Moderns*, 139); the social reformer Josephine Butler (Jane Jordan, *Josephine Butler* (2001), 277–8); Mary Berenson (Samuels, *Bernard Berenson*, 218); Burne-Jones (Ellmann, 450); 'C.S.M', *Reynolds's Newspaper*, 29 May 1895 (*Wildean*, 22 (2003), 5–6). See also Mark Samuels Lasner, 'In Defence of Oscar Wilde', *Wildean*, 40 (2012), 2–5; Yasha Bereisner, 'Oscar Wilde: A University Mason', at www.freemasons-freemasonry.com; Anne Anderson, 'Private View', *Wildean*, 52 (2018), 10.

13 R. B. Haldane, *An Autobiography* (1929), 177–9; *CL*, 653n. Haldane had been a member of the Gladstone Committee, set up by Herbert Asquith in July 1894. Although the committee delivered its report in April 1895, Haldane preserved an interest in prison reform. Ellmann, 456.

14 Haldane to his mother, in McKenna, 540; CMW to Arthur Clifton, in Moyle, 277; *PMG*, 4 June 1895; *Daily Chronicle*, 5 June 1895; Asquith to Prison Commissioners, 5 June 1895, in Robins, *Oscar Wilde: The Great Drama of His Life*, 25.

15 Hyde, *Aftermath*, 7. Haldane met with Rosebery on the morning of his conference with Wilde's 'family'; see McKenna, 540; Harris, 192; Haldane to More Adey, 8 January 1896 (Clark).

16 Maguire, 53–5; RR to LAD, 23 June 1897 (Clark): 'Before the Queensberry trouble More was not a friend of Oscar's at all. I do not think he ever liked Oscar particularly. He certainly disapproved of him very much, & I don't think he had read any of Oscar's works. He was however very fond of you & admired you very much. Directly Oscar was in low water, he became as fond of Oscar

I believe as any friend of Oscar's could be, because that is More's nature. Partly owing to this, and for other reasons which I will not enter into, he gave £200 to Humphreys for Oscar's defence.'

17 Sir Matthew Ridley to Evelyn Ruggles-Brise, 30 September 1895 (PRO). See LAD to Percy Douglas, 11 July 1895 (BL): 'Do old chap see if you can't do something about bribing the warders at Pentonville. I hear that much can be done, in the way of getting food et cet. sent in.'

18 Harris, 194, 198: Ellmann, 456; Harris 194, 214; Haldane to Ruggles-Brise, 10 October 1895 (PCOM 8/432 (13629) PRO); Wandsworth Prison, 'Nominal Register' (London Metropolitan Archives) OW's entry can be viewed online at https://search.lma.gov.uk. It does not list his weight, only age (40), height (6.0) and hair colour ('Drk brown'). It gives his occupation as 'Author', his education as 'Sup[erior]', his religion as 'C of E' and his conviction as 'Misc'. The other prisoners listed on his page are almost all 'labourers', and all were serving shorter sentences; W. D. Morrison to Haldane, 11 September 1895 (PCOM 8/432, PRO); Dr Quinton report to Prison Commissioners, 18 September 1895; Captain Helby to Prison Commissioners (PCOM 8/432, PRO). Helby indicates that OW's weight on arrival at Wandsworth (4 July) was 175 lbs, and that he had lost only a further 8 lbs by 18 September 1895.

19 Maguire, 54; *PMG*, 22 August 1895.

20 More Adey, 'Notes on OW's ms' (Clark): 'O's answers 6 Sept '95'.

21 *CL*, 716.

22 Sherard, *SUF*, 197–8; the newspaper article that Sherard quotes seems to conflate this visit and the one he made on 23 September 1895.

23 And in August the young poet Hugues Rebell would publish 'Defense d'Oscar Wilde' in the *Mercure de France*, Richard Hibbitt, 'The Artist as Aesthete' in Evangelista, ed., *The Reception of Oscar Wilde in Europe*, 77; LAD to Percy Douglas from Hôtel de la Poste, Rouen, 20 June 1895 (BL).

24 Ellmann, 462; Moyle, 278.

25 Sherard, *SUF*, 200; Otho Holland Lloyd to Mary Lloyd, 9 September 1895, in R. Hart-Davis, ed., *Letters of Oscar Wilde* (1962), 872.

26 *CL*, 715; Otho Holland Lloyd to Mary Lloyd, 9 September 1895, in R. Hart-Davis, ed., *Letters of Oscar Wilde*, 871–2; it is doubtful that CMW's letter to OW, from which Otho quotes, would have been delivered to him, as he had already received his allowed quarterly letter (from Otho); see Otho Lloyd to Mary Lloyd, 12 September 1895, in Moyle 279–80; quoted in Sherard, *SUF*, 201–2.

27 Sherard, *SUF*, 202–4.

28 *CL*, 666; Sherard, *SUF*, 204–6.

29 Maguire, 57; *PMG*, 24 September 1895; Adela Schuster had promised £250, but the other substantial commitments were £500 from Trelawney Backhouse, a young fantasist, and the same amount from Percy Douglas, who also had no money of his own. Stewart Headlam was, meanwhile, 'going to write to some people'. Ada Leverson to More Adey, 19 September [1895] (Clark).

30 A. Clifton to Carlos Blacker, 8 October 1895, in Maguire, 58–9.

31 W. D. Morrison to Haldane, 11 September 1895 (PRO); McKenna, 545–6.

32 McKenna, 547–8; Sir Matthew Ridley to Haldane, 7 October 1895 (PRO).

33 Dr Gover to Ruggles-Brise, 28 September 1895; Gover followed up his comment about OW not working with 'London thieves' by observing, 'With reference to his matter, I propose shortly to pay another visit to the prisoner, and to submit a recommendation for your consideration.' Gover's letter/report of 28 September had been requested by Ruggles-Brise to replace his first letter/report of 23 September. See Robins, 31. Haldane's suggestion that 'bookbinding' might be 'good work to put Wilde to' is in Haldane to Ruggles-Brise, 13 September 1895 (PCOM 8/432 (13629) PRO); [anon senior official at Home Office] 1 October 1895, quoted in Robins, 34.

34 Harris, 196.

35 R. H. Sherard to More Adey, 18 October 1895 (Clark); Lily Wilde to More Adey, 18 October 1895 (Clark).

36 The *Daily Chronicle* began its campaign in 1894 with a series of anonymous articles on prison conditions titled 'Our Dark Places'. There were some who suspected Rev. Morrison of being the author. It was these articles that prompted the setting up of the so-called 'Gladstone Committee' (chaired by the former prime minister's son, Herbert Gladstone MP) on which Haldane had served. PCOM 8/433 (PRO), quoted in Maguire, 60–1.

37 Robins, 36–8.

38 Harris, 192; W. D. Morrison (chaplain at Wandsworth Prison) to Haldane, 11 September 1895 (PRO).

39 David Nicolson and Richard Bryan, report, quoted in full in Robins, 41–5.

40 Report of Drs D. Nicholson and R. Bryan, 29 October 1895, HO 45/24514 (PRO).

41 Robins, 47; the choice of Reading was made by the prison commissioners.

42 Ellmann, 461; RR to Oscar Browning, 13 November 1895, in Maguire, 62.

43 *CL*, 722: OW describes himself at the bankruptcy court as 'handcuffed' and

'between two policemen' – but the contemporary press reports make no mention of handcuffs, and describe his two attendants as 'warders', one walking in front, and one behind; *Daily News* (London), 13 November 1895; *Freeman's Journal*, 13 November 1895; *Star* (Saint Peter Port), 12 November 1895; *Reynolds's Newspaper*, 17 November 1895.

44   RR to Oscar Browning, 12 November 1895, in Ellmann, 461n.

45   *CL*, 757 where the date of his transfer is mistakenly given as 21 November; the incident of the man spitting at OW is in Sherard, *SUF*, 212.

Chapter 2: The System

1   'In the Depths: Account of Oscar Wilde's Life at Reading. Told by his Gaoler', *Evening News and Evening Mail* (London), 1 March 1905, in Mikhail, 328–9; *CL*, 1002.

2   Peter Stoneley, '"Looking at the Others": Oscar Wilde and the Reading Gaol Archive', *Journal of Victorian Culture*, 19 June 2014, 457–80, provides an interesting breakdown of the Reading prison population during the time of Wilde's incarceration. He was, throughout his stay, the only inmate serving time for a sexual offence with another male.

3   *CL*, 983; Harris, 197; Gide, *Oscar Wilde*, 65; F. Harris, *Oscar Wilde, His Life and Confessions* (1918 edition), 2:606; Harris, 193–4.

4   *CL*, 983; Ross, ed., *Robbie Ross – Friend of Friends*, 39.

5   More Adey to LAD; LAD, *Oscar Wilde and Myself*, 163–4; R. Haldane to M. Adey, 23 January 1896 (Clark).

6   R. Haldane to M. Adey, 23 January 1896 (Clark); *CL*, 653n.

7   More Adey, draft petition (Clark); O'Sullivan, 63.

8   *CL*, 721.

9   PCOM 8/433 (PRO); *CL*, 816–18, 766.

10   *CL*, 652.

11   OET V, 474–81. The performance took place in a double bill with Romain Collus's *Raphaël*, in the hired Comédie-Parisienne theatre on 11 February 1896, with Lina Munte in the title role; *CL*, 653–4.

12   *CL*, 652n; RR to More Adey, in Ross, ed., *Robbie Ross – Friend of Friends*, 39–43.

13   Ross, ed., *Robbie Ross – Friend of Friends*, 39–43; Robins, *Oscar Wilde: The Great Drama of His Life*, 53.

14   PCOM 8/433, National Archives (Kew); Frank Harris to More Adey, 4 January 1896 (Clark): Harris has to go to S. Africa 'for some months'.

15   Harris, 197; Robins, 101; Robins argues convincingly against accepting all the details of Harris's account, regarding OW's ear infection.

16   OW to home secretary, 2 July 1896, *CL*, 656–60.

17   Robins, *Oscar Wilde: The Great Drama of His Life*, 57–60; Dr Maurice medical report, National Archives (Kew), HO 45/24514; RR to More Adey, [May 1896], in Ross, ed., *Robbie Ross – Friend of Friends*, 39–43; More Adey, draft petition, November 1895 (Clark); also RR to O. Browning [November 1895] (King's College, Cambridge); Visiting Committee Book of Reading Prison (Berkshire Record Office); National Archives (Kew) PCOM 8/433; HO 45/24514.

18   *Reading Mercury*, 16 July 1896, in Hyde, *Oscar*, 395; 'In the Depths: Account of

Oscar Wilde's Life at Reading. Told by his Gaoler', *Evening News and Evening Mail*, 1 March 1905, in Mikhail, 331; 'Oscar Wilde's Prison Life' ms (Clark).

19 It is sometimes suggested that Isaacson's removal had been prompted by Home Office concerns about his role in OW's decline, and was perhaps even initiated by the influence of Frank Harris (see Robins, *Oscar Wilde: The Great Drama of His Life*, 63). But R. H. Sherard, *Bernard Shaw, Frank Harris & Oscar Wilde* (1937), 212, demonstrates that his transfer to Lewes had been arranged before the Home Office inquiry into OW's condition at Reading, and that it was a significant promotion in a stellar career that led from Reading to Lewes, to Brixton and, finally, to the 'red ribbon of the Prison Service', Strangeways gaol in Manchester.

Chapter 3: From the Depths

1 Wilfrid Hugh Chesson, 'A Reminiscence of 1898', in Mikhail, 376; *CL*, 854, 667; 'Oscar Wilde's Prison Life' ms (Clark); Robins, *Oscar Wilde: The Great Drama of His Life*, 103–4.

2 *CL*, 660n, 743; Robins, 63; *CL*, 666; *Manchester Guardian*, 13 October 1914.

3 M. Adey to CMW, 22 September 1896 (Clark); M. Adey to Adela Schuster, 16 March 1897 (Clark); *CL*, 669; 'Wilde's Prison Life' [anonymous holograph by 'A Prison Warder'] (Clark).

4 'Wilde's Prison Life'.

5 Rothenstein, *Men and Memories I*, 311.

6 'Wilde's Prison Life'. The author laments that the fifty or so sheets of paper that he preserved, with OW's 'views on almost every conceivable subject, written in his beautiful hand' were lost 'in South Africa during the late war'.

7 Sturge Moore, ed., *Self-Portrait*, 112.

8 'In the Depths: Account of Oscar Wilde's Life at Reading. Told by his Gaoler', *Evening News and Evening Mail*, 1 March 1905, in Mikhail, 331.

9 *CL*, 754.

10 *CL*, 1048, 174; A. Gide, *Recollections of Oscar Wilde* (1906), 54–6; in *CL*, 762, OW suggests that his encounter may have occurred while he was still at Wandsworth.

11 'Wilde's Prison Life'.

12 *CL*, 887, 830, 976.

13 'Oscar Wilde's Prison Life'; *CL*, 852–3.

14 *CL*, 654–5.

15 LAD to RR, 4 June 1896, in Ellmann, 470.

16 LAD to More Adey, 20 September 1896, in Ellmann, 480.

17 LAD, 'Une introduction à mes poèmes, avec quelques considérations sur l'affaire Oscar Wilde', *La Revue Blanche*, 10, no. 72 (1 June 1896), 484–90.

18 *CL*, 669.

19 *CL*, 786, 671–2.

20 *CL*, 819.

21 *CL*, 728; LAD eagerly supported the scheme, when told of it, hoping that it might be a way of restoring his relationship with OW. He wrote to his brother Percy from Capri, 'I hope you will see More Adey about poor Oscar's life interest, it is the only thing in the world left him & the only hold he has over his beastly wife who has behaved infamously. Her sollictors [*sic*] want to buy it, but it could be secured for £100. If you could possibly afford it, & as the money you offered for the bankruptcy was not required, it would be splendid of you to buy it & give it to me. I of course should give it back to Oscar but

it would be an enormous pleasure to me to be able to give it to him as a gift, especially as I fear that the poor fellow has been set against me by Mrs Wilde's party, George Lewis & Co & others. I think I should die of misery if after all this when Oscar came out there was to be a complete estrangement between us. It is so utterly unjust after all I did & suffered that it seems incredible, but the real truth is that he is (temporarily) mad, & no wonder, both Adey and Ross have now no doubt of it.' (BL).

22 CL, 704; For the law on divorce, see Matrimonial Causes Act 1857, section 27 (20 & 21 Vict., c. 85).

23 Robins, 93–4. The case was heard in chambers in the Court of Chancery on 1 March 1897; OW was not present.

24 CL, 678.

25 Martin, in Mikhail, 333.

26 RR to Adey, in Ross, ed., Robbie Ross – Friend of Friends, 40.

27 Henry Salt to Edward Carpenter, 7 July 1897, in George Hendrick, Henry Salt, Humanitarian, Reformer, and Man of Letters (1977), 79; Henry Salt, Seventy Years Among Savages (1921), 181–2.

28 Daily News and Leader (London), 11 December 1913, in Mikhail, 325.

29 Sherard, Life, 377–83: Sherard does not name OW's interlocutor but the possible field is a small one, and the chaplain the most likely candidate; CL, 741–53.

30 Sherard, Life; CL, 750.

31 The full text is at CL, 683–781; the ms is at the BL.

32 CL, 781–2; LAD had been primed by Adey and Ross to expect a letter from OW. On 8 February 1897, he wrote to Adey (from Villa Lucullo, Rome):

'I look forward without excitement to Oscar's letter. Indeed I wonder he writes. What he can have to say to me unless one thing I cannot understand, & if he is going to abuse me I would rather not see it. In all his life he has never written me a letter that was unkind or at least unloving and to see anything terrible in his writing written directly to me would almost kill me. However he must do as he pleases, & I will write again only what I think will be agreeable to him. Please let me know if possible by return –

When exactly may I expect his letter? When exactly will Oscar be released?

I suppose you will let me know any other necessary directions about writing the letter. I suppose it would be inadvisable to put more than My dear Oscar at the beginning, or might I put Dearest? Forgive what seems harsh or disagreeable in this letter. My nerves are much unstrung by this incident & you know I am truly fond of you dear More & appreciate you kindness, though your ways are not my ways & I can't see with your eyes. Yours always, Bosie.' (Clark).

33 Daily News and Leader (London), 11 December 1913, in Mikhail, 329.

34 RR to M. Adey, CL, 1212.

35 Ricketts, 49.

36 CL, 669.

37 CL, 812; in 1892 RR and Adey had collaborated on a new edition of Melmoth the Wanderer for the publisher Richard Bentley. In their joint introduction (dated February 1892) they recorded 'their best thanks to Mr Oscar Wilde and Lady Wilde (Speranza) for several details with regard to Maturin's life'. Michael Seeney, More Adey (2017), 31.

38 CL, 812.

39 CL, 800.

40 CL, 802.

41 CL, 677.

42 CL, 812.

43 Harris, *Oscar Wilde, His Life and Confessions* (1918 edition), 2:577.

44 Martin, in Mikhail, 335.

45 *CL*, 754.

46 *CL*, 759; Ricketts, 48–9, mentions plans for his play about 'Pharaoh'; O'Sullivan, 220, on OW evolving new plot-lines from his Bible-reading in prison.

47 *CL*, 798.

48 *CL*, 680, 811.

49 *CL*, 677–8.

50 *CL*, 827.

51 *CL*, 806.

52 *CL*, 800, 813; Harris's memory of the interview, in the 'Appendix' to Harris, *Oscar Wilde: His Life and Confessions* (1918 edition), 577, suggests that he simply offered to pay Wilde for any contributions he made to the *Saturday Review* at a higher rate to that which he gave Bernard Shaw.

53 *CL*, 791, 811.

54 *CL*, 828.

55 *CL*, 809.

56 *CL*, 809.

57 *CL*, 829, 831.

58 *CL*, 807.

59 *CL*, 813.

60 *CL*, 814.

61 *CL*, 827–8.

62 *CL*, 823.

63 *CL*, 837.

64 *CL*, 789.

65 *CL*, 808.

66 Hansell visited OW at Reading in March 1897 to propose the plan. On 10 April 1897 he sent the terms for such an arrangement as drawn up by himself and Hargrove. OW accepted them, and signed the 'deed of separation' at Reading on 17 May 1897; Robins, *Oscar Wilde: The Great Drama of His Life*, 95–7.

67 'In the Depths', in Mikhail, 330.

68 Arthur Hansell to More Adey, 11 May 1897 (Clark): 'I have learned today that Mrs Wilde will make the allowance of £150 run as from 20th Feby. last so that there will be an quarter to receive on the 20th inst.'

69 J. G. Adderley, *In Slums and Society* (1916), 178–9.

70 *CL*, 828. Ernest Leverson to More Adey, 11 May 1897 (Clark) had given the account balance as £168 11s 6d. The reduction in this amount was probably the result of a payment to the solicitor, Humphreys.

71 A. Schuster to More Adey, 30 April 1897 (Clark).

72 *CL*, 831 + n.

73 *CL*, 829.

74 *CL*, 831.

75 Adderley, *In Slums and Society*, 178–9; see Robins, 68–9, for details of Adderley's application to the prison commissioners. Adderley (1861–1942), when at Oxford, had been a founder member of the University Dramatic Society, and OW had praised his performance in the society's production of *Twelfth Night* (OET VI, 64). He was also a friend of OW's cousin, Fr Basil Maturin.

76 'News of the World', *Evening News* (Sydney), 3 July 1897.

77 Lena Ashwell, *Myself A Player* (1936), 80.

78 Ricketts, 46.

79 Shane Leslie, 'Oscariana', *National Review*, 15 January 1963, in Ellmann, 492.

80 Leverson, *Letters to the Sphinx*, 46.

Part X: *The Fisherman and his Soul*
Chapter 1: Asylum

1   Hyde, *Aftermath*, 140; Bettany, *Stewart Headlam*, 131; *CL*, 832–3. OW's bath is conjectural, based on his stated desire to cleanse himself of all trace of prison, and the fact that (when he thought he would be going to a hotel, rather than to Headlam's) he told Turner, 'Try and find a hotel with a good *bathroom* close to bedroom: this most essential' (*CL*, 833).

2   Leverson, *Letters to the Sphinx*, 44–7; Maude M. Ffoulk, *My Own Past* (1915), 213. Ada Leverson said that Wilde 'made most of the other men look like convicts'.

3   Bettany, *Stewart Headlam*, 131.

4   There are four slightly conflicting versions of this incident. Bettany, *Stewart Headlam*, 131, quotes Headlam as saying, 'at length he asked me to send for one of the Farm Street priests I sent off a message, but they would have nothing to do with him there'. Ada Leverson, in her 'Reminiscences' (in *Letters to the Sphinx*, 45), describes how '[OW] wrote a letter, and sent it in a cab to a Roman Catholic Retreat, asking if he might retire there for six months'. LAD, *Autobiography*, 141, reports that OW, on the day of his release, 'went to the Brompton Oratory and asked to see one of the Fathers' (perhaps Fr Bowden). Reggie Turner, in a letter to John H. Hutchinson, 27 February 1937 (Clark), corrects this version, saying that 'when Oscar came out of prison he didn't go to the Brompton Oratory, but sent to ask one of the priests to come to him. The priest was either out, or – as I was told [probably by Adey, or Ada Leverson] declined to come.' Given that OW's existing Catholic connections were all with the

Brompton Oratory it seems the most likely place for him to have directed his inquiries. Schroeder, 191, suggests that OW's application for a six-month retreat is 'a myth invented by Ada Leverson', and Holland and Hart-Davis (*CL*, 842 n1) also find it 'implausible'. But it seems to me that OW's anxieties about money, and about Dieppe (*CL*, 135–6), and his general state of nervous agitation, might well have prompted him to scout such a plan on the spur of the moment.

5   Leverson, *Letters to the Sphinx*, 45–7.

6   Hyde, *Aftermath*, 146.

7   *CL*, 844.

8   Ross ms of unfinished preface to projected collection of OW letters, *CL*, 842; R. Turner to Christopher Millard, 29 October [1920] (Clark).

9   Hart-Davis, ed., *Max Beerbohm's Letters to Reggie Turner*, 118.

10 *CL*, 845; Douglas, *Autobiography*, 145, claimed that when Wilde left England 'a sum of £800 was subscribed for him by various friends', and this figure has been re-used by biographers (e.g. Ellmann, 496). But there is no evidence to support it. Although there were reports in the press that a subscription among 'several gentlemen of the highest respectability' had raised £500 to give Wilde 'a fresh start in life' (*Western Mail*, 3 June 1897), these, like many articles published in the wake of Wilde's release, were pure invention. At the Clark Library there is a small accounts notebook, inscribed with the name 'Melmoth' – perhaps given to OW by RR to encourage habits of economy. The amounts listed to 'Credit' on page 1 are: 'Cheque – Leverson [the residue of Adela Schuster's fund] – £111.11s.6d;

Notes – Leverson – £80; More [Adey] Collection – £50; Anonymous [Adela Schuster] £25; cheque Harris – £50; Mrs Wilde's cheque – £37.10s.' This gives a total of £354 1s 6d. Ricketts did raise £100 to give to Wilde, but RR – aware of the artist's own straightened circumstances – returned the money. RR, aware of OW's tendency to excess, seems to have kept back some of the money due to Wilde, so that it would not all be spent at once (by 2 June OW was asking him to send a further £40). Listed on page 3 of the accounts notebook are further small, undated, credits apparently received up until the end of July. They total £90 16s and include contributions from Vincent O'Sullivan, Rothenstein, Lady Queensberry, Smithers, Bosie and a 'Miss Martin' [?].

11 CL, 858.
12 CL, 844n.
13 CL, 848.
14 CL, 870.
15 CL, 847.
16 CL, 873.
17 CL, 855.
18 CL, 858.
19 Harris, 226; John Rothenstein, The Life and Death of Conder (1938), 118.
20 Simona Pakenham, Sixty Miles from England: The English at Dieppe, 1814–1914 (1967), 168.
21 CL, 922; Blanche, Portraits of a Lifetime, 99–100; Sherard, Life, 406; Pakenham, Sixty Miles from England, 168.
22 CL, 881n.
23 CL, 882, 1089.
24 Rothenstein, Men and Memories I, 90.
25 CL, 883, 908, 901, 906.
26 CL, 891, 892–3, 885; Gide, Oscar Wilde, 55–63.
27 Stuart Merrill, in La Plume (15 December 1900), in Mikhail, 466.
28 A. Gide, Oscar Wilde, 57.
29 Ernest Dowson to H. Davray, 11 June 1897, in Flower and Mass, eds, The Letters of Ernest Dowson, 386.
30 CL, 892.
31 Alin Caillas, Oscar Wilde, tel que je l'ai connu (1971), translated in Padraig Rooney, 'Feasting with Cubs: Wilde at Berneval', Harp, vol. 11, 1996
32 John Fothergill, ms memoirs, quoted in David Sox, Bachelors of Art (1991), 140.
33 CL, 861–2.
34 Georgette Leblanc, Souvenirs, My Life with Maeterlinck (1932), 127–8.
35 CL, 886.
36 CL, 894.
37 A. Gide, Oscar Wilde 65.
38 CL, 879; Harris, 214; CL, 880.
39 CL, 865n; Maguire, 85–6.
40 CL, 865, 909.
41 CL, 872, 861.
42 CL, 865.
43 H. Martin Holman to More Adey, 10 May 1897 Clark).
44 CL, 876.
45 CL, 873.
46 CL, 880.
47 Lady Queensberry to More Adey, 9 June 1897 (Clark).
48 CL, 901–2; LAD, Autobiography, 151.
49 Sox, Bachelors of Art, 141. Sox suggests that the couplet referred to Fothergill and Douglas, but this seems unlikely. It is perhaps possible that Wilde's comforting dark-haired 'love' was Constance. He may even have fashioned it so that it could taken for either Constance or Ross.

Chapter 2: Artistic Work

1   CL, 865, 869.

2   CL, 874, 923; Harris, 227.

3   CL, 928.

4   CL, 952, 926, 937.

5   CL, 873; Gide, Oscar Wilde, 72; O'Sullivan, 220.

6   John Fothergill's ms memoirs, quoted in Sox, Bachelors of Art, 139.

7   PMG, 9 August 1897; LAD to More Adey, 24 October 1896 (BL); Octave Mirbeau was said to be the moving force behind the idea of OW's inclusion.

8   CL, 928–9; when the American producer Augustin Daly approached him, offering an advance for a new work, OW felt obliged to put him off until he had fulfilled these existing obligations.

9   NYT, 12 December 1897, reported a comment in the St James's Gazette regarding a 'prominent manager' (probably Wyndham) 'preparing to produce [OW's] latest play under a thinly veiled pseudonym': 'The manager has failed to grasp the fact that this dramatist's career at respectable London playhouses must be considered closed.'

10 CL, 873.

11 CL, 876, 912.

12 CL, 867 and n. Although OW did not mention the plot details of his planned 'play' during his time at Berneval, his various references to the piece suggest that it was a commercially viable, English-language, modern comedy-drama about marital relations. And, in view of his subsequent attempts to promote the Alexander scenario, it seems certain that this was the story he was envisaging. The proposed title 'Love is Law' was first mentioned in OW's letter to Harris, 20 June 1900, but is used here for convenience.

13 CL, 915; 918–19.

14 CL, 897; A. Gide, Oscar Wilde, 62; O'Sullivan, 25.

15 OW to LAD, 23 June 1897, CL, 906–7; OW in his letter says the children 'chose' their own instruments ('6 accordions, 5 trompettes, 4 clarions'), but Alin Caillas, in his memoir of the event, recalls: 'In a large chest was a pile of musical instruments: accordions, trumpets, bugles, a drum and a kettledrum. We drew lots, and whatever the outcome everybody was perfectly satisfied. Félicien Bellêtre got an accordion – which he didn't know how to play – and I got a magnificent kettledrum which was much easier to play!'

16 CL, 916.

17 CL, 925.

18 CL, 930–1; the publisher was Grant Richards.

19 Pakenham, Sixty Miles from England, 166. Pakenham links this incident to the first days of OW's exile, but this seems unlikely. At that time he was under the care of Ross and Turner, and was anxious not to draw attention to himself. Moreover Gide, who visited OW on 19 June, claimed that he was the first French writer to see OW after his release.

20 Flower and Mass, eds, The Letters of Ernest Dowson, 390.

21 CL, 355.

22 CL, 924.

23 CL, 926.

24 CL, 919.

25 J-E. Blanche, Dieppe (Paris, 1927), 1–2.

26 CL, 921.

27 Sox, Bachelors of Art, 140; John Fothergill, Confessions of An Innkeeper (1938), 134.

28 Sox, Bachelors of Art, 141; John Fothergill to A. J. A. Symons, [1933?] (Clark).

29 Sox, *Bachelors of Art*, 141; Sherard, *Life*, 405.

30 O'Sullivan, 72.

31 Pakenham, *Sixty Miles from England*, 168.

32 Caillas, *Oscar Wilde, tel que je l'ai connu*.

33 Blanche, *Portraits of a Lifetime*, 98.

34 O'Sullivan, 87.

35 *CL*, 1229.

36 *CL*, 920.

37 *CL*, 921, CMW to Otho Lloyd, 5 August 1897, at *CL*, 865n.

38 Yeats, *Autobiographies*, 404.

39 *CL*, 880; in this and several other letters to friends OW asserted, 'I do not accept the British view that Messalina [a byword for heterosexual vice] is better than Sporus [the infamous catamite of Nero]; these things are matters of temperament' – while allowing that, as purely 'sensual pleasures', they lacked nobility.

40 *CL*, 887.

41 R. H. Sherard to A. J. A. Symons, 3 June [1937] (Clark). Sherard suggests the incident took place in 'June 1897', but as neither he nor RR was at Berneval in that month, and both were staying there in mid-August, the latter date is to be preferred.

42 *CL*, 922.

43 *CL*, 953.

44 Smithers to OW, 2 September 1897, in *CL*, 931n.

45 *CL*, 922.

46 *CL*, 929.

47 *CL*, 861; 893.

48 *CL*, 936.

49 *CL*, 923.

50 Sox, *Bachelors of Art*, 142.

51 LAD, *Autobiography*, 151; Hyde, *LAD*, 109–10, suggests that OW's invitation to meet LAD at Rouen was issued in late July/early August; *CL*, 930.

52 *CL*, 934.

53 LAD, *Autobiography*, 152.

54 Douglas Murray, *Bosie* (2000), 104, mentions LAD's gift of a cigarette case inscribed with some lines from Donne's 'Canonisation', but Don Mead, in *The Oscar Wilde Society Newsletter*, November 2018, raises legitimate doubts about its authenticity.

55 LAD wrote to his mother asking for £75, claiming it was needed to repay a debt of 'honour' that he and Percy owed. She sent £10 as a first instalment via Adey. Sybil Queensberry to More Adey, 1 August 1897 (Clark).

56 *CL*, 935; 1029.

57 *CL*, 936.

58 *CL*, 932–3.

59 LAD, *Autobiography*, 152.

60 Max Beerbohm to Reggie Turner, 5 September 1897, in Hart-Davis, ed., *Max Beerbohm's Letters to Reggie Turner*, 122.

61 *CL*, 934.

62 *CL*, 935.

63 *CL*, 937.

64 *CL*, 937; Arthur Hansell to OW, 31 August 1897 (Clark); *CL*, 936.

65 Caillas, *Oscar Wilde, tel que je l'ai connu*; O'Sullivan, 194–7.

66 W. H. Chesson, in Mikhail, 376.

67 *CL*, 935, 936.

68 *CL*, 935.

69 *CL*, 932–3.

Chapter 3: Outcast Men

1 The hotel, like the other grand waterfront hotels, filled the block between the via Partenope and via Chiatamone, and had entrances on each street. It has since been replaced by the Royal Continental Hotel.

2   *CL*, 947.

3   *CL*, 947.

4   *CL*, 943; *CL*, 947.

5   LAD, *Autobiography*, 152.

6   *CL*, 949.

7   *CL*, 952.

8   *CL*, 952.

9   *CL*, 947.

10 CMW to Carlos Blacker, 26 September 1897, in Maguire, 94.

11 Vyvyan Holland to Frank Harris, quoted in Ellmann, 513; Vyvyan left for his school in Monaco shortly before the end of the month. CMW to Carlos Blacker, 30 September 1897, BL RP3291.

12 CMW to Carlos Blacker, 26 September 1897, in Maguire, 94.

13 CMW to Carlos Blacker, 26 September 1897, *CL*, 955n.

14 OW to RR, *CL*, 942–3.

15 OW to Reggie Turner, *CL*, 948.

16 OW to Reggie Turner, *CL*, 948.

17 Paton to Carlos Blacker, 29 October 1897, quoted in Maguire, 96.

18 Quoted in Maguire, 96.

19 *CL*, 962, Sherard, *SUF*, 258.

20 *CL*, 961.

21 *CL*, 1006.

22 *CL*, 949.

23 *CL*, 963.

24 Wintermans, *Alfred Douglas*, 87.

25 *CL*, 994. CMW's letter was written on 29 September 1897.

26 *CL*, 955.

27 OW to More Adey, *CL*, 994.

28 RR to Schuster, *CL*, 1229.

29 CMW to Carlos Blacker; 1 October 1897, in Moyle, 311.

30 *CL*, 954–5.

31 LAD, *Autobiography*, 154; OW to RR, *CL*, 955.

32 *CL*, 943, 945, 948, 949.

33 *CL*, 957.

34 *CL*, 945.

35 *CL*, 956.

36 'Arnoldo de Lisle' (G. G. Rocco) in Miracco, *Verso il Sole (Naples, 1981)*, 23, refers to OW moving to a 'grazioso appartamento' at the 'Villa del Giudice [sic]'; *CL*, 968. LAD to George Ives, 22 October 1897, Clark: 'We shall be here to the end of January, we have taken this place till then.' Although it is sometimes stated that LAD paid for the villa, the money must have come from Young's £100. OW told Ross that since the opera libretto was to be a collaboration, LAD had 'had half of the £100 provided by Dal Young' RR to Clement Shorter, 27 December 1916 (Clark). And LAD, describing the villa to Percy, wrote, 'Oscar Wilde is with me, and we have taken the place between us. LAD to Percy Douglas, 5 November 1897 (BL).

37 *Il Pungolo parlamentare*, 9–10 October 1897, in Miracco, *Verso il Sole*, 30–1; LAD, *Autobiography*, 158.

38 *CL*, 950.

39 P. Borelli, *Esperia* (1903), in Miracco, *Verso il Sole*, 46–7.

40 LAD, *Autobiography*, 158. The ms of LAD, 'Autobiography' (Morgan) gives the servants' names as 'Peppino and Ettore'; *Il Pungolo Parlamentare*, 9–10 October. The Villa [del] Giudice is now No. 37 via Posillipo. There is some doubt as to exactly where OW and LAD stayed as there are several buildings on the site. LAD, *Autobiography*, 158, recalled 'the cost of feeding Wilde and myself and the servants was about 12 francs a day' (ms 10 francs) This converted to 9s 2¼ d – a modest, but not negligible amount.

41 LAD to More Adey, 15 Oct 1897 (BL).

42 LAD, *Autobiography*, 158, says 'house opposite'; 'Arnoldo de Lisle' (G. G. Rocco) names it as the Hotel della Riviera di Chiaja. Miracco, *Verso il Sole*, 35.

43 LAD to More Adey, 15 October 1897 (BL).

44 Borelli, *Esperia*, in Miracco, *Verso il Sole*,

46–7.

45 LAD, *Autobiography*, 158.

46 LAD, *Autobiography*, 158.

47 LAD to More Adey, 15 October 1897 (BL).

48 *CL*, 944, 952; also Harris, 252.

49 *CL*, 949.

50 *CL*, 946.

51 *CL*, 950.

52 *CL*, 953.

53 *CL*, 996.

54 LAD, *Autobiography*, 156.

55 *CL*, 947.

56 RR to Smithers, 17 April 1898, *CL*, 1055n.

57 *CL*, 957.

58 LAD, *Autobiography*, 158. Douglas's unpublished poem contained the line, 'Into the dreadful town through iron doors, / By empty stairs and barren corridors.'

59 *CL*, 996.

60 *CL*, 950.

61 *CL*, 959.

62 *CL*, 956.

63 Norman Douglas, *Looking Back* (1936), 461–2. Douglas suggests that the first false report appeared in *Il Mattino*, but it seems to have been in the *Corriere di Napoli*. That certainly was where it was corrected on 11 October 1897, 1.

64 *Star*, 9 October 1897; *La Patrie*, quoted in *Star*, 14 October 1897; Douglas, *Looking Back*, 461–2.

65 According to Miracco, *Verso il Sole*, 32, OW was mentioned in *Naples Echo*, *Journal des Etrangers*, *Captain Fracassa*, *Corriere di Napoli* and *Il Mattino*.

66 *Il Mattino*, 7/8 October 1897, p. 1.

67 'Arnoldo de Lisle' quoted in Miracco, *Verso il Sole*, 35.

68 *Il Pugnolo parlamentare*, 9–10 October, 1897, reprinted in Miracco, *Verso il Sole*, 30–3. For an English translation see Masolino D'Amico, 'Oscar Wilde in Naples', in Sandulescu, ed., *Rediscovering Oscar Wilde*, 79.

69 *Il Mattino*, 7 October 1897, 1.

70 *CL*, 950.

71 'Arnaldo de Lisle', in Miracco, *Verso il Sole*, 35.

72 *CL*, 955.

73 *CL*, 962.

74 *Comoedia*, 21 April 1923, in Miracco, *Verso il Sole*, 35–7; a fictionalized echo of this incident also appears in Roger Peyrefitte's novel, *L'Exile de Capri* (1959).

75 LAD to Lady Queensberry, quoted in Bengt Jangfeld, *The Road to San Michele* (2008), 157.

76 *Comoedia*, 21 April 1923, in Miracco, *Verso il Sole*, 35–7.

77 *CL*, 965.

78 *CL*, 965.

79 Leonard Green to Charles Kains Jackson, 11 August 1919, quoted in Wintermans, *Alfred Douglas*, 88.

80 Harry de Windt, *My Restless Life* (1909), 232; LAD, *Autobiography*, 154.

81 Wintermans, *Alfred Douglas*, 88; LAD, *Autobiography*, 154.

82 *CL*, 950; G. G. Rocco had edited the literary magazine *Stenna Margherita* in 1894. Although OW referred to him as a 'poet', he does not appear to have published a volume of poems.

83 Rita Severi, '"Astonishing in my Italian": Oscar Wilde's First Italian Editions', in Evangelista, ed., *The Reception of Oscar Wilde in Europe*, 109.

84 *CL*, 959.

85 *CL*, 961.

86 A contract letter was deposited with the Neapolitan notary, Sodano, dated 25 October 1897: 'Dear Mr Rocco, I authorize you with great pleasure to translate and arrange for the performance of my play *Salomé* on the Italian stage. Oscar Wilde.' Rita Severi, 'Astonishing in my Italian', 111.

87 *CL*, 959.

88 *CL*, 967–8.

89 *CL*, 959.

90 'Arnaldo de Lisle', quoted in Miracco, *Verso il Sole*, 55–6.

91 Severi, 'Astonishing in my Italian', 111.

92 *CL*, 958.

93 *Baedeker Southern Italy* (1896 edition), 67–8.

94 *CL*, 958.

95 A. Sper, *Capri Und Die Homosexuellen* (1902), quoted in Robert Aldrich, *The Seduction of the Mediterranean* (1993), 163.

96 R. Ross, 'Statement of Evidence in His Case Against Douglas' (Clark).

97 Harris, 300.

98 Miracco, *Verso il Sole*, 23; *CL*, 979; 1118.

99 Miracco, *Verso il Sole*, 23; *CL*, 967. Nothing is known of the Falstaffian 'Sir John' Ashton, though he is perhaps the mysterious 'X' in LAD's comically coded letter to the secretive George Ives: 'We met a charming fellow here yesterday. I wonder if you know him; his name is X and he lives at Z. He was obliged to leave R on account of a painful scandal involving H & T.' LAD to George Ives, 22 October 1897 (Clark).

100 'Arnoldo de Lisle' in Miracco, *Verso il Sole*, 35.

101 Miracco, *Verso il Sole*, 39.

102 LAD, *Oscar Wilde and Myself*, 127–8.

103 *CL*, 976.

104 *CL*, 978, 981.

105 LAD to Edward Strangman, 29 November 1897, in Ellmann, 520.

106 *CL*, 968.

107 *CL*, 971.

108 *CL*, 978.

109 *CL*, 976.

110 *CL*, 981, 990.

111 *CL*, 971.

112 *CL*, 980.

113 *CL*, 972.

114 *CL*, 953.

115 *CL*, 954, 957; 966.

116 James G. Nelson, *Publisher to the Decadents* (2000), 181–2.

117 *CL*, 972.

118 *CL*, 975.

119 *CL*, 984.

120 *CL*, 994–5, 965, 959.

121 *CL*, 988, 969, 983.

122 *CL*, 1003.

123 *CL*, 984.

124 *CL*, 1011.

125 *CL*, 973.

126 RR to Leonard Smithers, 16 November 1897 (Fales).

127 *CL*, 956; *Publisher to the Decadents*, 200–1.

128 Harris, 252.

129 LAD to Lady Queensberry, 7 December 1897, quoted in Wintermans, *Alfred Douglas*, 90.

130 LAD, *Autobiography*, 154.

131 V. O'Sullivan to A. J. A. Symons, [?1932] (Clark).

132 Harris, 252.

133 Harris 252–3; Miracco, *Verso il Sole*, 39.

134 *CL*, 1004.

135 *CL*, 979, 995.

136 Percy Douglas to LAD, BL RP 5487.

137 LAD to Edward Strangman, in Ellmann, 520.

138 *CL*, 991.

139 LAD to Edward Strangman, in Ellmann, 520.

140 Lady Queensberry to M. Adey, 18 December 1897 (Clark).

141 LAD to Lady Queensberry, 7 December 1897, in Hyde, *LAD*, 117.

142 *CL*, 997.

143 *CL*, 983.

144 *CL*, 1003.

145 *CL*, 993.

146 R. Croft-Cooke, *Bosie*, 163–4: LAD, having learnt that Ross had expressed a doubt to Smithers about whether the US serial rights would have any value, had written to a common friend (More Adey) claiming that Ross was trying to prevent Wilde earning money from the poem.

147 *CL*, 1006.

Chapter 4: Bitter Experience

1   CL, 998; Joseph Francis Daly, *The Life of Augustin Daly* (1917), 626; OW hoped for '£100 down, and £100 for each completed act'.

2   CL, 961; 969, 976.

3   CL, 958. A letter from L. Smithers to OW, 26 January 1898 (Bodleian), stating 'I hear that you are within an ace of completing your play, "Pharaoh"' seems to have been based on an overoptimistic report.

4   'Arnoldo de Lisle' (G. G. Rocco), quoted in Miracco, *Verso il Sole*, 23. The anecdote recorded by Rocco related to LAD, trying to imitate OW's 'system', taking too many pills, and becoming violently sick.

5   CL, 972–3.

6   CL, 1005–6; Severi, 'Astonishing in my Italian', 113. Chiara had a copy of Eugene Tardieu's French translation (published in 1895) to start from; Wilde's own copy, sent down to Naples with his other books from Berneval, was impounded awaiting a customs payment he was unable make. CL, 992, 1005. Chiara's translation, *Dorian Gray Dipinto*, was finally published in 1905.

7   CL, 992.

8   Sturge Moore, ed., *Self-Portrait*, 137; D'Amico, 'Oscar Wilde in Naples', 80. She performed at the Teatro Mercadante in Suderman's *Magda* and *La Seconda Moglie* (as Pinero's *The Second Mrs Tanqueray* was known in Italy).

9   CL, 1006.

10 Severi, 'Astonishing in my Italian', 11; Sturge Moore, ed., *Self-Portrait*, 137.

11 'Arnoldo de Lisle', quoted in Severi, 'Astonishing in my Italian', 111.

12 Rocco's translation was published in 1901 in Neapolitan journal *Rassegna Italiana*. The first Italian production of *Salomé* was on 30 December 1904 at the Teatro dei Filodrammatici, Milan. Severi, 'Astonishing in my Italian', 112.

13 CL, 1006.

14 O'Sullivan, 69–70.

15 CL, 983; V. O'Sullivan to A. J. A. Symons [1932?] (Clark).

16 O'Sullivan, 64.

17 O'Sullivan, 161–2.

18 RR, 'Statement of evidence in his case against Douglas' (Clark).

19 Samuels, *Bernard Berenson*, 292. Blaydes, a twenty-five-year-old doctor and would-be philosopher, had been in Tuscany (where he had begun an affair with Mary Berenson, or Costelloe as she then still was) and was heading to North Africa when he stopped in Naples that December.

20 Edwin Tribble, ed., *A Chime of Words: The Letters of Logan Pearsall Smith* (1984), 102; see also Samuels, *Bernard Berenson*, 292. 'Rumour had it that Smithers was paying him a pension of sorts to write indecent books to sell at thirty or fifty pounds a copy.' The rumours did not prevent Blaydes touching the ever-generous Wilde for a small loan. W. Blaydes to OW, 28 January 1898 (Clark).

21 Samuels, *Bernard Berenson*, 292.

22 Samuels, *Bernard Berenson*, 292; Tribble, ed., *A Chime of Words*, 102.

23 Samuels, *Bernard Berenson*, 292.

24 CL, 1008; OW's friend may have been the photographer Baron Rudolf von Transéhe-Roseneck. There is a letter at the Clark from the Baron to OW (10 January 1898) reminding OW of their recent time together in Taormina, asking for the repayment of 1,000 lire that Wilde had borrowed in Naples, and mentioning 'Guglielmo' who speaks every day of a red silk handkerchief that Wilde had promised him.

25 http://www.italiannotebook.com/
    local-interest/florence-trevelyan-taor-
    mina/.

26 *CL*, 1032; Nicholas Frankel, *Oscar Wilde:*
    The Unrepentant Years (2017), 165.

27 See the not very reliable commemora-
    tive plaque outside the Hotel Victoria,
    Corso Umberto 81, Taormina. Among
    its various clear errors, it describes
    Wilde as staying a whole month in
    the town, and not leaving until 13
    February. It also contains a quote from
    an otherwise unknown letter to LAD
    suggesting that they might come and
    live together in Taormina. But the
    Gloeden references may preserve local
    memories of Wilde's visit.

28 J. G. Nelson, *Publisher to the Decadents*,
    199–200: after Miss Marbury deducted
    her commission and expenses, she
    sent a cheque for $88.59 to be divided
    equally between Wilde and Smithers.

29 *CL*, 1011–12.

30 *CL*, 1012–13 +n.

31 L. Smithers to OW, 26 January 1898
    (Bodleian); *CL*, 1013.

32 Graham Greene, *A Sort of Life* (1971), 26.

33 *CL*, 1013.

34 W. Blaydes to OW, 28 January 1898
    (Clark); *CL*, 1013.

Part XI: *The Teacher of Wisdom*
Chapter 1: The Parisian Temple of Pleasure

1   *Athenaeum*, 12 February 1898.

2   'New Poem by Oscar Wilde', *Reyn-*
    olds's Newspaper, 13 February 1898.

3   *Sunday Special*, 13 February 1898, quot-
    ed in *CL*, 1030.

4   G. S. Layard, *Mrs Lynn Linton: Her Life,*
    Letters, and Opinions (1901), 356.

5   Ivor C. Treby, *Binary Star* (2006), 140;
    diary entry 3 April 1898.

6   *CL*, 1019.

7   Mason, 417; Karl Beckson, ed., *Oscar*
    Wilde: The Critical Heritage (1970),
    211–22. RR to L. Smithers, 'Saturday'
    [1898] (Fales) also mentions 'a favour-
    able note about the Ballad' on 'page 57
    of the current *Outlook*' (Henley's un-
    favourable review appeared on page
    146, in the issue of 5 March 1898).

8   *CL*, 1036.

9   *CL*, 1037.

10 *CL*, 1024, 1027; Laurence Housman's
    brother, A. E. Housman, considered
    'parts' of the poem 'above Wilde's aver-
    age' but suspected they had been writ-
    ten by LAD. Archie Burnett, ed., *The*
    Letters of A. E. Housman (2007), 2:77.

11 *CL*, 1021; John Rothenstein, *Summer's*
    Lease (1965), 145.

12 Ross, ed., *Robbie Ross – Friend of Friends*,
    50; CMW to Carlos Blacker, 4 February
    1898 (BL); CMW to Carrie Blacker,
    5 March 1898 (BL); Major Nelson, to
    whom Ross had sent a proof copy,
    was not entirely won by the poem.
    He wrote back: 'I quite concur in your
    criticism and altho' thinking some
    stanzas very fine am of the opinion that
    the work is not worthy of the writer's
    best effort. It is a terrible mixture of
    good bad and indifferent.' Though dis-
    tressed to learn that 'Mr. Wilde has
    not succeeded in rescuing himself
    completely from the slough of the past
    two years', he had hopes that 'we shall
    someday see something really worthy
    of so brilliant and so unique a pen'.

13 Lily Wilde to More Adey, 14 March
    1898 (Bodleian).

14 *CL*, 1026.

15 Mason, 420; J. G. Nelson, *Publisher to*
    the Decadents, 202.

16 *CL*, 1045; 1053.

17 *CL*, 1063; J. G. Nelson, *Publisher to the Decadents*, 207.

18 J. G. Nelson, *Publisher to the Decadents*, 208; curiously the scheduled appearance of the poem in the *New York Journal* on 13 February never occurred. It seems that the sinking of a transatlantic steamship on the previous day had resulted in the clearing of the paper's pages to give full coverage of the disaster. For copyright purposes Smithers did produce a special edition of just six copies in the US. G. F. Sims Catalogue No. 78. (March 1971), item 438.

19 *CL*, 1022.

20 P. Valéry to P. Louÿs, 31 March 1898, in Fawcett and Mercier, eds, *Correspondances À Trois Voix*, 852.

21 David Charles Rose, *Oscar Wilde's Elegant Republic* (2016); 415; Niederauer and Broche, eds, *Henri de Régnier*, 449, March 1898 entry.

22 *CL*, 1079.

23 *CL*, 1057; OW to Henry Davray [June 1897], (Christie's sale 6973, 3 March 2004); *CL*, 1028; J. G. Nelson, *Publisher to the Decadents*, 208.

24 RR to OW, 'Monday evening' [May 1898] (Clark).

25 *CL*, 1030.

26 *CL*, 1078, 1079; Georgette Leblanc, *Souvenirs, My Life with Maeterlinck* (1932), 127–8.

27 Healy, *Confessions of Journalist*, 157, 165.

28 *CL*, 1051.

29 Maguire, 120–6.

30 Healy, *Confessions of a Journalist*, 125–6.

31 Maguire, 120.

32 Maguire, 127.

33 Healy, *Confessions of a Journalist*, 125, 136. Healy claims that Wilde refused to visit Zola 'on the curious ground that Zola was a writer of immoral romances'. But given Wilde's oft-stated

views on art and morality this seems scarcely credible. His objection was far more likely to have been artistic.

34 Ernest La Jeunesse, 'Oscar Wilde', *Revue Blanche*, 15 December 1900, in Maguire, 111.

35 Vance Thompson, 'Oscar Wilde: Last Dark Poisoned Days in Paris', *New York Sun*, 18 January 1914, 18.

36 Newman Flower, ed., *The Journal of Arnold Bennett, 1896–1910* (1932), 215; *CL*, 1051 n1.

37 Robert Sherard, *Twenty Years in Paris* (1905), 443; Healy, *Confessions of a Journalist*, 165.

38 *CL*, 1105; 1019, 1044.

39 *CL*, 1104.

40 Harris, 300.

41 *CL*, 1078, 1106, 1104.

42 Harris, 269; Harris's rather fanciful verbatim account of OW's meeting with the 'little soldier' does not mention Gilbert by name, and although the dates he gives do not correspond exactly with references in OW's letters, the identification seems all but certain.

43 *CL*, 1030–1; Harris, 270.

44 *CL*, 1036, 1041, 1037. On 15 March 1898 – a month after publication – he received a first modest cheque for £4.

45 Maguire, 119; for 200 francs and 100 francs.

46 CMW to Carrie Blacker, 26 March 1898 (BL RP 3291).

47 *CL*, 1050.

48 *CL*, 1038–9.

49 CMW to Carlos Blacker, 20 March 1898, in Maguire, 119.

50 CMW to Carrie Blacker, 26 March 1898 (BL RP 3291).

51 Frank Harris to Henry Davray, 24 November 1926 (Austin).

52 LAD, *Oscar Wilde, A Summing Up* (1940), 100–1.

53 *CL*, 1054, 1229; Maguire, 121, 127.

54 Vyvyan Holland, *Time Remembered after Père Lachaise* (1966), 10–12, in Mikhail, 361–2.
55 *CL*, 1040.
56 *CL*, 1062; Robins, *Oscar Wilde: The Great Drama of His Life*, 101.
57 *CL*, 1056.
58 Stuart Merrill, 'Oscar Wilde', trans. H. M. Hyde (1912) (Clark); Vincent O'Sullivan to A. J. A. Symons, 26 October 1931 (Clark).
59 O'Sullivan, 54.
60 *CL*, 1058.
61 *CL*, 1065; 1077–8.
62 Noel Arnaud, *Alfred Jarry* (1974), 418.
63 *CL*, 1057.
64 Sherard, *SUF*, 263.
65 *CL*, 1057; LAD, *Oscar Wilde and Myself*, 130.
66 RR to L. Smithers, [April 1898] (Fales).
67 *CL*, 1058.
68 *CL*, 1066.

69 RR to L. Smithers, [9 May 1898] (Fales).
70 *CL*, 1090.
71 Rowland Strong, *Sensations of Paris* (1912), 187.
72 W. H. Chesson, in Mikhail, 377.
73 Carlos Blacker's visit was on 7 June; Maguire, 125; *CL*, 1085–6.
74 H. Bauër to Carlos Blacker, 2 August 1898, in Maguire, 137. OW seems to have been unaware of Bauër's animosity. In July 1899 he sent him a copy of *AIH*.
75 Maguire, 150.
76 *CL*, 1094, 1092, 1093.
77 Conder to Mrs Dalhousie Young, quoted in Ellmann, 533.
78 Conder to Mrs Dalhousie Young, quoted in Ellmann, 533.
79 Kessler, *Journey to the Abyss*, 329.
80 Conder to Mrs Dalhousie Young, quoted in Ellmann, 533; RR to Adela Schuster, *CL*, 1229.

Chapter 2: Going South

1   *CL*, 1028, 1080.
2   *CL*, 1035.
3   *CL*, 1068.
4   RR to L. Smithers, 19[?] February 1898 (Fales).
5   Ellmann, 528.
6   *CL*, 1101.
7   Wilfrid Hugh Chesson, 'A Reminiscence of 1898', *Bookman*, 34 (1911), in Mikhail, 376. Chesson's Christian name is wrongly given as 'Wilfred'.
8   Chris Healy, in Mikhail, 385.
9   W. H. Chesson, in Mikhail, 380.
10 OW's enthusiasm for absinthe was something new. In the early 1890s he had told Bernard Berenson that 'absinthe has no message for me'. Samuels, *Bernard Berenson*, 155.
11 Fothergill, *Confessions of An Innkeeper*, 134, 272; Leverson, *Letters to the*

Sphinx, 39–40.
12 O'Sullivan, 54.
13 J. Joseph-Renaud, 'The Last Months of Oscar Wilde in Paris', 3, ts (Clark).
14 The bill, dated 29 and 30 August, is at the Clark.
15 *CL*, 1061–2n; RR also tried to set up a fund contributed to by OW's friends. But, though Ernest Leverson pledged '£5 a year for two years', it failed to get off the ground. E. Leverson to RR, 2 June 1898 (Clark).
16 *CL*, 1102; Harris, 265–6.
17 *CL*, 1098; the contract – 24 October 1898 (BL) – offered an advance of £50 on signature, 150 francs a week for eight weeks, and £100 on delivery 'on or around January 1st'.
18 Harold Acton, *Confessions of an Aesthete* (1948), 381.

19 Stratmann, *Marquess of Queensberry*, 264.

20 *CL*, 1103, 1106, 1109.

21 Sherard, *Life*, 418–19; O'Sullivan, 53; La Jeunesse, 'Oscar Wilde', *Revue Blanche*, 15 December 1900; Mikhail, 478.

22 Shane Leslie, *Memoir of John Edward Courtenay Bodley*, 18.

23 *CL*, 1108. Wilde gives the name of the bar as Kalisaya; O'Sullivan as 'Calsaya'; J. Joseph-Renaud as 'Calysaya'; and Leonard Carlus (in a letter to OW at Clark) as 'Calizya'; but 'Calisaya' is the spelling preferred by Marcel Boulestin and Gustave Le Rouge, and has been adopted here.

24 Rose, *Oscar Wilde's Elegant Republic*, 407.

25 Gustave Le Rouge, 'Oscar Wilde' [1928], in Mikhail, 460–1.

26 John Stokes, *Oscar Wilde: Myths, Miracles and Imitations* (2006), 23–38.

27 La Jeunesse, 'Oscar Wilde', in Mikhail, 479.

28 Stuart Merrill, *La Plume*, 15 December 1900, in Mikhail 466; Ernest La Jeunesse, 'Oscar Wilde', in Mikhail, 479. O'Sullivan also noted that although OW 'would borrow a few francs from his landlord or his washerwoman' he did not apply to his French literary friends. But this was not quite true: Davray recalled OW touching him for a few sous (offering his own inscribed copy of *The Duchess of Malfi* as security); and Stuart Merrill received a note from OW asking for a very small sum, 'afin de finir ma semaine'. O'Sullivan, 56; H. Davray to Walter Ledger, 26 February 1926 (Ross Collection, Univ Coll, Oxford); Ransome, 198.

29 Gustave Le Rouge, in Mikhail, 461.

30 *CL*, 1108.

31 Vincent O'Sullivan to A. J. A. Symons [1931] (Clark).

32 *CL*, 1157.

33 Gide, *Oscar Wilde*, 82–8.

34 Rose, *Oscar Wilde's Elegant Republic*, 419. Sibleigh's translation was published in Ohio in 1900; he also contributed to a privately printed 1901 volume of *Verses Written in Paris by Members of a Group of Intellectuals*.

35 Kessler, *Journey to the Abyss*, 351.

36 Reggie Turner to G. F. Renier, 22 March 1933 (Clark).

37 *CL*, 1105.

38 Gustave Le Rouge, 'Oscar Wilde' [1928], in Mikhail, 461–2; Thomas Beer, *The Mauve Decade* (1926), 130–1; Sue Prideaux, *Strindberg: A Life* (2012), 106; *CL*, 1157.

39 Wilfrid Scawen Blunt, *My Diaries – Part Two* (1932), 122.

40 Harris, 277.

41 *CL*, 1118.

42 *CL*, 1119.

43 *CL*, 1112.

44 *CL*, 1116.

45 Harris, 281–2; 287.

46 *CL*, 1115.

47 Neil Titley, *The Oscar Wilde World of Gossip* (2011).

48 *CL*, 1116.

49 Harris, 294–5.

50 *CL*, 1128.

51 *CL*, 1130, 1138.

52 *CL*, 1154; James G. Nelson, *Publisher to the Decadents*, 212; Mason 423 – the new edition of *BRG* was published on 23 June 1899.

53 See 'Theatrical Gems', *Bristol Mercury and Daily Post*, 7 March 1899; *CL*, 1128.

54 *CL*, 1131, 1129, 1139.

55 *CL*, 1139.

56 *CL*, 1142.

57 *CL*, 1149. In May 1899 Sedger was sued by the mother of one of the child actors in *Alice* and had to pay £16 10s plus costs (*Era*, 6 May 1899); on 5 July 1899 Sedger was declared bankrupt – for the second time in his career –

putting his failure down to 'excesses of expenditure over his income'. *Era*, 8 July 1899.

58 L. Smithers to OW, 4 May 1899 (Bodleian); the identity of 'Roberts' remains obscure. He could, perhaps, have been the Sir Randall Roberts against whom OW had warned Elizabeth Robins.

59 *CL*, 1225.

60 OW settled at the Hôtel de la Neva on the rue de Monsigny, not far from the Cailsaya; and then moved to the nearby Hôtel Marsollier.

61 *CL*, 1143, n, 1145, 1146, 1147, 1150; L. Smithers to OW, 30 May 1899 (Bodleian).

62 *CL*, 1150.

63 Robertson, *Time Was*, 230–1.

64 *CL*, 1154, 1152.

65 Robertson, *Time Was*, 231.

66 K. Bellew to OW, 20 April 1899 (Clark).

67 *CL*, 1143; Kyrle Bellew to OW, 12 June 1899; 6 July 1899; 7 July 1899; (Clark). Wilde was at both Le Havre and Trouville at the end of June.

68 *CL*, 1202; 1195.

69 OW asked for money from, among others: Harris, Smithers, Ross, Arthur Humphreys and Morton Fullerton. *CL*, 1154–63.

70 Kessler, *Journey to the Abyss*, 351; OW's ms list of people to receive copies of *AIH* (Clark) gives the name as 'Lautrec' – which could also refer to Henri's cousin Gabriel Lautrec.

71 Sherard, *Life*, 410, 418; Sherard claims that Dupoirer 'discharged' OW's bill at the Marsollier, but the payment was surely made with money provided by OW.

72 Testimony about OW's drunkenness during his last years in Paris is contradictory, with Sherard suggesting that he was never 'the slightest the worse for drink' (Sherard to A. J. A. Symonds, 13 Mary 1937 (Clark)) and Douglas claiming that he was 'over and over again so drunk that he couldn't walk' (LAD to A. J. A. Symonds, 8 March 1937 (Clark)). But the most reliable assessments would seem to be provided by Reginald Turner in a letter to Sherard, 3 January 1934 (Reading), quoted in Frankel, *Oscar Wilde: The Unrepentant Years*, 349; and RR to A Schuster, quoted in *CL*, 1225.

73 Frédéric Boutet, 'Les Dernières Années d'Oscar Wilde' (unidentified newspaper clipping), 3 December 1925 (Clark), in Ellmann, 531; the author suggests that OW sat there because he was unable to pay his bill, but this must be conjecture. He could, simply, have been reluctant to return to his hotel room.

74 *CL*, 1025.

75 [LAD] 'Oscar Wilde's Last Years in Paris', *St James's Gazette*, in *The Trial of Oscar Wilde: from the Shorthand Reports* (1906), 117.

76 Augustus John, *Chiaroscuro* (1954), 34.

77 Augustus John, *Finishing Touches* (1964), 145.

78 Laurence Housman, *Echo de Paris* (1923), 49–59.

79 George Charles Williamson to RR [n.d.] (Clark).

80 RR, 'Introduction', *Miscellanies*, 13; Speedie, *Wonderful Sphinx*, 116.

81 Housman, *Echo de Paris*, 37.

82 [LAD] 'Oscar Wilde's Last Years in Paris', in *The Trial of Oscar Wilde: from the Shorthand Reports*, 118–9; Harris, 256.

83 Housman, *Echo de Paris*, 28–30, 37, 49–59; L. Housman to Hesketh Pearson, 4 April 1944 (Austin), listing the passages in the book that are closest to OW's speech.

84 *CL*, 1175, 1169.

85 Robins, 110–11.

86 Louis Nethersole to OW, 27 December 1899 (Clark).

87 *CL*, 1200: Eliot, who was Sedger's part-

ner in the production of *Alice in Wonderland* and *Great Caesar*, was described in the press as 'nephew of Lord Wimborne and Earl St Germans'. 'The Theatres', *Daily News*, 5 December 1898.

88 *CL*, 1173: other causes have also been put forward, including secondary stage syphilis (although such a rash would not itch), and an allergic reaction to hair dye. Robins, 112.

89 *CL*, 1176; Robins, 101.

90 *CL*, 1173–4, 1176.

91 *CL*, 1173.

92 Sherard, *Real*, 419–20.

93 LAD, *Autobiography*, 161; Stratmann, *Marquess of Queensberry*, 271–2.

94 *CL*, 1173.

95 LAD to Percy Douglas, 7 March 1900, Hotel Victoria, London: 'I wish you would seriously make some arrangements about the £125 for OW. He keeps on writing to me about it. I thought you had settled to pay it to More Adey, or someone. As you know I paid my half & some more besides a fortnight ago' (BL). It seems, though, that Percy never did make the payment. A later letter from LAD to Percy (19 December 1900 (BL)) asks where 'the £125' is. This perhaps suggests that LAD also paid his brother's share, in a series of instalments. LAD's next three payments to OW were: £12 (27 February); £25 (16 March); £25 (10 May). LAD, *Autobiography*, 323.

96 *CL*, 1170+n; Guy & Small, 205–7.

97 Elisabeth Marbury to OW, 30 April 1900 (Clark); Marbury, in October 1899, had also sold the American performing rights for 'a modern comedy drama', to be written by OW 'before' 1 June 1900, to Charles Frohman. OW received £100 advance on signature, with £200 due on delivery (BL).

98 H. Beerbohm Tree to OW, 17 February 1900 (Clark). Mrs Waller's company performed *WNI* on 30 November 1899 at the Coronet Theatre, London.

99 Michael Seeney, *From Bow Street to the Ritz* (2015), 127ff.

100 Aubrey C. Smith to OW, 20 March 1900, St James's Theatre (Clark): 'Mr Alexander wishes me to enclose you a letter he has received from French's people with regard to putting *Lady Windermere's Fan* and *The Importance of Being Earnest* into book-form. He is of opinion that doing so is a far better advertisement for the play among Amateurs than in manuscript as the reading fee is done away with. I note your wishes to hold cheques back for the present – you will doubtless let me know when & where you wish them sent next!'

101 *CL*, 1176, March 1900; Ransome, 197.

102 *CL*, 1185.

103 *CL*, 1179.

104 *CL*, 1185.

105 Ransome, 197.

106 *CL*, 1182.

107 'Michael Field', 'Works and Days', BL Add MS 46798 f.202 (notebook 23, page 414).

108 *CL*, 1225–6.

109 Ransome, 197; *CL*, 1183.

Chapter 3: All Over

1 *CL*, 1187.

2 John Farrington to OW, 9 July 1900 (Clark).

3 Harris, 308; RR to Vyvyan Holland, 1918, in Mary Hyde, ed., *Bernard Shaw & Alfred Douglas: A Correspondence* (1989), xxiv.

4 *CL*, 1192.

5   CL, 1188.

6   Harris, 305; the unfortunate dinner with LAD occurred at the end of May. LAD gave OW cheques for £25 on 30 June, for £50 and £25 on 17 July; LAD, *Autobiography*, 323.

7   CL,1193; 1226+n., Ross told Adela Schuster that OW, during the course of 1900, received '£100 from a theatrical manager' – almost certainly Alexander.

8   CL, 1189–90+n; Harris, 301–2.

9   La Jeunesse, 'Oscar Wilde', *Revue Blanche*, 15 December 1900, in Mikhail, 480.

10 CL, 1194.

11 Paul Fort, quoted in Ransome, 198.

12 Stuart Merrill, 'Some Unpublished Recollections of Oscar Wilde', in Mikhail, 470.

13 Frederic V. Grunfeld, *Rodin: A Biography* (1988), 411.

14 CL, 1192; La Jeunesse, 'Oscar Wilde', *Revue Blanche*, 15 December 1900, in Mikhail, 478.

15 CL, 1191; Ransome, 198–9; Ellmann, 543. Raoul le Boucher was the ringname of Raoul Musson.

16 The lurid account of this incident given in Marjoribanks, *Life of Lord Carson*, in which Carson inadvertently knocks 'the wretched painted' Wilde into the gutter, has long been discredited. See Vincent O'Sullivan to A. J. A. Symons, [1932] (Clark), and Mrs C. S. Pell, *Life's Enchanted Cup* (1933), 103.

17 Rothenstein, *Men and Memories*, 362.

18 CL, 1190–1.

19 Steen, *A Pride of Terrys*, 206n.

20 Her verbatim account of their conversation, Anna, comtesse de Brémont, *Oscar Wilde and His Mother* (1911), 176–88, in Mikhail, 450, seems implausible.

21 Sir Peter Chalmers Mitchell, *My Fill of Days* (1937), 183–4, in Mikhail, 366–7.

22 [LAD], 'Oscar Wilde's Last Years in Paris', in *The Trial of Oscar Wilde from the Shorthand Reports*, 125; Hyde, LAD, 127; LAD, *Autobiography*, 323.

23 CL, 1194.

24 Ellmann, 543.

25 CL, 1163–4. OW's letters to Lowther are dated by the editors to 'August 1899', but 1900 seems more likely, as Lowther and Terry were described as visiting OW at the time of the Exhibition. Vance Thompson records (in 'Oscar Wilde: Last Dark Poisoned Days in Paris', in the *New York Sun*, 18 January 1914) that Thadée Nathansen, the proprietor of the *Revue Blanche*, urged OW to write for his publication, and OW even began 'putting down a few French phrases'.

26 CL, 1198.

27 Ransome, 199.

28 Dr Maurice A'Court Tucker was born in Paris in 1868 to an English father; he qualified as a doctor in 1896.

29 CL, 1212; TLC Mrs Mamie Ella Christie to R. H. Sherard, 22 January 1937 (Clark): 'I was studying in Paris at the time of Wilde's death, and Dr. Tucker came in one day saying, "You English don't deserve to have great men, when you allow them literally to starve to death."'

30 CL, 1223.

31 CL, 1212, 1127; RR gives the name of the 'well known specialist' as Hobean – though it may well be that the name was mis-transcribed. Ashley Robins has been unable to find any doctor named 'Hobean' listed in the French medical records.

32 For the best and most convincing account of OW's illness see Robins, 104–8; CL, 1206.

33 CL, 1200; OW, having been accommodated in several different sets of rooms at the Hôtel d'Alsace during the course

of the past fourteen months, was currently installed in a 'big room on the ground floor... to which access was through the courtyard'. Reggie Turner to Thomas H. Bell [1935] (Clark).

34 CL, 1199, 1200, Robins, op. cit. 106–9.

35 CL, 1199.

36 CL, 1207.

37 CL, 1199–1200.

38 CL, 1195, 1202.

39 CL, 1199–1200.

40 CL, 1199–1200.

41 CL, 1212.

42 CL, 1212, 1226.

43 CL, 1212; Robins, 109.

44 Harris, 314.

45 CL, 1212–13, 1227.

46 CL, 1212; RR merely records that OW made the witticism about 'dying above his means'. Turner (see Harold Acton, *Memoirs of an Aesthete* (1948), 63) reported that OW made the remark 'when he called for champagne'. J. Joseph-Renaud ('The Last Months of Oscar Wilde in Paris', ts 5 (Clark)) suggests – less convincingly – that it was said after OW had overheard his 'two English doctors [*sic*] whispering – not unkindly – about their fees in a window recess'. It is, of course, possible that OW, having coined the remark, repeated it on several occasions.

47 CL, 1213. According to RR, OW's debts included £50 to Tucker and £96 to the hotel; CL, 1228.

48 CL, 1213.

49 CL, 1201–8, 1213.

50 CL, 1212, Harris, 314.

51 CL, 1212.

52 CL, 1212; Harris, 315.

53 CL, 1213.

54 CL, 1213.

55 Ricketts, 59.

56 Clifford Millage (Paris office of the *Daily Chronicle*) to OW, 5 November 1900 (Clark); Millage's report was

widely syndicated: e.g. *Northern Echo*, 4 December 1900.

57 CL, 1220; Blunt, *My Diaries – Part Two*, 121–2.

58 CL, 1213.

59 CL, 1227.

60 CL, 1213, 1227.

61 CL, 1213.

62 CL, 1214.

63 Reggie Turner to Thomas H. Bell [1935] (Clark); R. H. Sherard, *Modern Paris* (1911), 160, says the move occurred 'within a fortnight of [OW's] death', i.e. around 16 November.

64 CL, 1215–16.

65 RR to Will Rothenstein, 11 December 1900 (Houghton); CL, 1218.

66 Ellmann, 550. The poets Raymond de la Tailhède and Jehan Rictus visited daily; Claire de Pratz, in G. de Saix, *Souvenirs inédits*, in Ellmann, 456; CL, 1228.

67 CL, 1228.

68 Mrs Will Gordon, *Echoes and Realities* (1934), 83–4.

69 CL, 1227, where RR gives Dr Claisse's name as 'Kleiss'; CL, 1214; Drs Tucker and Claisse, medical certificate, 27 November 1900, repr. in Robins, 106–7.

70 Drs Tucker and Claisse, medical certificate, 27 November 1900, in Robins, 106–7. In the decade after OW's death, the idea was put forward, apparently by RR, that OW's final illness was 'the legacy of an attack of tertiary syphilis'. Rumours to this effect began to circulate from as early as 1906. At the beginning of that year Harry Kessler recorded in his diary (12 January) that Conder had told him 'Wilde died of syphilis, aggravated by his consumption of absinthe'. The first published assertion of the fact was in Arthur Ransome's 1912 book *Oscar Wilde: A Critical Study* (for which RR provided the biographical information, and from

which the initial quotation derives). The page proofs of the book mentioned that OW had contracted the disease while at Oxford, but was convinced that it had passed by the time of his marriage. These details, however, were not included in the published edition of Ransome's book, although they seem to have been circulated by RR to Sherard and others (Robins, 113). Since then biographers – from Frank Harris (1916) to Richard Ellmann (1987) – have been apt to claim that OW was suffering from the disease throughout his adult life, and that it contributed in some way to his death. The point, however, is contentious. That RR thought he was correct in making the claim can probably be assumed. But laymen are notoriously ready to come up with fanciful diagnoses when assessing their own, and others', ailments. Against his assertion it should be noted that there is not a single reference in letters from, to, or about Wilde during his lifetime to suggest that he had contracted syphilis, or that he felt he was living under the shadow of some terrible, unnamed disease. The extensive medical records available from OW's time in prison are similarly silent upon the subject. LAD dismissed the notion out of hand (*Oscar Wilde: A Summing Up*, 96). And, as to the specifics of his final illness, Ashley Robins – in his medically informed 2011 book, *Oscar Wilde: The Great Drama of His Life* – finds nothing to support the involvement of syphilis. There is certainly no evidence to confirm that he had the disease. And there is almost nothing in the incidents of his life to suggest that he was suffering from it. As John Stokes has sagely noted, even Ellmann's claim that the disease 'is central to my conception

of Wilde's character and my interpretation of many things in [his] later life' is not sustained in his book (Schroeder, 35). In light of the above it would seem wisest to assume that OW was *not* suffering from syphilis throughout his life. Certainly his 1900 illness was not the tertiary manifestation of the disease.

71 *CL*, 1218.

72 *CL*, 1216.

73 *CL*, 1218.

74 *CL*, 1216.

75 *CL*, 1216.

76 *CL*, 1218+ n.

77 *CL*, 1219: R. Turner to Thomas H. Bell, [1935] (Clark), states that OW's hair was shaved, and the leeches applied, 'two days before his died' – i.e. on 28 November.

78 Fr Cuthbert Dunne (1869–1950), 'Extracts from the Memoir of Father Cuthbert Dunne, C.P.', ts (Austin); Rev. Edmund Burke, 'Oscar Wilde: the final scene', *London Magazine*, 1, no. 2 (May 1961). *CL*, 1219–20.

79 *CL*, 1220.

80 RR to A. Schuster, mentions that OW was given 'the last sacraments' on 'the morning before he died', *CL*, 1226; Fr Dunne's own account, 'Extracts from Memoir of Father Cuthbert Dunne, C.P' and *CL*, 1223–4, indicate that he made at least one return visit to Wilde's sick-chamber, and possibly more.

81 *CL*, 1220.

82 *CL*, 1225.

83 *CL*, 1229.

84 *CL*, 1229.

85 [LAD] 'Oscar Wilde's Last Years in Paris', in *The Trial of Oscar Wilde: from the Shorthand Reports*, 117.

86 *The Times*, 1 December 1900.

87 *The Sunday Times*, 2 December 1900.

88 *CL*, 1229, *PMG*, 1 December 1900.

Image Credits

Every effort has been made to trace copyright holders and gain permission to reproduce images. We apologise if there are any errors or omissions and would be happy to make any amendments in future editions.

We would particularly like to thank Merlin Holland for his help in sourcing many of the images in this book.

Part openers
p. 2 The William Andrews Clark Memorial Library, University of California, Los Angeles; p. 60 Shutterstock Premier; p. 134 Hulton Archive/Getty Images; p. 198 Library of Congress; p. 270 The William Andrews Clark Memorial Library, University of California, Los Angeles; p. 378 Courtesy of Robert Whelan; p. 462 Bridgeman Images; p. 530 *London Evening News*, May 1895; p. 586 *The Standard*, Vol. XIII, September 1895, New York; p. 626 Topfoto.co.uk; p. 672 ullstein bild/Getty Images; p. 716 Hulton Archive/Getty Images.

Plate sections
1, 2, 3, 12, 15, 23, 31, 32, 35, 36, 38, 45, 46, 49, 50, 53, 54, 59, 61, 62 Private collection of Merlin Holland; 11, 47 The William Andrews Clark Memorial Library, University of California, Los Angeles; 9, 10, Magdalen College, Oxford; 42 © Ashmolean Museum, University of Oxford/Estate of Max Beerbohm; 22 *Punch Magazine*; 52 National Archives; 4, 29, 30, 60 Library of Congress; 57 Berkshire Record Office; 40 Courtesy of C. Barlas and Rivendale Press; 5 Portora Royal School; 7, 16, 18, 19, 24, 25, 27, 28, 34, 48, 50 Getty Images; 8, 13, 17, 21, 39 Bridgeman Images; 6, 33, 41, 44, 58 Alamy Stock Photo; 43 Shutterstock Premier; 14 Google Art Project.

Index

OSCAR

MATTHEW STURGIS is a writer with a deep knowledge of the late Victorian cultural world. He is the author of acclaimed biographies of Aubrey Beardsley and Walter Sickert, as well as *Passionate Attitudes – The English Decadence of the 1890s*. He has contributed book reviews to the *Times Literary Supplement*, art criticism to *Harpers & Queen*, and football reports to the *Independent on Sunday*. He is on the editorial board of *The Wildean*, the journal of the Oscar Wilde Society.